FUNDAMENTALS OF CHRISTIANITY

A BIBLE STUDY AND GUIDE

Fourth Edition

Andrew V. Barber, PhD

Dedicated to Jesus Christ

Christ at 33 – Painting by Heinrich Hofmann (1824–1911)

Fundamentals of Christianity: A Bible Study and Guide (Fourth Edition)

© Copyright 1999, 2016, and 2020 by Andrew V. Barber

Published by Special Delivery Press
7121 Tierra Alta Ave.
El Paso, TX 79912
(915) 600–5039

All rights reserved. No part of this publication may be reproduced, transmitted, or distributed in any form or by any means without expressed written permission from the copyright owner.

The following components of this text are public domain and not subject to this copyright:
- Scriptural references paraphrased from the King James Version (KJV) of the Holy Bible;
- Lyrics from favorite hymns;
- Photocopies of famous paintings;
- Clipart used by permission from Microsoft Corp.

ISBN: 9780966970234

LCCN: 2020936058

Author: Andrew V. Barber

Cover Design, Interior Design, Photography, and Original Illustrations: Andrew V. Barber.

Subjects:
1. Christianity
2. Holy Bible
3. Word of God
4. Holy Trinity
5. Christian Apologetics
6. Religious Education

TABLE OF CONTENTS

CHAPTER ONE ~ WHAT IS THE BIBLE?

VALIDITY OF THE BIBLE — 1

- History — 1
- Authenticity — 3
- Reliability — 3
- Prophecy — 4
- The Canonization of Scripture — 6

- Lesson: Biblical Hermeneutics — 7
- Lesson: Synopsis of the Bible — 13

INSTRUCTIONS ON HOW TO LIVE — 14

- Seek God and His Love; Study His Word — 14
- Obey God's Laws and Pray to Him Always — 14
- Trust in the Salvation of Jesus Christ — 15
- Honor the Father, the Son, and the Holy Spirit — 15

- Lesson: Understanding God, Ourselves, and Our Relationship with God — 16
- Lesson: Communicating with God — 26
- Lesson: The Facts of Life — 32
- Lesson: Living by Example — 36
- Lesson: Stewardship — 41
- Lesson: Tools for Change — 47

CHAPTER TWO ~ WHO IS GOD?

THE ALMIGHTY — 51

- God Is Omniscient — 51
- God Is Omnipotent — 52
- God Is Omnipresent — 52
- God Is the One and Only God — 53
- Powers of God — 54

- Lesson: Awesome God — 55
- Lesson: Glory Be to God — 60
- Lesson: The Wisdom of God — 65

THE HOLY TRINITY — 69

- God Exists in Three Persons — 69
- Jesus Christ and the Almighty Father Are One — 69

CONTENTS

The Holy Spirit Is One with the Father and the Son	71
Direct References to the Trinity	71
Melchizedek	72
Immaculate Conception	73
Lesson: God in Three Persons	74
Lesson: Characteristics of Our Triune God	77
Lesson: God Is	79

GOD'S COVENANT — 82

God's Covenant with Noah	82
God's Covenant with Abraham	82
God's Covenant with Moses	83
God Revealed His New Covenant to Moses	83
God Revealed His New Covenant to David and Nathan	83
God Revealed His New Covenant to Isaiah	84
God Revealed His New Covenant to Jeremiah	84
God Revealed His New Covenant to Ezekiel, Daniel, Zechariah, Malachi	84
Jesus Explained the New Covenant to His Apostles	85
God Explained the New Covenant through Luke	85
God Explained the New Covenant through Paul and His Companions	85
Lesson: The New Covenant	87
Lesson: The Free Gift	91
Lesson: Holy Week	98
Lesson: God's Chosen People	100
Lesson: The Seed of Abraham	104
Lesson: The Apostles	110

CHAPTER THREE ~ WHO IS JESUS CHRIST?

OUR REDEEMER — 114

Jesus Christ Is the New Covenant	114
Old Testament References	115
New Testament References	120
The Word	125
Atonement	126
Forgiveness	128
Justification and Sanctification	129
Salvation	132
Lesson: Redemption and Reconciliation	134
Lesson: Once Saved Always Saved?	136
Lesson: Why a Messiah?	139

CONTENTS

    Lesson: Jesus Christ Is the Messiah 142
    Lesson: The Word as Truth 145

THE GOSPEL OF JESUS CHRIST **148**

    Jesus's Lineage 148
    Jesus's Birth 149
    Jesus's Initiation into the Ministry 151
    Jesus Feeds His People 157
    Jesus's Final Journey to Jerusalem 165
    Maundy Thursday and Good Friday 174
    Easter and Jesus's Ascension 179
    The Birth of the Christian Church 182
    Jesus's Travels 183

    Lesson: The Branch 184
    Lesson: The Sacrificial Lamb 187
    Lesson: Imagine 192
    Lesson: The Image of Life 196
    Lesson: The Gospel Message 200

THE SECOND COMING OF CHRIST . . . **205**

    The Latter Days 205
        Jesus's Personal Account 205
        Old Testament Accounts 206
        New Testament Accounts 210
    Predicting the End of Time 214
    Evil Generations 214
    The New Babylon 215
    The Rapture 216
    The Resurrection 217
    The Judgment 220

    Lesson: Introduction to Revelation 223
    Lesson: Signs of the Second Coming 234
    Lesson: The Tribulation and the Beast 240
    Lesson: The Rapture, the Resurrection, and the Judgment . . 245
    Lesson: Promises, Promises 251
    Lesson: Newness of Life 255
    Lesson: The Final Word 259

CONTENTS

CHAPTER FOUR ~ WHO AM I?

LIVING SPIRITS **260**

    Humans Were Created in the Image of God 260
        Heart 261
        Mind 262
        Spirit 262
        Soul 264
    All People Are Created Equal 265
    Heirs with Christ but Not Gods 267
    Powers of Humans 268
    Revelations and Visions 269
    Life 270
    Death 271
    The Church 273

    Lesson: Making Decisions and Solving Problems . . . 277
    Lesson: Endurance and Patience 280
    Lesson: Onward Christian Soldiers 283
    Lesson: The Priesthood of Believers 289
    Lesson: Unity in the Body of Christ 294
    Lesson: Parenthood 299

OTHER SPIRITUAL BEINGS **305**

    Angels 305
    Spirits, Powers, Devils, Dominions, and Principalities . . . 307
    Satan 308
    Powers of Satan 309

    Lesson: The Powers that Be 310
    Lesson: Angels and Spirits 313
    Lesson: Discerning Spirits 318
    Lesson: Weapons for Fighting Demons 321
    Lesson: Keeping Your Head 323
    Lesson: Choices 327

CONTENTS

CHAPTER FIVE ~ HOW CAN I BE SPIRITUAL?

SPIRITUAL TREASURES — **331**

- Love and Charity — 332
- Grace and Mercy — 334
- Faith and Works — 335
- Hope and Trust — 337
- Peace and Joy — 338
- Truth, Wisdom, Knowledge, and Understanding — 340

- Lesson: Freedom — 343
- Lesson: Healing — 346
- Lesson: Unconditional Love — 350
- Lesson: Home Sweet Home — 356
- Lesson: Prosperity — 359
- Lesson: Responsibility — 364

SPIRITUAL ACTS — **367**

- Repentance and Confession — 367
- Discipleship and Witnessing — 368
- Teaching — 370
- Evangelism — 371
- Holy Sacraments — 373
  - Holy Baptism — 373
  - Holy Communion — 375
- Other Holy Practices — 376
  - Confirmation — 376
  - Marriage — 377
- Worship, Praise, Thanksgiving, Offerings, and Service — 378
- Prayer — 381
  - Prayer Guide — 384
- The Creed — 387

- Lesson: Gone but Not Forgotten — 389
- Lesson: Bearing Good Fruit — 393
- Lesson: Using Our Talents — 396
- Lesson: The Holy Sacraments — 401
- Lesson: Sacrifice — 407
- Lesson: The Witness as Preacher — 412

CONTENTS

CHAPTER SIX ~ WHAT IS EVIL?

SIN AND TEMPTATION **415**

    What Is Sin? 415
    Original Sin 415
    People Are Sinful by Nature 416
    People Can Resist Temptation 416
    The Result of Sin Is Death 417
    Satan Appeals to Our Desires when Tempting Us to Sin . . 418
    Greed and Riches 419
    Lust 420
    Sexual Deviancy 422
    Abortion 423
    Pride versus Humility 424
    Hatred and Anger 426
    Lying and Deceit 429
    Gluttony 430
    Laziness and Idleness 432
    The Eight Deadly Sins 432

    Lesson: The Ten Commandments 434
    Lesson: Sinfulness 442
    Lesson: Five Unnatural Sins 447
    Lesson: Bad Habits 453
    Lesson: Suffering 457

FALSE DOCTRINE **463**

    False Teachers and Fake Prophets 463
    The Occult 465
    Idolatry 465
    Swearing Oaths and Allegiances 466
    Secrecy 466
    Traditions 467

    Lesson: False Doctrine and Cults 469
    Lesson: Distortions of Christianity 475
    Lesson: World Religions 478
    Lesson: Mormonism versus Christianity 485
    Lesson: Islam versus Christianity 494
    Lesson: The Rise of Satanism 503

CONTENTS

GOOD VERSUS EVIL — 508

    Darkness of Evil versus Light of Righteousness — 508
    Fear — 509
    The Kingdom of Heaven — 512
        Paradise — 513
        Zion and the New Jerusalem — 515
    Hell — 517
    The Inheritance of the Righteous — 519
    The Fate of the Wicked — 521

    Lesson: The Salt of the Earth — 523
    Lesson: Science and Religion — 526
    Lesson: Politics and Religion — 533
    Lesson: Dreams and Visions — 537
    Lesson: Where Do We Go from Here? — 542
    Lesson: Crown of Life — 546

CHAPTER SEVEN ~ BIBLE OUTLINE

    Old Testament Books — 553
    New Testament Books — 580

    Lesson: The Trinity Revisited — 599
    Lesson: The Seven Spirits of God — 607
    Lesson: Counseling for Christ — 612
    Lesson: Mending the Broken Heart — 620
    Lesson: Remember — 623
    Lesson: Answers — 627
    Lesson: No Excuses — 630

CHAPTER EIGHT ~ BIBLE FEATURES

IMPORTANT NUMBERS — 635

    Number 2 — 635
    Number 3 — 636
    Number 4 — 639
    Number 6 — 640
    Number 7 — 641
    Number 8 — 644
    Number 10 — 645
    Number 12 — 646

CONTENTS

    Number 20 647
    Number 40 647
    Number 70 648
    Number 1000 649

FOR FURTHER STUDY 651

    Bible Study: Is Jesus God? 652
    Bible Study: How Do We Listen to God? 653
    Bible Study: Why Do People Go to Hell? 656
    Bible Study: Does Science Disagree with the Bible? . . 659
    Bible Study: Did Christ Really Rise from the Dead? . . 664
    Bible Study: How Are God and Light Alike? . . . 668
    Bible Study: Is There Proof of God? 670
    Bible Study: Is the New Testament True? 675
    Bible Study: Fulfillment of Biblical Prophecy . . . 688

DEEPER INTO THE WORD 691

    Empirical Proof that the Holy Bible Is True . . . 691

    Lesson: Lord of the Sabbath 694
    Lesson: Jesus's Last Words 699
    Lesson: Receiving the Holy Spirit 704
    Lesson: Can Spirits Be Dead? 710
    Lesson: Has Anyone Seen Heaven? 716
    Lesson: The Key to Three 720
    Lesson: Babylon: Past, Present, and Future . . . 726
    Lesson: The Great I AM 736
    Lesson: Steadfastness 739
    Lesson: The Golden Rule 743
    Lesson: If You Could Choose Your Job in Heaven . . 747

GLOSSARY OF NAMES, PLACES, AND TERMS . 752

BIBLICAL TIMELINES 769

INDEX OF KEYWORDS 773

Foreword

This study guide was compiled to teach the basic tenets of what it means to be a child of God and how to become one. The goal is to spread the Good News of Jesus Christ. It is hoped that those who are unsure about God or Christ especially would find the book helpful. This text will point at verses in the Bible to encourage you to continue reading your Bible. You probably will begin studying the Bible regularly once you realize how much you can learn.

Fundamentals of Christianity was written to be a teaching and learning tool, and a devotional and inspirational guide. The book is intended to be a resource for individuals, families, Bible School teachers, ministers, and anyone who wants to understand the Bible better or who would instruct others about God's Word. Thus, it is for anyone and everyone who seeks God's knowledge and truth. This is the fourth edition of the book which was first published in 1999. Continuous updates have been made to add clarification and material, and to correct minor errors. The book has grown from 500–800 pages over the course of twenty years and incorporates over forty years of biblical analysis and consolidation. The Keyword Index is especially helpful to rapidly conduct scriptural research on a variety of topics.

A scholarly review of fundamental biblical concepts has been organized in a logical sequence for maximum understanding. The book enables rapid cross-referencing of spiritually relevant topics to several essential Bible verses. Each section reviews important Christian issues, doctrines, or prophecies and provides numerous Old and New Testament passages defining them. In essence, a Bible study is provided for every subject. Scriptural references are ordered from Genesis to Revelation. Organized lessons summarizing important doctrines and referencing key scriptures are provided as a review. The book arranges and discusses various Bible passages in such a way as to make a point or teach a principle. The author makes no attempt to introduce new theologies, doctrines, prophecies, or beliefs, or to belabor trivialities.

The Holy Bible is regarded to be the Word of God in its entirety because the authors of the Bible were directed by God Himself to record His thoughts. While the Bible may be infallible, this text is not. Although Dr. Barber was inspired by the same Holy Spirit that moved the biblical prophets and patriarchs, he does not claim inerrancy. This book is not meant to be a substitute for studying God's Word. Readers are encouraged to compare everything they see, read, and learn with what the Holy Bible says. The Bible provides all we need to know to be a solid Christian (*sola scriptura*).

Scripture references are based on the King James Version (KJV) of the Bible; they have been paraphrased in modern English for ease of reading. The KJV is an excellent word-for-word translation from the original Greek. There are many modern translations of the Bible that are highly regarded and accepted; it is recommended that the reader obtain a few of these Bibles and compare the scriptures cited in this book. In this text, the term "Bible" is never used generically, but refers to the orthodox Christian Bible comprising the sixty-six canonical books of the Old and New Testaments.

Scriptural interpretations follow some basic rules of biblical study to include the following.

1. Translation employed must be accurate and reliable.
2. Passages are understood within context.
3. Scripture is used to interpret scripture.
4. Interpretations of all relevant scriptures must be in agreement.
5. Prophecy sometimes can be fulfilled more than once.

BOOKS OF THE BIBLE AND ABBREVIATIONS

Old Testament

BOOK	ABBREV.	BOOK	ABBREV.
Genesis	GEN	Ecclesiastes	ECC
Exodus	EXO	Song of Solomon	SOS
Leviticus	LEV	Isaiah	ISA
Numbers	NUM	Jeremiah	JER
Deuteronomy	DEU	Lamentations	LAM
Joshua	JOS	Ezekiel	EZE
Judges	JDG	Daniel	DAN
Ruth	RUT	Hosea	HOS
1 Samuel	1 SA	Joel	JOE
2 Samuel	2 SA	Amos	AMO
1 Kings	1 KI	Obadiah	OBA
2 Kings	2 KI	Jonah	JON
1 Chronicles	1 CH	Micah	MIC
2 Chronicles	2 CH	Nahum	NAH
Ezra	EZR	Habakkuk	HAB
Nehemiah	NEH	Zephaniah	ZEP
Esther	EST	Haggai	HAG
Job	JOB	Zechariah	ZEC
Psalms	PSA	Malachi	MAL
Proverbs	PRO		

New Testament

BOOK	ABBREV.	BOOK	ABBREV.
Matthew	MAT	1 Timothy	1 TI
Mark	MAR	2 Timothy	2 TI
Luke	LUK	Titus	TIT
John	JOH	Philemon	PHM
Acts	ACT	Hebrews	HEB
Romans	ROM	James	JAM
1 Corinthians	1 CO	1 Peter	1 PE
2 Corinthians	2 CO	2 Peter	2 PE
Galatians	GAL	1 John	1 JO
Ephesians	EPH	2 John	2 JO
Philippians	PHP	3 John	3 JO
Colossians	COL	Jude	JDE
1 Thessalonians	1 TH	Revelation	REV
2 Thessalonians	2 TH		

Resources

The Holy Bible in the King James Version (1984). New York: Thomas Nelson Publishers.
The Lutheran Hymnal (1982). St. Louis: Concordia Publishing House.
Service Book and Hymnal (1958). Minneapolis: Augsburg Publishing House.

Lyrics from the following hymns are provided in this book.

Abide oh Dearest Jesus (Josua Stegmann, 1588–1632)

All Glory, Laud, and Honor (John Neale, 1818–1866)

Amazing Grace (John Newton, 1725–1807)

A Mighty Fortress is Our God (Martin Luther, 1483–1546)

Beautiful Savior (Author unknown)

Blest Be the Tie that Binds (John Faucett, 1740–1817)

Built on the Rock the Church Doth Stand (Nikolai Grundtvig, 1783–1872)

Chief of Sinners Though I Be (William McComb, 1793–1873)

Crown Him with Many Crowns (Matthew Bridges, 1800–1894)

Go to Dark Gethsemane (James Montgomery, 1771–1854)

Hark, the Voice of Jesus Crying (Daniel March, 1816–1909)

Holy Ghost with Light Divine (Andrew Reed, 1788–1862)

Holy God, We Praise Thy Name (Clarence Walworth, 1820–1900)

Holy, Holy, Holy, Lord God Almighty (Reginald Heber, 1783–1826)

I Am Trusting Thee, Lord Jesus (Frances Havergal, 1836–1879)

I Know that My Redeemer Lives (Samuel Medley, 1738–1799)

I Love to Tell the Story (Katherine Hankey, 1834–1911)

Just as I Am, Without One Plea (Charlotte Elliott, 1789–1871)

Let Us Ever Walk with Jesus (Sigismund von Birken, 1626–1681)

My Faith Looks Up to Thee (Ray Palmer, 1808–1887)

Now Thank We All Our God (Martin Rinckart, 1586–1649)

Onward Christian Soldiers (Sabine Baring-Gould, 1834–1924)

Rock of Ages, Cleft for Me (Augustus Toplady, 1740–1778)

Savior, Thy Dying Love (Sylvanus Phelps, 1816–1895)

Stand Up, Stand Up for Jesus (George Duffield, 1818–1888)

Take My Life and Let It Be (Frances Havergal, 1836–1879)

The Church's One Foundation (Samuel Stone, 1810–1876)

What a Friend We Have in Jesus (Joseph Scriven, 1820–1886)

When I Survey the Wondrous Cross (Isaac Watts, 1674–1748)

Giving It All

© 1995 by Andrew Barber (PAu 1–986–264)

CHORUS
```
           A        D      A      D          A        D      E
I'm giving everything to Jesus, giving Him it all; I'm giving everything to the Lord.
      G          A       D         G           D     A        D
Every night and day He sees us, He protects us, and He frees us, so I'm giving it all to the Lord.
```

VERSE 1
```
      G         A        D              G
God gave to us His Word, that through faith we could afford
       D            G     A
To be spared from His mighty sword.
        G            A         D             G
Let us heed the sacred birth, and the death that saved the earth!
       D           G          D            G
Let us sing with joy and mirth, "Now my life has good and worth,"
         D      A        D
"Since I'm giving it all to the Lord."
```

CHORUS
I'm giving everything to Jesus, giving Him it all; I'm giving everything to the Lord.
Every night and day He sees us, He protects us, and He frees us, now let's give it all to the Lord.

VERSE 2
I was lost but now I'm found, so when Judgment comes around,
I'll be glad I'm heaven bound.
Let us sing with the chorus, "I know He won't ignore us."
"He paid the ransom for us; from death He will restore us,"
"And, I'm giving it all to the Lord."

CHORUS

VERSE 3
Well your faith and hope will grow, and the love inside will show.
You'll defeat the evil foe.
From your heart remove all greed. Help your fellow man in need.
Be fruitful, sow God's seed; you will reap above indeed,
If you've given it all to the Lord.

REPEAT CHORUS

EPILOGUE (Repeat and/or Fade)
```
           A        D A D         A         D A D
I'm giving everything to Jesus. I'm giving everything to Jesus.
```

CHAPTER ONE

WHAT IS THE BIBLE?

VALIDITY OF THE BIBLE

There is considerable proof available concerning the validity of the Holy Bible. There are four different categories of evidence that are easy to remember—just think of the word *HARP*: History, Authenticity, Reliability, and Prophecy. No other religious or spiritual account has such a vast amount of supporting evidence, yet many people still do not believe that the Bible is true. Conversely, some books on religion have no supporting evidence, yet many believe passionately in them. No written work has been interpreted and translated as many times as the Bible, indicating that the Bible is held in more esteem than any other book known to humankind. Obviously, God has a purpose that is fulfilled by His written Word, and this underlying purpose is communicated in every accepted and validated translation or interpretation of the Holy Bible.

The Bible, comprising both the Old and New Testaments, is the most important reference available to learn about God, His plans, and His will. Those who believe that God has revealed Himself in any other prophetic work are pursuing false prophets and doctrines. There is insufficient proof to suggest that any book other than the Bible is the indisputable Word of God. Certainly, there are books that provide factual information and even corroborate the truth found in the Holy Bible; but the Bible is set apart because God Himself directed the patriarchs and prophets to write His words. *Fundamentals of Christianity* is to be counted among the former group of books; in other words, it can be validated or invalidated using the words of God, but not the other way around.

History

Historical support for the Bible includes written historical records, including geological, geographical, and astronomical data and archaeological evidence.

The fact that the Bible is an accurate history book is corroborated in numerous historical accounts. For example, the Bible correctly describes the progression of empires and the reigns of monarchs, such as pharaohs of the Egyptian empire including Rameses I and II; Kings David and Solomon who ruled prior to the Assyrian era which introduced Kings Shalmaneser and Sennacherib; Kings Nebuchadnezzar and Belshazzar from the Babylonian empire; Kings Darius, Cyrus and Xerxes of the Medio-Persian empire; and Kings Augustus, Tiberius, and Nero of the Roman empire. Further, many wars and campaigns recorded in the Bible are recorded elsewhere. The achievements of the Israelites in battle were well known in other cultures. In fact, the reputation of the Israelites in battle preceded them wherever they campaigned carrying the Ark of the Covenant. Many of the events in the Bible have been documented in ancient cultures such as the Chinese and Persians to include a huge deluge and flood. Jewish and Roman historians such as Josephus and Tacitus also corroborate many occurrences in the Holy Land to include the life and death of the one called Christ.

When the Bible was written, accurate and comprehensive maps were scarce. However, the geographical and geological descriptions in the Bible are extremely precise, suggesting that they were documented by people who were there. Good examples exist in the records of the travels of Abraham, Jacob, Moses, Joshua, Paul, and Jesus.

Scientists, often in an attempt to refute the Bible, have identified natural phenomena to account for some of the cataclysmic events recorded in the Bible. Data collected via natural sciences (geology, meteorology, astronomy, etc.) have been employed to explain events including a worldwide flood, the destruction of Sodom and Gomorrah, the parting of the Red Sea, and the Star of Bethlehem. Although these were acts of God, it is possible that God employed the forces of nature to produce them. Thus, the scientific findings do not serve to refute the Bible but rather support it, because they prove that such phenomena were not only possible but indeed occurred. The following list is but a sampling of historical findings that are in agreement with biblical accounts.

- Discovery of Noah's Ark on the mountains of Ararat
- Large shelf of silt along the Euphrates River near Ur, evidence of a great ancient flood
- Baked sulfur deposits along the Jordan River where cities were hit by fire and brimstone
- Archaeological discovery of the ruins of Jericho
- Moabite stone recording the defeat of Omri in Israel
- Cuneiform from Assyrian capitol of Nineveh recording Sennacherib's conquest of Judea
- Ivory relics from the reign of King Ahab
- Archaeological discovery of the palace of Darius I at Persepolis
- Frieze from the reign of Artaxerxes depicting a lion, indicating royalty
- Archaeological discovery of ruins and artifacts from the palace of King Saul
- Jewish historian Josephus's review of the early Christian church
- Roman historian Tacitus's account of the crucifixion of Jesus by Pontius Pilate

The archaeological evidence supporting the Bible is overwhelming. Most scholars believe that humankind originated in the region of the Tigris and Euphrates Rivers, also the site of the Garden of Eden according to the book of Genesis. The theorized spread of civilization from that area is consistent with biblical accounts. An enormous, ancient ark, with several levels and partitions, has been spotted on numerous occasions on the mountains of Ararat (which spread from Turkey to Iran). The book of Genesis tells the story of Noah, whose ark came to rest in that location. Ancient stone ruins called the ziggurat at Ur is a popular attraction near the Euphrates River; Ur was the original homeland of renown patriarch Abraham. These ruins are among the oldest and most intact ever discovered and resemble a giant, multilevel structure, similar to the Tower of Babel described in Genesis which was referred to as the House of Nimrod in Jewish culture. Archaeologists have uncovered cities along the Jordon River banks which were destroyed by fire and brimstone, and likely include the remains of Sodom and Gomorrah. A number of stone structures in Egypt have been associated with the reigns of the pharaohs Rameses I and II which occurred coincident with the life of Moses. No doubt, many of these edifices were built by the Hebrews who were enslaved there. Ruins of the ancient city of Jericho have been examined, and archaeologists have concluded that the walls of the city collapsed and fell, consistent with the biblical account in the book of Joshua. These are but a few of the countless archaeological finds that can be linked to events recorded in the Bible.

Authenticity

Thousands of manuscripts and documents have contributed to the development of the Bible as we know it. These written accounts have been studied extensively by theologians and scholars. The origin of these documents can be traced with reasonable accuracy, revealing location, date, and oftentimes, author. There is a great deal of consistency among the various authors who recorded events in the Bible. Many of these authors were eyewitnesses to the events they recorded. This has been verified by placing the authors and manuscripts at the appropriate time and location that the events took place.

The Bible is set apart from other books in that it is a compilation of sixty-six books, produced by a multitude of authors (forty or so), from different eras of history, in a number of different languages including Hebrew, Greek, and Aramaic. Biblical manuscripts were aggregated by large groups of religious scholars who agreed on the authenticity, authorship, and interpretations of the various works. Those compiling the canon of scripture found considerable consistency between the authors and among the various books comprising the Bible. This redundancy allowed scholars to accurately aggregate the available information and reach a consensus concerning its meaning, relevancy, and origin. Other religions, such as Islam, Buddhism, and Mormonism, are based on the teachings or writings of a single individual. Unfortunately, their supposed connection to God cannot be corroborated elsewhere in historical databases, or by other prophets and authors; further, there is little if no supporting physical evidence for purported events recorded by their so-called prophets. These texts also have undergone numerous revisions since their inception. If the works were truly ordained by God, why would He provide no additional support for their authenticity as He has with the Bible? And why would the works need to be modified at all?

The discovery of ancient scrolls has occurred several times throughout history. Many of these manuscripts were transcribed by Jews who lived in the region of Palestine. The discovery of the Dead Sea Scrolls was among the most significant in recent history. Some of the scrolls were written around the time of Christ and describe the arrival of a messianic prophet. They appear to describe the ministry of Christ, adding further credibility to the New Testament. Among these scrolls is the entire book of Isaiah without revisions, proving that reproductions were meticulously accurate. Though this manuscript is over two thousand years old, it is virtually identical in content to the book of Isaiah found in modern Bibles. Arguments that the Bible has lost its meaning over time due to retranslation are therefore unsupported by the facts. A great number of additional discoveries have added to the authenticity of the Bible. For more information, it is recommended that the reader research the available literature on biblical archaeology and history, Christian dogmatics, hermeneutics, and the canonization of scripture. These topics are discussed in detail in this text (refer to the Index of Keywords).

Reliability

Numerous authors reported biblical events independently of each other, yet their accounts are remarkably similar. A good example is found in the first four books of the New Testament. Some of the events recorded by these Gospel writers were witnessed firsthand and some were described as a result of interviews with eyewitnesses. Although each author had his own writing style and independently provided specific details about the life and ministry of Christ, they were in agreement with their accounts, particularly concerning some very momentous events. There are extensive cross-references in the Bible that add to its reliability, which this book illustrates.

For example, visions concerning the latter days, provided by prophets such as Isaiah, Jeremiah, Ezekiel, Daniel, John, Paul, Jesus, and others fit together. One cannot easily comprehend the events leading up to Christ's return without reading all the biblical excerpts, both from the Old and the New Testaments. Each prophet visualized the events differently, and it is obvious in their writings that they didn't merely copy their ideas from another. Yet, each prophet provided separate pieces to a puzzle that collectively produce a greater picture or vision. A good example relates to the progression of kingdoms prophesied by Daniel (the four kings) and completed in John's Revelation (the eight kings). Another example can be found in the descriptions of heaven by Ezekiel and John (Revelation).

It is amazing how a book comprised of thousands of texts, produced over thousands of years, by authors of different regions, languages, and times could be so perfectly integrated. If a room full of independently enlightened prophets congregated over several years, they would not be able to collectively produce an anthology as cohesive as found among the books of the Bible.

Of primary significance is the agreement between the Old and New Testaments. In fact, the two cross-validate each other, resulting in the great mysteries of God being revealed to humanity. The Old Testament, which is based on the original covenant founded in God's Law, provides the transition and promise of the New Testament, which is based on the New Covenant of Grace founded in Jesus Christ. That is, the entire Old Testament points to the coming of a Messiah, and that prophecy is fulfilled in the New Testament, which documents the life and purpose of Christ the Messiah. Thus, the New Testament (NT) validates the Old Testament (OT), and vice-versa. Those who assert that there are conflicts in the Bible are mistaken. In fact, the internal consistency in the Bible exceeds statistical significance. It takes several readings to grasp the intricate workings of scripture, but with careful study, the reader will find that everything congeals perfectly.

Prophecy

The most compelling evidence for the validity of the Bible is the accuracy of the prophecies. Prophecies in the Bible are extremely specific and detailed. No other religious work is this accurate. Other so-called prophetic works provide vague and general statements like those of Nostradamus. Such imprecise predictions can be attributed to any number of events in history.

However, biblical prophecy leaves nothing to the imagination. A good example exists in the prophecies of Elijah concerning the deaths of King Ahab and his wife Jezebel. Elijah's prophecies were accurate to the finest detail, and all came true just as he predicted. Elijah declared that dogs would lick the blood of Ahab's corpse at the same location in which dogs had licked the blood of Naboth, who was murdered by the order of Ahab and Jezebel. He also declared that dogs would eat and scatter the dead remains of Jezebel. What a way to go, huh? Another example is the prophecy of Daniel who accurately declared that Babylon would fall and further named the empires that would follow including Media-Persia and Greece. Each of these prophecies can be linked to one, and only one, event or phase in history. Foreseen events often occurred hundreds of years after the prophet's death.

OT prophecies concerning the birth, life, ministry, suffering, and death of Messiah are amazingly precise and detailed. Abraham, Moses, David, Isaiah, Jeremiah, Micah, and Zechariah were noted messianic prophets. These and other OT prophets provided several reconcilable truths about Messiah's coming (see Chapter Three). Their prophecies were fulfilled in Jesus Christ as recorded in the NT. Further, Jesus Himself gave a complete and accurate account of His future fate to the apostles, prior to His death and resurrection.

Messiah was foretold to be born of a virgin in a town called Bethlehem. His ancestors would include Abraham, Isaac, Jacob, Judah, Jesse, David, and Solomon. Kings from the east bringing gifts of gold and incense would worship Him. Messiah would be called the Prince of Peace, the only Son of God, and the right hand of God. He would heal the lame and the blind. He would show the way of salvation to the Gentiles (non-Jews). He would ride triumphantly yet humbly on a donkey's colt. He would be betrayed for the price of thirty pieces of silver, which would be paid to purchase a potter's field that would become a graveyard for paupers. He would suffer and die to save humankind from sin and death. His hands and feet would be pierced and He would be tortured to death. People would gamble for His clothes. He would live as a poor man, yet He would be buried in a rich man's grave. He would arise from the dead and his life would be prolonged. All these prophecies came true in Christ the Lord. The mathematical probability that some other Messiah could fulfill all Old Testament prophecies (over three hundred) is astronomically small (estimated in scholarly probability studies to be one over a trillion times a trillion), thereby rendering the probability that Christ is the Messiah to be a statistical certainty.

There is no way that humans could produce such a truthful, prophetic, inspirational, and reliable work as the Holy Bible without God's intervention. And the Bible has withstood the test of time, presenting the exact truth and providing spiritual guidance to all people of the world: past, present, and future. That is why Christianity is the primary religion of the world today. People want the truth because truth always prevails in the end; and they find that truth in the words of God.

Religion and Geography

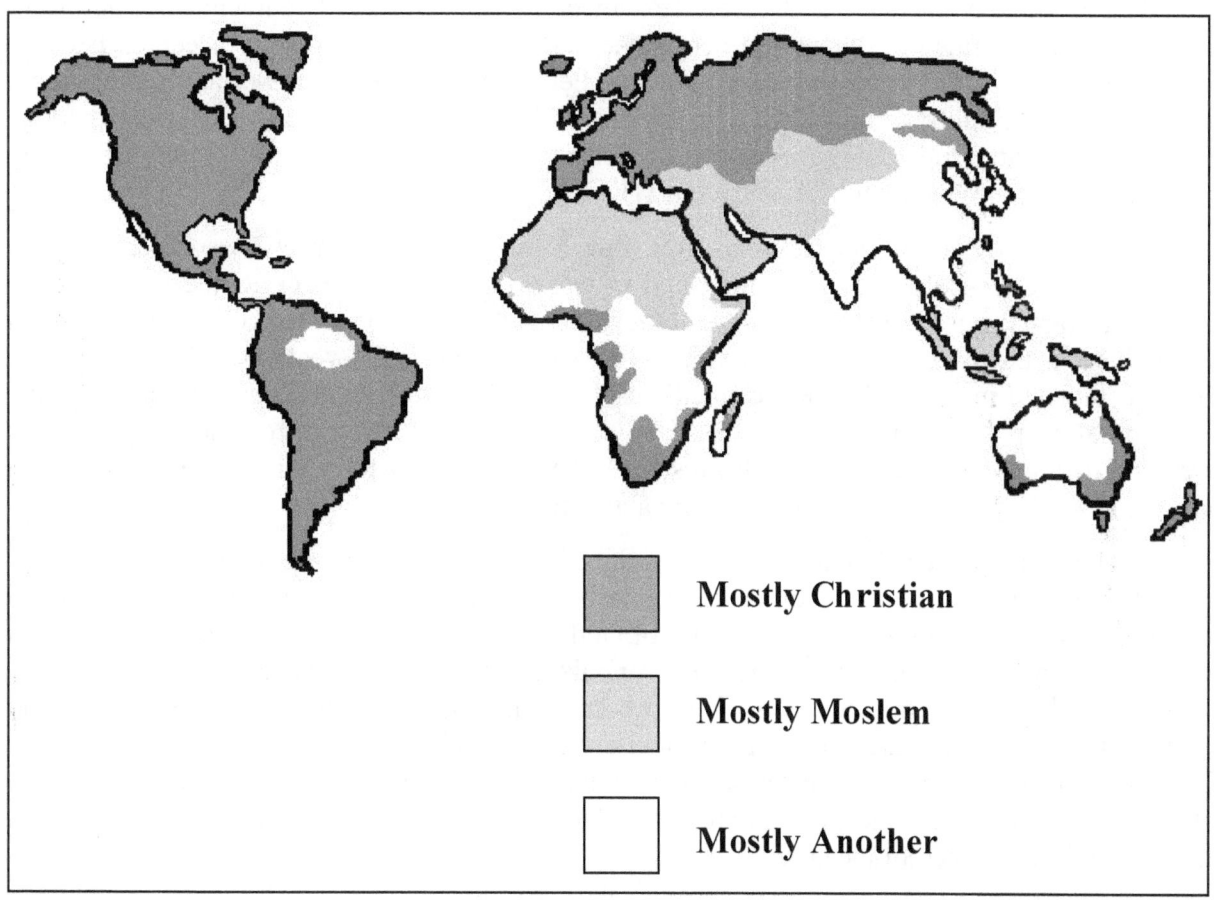

The Canonization of Scripture

The word "canon" comes from the Greek *kanon*, which means standard or rule. There was a need for such a standard in the early church, since a large number of supposed "inspired" works were circulating. The apostles were dead, as well as other eyewitnesses that could attest to the truth. Christians were being persecuted, and secular governments were determined to destroy all knowledge of and references to Jesus Christ. In order to establish the true Word of God, identify false teachers and prophets, and preserve the truth for everyone, standards were needed for distinguishing works inspired by God from those that were not.

In addition to the proliferation of apocryphal works that imitated scripture, numerous false prophets and teachers began infiltrating the church. It seems that divine revelation was the popular platform for anyone claiming to be sent by God. Many of these heretics were gaining followers adding further to the confusion. Church leaders realized that they had to agree on what was truly scriptural. Such a standard would be required in order to refute the words of the false teachers and fake messiahs. Besides, reading from scripture was an essential part of Christian worship, so it was necessary to identify those passages that could be classified as doctrinal.

A number of criteria were established that were applied to the various works being considered for inclusion into the canon of scripture. The Old Testament, itself having been scrutinized by the Jews during its canonization, was accepted in due course. Since divine inspiration was the goal, and since the apostles were eyewitnesses commissioned by Christ Himself, any treatise that could be verified as being authored by an intimate companion of Christ (such as an apostle) was deemed worthy of inclusion into the New Testament. Another critical element was consistency with other scripture and with accepted doctrine. The Gospels were the first documents to be included in the New Testament, as they were easily authenticated and were in agreement in terms of content and consistency. The Epistles were readily accepted because they either were written by apostles such as Paul, Peter, and John, or by important leaders in the early Christian church including the companions of Paul (e.g., Luke) and the half-brothers of Christ (James and Judah). These writings were in concert with other scriptures, endorsing authorship by close companions of Christ and His inner circle.

The twenty-seven books comprising our New Testament largely were accepted by theologians of the early church, as indicated in works dating as far back as the first century. Then, an extensive canonical process was undertaken within the Roman Catholic Church. Seven ecumenical councils were convened, with the first occurring in the year AD 325 and the last being completed in AD 787. These councils resolved such issues as the nature of humanity, the divinity of Christ, sanctification by the Holy Spirit, and the doctrine of the Holy Trinity. Development of statements of faith also resulted, such as the Apostolic, Nicene, and Athanasian creeds. In total, some 4700 manuscripts were authenticated.

The Old and New Testaments have remained intact since their original inception into the Holy Bible. That is, the Holy Bible continues to be recognized by all Christians and associated evangelical denominations as the true Word of God. However, the Catholic Bible often includes certain apocryphal works that were not canonized and are not recognized as scripture, particularly by Protestants. Some of these works supported doctrines such as purgatory and praying to saints which are not scriptural and are exclusively Catholic. In fact, the Protestant Reformation spawned precisely because the church had elevated some of its own traditions to the stature of doctrine, with the main premise of Martin Luther being that scripture alone should determine doctrine and not the church leaders.

Lesson: Biblical Hermeneutics

Definitions

Canonization of scripture is the process whereby the thirty-nine books of the Old Testament (OT) and the twenty-seven books of the New Testament (NT) were authenticated. The word canon means standard or rule; to be included into the canonical books of the Bible, a manuscript underwent intense scrutiny during which rules of authenticity and reliability were applied to determine if the document adhered to very strict standards. For example, the twenty-seven canonical books of the New Testament were verified as authentic, complete, and homogenous in their entirety. They were not viewed as an assemblage of disparate independent works, even though they were written by different people some five to fifty years after Jesus Christ's resurrection. New Testament analysis incorporated an examination of relevant OT scriptures as a means of further validating meaning, intent, and usage of the NT.

Hermeneutics is the science of properly deriving meaning from written works using sound principles of interpretation. ***Biblical Hermeneutics*** are applied to derive the intended meaning of scripture from the perspective of the Holy Spirit who inspired it. ***Exegesis*** is an analytical explanation or clarification of written material, especially of a religious nature. Regarding the Holy Bible it must be emphasized that God does not contradict Himself, enabling one scripture to be interpreted in light of similar scriptures.

Hermeneutics uses reasonable investigative methods to uncover the truth by ascertaining answers to basic questions concerning written material: who, what, why, when, where, how.

- What do we know about the author (can the author be identified)?
- When was the work written?
- Where did the author live?
- What did the author have to say (what is the message)?
- Who was the intended audience?
- Why was the author writing to this particular audience?
- How did the author present the message (linguistics, genre, style)?
- Why did the author present it that way?
- What was noteworthy about the cultural influence, the sociopolitical climate, and the pivotal events at the time the work was written?

Sound Hermeneutic Principles

1. Historical and Cultural Perspectives: The evaluator will develop an understanding of the author's background, timeline, culture, government, geography, historical data, customs, laws, and situational conditions underlying the original text as well as the life and times of the peoples and places. Thorough research of the secular literature, archaeology, geology, and archives from history and science may corroborate many of the facts found in the work. Not only does such investigation add to the meaning, it provides elaboration and context. Interestingly, many events recorded in the Bible are supported by ancient literature from a variety of cultures and by secular historians, thereby contributing to the authentication and interpretation of scripture. For example, many modern historians regard the book of Luke to be an extraordinary exposition of the life, events, figures, and times of first century Palestine. This is because of the amazing degree of applicable detail that Luke provides, most of which has been proven to be historically accurate (LUK 1:1–5; LUK 2:1–3; LUK 3:1–3).

2. Linguistic Construction: This rule utilizes the grammar, syntax, vocabulary, word usage, definitions, sentence construction, punctuation, tense, and other characteristics of the language of the original text to generate insight and understanding from the written words (read ACT 17:18–34). Note that the Old Testament was written primarily in Hebrew and the New Testament was written primarily in Greek. It is helpful to understand how people formed and communicated ideas, what certain words and phrases meant, and how it all translates into modern English. Anyone that has ever learned a foreign language or other communication system (even a computer language) knows that precise translation to or from English is not possible. This is because words and phrases may not transfer directly from one language to the other in a word-for-word manner; context, consistency, authorship, and intent help to rectify such differences.

3. Contextual Translation: Before interpreting a word, phrase, statement, or concept one must examine the entire context, to include passages before, surrounding, and after the passage being examined, as well as the section, chapter, book, and testament in which the passage is located. The *Threefold Principle* (Hartill, 1947) infers that some biblical truths are presented in sets of three: past (justification), present (transformation), and future (consummation) (read 2 CO 1:9–13; TIT 2:11–15). In the case of repeated themes dealing with the same idea or topic, one can apply *Subdivided Context Principles* as follows (ibid).

    - The First Mention Principle states that the particular truth implicit in the first occurrence connects additional passages addressing the subject. A great example is our initial introduction to the character and methods of Satan (GEN 3:1–15).
    - The Progressive Mention Principle infers that God makes the revelation of any given truth increasingly clearer as the idea or concept progresses into an inevitably comprehensive explanation. A wonderful example is the progression of OT prophecies that point to the Messiah, all of which were fulfilled during the course of Christ's birth, life, ministry, death, and resurrection as documented in the NT (ISA 53).
    - The Comparative Mention Principle is applied to compare and contrast passages by examining similarities or differences, respectively, as well as their magnitude. Careful analysis reveals sufficient commonality or diversity to either connect or disconnect one passage from another. For example, an interesting connection is made when comparing the four kings discussed in Daniel (DAN 2; DAN 7:17) with the eight kings discussed in Revelation (REV 17:9–11).
    - The Full Mention Principle asserts that God makes vital concepts entirely coherent. For example, Jesus affirmed repeatedly that He would be killed and would rise from the dead after three days (MAT 12:39–40; MAT 26:31–32; MAT 27:62–63; MAR 10:33–34; JOH 2:18–21).

4. Literal and Symbolic Interpretations: It is important to consider who is saying what, and how, and why they are saying it. Literal translation follows the common sense rule. Most words used in the Bible have a common meaning (depending on context); when symbolism, metaphor, or exaggeration is used it is relatively obvious. For example, is Satan a snake (GEN 3:1–15), a dragon (REV 12), or a fallen angel (ISA 14:12–15)? Did Jesus really mean you should pluck out your eye if you sin in what you see (MAT 18:9)? Keep in mind that the use of symbolism doesn't necessarily mean that the passage cannot be taken literally (JOH 2:18–21). Certain presentations or sayings connote symbolism such as the use of numbers, parables, depictions, and illustrations. These may teach a lesson, provide a comparison, or establish a conceptualization. On the other hand, some demonstrations are very precise and detailed as in the case of histories and prophecies.

5. Application Rule: Although every verse in the Bible may have a unique meaning, it also may have several possible applications. But an application only can be drawn given the correct interpretation; otherwise, all such applications will be false. Further some truths or concepts are deliberately repeated and each adds substantiation and detail to the thought, making the application quite straightforward. Obviously, if the Lord Jesus is making an application it is because He wants us to do the same; that is, we can apply it to our own lives just as He was applying it to others at that time (MAT 22:15–22). This principle also would hold true if God, a prophet of God, an apostle, or any writer of scripture inspired directly by the Holy Spirit was presenting such an application (1 JO 4:1–4).

6. Cross Validation Rule: The first tenet of this rule is that the Old and New Testaments cross validate one another (GAL 3:24; ROM 3:21–26; HEB 8; HEB 10:14). For example, sometimes a prophecy given in the OT is fulfilled in the NT (especially the prophecy concerning Messiah). And the Old Covenant of the Law points to the New Covenant of Grace that succeeds it. We also see extensive quoting of the OT by Jesus, NT authors, and witnesses. An exciting progression of scriptural illumination proceeds from Genesis to Revelation. In short, we cannot understand completely one testament without the other. Secondly, the entire Bible has internal consistency and reliability. Relationships exist among passages and events presented throughout the Bible that address the same topic or illustrate the same principle. This harmony and trustworthiness found in the Bible allows one scripture to be interpreted by the rest of scripture (2 TI 3:15–16; 2 PE 3:13–16).

7. The Perfect Standard Rule: The purpose of the Bible is for God to communicate real truth to whoever reads it (JOH 1:1; JOH 4:14; JOH 14:16–17; JOH 16:12–16; 1 JO 5:6). There is no such thing as relative truth, since a proven fact is absolutely true for everybody, anytime, anywhere. God's Word is never vague when it comes to establishing absolute truth or an essential doctrine of the faith. Such wisdom is clearly presented and continuously supported. An essential truth, doctrine, or theological argument is not going to hang on one ambiguous passage taken out of context; but the unambiguous passages can be used to interpret the ambiguous ones. Additionally, God's perfect standard of morality is clearly outlined in His laws, statutes, and precepts (PSA 100:5; ECC 7:20; MAR 10:17–18; ROM 13:8–10; GAL 5:14). The foundation of our human morality is God's unconditional love which He has bestowed upon all people and which is patently seen in Jesus Christ (MAT 22:35–40; JOH 13:34; JOH 15:13). Note that there is an implied hierarchy within the moral law that focuses on the greater good; this is evident in the Ten Commandments. Additional examples would be taking a life during the course of saving or protecting the innocent, or declaring war on evil (for example, against the Third Reich). Remember this: scripture will never violate God's perfect will (ISA 8:20; JER 23; ROM 8:28).

8. Law of Non-Contradiction: Scriptural interpretations must be consistent with the rest of scripture. Inconsistency in timeframe, location, intention, or application could negate connection among passages, as that might alter the intended meaning of a passage. For example, established prophecy cannot contradict other prophecy referring to the same event; otherwise it would be impossible to determine which is true. If two prophecies seem in conflict it is likely because they are not addressing the same topic. God's declared will and promises are not subject to debate or scrutiny. Therefore, any derived interpretation that is incongruent with God's message is necessarily false (ISA 44:25; JER 14:14; GAL 1:6–12; 2 TH 2:9–11; 2 TI 4:3–4). That includes sayings, beliefs, or assumptions contradicting what Christ and the apostles taught, or opposing established dogmas and doctrines advanced within the canonical books of the Bible and practiced by Bible-based denominations. Proper application of biblical hermeneutics helps to resolve supposed conflicts and ambiguities.

9. Inerrancy Standard: Related to the above principle, Christian dogmatics addressing essential doctrines of the faith will never change. Therefore, in order for purpose and meaning to be entirely unalterable, the Bible must be without any errors that could confuse the truth. Thoughts, interpretations, or ideas that deny or obscure the fundamentals of the Christian faith are, by definition, blatantly untrue. For example, numerous extra-biblical sources deny the deity of Christ (ISA 7:14; ISA 9:6; ISA 43:10–11; JOH 10:30,38; COL 2:9) and that Christ is the author of eternal life (JOH 3:16; JOH 5:25; JOH 11:25–26; JOH 14:6; ROM 6:23; COL 3:4); some deny that Christ is the voice of God's Word (JOH 1:1,14; JOH 5:19–47; JOH 6:30; JOH 10:25–30) and the finisher of God's work (MAT 5:17; JOH 19:30; ROM 5:6–11; 2 CO 5:21; COL 1:1–20; HEB 12:1–3). Note that one may discover copyist errors, variations in word usage or spelling, and other inconsistencies in manuscripts or translations, all of which are irrelevant if the meaning of the text and the accuracy of the account remain clear and unchanged; such examples do not violate the inerrancy principle. God guided His appointed ones to write down His true thoughts, which are recorded in the style and understanding of the authors; that is, the Bible was inspired by God not induced by Him (2 PE 1:20–21). However, God ensured that each author properly transcribed His message, and God ensured that the meaning would not change over time. In the Holy Bible, God has produced and preserved the truth for all people that desire to know it.

10. Literary Genre Analysis: Different types of literature can have implications or intentions, such as prose contrasted with poetry. For example, poetry is frequently associated with songs of praise, worship, and inspiration, while prose is commonly used in historical narratives, prophecy, and letters. Look for the use of figurative language, allegory, metaphor, analogy, irony, or hyperbole before interpreting a passage literally as opposed to symbolically. Be careful not to make an inference of revelation when the purpose is illumination. Recognize the difference between a suggestion and a conviction. Some genres and their possible applications are listed below.

    - Pentateuch (Torah): Genesis, Exodus, Leviticus, Numbers, Deuteronomy
    - Gospels: Matthew, Mark, Luke, John
    - Epistles: Romans, 1st and 2nd Corinthians, Galatians, Ephesians, Philippians, Colossians, 1st and 2nd Thessalonians, 1st and 2nd Timothy, Titus, Philemon, Hebrews, James, 1st and 2nd Peter, 1st, 2nd, and 3rd John, Jude

    - History: Genesis, Exodus, Numbers, Joshua, Judges, Ruth, 1st and 2nd Samuel, 1st and 2nd Kings, 1st and 2nd Chronicles, Ezra, Nehemiah, Esther, Job, Hosea, Jonah, Gospels, Acts
    - Biography/Genealogy: Genesis, Exodus, Numbers, 1st and 2nd Samuel, 1st and 2nd Kings, 1st and 2nd Chronicles, Ruth, Esther, Matthew, Luke, Acts
    - Law: Exodus, Leviticus, Gospels, Romans, Hebrews, James
    - Wisdom/Teaching: Deuteronomy, Job, Proverbs, Ecclesiastes, Gospels, Epistles
    - Songs/Poetry: Psalms, Song of Solomon, Lamentations
    - Prophecy/Eschatology: Isaiah, Jeremiah, Ezekiel, Daniel, Hosea, Joel, Amos, Obadiah, Jonah, Micah, Nahum, Habakkuk, Zephaniah, Haggai, Zechariah, Malachi, Gospels, 1st Corinthians, 1st Thessalonians, Revelation

Common Mistakes (bad exegesis)

1. Investigator Bias: Everyone interprets information based on their individual worldview. Therefore, the beliefs one brings into the examination of information can limit the possible interpretations or skew the analytical results. A common fallacy is when we assume objectivity; the reader may suppose he or she is completely unbiased and not incorporating his or her personal views when drawing conclusions. Unfortunately, it is impossible to completely disregard preexisting assumptions or opinions, which is why we must ensure that all presuppositions are scripturally supported. Anyone can make the Bible say whatever they want it to say, as people often do. They tend to force messages into their internal models rather than allowing the words to guide their understanding and shape their beliefs (PSA 37:23; PSA 119:105; PRO 3:5–6; PRO 16:1; PRO 19:21).

2. Misapplication: This includes reading into the Bible rather than reading out of it, like trying to discount what the Bible is reiterating in order to justify a lifestyle, behavior, or worldview. Over-allegorizing can occur when the reader/interpreter takes figurative language too literally; analogy, irony, symbolism, characterization, and figures of speech are examples of figurative language. Taking things too literally can happen when one interprets a metaphor or allegory as a command or precept (again MAT 18:9). Reading something into scripture might occur when one places emphasis on a possible interpretation or explanation instead of the probable one. Some people erroneously assume that every passage of scripture has a hidden spiritual truth; the individual peruses the Bible in search of spiritual revelation alone and not for content. Another common mistake is assuming that some theological beliefs are outdated and no longer apply, wherein an important precept is ignored (MAT 5:17–18). Occasionally, the reader overlooks why the Bible is saying something and focuses only on what is said, missing how it is to be applied.

3. Misinterpretation: Scripture affirms certain truths implicitly and explicitly. Mistakes in interpretation result when the implicit is used to explain the explicit, or the possible is used to explain the probable, or the uncertain is used to explain the certain. It has to be the other way around, whereby concreteness in meaning unpacks ambiguity. Common misinterpretations happen when assuming there is a contradiction when there is not (PRO 26:4–5), viewing a proverb as a promise (PRO 22:6), and taking words or phrases out of context (JAM 2:17). Neglecting to recognize what the Bible has constantly affirmed can have dire consequences when it comes to salvation (EPH 2:8–9; COL 2:8). And when it is not crystal clear, God may have a reason for that; we may not have a "need to know." For example, Christ told us bluntly that nobody knows the time of His return (MAR 13:32); John also was instructed by Christ not to reveal everything that was revealed to him (REV 10:4).

4. Fabrication: This is when deductions are based on references outside of scripture, or they are based on scriptural events or passages taken out of context. Skeptics often challenge the historical or theological accuracy of the Bible by introducing a poor or inaccurate foundation of evidence. They will refute the inerrancy of the Bible without sufficient knowledge of what it says, often because they never actually studied it thoroughly. Such imposters are ignorant of the historicity of the Bible, the overwhelming proof of its accuracy, and the corroborative evidence from the secular world. It is really strange when learned scholars try to discredit the Bible by drawing illogical conclusions, presenting irrelevant findings, or using circular reasoning to bolster their case. These are a total violation of the scientific method, the practice of hermeneutics, and the very fundamentals of pragmatic study that are supposed to guide such conclusions (MAT 28:11–15).

5. New Revelation: Imposters and deceivers invent new scripture or testaments, and proclaim extra-biblical works as being inspired by God. They may attempt to introduce non-authenticated works as canonical or interpret biblical concepts or events using non-biblical sources. If it does not agree with what the Bible says, it is not inspired by God (1 TH 5:21; 2 TH 2:11–13). Many recently formed cults (within the past two centuries) are based on different translations or significant alterations of the Bible, rendering their entire philosophy as false and contrary to Christianity. Their leaders and teachers are mistaken, they are following the wrong path, and/or they are attempting to lead others astray (DEU 4:2; PRO 30:5–6; REV 22:18–19). Such are the tactics of Satan whose primary motive is to deceive (REV 12:12).

Talmudical Hermeneutics

The Talmud consists of rabbinical teachings of the historic Jewish faith. Hermeneutical methods were used by scholarly Jews to ascribe meaning to scripture. Rabbis obtained and passed along oral and written material that were accepted interpretations of Jewish doctrine and history. This knowledge was delivered to successive generations in order to maintain consistency. The objectives were to establish the precise meaning of original works at the time they were written, and maintain the integrity of that meaning for generations to follow. Some of the principles they used are listed below (*Jewish Encyclopedia*, 1901–1906). Note that word play and letter counting were employed to validate meaning already determined through tradition or rabbinic rulings.

- Interpretation of certain words and letters, missing words or letters, prefixes and suffixes
- Interpretation of those letters which, in certain words, are provided with points
- Interpretation of the letters in a word according to their numerical value
- Interpretation of a word by dividing it into two or more words
- Interpretation of a word according to its consonantal form or according to its vocalization
- Interpretation of a word by transposing its letters or by changing its vowels
- Interpretation of Jewish laws from a scriptural text or other Jewish teaching

References

Hartill, J. E., (1947). *Principles of Biblical Hermeneutics.* Grand Rapids, MI: Zondervan Publishing House.

Jewish Encyclopedia (1901–1906). New York: Funk and Wagnalls.

http://www.forananswer.org

http://www.theopedia.com

Lesson: Synopsis of the Bible

God gave Adam and Eve the ability to discern good and evil. They ate the forbidden fruit and were expelled from the Garden of Eden. God placed cherubim and a flaming sword to guard the entrance to the garden. And God knew He would have to abolish sin someday, once and for all.

God was disappointed with humans. They were sinful to the core. He destroyed the earth with a flood because of the wickedness that existed. However, he saved Noah and his family because of Noah's faith, and made a covenant with him.

The Sword of Justice

After freeing the Hebrew slaves from Egyptian rule, God decreed to them His Covenant of the Law through Moses. That Old Covenant included the promise of a New Covenant.

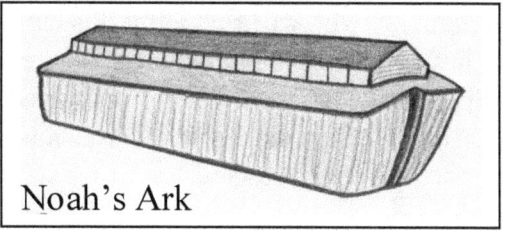

Noah's Ark

The Holy Bible reveals the mystery of salvation based on God's Grace and our Faith. The Old Testament declared a New Testament which is Jesus Christ. God sent His only Son into the world to be the light that shows us the pathway to heaven; all that is required is to follow Him.

God's Word is a lamp that lights the Way home.

The Law

Jesus Christ is the source of our faith and the anchor to our soul. If we become grafted to Him, we will bear good fruit.

Jesus Christ is the Messiah, the New Covenant spoken of by prophets such as Abraham, Moses, Isaiah and others. Christ died for our sins and rose from the dead, thereby overcoming this world of sin, and reconciling God's people unto Himself forever.

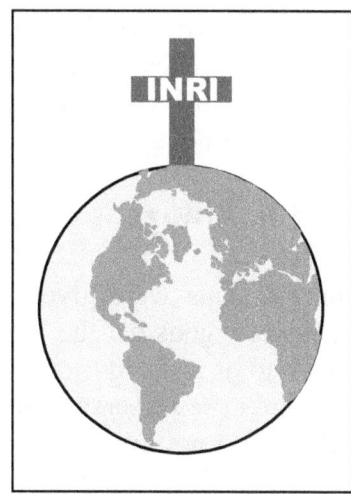

CHAPTER ONE

INSTRUCTIONS ON HOW TO LIVE

Although written by men, the Holy Bible is God's Word, inspired by the Holy Spirit. Therefore, it is important to read the Bible constantly, because every time the Bible is studied new insights are sure to emerge. This is because it is God's Holy Spirit speaking through the written Word. You always can read the Bible and learn something, even if you have read it ten thousand times.

The Holy Bible has been given to us by God to learn about Him. The Bible also provides guidelines about how we should conduct our lives. When it comes to God and our spiritual health, there is much to learn. However, the principal concepts of Christianity have been summarized in this study guide. The reader is encouraged to continue absorbing the scriptures daily. The following are imperative things a person should understand from the Bible and from this text.

- Seek God and His love, and you will find Him; this can be done by studying His Word.
- Try to obey God's laws and pray to Him always.
- Believe in God's Son Jesus Christ and you will be saved.
- Understand that Jesus Christ, the Holy Spirit, and God the Father Almighty are components of the one and only true God.

Seek God and His Love; Study His Word.

- DEU 4:29–31 ~ If you seek God with all your heart and soul you will find Him. If you are distressed, even in the latter times, turn to God and obey His commandments. God is merciful and He will never abandon you or destroy you; He will never forget the covenant He made with your forefathers.
- ISA 55:6–7 ~ Seek the Lord while He may be found; call upon Him while He is near. Let the wicked forsake their evil ways and their unrighteous thoughts, and return to the Lord; and He will have mercy on them and will pardon them abundantly.
- MAT 7:7 ~ Jesus taught: Ask and you will receive. Seek and you will find. Knock and the door will be opened.
- 2 TI 3:16 ~ All scripture is inspired by God. God's Word provides the doctrine of truth, refutes that which is false, and instructs all people in the ways of righteousness.
- 1 JO 4:11–12,18–19 ~ Since God loved us, we should love one another. Although nobody has seen God, if we love each other God's love will live inside us to be perfected in us. There is no fear in love, but perfect love repels fear, because fear has torment. We love God because He loved us first; but you cannot love God and hate your neighbor. For how can you love someone you haven't seen if you can't even love someone you have seen?

Obey God's Laws and Pray to Him Always.

- EXO 20:3–17 ~ The Ten Commandments were given to Moses on our behalf by God Himself. 1. Do not worship or honor any gods but the Lord God Almighty; 2. Do not make graven images and do not bow down to or serve idols; 3. Do not take God's name in vain; 4. Remember the Sabbath and keep it holy (i.e., reserved for worshipping God); 5. Honor your father and mother; 6. Do not kill; 7. Do not commit adultery; 8. Do not steal; 9. Do not commit perjury or falsely accuse anyone; 10. Do not be envious or jealous of someone else, desiring what belongs to them (including their home, spouse, belongings, etc.).

- MAT 6:9–13 ~ Jesus taught us to pray: Our Father in heaven, your name is holy. Bring us to your kingdom. Let your will be done on earth as it is in heaven. Provide us our daily needs. Forgive our sins, as we forgive others who sin against us. Lead us away from temptation and deliver us from evil. For the kingdom, power, and glory are yours forever, Amen.
- MAT 22:37–40 ~ Jesus said, "Love the Lord your God with all your heart, mind, and soul: this is the first and greatest commandment. The second is like unto the first: Love your neighbor as yourself. All the laws and the prophets depend on these two commandments."
- ROM 8:4–6 ~ Live, not according to the flesh but according to the spirit. Those who live according to the flesh set their minds on evil, but those who live according to the spirit set their minds on God. To set the mind on flesh results in death, but to set the mind on God results in peace and life.

Trust in the Salvation of Jesus Christ.

- ISA 53:10–12 ~ Yet God was pleased to bruise and grieve His Son, making His soul an offering for sin. God will prolong His days and God's pleasure will prosper in His hands. He will see the travail of His soul and be satisfied, and through knowledge of His righteous servant many will be justified, for He will bear their iniquities. God will render to Him a position of greatness and the best of the spoils, because He poured out His soul unto death. Though numbered with the transgressors, He bore their sins, interceding for them.
- MAR 16:16 ~ Jesus said, "Whoever believes and is baptized will be saved, but unbelievers will be damned."
- JOH 3:16–17 ~ Jesus said, "God loved the world so much that He sacrificed His only Son, so that anyone could believe in Him and not die, but live forever. For God sent His only Son into the world to save it not to condemn it."
- ROM 3:23; ROM 6:23 ~ Everyone has sinned and come short of God's glory. The risk of sin is death. But God's gift of eternal life is available to all through Jesus Christ our Lord.
- 1 PE 1:18–22 ~ You are not redeemed with corruptible things like gold or silver, you are redeemed with the precious blood of Christ, who was like a lamb without blemish or spots. He, who was ordained before the foundation of the world, was made manifest in these past days just for you. Believe in Him who God raised from the dead and gave glory, so that your faith and hope can remain in God. Your souls will be purified by obeying the truth that the Holy Spirit has shown you; so fervently love your brothers and sisters with a pure heart.

Honor the Father, the Son, and the Holy Spirit.

- ISA 11:1–2 ~ A descendant of Jesse called "The Branch" will be born. The Spirit of God will be upon Him: the Spirit of wisdom, understanding, counsel and might; the Spirit of knowledge and the fear of God.
- MAT 28:18–20 ~ Jesus said to His apostles just before leaving them, "All power in heaven and earth is given to me. Go and teach all nations the things I have taught you, baptizing them in the name of the Father, Son, and Holy Spirit. And remember, I will be with you always, even until the end of time."
- JOH 1:1,14 ~ In the beginning was the Word, and the Word was with God, and the Word was God. And the Word became flesh and lived among us; and we saw His glory, the glory of the Father's only Son, full of grace and truth.
- 1 JO 5:7 ~ There are three in heaven who reveal themselves to us: the Father, the Word (Christ), and the Holy Spirit; and these three are one.

CHAPTER ONE

Lesson: Understanding God, Ourselves, and Our Relationship with God

To understand God and our relationship with Him, it is necessary to grasp basic biblical principles. It is important to get used to studying God's Word and to dig deep into the scriptures. First, let us review several passages revealing what <u>the Bible tells us about God</u>.

- GEN 1:1–27 ~ God created the heavens and earth, day and night, oceans and land, and all living creatures, and He created humankind in His image.
- DEU 6:4 ~ Listen Israel, the Lord your God is one Lord.
- PSA 110:1,4 ~ The Lord said to my Lord, "Sit at my right hand and I will make your enemies your footstool." He is priest forever, after the order of Melchizedek.
- ISA 6:3 ~ They shouted, "Holy, Holy, Holy is the Lord of hosts; the whole earth is full of His glory." [Note that the word holy is repeated three times for a reason.]
- ISA 33:22 ~ The Lord is our judge, lawgiver, and king.
- ISA 48:16 ~ Come and listen. I have not spoken in secret since the beginning. I was there all along, and now, the Lord God and His Spirit have sent me.
- JER 10:10 ~ The Lord is the only true, living God.
- JOH 1:1–4,14 ~ In the beginning was the Word, and the Word was with God, and the Word was God. All things were made by Him. In Him was life, and that life was the light of humankind. The Word was made flesh and lived among us; and we saw His glory, like the glory of the only Son of the Father, full of grace and truth.
- JOH 14:6,9–11 ~ Jesus said, "I am the way, the truth, and the life; nobody comes to the Father but by me. If you have seen me, you have seen the Father, because the Father lives in me and I in Him."
- ACT 17:24 ~ God made the world and everything in it; He is Lord of heaven and earth.
- 1 CO 2:10–13 ~ God reveals His mysteries to us through His Spirit, for the Spirit searches all things, even the deepest things of God. Nobody can know the deepest thoughts of another, only the spirit within that person can know them. Similarly, nobody can know the deepest thoughts of God except His Holy Spirit. We have received the Spirit of God, not the spirit of the world, so that we might know the things that God has given to us for free. This is why we teach in accordance with the wisdom of the Spirit, not the wisdom of this world, for you cannot compare spiritual things with worldly things.
- GAL 3:20 ~ Christ, is not a mediator of one, but of many, and He is our mediator with God, who is one being.
- COL 1:12–20 ~ Give thanks to the Father, who has allowed us to partake of His inheritance, given to the saints who abide in His light. He has ransomed us from the power of darkness and delivered us to the kingdom of His dear Son Jesus Christ, who has redeemed us and forgiven us through His own precious blood. Christ is the very image of the invisible God; He is the firstborn of all living creatures. Through Him, all things were created on earth and in heaven, whether visible or invisible, including all thrones, dominions, principalities, and powers. All things were created by Him and for Him. He is before all things, and because of Him all things exist. He is the head of the body, which is the church. He is the beginning, the firstborn of the dead, and the Supreme Being above all things. God was pleased to allow His fullness to live in Christ. Christ established an everlasting peace through His blood which was shed on the cross, thereby causing all things on earth and in heaven to exist together in harmony with Him.
- COL 2:9 ~ In Jesus Christ the whole deity of God lives.

- 1 TI 2:5 ~ There is only one God, and the only mediator between Him and humankind is Jesus Christ.
- 1 JO 5:6–8,20 ~ There are three that are recorded in heaven: the Father, the Word, and the Holy Spirit. These three are one. The same three bear witness: the Spirit, the Water, and the Blood. The Spirit is the witness, because the Spirit bears the truth. We know Jesus Christ who is true so that we may know God who is true. We live in Him who has shown us His Son, the source of eternal life.

God has created people in His image, meaning <u>we are like God in many ways</u>. The Bible tells us how we are like God and how we can communicate with Him. One way we are not like God, however, is that we are sinful.

- GEN 1:26:3,22 ~ God said, "Let us make a man in our image, like us." God said, "Man is like us, able to discern good and evil. He knows not to eat the forbidden fruit."
- GEN 2:7 ~ God formed man from the dust of the earth, and breathed into his nostrils the breath of life, and man became a living soul.
- GEN 3:22 ~ God said, "Humans are like the higher-order beings because they have the knowledge of right and wrong. They can eat from the tree of life and they can live forever."
- DEU 30:19–20 ~ Moses said, "I have presented you with life and death, blessing versus cursing. I recommend that you choose life so that you and your descendants may live. I hope you choose to love God, obey his Law, and cling to Him; for He is your life and He is your time; and you will live in the land which He promised to you and your ancestors."
- JOB 12:10 ~ In His hand is every living soul.
- JOB 32:8 ~ It is the spirit in a man, the breath of the Almighty, that makes him understand.
- ECC 8:8 ~ Nobody has power over the spirit to retain it when they die, neither does anyone have any power over death. Nobody can escape death, neither can anyone be delivered from death through wickedness.
- ECC 12:7 ~ Upon death, the dust will return to earth, and the spirit will return to God who gave it.
- ZEC 12:1 ~ The Lord formed the spirit of man within him.
- MAL 2:15–16 ~ God has made and sustained for us the spirit of life.
- MAT 10:28 ~ Jesus said, "Don't fear anyone who can kill your body but not your soul; fear the One who can destroy both your body and your soul in hell."
- MAT 26:41 ~ The spirit is willing but the flesh is weak.
- JOH 6:63 ~ Jesus said, "It is the spirit that gives life, not the flesh." Jesus spoke the words of spirit and life.
- JOH 11:25 ~ Jesus said, "I am the resurrection and the life; whoever believes in me, though they were dead, yet shall they live."
- ROM 8:26–27 ~ God's Spirit helps us in our weakness; His Spirit intercedes for us when we pray. The mind of the Spirit intercedes for the saints according to God's will.
- 1 CO 3:16 ~ You are the temple of God for the Spirit of God lives in you.
- 1 CO 7:37 ~ People have the power over their own will (power to do God's will).
- 1 CO 15:20–26,44 ~ Christ arose from the dead, becoming the first to rise. Just as death came by a man, by a man has come the resurrection of the dead. Like Adam, we die, and like Christ, we will rise from the dead, Christ being the first. Christ will reign, and all His enemies will be destroyed; the last enemy to be destroyed will be death. It is our natural body that dies, it is our spiritual body that lives on after death.

- 2 CO 5:1,6–8,10,15 ~ We know that when this temple, which is our body, is dissolved, we will have a home in heaven; not a house made by hands but one that is eternal. This gives us the confidence we need, for we are living here in the flesh and absent from the Lord. We must walk by faith not by sight. I am not afraid; indeed, I yearn to be absent from this body and present with the Lord. We will appear before the judgment seat of Christ, to receive back the things we did with this body, whether good or bad. Since Jesus Christ died for all, we should dedicate our entire lives to Him who died and rose again.
- GAL 5:17–18,22–23 ~ The desires of the flesh are against the spirit, and vice-versa, for they are opposed to each other. If you are led by the Holy Spirit, you are not under the Law. The fruits of the spirit include love, joy, peace, patience, kindness, goodness, faithfulness, gentleness, and self-control.
- 1 TH 5:23 ~ May the God of peace sanctify you wholly, so that your entire spirit, soul, and body can be preserved blameless until the coming of our Lord Jesus Christ.
- HEB 4:12 ~ The Word of God is living and active, sharper than any double-edged sword, dividing the soul and spirit, and discerning the thoughts and intentions of the heart.
- JAM 1:15 ~ Lust brings forth sin. Sin, when finished, brings death.
- JAM 2:26 ~ Just as the body apart from the spirit is dead, faith apart from works is dead.
- 1 PE 2:11 ~ Abstain from the passions of the flesh, which wage war against your soul.

God communicates His love to all people through His Holy Spirit. In the Bible, God has explained the way of redemption through faith in Christ. The Bible outlines an insurance contract for eternal life in accordance with the New Covenant as described in the following passages.

- GEN 14:18–20 ~ Melchizedek, King of Salem (meaning Peace), brought wine and bread to dine with Abraham. Melchizedek was the priest of the most-high God. He blessed Abraham, and Abraham gave him a tenth of all he owned.
- GEN 17:1–7; GEN 22:1–17 ~ God made a covenant with Abraham, who loved God so much he was willing to sacrifice his first and only legitimate son and heir. Abraham's willingness to sacrifice Isaac showed he had a strong faith in God. When Isaac asked his father where the lamb was that would be used as the offering, Abraham told his son that God would provide the sacrifice. God spared Isaac because of Abraham's trust, and provided a ram to replace Isaac as the offering. God rewarded Abraham with descendants as numerous as the stars. Isaac became the father of Israel (Jacob). God's covenant with Abraham resulted in Israel becoming a great nation, chosen by God.
- GEN 18:1–3 ~ The Lord appeared to Abraham along the plains of Mamre as he sat in his tent. Abraham looked up and saw three men standing there at the tent door. When Abraham saw them, he bowed before them and said, "My Lord, if I have found favor in your sight, please promise me, I pray, that you would never leave me."
- EXO 12:3–13 ~ God renewed the covenant with Moses and the Israelites. The Israelites were commanded by God to sacrifice an unblemished male lamb and sprinkle the lamb's blood on the door. This act of faith spared the first born of Israel from God's curse on the Egyptians. The lamb's blood signified that God would protect the righteous from the angel of death on this the first Passover.
- EXO 24:7–8 ~ Moses preached about the everlasting covenant that God was going to make with all believers. After the peace offerings and burnt offerings were sacrificed, Moses sprinkled the blood of the offering on the alter and the people, to signify that their sins would be cleansed by the blood of the Lamb of God, the New Covenant.

- DEU 7:6–9 ~ You are a holy people to God, for He has chosen you to be a special people to Him, above all people on the earth. God didn't choose you and love you because you were greater in number than the others, for you were actually fewer in number. He loves you, and He keeps his holy covenant with you; He brings you out with His mighty hand and redeems you from slavery. Know then that He is God, faithful and just, who keeps His covenants and gives mercy to those who love Him and obey His commandments.
- 2 SA 7:12–13 ~ God said to David through Nathan the prophet: I will raise up one of your descendants to build my kingdom. He will be my Son and I will be His Father; and my throne will be established forever.
- ISA 2:3; ISA 11:1–4,10; ISA 42:1,6 ~ God said to Isaiah: From Zion (heaven) I have sent the Law. From Jerusalem I will send the Word. I will raise up a descendant of Jesse, and the Spirit of the Lord will be upon Him. He will possess the Spirit of wisdom, understanding, counsel, and might. He will be faithful to God and will judge with righteousness. I have given Him to you as a covenant to the people, to be a light to all nations; and all nations, including Jews and Gentiles alike, shall seek Him.
- ISA 9:6 ~ A child is born for us; a Son is given to us. The government will be upon His shoulders. His name will be called Wonderful Counselor, Mighty God, Everlasting Father, and Prince of Peace.
- ISA 53:1–12 ~ Isaiah's prophecy of the coming of the Messiah was most profound: He was despised and rejected by His own kind, a man of sorrow and grief, yet He has taken our grievances and sorrows upon Himself. We regarded Him as an outcast to God, but His wounds and afflictions were because of our sins and provided healing power to our souls. He never sinned, though He was slaughtered anyway as if a criminal, then He was buried in a rich man's grave. It was God's will to let Him be the offering for the sin of the world, and to prolong His days on earth. He, the greatest of all, bore His soul unto death to intercede for sinners and pay their penalty.
- JER 23:5–6; JER 31:31–34; JER 33:15; JER 50:4–5 ~ God said to Jeremiah: The days are coming when I will make a New Covenant with my people. It will not be like the covenant I made when I brought the Israelites out of Egypt, which they broke. The New Covenant will be this: Instead of writing my laws on stone, I will write them into the hearts of my people. They will not have to instruct others to know me, because everyone will know me, for I will forgive their sins and remove those sins forever. I will raise up a descendant of David. He will be a king and will reign with wisdom. His name will be called "The Lord our Righteousness" and He will come to save His people. The children of Israel will come weeping, seeking the Lord. They will ask the way to Zion saying, "Let us join with the Lord in a perpetual covenant that will never be forgotten."
- MAT 5:17 ~ Jesus said, "I didn't come to abolish the Law, I came to fulfill it."
- MAT 22:32 ~ Jesus said, "God said, I AM the God of Abraham, Isaac, and Jacob," implying that He is a God of the living, not a God of the dead.
- LUK 1:68–73,79 ~ The New Covenant is Jesus Christ.
- JOH 3:16 ~ God loved the world so much that He sacrificed His only begotten Son, so that anyone could believe in Him and not die, but receive eternal life.
- ROM 3:9,23–25,29 ~ Are the Jews better than the Gentiles? No! Everyone has sinned and fallen short of God's glory, and everyone is justified by the grace of Jesus Christ who died for the sins of the world. Therefore, God is not only a God of the Jews but of the Gentiles as well.
- ROM 7:7,14 ~ The Law told me what not to do, thereby revealing sin to me. So, is the Law sin? No, it is the opposite of sin. For the Law is spiritual, but I am carnal because I sin.

- 2 CO 5:19–21 ~ God was in Christ, and reconciled the world to Himself. He has not imputed our sins upon us, but rather has given us the message of reconciliation. So now we have become ambassadors for Christ, as though God was speaking His message through us, so that you too may be reconciled to Him. For He gave us His Son Jesus Christ, who knew no sin, to bear our sins, so that we could receive the righteousness of God that was in Him.
- GAL 3:16 ~ God made His promises concerning Christ to Abraham and his descendants.
- GAL 3:8–13,21–24 ~ The scriptures foretold that God would justify sinners through faith, announcing the Gospel in advance to Abraham, and promising him many descendants, one of whom would be a blessing to all nations. Those who live by faith will be blessed as Abraham was. But nobody is justified in God's sight by works of the Law, for it is written that the just will live by faith. Christ has redeemed us from the curse of the Law, being made a curse in our place, for it is written that cursed is He who is crucified on a cross. Is the Law, therefore, in opposition to God's promise? Absolutely not! For no law was given that could bring life. The scriptures tell us that the world is a slave to sin, and that the promise of life is given to all believers in Jesus Christ. Before faith in Christ came, everyone was a prisoner to the Law, kept there until faith was revealed in Christ. Hence, the Law is our teacher to bring us to faith in Christ, so that we might be justified by that faith.
- GAL 3:26,29 ~ You are the children of God because of your faith in Jesus Christ. If you belong to Christ then you are part of Abraham's chosen seed, and heirs according to God's covenant.
- GAL 4:4–7 ~ When the time was right, God sent His Son, who was born of a woman under the Old Covenant of the Law, to redeem those who were under the Law. He did this so that everyone could receive the honor of becoming adopted children of God. If you are a child of God you are no longer His servant, but a fellow heir of God through Christ.
- EPH 2:18 ~ Through Jesus Christ we have access, by one Spirit, to God.
- COL 1:19–22 ~ God was pleased to have His fullness living in Christ, so that through Him, everything on earth and in heaven could be reconciled to Himself, by the peace that came through the shedding of Christ's blood on the cross. Before, you were separated from God; you were His enemies because of your sinful minds and evil deeds. But now, God has reconciled you by the body of Christ through His death, to be presented holy, blameless, and pure in the sight of God.
- HEB 5:9–10; HEB 6:19–20; HEB 8:10 ~ God made Christ perfect, and the author of eternal salvation for all who obey Him. He was called by God to be the high priest, like the forerunner Melchizedek. We have Jesus as a sure and steadfast anchor for our souls. According to His covenant, the Lord has placed His Law into our minds and written it upon our hearts.
- HEB 7:1–28 ~ Melchizedek was the first King of Righteousness, and the King of Salem, meaning Peace. Melchizedek had no parents or ancestors, no beginning or end. Melchizedek was made like the Son of God, being a priest and king continually. Consider how great He was, for Abraham paid tithes to Him, and always counted on His promises. Under the Levitical priesthood, the people received the Law. But the priesthood was changed, and this required a change in the Law. The new priesthood was fashioned by the power of eternal life, not the Law over sinful man. The Law made nothing perfect, but the bringing of a better hope did; that hope draws us to God through the testament of Jesus Christ, who is priest forever after the order of Melchizedek. Since Christ lives forever, the priesthood will never again change, for He is the holy, pure, and perfect high priest. The daily sacrifice of the Levitical priesthood has been replaced with the sacrifice of Christ, once and for all.
- HEB 9:11–15,18–22 ~ Christ came as the high priest and king over all good things to come, to prepare a greater and more perfect church, not made by hands like a building. Christ

obtained eternal redemption for us, not by the blood of burnt offerings but by His own precious blood. If the blood of burnt offerings purified the hearts of men, how much more will the blood of Christ purify us! Through the Holy Spirit, Christ offered Himself, who was without blemish (sinless), and who purged our consciences from dead works to serve the living God. By this cause, Christ has become the mediator of the New Testament (Covenant). By His death, we are redeemed from the sins committed under the first (old) covenant, so that those who are called might receive the promise of God's eternal inheritance. Even the first covenant included blood, for after Moses read from the Book of the Law, He sprinkled blood from the offering on the book and the people, saying, "This is the blood of the covenant which God has commanded for you to keep." Moses also sanctified the tabernacle in this manner. Under the Law, all acts of disobedience are purged with blood, for without the shedding of blood there is no remission of sins.

- HEB 10:39 ~ We do not shrink back and we are not destroyed, because those who have faith keep their souls.
- 1 PE 1:2 ~ You have been chosen in advance by God the Father, and sanctified by His Holy Spirit, through the shedding of the blood of His Son Jesus Christ, to whom you have become obedient. May God bless you with His abundant grace and peace.
- 1 PE 1:18–22 ~ You are not redeemed with corruptible things like gold or silver, you are redeemed with the precious blood of Christ, who was like a lamb without blemish or spots. He, who was ordained before the foundations of the world, was made manifest in these past days just for you. Believe in Him who God raised from the dead and gave glory, so that your faith and hope can remain in God. Your souls will be purified for obeying the truth that the Holy Spirit has shown us; therefore, you must fervently love each other with a pure heart.

Once you start to understand God's covenant, and the guarantee of eternal life that goes with it, you begin to realize how to react to His promises. Peruse these verses on how one should <u>respond to God's loving kindness</u>.

- DEU 6:2–7 ~ Fear the Lord and keep all His commandments and laws. Ensure that your children and your children's children obey God. Do this and you will prosper and your life will be prolonged. Love God with all your heart, soul, and might. Keep God's Word in your heart and teach His ways carefully and thoughtfully to your children. Talk with your family all the time about God, every day and night, whenever you are together.
- PSA 51:10–12 ~ Create in me a clean heart, Lord, and renew an upright spirit within me. Don't remove me from your presence and don't take your Holy Spirit from me. Restore to me the joy of your salvation, and uphold me with your free Spirit.
- PSA 95:2 ~ Let us go before God with thanksgiving; make a joyful noise to Him with singing.
- PSA 96:8 ~ Give God the glory He deserves. Bring your offerings to church and worship Him.
- MAT 6:33–34 ~ Jesus taught: Seek first the kingdom of God and His righteousness, and everything else will be yours. Don't be anxious about tomorrow, because God will provide your needs.
- MAT 22:37–40 ~ Jesus said, "Love the Lord your God with all your heart, mind, and soul: this is the first and greatest commandment. The second is like unto the first: Love your neighbor as yourself. All the laws and the prophets depend on these two commandments."
- MAT 28:19–20 ~ Jesus said, "Go into the world and teach all nations what I have taught you. Baptize them in the name of the Father, Son, and Holy Spirit. Remember, I will always be with you, even until the end of time."
- JOH 4:24 ~ Jesus said, "God is Spirit and should be worshipped in spirit and in truth."

- JOH 8:31–32 ~ Jesus said, "If you continue in my Word, then you are indeed my disciples, and you will know the truth, and the truth will set you free."
- ROM 6:23 ~ The wages of sin is death, but God's gift of eternal life is available through Jesus Christ our Lord.
- ROM 8:4–6 ~ Walk, not according to the flesh, but according to the spirit. Those who live according to the flesh set their minds on evil, but those who live according to the spirit set their minds on God. To set the mind on flesh results in death, but to set the mind on God results in peace and life.
- ROM 9:4–8 ~ Who are the Israelites, to whom God gave the Law and granted the adoption, and with whom God made the covenants and promises? Christ came for them and for all people. It's not as if God's Word had no effect, for they who are of Israel are not all from Israel. Those who are of Abraham's seed are not all his children. In other words, those who are the children of the flesh are not children of God; only those who cling to God's promises are counted as children.
- ROM 13:10 ~ Love is the fulfilling of the Law.
- PHP 4:6–7 ~ Don't have anxiety about anything, but pray for everything. With thanksgiving let your requests be known to God. And the peace of God which passes all understanding will keep your heart in mind in Jesus Christ.
- PHP 4:8 ~ Focus your mind on things that are true, honest, just, pure, lovely, admirable, virtuous, and praiseworthy.
- GAL 6:8 ~ Those who sow to the flesh will reap corruption to their flesh; those who sow to the Spirit, will from the Spirit reap eternal life.
- COL 2:2 ~ My (Paul's) hope is that people's hearts will be comforted, being bound together in love, and that they receive the riches of understanding and acknowledgement of the mystery of God, and of the Heavenly Father, and of Jesus Christ.
- 1 JO 2:6 ~ Whoever says they are a Christian should show they are following Christ by the way they conduct their lives.
- 1 JO 4:8 ~ If you don't love, you cannot know God, because God *is* love.

The previously reviewed scriptures tell us about the nature of God, the nature of people, and the relationship between God and people. They teach us how we are created in God's image and how we can please Him by being more like Christ. We can become sanctified in His Spirit unto life everlasting. There is much we can learn from the Holy Bible, and we can apply the information to our everyday lives. The scriptures draw us closer to God until that day when we will live with Him forever as adopted children.

In this book a lot of scripture will be reviewed. Each topic will be loaded with relevant Bible passages so that the subject matter can be understood in light of God's own Word. Many scriptures are repeated throughout this study guide because they can be applied to multiple topics. Such repetition helps the reader to remember and to memorize key sayings coming directly from God. I implore all who open this book, and read, to spend twice as much time rereading the scriptures that are cited, using multiple translations of the Bible. Commentary has been provided, but one should always verify interpretations and discussions with the unchanged words of God. He explains things better than any human can, enabling the reader to comprehend within his or her spirit by the power of the Holy Spirit.

- 1 CO 2:14 ~ Worldly people do not receive the things of the Spirit of God, for these things are foolishness to them; neither can they know these things for they must be discerned spiritually.

How We Experience God

To acknowledge God is to accept all three personifications in which God manifests Himself to us. Those who cannot comprehend the Holy Trinity or accept it need to understand the way the three persons interact. To comprehend God, we can begin by looking at ourselves, through the human experience. Our experience follows three basic steps. First, we sense stimuli and perceive that something is there. Second, we perform some mental manipulation in which sensory-perceptual data are evaluated, and a decision is reached as to the proper action to take. Third, we execute a deliberate response, periodically modifying it to achieve the desired results. This process is depicted in the human performance model shown below. Notice that there is a perceptual, cognitive, and psychomotor component to human behavior. These processes comprise the essence of human interaction with the environment, other people, and God.

Sense/Perceive → Evaluate/Decide → Respond/React

The sensory-perceptual component is our physical link to God. People can be selective in what they sense and the way they perceive it which requires mindfulness before deciding. The cognitive component is our mental link to God, who gave us His Word. The Word or Holy Bible defines who God is and what His desire is for us. Our power of discernment is what makes us different from any other earthly creature. However, it is up to each individual to choose to seek and obey God or not, as demonstrated by words, actions, and emotions. When we express ourselves, we are exercising our spiritual component. We can follow Christ in our lives, or we can be led astray by worldly pursuits. Christ provides a direct, spiritual link to God. He is the author and finisher of our faith, and the mediator between us and the Almighty Father. We can approach the Father, in spirit, through Christ the Lord.

It is the Spirit of God that energizes us, thereby providing us the means to enjoy the creation, each other, and God. The spirit God gave us vitalizes our bodies and minds to experience the sensations, interactions, and imaginations that are life itself. He gave us the ability to discriminate between right and wrong, and the freedom to choose what is good or evil. We are motivated to express ourselves in thought, word, and deed, either in a way that is pleasing to God or offensive to Him. Thus, in His own image, God has given us a body, mind, and spirit. If we use our faculties to search for God, we will find Him. If we choose righteousness over wickedness, and have faith in Christ, we can live forever in His kingdom. Thus, the aspects of human existence include the body that enables us to sense and feel, the mind that helps us analyze and decide, and the spirit that allows us to express what we think and feel. Notice how these components are separate yet interconnected. Holistic health means to exercise and nurture all three domains.

Body/Physical ←→ Mind/Mental ←→ Spirit/Spiritual

God has the same three dimensions. The physical form of God is Christ in the flesh, in whom God showed the way to heaven by setting the example of obedience and ultimately paying the price of disobedience for all believers. The mental component of God is the Father, who created us, directs us, and sustains us in His grace and mercy. He established the universe, and its laws and precepts which we are compelled to obey. The spiritual component of God is the Holy Ghost, who directly communicates to us God's love, truth, and knowledge via the Holy Bible and Jesus Christ. Now we can begin to understand the three persons of God comprising the Holy Trinity. Note that these three are interrelated, interact, and are totally inclusive.

__/ Almighty Father __
Jesus Christ   ← | →   Holy Spirit

God the Father gave us a piece of His mind, so that we could tell the difference between good and bad. Using our minds, we can study His Word, and know the truth, for the truth is always right and good. To do what is good is to be guided by one's spirit; to do what is evil is to be guided by one's sinful flesh. If you live in truth you will always live in the spirit, but living for the flesh can only lead to death. God the Spirit is the Word, which gives us the covenants of the Law and of God's promise of the Way: the way to be ransomed from the grave and to live with God forever—the Way to heaven! That Way is through Jesus Christ who is God the Son, our prophet, priest, and king; He is the New Covenant. The Old Covenant of the Law, described in the Old Testament, was communicated directly to Abraham and Moses via the high priest and king, God's Holy Spirit. The entire priesthood, kingdom, and authority were transferred to Christ, the promised Messiah, as fulfilled in the New Testament. All believers are benefactors of God's faith covenant; they will receive an inheritance in God's kingdom that endures forever.

Through Christ, we can experience God Himself, for God will freely give His Holy Spirit to those who seek the Lord in spirit and truth. In other words, because of the grace of God, we can receive the free gift of His Holy Spirit by simply believing His promises. But we can only be justified by our faith not by our actions, for we are unable to obey the Law perfectly and are otherwise condemned. With God's Spirit living in us, we can communicate God's love back to Him and toward one another. We are linked to God's Spirit by studying the Holy Bible, believing in Christ, praying through Him, worshipping God (the Holy Trinity), attending church, witnessing Jesus in our lives, and expressing His perfect love.

Summary: This analysis can be summarized by consolidating what we have learned into two conceptual models, one describing ourselves, and another describing God in whose image we are created. Note that all three personifications of God equally share the attributes ascribed to Him. That is, there are three persons integrated into one being, not one divided into three; the persons of God are not mutually exclusive. Similarly, the three components of man are integrated, but unlike God, the body can be separated from the spirit, and the spirit from the mind or soul.

GOD (the Way, for man)	MAN (the way to God)
Father >> Holy Spirit >> Son (Christ)	Body >> Mind >> Spirit
Prophet – Priest – King	Sensation – Cognition – Action
Truth – Life – Way	Feel – Think – Express
Creator – Sustainer – Savior	Seek – Understand – Obey
Law (faith) – Word – Grace (faith)	
Lawmaker – Enforcer – Judge	

In conclusion, God the Father has given us life and wants us to be with Him. By studying the Bible, we begin to understand who God is and what He expects of us. He gave us the covenants of the Law and Grace that through faith we might seek Him and come to the knowledge of salvation by way of His Son, our Redeemer. God's Law is His will, communicated to us by the Holy Spirit, which conveys the truth that leads to life via the written Word and the Word made flesh which is Christ the Lord. We find God through the Holy Spirit, given to us in Jesus Christ, who shows the way to heaven. Our faith in the atonement of Christ is demonstrated by our obedience to God and willingness to improve. This is a lifelong process in which we become sanctified by the Holy Spirit and reconciled with our Creator. Note that examination of scriptural references concerning the Holy Trinity occurs throughout this textbook.

HOW WE RELATE TO GOD

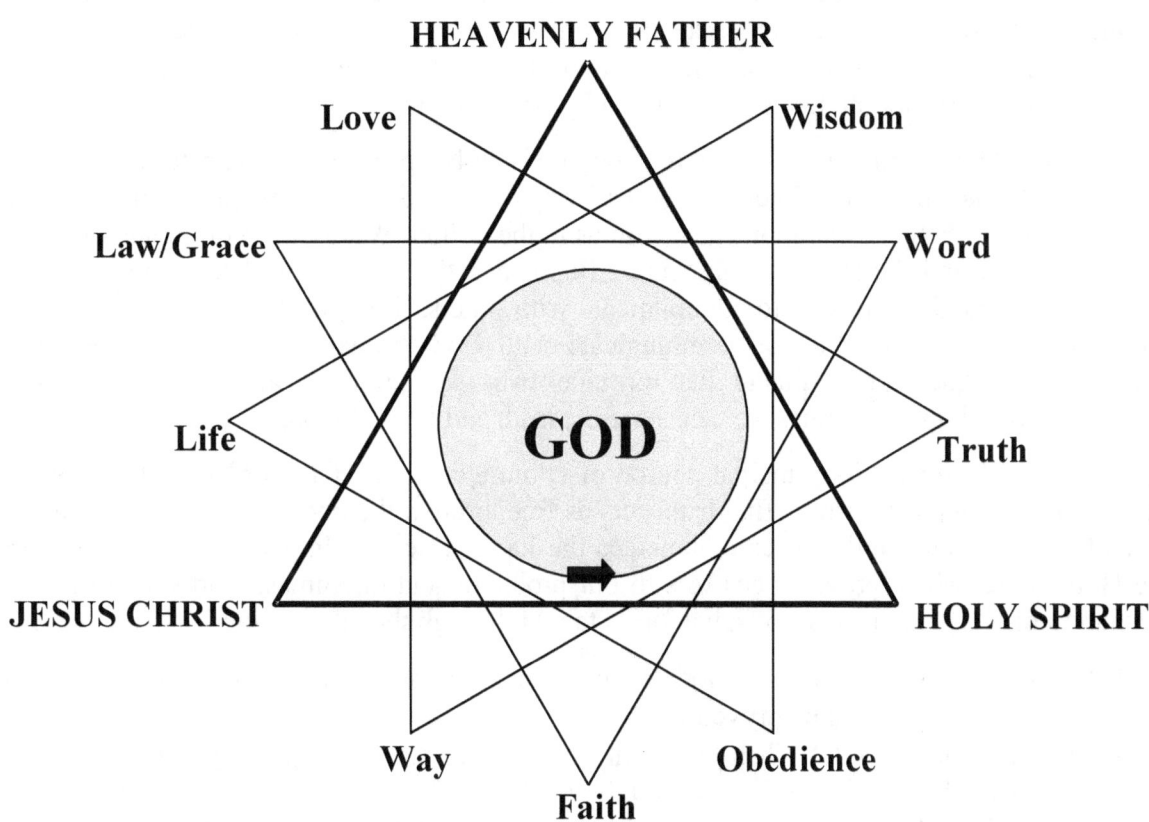

Lesson: Communicating with God

Text: ISA 55:10–12 ~ The rain and snow that fall from heaven do not return to heaven but water the earth, causing the plants to bud and to seed and providing food. So also, God's Word does not return to Him void, but accomplishes what He wishes, and prospers wherever He sends it. We joyfully go out, being led in peace. The mountains and hills sing before you and the trees clap their hands; all the world will rejoice around you. Instead of a thorn bush, a tree will grow. And the name of the Lord will be magnified as an everlasting sign of the nurturing He provides.

God's Holy Spirit gives life, and His love nourishes every living thing. Without His Spirit nothing could live. Not only does the Holy Spirit give us life but it also gives us knowledge and understanding. God is the source of all wisdom and truth, and He communicates that wisdom and truth with all people through His Holy Spirit.

- JOB 32:8 ~ It is the Spirit in a man, the breath of the Almighty, that makes him understand.
- ZEC 12:1 ~ The Lord formed the spirit of man within him.
- MAL 2:15–16 ~ God has made and sustained for us the spirit of life.
- 1 CO 2:10–12 ~ God reveals His mysteries to us through His Spirit, for the Spirit searches all things, even the deepest things of God. Nobody can know the deepest thoughts of another, only the spirit within that person can know them. Similarly, nobody can know the deepest thoughts of God except His Holy Spirit. We have received the Spirit of God, not the spirit of the world, so that we might know the things that God has given to us for free
- 2 CO 3:6 ~ God has made us able ministers of the new testament, not of the letter of the Law, but of the Spirit, for the letter kills, but the Spirit gives life.

Since God communicates with us through His Holy Spirit, we also can communicate with God through His Holy Spirit. There are several ways that God and His people communicate with one another. God's Spirit communicates with us in the written Word, the Word made flesh which is Jesus Christ, and the Holy Sacraments of Baptism and Communion. We communicate with God's Spirit, and God uses us to communicate with others, through our love, acts of faith, and witnessing of the truth. We also communicate with God through the act of prayer. Thus, a number of avenues are available that provide two-way communication between God and humans. Through these avenues we can share the truth and love of God.

God's Word is His principal source of communication. His Word is truth; it is God's Spirit that communicates truth. That truth sets us free through the knowledge of God's only Son, Jesus Christ. God's Word also communicates the Law, which is His will. The written Word is the Holy Bible, which provides answers to our problems and dilemmas. God's Word gives the revelation of His great mystery of salvation obtained through the atoning sacrifice of Christ.

- PRO 30:5–6 ~ Every word of God is true. Don't attempt to add to His words or He will rebuke you and you will be proven false.
- JOH 16:13 ~ Jesus said, "When the Spirit of truth comes, He will guide you in truth. He will not speak of Himself, but will show you things to come."
- 1 CO 2:13 ~ We teach using words taught by the Holy Spirit, not by human wisdom. Spiritual truths must be interpreted by those who possess the Spirit.
- 2 TI 3:16 ~ All scripture is inspired by God. God's Word provides the doctrine of truth, refutes that which is false, and instructs people in the ways of righteousness.

God's Word became flesh so that He could communicate with His people face to face. The Word in human form is Jesus Christ. Those who saw Christ were seeing God. God communicated to humankind through His Son Jesus Christ, so that all would know Him. God became a man to set an example for everyone to follow and that example, Jesus Christ, leads us to heaven. Christ fulfilled God's covenant of Grace, so that anyone who seeks God can be with Him forever, through faith in Christ.

- EXO 25:22 ~ The Lord said to Moses, "I will commune with you from heaven, from between the two cherubim that are on the Ark of the Covenant. I will tell you all the commandments that I have for Israel."
- JOH 1:1,14,17–18 ~ In the beginning was the Word, and the Word was with God, and the Word was God. And the Word became flesh, and lived on earth; and we saw His glory, the glory of the only Son of the Father. God's grace and truth came to us through Christ. God revealed Himself to us through Christ.
- JOH 8:31–32 ~ Jesus said, "If you continue in my Word, then you are indeed my disciples, and you will know the truth, and the truth will set you free."
- JOH 14:6,9–11 ~ Jesus said, "I am the way, the truth, and the life; nobody comes to the Father but by me. If you have seen me, you have seen the Father, because the Father lives in me and I in Him."
- ACT 10:36–41 ~ Peter preached, "The Word that God sent to Israel is Jesus Christ; in Him God's peace can be found. That Word began in Galilee and became known throughout Judea, after the baptism preached by John. God anointed Jesus Christ of Nazareth with the Holy Spirit and with His power. Jesus spent His time doing good and healing the demon possessed, for God was with Him. We are witnesses of all the things He did in the land of the Jews, and in Jerusalem where He was killed on a cross. God raised Him from the dead after three days. Many people chosen by God to be witnesses saw Him, and we are among those witnesses."

We go to church to hear the Word of God and to worship Him. Our hymns of praise and our thank offerings are the means by which we communicate our appreciation for all that He has done for us. To neglect going to church and studying God's Word is to rob Him of the glory, praise, and adoration He deserves.

- 1 CH 16:8–12,23–25,29–31,35–36 ~ Give thanks to the Lord; call upon His name; make known His wondrous deeds to everyone. Sing praises to Him and rejoice. Continuously seek the Lord with all your strength. Remember all the great things He has done. Sing to the Lord all the earth; tell others about His salvation. Declare His glory to the nations. For great is the Lord and greatly is He to be praised. He is to be held in awe above all gods. Give to the Lord His due glory, with praise and offerings. Worship the Lord in holy array; tremble before Him all the earth. Let the heavens be glad and the earth rejoice, and let everyone say, "The Lord reigns." Give thanks to the Lord for He is good and His steadfast love endures forever. Ask God to deliver, gather, and save you, so that you may give eternal thanks and glory to Him. Blessed be the Lord from everlasting to everlasting.
- PSA 50:23 ~ God says that whoever offers Him praise, glorifies Him. To those who do this, He will show His salvation.
- MAL 3:8 ~ Can you rob God? Yes, you can, for people have robbed Him by not presenting their offerings and tithes.
- JOH 4:24 ~ Jesus said, "God is Spirit and should be worshipped in spirit and in truth."

- COL 3:16–17 ~ Remember what Christ taught you and let His words enrich your lives and make you wise. Teach His words to each other. Sing them openly and spiritually in psalms and hymns with thankful hearts. Whatever you do or say, do it in Jesus's name, and give thanks to God in Jesus's name.
- HEB 13:15 ~ Let us continually offer to God the sacrifice of praise; praise and thanks are the fruit of our lips.

God is communicating with us as we study the Holy Bible and listen to the teachings of Christ. It is necessary that we bring our children to church and Sunday School so they too can hear the Word of God. We are commanded to teach God's Word to our children and to share His Word with others that we know or meet.

- DEU 4:9–10,36 ~ Don't forget what God has done for you. May His works have a lasting impression on your lives. Teach your children and grandchildren about His glorious miracles. Especially remind your children of God's instructions given to Moses at Sinai about reverencing Him and about teaching His laws from generation to generation. From heaven, God enabled you to hear His voice so that He could instruct you. On earth He spoke to all people from the great fire, giving us His laws.
- MAT 28:19–20 ~ Jesus told His disciples, "Go into every nation and teach the people everything I have taught you. Baptize them in the name of the Father, Son, and Holy Spirit. Remember, I'll always be with you even until the end of time."

At church we also communicate with God through His Holy Sacraments which Christ Himself taught us through His example. Christ showed us how we could receive God when participating in these sacraments. The sacraments provide a unique way for God's Spirit to communicate directly with ours. The sacraments are a means for us to open our hearts and minds to receive God's Holy Spirit. Both sacraments purify us, thereby allowing the Spirit of the Lord to dwell within us. Communing with God by way of the Holy Sacraments is an intimate communication between our spirit and His.

- MAT 3:11 ~ John the Baptist said, "I baptize you with water to fulfill your desire for repentance. But One comes after me, who is mightier than I, and whose shoes I am not worthy to carry. He will baptize you with the Holy Spirit, and with fire."
- JOH 3:3–6 ~ Jesus said, "Unless a person is born again, he cannot see God's kingdom." Nicodemus asked, "How can someone be born when they are old?" Jesus answered, "Unless a person is born of water and of the Holy Spirit he cannot enter into God's kingdom. Those who are born of the flesh are flesh, and those who are born of the Spirit are Spirit."
- 1 CO 10:16–17,21 ~ The cup of blessing that we bless, doesn't it represent our communion with the blood of Christ? The bread that we break, doesn't it represent our communion with the body of Christ? Although we are many, we have become one body for we all are partakers of that one bread. You can't drink from the cup of the Lord and from the cup of devils (you can't be one with Christ if you commune with devils).
- 1 CO 11:25–29 ~ Jesus commanded the apostles on the first Holy Communion to partake of the sacrament often to remember Him. Thus, as often as you eat the bread and drink the wine of Holy Communion, you proclaim the death of Christ until His return. But if you participate in this holy sacrament unworthily (without sincerely repenting of your sins and desiring a communion with Christ), you will become one of those who are found guilty of Christ's crucifixion. Examine yourself before partaking of Holy Communion, because if you partake unworthily, you will be eating and drinking damnation upon yourself.

When we receive the sacraments, we are cleansed of unrighteousness, thereby allowing the Holy Spirit to live within us. In Holy Baptism, the Holy Spirit interacts with us in the form of water, cleansing our sinful flesh of all unrighteousness. In Holy Communion, the Holy Spirit interacts with us through the body and blood of Christ, cleansing our sinful minds of all unrighteousness. We need this intimate joining with God so that we can remain in the Spirit and not be influenced by our sinful flesh and the temptations of the material world.

- 2 CO 6:14 ~ Do not be joined with unbelievers, for what fellowship can there be between righteousness and unrighteousness? What communion can there be between light and darkness?
- 2 CO 13:14 ~ The grace of the Lord Jesus Christ, the love of God, and the communion of the Holy Spirit be with you.
- TIT 3:5 ~ Christ has saved us, not because of our works of righteousness, but because of His mercy, through our spiritual washing by the Holy Spirit.

Going to church, participating in the sacraments, sharing the good news with others, these are ways in which we publicly witness the truth and communicate to God our love for Him. Additionally, being God's witnesses is an excellent way in which God communicates through us to others. There are a number of ways we can witness for Him including confessing, serving, giving, helping, and living a Christian lifestyle.

We always should be willing to confess our faith when there is a reasonable opportunity to do so. However, we must not be forceful or aggressive when we witness to others, but rather gentle and compassionate. Whenever we confess God publicly, God's Spirit tells us what to say and do.

- MAT 10:19–20 ~ Jesus said, "When they arrest you and bring you before the authorities, don't worry about what to say, for you will know what to say when the time comes. And it will be the Holy Spirit inside you doing the talking."
- MAT 10:32–33 ~ Jesus said, "If any person confesses me to other people, I will confess them to my Father in heaven. If any person denies me to other people, I will deny them to my Father in heaven."
- 2 TI 2:24–26 ~ A servant of the Lord doesn't waste time arguing, but is gentle to everyone, able to teach, and not resentful. Such disciples gently instruct those who are in opposition to them, hoping that God will grant repentance for acknowledging His truth, so that they may escape the devil's traps who would otherwise capture them for his own purpose.
- 1 PE 3:15 ~ Sanctify the Lord in your hearts, and always be ready to give an answer, with humility and respect, to anyone who asks about the hope that is within you.

Unless we act on our faith, that faith will become stagnant. God gave everyone special abilities, and we should exercise these talents to the glory of His holy name. Serving God by using the gifts He has given us is a wonderful way of communicating that special love that brightens our spirit for others to see.

- ROM 12:4–8 ~ Just as our body has many members, each with a separate purpose, so we, being part of the body of Christ, have different responsibilities. We all have different gifts that the Lord our God in His grace has given us. Some people can minister, some can teach, some can provide guidance and counseling. If you have the gift of prophecy do so in proportion to your faith. If you have the gift of giving, do so generously. If you have the gift of governing, do so with diligence. If you have the gift of mercy, show it cheerfully.

- 2 CO 4:6 ~ God, who commanded the light to shine out of darkness, has shined in our hearts, so that we can share the light of the knowledge of God's glory in Jesus Christ.
- HEB 12:28 ~ Since God has given us the kingdom, let us please Him by serving Him with thankful hearts, with holy fear, and with awe.
- 1 PE 4:10–11 ~ Whoever has received the gift of salvation in Christ should share that gift with others, as a steward of God's eternal grace. If you preach, do so as a messenger of God. If you minister, do so with the ability God gives you. Do this to glorify God through His Son Jesus Christ.

Giving is not limited to providing financial support to the church at large. Giving of oneself is the most important way we can serve God and communicate His love to others. Time is a precious commodity, more valuable than money, for time represents life. Giving one's time to God is the least we can do, since He gave us all our time, both on this earth, and forevermore in His heavenly realm.

- MAL 3:10 ~ The Lord says, "Bring tithes of your income to the storage room, so that there will be plenty in my house, and prove to yourself that I will open the windows of heaven and pour upon you so many blessings that you will not have room for them."
- MAT 25:40,45 ~ Jesus said, "Whenever you have done something to help another person, you have done it to me as well; whenever you have not done something to help another person, you have not done it to me either."
- 2 CO 3:5–6 ~ We owe everything we are to God who has made us ministers of the New Testament. We don't tell people that they must adhere to the very letter of the Law, but to the Spirit; for the Law kills but the Spirit gives life.
- COL 3:24 ~ If you help others you are really serving Christ.

Maybe you don't have much money or time, but you still can be God's witness simply by the way you live. The way we conduct ourselves should show others that we have the light of God's Spirit living within us.

- ROM 12:1 ~ Give yourselves to God. Let yourself be a living sacrifice. After all He has done for you, is that too much to ask?
- 1 JO 2:6 ~ Whoever says they are a Christian should show they are following Christ by the way they conduct their lives.

The methods described thus far are effective ways that God communicates to us and through us. God has also given us an effective way of communicating directly to Him through the gift of prayer. In prayer, we can bring our ideas, needs, desires, troubles, pains, fears, doubts, and frustrations to God. Of course, He already knows what we want and what we need, and He answers our prayers according to what is in His, and our, best interest. If we seek God and His righteousness, praying for His Spirit to strengthen us, He will listen, and He will provide everything we need. God's Holy Spirit intercedes for us when we pray, ensuring that our prayers are answered to our benefit. You may not always get what you want but you always get what you need.

- MAT 6:6–7 ~ Jesus taught: When you pray, do so in private. Pray to the Father in your mind and He will know what you are thinking. Pray to Him secretly, and He will reward you openly. Do not use vain repetitions like the unbelievers do, for they think they will be heard for their many words.

- MAT 6:33–34 ~ Jesus taught: Seek first the kingdom of God and His righteousness, and everything else will be yours. Don't be anxious about tomorrow, because God will provide your needs.
- ROM 8:26 ~ The Holy Spirit intercedes for us when we pray. We don't know what we should pray for all the time. But through the act of prayer, God analyzes our needs and answers our prayers in the best possible way.
- EPH 6:18–19 ~ Pray all the time in the Spirit. Keep alert and persevere. Pray for Christians, prophets, and priests, that their words will proclaim the mystery of the Gospel.
- PHP 4:6–7 ~ Don't have anxiety about anything, but pray for everything. With thanksgiving let your requests be known to God. And the peace of God which passes all understanding will keep your heart and mind in Jesus Christ.
- COL 4:2 ~ Continue to pray and wait for the answer, giving thanks for the result.

Let us exercise these tools God has given us to remain constantly connected to His Holy Spirit so that Satan will have no power over us. Not only will we be able to resist temptation and repel evil, we will be able to show others, by our example, the way to heaven, just as Christ revealed it to us by His example. God's Spirit is a free gift to all that ask for it; it is a gift to be shared and appreciated. This is something to always be cognizant of, His ever-present Spirit. We should talk to Him in our thoughts whenever He comes to mind. For He is there, and He wants you to acknowledge Him. And He will never leave you or forsake you (DEU 31:8; HEB 13:5).

- PSA 51:10–12 ~ David prayed: Create in me a clean heart, Lord, and renew an upright spirit within me. Don't remove me from your presence and don't take your Holy Spirit from me. Restore to me the joy of your salvation, and uphold me with your free Spirit.
- EPH 2:8–9 ~ You are saved by the grace of God because of your faith in Jesus Christ. Salvation is a gift of God, it cannot be earned through good works, so nobody should brag.
- 1 PE 4:10 ~ As everyone has received the gift of love, even so minister the same to one another, as good stewards of the manifold grace of God.

Isn't it amazing that we can come to God our Father in prayer in the manner Christ taught us to do (LUK 11:1–4)? Prayer is a great way to imitate Christ, to connect with God, and to become conformed into His image through sanctification by the Holy Spirit (ROM 8:15; HEB 2:11). If you don't know what to pray for when you are in a bind, afraid of what may happen, or overcome with despair, pray for the same thing Christ prayed for as He anticipated His trial and execution: "Oh heavenly Father, let your will be done and not my own" (LUK 22:42).

Christ in the Garden of Gethsemane
Painting by Heinrich Hofmann
(1824–1911)

Lesson: The Facts of Life

The FACTS of life refer to eternal life and the requirements for obtaining eternal life.

F = Faithfulness/Forgiveness
A = Atonement/Amends
C = Contrition/Confession
T = Testimony/Teaching
S = Steadfastness/Supportiveness

F = ACTS: Faith is an action in and of itself, insofar as one must choose what they will believe, and those beliefs influence thoughts which produce associated behaviors. Actions based on genuine faith exemplify that faith and the results reflect it. For example, to seek forgiveness one must have faith in God, and He will react accordingly. Our faith in Jesus is demonstrated by acts of faith such as those listed above, which is our response to God's actions. We should follow the example of Jesus Christ whose entire life teaches us how to act on our faith and to bear fruit of the Spirit.

- MAT 5:15–16 ~ Don't hide the light that's inside you but let it shine before others.
- ROM 12:1–2 ~ Let your body be a living sacrifice to God; this is the least you can do. Conduct yourself according to the will of God, not according to the world.
- TIT 2:12 ~ Avoid ungodliness and the lusts of this world, and live a life of sobriety, righteousness, and godliness.
- JAM 2:17–26 ~ Faith without works is dead. For example, Abraham's faith was demonstrated by his willingness to sacrifice Isaac. Thus, faith became active first, and Abraham's works demonstrated that faith in action.
- 1 JO 2:6 ~ Whoever says they are a Christian should show they are following Christ by the way they act.

F = <u>Faithfulness/Forgiveness</u>. The first thing that must happen is to seek God in faith and ask Him for forgiveness. He will forgive anyone who sincerely repents. However, to be forgiven, you must be willing to forgive others as God has forgiven you. God's action is forgiveness and our reaction should be the same.

- PSA 37:5–6 ~ Commit yourself to God and trust in Him, and He will forgive you.
- MAT 6:14–15 ~ Jesus said, "If you forgive others, God will forgive you. If you don't forgive others, God won't forgive you."
- JOH 1:12 ~ God gave us the choice to become children of God through faith in Christ.

A = <u>Atonement/Amends</u>. The supreme act of faith for all time was the atoning sacrifice made by Jesus Christ. Without His sacrifice, nobody could be saved. While the blood of Christ washes away our sins, we must make an earnest effort to resist temptation in the future, and to stop committing the sins we've committed in the past, making amends to the extent possible. In short, if we come to God with a contrite heart it implies that we wish and intend to do better. To not try is a denial of sincerity; or put another way, to request forgiveness and not act is dishonest.

- GEN 17—22 ~ Abraham was prepared to atone for his sinfulness by sacrificing his only son Isaac. Abraham's act of faith, demonstrated by his willingness to please God at the cost of his own son, was sufficient for God to spare Abraham and Isaac, and to make a covenant with them.
- EXO 12 ~ The Jews' act of faith in observing God's rules during the first Passover saved their first born from being sacrificed.

- LEV 1—5 ~ Atonement was made for sin by offering sacrifices in accordance with God's laws given to Moses. Thus, the first covenant was the Law.
- HEB 7—8 ~ However, the law was imperfect, which is why God promised humanity a New Covenant, which would be faultless.
- ROM 11:25–32 ~ Jesus Christ is the New Covenant promised by God for the redemption of our sins.
- HEB 10:10–18 ~ Jesus's sacrifice is the last sacrifice that will ever need to be made to atone for sin. Under the Old Covenant, sacrificial offerings were made as an atonement for sin. Under the New Covenant, we are made clean by the blood of Christ in one final sacrificial offering. This sacrifice will stand for all time, so there is no longer any need for sin offerings or sacrifices.
- 1 JO 2:1–2 ~ If you sin, you have an advocate with the Father; this advocate is Jesus Christ the righteous, who eliminated the sin of the world.

C = <u>Contrition/Confession</u>. By the grace of God, we are saved through faith in Christ. However, to obtain God's forgiveness, we must repent of our sins, confessing them before God with remorse for what we have done. Through this act of faith, we acknowledge Jesus Christ as our Lord and Savior, and the fact that we need His forgiveness, redemption, and salvation. It is an admission of guilt whereby our conscience has convicted us; but God will exonerate us.

- LEV 26:40–44 ~ Repent and confess, and God will remember the covenant He made with your forefathers.
- PSA 32:5 ~ I confessed my sins to God, I did not try to hide them, and He forgave me.
- MAT 10:32–33 ~ If anyone confesses Jesus Christ to others, He will confess them to God in heaven.
- ACT 2:38–39 ~ Peter said, "Repent and be baptized every one of you. For the gift of Christ's redemption is for all people, including children."
- ROM 10:10 ~ Believe in your heart and be justified. Confess with your lips and be saved.
- 2 CO 7:9–10 ~ I am glad that you were sorry for your sins and repented. Spiritual sorrow for one's sins works repentance unto salvation; but the sorrow of the world works death.
- PHP 2:11 ~ Every tongue should confess that Jesus is Lord to the glory of God the Father.
- 1 JO 1:9 ~ If we confess our sins, God is faithful and just to forgive us our sins and cleanse us from unrighteousness.

T = <u>Testimony/Teaching</u>. Confessing our sins, repenting, asking for forgiveness, and forgiving others are not where an active faith stops. Our whole life should be a testament to Jesus Christ. Everyone has talents that they can use. Christ has appointed all people to serve in the world, using their individual abilities. He also places His witness, the Holy Spirit, into us as we testify to others and teach our families.

- DEU 4:9–10 ~ Teach your children and grandchildren what God has done for you.
- ISA 6:8 ~ When God asked who to send as His messenger, Isaiah replied, "Here I am, Lord, send me."
- MAT 28:19–20 ~ Jesus said, "Go into the world and teach all nations what I have taught you. Baptize them in the name of the Father, Son, and Holy Spirit. Remember, I will always be with you, even until the end of time."
- JOH 1:7 ~ Jesus Christ came to be a witness to the Light, so that all who believed in Him would be saved.
- 1 PE 4:10–11 ~ Whoever has received the gift of salvation in Christ should share that gift with others. Be a witness or a messenger with whatever abilities God has given you.

- EPH 6:1–4 ~ Teach your children and grandchildren what God has done for you.

    S = <u>Steadfastness/Supportiveness</u>. Be steadfast in the faith by continuing to act on your faith producing spiritual fruit. For example, pray to God frequently and constantly. Read His Word daily and meditate upon it. Steadfastness is also demonstrated in perseverance. Do not quit; do not get discouraged and do not give up. Further, strengthen others in their faith, and support their efforts to remain faithful. This is why it is necessary to commune with others in the faith. Collectively, we edify one another so that God's love is shared and grows in our community of faith.

- 2 SA 22:22–24 ~ Within each of us is the power to obey God.
- PSA 37:3–7 ~ Trust in the Lord. Commit yourself to the Lord. Wait patiently for the Lord.
- MAT 7:14 ~ Straight and narrow is the gate that leads to eternal life.
- JOH 8:31 ~ Jesus said, "If you continue in my Word you are truly my disciples, and you will know the truth, and the truth will set you free."
- LUK 18:1–8 ~ Jesus taught the parable about the unjust judge: There was a judge who neither feared God nor had a high regard for his fellow man. A widow appealed to him to avenge her of an enemy who had done her wrong. The judge did nothing. The widow continued to bother the judge until her persistence finally paid off and the judge awarded her a fair settlement. God also will avenge His elect who plead with Him day and night, even though He does it in His own time. However, when the Son of God returns, will He find such a persistent faith on the earth?
- 1 CO 15:58 ~ Be steadfast, immovable, and fruitful in the Lord; for your efforts will not be in vain.
- EPH 6:18 ~ Pray always in the Spirit, and continue to watch for the Lord with perseverance.
- 1 TH 5:17–18 ~ Pray without stopping. Give thanks for everything.
- 2 TI 3:14 ~ Continue in what you have learned and have firmly believed, keeping in mind from whom you learned it.
- JAM 4:7 ~ We have the ability to resist Satan.
- 2 PE 2:20–21 ~ If, after a person has escaped the wickedness of this world through the knowledge of the Lord and Savior Jesus Christ, they allow themselves again to be entangled and overcome by the world, their end will be worse than their beginning. For it would have been better for them not to have known the ways of righteousness, than to have understood and yet turned away from the holy commandments given to them.
- REV 2:10 ~ Jesus said, "Be faithful unto death, and I will give you a crown of life."

    What exactly is faith? It seems an intangible phenomenon and not easily quantified. Simply put, faith is the beginning of a new life dedicated to Christ with the foreknowledge that one is saved because of His atonement. What follows is the purification by the Holy Spirit via the faith He has placed within our hearts. That faith is our part of the contract God has made with all people who seek Him and desire His presence in their lives forever. God's part of the contract is eternal life in paradise.

- HEB 11:1,3,6 ~ Faith is the assurance of things hoped for, the evidence of things not seen. By faith we understand that the world was created by the Word of God, such that things we see were made from things which do not appear. Without faith, it is impossible to please God, for whoever would wish to come to Him must believe He exists and that He rewards those who seek Him.
- HEB 12:2 ~ Jesus Christ is the author and finisher of our faith.

Acts of faith are presented below with corresponding Bible verses which describe works worthy of repentance in response to a persistent faith in Christ: kindness, forgiveness, brotherly love, confession and repentance, witnessing and testifying, teaching, praying, participation in the sacraments, worship, praise, singing, thanksgiving, righteous living, service and sacrifice. These are spiritual acts which will produce fruit, meaning that our faith is cultivated and nurtured yielding positive returns. It's like an investment in God who guarantees great payoffs.

- 1 CH 16 ~ Thank the Lord. Call upon Him. Sing praises to Him. Continuously seek the Lord with all your strength. Declare His glory to all nations. Give Him praise and offerings. Worship Him.
- PSA 32:5 ~ Acknowledge (confess) the sin which always goes before you.
- EZE 18:30 ~ Repent and turn away from sin, or you will be ruined by sin.
- MAT 7:7 ~ Ask and you will receive. Seek and you will find. Knock and the door will be opened.
- ROM 12:1 ~ Give yourselves to God. Let yourself be a living sacrifice. After all He has done for you, is that too much to ask?
- 1 CO 11:26 ~ Take communion often to proclaim the Lord's death until His return.
- EPH 4:32 ~ Be kind to one another, tenderhearted, and forgiving, even as God for Christ's sake has forgiven you.
- EPH 6:4 ~ Raise (teach) your children in the nurture and discipline of righteousness.
- COL 3:16 ~ Remember what Christ taught you and let His words enrich your lives and make you wise. Teach His words to each other. Sing them openly and spiritually in psalms and hymns, with thankful hearts.
- 1 TI 2:1–8 ~ Pray and give thanks always and everywhere.
- HEB 10:25 ~ Remember to assemble together in church, as some others have quit doing.
- HEB 12:28 ~ Since God has given us the kingdom, let us please Him by serving Him with thankful hearts, holy fear, and with awe.
- 2 PE 1:5–8 ~ Supplement your faith with virtue, knowledge, self-control, steadfastness, godliness, and brotherly love.

The result of our faith is salvation of the soul and eternal life with Jesus. This is our reward for staying steadfast in our faith, ever trusting in God, and being faithful stewards of His gifts and blessings by being a blessing to others through our gifts and service, as well as in our daily living, attitude, and character.

- JOH 11:25–26 ~ Jesus said, "I am the resurrection and the life. Those who believe in me, though they were dead, yet shall they live. Whoever believes in me will never die."
- ROM 6:23 ~ The wages of sin is death. But the gift of eternal life is available to everyone through Jesus Christ our Lord.
- 1 CO 15:52–54 ~ Christians will be raised incorruptible, to be changed into new beings, becoming immortal.
- 1 PE 1:9 ~ The outcome of our faith in Jesus Christ is salvation of the soul.
- REV 20 ~ Those who stayed righteous came to life again and reigned with Christ.
- REV 22 ~ Blessed are those who keep God's commandments for they will be allowed to enter the gates of heaven and partake of the everlasting waters and of the tree of life. And they will never die again.

Lesson: Living by Example

God's Word is our guide to life. It provides instructions on what to do and what not to do. It communicates to humankind God's plan of salvation, and the way to obtain this free gift. The Bible is our handbook on how to act, when to speak, and what to think. In essence, God has given all people an example to follow and that example is Himself.

The Old Testament is based on God's Law and is a testimony of how His people demonstrated their faith through obedience. The Ten Commandments provided the foundation upon which all other laws are based. The first five books of Moses (the Torah) delineate a great number of additional laws and statutes. Modern judicial systems are founded on the very laws, ordinances, and statutes that the Lord handed down to Israel through the prophets. God further communicated His will through the New Testament of Jesus Christ. God's precepts represent a standard of conduct that all people should embrace. Those precepts are stated clearly and precisely in both testaments of the Holy Bible. Furthermore, God's moral code is implanted in the conscience of all people.

- EXO 18:20–21 ~ Moses's father-in-law advised Moses to teach the people God's laws and doctrines, and tell them the way to live and what duties to perform. He further advised Moses to select capable men to help him govern the people, men who feared God and were trustworthy and honest.
- LEV 19:37; LEV 26:46 ~ God commanded the Israelites to obey all His laws and statutes, which He communicated to Moses on Mt. Sinai.
- NEH 9—10 ~ Nehemiah spoke a great prayer of worship and thanksgiving to God for bringing the Israelites back home. A written agreement was prepared binding the people in obedience to God and His rules. The leaders and priests affixed their seal to this agreement, and all the people swore an oath of allegiance to the Lord.
- PSA 119 ~ Blessed are those who walk in the ways of the Lord, who seek Him, and who keep His commandments. God has laid down His precepts and they are to be obeyed completely. Oh, that my ways were steadfast in obeying your decrees, Lord. I will praise you as I learn your righteous ways and obey your regulations. How can anyone keep his or her ways pure, but by living according to God's demands? Never let me stray from your commands, Lord. I will meditate upon your precepts; I will delight in your decrees; I will not neglect your Word. Open my eyes so I may see clearly the wonders of your Law. Teach me your ways and help me to understand your teaching and the meaning of your precepts. Turn me away from worthless things and preserve my life. May your unfailing love always be a comfort to me. I will walk in freedom, for I seek your wisdom and speak of your decrees. I know that your laws are righteous. Your Word is a lamp to my feet and a light to my path. If your Law had not been my delight, I would have perished in my affliction. Look upon my suffering and deliver me, for I have not forgotten your Law. How I love your Law; I meditate upon this night and day. I wait for your salvation, Lord, as I follow in your footsteps. [Note that PSA 119 is the longest chapter in the Bible; the above is a brief synopsis of that book.]
- JER 10:23–25 ~ Lord, I know that a man's life is not his own; it is not for man to direct his own steps. Correct me Lord, in your justice not in your anger, lest you reduce me to nothing. Pour your wrath out upon the nations that do not acknowledge you, and on the people that do not call upon your name.

God rewards those who are obedient to His Law and punishes those who are not. Those who are disobedient will be made examples of, so that others may be warned. Adopt the standards set by God or suffer the consequences.

- GEN 17,26 ~ God promised Abraham that his descendants would be as numerous as the stars because of his obedience. This promise also was made to Abraham's son Isaac.
- EXO 15:26 ~ God said, "If you listen carefully to the voice of the Lord and do what is right in His eyes, if you pay attention to His commands and keep all His decrees, then I will not bring upon you any of the diseases I brought upon the Egyptians, for I am the Lord who heals you."
- DEU 4:1–2,5–6 ~ God said, "Listen Israel to the laws and statutes I am about to teach you. Follow them so you can live and take possession of the land I am going to give to you. Do not add to my commands and do not subtract from them. Keep these laws carefully, for this will demonstrate to other nations your wisdom and understanding."
- ISA 24:4–6 ~ The earth is defiled and withers; the exalted of the earth decline. The earth is defiled by its people for they have disobeyed the laws, violated the statutes, and broken the everlasting covenant. Therefore, a curse consumes the earth; its people must bear their guilt. Earth's inhabitants are being burned up and very few are left.
- ISA 29:13–14,20 ~ God says, "Those people speak of me but their hearts are far from me. Their worship of me is made of rules taught by men. Therefore, I will take vengeance upon them, and turn their wisdom into foolishness. The ruthless will vanish, the mockers will disappear, and all who have an eye for evil will be cut down."
- EZE 5:5–8 ~ The Lord says, "Behold Jerusalem, which I have set in the center of the nations. In her wickedness she has rebelled against my laws and decrees, even more than the surrounding nations. She has been more unruly than they, conforming to their standards and not mine. Therefore, I am against you Jerusalem, and I will inflict punishment upon you for all the world to see."
- DAN 9 ~ Daniel prayed a great prayer of confession and repentance to the Lord regarding the sinfulness of the people. He recognized that disaster had befallen the Israelites because of their disobedience to God. Daniel pleaded with God to turn away His vengeance and forgive them. And God immediately answered Daniel's prayer by sending to him the angel Gabriel, who revealed the coming of the Anointed One.
- 1 CO 10:1–12 ~ Paul explained how our forefathers in the faith were founded on the same spiritual rock which is Christ. He further explained how those who were disobedient were made examples of as a warning to everyone else.
- HEB 4:11 ~ Let us make every effort to enter our rest without having failed by being an example of disobedience.
- JDE 1:6–7 ~ The angels that did not keep their positions of authority but abandoned their home in heaven, they have been kept in darkness, bound in eternal chains and awaiting Judgment Day. In the same manner, Sodom and Gomorrah, and the cities around them, gave themselves over to sexual immorality and perversion. They are examples of those who must suffer the vengeance of eternal fire. (also 2 PE 2:6; REV 20:10–15)

The laws and statutes of God were established to guide us to Him and to His truth, wisdom, and righteousness. God is our righteousness, and our obedience through faith in Him is counted as righteousness. By being obedient to God, a person becomes conformed to the likeness of Christ.

- LEV 20:7–8 ~ God said, "Consecrate yourselves and be holy, because I am the Lord your God. Keep my decrees and follow them. I am the Lord who makes you holy."
- DEU 6:4–25 ~ God said, "Listen Israel, the Lord our God is one Lord. Love Him with all your heart, with all your soul, and with all your strength. Talk about God's laws frequently and openly with your children. Fear the Lord and serve only Him; take your oaths in His name. Never follow other gods, for there is only one Lord among you and He is a jealous God; His anger will burn against you and He will destroy you if you follow false gods. Do not test God and make sure you continue to keep His commandments. Do what is good and right so everything may go well with you, and you will take the land that has been promised and drive away your enemies. When your children ask the meaning of these statutes and laws, explain to them what happened to you in the land of Egypt, and how God rescued you and performed all the wonderful miracles. Tell them that the Lord commanded you to obey His decrees and to fear Him, so that the people could prosper and live, as is still the case today. And if you are careful to obey God's Law, He will count that as righteousness."
- PSA 31:3; PSA 32:8; PSA 48:14; PSA 73:24 ~ The Lord is my rock and my fortress. Lord, lead me and guide me for the sake of your name. The Lord says, "I will teach you and lead you in the way you should go; I will give you advice and I will watch over you." This is our God and He will be our God forever; He will guide us and lead us until we die. Therefore, guide me with your counsel Lord, and afterward receive me into your glory.
- PRO 3:5–6 ~ Trust in God with all your heart and do not depend on your own understanding. In all your ways acknowledge God and He will direct you in the way to go.
- JOH 16:13 ~ Jesus said, "When the Spirit of truth comes, He will guide you into all truth."
- ROM 4:5 ~ Trust God who justifies sinners and your faith will be credited as righteousness.
- COL 3:15 ~ Let the peace of Christ rule in your hearts, since by members of one body you were called to peace.
- 2 TH 3:5 ~ May the Lord direct your hearts into God's love and Christ's perseverance.

God has revealed to all people the way of salvation through His only Son Jesus Christ (TIT 2:11–14). Jesus is the example of God in human form; if we follow His example, we will become like Him, perfect in righteousness. Through the act of sanctification, followers of Christ are gradually conformed to bear His image and name. Thus, Christ is the image of God, and those who follow Him are the image of Christ.

- GEN 1:26–27 ~ God said, "Let us make humans in our image, after our likeness. And let them have dominion over the fish of the sea, over the fowl of the air, over the cattle, and over all the earth and everything that creeps upon the earth." So, God created humankind in His own image; in the image of God He created us all, males and females alike.
- JOH 13:14–15 ~ Jesus said, "Now that I, your Lord and Teacher, have washed your feet, even so you should wash one another's feet. I have given to you an example that you should do for others as I have done for you."
- ROM 8:29; ROM 12:2 ~ For those He foreknew He also predestined to be conformed to the image of his Son, that He might be the firstborn among many more brothers and sisters. Do not conform to this world, but become transformed by the renewing of your mind. Then you will be able to test and prove God's good, acceptable, and perfect will.
- 1 CO 2:16 ~ Who has known the mind of God that they can instruct Him? But we have the mind of Christ.
- 2 CO 3:18 ~ But we, as if looking in a mirror and seeing the glory of the Lord, are changed into the same image from glory to glory by the Spirit of the Lord.

- PHP 2:6–10 ~ Jesus Christ, who was the image of God and was deserving of God's glory, was made in the likeness of a man. However, instead of glorifying Himself He became a humble servant, obedient unto death on the cross. Therefore, God exalted Him, giving Him a name above all other names, so that everyone on earth and in heaven would bow before the name of Jesus Christ.
- COL 1:12–20 ~ Give thanks to the Father, who has allowed us to partake of His inheritance, given to the saints who abide in His light. He has ransomed us from the power of darkness and delivered us to the kingdom of His dear Son Jesus Christ, who has redeemed us and forgiven us through His own precious blood. Christ is the very image of the invisible God; He is the firstborn of all living creatures. Through Him, all things were created on earth and in heaven, whether visible or invisible, including all thrones, dominions, principalities, and powers. All things were created by Him and for Him. He is before all things, and because of Him all things exist. He is the head of the body, which is the church. He is the beginning, the firstborn of the dead, and the supreme being above all things. God was pleased to allow His fullness to live in Christ. Christ established an everlasting peace through His blood which was shed on the cross, thereby causing all things on earth and in heaven to exist together in harmony through Him.
- HEB 1:3 ~ The Son is the radiance of God's glory and the exact image of His person, who sustains all things by His powerful Word...

God provides an example of Himself in Christ. Just as God sent His Son to be a model for us, Christ sends us to be a model of behavior for others. That is, if you are a Christian, people should be able to see Christ in you and follow you to Him, even as you are following Him to your heavenly home. Christ is the only way to the Father; you can assist others in finding their way by radiating His love.

- PHP 3:13–17 ~ Brothers and sisters, I (Paul) have yet to take hold of the prize, but I have forgotten the past and focused on what lies ahead. I continue to press onward toward the goal for which God has called me heavenward through Jesus Christ. Those of us who are mature in the faith should share this viewpoint. And if you have a different opinion, God will clarify it for you. Let us live up to what we have already attained. Join with others in following my example, and take note of those who live in accordance with the standards we set for you.
- 1 TH 1:4–8 ~ We know, brothers and sisters who are loved by God, that He has chosen you. Because the Gospel of Christ came to you, not just with words, but with the power of the Holy Spirit and with deep conviction. Remember how we lived with you and how you came to imitate us and our Lord? Despite your sufferings, you welcomed the message with a joy that only the Holy Spirit can give. And now you have become a model to other believers, not just in your land, but everywhere your faith has become known.
- 2 TH 3:7–10 ~ You know that you are supposed to follow our example. We were not idle and we paid our way. We worked day and night, laboring and toiling, so that we would not be a burden to you. This we did, not because we had no right to your help, but in order to present ourselves as models for you to follow.
- 1 TI 1:15–17 ~ The truth is, Jesus Christ came to earth to save sinners, of whom I (Paul) am the worst. But for that very reason I was shown mercy, so that in me, the worst of sinners, Christ could reveal His unlimited patience as an example for those who would believe in Him and receive everlasting life. To the eternal, invisible, and immortal King, the only God, be all honor and glory forever and ever, Amen!

- 1 TI 4:12–16 ~ Paul wrote to Timothy: Do not let anyone put you down because you are young, but set an example for the believers through your speech, life, love, faith, and purity. Devote yourself to the public reading of scripture, and preaching and teaching. Never neglect your gift, which was given to you in a prophetic message when the elders laid their hands upon you. Be diligent in these matters, and give yourself completely to them, so that everyone may see your progress. Keep a close watch on your life and your doctrine and persevere in them, for you will prove yourself as well as those who will listen.
- JAM 5:10–11 ~ Remember the prophets as examples of patience in the face of suffering. We consider those who have persevered to be blessed by God.
- 1 PE 2:19–21 ~ It is commendable if a man suffers unjustly because he is conscious of God. If you suffer for doing good and you endure it, you are favored by God. This is one reason you are called, because Christ suffered for you, giving you an example to follow.
- 1 PE 5:1–4 ~ Peter wrote to the elders as a fellow elder and witness of Christ's sufferings: Be shepherds to the flock that God has placed under your care, serving as overseers. Do this, not because you must or for money, but because you want to, as God desires. Be eager to serve, not lording over those God has entrusted to you, but as an example to the flock. And when the Chief Shepherd appears, you will receive a crown of glory that will never fade.

God's Word is a testimony to Himself and Jesus Christ. God showed us the way by sending Himself in human form, as an example of His righteousness through the perfect obedience of a Son to His Father. Having fulfilled the Law on our behalf, that Son was sacrificed as a blood offering for sin, paying the punishment for crimes He never committed. Because He was blameless under the Law, Christ could pay the penalty for death and still live again eternally with God. This reward Christ has passed onto all believers, that He has paid the ransom for sin and redeemed our souls from the grave. By the obedience of Christ anyone can be saved. However, we are unable to earn salvation on our own, as it requires the perfection which only Christ can offer. Once we have accepted these truths, we must reject our sinful nature, so we can become transformed into the image of God by following the example of His Son.

Even as children imitate their parents, so we can imitate God. God has enabled us to do so by creating us in His image, with a mind that can discern right from wrong and the truth of His Word. Through knowledge of the Law, we come to recognize our sinfulness when we disobey our Father in heaven. God's Son is our example of obedience to the Father, and that standard is what a Christian should strive to emulate. By exemplifying Christ, others can detect God's love, our faith, and the living hope within us. A Christian lifestyle and worldview present the patterns our children, spouses, relatives, and neighbors should see and admire (1 PE 3:5; 1 JO 2:6). Sanctification will continue throughout a Christian's life until he or she dies. Then at the resurrection, believers will assume the very image of righteousness and receive a glorified body like Christ's. All adopted children of God will share in His kingdom, as rightful heirs to an inheritance that will last forever.

- JOH 14:2–3,6,19 ~ Jesus said, "In my Father's house are many mansions; I go to prepare one for you. I will return for you, so that where I am you can be also. I am the way, the truth, and the life; nobody can come to the Father without coming through me. In a little while, the world will see me no more, but you will see me again; and because I live, you will live also."
- COL 3:4,10–11 ~ When Christ appears, who is our life, all Christians will appear with Him in glory. For we have become new people, renewed in God's image, by our knowledge of Him through Christ. There are no longer Jews or Greeks, circumcised or uncircumcised, civilized or uncivilized, slave or free, because Christ is all and in all.

Lesson: Stewardship

Stewardship means to serve or to minister. For example, a steward or stewardess on an airliner serves the people who are traveling. A steward for God is a person who serves God, and who serves others in a way that glorifies God. Stewardship implies offering one's services for the wellbeing of others. Everyone should offer his or her services to God, for everything we are and everything we have we owe to Him. And by serving others, we are serving God.

- 2 CO 3:5–6 ~ We owe everything we are to God who has made us ministers of the New Testament. We don't tell them that they must adhere to the very letter of the Law, but to the Spirit; for the Law kills but the Spirit gives life.
- HEB 12:28 ~ Since God has given us the kingdom, let's please Him by serving Him with thankful hearts, with holy fear, and with awe.

Jesus Christ, although He was God, came to earth as a man to be the servant of all. Although He was the King of kings, He humbled Himself, becoming the Servant of servants. Just as He served us, we are to serve Him, and others.

- DAN 7:13–14 ~ From the clouds of heaven there came One like the Son of Man, and to Him was given all dominion, glory and kingdom, so that all people, nations, and cultures should serve Him.
- PHP 2:3–8 ~ Do not do anything through strife or vanity; instead, be humble and regard others as better than yourselves. Do not focus on yourself; focus on others just like Christ did, who although He was equal with God, He took on the form of a man. Instead of exalting Himself, He became the servant of all. He humbled Himself before others and was obedient unto death, even death on the cross.
- 1 PE 5:5 ~ Show respect to your elders. Serve each other. Clothe yourselves in humility. For God resists the proud and gives grace to the humble.

Everyone should give of themselves to the Lord in any way they can, for the Lord has been generous to us in a most extraordinary way. By giving His only Son to die for us, God has given Himself to each and every one of us, for all time. Since God has given Himself to us, and given us a lifetime that will last for eternity, we should offer ourselves to Him and we will last for eternity.

There are six major categories in which we are called by God to be stewards of His love and mercy. I call them the Six T's of Stewardship: Time, Treasure, Talent, Tribute, Tenderness, Testimony.

In each of these six ways we can minister to others and serve God at the same time. Everyone can and should participate; there are no exceptions. If you are too busy to give of your time, you can give of your wealth. If you have no money you can use your talents to serve. If you haven't the time or the money, then be prepared to give testimony at every opportunity, and set an example of God's love by your conduct and attitude.

It is written that a faith without works is a dead faith (JAM 2:17,26). Stewardship is a way of proving you are a Christian through your actions. It is a way of keeping your faith alive.

<u>Offering our Time</u>. Time seems to be a hot commodity these days. Who is willing to stop what they are doing to help others? Who volunteers monthly in the church or the community? Who serves in church every week? Who sets aside time every day to study the scriptures? Who prays without ceasing and is constantly mindful of God?

When God created the universe, He rested on the seventh day and admired His creations. We are to follow His example and set aside a day each week to admire God and His creations. That is what God has instructed in the Ten Commandments (EXO 20:8–11). Therefore, the very least we should do is be willing to give to God one seventh of our time, or one day a week.

You may not have a lot of money to give, but giving your time is even more valuable than money. Time is life, and by giving your time in service to the Lord you are in essence giving yourself. And that is precisely what God has given to us—Himself. Your time is considerably more valuable than any money you could give.

- MAT 25:40,45 ~ Jesus said, "Whenever you have done something to help another person, you have done it to me as well; whenever you have not done something to help another person, you have not done it to me either."
- ROM 12:1 ~ Give yourselves to God. Let yourself be a living sacrifice. After all He has done for you, is that too much to ask?
- COL 3:24 ~ If you help others you are really serving Christ (also EPH 6:7).

Offering our Talents. In addition to giving our time, we should be willing to exercise our talents to the glory of God. Sure, we should spend time studying the Bible, going to church, and helping others. Anybody can do those things. But everyone has special abilities that they can exercise to God's glory.

- ROM 12:6–8 ~ Use those gifts God has given you. If you have the gift of prophecy, exercise that gift according to the proportion of your faith. If your gift is ministry, then minister; if it is teaching, then teach; if it is encouraging, then encourage; if it is giving to the needy, then give generously; if it is leadership, then lead diligently; if it is showing mercy, then do so cheerfully.
- 1 CO 12:4–12,26 ~ There are a variety of spiritual gifts, but only one Spirit. There are different ways of administering but only one Lord. There are different operations, but the same God who works through them. The Spirit is manifested in some way for everyone to use productively. Some people have received wisdom, some knowledge, some faith, all from the same Spirit. Some people have the ability to heal, others to work miracles, others to prophesy, others to discern spirits, others to speak foreign tongues. But all of them are working with the same Spirit, who divides power among His people as He chooses. Just as one body has many members so is Christ one body with many members. When one member suffers, all suffer; when one member is honored, all are honored.
- EPH 4:11–13 ~ God gave some the abilities of apostles, prophets, evangelists, pastors and/or teachers for the work of the ministry, the edifying of the saints, the perfecting of the body of Christ, and the unity of faith. Each can impart the knowledge of the Son of God, who was a perfect man, so that we could take on the characteristics of Christ.

We are blessed with individual gifts: spiritual, mental, and physical. Those who have the talent for teaching, a spiritual gift, can help in Sunday School. Those who have the ability of leadership, a mental gift, can chair a church committee. Those who have a beautiful voice, a physical gift, can sing in the choir. All the talents that exist in the world can and should be used to glorify God. The following are a few examples from a very large list:

- The Arts: Art, Music, Drama
- Business: Accounting, Administration, Management, Clerical
- Social Sciences: Nursing, Counseling, Ministering
- Technical: Maintenance, Construction, Engineering

- Analytical: Decision Making, Research, Problem Solving
- Spiritual: Preaching, Teaching, Discerning Spirits.

<u>Offering our Tribute</u>. Why do we go to church? Is it to honor the Sabbath? Is it to hear and study the Word of God? Those answers would be incomplete. The primary reason we go to church is to show tribute to our Lord for His many blessings and mercy. We do this by offering our thanks, praise, and adoration.

Just as our obedience to God's commandments should not be limited to church attendance on the Sabbath, and just as the study of God's Word should not be limited to Sunday School, so also our worship and praise should not be limited to a day each week or an hour each day. We should praise and glorify God at all times, in all places, and in every aspect of our lives. God has done wonderful things for us. The least we can do is thank and praise Him for it. This requires very little effort on our part, yet it is very enjoyable to God.

- 1 CH 23:30 ~ Give thanks and praise to the Lord every morning and every evening.
- PSA 9:1–2 ~ I will praise you Lord with all my heart; I will show your marvelous works. I will be glad and rejoice. I will sing praises to your holy name.
- PSA 50:23 ~ God says that whoever offers Him praise, glorifies Him. To those who do this, He will show His salvation.
- PSA 96:8 ~ Give God the glory He deserves. Bring your offerings and worship Him.
- PSA 100:4 ~ Enter into God's gates with thanksgiving and into his courts with praise. Be thankful and bless His name.
- PSA 147:1 ~ It is good to sing praises to God, for this is pleasant and beautiful.
- JOH 4:24 ~ Jesus said, "God is Spirit and should be worshipped in spirit and in truth."
- HEB 13:15 ~ Let us continually offer to God the sacrifice of praise; praise and thanks are the fruits of our lips.

<u>Offering our Tender Loving Care</u> (or <u>Tenderness</u>). Part of showing tribute to God is radiating His love. Our lives should be a constant example of the love God has for us. By showing others that we love God, and that we love them as much as we love ourselves, God's love becomes perfected in us. Expressions of love will flourish around you; and that love will rub off on those with whom you come in contact (1 JO 4). In other words, godly love is contagious.

- MAT 5:15–16 ~ Jesus said, "You don't light a candle and then cover it, because it is supposed to give light. So, let the light inside you shine before others; let people see in your actions that you live to glorify your Father in heaven."
- MAR 12:33 ~ It is more important to love God and to love others than to offer different kinds of sacrifices on the alter.
- 1 CO 10:31 ~ Whenever you eat, drink, or do anything, do it for the glory of God.
- 1 CO 13:2–8,13 ~ Even if you have the gift of prophecy, can understand all mysteries, and have a faith to move mountains, you are nothing without love. Even if you give all you have to the poor, you profit nothing if you don't have love. Love is patient. Love is kind. Love is never envious or conceited. Love is not rude, self-seeking, or angered, nor does it find pleasure in sin. Love does not think of sinful things nor is it provoked by evil. Love rejoices in the truth. Love always protects, always trusts, always hopes, and always endures. Love never fails... Faith, hope, and love abide; but the greatest of these three is love.
- 1 PE 3:8 ~ Have unity of mind, sympathy, love for one another, a tender heart, and a humble mind.

- 1 JO 2:6 ~ Whoever says they are a Christian should show they are following Christ by the way they conduct their lives.

Offering our Testimony. Christ came to be God's witness, and Christ has commissioned us to be witnesses. We should share the good news of salvation whenever possible, especially to those who do not believe or who are lost. Jesus Christ, an innocent man, was judged guilty by the Jews and Romans of His time and was put to death for sins that all humans have committed. We have been called as witnesses to testify on His behalf; for He was innocent and we are the guilty ones. We must communicate to others that God is the source of all laws, He is the judge, and He is the enforcer. But we can be found not guilty of our transgressions by placing our trust and hope exclusively in Christ for our absolution and reconciliation. If we confess Christ, then He will testify on our behalf when the day of judgment comes. He will claim us as His because we claimed His blood in order to receive His righteousness, and God gladly will accept us into His kingdom.

- MAT 10:32–33 ~ Jesus said, "If any person confesses me to other people, I will confess them to my Father in heaven. If any person denies me to other people, I will deny them to my Father in heaven."
- MAT 28:19–20 ~ Jesus told His disciples, "Go into every nation and teach the people everything I have taught you. Baptize them in the name of the Father, Son, and Holy Spirit. Remember, I'll always be with you, even until the end of time."
- JOH 20:21 ~ Jesus said, "Peace, brothers. Just as the Father sent me, now I am sending you."
- ACT 20:22–24 ~ Paul wrote: I go forward to Jerusalem, bound in the Spirit, not knowing what will happen except that the Holy Spirit witnesses in every city, and that bondage and affliction go with me. But these things do not move me, neither do I count my life dear to myself, in order that I can finish my course with joy, and complete the ministry which I have received from the Lord Jesus Christ to testify concerning the Gospel of the grace of God.
- 1 CO 11:23–26 ~ Jesus commanded the apostles on the first Holy Communion to partake of the sacrament often to remember Him. Thus, as often as you eat the bread and drink the wine of Holy Communion, you proclaim the death of Christ until His return.
- PHP 2:11 ~ Every tongue should confess that Jesus Christ is Lord, to the glory of God the Father.
- 1 PE 3:15 ~ Sanctify the Lord in your hearts, and always be ready to give an answer, with humility and respect, to anyone who asks about the hope that is within you.
- 1 PE 4:10–11 ~ Whoever has received the gift of salvation in Christ should share that gift with others, as a steward of God's eternal grace. If you preach, do so as a messenger of God. If you minister, do so with the ability God gives you. Do this to glorify God through His Son Jesus Christ.

Offering our Treasure (or Tithe). God prospers those who follow Him. He wants us, who have prospered by His grace, to give back some of our bounty to the church and to the poor. Although we are commanded in the Law to give of our "first fruits," God wants us to give voluntarily and without reservations. Remember the story of the widow who gave all the money she had in the world, even though it was only two mites (MAR 12:41–44)? She gave far more than was required. If we share our profits with the Lord we will continue to prosper.

- DEU 16:17 ~ Everyone should give as they are able, in accordance with the blessings which God has given them.
- PRO 3:9–10 ~ Honor the Lord with your profits, and with the first fruits of your income, and your barns be filled and your winepresses will burst with new wine.

- MAT 6:1–4 ~ Jesus said, "Remember that you shouldn't give to the poor just so others can see you do it; otherwise you will receive no reward from your Father in heaven. In other words, don't sound your horn when you give, like the hypocrites do, who do it only so that others will see them and praise them for it. Truly, this is the only reward they will ever receive for their good deeds. Give generously, but do so in secret; and your Father in heaven will see it and He will reward you openly."
- ACT 20:35 ~ In your labors, give to the needy, remembering the words of Jesus Christ, "It is more blessed to give than to receive."
- 1 CO 16:1 ~ On the first day of each week everyone should set aside something for the Lord in accordance with the degree to which they have prospered by His grace, so it will not be necessary to take a collection.
- 2 CO 9:7 ~ Everyone should give whatever they think is fair in their heart. Giving should be done voluntarily, not out of obligation, for God loves a cheerful giver.

The Bible suggests that we tithe, or give one tenth of our income back to God (LEV 27:30–32). The precedent for tithing was set by Abraham (GEN 14:18–20), who gave tithes to the King of Peace. The tradition continued under Moses (NUM 18:26); in fact, tithing to the church was part of God's instructions to the Israelites (LEV 14:28). The church of Israel was administered by the Levites, who also were commanded to return ten percent of the tithes they were collecting to support themselves (HEB 7:5,9).

- LEV 27:30 ~ Tithe of all your increase to the Lord, for He considers that portion to be holy.
- DEU 14:22 ~ It is God's command that you tithe of your increase to Him.

God assures us that we will be rewarded greatly for tithing. God will bestow abundant blessings on those who share their wealth with others who are in need.

- MAL 3:10 ~ The Lord says, "Bring tithes of all your income to the storage room so that there will be plenty in my house, and prove to yourself how I will open the windows of heaven and pour upon you so many blessings that you will not have room for them."
- LUK 6:38 ~ Give and it shall be given to you in abundance, overflowing; for the same measure that you give is returned unto you.

Summary: Since God has been very generous to us, we should be generous to others. God has given us our lives, and has promised us everlasting life as well. We owe Him our lives, and a life of service; and we will have the privilege of serving Him forever in a state of innocence, purity, and holiness. God has blessed us with special knowledge, skills, and abilities that we can use to serve Him and others, to demonstrate the love He has for us, and to testify that He is the source of all good things. God has bestowed upon us an abundance of treasures, not only spiritual riches and material wealth, but also physical and mental capabilities. We are commissioned to share these treasures with others.

Just as God has been a blessing to us, we should be a blessing to others. Just as God has prospered us, we must share our wealth and belongings with others. Just as God will glorify us with His Son Jesus Christ, we must glorify Him in everything we say and do. Just as God has offered Himself, so we must offer ourselves, sacrificing our time and services. This is what stewardship is all about. To not serve God and others is to rob God of what rightfully belongs to Him: all praise, glory, adoration, knowledge, honor, and wealth. If you are not doing these things you might consider developing a list of activities that you can fit into your schedule; by planning in advance, you will find you have plenty of time for everything to include your work, play, and service. If you claim you don't have the time, you're probably wasting a great deal of it.

- MAL 3:6–8 ~ God says, "I am the Lord, I never change. But you have not kept my commandments. Return to me and I will return to you. Will you rob God? Yet you have robbed me. You ask how you have robbed me? By not presenting your tithes and offerings."
- LUK 12:48 ~ Jesus said, "To whomever much is given, much will be required. To those who have committed much, of them more will be asked."

Methods of Being a Good Steward

Commodity	Avenues of Service
Time	Helping others in need. Reserving individual time for studying God's Word, and attending Church and Sunday School. Praying in the Spirit and reserving time for spiritual meditation.
Talents	Using spiritual gifts, special talents, and innate abilities in service to your church and community. Exercising your gifts to the glory of God. Acknowledging God in all your achievements.
Tribute	Offering praise and adoration. Attending worship service; singing hymns of praise; reciting psalms; giving thanks. Glorifying God in all that you say and do.
Tenderness	Living a Christian lifestyle. Being loving, kind, compassionate, and humble to others. Radiating God's love.
Testimony	Witnessing the truth. Sharing the good news of the Gospel. Confessing Christ. Participating in the Holy Sacraments. Evangelizing in the home, community, nation, and the world.
Treasure (Tithe)	Being charitable to orphans, widows, the poor, etc. Providing financial support to the church. Supporting missions.

Let Us Ever Walk with Jesus

Let us ever walk with Jesus, follow His example pure,
Flee the world, which would deceive us, and to sin our souls allure.
Ever in His footsteps treading, body here, yet soul above
Full of faith and hope and love, let us do the Father's bidding
Faithful Lord, abide with me; Savior lead, I follow Thee.

Let us also die with Jesus and avoid the second death;
From our soul's destruction frees us, quickens us with life's glad breath.
Let us mortify while living, flesh and blood and die to sin;
And the grave that shuts us in shall but prove the gate to heaven.
Jesus here I die to Thee, there to live eternally.

Let us gladly live with Jesus; since He's risen from the dead,
Death and grave must soon release us, Jesus, Thou art now our Head,
We are truly Thine own members; where Thou livest, there live we.
Take and own us constantly, faithful Friend, as Thy dear brethren.
Jesus, here I live to Thee, also in eternity.

Lesson: Tools for Change

In order to change behavior, a person must change his or her thinking; in order to change thoughts, that person must have a change of heart. You've probably heard it said: "You can't change anybody but yourself, and you have to make the effort to change." It's true isn't it? Wanting to change requires caring about yourself; and caring requires love. And the love of God can change anybody.

God is the source of all love; in fact, God is love. The Lord said that the most important commandment is to love God first, and the second most important is to love others as yourself. Notice that the second part includes you and implies that you should love yourself as you do others. All too often, people neglect themselves when it comes to distributing their love; they become too wrapped up trying to satisfy everyone else and end up neglecting their own needs.

- PRO 3:5–7 ~ Trust in the Lord with all your heart and don't rely on your own insight. In all your ways acknowledge Him and He will make your paths straight.
- ECC 10:2 ~ A wise heart inclines a person to do what is right.
- MAT 22:35–40 ~ A lawyer in the gathering, in an attempt to trick the Lord, asked, "Master, what is the greatest commandment of the Law?" Jesus replied, "Love the Lord your God with all your heart, soul, and mind: this is the first and most important commandment. And the second most important commandment is similar to the first: love your neighbor as yourself. If you obey these two commandments, you will fulfill all the Law and the prophecy."
- 1 CO 13:2–8,13 ~ Even if you have the gift of prophecy, can understand mysteries, and have a faith to move mountains, you are nothing without love. Even if you give all you have to the poor, you profit nothing if you don't have love. Love is patient. Love is kind. Love is never envious or conceited. Love is not rude, self-seeking, or angered, nor does is it find pleasure in sin. Love does not think of sinful things nor is it provoked by evil. Love rejoices in the truth. Love always protects, always trusts, always hopes, and always endures. Love never fails. Faith, hope and love abide, but the greatest of these three is love.
- COL 3:15 ~ Let the peace of God rule in your heart.

One of the major roadblocks to change is fear, like being afraid of failing, or of the past coming back to haunt you, or of what you have become, or that nothing will change, or that it will be too hard. People worry endlessly about unimportant or trivial matters; they seem preoccupied dwelling on life's stumbling blocks. If they expended the same amount of energy working the problem that they did worrying about it, then it probably wouldn't be a problem anymore.

Love conquers the fear that torments our minds. Since the power of love comes from God, it follows that fear must be the power of evil, because the two cannot coexist. Love consumes fear just as light consumes darkness.

- 1 JO 4:7–12,16–21 ~ Let us love one another, for love is from God, and those who love are born of God and know Him. If you don't love God you can't know Him because God is love. The love of God was manifested among us through His only Son, so we might live through Him. If God loves us so much, we should love one another; if we love one another, God lives in us and His love is perfected in us. If you abide in love you abide in God, and God abides in you. This perfect love gives us confidence on the day of judgment, because there is no fear in love but perfect love destroys fear, because fear brings torment. We love because God loved us first. You can't say you love God and hate your brother without being a liar, because you can't hate someone you have seen and still love God who you have never seen. So, you should love God and your brother (neighbor).

- 2 TI 1:7 ~ God did not give us a spirit of fear, but of power, love and a sound mind.

Fear causes us to have a tormented mind, but love enables us to have a sound mind. If you want to think clearly, and stay focused on the positive, you need God's love living in your heart. Otherwise, fear will block your way and you may veer from the path. Thus, the first and most important tool for change in your toolbox is love, which will overcome the obstacle of fear that the devil will use to infiltrate your thoughts.

Once the person cares enough to amend his or her life, they begin to believe that such change is possible. But you can be sure that Satan will try to destroy your faith by bombarding you with doubt. When it comes to God, we don't doubt Him because He never goes back on His Word. But when we place our faith in ourselves or others, there is a chance that we will be disappointed. Therefore, your faith and confidence should be placed on God, who changes everything in your life once you have experienced that change of heart. You cannot succeed without Him; indeed, without God you will fail. Faith is an important tool in the toolbox, because it helps us overcome doubt, which constantly tries to dominate our thoughts and leave us with uncertainty. Doubt comes from the weakness of our flesh, but faith comes from the Holy Spirit and assures us of the truth which eliminates uncertainty.

- 2 CO 5:17 ~ If anyone lives in Christ, he or she becomes a new creation; old ways have passed away, and behold, all things have become new.
- HEB 12:2 ~ Jesus Christ is the author and finisher of our faith.
- JOH 15:3–5 ~ Jesus said, "Now that you have been cleansed by the Word which I have spoken to you, you can live in me as I live in you. Just as a branch cannot bear fruit when separated from the vine, neither can you unless you stay connected to me. I am the vine and you are the branches. If you stay connected to me you will bear much fruit, but apart from me you can do nothing."

God promises to give us everything we need, in addition to the kingdom. That is our hope, and because we have faith, we do not doubt Him. If you cling to His promises, you will succeed in achieving the changes you desire, without depending on your own strength, but letting the Lord be your strength and guide. When you follow in the ways of righteousness, you will always be heading in the right direction. God will illuminate the route for you for His light is ever-present; if you do not see the light, you are off the beaten track or going in the wrong direction.

- PSA 119:105 ~ God's Word is a lamp unto my feet and a light unto my path.
- PSA 145:14–16 ~ The Lord raises those who fall and lifts those who are down. The eyes of all wait for Him and he gives them what they need when they need it. He opens His hand and satisfies the desires of every living thing.
- MAT 6:31–34 ~ Jesus said, "Don't worry about your worldly needs; your Father in heaven knows what you need. Instead, seek first the kingdom of heaven and the righteousness of God, and this you will receive, as well as all your earthly needs. Don't be concerned about tomorrow for it will bring its own problems; you have enough to deal with today without worrying about tomorrow."
- HEB 11:1 ~ Faith is the assurance of things hoped for, the evidence of things not seen.

Looking forward to the possibilities that lie ahead gives us purpose, courage, and direction. If you keep focused on the big picture, you will see the Lord waiting at the finish line. And He will give you everything you need and you will prosper, because that's what He said would happen if you remain connected to Him. However, we don't know exactly what His plan is or when it will happen because if we did, we could anticipate everything and life would be awfully boring. So, we must never give up hope, and that hope leads to glory.

When one feels hopeless, they become desperate, behave irrationally, and take unnecessary risks. Hope is a powerful tool because it enables us to conquer despair, another one of those obstacles that the evil one uses to distract us from seeing the big picture. Hope becomes the model of change, whereby we can envision what lies ahead, the opportunities available to us, and what positive growth might look like.

- PSA 130:5 ~ I wait for the Lord; my soul waits for Him and in His Word I will hope.
- ECC 8:6–7 ~ For every purpose under heaven there is a season, a time designated by God, although misery and trials may continue to occur. Since we do not know what that purpose is, who (but God) will be able to tell us when?
- ROM 5:1–5 ~ Being justified by faith we achieve peace with God through Christ, in whom we have access by that faith to the grace in which we stand, rejoicing in the hope of glory. Therefore, we rejoice in time of tribulation, knowing that it teaches us patience, it strengthens our hope, and we gain experience.
- ROM 8:24–25 ~ We are saved because we hope. But hope that is seen is not hope, for who hopes for things they can see? However, if we hope for what we cannot see, we must be patient.
- GAL 5:5–6 ~ Through the Spirit, by faith, we wait for the hope of righteousness. Circumcision is of no avail; instead, it is faith working through love.

Clearly, it follows that patience is another valuable tool. Never give up, quit, or not try, because that is the only way to guarantee failure. Even if we do not succeed the first, second, or tenth time, this does not constitute failure, because once you succeed in a given challenge then failure is no longer possible, and you will be ready to move onto the next challenge. Unfortunately, it takes time; but our timeframe is usually not in concert with God's. If you trust in Him, you know that good things will come your way; you just aren't sure what or when.

Patience overcomes exasperation, giving up, quitting. The more you try the better you get, and when you triumph, you'll have a new skill set to bring with you as you take a giant step forward.

- PRO 1:21 ~ People develop their own plans, but it is the Lord's purpose that will prevail.
- LUK 21:19 ~ Jesus said, "The result of your patience is to possess your soul."
- JAM 1:3 ~ The trying of your faith produces patience.
- ROM 12:12 ~ Rejoice in hope, be patient in tribulation, and be constant in prayer.

Like a skilled Olympic athlete, you can run this race and win the crown if you stay focused on the road ahead and never lose sight of the finish line. You will notice the hurdles that you must breach, but they will not mask your view of what lies beyond. And you will leap over them with ease because you have trained hard for the event and in the process developed the patience and ability to persevere.

Before, you may have considered the hurdles as obstacles that often obscured your vision of the goal. But they were not obstacles at all, just challenges that you faced head-on and eventually overcame, thereby providing additional knowledge and ability. In fact, these challenges became opportunities for further success, each of which got you closer to the objective, which strengthened your resolve, confidence, and character.

These gifts of love, faith, hope, and patience, they are freely given and form the basis of your relationship with God. They provide the inner strength that enables you to overcome adversity and periodic setbacks. The key to employing these tools effectively is staying united with God in spirit. We connect with God the same way we connect with others: communication. Speak to Him often in prayer; listen to Him as you read and meditate on His Word, and when the Holy Spirit speaks to you through ministers of the Word.

Let Christ live in you and He will show you the way for He is the key to opening your heart. Always look forward, not backwards, expecting only that God's purpose in your life will be revealed in due time and the timing will be impeccable. Stay on the highway that takes you to the ultimate destination, which is heaven, where the reward of eternal life with the Lord awaits you. Meanwhile, enjoy the journey as you explore all the possibilities, because you will discover meaning in your life, purpose to everything that happens, and guidance at every crossroads.

- ISA 64:4 ~ Nobody has ever heard, seen, or even perceived the wonderful things that God has prepared for those who love Him. (also 1 CO 2:9)
- LUK 17:20–21 ~ Jesus said, "The kingdom of heaven will not appear while you are looking around for it, because the kingdom of heaven is found within you."
- JOH 14:2 ~ Jesus said, "In my Father's house are many mansions; I'm going ahead to prepare one for you."
- GAL 5:22–23 ~ Fruits of the Spirit include love, joy, peace, patience, kindness, goodness, faithfulness, gentleness, and self-control. There is no law against these things.
- PHP 4:8 ~ Whatever is true, honest, just, pure, lovely, uplifting, virtuous, and praiseworthy—think about these things.

Remain positive in your outlook. Don't let the negativity rule your mind; such thoughts will only bring you down, and usually have no semblance of truth. There is no challenge too menacing or temptation too great that you cannot overcome with the Lord on your side. Bring your troubles to Him and He will give you peace, assurance, and conviction. All your dreams will come true and you will become the person you strive to be, and were meant to be.

- LUK 1:37 ~ Nothing is impossible with God.
- PHP 4:13 ~ I can do all things through Christ who strengthens me.
- JAM 4:7 ~ Submit to the Lord. Resist the devil and he will flee from you.
- 1 JO 4:4 ~ You are from God my children, and have overcome the world; because greater is He that is in you (Christ) than he that is in the world (Satan).

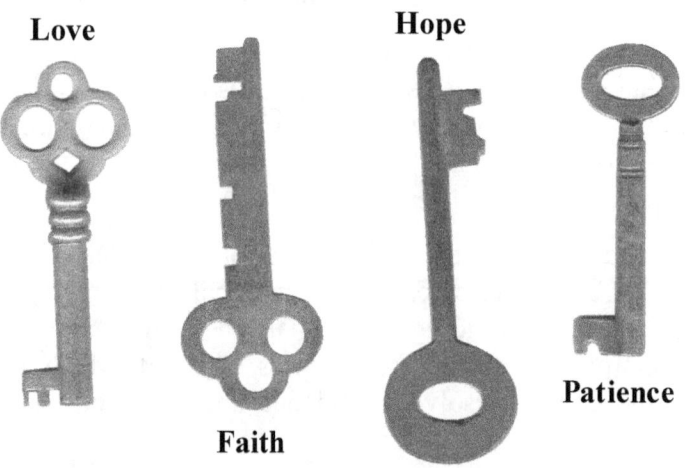

CHAPTER TWO

WHO IS GOD?

THE ALMIGHTY

There is only one God. He is the creator of everything, both visible and invisible. God is our heavenly Father. God exists in three persons: Father, Son, and Holy Spirit. While God manifests Himself to us in three ways, He is still one being. Thus, there is only one God, and there are no other gods. The concept of more than one god is an invention of people. Those who worship other gods might as well be worshipping Satan or demons. God is King of kings and Lord of lords. He is the first, last, and is everlasting. He always existed and always will: He is the Ancient of Days. He is omniscient (all-knowing), omnipotent (all-powerful), and omnipresent (always present). God exists in all things: physical, mental, and spiritual, seen and unseen. God is light and God is love.

- 1 CH 29:11 ~ Yours, oh Lord, is all greatness, power, glory, victory, and majesty. Everything in heaven and earth is yours, including the everlasting kingdom. You are exalted as head above all creatures.
- PSA 102:27 ~ God is always the same and His existence is eternal.
- PSA 145:17 ~ God is righteous in all His ways and Holy in all His works.
- ISA 33:22 ~ The Lord is our judge, lawgiver, and king.
- ISA 46:9 ~ There is nothing and nobody like God.
- 2 TI 2:13 ~ Although we are often faithless, He remains faithful, for He cannot deny Himself.
- JAM 1:17 ~ Every good thing comes from God; every perfect gift comes from above, from the Father of lights. God never varies, and in Him there is no darkness, not even a shadow.
- 1 JO 4:8 ~ If you don't love you can't know God, because God is love.
- REV 1:17; REV 22:13 ~ He is the first and last, the beginning and the end.

God is Omniscient.

- JOB 37:16 ~ Do you know the way the clouds are balanced, and the other wondrous works of Him who is perfect in knowledge?
- JOB 42:1–2 ~ Job said to the Lord, "I know you can do anything, and that no thought can be hidden from you."
- PSA 94:11 ~ God knows all the vain thoughts of humankind.
- PSA 139:1–6 ~ Lord, you have searched me and you know everything about me. You discern my thoughts, and are familiar with all my ways. I could never attain such knowledge. Even before I speak, you know what I will say.
- PSA 147:4 ~ God knows how many stars there are, and has given each one a name.

CHAPTER TWO

- PRO 15:3 ~ The eyes of the Lord are everywhere, seeing all the evil and all the good.
- MAT 10:30 ~ God even knows the number of hairs on your head.
- JOH 16:30 ~ The disciples said to Jesus, "We know that you are all-knowing and that you came from God."
- 1 CO 2:10 ~ The Holy Spirit searches everything, including the depths of God.
- HEB 4:13 ~ There isn't a single creature that God doesn't see; nothing can be hidden from Him for He sees everything we do.

God is Omnipotent.

- GEN 1:1–27 ~ God created the heaven and earth, day and night, oceans and land, and all living creatures, and He created man in His image.
- DEU 4:35,39 ~ Has any other God demonstrated such wonders, signs, and might? The Lord is God in heaven and earth; there is no other God.
- ISA 45:5,7 ~ God says, "I am the Lord; there are no other gods besides me. I created the light and the dark; I created peace and despair."
- DAN 7:9,22 ~ The Ancient of Days sat on His throne. The Ancient of Days came for judgment.
- MAL 2:10 ~ Don't we all have the same Father? And didn't God create all of us? Then why do we profane the covenant God made with our forefathers by corrupting the faith among one another?
- JOH 1:1–4 ~ In the beginning was God. All things were made by Him.
- ACT 17:24 ~ God made the world and everything in it; He is Lord of heaven and earth.
- COL 1:16–17 ~ He created all things on heaven and earth, visible and invisible. He is before all things, and holds all things together.
- HEB 3:4 ~ A house may be built by a man, but God built everything.
- JDE 1:25 ~ To the only God, our Savior through Jesus Christ our Lord, be all glory, majesty, dominion and authority, now and forever.
- REV 17:14; REV 19:16 ~ He is Lord of lords and King of kings.
- REV 19:6 ~ I heard the voice of a great multitude which sounded like the voice of many oceans or like thunder, and which said, "Alleluia! For the omnipotent Lord God reigns."

God is Omnipresent.

- 1 KI 8:27 ~ Will God live on earth? Behold, even the highest heavens cannot contain God.
- PSA 90:2 ~ You are God since before the earth was created, and even from eternity to eternity.
- PSA 139:7–8 ~ I cannot go anywhere without God being there, for He occupies all of heaven and earth.
- JER 23:24 ~ The Lord says, "Can anyone hide from me? Do I not fill heaven and earth?"
- MAT 18:20 ~ Jesus said, "When two or more are gathered in my name, I am there."
- MAT 28:20 ~ Jesus said, "I am with you always, even forever".
- 1 CO 12:5 ~ God is always the same.
- EPH 4:5–6 ~ There is only one Lord, one faith, one baptism, one God and Father of us all, who is above all, through all, and in all.
- HEB 1:8 ~ His throne is forever.
- HEB 13:8 ~ Jesus Christ is the same yesterday, today, and forever.

God is the One and Only God.

- DEU 6:4 ~ Listen Israel, the Lord your God is one Lord.
- DEU 32:17,39 ~ Those pagans were sacrificing to demons, not gods; new gods were invented by people. Besides God, there are no others.
- PSA 96:5 ~ The mythological gods of the people are nothing but idols.
- ISA 37:19–20 ~ Their gods will be cast into the fire, for they weren't gods at all but an invention of humans. Let all the kingdoms know that you alone are God.
- ISA 41:23–24 ~ Let's see if these other gods can tell us the future, do good, and impress us with their might. Those who choose such gods are an abomination.
- JER 2:11; JER 5:7 ~ These other so-called gods are not gods.
- JER 10:10 ~ The Lord is the only true, living God.
- JER 16:20 ~ Man cannot produce gods.
- MAR 12:29 ~ Jesus said, "The Lord God is one."
- JOH 20:17 ~ Jesus said, "I am ascending to my Father and your Father, to my God and your God."
- ROM 16:27 ~ To the only wise God be glory forevermore.
- 2 CO 4:4 ~ The prince of this world (Satan) prevents people from seeing the true God.
- 2 CO 10:20 ~ What pagans offer as a sacrifice they sacrifice to demons.
- GAL 4:8 ~ You were in bondage to beings who were not gods.
- 1 TH 1:9 ~ Turn from worshipping idols to worshipping the living and true God.
- 2 TH 2:3–4 ~ Beware of the son of hell, who exalts himself and proclaims to be God.
- 1 TI 1:17 ~ To the only wise God, immortal King of ages, be all glory and honor forever.
- 1 TI 6:15–16 ~ To the only sovereign God, immortal King of kings and Lord of lords, be all honor and dominion.
- JAM 2:19 ~ Even the demons believe in one God, and they tremble.

The first and last letters of the Greek Alphabet are often used to symbolize God who was, is, and will be the only true God (ISA 44:6). Jesus Christ, who has been with God since the beginning, is also described as the Alpha and Omega for they are one (REV 1:8).

Powers of God

God is omnipotent, meaning all powerful. He created everything. Nothing is impossible for Him. God the Father's power is manifested through the Holy Spirit. God's Holy Spirit communicates God's Word to us. The Holy Spirit became a human being to help us know God better and learn about His righteousness firsthand. Jesus Christ is God in the flesh. Since Jesus Christ possessed the Holy Spirit, He had access to the powers of God the Father. Thus, Christ exhibited the same powers as God, proving that He was God.

God and Christ also can bestow their power on humans. The Bible presents many examples of the powers exhibited by God's people because of their faith (MAT 10:1; LUK 10:19; HEB 11:7–38).

- 2 CH 25:8 ~ God has the power to help people and to cast them down into hell.
- JOB 26:7–14 ~ God spreads the sky over the empty space and suspends the earth upon nothing. He holds the water in the clouds but the clouds do not burst under the weight. He covers the face of the moon. He marks the horizon over the waters for a boundary between darkness and light. The heavens quake at His voice, and His breath turns the sky into brightness. His was the hand that pierced the slithering snake. And these are among the least of His great works.
- PSA 49:15 ~ God has the power to redeem a person's soul from the power of the grave.
- MAT 9:6 ~ Jesus Christ has the power to forgive sins.
- MAT 28:18 ~ Jesus Christ said, "All the power in heaven and in earth belongs to me."
- LUK 1:35 ~ God had the power to allow His Holy Spirit to come upon Mary and conceive a child.
- LUK 4:32 ~ The people were astonished at the power Jesus displayed in His words.
- LUK 12:5 ~ Jesus Christ has the power to kill people and cast them into Hell.
- JOH 1:12 ~ God has the power to give us the choice to become His children if we believe.
- JOH 10:18 ~ Jesus Christ has the power to lay down His life and to take it back again.
- JOH 16:30 ~ The disciples told Jesus, "We know that you know everything and that nobody can tell you anything you don't already know. This is how we know that you came from God."
- JOH 17:2 ~ God has the power over all flesh, and the power to give eternal life.
- ROM 13:1 ~ There is no power but of God; all powers that exist are ordained by God.
- 1 CO 1:24 ~ Jesus Christ is the power of God and the wisdom of God.
- EPH 1:20–21 ~ God set Jesus at His right hand, with power greater than all principalities, powers, and dominions. His name is greater than every other name in this world and the world to come.
- COL 1:16 ~ All things in heaven and earth, visible and invisible, thrones, dominions, principalities, and powers were created by Him and for Him.
- HEB 4:12 ~ God's Word is swift, sharp, and powerful. Like a double-edged sword, it can pierce and divide the very soul and spirit, and it can discern the thoughts and intents of the heart.
- REV 1:18 ~ Jesus Christ said, "I am the living One. Behold, I died, and now I am alive forever. And I have the keys to Death and Hell."

Lesson: Awesome God

Our God is awesome, majestic, and marvelous. We cannot fully grasp the magnitude of His power, glory, and dominion. We only can wonder about His amazing creations, the intricacy of the universe, the miracles of life, and His overwhelming presence.

- EXO 15:11 ~ Who among the gods is like you, oh Lord? Who else is majestic in holiness, awesome in glory, and works such great wonders?
- 1 CH 29:11 ~ Yours, oh Lord, is all greatness, power, glory, victory, and majesty. Everything in heaven and earth is yours, including the everlasting kingdom. You are exalted as head above all creatures.
- JOB 5:9; JOB 37:5,22; JOB 40:10 ~ God performs wonders that cannot be fathomed and miracles that cannot be counted. His voice thunders in marvelous ways; He does great things beyond our understanding. He comes to us in golden splendor and in awesome magnificence. God is adorned with majesty and excellence, with glory and beauty.
- PSA 29:4; PSA 96:6: PSA 104:1; PSA 118:15–16 ~ The voice of the Lord is powerful and majestic. Splendor and grandeur are before Him; strength and glory are His sanctuary. Praise the Lord, oh my soul! He is awesome; He is clothed in brilliance and majesty. Shouts of joy and victory resound in the tabernacles of the righteous saying, "The right hand of the Lord is lifted high; His right hand has done mighty things."
- ECC 5:1–2,7 ~ Trod carefully when you enter God's house. Listen intently rather than offering the sacrifice of fools who do not realize their error. Do not hasten to speak and when you do let your words be few. Much dreaming and many words are meaningless. Therefore, stand in awe of God.

Because God is so magnificent, we cannot help but marvel at Him. It is proper to fear God and His strength. However, His people fear Him because He is great and powerful, not because they are scared. We are not afraid, for God is our faith and our hope. His great love preserves us and comforts us. In His hands we feel safe, not fearful.

- 1 SA 12:24 ~ Fear only the Lord and serve Him in truth with all your heart. Consider the wonderful things He has done for you.
- JOB 4:6–7 ~ Eliphaz, who surmised that God was punishing Job, asked Job "Isn't the fear of God your confidence, hope, and righteousness? Did the innocent ever perish? Were the upright ever destroyed?"
- MIC 5:4–5 ~ He will stand and feed His flock in the strength of the Lord and in the majesty of His name. And His sheep will live securely and in peace, for His greatness will extend to the ends of the earth.
- 1 JO 4:16,18–19 ~ We know and believe in God's love for us, because God is love. Those that live in love live in God and He lives in them. There is no fear in love, but perfect love casts out fear, because in fear there is torment. Those who fear are not made perfect in love. We love God because He loved us first.

God has promised us so many wonderful things, and only He can make them happen. Those who believe in God's promises will live forever. If we trust in Him for our salvation, we needn't fear His wrath. Since He is on our side, we have nothing to fear at all. For those who lead a life of sin without repentance there is much to fear, for God will destroy their bodies and souls in hell.

CHAPTER TWO

- DEU 28:58–59 ~ If you do not observe God's Law or revere His glorious and awesome name, He will send horrible plagues, harsh and prolonged disasters, and severe and lingering illnesses upon you and your descendants.
- PSA 23:4 ~ Even when I walk through the valley of the shadow of death, I will not be afraid of any evil, for God will be with me to comfort me.
- PSA 33:8,10 ~ Let all the earth fear the Lord; let all the inhabitants of the world stand in awe of Him. Many are the woes of the wicked, but the Lord's unfailing love surrounds those who trust in Him.
- PRO 1:7,33 ~ The fear of the Lord is the beginning of knowledge, but fools despise knowledge and wisdom. Those who seek God will be safe and sound from the fear of evil.
- MAT 10:28 ~ Jesus said, "Don't be afraid of those who can kill the body but not the soul. Fear only God who can destroy both your body and soul in hell."

If you do not trust in Christ for your salvation you will experience God's wrath in a big way. What a terrible fate awaits the ungodly and the wicked. God is both awesome in the magnitude of His love as well as in the gravity of His vengeance.

- ISA 2:10,19,21 ~ Hide in the rocks for fear of the Lord and for the glory of His majesty. For He has risen to shake the earth.
- ISA 28:15,18–19 ~ You brag that you have entered into a covenant with death, and have made an agreement with the grave. Do you think you will escape the overwhelming scourge by making a lie your refuge and a falsehood your hiding place? But your covenants with death and your agreements with hell will be null and void. You will be beaten down by the overwhelming scourge. Then you will understand this message and it will bring sheer terror unto you.
- ROM 13:4 ~ If you do what is evil, be afraid, for God's minister will not bear the sword in vain, because he is sent to execute wrath upon those who do evil.
- HEB 10:26–27,31 ~ If you deliberately continue sinning after you have received the knowledge of truth, there will remain no sacrifice for sins. All you will receive is the fearful expectation of judgment and a raging fire that will consume the enemies of God. Yes, it is a dreadful thing to fall into the vengeful hands of the living God.
- REV 21:8 ~ The fearful, the unbelieving, the murderers, prostitutes, sorcerers, idolaters, and liars will take part in the lake of fire which is the second death.

We know that God has shown Himself to us through Jesus Christ and that Christ is the instrument of God's Holy Spirit. He is our Savior who will return someday and bring us home to our Heavenly Father. Christ revealed to all people the salvation God grants to anyone that follows Him. What a fabulous plan God developed to ensure that we could live with Him forever in a state of purity, righteousness, and blessedness.

Christ, then, is the administrator of God's plan of salvation. He is the right hand of God who performed God's will and wielded His mighty power here on earth. And His Holy Spirit remains with us to ensure we continue our mission on earth and emerge victorious.

- PSA 17:7; PSA 45:4; PSA 98:1 ~ Show us your wonderful loving kindness, Lord, who saved us by your right hand, those who trust in your protection. In your majesty, Lord, ride forth victoriously on behalf of truth, humility, and righteousness. Let your right hand display your awesome deeds. Sing unto the Lord a new song, for He has done marvelous things. The right hand of His holy arm has won for Him the victory.
- PSA 80:14–19 ~ Return to us Almighty God! Look down from heaven and see! Watch over this vineyard that your right hand has planted, and the Branch you have raised up for

yourself. The vine has been cut down and burned in the fire; at your rebuke your people perish. Let your hand rest on the man at your right, the Son of Man who you have raised for yourself. Do this so we will not turn our backs on you. Revive us so we can call on your name. Turn us back, Lord of hosts, and let your face shine on us so we can be saved.

- PSA 110:1 ~ The Lord said to my Lord, "Sit at my right hand and I will make your enemies your footstool." [This verse is quoted many times in the New Testament by Christ and the apostles. For example, see MAR 12; ACT 2; HEB 1.]
- ISA 41:10 ~ God says, "Fear not for I am with you; do not be dismayed for I am your God. I will strengthen and help you; I will hold you up with my righteous right hand."
- MAR 12:35–37 ~ Jesus was teaching in the temple. He asked the people why the teachers of the law insisted that Christ was the son of David. David himself, speaking by the Holy Spirit, declared: The Lord said to my Lord, "Sit at my right hand and I will make your enemies your footstool." Jesus continued, "If David calls him Lord, then how can He be David's son?"
- MAR 14:61–62 ~ The high priest asked Jesus, "Are you the Christ?" Jesus replied, "I am. And you will see the Son of Man sitting at the right hand of power, and coming in the clouds of heaven."
- ACT 2:22–35; ACT 5:31–32 ~ Peter preached to the crowds about the miracles of Christ, including His resurrection. Peter reminded them about the prophecies of David concerning Christ. Peter taught them, "God raised Jesus to life, and we are witnesses of that fact. He has been exalted to the right hand of God. God exalted Him as Prince and Savior to His own right hand, so that He might give repentance and forgiveness to Israel. We are witnesses to these things, and so is the Holy Spirit whom God has given to those who obey Him."
- ACT 7:55–56 ~ Stephen, being enthralled by the Holy Spirit, gazed into heaven and saw the glory of God, and Jesus standing at His right hand. And Stephen proclaimed, "Behold, I see an opening in the heavens and the Son of Man standing at God's right hand."
- ROM 8:34 ~ Who is He that condemns? It is Christ who died, and more than that, who rose from the dead and now sits at the right hand of God, and who also intercedes for us.
- EPH 1:19–20 ~ God's incomparably great power, like the working of His mighty strength, was exerted through Christ when He arose from the dead, and took the seat at God's own right hand in the heavenly places. His reign is far above all rule and authority, power and dominion, and every title that can be given in the present age and in the age to come.
- HEB 1:3; HEB 8:1–2; HEB 10:12; HEB 12:2–3 ~ The Son is the radiance of God's glory and the exact representation of His being, sustaining all things by His powerful Word. After He had provided purification for sins, He sat down at the right hand of His Majesty in heaven. To summarize, we have a High Priest, who sits at the right hand of God's throne in heaven and who serves in the sanctuary, the true tabernacle, set up by the Lord and not by man. This Priest offered one sacrifice for sins that will last forever. Let us fix our eyes on Jesus Christ, the author and finisher of our faith, who for the joy set before Him endured the cross, scorning the shame, and now sits at God's right hand. Consider Him who endured such opposition from sinful men, so that you will not grow weary and lose heart.

Because we have claimed Christ as our Lord and Savior, God has claimed us as His people. It is our duty to declare Him to the world, and to be witnesses in our lives for Him. We show our appreciation for His many blessings by giving Him the credit, the thanks, the praise, and the glory. Even as Christ was the instrument of God's right hand, so are we to be His instruments. He is the conductor and we are the orchestra, and together we will make beautiful music in His name. Like a perfectly calibrated machine, the body of Christ collectively turns out works of praise which will bring greater glory to the Father, who will glorify us in the end along with His Son.

- 1 CH 16:12,24–25 ~ Remember God's marvelous works, His wonders, and His judgments. Declare His glory among the heathen, and His amazing works among all nations. For the Lord is great, and He is worthy of our praise.
- PSA 9:1–2 ~ I will praise you, Lord, with all my heart. I will speak of all your wonders. I will be glad and rejoice. I will sing praises to your name.
- 1 PE 2:9 ~ You are a unique, chosen generation, a priesthood and holy nation, because you praise Him who called you from darkness into His marvelous light.
- JDE 1:25 ~ To the only wise God our Savior be glory and majesty, dominion and power, now and forevermore, Amen.
- REV 15:3 ~ They sing the song of Moses, God's servant, and the song of the Lamb, saying, "Great and marvelous are your works, Lord God Almighty; just and true are your ways, oh King of saints."

God has promised us many things, including the kingdom, if only we believe. He gives us the power to do His will, to minister to others, to overcome the world, and to possess the kingdom. The forces of evil, as well as certain unbelievers, will be obstructions in our path. However, no impediment is too great that we cannot achieve what God has guaranteed. It is His Spirit living in us which gives us the power to make things happen; we can do nothing without Him. With Him, we can do everything. Therefore, we needn't be afraid or dismayed when we are threatened or the odds are against us, because God and His angels will be fighting on our side.

How awesome is our God who performs mighty deeds, and enables us to do amazing things according to His purpose and desire. The following is but a sampling of the great things God did through the lives of His people.

- GEN 6—7 ~ Noah built the great ark and gathered all the animals.
- EXO 14; EXO 17; NUM 20 ~ Moses parted the Red Sea and brought water from the rocks.
- NUM 13—14; JOS 14 ~ Moses sent spies into the land expecting them to return and report on their findings. Of the twelve spies, ten returned with an unfavorable report that generated fear concerning the strength of the inhabitants there. Two returned with a favorable report, namely Caleb and Joshua. They believed God's words and were eager to take the land that God had promised Israel. Caleb quieted the people and said, "Let's go immediately and possess the land, for we can overcome those people." But the others were afraid, and saw themselves as grasshoppers compared to the mighty giants that lived in the land. Joshua and Caleb pleaded with the people saying, "This is a great land, flowing with milk and honey. Let us not rebel against the Lord or be afraid of the inhabitants there, for we will eat them alive." But the people did not listen. And God cursed Israel, telling Moses how the adults would never make it to the Promised Land except for Joshua and Caleb. God said, "My servant Caleb has another Spirit within him, and because he followed my advice completely, he will enter the land and possess it." And forty-five years later at the age of eighty-five Caleb was still eager for the Lord, and in his patience, he inherited the land God promised.
- 1 SA 17:36–37,45–47 ~ David told King Saul, "I have killed a lion and a bear, and this uncircumcised Philistine (Goliath) will join them, since he has defied the armies of the living God. The Lord that delivered me from the lion and the bear will deliver me from this Philistine." And Saul said to David, "Go, and may the Lord be with you." Upon arriving at the battleground, David told Goliath, "You have come with a sword, a spear, and a shield, but I come in the name of the Lord of hosts, the God of the armies of Israel, whom you have defied. Today the Lord will deliver you into my hand, for I will strike you down and take your head as a trophy. And everyone will know that there is a God in Israel who saves, not with a sword or spear. This battle belongs to the Lord, for He will give you to us."

- 1 KI 17—18 ~ Elijah raised a boy from the dead and brought fire down from heaven.
- ACT 3; ACT 9; ACT 14; ACT 20 ~ The apostles healed the lame and raised the dead.
- HEB 11:7–38 ~ Because of their great faith, men of God were able to endure anything and performed remarkable feats, such as subduing kingdoms, escaping certain death, overcoming incredible odds, healing the sick, and even raising the dead.

Believers have nothing to fear, for our trust is in the Lord. God gives us the power of His Holy Spirit to subdue our enemies, both physical and spiritual. With Christ living within us, we can thwart the devil and drive out the evil from our midst. Without His power and presence in our lives we become vulnerable to a myriad of worldly and spiritual threats.

- LUK 10:19–20 ~ Jesus said to His disciples, "I have given you power over snakes and scorpions, and over all the strength of the enemy. Nothing can hurt you. But do not rejoice because the spirits are subject to you, but rather rejoice because your names are written in heaven."
- JAM 4:7 ~ Submit to God and resist the devil, and he will run from you.
- 1 JO 4:2–6 ~ Every spirit that confesses that Jesus Christ is God in the flesh is of God. Those spirits that do not confess are not of God, but are spirits of the antichrist, which you have heard about and which is in the world. You belong to God and have overcome these spirits of malice. For greater is He that is within you than he that is in the world. They are of the world, and therefore speak of worldly things, and the world listens to them. We are of God. Those who know God will listen to His messengers, and those who are not of God will not listen. We know the difference between the Spirit of truth and the spirit of untruth.

We depend on God for everything, and because of Him we lack nothing. We are covered by His righteousness like a blanket (ROM 4), protected from all evil like a suit of armor (EPH 6), and given a freedom that will last for eternity (ISA 61; ROM 8). Indeed, it would take a lifetime to count the many blessings the Lord has poured out upon us. It is unfortunate that so many people waste their lives away enumerating their hardships and absorbed in their sorrows.

Take a few minutes to ponder some of the miracles God has performed in your life, such as delivering you from danger or certain death; curing a loved one of a fatal disease or injury; converting a lost soul by changing his or her heart; opening a window of opportunity when you least expected it; or making your dreams come true when everything seemed hopeless. If you ever have found yourself amazed at the wonders of life, astounded at the accomplishments of humanity, or bewildered about how miracles happen, just remember they never could have occurred without God's intervention.

- JER 32:27 ~ Behold, I am the Lord, the God of all flesh. Is there anything too hard for me?
- MAT 17:20 ~ Jesus told them, "I tell you the truth, if you had faith the size of a mustard seed you could command the mountain to move; nothing would be impossible for you."
- ACT 3:12,16 ~ Peter answered them, "Men of Israel, why do you marvel at this, and look with earnest upon us as if, by our own power, we enabled this lame man to walk. By faith in the name of Jesus was this man healed, a man whom you have seen and known. Yes, it was faith in Christ which made him whole in the presence of you all."
- PHP 4:13 ~ I can do all things through Christ who strengthens me.

Lesson: Glory Be to God

God created everything, and everything belongs to Him. God created humankind in His image so that He could have children that would look up to Him, just as children should be able to revere their earthly parents. God is our heavenly Father who loves us and cares for us. He is an omnipotent God, the ruler over heaven and earth. His name is to be exalted at all times and in all places.

- 1 CH 29:11 ~ Yours, oh Lord, is the greatness, the power, the glory, the victory, and the majesty; for all that is in heaven and on earth is yours. Yours is the kingdom, Lord, and you are to be exalted as head above all.
- PSA 97:9 ~ You, oh Lord, are high above all the earth; you are exalted far above all gods.
- ISA 6:3 ~ The angels cried to one another, saying, "Holy, Holy, Holy is the Lord of hosts; the whole earth is full of His glory."
- HEB 12:9 ~ The fathers of our mortal flesh corrected us, and we gave them reverence. Shouldn't we be in subjection to the Father of spirits even more, and live?
- REV 4:11 ~ You are worthy, oh Lord, to receive glory, honor, and power; for you have created all things, and for your pleasure they were and are created.

Not only does God deserve the glory, He demands it. He cannot and will not share His glory with another. There can be only one Supreme Being, and He is the Creator of everything that exists.

- EXO 34:14 ~ You must worship no other god, for the Lord, whose name is Jealous, is a jealous God.
- 2 CH 7:19 ~ But if you turn away from me, and forsake the statutes and commandments that I have set before you, and go and serve other gods and worship them, I will uproot Israel from the land that I have given them, and I will reject this temple I have consecrated for my name. I will make it a byword and an object of ridicule among all nations.
- ISA 42:8 ~ I am the Lord, that is my name. I will not give my glory to another or my praise to graven images.

God sent us His Son to show us the way home. Christ is the only way there so we should follow Him, and demonstrate commitment our entire life to Him. He is our Savior and He is our brother. Christ is God's perfect witness since He is God. Therefore, He will be exalted as the King above all people when He returns in glory to receive the elect into His kingdom. Everyone will behold His glory, regardless as to whether they believed in Him or not.

- JOB 19:25–26 ~ I know that my Redeemer lives, and that He will stand over the earth on the last day. And though worms will have destroyed my body in the grave, yet in my flesh I will see God.
- ISA 40:5 ~ The glory of the Lord will be revealed, and all human flesh will see it together, for the Lord has said so.
- MAT 25:31–32 ~ Jesus said, "When the Son of Man comes in glory, and the holy angels with Him, He will sit upon the throne of His glory. And all nations will be gathered before Him. And He will separate them like a shepherd divides the sheep from the goats."

Christ, though He lived the humble life of a servant, was equal with God. Christ shared the kingdom, the power, and the glory of God in His sufferings as well as in His victory. After His resurrection, Jesus ascended into heaven and reassumed His position at God's right hand. He left His Holy Spirit behind to continue teaching us and preparing us to witness and serve. And when we speak of Him, He will speak through us.

- JOH 1:14 ~ And the Word became flesh and lived among us. And we witnessed His glory, the glory of the Father's only Son, full of grace and truth.
- JOH 12:23,27–28 ~ Jesus answered them, saying, "The hour is nigh for the Son of Man to be glorified. My soul is troubled, but what can I say, Father save me from this hour? Father, glorify your name!" Then a voice came from heaven, saying, "I have glorified it, and I will glorify it again."
- JOH 17:1–5 ~ Jesus lifted His eyes to heaven and prayed, "Father, the hour has come; glorify your Son so that your Son may glorify you. You have given me power over all people to grant eternal life to all those who are mine, so that they may know the only true God and Jesus Christ whom you have sent. I have glorified you here on earth and I have finished the work you gave me to do. And now, oh Father, glorify me in your presence with the glory I had with you before the world began."
- PHP 2:9–11 ~ God has exalted Christ and placed His name above every other name, so that everyone in heaven and on earth should kneel and every tongue confess that Jesus Christ is Lord to the glory of God the Father.

Those who would exalt themselves and boast about their great achievements will be disgraced. Those who argue that Christianity is for the ignorant and weak will be embarrassed. God will expose them, and will enlist the help of believers to do it.

- ISA 2:11–12 ~ The eyes of the arrogant ones will be humbled, and their pride will be torn down. The Lord alone will be exalted in that day. He has reserved a day for the proud and conceited ones; and these so-called exalted ones will be disgraced.
- ISA 5:14 ~ Hell has enlarged herself, and opened her mouth wide. And into the grave will descend those pompous and arrogant people (also ISA 23:9).
- ISA 10:15–17 ~ Should the axe boast itself as greater than the one who uses it to chop the wood? Should the saw magnify itself over the one who uses it to shape the wood? It's as if the rod could strike the one that that lifts it up, or the club could lift up by itself and beat the one holding it, who is not made of wood but of flesh. Therefore, the Almighty will send a wasting disease among the great warriors; under their pomp a fire will be kindled like a blazing inferno. The Light of Israel will become a fire, and their Holy One a flame. In a single day this fire will burn away all the thorns and briers.
- OBA 1:4 ~ The Lord says, "After you exalt yourself as the eagle, and build a nest among the stars, then I will knock you down."
- LUK 18:9–14 ~ Jesus told the parable of the Pharisee and the publican. Two men went to the temple to pray: a Pharisee and a publican. The Pharisee said, "Thank you Lord that I am not a sinner like other men, such as that tax collector, because I give tithes and I fast twice a week." The publican bowed low before the altar and beat on his breast saying, "God be merciful to me a sinner." Only the publican returned home justified by God. Those who exalt themselves will later be humbled, and those who humble themselves will later be exalted.
- 1 CO 1:31; 1 CO 3:21; 1 CO 10:31 ~ Whoever would offer praise, let them offer it to the Lord. Therefore, do not glorify men, because God has given all things to you. Whether you eat, drink, or whatever you do, do it to the glory of God.

God deserves the credit for everything He has done for us. God also deserves the credit for what we accomplish using the wonderful gifts and talents He has given to us. If not for Him, we could do nothing, and we would be nothing. We must never exalt ourselves, but instead boast about His mighty works. Because any mighty works done by our own hand was done by the power of His Holy Spirit working through us.

- 1 CH 16:29 ~ Give to the Lord the glory due His name. Bring an offering and come before Him. Worship the Lord in the beauty of holiness.
- ISA 12:2–5 ~ God is my salvation. In Him I put my trust; I am not afraid for He is my strength and my song. With joy, the righteous will draw water from the well of His salvation. Give thanks to the Lord and call upon His name. Make known among the nations all He has done and proclaim that His name is exalted. Sing to the Lord for He has done glorious things; let everyone in the world know that He alone is God.
- JER 9:23 ~ God says, "The wise man must not glory in his wisdom, neither the mighty man glory in his might, nor the rich man glory in his riches. But let him that glorifies, glory in this: that he understands and knows me, and that I am the Lord that exercises loving kindness, judgment, and righteousness on the earth, for in these things I delight."
- MAT 6:2 ~ When you help the needy, don't sound your trumpet as the hypocrites do in the churches and in the streets, so that they can receive praise from others. The truth is, that's all the reward they will ever receive.
- ROM 5:3–4 ~ We rejoice in our sufferings, knowing that suffering produces patience, and patience, character, and character, hope.
- 2 CO 12:6–10 ~ Even if I (Paul) had something to brag about I wouldn't. I don't want people to think more highly of me than they ought. To keep me from getting self-centered, I was given a thorn in the flesh. I asked God three times to take it from me, but He replied, "My grace is enough for you, for my power is made perfect in weakness." Therefore, I boast gladly about my weaknesses, so that the power of Christ may rest upon me. I delight in my hardships, insults, persecutions, and difficulties, because when I am weak, then I become strong.
- GAL 6:14 ~ God forbid that I should glory, except in the cross of our Lord Jesus Christ, by whom the world is crucified unto me, and I unto the world.
- 1 PE 4:13–14 ~ Rejoice when you partake of Christ's sufferings, so that you can be filled with joy when His glory is revealed. If you are insulted because you carry the name of Christ, be happy, for the Spirit of Glory and of God rests upon you. On their part He is despised, but on your part, He is glorified.

As disciples of Christ, we will do great things for the Lord. But it is not for us to brag about our abilities or accomplishments. Instead, we give the glory to God who equips us with the power and the tools. By giving the glory to God, we set an example for others, so that they too can glorify God and thank Him for their many blessings and achievements.

- MAT 5:16 ~ Let your light shine before others, so they may see your good works and glorify your Father who is in heaven.
- MAT 15:31 ~ The people were amazed when they saw the mute speaking, the crippled walking, and the blind seeing. And they praised God.
- ACT 3:11–16 ~ After Peter healed the lame man the people marveled. And when Peter saw this he responded, "Men of Israel, why does this amaze you? Why do you look at us as if, because of our own holiness or power, we were able to make this man walk? The God of Abraham, Isaac, and Jacob, yes, the God of our fathers has glorified His Son Jesus, the same man you delivered to Pilate to be crucified. It was by the name of Jesus Christ, and through faith in His name, that this man became strong. Faith in Christ has healed this man before your very eyes."

- 2 CO 4:6 ~ For God, who commanded the light to shine out of darkness, has shined in our hearts to give the light of the knowledge of the glory of God in the face of Jesus Christ.
- 2 CO 10:3–5 ~ Although we abide in this world, we do not fight its wars. For our weapons are not of a physical nature, yet they are far more powerful, able to demolish the strongholds of the enemy. We destroy the arguments and pretensions that are raised against the knowledge of God, and bring captive every thought into the obedience of Christ.
- 1 TH 2:6 ~ We did not seek praise from you or anybody else. As apostles of Christ, we could have been a burden to you, but we chose to be gentle and caring like a mother is with her children.

We believe in God's promises, made clear through the Gospel of Jesus Christ. It is our duty to act on this faith and bear good fruit. And the spiritual fruits that we bear will bring glory to His holy name, proving to others by our acts of faith that we are His.

- PSA 86:12 ~ I will praise you, Oh Lord my God, with all my heart, and I will glorify your name forevermore.
- JOH 14:13 ~ Jesus said, "Whatever you ask in my name, that I will do, so that the Father may be glorified in the Son."
- 2 CO 4:13–15 ~ It is written: I believed therefore I have spoken. With that same spirit of faith, we also believe and therefore speak; because we know that the One who raised Jesus from the dead will raise us and you to be with Him. This is for your benefit, so that the grace that is reaching more and more people may cause thanksgiving to overflow, to the glory of God.

Even as we glorify our Lord and Savior here on earth, so He will glorify us when He brings us home to be with our heavenly Father. The reward for dedicating our lives to His Son is to live forever in a glorified state in the likeness of Jesus Christ, having been made holy by His righteousness not through any righteousness of our own.

- JOH 17:22–24 ~ Jesus prayed to God, "The glory that you gave me I have given to them, so that they may be one even as we are one. Just as you are in me and I in you, may they also be in us so that the world will see that you have sent me. Father, it is my wish that they also, whom you have given to me, would be with me wherever I am, so that they may behold the glory that you have given me; for you loved me before the foundation of the world."
- ROM 8:16–18 ~ The Holy Spirit testifies with our spirits that we are God's children. If we are His children, then we are heirs: heirs of God, and joint-heirs with Christ, if indeed we share in His sufferings in order that we may later share in His glory. For I consider the sufferings of this present time to be nothing compared to the glory that will be revealed in us.
- ROM 8:28–31 ~ We know that all things work together for good to those who love God and are called according to His purpose. For God knew them in advance and predestined them to be conformed to the image of His Son, and to be among the firstborn of His brothers. Whomever He predestined, He called; and whomever He called He justified; and whomever He justified, He also glorified. Therefore, if God is with us, who can be against us?
- 1 CO 15:42–44 ~ Regarding the resurrection, the body that is sown is perishable but it is raised imperishable. It is sown in dishonor but it is raised in glory. It is sown in weakness but it is raised in power. It is sown a natural body but it is raised a spiritual body.
- COL 3:4 ~ When Christ, who is our life, appears, then you also will appear with Him in glory.
- 2 TH 2:14 ~ God called you by the Gospel to obtain the glory of our Lord Jesus Christ.

This wonderful scriptural prayer captures the basic message conveyed in this lesson.

- JDE 1:24–25 ~ To Him that is able to keep you from falling, and to bring you blameless into His glorious presence with endless joy, to the only God our Savior be glory, majesty, power, and authority, through Jesus Christ our Lord, timeless throughout the ages, now and forevermore, Amen.

All Glory, Laud, and Honor

All glory, laud, and honor to Thee, Redeemer, King,
To whom the lips of children made sweet hosannas ring.
To Thee, before Thy Passion, they sang their hymns of praise;
To Thee, now high exalted, our melody we raise.

Holy God We Praise Thy Name

Holy God, we praise Thy name; Lord of all we bow before Thee.
All on earth Thy scepter claim, all in heaven above adore Thee.
Infinite Thy vast domain, everlasting is Thy reign.

Hark! The glad celestial hymn, angel choirs above are raising;
Cherubim and seraphim, in unceasing chorus praising,
Fill the heavens with sweet accord: Holy, holy, holy Lord.

Holy Father, holy Son, Holy Spirit, three we name Thee;
Though in essence only one, undivided God we claim Thee
And adoring, bend the knee while we own the mystery.

Lesson: The Wisdom of God

God's wisdom is infinite; His knowledge has no boundaries. We can never approach Him with full understanding, but we can continuously grow in our wisdom and knowledge by studying the Holy Bible, going to church, and fellowshipping with other believers. God's Word is fact and therefore an extension of His wisdom. The Bible provides the stepping stones of our faith: law, gospel, truth, and purpose.

The Bible, especially the Old Testament, provides knowledge of the Law. All people are given the power to discern good from evil, but God's Law spells it out for us in detail.

- GEN 2:9,16–17 ~ And God allowed every tree that is pleasant to the sight and good for food to grow out of the ground. This included the Tree of Life which was in the middle of the garden, and the Tree of Knowledge of good and evil. And God commanded the man saying "You may eat from any tree in the garden except the Tree of Knowledge; for if you eat from it you will surely die."
- HOS 4:6 ~ My people are destroyed from lack of knowledge. Because you rejected knowledge, I will reject you, and you will not serve as priests. Since you have ignored God's Law, I will ignore your children.
- ROM 3:20 ~ Nobody can be justified in His sight by works of the Law; rather, through the Law we become conscious of sin.

God's Word gives knowledge of Himself: Father, Son, and Holy Spirit. God the Father passed onto us His Law, His will, and His mysterious plan of redemption. The Holy Spirit establishes and strengthens our faith in God and compels us to perform acts of obedience. In His grace, God sent His only Son Jesus Christ, the way of salvation upon which our faith is founded. To know and fear God is to believe in Him and in His promises, and that is very wise indeed.

- JOB 28:28 ~ God declared to humanity, "The fear of the Lord is the beginning of wisdom, and to shun evil is understanding."
- PRO 24:14 ~ Wisdom is sweet to the soul, and if you find it you will have hope, and that hope will not be removed.
- ROM 11:33–35 ~ Oh how deep are the riches of the wisdom and knowledge of God. How unsearchable are His judgments; how untraceable are His steps. For who knows the mind of the Lord, and who has been His counselor? Who has ever sacrificed to God, that God should repay them?
- 2 CO 10:4–5 ~ The weapons we fight with are not of this world, but have divine power to demolish strongholds. We cast down vain imaginations, and every pretension that is raised against the knowledge of God, capturing every thought to make it obedient to Christ.
- EPH 1:17 ~ I pray that the God of our Lord Jesus Christ, the Father of glory, may give you the Spirit of wisdom and revelation, so that you may know Him more completely.
- 2 PE 1:2–8 ~ Grace and peace be multiplied to you through the knowledge of God, and of Jesus our Lord. His divine power has given us everything we need for life and righteousness through our knowledge of Him who called us by His own glory and goodness. He has given us His very great and precious promises, so that through them we may participate in the divine nature and escape the corruption of this world and its evil desires. So, add to your faith goodness, knowledge, self-control, perseverance, godliness, kindness, and love. For if you possess these qualities, you will not be unproductive or ineffective in your knowledge of our Lord Jesus Christ.

The Holy Bible reveals God's elaborate plan by which we attain the knowledge of salvation through faith in Jesus Christ. This is the message of the Gospel, and the New Testament, which was foretold in the Old Testament.

- ISA 53:4–5,10–11 ~ Surely, He bore our grief and carried our sorrows. Yet we treated Him as an outcast, as if stricken, smitten, and afflicted by God. But He was wounded and bruised because of our sins. Our punishment was given to Him, bringing us peace, and through His suffering, we have been healed. It pleased the Lord to bruise Him and to make Him suffer. His life was given as an offering for sin, and God will see His Son and will prolong His days; the will of God will flourish in Him. After His soul has suffered enough, He will be able to look back with satisfaction. By knowledge of Him many will become justified, for He took their sins upon Himself.
- LUK 1:76–77 ~ John the Baptist, a prophet of the Most High, went before the Lord to prepare the way for Him, and to give His people knowledge of salvation through forgiveness of sins.
- 1 TI 2:4–6 ~ God wants all people to be saved and to come to know the truth. For there is one God and one mediator between God and humankind, the man Jesus Christ, who gave Himself as a ransom for all, and whose testimony will be heard in due time.
- TIT 2:11–14 ~ The grace of God that brings salvation has appeared to all people. It teaches us to refrain from ungodliness and worldly passions, and to live our lives in an upright, godly, and self-controlled manner. This we do as we await the blessed hope for the glorious appearing of our great God and Savior Jesus Christ, who gave Himself for us to redeem us from sin and to purify His people for Himself.

God's plan of salvation existed from the very beginning; God didn't make it up as He went along. This plan has been established and validated throughout the Old and New Testaments, that God would save humanity from sin.

- PRO 8:1,14,22–23 ~ I, wisdom, call to you. Counsel and sound judgment are mine; I understand all things and I have great power. The Lord possessed me in the beginning of His way, before His works of old. I was set up from everlasting, from the beginning, before the earth existed.
- ISA 48:16 ~ Come and listen. I have not spoken in secret since the beginning. I was there all along; and now the Lord God and His Spirit have sent me.
- JOH 1:1 ~ In the beginning was the Word, the Word was with God, and the Word was God.
- JOH 17:4–5,24 ~ Jesus prayed, "Father, I have glorified you here on earth and I have finished the work you gave me to do. And now, oh Father, glorify me in your presence with the glory I had with you before the world began. Father, it is my wish that they also, whom you have given to me, would be with me wherever I am, so that they may behold the glory that you have given me; for you loved me before the foundation of the world."
- 1 CO 2:6–7 ~ We speak a message of wisdom among the mature, but not using the wisdom of this age or of its rulers who will come to nothing. No, we speak of God's secret wisdom that was previously hidden, which God destined for glory before the world began.
- 1 PE 1:18–20 ~ You were redeemed by the blood of Christ who was ordained before the foundation of the world.
- REV 13:8 ~ The Lamb was slain since the creation of the world.

The Holy Spirit is the wisdom of God; He passes that wisdom to human beings through the Word, and the Word made flesh who is Christ the Lord. Thus, Christ, who was filled with the Holy Spirit, is the wisdom of God. Through Him God's plan of salvation is realized.

- ISA 11:2 ~ The Spirit of the Lord will rest upon Him (the Messiah), the spirit of wisdom and understanding, the spirit of counsel and might, the spirit of knowledge, and the fear of God.
- 2 CO 4:6 ~ God, who commanded the light to shine out of darkness, has shined in our hearts to give the light of the knowledge of the glory of God in the face of Jesus Christ.
- COL 2:9–10 ~ The complete fullness of God lives bodily in Jesus Christ. And you live completely in Christ, the head of all principalities and powers.

Becoming a Christian should be a lifelong process whereby we mature in God's wisdom. The Spirit of God's wisdom is available to all people. There are many examples in the Bible in which God freely gave His wisdom to those who sincerely desired it and actively pursued it. Here is a list of some men who possessed a great deal of spiritual understanding: Joshua (DEU 34:9), David (PSA 49:3), Solomon (1 KI 3:28), Ezra (EZR 7:25–26), Daniel (DAN 1:17–20), and Paul (1 CO 1:17–25; 1 CO 3:16–23). The more we study God's Word, follow Christ, and cultivate our faith, the more spiritual wisdom we will obtain. That is, the more we seek God and His righteousness, the more we understand God and our universe, and the greater is our grasp of absolute truth.

- ISA 7:14–17 ~ The Lord Himself will provide the sign: A virgin will become pregnant and bear a son, and will call His name Immanuel. He will eat curds and honey until He knows enough to reject the wrong and choose the right. But before the boy shall know to refuse the evil and choose the good the land will be laid to waste.
- EPH 3:10; EPH 4:12–13 ~ His intent was that now, through the church, the manifold wisdom of God could be known to the rulers and authorities in the heavenly realms. The objective is to prepare God's people for works of service in order to edify the church. This will continue until we reach unity in the faith and in the knowledge of the Son of God, and become mature, attaining the whole measure of the fullness of Christ.
- COL 1:9–10 ~ We have not stopped praying for you and asking God to fill you with the knowledge of His will, through all spiritual wisdom and understanding. This is so you might live your lives worthy of the Lord and may please Him in every way, bearing good fruit and growing in the knowledge of God.

The wisdom of humanity is insignificant when compared to God. To rely exclusively on one's own understanding is to miss the point entirely, but to rely on God is to find truth and life (JOH 14:6). In this life, we cannot begin to understand God or be convinced of His promises without the help of God's Holy Spirit. But when we meet the Lord face to face, we will understand all things.

- 1 CO 1:19–25; 1 CO 2:4–5; 1 CO 3:19 ~ It is written: I will destroy the wisdom of the wise, and I will bring to nothing the understanding of the prudent. Where is the wise person? Where is the scholar? Where is the philosopher of this world? Hasn't God made foolish the wisdom of this world? The world through its wisdom did not know God, but through simple preaching, God enabled people who would believe to be saved. The Jews required signs and miracles and the Greeks searched for wisdom and truth. We preach about the crucified Christ, which to the Jews is an obstacle and to the Gentiles is foolishness. But to those whom God has called, both Jews and non-Jews, Christ is the power of God and the wisdom of God. For the foolishness of God is wiser than the wisdom of humanity, and the weaknesses of God are stronger than the might of men. My message and my preaching were not with wise and persuasive words but with the power of the Spirit, so that your faith would be based, not on the wisdom of the world but in the power of God. For the wisdom of this world is foolishness to God. As it is written, He catches the wise in their own craftiness.

- 2 PE 2:20–21 ~ If a person has escaped the corruption of the world through the knowledge of our Lord and Savior Jesus Christ, and becomes entangled again and overcome, the person is worse off in the end than the beginning. It would have been better for them not to have known the way of righteousness, than to have known it and turned their backs on the sacred instructions given to them.

The wisdom of God is the Holy Spirit who lived fully in Jesus Christ, and proclaimed God's truth directly to all people. This is the wisdom which God has given to humanity, that He gave us His Son who has given us eternal life. The magi that visited the Christ child were bearers of gifts; now these were truly wise men for they acknowledged His kingship. Christians likewise share gifts when we celebrate Jesus's birth on Christmas Day; it is an annual festival with singing and laughter. This celebration will continue without end when we arrive in the Promised Land. Then, God will give away the bride at the wedding feast of His Son. That bride is His Church, for God the Father has given it to Jesus Christ who will reign forever as the King of kings and our friend.

- SOS 2:1 ~ I AM the rose of Sharon among the lilies of the valleys. Like a lily among thorns is my beloved among the daughters.
- ISA 7:14 ~ The Lord Himself will give you a sign: Behold a virgin will bear a son and will call His name Immanuel.
- ISA 11:1–2 ~ There will come forth a shaft from the stem of Jesse; a Branch will grow from his roots. And the Spirit of the Lord will rest upon Him...
- ISA 35:1 ~ The wilderness and its arid land will be glad; the desert will rejoice and blossom as a rose.

An old German Christmas carol from the fifteenth century, still heard to this day is entitled, *Lo, how a rose e'er blooming*. It was translated into English by T. Baker (1894). The original music was composed by M. Praetorius (1571–1621).

The theme is based on verses from Isaiah (above) explaining how a flower would spring from the lineage of Jesse, born of a virgin, truly human and truly God. He would bring pure light into the world to dispel the darkness of evil. And He would be made an offering for sin, but rise from the dead, conquering death for all people (ISA 53). Christ is the rose which blooms in the hearts of all who receive Him.

THE HOLY TRINITY

In the Bible, God is described in three ways: as the Father, Son, and Holy Spirit. Thus, Jesus Christ, the Holy Spirit, and the Almighty Father are all components of the same God.

God Exists in Three Persons.

- GEN 1:26; GEN 3:22 ~ God said, "Let *us* make a man in *our* image, like *us*"... God said, "Man is like *us*, able to discern good and evil. He knows not to eat the forbidden fruit."
- GEN 18:1–3 ~ The Lord appeared to Abraham along the plains of Mamre as he sat in his tent. Abraham looked up and saw three men standing there at the tent door. When Abraham saw them, he bowed before them and said, "My Lord, if I have found favor in your sight, please grant me, I pray, that you would never leave me." [While two of the visitors may have been angels, the number three is still relevant.]
- ISA 6:3 ~ They shouted, "Holy, Holy, Holy is the Lord of hosts; the whole earth is full of His glory." [Note that the word holy is repeated three times for a reason.]
- 1 TI 3:16 ~ Without question, the mystery of God is great. For God has appeared in the flesh and He is justified in the Spirit. He is worshipped by angels, is preached to the nations, is believed all over the world, and is glorified above all others.
- 1 PE 1:2 ~ You have been chosen in advance by God the Father, and sanctified by His Holy Spirit, through the shedding of the blood of His Son Jesus Christ, to whom you have become obedient. May God bless you with His abundant grace and peace.

Jesus Christ and the Almighty Father Are One.

- ISA 9:6 ~ A child is born for us; a Son is given to us. The government will be on His shoulders. His name will be called Wonderful Counselor, Mighty God, Everlasting Father, and Prince of Peace.
- ISA 11:1–2 ~ A descendant of Jesse, a Branch, will be born. The Spirit of God will be upon Him: the Spirit of wisdom, understanding, counsel, and might, the Spirit of knowledge and the fear of God.
- ISA 43:10–12,15 ~ There are no gods before Him or after Him. God says, "You are witnesses to what I have said. My servant whom I have chosen is also sent to be a witness so that you can know me and believe; and even so, I am He. I am the Lord and there is no other savior besides me. I have declared myself to you and I have saved you whenever you have forsaken all other gods for me. You are witnesses that I am God, the Holy One, the creator of Israel, and your King."
- ISA 44:6,24 ~ God and His Redeemer the Lord of hosts say, "I am the first and last; there are no other gods besides me. I am the Lord who makes everything, who stretches the heavens above and who spreads the earth abroad."
- ISA 45:11–13,21–22 ~ The Lord the Holy One of Israel and His Maker say, "I created the earth and humankind, the heavens, and the heavenly hosts. I have raised up a righteous One and I will direct Him in all His ways. He will build my city and free my people, expecting nothing in return. Look to me and I will save you for I am God and there are no others."
- ISA 49:7 ~ The Lord, the Redeemer of Israel, and His Holy One that humankind hates say, "Kings and princes will see and come to worship, because the Lord is faithful as is His Holy One."

- MIC 5:2 ~ From Bethlehem will come forth a ruler, whose origin is from ancient days.
- JOH 1:1–4,14 ~ In the beginning was the Word, and the Word was with God, and the Word was God. All things were made by Him. In Him was life, and that life was the light of humankind. The Word was made flesh and lived among us; and we saw His glory, like the glory of the only Son of the Father, full of grace and truth.
- JOH 1:15,18,30 ~ John the Baptist said that Jesus would come after him, that He ranks before him, and that He came before him as well. He said that only the Son, who is in the Father's bosom, knows the Father.
- JOH 8:19,42,58 ~ Jesus said, "If you know me you know the Father. I came from the Father. I tell you the truth, before Abraham was, I AM."
- JOH 10:30 ~ Jesus said, "The Father and I are one."
- JOH 14:6,9–11 ~ Jesus said, "I am the way, the truth, and the life; nobody comes to the Father but by me. If you have seen me, you have seen the Father, because the Father lives in me and I in Him."
- JOH 17:3–5,20–21 ~ Jesus referred to God as the only true God. He also referred to the glory He had before the world was made. Then Jesus prayed for believers that they may be one, even as He is one with God.
- JOH 20:28 ~ Thomas called Jesus Lord and God.
- ACT 4:12 ~ There is no salvation in any other; for there is no other name under heaven, given to us, whereby we can be saved.
- ROM 9:5; ROM 10:12 ~ Jesus Christ is over all of us.
- 1 CO 8:4–6 ~ An idol has no existence. There is only one God the Father, and one Lord Jesus Christ. Christ is in us and we are in Him; God is in us and we are in Him.
- GAL 3:20 ~ Although an intermediary (Christ) implies more than one, God is still only one being.
- PHP 2:5–11 ~ Keep your thoughts on Jesus Christ who, although He was God in the flesh, did not glorify Himself but became a servant. In the form of a man, He humbled Himself, becoming obedient unto death even death on a cross. Therefore, God has exalted Him and given Him a name above all other names. Everyone should bow at the name of Jesus Christ, whether they are in heaven or on earth. Every tongue should confess that Jesus Christ is Lord, to the glory of God the Father.
- COL 1:13–15 ~ God's Son Jesus Christ, in whom we have redemption and forgiveness, is the image of the living God and the firstborn of every creature.
- COL 2:9 ~ In Jesus Christ the whole deity of God lives.
- COL 3:11 ~ Christ is all and in all.
- 1 TI 2:5 ~ There is only one God, and the only mediator between Him and humanity is Jesus Christ.
- HEB 1:3 ~ The Son is the very image of the Father, having His radiance and sharing His glory.
- HEB 13:8 ~ Jesus Christ is the same today, yesterday and forever.
- JAM 2:19 ~ Even the demons believe that Jesus Christ is one with God (references: MAT 8:29; MAR 3:11; LUK 4:34).
- 2 PE 1:1,11 ~ Peter called Jesus his God and Savior and referred to His eternal kingdom.
- 1 JO 2:23 ~ Whoever denies the Son denies the Father. Whoever acknowledges the Son acknowledges the Father.
- REV 1:8 ~ Jesus said, "I am the Alpha and the Omega, the beginning and the end; which is, was, and which always will be—the Almighty."

The Holy Spirit is One with the Father and the Son.

- DAN 3:12–27 ~ The king of Babylon had Shadrach, Meshach, and Abednego thrown into the fiery furnace for not worshipping his false idol. The king looked into the fire and said, "I see four men in the fire and none of them have been affected in the least. And the fourth man looks like the Son of God." The king ordered, "You men, who serve the most-high God, come out of the furnace," and three men came out unscathed.
- MAT 3:16–17; MAR 1:10–11 ~ And Jesus, after He was baptized, emerged from the water, and the heavens were opened, and He saw the Spirit of God descending like a dove and resting upon Him. Then a voice from heaven said, "This is my beloved Son who pleases me very much."
- LUK 4:1 ~ Jesus was filled with the Holy Spirit.
- JOH 4:24 ~ God is Spirit and should be worshipped in spirit and in truth.
- JOH 14:26; JOH 15:26 ~ Jesus informed the apostles, "The Comforter, the Holy Spirit, who the Father will send in my name..." and, "I will send the Comforter, the Holy Spirit." [If the Father will send the Holy Spirit and Jesus will send the Holy Spirit, then the Father, Jesus and the Holy Spirit must be together.]
- ACT 20:28 ~ Paul referred to the Holy Spirit as the divine overseer of those purchased by the shedding of His own blood through Jesus Christ.
- EPH 2:18 ~ Through Jesus Christ we have access, by one Spirit, to God.
- COL 2:9 ~ The complete fullness of God lives bodily in Jesus Christ.

Direct References to the Trinity

- ISA 11:2 ~ The Spirit of the Lord shall rest upon the Messiah: the Spirit of wisdom, understanding, counsel, might, knowledge, and the fear of the Lord.
- ISA 48:16 ~ Come and listen. I have not spoken in secret since the beginning. I was there all along; and now the Lord God and His Spirit have sent me. (JOH 1:1–14)
- MAT 28:18–20 ~ Jesus said, "All authority in heaven and earth is given to me. Go and teach everyone what I have taught you; baptize them in the name of the Father, Son, and Holy Spirit."
- 2 CO 13:14 ~ Paul referred to the Trinity: May the grace of Jesus Christ, the love of God, and the communication of the Holy Spirit be with you.
- COL 2:2 ~ My (Paul's) hope is that their hearts will be comforted, being bound together in love, and that they receive the riches of understanding and acknowledgment of the mystery of God, and of the Heavenly Father, and of Jesus Christ.
- 1 JO 5:6–8,20 ~ There are three that are recorded in heaven: the Father, the Word, and the Holy Spirit. These three are one. The same three bear witness: the Spirit, the Water, and the Blood. The Spirit is the witness, because the Spirit bears the truth. We know Jesus Christ who is true so that we may know God who is true. We live in Him who has shown us His Son, the source of eternal life.
- 1 PE 1:1–2 ~ Peter, an apostle of Jesus Christ, was elected according to the prior knowledge of God the Father, through sanctification by the Spirit, unto obedience and cleansing by the blood of Christ.
- REV 1:4–5 ~ John greeted the seven churches saying, "Grace and peace to you from the One who is, was, and is to come, and from the seven spirits before His throne, and from Jesus Christ the faithful witness, the firstborn of the dead, and the ruler over all earthly kings..."

Melchizedek

Melchizedek was the "King of Righteousness." He was the great high priest and king who appeared to Abraham and with whom Abraham communed and gave tithes (note: this is the first reference to both communion and tithing in the Bible). Jesus Christ, the great high priest and king, is the only one to follow from that priestly order, which is a perfect and everlasting priesthood. Jesus told the Pharisees and others in the temple that Abraham knew Christ and praised Him. Abraham likely learned about Christ through Melchizedek, who was probably a manifestation of the Holy Spirit. If Melchizedek was a physical (human) appearance of the Holy Spirit, He was the pre-incarnate Christ who is God in the flesh. Melchizedek was called the King of Peace (Salem or "shalom" in Jewish); Christ is called the Prince of Peace. Christ is the only begotten Son of God, conceived by the Holy Spirit. Thus, the story of Melchizedek and Abraham provides a unique example of the link between the Heavenly Father, Christ, and the Holy Spirit.

- GEN 14:18–20 ~ Melchizedek, King of Salem (meaning peace), brought wine and bread to dine with Abraham. He was the priest of the most-high God. He blessed Abraham and Abraham gave Him tithes of all his goods.
- PSA 76:2 ~ In Salem (city of peace) is God's tabernacle; in Zion is His home.
- PSA 110:1,4 ~ The Lord said to my Lord, "Sit at my right hand and I will make your enemies your footstool." He is priest forever, after the order of Melchizedek.
- ISA 9:6 ~ Unto us a child is born; unto us a Son is given. The government will be on His shoulders. His name will be called Wonderful Counselor, Mighty God, Everlasting Father, and Prince of Peace. [Melchizedek was the King of Peace; Christ was the Prince of Peace.]
- JOH 8:56–58 ~ Jesus said, "Abraham saw my day and rejoiced." The Jews replied, "You're not even fifty years old and you claim to have seen Abraham." Jesus declared, "I tell you the truth, before Abraham was, I AM."
- HEB 5:9–10 ~ God made Christ perfect and the author of eternal salvation for all who obey Him. He was called by God to be the high priest after the order of Melchizedek.
- HEB 6:20; HEB 7:1–28 ~ Jesus is the high priest like the forerunner, Melchizedek, who was the first King of Righteousness, and the King of Salem meaning peace. Melchizedek had no parents or ancestors, no beginning or end. Being like the Son of God, Melchizedek remains priest and king forever. Consider how great He was, for Abraham paid tithes to Him and always counted on His promises. If perfection could have been attained through the Levitical priesthood, which was based solely upon the Law, why was there a need for another priest to come through the order of Melchizedek? Because a change in the priesthood requires a change in the Law. The new priesthood was fashioned by the power of eternal life, not the law over sinful man. Law made nothing perfect, but the bringing of a better hope did. That hope draws us to God through the testament of Jesus Christ, who is priest forever after the order of Melchizedek. Since Christ lives forever, the priesthood will never again change, for He is the holy, pure, and perfect high priest. The daily sacrifice of the Levitical priesthood has been replaced with the sacrifice of Christ, once and for all.
- HEB 9:1–15 ~ The first covenant had regulations of divine service performed in an earthly sanctuary, such as the offering of gifts and sacrifices. But Christ, who became the high priest, was a more perfect sanctuary, shaped by God's Spirit, not built by human hands; and His own blood was shed as the sacrifice, not the blood of animals. How much more the blood of Christ, who offered Himself as the unblemished sacrifice, will purify our flesh and restore our consciences to serve the living God! For this reason, Christ has become the mediator of the New Covenant, because through His death He redeemed us from sin committed under the Old Covenant, so that we may receive our eternal inheritance.

Immaculate Conception

Jesus Christ was born of the Virgin Mary, and was begotten by the Holy Spirit of God, making Christ God's only begotten Son. He is the Godman: His father being God and His mother being human; He was by nature both a human and a deity. This Immaculate Conception provides another unique example of the link between the Heavenly Father, Christ, and the Holy Spirit, and the limitless power of God.

- PSA 2:6–7,11–12 ~ God says, "I have set my King on the holy mountain Zion. I will declare to the world that you are my Son for this day I have begotten you. Serve the Son with fear and joy. Kiss the Son, because you will die if you get in the way of His wrath."
- ISA 7:14 ~ God Himself will provide the sign: A virgin shall conceive and bear a son. His name will be called "God with us."
- MAT 1:18,20,24–25 ~ Mary, before she had come together with Joseph, became pregnant by the Holy Spirit. God made this fact known to Mary's fiancé Joseph in a dream. Joseph took Mary to be his wife, but didn't consummate their marriage until after Jesus was born (1 KI 1:4).
- LUK 1:34–35 ~ Mary said to the angel, "How can I bear a son when I've never been with a man?" The angel said, "The Holy Spirit will come upon you. Therefore, your child will be called the Son of God."

Imagine the faith of Joseph and Mary who gladly accepted the role as foster parents to God's only Son. They believed God's messenger that they had been chosen for this marvelous work. At the decree of Caesar Augustus, they traveled to Bethlehem for the tax census, though Mary was close to delivering her child. This was part of God's elaborate plan provided in OT prophecy that Messiah would be born in Bethlehem (MIC 5:2). After Jesus was born, they had to flee into Egypt to escape Herod's evil decree to murder all the babies in Bethlehem (JER 31:15). Once Herod died, they were allowed to return to their homeland (PSA 80:8–17). Such a humble way for our Lord to enter the world, which should humble us to kneel before Him and present ourselves as a gift.

Lesson: God in Three Persons

In the Bible, God manifests Himself to us in three ways: as the Father, Son, and Holy Spirit. The Holy Spirit impregnated the Virgin Mary who gave birth to Jesus Christ. Thus, Christ became God in the flesh so He possessed the power of the Holy Spirit. The Almighty Father's power is channeled through His Holy Spirit. Jesus Christ was filled with this Spirit, thereby giving Him powers of Almighty God. Thus, Jesus Christ, the Holy Spirit, and the Almighty Father are components of the same triune God and are equal in power, presence, and holiness.

There is only one God (not more than one). There are not three separate gods, but one God with three personages. Some people interpret the Trinity as God having three facets, personalities, or expressions. However, it is important to understand that there are three persons in the godhead which equally reveal the deity and glory of our only, universal, sovereign Lord. Those placing their faith in any other god have not found God at all.

- DEU 6:4 ~ The Lord God is one God.
- MAR 12:29 ~ The Lord God is One.

Jesus Christ is the way to God. He is God's mediator.

- JOH 14:6 ~ Jesus said, "I am the way, the truth, and the life; nobody comes to the Father but by me."
- ACT 4:12 ~ There is no salvation in any other; for there is no other name under heaven, given to us, whereby we can be saved.
- 1 CO 8:4–6 ~ An idol has no existence. There is only one God the Father and one Lord Jesus Christ.
- EPH 2:18 ~ Through Jesus Christ we have access, in Spirit, to God.
- GAL 3:20 ~ An intermediary implies more than one, but God is one being.
- 1 TI 2:5 ~ There is only one God, and the only mediator between Him and humankind is Jesus Christ.

Although Jesus represents a unique person from the Father, Jesus is God just like the Father is God.

- ISA 9:6 ~ A child is born for us; a Son is given to us. The government will be on His shoulders. His name will be called Wonderful Counselor, Mighty God, everlasting Father, and Prince of Peace.
- JOH 20:28 ~ Thomas called Jesus Lord and God.
- PHP 2:5–11 ~ Keep your thoughts on Jesus Christ, who, although He was God in the flesh, did not glorify Himself, but became a servant. As a man He humbled Himself, becoming obedient unto death even death on a cross. Therefore, God has exalted Him giving Him a name above all others. Everyone should bow before Jesus Christ, whether they are in heaven or on earth. Every tongue should confess that Jesus Christ is Lord, to the glory of God the Father.
- COL 2:9 ~ In Jesus the whole deity of God lives.
- 2 PE 1:1,11 ~ Peter called Jesus God and Savior and referred to His eternal kingdom.
- 1 JO 2:23 ~ Whoever denies the Son, denies the Father. Whoever acknowledges the Son, acknowledges the Father.

Jesus Christ and the Almighty Father are one in the same.

- ISA 43:10–12,15 ~ There are no gods before Him or after Him. God says, "You are witnesses to what I have said. My servant whom I have chosen is also sent to be a witness so that you can know me and believe; and even so, I am He. I am the Lord and there is no other savior besides me. I have declared myself to you and I have saved you whenever you have forsaken all other gods for me. You are witnesses that I am God, the Holy One, the creator of Israel, and your King."
- ISA 44:6,24 ~ God and His Redeemer the Lord of hosts say, "I am the first and last; there are no other gods besides me. I am the Lord who makes everything, who stretches the heavens above, and who spreads the earth abroad."
- ISA 45:11–13,21–22 ~ The Lord the Holy One of Israel, and His Maker say, "I created the earth and humankind, the heavens and the heavenly hosts. I have raised up a righteous One and I will direct Him in all His ways. He will build my city and free my people, expecting nothing in return. Look to me and I will save you, for I am God and there are no others."
- JOH 1:1–4,14 ~ In the beginning was the Word, and the Word was with God, and the Word was God. All things were made by Him. In Him was life, and that life was the light of humankind. The Word was made flesh and lived among us; and we saw His glory, like the glory of the only Son of the Father, full of grace and truth.
- JOH 1:15,18,30 ~ John the Baptist said that Jesus would come after him, that He ranks before him, and that He came before him as well. He said that only the Son, who is in the Father's bosom, knows the Father.
- JOH 8:19,42,58 ~ Jesus said, "If you know me you know the Father. I came from the Father. I tell you the truth, before Abraham was, I AM."
- JOH 10:30 ~ Jesus said, "I and the Father are one."
- JOH 14:9–11 ~ Jesus said, "If you have seen me, you have seen the Father, because the Father lives in me and I in Him."
- JOH 17:3–5,20–21 ~ Jesus referred to God as the only true God. Jesus referred to the glory He had before the world was made. Then Jesus prayed for all believers that they may be one, even as He is one with God.

Jesus and the Father have been and will be together forever.

- COL 3:11 ~ Christ is all and in all.
- HEB 13:8 ~ Jesus Christ is the same today, yesterday, and forever.
- JAM 2:19 ~ Even the demons believe that Jesus is one with God (MAT 8:29; MAR 3:11; LUK 4:34).
- REV 1:8 ~ Jesus said, "I am the Alpha and the Omega, the beginning and the end; which is, was, and which always will be—the Almighty."

The Holy Spirit is God. Both the Almighty Father and His Son Jesus Christ possess this Spirit.

- ISA 11:2 ~ The Spirit of the Lord shall rest upon the Messiah: the Spirit of wisdom, understanding, counsel, might, knowledge, and the fear of the Lord.
- LUK 4:1 ~ Jesus was filled with the Holy Spirit.
- JOH 4:24 ~ God is Spirit and should be worshipped in spirit and in truth.
- JOH 14:26; JOH 15:26 ~ Jesus informed the apostles, "The Comforter, the Holy Spirit, who the Father will send in my name..." and, "I will send the Comforter, the Holy Spirit."

- ACT 20:28 ~ Paul referred to the Holy Spirit as the divine overseer of those purchased by the shedding of His own blood by Jesus Christ.

God the Father is the Creator who gave us a discerning mind so we could tell the difference between good and evil, and so we could find Him and know His love. God the Spirit is the person through whom God expresses Himself. He is the witness, sharing God's truth and love. God the Son is He who suffered, died, and rose again. He knew, saw, and felt the pain, guilt, and shame of sin. Through Christ, God can hear us and touch us, just as He was heard and touched by many people. Thus, like God we can feel, think, and express, for we are created in His image. God is able to think, feel, and experience everything that humans do, so you can be sure, He felt every bit of Jesus's pain and suffering and He understands your hurting as well. For He has taken all of our trials, tribulations, and sorrows upon Himself so you can be free of them.

The following are direct references to the Holy Trinity, found in both testaments of the Bible.

- ISA 48:16 ~ Come and listen. I have not spoken in secret since the beginning. I was there all along, and now, the Lord God and His Spirit have sent me.
- MAT 28:18–20 ~ Jesus said, "All authority in heaven and earth is given to me. Go and teach everyone what I have taught you, baptizing them in the name of the Father, Son, and Holy Spirit." [Note that the word "name" is singular but three persons are mentioned.]
- 2 CO 13:14 ~ Paul referred to the Trinity: The grace of Jesus Christ, the love of God, and the communication of the Holy Spirit be with you.
- COL 2:2 ~ My (Paul's) hope is that their hearts will be comforted, being bound together in love, and that they receive the riches of understanding and acknowledgment of the mystery of God, and of the Heavenly Father, and of Jesus Christ.
- 1 JO 5:6–7,20 ~ There are three recorded in heaven: the Father, the Word, and the Holy Spirit; these three are one. The Spirit is the witness, because the Spirit bears the truth. We are in Jesus Christ who is true, so we are in God who is true; He is the source of eternal life.
- REV 1:4–5 ~ John greeted the seven churches saying, "Grace and peace to you from the One who is, was, and is to come, and from the seven spirits before His throne, and from Jesus Christ the faithful witness, the firstborn of the dead, and the ruler over all earthly kings..."

Read or sing this hymn to yourself as you pray these words to the Lord (ISA 6:3).

Holy, Holy, Holy

Holy, Holy, Holy! Lord God Almighty!
Early in the morning our song shall rise to Thee.
Holy, Holy, Holy! Merciful and mighty;
God in three persons, blessed Trinity!

Holy, Holy, Holy! Though the darkness hide Thee,
Though the eye of sinful man, Thy glory may not see,
Only Thou art Holy; there is none beside Thee,
Perfect in power, in love, and purity.

Holy, Holy, Holy! Lord God Almighty!
All Thy works shall praise Thy name in earth, and sky, and sea.
Holy, Holy, Holy! Merciful and mighty;
God in three persons, blessed Trinity!

Lesson: Characteristics of Our Triune God

Each component of the Trinity has individuality, responsibilities, and characteristics that are distinctive, yet all persons of the Trinity share equally the power, deity, and supremacy. Thus, the Father, Son, and Holy Spirit are fully God, independently and collectively. God's marvelous plan of salvation requires involvement by each person of the Trinity, and without the existence and participation of any one, the plan fails. The attributes that can be ascribed to the three persons of God are provided in scripture, and all three equally share those attributes, though each person also exhibits distinguishing qualities and positions. Notice the interplay between the three members of the Godhead, how they relate to and complement each other, and how they collectively comprise the one and only true and triune God.

1. **God, our Almighty Father**: Out of love, our heavenly Father created us, protects us, guides us towards righteousness, delivers us from evil, and is always with us. He is the perfect Father, the ultimate example of parenthood. He reveals to us His will, He punishes us when we are disobedient, and He loves us unconditionally and perfectly.

- Our Father in heaven is Love (DEU 7:9; PSA 36:7–10; PRO 3:11–12; PRO 22:6; JOH 3:16; 1 JO 4:7–9)
- God is the Creator (GEN 1:1–27; ISA 40:28; ISA 45:5–13; MAL 2:10; COL 1:16–17; REV 4:11)
- He is our Protector and Defender (GEN 15:1; DEU 31:6; 2 SA 22:2–3; PSA 5:11; PRO 20:22; ISA 41:10; MAT 6:9–13; GAL 1:3–5)
- God is the Lawgiver (EXO 20:1–17; ISA 33:22; ROM 7:7,14,22–25; HEB 12:1–7; JAM 4:10–12)
- He is the I AM (EXO 3:2–14; ISA 43:10–11; ISA 44:6; MAT 22:31–32; MAT 28:19–20; JOH 8:56–58; REV 1:8,18)

2. **God's Son, Jesus Christ**: The perfect example of obedience to the Father is Christ. He brought the message of salvation, fulfilled the scriptures, and sacrificed Himself to atone for the sins of humanity. His resurrection shows us the way of redemption through faith. Christ will judge the wicked, but those who believe in Him will be saved, and will inherit a standing in His kingdom forever.

- Jesus Christ is our Prophet, Priest, and King (PSA 110:1–7; ISA 33:22; ZEC 6:12–13; JOH 18:37; HEB 9:11–14; REV 7:9–14; REV 17:14; REV 19:16)
- Christ is our Savior and Redeemer (ISA 53:4–12; MAT 1:21; JOH 10:17–18; GAL 4:4–5; HEB 10:14,18; 1 PE 2:24; 2 PE 1:1–11)
- Jesus is the New Covenant of Grace, the Messiah (GEN 22:7–13; DEU 18:18–19; JER 31:31–33; JOH 1:14–17; ROM 3:24; 2 CO 8:9; HEB 9:1–18)
- Jesus Christ is the Sacrificial Lamb of God (JER 11:19–23; JOH 1:35–37; EPH 5:2; 1 PE 1:18–19; 1 JO 2:1–2)
- Jesus is the Light that shows the Way (GEN 28:12; PSA 119:105; ISA 60:1–2; LUK 1:79; JOH 1:6–13; JOH 8:12; JOH 12:35; JOH 14:6; 2 CO 4:6; 1 JO 1:5)
- He is God's humble Servant, the Good Shepherd (PSA 23:1–6; EZE 34:23–24; ZEC 13:7; MAT 25:40–45; MAR 10:43–45; JOH 10:1–18; PHP 2:5–11; HEB 13:20–21)
- Jesus Christ is the Judge (1 CH 16:31–34; PSA 82:8; PSA 96:1,10,13; JOH 5:22–30; ROM 14:10; 2 CO 5:10; REV 19:11–13)

3. **God the Holy Spirit**: The Spirit energizes our bodies to become living souls, and that Spirit continues to preserve us in our lives. The Holy Spirit enlightens us with the knowledge of the truth, sustains us in our faith, sanctifies us and purifies us as we become conformed to the image of Christ. He is the witness who communicates to us God's Word and Law, and who connects us to God the Father through Jesus Christ.

- The Spirit is Life (PRO 8:34–36; ECC 12:7; JOH 6:63; ROM 8:2; 2 CO 3:6)
- God's Spirit is our Comforter and Healer (PSA 51:10–12; PSA 94:19; MAR 9:17–27; JOH 14:16–26; JOH 15:26; JOH 16:7; ACT 3:12–16; 1 CO 12:7–10,28; 2 CO 1:3–6)
- The Holy Spirit is the Word, the Witness, the Truth (NEH 9:20,30; JOH 1:1; JOH 4:24; JOH 8:31–32; ROM 8:16; HEB 4:12; 1 JO 5:6–10)
- The Spirit is Wisdom and Understanding (JOB 32:8; ISA 11:2; PRO 2:2–12; MAT 13:11–23; 1 CO 2:10–13)
- The Holy Spirit is our Faith (HAB 2:4; ISA 25:1; ROM 3:20–22; ROM 8:26–28; GAL 5:5–6; TIT 3:5–8; HEB 11:1–6)
- God's Spirit is our Sanctifier and Preserver (LEV 20:7–8; ACT 26:13–18; ROM 8:29–30; ROM 15:13–16; 1 CO 6:11; 1 TH 5:23; 2 TH 2:13–14; HEB 2:11; 1 PE 1:1–5)

Our triune God is gracious, merciful, compassionate, loving, holy, righteous, glorious, awesome, and wonderful. More of His extraordinary traits are reviewed in the next lesson.

- EXO 15:11 ~ Who among the gods is like you oh Lord? Who is majestic, holy, glorious, and wonderful like you?
- EXO 34:6 ~ The Lord passed before Moses who proclaimed, "The Lord! The Lord! He is merciful, gracious, slow to anger, abounding in love and truth, and forever faithful."
- DEU 4:31 ~ The Lord God is merciful; He will never abandon you or destroy you. He will never forget His covenant given to your forefathers by promise.
- PSA 116:5 ~ The Lord is gracious, righteous, and compassionate.
- JOE 2:13 ~ Return to the Lord for He is gracious and compassionate, slow to anger and abounding in love; He will protect you from calamity.

Lesson: God Is

God is alive and well. He is the source of all that is good. He is our creator and redeemer. God is love and God is truth. God is light and God is life. God is the lawgiver and the judge. Our Father in heaven nurtures us and disciplines us, as a loving father should. He loves us absolutely whether we are right or wrong. He will punish those who are evil and reward those who seek His righteousness by acknowledging His Son.

- GEN 1:1–27 ~ God created all things. He created humankind in His image.
- PSA 36:7–9 ~ How excellent is your unending love, Lord! Therefore, all people can feel safe under your wings. They will be abundantly satisfied from the bounty of your house, and they will drink from your river of delights. For you are a fountain of life, and in your light we can see.
- PSA 94:1 ~ Show yourself to us, Lord, to whom all vengeance belongs.
- PRO 2:1–6 ~ My child, if you would receive my words and hold fast to my commandments, so that you listen to wisdom and desire understanding; if you seek knowledge and truth instead of worldly riches; then you will understand the fear of the Lord and you will find the knowledge of God, for only He can provide wisdom and from Him comes all knowledge and understanding.
- PRO 3:5–6,11–12 ~ Trust in the Lord with all you heart and do not depend on your own understanding. In all you do acknowledge Him and He will direct you in the way you should go. Do not despise the Lord's discipline and do not resent His correction, for the Lord corrects those He loves just as any father who delights in his child.
- ISA 33:22 ~ The Lord is our judge, our lawgiver, and our king.
- NAH 1:2–3 ~ God is a jealous and avenging God; He is angry at the wicked and will unleash His wrath upon them. God is slow to anger and great in power, but His enemies will suffer the consequences for their actions.
- JOH 4:24 ~ Jesus said, "God is Spirit and should be worshipped in spirit and in truth."
- 1 JO 4:7–12,16–21 ~ Let us love one another, for love is from God, and those who love are born of God and know Him. If you don't love God you can't know Him because God is love. The love of God was manifested among us through His only Son, so we might live through Him. If God loves us so much, we should love one another; if we love one another, God lives in us and His love is perfected in us. If you abide in love you abide in God, and God abides in you. This perfect love gives us confidence on the day of judgment, because there is no fear in love but perfect love destroys fear, because fear brings torment. We love because God loved us first. You can't say you love God and hate your brother without being a liar, because you can't hate someone you have seen and still love God who you have never seen. So, you should love God and your brother (neighbor).

Jesus Christ is Lord. He came from heaven to reveal Himself as our Savior. He is our prophet, priest, and king. He is God's Messiah foretold in the OT and revealed in the NT.

- JER 31:31–33 ~ The days are coming when I will make a New Covenant with my people. It won't be like the covenant I made when I brought my people out of Egypt, which they broke. The New Covenant will be this: Instead of writing my laws on stone, I will write my laws inside the hearts of my people. They will not have to teach others to know God because everyone will know me, for I will forgive their sins and remove those sins forever.
- MAT 12:39–41 ~ Jesus answered, "An evil and adulterous generation seeks a sign, but will receive none, except the sign of the prophet Jonah. For just as Jonah was three days and three nights in the whale's belly, so shall the Son of man be three days and three nights in the heart

of the earth. The men of Nineveh shall rise in judgment of this generation, and shall condemn it, because they repented at the preaching of Jonah; and, behold, a greater one than Jonah is here."

- JOH 10:17–18 ~ Jesus said, "Therefore, my Father loves me, because I lay down my life so that I might take it back again. Nobody takes it from me but I lay it down of my own free will. I have power to lay it down and I have power to take it back again. This commandment I have received from my Father."
- JOH 18:33–37 ~ Jesus was taken before Pilate who asked Him if He was the King of the Jews. Jesus replied, "My kingdom is not of this world; if it were, then my people would fight for me. I was born to give testimony to the truth. Anyone who is interested in the truth will listen to me."
- EPH 1:19–22 ~ God's incomparable power and strength was shown to all believers through Christ, whom He raised from the dead and set Him at His own right hand in heaven. The power of Christ is far greater than any other ruler, dominion, or empire; and His name is greater than any other name in heaven or on earth.
- COL 1:12–20 ~ We give thanks to the Father who has given us an inheritance with the saints in the kingdom of His dear Son, in whom we have received redemption and forgiveness. He is the very image of the invisible God, and the firstborn of every creature. By Him all things were created in heaven and earth, visible and invisible, including thrones, powers, and kingdoms. All things were created by Him and for Him; He is before all things and He holds all things together. He is the head of the body which is the church. He has been with God since the beginning, and God was pleased to allow His greatness and supremacy to be demonstrated through Him.
- HEB 9:11–14 ~ Christ has come, the high priest of all good things, into a perfect temple; not a temple made with hands like a building. He entered the sanctuary, not by the blood sacrifice of animals, but through the perfect sacrifice of His own blood. He obtained, not temporary forgiveness for us, but eternal redemption. Therefore, if the blood of animals could sanctify those who are unclean, how much more will the blood of Christ, who offered Himself unblemished to God, cleanse our consciences from sin that leads to death so that we may serve the living God.

God refers to Himself as *I AM* and so does Jesus Christ. This is because Christ was, is, and always will be with God and part of God.

- GEN 15:1; GEN 26:24 ~ God's Word came to Abraham in a vision, saying, "I am your shield and your great reward. I am always with you and I will bless you and your seed.
- EXO 3:2–14 ~ The angel of the Lord appeared to Moses in the burning bush. God called to Moses from the bush saying, "I am the God of your father, and of Abraham, Isaac, and Jacob. I will deliver the Israelites from the Egyptians and give them the Promised Land. You will lead them there." Moses replied, "Who am I to do such a great thing?" God said, "I'll be with you to help you." Moses asked, "When I tell the Israelites this, who am I going to say spoke to me?" God replied, "I AM that I AM. Tell them I AM has sent you."
- DEU 32:39–40 ~ God says, "Understand that I, even I, am He, and there is no other god with me. I kill and I make alive; I wound and I heal. Nobody can be delivered out of my hand. I live forever."
- ISA 43:10–11 ~ God says, "You are my witnesses, and so is my servant whom I have chosen so you can know me and believe in me; and understand that I am He. There have never been any gods before me, nor will there be any after me. I am the Lord; there are no other saviors."

- ISA 44:6 ~ The Lord the King of Israel, and His Redeemer the Lord of Hosts, say, "I am the first and the last; there are no other gods except me."
- ISA 48:16 ~ Come here and listen; I have not spoken in secret from the beginning. From the time that was, there am I; and now the Lord God, and His Spirit, have sent me.
- ISA 65:1 ~ God says, "I am being sought by those who never asked for me. I am being found by those who never looked for me. I am here for the nation that never called upon my name. Here I am."
- JOE 2:27–28 ~ God says, "You will know that I am with Israel, that I am the Lord your God, and that there is nobody else. And my people will never be ashamed of me. Then I will pour my Spirit out upon all people. Your sons and daughters will prophesy, the old men will dream dreams, and the young men will see visions."
- MAT 22:31–32 ~ Jesus instructed the crowd: Regarding the resurrection of the dead, haven't you read the Word of the Lord who said, "I am the God of Abraham, Isaac, and Jacob?" God is not a God of the dead; He is a God of the living.
- MAT 28:19–20 ~ Jesus said, "Go into every nation and teach them everything I have taught you. Baptize them in the name of the Father, Son, and Holy Spirit. Remember, I am always with you, even until the end of time."
- MAR 14:61–62 ~ The chief priest asked Jesus, "Are you the Christ, the Son of God?" Jesus replied, "I am. And you will see the Son of God sitting at His right hand, and returning in the clouds from heaven."
- JOH 4:25–26 ~ The woman said to Jesus, "I know that the Messiah comes, who is called Christ. When He comes, He will explain everything." Jesus replied, "I who speak to you am He."
- JOH 6:35 ~ Jesus said, "I am the bread of life. Whoever comes to me will never hunger or thirst."
- JOH 7:28–29 ~ Jesus said, "You know who I am and where I came from. I am not here on my own, I am here because my Father in heaven sent me. I know Him because I am from Him and He sent me."
- JOH 8:12 ~ Jesus said, "I am the light of the world. Whoever follows me will never be in darkness, but will have the light of life."
- JOH 8:56–58 ~ Jesus said, "Abraham rejoiced to see my coming; it made him very happy." The Jews replied, "Sure, you aren't even fifty years old, and you're claiming to have seen Abraham." Jesus answered, "I tell you the truth, before Abraham was, I AM."
- JOH 10:11 ~ Jesus said, "I am the Good Shepherd who lays down His life for His sheep."
- JOH 11:25 ~ Jesus said, "I am the resurrection and the life. Whoever believes in me, though they were dead, yet shall they live."
- JOH 13:13 ~ Jesus said, "You call me Teacher and Lord, and you are right, because that is what I am."
- JOH 14:6,11 ~ Jesus said, "I am the way, the truth, and the life. Nobody gets to the Father without going through me. Believe me, I am in the Father and He is in me; if you cannot believe this, at least believe in the work I do as evidence that He sent me."
- REV 1:8,18 ~ Jesus said, "I am the Alpha and the Omega, the first and the last, who was, is, and who always will be—the Almighty. I am the living One; although I died once, I am still alive, forever. I hold the keys to death and hell."

GOD'S COVENANT

God has acknowledged righteousness and faith in His people by making covenants with them. A covenant is like a contract. God's covenants are a means of demonstrating His love and encouraging all people to seek Him and His righteousness. God made a covenant with Noah in recognition of his willingness to do God's will and comply with His extraordinary request to build the ark. God made a similar covenant with Abraham, who intended to obey God even if it meant sacrificing his son Isaac. God also made a covenant with the nation of Israel when He gave to Moses the Law and assorted commandments and regulations.

In the Old Testament, people showed their desire to please God by adhering to His laws and by offering sacrifices to Him as an atonement for sin. Because of our sinful nature, God knew that people could never be made perfect in righteousness by simply obeying the Law and making sacrifices. Therefore, He promised humankind a Redeemer, a Messiah, to set all people free: not freedom from slavery or oppression but freedom from sin and death. In the New Testament, this New Covenant was realized through Jesus Christ. Jesus, who was perfect in righteousness, became the sin offering for all of humanity. Never again will such a sacrifice be necessary to obtain salvation or to atone for sin.

God provides salvation to anyone who believes in and follows Christ. Although we must do our best to abide by God's commandments, nobody is capable of adhering perfectly to the Law except Christ. Therefore, we are saved through faith in Christ, by the grace of God, not by works of the Law. All of this can be summarized in the words of Jesus (MAT 5:17) when He said, "I did not come to abolish the Law but to fulfill it." In conclusion, the Old Testament presents the first covenant of the Law, and the New Testament presents the New Covenant of Grace, bestowed upon all people who are faithful to Christ.

God's Covenant with Noah (GEN 6:18; GEN 9:15–16)

God (to Noah): I will establish my covenant with you, and you will come into the ark with your wife, your sons, and their wives... The rainbow in the clouds will be a reminder of the everlasting covenant between me and all living things upon the earth, that I will never again send a flood to destroy the earth.

God's Covenant with Abraham (GEN 17:1–15; GEN 22:2–13; ACT 3:25)

God (to Abram): Walk in righteousness and be blameless and I will make a covenant with you. I will multiply you exceedingly, and the everlasting covenant will be with your descendants from generation to generation. As evidence of this covenant, males shall be circumcised. Your name is now Abraham, and your wife's name is now Sarah. And she will bear you a son.

Abraham (laughing): Shall a hundred-year-old man have a son by his ninety-year-old wife?

God: Yes! You will call his name Isaac, and my covenant will be with him and his descendants.

Narrator: Several years passed, and Isaac was a young boy.

God: Abraham, take your only son Isaac and sacrifice him on the mountain that I will show you.

Narrator: So, Abraham traveled to Moriah as instructed, took his son to the mountain, prepared an altar and lit the fire.

Isaac: Where is the lamb for the offering?

Abraham: God Himself will provide the lamb.

Narrator: Abraham lifted the knife to slay his son when suddenly an angel appeared.

Angel: Abraham!

Abraham: Here I am!

Angel: Stop! Do not hurt your son in any way. God is satisfied knowing you would sacrifice your only son, who you love, to honor God who you love even more. Because you have not withheld your only son, God will bless you. He will multiply your descendants as the stars in heaven and as the sands on the seashore. Because you have obeyed God, you will be the father of many nations, and from your seed all the nations of the world will be blessed.

Narrator: God allowed a ram that was trapped in the bushes to become the sacrifice.

God's Covenant with Moses (EXO 12:3–12; EXO 24:6–8; LEV 26:45; DEU 9:9–10)

God (to Moses): Instruct the Israelites to sacrifice an unblemished male lamb, to take the blood of the lamb and sprinkle it around the door frame of their houses, and to eat the lamb for dinner.

Narrator: When God sent the angel of death to kill the first born in Egypt, the angel avoided (passed over) the homes of those who had done as God commanded...

Narrator: Years later, Moses took the book of the covenant (the Book of the Law and the Ten Commandments) and read it to the people. Then he took blood from the sacrifice and sprinkled it on the altar and on the people.

Moses (to the people): This is the blood of the everlasting covenant made by the Lord in these His words.

God Revealed His New Covenant to Moses. (DEU 18:15–19)

God (to Moses): I will raise up a prophet from among you, and I will put my words in His mouth. He shall speak in my name and His words will be true. He is your deliverer just as your people requested of me at Horeb (Mt. Sinai).

God Revealed His New Covenant to David and Nathan. (2 SA 7:12–13; PSA 80:17; PSA 110:1)

Nathan (to David): God says, "I will raise up one of your descendants to build my kingdom. He will be my Son and I will be His Father; and my throne will be established forever."

David (to God): Let your right hand be upon the Son of Man whom you have made strong.

David: God said to my Lord, "Sit at my right hand. The Lord will rule in the midst of His enemies, who will become His footstool."

God Revealed His New Covenant to Isaiah. (ISA 2:3; ISA 11:1–4,10; ISA 42:1,6; ISA 55:3)

God (to Isaiah): I will make an everlasting covenant with humankind. From Zion (heaven) I have sent the Law. From Jerusalem I will send the Word. I will raise up a descendent of Jesse, and the Spirit of the Lord will be upon Him. He will possess the Spirit of wisdom, understanding, counsel and might. He will be faithful to God and will judge with righteousness. I have given Him to you as a covenant to the people, to be a light to all nations; and all nations, including the Gentiles (foreigners), will seek Him.

God Revealed His New Covenant to Jeremiah. (JER 23:5–6; JER 31:31–34; JER 32:40; JER 33:15; JER 50:4–5)

God (to Jeremiah): The days are coming when I will make a New Covenant with my people. It will not be like the covenant I made when I brought my people out of Egypt, which they broke. The New Covenant will be this: Instead of writing my laws on stone, I will write my laws inside the hearts of my people. They will not have to teach others to know God because everyone will know me, for I will forgive their sins and remove their sins forever. I will raise up a descendent of David. He will be a king and will reign with wisdom; His name will be called "the Lord our Righteousness," and He will come to save His people. The children of Israel will be weeping, seeking the Lord. They will ask the way to Zion saying, "Let us join with the Lord in a perpetual covenant that will not be forgotten. It will be, therefore, an everlasting covenant."

God Revealed His New Covenant to Ezekiel. (EZE 16:60; EZE 34:23–25; EZE 37:26)

God (to Ezekiel): I will remember the covenant that I made, and I will establish with humanity an everlasting covenant. I will make a covenant of peace with my people, and I will be their God. And they will have one shepherd who will feed all of them, even my servant David.

God Revealed His New Covenant to Daniel. (DAN 7:13–14; DAN 9:27)

Daniel: I saw in a dream the Son of Man descending from the heavens. He was given all dominion and glory, to rule all peoples, nations, and languages. His kingdom was everlasting. In one week, His sacrifice was completed confirming God's covenant to His people.

God Revealed His New Covenant to Zechariah. (ZEC 6:12–13)

Zechariah: The Lord says that the Son of Man will build God's temple. He will bear the royal honor and will be ruler and priest.

God Revealed His New Covenant to Malachi. (MAL 3:1)

God (to Malachi): I will send a messenger to prepare the way for me. Then the Lord, whom the people seek, will come to the temple. He will be the messenger of a New Covenant; and He will make the people happy again.

Jesus Explained the New Covenant to His Apostles. (MAT 26:27–28; MAR 14:24; LUK 22:20)

Jesus (to the apostles during the first Holy Communion): Take this cup and drink from it all of you, for this cup represents the New Covenant in my blood which is shed for you and many others for the remission of sins.

God Explained the New Covenant through Luke. (LUK 1:68–79)

The Lord God has redeemed His people just like He said He would by the words of the prophets. This mercy that He has shown to us was promised to our ancestors, when He told everyone to remember His holy covenant which He swore to Abraham. He gave knowledge of salvation to His people through the remission of their sins. This was done to provide light to those who sit in darkness and in the shadow of death. It was done to guide all people who would follow Him into the paths of righteousness for the sake of His Son Jesus Christ, who was sent for this purpose, and who possessed the Spirit of God.

God Explained the New Covenant through Paul and His Companions. (ROM 10:4–5; ROM 11:26–27; GAL 2:16; GAL 4:28; HEB 7:15–19; HEB 8:6–13; HEB 9:14–22; HEB 10:1–2)

It was written that a deliverer would come to take away our sins, for this was the covenant of God. It was a New Covenant, which was based on God's most excellent promise. For if the first covenant which was based on the Law had been perfect, there would have been no need for a second covenant. But because of the evil nature of humankind, God decided to make a New Covenant, not according to the one He made when He freed Israel from captivity to the Egyptians, because they did not continue in that covenant, and were therefore disregarded by God. The Old Covenant was designed to put God's Law into our minds, but God knew that His Law must also be written into our hearts.

The blood of Christ, who was blameless before God, was offered to purge our hearts and minds of evil and the power of death. For God knew that the weakness of our flesh precluded us from justification by works of the Law; therefore, we are now justified by faith in Christ. Now we, like Isaac, have become God's children through His sacred promise. Through Christ we receive the promise of eternal life; thus, Christ is the mediator of the New Covenant. Through Christ's death we have redemption from our sins which were committed from disregard of God's Law (the first covenant). In fact, the first covenant was not without blood, because after Moses read the Law to the people, he took the blood of the sacrifice and sprinkled it on the book and the people, saying, "This is the blood of the everlasting covenant that God has made with you." For the Law, with its sacrifices, would never have been sufficient to make us perfect before God, so Christ made a single, perfect sacrifice for sins that would last forever.

God Further Explained the New Covenant Through Paul. (ROM 4:13–16; GAL 3:13–20,23–24; COL 2:13–14)

Although it is a covenant of man, it will surely be confirmed, and nobody can add to it or nullify it, any more than a person can change or nullify a contract made between people. The promise that Abraham would produce an heir for the entire world was not made only to Abraham, or to his seed according to the Law, but was made to all people according to our faith.

If heirs were made in accordance with the Law, there would be no need for faith, because the Law works wrath, and where there is no Law there is no sin. Therefore, the promise is one of faith, given by His grace to all the seed, not only to those who are under the Law, but also to those who have the same faith that Abraham displayed. The promises were made to Abraham and his seed; notice the word "seed" is singular, not plural. The scriptures do not say "seeds" meaning many, but "seed" meaning one person, which is Jesus Christ. What, then, was the purpose of the Law? It was added due to sin, until the seed promised to Abraham had come. Thus, although the covenant is made for all people, it refers to one descendant, who is Jesus Christ. The New Covenant, which came into effect 430 years after Abraham, does not nullify the original covenant made between God and Abraham. We were under the Law until faith was revealed in Christ. The Law is our teacher to bring us to Christ so we can become justified by faith in Him. We were dead in our sins, but Christ brought us back to life, forgiving us of our sins. He took the laws that were against us and removed them, nailing them to the cross.

Summary: God's Covenant is unquestionably for all people demonstrating an unyielding faith in God and complete trust in His promises. Abraham was the Old Testament example of devout faith coupled with godly obedience, and Christ is the New Testament example of perfect faith coupled with impeccable obedience. Since we are not flawless, God will accept anyone exhibiting faith like that of Abraham. Remember, both the old and the new covenants have been based on God's promise of Messiah, the Lamb of God who takes away the sin of the world (GEN 22:7–8; JOH 1:29). Jews and Christians alike are awaiting the arrival of Messiah who is the Christ. Those who proclaim to be people of faith but are not looking forward to Christ's coming, or do not believe in His resurrection, or do not recognize the deity of God's Messiah and Redeemer, or are not prepared to witness to others about the many blessings bestowed on them via the Holy Spirit (such as faith, hope, and trust), are not fulfilling their part of the deal. We have the easy part of the bargain; God had the hard part by sacrificing His only Son. If you believe in God but are not committed to His Son, you are wasting your time and leaving behind an eternity of time that will have gone to waste.

Star of David and Cross of Christ

Lesson: The New Covenant

A covenant is like a treaty or a contract. The Old Testament has many examples of how God made covenants with those who, out of faith, sought Him and His wisdom. In OT days, faith was demonstrated by obedience to God's will; this was the covenant of the Law. In the New Testament, God revealed an eternal covenant with all people who showed this same faith. Jesus Christ is this New Covenant; it is the covenant of Grace. Consequently, all people are justified through faith, by the grace of God. That is, God will reward those who demonstrate a strong faith, both here on earth and again in heaven.

Old Covenant. The Old Covenant was based on the Law: God's will and God's commandments. A willingness to obey the Law is what guided God's people in their faith during Old Testament times; and that included offering sacrifices as an atonement for sin.

- GEN 6:18; GEN 9:15–16 ~ Noah believed God when He said He would destroy the earth by flood. Noah was rewarded, being the sole survivor of that flood, along with his family.
- GEN 17:1–2,7,15–16; GEN 22:1–3,7–12 ~ Abraham loved God so much that He was willing to sacrifice his only legitimate son and heir. God spared Abraham's son. Abraham was rewarded by being the father of many nations.
- EXO 12:3,7–8,12–13; EXO 20:1–17; EXO 24:7–8 ~ Moses was the next to receive God's covenant, in response to the faith and prayers of the Israelites. The firstborn of the entire nation of Israel was spared during the great Passover. Then Moses led them out of the bondage of Egyptian slavery and oppression. Next, Moses was chosen by God to deliver God's laws and commandments to the people.

New Covenant. Unfortunately, God's people broke the sacred covenant with Moses. God knew that His people needed to be delivered from the bondage of sin and death. Therefore, God gave His promise of a New Covenant, a Messiah that would save humanity from their sins. God revealed the great mystery of the New Covenant to all the major Old Testament prophets. God's promise of a Messiah was fulfilled through the life, ministry, death, and resurrection of God's only begotten Son, Jesus Christ. Thus, God's purpose is communicated to us through His Word. The prophecy of the Messiah, as documented in the OT, was fulfilled in Christ, as documented in the NT. Abraham was the patriarch to whom God revealed His New Covenant, and Abraham, in turn, glorified God.

- GEN 14:18–19 ~ The first recorded physical manifestation of the Holy Spirit was when King Melchizedek (the King of Salem or Peace) appeared to Abraham. Abraham communed with this priest and king, and gave tithes to Him (JOH 8:56–58).
- DEU 18:18–19 ~ Moses was aware of the New Covenant when he sprinkled the blood of the sacrifice on the Book of the Law and the people saying, "This is the blood of the everlasting covenant made by God through this His Word."
- 2 SA 7:12–13; PSA 80:17; PSA 110:1,4 ~ David's faith and repentance ensured him a place in history, not just as a king of Israel, but also an ancestor of the Messiah who is the only other priest and king from the order of Melchizedek.
- ISA 11:1–2,4; ISA 42:1,6 ~ Isaiah is considered the greatest of the Hebrew prophets; his prophecies concerning the coming Messiah are extremely profound. He describes the purpose, the persecution, the death, and the resurrection of Messiah.
- JER 23:5–6; JER 31:31–34 ~ Jeremiah knew that the Messiah would be the one to write God's Word into our hearts and not just our minds.

- EZE 34:23–25; EZE 37:26 ~ Ezekiel understood the Messiah to be the Good Shepherd who feeds God's people, including those who lived during the Old Testament era.
- DAN 7:13–14; DAN 9:27 ~ Daniel saw the Messiah as the One to whom all dominion and glory would be given forever.
- ZEC 6:12–13 ~ Zechariah described the Messiah as our royal priest and king.
- MAL 3:1 ~ Malachi informed that the Messiah would be the messenger of the New Covenant.
- JOH 8:56–58 ~ Jesus said, "Abraham rejoiced to see my day... Truly I tell you, before Abraham was, I AM."

Why was a New Covenant necessary? Ever since Adam and Eve people have known right from wrong, for God revealed His will in His laws and commandments. Through God's Law, everyone will learn the difference between good and evil. We know that God created everything (GEN 1), including good and evil (ISA 45:7). God gave us a discerning mind and the choice to obey Him or not, thereby opening the door for evil. However, God did not create sin, for we create our own sin; in fact, God is incapable of sin. Every human being, except Jesus Christ, has committed sin. God intends to destroy evil, the devil, sin, and death. This is the purpose of the Messiah, God's Son Jesus Christ.

- GEN 3:22 ~ God said, "Now man is like us, able to discern good and evil. He knows not to eat the forbidden fruit."
- ISA 45:7 ~ God created light and darkness; He created peace and He created evil (KJV).
- 1 JO 3:8 ~ Whoever commits sin is of the devil, who sinned from the very beginning. The Son of God was manifested to destroy the works of the devil.
- ROM 3:20 ~ Nobody can be justified by works of the Law, for by the Law comes the knowledge of sin.
- ROM 5:13,18–19 ~ Sin existed in the world before the Law was given; but nothing can be attributed to sin where there is no Law. By the sin of one (Adam) came the judgment of all, unto condemnation of death. By the righteousness of one (Christ) came the free gift of justification, unto eternal life. As by the disobedience of Adam are many people made sinners, so by the obedience of Christ are many people made righteous.
- 2 CO 5:21 ~ Christ, who never sinned, became sin for us so that we could become righteous before God through Him.

Messiah was foretold to be the Son of God, filled with the Holy Spirit. Jesus Christ is that Messiah. He is the source of our faith and salvation. It was too difficult for sinful people to adhere perfectly to the Law and God knew this. Jesus Christ was without sin, the only human who could ever be perfect under the Law. His perfection in life resulted in His being condemned to death. That death resulted in the atonement for the sin of all people. His death was overcome by His victorious resurrection, the result of being blameless before God. His resurrection results in the resurrection of humankind, and the salvation of those who believe these things to be true.

- MAT 26:27–28 ~ Jesus presented the first Holy Communion to His apostles, informing them that the shedding of His blood was the New Covenant, and that His blood cleansed everyone from all unrighteousness.
- JOH 1:1,14 ~ The Old Covenant came from the Word of God, provided in the Book of the Law. The New Covenant is the Word made flesh, which is Jesus Christ.
- LUK 1:68–79 ~ The Holy Covenant sworn to Abraham was made manifest in Jesus Christ. Now we can follow Christ and find our way to heaven.

There is an interesting and unique relationship between the Old and New Covenants as revealed in the following scriptures paraphrased below (ROM 10:4–5; GAL 2:16; GAL 3:13–17,23–26; HEB 7:15–19; HEB 8:6–13; HEB 9:14,20,22).

It was written that a deliverer would come to take away our sins, and He represents the New Covenant of God. This covenant was based on God's most excellent promise. For if the Old Covenant which was based on the Law was perfect, there would have been no need for a New Covenant. The Old Covenant was designed to put God's Word into our minds, but God knew that His Word must also be written upon our hearts.

The blood of Christ, who was blameless before God, purges our hearts and minds of evil and gives us power over death. God knew that the weakness of our flesh precluded us from justification by works of the Law. Therefore, we are now justified by faith in Christ. Through Christ's death we have redemption from our sins which were committed from disregard of God's Law (the Old Covenant).

In fact, the Old Covenant included blood, because after Moses read the Book of the Law to the people, he took the blood of the sacrifice and sprinkled it on the book and the people, saying, "This is the blood of the everlasting covenant that God has made with you." For the Law, with its sacrifices, would never have been sufficient to make us perfect before God. But Christ made a single, perfect sacrifice for sins that would last forever.

God will never break His covenant. Nobody can add to this covenant or nullify it, any more than a person can change or nullify a legal contract made between people. God made His promises to Abraham and later to the entire world. However, the New Covenant, which came into effect 430 years after Abraham, does not nullify the Old Covenant made between God and Abraham. In the Old Covenant, people were justified by faith under the Law, until faith was revealed in Christ in accordance with the New Covenant. Thus, the Law now becomes our teacher of God's New Covenant which brings us to faith in Christ.

The Old Covenant was based on faith through obedience to the Law. The New Covenant is based on obedience through faith in Christ. The Law was given by Moses, but grace and truth came by Jesus Christ (JOH 1:17). Now, sin has no hold over the believer, for the believer is no longer under the Law but under God's grace. (ROM 6:14; ROM 10:4)

Summary: The penalty for sin is death. Condemnation to death means total separation from God. God does not want us to be separated from Him, so He has given us a chance to be redeemed from sin and reconciled unto Him. That is, our sin has to be removed from us to enable us to be with God for He is righteous. Otherwise, we could never come near Him since sin and righteousness are incompatible, just as darkness and light do not mix.

Because of our sinful nature, people could never become perfect in righteousness by works of the Law. Therefore, God promised His people a New Covenant, a Redeemer, a Messiah. The Messiah sets people free: not freedom from slavery or oppression, but freedom from sin and death. Jesus Christ, who was perfect in righteousness, is that Messiah. He perfectly obeyed the Law on our behalf, and He paid the penalty for sin on our behalf. The shedding of His blood cleanses us from unrighteousness, allowing us to be reconciled with God. His resurrection proved His victory over death, thereby enabling us to live forever with Him.

In the Old Testament, under the Old Covenant, faith was demonstrated by adherence to God's Law, through personal sacrifice, and with burnt offerings. In the New Testament, under the New Covenant, faith in Christ is the only means of salvation. Of course, we are still supposed to abide by God's Law and be willing to make personal sacrifices for Christ. But burnt offerings are no longer a requirement, because Christ offered Himself as a single sacrifice to last for all time. In conclusion, remember the words of Christ (MAT 5:17), "I did not come to abolish the Law, I came to fulfill it."

The Old Covenant was based on the Law; the New Covenant is based on God's amazing Grace. We are saved through faith because of the grace of God, not from any merit of our own. Only Jesus Christ can save us; we can never earn it by ourselves.

Amazing Grace

Amazing Grace! How sweet the sound that saved a wretch like me!
I once was lost but now am found, was blind but now I see!

The Lord has promised good to me, His Word my hope secures;
He will my shield and portion be as long as life endures.

Through many dangers, toils, and snares, I have already come;
His Grace has brought me safe so far, His Grace will see me home.

Yes, when this flesh and heart shall fail and mortal life shall cease,
Amazing Grace shall then prevail in heaven's joy and peace.

I Know That My Redeemer Lives

I know that my Redeemer lives; what joy this blest assurance gives!
He lives, He lives who once was dead; He lives my ever-living Head!

He lives, to bless me with His love, He lives, to plead for me above,
He lives, my hungry soul to feed; He lives, to help in time of need.

He lives, and grants me daily breath; He lives, and I shall conquer death;
He lives, my mansion to prepare; He lives, to bring me safely there.

He lives, all glory to His name; He lives, my Savior, still the same;
What joy this blest assurance gives; I know that my Redeemer lives!

Lesson: The Free Gift

God has given us His Holy Spirit. It is given to us solely because of His bountiful grace and mercy. God wanted to have children to live with Him and gave us life and breath. He breathed into our bodies His life force which is His Spirit; that is, the Holy Spirit gives us life and sustains us. This is the same Spirit that lived in fullness in Jesus Christ. Just as Christ was the seed of the Holy Spirit, so are human beings God's offspring. However, Christ is equal with God; we are not gods and never will be. In Christ, and through God's Word (the Holy Bible), God has shown us the way to eternal life with our Father in heaven. If we place our faith, trust, and hope in Christ, the Rock of our salvation, we will be allowed to retain God's breath of life within us for eternity. Thus, we have the option of accepting the free gift, or rejecting it. Accepting it means we are obligated to God and His Son, as shown by our obedience, worship, prayers, and our actions toward others. Sharing God's gift with others is the best way of demonstrating our faith through our behavior.

- ACT 2:38–39 ~ Peter said, "Repent and be baptized every one of you, in the name of Jesus Christ for the remission of your sins, and you will receive the gift of the Holy Spirit. This promise pertains to you, to your children, and to people everywhere: to whomever the Lord calls."
- 1 CO 2:10–13 ~ God reveals His mysteries to us through His Spirit, for the Spirit searches all things even the deepest things of God. Nobody can know the deepest thoughts of another, only the spirit within that person can know them. Similarly, nobody can know the deepest thoughts of God except His Holy Spirit. We have received the Spirit of God, not the spirit of the world, so that we might know the things that God has given to us for free. This is why we teach in accordance with the wisdom of the Spirit, not the wisdom of this world, for you cannot compare spiritual things with worldly things.
- 1 PE 4:10 ~ As everyone has received the gift, likewise they should share it with others, as good stewards of the manifold grace of God.

God's Holy Spirit is life; that is, the spirit which has given life to you and me came from God's Spirit, and He continues to give it freely to preserve us. It is the spirit within a person that makes him or her a living soul. God breathed into us His Holy Spirit, the breath of life. And it will sustain you forever if you want to be His adopted child. But the Spirit cannot reside in you if you allow your spirit to become infected. Remember, your body is the temple of the Holy Spirit so do not defile that body.

- GEN 2:7 ~ God formed man from the dust of the earth and breathed into his nostrils the breath of life, and man became a living soul.
- JOB 32:8 ~ There is a spirit in a man, through which the inspiration of the Almighty gives him understanding.
- PSA 51:10–12 ~ Create in me a clean heart, Lord, and renew an upright spirit within me. Don't remove me from your presence and don't take your Holy Spirit from me. Restore to me the joy of your salvation, and uphold me with your free Spirit.
- ZEC 12:1 ~ The Word of God stretches across the heavens and lays the foundation of the earth, and forms the spirit within a man.
- MAL 2:14–16 ~ The Lord has formed a husband and wife into one flesh. In flesh and spirit, they belong to God. But why is this so? Because God wishes godly offspring from them. So guard your spirit, and do not break the covenant with your wife or husband by getting divorced.

- JOH 6:63 ~ Jesus said, "It is the Spirit that gives life; the flesh by itself is worthless. I speak to you the words of the Spirit, and those words bring life."
- 1 CO 3:16–17 ~ Don't you realize that you are the temple of God and that His Spirit lives in you? Therefore, do not defile the temple of the Lord or you will be destroyed. A temple of God must be holy, and you are such a temple.
- 1 CO 6:19–20 ~ Don't you realize that your body is the temple of the Holy Spirit that lives within you which God has given to you? Therefore, you belong to Him; you were bought with a great price. So, glorify God in your body as well as in your spirit, both of which belong to God.

Upon death, the spirit that gives us life returns to God. He gave it to us and it belongs to Him. He will keep it safe until Judgment Day. If you have loved Him with your heart you will be allowed to keep it after that, for the rest of eternity.

- ECC 8:8 ~ Nobody has the power to retain the spirit when they die, and nobody has authority over death.
- ECC 12:7 ~ Upon death, the spirit returns to God who gave it.
- EZE 18:4 ~ God says, "All souls are mine, including the soul of the father and the soul of the son. The soul that sins shall die."

Those who accept the free gift should sow to the Spirit, living each day by faith, with the hope of inheriting a place in God's everlasting kingdom. Their bodies will be regenerated by the Holy Spirit and they will live again. God will renew their spirits within them, delivering their souls from the curse of the grave, and saving them to live forever as members of the household of the Father and His Son. It is the death and resurrection of Jesus Christ that has ransomed our souls from death and the grave. His blood has cleansed us from unrighteousness, thereby permitting His Holy Spirit to dwell within us. Otherwise, our corrupt bodies would not be made holy, thus preventing a communion with God's Holy Spirit and reconciliation with God the Father.

- PSA 86:4,13 ~ Gladden my soul, oh Lord, for to you I lift up my soul. For great is your steadfast love toward me; you have delivered my soul from the depths of hell.
- MAT 10:28 ~ Jesus said, "Don't fear anyone who can kill your body but not your soul; fear the One who can destroy both your body and your soul in hell."
- MAT 16:26 ~ Jesus said, "What does it profit a person who gains the world but loses the soul. What can a person give in return for their soul?"
- LUK 21:17–19 ~ Jesus said, "People will hate you because of me; but be patient and you will keep your soul."
- GAL 6:8 ~ Those who sow to the flesh will reap corruption to their flesh; those who sow to the Spirit will from the Spirit reap eternal life.
- TIT 3:5–7 ~ He has saved us, not because of our works of righteousness, but according to His mercy, through the washing of regeneration and renewing by His Holy Spirit, which He abundantly bestowed upon us through Jesus Christ our Savior. Being justified by grace, we have become heirs according to the hope of eternal life.
- HEB 10:39 ~ We do not shrink back and we are not destroyed, because those who have faith keep their souls.

God's Holy Spirit is the power of truth and love given freely to us, and bringing us from death into life. That Spirit nurtures us and maintains us, through the study of God's Word and through faith in Jesus Christ. God's Word is a seed, planted in the hearts and minds of people.

God wants that seed to grow into a flourishing tree of life that will live forever. God proved through the life, death, and resurrection of His Son how incorruptible is the seed of the Holy Spirit. If we do not cultivate His seed within us, we will become corrupted by the world, separated from the vine, and eventually wither away.

- GEN 3:14–15 ~ God told the serpent (Satan), "I will place a barrier of hostility between you and the woman and between her progeny and yours. The offspring from the woman will bruise your head, and you will bruise his heel."
- ISA 5:1–13 ~ Isaiah compared the house of Israel to a vineyard: My most beloved has a vineyard on a very fruitful hill. He fenced it, landscaped it, and planted the choicest vine. However, it bore wild grapes, despite the care that was taken. Therefore, the vineyard will be trampled down, and weeds and briers will grow; the rain will cease and the vineyard will wither. This vineyard belongs to the Lord of hosts, and the vineyard represents the house of Israel and those who have fallen from God's grace.
- REV 12:17 ~ The dragon was angry with the woman, and made war with the remnant of her offspring that kept God's commandments and held fast to the testimony of Jesus Christ.

Jesus Christ is the seed promised to Abraham. Christ was conceived by the Holy Ghost, which impregnated Jesus's mother Mary who was virtuous and chaste. God's seed was passed onto His only begotten Son through the descendants of holy men of God, who lived a life of obedience to their Lord such as Noah (GEN 9:8–9), Shem (GEN 9:26), Abraham (GEN 17:7), Isaac (GEN 21:12–13; GEN 26:4), Jacob (GEN 28:14), Judah (GEN 49:10), Jesse (ISA 11:1–2), and David (JER 23:5). Were these men perfect? Far from it, but they were faithful to the end. Perfection is found in Christ who will crown you with His perfection.

- ISA 7:14 ~ The Lord Himself will show you a sign: A virgin will conceive and bear a son, and His name will be called Immanuel.
- ISA 53:10 ~ The Lord saw His seed being made an offering for sin and He prolonged His days, and the pleasure of the Lord prospered in His hand.
- MAT 1:21–23 ~ She will bear a son and will name Him Jesus which means Savior, for He will save His people from their sins. This will be done to fulfill the prophecy of Isaiah (as stated above).

Christ became a man to show us the way to God. He offered Himself to us giving us that same Holy Spirit, so that we could be like Him, pure and perfect. Welcome Him to live in you and you will live perpetually without fear or sorrow. However, the Holy Spirit cannot abide in you if you have not accepted Christ as your personal Savior. Through repentance, and acceptance of the fact that the atoning sacrifice He made is the only basis of salvation, your spirit is regenerated and renewed, and your soul is purified. God has given us the sacraments of Holy Baptism and Communion as a means of refining ourselves, thereby inviting the Holy Spirit to remain with us.

- ISA 55:10–11 ~ The rain and snow fall from heaven, but do not return, but rather water the earth, making the plants bud and bloom, which provides seeds to the sower and bread to the eater. Likewise, God's Word proceeds from His mouth, and does not return to Him void, but rather accomplishes His will and prospers in the minds of those to whom it was sent.
- JOH 15:1–6 ~ Jesus said, "I am the true vine; others are branches of this vine. If you do not abide in the Branch you will die, just like a branch that is cut from the vine withers and dies. If you abide in the Branch you will bear much fruit. Branches of the vine that do not bear fruit are chopped away and burned in the fire."

The seed of God will grow and flourish if properly nourished. And that seed will become an unpolluted and incorruptible tree of life, worthy of forever abiding under the protective umbrella of God's love, grace and mercy.

- MAT 13:1–23 ~ Jesus told a parable about sowing to the Spirit: A sower of seeds left seeds by the wayside where the birds ate them. He left seeds in the rocky ground where there was insufficient soil for them to grow. He left seeds among the weeds and thorns where they were choked to death. He also left seeds on fertile ground where they grew and bore fruit. The seeds represent the Word of God. If the Word is left by the wayside, it will be snatched away by the wicked one. If the Word is given to those with a heart of stone, it will never take root in their hearts. If the Word is given to corrupt and worldly people, it will be choked out by the lusts of the flesh. But if the Word is received by someone who listens and understands, it will take root in his or her heart and that person will bear much fruit.
- MAT 13:31–32 ~ Jesus told a parable about sowing to the Spirit: The kingdom of heaven is like the mustard seed. It is one of the smallest of seeds yet it grows into one of the largest of trees. Then the birds come and make homes in its branches.
- ROM 4:13–16 ~ The promise that Abraham would produce an heir for the entire world was made not only to Abraham, or to his seed according to the Law, but also was made to all people according to their faith. If heirs were made in accordance with the Law, there would be no need for faith, because the Law works wrath, and where there is no Law there is no sin. Therefore, the promise is one of faith, given by His grace to all the seed, not only to those who are under the Law, but also to those who have the same faith that Abraham displayed.
- 1 CO 15:42–44 ~ The resurrection is like a special seed, sown in corruption and raised incorruptible; sown in dishonor and raised in glory; sown in weakness and raised in power. It is sown a natural body and raised a spiritual body.
- GAL 3:16,19–20 ~ The promises were made to Abraham and his seed; notice the word "seed" is singular, not plural. The scriptures do not say "seeds" meaning many, but "seed" meaning one person, which is Jesus Christ who is the mediator between God and us. What then was the purpose of the Law? It was added due to sin, until the seed promised to Abraham had come.
- 1 PE 1:22–23 ~ You have purified your soul by obeying the truth through the Spirit, and by fervently loving one another with a pure heart. You have been born again, not of corruptible seed but of incorruptible, by the Word of God which lives and abides forever.
- 1 JO 3:9–10 ~ Whoever is born of God does not sin, for God's seed remains in that person, preventing him or her from sinning. This is how you can tell who is of the seed of God and who is of the seed of the devil. Whoever does what is righteous is a child of God; whoever does what is wicked is a child of the devil.

God has planted His seed within us, and that seed is His Holy Spirit, revealed in His Word and in His Son Jesus Christ. It is God's Holy Spirit that creates, nurtures, and sustains us. His Holy Spirit strengthens us in the true faith unto life everlasting. From His Spirit, God's love and wisdom flow into our bodies and minds giving us life. Christ is that Rock from which springs living waters. That water quenches our spiritual thirst for God's love and wisdom.

- NUM 20:8–11 ~ God empowered Moses to bring water from a rock. That water flowed in abundance, sufficiently quenching the thirst of the Israelites in the desert.
- PSA 105:41; PSA 114:8 ~ God opened the rock and the water gushed out, creating a fountain of water which poured out over the dry land.

- ISA 48:21 ~ They did not thirst while Moses led them across the desert, for Moses struck the rock and God caused water to come gushing out.
- JOH 4:7–14 ~ Jesus told the Samaritan woman at the well that if she were to drink from His living water, she would never be thirsty again. His is living water that provides everlasting life.
- 1 CO 10:1–4 ~ You should know that our forefathers drank of the same spiritual drink, which came from the same spiritual Rock, and that Rock is Jesus Christ.
- REV 22:1–2 ~ In John's vision of heaven he saw a pure river of the water of life, clear as crystal, proceeding from the throne of God and the Lamb. The river nourished the Tree of Life which bore twelve different kinds of fruit each month, with leaves that provided enough medicine to heal all nations.

To repeat, the Rock upon which our faith is founded is Jesus. It is a solid base for our salvation that cannot be broken. The prophets erected altars and a temple upon that Rock (Zion): Abraham (GEN 22:11–17), Jacob (GEN 28:10–22), Gideon (JDG 6:19–26), David (1 CH 21:18–19), Solomon (2 CH 3:1).

- DEU 32:3–4,15,31 ~ God is the rock, perfect, just, righteous and true. He is the rock of our salvation.
- 2 SA 22:2–3 ~ David said, "The Lord is my rock, my fortress, and my deliverer. In him I place my trust. He is my shield, the horn of my salvation, my high tower, my refuge, and my Savior. He saves me from violence."
- PSA 18:2; PSA 28:1; PSA 31:2–3; PSA 62:2–7; PSA 89:26 ~ He is my fortress, my strength, my refuge, my defense, my deliverer; I trust in Him. Lead me and guide me, for my soul waits for you, my Father God, the rock of my salvation.
- ISA 17:10–11 ~ You, who have forgotten about the rock of your strength, will sow your seeds and they will flourish, but you will reap only grief and sorrow.
- MAT 7:24–27 ~ Jesus said, "A wise man builds his house upon a rock, not upon the sand. A house built upon a rock will stand against the elements, but one built upon the sand will fall."

The Rock became known to us when God sent His Son to Earth to save us. If your faith is established in Him it is rock solid. On that rock, the foundation of God's church also has been placed, Christ being the chief cornerstone; this church consists of the entire community of saints. From that rock will flow living water, continuously. We build our lives upon that rock because we are allied with Him, not the world. Those who refuse will be crushed by that same rock.

- EXO 17:6 ~ God told Moses, "I will stand before you upon the rock in Horeb, and you will strike the rock, and from it will flow pure water so that the people may drink. And the elders of Israel witnessed this (also NUM 20:8–11).
- PSA 118:22 ~ The stone rejected by the builders has become the chief cornerstone.
- ISA 8:12–14 ~ Do not call a scheme what others call a scheme or fear what they fear. The Lord of Hosts is holy; let Him be your fear. He will be a sanctuary, an offensive stone, a stumbling block to both houses of Israel, and a trap to ensnare the people of Jerusalem.
- ISA 28:16 ~ God says, "I have placed in Zion a tested and precious cornerstone to ensure a sure foundation."
- DAN 2:34–35 ~ A stone was cut but not by human hands, and it struck the image (the statue in Nebuchadnezzar's dream) on its feet of iron and clay and broke them into pieces. And they (the kingdoms) became like the chaff on the summer threshing floor, blown away by the wind.

- MAT 16:18 ~ Jesus told Simon, "You are Peter (from the Greek word *petra* meaning rock), and upon this rock I will build my church. And the gates of hell will not prevail against it." (Jesus named Simon Peter "the rock" upon his commission as an apostle: JOH 1:42).
- MAT 21:42; MAR 12:10; LUK 20:17–18 ~ Jesus quoted Isaiah (ISA 28) to the crowd saying, "Isn't it marvelous? But whoever falls on that stone will be broken, and whoever the stone falls on will be crushed."
- ACT 4:10–12 ~ Let everybody know that it was Jesus Christ, whom you crucified, but whom God raised from the dead, who has become the chief cornerstone. There can be salvation in nobody else, for there are no other names under heaven that can save us except Christ alone.
- ROM 9:33 ~ Behold, I am placing in Zion a stone that will make men stumble and fall. Those who believe in Him will never be put to shame (ISA 28:16).
- EPH 2:18–21 ~ We have access through Jesus Christ to God the Father. We are not foreigners, but fellow citizens with the saints in the household of God. His house is built upon the foundation placed by the apostles and prophets, with Jesus Christ being the chief cornerstone of that foundation.
- 1 PE 2:4–8 ~ He is a living stone, rejected by men, but chosen by God and precious to Him. That is the stone of offense that makes men stumble and fall (reference to ISA 28). You are also like living stones, built into a spiritual house to be a holy priesthood.

God's Law was written in stone, and was called the Ten Commandments (EXO 31:18; EXO 34:1–4). Likewise, our faith is firmly founded on the Rock of Ages. So also, will the names of the saints be written in stone, when the free gift of eternal life is granted to all believers.

- ZEC 3:8–9 ~ God says, "Listen all you high priests sitting before me, for I am going to bring my servant the Branch. See the stone I have set before you. There are seven eyes on that one stone; on that stone I have engraved an inscription which states that I have removed the sin of this land in a single day."
- REV 2:17 ~ This is what the Spirit has to say to the churches, "I will give the heavenly food to those who overcome. I will give each one of them a white stone (indicating "not guilty"). On the stone their new name will be engraved (their passport to heaven)."

Our sinful flesh is in constant conflict with our spirit. This is because the flesh connects us to the world while the spirit connects us to God. The Spirit of God gives us our conscience, where our knowledge of morality resides. Our flesh compels us to do and say wicked things; if we are guided by the flesh, we become corrupted. The spirit compels us to be like God, righteous and holy. If we are guided by the spirit, we will try to do what is right in the eyes of the Lord.

- ROM 8:4–6 ~ Live, not according to the flesh, but according to the spirit. Those who live according to the flesh set their minds on evil, but those who live according to the spirit set their minds on God. To set the mind on flesh results in death, but to set the mind on God results in peace and life.
- GAL 5:17–18,22–23 ~ The desires of the flesh are against the spirit, and vice-versa, for they are opposed to each other. If you are led by the Holy Spirit, you are not under the Law. The fruits of the spirit include love, joy, peace, patience, kindness, goodness, faithfulness, gentleness, and self-control.
- GAL 6:8 ~ Those who sow to the flesh will reap corruption to their flesh; those who sow to the Spirit will from the Spirit reap eternal life.

In conclusion, God has given His Holy Spirit to each and every one of us as a free gift. His Spirit conveys life, even life eternal, if only we receive Him. We can receive Him by studying His Word and by placing our trust in Jesus Christ. We invite Him to live in us through the Holy Sacraments, Bible study, and public worship. Using these means of grace, our spirit becomes joined with God's Holy Spirit. This communion can take place only if we have been cleansed of unrighteousness, through faith in the atoning sacrifice of Christ.

- ROM 4:4–8 ~ When people work, their wages are not considered a gift but an obligation. However, to those who do not work, but trust in God who justifies the wicked, their faith is credited as righteousness. If it could be earned, then it wouldn't be free (it is given to us; we do not work for it). This is what David said about God who blesses us with righteousness apart from works: Blessed are they whose sins are forgiven and whose sins are covered; blessed are they whose sins the Lord does not count against them.
- ROM 6:23 ~ The wages of sin is death, but the gift of eternal life is available through Jesus Christ our Lord.
- ROM 8:14–17 ~ Whoever is led by the Spirit of God becomes a child of God. They have not received a spirit of slavery or fear, but a spirit of adoption, which is why we refer to God as our Father. The Spirit of God is a witness with our spirits that we are the children of God. If we are children of God, then we are His heirs and joint heirs with Christ. So, if we suffer with Christ, we will be glorified with Him also.
- 2 TI 1:7 ~ God didn't give us a spirit of fear but a spirit of power, love, and a sound mind.
- 1 JO 5:4–6,9–10 ~ Whoever is born of God overcomes the world; the victory that overcomes the world is found in faith. Jesus Christ overcame the world; anyone believing in Him will also overcome the world. Christ is He, who came by water and blood. The Holy Spirit is He who bears witness, because the Spirit is truth. If we believe a person witnessing for another, we should believe God's witnessing even more; and God has given witness of His Son. Those who believe that Jesus is God's Son have God's witness in themselves; those who don't believe are calling God a liar, because they don't believe God's testimony concerning His Son.

Holy Ghost with Light Divine

Holy Ghost with light divine, shine upon this heart of mine;
Chase the shades of night away, turn the darkness into day.

Let me see my Savior's face, let me all His beauties trace;
Show those glorious truths to me which are only known to Thee.

Holy Ghost, with power divine, cleanse this guilty heart of mine;
In Thy mercy pity me, from sin's bondage set me free.

Holy Ghost, with joy divine, cheer this saddened heart of mine;
Yield a sacred, settled peace; let it grow and still increase.

Holy Spirit, all divine, dwell within this heart of mine;
Cast down every idol throne, reign supreme and reign alone.

See, to Thee I yield my heart; shed Thy life through every part;
A pure temple I would be, wholly dedicate to Thee.

Lesson: Holy Week

Holy Week is a good time to reflect on God's Covenant, which He promises to all who seek Him. A covenant is an agreement or contract; you can bet that when God makes a contract, He will never break that contract. God offers people salvation for free if they will be faithful to Him; and that faith leads to eternal life. It is the greatest deal anyone will ever offer you. Only a fool would reject such an offer.

In the Old Testament, God made covenants with Noah, Abraham, Isaac, Jacob, Moses, and David. Through these prophets, God also promised a New Covenant: His Messiah. The New Covenant was further confirmed through Isaiah, Jeremiah, Daniel, Zechariah, Micah, and other great prophets. The Old Covenant was based on faith in God as demonstrated by obedience to God's Law which required sacrificial offerings. God knew all along that humans were incapable of remaining obedient due to their sinful nature (ROM 3:20; ROM 7:7,14; JAM 2:10), so He promised a more perfect covenant based on faith in Christ's self-sacrifice (ROM 16:25–26; GAL 3:13–23; HEB 7:15–19; HEB 8:6–13).

Jesus Christ is the Messiah, the Redeemer, the New Covenant (LUK 1:68–79). Christ came to earth to perfectly fulfill the Law on our behalf (MAT 5:12–19), as well as to assume the punishment for our noncompliance with the Law (ISA 53:1–12; PHP 3:11–12). His sufferings and death paid the price of sin which is death (ROM 6:23), thereby conquering sin (1 JO 2:2). His resurrection from the dead brought with it the resurrection of all people (ROM 8:11), thereby conquering death (2 TI 1:10). By redeeming our bodies from the grave and washing our souls clean, we have been made spotless and unblemished like Christ (1 CO 1:8), making us acceptable to live with our perfect God in His kingdom forever (COL 1:29; HEB 10:14).

Interestingly, the Old and New Covenants have several things in common and this is not a coincidence. God's plan was repeatedly announced during Holy Week and upon God's holy mountain in the City of David which was Jerusalem.

Abraham was visited by King Melchizedek, an early manifestation of the pre-incarnate Christ. Abraham communed with Melchizedek, the great High Priest and the King of Salem (meaning peace), sharing bread and wine, and giving tithes of all he owned to the Lord (GEN 14:18–20). Later, Abraham was sent by God to the holy mountain to sacrifice his only son Isaac (GEN 22:1–8). Of course, Isaac was spared because Abraham remained faithful; a ram was sacrificed in Isaac's place (GEN 22:9–13). This ram represents the Sacrificial Lamb, God's firstborn and only Son, who was offered for the sin of the world (JOH 1:29).

Isaac's son Jacob slept on that same holy mountain and dreamed of a ladder to heaven with angels (GEN 28:10–22); this ladder represents Jesus Christ, who is the Way to the Father (JOH 14:6), and upon whom the angels in Jacob's dream were ascending and descending (JOH 1:51). This holy mountain (Zion) became the center of King David's holy city of Jerusalem (2 SA 5:7), and the site of the original temple built by his son Solomon.

God used Moses as a messenger of the Law as well as a messenger of the New Covenant (EXO 24:7–8). During the first Passover, God spared the firstborn of all who obeyed His commandment and sacrificed an unblemished young ram (EXO 12:3–13). Again, Christ is that Passover Lamb (1 PE 1:19), whose sacrifice saves us from the power of death. There are numerous references to Christ in the OT; each of these examples illuminates Christ who shined the light of God for all living souls to see. If you cannot see the light you will lose your way and end up in darkness.

God commanded His people to remember forever His great works when He freed them from the bondage of Egyptian oppression. This is the purpose of the Old Testament Feasts of Passover, Unleavened Bread, and First Fruits (LEV 23:5–10), which the Jews celebrate during Holy Week to this day. During these feasts, God's mighty deeds were celebrated by fasting, feasting, sacrificing, and tithing.

During this same Holy Week, Christians celebrate the breaking of Christ's body on the cross (Feast of Unleavened Bread), the shedding of His blood (Feast of Passover), and His Resurrection from the tomb on Easter Sunday (Feast of First Fruits). In accordance with Christ's commandment, we commemorate these wonderful acts of God every time we partake of Holy Communion (1 CO 11:25–26), in which we share the bread and wine in a spiritual communication with God's Holy Spirit just as Abraham did so long ago. This we do to remember forever that God has freed us from the slavery and bondage of sin (LUK 22:19–20).

As we reflect on the sacrifice of Christ and His resurrection, we cannot help but be moved. What a great time to express our gratitude by giving to the Lord the first fruits of our increase (2 CH 31:5; PRO 3:9; 1 CO 16:2). Christ is the first fruits of those who have been raised to live forever on God's holy mountain of Zion (1 CO 15:20–23,44). All believers will follow Christ in death, and be resurrected to live forever with Him and our heavenly Father in the New Jerusalem (EZE 34:12,23–24; EPH 1:10–11; PHP 3:20–21). What a marvelous gift God has given us; He gave us everything He owned, even Himself! And all He requires in return is gratitude. This we show by offering our worship and gifts through faith (LEV 27:30; DEU 14:22; MAL 3:6–8). Plus, God promises that if we give him our first fruits (tithe), He will further bless us with increased prosperity, so how can we lose (MAL 3:10; LUK 6:38)? Is there any limit to God's goodness, grace, and mercy? No, there is not (PSA 100:1–5)! Read or sing the following hymns of joy and celebration for everything the Lord has done for you.

Beautiful Savior

Beautiful Savior! King of creation! Son of God and Son of Man!
Truly I'd love Thee, truly I'd serve Thee, Light of my soul, my Joy, my Crown.

Fair are the meadows, fair are the woodlands, robed in flowers of blooming spring;
Jesus is fairer, Jesus is purer; He makes our sorrowing spirits sing.

Fair is the sunshine, fair is the moonlight, bright the sparkling stars on high;
Jesus shines brighter, Jesus shines purer, than all the angels in the sky.

Beautiful Savior! Lord of the nations! Son of God and Son of Man!
Glory and honor, praise, adoration, now and forevermore be Thine!

Chief of Sinners Though I Be

Chief of sinners though I be, Jesus shed His blood for me.
Died that I might live on high, lives that I might never die.

As the branch is to the vine, I am His, and He is mine.
Oh, the height of Jesus's love, higher than the heavens above,

Deeper than the deepest sea, lasting all eternity!
Love that found me wondrous thought; found me when I sought Him not.

Lesson: God's Chosen People

In the Old Testament, God's chosen people were the Jews. However, He did not choose them because of their race; He chose them because of their faith. Those people who sought God, who tried to obey Him, and who worshipped only God were considered God's people. The same is still true today. Thus, anyone who chooses God is chosen by Him as well.

- JOS 24:21–22 ~ The people said to Joshua, "We promise to serve the Lord." Joshua replied, "You are witnesses before me and your countrymen that you have chosen the Lord and have promised to serve him." They responded, "Yes, we are witnesses."

The Jews were an example of a people that chose to follow the Lord. Because of this, they were rewarded with prosperity and peace (LEV 26:3–7). However, they became corrupted by the idolatry, promiscuity, and spiritual infidelity of foreigners and unbelievers. They were punished by God, just like any loving father disciplines a disobedient child (LEV 26:27–33). Everyone who turns back to God will be forgiven and welcomed back with open arms, just as God welcomed the Jews whenever they repented.

- DEU 7:7–10 ~ The Lord did not pour His love upon you, or choose you because you were greater in number than other people, for you were the fewest of all people. But because the Lord loved you, and in order to keep the promise that He made with your fathers, He brought you out with a mighty hand, and redeemed you from bondage in the land of Egypt. Know therefore that the Lord is your God; He is faithful and keeps the covenant, and bestows mercy on those who love him and keep His commandments. But He repays those who hate Him to their face, and utterly destroys them for everyone to see.
- JDG 10:14 ~ Go and cry to the gods that you have chosen; see if they will deliver you in the time of your tribulation.
- 2 CH 6:38 ~ If they will return to God with all their heart and soul in the land of their captivity, and pray for their land that God gave to their fathers, and toward the city that He chose for Himself, and toward the house which was built in His name, God will hear them from the heavens, and He will answer their prayers, and He will champion their cause, and He will forgive His people who have disobeyed Him.
- NEH 1:9 ~ But if you turn to me, keep my commandments and obey, even though some of you were cast out of the uttermost part of the heavens, yet I will gather you all and bring you to the place that I have chosen which carries my name.

God's people include anyone who desires a relationship with Him, and who strives to be joined with His Holy Spirit. That relationship is based on God's love for us and our faith in Him. They are members of God's household that believe in Him. His children are equal heirs to the kingdom of heaven, regardless of nationality.

- ISA 14:1 ~ For the Lord will have mercy on Jacob; He still will choose Israel and place them in their own land. And strangers will be joined with them to be among the house of Jacob.
- ROM 4:13,16; ROM 9:6–7 ~ For the promise that he should be the heir of the world, was not to Abraham or to his seed through the Law, but through the righteousness of faith. Therefore, it is by grace through faith that the promise is given to all the seed; not only to those who obey the Law, but also to those who demonstrate the faith of Abraham who was the father of us all. Not everyone who is a descendant of Jacob is of the house of Israel. That is, just because someone is from the lineage of Abraham, it doesn't necessarily make them children or heirs.

- GAL 3:6–29 ~ Just as Abraham believed God, and it was accounted to him as righteousness, so also are those who have the same faith, children of Abraham. The scriptures foretold that God would justify the heathen through faith, as preached before the Gospel of Christ to Abraham himself in the words, "In you all nations will be blessed" (JOH 8:56–58). Therefore, those who have faith are blessed along with Abraham. Nobody is justified by the Law, but by faith. Christ redeemed us from the curse of the Law through His crucifixion on the cross. This He did to enable the blessing given Abraham to be given to the Gentiles as well, so that they too could receive the promise of the Holy Spirit through faith (ISA 49:6). I am talking about a contract that cannot be annulled any more than a contract between men can be nullified. Now to Abraham and his seed these promises were made. God didn't say, "seeds," as of many, but "seed" as in one. And that seed is Jesus Christ. If the inheritance was to be the Law, it wouldn't be in the form of a promise; but God gave it to Abraham by promise. Then what good is the Law? It was given to us to show us our sins until the promised Messiah would come who is the mediator of God's covenant. Is the Law contrary to the promise? Absolutely not! If there had been a law that could bring life, then righteousness could have been earned by obedience to that law. But the scriptures told us that, because of sin, faith in the promise of Jesus Christ would be provided to all who would believe. Before faith came, we were kept according to the Law until the time that faith would be revealed. Thus, the Law was our teacher of the promise of faith that would bring us to the knowledge of Christ. We are children of God by faith in Jesus Christ, because anyone who has been baptized by the Spirit bears the name of Christ. Therefore, there is no such thing as Jew or Greek, slave or free, male or female, for we all are equal in Jesus Christ. And if you belong to Christ then you are Abraham's seed, and heirs according to God's promise. (also LUK 16:19–31)

God chose the faithful who obeyed Him to be His own. He also chose their rulers (DEU 17:15; 1 SA 10:24; 1 KI 3:8), judges (JDG 2:16–18; JDG 13:5), ministers (NUM 1:50; DEU 21:5), and prophets (NEH 9:7; ISA 6:8; JER 1:5). Jesus Christ continued this tradition by choosing His apostles (JOH 6:70; ACT 1:2; ACT 9:15). Christ also chooses us to be His disciples and to serve one another (MAT 20:1–16).

Those people who set an example of God's love, understanding, fairness, and wisdom are placed in positions of authority over His sheep, so that others may follow His example. In the same way, God ordained His Son to be an example before all the world of His unconditional and steadfast love. Jesus Christ was ordained from the beginning of time to show all people who He was and how we could be like Him (JOH 1:1–14). If we follow Him, we shine His light, showing the way for others who are lost and cannot find their way (PSA 119:105; JOH 8:12).

- PSA 89:3–4,27,29,34 ~ I have made a covenant with my chosen people, and I have sworn to my servant David that the throne of my blessed servant (Christ) will be established forever before all generations. He will be my firstborn, higher than all of the kings of the earth, and His seed will live forever. And I will never break that covenant.
- ISA 42:1 ~ God said, "Behold, the Chosen One, my delight; my Spirit is upon Him."
- ISA 43:10–12,15 ~ There are no gods before Him or after Him. God says, "You are witnesses to what I have said. My servant whom I have chosen is also sent to be a witness, so that you can know me and believe; and even so, I am He. I am the Lord and there is no other savior besides me. I have declared myself to you and I have saved you whenever you have forsaken all other gods for me. You are witnesses that I am God, the Holy One, the creator of Israel, and your King."

- MAT 12:15–18 ~ Jesus Christ is the fulfillment of the prophecy of Isaiah (above) who wrote: Behold my servant, whom I have chosen; He is my beloved, who pleases my soul. I will put my Spirit upon Him, and He will show judgment to the Gentile nations.

God chose Christ who in turn chooses you. Everyone is called to be a child of God, but God chooses only those who call upon Him to be their Lord. If you choose to seek the Lord, you will find Him through His only Son Jesus Christ. If you follow Christ, He will lead you to the Promised Land, where all His chosen people will live in God's presence forevermore. Once called, however, it is important to remain faithful and to set an example for others to see. This is not an easy thing to do, because to be faithful to God is to be at odds with the world.

- DEU 14:2 ~ You are a holy people to the Lord, for He has chosen you to be a peculiar people unto Himself, above all the nations that are upon the earth. (also PSA 135:4)
- MAT 20:16 ~ Jesus said, "The last will be first, and the first last, for many are called but few are chosen."
- JOH 15:16,19 ~ Jesus said to His disciples, "You didn't choose me, I chose you and ordained you, so that you could bear fruit that would not wither. Anything you ask of the Father in my name will be given to you. If you were of the world, only the world would love you; but I have chosen you out of the world, and that is why the world hates you."
- 1 PE 2:9 ~ You are a chosen generation, a royal priesthood, a holy nation, a unique people; So, praise Him who has called you out of darkness into his marvelous light.

To be chosen by God is a wonderful thing indeed. What great rewards God has promised to those who love Him and earnestly try to keep His commandments. God's joy and peace are bestowed upon His people on earth and again in heaven. There is no end to His loving kindness, which can be enjoyed the moment one dedicates his or her life to the Lord and which endures for eternity. Therefore, to choose God, and to choose to follow His Son, is to choose life. To choose not to seek God and be with Him, choosing the world instead, is to choose death.

- DEU 30:19–20 ~ Moses said, "I have presented you with life and death, blessing versus cursing. I recommend that you choose life so that you and your descendants may live. I hope you choose to love God, obey his Law, and cling to Him; for He is your life and He is your time; and you will live in the land which He promised to you and your ancestors."
- PSA 33:12 ~ Blessed is the nation whose God is the Lord, and blessed are the people He has chosen for His own inheritance.
- ISA 66:4 ~ I (God) will choose their delusions; I will bring their fears upon them. Because when I called nobody answered; when I spoke, nobody listened. Instead, they were evil before my eyes, and they chose to do the things that I despise.
- EPH 1:4 ~ He has chosen us to be His own before the foundation of the world, that we should be holy and without blame as we come to Him in love.
- 2 TH 2:13 ~ We will give thanks to God always for you brothers, beloved of the Lord, because God chose you from the beginning to receive salvation through sanctification of the Spirit and belief in the truth.
- REV 17:14 ~ The devil's own will make war with the Lamb, but the Lamb will overcome them, for He is Lord of lords and King of kings. Those who are with the Lamb are those who were called, chosen, and faithful.
- REV 20:14; REV 21:8 ~ Death and hell will be thrown into the lake of fire, along with the cowardly, the unbelievers, the corrupt, the murderers, the immoral, the occultists, the idolaters, and the liars. Their place will be the eternal lake of fire and this is the second death.

In the Old Testament, the firstborn son was the one who was chosen to receive the father's blessing. This blessing was called the birthright, the right to receive a double portion of the father's estate as an inheritance (DEU 21). Of course, the first son didn't always earn the birthright. Isaac was not the firstborn of Abraham, yet he was the chosen son (GEN 21). Jacob was not the firstborn of Isaac, but he deceitfully obtained the birthright that his brother Esau despised (GEN 25). Although Reuben was Jacob's first son, Jacob awarded the birthright to Joseph (the eleventh son), yet it would be Jacob's fourth son Judah who would be of the royal lineage of Christ (GEN 49; 1 CH 5:1). Jacob blessed Ephraim, Joseph's second son, and not Manasseh, the firstborn (GEN 48), and the list goes on. Plainly, God gets to choose who He intends to carry on His legacy.

So, who is it that is supposed to receive the blessing, or birthright? It is everyone who belongs to Christ, the firstborn of God the Father. All believers will receive an equal inheritance with Christ in the kingdom of heaven. Christ is the first fruits of God and Christians are the first fruits of Christ. For this reason, we are compelled to offer ourselves and the first fruits of our income or produce to the church, to the needy, and to charities, preferably those motivated by true Christian love. This will serve to nurture people who are physically, mentally, and/or spiritually handicapped.

- PSA 89:19,22,27–29 ~ God said, "I have placed my strength on the mighty One, whom I have exalted above all the others. The enemy will never subordinate Him or oppress Him. I will appoint Him to be the firstborn, the greatest of the kings of the earth. I will love Him forever and my covenant with Him will be everlasting."
- ROM 8:28–31 ~ We know that all things work together for good to those who love God and are called according to His purpose. For God knew them in advance and predestined them to be conformed to the image of His Son, and to be among the firstborn of His brothers. Whomever He predestined, He called; and whomever He called He justified; and whomever He justified, He also glorified. Therefore, if God is with us, who can be against us?
- HEB 2:10–11 ~ In bringing many children to glory, it was appropriate that God would make the author of their salvation (Christ) perfect through His suffering. Both the One who makes us holy and those who are made holy are of the same family. Therefore, Jesus is not ashamed to call them His brothers and sisters.
- HEB 12:22–24 ~ You have come to the joyful assembly of millions of angels to the church of the firstborn, whose names are written in heaven. You have come before God the judge of the entire human race, among the spirits of the righteous who have been made perfect, to Jesus Christ the mediator of the New Covenant.
- 1 PE 3:8–9 ~ Live in harmony with one another with love, sympathy, compassion, and humility. Do not repay evil with evil or insult others, but repay with blessings. Be a blessing to others for you were called to inherit a blessing.

Every human being has value and should be treated with respect and love regardless of their ethnicity, creed, gender, age, party, color, or any other demographic. God loves all people unconditionally; this is our duty, to love them as much as ourselves. You and I are loved as much as the nest person, for all are precious to the Lord. So, when it comes to giving, everyone is qualified to give and to receive the blessings of our heavenly Father. Sharing these blessings is a blessing itself, and leads to more giving and more blessings. God has called every human being to be His and it is up to each individual to heed that call. Those who do are among God's chosen people.

Lesson: The Seed of Abraham

Abraham was one of the great patriarchs, not only for the Israelites, but also for all of God's chosen people. Abraham himself was chosen by God for his unyielding faith. He demonstrated this to God through his willingness to sacrifice Isaac, Abraham and Sarah's only legitimate son and heir. But God told Abraham that He would provide the sacrifice, and Abraham learned that the sacrifice would be God's only Son. Abraham's faith was strong, and he backed it up with his actions. For this, God made a promise to Abraham, that his descendants would be as numerous as the stars in heaven and as the sands on the seashore. That covenant was passed onto Abraham's son Isaac, and Isaac's son Jacob.

- GEN 15:5 ~ And God brought Abraham outside and said, "Look up to the heavens, and count the stars, if indeed you can. So will your offspring be."
- GEN 17:19 ~ God told Abraham, "Your wife Sarah will surely bear a son and you will name him Isaac. And I will establish my everlasting covenant with him, and his descendants."
- GEN 22:17 ~ God told Abraham, "I will bless you by multiplying your seed as the stars in heaven and as the sand along the seashore. Your descendants will possess the cities of your enemies."
- GEN 26:24 ~ God appeared to Isaac and said, "I am the God of your father Abraham. Do not be afraid for I am with you and I will bless you. I will multiply your seed for the sake of your father Abraham."
- GEN 32:12 ~ God told Jacob, "I will bless you and I will multiply your seed as the grains of sand in the sea, which cannot be counted."
- PSA 105:6 ~ Oh seed of Abraham, God's servant; you children of Jacob, God's chosen ones; He is the Lord our God, and His judgements are everywhere. (1 CH 16:13)
- ISA 41:8 ~ You Israel, are my (God's) servants, the children of Jacob whom I have chosen, and the seed of my friend Abraham.

We understand that God's agreement with Abraham guaranteed him descendants too numerous to count. The Jews would naturally interpret this as being the Hebrew race. We know that many other nations also came from Abraham; for example, Arabs and other Moslem peoples revere Abraham as their father by blood via Ishmael. Christians are among Abraham's spiritual descendants insofar as we exhibit the faith of Abraham and are therefore part of the "seed."

We find in scripture that "descendants of Abraham" does not refer to Jews or Arabs. Children of Abraham include anybody that demonstrates a saving faith. As the apostle Paul aptly pointed out, Abraham's seed refers to one, the term "seed" being in the singular. That one person is Jesus Christ. Thus, the children of Abraham comprise those who looked for, found, and belong to Christ. The promise of eternal life was made to Abraham and all believers; anyone who believes is counted among the children of promise.

- GEN 22:18 ~ God told Abraham, "In your seed all the nations of the world will be blessed because you have been obedient to me."
- MAT 3:7–10 ~ John was baptizing people in the Jordan River when many of the Pharisees and Sadducees came to observe. John spoke to them saying, "You snakes! Has anyone warned you of the judgement that awaits you? You'd better start bearing fruit that is worthy of repentance. You say to yourselves that you have Abraham as your father. I assure you that God can produce children of Abraham from these stones. The ax is ready to strike at the roots; any tree that does not bear good fruit will be chopped down and burned in the fire."

- JOH 8:31–47 ~ Jesus spoke to those Jews who believed in Him saying, "If you continue in my Word, you are indeed my disciples, and you will know the truth and the truth will set you free." Some of the bystanders answered, "We are descendants of Abraham, and we have never been slaves to anyone; how can we possibly be set free?" Jesus replied, "Whoever sins becomes a slave to sin. A slave has no position in the family, but a son does. If the Son sets you free, you will definitely be free. I know you descended from Abraham, yet you are ready to kill me because you have no room for my Word in your heart. I've been telling you what I have seen in the Father's presence." They responded, "Abraham is our father." Jesus announced, "If you were Abraham's children you would do as he did. Instead, you plot to kill me, a man who has given you the truth directly from God; Abraham would never do such a thing. You are only following the ways of your earthly father." They protested, saying, "We are not illegitimate children; God Himself is our Father." Jesus explained, "If God was your Father you would love me, for I came from Him and here I am; I have not come on my own but He has sent me. Why is this so hard for you to understand? I'll tell you why, because you belong to your father the devil, and your desire is to carry out his will. He was a murderer from the start and despised the truth, for there is no truth in him. He speaks only lies whereas he is the father of lies. I speak only the truth but you refuse to listen. Can you prove me wrong; if not, why do you not believe? Whoever belongs to God listens to Him. The reason you do not understand is because you do not belong to God."
- GAL 3:6–9,16,26–29 ~ Consider Abraham. He believed God and his faith was credited to him as righteousness. Understand then, that those who believe are the children of Abraham. The scriptures foresaw that God would justify the Gentiles by faith, and announced it in the Gospel to Abraham as it is written: All nations of the world will be blessed through your seed (GEN 22:18 above). Anyone having faith is blessed along with Abraham, a man of great faith. To Abraham and his seed, the promises were made. God didn't say "seeds" meaning many people, He said "seed" meaning one person, who is Christ. You are all children of God through faith in Jesus Christ, for you have been baptized unto Him and have clothed yourselves in His righteousness. There is neither Jew nor Greek, slave nor free, male nor female, for you are all one in the Lord. If you belong to Christ, then you are Abraham's seed and heirs according to His promise.
- GAL 4:23,28,31 ~ Abraham had two sons, one born in bondage after the flesh and the other born in freedom after the promise. Now brothers we, like Isaac, are born under the promise. We are not born in bondage but are born free.
- HEB 6:12–18; HEB 8:6–7,13; HEB 9:15; HEB 10:23,36; HEB 11:6 ~ Do not be lazy, but follow those who, through faith and patience, inherit the promise. When God made the promise to Abraham, God (who cannot lie) swore an oath saying, "I will bless you and give you many descendants." Abraham patiently endured and obtained the promise of Messiah, the New Covenant. The New Covenant of Christ is superior to the Old Covenant because it is founded on greater promises. If the first covenant had been perfect, there would have been no need for the second. By calling the second covenant "new" He has rendered the first obsolete, and things that are obsolete soon disappear. Christ is the mediator of the New Covenant, which declares that those who are called may receive the promised eternal inheritance, because He has ransomed their souls from the sins committed under the Old Covenant. Let us cling to our faith without wavering, for He that gave us the promise is faithful. Be patient, so like Abraham you may receive the promise, having remained obedient to God. Without faith it is impossible to please God, for you cannot come to God unless you believe that He exists and that He rewards those who earnestly seek Him.

Abraham was commanded by God to ensure that males were circumcised as a recognizable sign of their commitment to God's holy covenant. God wanted to set His people apart from the rest of the world. By having all men to be circumcised, Abraham's offspring would demonstrate to their enemies that they were different. Therefore, whenever one would fall in battle, the enemy would see that they were circumcised and would know they were loyal to the God of Abraham.

There was division among the early Christians regarding circumcision. In fact, Peter and Paul originally disagreed over the matter of circumcision, and for a time remained estranged from one another. On the one side, Peter argued that the Gentiles also must be circumcised, as written in the Law, in order to belong to the children of Abraham. On the other side, Paul argued that circumcision was not demonstrated outwardly in the physical sense, but inwardly in the spiritual sense. Paul correctly pointed out that nobody could be justified by works of the Law, only by faith in Christ. Hence, adhering to ancient Jewish customs was no longer required; what was required was genuine faith. It was Abraham's faith that justified him and his family, not their ability to conform to the Law. Their obedience was in response to faith. That faith has been exhibited by commitment to God through circumcision under the Old Covenant and through baptism under the New Covenant.

- GEN 17:7–11 ~ God told Abraham, "I will establish my covenant with you and your descendants, and it will be an everlasting covenant that will continue for generations to come. I will be your God and the God of your offspring. You and your descendants must not break this covenant. To prove your commitment to this covenant, every male among you must be circumcised."
- JER 4:4; JER 6:10; JER 9:25–26 ~ Circumcise yourselves to the Lord, and remove the foreskins of your hearts, you men of Judah and inhabitants of Jerusalem, or my fury will burn like an unquenchable fire because of your evil ways. Who can I speak to, and who can I warn that will take heed? Behold, their ear is uncircumcised, so they cannot listen. To them the Word of the Lord is offensive, and they do not delight in it. Thus, the circumcised will be punished along with the uncircumcised: Egypt, Judah, Edom, Ammon, Moab, and desert dwellers from distant lands who are uncircumcised in the literal sense, as well as the nation of Israel which is uncircumcised in the heart.
- ACT 7:51 ~ Stephen rebuked, "You stubborn and uncircumcised in heart and ears; you always resist the Holy Spirit just as your fathers did."
- ROM 2:25; ROM 3:2,30 ~ Circumcision has value if you obey the law, but it has no value if you are a lawbreaker. If those who are not circumcised obey the law they are regarded as obedient. That is, if a person who is not physically circumcised obeys the law, that person is worthier than someone who is physically circumcised but does not obey the law. A man is not a Jew if he is merely one outwardly; similarly, circumcision is not merely an outward sign. No, a man is a Jew if he is one inwardly; thus, circumcision should be of the heart, whereby a person is changed by the Spirit not by the written Law. Is there an advantage in being a Jew or in being circumcised? The advantage is in being entrusted with the Word of God. There is one God, and He will justify the circumcised by faith, and the uncircumcised by the same faith.
- ROM 4:9–13 ~ Is God's blessedness only for the circumcised, or is it also for the uncircumcised? We have said that Abraham's faith was credited to him as righteousness. Under what circumstances was it credited? Was it after he was circumcised or before? It was before! He received the sign of circumcision as a seal of the righteousness he received by the

faith he had before he was circumcised. Therefore, he is the father of all who believe, whether they have been circumcised or not, so that righteousness can be credited to believers. Abraham is the father of those who walk in the steps of that same faith which he displayed prior to being circumcised. It was not through the Law that Abraham and his offspring received the promise that he would be heir to the world, but through the righteousness that comes by faith.
- 1 CO 7:19 ~ Circumcision is nothing and uncircumcision is nothing; keeping God's commandments is what is important.
- GAL 5:6 ~ For in Jesus Christ neither circumcision nor uncircumcision matters. What matters is faith expressing itself through love.
- PHP 3:3 ~ They are the circumcision, those who worship God in the spirit, who rejoice in Christ Jesus, and who place no confidence in the flesh.
- COL 2:11 ~ In Christ you have been circumcised, not with a circumcision done by the hands of men, but done by Christ when He removed the sins from your flesh.
- TIT 1:10 ~ There are many rebellious and deceitful people, especially the group of people that demand circumcision (who believed that circumcision was necessary for sanctification to take place).
- JAM 2:17–26 ~ Faith without works is dead. Was Abraham justified by works when he offered his son Isaac? Faith was active before that and was completed by the works. So a person is justified also by works and not faith alone. Just as a body apart from the spirit is dead, so is faith apart from works.

God made His promises to Abraham, Isaac and Jacob, but the promises were for the entire human race. Messiah came for Jews and non-Jews alike. Anyone willing to listen and believe will receive the gifts God promised. Unfortunately, most Jews rejected Christ, while at the same time assuming they were still God's people, excluding others from that status. Feeling they had earned the right somehow, they expected everyone else to earn it by following their rules and obeying their laws. Such a religion is centered on works and not faith. However, we know that the gift is free, and needs only to be accepted; it cannot be earned. And that gift is to be shared, not hoarded. Once received, actions of obedience should follow.

It is like a father that has adopted another child and his natural child does not want to share a present he received. The father takes away the gift from the natural child and gives it to the adopted one. Those choosing to reject God's Messiah lose their right to be included in the household of the Lord, regardless of ethnicity or ancestry. The kingdom of heaven is the Promised Land. It is not a piece of real estate in Palestine, it is an inheritance shared among God's household. There is no paradise on earth, and no nation or race has exclusive right to heaven.

- ROM 11:1–32 ~ Did God reject His people? Absolutely not! I (Paul) am an Israelite, a descendant of Abraham from the tribe of Benjamin. God did not reject the Israelites whom He foreknew. Just like in the time of Elijah so it is now. God has set aside a remnant chosen by His grace. And since it is by grace, then it can't be by works; if it were, grace would no longer be grace. But that which Israel sought they did not obtain; only the elect did. The others hardened their hearts, as it is written: God gave them a spirit of slumber so they could not see or hear, even until now. The words of David also come to mind: May their table be a snare, a trap, and an obstacle, so they cannot see or hear, and their backs will be bent forever. I ask you: did they stumble and fall for good or is there still a chance for them? Through their fall, the knowledge of salvation became known to the Gentiles, in order to provoke Israel to jealousy. Their loss meant spiritual riches for the Gentiles. What an even greater reward their return could bring! Listen you Gentiles, I have been sent to you. And I am hoping it will make my own people jealous, so they too will strive for what you have and be saved. For if their apparent rejection of the gift and associated exclusion helped to reconcile the rest of the world, wouldn't their acceptance surely mean life? If the part of the bread which is offered is holy, then so is the entire loaf; if the root is holy then so are the branches. If some of the branches have been broken off, but you a wild olive shoot have been grafted in, then you can share the nourishment from that same root. But do not boast of your heritage, because you do not support the root, it supports you. Branches can be broken off due to unbelief, and branches can be grafted in because of faith. If God did not spare the natural branches that were broken off, He will not spare you either. God was stern with those that fell, but He will be kind to you if you continue in Him; if you don't you will be cut off as well. Anyone that refrains from disbelief will be grafted in. You were wild olive branches that, contrary to nature, were grafted into a cultivated olive tree. Imagine how readily the natural branches could be grafted back into their own tree! Israel, my brothers, I don't want you to be ignorant of this mystery. Israel has become hardened so that the Gentiles can enter. But Israel will be saved, as it is written: The deliverer will come out of Zion to turn godlessness away from Jacob; this is my covenant with them to remove their sins. As far as the Gospel is concerned, the Gentiles are enemies because of you. But as far as the elect are concerned, they are loved because of the patriarchs. For God's gifts and His call cannot be overturned. You were once disobedient but God showed you mercy after that disobedience. Now God is being merciful to the Gentiles just as He showed mercy to you when you humbly came to Him. For God has allowed everyone to fall so that He can show all of them His mercy.

In summary, those who are of the seed of Abraham are part of the body of Christ, because Christ has changed them on the inside. Whoever believes in Christ will live with Him forever, along with the rest of God's chosen people. If Christ lives in you, you are included in the household of God and the citizenship of heaven.

- LUK 16:19–31 ~ Jesus told the parable of the rich man and the poor man: There was a rich man who lived a life of pleasure and luxury. A poor man lay at the gate; he was weak, hungry, and afflicted, desiring just the crumbs off the rich man's plate. The two men died. The poor man was taken to Abraham's bosom, and the rich man was exiled in Hades. The rich man called out to Abraham asking if he would let the poor man dip his finger into water to wet his parched tongue. But Abraham reminded him how thoughtless and unmerciful he had been to the poor man before, and told him that nobody could pass through the chasm separating the two underworlds. The rich man implored that his family be warned, to prevent them from the same fate. Abraham informed the rich man that they would have to rely on the Word of God like everybody else; if they didn't, not even a visit from the dead would persuade them to change their ways.
- ROM 9:4–8 ~ Who are the Israelites, to whom God gave the Law and granted the adoption, and with whom God made covenants and promises? Christ came for them and for all people. It's not as if God's Word had no effect, for they who are of Israel are not all from Israel. Those who are of Abraham's seed are not all his children. In other words, those who are children of the flesh are not children of God; those who cling to God's promises, they are counted as children.
- ROM 9:25–26; ROM 10:20 ~ God spoke through Hosea (HOS 2:23) saying, "I will call them my people who were not my people, and I will call them beloved who were not my beloved. And at that place (Israel) where I told them they were not my people, others (Gentiles) will be called the children of the living God." God also spoke through Isaiah (ISA 65:1) saying, "I was found by them who did not seek me; I revealed myself to those who did not ask for me."

- 1 CO 1:24 ~ To those whom God has called, both Jews and Gentiles alike, Christ is the power of God and the wisdom of God.
- COL 3:15 ~ Let the peace of God rule in your hearts, since as members of one body you were called to peace. Be therefore, thankful. Let the Word of Christ live in you richly as you teach and admonish one another with wisdom, and as you sing psalms, hymns, and spiritual songs with gratitude in your hearts to God.

We should be compelled to sow the Seed, which is the Word, so that it may grow in the hearts of others. Remember, the Word is God; Christ is the Word made flesh (JOH 1:1–4,14; 1 JO 5:7–8). And since God is love (1 JO 4:7–8), we are sowing the seeds of love. And that Seed will flourish in the hearts of those who believe God and cherish His promises; and those people will be productive in Jesus Christ our Lord, for His love will multiply in them and in the world. This is what is meant in the following parable.

- MAT 13:1–23 ~ Jesus told a parable about sowing to the Spirit: A sower of seeds left seeds by the wayside where the birds ate them. He left seeds in the rocky ground where there was insufficient soil for them to grow. He left seeds among the weeds and thorns where they were choked to death. He also left seeds on fertile ground where they grew and bore fruit. The seeds represent the Word of God. If the Word is left by the wayside, it will be snatched away by the wicked one. If the Word is given to those with a heart of stone, it will never take root in their hearts. If the Word is given to corrupt and worldly people, it will be choked out by the lusts of the flesh. But if the Word is received by someone who listens and understands, it will take root in his or her heart and that person will bear much fruit.

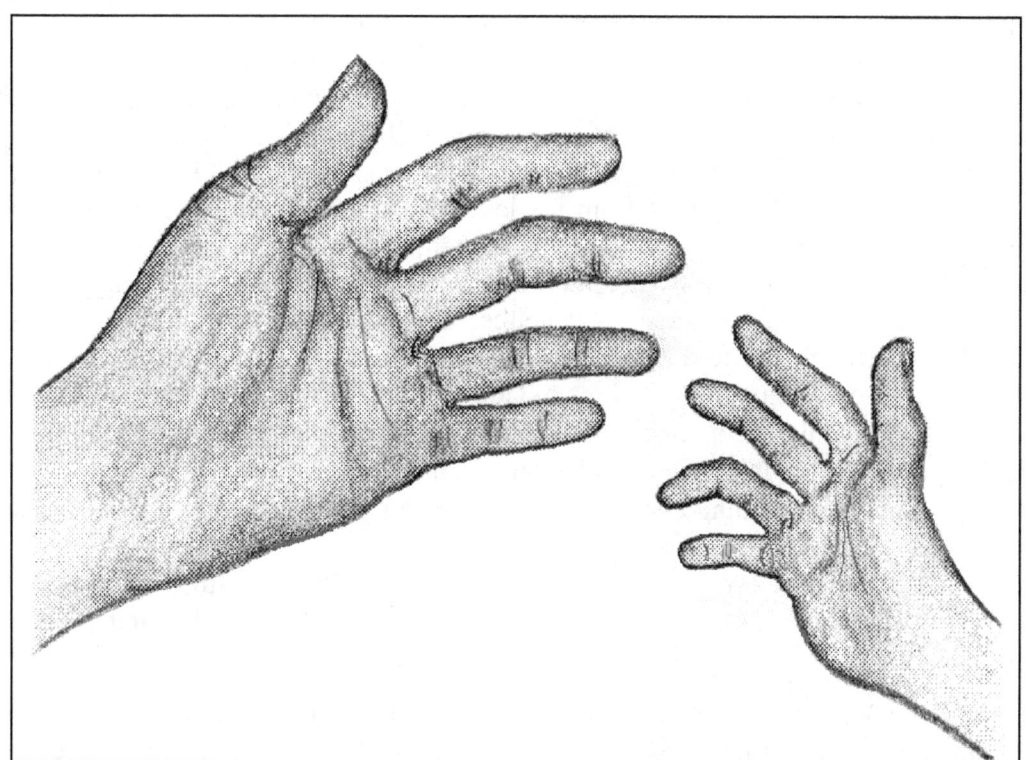

The seed of Abraham is Jesus Christ. Abraham knew this and rejoiced (JOH 8:56–58). Everyone who shows the same faith as Abraham will be welcomed home by our Heavenly Father as adopted sons and daughters (GAL 3:26,29).

Lesson: The Apostles

The term "apostle" was ascribed by Christ Himself to the twelve who lived with Him and to whom He gave the tools to become the first evangelists of the Christian faith. Often, this term is used interchangeably with the term "disciple" which literally means follower, or believer. Among His disciples, Jesus chose twelve apostles.

- LUK 6:12–16 ~ One day Jesus went up into a mountain to pray, and continued all night in prayer to God. When morning came, He called His disciples together, and He chose twelve whom He named apostles. They included Simon, (whom he later named Peter), Andrew his brother, James and John, Philip and Bartholomew (also called Nathanael), Matthew and Thomas, James the son of Alphaeus, Simon called Zelotes (the Zealot), Judas (known as Lebbaeus Thaddaeus) who was the brother of James (a different James than those above), and Judas Iscariot, who would become a traitor. (also MAT 10:2–4; MAR 3:13–19)

Clearly, the apostles were set aside from other disciples. They were chosen to perform great works of faith in their assigned function of spreading the Gospel to the ends of the earth and winning souls for Jesus Christ. During the conduct of that holy mission, the apostles would have to suffer many trials and tribulations.

- JOH 16:33 ~ Jesus said to the apostles, "I have told you these things so that you might have peace, because in the world you will have tribulation. But be of good cheer for I have overcome the world."
- ACT 2:43; ACT 4:33 ~ Fear came upon every soul, for many wonders and signs were performed by the apostles. And with great power the apostles bore witness of the resurrection of the Lord Jesus; and exceeding grace was bestowed upon them.
- ACT 5:12,29 ~ Peter and the other apostles asserted, "We must obey God rather than men."
- ROM 5:3; ROM 8:35–39 ~ We also rejoice in our tribulations, because we know that tribulation produces patience, and patience produces character, and character produces hope. And hope will not disappoint us, because God has poured out His love into our hearts by His Holy Spirit. What can separate us from the love of Christ: tribulation, distress, persecution, famine, nakedness, peril, or sword? As it is written, for your sake we face death on a daily basis; we are sent as sheep to the slaughter. But we have conquered these things through Him who loved us. For I am convinced that neither death nor life, neither angels nor demons, neither the present nor the future, nor any powers, neither height nor depth, nor anything in all creation can separate us from the love of God that is in Jesus Christ our Lord.
- 1 CO 4:9 ~ God put us, the apostles, on display, like those who die in the arena; for we were made to be a spectacle to the world, and to angels, and to men.
- GAL 1:8 ~ Anyone, including angels, who preaches anything contrary to what Jesus and the apostles preached are cursed.
- EPH 2:19–20 ~ You are no longer foreigners but fellow citizens with God's people and the members of His household, built upon the foundation of the apostles and prophets, with Christ being the chief cornerstone.

After Judas Iscariot became a traitor to the cause, the remaining eleven apostles drew lots to select someone to replace him; Matthias was the winner (ACT 1:15–26). However, it wasn't their place to appoint apostles, it was Christ's; and Christ chose Paul. In fact, the above passage is the only time Matthias is mentioned in the NT.

- ROM 1:1; ROM 11:13; 2 TI 1:11 ~ I Paul, a servant of Jesus Christ, was called to be an apostle, set apart to preach the Gospel of the Lord. I am the apostle to the Gentiles. I have been appointed to be a preacher, an apostle, and a teacher to the Gentiles.
- 1 CO 9:1–2 ~ Am I (Paul) not an apostle? Am I not free? Have I not seen Jesus Christ our Lord? Are you not the result of my work in the Lord? Though I may not be considered an apostle to others, doubtless I am to you; for you represent the proof of my apostleship in the Lord.
- 1 CO 15:3–11 ~ Christ died for our sins in accordance with the scriptures, He was buried, and He arose from the dead the third day, appearing to Peter and the twelve. After that, He was seen by over five hundred people at the same time most of whom are still alive. Then He appeared to James, and again to the remaining apostles. Eventually, He also appeared to me, the misfit of the family. For I am the least of the apostles; indeed, I am not worthy to be called an apostle because I persecuted the church of God. But by the grace of God I am what I am, and that grace which He bestowed upon me was not in vain. Because I worked harder than all of them; but it wasn't me, it was the grace of God which lived in me. Therefore, whether it was them or me, this is what we preached, and this is what you believe.

The following are brief descriptions of the twelve ordered alphabetically, excluding Judas Iscariot who betrayed Jesus and committed suicide.

Andrew: He was a fisherman from Bethsaida and brother to Simon Peter. He was possibly the first of the apostles to follow Christ. A disciple of John the Baptist, he was present when John identified Christ as the Lamb of God, and he followed Jesus thereafter. Andrew brought his brother Peter to meet Christ that same day (JOH 1:35–42).

Bartholomew: He also was known as Nathanael to the disciples. He was introduced to Jesus by Philip the day that he and Andrew left John the Baptist to follow Christ. Jesus told Nathanael how Philip had found him sitting beneath the fig tree, and Nathanael immediately became convinced that Jesus was the Christ (JOH 1:41–51).

James Alphaeus: This apostle is often referred to as James the lesser, probably because he was younger than James the son of Zebedee (MAR 15:40). Like Jesus and many others, James's mother was named Mary.

James Zebedee: He was the elder brother of John, both fishermen, and partners with Simon Peter. Salome, James's mother, was the wife of Zebedee. James was the first apostle to be martyred, beheaded by Herod Agrippa I (ACT 12:1–2). He and his brother were nicknamed the "sons of thunder" possibly because of their temperament.

John: He was the son of Zebedee and Salome and younger brother to James. He was an influential leader of the early Christian church and one of Christ's beloved followers (JOH 13:23–24). He is the author of the Gospel of John, the three epistles bearing his name, and the book of Revelation. He was exiled to the island of Patmos in the Aegean Sea because of his faith in Jesus, where he likely authored Revelation.

Matthew: He was called by Christ and immediately left his job as a tax collector (LUK 5:27–32). Referred to by Jesus as Levi (from that tribe), he was the author of the Gospel of Matthew, which probably began circulating around the same time as the Gospel of Mark, the earliest of the Gospels.

Paul: Paul (formerly Saul) was a Roman citizen from Tarsus, a city in Asia Minor. He was trained to be a Pharisee by Gamaliel, one of the principal teachers of Jewish Law. Zealous for the Lord, he was a persecutor and murderer of Christians, until Christ personally called him to bring the Gospel to the Gentiles (ACT 22:1–21). Paul subsequently endured many persecutions and abuse, on his way to becoming the most prolific evangelist of all time.

Peter: He was a fisherman and the brother of Andrew. Christ changed his name from Simon to Peter, meaning "the rock" (MAT 16:13–19). He became the leader and spokesman for the apostles, boldly speaking the Gospel to the Jews prior to taking his ministry to Babylon and Rome. Like Paul, he performed a number of miracles, including raising the dead. He wrote the two epistles bearing his name. He is regarded as the primary source for the Gospel of Mark.

Philip: Another follower of the Baptist, he also was from Bethsaida of Galilee, hometown of Andrew and Peter. Philip introduced his companion Nathanael to Christ, and became an evangelist to the Greeks (JOH 12:20–36).

Simon: He was a Canaanite (MAR 3:14–19). He also was a member of a religious group known as the Zealots (ACT 1:13), an extreme faction of Jews that zealously sought the removal of the Romans from Palestine, and protested the paying of taxes to Rome.

Thaddaeus: Thaddaeus was the surname for this apostle called Lebbaeus (MAT 10:3). He also was referred to as Judas (not Iscariot; see LUK 6:16).

Thomas: Also called Didymus, he was absent when Christ first appeared to the apostles following His resurrection. Famed as the one who doubted that Christ had arisen, he finally became convinced upon seeing and touching the resurrected Christ in the flesh (JOH 20:19–29).

All of the apostles met an untimely death except John, the only one that probably died of old age. The following accounts are documented elsewhere in historical texts indicating how apostles of Christ were martyred for their unrelenting faith in Jesus Christ.

APOSTLE	MINISTRY	DEMISE
Andrew	Russia; Ukraine	Crucified in Patras Greece on an X-shaped cross
Bartholomew	Armenia	Beheaded in Armenia
James A.	Palestine	Beat and cut to pieces in Jerusalem
James Z.	Palestine	Beheaded by Herod Agrippa I
John	Asia Minor	Died a natural death in Ephesus after his exile
Matthew	Ethiopia	Impaled with swords in Ethiopia
Paul	Asia Minor; Rome	Executed in Rome by Emperor Nero
Peter	Babylon; Rome	Crucified upside-down in Rome
Philip	Asia Minor	Executed in Asia Minor
Simon	Arabia	Beaten to death by an angry mob in Arabia
Thaddaeus	Assyria; Persia	Shot with arrows in Babylonia
Thomas	Persia; India	Impaled with a spear in India

In addition to the apostles, there were countless others that were leaders, spokespersons, and evangelists of the early Christian church. Among them were Barnabas, Silas, Apollos, Mark, Luke, Priscilla, Phoebe, and Timothy. Additionally, the maternal brothers of Jesus were renown disciples. His brother James was a revered elder of the Christian church in Jerusalem. The New Testament epistles of James and Jude are commonly attributed to Jesus's half-brothers. Note that some believers deny that Mary had children after Jesus, but the implication is that she did, as found in the words of Matthew, "and Joseph knew her not until she had brought forth her firstborn Son, and he called His name Jesus" (MAT 1:24–25). Further, Matthew lists four brothers of Jesus and mentions sisters as well in his Gospel (see MAT 13 below). Thus, Jesus was the eldest of many siblings. Some would argue against that fact, maintaining that Joseph had other children prior to marrying Mary; but if that were true, they also would have made the pilgrimage to Bethlehem during the census. Conclusively, Jesus was the member of quite a large family, and was the firstborn of many siblings. Theologians often assert that his brothers denied Jesus as the Christ until after the resurrection, at which time James became the leader of Christian Jews until he was stoned to death in Jerusalem because of his persistent faith. This event was reported by the historian Josephus.

- MAT 13:53–57; MAR 6:1–4 ~ After Jesus had finished telling the parables He departed into His own country. He taught in the synagogue, and the people were astonished saying, "Where does He get such wisdom, and the power for such mighty works? Isn't He the carpenter's son, and isn't His mother called Mary? And aren't his brother James, Joseph, Simon, and Judah, and aren't His sisters also with us? And many were offended. But Jesus said to them, "A prophet is dishonored only when he is in his own country or in his own house."
- ACT 1:12–14 ~ They returned to Jerusalem from the Mount of Olives, a Sabbath day's walk from the city. After arriving, they went to the upper room where they were staying. Those present included Peter, James, John, Andrew, Philip, Thomas, Bartholomew, Matthew, James Alphaeus, Simon Zelotes, and Judas the brother of James. Together they prayed constantly, along with the women, and Mary the mother of Jesus, and His brothers.
- GAL 1:15–19; GAL 2:9 ~ God, who had singled me (Paul) out since birth and called me by his grace, was pleased to reveal his Son to me, so I might preach about Him to the heathen. Immediately, without consulting anybody, and without going to Jerusalem to meet the apostles, I went into Arabia, and returned again to Damascus. Finally, after three years I went to Jerusalem to meet Peter, and stayed with him fifteen days. But I didn't see any of the other apostles except James, the Lord's brother. And when James, Cephas (meaning "rock" in Hebrew; namely Peter which is *Petra* in Greek), and John who were pillars of the Christian church, saw the grace that was given to me, they offered to me and also Barnabas the right hand of fellowship. It was agreed that we would preach to the Gentiles and they would preach to the Jews.
- JAM 1:1–4 ~ Greetings from James, a servant of God and of the Lord Jesus Christ, to the twelve tribes which are scattered abroad. My brothers, count it all joy when you fall into different temptations, for the trying of your faith produced patience. But let patience have her perfect work so that you may be perfect, and never wanting.
- JDE 1:1–2 ~ From Jude (Judah), the servant of Jesus Christ and brother of James, to those who are sanctified by God the Father, preserved in Jesus Christ and called to be His disciples: Mercy to you; peace and love be multiplied unto you.

CHAPTER THREE

WHO IS JESUS CHRIST?

OUR REDEEMER

Jesus Christ is the Messiah, the Son of God, the Word made flesh, the New Covenant, and the central figure of the New Testament. He is the human manifestation of the only living God and is part of the Holy Trinity. He is our Lord and God. Christ is the Savior of the human race, the Judge, the Redeemer, the High Priest, the Prince of Peace, God's messenger and prophet, and the King of kings.

Jesus Christ made the ultimate sacrifice; this is the New Covenant. Not by coincidence, the sacrifice of the Lamb of God was made during the celebration of Passover. Because of His sacrifice, all people can be saved from sin and death, for God promised this faith covenant to all believers. Through God's Covenant, everyone can come to God in faith, become one of His chosen people, and obtain the everlasting protection of the Good Shepherd.

God's Covenant of Grace is the sacrifice of His firstborn and only Son Jesus Christ. This event provides atonement for the sin of the whole world. Because of Christ's offering of Himself, never again will any blood offering need to be made to atone for sin. Therefore, sacrificial offerings made in accordance with God's Old Covenant of the Law are no longer necessary, because Christ made a blood atonement that would last for the duration of humanity.

Jesus Christ Is the New Covenant.

The Old Testament tells us about God's laws and commandments, and a covenant promise between Himself and Israel, including anyone who likewise sought God and His righteousness. God desired obedience and sacrifice, and in return offered the gift of eternal life. This was a temporary covenant that God established under the Law. However, God knew that sinful humans were incapable of perfect adherence to His laws. That's why the Old Covenant came with the promise of a New Covenant which would last for all time. The New Covenant is the promised Messiah sent to earth to free people from sin and death. Jesus Christ is that Messiah, who brought with Him the good news of salvation through faith in Him.

Recall that the Old Testament provided numerous examples of prophecy about the coming Messiah, which came true in Jesus Christ. The fulfillment of this prophecy is documented in the New Testament. Therefore, these two testaments of God cross-validate each other. The OT made it clear who the Messiah was, what He was coming for, and how He would live, serve, die, and rise again from the dead. The NT reveals how these things actually happened when God's Son came to Earth. In this section, a sampling of OT verses referring to the coming Messiah are provided, followed by the NT verses that confirm them. In other words, OT verses are referenced to NT verses that describe the fulfillment of prophecies about God's Messiah.

Old Testament References

- GEN 3:14–15 ~ (God to Satan) You and your offspring will hate the woman and her offspring. He (Christ) will crush your head and you will strike His heel.
- GEN 9:26 ~ Shem is blessed of God, and Canaan will be his servant (Jesus descended from Shem: LUK 3:36).
- GEN 12:3 ~ Through the seed of Abraham all nations will be blessed (MAT 1:1; LUK 3:34).
- GEN 17:7,19 ~ God told Abraham He would establish an everlasting covenant between Him and Abraham, Abraham's descendants, and the generations to come (LUK 1:55).
- GEN 18:18; GEN 26:4; GEN 28:14 (also ISA 49:6) ~ God said to Abraham, then Isaac, and then Jacob, "From your seed all nations on earth will be blessed." (Jesus was a descendant of those three men of God: see MAT 1:2–16; LUK 3:23–38; GAL 3:16).
- GEN 22:1–12 ~ Abraham was commanded by God to sacrifice Isaac, who was Abraham's only legitimate heir. Abraham was in the process of doing so when God commanded His angel to stop Abraham. Because of Abraham's loyalty, Isaac was spared; instead, Abraham sacrificed a ram to God. (God's plan was to sacrifice His only Son for sin, so Abraham did not have to sacrifice Isaac: see JOH 3:16).
- GEN 28:12 ~ Jacob dreamed about a ladder that stood on earth and reached into heaven, and angels of God were ascending and descending on the ladder (Jesus Christ is the ladder; He is the way to heaven: see JOH 1:51).
- GEN 49:10 ~ The royal scepter will not depart from Judah until the One to whom it belongs comes, who all people will obey (Jesus was a descendant of Judah: see MAT 1:2; LUK 3:33; HEB 7:14; REV 5:5).
- EXO 12:3–12 ~ Through Moses, God commanded the Israelites to sacrifice an unblemished male lamb, take the blood of the lamb and paint the door posts of their houses, then eat the lamb for dinner (refer to ISA 53; REV 5:11–12). When God sent the angel of death to kill the first born in Egypt, the angel avoided the homes of those who had done as God commanded.
- EXO 21:32 ~ The price of reimbursement for a slave was thirty pieces of silver (the same price Judas received when he betrayed Jesus: MAT 27:3).
- EXO 24:8 ~ Moses took blood from the sacrifice and sprinkled it on the people saying, "This is the blood of the everlasting covenant revealed by the Lord in these His words." (Jesus Christ is the Lamb of God, represented as the sacrificial lamb of the Israelites; Jesus became the sacrifice, removing sin and conquering death: see JOH 1:29; HEB 9:19–22; 1 PE 1:19; REV 5:12).
- LEV 16:8–10 ~ Aaron (the priest) shall present two goats and randomly select one to be for the Lord and the other to be the scapegoat. The first will be sacrificed to God and the second will be presented alive before the Lord for atonement, by sending it into the wilderness to be a scapegoat for sin. (Christ was made the scapegoat and the sacrifice for sin: see 2 CO 5:21).
- NUM 24:17 ~ I shall send Him, but not now. A star will rise out of Jacob (Israel), a ruler to strike down Moab and the children of Seth. (Possible reference to the Star of Bethlehem).
- DEU 18:15,18 ~ God said, "I will raise up a prophet like me from among your brothers. You must listen to Him. I will put my words in His mouth and He will tell the people everything I ask of Him" (see ACT 3:22–23).
- 2 SA 7:12–16 ~ God said to David, "I will make one of your descendants a strong king who will rule forever. I will be His Father and He will be my Son." (Jesus was a descendant of David: see MAT 1:6; LUK 2:4; REV 5:5).
- 1 KI 1:4 ~ The king knew her not (refers to the fact that King David never had sex with the concubine that kept him warm and ministered to him in his old age: see MAT 1:24–25).

- 1 CH 5:2 ~ From the tribe of Judah came the chief ruler, even though it was Joseph who received the birthright from their father Jacob. (Jesus was a descendant of Judah: see MAT 1:2; LUK 3:33; HEB 7:14; REV 5:5).
- PSA 22:1 ~ My God, my God, why have you forsaken me? (Repeated by Christ on the cross: see MAT 27:46).
- PSA 22:7–8 ~ They that look upon me laugh at me and scorn me. Shaking their heads, they say, "He trusted in the Lord for deliverance, let the Lord save him." (Jesus was scoffed in this manner as he hung on the cross: see MAT 27:41–43).
- PSA 22:16–18 ~ David prophesied: Evil men circle me like a wolf pack. They have pierced my hands and feet (also ZEC 13:6). They have bruised every bone in my body. They gloat and stare. They divide my clothes by casting lots. (Jesus was crucified in this manner, and the soldiers gambled for His robe by tossing dice: see MAT 27:35; JOH 19:37).
- PSA 23:1 ~ The Lord is my Shepherd who provides everything I need. (Jesus is the Good Shepherd: see 1 JO 1:1–18).
- PSA 31:5 ~ Into your hands I commit my spirit. (Spoken by Christ on the cross: LUK 23:46).
- PSA 34:20 ~ David prophesied: Not a bone of His will ever be broken. (The soldiers broke the legs of the two men crucified with Jesus, but did not break Jesus's legs: see JOH 19:36).
- PSA 41:9–10 ~ The trusted friend with whom I ate bread has betrayed me. Have mercy on me. Raise me up so that I can repay them. (Jesus was betrayed by Judas, his friend, during the Passover festival: see JOH 13:18,26).
- PSA 61:6–7 ~ You will prolong the king's life, for His years are as generations; He will abide before God forever, preserved in mercy and truth (see 1 PE 1:18–22).
- PSA 69:21 ~ They offered me gall when I was weak, and vinegar when I was thirsty (this drink was given to Jesus during His crucifixion; see MAT 27:34; JOH 19:28–29).
- PSA 78:2 ~ David prophesied: He will speak in parables and disclose hidden truths. (Jesus frequently taught hidden truths through parables: see MAR 4:33; JOH 18:37).
- PSA 80:8–17 ~ The vine, God's right hand, the Son of Man who God has made strong for Himself, will be called out of Egypt, and He will be cut down. (Reference to the flight to Egypt to avoid Herod's decree, and the subsequent death of Christ: see MAT 2:13–15).
- PSA 89:27,45 ~ I will make Him, my firstborn, higher than all the kings of the earth. The days of His youth will be shortened, and He will be covered with shame. (Jesus died a shameful death at an early age).
- PSA 110:1 ~ God said to my Lord, "Rule at my right hand and you will subdue your enemies" (also PSA 16:8,10). (David recognized that God would send His Son to be ruler over humankind, including those who lived before the birth of Christ, like David himself: see MAR 16:19; HEB 1:3).
- PSA 118:22 ~ The stone rejected by the builders became the main cornerstone of the foundation (i.e., the capstone of the arch; see also ISA 28:16). (The priests and Pharisees rejected Jesus as the Messiah, although He became the foundation of God's love, the church, and our faith: see MAT 21:42; LUK 20:17; ACT 4:11).
- PRO 30:4 ~ Who has ascended into heaven or descended? Who has established everything on earth? Do you know His name and the name of His Son? (Jesus was the Son of God who came down from heaven and then ascended: MAT 1:21–23).
- ISA 1:3–4 ~ The ox knows his owner and the ass his master's crib; but Israel does not know these things. This sinful nation has forsaken the Lord and provoked His Holy One into anger. (Indicates that Jesus was born in a stable and was rejected by His own people: see LUK 2:12; MAT 27:1).

- ISA 6:9–10 ~ God told Isaiah, "Go and speak to your people. They will hear but will not understand; they will see but will not perceive. For their heart is fat, and it makes their eyes heavy. They shut their eyes and ears so they cannot see or hear, and therefore they cannot understand in their heart, become converted, and be healed." (Jesus spoke in parables to reach those who would not just hear but listen; see MAT 13:10–17; ROM 11:7–8).
- ISA 7:14 ~ God Himself will provide a sign: A son will be born of a virgin; He will be called "God with us." (Christ was born of the Virgin Mary: see MAT 1:22–23; LUK 1:26–35).
- ISA 9:1–2,6–7 ~ In the future, this land (from Galilee to Jerusalem) will behold the glory of God, the light of life. For a Son will be born and the government will be upon His shoulders. He will be called Wonderful Counselor, Mighty God, Everlasting Father, and Prince of Peace. His eternal reign will bring truth and justice to all nations. (Isaiah declares what Jesus would be called and where He would preach: see MAT 4:12–16; MAR 1:9; ACT 5:31).
- ISA 11:1–2,10 ~ From the lineage of Jesse will come a branch who will possess the spirit of wisdom, understanding, knowledge, counsel and might, and the fear of God. Jesse's root will become the symbol of God's people, including the Gentiles. (Jesus descended from Jesse; see MAT 1:6; MAT 12:14–21; LUK 2:25–34).
- ISA 35:5–6 ~ The blind shall see and the lame shall leap. (Jesus and his apostles healed many blind and lame people: see MAT 15:30; ACT 4:9–10).
- ISA 40:3 ~ The one crying in the wilderness will prepare the way for the Lord; he will clear a straight path in the desert to be a highway for our God. (John the Baptist was that messenger: see MAT 3:1–3).
- ISA 42:1 ~ Behold, the chosen One, my delight; God's Spirit is upon Him. (Jesus had command of the Holy Spirit: see JOH 14:26; JOH 15:26).
- ISA 42:6 ~ I (God) called Him in righteousness to keep and watch over you, and to be a covenant for my people and a light for the Gentiles. (Simeon quoted this passage from Isaiah at the dedication of the baby Jesus: see LUK 2:25–34).
- ISA 49:7 ~ Kings and princes will see the sign and will come to worship. (The magi saw the star and followed it to Bethlehem where they worshipped the Christ child: see MAT 2:1–2,11).
- ISA 50:6 ~ I gave my back to be whipped; I gave my face to be mocked and spat upon. (These are accurate descriptions of Jesus's passion: see MAT 27:26–31).
- ISA 53:4–12 ~ He took upon Himself all of our grief and sorrows; yet we treated Him as an outcast. He was tortured for our sins and punished for our peace, and through His wounds we are healed. He was slaughtered like a lamb (EXO 12:3–12). He was buried like a criminal but in a rich man's grave. He was made an offering for sin, although He never committed a single act of sin or spoke an evil word. Therefore, His days will be prolonged and His name will be made great. He will be exalted, for He emptied his soul unto death. (Jesus Christ was tried and convicted, though Pilate himself admitted to Jesus's innocence. He bore our sins through His torture and crucifixion. He was treated like a criminal and was buried in a tomb donated by the wealthy Joseph from Arimathaea. His days were prolonged after His resurrection: see LUK 23:4,50–51; LUK 24:46; JOH 1:29; JOH 20:24–29; ACT 8:30–35; 2 CO 5:21; 1 PE 2:24).
- ISA 60:1–2 ~ Arise and shine, for your light has come; yes, the glory of God has come to you. Darkness covers the earth and great darkness covers its people. But the Lord will arise and come to you, and you will see His glory. And the Gentiles will come to His light, and kings will come to the brightness of His rising. (The light of Christ was marked by the Star of Bethlehem, which showed the three kings the way to the Christ child; see MAT 2:1–11).

- ISA 60:6 ~ They come with caravans of camels from Midian, Ephah, and Sheba, bringing gold and incense and praising God. (Reference to the visit of the wise men from the East, and the gifts they brought to the baby Jesus: see MAT 2:1,11).
- ISA 61:1–3 ~ The Spirit of God is upon me, because He has directed me to preach His good news to the humble, to heal the broken hearted, to free the slaves, and to release those who are bound in chains and in prison; to proclaim the Lord's favor and His vengeance, to comfort all who mourn, and to tell those who mourn to exchange their ashes for beauty; to replace mourning with joy, and to don the garment of praise in exchange for the spirit of sorrow, so that they may be trees of righteousness, planted by the Lord for His glorification. (Jesus quoted this passage when He began His ministry in his hometown of Nazareth; see LUK 4:14–20).
- ISA 65:9 ~ I (God) will bring forth a seed from Jacob and Judah; then my elect will inherit the mountains of the Holy Land. (Jesus was a descendant of Jacob and Judah).
- ISA 66:4–6 ~ I (God) will create their delusions and bring their fears upon them, because when I called, they didn't answer and when I spoke, they didn't listen. Instead, they chose evil before God. Listen to the Word of God and tremble. For His people hated Him and condemned Him in my name. Yet He will become your joy and they will become ashamed. (Jesus's own people, the Jews, ignored, rejected, hated, and condemned Him though He was received by the Gentiles: see MAT 11:20–21; MAT 12:9–14; MAT 27:1; MAR 8:31; JOH 15:23–25).
- JER 7:11 ~ Has my house become a den of robbers? (Jesus drove away the moneychangers in the temple and quoted this scripture: see MAR 11:17).
- JER 23:5–6; JER 33:15–17 ~ I (God) will place a righteous king to inherit David's throne; from David's lineage a king will come who will reign forever. (Jesus was a descendant of David: see MAT 1:6; LUK 2:4).
- JER 31:15 ~ In Ramah was heard the bitter weeping and mourning over the children who were killed. (Reference to Herod's failed attempt to kill the Christ child by butchering babies: see MAT 2:16–18).
- JER 31:31–34 ~ Jeremiah prophesied about the New Covenant, and how God would write His laws upon the hearts of His people (see HEB 8:7–13).
- DAN 7:13–14 ~ From the clouds of heaven there came one like the Son of Man, and to Him was given all dominion, glory and kingdom, so that all people, nations and languages should serve Him. (Jesus was sent to save all nations, not just the Jews: see ROM 3:29; GAL 3:28).
- DAN 9:27 ~ In one week the sacrifice was complete, confirming God's covenant to His people. As a result, all offerings and sacrifices ceased, and all abominations were desolated and consumed. (Jesus entered Jerusalem on Palm Sunday, preached, was arrested and crucified, and arose on Easter Sunday; this occurred in one week: see MAT 21–28; MAR 11–16; LUK 20–24; JOH 17–20. All further sacrifices became unnecessary: see HEB 9:14–22).
- AMO 8:9 ~ God says that in that day He will cause the sun to go down at noon, and will darken the earth in the middle of the day (see MAT 27:45 concerning Christ's crucifixion).
- JON 1:17 ~ God arranged for a whale to swallow Jonah, and he was in the belly of the whale three days and nights. (Jesus was in the grave three days and nights: see MAT 12:40).
- MIC 5:2–4 ~ Oh Bethlehem, you are such a small village but will be the birthplace of my king, who has been foretold from time eternal. God will forget Israel until the time has come for the chosen woman to bear the child; then the children of Israel will return. The Son will stand for and feed off the Lord, and will share His majesty. The children shall live in Him who is great, even to every corner of the earth. (Micah tells where Christ, God's Son, will be born and that He will be great among the nations: see MAT 2:5–6; JOH 7:42).

- MIC 6:6–7 ~ How am I to appear before God? Shall I come before Him with offerings and sacrifices? Will He be pleased with thousands and thousands of sacrifices? Shall I sacrifice my firstborn, the fruit of my body, to atone for the sin of my soul? (Indicates that we could never make enough sacrifices to atone for our sin, which is why Christ had to do it for us).
- HAG 2:23 ~ On that day, I (God) will take Zerubbabel my servant, and give him the royal ring, for I have chosen him. (Zerubbabel was of the royal lineage, and the ancestor of Joseph and Mary; see MAT 1:12–13, LUK 3:27).
- ZEC 3:8–9 ~ I (God) will bring forth my servant, the Branch. He will be the foundation stone; He will remove the sins of the world in a single day. (Christ removed all sin by dying on the anniversary of Passover: see JOH 1:29; 2 CO 5:21; 1 PE 2:24).
- ZEC 4:9 ~ The hands of Zerubbabel have formed the foundations of this house (i.e., the temple in Jerusalem), and his hands will finish it. Then you will know that the Lord has sent me to you. Note that both the lineage of Joseph (MAT 1:12) and Mary (LUK 3:27) include Zerubbabel (HAG 2:23).
- ZEC 6:11–13 ~ Make crowns of silver and gold and place them on the head of Joshua, the high priest, and declare, "The Branch will grow up from his place and He will build the temple of the Lord. He will bear the glory and will rule from His throne. He will be a priest and a king, both functions being guided by the council of His peace" (i.e., the Holy Spirit). (Note that "Joshua" essentially means "Savior;" it is an OT form of the name "Jesus").
- ZEC 9:9–10 ~ Rejoice, for here comes your righteous king riding on a donkey's colt. He will bring peace to all nations. (Jesus entered Jerusalem on Palm Sunday riding a donkey's colt: see MAT 21:7; JOH 12:14–15).
- ZEC 11:12–13 ~ His price was thirty pieces of silver, thrown down in the house of the Lord, and used to buy the potter's field. (Judas received this price for betraying Jesus, but he tossed the money at the feet of the high priests after realizing his terrible deed; they used the money to buy the potter's field for use as a paupers' graveyard: see MAT 27:6–10; ACT 1:17–19).
- ZEC 12:10 ~ I (God) will bless the house of David and all Jerusalem with the Spirit of grace, and they will look upon me whom they have pierced. They will mourn for Him, like a Father mourns the loss of His only Son (Jesus, God's only Son, was pierced in His hands, feet, and side: see JOH 3:16; JOH 19:31–37; JOH 20:24–29).
- ZEC 13:6 ~ Someone will say, "What are these wounds on your hands?" He will reply, "Those wounds I received in the house of my friends." (Accurate description of the wounds Jesus suffered and the fact that He was condemned by His fellow Jews, who claimed to be devout and righteous: see MAT 27:1,11–12,37; JOH 18:12,31).
- ZEC 13:7 ~ They will strike down the Shepherd and the sheep will scatter; but He will come back for His sheep. (Jesus repeated these words to His apostles during the Last Supper: see MAT 26:31. Jesus referred to Himself as the Good Shepherd who lays down His life for His sheep, and who returns to gather them to be with Him forever: see JOH 10:1–18).
- MAL 1:11 ~ My (God's) name will be great among the Gentiles (MAT 12:14–21).
- MAL 3:1–3 ~ I (God) will send a messenger to prepare the coming of the Lord; but who can endure His coming? For He is like a refiner's fire which completely removes all impurities and imperfections. (John the Baptist, the messenger referred to here, used the same analogy in describing Christ, for whom he was sent to prepare the way: see MAT 3:1–3,11).
- MAL 4:2 ~ The Star of Righteousness shall arise with healing in His wings. (Jesus arose from the dead and provided healing from our sins: see LUK 24:46–47).

Refer also to ISA 12:6; ISA 19:20; ISA 28:16; ISA 32:1; ISA 52:13–15; ZEP 3:15–18

New Testament References

- MAT 1:1–16 ~ The genealogy of Jesus from Abraham to Joseph (Jesus's earthly father) is provided.
- MAT 1:21–25 ~ God told Joseph that Mary would bear a son to be named Jesus (meaning Savior), for He would save His people from their sins. This took place to fulfill the prophecy that a virgin would bear a son who would be called Emmanuel, meaning "God with us."
- MAT 2:1–2,9–11 ~ Jesus was born in Bethlehem of Judea in the days of Herod the king. Wise men came from the east to Jerusalem asking Herod, "Where is He who is born king of the Jews? From the east we have seen His star and we have come to worship Him." After leaving Herod they followed the star. Finally, they stood directly under the star. They found the young Christ child with Mary, His mother, and worshipped Him. They opened their treasures and presented to Him gifts of gold, frankincense, and myrrh.
- MAT 2:4–6 ~ Herod gathered together the chief priests and scribes, demanding to know where the Messiah would be born. They replied that it would be Bethlehem of Judea, for it was written, "Bethlehem is not insignificant among the cities of Judea, for from there will come a governor who will rule my (God's) people Israel."
- MAT 2:13–15 ~ The angel of God told Joseph in a dream to take his family to Egypt to escape Herod's evil decree to kill all the male toddlers in Bethlehem. They stayed in Egypt until after Herod died, thereby fulfilling the prophecy: Out of Egypt God has called His Son.
- MAT 2:16–18 ~ Herod killed all the babies in Bethlehem who were two years old and younger. This fulfilled the prophecy of Jeremiah who wrote, "In Ramah was heard the bitter weeping and mourning over the children who were killed."
- MAT 3:1–3,11 ~ John the Baptist came preaching in the wilderness of Judea, saying, "Repent for the kingdom of heaven is near." This is the person spoken of by Isaiah who said, "The voice of the one crying in the wilderness will prepare the way of the Lord, making straight a pathway to Him." John told the people, "Indeed, I baptize you with water unto repentance. But He who comes after me is mightier than I; I am not even worthy of untying His shoes. He will baptize you with the Holy Spirit, and with fire."
- MAT 4:12–16 ~ Jesus lived and preached in the land of Capernaum, which is along the seacoast between Zebulun and Naphtali, thereby fulfilling the prophecy of Isaiah.
- MAT 11:20 ~ He (Christ) began to rebuke the cities where most of His mighty works were performed, because they did not repent.
- MAT 12:16–21 ~ Jesus asked the crowds not to expose Him in order to fulfill the prophecy of Isaiah saying, "Here is my servant whom I (God) have chosen, and who pleases me very much. I will put my Spirit in Him and He will show the way of judgment to the Gentiles; the Gentiles will trust in His name."
- MAT 12:38–40 ~ The scribes and Pharisees said, "We want a sign from you." Jesus replied, "An evil and adulterous generation seeks a sign, but the only sign they will see is that of Jonah. For just as Jonah was in the belly of a whale for three days and nights, so shall the Son of Man be three days and nights in the belly of the earth."
- MAT 13:10–17 ~ The disciples asked Jesus why he spoke in parables. Jesus replied, "You are able to know the mysteries of the kingdom but others are not so lucky. I speak to them in parables because they have eyes but don't watch and they have ears but don't listen. In them the prophecy of Isaiah is fulfilled: Their hearts have hardened; they hear but don't understand; they see but don't perceive. They have closed their eyes and ears so they cannot understand with their heart and become converted. You are blessed because your eyes and ears are opened to me. Many people have longed to hear and see what you have heard and seen."

- MAT 15:30 ~ The multitudes came to Jesus, bringing the lame, blind, dumb, maimed, and ill to Jesus, and Jesus healed them all.
- MAT 21:42; LUK 20:17 ~ Jesus said to them, "Have you read in the scriptures that the stone which the builders rejected has become the primary cornerstone. This is the Lord's doing, and isn't it marvelous?"
- MAT 27:1 ~ The chief priests and elders conspired against Jesus to put Him to death.
- MAT 27:3–10 ~ Judas who had betrayed Jesus, after recognizing he had condemned himself, relented and returned the thirty silver coins to the chief priests and elders saying, "I have sinned because I betrayed an innocent man." They replied, "Do you think we care?" Judas threw the money on the floor of the temple, and left to hang himself. The chief priests took the money, declaring that it was unlawful to place blood money in the treasury, so they decided to buy a field owned by a potter, and use the field as a graveyard for strangers. The graveyard was known thereafter as the field of blood. Thus, the Old Testament prophecy was fulfilled which stated, "They took the thirty silver coins, the price of Him that was valued, and bought the potter's field."
- MAT 27:26–30 ~ They released Barabbas. Then they whipped Jesus and delivered Him to be crucified. Soldiers gathered around Jesus, stripped Him, and put a scarlet robe on Him. They placed a crown of thorns on Jesus's head and a reed in His hand. They bowed before Him mocking Him, saying, "Hail, king of the Jews." They spat on Him and beat Him on the head.
- MAT 27:34–35 ~ During Christ's crucifixion, a soldier gave Him gall mixed with vinegar, but He would not drink it. The soldiers gambled for His garments by throwing dice, thereby fulfilling the prophecy, "They parted my garments among them, and they cast lots for my clothes."
- MAT 27:41–43 ~ The chief priests, scribes, and elders mocked Jesus saying, "He saved others but cannot save himself. If he is the king of Israel let him come down from the cross and we will believe him. He trusted in God to deliver him, let God deliver him now, if God wants him, for didn't he say he was God's son?"
- MAT 27:45 ~ Darkness came over the land from the sixth hour to the ninth hour.
- MAR 1:9 ~ Jesus came from Nazareth of Galilee, and was baptized by John in the Jordan River.
- MAR 4:33 ~ Jesus spoke the Word to the crowds with many such parables, for the benefit of those who would listen and understand.
- MAR 8:31 ~ Jesus explained that the Son of God had to suffer many things, be rejected by the elders, scribes, and chief priests, be killed, and rise from the dead after three days.
- MAR 11:17 ~ Jesus, while driving away the money changers, quoted Jeremiah, "Has my house become a den of thieves?"
- MAR 16:19 ~ After Jesus had spoken to them, He was received into heaven where He sat at the right hand of God.
- LUK 1:26–35 ~ God sent the angel Gabriel to the city of Nazareth in Galilee, to speak to a virgin named Mary, who was engaged to a man named Joseph a descendant of David. The angel came to her and said, "You are highly favored by God and He is with you; you will be blessed more than other women." Mary trembled with fear. Gabriel said, "Don't be afraid, for you please God very much. You are going to conceive and bear a son; you will call Him Jesus. Your son will be great, the Son of the Most High. God will give to Him the throne of his ancestor David. He will reign over the house of Jacob (Israel) forever; His kingdom will never end." Mary replied, "How can I bear a child since I've never had sex with a man?" Gabriel replied, "The Holy Spirit will come upon you and impregnate you. Thus, your child rightly will be called the Son of God."

- LUK 2:4–5 ~ Joseph took his pregnant wife Mary from the city of Nazareth in Galilee to the city of David which is called Bethlehem, because he was a descendant of David; it was there that he and his family were to be taxed by the Romans.
- LUK 2:25–35 ~ There was a man from Jerusalem named Simeon who was a devout and just man, and the Holy Spirit was with him. The Holy Spirit had revealed to him that he would not die until he had seen the Messiah. The Spirit led him to the temple where Jesus's parents had brought Jesus to be circumcised. Simeon took the baby Jesus in his arms and blessed God, saying, "Lord, you may now let me, your servant, die in peace according to your promise. For my eyes have seen your salvation which you prepared for all people: a light for the Gentiles and the glory of your people Israel." Joseph and Mary marveled at the things Simeon said. Simeon blessed them, saying to Mary, "In this child exists the fall and rising of many in Israel. He is the sign, which many will deny; and He will reveal the thoughts of many hearts. Yes, because of this child your very soul will be pierced like a sword."
- LUK 3:23–38 ~ The genealogy of Jesus from Adam to Joseph (i.e., Mary) is provided.
- LUK 4:16–20 ~ Jesus read from Isaiah the prophecy which identified Him as the Anointed One who would bring the good news of salvation.
- LUK 23:4 ~ Pilate said to the chief priests and to the people, "I see no fault in this man."
- LUK 23:50–53 ~ There was a man named Joseph from Arimathaea, who was a member of the Jewish high council; he was an upright and just man. He was against the decision of the council to condemn Jesus. He appealed to Pilate for the body of Jesus. Pilate allowed him to take the body, wrap it in linens, and place the body in his own tomb which was carved from solid rock, and in which no other dead bodies had ever been laid.
- LUK 24:46–48 ~ Jesus taught, "It was written that Messiah would suffer, but would rise from the dead in three days. It was written that He would preach repentance and forgiveness of sins among all nations, beginning with Jerusalem. You are witnesses of these things."
- JOH 1:29–35 ~ John the Baptist saw Jesus coming when he said, "Look, here comes the Lamb of God who takes away the sin of the world. He is the One of whom I spoke, who would come after me, though He is preferred over me, for He existed before me. I didn't know Him intimately, but He is the reason I have been baptizing people with water. He told me that I would see the Spirit of God descending upon Him and remaining there. I saw the Spirit of God descending upon Him like a dove, and it rested upon Him. He is the same One who will baptize with the Holy Spirit. I am a witness that He is the Son of God."
- JOH 1:51 ~ Jesus said, "Truly I tell you, from now on you will see the angels of God ascending and descending upon the Son of Man."
- JOH 3:16 ~ God loved the world so much that He sacrificed His only begotten Son, so that anyone could believe in Him and not die, but receive eternal life.
- JOH 7:41–43 ~ Some people said, "He is the Christ," while others said, "Will the Christ come from Galilee?" Others replied, "Didn't the scriptures tell us that God's Messiah would be a descendant of David and be born in Bethlehem, the city of David?" So, there was division among them concerning Jesus.
- JOH 10:1–18 ~ Jesus said, "Truly I tell you, whoever does not enter through my door, but attempts to enter some other way, is a thief and a robber. Whoever comes to my door will be allowed inside. The Shepherd will call His sheep by name, and they will recognize His voice and follow Him. The sheep will not follow strangers for they will not recognize the voice of strangers. I am the door to heaven; I am the Good Shepherd who gives His life for His sheep. I am not like the hired hand that runs away from the flock when the wolf comes, causing the sheep to scatter. I am the Good Shepherd; I know my sheep and they know me, just as the Father in heaven knows me and I, Him. And there will be one flock and one Shepherd. Thus,

- the Father loves me, for I will give my life so that I may take my life back again. Nobody takes my life away from me but I give it by myself. I have the power to give my life and to take it back again. I have received this mission from my Father in heaven."
- JOH 12:14–15 ~ Jesus sat on the young donkey just as it was written: Fear not daughter of Zion, for here comes your king, sitting on a donkey's colt (that had never been ridden).
- JOH 13:11,18,25–26 ~ Jesus, knowing that He would be betrayed, told His apostles, "Not all of you are clean. I am not talking about everyone; I know who I have chosen to be mine. But the scriptures must be fulfilled which say that the one who eats bread with me will betray me." An apostle leaning next to Jesus asked, "Lord, who is it?" Jesus replied, "It is the one to whom I give this bread after dipping it in the sauce." Then Jesus dipped the bread and gave it to Judas Iscariot.
- JOH 14:26 ~ Jesus said, "God will send the Comforter in my name, which is the Holy Spirit. He will teach you everything, and will help you remember all the things I have taught you."
- JOH 15:23–25 ~ Jesus said, "Those who hate me hate the Father. This is the fulfillment of the prophecy: They hated me without cause."
- JOH 15:26 ~ Jesus said, "I will send the Comforter from the Father, which is the Spirit of truth that proceeds from the Father, to testify about me."
- JOH 18:12–13,31–32 ~ The representatives of the Jews took Jesus, bound Him and took Him away. When Pilate told them to take Jesus back and judge Him themselves, they replied, "It is against the law for us to put a man to death" (implying that they wished for the Romans to put Jesus to death by crucifixion).
- JOH 18:37 ~ Pilate asked Jesus, "Are you a king?" Jesus replied, "You have said it. This is why I came into the world, to be a witness to the truth. Everyone who is interested in the truth will listen to me."
- JOH 19:28–29 ~ Jesus said, "I'm thirsty." They gave Him vinegar on a hyssop branch and raised it to His mouth to drink, which fulfilled prophecy.
- JOH 19:31–37 ~ The Jews didn't want bodies of the crucified to hang on their crosses into the Sabbath for that was a holy day. So, they asked Pilate to have the soldiers break the legs of the crucified to hasten death, and be taken away for burial. The soldiers broke the legs of the first two, but when they came to Jesus, they could tell He was already dead so they didn't break His legs. Then one of the soldiers pierced Jesus's side with a spear and out flowed blood and water, verifying that He was indeed dead. These things were done to fulfill the scriptures, "No bone of His will ever be broken," and, "They looked at Him who they had pierced."
- JOH 20:24–29 ~ Thomas was not with the other disciples when Jesus had appeared to them, so they told him about Jesus's visit. Thomas replied, "I will not believe until I myself have seen the nail prints in His hands and feet and touched His wounded hands and side." After eight days Jesus returned to His disciples, and this time Thomas was with them. Jesus said, "Peace to all of you." Then He turned to Thomas and said, "Look at me, see and touch my wounds, so that you might not be without faith but believe." Thomas answered, "My Lord and my God." Jesus replied, "Thomas, you have believed because you have seen; blessed are those who have not seen and still have believed."
- ACT 1:16–20 ~ Peter told the people, "The scriptures written by David had to be fulfilled concerning Judas who betrayed Jesus. Judas was with us and was part of this ministry. The reward for his sin was used to buy a field, and that field is called the *Field of Blood*. In Psalms it was written that his place in this ministry would become vacant and would have to be filled by another."

- ACT 4:9–11 ~ Peter told the people that it was by the power of Jesus Christ, whom the Jews had crucified, that he was able to heal the lame man. He said, "Christ was the stone which was rejected by the builders, and He became the chief cornerstone."
- ACT 5:31 ~ God has exalted Christ to be at His right hand and rule as Prince and Savior, and to give repentance to Israel and forgiveness of sins.
- ACT 8:27–38 ~ Philip asked a treasurer from Ethiopia if he understood what he had read from the book of Isaiah. The Ethiopian replied, "I need someone to guide me." The scripture of interest was this: He was led as a sheep to the slaughter, and like a dumb lamb before the sheerer. He was humiliated and denied justice. Who can identify His descendants, for His life was taken from Him? The Ethiopian asked Philip, "Who was the prophet talking about, himself, or someone else?" Philip began to explain to the man about Jesus. The man was converted and Philip baptized him.
- ROM 3:23–24,29 ~ All people have sinned and come short of God's glory. All are justified for free by God's grace through the redemption found in Jesus Christ. Is Christ the God of only the Jews and not the Gentiles? No, Christ is the God of both Jews and Gentiles alike.
- ROM 11:7–8 ~ The Israelites did not find what they were looking for; but God's elect found it. Thus it is written, "They have eyes that do not see and ears that do not hear."
- 2 CO 5:21 ~ God made Christ, who never sinned, to become sin for us so that we could be made righteous before God through Him.
- GAL 3:16 ~ God made His promises concerning Christ to Abraham and his descendants.
- GAL 3:28 ~ There is neither Jew nor Greek, slave nor free, male nor female, for we are all equal in Jesus Christ.
- HEB 1:3 ~ Christ is the brightness of God's glory and the image of God in the flesh. He upholds all things by the power of His Word, purges us of our sins, and now sits at the right hand of God.
- HEB 7:14 ~ Our Lord Jesus Christ was a descendant of Judah, a tribe which Moses said nothing concerning priesthood.
- HEB 9:19–22 ~ Moses sprinkled the blood of the sacrifice on the Book of the Law, the church, and the people, testifying of God's everlasting covenant. By the Law evil is purged with blood, and without blood there can be no remission of sins (see EXO 24:8).
- 1 PE 1:18–22 ~ You are not redeemed with corruptible things like gold or silver, you are redeemed with the precious blood of Christ, who was like a lamb without blemish or spots. He, who was ordained before the foundation of the world, was revealed in these past days just for you. Believe in Him who God raised from the dead and gave glory, so that your faith and hope can remain in God. Your souls will be purified for obeying the truth that the Holy Spirit has shown to us. Therefore, fervently love your brothers with a pure heart.
- 1 PE 2:24 ~ Christ bore our sins in His own body on the cross, so that we, who were dead in our sins, could live unto righteousness.
- REV 5:5 ~ One of the elders said, "Look, the Lion from the tribe of Judah the descendant of David; He has prevailed to open the book and loosen the seven seals which bind it."
- REV 5:11–12 ~ I (John) heard the multitude of angels and saints saying, "The Lamb who was slain is worthy to receive all the power, riches, wisdom, strength, honor, glory, and blessing."

The Word

The Word of God is communicated through God's Holy Spirit. It was the Holy Spirit who influenced the prophets to write the Holy Bible. Therefore, the Bible is inspired by God. The Holy Spirit, God's Word, was made manifest in human form through Jesus Christ. God figured that the best way to communicate His Word to humans was to become a human Himself.

God's Word is always true and never false. Therefore, the Holy Bible provides absolute truth; Jesus Christ never told a lie for He is truth as well. Anyone attempting to add to, subtract from, or otherwise change the words and/or meaning of God's Word are committing a great sin. Anyone claiming that the Bible is inaccurate and/or who preaches doctrine not preached by Jesus, His apostles, and the prophets, is mistaken and lost.

- DEU 12:32 ~ Do what I (God) have commanded you, and do not add to it or diminish from it.
- PSA 119:105 ~ God's Word is a lamp to our feet and a light to our path (it shows the way).
- PRO 30:5–6 ~ Every word of God is true. Don't attempt to add to His words or He will rebuke you and you will be proven false.
- ISA 2:3 ~ People will say, "Come, let us go to the mountain of the Lord to the house of the God of Jacob, and He will teach us His ways and we will walk in His paths. For out of Zion will come the Law; out of Jerusalem will come the Word." (also MIC 4:2)
- ISA 55:10–11 ~ The rain and snow fall from heaven and do not return, but rather water the earth making the plants bud and bloom, which provides seeds to the sower and bread to the eater. Likewise, God's Word proceeds from His mouth and does not return to Him void, but rather accomplishes His will and prospers in the minds of those to whom it was sent.
- MAT 13:1–23 ~ Jesus told a parable about sowing to the Spirit: A sower of seeds left seeds by the wayside where the birds ate them. He left seeds in the rocky ground where there was insufficient soil for them to grow. He left seeds among the weeds and thorns where they were choked to death. He also left seeds on fertile ground where they grew and bore fruit. The seeds represent the Word of God. If the Word is left by the wayside, it will be snatched away by the wicked one. If the Word is given to those with a heart of stone, it will never take root in their hearts. If the Word is given to corrupt and worldly people, it will be choked out by the lusts of the flesh. But if the Word is received by someone who listens and understands, it will take root in his or her heart and that person will bear much fruit.
- MAT 13:31–32 ~ Jesus told a parable about sowing to the Spirit: The kingdom of heaven is like the mustard seed. It is one of the smallest of seeds yet it grows into one of the largest of trees. Then the birds come and make homes in its branches.
- MAT 24:35 ~ Jesus said, "Heaven and earth will pass away, by my words will remain forever."
- JOH 1:1,14 ~ In the beginning was the Word, and the Word was with God, and the Word was God. And the Word became flesh, and lived on earth; and we saw His glory, the glory of the Father's only Son. (also PRO 8)
- JOH 17:17 ~ God's Word is truth.
- ACT 10:36–41 ~ Peter said, "The Word which God sent to Israel is Jesus Christ; in Him God's peace can be found. That Word began in Galilee and became known throughout Judea, after the baptism preached by John. God anointed Jesus Christ of Nazareth with the Holy Spirit and with His power. Jesus spent His time doing good and healing the demon possessed, for God was with Him. We are witnesses of all the things He did in the land of the Jews, and in Jerusalem where He was killed on a cross. God raised Him from the dead after

three days. Many people chosen by God to be witnesses saw Him, and we are among those witnesses."
- ROM 1:16 ~ I am not ashamed of the Gospel; it is the power of God which brings salvation to all who have faith, regardless of race.
- ROM 13:10 ~ Love is the fulfilling of the Law.
- 1 CO 2:13 ~ We teach using words taught by the Holy Spirit, not by human wisdom. Spiritual truths can be interpreted only by people who possess the Spirit.
- GAL 1:8 ~ Anyone, including the angels, who preaches anything contrary to what Jesus Christ and the apostles preached are cursed.
- EPH 5:26 ~ Jesus gave Himself for His people so He could sanctify them through the washing of water by the Word.
- 1 TH 2:13 ~ We thank God that you received His Word and accepted it as the Word of God and not the word of men. The Word of God is at work in believers like you.
- 2 TI 3:16 ~ All scripture is inspired by God. God's Word provides the doctrine of truth, refutes that which is false, and instructs all people in the ways of righteousness.
- HEB 4:12 ~ The Word of God is alive and powerful. It is sharper than any double-edged sword, piercing deep, so as to divide the very soul and spirit. It can discern the thoughts and intents of the heart.
- 2 PE 1:16,21 ~ We did not follow cleverly devised fables when we told people about the power and coming of Jesus Christ, for we were eye witnesses of His majesty. No prophecy ever came from the impulse of man, but holy men spoke as they were directed by God.
- 1 JO 5:6–8,20 ~ There are three that are recorded in heaven: the Father, the Word, and the Holy Spirit. These three are one. The same three bear witness: the Spirit, the Water, and the Blood. The Spirit is the witness, because the Spirit bears the truth. We know Jesus Christ who is true so that we may know God who is true; and so, we live in Him who has shown us His Son, the source of eternal life.
- REV 22:18–19 ~ For I testify to everyone who hears the words of the prophecy of this book, that if anyone adds to these words, God will add unto that person the plagues mentioned in this book. If anyone subtracts from the words of this prophecy, God will take away their name from the Book of Life, and they will not share in the inheritance.

Atonement

God gave everyone a mind to discern good and evil. We disobey God whenever we do, say, or think something evil. Unfortunately, everyone chooses to disobey God, for all people are influenced by their sinful nature which Satan preys upon. God is extremely displeased when we are sinful, the punishment being death. Thus, God intends to destroy everything evil, but He is going to save that which is good.

To commit a single sin is to disobey God; therefore, everyone is guilty. So how can anyone be saved? Even the most moral person is sinful at times. Well, God has separated good and evil, just as He separated light and darkness; likewise, God will separate believers from unbelievers. The atonement provided by Christ destroys sin, thereby removing the penalty of death. We are saved because we have become pure, cleansed of evil by the precious blood of Christ. In the Old Testament, God's faithful made sacrifices to atone for their sin; these sacrifices had to be made constantly since the people could not stop sinning. God knew that no number of sacrifices would ever be enough, so He sent His Son to make a single sacrifice to last for all time.

Christ's sacrifice atoned for the sins of all people. Faith in Christ's atonement leads to personal redemption and salvation. That is, everyone has been redeemed by Christ and we merely have to believe this to receive salvation. Thus, in His life Christ conquered the Law. In His death Christ conquered sin. In His resurrection Christ conquered death. Since Christ arose from the dead and lives eternally, those saved by Christ will arise and live eternally. This is the atonement that destroys all evil and allows us to be saved from the condemnation of death and reconciled with our most holy Father.

- LEV 1–5 ~ God commanded that certain sacrifices be offered for the purposes of atonement, reconciliation, and communion with God.
- LEV 17:11 ~ The life of all flesh resides in the blood, and I (God) have given it to you upon the altar to make atonement for your souls; for it is the blood that makes atonement for the soul.
- LEV 23:27 ~ The tenth day of the seventh month will be the day of atonement. It will be designated a holy day in which you will assemble together, denying yourselves, and presenting an offering made by fire to the Lord.
- MIC 6:6–7 ~ How am I to appear before God? Shall I come before Him with offerings and sacrifices? Will He be pleased with thousands and thousands of sacrifices? Shall I sacrifice my firstborn, the fruit of my body, to atone for the sin of my soul?
- ROM 5:8–11 ~ God showed His great love for us, for although we were sinners, Christ died for us. Therefore, we are justified by the blood of Christ, saved from God's wrath through Him. We were reconciled to God by the death of His Son and we were saved by His life. We find great joy in God through our Lord Jesus Christ by whom we now have received the atonement.
- ROM 5:12,18–19 ~ By one man, sin came into the world, bringing death with it; and death was subsequently passed along to everybody for all have sinned. Therefore, while the sin of one brought judgment and condemnation upon humankind, so the righteousness of one brought the free gift of justification and life. Thus, by the disobedience of one (Adam) we became sinful, and by the obedience of one (Christ) we can become righteous.
- HEB 9:11–15,18–22 ~ Christ came as the high priest and king over all good things to come, to prepare a greater and more perfect church, not made by hands like a building. Christ obtained eternal redemption for us, not by the blood of burnt offerings but by His own precious blood. If the blood of burnt offerings purified the hearts of men, how much more will the blood of Christ purify us! Through the Holy Spirit, Christ offered Himself, who was without blemish (sinless), and who purged our consciences from dead works to serve the living God. By this cause, Christ has become the mediator of the New Testament (Covenant). By His death, we are redeemed from the sins committed under the first (old) covenant, so that those who are called might receive the promise of God's eternal inheritance. Even the first covenant included blood, for after Moses read from the Book of the Law, He sprinkled blood from the offering on the book and the people, saying, "This is the blood of the covenant which God has commanded for you to keep." Moses also sanctified the tabernacle in this manner. Under the Law, all acts of disobedience are purged with blood, for without the shedding of blood there is no remission of sins.

CHAPTER THREE

Forgiveness

In the Old Testament, atonement was provided through faith, by obedience to God's laws and via sacrificial offerings. But nobody could become perfect under the Law; this is why Christ came. Christ was perfect under the Law, thereby fulfilling the Law on our behalf. Christ became the sacrificial offering, for He ransomed our souls from death by paying the penalty for our sins. That is why the Bible has a New Testament, to teach us that atonement can be obtained only through faith in Christ, not by works of the Law.

Christ is the only sacrificial offering that will ever need to be made for sin. God will forgive and forget our sins if we believe in His Son Jesus Christ, and humbly and sincerely repent of our sins in His name. So, while Christ has atoned for the sin of the world, we still must seek His forgiveness to obtain personal salvation. In other words, to believe in the atoning sacrifice of Christ is to rely entirely upon Him for forgiveness and salvation. If we are sincerely sorry for our wrongdoing and ask Him for mercy, God will forgive us through Christ. In response, we are commanded to forgive others.

- 2 CH 7:14 ~ God says, "If my people, who are called by my name, humble themselves, pray, seek my face, and turn from their evil ways, I will hear them and forgive their sins, and I will heal their land."
- PSA 32:5 ~ I acknowledged my sin to you Lord; I have not tried to hide my sinfulness. I confessed my sins and you forgave me all of them.
- PSA 86:5 ~ You are good, Lord, and ready to forgive. You bestow your bounteous mercy on those who call to you for help.
- PSA 130:3–4 ~ If you, Lord, counted our sins against us, who would be able to stand? But there is forgiveness with you that you may be feared.
- JER 31:34 ~ God says, "They won't have to teach others to know me anymore for they will all know me, from the least of them to the greatest. For I will forgive them and I will forget their sins."
- MAT 6:14–15; MAR 11:25–26 ~ Jesus said, "If you forgive others, your heavenly Father will forgive you. But if you do not forgive others, your heavenly Father will not forgive you."
- MAT 12:31–32 ~ Jesus said, "All manner of sin and blasphemy will be forgiven by God, except blasphemy against the Holy Spirit. Whoever speaks against the Son of Man can be forgiven. But whoever speaks against the Holy Spirit will not be forgiven, neither in this world nor in the world to come."
- MAT 18:18,21–22 ~ Jesus said, "Whatever you tie on earth will be tied in heaven, and whatever you untie on earth will be untied in heaven." Then Peter asked Jesus, "How many times should I forgive someone who has done wrong to me? Seven times?" Jesus answered, "Not seven times, but seventy-seven times."
- LUK 6:37 ~ Jesus said, "If you don't judge others, you won't be judged. If you don't condemn others, you won't be condemned."
- LUK 17:3–4 ~ Jesus said, "If someone sins against you, reprimand them. If they repent, forgive them. If they sin against you seven times in one day, and repent each time, then forgive them seven times."
- JOH 20:22–23 ~ Jesus appeared to His friends after His resurrection and said, "Receive the Holy Spirit. Anyone's sins that you forgive, they will be forgiven. Anyone's sins that you retain, they will be retained."
- ACT 13:38 ~ Through Jesus Christ all people can receive the forgiveness of sins.

- 2 CO 5:21 ~ Christ became sin for us, although He never sinned Himself, so that we could be made righteous before God through Him.
- EPH 4:32 ~ Be kind to each other, tenderhearted, and forgiving, even as God for Christ's sake has forgiven you.
- 1 JO 1:8–9 ~ If we say we do not sin we deceive ourselves and we are liars. If we confess our sins, God, who is faithful and just, will forgive our sins and cleanse us from all unrighteousness. Everyone has sinned, but everyone can seek salvation through faith in Christ who is our only source of salvation. There is no limit to the number of people who can receive salvation. All they have to do is seek God, believe in Christ as their Savior, love their neighbor, and above all, love God.

Justification and Sanctification

Christ was perfect under the Law, for He thoroughly fulfilled the Law on our behalf. While we have been made blameless by the atoning sacrifice of Christ, it is our belief in that atonement by which we are justified (found not guilty). That is, we are justified by our faith, because we believe that our souls have been purified by the blood of Christ. If the soul is redeemed from death it will live forever, for this is God's promise of eternal life given to all believers.

To be justified means to be absolved of sin and guilt. Jesus Christ paid the price of our punishment and His blood cleanses us from unrighteousness, thereby ransoming our souls from the grave. In other words, to be ransomed from death is to be redeemed by the blood of Christ. Because of His atoning sacrifice, our souls have been sanctified (made holy) by His Spirit. We have been made holy because Christ has taken our sins upon Himself, and has imputed His righteousness upon us.

Justification is the means, and sanctification is the end result. Abraham was justified by faith, which was proven by his actions. Abraham was willing to sacrifice Isaac as an atonement for sin, but it was his great faith in God and trust in God's judgment that justified him. In the OT, those who were faithful to God demonstrated their faith by obedience to His Law and belief in God's promise of a Messiah. In the NT, that obedience is still rooted in faith in God through trust in the salvation of Jesus Christ. Thus, we are now justified by faith in Jesus Christ. Faith always has been the avenue of justification, whether under the Law or under Grace.

Our faith is demonstrated by our works of love and our obedience to God. Anyone who places their faith and hope in the salvation bought by the blood of Christ is acceptable before God, and is no longer a condemned creature. Without the atonement, nobody could be saved, for all are guilty of sin and deserve to die. Works of the Law cannot save anyone, for those works are destroyed by a single sin. We are saved by the grace of God alone, whose only Son consecrated us through the shedding of His blood. However, we must continue to strive to become more like Him, which is a lifelong effort. A person cannot simply acknowledge the sacrifice of Christ and then continue to live a life of wickedness and debauchery. We come closer to God by studying His Word, participating in the sacraments, witnessing, tithing, and demonstrating our commitment to God through our obedience and service. Gradually, we become conformed to the likeness of Christ, until death when we are presented blameless before God the Father. Thus, the process of sanctification will continue throughout one's life once a person has accepted Christ. That is, once you have become a new person through Christ you cannot return to your previous evil ways.

- EXO 23:7 ~ Do not falsely charge anyone, and do not sentence an innocent person to death, for I (God) will not acquit the guilty.
- EXO 34:8–9 ~ Moses prayed: If I have found grace in your sight, Lord, let my Lord go among us, for we are a stubborn people. Pardon our sin and take us as your inheritance.
- 1 KI 8:32–34 ~ Judge your servants, Lord, and condemn the wicked; bring their evil back upon their own heads. But justify the righteous according to their ways. When your people are beaten down by the enemy because of their sin, and they turn back to you, confessing, praying, and humbling themselves before you, please listen to them and forgive them, and bring them back to the land you gave to their ancestors.
- JOB 9:20 ~ If I justify myself, my own mouth will have condemned me. If I say I am perfect, then I have proven myself to be perverse.
- JOB 25:4,6 ~ How can anyone be justified with God? Anyone born of a woman is nothing but a worm.
- PSA 143:2 ~ Lord, don't judge your servant harshly, for not a living soul is righteous before you.
- ISA 53:10–11 ~ It pleased the Lord to bruise Him (Christ) and to make Him suffer. His life was given as an offering for sin, and God will see His Son and prolong His days for the will of God will flourish in Him. After His soul has suffered enough, He will be able to look back with satisfaction. By knowledge of Him many will become justified, for He took their sins upon Himself.
- ISA 55:7 ~ Let evil and wicked people everywhere change their evil ways, forsake their immoral thoughts, and turn to the Lord, and He will have mercy on them; for the Lord will abundantly pardon those who seek Him.
- JER 33:8 ~ I (God) will cleanse them of their sin and pardon them.
- MIC 7:18 ~ Who is like you, God, who pardons sin and ignores the evil done by your people? God does not stay angry forever, but finds pleasure in giving mercy.
- MAT 5:17–19 ~ Jesus said, I didn't come to destroy the Law, I came to fulfill the Law. Not one little bit of the Law will be removed until heaven and earth have passed away. Whoever breaks even the least of the commandments will be considered among the least in heaven. Whoever obeys the Law and teaches others to do the same will be considered great in heaven.
- LUK 18:9–14 ~ Jesus told the parable of the Pharisee and the publican. Two men went to the temple to pray: a Pharisee and a publican. The Pharisee said, "Thank you Lord that I am not a sinner like other men, such as that tax collector, because I give tithes and I fast twice a week." The publican bowed low before the altar and beat on his breast saying, "God be merciful to me a sinner." Only the publican returned home justified by God. Those who exalt themselves will later be humbled, and those who humble themselves will later be exalted.
- ACT 13:37–39 ~ He, who God raised from the dead, was never evil. Therefore, everyone should realize that through this man is preached the forgiveness of sins. Whoever believes in Him will be justified from all the things that were done which could not be pardoned according to the law of Moses.
- ACT 26:14–18 ~ Jesus spoke directly to Paul, calling him to be an apostle. Jesus said, "I have appeared to you for a special reason, to be my minister and witness of things you have seen and things that I will show to you. I am sending you to the Gentiles to open their eyes, to turn them from darkness to light, and from Satan to God. I wish for them to receive the forgiveness that I offer, and the inheritance that is promised to those who are sanctified by faith in me."

- ROM 3:20,23–24,28 ~ By works of the Law will no person be justified in His sight, for with the Law comes the knowledge of sin. For all have sinned and come short of God's glory. We are justified freely by the grace of God through the redemption found in Jesus Christ. In conclusion, a person is justified by faith not by works of the Law.
- ROM 4:24–25 ~ We believe in Him who raised Jesus Christ, our Lord, from the dead. He was delivered over to death for our sins and was raised from the dead for our justification.
- ROM 5:8–11,18–21 ~ God showed us His great love for us, for although we were sinners, Christ died for us. Therefore, we are justified by the blood of Christ, saved from God's wrath through Him. We were reconciled to God by the death of His Son and we were saved by His life. We find great joy in God through our Lord Jesus Christ by whom we have now received the atonement. By one man, sin came into the world, bringing death with it; and death was subsequently passed along to everybody, for all have sinned. Therefore, while the sin of one brought judgment and condemnation upon humankind, so the righteousness of one brought the free gift of justification and life. Thus, by the disobedience of one (Adam) we became sinful, and by the obedience of one (Christ) we can become righteous.
- ROM 8:29–30 ~ Those who God called He knew before and predestined them to be conformed to the image of His Son, that He might be the firstborn of many other brothers and sisters. Whoever God predestined, He later called; and whoever He called, He also justified; and whoever He justified He also will glorify.
- ROM 12:1–2 ~ I implore you therefore, by the mercies of God, that you present yourselves as a living sacrifice, holy and acceptable to God, which is a reasonable response to His love. Do not conform to the ways of this world, but be transformed by the renewing of your mind, and you will be able to determine what is good, acceptable, and perfect according to God's will.
- 1 CO 6:9–11 ~ Don't you realize that the wicked will not inherit the kingdom of God? Don't be deceived, for sinners, to include fornicators, idolaters, adulterers, homosexuals, perverted people, thieves, greedy people, drunkards, slanderers, and swindlers, will not inherit the kingdom. Many of us were sinners just like them. But we have been washed clean, sanctified, and justified in the name of our Lord Jesus Christ, by the Spirit of our God.
- 2 CO 5:17 ~ Therefore, if anyone be in Christ, he or she is a new creature; old things have passed away and all things have become new.
- EPH 2:8–9 ~ You are saved by the grace of God because of your faith in Jesus Christ. Salvation is a gift of God, it cannot be earned through good works, so nobody should brag.
- GAL 2:16 ~ Nobody is justified by works of the Law but by faith in Jesus Christ. Therefore, in Him we will place our faith, and not in our ability to adhere to the Law.
- GAL 3:8–9,11,13,21–24 ~ The scriptures foretold that God would justify the unrighteous through faith, announcing the Gospel in advance to Abraham through whom God said all nations would be blessed. So those who live by faith will be blessed along with Abraham. But nobody is justified by the Law in God's sight, for it is written that the just will live by faith. Christ has redeemed us from the curse of the Law, being made a curse in our place; for it is written that one is cursed who is crucified on a cross. Is the Law, therefore, in opposition to God's promise? Absolutely not! For no law was given that would bring life. The scriptures tell us that the world is a slave to sin, and that the promise of life is given to all believers in Jesus Christ. Before faith in Christ came, everyone was a prisoner to the Law, kept there until faith was revealed in Christ. Hence, the Law is our teacher to bring us to faith in Christ, so that we might be justified by that faith.
- TIT 3:7 ~ Being justified by God's grace, we are made heirs according to the hope of eternal life.

- 2 TH 2:13 ~ We will always give thanks for our brothers and sisters in Christ, because from the beginning God chose them for salvation, through sanctification by the Spirit and belief in the truth.
- HEB 2:11 ~ Both He who does the sanctifying (Christ) and those who He has sanctified are of one Spirit. Therefore, He is not ashamed to call them brothers and sisters.
- HEB 10:10,18 ~ We are sanctified by the offering of the body of Jesus Christ, one sacrifice for all people. No more offering for sin will ever be needed again.
- JAM 2:21–22,26 ~ Was Abraham justified by works when he offered Isaac upon the altar? Don't you see that his faith was made perfect by his works? Just as the body apart from the spirit is dead, so is faith apart from works.
- 1 JO 2:1 ~ Refrain from sin. But if you do sin, remember that everyone has an advocate with the Father: Jesus Christ the righteous.

Salvation

God has told us that He will destroy evil. Thus, since all people have sinned, everyone needs to be redeemed. Anyone who seeks redemption and salvation through Christ can receive eternal life. To receive salvation, one must confess their sins before God and sincerely repent of them. This implies a real and active faith, demonstrated by the way one conducts his or her life. One cannot expect forgiveness if no attempt is made to seek God and to lead a godly life. That is, a true faith is an active one. You must not accept God's forgiveness after doing something evil, and then continue to do it; you must have genuine intent to change that behavior.

Therefore, all people must acknowledge that they are sinful and need to be redeemed, and all must trust in Christ for that redemption. Everyone who believes that Jesus Christ has the power to redeem their souls from the grave will be saved. Through His death and resurrection, Christ has paid the ransom for our souls.

- PSA 49:6–8,15 ~ They trust in their wealth, and brag about their riches; but none of them have the means to redeem anyone, or to give a ransom for another. The ransom is extremely costly, and no amount of money is enough to buy eternal life. Only God can redeem my life from the grave.
- PSA 51:5 ~ I was brought forth in sin, and in sin my mother conceived me.
- ECC 7:20 ~ Surely there is not a righteous person on earth who does good and never sins.
- ISA 53:4–5 ~ Surely, He bore our grief and carried our sorrows. Yet we treated Him as an outcast, as if stricken, smitten, and afflicted by God. But He was wounded and bruised because of our sins. Our punishment was given to Him, bringing us peace, and through His suffering, we have been healed.
- MAT 1:21 ~ God said to Mary, "You will call the child Jesus (meaning Savior) because He will save His people from their sins."
- MAR 16:16 ~ All who believe and are baptized will be saved.
- LUK 1:76–77 ~ You (John the Baptist) will prepare the way for the Lord, and give knowledge of salvation to His people for the forgiveness of their sins.
- JOH 3:16 ~ For God loved the world so much that He gave His only begotten Son, so that anyone could believe in Him and never die, but would receive everlasting life.
- JOH 11:25–26 ~ Jesus said, "I am the resurrection and the life. Those who believe in me, though they were dead, yet shall they live. Whoever believes in me will never die."
- ROM 3:23 ~ All have sinned and come short of the glory of God.
- ROM 11:11 ~ Through Christ, salvation has come to the Gentiles.

- 1 CO 15:3 ~ Christ died for our sins in accordance with the scriptures.
- 2 CO 5:21 ~ God made Him (Jesus), who knew no sin, to be sin for us, so we could be made righteous before God through Him.
- 2 CO 10:4–5 ~ We fight with spiritual weapons to break down the barriers of sin. We destroy the arguments and pretensions that oppose God's truth, and we take prisoner all thoughts so they may be obedient to God.
- GAL 5:17–18,22–23 ~ The desires of the flesh are against the spirit, and vice-versa, for they are opposed to each other. If you are led by the Holy Spirit, you are not under the Law. The fruits of the spirit include love, joy, peace, patience, kindness, goodness, faithfulness, gentleness, and self-control.
- EPH 4:30 ~ Do not grieve the Holy Spirit of God, who has sealed you for the day of redemption.
- 1 TH 5:9 ~ God has not destined us for wrath, but to obtain salvation through Christ our Lord.
- 1 TI 2:4 ~ God desires all people to be saved and to come to the knowledge of the truth.
- HEB 9:28 ~ Christ, who bore the sins of many, will appear a second time; not to deal further with sin, but to save those who have been waiting eagerly for Him.
- HEB 10:14,18 ~ By a single offering, Christ has perfected us to be sanctified forever. Where there is forgiveness, there is no longer any need for a sin offering.
- 1 PE 1:3–4,9 ~ Through God's mercy we have been born again to a living hope by the resurrection of Jesus Christ, to receive His inheritance which is imperishable, undefiled, unfailing, and kept in heaven for all believers. The outcome of faith in Jesus is salvation of the soul.
- 1 PE 2:24 ~ Christ bore our sins in His own body on the cross, so we could die in sin and still live in righteousness.
- 1 JO 2:1–2 ~ If anyone sins, we have an advocate with the Father: Jesus Christ the righteous who abolished the sin of the whole world.

Escape

(By Andrew Barber, 1983)

Escape the eternal void within; open your heart and mind to begin.
Abandon all foolishness, sorrow, and pride. Release your faith—let it be your guide.
And soar through enchanted bliss! Ecstasy awaits your kiss!

The body is a cell in which we exist. Virgin love unveiled! Can you resist?
Faith, hope, and charity beneath the mask; to set them free, you need but ask.

Admit to yourself you're lost; power and greed aren't worth the cost.
In the Lord and yourself believe, and the glory you will receive.

I leave you now in your innocent youth, the gifts of righteousness, wisdom, and truth.
Learn from these, and teach your neighbor. Strength be yours throughout your labor.

Lesson: Redemption and Reconciliation

We cannot live with God if we are sinful, because there cannot be any communion between evil and goodness (2 CO 6:14). This is why Christ has redeemed us with His blood, purifying us of all sin, so that we can be acceptable to God who is holy. Praise the Lord, we have been reconciled to God! He has brought us back to Himself, spiritually clean as when He first gave man His live-giving Spirit. All evil and corruption have been eliminated from our souls, and we have become pure, like Christ; for Christ imputed His righteousness upon us when He took our sins upon Himself. In short, we have been redeemed by the blood of Christ, who has ransomed our souls from the grave, so that we can be reconciled unto God our Father.

The Old Testament provides the foundation for this process, so that we can better understand God's plan, and the execution of this plan through Jesus Christ. Throughout the OT, a Redeemer is promised, who is Christ the Lord. The characteristics of this Redeemer are described in great detail. Abraham's willingness to sacrifice his son Isaac was the first witness of the atonement that God had planned.

The story of Moses and the freeing of the Hebrew slaves provides the next significant example (read EXO 12). Moses was the redeemer that God sent to Pharaoh to negotiate the freedom of the Hebrews from Egyptian slavery. Of course, this entire episode reflected the coming of the true Redeemer, Jesus Christ, sent by God to the world to set people free from the slavery of sin. The connection between the Passover lamb and the Lamb of God is most important, for it is the shedding of the blood of the Lamb that brings redemption, salvation, and freedom.

- 1 CO 5:7 ~ Get rid of the old yeast (sin) so that you can become a new dough without yeast (sin); for Christ, who is our Passover, is sacrificed for us.
- 1 PE 1:18–19 ~ You were redeemed, not with corruptible things such as gold and silver, but with the precious blood of Christ, a Lamb without any imperfections.

Other fine examples can be found in Jewish laws, one which permits a relative to redeem a fellow Jew from servitude (read LEV 25:23–55), and another which provides for the offspring of a deceased Jew to inherit the land of their ancestors (read GEN 38 and the book of Ruth). Again, we see the focus placed on freedom and inheritance, both of which are provided by the redemption bought by Christ: freedom from the slavery of sin and the penalty of death, and an inheritance in heaven as rightful heirs to God's kingdom. Note also in the above examples the fact that the lineage of Jesus Christ is interjected (RUT 4:11–22); this is to emphasize that Jesus is the kinsman who would redeem the Jews (as well as the rest of humankind), and Jesus also is our insurance that we will inherit the kingdom.

Redemption

Redemption is being ransomed, freed from sin and saved from the grave by the blood of Christ. It is an action whereby something of great value is bought back, like a soul; or a debt has been paid like the punishment of eternal death.

- LEV 17:11 ~ The life of the flesh is in the blood, and I have given you the opportunity to offer this upon the altar for atonement of your souls; for it is through the blood that atonement is provided.
- PSA 49:6–8,15 ~ Those who trust in their wealth and brag about their riches will never be able to redeem the life of another nor provide a ransom for them. For the redemption of their

soul is precious; no worldly payment will ever be enough. But God will redeem my soul from the power of the grave.
- GAL 3:13; GAL 4:4–5 ~ When the time was right, God sent His Son, born of a woman and established according to the Law, to redeem those who were under the Law, so that we could receive adoption as children of God. God has redeemed us from the curse of the Law, being made a curse in our stead.
- EPH 1:3–7 ~ Praise to God, the Father of our Lord Jesus Christ, who has chosen us before the foundation of the world to be holy and blameless before Him in love. We were destined to be God's adopted children, in accordance with His good will and grace, through Jesus Christ, in whom we have redemption and forgiveness through His blood.
- TIT 2:13–14 ~ Jesus Christ gave Himself for us to redeem us from all sin, and to purify His people unto Himself.
- TIT 3:5–6 ~ God has saved us, not because of our works of righteousness, but according to His mercy thorough the washing of regeneration and renewing by the Holy Spirit, which He abundantly bestowed upon us through Christ our Savior.
- HEB 9:22 ~ Almost everything under the Law can be purged with blood, and there can be no remission without the shedding of blood.

Reconciliation

Reconciliation is being accepted as you are, such as restoring a broken or estranged relationship, or being reunited with an esteemed loved one, or being welcomed with open arms like an adopted child.

- LUK 15 ~ The parables of the lost sheep and the prodigal son are great examples of how our Father in heaven desires for us to return to Him and live with Him forever. The father welcomed back the prodigal son after he squandered his inheritance on lustful pleasures. The father rejoiced and had a banquet for his wayward son, who had been lost and then was found again. Similarly, the shepherd left the ninety-nine sheep as he searched for the one that was lost, rejoicing when it was returned to the flock. Both examples reveal the love our Heavenly Father has for His sheep; He loves them whether they are good or bad, and rejoices when they return to the fold.
- 1 CO 6:19–20 ~ Don't you realize that your body is the temple of God's Holy Spirit which He has given to you? Your body no longer belongs to you for you were bought with a great price. Therefore, glorify God in your body and in your spirit, both of which belong to God.
- 2 CO 5:19–21 ~ God was in Christ, who reconciled the world to Himself. He has not imputed our sins upon us; instead, He has given us the message of reconciliation. So now we have become ambassadors for Christ, as though God was speaking His message through us, so that you too may be reconciled to God. For He made Christ, who knew no sin, to bear our sins so that we could receive the righteousness of God which was in Him.
- COL 1:19–22 ~ God was pleased to have His fullness living in Christ, so that through Christ, everything on earth and in heaven could be reconciled to Himself, by the peace that came through the shedding of Christ's blood on the cross. Before, you were separated from God; you were His enemies because of your sinful minds and evil deeds. But now, God has reconciled you by the body of Christ through His death, to be presented holy, blameless, and pure in the sight of God.
- 1 TH 5:23 ~ May the God of peace sanctify you wholly, so that your entire spirit, soul, and body can be preserved blameless until the coming of our Lord Jesus Christ.

CHAPTER THREE

Lesson: Once Saved Always Saved?

Once salvation has been gained, can it be lost again? This question has puzzled theologians for centuries. Many believe that a person can never lose their salvation; others believe that it is possible to forfeit salvation. Thus, there are two diametrically opposing viewpoints. But what do the scriptures say?

On the one hand, there are those who hold that you can lose your salvation if you do not remain steadfast in the faith. The argument here is that you can know Christ and believe, but later turn your back on the faith. To accept Christ and then to return to evil will result in condemnation. Support for this conjecture is found in the fact that sanctification continues throughout one's lifetime, as a person strives to become more like Christ. However, our sinful nature requires constant regeneration in the Holy Spirit. This is why Christ commanded His disciples to partake of Holy Communion frequently, because we need to be strengthened in the Spirit constantly. The following scriptures make a strong case for the notion that one can lose their salvation by turning away from God after having loved Him.

- EZE 18:24 ~ When a righteous person turns away from righteousness, commits sin, and is motivated by evil, can that person live? All the righteousness that occurred beforehand will never be remembered, but because of the sin he or she will die.
- EZE 28:14–19 ~ You (Lucifer) were the anointed cherub; you lived upon the holy mountain of God. You were perfect from the day you were created until evil was found in you. Your great wealth made you violent inside and you became sinful. Therefore, you were thrown off the holy mountain, and you will be destroyed. You exalted yourself because of your beauty, thereby corrupting yourself. You defiled the sanctuaries with your abominations. You will be destroyed by the fire within you, and your terrible deeds will come to an end.
- MAT 13:3–23 ~ Jesus told the parable of the sower of seeds. He explained that some people would receive the Word with joy, it will begin to grow, but it will not take root (the seed sown upon rocky places). Tribulations and persecutions associated with being a follower of Christ will offend those people and they will let the Word die in their hearts.
- HEB 6:4–6 ~ It is impossible for those who were once enlightened, who tasted of the heavenly gift and were made partakers of the Holy Ghost, who understood the good Word of God and the powers of the world to come, to be renewed unto repentance if they should fall away. They crucify the Son of God all over again, and put Him to open shame.
- JAM 5:19–20 ~ If a person strays from the truth, and another person converts him or her, the person who converted the sinner from the error of his or her ways will save a soul from death, and will cover a multitude of sins.
- 2 PE 2:20–22 ~ For if, after they have escaped the pollution of the world through the knowledge of the Lord and Savior Jesus Christ, they are again entangled therein and overcome, the latter end is worse for them than the beginning. For it would have been better for them not to have known the way of righteousness, than after they had known it, to turn from the holy commandment delivered to them. What will happen to them is like a true proverb: The dog has returned to his own vomit, and the pig that was washed is again wallowing in the mire.
- JDE 1:4 ~ False teachers have infiltrated the churches, claiming that once you become Christians you can do whatever you want without being punished.

Now, let us turn to the counterargument, that once gained, salvation cannot be lost. This view holds that people who turn away from the faith never really had Christ in their hearts to begin with. In other words, they had not fully accepted Christ as their personal Savior and hence, never were saved at all. Support for this supposition is found in the doctrine of predestination. God foreknew who would be saved and who would not be saved, because He is omniscient. Theoretically, if you have been sanctified by His Spirit you have been marked for salvation. The following scriptures make a strong case for the notion that one cannot lose their salvation once they have been claimed by Jesus.

- MAT 7:21–23 ~ Jesus informed the people that not everyone who says to Him, "Lord, Lord," will enter the kingdom of heaven, but only those who do the will of our heavenly Father. Many will say to Him, "Haven't we prophesied and done mighty works in your name?" Jesus will reply to them, "I never knew you; depart from me you who work iniquity."
- MAT 22:14 ~ Jesus said, "Many are called but few are chosen."
- JOH 10:14,26–28 ~ Jesus said, "I am the Good Shepherd. I know my sheep and they know me. But you do not believe, because you are not my sheep. My sheep hear my voice, and they recognize it's me, and they follow me. And I give them eternal life; and they will never perish, neither will anyone pluck them out of my hand."
- JOH 17:6,11–12 ~ Jesus prayed to God, "I have revealed you (God the Father) to those that you have given to me out of the world. They were yours and you gave them to me, because they obeyed your Word. I will remain in the world no longer, but they are still in the world while I am coming to you, Holy Father. Protect them by the power of your name, the name you gave me, so that they may be one as we are one. While I was with them, I protected them and kept them safe by that name you gave me. None have been lost, except those doomed to destruction, so that the scriptures can be fulfilled.
- ACT 13:47–48 ~ The Gentiles heard the prophecy that the Light was sent for them and they were glad and glorified God and loved His Word; and those who were ordained to eternal life believed.
- ROM 8:28–31,38–39 ~ We know that all things work together for good to those who love God and are called according to His purpose. For God knew them in advance and predestined them to be conformed to the image of His Son, and to be among the firstborn of His brothers. Whomever He predestined, He called; and whomever He called He justified; and whomever He justified, He also glorified. Therefore, if God is with us, who can be against us? Nothing can separate us from the love of God, not death or life, not angels or demons, not anything present or future, not any powers, and not anything in all creation.
- EPH 1:4–5,9–11 ~ For He chose us before the creation of the world to be holy and blameless in His sight. In love, He predestined us to be adopted children through Jesus Christ, in accordance with His pleasure and will, to the praise of His glorious grace which He has freely given to us in the One He loves. He made known to us the mystery of His will according to His good pleasure, which He purposed in Christ to be put into effect when the times reached their fulfillment, thereby bringing all things in heaven and on earth together under one head who is Christ. In Him we were chosen, being predestined according to His plan, ensuring that everything conforms to His purpose and will.
- EPH 2:10 ~ We are God's workmanship, created in Jesus Christ to do good works which God prepared in advance for us to do.
- 2 TH 2:13–14 ~ Give thanks always to God for choosing you from the beginning to be saved through sanctification of the Spirit and belief in the truth. He called you by His Gospel to share in the glory of our Lord Jesus Christ.
- 2 TI 1:9 ~ God saved us and called us to be holy, not by our works, but by His purpose and grace, given to us through Christ before the world began.
- 1 PE 1:2,4–5 ~ Christians are chosen by God in advance through sanctification of the Spirit, to be obedient to Christ and cleansed by His blood. Blessed be to God the Father of our Lord

Jesus Christ. According to His abundant mercy, He recreated in us the living hope, brought by the resurrection of Christ from the dead, to receive an incorruptible and undefiled inheritance reserved in heaven and lasting forever. Through faith, He has shielded us by His power until the coming of the salvation which is ready to be revealed on the last day. (Note that the disbelievers also were destined to become disobedient: see 1 PE 2:8).

Clearly, there is compelling evidence for both points of view. Then what can we conclude? First, we can conclude that a person cannot lose salvation simply by sinning, because it is by God's grace that we are saved. Nothing we do can save us, but our sin can condemn us if we do not depend on Christ alone for our salvation. Second, salvation can be lost by rejecting God, insofar as it cannot be gained without accepting Christ as Savior. However, to accept Christ implies a change of heart, mind, and spirit. Without undergoing such a change, the sinful flesh will prevail. If you are not positive where you stand, examine yourself (1 CO 11:28–29).

- ROM 6:1–2,12–16 ~ Shall we continue to sin, so that God's grace can continue to abound? God forbid it! How can we, who were dead in our sins, continue to live a life of decadence? Do not allow sin to reign in your mortal body, influencing you to pursue the desires of the flesh. Do not use your body parts as instruments of unrighteousness and sin; but yield to God and use your body to glorify Him. Sin cannot control you for you are no longer under the Law but under the Grace of God. Does that mean we can sin, because we are under Grace and not the Law? No way! A person obeys whomever they yield to; you can yield to sin unto death, or you can yield to obedience unto righteousness.
- 1 CO 5:7 ~ Get rid of the old yeast (sin) so that you can become a new dough without yeast; for Christ, who is our Passover, is sacrificed for us.
- 2 CO 5:17 ~ Therefore, if anyone is in Christ, he or she is a new creation; old things have passed away and all things have become new.
- 1 TH 5:23 ~ May the God of peace sanctify you wholly, so that your entire spirit, soul, and body can be preserved blameless until the coming of our Lord Jesus Christ.
- HEB 3:14 ~ We are partakers of Christ if we keep the same confidence that we had in the beginning, steadfast until the end.
- 2 PE 1:10–11 ~ Therefore, my brothers, be diligent to make your calling and election sure; for if you do these things (e.g., exercise your spiritual gifts), you will never fall, and you will receive a warm welcome into the eternal kingdom of our Lord and Savior Jesus Christ.

My Faith Looks up to Thee

My faith looks up to Thee, Thou Lamb of Calvary, Savior divine!
Now hear me while I pray; take all my guilt away.
Oh, let me from this day be wholly Thine.

May Thy rich grace impart strength to my fainting heart, my zeal inspire;
As Thou hast died for me, oh make my love to Thee,
Pure, warm, and changeless be, a living fire.

While life's dark maze I tread, and griefs around me spread, be Thou my guide;
Bid darkness turn to day, wipe sorrow's tears away
Nor let me ever stray from Thee aside.

When ends life's transient dream, when death's cold sullen stream shall o'er me roll;
Blest Savior, then in love, fear and distrust remove.
Oh, bear me safe above, a ransomed soul.

Lesson: Why a Messiah?

When the first six days of creation took place, God created the world as we know it (GEN 1). When God gave man and woman a choice to do good or evil, He made His will to be known. God's will can be found in the Holy Bible. Unfortunately, all people have disobeyed God's commandments, precepts, and directives. This goes against God's will, and everyone is guilty.

According to Isaiah, God created everything, including peace and evil (ISA 45:7, KJV translation). How can this be so? Well, God gave us a choice to obey Him or not. This choice is reflected in God's Law, which tells us what His will is for humankind. God is good, so everything that opposes God is evil. God has given us a discerning mind to tell the difference between good and evil. We know in advance whether our words and actions are in accordance with God's will; it is a voice in the conscience which alerts the person. And yet we sin; we can't help it. We are doomed to die but for the fact that Messiah died in our place.

- GEN 3:22 ~ God said, "Now man is like us, able to discern good and evil. He knows not to eat the forbidden fruit."
- ROM 3:20 ~ Nobody can be justified by works of the Law, for by the Law comes the knowledge of sin.
- ROM 4:15; ROM 5:13 ~ Sin existed in the world before the Law was given; but nothing can be attributed to sin where there is no Law. Where there is no Law, there is no sin.
- ROM 7:7,14 ~ The Law told me what not to do thereby revealing sin to me. So is the Law sin? No, it is the opposite of sin. For the Law is spiritual but I am carnal because I sin.
- 1 JO 3:4 ~ Whoever commits a sin disobeys the Law for that is the definition of sin.
- JAM 2:10 ~ Whoever keeps the Law, then disobeys but one point, is guilty of disobeying all the Law.

The Law tells us what is right. To disobey God's Law is to sin. Thus, God gave people the free will to obey His Law or not. The Law, therefore, represents obedience. Satan was the first to disobey God. Satan tempts others to do the same; thus, sinning is doing the devil's will and not God's will.

- 1 CO 7:37 ~ People have power over their own will (power to do God's will).
- 1 JO 3:8 ~ The devil sinned from the very beginning. Whoever sins, he or she is of the devil. God intends to destroy the works of the devil (to include evil, sin, and death).

In Genesis, God is pleased with the good things He created. Unfortunately, humanity fell from grace because of sin. God is not pleased with sin, for sin is evil and evil can never be good. Thus, God is determined to destroy evil forever. However, He wants to save that which is good. But how can God save us if we are both good and evil at the same time? By cleansing us of the evil inside and making us pure, that's how. God sacrificed His only Son to destroy the evil in this world and to save us from our sins. No other sacrifice will ever need to be made to atone for sin because Christ atoned for the sin of everyone. Would you be willing to make such a sacrifice as Abraham or Christ to atone for your own sin?

- MIC 6:6–7 ~ How am I to come before the Lord? Should I come with burnt offerings of yearlings? Will the Lord be pleased with thousands of rams, or ten thousand rivers of oil? Shall I sacrifice my firstborn for my sins?

Although God gave us the option of doing good or evil, He is incapable of sinning and He never tempts us to sin. Sin is a choice made by everyone. God does not choose for you to sin.

Neither can He sin; neither can Christ sin for He also is God. It is our own sin that leads to our death. Satan cannot force us to sin either; he tempts us to fall away but we can resist.

- ROM 6:23 ~ The wages of sin is death.
- 1 CO 10:13 ~ God will not allow us to be tempted beyond our ability to withstand it, and He will always provide us an escape from temptation.
- JAM 1:13,15 ~ God cannot be tempted to sin, neither does He tempt anyone. Sin brings forth death.

In the final analysis, Christ lived the perfect life on our behalf, He died to pay the punishment for the sinful life that we have led, and He rose again because sin and death had no power over Him. This He did so we would not be separated from God by our sin but live with Him forever, being made righteous through His Son.

- ISA 53:4–5 ~ Christ came to suffer for our sins.
- MAT 5:17 ~ Christ came to fulfill the Law.
- 1 JO 2:2 ~ Christ came to abolish sin.
- 2 TI 1:10 ~ Christ came to abolish death.
- 1 JO 3:8 ~ Christ came to destroy the works of the devil.
- HEB 2:14 ~ Christ came to destroy the devil.

The Old Testament makes reference to the Messiah, the New Covenant, throughout. Those prophecies came true in the New Testament of Jesus Christ. To repeat, the two testaments cross-validate each other; this is why we have two and only two testaments (OT and NT). Their connection to one another is found in the relationship between the Law and the fulfillment of the Law in Christ. The feasts of Unleavened Bread, Passover, and First Fruits, commemorative celebrations initiated under the Law of Moses, also reflect the sacrifice of the body and blood of Jesus Christ, and His resurrection, respectively.

Thus, the purpose of Messiah is well documented in both the OT and NT. In Jesus Christ, the mystery of God's New Covenant is unraveled. He is the one who died for our sins and arose from the dead to live again forever, so that we too could obtain the promise of eternal life. This is how much our Almighty Father loves us, that He would make the ultimate sacrifice so that we might live with Him.

- 1 KI 8:56 ~ Blessed is the Lord, who gives rest to His people according to all He promised them. For He didn't fail on a single word which He promised to Moses His servant.
- JER 33:14–15 ~ God says, "Soon the day will come when I will make good on the promise I made to Israel and Judah, for the Branch of righteousness is coming to execute judgment and righteousness throughout the land."
- MAR 4:11 ~ Jesus said to His disciples, "You have been given the ability to understand the mystery of the kingdom of God. To the unbelievers, God's mystery is seen in parables, for Isaiah wrote that they would see but not perceive, and they would hear but not understand."
- ROM 16:25–26 ~ By the power of God you have received the Gospel of Jesus Christ and the revelation of His mystery which was kept secret since the world began. This mystery has now become a reality through Christ, according to the scriptures and the commandment of the everlasting God, and is sent to every nation for all to understand the obedience of faith.
- 1 CO 2:7 ~ Paul wrote: We (the apostles) speak the hidden wisdom of God in a mystery, the mystery that brings us glory which He ordained before the world was made.
- 1 CO 15:51 ~ Look, I will show you a mystery: Not all of us will sleep but we will all be changed.

- GAL 3:28–29 ~ There is neither Jew nor Greek, slave nor free, male nor female, for everyone is made equal in Jesus Christ. And if you belong to Christ, then you are part of Abraham's seed and fellow heirs according to God's covenant.
- EPH 1:10–11 ~ When the time comes, He will gather together all who are in Christ, both in heaven and on earth, to receive an inheritance.
- EPH 3:3–6,9–11 ~ Paul wrote: In a revelation, God showed me the mystery of Christ, and I must share that mystery with the world. It is a mystery that was hidden but is now revealed through His apostles and prophets by the Holy Spirit. For the Gentiles will be fellow heirs with the Jews, and will partake of the promise that came true through Christ by the Gospel. All people can know the mystery which God hid from the beginning of the world, and the eternal purpose for which Jesus Christ our Lord has come.
- PHP 3:20–21 ~ We look to heaven as our home, the home of our Savior Christ the Lord, who will change our vile bodies into glorious bodies like His own.
- COL 1:26–27 ~ The mystery, hidden from ages past, has now been revealed to the saints, to whom God will give the riches of His glory. It is for anyone who turns to Christ for their hope including the Gentiles.
- COL 2:2 ~ Let your hearts be comforted for you are bound together in love. You have received the wealth of knowledge and understanding by acknowledging the mystery of God, the Father and the Son.
- 1 TI 3:16 ~ Without question, the mystery of godliness is great. For God was manifested in the flesh, justified in the Spirit, worshipped by angels, preached to the Gentiles, believed by the world, and has now ascended into heaven in His glory.
- JAM 1:12 ~ Blessed are those who endure temptation, for when they appear for judgment, they will receive a crown of life according to the promise God made to all who love Him.
- 2 PE 1:4 ~ We are given terrific and precious promises that we will partake of His divine nature, having escaped the corruption of this world.
- 1 JO 2:25 ~ The promise He made was eternal life.
- REV 10:7 ~ When the seventh angel sounds his trumpet, the mystery of God will be finished, as He declared to the prophets and the saints.
- REV 21:4 ~ God will wipe away everyone's tears; He will remove all death, sorrow, crying, and pain. All the unpleasant things of the previous life will be gone forever.

God's Holy Spirit is free. He gives it lovingly to people who accept Christ as their personal Savior. The Holy Spirit comes to us through Jesus Christ who was given to die for us. On Christmas Day we celebrate His arrival. During Passover we remember how He offered Himself as a sacrifice for our sins. On Easter we rejoice in His resurrection through which He guaranteed our victory over death and our inheritance in heaven. Share this gift with others, and keep Christ in Christmas.

Lesson: Jesus Christ Is the Messiah

Jesus Christ was, is, and always will be the Messiah. The Old Testament foretold the coming of Messiah, providing extraordinary detail about who He was and what He was going to do. The New Testament tells the story and purpose of God's Messiah in even more detail. In fact, the OT is cross-referenced by the NT and vice-versa. In this lesson, significant OT prophecy is presented concerning the coming Messiah, along with the NT scriptures that describe the fulfillment of that prophecy.

History of the Messiah, God's Covenant

Old Testament	Event	New Testament
GEN 3:14–15	The Son will crush Satan.	HEB 2:14
GEN 22:1–12	Isaac spared; ram sacrificed by Abraham.	JOH 3:16
EXO 12:3–12	Male lamb sacrificed on the first Passover.	JOH 1:29/1 PE 1:19/ REV 5:12
EXO 24:8	Blood is in the everlasting covenant.	HEB 9:19–22
ISA 53:4–12	Messiah is slaughtered like a lamb.	ACT 8:32–33,35
DAN 7:13–14	God's only Son.	MAT 1:21–23
PSA 30:4	God's only Son.	

Lineage of the Messiah

Old Testament	Ancestor	New Testament
GEN 9:26	Noah, Shem	MAT 1:2–16
GEN 12:3; 18:18	Abraham	LUK 3:23–38
GEN 26:4	Isaac	GAL 3:16
GEN 28:14	Jacob	HEB 7:14
GEN 49:10	Judah	REV 5:5
1 CH 5:2	Judah	
ISA 11:1–2	Jesse	
2 SA 7:12–14	David	
JER 23:5	David	
ZEC 12:10	David	
HAG 2:23	Zerubbabel	
ZEC 4:9	Zerubbabel	

WHO IS JESUS CHRIST?

Characteristics of the Messiah

Old Testament	Characteristic	New Testament
GEN 28:12	Ladder from earth to heaven with angels.	JOH 1:51
PSA 23:1	The Good Shepherd.	JOH 10:1–18
PSA 110:1	The right hand of God.	MAR 16:19/ ACT 5:31/HEB 1:3
PSA 118:22	Capstone of the arch (chief cornerstone).	MAT 21:42/ LUK 20:17/ACT 4:10–11
ISA 9:6	Wonderful Counselor, Prince of Peace.	ACT 5:31
ISA 42:1	Command of the Holy Spirit.	JOH 14:26; JOH 15:26
ISA 42:6	Light to the Gentiles.	MAT 12:18/LUK 2:32
ISA 53:3–12	Suffered and died for the sin of all.	JOH 1:29/ROM 3:29/ 2 CO 5:21/1 PE 2:24
MAL 3:1–2	Purifies the soul like a refiner's fire.	MAT 3:11; MAT 11:20

Birth of the Messiah

Old Testament	Description	New Testament
ISA 7:14	Born of a virgin.	MAT 1:21–23/LUK 1:26–35
MIC 5:2	Birthplace is Bethlehem.	MAT 2:5–6/JOH 7:42
ISA 49:7	Kings will see the sign and come worship.	MAT 2:1–2/LUK 1:26–35
ISA 60:6	Wise men bring gifts of incense and gold.	MAT 2:1–2,11
JER 31:15	Mourning over the butchered children.	MAT 2:16–18
PSA 80:8–17	The Branch is called out of Egypt.	MAT 2:13–15
ISA 40:3	A messenger will prepare the way.	MAT 3:1–3/JOH 1:29–35
MAL 3:1	A messenger will prepare the way.	

Ministry of the Messiah

Old Testament	Description	New Testament
ISA 9:1–2	A great light preaches in Galilee.	MAT 4:12–16/MAR 1:9/ JOH 7:42
PSA 78:2	Taught parables; disclosed hidden truths.	MAT 13:10–17/ MAR 4:33/JOH 18:37
ISA 6:9–10	People see and hear without understanding.	MAT 13:10–17/ ROM 11:7–8
ISA 35:5–6	Healed the sick, lame, and blind.	MAT 15:30
ISA 66:4–6	Not listening but conspiring against Him.	MAT 11:20; MAT 12:11/
ZEC 13:6	Rejected and condemned by friends.	MAT 27:1/JOH 18:12,31

Final Days of the Messiah

Old Testament	Description	New Testament
ZEC 9:9	Riding triumphantly on a donkey's colt.	JOH 12:14–15
PSA 41:9	Betrayed by a friend.	JOH 13:18/ACT 1:16–20
ZEC 11:12–13	Blood money used to buy a graveyard.	MAT 27:6–10
ZEC 13:7	The Shepherd is killed; the sheep scatter.	JOH 10:11–12

Death of the Messiah

Old Testament	Description	New Testament
ISA 50:6	Tortured to death.	MAT 27:26–35
ZEC 12:10; 13:6	Pierced and wounded.	JOH 19:37
PSA 22:16–18	Pierced hands and feet; gamble for clothes.	MAT 27:35
PSA 34:20	No broken bones.	JOH 19:36
ISA 53:8–9	Buried in a rich man's grave.	LUK 23:50–51
DAN 9:27	In one week the sacrifice was completed. (Holy Week)	JOH 1:29/2 CO 5:21/ 1 PE 2:24
ZEC 3:9	Removed the sin of the world in one day. (Passover)	LUK 22:15/1 CO 5:7–8

Resurrection of the Messiah

Old Testament	Description	New Testament
HOS 6:2	In three days the saints arise from grave.	MAR 8:31
JON 1:17	In the earth's belly three days and nights.	MAT 12:40
MAL 4:2	A star of righteousness will arise.	MAR 8:31
PSA 61:6–7	His days will be prolonged.	LUK 24:46
ISA 53:10	His days will be prolonged.	JOH 20:24–29

Jesus is the Lamb of God who takes away the sins of the world (JOH 1:29).

Lesson: The Word as Truth

God communicates His love to us through His Word. God's Holy Spirit is the means by which He shares His Word with us. In fact, the Holy Spirit and God's Word are one in the same. Jesus Christ, begotten by the Holy Spirit, is the Word made flesh. Christ was sent to personally give God's Word to human beings and His words are found in the New Testament. Thus, God's Word has been communicated to us through the Holy Bible, Jesus Christ, and true ministers of the Word. God's Word is truth. His Word provides comfort to believers. This is a principal reason why Jesus referred to the Holy Spirit as the Comforter; it is always comforting to be sure and to know the truth, for it will set you free.

- PRO 8:1,4,21,34–35 ~ God says, "Doesn't wisdom cry out and understanding speak? I call to you people; my voice speaks to everyone. I want those that love me to inherit something of substance, for I will fill their treasure troves. Blessed is the person who listens to me, watches daily at my gates, and waits at the door. For whoever finds me finds life and obtains my bountiful favor."
- JOH 8:31–32,36 ~ Jesus said, "If you believe in my words then you are indeed my disciples; and you will know the truth and the truth will set you free. If the Son of God sets you free, you will definitely be free."
- JOH 1:1,14 ~ In the beginning was the Word, and the Word was with God, and the Word was God. And the Word became flesh, and lived on earth, and we saw His glory, the glory the Father's only Son.
- JOH 15:26 ~ Jesus said, "I will send the Comforter to you and He will testify about me; the Comforter is the Spirit of Truth which proceeds from the Father."

God's Word was at work in the minds of the patriarchs, apostles, and prophets who wrote the scriptures that we call the Holy Bible. Thus, the Bible was authored by God, but written by holy men who were directed by the Holy Spirit concerning what to write.

- 1 CO 2:13 ~ We teach using words taught by the Holy Spirit, not by human wisdom. Spiritual truths can only be interpreted by those who possess the Spirit.
- 1 TH 2:13 ~ We thank God that you received His Word and accepted it as the Word of God and not the word of men. The Word of God is at work in believers like you.
- 2 TI 3:16 ~ All scripture is inspired by God.
- 2 PE 1:16,21 ~ We did not follow cleverly devised fables when we told people about the power and coming of Jesus Christ, for we were eye witnesses of His majesty. No prophecy ever came from the impulse of man, but holy men spoke as they were directed by God.

Since the Word comes from God, it is perfect. Therefore, everything in the Holy Bible is true, because God is incapable of telling a lie. Anyone attempting to change the words or meaning are committing a great sin. Blasphemy is when someone writes or says something to refute what God says, or otherwise change it to mean something else. To alter the meaning of God's Word, or to add or subtract from its purpose, is therefore, blasphemy.

- PRO 30:5–6 ~ Every word of God is true; don't attempt to add to His words or He will rebuke you and you will be proven false.
- MAT 24:35 ~ Jesus said, "Heaven and earth will pass away, by my words will remain forever."
- GAL 1:8 ~ Anyone, including the angels, who preaches anything contrary to what Jesus Christ and the apostles preached are cursed.

- REV 22:18–19 ~ For I testify to everyone who hears the words of the prophecy of this book, that if anyone adds to these words, God will add unto that person the plagues mentioned in this book. If anyone subtracts from the words of this prophecy, God will take away their name from the Book of Life, and they will not share in the inheritance.

Anyone claiming that the Bible is inaccurate or who preaches any doctrine not preached by Jesus and the apostles is committing blasphemy. If anyone calls God a liar or attempts to turn God's truth into lies, he or she has committed blasphemy against the Word of God. God's Word comes from His Holy Spirit, so those blaspheming the Word are potentially committing the one unpardonable sin.

- LEV 24:16 ~ Whoever blasphemes the name of the Lord will surely be put to death; the entire congregation will certainly stone that person whether a stranger or a native to the land.
- MAT 12:32 ~ Jesus said, "Whoever speaks against the Holy Spirit will not be forgiven, neither in this world nor in the world to come."
- ROM 1:25 ~ They changed God's truth into a lie and worshipped and served the creature rather than the Creator who is blessed forever, Amen.

Beware of false prophets and cults which rely on false prophecy and false visions, and which teach false doctrines. There are many cults in the world today which deviate from the true Word. The Holy Bible, including the Old and New Testaments, is the only true Word; all other so-called religious works are false for they have not been inspired by God and are often in disagreement with the Bible. Any teachings or practices that are not biblical should be avoided. People who appear to be devout and wise could be attempting to deceive others into following erroneous teachings. It is essential to learn the truth from God in order to recognize untruth.

- ISA 59:4,13 ~ They know they are being disobedient to God; they carefully plan their lies and mischief.
- JER 14:14 ~ False prophets tell lies in my (God's) name; I did not send them, command them, or speak to them. They receive false visions and make false predictions from the deceit of their lying hearts.
- JER 23:32 ~ Their lies lead many into sin. God did not send them and they have nothing of importance to say.
- LAM 2:14 ~ Your prophets have said foolish things and seen false visions.
- MAT 7:21 ~ Not everyone who acts or appears righteous is righteous.
- MAT 24:11,24 ~ Jesus said, "False prophets will come and lead many astray, performing wonders in an attempt to trick people. Even some of God's people could become deceived."
- MAR 7:7–9 ~ Jesus said, "Those hypocrites ignore God's laws and substitute their own traditions. They pray great prayers but they don't really love God and their worship is a joke. They claim that God commands them and their followers to adhere to their idiotic rules."
- ACT 20:30 ~ From among yourselves will come those speaking perverse things to gain followers.
- 2 CO 11:13–14 ~ They have fooled people into thinking they are Christ's apostles. But that is not surprising, for even Satan disguises himself as an angel of light.
- 2 TH 2:3–4 ~ Beware of Satan, who exalts himself, claiming to be a god.
- 2 TH 2:9–11 ~ Those false signs and fake miracles come from Satan. Such deceptions belong to the self-righteous who will die, for they did not believe the truth that could save them. God will let them believe their lies and perish.
- 2 TI 3:13 ~ Evil people and false teachers will get worse, deceiving many; they themselves have been deceived by Satan.

- 2 TI 4:3–4 ~ People will seek teachers who conform to their own likes and dislikes; they will turn away from the truth and wander into myths.
- JDE 1:4 ~ False teachers have infiltrated the churches, claiming that once you become Christians you can do whatever you want without being punished.

Test those who claim to be prophets, ministers, or teachers. They are not from God if they do not rely exclusively on the Holy Bible for inspiration, if they do not acknowledge Jesus Christ as God in the flesh, if they do not confess Jesus Christ alone for their salvation, or if they claim to be divine beings themselves.

- JOH 3:16 ~ God loved the world so much that He sacrificed His only begotten Son, so that anyone believing in Him would not perish but would live forever.
- 1 JO 4:1–3 ~ Test the prophets by asking them if they acknowledge Jesus Christ as God's Son who came as a human being to save humankind from sin.
- 1 JO 5:20–21 ~ Remain in Christ who is true. Stay away from anything or anyone who would distort God's truth or attempt to take God's place in your heart.

Jesus Christ is the New Covenant, the New Testament. Only Jesus can provide salvation, through His death which atoned for the sin of the world, and His resurrection which provides eternal life for all believers. If we believe in Christ as our Savior, we become cleansed by His blood, thereby washing away our sins and filling us with the Holy Spirit.

- ACT 4:12 ~ There is no salvation in any other; for there is no other name under heaven, given to us, whereby we can be saved.
- GAL 4:6 ~ Because you are God's children, He has sent the Spirit of His Son into your hearts.
- EPH 5:26 ~ Jesus Christ gave Himself for His people so He could sanctify them through a spiritual washing by the Word.
- 1 JO 5:6–8,20 ~ There are three that are recorded in heaven: the Father, the Word, and the Holy Spirit. These three are one. The same three bear witness: the Spirit, the Water, and the Blood. The Spirit is the witness, because the Spirit bears the truth. We know Jesus Christ who is true so that we may know God who is true; and so we can live in Him who has shown us His Son, the source of eternal life.

I Love to Tell the Story

I love to tell the story of unseen things above,
Of Jesus and His glory, of Jesus and His love.
I love to tell the story, because I know 'tis true;
It satisfies my longings as nothing else could do.
I love to tell the story, 'twill be my theme in glory,
To tell the old, old story of Jesus and His love.

I love to tell the story; for those who know it best
Seem hungering and thirsting to hear it, like the rest.
And when, in scenes of glory, I sing the new, new song.
'Twill be the old, old story that I have loved so long.
I love to tell the story, 'twill be my theme in glory,
To tell the old, old story of Jesus and His love.

CHAPTER THREE

THE GOSPEL OF JESUS CHRIST

The word "Gospel" literally means "Good News." Good News is found in the person of Jesus Christ. The New Testament to the Bible describes the life, ministry, teachings, and purpose of Jesus Christ. It documents His persecution, death, resurrection, ascension, and second coming. The first four books in the NT are known as the Gospels: Matthew, Mark, Luke, and John. These books focus exclusively on the life and ministry of Jesus Christ. Jesus's apostles and disciples preached the Gospel of Christ. Their testimonies and acts are described in NT books and epistles. In this section, the four Gospels have been consolidated and condensed into the form of a drama, or screenplay. It is not a comprehensive exposition but a general summary. Note that some sayings have been ascribed to individuals which were not explicitly recognized as the source.

Jesus's Lineage

The genealogy of Jesus Christ is described first. The lineage given in Matthew and the lineage given in Luke are presented below. Note that these two lineages are not identical. It is commonly recognized that the lineage in Matthew reflects the ancestry of Joseph, and in Luke, the ancestry of Mary. Interestingly, Old Testament references to the lineage of the Messiah from Adam to David fit the lineage of both of Jesus's earthly parents. The reliability and accuracy of the Messianic prophecies clearly point to their application to Jesus Christ.

Each of the three blocks below represents fourteen generations with forty generations counting from Abraham to Jesus (MAT 1:17).

Abraham > Isaac > Jacob > Judah > Phares[1] > > > > > Boaz[2] > Obed[3] > Jesse > David

David > Solomon[4] > > > > > > > > > > > Josias (fall of Babylon)

Josias > Jechonias > Zerubbabel > > > > > > > > > Joseph > Jesus

Lineage from Abraham (MAT 1:2–16)

Abraham - Isaac - Jacob - Juda - Phares - Esrom - Aram - Amindab - Naasson - Salmon - Boaz - Obed - Jesse - David - Solomon - Roboam - Abia - Asa - Josaphat - Joram - Ozias - Joatham - Achaz - Ezekias - Manasses - Amon - Josias - Jechonias - Salathiel - Zorobabel - Abiud - Eliakim - Azor - Sadoc - Achim - Eliud - Eleazar - Matthan - Jacob - Joseph - Jesus

[1] Mother was Tamar
[2] Mother was Rahab
[3] Mother was Ruth
[4] Mother was Bathsheba

Lineage from Adam (LUK 3:23–38)

God - Adam - Seth - Enos - Cainan - Maleleel - Jared - Enoch - Mathusala - Lamech - Noah - Shem - Arphaxad - Cainan - Sala - Heber - Phalec - Ragau - Saruch - Nachor - Thara - Abraham - Isaac - Jacob - Juda - Phares - Esrom - Aram - Amindab - Naasson - Salmon - Boaz - Obed - Jesse - David - Nathan - Mattatha - Menan - Melea - Eliakim - Jonan - Joseph - Judah - Simeon - Levi - Mathat - Jorim - Eliezer - Jose - Er - Elmodam - Cosam - Addi - Melchi - Neri - Salathiel - Zorabel - Rhesa - Joanna - Judah - Joseph - Semei - Mattathais - Maath - Nagge - Esli - Naum - Amos - Mattathias - Joseph - Janna - Melchi - Levi - Mattat - Heli - Joseph (e.g., Mary) - Jesus

Jesus's Birth

Narrator: The angel Gabriel appeared to Zechariah.

Gabriel: Your prayers have been heard. You and Elisabeth will have a son. You will call him John. He will never drink any alcohol. He will be filled with the Holy Spirit, even from the womb. He will have the power of Elijah to turn hearts toward the truth. He will make ready the way of the Lord.

Zechariah: How can this be? We're too old to have children.

Gabriel: I came to tell you this good news. Since you doubt it, you will not speak a word until this prophecy has been fulfilled.

Narrator: Six months passed. The angel Gabriel appeared to Mary.

Gabriel: You are favored by God. You will bear a son. You will call Him Jesus. He will be the Son of the Most High. There will be no end to His kingdom.

Mary: But I have never lain with a man!

Gabriel: The Holy Spirit will come upon you and you will bear the Son of God. Even your cousin Elisabeth has conceived in her old age. This proves that nothing is impossible with God.

Mary: I am the Lord's servant. Let it be as you have said.

Narrator: The prophet Isaiah had written that a virgin would conceive and bear a son, and His name would be called "God with us" (ISA 7:14).

Narrator: Mary confided in her fiancé, Joseph. He didn't believe her and wondered how to deal with her pregnancy honorably. He was going to divorce her quietly so that she would not be disgraced. That night the angel Gabriel appeared to Joseph in a dream.

Gabriel: Son of David, marry your betrothed anyway. Mary is carrying the child of the Holy Spirit. You will call Him Jesus for He will save His people from their sins.

Narrator: Joseph reconciled with Mary; for it was written: He knew her not until after her first born. Then Mary left to visit Elisabeth.

Mary: Hello, Elisabeth!

Elisabeth: My baby leaped inside me when he heard your voice! Blessed be the fruit of your womb.

Mary: My soul magnifies the Lord! He has put down the kings from their thrones. He has filled the hungry.

Narrator: Three months passed and John was born. The day of his circumcision had come.

Elders: What will be his name?

Elisabeth: John.

Elders (objecting): You have no relatives by that name.

Narrator: Zechariah wrote a note saying, "His name will be John," and handed it to the chief elder. Immediately his mouth was opened.

Zechariah: The Lord has visited and redeemed His people. Do you remember His holy covenant? He swore to Abraham that this child would go before the Lord to give knowledge of salvation.

Narrator: At that time, Caesar Augustus ordered a census taken for the purposes of tax assessment. Everyone had to go to his or her city of origin to be counted. Herod was the king of Judea, and Quirinius was the governor of Syria. Even though Mary was soon to deliver, Joseph and Mary had to leave Nazareth in Galilee, and travel to Bethlehem in Judea for the census, since their city of origin was the city of David.

Narrator: Upon arriving in Bethlehem, Joseph and Mary tried to find a place to stay, but all the rooms were filled. They were allowed to stay in a stable where Mary gave birth. Hence, the prophecies of Isaiah and Micah were fulfilled. Oh Bethlehem, such a small town in Judea to be the birthplace of the ruler of Israel, who will feed God's flock with the strength of the Lord, and who will be great forever to the ends of the earth (MIC 5:2). Unto us a Son is given who will be called Wonderful Counselor, Mighty God, and the Prince of Peace (ISA 9:6–7).

Narrator: There were shepherds watching their flocks that night. The angel Gabriel appeared to them.

Gabriel: Do not be afraid. I've got great news! A Savior is born this day in the city of David who is Christ the Lord! You'll find him wrapped in cloth and lying in a manger.

Heavenly Hosts: Glory to God in the highest, and on earth, peace and good will to all people.

Shepherds: Let's go witness this wonderful event.

Narrator: The shepherds found Mary, Joseph, and Jesus. They glorified and praised God, telling everyone what they had heard and seen. Everyone marveled at what the shepherds told them.

Narrator: The day of Jesus's dedication and circumcision had come. A righteous man named Simeon was present in the temple. That day God made good on his promise to Simeon that before his death he would see God's Messiah.

Simeon: Lord, now you can let me die in peace. For I have seen the salvation you prepared for all people. It is just like the prophet said, "A light of revelation to the Gentiles and the glory of your people Israel."

Narrator: Mary and Joseph were amazed at the wisdom and insight Simeon displayed.

Simeon (to Joseph and Mary): Your child will cause many in Israel to rise and to fall, for He will reveal their innermost thoughts. Even your very soul will be pierced to the core.

Narrator: An aging prophetess named Anna also was present at this sacred event. She thanked God for the Christ child and went her way, proclaiming the Messiah to others who had been looking forward to the redemption of Jerusalem.

Narrator: Meanwhile, wise men from the east came to Jerusalem to pay homage to Herod for traveling in Judea.

Herod: What brings you here?

Gaspar: We've been following the giant star.

Balthazar: We came to worship the Christ child.

Herod: Let me know when you find Him so I can worship Him too.

Narrator: For Isaiah wrote that kings shall see the sign, arise and worship (ISA 49:17). The wise men found Jesus and presented Him with gifts of gold, frankincense and myrrh. They were ready to leave when God warned them in a dream not to return to Herod.

Narrator: Herod ordered that all children in the region under two years old be murdered in order to eliminate the Christ child, thereby fulfilling the prophecy of Jeremiah: Wailing and loud lamentation was heard and weeping for the children (JER 31:15). The angel Gabriel appeared to Joseph in a dream and warned him that Herod wanted to destroy Jesus. They traveled to Egypt and stayed there until Herod died, at which time Gabriel told them they could return to Nazareth. This fulfilled the prophecy of David: Out of Egypt He is called (PSA 80:8).

Narrator: God became flesh and lived on earth. His Son was filled with grace and truth, and many observed His glory. Christ came according to God's promise, to save humankind from their sins.

Jesus's Initiation into the Ministry

Narrator: One day when Jesus was twelve years old, His family was visiting Jerusalem for the Passover. His parents didn't realize when they left that Jesus wasn't among them. They searched for him three days until they found Him studying in the temple. The elders and teachers were amazed at His understanding of the scriptures.

Joseph: We've been looking all over for you.

Jesus: Did you not know I would be in my Father's house?

Narrator: The Lord matured. Meanwhile, John the Baptist was preaching across the land.

John: I came to prepare the way which all people should follow.

John (to Pharisees): Every tree that doesn't bear fruit will be chopped down and thrown into the fire.

Crowd: What shall we do?

John: If you have two coats, give one to the poor.

John (to tax collector): Be fair and honest in your collections.

John (to soldiers): Be content with your wages. Do not misrepresent or lie.

Crowd: Are you Elijah?

John: No.

Crowd: Are you the Christ?

John: No.

Crowd: Who are you?

John: I am the voice of one crying in the wilderness. I baptize with water; but One greater than I will come, and He will baptize with the Holy Spirit, and with fire. I'm not worthy of tying His shoes.

Narrator: This fulfilled the prophecies of Isaiah and Malachi: I send my messenger to prepare the way, the messenger of the covenant who will follow. Nobody can endure His coming, for He is like a refiner's fire that will purify men's souls (MAL 3:1–3). The voice of one crying in the wilderness will show the way of the Lord (ISA 40:3).

Narrator: John was baptizing people in the Jordan River when Jesus approached. Jesus was about thirty years old.

CHAPTER THREE

John: Here comes the Lamb of God who takes away the sins of the world.

Jesus: I want to be baptized.

John: I need baptism from you.

Jesus: Let it be this way now, for we must fulfill all righteousness.

Narrator: John baptized Jesus. God's Holy Spirit descended from heaven in the form of a dove.

God: This is my beloved Son who pleases me very much.

Narrator: Jesus continued on His journey alone, into the wilderness. He fasted and meditated for forty days. Satan came to tempt Him while He was physically weak.

Satan: If you're hungry, why not turn these stones into bread?

Jesus: It is written, man cannot live by bread alone, but by God's Word.

Narrator: Satan took Jesus to the pinnacle of the temple.

Satan: Jump, for it is written that the angels will lift you up.

Jesus: It is written, do not tempt the Lord your God.

Narrator: Satan took Jesus to a high mountain. All the kingdoms of the world were visible before them.

Satan: I'll give all of this to you if you worship me.

Jesus: It is written, worship the Lord your God, and serve only Him.

Narrator: Satan, dejected, left Jesus. Jesus returned to the Jordan River. He came to Bethany where John the Baptist was with two of his followers.

John (to Andrew and Philip): Behold the Lamb of God. Trust in Him.

Narrator: John's disciples followed Jesus to Galilee, spending most of the day with Him. Then Andrew went to tell his brother Simon that he had found the Messiah.

Narrator: On the Sabbath, Jesus went to Nazareth to worship in the synagogue. He stood up to read from the book of Isaiah (ISA 61:1–2).

Jesus: The Spirit of the Lord is upon me to preach the good news. He has sent me to free the captives, to give sight to the blind, and to proclaim the year of the Lord.

Narrator: Jesus closed the book and returned to His seat.

Jesus: Today, that prophecy was fulfilled as you were hearing it.

Crowd (murmuring): Isn't this the son of Joseph the carpenter?

Narrator: The crowd rose up to remove Jesus from the synagogue.

Jesus: A prophet is never accepted in his hometown.

Narrator: Then Jesus disappeared among them as they sought to throw Him out.

Narrator: Jesus journeyed to Cana to attend a wedding. His mother was one of the hostesses. During the festival, they ran out of wine.

Mary (to Jesus): We have run out of wine; please help.

Mary (to servants): Do whatever He tells you to do.

Jesus: Fill those large water pots over there with water.

Narrator: The servants did as Jesus asked and then returned. Little did they know that Jesus had turned the water into wine.

Jesus: Dip some out and give it to the host.

Host (to groom): This wine is excellent. Most people save the cheap wine for the end, but you have saved the best for last.

Narrator: Jesus went to the Sea of Galilee where Simon and Andrew had been casting their fishing nets.

Jesus (by the seashore): Cast your nets.

Simon: We've been fishing all night and caught nothing. But if you say so we'll try it.

Narrator: They cast their nets and found so many fish that the nets began to break. It took two boats to pull in all the fish. They returned to shore with their substantial catch of fish.

Simon (to Jesus): Leave me Master, for I am a sinful man.

Jesus: From now on you'll be catching men instead of fish.

Narrator: Simon and Andrew followed Jesus immediately.

Jesus (to Simon): From now on you will be called Peter, the rock.

Narrator: As they journeyed along the shore, they came across James and John mending nets. Jesus called out to them and they also followed Him. Likewise, Philip encountered the group.

Jesus (to Philip): Come with me.

Philip: First let me find my companion Nathanael.

Narrator: Philip found Nathanael.

Philip (to Nathanael): We found the Messiah; the very person Moses and the prophets spoke of.

Narrator: Philip and Nathanael caught up with Jesus.

Jesus: Here comes an honest man.

Nathanael: How do you know?

Jesus: I saw you under the fig tree where Philip found you.

Nathanael: You are the Son of God, the King of Israel.

Jesus: You will see greater proof than this. You will see heaven open and God's angels descending and ascending upon the Son of Man.

Narrator: Meanwhile, John the Baptist was baptizing people in the Jordan River.

Crowd (to John the Baptist): Everyone is following Jesus now.

John: I told you before that I was not the Christ but I was here to prepare the way for Him. Therefore, He must increase and I must decrease. This is the joy of my life. Those of the earth belong to the earth and speak of earthly things. He that is from heaven is above all, and receives testimony directly from God. The Father loves the Son and has given Him dominion over all the earth. He who believes in the Son will receive eternal life.

CHAPTER THREE

Narrator: Jesus and his followers journeyed to Capernaum where Jesus continued to preach. Everyone was astonished by His knowledge and authority.

Jesus (to crowd): Repent for the kingdom of heaven is at hand.

Man (possessed with evil spirits): What have you to do with us, Jesus? Have you come to destroy us? We know you are the Holy One of God.

Jesus (to spirits): Be silent and depart from this man.

Narrator: The man went into convulsions and then relaxed as the spirits left.

Crowd (marveling): What authority He has! Why, He even commands the demons and they obey.

Narrator: Jesus and his disciples journeyed throughout Nazareth and Judea. They stopped in Bethsaida to visit Peter's sick mother-in-law. Jesus stood over her and her fever left. Word spread of Jesus's healing power and people brought the sick, lame, demon-possessed, and handicapped to Jesus.

Leper: Please cleanse me, Jesus.

Jesus (touching him): Be clean!

Narrator: Immediately the man was cleansed of his leprosy.

Jesus: Do not tell anyone but show yourself to the priest that you are clean.

Narrator: Multitudes from various foreign countries would follow Jesus to hear the Word of God and to be healed. One day some men brought a crippled and paralyzed man, but they could not make their way through the crowd. They went up on the roof of the place where Jesus was ministering and lowered the man down on his bed through the ceiling.

Jesus: Man, your sins are forgiven.

Pharisee: He speaks blasphemy; only God can forgive sins.

Jesus (to crowd): So that you know I have the power to forgive sins...

Jesus (to man): Rise, take your bed, and go home.

Narrator: The lame man rose and walked off with his bed. The crowd marveled and rejoiced. Jesus left and the crowd followed.

Narrator: One day on the Sabbath, Jesus and his disciples were gathering grain.

Pharisee: It is unlawful to work on the Sabbath.

Jesus: Even David took the holy grain and fed the hungry and himself. The Son of Man is Lord, even of the Sabbath.

Pharisee: Why don't you people wash your hands before eating?

Jesus: You hypocrites. You clean the outside while the inside is full of extortion and excess. You outwardly appear to be righteous, but inside you are full of hypocrisy and iniquity. What goes into the mouth does not defile the person, but what comes out of the mouth does. The things people say come from the heart; all too often, from the heart proceed evil thoughts that corrupt a person.

Judas: You offended the Pharisees.

Jesus: Any plant not planted by my heavenly Father will be uprooted.

Narrator: Jesus entered the synagogue at Capernaum to worship and teach. A man was there with a crippled hand.

Jesus (to Pharisees): Is it lawful to heal and save lives on the Sabbath?

Narrator: The Pharisees were silent.

Jesus (to man): Stretch out your hand.

Narrator: As he did, his hand was restored to normal. At that point, the Pharisees began to plot Jesus's demise with Herod.

Narrator: Jesus and His followers passed by Matthew, a tax collector.

Jesus: Follow me.

Narrator: Matthew left his tax-collecting job and followed Jesus. Matthew decided to have a celebration feast at his house.

Pharisee: Why does He eat with sinners?

Jesus (to Pharisee): Only the sick need a physician. I came to call sinners, not the righteous, to repentance.

Crowd: Why do the Pharisees and the disciples of John the Baptist fast, but not you and your disciples?

Jesus: Should the wedding guests fast while the groom is with them? When the groom goes away, then it will be time to fast.

Narrator: Jesus healed many people: the lame, blind, lepers, and the demon possessed. This fulfilled the prophecy of Isaiah: The blind shall see and the lame shall leap (ISA 35:5–6).

Narrator: Jesus's disciples went to Jerusalem for the Passover. Jesus didn't accompany them because people were already plotting to kill Him. Instead, He went after them, secretly taking an alternate route.

Narrator: Jesus came across a man by the pool of Bethzatha who was crippled. Others were waiting there to be healed by the pool when the waters became stirred.

Jesus: Do you want to be healed?

Man: Yes, but I have nobody to carry me to the pool.

Jesus: Get up and walk.

Narrator: The man got up and walked, telling everyone what Jesus had done. The Jews got upset because Jesus had healed the man on the Sabbath.

Jesus (to crowd): I cannot do anything without my Father's permission. He shows me what to do and I do it. Therefore, you should honor the Son even as you honor the Father. If you do not honor the Son, you do not honor the Father who sent Him. He who believes in me believes in Him who sent me, and receives eternal life. The Father gives the Son the authority to execute judgment. And when the time comes, the dead will hear His voice. Then the righteous will be resurrected to everlasting life, but the evil ones will be damned.

Jesus: There is another who has been a witness to the truth: John the Baptist. I am a greater witness than John. In fact, the Father Himself has told you through the scriptures that I would come, and be proclaimed by John the Baptist. If you believed Moses, John, and the other prophets, you would also believe me.

Crowd: Give us a sign, like when God sent manna to Moses to feed the multitude.

Jesus: I am the bread of life that comes from heaven. Those who come to me will never hunger. This bread is my flesh, which I give to the world so all people can live. Unless you eat the flesh and drink the blood of the Son of Man, you will die. However, he who partakes of my body and blood lives in me and I in him.

Narrator: Many of the people didn't like hearing this and left. Even the disciples found the teaching disturbing.

Jesus (to disciples): Would you leave me as well?

Peter: You have the words of eternal life. Who else can we turn to? We believe that you are the Son of God.

Narrator: Jesus called together the twelve apostles: Peter and his brother Andrew, James and his brother John (sons of Zebedee), Philip, Bartholomew (Nathanael), Thomas, Matthew, James (son of Alphaeus), Thaddaeus (Lebbaeus; possibly also called Judas), Simon (a Canaanite), and Judas Iscariot. He also solicited seventy others. He grouped the disciples into pairs.

Jesus: I am sending you ahead of me into various townships to prepare them to receive me and to find the lost sheep of Israel. If any two or more of you are gathered in my name, I will be there also. Preach that the kingdom of God is at hand. Heal the sick, raise the dead, and cast out demons. Take no money and travel light. Stay with folks who are worthy and bless their homes. At those towns that do not receive you gracefully, shake the dust off your feet while you leave. Do not worry about what to say for the Holy Spirit will provide the words. You will be hated, but do not be afraid of those that can kill the body, because they cannot touch your soul. Instead, fear Him who can destroy your body and soul in hell. Those who confess me, I will confess them to our Father in heaven. Those who deny me, I will deny them before our Father in heaven. He that loses his life for my sake will find it.

Narrator: Jesus departed through Samaria, stopping at Jacob's well. A Samaritan woman came for some water.

Jesus: How about a drink?

Woman: Since when do Jews converse with Samaritans?

Jesus: If you knew who I am you'd be asking me for living water.

Woman: How can you draw water from a deep well with no bucket?

Jesus: Whoever drinks this water will get thirsty again, but whoever drinks my water will never thirst again. It is a spring of everlasting life.

Woman: I'd like some of this living water.

Jesus: Go call your husband.

Woman: I have no husband.

Jesus: You've actually had five husbands, not including the man you are with now.

Woman: You are a prophet. Tell me, why do Jews insist on worshipping in Jerusalem, while we Samaritans are content to worship here on this mountain?

Jesus: The time will come when people will not be worshipping anywhere. People do not even know what they are worshipping these days. True worshipers worship the Father in spirit and in truth no matter where they are.

Woman: I have heard that the Messiah is coming. When He comes, He'll tell me what to do.

Jesus: I am He.

Narrator: The woman believed and went to tell everyone that a prophet had come who knew her life story, and that He must be the Christ. Jesus stayed two days. Many people believed and were saved. Meanwhile, the rest of the disciples caught up with Jesus.

Disciples: Even demons obey us!

Jesus: It was I who gave you the authority. Do not rejoice in this, but rather in the fact that your names are written in heaven.

Narrator: Herod the king, even though he respected John the Baptist as a prophet, had John thrown into prison because John was always tormenting him and his cohorts due to Herod's adulterous affair and other atrocities. John sent his disciples to find Jesus and ask Him if He was the true Messiah.

Jesus (to John's disciples): Tell John about the miracles. Tell John, blessed is he who is not offended by me.

Jesus (to crowd): John was the one who the prophets wrote about when they said that a messenger would come to prepare the way for Messiah. I tell you that nobody before him was greater than John the Baptist.

Jesus Feeds His People

Narrator: Multitudes followed Jesus wherever He went, so Jesus went up a mountain to preach.

Jesus (to Philip): Go buy bread to feed these people.

Philip: It would take more than two hundred days wages.

Narrator: A boy was nearby with his lunch of two small fish and five biscuits.

Jesus (to disciples): Have the people sit down.

Narrator: Jesus gave thanks and distributed the boy's lunch to the disciples.

Jesus (to disciples): Distribute this food to the multitude.

Narrator: Jesus's disciples distributed the food to everyone, numbering over five thousand, and they all ate until they were full.

Jesus (to disciples): Gather up the remains of the food.

Narrator: The disciples gathered twelve baskets of crumbs. Then Jesus got up to teach, and everyone became silent.

Jesus: Blessed are the poor in spirit, for theirs is the kingdom of heaven. Blessed are the mourners, for they shall be comforted. Blessed are the meek, for they shall inherit the earth. Blessed are those who hunger and thirst for righteousness, for they shall be satisfied. Blessed are the merciful, for they shall obtain mercy. Blessed are the pure in heart, for they shall see God. Blessed are the peacemakers, for they shall be called the sons of God. Blessed are those who are persecuted for righteousness sake, for theirs is the kingdom of heaven. Blessed are those who are persecuted because of me, for their heavenly reward will be great.

Jesus: You are the salt of the earth, but salt with no taste is thrown out. You are the light of the world. Let your light shine before everyone, do not hide it. You are still bound by the Law. I did not come to abolish the Law I came to fulfill it. Reconcile yourself with your neighbor; then reconcile yourself with God. If your hand causes you to sin, cut it off; if your eye causes you to sin, pluck it out. Better to go to heaven maimed than to go to hell with your whole body. You have heard, do not commit adultery. I say do not divorce your wife except for unfaithfulness; otherwise you will be guilty of adultery and so will she if you have sex with anyone else. Whatever God has joined together, let no man split apart. Do not even look upon a member of the opposite sex with lust, for you will have committed adultery in your heart. You have heard that it is wrong to swear falsely. I say, do not swear at all. A simple yes or no will suffice. You have heard: an eye for an eye, a tooth for a tooth. I say, if someone slaps your cheek, turn to them your other cheek also. If someone sues you for your coat, let them take your cloak as well. If someone forces you to go with them one mile, go two miles. If someone is in need, give them what they need and expect nothing in return. Do not refuse anyone anything. Anybody can love those who love them. But I say, love your enemies also. Pray for those who persecute you. Try to be perfect in love, just like your heavenly Father is perfect. God will reward you for being loving, unselfish, and merciful to others.

Jesus: Do not display your piety to others to gain approval; you receive no reward in heaven for this. Those who desire recognition for their dedication or for their gift will receive no further recognition or reward. When you pray, do not be like the hypocrites who like to pray openly so others may observe them. Instead, pray by yourself in secret. And when you pray, do not heap together long dissertations of words, for the length of the prayer has no bearing on its meaning.

Mark: Teach us to pray.

Jesus: Pray like this: Our Father in heaven. Your name is Holy. Let your kingdom come to us. Let your will be done here on earth as in heaven. Provide us with our daily needs. Forgive us our sins, as we should forgive others who sin against us. Protect us from temptation and evil. For the kingdom, power, and glory are yours forever, Amen.

Jesus: Remember, if you forgive others, God will forgive you. Do not strive for earthly wealth, but save up spiritual gifts so that your wealth will reside in heaven. For where your treasure is, there your heart will be. You cannot serve two masters. You cannot serve God and money. Do not be anxious about your life, and do not worry about your next meal or what to wear. Look at the birds. They neither sow nor reap, but God feeds them just the same. Look at the lilies. They do not work or worry, but Solomon himself was not clothed in such beauty. And are you not more important to God than birds and flowers? Besides, will being anxious about tomorrow add one second to your life? Seek first the kingdom of heaven, and God will give it to you, and all of your earthly needs will be provided in addition. And who knows better than God what your needs are?

Jesus: Treat others the same way you want to be treated. Do not associate holy things with filth. Do not judge others unless you want to be judged yourself, for you will be judged by the same standards as you judge others. Do not attempt to remove the speck in your brother's eye until you remove the plank from your own eye. A blind man cannot lead another blind man, or they will both fall into the ditch. A disciple is not above his teacher; once taught, however, he will become a teacher himself.

Jesus: Ask and you shall receive. Seek and you shall find. Knock and the door shall be opened. The narrow gate where the way is hard leads to life; the gate to destruction is the one that is wide and easy. Beware of false prophets; they are like wolves in sheep's clothing. Only strong trees can bear good fruit. Every tree that does not bear good fruit will be chopped down and thrown into the fire. You must obey the Father to enter the kingdom of heaven. Those who hear my words and obey are like the man who built his house upon the rock. His house remained standing despite the rains, winds, and floods. Those who hear my words and ignore them are like the man who built his house upon the sand. That house was destroyed completely.

Narrator: The crowds were astonished at the wisdom and authority of Jesus's sermon. Jesus came down from the mountain. He journeyed to Capernaum. At the outskirts of the city a centurion approached.

Centurion: Can you heal my servant?

Jesus: Lead me to him.

Centurion: I am not worthy to have you in my home. But I know if you say the word he will be healed, just like when I give an order to a subordinate they obey.

Jesus (to crowd): I have not seen so great a faith in Israel.

Jesus (to centurion): As you have believed, so it will be.

Narrator: Jesus and the crowd passed a funeral procession. A mother had lost her only son. Jesus had compassion on her.

Jesus (to corpse): Rise.

Narrator: The dead boy arose and started talking. The crowd was stunned. Jesus was mobbed.

Jesus (to disciples): Notice how the harvest is plentiful but the laborers are few. Pray that the Lord will send laborers to help with the harvest.

Narrator: Jesus freed a man from demon possession.

Pharisee (concerning Jesus): This man gets his power from Satan.

Jesus: How can a kingdom divided against itself stand? How can Satan cast out Satan? Remember this: all sins are forgiven for those who repent. However, he who blasphemes against the Holy Spirit will not be forgiven. The day is coming when an evil spirit will be sent out of a person and it will find seven more spirits even more evil, then come back to possess that person making the person worse off than before.

Narrator: The crowd followed Jesus to the Sea of Galilee. Jesus preached from a boat while the crowd stood alongside the banks of the sea.

Jesus: A man was sowing his seeds. Some seeds fell on the path and the birds came and ate them. Some seeds fell on the rocks, where there was insufficient soil for them to take root, and the seedlings died. Some seeds fell upon the thorns, where the seedlings were choked to death. Some seeds fell on good soil, took root, and grew. And the harvest was great. You who have ears should listen.

Voices from the crowd: Why do you speak in parables?

Jesus: I speak in parables because those who have eyes do not always see, and those who have ears do not always hear. This is exactly what the prophet Isaiah said (ISA 6:10). You have been given the secrets of heaven. Everything that was hidden will be brought into the open. The measure you give will be the measure you receive and more. Those who have will receive more; those who do not have will have what little they possess taken away. The parable means that the Word of God will be given to everyone. Some will not grasp it, allowing the evil one to snatch it away from them. Some will receive the Word but it will not take root in their hearts. Some will hear the Word but will be distracted by earthly riches and pleasures. However, those who hear the Word of God, understand it, and share it with others will bear much fruit.

Jesus: Similarly, a man sowed seeds of grain, but while he was sleeping, his competitors sowed seeds of weeds in his fields. Therefore, both grain and weeds sprouted and grew. The man's servants questioned him and the man surmised that his enemies had done the evil deed. The servants asked if they should pull the weeds, but the man told them not to because the gathering of the weeds could cause some of the wheat to be uprooted as well. So, the weeds grew along with the grain. At harvest time, the wheat was separated from the weeds. The grain was stored in the barn, and the weeds were burned. He who sows the good seed is the Son of Man sowing God's Word. The field is the world. The seed will flourish in good people but will die in evil ones. The harvest is the end of the world and the reapers are the angels of heaven. Righteous people will be collected to live in heaven, but evil people will be thrown into the fire.

Jesus: The kingdom of heaven is like a small seed which grows into a giant tree. And the birds make their nests in its branches. The kingdom of heaven is like a magnificent pearl for which the merchant sold all he had to purchase it. The kingdom of heaven is like a net of fish that the fishermen brought in. There were all kinds of different types of fish, the good ones were kept and the bad ones were thrown out.

Narrator: Jesus often spoke in parables, fulfilling the prophecy of David: I will speak in parables and disclose hidden truths (PSA 78:2).

Jesus: Now let's go to the other side of the sea.

Narrator: During the journey, a great storm arose while Jesus slept. Jesus's disciples were afraid and awoke Him.

Jesus (to disciples): What little faith you have.

Jesus (to storm): Be still.

Narrator: The storm ceased.

Disciples: What kind of man is He, that even the wind and sea obey Him?

Narrator: They arrived at the other side of the Sea of Galilee near Gadara. Immediately word spread that Jesus had come. As they were disembarking, a possessed man who lived in the catacombs approached. Nobody could subdue this man so he did whatever he wanted.

Man: Do not torment me Son of the Most High.

Jesus: What is your name?

Man: Legion, for we are many. Please do not send us out of the country; send us instead into that herd of swine.

Jesus: Very well. Now be gone!

Narrator: The evil spirits left the possessed man and entered the swine. The entire herd of swine ran toward the cliffs, and jumped into the sea to their deaths. Everyone marveled, and word spread of this extraordinary event.

Man: Let me go with you.

Jesus: Instead of going with me, go tell everyone what great things the Lord has done for you.

Narrator: As they journeyed, another man approached Jesus.

Head of synagogue: Please come heal my daughter.

Narrator: They went to the man's house so Jesus could heal his daughter. Along the way a woman approached who had been hemorrhaging for twelve years. She touched Jesus's garment and was immediately healed.

Jesus: Who just touched my garment?

Woman: I did.

Jesus: Go your way; your faith has healed you.

Narrator: Just then, a family member approached the man to tell him that his daughter already had died.

Jesus: Have no fear; she is only sleeping.

Narrator: They came to the man's house. Jesus made everyone stay outside except Peter, James, John, and the girl's parents. The crowd rebuked Jesus, repeating that the girl had died. Jesus entered the house, found the girl and held her hand.

Jesus (to girl): Arise.

Narrator: The girl arose as Jesus requested. The people were amazed. Jesus also healed two blind men that day.

Narrator: Jesus told his disciples to prepare a ship to go back across the sea. Meanwhile, he went up into the mountain to pray. When he returned, a big storm was brewing. Jesus began walking across the water to the ship. The disciples became afraid and cried out in fear.

Jesus: Fear not, it is I.

Peter: If it's you, tell me to come to you.

Jesus: Come.

Narrator: Peter began to walk on the water toward Jesus, but he was distracted by the waves and turbulence and began to sink. Jesus pulled him up.

Jesus: Why did you doubt?

Narrator: They climbed aboard the ship and the storm ceased. Their journey took them all the way to Tyre and Sidon in Syria. A woman from Canaan approached Jesus.

Woman: Can you help my daughter, she's possessed?

Jesus: It is not right to give the children's food to the dogs.

Woman: But even the dogs eat the scraps from the table.

Jesus: How true. Go home, your daughter is clean.

Narrator: Further along, Jesus encountered a deaf and dumb man. Jesus put His finger in the man's ear, spat on his finger, and touched the man's tongue. Immediately the man began to hear and speak. Everyone thought Jesus was wonderful. Jesus and His disciples journeyed back towards the Sea of Galilee. The ever-present crowds gathered and Jesus preached three days. The people had become very hungry. Jesus fed the entire multitude (over four thousand people) with seven small loaves of bread.

Jesus: If you want to be my disciples, you must reject your own desires and take up your cross. You must love me more than anyone else, even yourself. If a person expects to build a tower, he considers in advance the costs to ensure he can finish it. If not, he will never finish it and he will become the laughing stock of the town. If a king expects to go to war, he plans his strategy. If he cannot defeat his enemy, he will send an emissary to establish terms of peace. Therefore, you must renounce everything in advance and follow me. What do you gain if you inherit the world but lose your soul? Is anything worth more than your soul?

Narrator: Jesus sent the crowds away to continue his ministry elsewhere.

Jesus (to disciples): Who do the people say I am?

James: John the Baptist.

Simon: Elijah.

Jesus: Who do you say I am?

Peter: You are the Christ, the Son of the living God!

Jesus: You are blessed among men, Peter. You will help me build my church. I will give to you the keys to heaven. Whatever you lock on earth will be locked in heaven, and whatever you unlock on earth will be unlocked in heaven.

Jesus (to disciples): The chief priests and elders will reject me. I'll be handed over to the Gentiles. I will be mocked and beaten. I will suffer and die. I will arise three days later. When we get to Jerusalem, these prophecies of old will come true.

Peter: This can't happen to you; you shouldn't say such things.

Jesus: Satan, get behind me! You people cannot comprehend the things of God, only of men.

Narrator: Meanwhile, it was Herod's birthday and was having a stag party where he asked his illegitimate daughter to dance. Herod told her he'd give her anything she wanted if she would dance. She consulted her mother who talked her into asking for the head of John the Baptist on a silver platter. To save face, Herod had John beheaded. Word got back to Jesus and His disciples; they mourned for John as they continued their travels.

Narrator: Jesus took Peter, James, and John to a high mountain to pray. Jesus became transfigured, glistening with intense white, while Elijah and Moses appeared with Him. Jesus was talking with Elijah and Moses.

Peter: I'll make three shelters, one for each of you.

Narrator: A cloud overshadowed the mountain enclosing them in its mist.

God: This is my beloved Son. Listen to Him.

Narrator: Then Elijah and Moses disappeared.

Jesus: Do not tell anybody about this until the Son of Man has risen from the dead.

Narrator: They came down the mountain where a crowd was waiting to see Jesus.

Jesus (to crowd): Nobody but the Son knows the Father sufficiently to approach Him, except those who the Son refers to Him. Therefore, I welcome all to come to me who feel overloaded or fatigued and I will give you rest.

Man: Teacher, please help my son; he is possessed. He foams at the mouth and convulses.

Jesus: Bring him here.

Narrator: The man's son began convulsing in front of Jesus.

Jesus: All things are possible to those who believe.

Man: I believe, Lord. Help me overcome my unbelief.

Jesus (to demon): Come out of him and never return.

Narrator: The boy became like a corpse as the evil spirit left.

Crowd: The boy is dead.

Narrator: Jesus lifted the boy to his feet.

Woman: Blessed be the womb that bore you and the breast that nursed you.

Jesus: Rather, blessed be those who hear the Word of God and keep it.

Disciples: We tried to heal the boy while you were gone but were unable. Why couldn't we cast the demon out?

Jesus: If you had faith the size of a mustard seed you could uproot trees and move mountains; nothing would be impossible. However, that kind of demon cannot be driven out by anything but persistent prayer.

John: We saw someone casting out demons in your name but we told him to stop because he was not with us.

Jesus: Do not forbid anyone who does miracles in my name. He that is not against us is for us.

Narrator: People brought children to Jesus for Him to bless. The disciples tried to prevent them from coming forward.

Jesus: Do not prevent the children from coming to me, for such as these will inherit the kingdom of God. You must receive the kingdom of God like a child if you expect to enter there.

Jesus (taking a child in His hands): Whoever receives a child in my name receives me. Whoever receives me, receives Him who sent me. Whoever causes one of these little ones to sin, that person would be better off if he was tied to a millstone and thrown into the sea.

Man: What should I do to inherit eternal life?

Jesus: What is written in the Law?

Man: Love the Lord with all your heart, mind, soul, and strength, and love your neighbor as yourself.

Jesus: That is correct.

Man: Who exactly is my neighbor?

Jesus: A man was mugged and left by the side of the road for dead. A priest approached, saw the man, and passed along the other side of the road. A Levite also passed by, avoiding the man. Later a Samaritan came, took pity on the man, placed him upon his donkey, and took him to the nearest inn to recuperate. The next day the Samaritan gave some money to the innkeeper to continue to care for the injured man until he recovered. Who was a neighbor to the man?

Man: The one who was merciful.

Jesus: Go and do likewise. Sell your belongings and give the money to the poor.

Narrator: The man left feeling depressed, for he had great riches and didn't like the thought of giving everything away.

Jesus: I am telling you that it is easier for a camel to pass through the eye of a needle than for a rich man to get into heaven. There was a rich man who lived a life of pleasure and luxury. A poor man lay at his gate who was weak, hungry, and afflicted, desiring just the crumbs off the rich man's plate. The two men died. The poor man was taken to Abraham's bosom, and the rich man was exiled in Hades. The rich man called out to Abraham asking if he would let the poor man dip his finger into water to wet his parched tongue. But Abraham reminded him how thoughtless and unmerciful he had been to the poor man, and informed him that nobody could pass through the chasm separating the two underworlds. The rich man implored that his family be warned, to prevent them from the same fate. Abraham told the rich man that they would have to rely on the Word of God like everybody else; otherwise, a visit from the dead would not persuade them to change their ways.

Crowd: Then who is saved?

Jesus: With men it is impossible, but with God all things are possible. Whoever leaves his possessions and loved ones to follow me will receive a hundred times that.

Jesus: There was a rich man who had a plentiful harvest. He decided to tear down his old barns and build larger ones to store the grain. He had stocked up so much grain and goods that he decided to take it easy and to eat, drink, and be merry. But God said to him, "Fool! Tonight, your soul is required of you. All the things you have will no longer be yours." Remember this: those who lay aside only earthly treasures have no heavenly treasures.

Jesus: A king gave ten shares of gold to three servants to invest during his absence. Upon his return he gathered the three servants together. The first proclaimed he had made an extra ten shares with his investment. The king was pleased and gave him ten cities to govern. The second servant had made five extra shares so he was given five cities to govern. The third told the king, "Knowing what a stern man you are, I hid my shares in the ground so as not to lose anything, and here they are." The king said, "You could have invested the money in the bank at the very least. As you have called me a stern man so I will deal with you sternly." The king ordered that the third servant's shares be given to the first servant who had invested the wisest, and ordered the wicked servant to be taken to the dungeon. Therefore, to those who have, more will be given, and to those who have not, the little they have will be taken away. Of those who have been given much, much will be required, and of those who have been guaranteed much, more will be demanded.

Jesus: Be like the man who awaits his master to come home from the marriage feast, so that he may open the door when his master arrives. Blessed are those who the master finds awake when he returns. If the homeowner knew the time that the thief would rob him, he would have been prepared. Be ready at all times for the Son of Man to come, because no-one knows the exact hour.

Narrator: Jesus and His followers continued their journey into Galilee. The apostles were arguing about who was the greatest among them. Jesus gathered everyone together.

Jesus: What are you bickering about?

Mrs. Zebedee: I would like my sons James and John to sit at your right and left hands in heaven.

Jesus: Get serious. Can anyone take my place? I tell you the truth, anyone who wants to be first will be last. Remember, many are called but few are chosen.

Jesus: A Pharisee and a publican were both praying in the temple. The Pharisee prayed, "I am grateful to you Lord that I am not like the publican. I fast and I tithe." The publican beat his breasts and prayed, "Oh Lord, be merciful to me a miserable sinner." I tell you, only the publican left the temple forgiven and justified in his faith. Those who exalt themselves will be humbled and those who humble themselves will be exalted.

Jesus: The kingdom of heaven is like the landowner hiring laborers for his vineyard. The employer went to town where he found people looking for work. He hired them, agreeing on a wage of a dollar a day. At the marketplace he found more idle laborers so he hired them at the same wage. Later still he found more people looking for work and sent them to the vineyard. When the evening came, he called the laborers together. He paid all of them a dollar, even though most had only worked part of the day. Those who were hired first were angry because they had worked all day, while some had only worked a few hours. The employer told them, "You received the agreed-upon wage and should be content. I chose to pay the last as I have paid you, and that is my prerogative. Do you begrudge my generosity?" For the last will be first and the first will be last.

Peter: How often should I forgive someone who did me wrong? Seven times?

Jesus: No, seventy-seven times. A man who owed a large sum of money was brought before the king to pay his debt. The man could not pay so the king ordered him and his family to be sold as slaves, and for his possessions to be sold as well. The man fell on his knees and begged for mercy, assuring the king that he would pay the debt. Out of pity the king released him, forgiving the debt. The same man accosted another who was indebted to him, demanding the debt be paid. The other man fell on his knees and begged for mercy, but the man had him thrown into prison until he could pay the debt. Word of this got back to the king who had the unmerciful man brought to the palace. The king scolded him for being wicked and unforgiving. In his anger, the king had him jailed until he could repay the entire debt. This is what the heavenly Father will do if you do not forgive others from your heart.

Jesus's Final Journey to Jerusalem

Narrator: Jesus and His disciples continued their travels. At the border of Samaria were ten lepers.

Lepers: Master, have mercy on us.

Jesus: Go to the priest and show him you are healed.

Narrator: As the lepers were walking to the synagogue they were healed. After showing themselves to the priest, one of them returned to find Jesus and fell at Jesus's feet.

Man: Glory be to God.

Jesus: Did I not heal ten lepers? Where are the other nine? Only this foreigner returns to glorify God! Man, your faith has made you well.

Narrator: The journey brought them to Jericho. A blind beggar noticed a commotion when Jesus entered the city; this man had been blind since birth.

Beggar: What is happening?

Others: It's Jesus of Nazareth.

Beggar: Jesus, Son of David, have mercy on me.

Jesus (to disciples): Bring him here.

Jesus (to beggar): What can I do for you?

Beggar: I would like to receive my sight.

Jesus: Your faith has given you your sight.

Narrator: Jesus also healed a hunchback woman.

Pharisee: Why do you work on the Sabbath? Healing should be reserved for the other six days in the week.

Jesus: Hypocrite! Do you not water your cattle and feed your goats on the Sabbath? Is it wrong to help others on the Sabbath?

Narrator: Most of the people sided with Jesus on the issue.

Pharisee: Why do you associate with sinners?

Jesus: I am here to bring sinners, not the righteous to repentance. A man with one hundred sheep lost one. He left the other sheep and searched until he found the one that strayed. He rejoiced more for finding the one that was lost, than for the ninety-nine that did not go astray.

Jesus: There was a man who had two sons. The youngest one decided he wanted to make it on his own and asked his father for his inheritance. The man gave his son the inheritance. The son packed up and left to another country, where he squandered all of his inheritance on wine and women. Meanwhile, a great famine arose in that country. The son had to feed pigs to make a living. He realized that even his father's servants had it better than this, so he decided to return home, confess everything to his father, and apologize to his father for being so stupid. While the son was still at a distance approaching his home, his father noticed him coming, ran out to meet the son, and embraced him. The son told his father that he was not worthy of being called a son and wished to be treated as a servant. But the father summoned his servants to prepare a great feast to celebrate the son's return. The elder son came home and noticed the singing and dancing and found out from a servant what the celebration was all about. In anger he refused to enter the house. The father came outside to get the elder son, who complained, "You've never had a party for me, yet I've remained here to serve you, while my brother ran off and spent his inheritance." The father replied, "You are always with me and all that is mine is yours. It was fitting to celebrate, because your brother was lost, but now he is found; he was dead but now he is alive."

Jesus: I am the Good Shepherd. My sheep recognize my voice and they follow me. I know my sheep and they know me, just as the Father knows me and I know Him. The Good Shepherd lays down His life for His sheep. The Father loves me for laying down my life and restores my life to me. No-one takes my life from me, but I give it voluntarily. My Father has given me the power to sacrifice my life and to take it back again. In fact, the Father and I are one. I am the door. Those who enter by me are saved, and I will give them eternal life.

Others: He is mad. Stone him.

Jesus: You would stone me even after seeing the miracles?

Others: We stone you for your blasphemy. You make yourself out to be God.

Jesus: If you do not believe in me, at least believe in the works that I do, which demonstrate that the Father is in me and I in Him.

Pharisee: It seems you have angered the crowd.

Jesus: I did not come to give peace to the earth, but rather strife and division. Families will split apart. A wicked generation will rise. They will be evil and will fall from God's grace. People will seek a sign and a messiah that will never come. You can read the signs in the sky to predict the weather, but you refuse to take notice of the warning signs around you concerning the crisis ahead.

Jesus: A certain rich man had a trustee who was accused of embezzlement. The trustee was called to give account of his actions or be fired from his job. The trustee explained that if he lost the job, he would not be able to work elsewhere since he had no other job skills. Therefore, he was preparing for that day by fixing the books in the favor of the rich man's clients, who later would help him if he became unemployed. The rich man commended the dishonest trustee for his shrewdness. In fact, the dishonest people of the evil generation are cleverer than the honest ones. Go ahead and become friends with materialism instead of righteousness and see if it earns you a trip to heaven. Those who are honest regarding insignificant things also will be honest in important things. Those who are dishonest in insignificant things also will be dishonest in important things. If you have been dishonest regarding earthly riches, who will entrust you with the riches of heaven? If you cannot be trustworthy with other people's money why should you be allowed to have money of your own? You cannot serve two masters, for you will end up serving one over the other; you cannot serve God and money at the same time.

Jesus (to Pharisees): You people justify yourselves before others, but God knows what is in your hearts. Those things that are regarded highly on earth are an abomination to God.

Jesus: A man planted a fig tree that bore no fruit, so he ordered his gardener to chop it down. The gardener asked the man to give it one more chance. "I will fertilize it and give it special attention" the gardener assured the man, "If it does not bear fruit next year, then I will chop it down." The door to heaven is narrow; work hard to get in. Many will try to enter after the door is locked. There will be weeping and gnashing of teeth. Some who are despised now will be honored then, and some who are important now will be nobody then.

Pharisee: You'd better get going before Herod gets his hands on you.

Jesus: You are a generation of snakes. How can you escape the damnation of hell? I send you prophets; some of them you mock and torture in your synagogues, some you persecute, some you murder. Tell Herod I will continue the miracles for three days until I reach Jerusalem. A prophet of God should die in Jerusalem where all the prophets get murdered.

Narrator: Jesus slipped through the crowd unharmed. He and His followers continued onward toward Jerusalem. Zacchaeus, a tax collector, was trying to get a glimpse of Jesus, but he was too short to see over the crowd so he climbed a tree.

Jesus (looking up): Zacchaeus, come down. I'm going to be a guest in your home.

Narrator: Zacchaeus climbed down and they went to his house.

Zacchaeus: From now on I'm going to give half of my wealth to the poor. Anyone who I've overcharged in the past will be reimbursed four times over.

Jesus: Salvation has come to this house today.

CHAPTER THREE

Narrator: They proceeded to Bethany where they met up with Mary and Martha, who informed Jesus that their brother, Jesus's friend Lazarus, had died.

Jesus: Lazarus is just sleeping. I have returned to Judea to wake him. Your brother will rise.

Martha: Of course, he'll rise at the resurrection.

Jesus: I am the resurrection and the life. He who believes in me, though he was dead, will live yet again. Whoever believes in me will never die. Do you believe this?

Martha: Yes. You are the Christ, the Son of God.

Narrator: They went to the tomb of Lazarus. Jesus wept.

Jews: Jesus must have really loved Lazarus.

Jesus: Take away the stone.

Martha: He probably stinks by now; it's been four days.

Jesus: Did I not say if you believe you will see the glory of God?

Jesus (looking upward): Thank you for hearing me heavenly Father.

Jesus: Lazarus come forth!

Narrator: Lazarus came out of the tomb, still wrapped in burial linens.

Jesus: Unwrap him and release him.

Narrator: Everyone was amazed. They went to tell the Pharisees.

Sadducees: If we don't arrest Jesus, the Romans will get mad and take everything we own.

Caiaphas (high priest): Can't you see that it would be expedient for him to die if it spares the rest of the Jews?

Narrator: Mary and Martha received Jesus into their home. As Martha served the guests, she complained that her sister Mary was not helping out.

Jesus: There is only one thing you should be concerned about; Mary has discovered it and I cannot take that away from her.

Narrator: Mary anointed Jesus's head with fine oil.

Judas: This oil should have been sold and the money given to the poor.

Jesus: Never mind that; be content while I am still around. Besides, this is part of my preparation for what lies ahead.

Narrator: Judas left to plot his betrayal of Jesus. The next day Jesus and His disciples proceeded towards Jerusalem, with Jesus preaching and telling parables along the way. As they neared Jerusalem, Jesus told a few of his disciples to go into town. They were to find a donkey with its colt tied alongside the road, and to bring the colt to Jesus; if anyone questioned them, they were to say that the Lord needed it. They did as Jesus asked. A man stopped them; they told the man what Jesus said and the man released the colt to them. They brought the colt to Jesus and put their coats over its back so Jesus could ride it into Jerusalem. This fulfilled the prophecy of Zechariah: Rejoice, for your King comes triumphant, riding on a donkey's colt (ZEC 9:9–11). As Jesus approached, the crowds saw Him coming and began spreading their coats and palm branches in His path.

Crowd: Hosanna to the Son of David! Blessed is He who comes in the name of the Lord! Glory to God in the Highest!

Narrator: Jesus entered the temple, where He found merchants selling animals for sacrifice and moneychangers who collected the fees. Jesus was indignant; He turned over tables and chased them out with a twine whip.

Jesus: Get this stuff out of here. Do not turn my Father's house into a marketplace!

Pharisees: What right do you have to order them out?

Jesus: Did John the Baptist act on his own authority, or was he sent from heaven?

Jesus: A man planted a vineyard and leased it to tenants. He left the country for a while, and upon returning, sent his servant for some of the fruit of the vineyard. The tenants beat the servant and ran him off. The man sent another servant, who was again beaten and driven away. The man sent yet another servant who was severely wounded and left to die. Then the man sent his only son, thinking the tenants would respect him. The tenants decided to kill the son, who was the man's only heir, thinking they could inherit the vineyard in his place. What do you think the man did next? He came and destroyed the tenants and leased the vineyard to others. This is what is meant by the scripture of David: The very stone which the builders rejected became the cornerstone of the foundation (PSA 118:22).

Narrator: The Pharisees knew Jesus was referring to them in the parable. They wanted to arrest Jesus but they were afraid of the crowd.

Jesus: Destroy this temple and in three days I will raise it up.

Pharisee: It took forty-six years to build it; I'd like to see you try to rebuild it in three days.

Narrator: But Jesus was referring to Himself.

Nicodemus (a Pharisee): We know you are a teacher and prophet because nobody can perform those miracles without God's power. Tell us, is it right to pay taxes to the Roman government?

Jesus (after asking for a coin): Whose face is on this coin?

Nicodemus: Caesar's.

Jesus: Give to Caesar the things that are Caesar's, and to God the things that are God's.

Sadducees: The laws of Moses say that if a man dies without children, his brother should marry the widow so that the man can have heirs. What if each of seven brothers dies without children? Who will be the husband in heaven?

Jesus: In heaven, people do not get married. They will be like the angels and will never die. You Sadducees do not believe in the resurrection. What you are really asking is this: Can you prove there is a resurrection? Moses quoted God as saying, "I am the God of Abraham, Isaac, and Jacob" implying that these prophets were alive.

Nicodemus: Well said!

Scribes: How can He be so learned without having studied?

Narrator: Nicodemus came under the shield of darkness to consult with Jesus and His disciples.

Jesus: My teaching comes from the Father who sent me. Those who speak on their own authority seek self-glory. I seek not my own glory; I seek to glorify my heavenly Father. Those who seek only the glory of Him who sent them will speak the truth. Listen to the truth. Unless you are born again, you cannot enter the kingdom of heaven.

Nicodemus: How can a man be born again?

Jesus: You must be born of water and the Spirit. That which is born of the flesh is flesh, and that which is born of the Spirit is Spirit.

Nicodemus: How is this so? Can a man reenter his mother's womb?

Jesus: If you cannot understand earthly things, how can you understand spiritual things?

Jesus: God loved the world so much that He sacrificed His only begotten Son, so that whoever believed in His Son would never die, but would live forever. God sent His Son into the world to save it, not to condemn it. If you believe, you are saved; if not, you have already been condemned. He who does what is true comes to the light so that everyone can see that his deeds are sanctioned by God. I am the light of the world; those who follow me will not walk in darkness.

Narrator: Later the next day Jesus was preaching in the synagogue.

Pharisees: This man has a demon.

Others: If He is not the Christ, will the real Christ do more than He has done?

Narrator: Jesus watched the rich people pass by the collection plate and drop in some money. Then a poor widow passed by and dropped in two cents.

Jesus (to crowd): This poor woman has given more than all of these rich folks combined. For they have an abundance of wealth and gave but a small portion of it, while this widow gave all the money she had in the world.

Jesus: Woe to you Pharisees, for you tithe but neglect the love of God, and do injustice to your neighbors. You enjoy the front seat, and all the salutations, but you are like an unknown grave that everyone walks over.

Jesus (to crowd): Beware of these people who would cheat a widow out of her money, and then for show recite long prayers. Those who exalt themselves before others shall receive the greater damnation.

Narrator: The Pharisees decided to have Jesus arrested.

Jesus: Moses gave you the Law, why do you disobey the Law? For example, why do you want to arrest and kill me? Regardless, I will be here a little longer and then I will leave. You will look for me but not find me, because I go to Him who sent me. Those who believe in me, from their hearts will flow rivers of living water. Those who do not believe will die in their sin. Those who are of God will hear these words because they come from Him. Those who keep my words will be my disciples, and they will know the truth, and the truth will set them free.

Sadducees: We are not slaves; how could we possibly be set free?

Jesus: Everyone who commits sin becomes a slave to sin. If the Son sets you free, you will be free indeed. If you do not listen to the Son it is because you cannot bear the truth. Instead you believe lies which come from Satan, the father of lies. Those who hear the Word of God and keep it will never die.

Pharisee: Now we know he's possessed. Even Abraham and the prophets died.

Jesus: Your father Abraham rejoiced to see my day.

Scribes: Abraham was dead before you were even born.

Jesus: Truly I say, before Abraham was, I am.

Crowd: He is the Christ!

Others: No, He isn't.

Narrator: They tried to stone Jesus as He left the temple but He slipped through the crowds.

Pharisees (to Scribes): Why didn't you arrest him? Are you led astray as well?

Nicodemus: Do you judge someone without hearing him out?

Pharisees: We don't have to. Besides, prophets don't come from Galilee.

Narrator: Jesus and his disciples passed by a blind man asking for alms.

Thaddaeus: Rabbi, who sinned, this man or his parents, to cause him to be blind?

Jesus: Neither, but that the works of God might be made manifest in him.

Narrator: Jesus spat on the ground, made clay, and put the clay over the blind man's eyes.

Jesus: Go wash yourself in the pool of Siloam.

Narrator: The man returned with perfect vision.

Others: It's the blind beggar. No, it can't be.

Man: It's me all right.

Others: How is it that you can see now?

Man: Jesus healed me.

Narrator: They took the formerly blind man to the Pharisees.

Pharisee: How were you healed?

Narrator: The man told them what Jesus had done.

Pharisees: What do you have to say about Jesus?

Man: He is a prophet.

Pharisee: Jesus can't be of God because he doesn't keep the Sabbath.

Others: How could a sinner perform such miracles?

Narrator: There was division among those present on this issue. The Pharisees sent for the man's parents.

Pharisee: Is this your son who was blind?

Parents: Yes.

Pharisee: We know only Moses. We don't know anything about this Jesus.

Man: Have you ever heard of anyone else healing the blind? If He wasn't from God, He couldn't have done it.

Pharisee: Who are you to teach us?

Narrator: The Pharisees had the man escorted out of the synagogue. Jesus heard about it and found the man.

Jesus: Do you believe in the Son of Man?

Man: Show me who He is so I can believe.

Jesus: I am He.

Man: Lord, I believe.

Jesus: For judgment I came into the world, to make the blind see and to make the sighted blind.

Narrator: Jesus went to the Mount of Olives to preach. On the way he encountered a mob that was going to stone a woman accused of adultery.

Pharisees (to Jesus): According to our law the penalty for adultery is death.

Jesus (picking up a stone): Very well, whoever is without sin may throw the first stone.

Narrator: Slowly, the mob dwindled away from the eldest to the youngest.

Jesus (to woman): Where are your accusers now? Since they will not condemn you, neither will I. Go and sin no more.

Jesus (at Mount of Olives): The people have hidden their eyes, and avoided me upon my visit. The time is coming when their enemies will crush them and destroy this city. Not even one stone will remain standing upon another, because they did not acknowledge my coming.

Crowd: When will this be? What sign will reveal that the time is near?

Jesus: Do not be deceived, for many will claim to be the Messiah or to be a prophet. They will perform feats of magic and will fool many people. You will hear about wars and rumors of wars. There will be earthquakes all over the place. There will be famines, afflictions, and pestilence. The righteous will be persecuted, interrogated, thrown into jail, and crucified. People will betray one another, and wickedness will abound. It will be like the days of Noah and Lot, only worse. The philosophy will be, eat, drink, and be merry. You will be hated for following me. This is the beginning of the time of sorrows, the beginning of the end. A time of great tribulation will come; worse than the world has ever known before or will ever know again.

Jesus: When you see Jerusalem surrounded by its enemies, the desolation is nigh. I am talking about the abomination that makes desolate spoken of by Daniel (DAN 11:31). When this happens, you should head for the hills; there will be no time to pack. Hope it does not happen in winter; it especially will be tough for those who have babies. It will be a time of great mourning. Two men will be working in the field, but just one will be taken. Two women will be weaving, one will be taken and one will not. There will be signs in the heavens also. The sun will be darkened, the moon will be dim, and stars will fall from the sky.

Jesus: The Gospel will need to be preached throughout the world. Do not worry about what to say or do, because the Holy Spirit will provide you with the information when you need it. When you see these things happen, be prepared for my return. Just as trees blossom as a sign that springtime is nigh, so will these signs proclaim the second coming of your Messiah. That generation will not pass until everything I just told you has taken place. Those enduring until the end will be saved.

Jesus: Finally, a sign in heaven will proclaim the return of the Son of Man. You will see Him in the clouds of heaven in all His power and glory. He will send angels to gather the righteous into heaven. Nobody but the Father knows when this will happen, not even the angels, not even the Son of Man. Heaven and earth will eventually pass away, but my words will remain true forever.

Jesus: Then all people will be gathered together. They will be separated like dividing the sheep from the goats, with the sheep on the right and the goats on the left. To those on the right I will say, "Come inherit the kingdom prepared in advance for you, for when I was hungry you fed me, when I was thirsty you gave me a drink, when I was naked and cold you clothed me." The sheep will say, "When did we do this?" I will say, "Whenever you did it to someone else you did it to me." To those on the left I will say, "Depart you cursed ones into the everlasting fire prepared for the devil and his angels, because you did not help your fellow man in need." The goats will inherit eternal torment, and the sheep will inherit eternal bliss.

Narrator: Simon, a Pharisee, invited Jesus to dine with him. Mary (Martha's sister) came with some ointment. She cried on Jesus's feet and wiped them with her hair. Then she kissed His feet and put some of the ointment on them.

Simon: A prophet would know that this is a sinful woman.

Jesus (to Simon): A creditor had two debtors. One owed ten times that of the other. The creditor forgave both their debts. Who was forgiven the most?

Simon: The one who owed the most.

Jesus: Correct. Now, when I entered your house you gave me no water to wash with, yet this woman has washed my feet with her tears and dried them with her hair. You gave me no kiss, yet she has smothered my feet with kisses. You did not anoint my head with oil, yet she has anointed my feet. Therefore, her sins, which are many, are forgiven, for she has shown me great love. Those who are forgiven very little, have little love to show for it.

Jesus (to Mary): Your sins are forgiven.

Narrator: Several people tried to sit at the head of the table.

Jesus: When you are invited to a marriage feast, do not sit at the place of honor. When the host comes to ask you to move to another place of lower honor you will feel humiliated. Instead, choose the place of least honor. When the host comes to ask you to move to another place of greater honor you will be honored before the other guests. For those who exalt themselves will be humbled, and those who humble themselves will be exalted.

Jesus: A king was giving a banquet for his son who was engaged to be married. The king sent his servants to the cities to invite important people. But most of them had some lousy excuse not to attend. Others beat and even killed the servants. The king became angry and had the murderous scoundrels executed and their cities burned. The king told his servants that the others were not worthy to attend the feast, so he sent them all over the country to invite the commoners, the poor, and the handicapped. None of the people on the original guest list were allowed to attend the banquet, but the wedding hall and banquet room were filled nevertheless. For many are called but few are chosen. And when you give a feast, invite people who cannot return the favor such as the lame, maimed, poor, and blind. You will be blessed for your generosity, and will be repaid at the resurrection of the just.

CHAPTER THREE

Maundy Thursday and Good Friday

Narrator: Jesus and the twelve apostles were preparing to celebrate the Passover meal together. Meanwhile, Judas Iscariot already had made a deal with the chief priests to deliver Jesus into their hands for thirty pieces of silver. This fulfilled the prophecy of Zechariah: His price was weighed at thirty pieces of silver (ZEC 11:12).

Jesus: In two days is the feast of Passover and the Son of Man will be betrayed.

Andrew: Where should we prepare the feast?

Jesus: Go to Jerusalem and find a man with a pitcher of water. Tell him, "Our Master's time is nigh and He wants to celebrate Passover in your guest chamber." He will show you a furnished upper room where you will prepare the feast.

Narrator: They did as Jesus instructed. After the twelve apostles had gathered, Jesus poured water into a basin and began to wash and dry each of the apostles' feet.

Peter: You needn't wash my feet.

Jesus: You may not understand why I am doing this, but you will someday. If I do not wash your feet you have no part of me.

Peter: Then wash my hands and head also.

Jesus: If you've washed for supper, then only your feet are dirty. If I wash your feet, you'll be clean all over, but not all of you. Henceforth, you will follow my example and wash each other's feet. Always love one another as I have loved you. If you love me, keep my commandments.

Narrator: Jesus and the twelve were having dinner.

Jesus: I have been anxious to participate in this Passover feast with you. This is the last time I will celebrate Passover until the kingdom of God has come. However, one of you will betray me. Woe to him; he would have been better off never being born.

Disciples: Not me. I would never do such a thing.

Narrator: Jesus dipped a bagel in sauce and gave it to Judas.

Judas: Who, me?

Jesus: You said it yourself. Hurry and get it over with.

Narrator: Judas left. The rest of the apostles were not sure why, but thought he might be running an errand. The disciples were arguing about who was the greatest disciple.

John: Who will be the greatest in your kingdom?

Jesus: I have told you before, the first will be last and the last will be first. Whoever should be first will be the servant of all, for the Son of Man came to serve not to be served.

Jesus: In my Father's house are many mansions. I am going to prepare a place for you. I will appoint you a kingdom as my Father appointed me. You will eat and drink at my table, and you will sit on thrones and judge the twelve tribes of Israel. Do not be troubled. I will return and receive you, so that where I am, there you will be also.

Thomas: We don't know where you're going, so how can we follow?

Jesus: Where I go you cannot go, but you will follow me later. I am the way, the truth and the life. Nobody comes to the Father but by me. If you know me you also know my Father. I will not leave you without hope.

James: How so?

Jesus: The Father will send the Comforter which is the Holy Spirit. The Holy Spirit will tell you everything you need to say and do. He will bring to memory all I have taught you. Do not be afraid, for my peace I leave with you.

Philip: Show us the Father so we'll recognize Him.

Jesus: Have you not been with me long enough to know that you have seen the Father in me? I must leave, and then I'll return for a while, and then I'll leave again to be with the Father. But the Comforter will remain with you. However, the devil, who is the prince of this world, will persist; but abide in me and you will not falter. The branch cannot bear fruit when severed from the vine. Abide in me and you will bear much fruit. Ask the Father anything in my name and it is yours. I have chosen you, and you will be persecuted because of me. You will bear witness to the truth. Although I am leaving, you should rejoice because you know I am going to be with the heavenly Father. I told you about this in advance so when it happened, you'd believe; and you could find peace in a world of tribulation. You'll weep and lament for a while, but your sorrow will turn to joy. You will be glad because you will realize that I overcame the world. And no-one will be able to take that joy from you.

Jesus (looking upward): Father, the hour is come when you glorify the Son so the Son may glorify you. You have given Him power over all flesh. Please help my disciples and your sheep so that they may be one as we are. Keep them from evil, and do not let them lose their way.

Narrator: Then Jesus took a loaf of unleavened bread, blessed it, broke it into pieces, and distributed it to each disciple.

Jesus: Take and eat. This is my body which is given for you. Do this to remember me.

Narrator: Then Jesus took a cup of wine and gave thanks to God.

Jesus: Drink from this cup all of you. This is the New Testament in my blood that is shed for many for the remission of sins. I will not drink wine again until I drink it new with you in my Father's kingdom. There is no greater demonstration of love than when a man lays down his life for his friends.

Jesus: All of you will be offended because of me tonight. This fulfills the prophecy of Zechariah: The shepherd will be struck down and the flock will scatter (ZEC 13:7).

Peter: I will never be offended of you.

Jesus: Tonight, before the rooster crows twice, you will deny knowing me three times.

Peter: I would sooner die. I will never deny you.

Jesus: Satan wanted you, Peter, but I have prayed for you that your faith will not fail. You must continue to strengthen your brothers.

Narrator: After the Passover meal was over, Jesus took Peter, James, and John with him to pray in the Garden of Gethsemane.

Jesus: Watch with me. My soul is exceedingly sorrowful. Wait here while I pray.

Narrator: Jesus went a little further, fell on His knees, hands clenching His face, and prayed.

Jesus: My Father, if possible, let this cup pass from me. But let it be in accordance with your will not mine.

Narrator: Jesus found the apostles sleeping and roused them.

Jesus: Watch and pray that you do not enter into temptation. The spirit is willing but the flesh is weak.

Narrator: Jesus went to pray again. He was deeply distressed, and His sweat became drops of blood. An angel arrived to strengthen and comfort Him.

Jesus: My Father, if this cup cannot pass from me, then let it be so.

Narrator: Jesus found the apostles sleeping again.

Jesus: Sleep now and rest. Behold, the time has come for me to be betrayed into the hands of evil men.

Narrator: Judas approached with a band of vigilantes carrying swords and clubs.

Judas (to army): Arrest the one who I kiss.

Judas (kissing Jesus): Hello, Master.

Jesus: Why are you here Judas? Would you betray me with a kiss?

Narrator: Peter drew his sword and slashed off the ear of the high priest's bodyguard. Jesus picked up the man's ear and placed it back on the man's head, completely healing it.

Jesus: Put your swords away; those who live by the sword will die the same way. Don't you realize I could easily call an army of angels to deliver me? But how could the scriptures be fulfilled then? Do you not see that I must drink this cup? You came with swords and clubs to arrest me as if I was a common thief. Yet I sat daily and preached in the temple and you did not lay a hand on me.

Narrator: The apostles got paranoid and ran off. The mob took Jesus before Caiaphas (the chief priest), the scribes, and the elders. Peter followed them from afar, and sat with the servants in the courtyard so he could see what was going on. They brought several false witnesses to testify against Jesus.

Annas: What about your doctrine?

Jesus: I spoke openly in the synagogues and temples. I have kept nothing secret. If I spoke evil, prove it. If not, why am I being abused?

Witness: He said, "Destroy the temple and I'll rebuild it in three days."

Caiaphas: Why did you say that?

Narrator: Jesus was silent.

Caiaphas: Are you the Christ, the Son of God?

Jesus: You've said it yourself. Hereafter you will find me sitting at God's right hand.

Caiaphas (ripping his clothes): Blasphemy!

Scribes: He deserves the death penalty.

Narrator: They mocked Jesus, spit on Him, and beat Him. Meanwhile, a woman approached Peter outside the gate.

Woman: You were with Jesus of Nazareth.

Peter (walking away toward the porch): You don't know what you are talking about.

Another woman: I've seen you before; you're one of His followers.

Peter: No, I am not.

Malchus (the guy whose ear was chopped off): Surely you were with Jesus. You're from Galilee.

Peter (cursing): I swear I don't know the man.

Narrator: Just then a rooster crowed and Peter realized what he had done. He ran away and wept bitterly. Meanwhile, Judas was returning the money the priests paid him to betray Jesus.

Judas: I've betrayed innocent blood.

Priest: We don't care.

Narrator: Judas threw the money on the floor, went away and hanged himself. The priests would later use the money to buy a potter's field that would become a graveyard for paupers, thereby fulfilling the prophecy of Zechariah (ZEC 11:12–13). After sunrise, Caiaphas led Jesus to Pilate the governor.

Pilate: What is He accused of?

Caiaphas: We wouldn't have brought Him here if he wasn't a troublemaker. He's caused trouble from Galilee to Jerusalem.

Pilate: If He is from Galilee, He's under Herod's jurisdiction, so take Him to Herod.

Narrator: They took Jesus to Herod.

Herod: Let's see a miracle.

Narrator: Jesus was silent. They mocked Jesus, placing a purple robe on Him, pretending He was a king. After they had their fun, they returned Jesus to Pilate.

Pilate: Judge Him according to your Jewish law.

Caiaphas: We're not authorized to put Him to death.

Pilate (to Jesus): Are you the king of the Jews? That's what everyone is saying.

Jesus: My kingdom is not of this world.

Pilate: Then you are a king?

Jesus: You said it yourself. I came to this world to bear witness of the truth. Whoever seeks the truth will listen to me.

Pilate (walking away): What is truth?

Pilate (to Jews): I see no fault in Him. I'll have Him flogged and then turn Him loose. After all, isn't it the custom to free one prisoner this time of year?

Jews: Release Barabbas instead.

Narrator: Pilate took Jesus to the soldiers to have Him flogged. They made a crown of thorns and placed it on Jesus's head. They mocked, spit upon, flogged and beat Him before bringing Him back to Pilate.

Pilate (to Jews): Here He is. What shall I do now?

Jews: Crucify Him!

Pilate: Why? What evil has He done?

Jews: Crucify Him!

Pilate (to Jesus): Who are you anyway?

Narrator: Jesus was silent.

Pilate: Don't you know I have the power to release you or to have you put to death?

Jesus: You have no power against me. The only power you have has been given to you from above.

Pilate (to Jews): He has done nothing that warrants death.

Jews: He claims to be a king. Doesn't that go against Caesar and Rome?

Pilate (washing his hands): Shall I crucify your king?

Jews: Caesar is our king.

Narrator: So, Pilate delivered Jesus to them for crucifixion and released Barabbas. They made Jesus carry His cross until He was too weak and He fell. Then they ordered Simon of Cyrene to carry the cross the rest of the way to Golgotha, which was a hill that resembled a skull. Two thieves were going to be crucified alongside of Jesus. This sign was placed on the cross of Jesus: Jesus of Nazareth, king of the Jews. The soldiers took Jesus's garment and divided it into quarters. They also took His seamless coat and threw dice to see who would win it. This fulfilled the prophecy of David saying that they would cast lots for His clothes (PSA 22:18).

Jesus (to crowd): Do not cry for me, but for your children.

Narrator: They nailed Him to the cross. The third hour passed.

Jesus (to his mother): Behold your son.

Jesus (to John): Behold your mother.

Narrator: Hour four passed.

Jesus: Father, forgive them for they know not what they do.

Jesus: I'm thirsty.

Narrator: They took some vinegar and wet a sponge, and lifted it on a stick to Jesus's mouth. Hour five passed.

Priests (laughing): He saved others and can't even save Himself.

First Thief (to Jesus): If you're the Christ, save yourself and us.

Second thief: Don't you fear God? We deserve our punishment but He is innocent.

Second thief (to Jesus): Lord, remember me when you enter your kingdom.

Jesus: Truly I tell you, today you will be with me in paradise.

Narrator: Hour six passed and it was already dark.

Jesus: My Father, why have you forsaken me? It is finished! Father, into your hands I commend my Spirit.

Narrator: Hour eight passed. The temple veil was ripped from top to bottom. An earthquake trembled and graves were opened. Saints arose from the dead and walked the streets.

Centurion: Surely, He was the Son of God.

Narrator: They broke the legs of the thieves to hasten death, which was the custom, but in Jesus's case they jabbed Him with a spear. Blood and water seeped out signifying that He was already dead, thereby fulfilling the prophecies of David and Zechariah: Not a bone in His body shall be broken (PSA 34:20); and they looked upon Him who was pierced (ZEC 12:10). A righteous Pharisee named Joseph of Arimathaea asked Pilate for Jesus's body. He was given the body of Jesus, which he and Nicodemus had wrapped in linen and embalmed with spices. They laid Jesus's body in an unused sepulcher, accompanied by Mary (Jesus's mother), Mrs. Zebedee, and Mary Magdalene.

Narrator: Jesus was treated shamefully, tortured and murdered so that all people could be freed from sin, thereby fulfilling the prophecies of David (PSA 22) and Isaiah (ISA 53).

Easter and Jesus's Ascension

Narrator: Jesus's triumph was realized during that most holy week in Jerusalem beginning with Palm Sunday and ending with Easter. This fulfilled the prophecy of Daniel: In one week the sacrificial offering was complete, confirming God's covenant to His people and His victory over the one who makes desolate (DAN 9:27).

Narrator: Mary Magdalene, Mary (mother of James and Joses), Salome, Joanna, and others collected spices for they planned on visiting the tomb. Meanwhile, the chief priests and Pharisees went to Pilate.

Pharisee: Jesus said he'd rise from the dead in three days. Seal the grave so His disciples won't steal Him and claim that He arose.

Pilate: Let it be done.

Narrator: A giant stone was rolled in front of the sepulcher and was sealed, blocking the entrance. However, two days later on Easter Sunday, an earthquake moved the stone. The guards shook with fear and became pale. That morning, some women had gone to the cemetery. They found the tomb and saw the stone had been removed. There appeared an angel, with a beaming countenance.

Angel: Do not fear. You seek Jesus? He is not here. He has risen from the dead. Come and see.

Narrator: They went to tell Jesus's disciples who couldn't believe their ears. Peter, John and some of the others ran to the cemetery and checked the grave. They were amazed. Word spread of the extraordinary event, reaching the chief priests and elders. They tried to claim that the body was stolen and even bribed the soldiers to say this to the governor. Meanwhile, Mary Magdalene (whom Jesus had cleansed of seven demons) stayed at the cemetery, and sat by the grave weeping.

Jesus: Why are you crying?

Mary: Where did you place the body of my Master?

Jesus: Mary.

Mary: Master!

Jesus: Do not touch me, because I have yet to return to my Father. Go tell my friends you saw me.

Narrator: Meanwhile, two of Jesus's disciples were traveling to Emmaus to meet with fellow believers there. On the way they were met by a stranger.

Jesus: You look sad.

Cleopas: You must not be from around here. Haven't you heard about Jesus?

Jesus: What about Him?

Narrator: They related the story.

Jesus: Christ had to suffer and die to enter His glory, did He not?

Narrator: Jesus proceeded to quote the scriptures and teach them along the way.

Simon: Stay with us.

Narrator: When they began to dine together, their eyes were opened and they realized it was Jesus with them. As soon as they recognized Him Jesus disappeared.

Cleopas: Weren't our hearts ablaze while He spoke with us and explained the prophecies?

Narrator: They went to tell Jesus's disciples that the Lord had appeared to them. As they were speaking, Jesus appeared among them.

Jesus: Peace be with you.

Narrator: They were afraid.

Jesus: Why are you afraid? Look, I am Jesus. See my hands, my feet, and my side? Do you have anything to eat?

Narrator: They prepared a meal of fish and honeycomb, and they ate.

Jesus: Heed the words of Moses, David, and the prophets, of which I have spoken often, and which had to be fulfilled. I suffered, died, and arose so that all people could be remitted of their sins. You are witnesses that it happened as the prophets said it would. Even as I was sent, so now I am sending you.

Narrator: Jesus breathed on each one.

Jesus: Receive the Holy Spirit. Whoever's sins you forgive they will be forgiven. Whoever's sins you retain they will be retained.

Narrator: Then Jesus vanished. Later that same night, Thomas showed up and they told him what happened.

Thomas: Unless I see Jesus and touch his wounded body, I cannot believe.

Narrator: Eight days later Jesus reappeared to the disciples.

Jesus: Hello Thomas. Do you believe now?

Thomas: My Lord and my God.

Jesus: Blessed are those who have not seen and still believe.

Narrator: Then Jesus vanished again. The disciples went to Galilee by the sea like Jesus had instructed them.

Peter: I'm going fishing.

Narrator: They were fishing all day but had not caught anything. They stayed overnight aboard the boat.

Jesus (on shore): Catch anything?

Peter: No.

Jesus: Cast your net on the other side of the boat.

Narrator: They did this and were overwhelmed with fish. They couldn't even pull the nets aboard. Peter knew it had to be Jesus. He grabbed his coat and swam ashore. The others came in a boat, dragging the nets behind them. They made a fire and roasted some fish.

Jesus: Count the fish.

Peter: The total is 153, all different varieties. Lucky the net didn't break.

Narrator: They ate breakfast.

Jesus (to Peter): Do you love me more than anyone or anything?

Peter: Yes, Lord, you know I do.

Jesus: Feed my lambs. (pause) Do you really love me?

Peter: Of course, I do.

Jesus: Feed my sheep. (pause) Do you love me above all?

Peter (anxiously): Yes, I do, you know I do.

Jesus: Feed my flock. (pause) When you were young you did whatever you pleased. When you are old, you will be carried off as I was.

John: Jesus, who was your betrayer?

Peter: Yes. What will happen to him?

Jesus: If I let him tarry until my return, what is this to you? Just follow me.

John: So, he doesn't have to die?

Jesus: It is not important. Just follow me.

Narrator: Jesus led them to a high mountain.

Jesus: I want you to return to Jerusalem and there you will wait to be baptized by the Holy Spirit. You will receive spiritual power and will witness to all of Judea, Samaria, and the uttermost parts of the earth. You will cast out demons, speak in tongues, and heal the sick. Serpents and poison drink will not harm you.

Narrator: At that time Jesus began to ascend slowly into heaven.

Jesus: All power in heaven and earth is given to me. Go and teach everyone in the world what I have taught you. Baptize them in the name of the Father, Son, and Holy Spirit. Instruct them on the commandments. And remember, I will always be with you, even until the end of time.

Narrator: Jesus disappeared into the clouds. The disciples continued gazing into heaven as two angels appeared with them.

Angel: Why are you staring into heaven? Jesus will return in the same manner in which He just departed.

The Birth of the Christian Church

Narrator: Soon, the day of Pentecost came and the apostles were gathered together preaching in the village square. Suddenly, tongues of fire appeared on each of their heads, and they began to preach in foreign languages. The crowd marveled when hearing the words in their native tongue. Some accused the apostles of being drunk.

Peter: We haven't been drinking. We are fulfilling the prophecy of Joel who testified that God will pour out His Holy Spirit on all people, and your sons and daughters will prophesy; and there will be wonders in heaven and on earth (JOE 2:28–30). We are here as witnesses to Jesus Christ, the Son of God who you crucified, and who God raised from the dead. Remember the words of David: I always saw the Lord before me, and my flesh can now dwell in hope for my soul will not be condemned to death. God said to my Lord, sit at my right hand (PSA 16:9; PSA 110:1). Yes, David your father knew Christ and rejoiced in Him.

Crowd: What should we do?

Peter: Repent and be baptized, every one of you, in the name of Jesus Christ.

Narrator: About three thousand souls were saved that day. The apostles continued in their teaching and fellowship, in the breaking of bread, and in prayer. Many miracles were performed in Jesus's name. And the prophecy of Haggai was fulfilled: I will pour out my Holy Spirit upon them, and I will shake the heavens and earth (HAG 2:6–9).

Narrator: Meanwhile, a particular scriptural scholar who was a Pharisee named Saul, was persecuting Christians all over the region. He was very zealous for God but did not know Jesus and was responsible for murdering His followers, most notably Stephen. One day Saul was traveling on the road to Damascus where he intended to continue terrorizing Christians. He was struck by lightning and the voice of the Lord called to Him. He dropped to the ground, completely blind.

Jesus: Saul, why do you persecute me?

Saul: Who are you?

Jesus: I am Jesus.

Narrator: For three days Saul could not see. The Lord sent Ananias to Saul to baptize him. After being baptized, Saul regained his sight. He then became Paul, a devoted teacher and evangelist, replacing Judas as the twelfth man called personally by Christ to be an apostle. Paul later wrote many treatises in the New Testament and spread the good news of the Gospel of Jesus Christ to the Gentiles.

Jesus's Travels

CHILDHOOD: Bethlehem, Egypt, Nazareth, Jerusalem

MINISTRY:

Jordan River (John the Baptist)

Wilderness (Satan's temptations)

Nazareth (Jesus rejected by fellow Jews)

Cana (Jesus's first miracle)

Capernaum (Jesus recruits Peter, Andrew, James, John, Philip)

Bethsaida (homes of Peter, Andrew, Philip, Nathanael)

Capernaum (Jesus recruits Matthew)

Jerusalem (Jesus embarrasses the Pharisees)

Samaria (woman at Jacob's well)

Galilee (Sermon on the Mount, and feeding of five thousand)

Capernaum (centurion's servant healed)

Sea of Galilee (Jesus calms the storm)

Gadara (Jesus casts out Legion)

Sea of Galilee (Jesus walks on water)

Tyre and Sidon (spreading the good news)

Sea of Galilee (feeding of four thousand)

Decapolis, Dalmanutha, Bethsaida

Caesarea Philippi (Peter confesses Christ)

Galilee (Jesus's transfiguration)

Samaria border (ten lepers healed)

Jericho (Jesus heals the blind)

Bethany (Jesus raises Lazarus)

Jerusalem (Last Supper and Jesus's trial)

Sea of Galilee (Ascension of Christ)

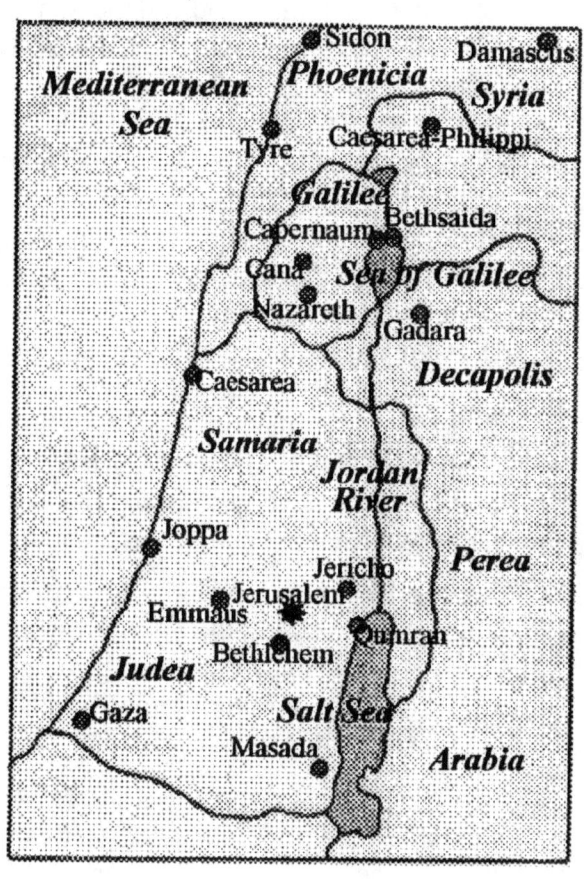

Lesson: The Branch

The Vineyard. The kingdom of God is often compared to a vineyard in the Bible. We are all vines in God's vineyard. He planted the primary Branch on Earth to connect us to Himself and His righteousness. Unfortunately, many people, including God's chosen Israel, did not cling to the Branch; anyone letting go of it will wither in die like a broken limb.

- ISA 5:1–13 ~ Isaiah compared the house of Israel to a vineyard: My most beloved has a vineyard on a very fruitful hill. He fenced it, landscaped it, and planted the choicest vine. However, it bore wild grapes, despite the care that was taken. Therefore, the vineyard will be trampled down, and weeds and briers will grow; the rain will cease and the vineyard will wither. This vineyard belongs to the Lord of Hosts; the vineyard represents the house of Israel and those who have fallen from God's grace.
- JER 2:21 ~ God planted a noble vine, a wholly perfect seed. Why then, have you grown into a degenerate plant from a strange vine?

The Branch. The main Branch of the vineyard is God's only Son who became a human to communicate to us God's wisdom. Thus, the Branch is Jesus Christ, God in the flesh to whom we must remain connected to stay alive forever. If we become grafted to Jesus Christ, we will become like Him and bear good fruit, sowing His seed and increasing the harvest.

- PSA 80:15–18 ~ King David praised God for the vineyard which He planted, and for the Branch, God's right hand and the Son of Man, who God made strong for Himself.
- ISA 4:2 ~ Isaiah spoke of a Branch, beautiful and glorious, bearing excellent fruit of the Spirit.
- ISA 11:1; ISA 27:6; ISA 37:31; JER 23:5 ~ We are informed by Isaiah and Jeremiah that the righteous Branch or Root would be a descendant of Jacob, Judah, Jesse, and David.
- ZEC 3:8–9 ~ The Branch is God's servant who will build God's temple, who will bear God's glory, and who will sit on God's throne as ruler and priest.
- JOH 15:1–6 ~ Jesus said, "I am the true vine; others are branches of this vine. If you do not abide in the Branch you will die, just like a branch that is cut from the vine withers and dies. If you abide in the Branch you will bear much fruit. Branches of the vine which don't bear fruit are chopped away and burned in the fire."
- ROM 11:16 ~ If the root is holy, so are the branches.
- GAL 5:18,22–23 ~ If you are led by the Spirit you are not under the Law. The fruits of the Spirit include love, joy, peace, patience, kindness, gentleness, goodness, self-control, and faith. Against these things, there is no law

The Harvest. God's seed is Jesus Christ. Those sowing God's seed will be sharing the good news and working the vineyard which is the mission field, and will reap what they sow. The vine will be replenished and grow into a larger vineyard, also illustrated as the body of Christ. Those who are not enjoined with Christ and bearing good fruit will perish; they will become severed from the vine.

- MAT 7:17–19 ~ A good tree bears good fruit; a corrupt tree bears evil fruit. A good tree cannot bear bad fruit and a bad tree cannot bear good fruit. Any tree that does not bear good fruit will be cut down at the roots and burned in the fire.
- MAT 20:1–16 ~ Jesus told a parable about the vineyard: The kingdom of heaven is like the owner of the vineyard who went to hire laborers. He agreed to pay them the usual wages for a full day of work. He continued to hire laborers all day, agreeing to pay them a fair wage for the time they worked. When evening came, the owner brought the laborers together and paid

them wages for a full day of work. Those who had worked all day were angry because they felt they deserved more than those who had worked only part of the day. The owner replied, "You received the agreed salary, so you have no room to complain. Am I not free to do what I want with what is mine? Do you have an evil eye for the others because I was generous to them?" In summary, the first will be last and the last will be first, for many are called but few are chosen.

Everyone is called to work in God's vineyard. That is, we all are called to faith in Christ. Everyone who accepts the call will receive the same reward, which is salvation through faith in Jesus Christ, regardless of when they repented and became true to God. Jesus Christ is the source of our faith, life, sustenance, and salvation. He had to die, but was resurrected to live again forever, so that we too could be raised from the dead and inherit eternal life. In response to these gifts, we should sow the seed of righteousness, and nurture and cultivate the vineyard.

- JER 11:19–23 ~ I was taken like a lamb to the slaughter. They had plotted against me, saying, "Let's destroy the tree that bears the fruit; let's cut him down, so that he will not be remembered." But they will be the ones who are destroyed and forgotten.
- MAR 12:1–9 ~ Jesus told the parable of the vineyard owner: The owner of the vineyard traveled to a far country and leased his vineyard to others. At harvest time, the owner sent a servant to collect some of the profits of the vineyard. The servant was beaten and sent away. The owner sent other servants that either were beaten and sent away or killed. Then the owner sent his only beloved son to the tenants, thinking that they would treat him with more respect. The tenants killed the son, figuring that if they killed the only heir, they would inherit the vineyard. What do you think the owner will do to the tenants? He will destroy the tenants and lease his vineyard to others. This parable reveals the meaning of the prophecy, "The stone that was rejected became the chief cornerstone."

The First Fruits. Jesus Christ represents the vineyard owner's only son who was rejected and killed. Those who killed Him will be destroyed. Those who work faithfully in God's vineyard and share their first fruits with Him will become children of God, and hence, the heirs of the vineyard. Jesus Christ is the first fruits from the harvest of God's vineyard. That is, Christ is the resurrection, the first to conquer death. His resurrection results in the resurrection of the rest of the vineyard, including all human beings. The righteous who stayed faithful and fruitful will be raised to inherit eternal life; the wicked who were cut off will be raised to inherit eternal fire.

- JOH 11:25–26 ~ Jesus said, "I am the resurrection and the life. Those who believe in me, though they were dead, yet shall they live. Whoever believes in me will never die."
- 1 CO 15:20,23 ~ Now is Christ raised from the dead, becoming the first fruits of those who have died. The next to be raised will be Christ's own, when He returns.
- GAL 4:6–7 ~ Because you are His children, God has sent the Spirit of His Son into your hearts. Therefore, you are no longer servants but children of God, and heirs with Christ.
- REV 14:18–20 ~ The angel was commanded to take his sickle and gather all the clusters on the vine, for the grapes were fully ripe. And he put the grapes into the winepress of God's wrath. And blood came out of the winepress, enough to fill a two hundred-mile valley up to the bridles on a horse.
- REV 20 ~ When Christ returns, the first fruits of God's chosen people will be resurrected. The next resurrection will occur after the millennial reign. Everyone will be judged according to the fruit that they produced, and whether it was good fruit or bad fruit.

The first fruits of the harvest belong to God. We should, therefore, present the first fruits of our profits or increase to the church and to the needy. This is the least we can do to assist in God's work here on earth in His vineyard. By serving them we are serving God.

- EXO 23:19 ~ The first fruits of your harvests shall be given to God.
- PRO 3:9 ~ Honor the Lord with the first fruits of all your income.
- MAL 3:10–11 ~ Bring your tithes to God, and He will pour His blessings upon you, to the degree that you will not have enough room for them all. And He will rebuke the evil one and those parasites that would devour or destroy the fruits of your labor.
- MAT 25:14–31 ~ Jesus told a parable about God's kingdom: The kingdom of heaven is like an investor who called his servants together and gave each of them some of his fortune to invest for him. He gave them varying amounts, depending on their abilities. After a year or so, the investor returned to see how his money had been invested. The man who had received five portions doubled his money, as did the man who had received two portions. The boss was very happy saying, "Since you have been faithful with but a few things, I will make you both rulers over many things." The man who had received one portion didn't invest it but kept it hidden away for fear of losing it. The investor was irate saying, "The least you could have done is put it in the bank where it would have yielded a modest amount of interest." Then he ordered his portion to be taken away and given to the man who had made the most of the boss's investment, saying, "To those that have, more will be given; to those that don't have, the rest will be taken away." Then, the unwise servant was thrown into the dungeon.

Therefore, don't hide what God has given to you, especially your knowledge of salvation. Let God's love shine in you and spread the good news of the Gospel whenever you can. Share God's love and truth with others and these will grow in them, and they will share their gifts. And the harvest will multiply in accordance with God's will into every corner of the globe.

There are many people who are hungry, not just for food but for love. Let us, who are richly blessed, provide for others who are in need of sustenance, not just physically, but also spiritually. And for your acts of service God will preserve you in body, mind, and spirit until the end of time. We are in this together, joined in Spirit by God's never-ending love.

- LUK 6:38 ~ Give and it shall be given to you in abundance, overflowing; for the same measure that you give is returned unto you.
- PHP 4:19 ~ God will supply all of your needs according to the riches of His glory through Jesus Christ.

Blest Be the Tie that Binds

Blest be the tie that binds our hearts in Christian love;
The fellowship of kindred minds is like to that above.

Before our Father's throne we pour our ardent prayers;
Our fears, our hopes, our aims are one, our comforts and our cares.

We share each other's woes, each other's burdens bear;
And often for each other flows the sympathetic tear.

When we are called to part it gives us inward pain;
But we shall still be joined in heart, and hope to meet again.

Lesson: The Sacrificial Lamb

<u>The Old Covenant was the Law</u>. In Old Testament times, God's people demonstrated their faith by obeying God's commandments. But His people were imperfect; even the most righteous people disobeyed God. Therefore, sacrificial offerings were made as a demonstration of repentance and thankfulness, and as an atonement for sin. God made covenants with those that eagerly sought Him, were faithful, and obeyed His Law.

- GEN 6:18; GEN 9:15–16 ~ God made a covenant with Noah, whose family was spared because of his great faith.
- GEN 17:1–2,7; GEN 22:1–3,7–13,16–17 ~ God made a covenant with Abraham, who loved God so much he was willing to sacrifice his first and only legitimate son and heir. Abraham's willingness to sacrifice his only son showed he had a strong faith in God. When Isaac asked his father where the lamb was that was to be sacrificed, Abraham told him that God would provide a lamb, hiding the fact that Isaac was to be the offering. God spared Isaac, however. Instead of sacrificing Isaac, Abraham sacrificed a ram that was caught in the underbrush. God rewarded Abraham's faith with descendants as numerous as the stars. Isaac become the father of Israel (Jacob). God's covenant with Abraham resulted in Israel becoming a great nation, chosen by God.
- EXO 12:3,7–8,12–13 ~ God made a covenant with Moses and the Israelites. The Israelites were commanded by God to sacrifice an unblemished male lamb (ram) and sprinkle the lamb's blood on the door. This act of faith spared the firstborn of Israel from God's curse on the Egyptians. The lamb's blood signified that the God would protect the righteous from the Angel of Death on this the first Passover.
- EXO 24:7–8 ~ Moses preached about the everlasting covenant which God was going to make with all believers. After the peace offerings and burnt offerings were sacrificed, Moses sprinkled the blood of the offering on the alter and on the people, to signify that their sins would be cleansed by the blood of the New Covenant.
- EXO 29:15–35 ~ Sanctification of the priest required sacrificing a bull and two rams without blemish, as well as unleavened bread.
- LEV 1:2–4 ~ An atonement offering was an animal from the herd (bovine) and the flock (sheep).
- LEV 4 ~ God's Law to Moses directed the Israelites to frequently make sacrificial offerings as an atonement for sin.

God revealed the New Covenant to Abraham, Moses, David, Isaiah, Jeremiah, Ezekiel, Daniel, Zechariah, Malachi, and others. God told these prophets that the New Covenant would take the form of a Messiah, who would lead all people to God. The blood of the Messiah would be shed to atone for the sin of the world. Thus, Messiah was foretold to offer Himself as a sacrifice unto death.

- LUK 1:68,71–73,79 ~ <u>The New Covenant is Jesus Christ.</u>

Jesus explained His mission to His apostles, and their testimony comprises the New Testament which is a testimony of the New Covenant.

- ROM 10:4,9; ROM 11:26–27; HEB 8:7; HEB 9:22 ~ The New Covenant in Jesus Christ replaced the Old Covenant of the Law. This is because the Law was imperfect. Jesus, who was perfect under the Law, sacrificed Himself. His blood now provides the perfect atonement that cleanses us from sin and makes us pure.

- HEB 9:1–10,18 ~ The first covenant included rules concerning service to the Lord and the operation of a sanctuary for worship and prayer. This was a facility made by man. Part of the covenant provided for the offering of gifts and sacrifices. But such sacrifices were insufficient to make the offerer's conscience perfect before God. This is why Christ the High Priest came. He was a divine and perfect sanctuary, not a sanctuary made by man but by the Holy Spirit. Christ obtained eternal redemption for us, not by the blood of sacrificial offerings but by His own blood. If the blood of sacrifices could sanctify and purify, in accordance with the Old Covenant, how much more the blood of Christ can purify and sanctify! Christ, who was without blemish (sin) offered Himself, to purge our consciences from dead works to serve the living God. Therefore, He is the mediator of the New Covenant; for by His death, the redemption and inheritance promised in the Old Covenant is realized. The Old Covenant was also dedicated with blood, for when Moses had finished reading from the Book of the Law, he took the blood of the sacrifice and sprinkled it on the book, the altar, and the people saying, "This is the blood of the everlasting covenant which God has prescribed for all people." Almost everything under the Law can be purged with blood, and without the shedding of blood there can be no remission. Christ must have suffered often since the beginning of time, but now He has abolished sin once and for all through His self-sacrifice. Just as it is necessary for all to die and then to be judged, so is it possible to be saved because Christ has taken our sins upon Himself. So, the Law, which pointed to the good things that were to come, could never with its continuous sacrifices make the offerer perfect before God; otherwise, the people would have been able to cease the offerings. The blood of such sacrifices could not cleanse the entire soul. God did away with the first covenant so He could establish the second, which provides for the sanctification of all people for all time, through the offering of the body of Jesus Christ. Christ offered one sacrifice for sins that would last forever, and now He sits at the right hand of God. Through that one offering, He has made eternally perfect those He has sanctified. The Holy Spirit has been a witness of this fact in both covenants. This is the meaning of the scripture, "This is the covenant I will make with my people after those days: I will put my laws in their hearts and write them in their minds, and I will remember their sins no longer." Hence, never again will a sacrificial offering need to be made to atone for sin, for Christ paid the price for humankind to last for all time.

Relationships between the Old and New Covenants

Satan tried to destroy both the Old and the New Covenants. He wanted to steal away the free gift that God gave us by His grace, namely our salvation. He wanted to destroy those sent by God to deliver this message to His people.

- EXO 2 ~ Pharaoh tried to destroy all the male babies born of the Israelites. Moses lived to establish with God the Old Covenant of atonement by obedience to the Law.
- EXO 12 ~ Pharaoh experienced the very curse He imposed on the Israelites, when his first born was taken by the Angel of Death.
- MAT 2 ~ Herod tried to destroy Jesus by killing all the babies in Bethlehem. Jesus lived to establish the New Covenant of Grace. Herod was cursed to die for his wicked and unsuccessful decree.
- REV 12:4–5 ~ The dragon stood before the woman, in an attempt to devour the child that she was about to deliver. She gave birth to a Son, who would rule all nations; and her child was brought up to God to sit on His throne.

Justification by faith in the Old Testament was obtained by observing the Law and by presenting burnt offerings to God. With the New Testament, justification can only be obtained through faith in Jesus Christ. In Abraham's covenant, Abraham's son and heir Isaac was spared, resulting in the birth of the nation of Israel. In Moses's covenant, the firstborn of Israel was spared during the first Passover. In the New Covenant, believers are spared, because the firstborn and only Son of God was sacrificed.

Christ became the blood offering instead of Isaac, and instead of the Passover lamb. The blood of Christ now provides the atonement previously offered by the blood of burnt offerings. His blood cleanses our hearts like laundry soap cleans clothes; His blood purifies our souls like a refiner's fire purifies gold. Christ's blood will subsequently become the fire that tests all men's souls for purity.

- PSA 66:10 ~ You, Lord, have proven us; you have tried us like silver is tried.
- ISA 48:10 ~ Behold, I have refined you, but not as silver; I have chosen you in the furnace of affliction.
- ZEC 13:9 ~ I will bring the third part through the fire and refine them as silver, and try them as gold. They will call upon my name and I will hear them. I will say, "These are my people," and they will say "the Lord is my God."
- MAL 3:1–3 ~ Messiah is compared to the refiner's fire and the fuller's soap. And He will sit as a refiner and purifier of silver, and purify the sons of Levi, and purge them as gold and silver that they may offer to the Lord an offering in righteousness.
- MAT 3:11 ~ The blood of Christ represents the refiner's fire that purifies one's very soul.
- 2 CO 5:17,21 ~ If we believe in the atonement provided in the blood of Christ, we are saved from sin and death and we become new creatures.

Holy Week. Interestingly, many significant sacrifices (all using young male sheep) have occurred during the same Holy Week. In the Old Testament, this week included the feasts of the Passover, Unleavened Bread, and First Fruits, lasing a total of eight days; Jews have celebrated these feasts annually by eating the Passover meal (also called Seder supper) of which the main course was lamb; unleavened bread and wine also were served with this meal. In the New Testament, Holy Week included Palm Sunday, Maundy Thursday, Good Friday, and Easter Sunday. Christ, who is the Passover Lamb, is celebrated in like manner by Christians for eight days.

- MAT 26:2,17–20 ~ Jesus said, "You know that in two days will be the feast of the Passover, and the Son of Man will be betrayed to be crucified." Now the first day of the feast of Unleavened Bread, the disciples asked Jesus where they should prepare the feast of the Passover, so Jesus directed them where to make everything ready. That evening, Jesus and the twelve assembled for the feast. (Later that night Jesus was betrayed, and the next morning He was tried and crucified).

In the OT, the body of Christ is reflected in the feast of Unleavened Bread and the blood of Christ is reflected in the feast of Passover. Unleavened bread, or bread without yeast, signifies the body without sin, representing Jesus Christ. Christ purged us of our sin, making us pure like Him. In the NT, the body and blood of Christ were offered to the apostles during the first Holy Communion, and then offered to the world during Jesus's crucifixion, just as the blood of the lamb was offered during the first Passover. Jews and Christians celebrate every anniversary of Holy Week, often with a Seder supper. Unmistakably, this is not a coincidence; it is a commemoration of the covenants made by God with His people. All who celebrate God and His Son are among His people; and this celebration will continue without end.

- LEV 23:5–6 ~ The feasts of the Passover and Unleavened Bread are described, during which faith offerings are to be made.
- MAT 26:26–28 ~ The Eucharist is described which occurred subsequent to the Last Supper. Jesus said, "Take and eat, this is my body; take and drink, this is my blood of the New Covenant, shed for you for the forgiveness of sins."
- JOH 6:30–35,51–58 ~ The people said to Jesus, "Can you show us a sign to convince us that we should believe you, like when our fathers ate manna in the desert?" Jesus answered, "The manna from heaven didn't come from Moses; it came from God who gives you the true bread from heaven. The bread of life comes from heaven and gives life to the world. I am the bread of life; whoever comes to me will never hunger again and whoever believes in me will never thirst again. The bread I give is my flesh, and I will give it for the life of the world. Unless you eat the body and drink the blood of the Son of Man, you have no life. If you eat my body and drink my blood, you live in me and I in you; and you will have eternal life, for I will raise you up the last day. Mine is not like the manna from heaven, for whoever eats the bread I give will live forever."
- 1 CO 5:7 ~ Throw out the old leavened dough and become a new dough, without yeast; for that is what you have become because of the sacrifice of Christ who is the Passover Lamb.
- EPH 5:26 ~ We are cleansed from sin by the washing of water and the Word who is Christ.

In the OT, the resurrection of Christ is reflected in the feast of the First Fruits, Christ being the first fruits of those raised from the dead to live forever with God. Christ's resurrection occurred on the first Easter, in conjunction with the feast of the First Fruits. His resurrection signifies that all believers will, like Christ, be raised from the dead to inherit eternal life in the kingdom of heaven.

- LEV 23:10–12 ~ The feast of the First Fruits is described in which offerings and tithes are given. During that feast, a male lamb is sacrificed.
- JOH 11:25–26 ~ Jesus said, "I am the resurrection and the life. Those who believe in me, though they were dead, yet shall they live."
- 1 CO 15:20–23,44 ~ Christ has been raised, the first fruits of those who have died, so that we too may obtain a new life.
- GAL 4:5–7 ~ Believers in Christ will become children of God and fellow heirs to His kingdom.

The Lamb of God. Jesus is the unblemished male, sacrificial lamb. He is represented by the ram sacrificed by Abraham, and He is represented by the unblemished lamb sacrificed by the Israelites during the first Passover. Instead of Abraham sacrificing his only son and heir, and instead of the Israelites sacrificing a lamb to save their first born, it was God's first and only son, the Lamb of God, who would be sacrificed to atone for the sin of the world. Thus, all these sacrifices in the OT are a shadow of Jesus Christ who is the Passover Lamb.

- JOH 1:15,25–29,32–36 ~ John the Baptist preached about the coming of Christ and addressed Him as the Lamb of God.
- ACT 8:32 ~ Jesus Christ was led as a sheep to the slaughter.
- 1 PE 1:19 ~ Peter describes Christ as a sacrificial lamb without blemish.
- REV 5–22 ~ Jesus Christ is depicted throughout the book of Revelation as the Lamb who was slain, and who now sits upon the throne of God.

<u>The Good Shepherd</u>. In addition to being the sacrificial lamb, Jesus Christ is also the Good Shepherd who dies to save His sheep. Then He returns to gather His sheep together. The Good Shepherd is the protector. He protects us from evil and death just like the Israelites were protected by the blood of the lamb during the first Passover (EXO 12). Note that King David was originally a shepherd, and his descendant Jesus Christ inherited David's throne and is our King and Shepherd forever.

- PSA 23 ~ The Good Shepherd is the one who always protects and cares for His sheep.
- ISA 44:28 ~ He is my appointed Shepherd and He will do everything I (God) ask. He will build Jerusalem, and lay the foundation of the temple.
- EZE 34:5–12,23–24 ~ The sheep were scattered because there was no shepherd. The sheep were hunted and killed. Beware you shepherds, for I (God) will require my flock, and I will deliver them. I will find every last one of them. As a shepherd searches for His flock when they become scattered, so I will find my sheep and deliver them from danger on that dark and cloudy day. I will set one Shepherd over them and He will feed them. I will be their God and my servant David will be their prince (referring to the ancestor of David who will inherit the throne, namely Messiah).
- ZEC 13:7 ~ They will strike down the Shepherd and the sheep will scatter. (also MAT 26:31).
- MAT 25:32,46 ~ The Son of God will gather everyone together, and will separate them, as a shepherd separates the sheep from the goats. The sheep will inherit eternal life, but the goats will inherit eternal punishment.
- JOH 10:1–2,7,14–18; JOH 10:27–28 ~ Jesus described Himself to the apostles as the Good Shepherd who lays down His life for His sheep, and who comes back to find His lost sheep, gathering them together to live under His protection and care forever.
- JOH 21:16–17 ~ Jesus implores Peter three times to feed His sheep and to feed His lambs.
- HEB 13:20 ~ Jesus is the Great Shepherd who brings salvation to His sheep.

Are further sacrifices to God necessary? Not for sin. But we still are supposed to give of ourselves to others and to God, offering the first fruits of our income to the church and sacrificing ourselves to Christ. Further, we still are obligated to abide by God's laws. However, we cannot be saved by doing these things; only by faith in Christ can we come to the knowledge of salvation, through which we give generously of ourselves in gratitude.

- GEN 14:18–20 ~ Abraham was the first to give tithes.
- EXO 23:19 ~ Moses instructed the Israelites to give to God the first fruits of their labor.
- PRO 3:9 ~ Honor the Lord by giving Him the first part of your income.
- MAL 3:10 ~ The Lord says, "Bring tithes of all your income to the storage room so that there will be plenty in my house, and prove to yourself that I will open the windows of heaven and pour upon you so many blessings that you will not have room for them all."
- MAT 5:17–19 ~ Jesus said, "I didn't come to destroy the Law, I came to fulfill the Law. Not one little bit of the Law will be removed until heaven and earth have passed away. Whoever breaks even the least of the commandments will be considered among the least in heaven. Whoever obeys the Law and teaches others to do the same will be considered great in heaven."
- LUK 6:38 ~ Give and it shall be given to you in abundance, overflowing; for the same measure that you give is returned unto you.
- ROM 12:1 ~ Give yourself to God. Let yourself be a living sacrifice.
- 2 CO 9:7 ~ Give, not reluctantly or out of necessity, for God loves a cheerful giver.

Lesson: Imagine

In this lesson you must use your imagination. We are going to play a little game of make-believe. It is very easy to do, especially for children.

First, try to imagine that you are a shepherd living some two thousand years ago. Imagine that it's late at night. There you are, reclining on a grassy hill next to a fellow shepherd. Your flock is congregated on one side of the hill and your colleague's flock is on the other side of the hill. It's been a long day and you are close to nodding off. As you gaze heavenward at the stars you observe an unusual astronomical phenomenon. Perhaps there are a few planets that appear clustered together in the sky, or a comet passing overhead. It is a beautiful thing to behold.

Suddenly, an intense light appears directly above you. The ground seems to glow around you as the light descends upon you and your companion. You sit up in wonderment, trying to determine if this is really happening or if it is a dream. As the light comes closer you become afraid. You look at your companion who has the same fearful look in his eyes. Then, an angel appears with spectacular radiance and speaks to you both, saying, "Don't be afraid, I have come to tell you some terrific news." You know it must be something important so you listen with undivided attention and anticipation. The angel declares, "At this moment, a Savior is being born in that little town nearby, and He is Christ the Messiah." Immediately, the entire sky is illuminated by the presence of thousands of angels and your ears are filled with beautiful music as the massive heavenly choir sings praises to God.

Were you able to conjure this vision in your mind? The interesting thing is, this really happened to some lowly shepherds on the first Christmas Day. It was the miracle of Christ's First Advent.

- LUK 2:8–14 ~ There were shepherds watching their flocks that night in the hills nearby. An angel of the Lord appeared to them, and the glory of God shined all around them. The shepherds were terrified. The angel told them, "Don't be afraid, I bring you good news that will be of great joy to all people on earth. Today, in the city of David, a Savior is born who is Christ the Lord. This is a sign to you: You will find a baby wrapped in cloths and lying in a manger." Suddenly, a great multitude of angels appeared in the heavens, praising God and singing, "Glory to God in the highest, and on earth peace and goodwill to all people."

After the shepherds received this news, they rushed down to Bethlehem and witnessed a very momentous event. Put yourselves in their shoes, or sandals, for a moment. Imagine that, for generations you and your people have been praying for God's Messiah to come, and now you receive notice that He has arrived. Who wouldn't drop everything and run to see Him? Nobody told them where to go, but you can bet that the Star of Bethlehem and the Holy Spirit guided them directly to the stable where Christ was born. And there they found the Christ child, just as the angel had told them. And what did they do next? They went all over town proclaiming the great news that they had been informed about and had witnessed firsthand.

- LUK 2:15–18,20 ~ When the angels left, the shepherds said to each other, "Let's go to Bethlehem and see this great miracle which the Lord has made known to us." They hurried to Bethlehem and found Mary and Joseph, and the baby lying in a manger. Afterwards, they spread the word to everyone they met concerning the marvelous things they had seen and experienced. And everyone who heard it was amazed at what the shepherds said. The shepherds returned to their flocks, glorifying and praising God for all that they had heard and seen, just as the angel had revealed.

Did you ever have great news, and you just couldn't wait to tell someone? Suppose there was a marriage or a birth in your family; or suppose you got promoted or you received a raise in salary; maybe you passed a difficult exam or you made good grades at school; or maybe you landed a big deal or got the job you've always wanted. At the moment you receive the fabulous news you can't wait to tell everyone. You'll even tell total strangers because you are so excited.

Shouldn't it be the same way concerning the good news of Jesus Christ? Is not the birth of Christ, His life, death, and resurrection the greatest news you ever received in your entire life? "Go tell it on the mountain, over the hills, and everywhere," like the Christmas carol states. Tell everyone you meet that Jesus Christ is alive! And they will marvel just as those who heard the shepherds' announcement. Imagine, if everyone who heard the good news shared it with someone. It wouldn't take long for everyone to know that Jesus Christ is Lord, to the glory of God the Father.

- MAT 28:19–20 ~ Jesus told His disciples, "Go into every nation and teach the people all that I have taught you. Baptize them in the name of the Father, Son, and Holy Spirit. Remember, I'll always be with you, even until the end of time."
- ROM 8:16 ~ The Holy Spirit is a witness with our spirits that we are the children of God.
- 1 PE 4:10 ~ Whoever has received the gift of salvation in Christ should share that gift with others, as a steward of God's eternal grace.

Besides, it's not hard to find God; you don't need directions or a road map. You can reach out for Him wherever you are and He is there. In fact, if you seek Him, He'll find you. You can knock, and as your knuckles rap on the door it will swing open. You can ask anything of God, and before you speak the words, He will have answered your call. He so eagerly wants you to find Him that all you need to do is say His name. If your desire is in God, you will never feel alone because He will never leave you.

- DEU 4:29–31 ~ If you seek God with all your heart and soul you will find Him. If you are distressed, even in the latter times, turn to God and obey His commandments. God is merciful and He will never abandon you or destroy you; He will never forget the covenant He made with your forefathers.
- ISA 55:6–7 ~ Seek the Lord while He may be found; call upon Him while He is near. Let the wicked forsake their evil ways and their unrighteous thoughts, and return to the Lord; and He will have mercy on them and will pardon them abundantly.
- MAT 7:7 ~ Jesus taught: Ask and you will receive. Seek and you will find. Knock and the door will be opened.
- JOH 10:1–2,7,14–18; JOH 10:27–28 ~ Jesus described Himself to the apostles as the Good Shepherd who lays down His life for His sheep, and who comes back to find His lost sheep, gathering them together to live under His protection and care forever.

Now let us visualize another scenario. Imagine that you are going about your daily routine, and you take a moment to stop and "smell the roses." Suddenly you feel light as a feather. It seems like you are floating on air. You gaze into heaven and notice the clouds are stirring. An eerie glow appears clear across the sky. Next, you hear voices of angels and trumpets blaring. An intense light descends from the clouds coming closer and closer. And if that isn't weird enough, you observe bodies of the dead arising from the grave. While they ascend into heaven, you begin to ascend. And you meet the Lord Jesus Christ face-to-face high up there in the bright sky. Next, you join with the entire multitude of saints and heavenly angels singing praises to God.

Is this not a strange scene? Yet, it is going to happen, perhaps not exactly in the way just envisioned. It is the miracle of Christ's Second Advent. This is why we celebrate the season of advent prior to Christmas. We anticipate Christ's return, and cherish the promise that He will come for us and carry us with Him to heaven.

- MAT 24:31 ~ Jesus said, "At the great sound of the trumpet, God will send His angels to gather His elect together from the four winds and one end of heaven to the other."
- ACT 1:11 ~ The angel said, "Men of Galilee, why do you gaze into heaven. Jesus, who you just saw ascend into heaven, will return the very same way."
- 1 TH 4:16–17 ~ The Lord will descend from heaven with a shout, with the voice of the archangel, and with a blast from the trumpet of God. Then the dead in Christ will rise first. Those who remain alive in Christ will rise to join the others in the clouds, meeting the Lord in the sky. Those chosen by Christ will live with Him forevermore.
- 1 CO 15:51–52,54 ~ Here is a mystery of God: We will not all sleep (die) but we will all be changed. Suddenly, when the last trumpet sounds, Christ's own, whether dead or alive, will arise without corruption and be changed. Hence, the corruptible will have become incorruptible and the mortal will have become immortal. Then the statement "death is swallowed up in victory" will be true.
- REV 10:7 ~ In the days when the seventh angel is about to sound his trumpet, the mystery of God will be accomplished, just as He announced through His servants the prophets.

There are three significant things that occur during this great day, which marks the end of time as we know it. First, Christ descends from heaven. Then those who are dead in Christ arise from the grave. Next, those who are alive in Christ are joined with them in the sky. Thus, Christ's Second Coming, the Resurrection, and the Rapture each will occur in rapid succession before our very eyes whether alive or dead in a single moment of time. Can you imagine that? It will be every bit as astonishing as when Christ showed Himself the first time.

- ISA 26:19 ~ The dead will live; along with my dead body they will arise. Awake and sing all of you who abide in the dust, for the earth will toss out its dead.
- DAN 12:1 ~ Michael the great prince will stand for God's people. There will be a time of tribulation worse than ever before or ever again. But God's elect will be delivered, all whose names are written in the Book of Life.
- MAT 24:22,31,40–42 ~ Unless those days (of tribulation) are shortened, none will survive. But only for the elect's sake, those days will be shortened. And He will send His angels when the great trumpet sounds, to gather His elect from all across heaven and earth. Two men will be working in the field, one will be taken; two women will be grinding at the mill, one will be taken. Watch and be ready, for you never know when the Lord may come.
- JOH 5:28–29 ~ The time is coming when all who are in the grave will hear His voice and come forth. Those who have been faithful and good will arise to everlasting life, and those who have been evil will arise to receive judgment.

Not only is Christ going to return again, you will experience it firsthand in a very personal way. In fact, everyone will witness this extraordinary event.

- JOB 19:25–26 ~ I know that my Redeemer lives and that He will stand upon the earth. And although my flesh will have been destroyed, yet in my flesh I will see God.
- ISA 40:5 ~ The glory of God will be revealed and humankind will see this together.
- MAT 24:30–31 ~ Jesus said, "At that time, the sign of the Son of Man will appear in the sky, and all the nations of the earth will mourn. They will see me riding on the clouds with power

and great glory. God will send His angels with a loud trumpet call, and they will gather His elect from the four winds, and from one end of heaven to the other."

Just as in Christ's first coming, there will be great rejoicing in heaven during His second coming. Don't you want to be among those numbered with the angels and saints, who live eternally with our Lord in heaven, forever praising His name? In the same manner in which Christ called Lazarus from the grave, He will call believers to come to Him (read JOH 11). Only this time it will be with a glorified body like His.

- JOH 11:25–26 ~ Jesus said, "I am the resurrection and the life. Those who believe in me, though they were dead, yet shall they live. Whoever believes in me will never die."
- COL 3:4 ~ When Christ, who is our life, appears again, you also will appear with Him in glory.
- REV 5:11–12 ~ Then I looked and saw a multitude of angels, numbering thousands upon thousands, literally millions of angels encircling the throne. And they sang aloud with one voice, "Worthy is Christ the Lamb who was slain, to receive power and wealth, and wisdom and strength, and honor, glory and praise."

How often do you consider God's promises and ponder them? Are you able to imagine what it was like when He came to earth and what it will be like when He returns again? Isn't it fun to wonder about these things and discuss them with fellow Christians? And finally, don't you feel compelled to share the good news of Jesus Christ with others who do not believe or cannot understand this great mystery?

God's promises are for real, and His Word is true. Christ came once and He will come again in glory. And this is not a figment of anyone's imagination.

CHAPTER THREE

Lesson: The Image of Life

God created all people in His image, giving them a living spirit and a discerning mind. He also gave us free will to do or not to do what is proper. Unlike Jesus, however, humankind chose sin instead of righteousness. Although we have the power to resist evil, we do not have the will. But God loves us just the same and wants us to be with Him; the only way that can happen is through Christ.

- GEN 1:26–27 ~ God said, "Let us make man in our image, after our likeness. And let them have dominion over the fish of the sea, over the fowl of the air, over the cattle, and over all the earth and everything that creeps upon the earth." So, God created humans in His own image; in the image of God He created us all, males and females alike.
- GEN 2:7 ~ God formed man from the dust of the earth, and breathed into his nostrils the breath of life, and man became a living soul.

To reconcile His children unto Himself, God sent Jesus Christ into the world to redeem us from sin and death. In order for us to know Him, God became the image of a man, with real flesh and blood. To be sure, God presented Himself to the world so that we could see Him through our own eyes and understanding. But the people executed Jesus, the only truly righteous person. Though a man, He was the perfect image of God, both consciously and spiritually. He was the perfect example of how we can mix morality with liberty and be happy all the time.

- ISA 9:6 ~ A child is born for us; a Son is given to us. The government will be on His shoulders. His name will be called Wonderful Counselor, Mighty God, Everlasting Father, and Prince of Peace.
- JOH 14:6,9–11 ~ Jesus said, "I am the way, the truth, and the life; nobody comes to the Father but by me. If you have seen me, you have seen the Father, because the Father lives in me and I in Him."
- COL 1:15–17 ~ Christ is the image of the invisible God, and the firstborn of every creature. By Him all things were created in heaven and earth, visible or invisible, including thrones, powers, rulers, and authorities. All things were created by Him and for Him. He is before all things, and only because of Him does anything exist at all.
- HEB 1:3 ~ Christ the Son is the brightness of God's glory, and the expressed image of His person. He sustains all things by the power of His Word. After He had purged our sins, He sat down at the right hand of His Majesty on high.

Christ intended to sacrifice Himself, and then to arise from the dead so that we could live. Therefore, it was God's plan all along to send His Son to die for us. He wanted His children to know Him and to love Him. He gave us His Word and His Law so that we could find Him and learn of His promises and His commandments. And every word, law, and promise were fulfilled through Jesus Christ, who is the Word made flesh, who obeyed the Law in its entirety, and who made good on God's promises of salvation and eternal life. God humbled Himself through Christ, who descended to earth to serve and to save humankind.

- ROM 8:3–4 ~ For what the Law could not do because of the weakness of human flesh, God accomplished by sending his own Son in the likeness of sinful flesh to be a sin offering. Thus, He condemned the sin of the flesh so that the righteous requirements of the Law could be found in those who do not live according to the flesh but according to the spirit.
- PHP 2:3–8 ~ Don't do anything through strife or vanity; instead, be humble, and regard others as better than yourselves. Don't focus on yourself, focus on others just like Christ did, who although He was equal with God, He took on the form of a man. Instead of exalting

Himself, He became the servant of all. He humbled Himself before others, and was obedient unto death, even death on the cross.

With Christ came the promise of eternal life, and the only requirement was to place our trust, hope, and faith in Him alone. Those who believe in Him and give their lives to Him just as He did for us, will live with Him forever in heaven. Little by little, through the process of sanctification, believers become transformed into His image. We become progressively better at listening to our conscience and making proper moral decisions. When we finally make it to heaven, we will be perfect in righteousness, the very image of Christ. And from that point on we will never sin again; we won't even think of sinning though we will still have free will.

- ROM 8:29; ROM 12:2 ~ For those He foreknew He also predestined to be conformed to the image of his Son, that He might be the firstborn among many more brothers and sisters. Do not conform to this world, but become transformed by the renewing of your mind. Then you will be able to test and prove that which is God's good, acceptable, and perfect will.
- COL 3:8–11 ~ You must rid yourselves of all evil, such as anger, rage, malice, slander, profanity, and lying. For you have removed the old self and put on the new self, which is being renewed in knowledge through the image of our Creator. There is no such thing as Jew or Greek, circumcised or uncircumcised, slave or free, civilized or uncivilized, because Christ is all and is in all.

Unfortunately, many have not and will not accept Christ as their personal Savior. They deny the fact that our Lord alone is true God, while they pursue worldly gods and treasures. Some even invent false gods or defile God's house with idol worship. Others worship themselves, in the image of Satan who was exiled from heaven for trying to steal worship from God, exalting himself in his own eyes. God will not permit the worship of anyone or anything but Him. They will be sorry, those who worship images of false gods created by human hands, those worshipping angels, and those following in Lucifer's footsteps trying to be their own gods.

- PSA 10:4 ~ The wicked through the pride do not seek God; He is never in their thoughts.
- EXO 20:4 ~ God commanded, "You shall not make for yourselves any graven image, or any likeness of anything that is in heaven above, or the earth below, or the water beneath the earth."
- HAB 2:18–19 ~ What value does a graven image have since it was a human that carved it? And what good is an image that teaches lies? For the one who makes it puts his trust in his own creation; he makes idols that cannot speak. Woe to him that says to the wood or to the stone, "Wake up and come to life." Can it give him guidance? It may be covered with gold and silver but it has no life in it.
- MAT 23:12 ~ Those who exalt themselves will be humbled...
- GAL 6: 2–3 ~ Bear each other's burdens, thereby fulfilling the law of Christ. If people think they are something when they are nothing, they deceive themselves.
- 2 TH 2: 3–4 ~ Do not let anyone deceive you, for there will be a falling away prior to the revealing of the son of perdition who opposes God and exalts himself above all others including God. Pretending to be a god he sits at the temple in his pompous arrogance.

The belief in false doctrine and the worship of false gods are traps that the devil sets to pull people away from our living Lord. Satan would love to take God's children with him to hell. That's been Satan's mission ever since he was banished from heaven. The final showdown will be prior to the return of Christ. Satan's opposition to God will culminate with the ultimate abomination of desolation whereby Satan exalts himself, defiling the holy temple. People will begin serving the image of the beast, influenced by the devil. But Satan and his followers will be defeated once and for all at the Battle of Armageddon. Then the Lord will come and claim His children as His own to live with Him forever. Satan and his followers will be cast into the lake of fire to be consumed.

- REV 13:11–15 ~ A beast came out of the earth and this beast had the authority of Satan (the original beast). And he deceived people into worshipping the beast by performing miraculous feats. The beast ordered the people to construct an image of the beast, who was wounded and yet lived. He was able to invigorate the image of the beast, so that the image could speak. Everyone was expected to worship the image of the beast; the penalty for not worshipping it was execution.

A terrible fate awaits those who reject Christ and His righteousness in favor of Satan and his wickedness. Only those who remain in Christ until the end will receive the promise of everlasting peace and joy in our Father's heavenly realm. It makes you wonder why anyone would choose evil over God, especially when they know full well the consequences.

- EZE 8:3–18 ~ The Lord grabbed Ezekiel by the hair and lifted him up between the earth and heaven, and showed to him visions of Jerusalem, and the door to the inner gate that looks northward. Ezekiel saw the seat of the image of jealousy. God told him to face toward that gate where he saw the idol of jealousy saying, "Do you see what they are doing, these utterly detestable things that the house of Israel is doing to drive me away from this sanctuary?" And Ezekiel witnessed a number of sacrileges that were occurring there. God said, "I will deal with them in anger, I will not pity them and I will not spare them. They can shout into my ears but I will not hear them anymore."
- REV 14:9–10 ~ The angel warned them that anyone worshipping the beast or receiving the mark of the beast would face God's wrath.
- REV 15:2–4 ~ Those that resisted the beast were victorious over him; they did not worship the beast or receive his mark, but were singing praises to God in heaven.
- REV 19:20; REV 20:10 ~ The beast (antichrist) was taken, and with him the false prophet that had performed miracles before him and through which he had deceived those who had received the mark of the beast. Also taken were those who worshipped the image of the beast, and all were thrown alive into the lake of fire. Then Satan was thrown into the lake of fire along with them.

God created humans in His image giving us a discerning mind and freedom of choice. Although we are able to distinguish right from wrong, our minds are feeble, and they do not easily comprehend God though we can tell the difference between good and evil quite easily. Therefore, God gave us His Word so that we could understand Him better and so that we could learn about His great plan of salvation. As a further witness to that truth, God sent the image of Himself into the world, His only begotten Son Jesus Christ. Christ was the image of God presented to humanity in the image of a man. But many have rejected God and Christ. Some would prefer to invent images of false gods and worship them if not themselves. Even in the latter days, Satan will produce an image of himself, and many will worship it. And by doing so, they will become conformed to the image of evil, and will inherit eternal damnation along with Satan. But for those who believe, follow, and worship the Lord God, they will be conformed to the image of Christ, who removed all their sin and replaced it with His righteousness. Christians will inherit God's kingdom, forever transformed into the image of life in His Spirit.

In summary, the resurrected Christ is the image of life: eternal life. When Christ arose from the dead, nobody recognized Him at first (LUK 24; JOH 20), possibly because He appeared in His glorified body. Similarly, when Christians are resurrected, we will become glorified with

Him (ROM 8:17,30), receiving bodies like His that will never die (PHP 3:20–21). Then we will be able to see Him as He really is, our eternal Lord and Savior.

- PSA 17:15 ~ In righteousness I will see God's face; when I awaken, I will be satisfied because I will recognize Him.
- 1 JO 3:2 ~ Dear friends, now we are the sons of God, and what we will become is not yet known. But we do know this: when He returns for us, we will become like Him, for we shall see Him as He really is.

Christ dying on a cross is the image of life, for His temporary death bought for us eternal life. Christians do not worship the image of the cross, however. It is a reminder of the sacrifice made by God on behalf of humanity. If we follow in His death, we will be raised to His life. It is unnecessary to remove from churches, homes, public places, or persons all images of Christ, to include crosses, and other biblical pictures or statues. I suppose some regard possessing these things as idolatrous; but it is, only if we idolize or adore them. They are, in fact, worldly things like everything else on this planet. True Christians worship one otherworldly, omnipotent, and trustworthy God: Father, Son, and Holy Ghost. If anyone allows a material object to capture their heart, by all means, they should get rid of it. For many, it shows they bear the image of Christ.

- ROM 6:8 ~ If we die with Christ, we believe we also will live with Him.
- REV 14:13 ~ The Spirit says, "Blessed are those who die in the Lord henceforth, for they will rest from their labors which will follow them."

CHAPTER THREE

Lesson: The Gospel Message

God is the source of all truth and the messenger of that truth is the Holy Spirit. The Spirit speaks to us through the Holy Bible and through Christ who became a man so that humanity could receive absolute truth directly from the source. The Old and New Testaments unveil to us the wisdom of God and His plan of salvation which leads to eternal life. The bottom line is this: the punishment for sin is death. Christ fulfilled the Law and took our place in death so that we could live. Those who believe these truths are forgiven and are saved. Disbelief is the only sin that cannot be forgiven and will seal the tomb for those who do not choose truth and life.

- PRO 30:5–6 ~ Every word of God is true; don't attempt to add to His words or He will rebuke you and you will be proven false.
- MAT 12:31–32 ~ Jesus said, "All manner of sin and blasphemy will be forgiven, except blasphemy against the Holy Spirit." Jesus continued, "Whoever speaks against the Holy Spirit will not be forgiven, neither in this world nor in the world to come."
- 2 TI 3:16 ~ All scripture is inspired by God. God's Word provides the doctrine of truth, refutes that which is false, and instructs all people in the ways of righteousness.
- 2 PE 1:16,21 ~ We did not follow cleverly devised fables when we told people about the power and coming of Jesus Christ, for we were eye witnesses of His majesty. No prophecy ever came from the impulse of man, but holy men spoke as they were directed by God.
- REV 22:18–19 ~ For I testify to everyone who hears the words of the prophecy of this book, that if anyone adds to these words, God will add unto that person the plagues mentioned in this book. If anyone subtracts from the words of this prophecy, God will take away their name from the Book of Life, and they will not share in the inheritance.

The cornerstone of our faith is Christ, the means by which we come to God and through whom eternal life is sought and guaranteed. The Gospel message connects the OT and NT, which together paint a picture of the purpose and promise in God's Messiah. This is the truth upon which eternal life is founded and the way that we find our direction home.

- JOH 14:2–3,6,19 ~ Jesus said, "In my Father's house are many mansions; I go to prepare such a place for you. I will return for you, so that where I am you can be also. I am the way, the truth, and the life; nobody comes to the Father but through me. In a little while, the world will see me no more, but you will see me again; and because I live, you also will live."

The strongest enemy of faith, perhaps, is doubt. In Old Testament times, people of God came to the prophets for answers to their questions about what God was going to do and when. They were constantly looking for signs that would prove to them that God's words were true. People want to be sure before making a commitment. A lack of confidence equates to uncertainty, which is risk. When risk is high fear is too, because we fear what we do not know. Uncertainty is reduced when there are facts, because the way to mitigate risk is with reliable and concrete information. God gave us His Word so that we would trust in the truth and believe, never doubting Him.

- MAR 9:17–27 ~ A man brought his son who was demon possessed to Jesus asking that He cast the demon out. Jesus asked the man, "If you have faith, all things are possible to those who believe." The man replied, "I believe Lord; help me in my unbelief." Then Jesus cast the demon out of the child.
- HEB 3:12,19; HEB 4:6 ~ Brothers beware, in case any of you have an evil heart of unbelief that strays from the living God; for they will not enter the kingdom because of their unbelief.

God's promise that a Redeemer would come and lead them to the Promised Land was centermost in the minds of the prophets and the hearts of God's people Israel. This was their hope and it is ours as well. We find references throughout the Bible of a flock trusting in their shepherd to lead them to safety. Isaiah is one of the most profound of the OT messianic prophets; he describes the promised Messiah in extraordinary detail. Many of the writings of lesser prophets also shed a great deal of light upon the coming of Messiah. Thus, God revealed the coming of Christ in the OT and showed Him to us in the NT.

- ISA 7:14; ISA 49:7; ISA 60:6 ~ God Himself will provide a sign: A son will be born of a virgin; He will be called "God with us." Kings and princes will see the sign and will come to worship. They come with caravans of camels from Midian, Ephah, and Sheba, bringing gold and incense, and praising God.
- ISA 9:1–2,6–7 ~ Someday this land will behold the glory of God, the light of life. For a Son will be born to us and the government will be upon His shoulders. He will be called Wonderful Counselor, Mighty God, Everlasting Father, and Prince of Peace.
- ISA 53:4–12 ~ He took upon Himself all of our grief and sorrow; yet we treated Him as an outcast. He was tortured for our sins and punished for our peace, and through His wounds we are healed. He was slaughtered like a lamb. He was buried like a criminal but in a rich man's grave. He was made an offering for sin, although He never committed a single act of sin or spoke an evil word. Therefore, His days will be prolonged and His name will be made great. He will be exalted, for He emptied his soul unto death.
- ISA 61:1–3 ~ The Spirit of God is upon me, because He has directed me to preach His good news to the humble, to heal the broken hearted, to free the slaves, and to release those who are bound in chains and in prison; to proclaim the Lord's favor and His vengeance, to comfort all who mourn, and to tell those who mourn to exchange their ashes for beauty; to replace mourning with joy, and to don the garment of praise in exchange for the spirit of sorrow, so that they may be trees of righteousness, planted by the Lord for His glorification.
- MIC 5:2–4 ~ Oh Bethlehem, you are such a small village but will be the birthplace of my king, who has been foretold from time eternal. God will forget Israel until the time has come for the chosen woman to bear the child; then the children of Israel will return. The Son will stand for and feed off the Lord, and will share His majesty. The children shall live in Him who is great, even to every corner of the earth.

Recognizing the connection between OT prophecy and NT eyewitness accounts, one can only be awestruck at the amazing accuracy, correlation, and reliability found in the Bible. This alleviates the doubt and certifies that God's words are true, removing all fear and risk, and creating complete confidence that Christ is Lord and God.

- PHP 2:5–11 ~ Jesus Christ, though equal with God, took upon Himself the nature of man and became a humble servant. He was obedient unto death, even a humiliating death on a cross. God has therefore exalted the name of Christ above all others; so, everyone should bow before His name and everyone should confess that He is Lord, to the glory of God the Father.

The apostle John had keen insight into this mystery and explained it quite eloquently in his gospel and epistles. He understood that Christ was always with God and was equal with God, and that through Christ, God could be found via the power of faith given us by the Holy Spirit. That power enables us to know the truth that sets us free. Hence, with the help of John, the doctrine of the Holy Trinity can be understood.

- JOH 1:1,14 ~ In the beginning was the Word, and the Word was with God, and the Word was God. And the Word became flesh and lived among us; and we saw His glory, the only begotten of God, full of grace and truth. (Notice the similarity to ISA 48:16 which states: Come and listen. I have not spoken in secret since the beginning. I was there all along, and now, the Lord God and His Spirit have sent me.)
- JOH 8:31–32 ~ Jesus said, "If you believe in my words then you are indeed my disciples; and you will know the truth, and the truth will set you free."
- 1 JO 1:1–3 ~ That which was from the beginning, the very Word of life, we heard, we saw, and we touched. For life was revealed, and we have seen it, and bear witness, and show you that eternal life, which was with the Father, visited us. That which we have seen and heard we declare to you, so that you can become one of us; for truly our fellowship is with the Father, and with his Son Jesus Christ.
- 1 JO 5:6–8,20 ~ There are three that are recorded in heaven: the Father, the Word, and the Holy Spirit. These three are one. The same three bear witness: the Spirit, the Water, and the Blood. The Spirit is the witness, because the Spirit bears the truth. We know Jesus Christ who is true so that we may know God who is true; we live in Him who has shown us His Son, the source of eternal life.

We get another perspective from Paul, who was not one of the original twelve apostles, but was recruited by Christ Himself after His ascension. Paul clarifies the association between the Law and the Gospel in a way that only he could. Being an avid student and enforcer of the Jewish Law prior to his conversion, Paul opens our eyes to God's great mystery and provides another view of the big picture. From Paul we learn the importance of justification by faith and not by works.

- ROM 3:23; ROM 6:23 ~ Everyone has sinned and come short of God's glory. The risk of sin is death. But God's gift of eternal life is available to everyone through Jesus Christ our Lord.
- ROM 8:1–2 ~ Those who are in Christ are no longer condemned, because through Him, the law of the Spirit of life sets us free from the law of sin and death.
- GAL 4:4–7 ~ When the time was right, God sent His Son, who was born of a woman under the Old Covenant of the Law, to redeem those who were under the Law. He did this so that everyone could receive the honor of becoming adopted children of God. If you are a child of God you are no longer His servant, but a fellow heir of God through Christ.
- EPH 2:8–9 ~ You are saved by the grace of God because of your faith in Jesus Christ. Salvation is a gift of God, it cannot be earned through good works, so nobody should brag.
- HEB 7:19; HEB 8:7 ~ The Law made nothing perfect, but the bringing of a better hope through Christ did; by that hope we are drawn to God. For if that first covenant (Law) had been faultless, there would have been no need for a second covenant (Grace).
- HEB 9:11–15,18–22 ~ Christ came as the high priest and king over all good things to come, to prepare a greater and more perfect church, not made by hands like a building. Christ obtained eternal redemption for us, not by the blood of burnt offerings but by His own precious blood. If the blood of burnt offerings purified the hearts of men, how much more will the blood of Christ purify us! Through the Holy Spirit, Christ offered Himself, who was without blemish (sinless), and who purged our consciences from dead works to serve the living God. By this cause, Christ has become the mediator of the New Testament (Covenant). By His death, we are redeemed from the sins committed under the first (old) covenant, so those who are called might receive the promise of God's eternal inheritance. Even the first covenant included blood, for after Moses read from the Book of the Law, He sprinkled blood

from the offering on the book and the people, saying, "This is the blood of the covenant which God has commanded for you to keep." Moses also sanctified the tabernacle in this manner. Under the Law, all acts of disobedience are purged with blood, for without the shedding of blood there is no remission of sins.

- HEB 10:1–2,10–18 ~ The Law, even with sacrifices for sin offered continuously throughout the year, could never make anyone perfect; otherwise the practice could have been discontinued as they would have rid themselves of the knowledge of sin. By one complete offering Christ has made perfect those who will be sanctified. We are sanctified by the offering of the body of Jesus Christ, one sacrifice for all people. No offering for sin will ever be needed again.

Peter was a constant companion of Jesus and paid close attention to every word He said. Peter was weak initially, but Jesus's resurrection strengthened and emboldened him to stand as leader of the apostles. Peter provides a straightforward summary of what all who would believe need to know. As in his life and in his teachings, Peter maintained Christ as the focus and center of his life, and gladly died on a cross like His Lord and friend.

- JOH 6:68–69 ~ Simon Peter answered Jesus, "Lord, who else can we turn to? You alone have the words of eternal life. We believe and we are positive that you are the Christ, the Son of the living God."
- ACT 4:9–12 ~ Peter informed the spectators and the elders of the church after healing the lame man (ACT 3) that it was not by the apostles' power but by the power of Christ that the man was healed, saying, "Salvation can be found in nobody but Christ, for there is no other name under heaven given among men that can possibly save us."
- 1 PE 1:3–4; 2 PE 2:9 ~ Blessed be God the Father, who by His mercy has given us new life through the resurrection of His Son Jesus Christ. Therefore, we will be raised with Christ to enjoy an incorruptible and undefiled inheritance, reserved in heaven for all believers. The Lord knows how to deliver the godly from temptation and to reserve the ungodly until the day of judgment to be punished.
- 1 PE 3:18 ~ Christ suffered once and for all, for the sins of the just and the unjust, in order to bring us to God. He was put to death in the flesh but raised by the Spirit.

The Gospel message can be found in both testaments of the Bible and provides the quintessential doctrine of the Christian faith (JOH 3:16). The scriptures quoted in this lesson provide the core beliefs that are vital if one wishes to be saved. Any religion or church that deviates from these basic teachings is flawed and should be avoided. There may be slight differences among various Christian (Protestant and/or Catholic) denominations regarding interpretations, traditions, and teachings, but they all agree on one important point: the good news of the Gospel of Christ is central to a saving faith.

- GAL 1:8 ~ Anyone, including angels, who preaches anything contrary to what Jesus and the apostles preached is cursed.
- COL 2:8 ~ Beware of those who would lead you astray with their errant philosophies and vain deceptions, following traditions fashioned by the world and not Christ.
- 1 TI 1:3–7 ~ Do not teach false doctrine, or recognize any myths or irrelevant genealogies, which only serve to raise questions not to provide answers concerning the faith. The goal is to love with a pure heart, a right conscience, and a sincere faith. Some have wandered away from these principles and turned to meaningless jabber; desiring to be teachers of the Law yet knowing nothing about the Law or about what they purport to be true.

Easter's Song

© 1981 by Andrew Barber (PAu 321–648)

```
     A        G       D       A    E
Anytime was perfect once, it only lasted for awhile.
     A        G       D        A     E
Being alive was easy once, but suddenly it's not my style.
     A       G   C G A A        G C  G A
Searching for some peace. Needing some release.
```

.... A. G C. G. A. A. G C. G. A. A. G C... C. G... C.

VERSE 1
```
          A    G C   G       A           G C G
The sky was clear, it echoed BLUE; like untold dreams, as yet untrue.
         A      G C  E.  A    B    G    A  F. G.
The broken, dusty avenue distracted me from feeling you.
```

VERSE 2
The pathway narrowed at midnight BLACK. I wandered from the beaten track.
I wrestled there with frozen death; I wondered who restored my breath.

A... G C G. A... G C G. A... G C G.

```
     D     A    E       B C. G                A   G C. C A.
Vague impressions, phantoms, ghosts? Shadows from the Lord of Hosts!
```

.... A. G C. G. A. A. G C. G. A. A. G C... C. G... C.

VERSE 3
The agony wore stripes of RED, but still some followed what He said.
A fugitive from worlds unknown? They wondered who removed the stone.

A... G C G. A... G C G. A... G C G.

D A. E B. C G...

```
     A       G   C G A A        G C  G A
Searching for some peace? Needing some release?
```

A... C D. A... C D G. A... C D G. A... C D G. A... E. G D A...

THE SECOND COMING OF CHRIST

The Latter Days

The Bible gives numerous accounts concerning the latter days prior to Christ's triumphant return. It will be a time of tribulation and sorrow. Christians will be persecuted and evil will flourish. It will worse than Sodom and Gomorrah when they were destroyed by God. Iniquity will triumph over goodness and deceit over truth. It will be a dangerous world, but those clinging to the cross will be protected despite attempts to bring them down. Terror, torment, trials, and temptations will be rampant, a warning the Savior's arrival is near. The numbers choosing to join in Satan's fall will increase exponentially. The Lord obliterated the evil ones during the time of Noah and Lot, and so will His vengeance rain upon the wicked once again when He returns in judgment. When asked when this would happen, Jesus responded as follows.

Jesus's Personal Account

(A synopsis of the Olivet Discourse: MAT 24; MAR 13; LUK 21)

Don't be deceived, for many will claim to be the Messiah or a prophet from God. They will perform magic tricks and will fool many people. There will be wars and rumors of wars. There will be earthquakes in different places. There will be famines, afflictions, and pestilence. The righteous will be persecuted, interrogated, imprisoned, and crucified. People will betray one another and wickedness will abound. It will be like the days of Noah and Lot, only worse; the philosophy will be: eat, drink, and be merry. You'll be hated for following me. This is the beginning of the time of sorrows; the beginning of the end. A time of great tribulation will come, worse than the world has ever known before or will ever know again.

When you see Jerusalem surrounded by its enemies, the desolation is nigh. This is the abomination that makes desolate spoken of by Daniel. When this occurs, head for the hills; there will be no time to pack. Hope it doesn't happen during winter; it will be especially tough for those with babies. It will be a time of great mourning. Two men will be working in the field; only one will be taken. Two women will be weaving; only one will be taken. There will be signs in the heavens. The sun and moon will be darkened and stars will fall from the sky.

The Gospel will need to be preached around the world. Don't worry about what to say or do, because the Holy Spirit will provide you with the information when you need it. When you see these things happen, be prepared for my return. Just as trees blossom as a sign that springtime is nigh, so will these signs proclaim the Second Coming of Messiah. That generation will not pass until everything I just told you has taken place. Those enduring until the end will be saved. Finally, a sign in heaven will proclaim the coming of the Son of Man. You will see Him in the clouds of heaven, in all His power and glory. He'll send angels to gather the righteous into heaven. Nobody but the Father knows when this will happen, not even the angels. Heaven and earth eventually will pass away, but my words will remain true forever.

Then all people will be assembled together but separated like dividing sheep from goats, with sheep on the right and goats on the left. To those on the right I will say, "Come inherit the kingdom prepared in advance for you, for when I was hungry you fed me, when I was thirsty you gave me drink, and when I was naked and cold you clothed me." The sheep will say, "When did we do this?" I will say, "Whenever you did it for someone else you did it for me." To those on the left I will say, "Depart you cursed ones into the everlasting fire prepared for the devil and his angels, because you did not help your neighbor in need." The goats will inherit eternal punishment; the sheep will inherit eternal bliss.

Chapter Three

Old Testament Accounts

- DEU 28:21–28 ~ God will send diseases, plagues, and war to destroy you. The heavens and earth will be unyielding as iron; a blight will destroy your crops. The land will become dry as dust from lack of rain; dust storms will destroy you. You will be defeated by your enemies. You will go to battle in glory but will run from your enemies in seven different directions, and you will be scattered all across the earth. Your dead bodies will become food for wild animals. God will send boils, tumors, and various diseases to crush you. You will become mad, blind, and confused.
- DEU 32:17,24 ~ They angered Him with strange gods, idols, and abominable practices. They sacrificed to demons. They shall be wasted with hunger and devoured with fire and pestilence. For they are a nation void of counsel and there is no understanding in them.
- PSA 137:1,8 ~ By the waters of Babylon they wept. Oh, daughter of Babylon, you devastator. What have you done to us? Happy is He who will repay you.
- ISA 2:6,11,19 ~ The people practice divination and fortunetelling. They please themselves with children of strangers. The pride of men will be humbled, and the Lord alone will be exalted on that day. And people will hide from the terror of the Lord when He comes.
- ISA 3:5,9,11 ~ The people will oppress each other. Youth will be insolent to their elders. They proclaim their sin like Sodom, they don't hide it. Woe to them. What they have done to others will be done to them.
- ISA 3:16 ~ The daughters of Zion are haughty and glance with their eyes wantonly.
- ISA 5:20–23 ~ Woe to those who call evil good and good evil. They seize their prey that nobody can rescue. Woe to those who are heroes at drinking alcohol, who acquit the guilty for a bribe, and who deprive the innocent of their rights.
- ISA 13:19 ~ Babylon will be like Sodom and Gomorrah when God overthrew them.
- ISA 28:15 ~ You have made a covenant with death, an agreement with hell, and hidden behind your lies.
- ISA 31:8 ~ The Assyrian will fall by the sword, only not of man, and his army will be overthrown.
- ISA 32:6–7 ~ The vile person speaks villainy, plots evil, practices ungodliness, and deprives the needy. His instruments are evil. He devises wicked plans to destroy the poor and the just with his lies.
- ISA 45:16 ~ They are put to shame, confounded and confused.
- ISA 59:3–7 ~ Your hands are defiled with blood and sin. Your lips have spoken lies and wickedness. They conceive evil and rely on foolishness and lies. They run to evil and hasten to shed innocent blood. Desolation and destruction ride their highways.
- JER 1:14 ~ From the north, evil will break forth upon the inhabitants of the land.
- JER 7:32–33 ~ In the valley of slaughter, their dead bodies will become food for the birds and beasts.
- JER 8:12 ~ They shall be punished, for they were not ashamed when they committed their abominations.
- JER 18:12 ~ They acted according to the abominations of an evil heart.
- JER 23:14,17 ~ I have seen horrible things. They commit adultery, tell lies, and support evildoers so that nobody returns to being good. They have become like Sodom and Gomorrah. They say you will find peace for being evil and following your fantasies.
- JER 47:2 ~ Waters arise from the north and become an overwhelming torrent. Men will cry and everyone will wail at the sound of the rushing horses and chariots coming to destroy the Philistines.

- JER 48:2–10 ~ The madmen will be silenced. Desolation and destruction abound. Flee! Save yourselves! The destroyer will come to all cities. Cursed are those who are deceptive in God's name, as well as those who spare the sword from bloodshed.
- JER 49:4,13,17 ~ There is the faithless daughter who trusted in her treasures. Her cities will become a horrible disaster, a wasteland, a curse like Sodom and Gomorrah.
- JER 51:6 ~ Flee from Babylon and save your lives. Don't get caught in her punishment, for this is the time of the Lord's vengeance.
- LAM 1:18–19 ~ Virgins and young men have been taken captive. Lovers deceive each other. Priests and elders perish searching for food for the soul.
- LAM 2:14 ~ Your prophets have seen false and deceptive visions.
- LAM 4:6,10,13 ~ Their punishment will be greater than that of Sodom. Women have boiled their children. Prophets and priests shed innocent blood.
- EZE 5:17 ~ I will send famines, pestilence, and wild beasts; and you will be destroyed by the sword.
- EZE 9:4–6 ~ God commanded His servant to set a mark on the foreheads of those who grieved because of the wickedness around them. The others were to be slain by the sword; all were to be slain except those with God's mark.
- EZE 13:19 ~ They will pollute me (God) among my people for a piece of bread. They will kill people that should not have to die and save others that should not live, and lie to people about it.
- EZE 16:15–20 ~ You trusted in your beauty and fornicated with anybody and everybody. You played the harlot more than ever before or ever again. You made images of men and played the harlot with them. You sacrificed your sons and daughters.
- EZE 38—39 ~ Face northward, toward Magog, and prophesy: God is against you Gog. You will mobilize armies of the distant north, as well as from Africa and Asia. You will invade Israel in an attempt to obtain her wealth and conquer her, Israel who has been at peace after having returned home from all over the world. This will happen in the latter years. There will be a great earthquake. You will end up fighting yourselves in the confusion. I will send animals to eat you, death, disease, and calamities. I will destroy five-sixths of your armies. I will rain fire and brimstone upon Magog and your allies to include the islands and coastlands, and places east of the Dead Sea. It will take seven months to bury the bodies. It will be a glorious victory for Israel. I will be their Lord from that day on, and forever.
- EZE 39:6,11 ~ I will send fire upon Magog and those who live securely along the coast. Gog and its multitude will be buried in the valley east of the sea in Israel.
- EZE 40—44 (especially EZE 44:1–15) ~ In a vision, God brought me (Ezekiel) into the land of Israel. The angel told me to pay close attention to the events occurring in the sanctuary, and to tell the rebellious house of Israel about the abominations I witnessed there. For they brought unclean strangers into the sanctuary to pollute it, and they broke God's covenant, and they didn't keep His holy things sacred. The priests strayed far away from God and pursued idols. Yet they were ministers in God's sanctuary and were in charge of the house of Israel; they killed the burnt offerings and made sacrifices of lambs without blemish. Because they ministered to the house of Israel before their idols, and caused Israel to fall into sin, they will be punished. They will not come near to God and His holy things. They will bear the shame of their abominations. But those priests that faithfully kept charge of God's sanctuary when the children of Israel went astray, they will be the ones who will come near to God and minister to Him. They will teach God's people the difference between what is holy and what is profane, so that they can learn what God considers clean and unclean.

- DAN 2:39–41,44 ~ After the king of Babylon (speaking of Nebuchadnezzar), will come an inferior kingdom, and then a third kingdom of bronze, which will rule the earth. Then will come a fourth kingdom of iron, which will crush the others. It will be a divided kingdom (iron mixed with clay) and eventually will fall apart (iron and clay don't mix). Eventually, God will set up a kingdom which will never be destroyed, and whose sovereignty will never change.
- DAN 7:3–13 ~ Four beasts arose from the sea. The first was like a lion with eagle's wings, which were plucked; the second was like a devouring bear; the third was like a leopard, with four wings of a bird and four heads. The fourth was dreadful, with iron teeth and ten horns; one horn rose up and replaced three. I (Daniel) watched until these thrones were thrown down before the Ancient of Days, who was dressed in pure white and sat on a throne of fire (see REV 13:1–4).
- DAN 7:14–27 ~ The four beasts represent four kings who will come (see REV 17). The fourth beast, representing the fourth kingdom that will come, is different, exceedingly terrible. The ten horns represent ten kings; three will fall overtaken by one. This one will speak bold things against God and will make war with the saints, defeating them. He will change the times and the rules. He will reign for a time, times, and half a time (i.e., 3 ½ years). Then the heavens will open and the Ancient of Days will come. And the glory and kingdom will be given to Him, and all people will serve Him. His will be the only kingdom, unified and everlasting. The books will be opened and all will be judged. The beast will be slain, its body destroyed, and thrown into the fire. The other beasts will be stripped of everything and allowed to live for a season and a time. Everything will be given to the saints who will reign with Christ in His everlasting kingdom.
- DAN 8:13–14 ~ The transgressions that make desolate will continue, and the sanctuary will be destroyed. After 2,300 days (6 ½ years) the sanctuary will be restored.
- DAN 8:20–25 ~ Daniel explained his vision: The ram with two horns represents the kings of Media and Persia. The male goat with one horn represents the first king of Greece. The goat's horn breaks, and is replaced by four others, representing four kingdoms. At the end of their rule will begin the rule of the terrible king, who understands riddles, and possesses great power. Through his cunning, he will cause the destruction of mighty men and saints. He will magnify himself and deceit will prosper. He will even rise up against the King of kings, but will be defeated.
- DAN 11:6–39 ~ The daughter of the king of the south (MAT 12:42) will make an agreement with the king of the north. Neither will stand. A branch from her roots will enter the fortress of the king of the north and will prevail. The king of the north will raise an army and defeat the south. Then he will turn towards the coastlands, but a commander will stop him. In his place will arise a contemptible person, without warning, and obtain the kingdoms through flatteries and deceit. He will overthrow armies. He will make alliances deceptively, and will plunder. He will corrupt people. He will forecast devices against his enemies. He will employ the power of forces. He will honor with money, pleasure, and luxury. He will exalt himself and speak against the Lord. He will profane the holy temple and honor those who forsake the holy covenant. He will set up in the holy place the abomination that makes desolate. He will give no heed to God or to the love of women. He will honor with riches and divide the land for a price. He will destroy many. He will prosper until the indignation is finished, but only for a short time.
- DAN 12:2 ~ Some will arise to receive everlasting life and some will arise to everlasting shame and contempt.

- DAN 12:11–12 ~ The abomination that makes desolate will be set up for 1,290 days (3 ½ years). Blessed are those who withstand the corresponding 1,335 days of tribulation.
- HOS 6:9 ~ The priests commit murder by giving their consent, and they commit lewdness.
- JOE 1:6,11–12 ~ A powerful nation has emerged. They have allowed the harvest of the fields and the groves to perish, and all gladness has perished with them.
- JOE 2:28–32 ~ I will pour out my Spirit on humankind. Your sons and daughters will prophesy and will see visions; old men will dream dreams. There will be signs in the heavens and earth: blood, fire, and smoke. The sun will turn dark and the moon will turn to blood, before the great and terrible day of the Lord. All who call upon the Lord will be delivered.
- JOE 3:3–4 ~ They gamble for my people, and trade a boy for a harlot, and sell a girl to get intoxicated. What are you doing? Are you paying me back? It will all come down upon your heads.
- AMO 1:11,13 ~ For three sins of Edom and for four I will invoke the punishment, because they never withdrew their anger. For the three sins of Ammon and for four I will invoke the punishment, because they ripped open pregnant women.
- AMO 2:1–6 ~ For three sins of Moab and for four I will invoke the punishment, because they burned their king's bones. For three sins of Judah and for four I will invoke the punishment, because they rejected the Law of the Lord, and their lies led them astray. For three sins of Israel and for four I will invoke the punishment, because they sold out the righteous and poor.
- AMO 2:16 ~ The mighty will flee away naked.
- AMO 4:10–11 ~ I will send pestilence like I did on Egypt. You will be overthrown as with Sodom and Gomorrah.
- AMO 8:11–13 ~ I will send a famine of the Word. They will seek the Word of God and not find it. The virgins and young men shall faint of thirst for the Word. Sundown will occur at noon; the clear day will be darkened.
- MIC 3:2–3,5 ~ You hate good and love evil. You skin people and eat their flesh. You chop their bodies into pieces. You talk of peace but make war.
- MIC 5:12–15 ~ All the sorcerers and fortune-tellers will be cut off. Their cities will be destroyed. I will execute vengeance on people that do not obey.
- MIC 6:12 ~ The rich men are full of violence and lies.
- MIC 7:2–6 ~ All the godly and upright men are gone. The wicked lie in ambush for blood. They do evil with diligence. Princes and judges ask for bribes. Great men speak of and pursue the evil desires of their souls. Even the best of them is like a thorn. Their confusion and punishment await them. Nobody can be trusted; even family and friends become the enemy.
- NAH 1:12–14 ~ They will be cut off. The afflictions will cease. They and their gods will be thrown into the grave for they are vile.
- NAH 3:1–6 ~ Woe to the bloody city full of lies, atrocities, prostitution, and the countless lewdness of that harlot who betrays nations and families. Heaps of slain corpses, dead bodies without end: that will be their reward. God will throw abominable filth on them for all to see.
- HAB 1:4 ~ Law and judgment are loosened, for the wicked encompass the righteous. Therefore, wrong judgment proceeds.
- ZEP 1:15–18 ~ A great day of wrath, distress and anguish, ruin and devastation, darkness and gloom is coming. Their blood will be poured out like dust and their flesh like dung. Their riches will do them no good then. All the earth will be consumed at once.
- ZEC 1:18–21 ~ Zechariah had a vision of four horns. The four horns represented the four kingdoms that would scatter Judah, Israel, and Jerusalem. Then Zechariah had a vision of

four carpenters. The four carpenters would come against the four kingdoms that scattered Judah and dismantle them.
- ZEC 2:6–7 ~ Escape from the north to Zion, those who dwell with the daughter of Babylon.
- ZEC 6:1–7 ~ Zechariah had a vision of four chariots emerging from between two mountains of brass. The first chariot was driven by red horses, the second by black horses, the third by white horses, and the fourth by brown and gray (or pale) horses. The chariots represented the four spirits of heaven which stand before the Lord of the earth. The black horses will go north, and the white horses will follow them. The pale horses will go south. The red horses will go back and forth across the earth (these are likely the four horsemen of the Apocalypse in REV 6).
- ZEC 14:11 ~ Never again will there be such a curse, and Jerusalem will finally dwell in security.

New Testament Accounts

- MAT 10:21,36; MAR 13:12; LUK 12:52–53 ~ People will betray their own family members to death. A person's enemy will be living in the same house.
- MAT 12:39,43–45 ~ An evil and adulterous generation will seek a sign that will never come. An evil spirit will go out of a man, find seven more evil than itself, and then return. That's how bad this evil generation will be.
- MAT 12:42 ~ The queen of the south will rise in defiance of this evil generation.
- MAR 13:14,19,22 ~ When you see the desolating sacrilege set up in the holy place, flee to the mountains and don't turn back (LUK 17:31). There will be tribulation such as the world has never seen before or ever will again. False prophets and false messiahs will arise and perform magic. Many will be led astray.
- LUK 16:8 ~ The dishonest people of this evil generation are smarter and trickier than the honest people.
- LUK 21:12 ~ They will persecute you for being Christians.
- ACT 20:30 ~ From among yourselves people will come speaking perverse things to draw disciples after them.
- ROM 1:25–32 ~ They exchanged God's truth with lies and worshipped and served the creation rather than the Creator. They performed dishonorable passions. Women gave up natural relations for unnatural. Men gave up natural relations with women in favor of passion for each other. Men performed shameless acts with other men, thereby receiving in their own persons the due penalty for these evil deeds. They were filled with all kinds of wickedness, evil, disobedience, covetousness, boastfulness, insolence, malice, murder, deceit, slander, strife, and malignity. They were faithless, heartless, ruthless, and foolish. They enjoyed doing evil, even though they were warned that such wickedness would lead to death.
- EPH 5:11–12 ~ Don't take part in their evil schemes but expose them instead. It is shameful to even speak about the evil that they do in secret.
- EPH 6:12 ~ You will be contending, not against flesh and blood, but against wickedness in high places and rulers of darkness.
- 2 TH 2:3–4,9–12 ~ The man of lawlessness comes, who is the son of perdition. He exalts himself to be a god or an object of worship, taking the seat in the temple of God. He brings about the acts of Satan through deception and magic. People will deceive themselves, and will be condemned for not believing the truth.
- 1 TI 4:1 ~ Some will depart from the faith by recognizing evil spirits and demons.

- 1 TI 6:10–11 ~ The love of money is the root of all evil; through the craving for worldly riches many have wandered away from the faith and pierced their hearts. Strive for righteousness, godliness, faith, love, steadfastness, and gentleness.
- 2 TI 3:1–6,13 ~ There will be a time of great distress. People will love themselves and money. They will be abusive, arrogant, conceited, disobedient, treacherous, slanderous, ungrateful, unholy, inhumane, haters of good and lovers of pleasure. They will capture weak and wayward women, swayed by impulses. Evil people and impostors will progress from bad to worse, as will the deceivers and the deceived.
- 2 TI 4:3–4 ~ People will seek teachers who conform to their own likes and dislikes; they will turn away from the truth and wander into myths.
- TIT 1:10–11 ~ There are many insubordinate ones; filthy abominators, empty talkers, and deceivers, especially regarding circumcision. They must be silenced, for they disrupt homes by teaching, for ill-gotten gain, what they know nothing about.
- HEB 9:28 ~ Christ was offered once to bear the sins of many; He will appear the second time, bringing salvation to those who look for Him.
- JAM 5:5 ~ People will live in luxury and pleasure and kill righteous men.
- 2 PE 2:1–3,14,18–19 ~ False prophets come to bring damnable heresies and to deny the Lord, deceiving many. They will exploit with false words and attract you with lusts of the flesh. They have eyes full of adultery, insatiable for sin. Their hearts are trained in greed, and they gain through wrongdoing. They promise freedom but are themselves slaves to corruption, and are condemned. They will get perpetually worse.
- 2 PE 3:3–4 ~ Scoffers will come, following their own passions and saying, "Where is the promise of His coming?"
- 1 JO 2:18 ~ You have heard that the antichrist comes, and many will.
- 2 JO 1:7 ~ Many deceivers will come who do not acknowledge the coming of Christ. One of them will be the antichrist.
- JDE 1:7–8,18–19 ~ It will be just like Sodom and Gomorrah, indulging in unnatural lust. In their dreams they defile the flesh, reject authority, and abuse the righteous. They are complainers, boasters, scoffers, deceivers, lewd and disgusting, and devoid of the Spirit.
- REV 1:7 ~ Behold, the Lord comes in the clouds, and everyone will see Him, including those who pierced Him. All races of people will mourn when they see Him.
- REV 2:10 ~ The devil will throw you into prison to test your faith; you will be tormented in captivity for ten days.
- REV 1—3 ~ John documented his vision which was revealed to him by the angel (probably Gabriel who gave a similar vision to Daniel). Christ Himself commanded him to provide copies to the seven churches of Asia, which were basically good but had fallen short. Seven candlesticks are portrayed first; one is like Jesus Christ, and holds seven stars reflecting the seven churches.

1. Ephesus: left their first love and must repent.
2. Smyrna: some will be cast into prison; many will have ten days of tribulation. Those who are faithful until the end will receive a crown of life (see LUK 21:12).
3. Pergamos: some teach false doctrine; those who repent will be saved.
4. Thyatira: allowed the harlot to seduce them and committed fornication; those who don't repent will be punished.
5. Sardis: faith is dead, wake up; keep watch and strengthen those who remain.
6. Philadelphia: a door is opened and there is protection; hold onto faith and overcome, and be rewarded in heaven. Those liars who claim to be Jews will make a synagogue of Satan.

7. Laodicea: lukewarm; claiming material riches instead of spiritual; those who repent will be saved.

- REV 4—10 ~ Twenty-four elders and four winged beasts are then portrayed. Seven seals on the sacred book are opened one at a time. Four horsemen of the apocalypse arrive in turn (also ZEC 6:1–7).

    1. White horse with conquering knight (they talk of peace but mean war; see MIC 3:5).
    2. Red horse with peace taker (i.e., the warmonger; see ISA 31:8).
    3. Black horse with rider holding balances (economic imbalance).
    4. Pale horse with death-rider, followed by four punishments: war, famine, pestilence and plagues, wild beasts (also EZE 5:17); one quarter of all people are destroyed.
    5. Those slain for believing the Word are given white robes and rest; they await the tribulations to come
    6. Earthquake, blackened sun, bloody moon, falling stars, hiding and fear; gloom and despair (see JOE 2:28–32). Sealing of 144,000 of God's servants with His mark (see EZE 9:4–6). Gigantic choir of survivors of much tribulation, washed by the blood of Christ.
    7. Seven angels get ready to sound their trumpets one at a time:

        1. Hail and fire mingled with blood burns one-third of the trees and all the grass.
        2. Mountain burning with fire cast into the sea killing one-third of the sea creatures and turning one-third of the sea into blood; one-third of the ships are destroyed as well.
        3. Star (called Wormwood) falls from heaven, glowing like a lamp and contaminating one-third of the fresh water.
        4. Darkening of one-third of the sun, moon, and stars; day shortened by one-third. Coming of the three woes.
        5. First woe. Star falls from heaven with key to bottomless pit, which is opened and releases smoke and stinging locust that torture those without God's mark for five months.
        6. Second woe. Loosing of four bound angels of death to kill one-third of humankind; 200,000,000 horsemen invade wearing breastplates of fire, jacinth, and brimstone (red, blue, and yellow, the colors of fire).
        7. God's mystery is finished. Third woe.

- REV 11 ~ Two witnesses prophesy for 3 ½ years, sending plagues, etc.; beast kills them but they rise from the dead in 3 ½ days, ascending into heaven (possibly during the first resurrection). The two witnesses are the two anointed ones, or olive trees; possibly angels (see PSA 99:1; ZEC 4:11–14).
- REV 12—13 ~ Satan tries to destroy the Son of God. War in heaven is portrayed; Michael and his angels fight the dragon and his angels. The devil (e.g., dragon or beast) is cast out, overcome by the Lamb. The beast has seven heads with ten horns (also DAN 7:3–27).
- REV 13—15 ~ The devil makes war with God's people for 3 ½ years. The beast is joined by a second beast who performs fake miracles (the son of hell: 2 TH 2:3–4,9–12). An image of the beast is brought to life; the mark of the beast is given to those that worship it; the beast's number is 666.
- REV 16 ~ Seven plagues are sent and the sinners still do not repent.

    1. Those with mark of beast given sores.
    2. Sea creatures die and sea becomes blood.
    3. Rivers and fountains become blood.

4. Scorching with heat and fire.
   5. Darkness and pain.
   6. Water dries up. Dragon, beast, and false prophet gather armies at Armageddon.
   7. Earthquakes destroy Babylon; giant hail falls.

- REV 17 ~ The beast's whore is described (i.e., Babylon) which sits on seven mountains and governs many waters (many nations or tongues). There are seven kings. Five kings are fallen, one is alive (sixth), and one is coming (seventh) having a short reign. The beast is number eight but was also one of the seven. Ten kings reign with the beast for one hour and make war with the Lamb.

  Note: Daniel predicted the progression of empires beginning with Babylon (DAN 2:39–44; DAN 7:3–27; DAN 8:20–25; see also ZEC 1:18–21), followed by Media-Persia, Greece the kingdom of bronze, and a kingdom of iron (namely Rome). As noted by John, there had been five great empires ("five are fallen"): Egyptian, Assyrian, Babylonian, Persian, and Greek. During the time of John was the Roman, or sixth great empire ("one is"). The next great empire (possibly the "seventh") to rule the Mediterranean, Holy Land, and Europe, was Nazi Germany ("having a short reign"). The eighth kingdom ("also one of the seven") will be that of the beast (sometimes referred to as the revived Roman Empire or the new Babylon).

- REV 18 ~ Babylon will fall because of its many abominations (ISA 13:1,9–10,19; JER 50:13,23–24,28,46; JER 51:6,29,35–37,49,64; NAH 3:1–6).
- REV 19 ~ The beast and those with his mark are cast into lake of fire (see ISA 28:18). The rest are slain by the sword and left as carrion.
- REV 20 ~ The devil is bound one thousand years while chosen saints who did not follow the beast reign with Christ. After the thousand years, the devil is set free. Satan is defeated a final time and is thrown into the lake of fire to be tormented eternally. The Book of Life is opened and everyone is judged (also DAN 7:10). Death and hell are cast into lake of fire as are those condemned to death.
- REV 21—22 ~ There is a new heaven and earth with no sea, and a new Jerusalem with twelve foundations: three gates at N, S, E, and W (twelve in all) in foursquare configuration (e.g., cubic, or a pyramid with four sides). The city is eternally lit by the Lamb and is always open to those redeemed by the Lamb. The new heaven has the Tree of Life and the River of Life (also ISA 65:17–19; EZE 47:1,5,9,12–13,22).

Predicting the End of Time

Although there are many signs indicating the return of Christ is near, nobody can accurately predict the end of the age and the Second Coming of Christ. Those claiming they are privy to that knowledge are gravely mistaken. Given that the signs appear to be happening already, we always must be watchful and prepared for His coming.

- MAT 24:36,44,50 ~ Nobody knows the day and hour, not even the angels; not even the Son of Man knows, but only the Father in heaven. For the Son of Man will come when you least expect Him.
- MAT 25:13 ~ Watch therefore, because you know neither the day nor the hour.
- 2 PE 3:10 ~ The day of the Lord will come as a thief in the night.
- REV 3:2–3 ~ Jesus said, "Be watchful and strengthen each other in the truth, for I have found imperfection on the earth. Remember everything you have heard, hold fast to it, and repent. If you are not watchful, I will surprise you like a thief, for you never know when I might come upon you."

Evil Generations

The Bible describes a number of evil generations in which wickedness prevailed over godliness. This is also the way it will be in the latter days, prior to Christ's return.

- GEN 7:1 ~ The Lord said to Noah, "You and your family must come into the ark, for you alone do I find righteous in this generation."
- EXO 32; DEU 8 ~ The Lord's anger against Israel was provoked by their worshipping of the golden calf. God made them wander in the wilderness for forty years, until the adults from that generation which committed evil before God had died.
- DEU 1:35 ~ Surely, not one person from this evil generation will see the good land which God promised to their fathers.
- PSA 78:8 ~ Listen everyone, don't be like your fathers, a stubborn and rebellious generation that did not possess an upright heart and a steadfast spirit.
- PRO 30:11–14 ~ There is a proud and arrogant generation that thinks they are pure and guiltless, yet they curse their parents and they take advantage of those less fortunate.
- MIC 7:3 ~ They are skilled at doing evil. Rulers require gifts and judges require bribes for their services. Those in power dictate their desires; together they conspire against others.
- MAT 12:39–40 ~ Jesus replied, "An evil and adulterous generation will look for a sign, but the only sign they will see will be that of Jonah. Just as Jonah was in the whale's belly three days and nights, so will the Son of Man be in the heart of the earth for three days and nights."
- MAT 12:43,45 ~ Jesus said, "When an evil spirit leaves a person, it roams the land, looking for rest but finding none. Then it finds seven other evil spirits that are even worse and returns to the person, leaving the possessed person worse off than before. This is the way it will be for this wicked generation to come."
- MAT 23:33 ~ Jesus said, "You, generation of snakes. How can you escape the damnation of hell?"
- MAT 24:5–34; MAR 13:30; LUK 21:32 ~ Jesus said, "Many shall come in my name, claiming to be me, and deceiving many. There will be wars, famines, pestilence, and earthquakes. These are only the beginning of sorrows. They will capture you, torture you, and kill you; you will be hated for following me. People will offend, betray, and despise each other. When you see the abomination of desolation stand in the holy place, as prophesied by

Daniel, escape into the mountains. There will be great tribulation, worse than ever before or ever again. Then a sign in heaven will appear. The whole earth will be in mourning when the Son of God returns in a cloud, with all His power and glory. This generation will not pass away until these things have happened."
- LUK 16:8–10,13 ~ Jesus summarized His parable about the dishonest bookkeeper saying, "The rich man commended the dishonest bookkeeper's shrewd tactics. He thought it was wise that this employee had made friends through greed and deceit. He thought it was smart to prepare for his retirement, because then he would have some means of external support when his job was over. That type of behavior will be considered wisdom to this evil generation. In fact, the evil children in that wicked generation will be wiser than the children of light. Those who are faithful in a little will be faithful in a lot, and those who are dishonest in a little will be dishonest in a lot. Nobody can serve two masters; they will be loyal to only one, honoring the one and despising the other. In other words, you can't serve God and money at the same time."

The New Babylon

In the latter days a new Babylon will emerge. Not unlike the old Babylon, the new Babylon will be represented by a world power that becomes a major source of evil and corruption in the world. Eventually, Babylon will fall and evil will be destroyed.

- 2 KI 20:17–18 ~ The days come when everyone in your house and your belongings will be carried away into Babylon, leaving nothing behind. And all your children will be taken to the king's palace. (also ISA 39:6–7)
- PSA 137:1,8 ~ We sat down by the rivers of Babylon and cried when we remembered Zion. Oh, daughter of Babylon, you will be destroyed; happy are we who will see you rewarded as you have done to us.
- ISA 13:1,9–10,19 ~ Isaiah foresaw the abominations of Babylon: The day comes when the Lord's wrath and anger will result in the desolation of Babylon and the destruction of the sinners there. The stars in heaven will not give light, and the sun and moon will be darkened. And the glory of Babylon will be like Sodom and Gomorrah when God destroyed those cities.
- JER 27:14 ~ Don't listen to the prophets who say you will not serve the king of Babylon, for they lie.
- JER 42:11 ~ Don't be afraid of the king of Babylon for I (the Lord) will deliver you.
- JER 50:13,23–24,28,46 ~ Babylon will be destroyed; everyone who goes there will be astonished at the plagues and destruction. Babylon will become a desolation. They were not aware that God would catch them and punish them for continuing to sin. They flee from Babylon as the vengeance of the Lord is declared in Zion. The earth will be moved for the cry of Babylon's fall will be heard around the world.
- JER 51:6,29,35–37,49,64 ~ Get out of Babylon and save your soul, don't get caught in her sin, for the Lord comes to pay them back for their sins. The land will tremble and mourn when God comes, making the land desolate, and eliminating its inhabitants. Their violence to innocent people will be upon their heads. As Babylon has killed the people of Israel, so shall everyone in Babylon be killed.
- EZE 16:15–20 ~ You trusted in your beauty, and played the harlot, fornicating with anyone and everyone. You took all the riches and fine things, made images and had sex with them. You sacrificed your sons and daughters to idols. Do you think this is a small matter?

- NAH 3:1–6 ~ Woe to the bloody city, full of lies and robbery. You prey on everyone; always you can hear the sounds of battle. Look at all the corpses. Because of the multitude of your abominations with the well-known prostitute, that witch that buys and sells nations and families, I will pour abominable filth upon you for all to see.
- ZEC 2:7 ~ Deliver yourselves, Zion, you who live with the daughter of Babylon.
- REV 14:8 ~ The angel said, "The great city of Babylon has fallen, because she caused all nations to drink the wine of the wrath of her fornication."
- REV 16:19 ~ The great city was divided into three parts and the cities of the nations fell. God remembered what they had done; their sin did not go unpunished.
- REV 17:5,9,18 ~ On her head was written: Mystery, Babylon the great, the mother of prostitutes and all earthly abominations. This is the great city that sits on seven mountains and over many waters, nations, and peoples.
- REV 18:2,10 ~ The angel cried, "Babylon has become the habitation of devils and of every foul spirit. That mighty city will receive judgment in one hour."

The Rapture

Both the Old and New Testaments refer to a time when God will call His people to be with Him in heaven. If this occurs when the person is still alive, this person is said to be raptured. In the Old Testament, Enoch and Elijah were possibly raptured (GEN 5:24 and 2 KI 2:11, respectively). That is, they went to heaven without ever being recorded or verified as having died. The verses listed below are evidence that a future rapture will occur and when this might happen. God can rapture anyone anytime He wants, but there is a particular time when Christ's elect will be raptured. This may occur in concert with the resurrection (1 TH 4:16–17).

During the tribulation, the devil will persecute, jail, and torture Christians (REV 2:10). The devil will make war with God's people and two witnesses will prophesy for 3 ½ years (REV 13:5). The abomination of desolation also will be set up for 3 ½ years (DAN 12:11–12). When this happens, people are instructed escape to the hills (MAR 13:14–22) and those who withstand that time will be blessed (DAN 12:12). One could infer that the rapture does not occur prior to the tribulation, because many Christians and Jews are persecuted first; but it seems the more popular view is the rapture does occur before the tribulation, because many Christians will be saved out of it. The mark of the beast will be given during the tribulation, but not to those who have received God's mark, of which 144,000 will be descendants, or more accurately "children" of Israel or Abraham (REV 7:4). The 144,000 will be redeemed from humankind (REV 14:3); perhaps this means they are among those who are raptured. They will be with Christ when the seven plagues are sent to earth near the end of the tribulation, coincident with the last trumpet and the third woe.

In summary, during the tribulation, the beast makes war with the righteous, the abomination of desolation is set up, the mark of the beast is given, and the two witnesses prophesy. The rapture and resurrection appear to occur simultaneously or in rapid succession upon Christ's return (2 TH 4:16–17). These events may occur either before, during, or at the end of the tribulations, war, and the abomination of desolation.

- ISA 27:12–13 ~ In that day a great trumpet will sound, and those who were about to perish in Assyria, and the outcasts in Egypt, will be rescued and will worship the Lord at the holy mountain of Jerusalem.
- JER 30:7 ~ That will be a great time (the tribulation); there will be no others like it. It is the time of Jacob's trouble; but he (Israel) shall be saved out of it.

- DAN 12:1,12 ~ Michael the great prince will stand for God's people. There will be a time of tribulation worse than ever before or ever again. But God's elect will be delivered, all whose names are written in the Book of Life. Blessed are those who endure the 1335 days during the time the abomination brings desolation.
- MAT 24:22,31,40–42 ~ Unless those days (of tribulation) are shortened, none will survive. But only for the elect's sake, those days will be shortened. And He will send His angels when the great trumpet sounds, to gather His elect from across heaven and earth. Two men will be working in the field, one will be taken; two women will be grinding in the mill, one will be taken. Watch and be ready, for you never know when the Lord may come.
- LUK 17:34–37 ~ Jesus said concerning His Second Coming, "Two men will be in bed, one will be taken and the other will be left behind; two women will be grinding grain together, only one will be taken; two men will be working in the field, only one will be taken."
- 1 CO 15:51–52,54 ~ Here is a mystery of God: We will not all sleep (implies death) but we will all be changed. Suddenly, when the last trumpet sounds, Christ's own, whether dead or alive, will arise without corruption and be changed. Hence, the corruptible will have become incorruptible and the mortal will have become immortal. Then the statement "death is swallowed up in victory" will be true.
- 1 TH 4:16–17 ~ The Lord will descend from heaven as the voice of the archangel, the shout of the Lord, and the trumpet of God are heard. And the dead in Christ will rise first. Then those who are alive in Christ will be caught up with the others and meet Christ in the sky to be forever with Him.
- HEB 11:5 ~ Enoch never saw death, because God brought him home when his testimony had been completed.
- REV 3:10 ~ Jesus said, "Because you have patiently kept my commandments, I will deliver you from the hour of temptation, when the patience of the entire world will be tested."
- REV 6:9,11 ~ I saw an altar, and beneath it were the souls of those who were slain because of their faith and their testimony. They were given white robes and told to wait a little longer before God avenged their death; for some of their fellow members in the faith were yet to perish as they did.
- REV 14:3–4 ~ The 144,000 sang a new song; nobody could learn the song except them. They were the ones who were undefiled. They were redeemed from humankind as the first fruits of God and the Lamb, for they were blameless.

The Resurrection

Jesus will come again in the flesh, the same way He departed. Just as Jesus was resurrected from the dead, so also will humankind be raised. Those who are evil will arise to everlasting contempt and condemnation. Those who are redeemed and saved will arise to everlasting bliss and peace. Christ was the first fruits of those to ascend into heaven to be with God the Father (1 CO 15:20). The next bodily resurrection will occur when Christ returns (1 CO 15:23; REV 20:4–5).

God will send his two witnesses who will prophesy for 3 ½ years during the tribulation (REV 11:3). They will rise from the dead in 3 ½ days after being murdered by the beast (REV 11:11–12). It is possible that the resurrection will occur at that time to coincide with their resurrection. Further evidence of this is as follows: The seventh angel sounds the trumpet and the temple of God in heaven is opened (REV 11:15,19). Then comes the third woe (REV 11:14). It is unclear if this occurs during or at the end of the tribulation. There may be a time of tribulation for the righteous, followed by a time of tribulation for the wicked.

- JOB 19:25–26 ~ I know that my Redeemer lives and that He will stand upon the earth. And although my flesh will have been destroyed, yet in my flesh I will see God.
- ISA 26:19 ~ The dead will live; along with my dead body they will arise. Awake and sing all of you who abide in the dust, for the earth will toss out its dead.
- EZE 37:1–5,12–14 ~ The hand of the Lord touched me (Ezekiel), carried me out with His Spirit, and set me down in the middle of a valley full of dry bones. And God said to me, "Can these bones live?" I answered, "Lord, surely you know." Then He said to me, "Prophesy upon these bones, and tell them to listen to the words of the Lord, for I will cause breath to enter into these dry bones and they will live again." I (God) will open your graves and cause you to come out, and bring you into the land of Israel. And you will know I am the Lord. I will put my Spirit into you and you will live in your own land.
- DAN 12:2 ~ Some will arise to everlasting life and some will arise to everlasting shame and contempt.
- MAT 24:29–31,42–44 ~ Jesus said, "After the tribulation there will be darkness over the world. Then a sign will appear in heaven, and everyone on earth will mourn, and they will see the Son of God coming in the clouds with all His power and glory. And He will send His angels at the sound of the great trumpet, and they will gather His elect from the four winds, and from one end of heaven to the other. So be watchful, for nobody knows when the Lord will return. If the man knew when the thief was going to burglarize his house, he would have been able to prevent it. Likewise, you must be ready, for the Son of God will come at a time when you least expect Him."
- MAT 25:30,41,46 ~ He will cast the worthless people into outer darkness where there is weeping and gnashing of teeth. They will depart into the eternal fire prepared for the devil and his angels. And they will go away into eternal punishment, but the righteous into eternal life.
- LUK 14:14 ~ If you help others who cannot repay you, you will be blessed, and you will be repaid at the resurrection of the just.
- JOH 2:18–22 ~ The Jews asked Jesus to show them a sign to verify that He had the authority to disrupt the temple merchants. Jesus replied, "Destroy this temple and I will raise it in three days." They exclaimed, "It took forty-six years to build it, how can you rebuild it in three days?" But Jesus was talking about the temple of His body. The disciples remembered this when Jesus's own prophecy had become fulfilled, proving that the scriptures and the words of Jesus were true.
- JOH 5:28–29 ~ The time is coming when all who are in the grave will hear His voice and come forth. Those who have been faithful and good will arise to everlasting life, and those who have been evil will arise to receive judgment.
- JOH 11:25–26 ~ Jesus said, "I am the resurrection and the life. Those who believe in me, though they were dead, yet shall they live. Whoever believes in me will never die."
- ACT 1:3 ~ Jesus Christ showed himself alive for forty days, after being crucified to death, and spoke of the kingdom of God. He proved to us many times that He had unquestionably risen from the dead.
- ACT 1:11 ~ The angel said, "Men of Galilee, why do you gaze into heaven? Jesus, who you just saw ascend into heaven, will return the very same way."
- ACT 10:40–41 ~ God raised Jesus on the third day, and many people saw Him; and we ate and drank with Him after He arose.
- ACT 24:15 ~ There is hope in God that there will be a resurrection of both the just and the unjust.
- 1 CO 15:12–58 ~ If Christ has risen from the dead, how can some of you say there is no resurrection? If there is no resurrection from the dead, then Christ was not raised either. If

Christ was not raised, we would be preaching in vain and your faith would also be in vain. But, in fact, Christ has been raised forever, the first to be brought back in the body from among those who have died; and He has brought with Him the resurrection. Just as death came by a man, by a man has come the resurrection of the dead. Like Adam we die, and like Christ we will rise from the dead, each in the proper order with Christ being first. After that, the end will come when He hands the kingdom over to God the Father. In Christ you also will be made alive after death. In a single moment, when the great trumpet sounds, the righteous, whether alive or dead, will arise into heaven to receive new, incorruptible bodies. The godly will receive spiritual bodies that never die. The flesh is of the earth, the spirit is of heaven; thus, flesh and blood will not inherit the kingdom of heaven. It is our natural body that dies; it is our spiritual body that lives after death. At Christ's coming will be the first resurrection of those who belong to Him. Then at the end, when He delivers the kingdom of God to the Father, He will destroy His enemies; the last enemy to be destroyed will be death. So, be confident in your faith because your labor is not in vain.

- PHP 3:10–11 ~ To know Him and the power of His resurrection is to share in His suffering, becoming like Him in death to attain the resurrection from the dead.
- COL 1:18 ~ Jesus Christ is the head of the body that is the church. He is the beginning, the firstborn of the dead, who is above all and is ruler over all the kings on earth (also REV 1:5).
- COL 3:4 ~ When Christ, who is our life, appears again, you also will appear with Him in glory.
- 1 TH 1:8–9 ~ He will inflict vengeance upon those who do not know and obey God and the Gospel of Jesus Christ. They shall suffer the punishment of eternal destruction, and exclusion from the glory of God.
- 1 TH 4:16–17 ~ The Lord will descend from heaven with a shout, with the voice of the archangel, and with a blast from the trumpet of God. Then the dead in Christ will arise first. Those who remain alive in Christ will rise to join the others in the clouds, meeting the Lord in the sky. Those chosen by Christ will live with Him forevermore.
- REV 7:9–10,13–14 ~ I (John) saw a giant multitude, too many people to even count; there were people from every nation, race, and tongue standing before the throne and the Lamb who was clothed in white. They held palm branches and sang, "Salvation to our God who sits on the throne, and to the Lamb." One of the elders asked me who these people were. I replied, "Tell me sir." He said, "These are the ones who came from great tribulation; they have washed their robes and made them white with the blood of the Lamb."
- REV 11:11–12,14–15,19 ~ After 3 ½ days, the Spirit of God entered into the two witnesses and they came to life again. And a voice from heaven called them and they ascended into a cloud as their enemies watched. The second woe had passed and the third woe was coming as the seventh angel sounded the trumpet. Voices in heaven were saying, "The kingdoms on earth now have become Christ's, and He will reign forever." Then the temple in heaven was opened.
- REV 19:11–16 ~ I saw heaven open and Jesus riding on a white horse. He is the one they call Faithful, True, and the Word of God. His eyes were like flames of fire and on His head were many crowns. He was clad in a robe covered with blood. He is the one called Lord of lords and King of kings. [Jesus must return in the flesh if He has eyes, a head, and wears a garment.]
- REV 20:4–5 ~ I saw thrones, and sitting on them were judges. I saw the souls of those who had been beheaded for their testimony of Jesus, who had not worshipped the beast or its image, nor received its mark on their foreheads or hands. They came to life again and reigned with Christ one thousand years. This was the first resurrection. The rest of the dead didn't come to life again until after the thousand years had ended (i.e., the second resurrection).

CHAPTER THREE

The Judgment

All people will be judged by the Lord Jesus, for judgment belongs to Him. Therefore, it is senseless for us to attempt to judge one another, particularly since we are guilty of the same things for which we condemn others. Everybody is guilty of something, some more than others, perhaps. But the number of sins one has committed has little bearing seeing how it takes only one to be guilty and worthy of death. And all it takes is godly faith to be rescued from a multitude of sins. But to be true to one's faith implies a change of heart.

Those who are redeemed according to the New Covenant in Christ will be judged righteous, for their sins will have been washed away by His blood. These could be the ones who experience the first resurrection. The rest of the people will possibly be judged according to the Law. All their deeds will be recorded in books; the books will be opened and those people will be judged appropriately in accordance with the Law. Whoever's names are written in the Book of Life will live with God in peace forever; the others will die in hell eternally (the second death). Actually, the easier way is to follow Christ, because if you rely on His atonement you will not be judged according to God's Law; for by His Grace you will be judged not guilty having received the righteousness of Jesus.

- EXO 12:12 ~ God said, "I will pass through the land of Egypt tonight and will kill the firstborn of humans and beasts, and I will execute judgment on all the gods of Egypt."
- DEU 32:35,41 ~ God said, "Vengeance and recompense are mine. The wicked will fall, for the day of their calamity is near. I will sharpen my sword and render vengeance upon my enemies."
- PSA 7:16 ~ The mischief and violence of the wicked will come back on their own heads.
- PSA 50:3–5 ~ God will come with a terrible fire burning all around Him. He will call everyone from heaven above to the earth below for judgment. He will gather the saints unto Himself.
- PSA 96:12–13 ~ Blessed are the people that you chastise, Lord, teaching them your Law, so that you can give them rest from days of adversity, until the pit is dug for the wicked.
- ECC 12:14 ~ God will judge each act of every person, every secret thing, to determine whether it is good or evil.
- ISA 14:15,20–21 ~ Satan will be thrown into hell; he will never join his followers in the grave and he will never have any successors. Slaughter awaits his followers; they will not rise again to possess the land or to prosper.
- ISA 26:14 ~ The wicked will die, never to live again; they will be destroyed completely, along with any memory of them.
- ISA 28:18 ~ Those who have made a contract with death and hell will find their agreement to be null and void. They will be trampled into the dust when the avenger passes through.
- ISA 29:20 ~ The evil foe will come to nothing; the foe will be consumed and the wicked will be cut off from God.
- ISA 40:5 ~ The glory of the Lord will be revealed, and all human flesh will see it together, for the Lord has said so.
- EZE 7:3 ~ God will judge everyone according to their ways, and will recompense the abominations of the wicked back upon them.
- EZE 34:16 ~ God said, "I will gather the lost sheep, I will mend the broken, and I will strengthen the sick; but I will destroy the fat and strong, and I will feed them judgment."
- DAN 7:10 ~ A stream of fire flowed before Him. Millions ministered to Him. Hundreds of millions stood before Him. The judgment was set and the books were opened.

- DAN 12:1 ~ Michael the great prince will arrive, who stands up for the righteous; and there will be a time of trouble worse than ever before or ever again. At that time the righteous will be delivered, everyone whose name is written in the Book of Life.
- HOS 6:2 ~ After two days He will revive us, and the third day He will raise us up to live in His presence.
- JOE 3:14 ~ There were multitudes in the valley of decision, for the day of the Lord was near.
- OBA 1:15 ~ The day of the Lord is near for the wicked. As they have done, so shall it be done to them; it will come back upon their heads.
- MAT 7:1–2 ~ Jesus said, "Don't judge another or you will be judged yourself; and you will be judged according to the same standards that you set for others; and whatever punishment you give is the punishment you will get."
- MAT 12:36 ~ Jesus said, "On Judgment Day, people will have to give account for every foolish word they spoke."
- MAR 16:16 ~ Jesus said, "Whoever believes in me and is baptized will be saved; whoever doesn't believe will be damned."
- LUK 6:37 ~ Jesus said, "Don't judge others and you will not be judged; don't condemn others and you will not be condemned. Forgive others and you will be forgiven."
- LUK 12:37 ~ Jesus said, "Blessed are those who the Lord finds watching for Him when He returns; like a waiter, He will seat them at the table and serve them a banquet."
- JOH 5:22,30 ~ Jesus said, "The Father judges nobody, but He has given this responsibility to the Son. I judge whatever I see and hear, and my judgment is fair because I seek the Father's will and not my own."
- JOH 5:24–25 ~ Jesus said, "Truly I tell you, whoever hears my Word and believes in Him who sent me will receive eternal life. They will not be condemned, but will pass from death into life. Truly I say that the hour is coming when the dead will hear my voice, and those who listened to me will live."
- ROM 1:32 ~ People commit evil acts, knowing full well that their acts are worthy of the death penalty. Yet they continue to be evil and to find pleasure in others who do the same.
- ROM 2:1 ~ It is inexcusable to judge another person, for by judging another you condemn yourself, because you are guilty of the same things.
- ROM 2:12–13 ~ All who sin apart from the Law will perish apart from the Law. All who sin under the Law will be judged according to the Law. Hearing the Law does not make you righteous in God's eyes, you must obey the Law to be declared righteous.
- 1 CO 4:3–5 ~ To be judged by another person is insignificant to me. In fact, I don't even judge myself because I don't know me as well as the Lord does. Therefore, don't judge anyone before the Lord returns. He will bring to light all that is hidden, even the secrets of our hearts. Then everyone will praise God.
- 2 CO 5:10 ~ We all shall stand before the judgment seat of Christ. We will be judged for everything we did, whether it was right or wrong, and we will be punished accordingly (also ROM 14:10).
- 2 TH 1:8 ~ With flaming fire God will take vengeance on those that don't know Him and that don't obey the Gospel of Jesus Christ.
- 2 TH 2:8,12 ~ The evil foe will be revealed, and the foe will be consumed by the Spirit of God and the brightness of His presence when He comes. Those who did not believe the truth but found their pleasures in unrighteousness will be damned.
- 1 TI 5:24–25 ~ Some people's sins will be exposed and they will be punished; for others, their punishment will come later. Likewise, some people's good deeds will be exposed and they will be rewarded; others will be rewarded later.

- HEB 9:27–28 ~ It is necessary for us to die once, and after this comes judgment. Christ was offered to bear the sins of many once, and then He will return, not to bear sins but to bring salvation.
- JAM 2:13 ~ Whoever shows judgment without mercy will receive no mercy. Whoever shows mercy will receive mercy, because mercy prevails against judgment.
- JAM 4:11–12 ~ Don't speak evil about others, because whoever speaks evil against another or judges another speaks evil against the Law and judges the Law. If you judge the Law you are not abiding by the Law. There is only one Lawmaker, who can save and destroy, and you don't want to be judging Him.
- 1 PE 4:17 ~ Judgment begins with God's people (i.e., God's people are judged first). Then God will judge the wicked, and what do you think will happen to them?
- 2 PE 2:4,9 ~ God didn't spare the angels that sinned, but imprisoned them in hell to await judgment. God knows how to deliver the righteous from temptation, and how to deliver the unrighteous to judgment for punishment.
- 1 JO 2:17 ~ The world will pass away along with its sinfulness; but whoever does the will of God will live forever.
- JDE 1:7 ~ Sodom and Gomorrah, and other cities and peoples who were destroyed because of their wickedness, are examples of the vengeance of eternal fire that awaits the wicked.
- REV 7:9–10,13–14 ~ I (John) saw a giant multitude, too many people to even count. There were people from every nation, race, and tongue standing before the throne and the Lamb who was clothed in white. They held palm branches and sang, "Salvation to our God who sits on the throne, and to the Lamb." One of the elders asked me who these people were. I replied, "Tell me sir." He said, "These are the ones who came from great tribulation, who have washed their robes and made them white with the blood of the Lamb."
- REV 19:11 ~ John had a vision of heaven opening and a white horse emerging, upon which rode the One called Faithful and True. He had come in righteousness to judge and to make war.
- REV 20:12,15 ~ In John's vision he saw the dead, both small and great, standing before God. The books were opened, along with another book called the Book of Life. And everyone was judged according to the things written in the books about their actions during their lifetimes. Whoever's name was not found in the Book of Life was thrown into the lake of fire.

Summary: To conclude this section, it should be pointed out that a person's view about the timeframe or sequence of the rapture, resurrection and judgment is not essential to anyone's salvation. Many theologians and evangelists preach about the end times as if they had a perfectly clear understanding of the entire scenario. But there are different theories being put out, all based to some degree on scripture. A precise calendar of end time events does not exist; if God intended it to be clear the Bible would clarify it. For this reason, many evangelicals avoid belaboring this subject because the primary message is to acknowledge that Christ is coming soon. Exactly when the rapture, resurrection, and judgment occur is not for us to know; otherwise people would wait until the last minute and possibly miss out.

To repeat, it is our duty to listen, watch, and prepare for our Lord to return. If we knew when, people might be inclined to put it off. Patience for the return of Messiah enables one to be ready at all times, trusting His Spirit to take the lead. We do not have a "need to know" until God let's us know, after which we can be sure and there will be no debate about it. In the meantime, it is wise to remain vigilant (1 PE 5:8), like a soldier in a foxhole awaiting an invasion from unseen enemies; daily fighting the good fight (1 TI 6:12) with victory already in sight (DEU 20:4; JOH 16:33; 1 CO 15:55–57).

Lesson: Introduction to Revelation

The Revelation of Jesus Christ related to St. John provides insight into the events surrounding the return of Christ and the subsequent Day of Judgment. John was not the only one to receive such a revelation. Many OT prophets received similar visions. In fact, one cannot begin to understand the book of Revelation without studying other latter-day revelations and prophecies found in both the Old and New Testaments. Those who have spoken about the end times include Ezekiel, Daniel, Paul, John, and Jesus Christ (to name but a few).

The Holy Bible is like an enormous jigsaw puzzle. Each book of the Bible, OT and NT included, provides a piece to that puzzle. Collectively, the pieces create a giant picture, which represents God's great mystery revealed to all people. You cannot focus on just one section of the puzzle and understand this mystery, just as you cannot visualize the entire picture to a jigsaw puzzle when different sections are missing.

The book of Revelation is no exception. Revelation cannot be understood by studying it in isolation; this is a common mistake. Modern day cult teachers lead many people astray with their wayward interpretations of Revelation. Many people fall prey to such false teachers because they have not studied the Bible sufficiently to visualize the entire picture.

Even traditionally accepted interpretations are often based upon an isolated view of the book of Revelation, separating it from the rest of the Bible. The mainstream typically views Revelation as being totally symbolic. Although some interpret the rest of the Bible literally, they treat Revelation as being different somehow. While there are indeed many symbolic concepts in Revelation, as well as elsewhere in the Bible, these concepts often can be interpreted literally, since there is nothing in the Bible that is false. However, it is very easy to become confused. Meaningful interpretations can be derived only as a result of searching all the scriptures and consolidating them by putting the pieces together one by one. In this way, the big picture becomes revealed, rather than some obscure part of that picture.

For example, Revelation presents concepts such as the tribulation, the evil beast, and the millennial reign. Traditional theologians consider these concepts to be purely symbolic, and not representative of actual events or characters. The tribulation is frequently interpreted as referring to troubles and tribulations in general, and not a specific period of time when evil reaches its peak; or as Jesus put it, "a time of affliction worse than ever before or ever again." The beast is often interpreted as referring to the works of Satan in general, and not the "son of perdition" spoken of by St. Paul, "who will be revealed during the last days." The millennial reign is interpreted in a variety of ways. Some say it is the period of time following Christ's ascension and prior to His return; some say it represents a period when Christians reign with Christ on earth; some say it refers to a heavenly reign. None of these views are completely supported by scripture, but neither are they refuted by it. We do know that the thousand years represents "a time when Christ and His people reign and Satan is bound in chains," as described by St. John. One thing for certain, Satan currently does not appear to be bound in chains (1 PE 5:8); instead, he is wreaking havoc all over the world. Since one thousand may be an indefinite number, it could refer to the infinite reign of Christ, the promise that Satan has no more power over those who have received the Holy Spirit through Christ, and the fact that Satan cannot prevent the Gospel message from reaching the world.

The various views on the above controversies are explored in this lesson in light of the scriptures. It is the position of this author that the events and characters in Revelation are real, and the days in which we live could be their fulfillment. Revelations about the latter days are not intended to lead people through the entire final scenario event by event. They can, however, be viewed as a warning, or an alarm, for people to awaken and prepare for their Savior to return. The point of Revelation can be summarized in the final quote from Christ at the end of the book, "Surely I come quickly," and St. John's response, "Amen, come Lord Jesus" (REV 22:20). Here is a warning that everyone should heed: prepare for the end since nobody knows when it will come, whether by one's death or by the return of Christ. Either way, it could happen tomorrow so we must not wait any longer because time could run out any day now. Don't put off Christ another minute; instead, put Him on like a suit of armor (ROM 13:14; EPH 6:10–11).

Nobody can know when the day or hour of Christ's coming will happen, but anyone can read the signs and see that the time might be rather soon. It may or may not occur in our lifetime, but it is still wise to remain alert and be ready to receive Him. Be like the watchman who is there to open the door when the master returns from the wedding feast. Jesus said, "Watch for the signs and pray that you have the strength to escape the terrible things that will take place, and to stand before the Son of Man" (LUK 21:36).

The book of Revelation will now be reviewed. The intent of this review is not to persuade the reader but to enlighten the reader. An effort has been made to consolidate various scriptures dealing with the latter days, and identify underlying themes. The overall sequence of events presented below has been provided by a number of Old and New Testament prophets, including Jesus Christ Himself. Interpretations for the scriptures in this lesson adhere to the five basic rules offered in this text:

1. Translation employed must be accurate and reliable.
2. Passages are understood within context.
3. Scripture is used to interpret scripture.
4. Interpretations of all relevant scriptures must be in agreement.
5. Prophecy sometimes can be fulfilled more than once.

<u>Summary of Events Recorded in Revelation:</u>

Peace – War – Economic Collapse – Mass Death via Four Judgments (famine, pestilence, wild beasts, war) – Persecution – Gloom and Despair – Sealing of God's People – New Babylon – Abomination of Desolation – Rapture and First Resurrection – Wrath of God (plagues) – Final Armageddon – Satan's Last Stand – Millennial Reign of Christ – Second Resurrection – Judgment – Second Death – Eternity (either in Heaven or the Lake of Fire)

<u>Introduction</u>. The apostle John was directed by Jesus Christ Himself to share this revelation with the seven churches. The angel of the Lord provided the information and John recorded it (REV 22:16). John's revelation was a view of things past, present, and future, with the focus being the future and the end times.

<u>The Seven Churches</u>. John sent Christ's message of the Revelation of Jesus Christ to seven churches which were prominent late in the first century. These Christian churches were in strategic locations, and were among the largest in Asia Minor. In addition to communicating his visions, John sent a special message to each church. While the seven churches are addressed in turn, there is no sequence implied, since all seven churches received notice of the revelation at about the same time. Interestingly, the problems and variations existing in churches during that period still exist today. It is likely that this parallelism between the past and present is not a coincidence.

The Seven Churches

Church	Characteristics and Warnings	Current Parallels
Ephesus	Love and faith were waning; warned to become strong like before	Some churches and members have become quite aloof
Smyrna	Endured suffering and persecution; encouraged to persevere in the faith	Many foreign countries persecute and torment Christians; Christians often portrayed as crazy by media
Pergamos	Compromised true doctrine; mixed politics and truth; warned to refrain from idolatry and worldly views	Cults distort Christian doctrine, introducing own ideas; striving to be politically correct; not scriptural
Thyatira	Followed false prophets and engaged in sexually deviant behavior; warned to refrain from immorality	Some churches claim Christ but are far from Him; corrupt leaders
Sardis	Hypocrites in the faith claim to be righteous and worthy but are not; their works will not save them; warned to wake up (their faith is dead and their hearts are empty)	Reflects the pious attitude of some (like the Pharisees then, the church at Reformation, and the Inquisition)
Philadelphia	A door is opened to all corners of the earth; tasked to perform the work of evangelism; encouraged to remain steadfast; warning given about Satan's temple	Many ministries have not faithfully shared the Good News abroad and at home (missionaries, evangelists)
Laodicea	Became too worldly; are lukewarm in the faith; rich in worldly terms, not spiritual; warned to seek the Spirit	Indicative of new-age mentality; emphasis is on experience, not faith

The Seven Seals. Each seal presents a phase that passes, and each phase seems to be progressively more unbearable. The seals reveal the future fate of this world. According to Christ, we can expect wars, famine, pestilence, earthquakes, persecution, false prophets, wickedness, abominations, and destruction (MAT 24:7–20). The seven seals could represent the seven presumed years of the tribulation, the seventy years of desolation (DAN 9), the forty-nine weeks (or years) associated with Pentecost (LEV 23; LEV 25:8), or something entirely different. The last seal presents the seven trumpets, the seventh trumpet representing the end of suffering for the saints.

First Seal: The white horse appears to bring peace, but it is a false peace. The white knight comes to conquer and is awarded a crown, but close behind follows the warmonger on the red horse. This notion of a false peace seems to fit the concept of a "new world order" in which the powerful countries of the world pledge to defend the weaker ones. It will likely become a global police force ("big brother") that controls rather than protects (i.e., globalism). World powers consolidating military might with economic strength easily would be able to dictate the rules of trade and growth ("holding companies"), as well as thwarting any serious opposition.

- PSA 55:21 ~ His words were as smooth as butter, but war was in his heart. His words were softer than skin cream, but they were drawing their swords.
- JER 6:14; JER 8:11,15 ~ They kept saying "peace, peace" but there was no peace. We looked for peace but none came; we hoped for health but got trouble instead.
- DAN 8:25 ~ He (the evil king) will exalt himself. He will destroy many in the name of peace. He will oppose the Prince of princes but will be destroyed.
- MIC 3:2,5 ~ You hate good and love evil. You talk of peace but make war.
- MAT 24:6 ~ Jesus said, "You will hear of wars and rumors of wars, but the end is yet to come."
- 1 TH 5:3 ~ When they talk of peace and safety, total destruction will come.

Second Seal: The red horse brings war. The false peace likely will turn to oppression, resulting in bloodshed. An evil empire eventually will rule, which will require gaining control of the world by force.

- DAN 9:26 ~ The followers of the evil prince will destroy the city and the sanctuary. The end will come like a flood; the wars will continue until the desolations have run their course.
- DAN 11:38 ~ He will honor the power of forces.
- MAT 24:7 ~ Jesus said, "Nations and kingdoms will be at war. This is only the beginning of sorrows."
- LUK 21:24 ~ They will be slain by the sword, and captured. Jerusalem will be trampled down by the Gentiles until their kingdom has reached its peak.

Third Seal: The black horse is next, carrying a rider with scales. The scales are tipped causing economic imbalance, followed by financial collapse. The world will become divided, with the affluent prospering at the expense of the poor. A ration of bread will cost a day of wages, and only the rich will be able to afford the oil and wine (REV 6:6).

- MAT 4:4 ~ Jesus told Satan, "Man does not live by bread alone, but by every word that proceeds out of the mouth of God."
- JOH 6:26–27 ~ Jesus said, "Truly I tell you, you sought me, not because you saw miracles, but because you ate the bread and were filled. Labor not for the meat that perishes but for the meat that endures unto everlasting life, which the Son of Man will provide for those who God the Father has sealed."

Fourth Seal: The pale horse arrives carrying the death rider. Many will die from the four judgments of the Lord: famine, pestilence, wild beasts, and the sword (LEV 26:20–25; JER 14:12; JER 24:10; REV 6:8).

- DEU 28:21–28 ~ God will send diseases, plagues, and war to destroy you. The heavens and earth will be unyielding as iron; a blight will destroy all your crops. The land will become dry as dust from lack of rain; dust storms will destroy you. You will be defeated by your enemies. You will go to battle in glory but will run from your enemies in seven different directions, and you will become scattered across the earth. Your dead bodies will become food for wild animals. God will send boils, tumors, and various diseases to destroy you. You will become mad, blind, and confused.
- 2 CH 20:9 ~ If evil comes upon us, like the sword, judgment, pestilence, or famine, and we stand before God's house and in His presence (for His name is spoken there), and we cry to the Lord in our affliction, He will hear us and help us.
- EZE 5:17; EZE 14:21 ~ God will send the four terrible judgments upon Jerusalem: sword, famine, evil beasts, and pestilence.

Fifth Seal: The saints in heaven must witness further persecution of God's people. As the evil one gains power, the righteous will become more of a threat. Christians everywhere will be tormented, jailed, and murdered. There will be a great famine of the Word, a thirsting for the truth. This will be a time of great tribulation for the righteous.

- AMO 8:11–13 ~ The time is coming when there will be an unquenchable thirst to hear the Word of God. People will seek the Lord everywhere but will not find Him.
- MAT 24:21,29 ~ Jesus said, "There will be a time of great tribulation, worse than ever before or ever again."
- LUK 21:11 ~ Jesus said, "They will capture you, persecute you, and bring you before their judges to be tried."

- 2 TI 3:12–13 ~ All the righteous people will suffer persecution. The evil people will get perpetually worse.
- 1 PE 4:17–18 ~ The time is coming when judgment will begin at God's house. But if judgment begins with us, imagine what will happen to those who are evil.

Sixth Seal: The persecution of Christians is followed by a time of gloom, accompanied by wonders in the heavens.

- ISA 13:10 ~ The stars in heaven will not give light, and the sun and moon will be darkened.
- EZE 32:7–8 ~ I (God) will cover the heavens and make the stars dark; I will cover the sun with a cloud, and the moon will not shine.
- JOE 2:2,10,30–31 ~ A day of great darkness and gloom is coming. The earth will quake and the heavens will tremble. There will be wonders in the sky and on the earth: blood, smoke, and fire. The sun will become dark and the moon will become like blood.
- AMO 8:9 ~ God says, "On that day, I will make the sun set at noon and I will darken the world in broad daylight."
- ZEP 1:14–15 ~ The day of the Lord is coming quickly, the day when the mighty ones will cry. It is a day of darkness, gloom and destruction.
- MAT 24:29 ~ Jesus said, "Immediately after the time of tribulation, the sun will become dark, the moon will be shrouded in gloom, and stars will fall from the sky."
- REV 6:12–15 ~ There was a great earthquake; the sun became black and the moon became like blood. The stars fell from the sky. Everyone tried to hide and take cover, even the rich and mighty ones.

Seventh Seal: The seventh seal is the last seal and comprises the seven trumpets. Four angels of doom have been preparing for this moment; they will be turned loose to deliver God's wrath all over the world. Before they begin their mission, however, God will mark (seal) His servants so that they will not be harmed; 144,000 recipients of His seal will be children of Israel (God's chosen and/or the children of Abraham). Millions of people of all nations who had suffered tribulation but were redeemed by the Lamb of God will be worshipping the Lord in heaven.

- EZE 9:3–6 ~ God told the cherub to mark the foreheads of those that cried over the terrible abominations they had witnessed. Then God told the angel to terrorize and kill all the other people, old and young alike. I pleaded to the Lord not to destroy all of Israel, but He said that they had become evil and perverse.
- REV 14:1–4 ~ The 144,000 (children of Israel) are the first fruits of the Lamb.

The Seven Trumpets. Each trumpet sounds a warning to repent and turn to God. Each warning blast is accompanied by a cataclysmic event. The trumpets occur, it seems, more rapidly than the seals. The seventh seal includes all seven trumpets, each trumpet representing an event occurring as a result of removing the last seal from the scroll.

First Trumpet: Hail and fire mixed with blood falls from the sky. One third of the earth is scorched, a third of the trees and all the grass are burned.

- JOE 1:19–20 ~ I will cry to the Lord, for fire has burned the pastures and the trees of the field. The animals cry, for the rivers are dried up and there is no grass in the wilderness.

Second Trumpet: A burning mountain falls into the sea. One third of the sea is scorched. A third of the sea life die, turning the sea into blood. A third of the ships are destroyed.

Third Trumpet: A great star ("Wormwood") falls from heaven contaminating one third of the water. Many people die from drinking poisoned water.

Fourth Trumpet: A third of the sun, moon, and stars are darkened. The daylight hours are shortened by one third. The three terrible woes follow. (Refer again to scriptures associated with the sixth seal).

Fifth Trumpet: An angel falls from heaven with the key to the bottomless pit. Evil creatures are freed which torment the earth for five months. This is the first woe. Earth's inhabitants yearn for death. The creatures prepare for the battle ahead, their ruler being the angel of the pit (Lucifer).

Sixth Trumpet: Four angels are set free to destroy one third of humankind. A cavalry of two hundred million monsters are among the slayers. This is the second woe. Those who remain alive will not repent.

- EZE 5:2,12 ~ A third will be burned with fire in the city, when the days of the siege have been fulfilled. A third will be stabbed with a knife. A third will be scattered to the wind, and I will draw out a sword after them. A third will die from pestilence, and from famine they will be consumed. A third will fall by the sword; I will scatter a third to the four winds, and I will draw out a sword after them.

Seven thunders utter their voices (but the message is not recorded by John). The seventh angel holds a little book that is sweet to eat but sours the stomach. Before that angel blows the last trumpet, two witnesses prophesy for 3 ½ years. They have unusual powers. They turn water into blood, send plagues, and stop the rain; they also breathe fire. Eventually, they are killed and then rise from the dead 3 ½ days later.

The two witnesses are described as two olive trees and two candlesticks. These are the same two described in Zechariah as the anointed ones that stand over the earth (ZEC 4:11–14). They could be the two cherubim that stand on either side of the throne of the Lord (EXO 25:10,18,22; PSA 99:1). The fact that the two witnesses breathe fire implies that they have the power of high-ranking angels. Perhaps they were the same two witnesses who warned Lot before destroying Sodom and Gomorrah (GEN 19:1). Many people believe the witnesses to be Moses and Elijah, Moses having turned water into blood (EXO 7:20), and Elijah having controlled the rain for 3 ½ years (1 KI 17–18 and JAM 5:17–18). The fact that it was Moses and Elijah who were transfigured with Christ (MAT 17:1–3) also supports that theory. Further, the prophet Malachi mentions that Elijah will return before the "dreadful day of the Lord" (MAL 4:5), just like he did the first time Christ came in the flesh (MAT 11:12–14; LUK 1:17).

Seventh Trumpet: When the seventh angel sounds the trumpet, the mystery of God is completed (REV 10:7) and the kingdom is turned over to Christ (REV 11:15). The temple of heaven is opened (REV 11:19) to receive the faithful who are participants in the rapture and the resurrection. The wrath of God is then poured out on the earth in judgment, to punish the wicked. This is the third woe. All these events are associated with the last trumpet. Perhaps this trumpet represents the final stage of the tribulation in which the "days are shortened for the elect" (MAT 24:22,31; REV 3:10). Some consider the seven trumpets to coincide with the years of tribulation; others associate the tribulation with the seventh trumpet which begins the seven vials of wrath.

- ISA 27:13 ~ The great trumpet will be blown, and those who were about to die in the land of Assyria and the outcasts in Egypt will come to worship on God's holy mountain.
- DAN 12:1 ~ Michael the great prince (the archangel), who stands for the righteous, will come; and there will be a time of trouble worse than ever before or ever again. Then the righteous will be delivered, those whose names are written in the Book of Life.

- JOE 2:1,15 ~ Blow the trumpet and sound the alarm; let everyone tremble, for the day of the Lord is at hand (also ZEP 1:16).
- 1 CO 15:51–52 ~ We will not all sleep, but we will all be changed. In a brief moment, the last trumpet will sound and the saints will arise, incorruptible.
- 1 TH 4:16–17 ~ The Lord will descend from heaven with a shout, with the voice of the archangel, and with a blast from the trumpet of God. Then the dead in Christ will arise first. Those who remain alive in Christ will rise to join the others in the clouds, meeting the Lord in the sky. Those chosen by Christ will live with Him forevermore.

<u>War Between Good and Evil</u>. The next part of John's vision depicts the war matching Satan and his angels against Michael and his angels. Satan is summarily defeated and thrown out of heaven along with one third of the angels, only to begin his campaign on earth. Satan is frustrated, knowing the end is near.

- ISA 14:12–15 ~ You have fallen from heaven and have been cut down to the ground, Lucifer, who brought down the nations. For you deceived yourself, wanting to be exalted, even above God. Instead, you will be brought down into the depths of hell.
- ISA 34:2–4 ~ The Lord's anger is upon all nations and armies; He will utterly destroy and slaughter them. Their dead bodies will be scattered and will stink; the mountains will flow with their blood. Their hosts in heaven will be dissolved and thrown down.
- EZE 28:14–19 ~ You (Lucifer) were the anointed cherub; you lived upon the holy mountain of God. You were perfect from the day you were created until sin was found in you. Your great wealth made you violent inside and you became evil. Therefore, you were thrown off the holy mountain, and you will be destroyed. You exalted yourself because of your beauty, thereby corrupting yourself. You defiled the sanctuaries with your abominations. You will be consumed by the fire within you, and your terrible deeds will come to an end.
- LUK 10:18–20 ~ Jesus said, "I saw the devil, like a star falling from heaven. I have given you power over that enemy, so nothing can harm you. But don't rejoice because the demons submit to you; rather rejoice because your names are written in the Book of Life."
- EPH 6:12 ~ You will be contending, not against flesh and blood, but against wickedness in high places and rulers of darkness.
- REV 12:4,9 ~ His (Lucifer's) tail swept the third part of the stars (angels) of heaven, which fell to the earth. And the dragon stood before the woman which was ready to be delivered to devour her child as soon as it was born. The great dragon was cast out, that old serpent called the Devil and Satan who deceived the world; he was thrown down to the earth and his angels with him.

Satan is the dragon that tried to devour the Christ child. Satan has attempted time and again to defeat the Holy Spirit, by going after the baby Moses, by going after the baby Jesus, in attempting to entice Jesus to sin, and in declaring war in heaven. He has been unsuccessful, so he has decided to go after God's people on earth. Satan will possess a human being (literally, the son of perdition or hell, also known as the beast), enabling that person to perform great feats (2 TH 2:3–4,9–11).

The beast will make war with the saints for 3 ½ years (REV 13:5–7; DAN 7:25; DAN 12:7). During this time, he will build a great empire. He seems to establish his headquarters in the Holy Land. At the holy temple, the beast will set up the abomination of desolation. There, Satan will exalt himself as an object of worship, defiling the temple with the sacrifice of burnt (blood) offerings. He will require everyone to receive his mark on their forearm or forehead (REV 13:15–18). Nobody will be able to buy or sell anything without that mark. The number of the beast is 666 (six hundred sixty-six per the KJV). The desecration of the temple also will last about 3 ½ years, presumably the last phase of the tribulation (DAN 9:27).

- DAN 12:11–12 ~ The abomination that makes desolate will be set up for 1,290 days (3 ½ years). Blessed are those who withstand the corresponding 1,335 days of tribulation. (Note the extra forty-five days of tribulation.)
- JOE 2:3 ~ A fire devours everything in its path, leaving behind a wasteland. Nobody can escape.
- MIC 7:2–6 ~ All the godly and upright people are gone. The wicked lie in ambush for blood. They do evil with diligence. Princes and judges ask for bribes. Great people pursue their evil desires. The best of them is like a thorn. Their confusion and punishment await them. Nobody can be trusted; even family and friends become the enemy.
- MAT 10:21,36; MAR 13:12; LUK 12:52–53 ~ People will betray their own family members to death. A person's enemy will be living in the same house.
- LUK 21:24 ~ They continue to destroy everyone until their kingdom has reached its peak.
- 2 TH 2:3–4,9–12 ~ The man of lawlessness comes, who is the son of perdition. He exalts himself to be a god, or an object of worship, taking the seat in the temple of God. He brings about the acts of Satan through deception and magic. God will let them believe these lies and carry on with their wickedness, and be condemned to hell.
- REV 14:13 ~ Blessed are those who die in the Lord henceforth; they will find rest, for their actions precede them.

The Seven Vials. The seven vials or bowls are related to the last trumpet. Each vial represents the wrath of God poured out upon the wicked. This may reflect the days of desolation that follow Satan's abomination (DAN 12:11–12). It may reflect a seven-year period of tribulation for the wicked (i.e., the pre-tribulation rapture viewpoint) or the final year of a seven-year tribulation. Seven plagues are sent upon Satan and those who received his mark and worshipped his image. The saints in heaven watch from above. In the end, Satan and his army are defeated by the Son of God in the valley of slaughter (Armageddon). That valley (about two hundred miles long like the valley of Jezreel) will be filled with blood up to the bridle on a horse (REV 14:18–20). The redeemed in Christ will praise the Lord in heaven, while the followers of Satan will be tormented.

- ISA 28:15–19 ~ All covenants of death and agreements with hell will be null and void. Those that trusted in these lies will be trampled by the overwhelming scourge that passes through.
- DAN 9:27 ~ During the last half of the week (interpreted as half of seven years) the abomination that causes desolation will continue, until the terrible end that awaits is poured out upon them.
- REV 6:15–17 ~ They tried to hide in the rocks and caves, praying that the mountain would fall on them, for the great day of God's wrath had come upon them.

First Vial: Terrible sores.

Second Vial: Sea turns to blood and all sea life expires.

Third Vial: All drinkable water turns to blood.

Fourth Vial: Sun gets terribly hot, scorching everyone.

Fifth Vial: The beast's kingdom is thrown into darkness; the wicked chew their tongues in painful agony, cursing God.

<u>Sixth Vial</u>: Euphrates River dries up; kings come from the east. Evil spirits emerge from the dragon (Satan), the beast (antichrist, or son of hell), and the false prophet. The demons gather their evil hosts for the final battle at Armageddon (mountains of Megiddo).

<u>Seventh Vial</u>: Great earthquakes and floods; large balls of hail fall. The destruction of Babylon occurs.

<u>The Rise and Fall of Babylon</u>. This is the evil city that sits on seven mountains. It is called the whore because it seduces the nations with its riches and pleasures of the flesh, enticing people to perform acts of wickedness and immorality. Babylon is the center of the kingdom of the beast, the final great empire to rule the Holy Land (Israel, Judea, and Jerusalem).

St. John writes of eight kingdoms, five past, one present, one future (having a short reign), and then the last which is that of the beast. John states that the kingdom of the beast will be a repeat of the other seven. Revelation refers to the final kingdom as Babylon. Many people also refer to the kingdom of the beast as the revived Roman Empire, based on the assumption that Rome was similarly influenced by Satan; emperors such as Nero, Caligula, and Antiochus Epiphanes pretended to be gods themselves, persecuted people of God, and desecrated the temple with their self-worship. Based on this assumption, the kingdom of the beast could be a repeat of any or all of the seven previous empires which fell because of greed, self-indulgence, immorality, and the oppression and genocide of other nations.

The prophet Daniel also wrote of the progression of kingdoms, accurately identifying the empires that would follow ancient Babylon (DAN 7—8). Part of that prophecy came from Daniel's interpretation of the dream of Nebuchadnezzar, king of Babylon (DAN 2). The dream was of a statue: head of gold, breast and arms of silver, belly and thighs of bronze, legs of iron, and feet of iron mixed with clay. The prophet Zechariah also spoke of four kingdoms. Zechariah referred to the Gentile kings that would scatter Israel, Judea, and Jerusalem, and the fact that God would have his four carpenters (angels) dismantle each one of those empires (ZEC 1:18–21).

The chart below represents the great empires written about by John and Daniel. These kingdoms each ruled over the Holy Land and the region surrounding the Mediterranean Sea. They were notorious for their evil, decadence, and waging war against God's people. Notice how the prophecies of Daniel line up with those of John.

The Great Empires

Reference	Egypt	Assyria	Babylon	Media-Persia	Greece	Rome	(Nazi)	Beast
DAN 2			Gold	Silver	Bronze	Iron		Iron-Clay
DAN 2			Head	Chest-Arms	Torso	Legs		10 Toes
DAN 7			Lion	Bear	Leopard	Dreadful		10 Horns
DAN 8			King 1	King 2	King 3	King 4		Terrible
REV 13			Lion	Bear	Leopard	Beast		10 Crowns
REV 17		<<------------- Five Have Fallen			------------->>	One Is	Short Reign	10 Kings
REV 17	King 1	King 2	King 3	King 4	King 5	King 6	King 7	King 8

The kingdom of the beast is comprised of ten kings that rule one "hour" with the beast. They become of one mind with Satan, joining him in strength and power in his war against Christ the Lamb. There are several references in Revelation about this hour: the hour of temptation (REV 3:10); the hour of power (REV 17:12); and the hour of Babylon's destruction (REV 18:10,17,19). When evil has reached its peak, God will destroy the new Babylon and all its inhabitants. Plagues, death, destruction, and fire will fall upon the evil city within the span of one "day" (REV 18:8). God's judgment upon the great whore is the end of the evil empire.

Many theorists have likened the new Babylon with Rome the seat of the Catholic Church, or Istanbul the seat of the Byzantine Church. Both cities encompass seven hills, and both represent denominations that have maintained their own traditions and not remained focused on orthodox Christian principles. In fact, Martin Luther accused the Roman Catholic Church during his time of distorting the truth and emphasizing their own traditions, and it was he who likened the Catholic Church of his era to a harlot. These incidents are presented only for information. It is not the intention of this review to implicate any church or denomination with the kingdom of the beast.

<u>The Millennial Reign and the Judgment</u>. A huge celebration takes place in heaven. The Lamb of God rides triumphantly on a white horse (not the same white horse as the first seal and the first horseman of the Apocalypse). The evil hordes make war with the Lamb. The beast (antichrist), the false prophet, and those that worshipped the beast and received his mark are thrown into the lake of fire. Satan is bound and thrown into the bottomless pit for one thousand years (an indefinite period). All those who remained faithful and witnessed for Jesus Christ will reign with Him eternally. These saints will be blessed for they are participants in the first resurrection.

After the thousand years, Satan is turned loose. The rest of the dead are resurrected at that time according to the millennialist point of view (the second resurrection). Satan tries to rally all the wicked souls once again to make war with Christ. Satan attacks the holy city and the saints, and fire pours out of the holy city devouring them. Satan is thrown into the lake of fire with the false prophet and the antichrist, to be tormented day and night forever.

- JDE 1:6–8 ~ The fallen angels who left heaven have been kept in chains and darkness until the day of judgment. Sodom, Gomorrah and other cities like them engaged in wickedness, and were made an example of God's wrath by suffering the eternal fire. In like manner, God will deal with these filthy dreamers who defile their bodies, despise authority, and speak evil of honor.

Finally, the dead are judged by God. The books that tell their life stories are opened, and the people are judged according to their conduct during their lives. The Book of Life is opened which has the names of those who will be allowed to live with God. They are judged not guilty because they are clothed in the righteousness of Christ. Death, hell, and all of those whose names are not recorded in the Book of Life are thrown into the lake of fire.

- ISA 33:14 ~ The sinners in Zion are afraid; fear has surprised the hypocrites. Who among us will live with the devouring fire? Who among us will burn forever?
- PSA 69:27–28 ~ By adding more sin to sin, one can never know righteousness. Let their names be obliterated from the Book of Life.
- REV 20:15 ~ Those whose names were not written in the Book of Life were thrown into the lake of fire.
- REV 21:8 ~ The fearful, unbelieving, abominable, murderous, promiscuous, idolatrous, lying, and satanic will have their part in the lake that burns with fire and brimstone; this is the second death.

<u>New Heaven and Earth</u>. Heaven will be a lovely place where there is never any sadness, death, pain, or sorrow. All that is evil will have been condemned to the lake of fire which is the second death. Heaven will be lit forever by the light of God, so never will there be darkness again. The New Jerusalem will be the holy city, arranged in a foursquare configuration (possibly a four-sided pyramid or cube) with three gates at each side (twelve in all). The city will be made of precious stones and metals, and the gates will be made of pearl. The River of Life will flow through heaven nourishing the Tree of Life and the saints. The tree will bear twelve kinds of fruit each month and the leaves will provide healing medicine. Note the similarities between the description of heaven by Ezekiel (EZE 47) and that of John (REV 22).

- ISA 65:17–19 ~ I (God) will create new heavens and a new earth; the former heaven and earth will never be remembered or recalled. You will be glad and rejoice forever, for I will make Jerusalem a place of happiness. I will rejoice in Jerusalem for I will be happy with my people, and there will nevermore be the sound of crying among my people.
- EZE 47:1,5,9,12–13,22 ~ Later, God brought me (Ezekiel) again to His house, and I saw waters flowing out from it which formed a river that I could not pass over. Everything that the water touched flourished. On both sides of the river grew all kinds of trees that never died. The trees produced new fruit every month; the fruit of the trees provided food and the leaves provided medicine. God told me that the river bordered the land promised to the twelve tribes of Israel. The land bordering the river was to be divided as an inheritance for God's chosen people, including the twelve tribes and the strangers who lived among them.
- JOE 3:18 ~ The mountains will flow with wine and the hills will flow with milk. The valleys will flow with water from a fountain in the center of the Lord's house.
- JOH 14:2 ~ Jesus said, "In my Father's house are many mansions. I go there to prepare such a place for you, so that where I am you can be also."
- 1 CO 2:9 ~ It is written: Nobody has ever heard or seen, or even imagined, the wonderful things God has prepared for those who love Him (ISA 64:4).
- REV 22:1–5 ~ I was shown a pure, crystal clear river of the Water of Life, proceeding from the throne of God and the Lamb. In the middle of the river, and on either side of it, was the Tree of Life. The tree bore twelve different fruits each month, and its leaves could be used as medicine for any ailment. The curse was gone forever. Everyone served the Lamb, and His name was on all of their foreheads. And His light shone constantly so that there was never any darkness, and nobody needed a lamp.

God has promised eternal life to all believers. Nobody has ever seen, heard, or imagined how happy, wonderful and beautiful it will be in paradise (ISA 64:4; LUK 23:43; 1 CO 2:9).

There is nothing on earth with which to compare heaven. The Bible does tell us, however, that never will there be any more suffering, sorrow, hunger, pain, or evil (ISA 35:10; REV 7:16; REV 21:4).

Lesson: Signs of the Second Coming

The Latter Days. Jesus gave His own account of the latter days occurring before His Second Advent, describing events surrounding His return (MAT 24–25; MAR 13; LUK 21). This is known as the Olivet Discourse (repeated here as an introduction).

Don't be deceived, for many will claim to be Messiah or His prophet. They will perform magic tricks and fool many people. There will be wars and rumors of wars. There will be earthquakes, famines, afflictions, and pestilence. The righteous will be persecuted, interrogated, imprisoned, and murdered. People will betray one another and wickedness will abound. It will be like the days of Noah and Lot, only worse. People will eat, drink and be merry. Christians will be hated for following Christ. This is the beginning of sorrows, the beginning of the end; a time of great tribulation will come, worse than any before or after.

Jerusalem will be surrounded by enemies when the desolation is nigh. This is the abomination spoken of by Daniel. When this happens, head for the hills; do not take time to pack. Hope it doesn't happen during winter; it will be especially tough for those with babies. It will be a time of great mourning. Two men will be working in the field; one will be taken. Two women will be weaving; one will be taken. There will be signs in the heavens. The sun and moon will be darkened and stars will fall from the sky. The Gospel will need to be preached around the world. The Holy Spirit will inform Christians what to say and do. When these things happen, be prepared for Christ's return. Just as blossoming trees will be a sign that springtime is nigh, so will these signs proclaim the Second Coming of Messiah. That generation will not pass until these things occur. Those enduring until the end will be saved.

Finally, a sign in heaven will proclaim the coming of the Son of Man. You will see Him in the clouds of heaven, in all His power and glory. He'll send angels to gather the righteous into heaven. Nobody but the Father knows when this will happen, not the angels, not even the Son of God. Heaven and earth will pass away, but God's Word will remain true forever. Then all people will be gathered and separated, like dividing sheep and goats, with the sheep on the right and the goats on the left. To those on the right Jesus will say, "Come inherit the kingdom prepared in advance for you, for when I was hungry you fed me, when I was thirsty you gave me a drink, and when I was naked and cold you clothed me." The sheep will say, "When did we do this?" Jesus will say, "Whenever you did it to anyone else you did it to me." To those on the left He will say, "Depart you cursed ones into the everlasting fire prepared for the devil and his angels, because you did not help your neighbor in need." The goats will inherit eternal torment; the sheep will inherit eternal bliss.

When will Christ return? It is impossible to predict with any accuracy exactly when Christ will come. However, significant events will happen within the span of a single generation. Those who purport to know the exact sequence or the timing are in error and should not be deemed reliable sources of truth.

- MAT 24:36,44,50 ~ Nobody knows the day and hour, not even the angels; not even the Son of Man knows, but only the Father in heaven. For the Son of Man will come when you least expect Him.
- MAT 25:13 ~ Watch therefore, because you know neither the day nor the hour.
- LUK 21:34 ~ That generation will not pass away until all these things have happened.
- 2 PE 3:10 ~ The day of the Lord will come as a thief in the night.
- REV 3:2–3 ~ Jesus said, "Be watchful and strengthen each other in the truth, for I have found imperfection on the earth. Remember everything you have heard, hold fast to it, and repent.

If you are not watchful, I will surprise you like a thief, for you never know when I might come upon you."

Israel was lost but then is found. The Jews were scattered around the world. However, Israel became an independent nation during the twentieth century (1948). Many Jews have been returning to Israel and continue to do so. During the end times, Israel will be surrounded by its enemies (LUK 21:20). This is actually the case now, with Moslem nations at every border (note that Israel and the Arab nations have been natural enemies since the death of Abraham).

- DEU 4:26–28 ~ I (God) call heaven and earth to witness against you this day, that soon you will perish from the land where you are going across the Jordan River. You will not possess it for long, but will be utterly destroyed. I will scatter you among the nations, and you will become a minority among the heathen where I shall lead you. And there you will serve other gods, the work of men's hands: wood and stone which cannot see, hear, eat, or smell.
- DEU 28:63–66 ~ Just as the Lord rejoiced over you, so He will destroy you. You will be taken from the land He gave you, and scattered from one end of the world to the other. You will never find peace or rest, and your life will hang in doubt day and night.
- DEU 30:3–5 ~ The Lord will have compassion on you, will gather you up, return you to your land, and allow you to multiply.
- 1 KI 14:15 ~ God will strike Israel down, uproot them, and scatter them abroad.
- ISA 11:11–12; JER 31:10 ~ He that scattered you from Israel will gather you again.
- EZE 20:34; EZE 36:24; EZE 37:24; EZE 39:27 ~ God will gather you from countries everywhere and bring you back to your homeland.
- MIC 5:8 ~ The remnant of Israel will be scattered among foreigners.
- ZEC 1:18–21 ~ Zechariah saw a vision of four horns that drive the Jews out of Israel, Judah, and Jerusalem, and then four carpenters which dismantle the horns that scatter the Jews.
- ZEC 7:14 ~ I (God) scattered them like a tornado among nations they did not know; and the land was laid to waste behind them.
- JAM 1:1 ~ I, James, a servant of God and the Lord Jesus Christ, send greetings to the twelve tribes which are scattered abroad.

An evil generation will come. It will be like the times of Noah and Lot, only worse (LUK 17:26). God destroyed civilization in Noah's time, and Sodom and Gomorrah during Lot's time. God allowed only the righteous people to escape these calamities. The same will happen in the last days: a time of wickedness, devastation, and deliverance. Sinfulness will flourish and evil will abound. The most heinous crimes possibly imaginable will occur, and the innocent will suffer.

- ISA 2:6 ~ The people practice divination and fortunetelling. They please themselves with the children of strangers.
- ISA 3:5,9,11 ~ The people will oppress each other. Youth will be insolent to their elders. They proclaim their sin like Sodom, they don't hide it. Woe to them, for what they have done to others will be done to them.
- ISA 5:20–23 ~ Woe to those who call evil good and good evil. They seize their prey which nobody can rescue. Woe to those who are heroes at drinking alcohol, who acquit the guilty for a bribe, and who deprive the innocent of their rights.
- ISA 59:3–7 ~ Your hands are defiled with blood and sin. Your lips have spoken lies and wickedness. They conceive evil and rely on foolishness and lies. They run to evil and hasten to shed innocent blood. Desolation and destruction ride their highways.
- JER 8:12 ~ They were not ashamed when they committed their abominations.

CHAPTER THREE

- JER 23:14,17 ~ I have seen horrible things. They commit adultery, tell lies, and support evildoers so that nobody returns to being good. They have become like Sodom and Gomorrah. They say you will find peace for being evil and following your fantasies.
- LAM 1:18–19 ~ Virgins and young men have been taken captive. Lovers deceive each other. Priests and elders perish searching for food for the soul.
- EZE 16:15–20 ~ You trusted in your beauty and fornicated with anybody and everybody. You played the harlot more than ever before or ever again. You made images of men and played the harlot with them. You sacrificed your sons and daughters.
- JOE 3:3 ~ They gamble for my people, and trade a boy for a harlot, and sell a girl to get intoxicated.
- MIC 3:2–3,5 ~ You hate good and love evil. You skin people and eat their flesh. You chop their bodies into pieces. You talk of peace but make war.
- MIC 6:12 ~ The rich men are full of violence and lies.
- MIC 7:2–6 ~ All the godly and upright people are gone. The wicked lie in ambush for blood. They do evil with diligence. Princes and judges ask for bribes. Great people pursue their evil desires. Even the best of them is like a thorn. Their confusion and punishment await them. Nobody can be trusted; even family and friends become the enemy.
- HAB 1:4 ~ Law and judgment are loosened, for the wicked encompass the righteous. Therefore, wrong judgment proceeds.
- MAT 10:21,36; MAR 13:12; LUK 12:52–53 ~ People will betray their own family members to death. A person's enemy will be living in the same house.
- MAT 12:39,43–45 ~ An evil and adulterous generation will seek a sign that will never come. An evil spirit will go out of a man, find seven more evil than himself, and then return. That's how bad this evil generation will be.
- LUK 16:8 ~ People are commended for being dishonest. The dishonest people of this evil generation are shrewder than the honest people.
- ROM 1:24–32 ~ They exchanged God's truth with lies. They worshipped and served the creation rather than the Creator. They performed dishonorable passions. Women gave up natural relations for unnatural. Men gave up natural relations with women in favor of passion for each other. Men performed shameless acts with other men, thereby receiving in their own persons the due penalty for these evil deeds. They were filled with all manner of wickedness, evil, disobedience, jealousy, boastfulness, insolence, malice, murder, deceit, slander, strife, and all manner of malignity. They were faithless, heartless, ruthless, and foolish. They enjoyed doing evil, even though they were warned that such wickedness would lead to death.
- 1 TI 6:10–11 ~ The love of money is the root of all evil; through the craving for worldly riches many have wandered away from the faith and pierced their hearts. Strive for righteousness, godliness, faith, love, steadfastness, and gentleness.
- 2 TI 3:1–6,13 ~ There will be a time of great distress. People will love themselves and money. They will be abusive, arrogant, conceited, disobedient, treacherous, slanderous, ungrateful, unholy, inhumane, haters of good and lovers of pleasure. They will capture weak and wayward women, swayed by impulses. Evil people and impostors will progress from bad to worse, as will the deceivers and the deceived.
- JDE 1:7–8,18–19 ~ It will be like Sodom and Gomorrah, indulging in unnatural lust. In their dreams they defile the flesh, reject authority, and abuse the righteous. They are complainers, boasters, scoffers, deceivers, lewd and disgusting, and devoid of the Holy Spirit.
- REV 18:23 ~ The businessmen were the most powerful men on earth, and through their cunning they deceived the nations.

False prophets will be everywhere. People will continue to stray from God, following Satan and others teaching lies. Christians will be persecuted. Prophets, priests, and politicians will be evil, addicted to power which they wield abusively. There will be a thirst for the truth but the Word of God will be stifled.

- ISA 32:6–7 ~ The vile person speaks villainy, plots evil, practices ungodliness, and deprives the needy. His instruments are evil. He devises wicked plans to destroy the poor and the just with his lies.
- LAM 4:13 ~ Prophets and priests shed innocent blood.
- EZE 13:19 ~ They will pollute me (God) among my people for a piece of bread. They will kill people that should not have to die and save others that should not live, then lie about it.
- HOS 6:9 ~ The priests commit murder by consent; they commit lewdness.
- AMO 8:11–13 ~ I will send a famine of the Word. They will seek the Word of God and not find it. The virgins and young men shall faint of thirst for the Word.
- EPH 6:12 ~ You will be contending, not against flesh and blood, but against wickedness in high places and rulers of darkness.
- 2 TH 2:3–4,9–12 ~ The man of lawlessness comes, who is the son of perdition. He exalts himself to be a god or an object of worship, taking the seat in the temple of God. He brings about the acts of Satan through deception and magic. People will deceive themselves, and will be condemned for not believing the truth.
- 2 PE 2:1–3,14,18–19 ~ False prophets come to bring damnable heresies and to deny the Lord, deceiving many. They will exploit with false words and attract you with lusts of the flesh. They have eyes full of adultery, insatiable for sin. Their hearts are trained in greed, and they gain through wrongdoing. They promise freedom but are themselves slaves to corruption, and are condemned. They will get perpetually worse.
- 2 PE 3:3–4 ~ Scoffers will come, following their own passions and saying, "Where is the promise of His coming?"

The New Babylon will thrive, representing an evil empire much like its predecessors which crumbled due to corruption, excess, and overall wickedness. It will be a final attempt at world domination by Satan, along with those who hunger for globalist control and power. But the empire will collapse quickly. The next destination for the conspirators and their mindless followers will be the lake of fire.

- ISA 13:19 ~ Babylon will be like Sodom and Gomorrah when God destroyed them.
- JER 49:4,13,17 ~ There is the faithless daughter who trusted in her treasures. Her cities will become a horrible disaster, a wasteland and a curse like Sodom and Gomorrah.
- JER 51:7 ~ Babylon got the world drunk with her wine, and they became crazy like her.
- EZE 16:15–20 ~ You trusted in your beauty, and played the harlot, fornicating with anyone and everyone. You took the riches and fine things, made images and had sex with them. You sacrificed your sons and daughters to your idols. Do you think this is a small matter?
- NAH 3:1–6 ~ Woe to the bloody city full of lies, atrocities, prostitution, and the countless lewdness of that harlot who betrays nations and families. Heaps of slain corpses, dead bodies without end: that will be their reward. God will throw abominable filth on them for all to see.
- 2 PE 2:14,18 ~ They have eyes full of adultery; they cannot cease from sin. Their souls are beguiling and unstable; their hearts are covetous and cursing. They are vain, and allure others with lust and promiscuity.
- REV 17:5,9,18 ~ The beast's whore (Babylon) is that great city that sits on seven mountains and over many waters, and rules over many nations and peoples.

- REV 18:2 ~ Babylon has become the habitation of devils and every foul spirit.

<u>The four judgements</u> will be brought upon the wicked. Because of the evil, God will send disease and pestilence, famine, wild beasts, and war (the sword) to devastate them. And there will be mass death.

- DEU 28:21–28 ~ God will send diseases, plagues, and war to destroy you. The heavens and earth will be unyielding as iron; a blight will destroy your crops. The land will become dry as dust from lack of rain; dust storms will destroy you. You will be defeated by your enemies. You will go to battle in glory, but you will run from your enemies in seven different directions, and you will become scattered across the earth. Your dead bodies will become food for wild animals. God will send boils, tumors, and various diseases to destroy you. You will become mad, blind, and confused.
- EZE 5:17 ~ I (God) will send famine, evil beasts, pestilence and the sword upon you.
- REV 6:8 ~ I saw a pale horse, and riding it was Death, and Hell followed him. And power was given to them to kill one quarter of the earth via the sword, hunger, death, and wild beasts.

<u>War</u>. There will be several conflicts, and then a great holocaust. It will not be a series of minor engagements or sporadic battles about the globe, it will be a worldwide campaign culminating in a siege lasting 3 ½ years (World War III, perhaps). The beast will be a conqueror in search of global power; the new Babylon will be his kingdom. Jerusalem will end up in the middle of this conflict, when the temple becomes desecrated by the beast's abomination. The aggression appears to come from the north, from Magog (GEN 10:1–2). For more information on this topic, refer to the lesson, *Babylon, Past, Present, and Future*, which discusses Gog and Magog in great detail (Chapter Eight).

- EZE 32:4–12 ~ I will toss you out upon the land where the beasts and fowl will feed on your carcasses. The land will be darkened beneath a gloomy sky. I will bring destruction upon all nations; the sword of the king of Babylon will terrorize you.
- EZE 38—39 ~ Face northward, toward Magog, and prophesy: God is against you Gog. You will mobilize armies of the distant north, as well as from Africa and Asia. You will invade Israel in an attempt to obtain her wealth and conquer her, Israel who has been at peace after having returned home from all over the world. This will happen in the latter years. There will be a great earthquake. You will end up fighting yourselves in the confusion. I will send animals to eat you, death, disease, and calamities. I will destroy five-sixths of your armies. I will rain fire and brimstone upon Magog and your allies to include the islands and coastlands, and places east of the Dead Sea. It will take seven months to bury the bodies. It will be a glorious victory for Israel. I will be their Lord from that day on, and forever.
- DAN 9:26 ~ The followers of the evil prince will destroy the city and the sanctuary. The end will come like a flood; the wars will continue until the desolations have run their course.
- DAN 11:6–45 ~ The daughter of the king of the south will make an agreement with the king of the north. Neither will stand. A branch from her roots will enter the fortress of the king of the north and will prevail (MAT 12:42). The north will raise an army and defeat the south. They will turn towards the coastlands, but a commander will stop them. In his place will arise a contemptible person, without warning, and obtain the kingdoms by flattery and deceit. He will overthrow armies, make alliances deceptively, and plunder. He will forecast devices against his enemies; he will employ the power of forces. He will corrupt people. He will honor with money, pleasure, and luxury. He will exalt himself and speak against God. He will profane the holy temple and honor people who forsake the holy covenant. He will set up

in the holiest place the abomination that brings desolation. He will give no heed to God or to women. He will divide the land for a price. He will destroy many. He will prosper until the indignation is finished, but only for a short time. The king of the south will fight back, but the north will attack like a tornado by land and sea. He will invade the glorious land and many countries will be conquered; but some will escape including Edom, Moab, and Ammon. But reports from the armies of the east and north will trouble him, so with fury he will utterly destroy and enslave the nations. He will encamp between the seas below the holy mountain, but he will come to an end and nobody will help him.

- JOE 2:20 ~ I will remove far from you the northern army, and will drive them into a wasteland, facing toward the eastern sea and backed against the other sea. The stench will be penetrating.
- LUK 21:24 ~ They will continue to destroy everyone until their kingdom (the Gentiles) has reached its peak.
- REV 13:1,7 ~ I saw an evil beast rise from the sea. He was given power to make war with the saints and to subdue them. He gained power of all races, tongues, and nations.

The beast will devastate the Holy Land, setting up the abomination of desolation in the holy temple. The Jews will flee as their land is desolated and their holy temple defiled. But the evil conquerors will be dispatched quickly. It will be the third and final time that the temple and the land are desecrated; those responsible will have an immediate day of reckoning to account for their despicable behavior.

- JOE 3:1–2 ~ Judah and Jerusalem will again become captives in those days. The nations will gather in the valley of Jehoshaphat. The Gentiles prepare for war; let them gather their warriors and come. Shape your tools into weapons of war. The winepress is full. Multitudes gather in the valley of decision, for the day of the Lord is close. Flee into the hills.
- ISA 27:10 ~ The defended city will be devastated, and its inhabitants will flee into the wilderness.
- ZEC 14:1–5 ~ The day of the Lord is coming when they will divide the spoils. For all nations will gather for battle against Jerusalem, and the city will be taken, the houses ransacked, and the women raped. Then the Lord will fight against those nations. He will stand on the Mount of Olives which will split to form a great valley. The Jews will flee across this valley.
- MAT 24:15–20; LUK 21:20–21 ~ Jesus said, "When you see Jerusalem surrounded by its enemies the abomination of desolation is nigh. Flee into the mountains; don't go back for anything. Hope it is not in winter; it will especially be difficult for those with small children."
- LUK 19:43–44 ~ Jesus said, "The time is coming when your enemies surround you, and Jerusalem will be utterly destroyed; and they will not leave one stone sitting on top of another."
- REV 11:2 ~ The holy city will be trampled down by foreigners for forty-two months (3 ½ years).
- REV 20:7-9 ~ When the thousand years are over, Satan will be cut loose from his prison to deceive the nations in all four corners of the earth, Gog and Magog, and muster them for battle, the number of which is as the sand of the sea. They will surround the camp of the saints and the beloved city; but fire will come down from heaven and consume them all.

Lesson: The Tribulation and the Beast

<u>The Tribulation</u>. A time of great tribulation will occur prior to Christ's return. Many believe that this will last for seven years (DAN 9:24–27). It could be the final phase of a forty-nine-year cycle consisting of seven stages lasting seven years each (LEV 25:8). This period of tribulation might coincide either with the seven trumpets or with the seven vials of wrath. Or, the number seven may be inferred to symbolize the end of time as we know it (representing completion). There are varying points of view regarding this period called the Great Tribulation, and the occurrence of the rapture and the resurrection, all of which will be discussed in a subsequent lesson.

During the tribulation, the devil will persecute, jail, and torture Christians (REV 2:10). The devil will make war with God's people for 3 ½ years. The abomination of desolation will be set up, probably during that 3 ½ period (DAN 12:11–12). Perhaps a seven-year stretch is divided into a tribulation for the righteous and one for the wicked. The mark of the beast will be given to followers of the beast, but not to God's faithful who will be sealed with His mark (144,000 from the nation of Israel, or the children of Abraham, who are among the "first fruits of the Lamb").

- JER 30:7 ~ That will be a great time (of tribulation); there will be no others like it. It is the time of Jacob's trouble; but he shall be saved out of it.
- DAN 12:1 ~ Michael the great prince will stand for God's people. There will be a time of tribulation worse than ever before or ever again, but God's elect will be delivered, all whose names are written in the Book of Life.
- JOE 2:28–32 ~ I will pour out my Spirit on humankind. Your sons and daughters will prophesy and will see visions; old men will dream dreams. There will be signs in the heavens and on earth: blood, fire, and smoke. The sun will turn dark and the moon will turn to blood, before that great and terrible day of the Lord. All who call upon the Lord will be delivered.
- AMO 8:11 ~ There will be a famine of the Word; people will hunger to hear the Word but they will not be filled.
- ZEP 1:14–15 ~ The great day of the Lord is coming quickly, when mighty men will cry. It is a day of wrath, trouble, and distress, of destruction and desolation, gloom, clouds, and darkness.
- MAR 13:19,24 ~ There will be a time of affliction worse than ever before or ever again. After the tribulation, the sun will be darkened and the moon will be blotted out.
- 2 TI 3:1,13 ~ In the last days, perilous times will come. The evil ones will get continuously worse.
- REV 6:9,11 ~ I saw an alter, and beneath it were the souls of those who were slain because of their faith and their testimony. They were given white robes and told to wait a little longer before God avenged their death because some of their fellow members in the faith were yet to perish as they did.
- REV 7:2–4 ~ The angel called to four other angels, commanding them to hurt the earth and the sea, but not those with God's seal. Before they were released, they had to seal God's people by putting His mark on their foreheads. There were 144,000 from the tribes of Israel that were sealed.
- REV 7:9,14 ~ I saw a gigantic choir in white robes; they were from various nations, kindreds, and tongues, and had come from great tribulation. They had washed their robes in the blood of Christ.
- REV 8:13 ~ The angel said, "Woe, woe, woe to the earth." (The three terrible woes were about to be brought upon the earth).

<u>The Beast</u>. Satan is the original beast that will come into power during the final days. The second beast in Revelation is Satan in the flesh, or the son of Satan. This beast will perform fake miracles and will use the power of forces to deceive and to subdue the people (DAN 11:38; 2 TH 2:9–11). Satan will possess and invade a human being in opposition to the Son of God. Actually, Satan has contrived an unholy trinity or three entities that oppose God (REV 16:13–14; REV 20:10). There is the antichrist, the son of hell who makes himself out as a messiah; the false prophet who is the liar, opposing all that is true, especially the Holy Spirit which is God's Word and God's truth; and the Beast, who is Satan the dragon.

- ISA 32:6–7 ~ The vile person comes speaking blasphemy and working evil and hypocrisy, opposing God Himself. His instruments are wickedness, lies, and dishonor.
- DAN 7:17,23–25 ~ The four beasts represent four kings who will come (REV 17). The fourth beast representing the fourth king is different, exceedingly terrible. The ten horns represent ten kings; three of them fall, because one replaces them. This evil one will speak great things against God and will make war with the saints, defeating them. He will change the times and the rules. He will reign for a time, times, and half a time (1+2+½ = 3 ½ years).
- DAN 8:20–25 ~ The ram with two horns represents the kings of Media and Persia. The male goat with one horn represents the first king of Greece. The goat's horn breaks, and is replaced by four others representing four kingdoms. After their rule will begin the rule of the terrible king, who understands riddles, and possesses great power. Through his cunning he will cause the destruction of mighty men and saints. He will magnify himself and deceit will prosper. Using the guise of peace (MIC 3:5), he will destroy many. In his arrogance, he will take on the Prince of princes Himself, who will destroy him without raising a hand.
- DAN 11:21–37 ~ A wicked person without honor will obtain the northern kingdom deceitfully. He will succeed in plundering the richest countries more than anyone has before. He will raise a great army and defeat the king of the south. He will oppose the holy covenant, and will corrupt people with his flatteries. But the people who know God will be strong and will perform miracles. The king will do whatever he pleases, and he will exalt himself above all others. He will speak against God and will prosper until his time is up. He will disregard the Lord God and other gods. He will disregard the desire for women.
- 2 TH 2:3–4,9–12 ~ The man of lawlessness comes, who is the son of damnation (perdition). He exalts himself to be a god, or an object of worship, taking the seat in the temple of God. He brings about the acts of Satan through deception and magic. God will let the fallen believe these lies and carry on with their wickedness, and be condemned to hell.
- 1 JO 2:18,22 ~ You have heard that the antichrist comes; in fact, many antichrists are already here. This is a sign that the days are nearing an end. Whoever denies that Jesus is the Christ is a liar; whoever denies both Jesus Christ and the Father is an antichrist.
- 1 JO 4:3 ~ Anyone denying Jesus as the Christ, and God in the flesh, is an antichrist. Have you heard about the antichrist coming? Well the antichrist is here already.
- REV 13:1–18 ~ While standing on the seashore I saw a beast rise out of the sea, with seven heads and ten horns; a crown was on each horn, and on each head was the name of blasphemy. And the dragon gave him his power (DAN 7). One of the heads had a wound on it, but it healed itself. The world marveled at the beast and worshipped the beast, and they worshipped the dragon that gave its power to the beast. The people said, "Who is like the beast? Who can possibly oppose him?" The beast spoke blasphemy against God for 3 ½ years. He waged war against anyone who was holy, and defeated them. He gained power over all races, peoples, and nations. Everyone except the righteous honored the beast. Then another beast with two horns arrived, speaking like the dragon. He exercised the same power

as the first beast, performing magic feats such as bringing fire down from heaven. He convinced everyone to worship the first beast, and to make a graven image of it. And the second beast brought the image of the beast to life. He caused everyone to receive the mark of the beast on their right hand or forehead; only those with the mark could buy and sell goods. They tracked down and murdered anyone who didn't receive the mark and worship the beast. The beast's number is the number of a man: 666.
- REV 16:13–14 ~ I saw three evil spirits that looked like frogs come out of the dragon, the beast, and the false prophet. These were the demons that performed miracles, and coerced the kingdoms of the world to unite against God.
- REV 17:10–11 ~ There are seven kings (DAN 7): five are fallen, one is alive (six), and one is coming (seven), having a short reign; the beast is number eight and was also one of the seven. Ten kings reign with the beast for one hour and make war with the Lamb. [Note: at the time of John, there had been five great empires: Egyptian, Assyrian, Babylonian, Persian, and Greek; during the time of John was the Roman, or sixth great empire. The next great empire, possibly the seventh to rule the Mediterranean, Holy Land, and Europe was Nazi Germany, which was a short reign. The next great empire will likely be that of the beast].
- REV 17:12–14 ~ Ten kings will obtain power for one hour with the beast. They will give their power and strength to the beast and will make war with the Lamb of God, only to be defeated.

The Abomination of Desolation. The beast will set up the abomination that brings desolation in the holy temple. This refers to the beast's attempt to exalt himself by demanding that people worship him and make blood sacrifices for him. It represents the ultimate sacrilege because everything that God considers holy and sacred is blasphemed and dishonored.

- EZE 8:9–10,17–18 ~ In Ezekiel's vision he observed many abominations occurring in God's holy temple. Particularly loathsome was the abominable image of jealousy, which provoked God to anger.
- EZE 40—44 (especially EZE 44:1–15) ~ In a vision, God brought me (Ezekiel) into the land of Israel. The angel told me to pay close attention to the events occurring in the sanctuary, and to tell the rebellious house of Israel about the abominations I witnessed there. For they brought unclean strangers into the sanctuary to pollute it, and they broke God's covenant, and they didn't keep His holy things sacred. The priests strayed far away from God and pursued idols. Yet they were ministers in God's sanctuary and were in charge of the house of Israel; they killed the burnt offerings and made sacrifices of lambs without blemish. Because they ministered to the house of Israel before their idols, and caused Israel to fall into sin, they will be punished. They will not come near to God and His holy things. They will bear the shame of their abominations.
- DAN 8:13–14 ~ The transgressions that make desolate will continue and the sanctuary will be destroyed. After 2,300 days (6 ½ years) the sanctuary will be restored.
- DAN 9:27 ~ During the last half of the week (3 ½ years) the abomination that causes desolation will continue, until the terrible end that awaits is poured out upon them.
- DAN 12:11–12 ~ The abomination that makes desolate will be set up for 1,290 days (3 ½ years). Blessed are those who withstand the corresponding 1,335 days of tribulation.
- MAT 24:15–16 ~ Jesus said, "When the abomination that brings desolation which the prophet Daniel spoke of is standing in the holiest place, flee Judea into the mountains."
- 2 TH 2:3–4 ~ Don't be deceived by anyone, for that day will not come before there is a falling away from the faith, when that man of sin, the son of hell, is exposed. He opposes God, exalting himself, and sitting in the holy temple claiming to be God.

- REV 3:9 ~ Those liars that call themselves Jews are of the synagogue of Satan.

<u>Armageddon</u>. A final battle between good and evil will transpire at Armageddon. The Bible reveals very little about this battle. Apparently, at the end of the tribulation and before the judgment, Satan will gather his followers and make a final stand in the valley of Jezreel near Megiddo. This is an appropriate place for the battle to take place, since it was the site of a number of great skirmishes in the Old Testament (JDG 5:19; 2 KI 9:27; 2 KI 23:29–30; 2 CH 35:22). Many kings fought and died in this valley. It was on Mt. Carmel where Elijah defeated the prophets of Baal. There are two principal views as to when the battle of Armageddon takes place. One view is that the battle occurs at the end of the tribulation and prior to the millennial reign of Christ, during which Satan is bound in chains. The more likely possibility is that the battle occurs after the millennial reign when Satan is released, and again attempts to wage war against God, after which he is thrown into the lake of fire with the rest of the wicked.

- PSA 79:2–3,7 ~ The dead bodies will become meat for the wild birds and animals. Their blood has been shed like water and there is nobody to bury them. They devoured Israel and devastated the land.
- ISA 31:8–9 ~ The Assyrian will fall in battle, but not by mean or mighty man (perhaps the sword belonging to the angel Michael will be the one that slays him, as when 185,000 Assyrians were killed; see DAN 12:1). Their stronghold will crumble from terror when they see the battle standard approaching.
- ISA 34:2–4 ~ The Lord's anger is upon all nations and armies; He will utterly destroy and slaughter them. Their dead bodies will be scattered and will stink; the mountains will flow with their blood. Their host in heaven will be dissolved and thrown down.
- EZE 38—39 ~ Face northward, toward Magog, and prophesy: God is against you Gog. You will mobilize armies of the distant north, as well as from Africa and Asia. You will invade Israel in an attempt to obtain her wealth and conquer her, Israel who has been at peace after having returned home from all over the world. This will happen in the latter years. There will be a great earthquake. You will end up fighting yourselves in the confusion. I will send animals to eat you, death, disease, and calamities. I will destroy five sixths of your armies. I will rain fire and brimstone upon Magog and your allies to include the islands and coastlands, and places east of the Dead Sea. It will take seven months to bury the bodies. It will be a glorious victory for Israel. I will be their Lord from that day on, and forever.
- JOE 3:2,9–14 ~ I (God) will gather all nations together at the valley of Jehoshaphat, where I will plead with them on behalf of my people as well as for my heritage Israel, whom they have scattered throughout the world. Tell the Gentiles to prepare for war. Wake up the warriors; beat your tools into weapons of war. Let the weak say, "I am strong." Multitudes are gathering in the valley of decision, for the day of the Lord is coming when he will judge the pagans.
- ZEP 1:17–18 ~ I will bring calamity on them; they will become disoriented, for they have sinned. Their blood will be poured out like dust and their bodies like dung. Their riches will not save them on the day of the Lord's wrath. The land will be devoured with fire. The Lord will quickly rid the land of all of them.
- ZEC 12:2–3,9,11 ~ I (God) will make Jerusalem a menace to all the peoples surrounding them; they will lay siege to Jerusalem and Judah. On that day, when the nations are gathered against her, I will make her like a rock that cannot be moved. All who try to move it will be cut to pieces. I will destroy any nation that comes against Jerusalem. There will be great sorrow in Jerusalem as there was in the valley of Megiddo.

- REV 14:19–20 ~ The angel threw the earth into the winepress of God's wrath and a river of blood came out of the winepress, enough to cover a valley two hundred miles long up to the height of a horse's bridle.
- REV 16:12–17 ~ The Euphrates River dried up, creating a path for the army (kings) from the east. Three evil spirits came from the dragon, the beast, and the false prophet; they went throughout the earth gathering armies to battle against God Almighty. They gathered their armies together at a place called Armageddon near the mountain of Megiddo. Then the seventh angel poured out his vial, and a voice from heaven said, "It is over."
- REV 19:19 ~ I saw the beast, the kings of the earth, and their armies gathered for battle against the King of kings.
- REV 20:7–8 ~ Satan, when released after one thousand years of bondage, will deceive the nations in all four corners of the earth, Gog and Magog, for the final battle.

King Nebuchadnezzar's Dream about Kingdoms

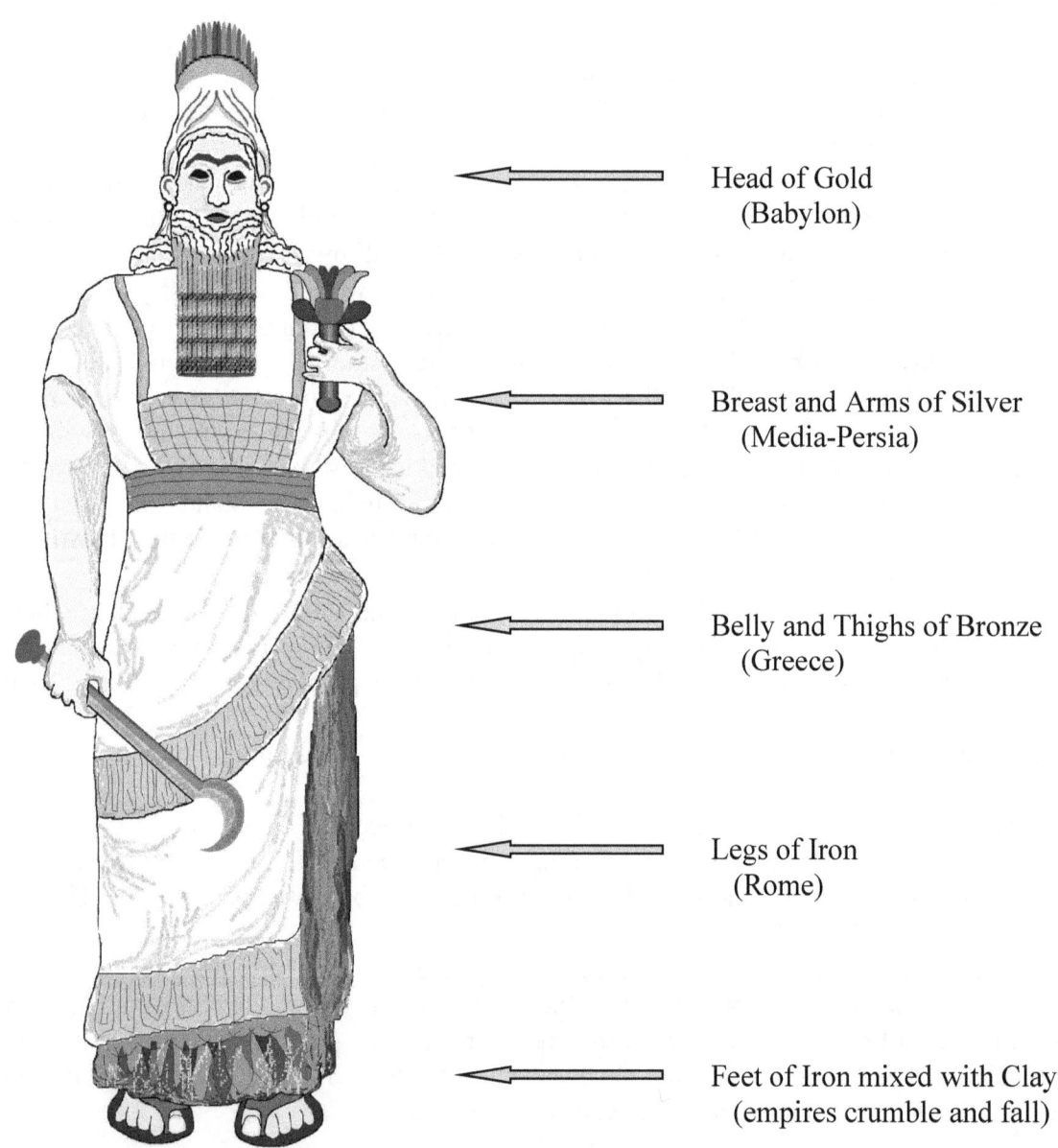

Head of Gold
(Babylon)

Breast and Arms of Silver
(Media-Persia)

Belly and Thighs of Bronze
(Greece)

Legs of Iron
(Rome)

Feet of Iron mixed with Clay
(empires crumble and fall)

Lesson: The Rapture, the Resurrection, and the Judgment

The Rapture. To be raptured means to be transported from one place to another. This usually refers to being translated from earth to heaven, as with Enoch and Elijah. Both the Old and New Testaments refer to a time when God will call His people to be with Him in heaven. God can rapture anyone, anytime, but there is a particular time when Christ's elect will be called to heaven. That will be the day Christ brings His church home.

During the tribulation, the beast makes war with the righteous, the abomination of desolation is set up, the mark of the beast is given, and the two witnesses prophesy. Then comes the sounding of the last trumpet, representing the seven vials of God's wrath. The rapture and resurrection occur simultaneously with Christ's return (2 TH 4:16–17). Depending on one's view of the tribulation, the rapture could occur before, during, or at the end of this period. Possibly, there will be a time of tribulation for the just and for the unjust; the rapture would occur at the midpoint with this view (after 3 ½ years).

- ISA 27:12–13 ~ In that day a great trumpet will sound, and those who were about to perish in Assyria, and the outcasts in Egypt, will be rescued and will worship the Lord at the holy mountain of Jerusalem.
- JER 30:7 ~ That will be a great time (the tribulation); there will be no others like it. It is the time of Jacob's trouble; but he (Israel) shall be saved out of it (REV 7:4; REV 14:3).
- DAN 12:1 ~ Michael the great prince who stands for the righteous will come; and there will be a time of trouble worse than ever before or ever again. Then the righteous will be delivered, those whose names are written in the Book of Life.
- MAT 24:22,31 ~ Unless those days (of tribulation) are shortened, none will survive. But only for the elect's sake, those days will be shortened. And He will send His angels when the great trumpet sounds, to gather His elect from across heaven and earth.
- 1 TH 4:16–17 ~ The Lord will descend from heaven with a shout, with the voice of the archangel, and with a blast from the trumpet of God. Then the dead in Christ will arise first. Those who remain alive in Christ will rise to join the others in the clouds, meeting the Lord in the sky. Those chosen by Christ will live with Him forevermore.
- REV 3:10 ~ Jesus said, "Because you have patiently kept my commandments, I will deliver you from the hour of temptation, when the patience of the whole world will be tested."
- REV 14:3–4 ~ The 144,000 sang a new song; nobody could learn the song except them. They were the ones who were undefiled. They were redeemed from humankind as the first fruits of God and the Lamb, for they were blameless.

The Resurrection. Because we are born sinful and lead sinful lives we are condemned to die. However, thanks to Christ we don't have to remain dead. Just as Jesus was resurrected from the dead, so also will humankind arise. Upon death, our body returns to the earth and our spirit returns to God who gave it to us (ECC 12:7). But some day all will be raised and will see God face to face, in the flesh. And God will separate the saved from the condemned.

- JOB 19:25–26 ~ I know my Redeemer lives and He will stand upon the earth. And though my flesh will have been destroyed, yet in my flesh I will see God.
- ISA 26:19 ~ The dead will live; along with my dead body, they will arise. Awake and sing all of you who abide in the dust, for the earth will toss out its dead.
- ISA 40:5 ~ The glory of the Lord will be revealed, and all human flesh will see it together, for the Lord has said so.

- EZE 37:1–5 ~ The hand of the Lord touched me (Ezekiel), carried me out with His Spirit, and set me down in the middle of a valley full of dry bones. And God said to me, "Can these bones live?" I answered, "Lord, surely you know." Then He said to me, "Prophesy upon these bones, and tell them to listen to the word of the Lord, for I will cause breath to enter into these dry bones and they will live again."
- HOS 6:2 ~ After two days He will revive us; the third day He will raise us up to live in His sight.
- LUK 16:19–31 ~ Jesus told the parable of the rich man and poor man who both died; the rich man was evil and went to Hades; the poor man was righteous and went to Abraham's bosom.
- JOH 11:25 ~ Jesus said, "I am the resurrection and the life. Those who believe in me, though they were dead, yet shall they live."
- ROM 8:11 ~ The Spirit of Him who raised Jesus Christ from the dead will abide in you, and also will restore your mortal bodies from the dead.

<u>The First Fruits</u>. Christ was the first fruits to be resurrected and to go to heaven to be with God our Father. The next to be resurrected will be His elect.

- 1 CO 15:12–58 ~ If Christ has risen from the dead, how can some of you say there is no resurrection? If there is no resurrection from the dead, then Christ was not raised either. If Christ was not raised, we would be preaching in vain and your faith would also be in vain. But, in fact, Christ has been raised forever, the first to be brought back in the body from among those who have died; and He has brought with Him the resurrection. Just as death came by a man, by a man has come the resurrection of the dead. Like Adam we die, and like Christ we will rise from the dead, each in the proper order with Christ being first. After that, the end will come when He hands the kingdom over to God the Father. In Christ you also will be made alive after death. In a single moment, when the great trumpet sounds, the righteous, whether alive or dead, will arise into heaven to receive new, incorruptible bodies. The godly will receive spiritual bodies that never die. The flesh is of the earth, the spirit is of heaven; thus, flesh and blood will not inherit the kingdom of heaven. It is our natural body that dies; it is our spiritual body that lives after death. At Christ's coming will be the first resurrection of those who belong to Him. Then at the end, when He delivers the kingdom of God to the Father, He will destroy His enemies; the last enemy to be destroyed will be death. So, be confident in your faith because your labor is not in vain.
- COL 1:18 ~ Jesus Christ is the head of the body which is the church. He is the beginning, the firstborn of the dead, who is above all and the ruler over all earthly kings (also REV 1:5).
- 1 PE 3:18 ~ Christ suffered for the sins of all, the just and the unjust, so He could bring us to God. He was put to death in the flesh, but raised to life in the Spirit.

Christ was the first fruits of God, the first to be raised from the dead and return to the Almighty Father. The Bible says that Jesus Christ will return in the flesh, the same way in which He departed. When Christ returns, it will be to gather the first fruits belonging to Him. The first fruits of Christ will be resurrected to meet Him in the sky, along with those who are raptured. These people represent Christ's chosen, who already have been judged righteous because they were cleansed of sin by His shed blood. That is, Christ has conferred His righteousness upon anyone who would believe in Him; these people represent His first fruits. They will be like virgins, perfect and chaste (2 CO 11:2). They will be reconciled with God the Father automatically, because they were justified by their faith in God's words and promises.

- JER 2:3 ~ Israel was holy to the Lord and represent the first fruits of His increase. Those who try to destroy God's elect will have evil come upon them.

- MAT 24:29–31,42–44 ~ Jesus said, "After the tribulation there will be darkness over the world. Then a sign will appear in heaven, and everyone on earth will mourn. They will see the Son of God coming in the clouds with all power and glory. He will send His angels at the sound of the great trumpet to gather His elect from the four winds, and from one end of heaven to the other. So be watchful, for nobody knows when the Lord will return. If a man knew when the thief was going to burglarize his house, he would have prevented it. Likewise, you must be ready, for the Son of God will come at a time when you least expect Him."
- JOH 5:28–29 ~ The time is coming when all who are in the grave will hear His voice and come forth. Those who have been faithful and righteous will arise to everlasting life, and those who have been evil will arise to receive judgment.
- ACT 1:11 ~ The angel said, "Men of Galilee, why do you gaze into heaven? Jesus, who you just saw ascend into heaven, will return the very same way."
- REV 7:9–10,13–14 ~ I (John) saw a giant multitude, too many people to even count; there were people from every nation, race, and tongue standing before the throne and the Lamb who was clothed in white. They held palm branches and sang, "Salvation to our God who sits on the throne, and to the Lamb." One of the elders asked me who these people were. I replied, "Tell me, sir." He said, "These are the ones who came from great tribulation; they have washed their robes and made them white with the blood of the Lamb."

In Revelation, John points out that there are two distinct resurrections. Two prevailing opinions exist about the first and second resurrections. The "Millennialists" believe that both represent a physical resurrection, the first occurring before and the second occurring after the millennial (thousand-year) reign. The first resurrection would be of Christ's elect and the second would be everyone else. The "Amillennialists" do not believe in a thousand-year reign per se, but hold that this period represents the time from Christ's ascension to His return (i.e., the era between the first and second advents of Christ). This school of thought asserts that the first resurrection is of the spirit (upon one's death) and the second is of the flesh (when Christ returns). The Millennial Reign paragraph below will expound further on this topic.

The scriptures indicate that people are resurrected at the proper time, when it is their turn (1 CO 15; 1 TH 4; REV 20). Let us review the scriptures and you can consider which of the above views best encompasses the facts.

- 1 CO 15:20,23–24 ~ In Christ we are made alive after death, each in the proper order, with Christ being the first fruits, and the next being those who belong to Christ when He returns. Then comes the end, when He has delivered the kingdom to the Father.
- 1 CO 15:42–44,46,50,53 ~ This is the way it will be with the resurrection of the dead. It is sown in corruption it is raised in incorruption. It is sown in dishonor it is raised in glory. It is sown in weakness it is raised in power. It is sown a natural body it is raised a spiritual body. The spiritual did not come first, but the natural came first and then the spiritual. Flesh and blood cannot inherit the kingdom, neither can corruption inherit perfection. For the perishable must clothe itself with the imperishable, and the mortal with immortality.
- 1 CO 15:51–52,54 ~ Here is a mystery of God: We will not all sleep (implies death) but we will all be changed. Suddenly, when the last trumpet sounds, Christ's own, whether dead or alive, will arise without corruption and be changed. Hence, the corruptible will have become incorruptible and the mortal will have become immortal. Then the statement "death is swallowed up in victory" will be true.
- 1 TH 4:16–17 ~ The Lord will descend from heaven with a shout, with the voice of the archangel, and with a blast from the trumpet of God. Then the dead in Christ will arise first.

Those who remain alive in Christ will rise to join the others in the clouds, meeting the Lord in the sky. Those chosen by Christ will live with Him forevermore.
- HEB 12:22–23 ~ You have come to God's holy mountain, to His holy city, to stay with the living God and His multitude of angels. You are part of the assembly and church of the firstborn, whose names are written in heaven. You are among the righteous that were redeemed, and whose spirits have been made perfect.
- REV 20:4–6,13–15 ~ I (John) saw thrones, and sitting on them were judges. I saw the souls of those who had been beheaded for their testimony of Jesus, who had not worshipped the beast or its image, nor received its mark on their foreheads or hands. They came to life again and reigned with Christ one thousand years. This was the first resurrection. The rest of the dead did not live again until after the thousand years. Blessed and holy are those who share in the first resurrection for they will not be victims of the second death. At the second resurrection the rest of the souls were raised to be judged by God. Death and Hell, and those not recorded in the Book of Life, were cast into the lake of fire; this was the second death.

The Millennial Reign. It is generally understood that the thousand-year reign is not a precise period of time, but is symbolic of a passing era. During that time Satan is bound in chains, meaning he cannot capture God's chosen or halt the spread of the Gospel. After this period will occur a bodily resurrection. Those belonging to Christ will be judged not guilty, to live forever in heaven. Technically, once a person dies, they are judged; so, the physical resurrection for the elect could be a glorified body that never dies (read LUK 16). The rest of the souls will be judged by the Law in accordance with what is written in the books concerning their conduct during their lifetimes (ROM 2; REV 20). They will suffer a second death, condemned by their sin. There may be levels of punishment commensurate with crimes against God, other people, and themselves (OBA 1:15).

Millennialists hold that one thousand years separate the first resurrection of Christ's saved and the second resurrection of the condemned, both a physical resurrection of the body. The elect will reign on earth with Christ during the thousand years, which end with the second resurrection when unbelievers will face judgment and a second death. Presumably, one gets another chance to be saved during the thousand-year interval; at least this is the position of many in the millennialist camp. Further, millennialists are more likely to believe in a literal thousand-year period.

Amillennialists hold that the millennial reign represents the era between the first and second coming of Christ. It is based on the notion that the dominion was turned over to Christ when He defeated Satan on the cross (DAN 7:9–14; JOH 12:28–32). The first resurrection is a spiritual one for anyone dying during this period, after which believers reside in Abraham's bosom and unbelievers reside in Hades. Thus, the righteous already have been judged not guilty and are in the presence of the Lord. Christ's second advent ushers in the second resurrection, a physical resurrection of all the dead. Whether dead or alive, everyone will see God. This is followed by either a pass to paradise for those claiming the blood of Jesus, or a second death for those preferring to be judged according to their deeds.

- DAN 7:14 ~ And there was given Him dominion, and glory, and a kingdom, that all people, nations, and languages, should serve Him. His dominion is everlasting which will never pass away, and His kingdom will never be destroyed.
- JOH 12:31–32 ~ Jesus said, "Now is the judgment of this world, wherein the prince of this world is cast out. And I am lifted up from the earth and will draw people unto myself."

- ROM 6:14,17–18 ~ Now sin has no hold over you, for you are not under the Law, you are under Grace. Thank God that we, who were servants of sin, have obeyed in our hearts the doctrine that delivers us, being made free from sin, and now serving righteousness instead.
- 1 CO 15:44 ~ There is a natural body and a spiritual body. It is born a natural body it is raised a spiritual body.
- 1 CO 15:25–26,44 ~ He must conquer until He has trampled all the enemies. The last enemy to be destroyed will be death.
- GAL 3:11,24–26 ~ No man is justified before God by the Law, but those who are righteous live by faith. Before faith came, we were under the Law. The Law was in effect until Christ came, so we could be justified by faith. In Christ we become children of God through faith.
- REV 20:6 ~ Blessed and holy are those who take part in the first resurrection, for the second death has no power over them. They will be priests of God and Christ, and will reign with Him a thousand years.

The Judgment. Everyone will rise from the dead to be judged, whether it is associated with the first or the second resurrection (1 PE 4:17). Those who believe in Christ, repent of their sins, and try to lead a godly life will be judged blameless and will never die again but will receive eternal life. However, those who choose not to believe, and who lead a life of sin without repentance, will die a second death never to arise again. Thus, those who choose evil or deny Christ will perish; they will face everlasting contempt and damnation. Those who choose righteousness and confess Christ are redeemed; they will enjoy everlasting bliss and peace.

- PSA 50:3–5 ~ God will come with a terrible fire burning all around Him. He will call everyone from heaven above to the earth below for judgment. He will gather the saints unto Himself.
- PSA 52:5 ~ God will destroy the wicked forever.
- PSA 69:28 ~ They will be blotted out from the Book of Life; their names will not appear with the righteous.
- ECC 12:14 ~ God will judge every person, every act and secret thing, whether good or evil.
- ISA 26:14 ~ The wicked will die never to live again; they will be destroyed completely along with any memory of them.
- ISA 29:20 ~ The evil foe will come to nothing; the foe will be consumed and the wicked will be cut off from God.
- ISA 38:18 ~ Those who go down into the pit can no longer hope to find His truth.
- EZE 7:3 ~ God will judge everyone according to their ways, and will recompense the abominations of the wicked back upon them.
- DAN 7:10 ~ A stream of fire flowed before Him. Millions ministered to Him. Billions stood before Him. The judgment was set and the books were opened.
- DAN 12:2 ~ Some will arise to everlasting life and some will arise to everlasting shame and contempt.
- OBA 1:15 ~ The day of the Lord is near for the wicked. As they have done, so shall it be done to them; it will come back upon their heads.
- JOE 3:14 ~ Multitudes gathered in the valley of decision, for the day of the Lord was at hand.
- MAT 12:36 ~ Jesus said, "On Judgment Day, people will have to give account for every foolish word that they spoke."
- MAT 25:30,41,46 ~ He will cast the worthless people into outer darkness where there is weeping and gnashing of teeth. They will depart into the eternal fire prepared for the devil and his angels. They will go away into eternal punishment, but the righteous into eternal life.

- MAR 16:16 ~ Jesus said, "Whoever believes in me and is baptized will be saved; whoever does not believe will be damned."
- JOH 5:22,30 ~ Jesus said, "The Father judges nobody, but He has given this responsibility to the Son. I judge whatever I see and hear, and my judgment is fair, because I seek the Father's will and not my own."
- 1 CO 4:5 ~ Don't be judgmental before the Lord returns. He will bring to light all that is hidden, even the secrets of our hearts. Then everyone will praise God.
- 2 CO 5:10 ~ We shall all stand before the judgment seat of Christ. We will be judged for everything we did, whether it was right or wrong, and we will be punished fairly (also ROM 14:10).
- 1 TH 1:8–9 ~ He will inflict vengeance upon those who do not know and obey God and the Gospel of Jesus Christ. They shall suffer the punishment of eternal destruction, and exclusion from the glory of God.
- 2 TH 2:12 ~ Those who did not believe the truth but found their pleasures in unrighteousness will be damned.
- REV 2:10–11 ~ Those who overcome persecutions will not be hurt by the second death.

Adoration of the Mystic Lamb – Painting by Jan van Eyck (@ 1395–1441)
Center panel of altarpiece, St. Bavo's Cathedral, Ghent Belgium

Lesson: Promises, Promises

God makes promises that He will keep as long as we believe in Him. And why wouldn't we believe, given that He is all powerful and never goes back on His Word? If we cling to His promises, we will have the assurance of obtaining all the wonderful things He has in store for us. Knowing this should give us the hope, willpower, and patience to persevere and overcome since this life is nothing compared to the next.

Clearly, the greatest of all God's promises is eternal life, complete with an inheritance in His kingdom and a share in His glory. In God's house we become equal heirs with Christ, His only begotten Son who has shown us the way home. All we have to do to receive this inheritance and heritage is believe that it is ours. Conversely, disbelief will ensure that you will not receive it. Reaching out to God is proof that you believe, or at least want to believe; otherwise you wouldn't even try. Such an eagerness to connect to Him will guarantee success, and create a link to the most powerful force in the universe, a link to last for all time.

- DEU 4:29–31 ~ If, from this time forward, you will seek the Lord, provided you seek Him with all your heart and soul, you will find Him. If you are in tribulation, even in the later days, and you turn to God and are obedient to Him, God who is merciful will not forsake you or destroy you. God will never forget the covenant He made with your ancestors.
- ISA 64:4 ~ Since the world began, nobody has heard, seen, or perceived, except God, the wonderful things He has prepared for those who wait for Him.
- JOH 14:2–3~ Jesus said, "In my Father's house are many mansions; I go to prepare such a place for you. I will return for you, so that where I am you can be also."
- EPH 1:13 ~ You were included with Christ when you listened to the word of truth and believed the good news of salvation, being marked by the Holy Spirit who has guaranteed your inheritance in God's kingdom.
- TIT 1:2 ~ Our faith and knowledge rests on the hope of eternal life which God, who cannot lie, promised before the beginning of time.
- 2 PE 3:13 ~ We, according to God's promise, look for new heavens and a new earth, wherein dwells righteousness.
- 1 JOH 2:25 ~ This is the promise that God promised us: eternal life.

The promise of everlasting life is administered through Jesus Christ, who grants forgiveness and salvation, making us worthy of absolution and acceptable to God our Father. It is based on the perfect sacrifice Christ made for sin and His subsequent resurrection, proving that He was without sin and a worthy offering for our transgressions. Our trust is founded on God's Son who was sent by the Father for that very purpose, and upon which the promise becomes ours through faith.

- PRO 3:5–8 ~ Trust in the Lord with all your heart; do not rely on your own understanding. Acknowledge God in everything you do, and He will direct you in your ways. Do not consider yourself wise, but fear the Lord, refrain from evil, and you will be healthy and strong.
- ROM 10:9 ~ If you confess with your mouth that Jesus is Lord and believe in your heart that God raised him from the dead, you will be saved.
- 2 CO 1:20 ~ No matter how many promises God has made, they all are affirmed through Christ who is the Amen.

- GAL 3:16,22,28 ~ To Abraham and his seed the promise was made. God didn't say "seeds" as in many, but "seed" as in one; and that seed is Christ who fulfills the promise. The scripture declares that all people are slaves to sin; but the promise is available to all who would believe they are redeemed. If you belong to Christ, then you are of Abraham's seed, and heirs according to the promise.
- 2 PE 1:3–4 ~ God's divine power provides us everything we need for life and righteousness through our knowledge of Him who called us in His glory and goodness. In these He has given us great and precious promises to participate in His divine nature and escape the corruption of the world caused by evil desires.

Once we have accepted these free gifts of salvation and eternal life, many more promises and gifts will follow. Of course, that requires a fervent response to God's loving kindness. Simply put, we must act on our faith in ways that are pleasing to God. He will prepare a path for us to follow that will further His kingdom, and will keep us focused on the way to heaven which is Jesus Christ. God will give us the power, strength, and motivation to become more like Him and to overcome temptation, sin, setbacks, suffering, and adversity. As we strive to be more like Christ, we continuously become stronger and purer in our thoughts and behavior. That is, striving to be like Jesus makes you more like Him, for His Holy Spirit is working in you.

- DEU 31:6 ~ Be strong and of good courage; do not fear or be dismayed. For the Lord God goes with you; he will never fail you or forsake you.
- JER 29:11 ~ I know the plans I have for you, says the Lord: plans for prosperity, protection, hope, and a bright future.
- MAT 11:28–30 ~ Jesus said, "Come to me all who are weary and burdened and I will give you rest. Take my yoke upon you and learn from me, for I am gentle and humble in heart; and you will find rest for your souls. For my yoke is easy and my burden is light."
- ROM 8:28 ~ All things work together for good to those who love God and are called according to His purpose.
- 1 CO 10:13 ~ The temptations before you are common to humanity. God is faithful and will not cause you to be tempted beyond your ability to endure, and He will always provide a way to escape the temptation.
- 1 CO 15:58 ~ Stand firm and remain steadfast, always abounding in the work of the Lord, knowing that your labor is not in vain.
- JAM 1:12 ~ Blessed are people who persevere when tempted and tried; because after they have stood the test, they will receive the crown of life which God promised to those who love him.
- 1 JOH 1:9 ~ If we confess our sins, God who is faithful and just will forgive our sins and cleanse us from all unrighteousness.
- REV 2:10 ~ Jesus said, "Don't be afraid of the things that you must suffer. Satan will throw some of you into prison to be tried; you will endure tribulation for ten days. Be faithful unto death and I will give you a crown of life."

Such dedication and perseverance as willing servants yield prosperity, provision, and protection. These promises bring a profound sense of peace, joy, and purpose which unbelievers cannot comprehend. Faithfulness gives us greater meaning, direction, and assurance in life, and this equates to happiness, confidence, and spiritual growth.

- PSA 37:4–5 ~ Find your delight in the Lord and He will give to you the desires of your heart. Commit yourself to the Lord and trust in Him, and He will make your desires come to pass.

- ISA 40:30–31 ~ Even youths faint and become weary, and young men stumble and fall. But those who trust the Lord will be renewed in their strength; they will soar on wings like eagles. They will run and not grow weary; they will walk and not feel faint.
- MAT 6:31–34 ~ Jesus said, "Don't worry about what you will eat or drink, or what you will wear; for your heavenly Father knows that you need these things. Instead, seek first the kingdom of God and His righteousness, and He will provide everything you need in addition to the kingdom."
- JOH 10:10 ~ Jesus came to give us abundant life.
- PHP 1:6 ~ The Lord who has begun a good work in you will bring it to completion until the day Christ returns.

God has promised us everything and the only requirements are that we seek Him and ask Him, just as a child asks a parent for something they need or desire. God will deliver on His promises each time we come to Him in prayer, often in ways that we do not understand, at least not immediately. But it makes sense once we have received His answer and His blessings. This process of asking and receiving helps us to remember the Lord is with us, to dedicate our lives to Jesus Christ in whom we bear fruit of the spirit, and to win others to Christ through our acts of witnessing, obedience, and worship.

- JOE 2:28 ~ I (God) will pour out my Spirit on humankind, and your sons and daughters will prophesy, your old men will dream dreams, and your young men will see visions.
- 2 CH 7:14 ~ God says, "If my people who bear my name would humble themselves, pray, seek my face, and turn from their evil ways, I would hear them from heaven, and I would forgive them of their sins and heal their land."
- MAT 7:7 ~ Jesus said, "Ask and you will receive; seek and you will find; knock and the door will be opened."
- MAT 21:22 ~ Jesus said, "If you believe, you can receive anything you ask through prayer."
- JOH 14:13 ~ Jesus said, "Whatever you ask in my name, I will do it so that the Son may bring glory to the Father."
- ACT 2:38–39 ~ Peter said, "Repent and be baptized every one of you, in the name of Jesus Christ for the remission of your sins, and you will receive the gift of the Holy Spirit. This promise pertains to you, to your children, and to people everywhere: to whomever the Lord calls."

Since we can have any good thing that we desire simply by going to our heavenly Father and asking, our response should be to generously give to others who ask for or who need our assistance and support. By cheerfully giving of ourselves and our time, we are sowing seeds of the spirit, and that will result in the reaping of more blessings from God. It's like an investment in which the interest is compounded each time we complete the cycle of accepting God's great gifts and sharing them with others. And one of those blessings which we should freely give is our forgiveness, which we have undeservedly obtained by the work of Christ on the cross. Each seed we sow is nurtured by the Holy Spirit, thereby multiplying His kingdom as the vineyard grows in leaps and bounds.

- MAL 3:8,10 ~ Bring tithes of all your income to the storage room, so that there will be plenty in my house, and prove to yourself that I will open the windows of heaven and pour upon you so many blessings that you will not have room for them all.
- MAT 6:14–15 ~ Jesus said, "If you forgive those who sin against you, your heavenly Father will also forgive you. But if you do not forgive others, your heavenly Father will not forgive you."

- LUK 6:38 ~ Give and it shall be given to you in abundance, overflowing; for the same measure that you give is returned unto you.
- LUK 12:8–9 ~ Jesus said, "Whoever confesses me to others, I will confess them before God and His angels; but whoever denies me to others, I will deny them before God and His angels."
- 2 CO 5:17–19,21 ~ Anyone who is in Christ has become a new creation; the old has been removed and everything has become new. God did this to reconcile us unto Himself through Christ. He has not counted our sins against us, but instead made Christ who knew no sin to become sin for us, so that we could receive the righteousness of God that was in Him.

If a person chooses not to believe, refuses to follow Christ, is not interested in being obedient to God or part of His kingdom, or refrains from accepting the blessings God wants all people to have—well there are promises which God makes to those people also. And those promises are not good news.

- ECC 5:10 ~ Those who love money will never be satisfied with it; those who love abundance will never have enough.
- AMO 8:11–13 ~ The day is coming when God will send a famine of the Word. Young people will faint from thirst of God's Word. They will wander to-and-fro seeking the truth but will not find it.
- OBA 1:15 ~ The day of the Lord is near for the wicked. As they have done, so shall it be done to them; it will come back upon their heads.
- ROM 6:23 ~ For the wages of sin is death; but the free gift of God is eternal life through Christ the Lord.
- GAL 6:7–8 ~ Do not be deceived; for God cannot be mocked. Whatever a man sows that will he also reap. People who sow to please their sinful flesh will reap destruction. People who sow to please the Holy Spirit will reap eternal life.

If you can't trust God, who can you trust? Which is to say, who can you trust but God, the only one able to make good on every promise every time? And He promises more than the world or anyone in it can deliver. If you do not trust in God then you are allowing the devil to have his way, and the only thing he can promise is death. Though he has no control over death, he is driven to show you a path that leads only to death and condemnation, which is where the devil also will find himself in the end. Such is the way of the world; but those who are saved are not of this world but are citizens of the Kingdom of Heaven.

God has told us that this world will end and pass away; for there will be a new Earth and a new Heaven. This world is perverse and evil; and those who place their reliance on earthly things will be destroyed along with the earth and all its depravity and sin. It is highly recommended that you focus on God's kingdom and His righteousness, and you will inherit a mansion in heaven, and He will add to that everything you need to sustain your body and life while you reside on this planet (MAT 6:33). This enables us to be happy, at peace, and hopeful, looking forward as we patiently await the return of Christ who is coming to take us home very soon. Just the thought of this should be uplifting to your spirit.

Lesson: Newness of Life

Once you have accepted Christ, everything changes in your life: your demeanor, attitude, desires, and deeds; your direction and destination. Your heart will change and your mind will change; and your spirit will be renewed each day through the power of God's Holy Spirit. And you will be a minister of the love and grace of God, guided by your spirit and not your flesh. For if you give God your works, He will give you His thoughts (PRO 16:3).

- PSA 51:10–12 ~ Create in me a clean heart, Lord, and renew an upright spirit within me. Don't remove me from your presence and don't take your Holy Spirit from me. Restore to me the joy of your salvation, and uphold me with your free Spirit.
- ROM 12:1–2 ~ I implore you therefore, by the mercies of God, that you present yourselves as a living sacrifice, holy and acceptable to God, which is a reasonable response to His love. Do not conform to the ways of this world, but be transformed by the renewing of your mind, and you will be able to determine what is good, acceptable, and perfect according to God's will.
- 2 CO 4:16 ~ Therefore we do not lose heart. Though outwardly we continue to deteriorate, yet inwardly we are constantly renewed.
- EPH 4:23–24 ~ With respect to your former ways, you were taught to put off your old self which was corrupted with deceitful desires, and be renewed in the spirit of your minds. So put on the new self, the one created to be like God in true righteousness and holiness.
- COL 3:9–10 ~ Do not lie to one another now that you have taken off your old self with its wayward ways, and have put on the new self which is renewed in knowledge after the image of our Creator.
- TIT 3:4–6 ~ With kindness and love, God our Savior appeared and saved us, not because of our works of righteousness, but because of His mercy; by the washing of regeneration, and renewing of the Holy Spirit, which He generously poured out for us through Jesus Christ our Savior.

Christ sacrificed Himself as a punishment for sin so that we could live for Him and not for ourselves. Thus, our mortal and corrupt bodies which were dead to sin can now live anew in the righteousness of Christ, bestowed upon us the instant He took our sins upon Himself. He created in us a new heart to share His love, and gave us a new mind to think His thoughts, in order to bear fruit worthy of repentance (LUK 3:8). The old self has become new because our past ways have been abandoned, and God's way has become clear. And though we exist in this world, we are no longer part of it, because we are part of Him. Now that He lives in us and we live in Him, we must also live for Him.

- ISA 53:10 ~ It was God's will to strike Christ down and cause Him to suffer, making Him a guilt offering for sin. And God will behold His progeny and prolong His days; and the will of the Father will thrive in the hand of the Son.
- JER 31:31–34 ~ God will make a New Covenant with Israel, not according to the covenant He made when He rescued Israel out of the land of Egypt, which they broke. With the New Covenant, God will write His Law into the hearts of His people. They will not have to teach each other to know God, for everyone will know Him, from the least to the greatest among them, because God will forgive all their sins and will forget their sins forever.
- 1 CO 15:20–22,44–45 ~ Christ has risen from the dead, and become the first fruits of those who have fallen asleep. By one man came death, and by one man came the resurrection of the dead. For in Adam we die, and in Christ we will be made alive. It is sown a natural body;

it is raised a spiritual body. There is a natural body, and there is a spiritual body. It is written: The first Adam became a living being; the last Adam became a life-giving spirit.
- 2 CO 5:14–21 ~ The love of Christ compels us, for we are convinced that if He died for all, then all have died. He died for all so that those who live would no longer live for themselves but for Christ who died for them and rose again. From now on, we will not look at others with a worldly point of view as we once viewed Christ. If anyone is in Christ, he is a new creature; old things have passed away and all things have become new. This wisdom is from God who reconciled us unto Himself through Christ, and commissioned us as ministers of reconciliation. God will not count our sins against us, those who have been reconciled unto Him. This is why we are committed to our mission as ambassadors for Christ's sake, so that God can appeal to you through us to be reconciled unto Him. For He made Christ, who knew no sin, to become sin for us so that we could receive the righteousness of God that was in Him.
- GAL 6:14–15 ~ God forbid that I should boast of anything but the cross of our Lord Jesus Christ, by whom the world has become dead to me, and I to the world. For in Christ it is not important whether or not you are circumcised, but that you are a new creation.

Being born again means to forsake who you used to be and become who you were meant to be. You died with Christ, and your sin was buried with Him. Newness of life means being made alive in Him and not allowing sin to control you anymore. You must not return to the old self or death will take hold of you and drag you into the grave. Since you were made alive again with Christ, let Him take control over your life; for you will never die if you trust in Him and follow Him. Your ways will be His ways, and His life will be your life.

- PSA 40:3; PSA 98:1 ~ He has put a new song in my mouth, a hymn of praise for our God. Many will notice, and will fear and trust in the Lord. Oh, sing to the Lord a new song, for He has done marvelous things. His right hand, which is His holy arm, has won for Him the victory.
- ISA 42:9–10 ~ God says, "Behold, the former things have come to pass, and new things I will declare; before they happen, I will tell you. Sing to the Lord a new song; sing His praises to the end of the earth…"
- EZE 18:31 ~ God says, "Forsake all your transgressions and get a new heart and a new spirit. Why should you die? I take no pleasure in anyone's death; I prefer that you repent and live!"
- JOH 3:1–12 ~ Nicodemus, a Pharisee and authority over the Jews, came to see Jesus at nighttime. And he said to Jesus, "Rabbi, we know that you are a teacher from God, for nobody can perform such miracles without God being with him." Jesus responded, "Truly I tell to you, unless a man is born again, he cannot enter the kingdom of God." Nicodemus asked, "How can a man be born when he is old? Can he enter his mother's womb a second time and be reborn?" Jesus answered, "I tell you the truth, unless a man is born of water and of the Spirit he cannot enter into the kingdom of heaven. That which is born of the flesh is flesh; and that which is born of the Spirit is spirit. Do not be astounded that I have told you that you must be born again. The wind blows wherever it wants; and you can hear it but you cannot see it or tell where it has come from or where it is going. It is the same with those who are born of the Spirit." Nicodemus wondered, "How can this be so?" Jesus replied, "Are you not a teacher in Israel? And yet do you not understand these things? Truthfully, we speak of what we know and we testify to what we see, but still there are many who do not receive our testimony. If I tell you about earthly things and you do not believe, how can you believe if I tell you about heavenly things?"

- ROM 6:1–23 ~ What shall we conclude? That it is okay to continue to sin so that Grace may abound? God forbid it! We are dead to sin; how can we possibly live any longer in it? Did you know that everyone baptized into Jesus Christ have been baptized into His death? Therefore, we are buried with Him by baptism unto death. And just as Christ was raised from the dead by the glory of the Father, so also, we receive newness of life. If we are united with Him in death, we will be united with Him in the resurrection. Our old self was crucified with Christ in order to destroy that body of sin and no longer be a slave to it. When you die you are freed from sin; and if you die with Christ you will live with Him as well. Christ, being raised from the dead, can die no more; death has no hold over Him. He died to sin once and for all; now He lives to God. Likewise, you are dead to sin, but alive to God through Jesus Christ our Lord. So do not allow sin to reign in your mortal body, or give into its lusts; and do not use the members of your body as instruments of unrighteousness. Instead, yield to God, along with those who are alive from the dead; and use your members as instruments of righteousness. And sin will have no hold over you, for you are no longer under the Law but under Grace. So, what shall we conclude? That it is okay to sin because we are not under the Law but under Grace? Of course not! When you give into something, you become a slave to it: whether to sin unto death, or to obedience unto righteousness. Thank God, that though you once served sin, you now obey wholeheartedly this teaching, being freed from sin to become a servant of righteousness. I speak in human terms to appeal to the weakness of your mortal flesh, as when you gave into its impurity and iniquity, hoping that you will now offer your bodies to serve righteousness which leads to holiness. For when you served sin you were liberated from righteousness. What reward does one receive for those shameful deeds but death? Only now you have been liberated from sin, to become servants of God and bear fruit that leads to holiness, the reward for which will be everlasting life. For the wages of sin is death; but the gift of God is eternal life through Jesus Christ our Lord.
- ROM 7:6 ~ Now we are delivered from the Law to which we were once held unto death, so we can serve in newness of spirit, instead of continuing in the old ways governed by the letter of the Law.
- GAL 2:18–21 ~ If I rebuild the things I destroyed, I am again a lawbreaker. If I have died to the Law I must live unto God. I have been crucified with Christ but yet I live; but it is not I who live but Christ who lives in me. This life that I now live in the flesh I live by faith in the Son of God who loved me and gave Himself for me. I will not frustrate the grace of God. For if righteousness could be received by works of the law then Christ would have died in vain.
- 1 PE 1:22–23 ~ Your souls have been purified for obeying the truth of God's Spirit, giving you a sincere love that you must share with your brothers and sisters. You have been born again, not of corruptible seed, but by the incorruptible Word of God which lives and endures forever.
- 1 PE 2:20–24 ~ He bore our sins in His own body on the cross, so that those who were dead to sins could live unto righteousness. By His wounds you have been healed.
- REV 20:6 ~ Blessed and holy are those who take part in the first resurrection, for the second death has no power over them. They will be priests of God and Christ, and will reign with Him a thousand years.

Second Coming

© 1981 by Andrew Barber (PAu 321–648)

VERSE 1
```
   G#           F#         G#            B
Listen to me everyone, I'm called upon to say,
    G#              F#        G#          F#
A warning sent from heaven is delivered here today.
    G#            F#        G#            B
Beware of certain strangers who say that they're the way,
    G#              F#          G#           F#
For servants come from darkness to lead many souls astray.
```

CHORUS 1
```
       G#          E      A     B   F#
So prepare for the Messiah, don't be fooled by clever hands;
       G#             E       A   B   F#   C#...
For the Judgment Day will burst upon our persecuted lands.
```

VERSE 2
Beware of these false prophets with their miracles and tricks;
They're led by Hell and Satan who these charlatans he picks.
Sodom and Gomorrah will become the style of life;
With suffering and slavery, the peak of human strife.

CHORUS 2
The earthquakes, floods, and famines, and the pestilence and war,
Will be a sign to everyone His coming lay in store.

C#... B... A. G#. F#...

INTERLUDE
```
      G#                F#    F#            G#
The sun will lose its radiance while darkness fills the world.
      G#              F#   F# G#
The stars will fall behind the gloom.
       G#             F#   F#             G#...
And fate—eternal life, not doom, to those who hold the pearl!
```

REPEAT VERSE 1 AND CHORUS 1

C#... B. B. B*b*. G#.

Lesson: The Final Word

The Greek word for Word is *Logos*. In the biblical context, logos means truth. The doctrine is spelled out very eloquently in the writings of St. John, and the prophets Moses and Isaiah. This doctrine refers to the fact that God spoke and the universe happened. He spoke it into existence by the power of His Word. Notice, in the first chapter of Genesis, the phrase "and God said," is used eight times. Every time God spoke, something wonderful happened. It was a miracle. Things came into being that had never existed before: things that could not occur naturally but only supernaturally by God's command (ISA 46:9–10; ROM 1:20; HEB 11:3).

Read Genesis 1:1—In the beginning, God created... Next read John 1:1–3—In the beginning was the Word... Now read John 1:14—And the Word became flesh... Finally, read ISA 48:16—I (Messiah) was there since the beginning and now God and His Spirit have sent me. Clearly, God the Father, God the Holy Spirit, and God the Son coexisted in unison before the beginning of time and space, and all three persons perform an integral role in creation and redemption (1 JOH 1:1–10; 1 JO 2:7–8; REV 1:8; REV 21:5–6). Absolute Truth came by God's Spirit through His spoken Word (MAR 16:19–20; JOH 4:24); and that Word became a man to deliver the truth personally to humanity (JOH 3:31–34; JOH 17:1–26). Thus, though Christ you can have a personal relationship with God Almighty by allowing His Spirit to dwell within you as it did in Jesus (1 CO 6:19–20; COL 1:19). How can you invite His Spirit? By receiving and ingesting His Word of Truth. God's Spirit has given us life just as the Spirit made the Word alive in Jesus Christ (REV 19:13; REV 22:18–19), who spoke wisdom to us in the written Word and the living Word (PSA 119:160; PRO 8:1–11,22–23,32–36; ROM 10:17).

Logos means Word, and the Word is Truth, and Truth comes by the Holy Spirit (JOH 15:26: JOH 16:13; 1 JO 5:6–7). And that Spirit gives Light and His Light shows us the Way (GEN 1:2–4; PSA 119:105; JOH 1:4–13; JOH 3:20–21; COL 1:10–18). And the Way is Jesus Christ (JOH 8:12; JOH 14:6–17) who gives us eternal Life (JOH 6:68; ROM 6:22–23; TIT 1:2; 1 JO 5:20). You see, Life is in the Spirit, not the flesh (ECC 12:7; JOH 6:63). The humanity of Christ was in the flesh: Son of Man (JOH 8:28–29; PHP 2:5–11). But the deity of Christ was in the Spirit: Son of God (JOH 20:30–31; 1 JO 5:8–13; 2 JO 1:1–3). Jesus is God, who came to Earth to be a witness of the Truth (JOH 1:17; JOH 2:22; JOH 5:36–38). But His works and His words cannot be clearly understood by way of our physical sensations, perceptual faculties, or mental reasoning (JOH 18:37–38; ROM 8:1–6). The Truth of God can only be discerned spiritually (LUK 10:22–24; 1 CO 2:12–14; 2 CO 4:17–18). Because, everything that God does is out of this world, since He exists outside of it. But He lives in us via the Holy Spirit if we desire Him, and Life is forever if we believe His Word (ROM 8:11,16; 1 CO 3:16; 2 TI 1:13–14).

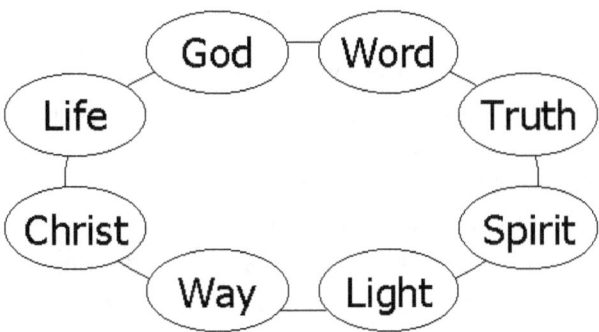

CHAPTER FOUR

WHO AM I?

LIVING SPIRITS

Like God, we exist physically, mentally, and spiritually. The Holy Spirit is God's spiritual being; this is the part of God that communicates His Word to us. In a way, everyone is born with a piece of God's Holy Spirit, for it is the Spirit which gives us life. When we die, our spirit and soul return to God for these belong to Him. Jesus Christ was God in a physical form, and God's only Son. God sent Jesus in human form as a means of communicating His Word in terms humans could understand. Since God could feel through Christ, everything that Christ felt was felt by God. Through Jesus, God fulfilled the New Covenant with His people.

Humans Were Created in the Image of God.

The mental component of God can be likened to the Almighty Father, who is the Lawmaker. God gave us a mind that can distinguish good from evil; He also gave us a choice to obey His laws and commandments, and to love Him. The soul (from the Greek word *psyche*) is often equated with the mind. The soul continues after death; only the body goes into the grave. Whoever believes in God and His Son Jesus Christ can possess their soul, which carries on; they will not experience the second death. Whoever chooses not to believe will have their body and soul destroyed in hell. The value of the soul is greater than anything on this earth. Our souls were ransomed from the grave through the great sacrifice made by Jesus Christ; that's how valuable we are to God who would rather all come to faith and live.

- GEN 1:26 ~ God said, "Let us make man in our image, like us..."
- GEN 2:7 ~ God formed man from the dust of the earth, and breathed into his nostrils the breath of life, and man became a living soul.
- DEU 4:9,29 ~ Keep your soul diligently. Don't forget the things your eyes have seen; teach these things to your children and your children's children. If you seek the Lord with all your heart and soul you will find Him.
- DEU 6:5 ~ You should love the Lord with all your heart, soul, and might.
- DEU 10:12–13 ~ The Lord requires you to fear Him, to walk in His ways, to love Him, to serve Him will all your heart and soul, and to obey His commandments (also JOS 22:5).
- 1 KI 8:48–49 ~ If they repent with all their minds and hearts, I will hear their prayers.
- 1 CH 28:9 ~ Know your God and serve Him with a whole heart and a willing mind. For the Lord searches all hearts and understands every thought and plan.
- MAT 10:28 ~ Jesus said, "Don't fear those who can kill the body but cannot kill the soul. Rather, fear Him who can destroy both the body and soul in hell."
- MAT 22:37 ~ Jesus said, "You must love the Lord with all your heart, soul, and mind."

- ROM 8:4–6 ~ Walk, not according to the flesh, but according to the spirit. Those who live according to the flesh set their minds on evil, but those who live according to the spirit set their minds on God. To set the mind on flesh results in death, but to set the mind on God results in peace and life.
- 1 CO 3:16 ~ You are the temple of God for the Spirit of God lives in you.
- 1 CO 6:17–20 ~ Those who are joined to the Lord are of one spirit. Refrain from fornication. Whoever commits sexual sin is sinning against his or her body. Don't you know that your body is the temple of God's Holy Spirit living in you? You do not own yourself, for you were bought with a great price. Therefore, glorify God in your body and spirit, both of which belong to God.
- 1 CO 14:15 ~ I will pray and I will sing, with the mind and with the spirit.
- 2 CO 3:18 ~ But we, as if looking in a mirror and seeing the glory of the Lord, are changed into the same image from glory to glory, by the Spirit of the Lord.
- 2 CO 5:8 ~ We would rather be away from the body and at home with the Lord (implying that to be absent from the flesh is to be present with the Lord, at least in spirit).
- 1 TH 5:23 ~ May the God of peace sanctify you wholly, so that your entire spirit, soul, and body can be preserved blameless until the coming of our Lord Jesus Christ.
- HEB 4:12 ~ The Word of God is living and active, sharper than any double-edged sword, dividing the soul and spirit, and discerning the thoughts and intentions of the heart.
- HEB 8:10 ~ According to His covenant, the Lord will put His laws into our minds and write them upon our hearts.
- 1 PE 3:8 ~ Have unity of mind, sympathy and love for one another, a tender heart, and a humble mind.

Heart

(emotion and feeling; the body's support system)

- 1 KI 8:61 ~ Let your heart be completely true to the Lord, walking in his statutes and keeping His commandments.
- 2 CH 30:18–19 ~ The good Lord pardons everyone who sets their heart to seek God, even if not according to the rules of the sanctuary.
- PSA 19:14 ~ Let the words of my mouth and the meditation of my heart be acceptable to you Lord.
- PRO 2:2 ~ Make your ear attentive to wisdom and your heart to understanding.
- PRO 3:5–7 ~ Trust in the Lord with all your heart and don't rely on your own understanding. In all your ways acknowledge Him and He will make your paths straight.
- PRO 4:23 ~ Keep your heart with diligence, for from it flows the springs of life.
- PRO 13:12 ~ Hope deferred makes the heart sick, but a desire fulfilled is a tree of life.
- PRO 17:22 ~ A cheerful heart is good medicine.
- PRO 23:17 ~ Don't let your heart envy sinners, but continue in the fear of the Lord all day.
- PRO 27:19 ~ The heart reflects the man just like a mirror.
- ECC 5:2 ~ Don't be rash with your mouth. Don't let your heart be hasty to utter a word before God; instead, let your words be few.
- ECC 10:2 ~ A wise heart inclines one to do what's right.
- ECC 11:9 ~ Rejoice in your youth and let your heart cheer you. Walk in the ways of your heart and the sight of your eyes. But remember, for all these things God will judge you.
- MAT 5:8 ~ Blessed are the pure in heart for they shall see God.

- MAT 15:18–19 ~ What comes out of the mouth proceeds from the heart and defiles the person. For out of the heart come evil thoughts and sinful acts.
- ACT 8:22 ~ Pray that the intent of your heart may be forgiven.
- ROM 10:10 ~ Those who believe with their hearts are justified. Those who confess with their lips are saved.
- COL 3:15 ~ Let the peace of God rule in your heart.

Mind

(thought, reasoning, imagination)

- 1 KI 3:9 ~ Give your servant an understanding mind to govern your people and to discern between good and evil.
- PRO 14:30 ~ A sound mind gives life to the flesh.
- PRO 14:33 ~ Wisdom abides in the minds of those with understanding, but it is not known in the minds of fools.
- PRO 15:28 ~ The mind of the righteous ponders how to answer, but the mouth of the wicked pours out evil.
- PRO 16:23 ~ The mind of a wise person makes speech judicious, and adds persuasiveness to words.
- PRO 22:17 ~ Incline your ear to hear the words of the wise and apply your mind to knowledge.
- PRO 23:19 ~ Hear and be wise, and direct your mind in the true way.
- ECC 7:25 ~ I turned my mind to know and to seek wisdom, and to know the wickedness of folly and the foolishness of madness.
- ECC 8:5 ~ Those who obey the commandments will meet no harm, and the mind of a wise man will know the time and the way.
- LUK 12:29 ~ Do not have a doubtful mind when it comes to God providing your every need.
- ROM 7:23 ~ The laws in the mind conflict with the desires of the flesh.
- ROM 12:2 ~ Don't conform to the world but be transformed by the renewal of your mind, to do the will of God.
- 1 CO 1:10 ~ By the name of Christ, be united in one mind and be of one opinion.
- PHP 4:8 ~ Whatever is true, honorable, just, pure, lovely, and gracious, if there is any excellence, if there is anything worthy of praise, think on these things.
- TIT 1:15 ~ To the pure all things are pure, but to the corrupt and unbelieving nothing is pure; their minds and consciences are corrupt and evil.

Spirit

(insight, communication with God, self-expression, conscience)

- EXO 31:3 ~ I have filled Him with the Spirit of God, with talent and intelligence, with knowledge and abilities.
- DEU 34:9 ~ Joshua was filled with the spirit of wisdom.
- 2 SA 23:2 ~ The Spirit of the Lord speaks by me; His Word is upon my tongue.
- NEH 9:20,30 ~ God gave His Spirit to instruct them. He warned them by the Spirit through the prophets, yet they did not listen.
- JOB 10:12 ~ I have been granted life and steadfast love; His caring has preserved my spirit.
- JOB 32:8 ~ It is the Spirit in a man, the breath of the Almighty, that makes him understand.

- PSA 51:10–12 ~ Create in me a clean heart, Lord, and renew an upright spirit within me. Don't remove me from your presence and don't take your Holy Spirit from me. Restore to me the joy of your salvation, and uphold me with your free Spirit.
- PSA 77:6 ~ I meditate and search my spirit.
- PRO 11:13 ~ He who is trustworthy in spirit keeps intimate things secret.
- PRO 15:4,13 ~ A perverse tongue breaks the spirit. A sorrowful heart breaks the spirit.
- PRO 16:18–19 ~ A proud spirit goes before a fall. It is better to have a humble spirit.
- PRO 17:27 ~ Those who exercise restraint (having a calm spirit) gain in understanding.
- PRO 18:14 ~ Who can bear a broken spirit?
- PRO 29:23 ~ A humble spirit will be honored but not a proud spirit.
- ECC 7:8 ~ It is best to have a patient spirit.
- ECC 8:8 ~ Nobody has the power to retain the spirit when they die, and nobody has authority over death.
- ECC 12:7 ~ Upon death, the spirit returns to God who gave it.
- ISA 30:1 ~ Woe to those who associate with a league of spirits that are not of the Lord.
- EZE 13:3 ~ Woe to the foolish prophets who follow their own spirit and have seen nothing.
- DAN 5:12 ~ Daniel had an excellent spirit, with the knowledge and understanding to interpret dreams, explain riddles, and solve problems.
- HOS 4:12 ~ A spirit of evil has led them astray.
- ZEC 12:1 ~ The Lord formed the spirit of man within him.
- MAL 2:15–16 ~ God has made and sustained for us the spirit of life.
- MAT 26:41 ~ The spirit is willing but the flesh is weak.
- LUK 8:55 ~ The girl's spirit returned to her when Jesus brought her back to life (implies separation of body and spirit upon death).
- LUK 24:39 ~ Jesus said, "The spirit does not have flesh and bones as I have."
- JOH 4:24 ~ Jesus said, "God is Spirit and should be worshipped in spirit and in truth."
- JOH 6:63 ~ Jesus said, "It is the spirit that gives life, not the flesh." Jesus spoke the words of spirit and life.
- ROM 1:9 ~ I serve God with my spirit.
- ROM 8:26–27 ~ The Spirit helps us in our weakness; the Spirit intercedes for us in prayer. The mind of the Spirit intercedes for the saints according to God's will.
- 1 CO 2:10–12 ~ God reveals His mysteries to us through His Spirit, for the Spirit searches all things, even the deepest things of God. Nobody can know the deepest thoughts of another, only the spirit within that person can know them. Similarly, nobody can know the deepest thoughts of God except His Holy Spirit. We have received the Spirit of God, not the spirit of the world, so that we might know the things that God has given to us for free.
- 1 CO 2:15 ~ The spiritual person judges all things except other people.
- 1 CO 15:44 ~ There is a natural body and a spiritual body. It is born a natural body it is raised a spiritual body.
- 2 CO 3:6 ~ God has made us able ministers of the new testament, not of the letter of the Law, but of the Spirit, for the letter kills, but the Spirit gives life.
- GAL 5:17–18,22–23 ~ The desires of the flesh are against the spirit, and vice-versa, for they are opposed to each other. If you are led by the Holy Spirit, you are not under the Law. The fruits of the spirit include love, joy, peace, patience, kindness, goodness, faithfulness, gentleness, and self-control.
- GAL 6:8 ~ Those who sow to the flesh will reap corruption to their flesh; those who sow to the Spirit will from the Spirit reap eternal life.

- EPH 4:23 ~ Be renewed in the spirit of your mind.
- EPH 6:18 ~ Pray at all times in the Spirit.
- 2 TI 1:7 ~ God didn't give us a spirit of fear but a spirit of power, love, and a sound mind.
- JAM 2:26 ~ Just as the body apart from the spirit is dead, faith apart from works is dead.
- 1 JO 4:6 ~ We know the spirit of truth and the spirit of error.
- 1 JO 5:8 ~ The Spirit is the witness, because the Spirit bears the truth.

Soul

(the essence and uniqueness of one's individual being or existence)

- GEN 35:18 ~ She died and her soul departed (implies separation of body and soul upon death).
- 2 CH 15:12 ~ They entered into a covenant to seek the Lord with all their heart and soul.
- JOB 12:10 ~ In His hand is every living soul.
- JOB 33:18,22,28 ~ He keeps back his soul from the pit, his life from perishing by the sword. His soul draws near the pit, and his life is drawn to those who bring death. He has redeemed his soul from the pit, and his life will see the light.
- PSA 24:4 ~ Those who have a pure heart, a truthful soul, and don't swear deceitfully will receive the Lord's blessing, and salvation for their souls.
- PSA 42:2 ~ My soul thirsts for God.
- PSA 49:7–8 ~ Nobody can ransom themselves, or give to God the price of their soul, for the ransom is costly and nothing can ever suffice.
- PSA 55:18 ~ He will deliver my soul safely from the battle that I wage.
- PSA 63:8 ~ My soul clings to God whose right hand holds me up.
- PSA 86:4,13 ~ Gladden my soul, oh Lord, for to you I lift up my soul. For great is your steadfast love toward me; you have delivered my soul from the depths of hell.
- PSA 119:167 ~ My soul keeps your testimonies for I love them exceedingly.
- PSA 130:5–6 ~ I wait for the Lord and in His words, I hope. My soul waits for the Lord more than those that watch for the morning.
- PSA 141:8 ~ My soul seeks refuge in the Lord.
- PRO 16:24 ~ Pleasant words are sweet to the soul and health to the body.
- PRO 21:10 ~ The soul of the wicked desires evil.
- PRO 24:14 ~ Wisdom is sweet to the soul. If you find it you have a future and you have hope.
- JER 31:25 ~ The Lord says, "I will satisfy the weary soul; I will replenish the languishing soul."
- EZE 18:4 ~ God says, "All souls are mine, including the soul of the father and the soul of the son. The soul that sins shall die."
- MAT 16:26 ~ Jesus said, "What does it profit a person who gains the world but loses his soul. What can a person give in return for his soul?"
- LUK 12:19–20 ~ The greedy man said to his soul, "Soul, you have ample goods. Take it easy; eat, drink and be merry." But God said to him, "Fool, tonight your soul is required of you. And all your goods, who will possess them now?"
- LUK 21:19 ~ Jesus said, "Be patient and you will possess your soul."
- HEB 4:12 ~ The Word of God is quick and powerful. It is sharper than any double-edged sword, piercing deep, even to divide the soul and spirit, and the joints and marrow. The Word discerns the thoughts and intents of the heart.

- HEB 6:19 ~ We have Jesus as a sure and steadfast anchor for our souls.
- HEB 10:39 ~ We do not shrink back and we are not destroyed, because those who have faith keep their souls.
- 1 PE 2:11 ~ Abstain from the passions of the flesh which wage war against your soul.
- 2 PE 2:7–8 ~ Lot was vexed in his righteous soul every day because of the lawlessness in the land.
- REV 18:14 ~ The fruit your evil soul longed for is gone, and all your luxuries and pleasures are lost forever.

All People Are Created Equal.

The principle of equality, upon which the USA was founded, is grounded in the Bible. All people are called by Christ, whether Jew or Gentile (non-Jew), regardless of sex, skin color, race, geography, chronology, and/or ancestry. While Israel is often referred to as God's people in the Bible, they were chosen for their faith, as are all people demonstrating godly faith and love. Biblical prophets warned the Jews and everyone else to turn away from evil and back to God. Whoever disobeys God and whoever falls from the true faith, regardless of religion, will end up facing judgment and condemnation. Whoever stays in the true faith and follows Christ will obtain an equal inheritance in God's kingdom as an adopted child of God.

- ISA 11:10 ~ A descendant of Jesse will be a sign for all people; and the Gentiles also will seek Him.
- ISA 25:6–9 ~ The Lord will prepare a feast for all peoples (LUK 14).
- ISA 42:1,6 ~ God said, "Behold my servant, in whom I delight. I have put my Spirit upon Him. He will bring judgment to the Gentiles. He will call everyone to righteousness. He will provide a covenant for all people, and a light for the Gentiles."
- ISA 49:6 ~ God said, "I will raise up the tribes of Jacob and restore the preserved of Israel. I will provide a light for the Gentiles who will receive my salvation unto the end of time."
- ISA 56:2–8 ~ Blessed are all people and their children if they obey God, avoid evil, keep the Sabbath, and cling to His covenant. Even those who are strangers to God's people Israel will be part of God's house if they obey Him. The righteous will be like God's sons and daughters, only better than that, with a name that will last forever. People of all walks of life will be joined together on His holy mountain to worship Him, for His house will be called a house for the righteous. (also 2 CO 6:17–18)
- EZE 47:22 ~ The land will be divided as an inheritance for the house of Israel as well as the strangers who lived among them and had children among them. Thus, the land will be shared by the twelve tribes as well as their companions.
- MAL 1:11 ~ God said, "My name will be great among the Gentiles, and among the heathen."
- MAT 8:5–13 ~ Jesus healed the centurion's servant. Jesus was impressed with the man's faith; he knew that all Jesus had to do was say the word and the servant would be healed. Jesus said to those who followed, "I tell you the truth, I have not found such a great faith in Israel. Many will come from the east and west, and shall sit down with Abraham, Isaac, and Jacob in the kingdom of heaven."
- MAT 13:47–48 ~ Jesus said, "The kingdom of heaven is like a net that caught a large quantity of many different kinds of fish. When the net was full it was pulled ashore and the fish were inventoried. The good fish were saved and the bad fish were thrown into the trash."
- LUK 14:16–24 ~ Remember the parable of the great banquet? Those on the initial guest list made up lousy excuses not to come, so invitations were sent out to the poor and physically handicapped, and to outsiders; and the banquet hall was filled.

- ACT 2:38–39 ~ Peter said, "Repent and be baptized every one of you, in the name of Jesus Christ for the remission of your sins, and you will receive the gift of the Holy Spirit. This promise pertains to you, to your children, and to people everywhere: to whomever the Lord calls."
- ACT 10:34–35 ~ Peter said, "Truly, God does not show favoritism for any person. Within every nation, anyone who fears the Lord and endeavors to be righteous is accepted by Him."
- ACT 11:18 ~ When the people heard Peter, they glorified God saying, "God has granted repentance unto eternal life to the Gentiles as well."
- ACT 26:20,23; ACT 28:28 ~ God asked me (Paul) to tell the truth to Damascus, Jerusalem, throughout the coast of Judea, and then to the Gentiles. I came to tell them that they should repent and turn to God, that they should perform good deeds, and that Christ had to suffer and rise from the dead to show everyone the way of righteousness. Know this: that the salvation of God has been sent to the Gentiles and they will hear it.
- ROM 2:29 ~ A real Jew is anyone who is right with God. God is not looking just for people who are circumcised, but for anyone who has changed for the better in their heart and mind.
- ROM 3:9,23–25,29 ~ Are the Jews better than the Gentiles? No! Everyone has sinned and fallen short of God's glory, and everyone is justified by the grace of Jesus Christ who died for the sins of the world. So, God is not only a God of the Jews but of the Gentiles as well.
- ROM 9:4–8 ~ Who are the Israelites, to whom God gave the Law and granted the adoption, and with whom God made the covenants and promises? Christ came for them and for all people. It's not as if God's Word had no effect, for they who are of Israel are not all from Israel. Those who are of Abraham's seed are not all his children. In other words, those who are the children of the flesh are not children of God; those who cling to God's promises, they are counted as children.
- ROM 10:12 ~ There is no difference between a Jew and a Greek when it comes to the spiritual riches they can obtain through Christ.
- 1 CO 1:24 ~ The apostles preached that the power and wisdom of God is for all who are called by Christ, whether Jews or Greeks.
- 1 CO 12:13 ~ By one Spirit we are baptized into one body. Whether Jews or Gentiles, free men or slaves, all Christians have become members of one Spirit.
- GAL 3:28 ~ There is no such thing as Jew or Greek, slave or free, male or female, for we are equal in Jesus Christ.
- EPH 3:6 ~ The Gentiles will be fellow heirs, members of the same body, and partakers of God's promise through Christ.
- COL 3:4,10–11 ~ When Christ appears, who is our life, all Christians will appear with Him in glory. For we have become new people, renewed in God's image by our knowledge of Him through Christ. There are no longer Jews or Greeks, circumcised or uncircumcised, civilized or uncivilized, slave or free, because Christ is all and in all.
- JAM 1:12 ~ Whoever endures temptation will be blessed by God, for God will judge them favorably and they will receive a crown of life which God promises to all who love Him.
- JAM 2:1–9 ~ Do not be partial to people just because you like the way they look or act. Do not give the rich or the famous more respect than anyone else, and do not give the poor and lowly less respect. If you abide by the royal law according to the scripture, "Love your neighbor as yourself," you are doing the right thing. But if you show favoritism to certain persons you commit sin, and are convicted of the law as a lawbreaker.
- REV 5:9 ~ They sang, "Only you, Lord, are worthy to open the book and its seals. For you were slain, thereby redeeming people of every kindred, tongue, race, and nation by your blood."

- REV 7:9,14 ~ The giant choir who had washed their robes in the blood of Christ came from a variety of nations, peoples, and tongues.

Heirs with Christ but Not Gods

We were created in God's image, but that does not make us gods. Only Jesus Christ can claim to be God because He is our Lord. Christians will become heirs with Christ as adopted children of God, and conformed to the likeness of His image. However, we will not become gods like Jesus is God, because there are no other gods but one, and there is nobody equal to Christ. Further, there have been no prophets, neither will there ever be any who are equal to Jesus Christ. If you want to be an heir and obtain an inheritance in heaven there is one way: faith in Jesus Christ.

- GEN 3:1–6 ~ The serpent was cleverer than the other animals. One day he tricked Eve into trying some fruit from the Tree of Knowledge, even though she knew it was forbidden by God. The serpent told her that whoever ate the fruit would become like a god, possessing the knowledge of good and evil, and that it would not lead to death as God had said. Eve ate the fruit and gave some to Adam who was with her, and he ate some too. Thus, Adam and Eve believed Satan's lie that eating the fruit would make them like gods. Instead, it made them sinful like Satan.
- DEU 32:17,39 ~ Demons are not gods; new gods were invented by people. Besides God, there are no other gods.
- ISA 37:19–20 ~ Their gods will be thrown into the fire, for they weren't gods at all but man's invention. Let all the kingdoms know that you alone are God.
- ISA 43:10; ISA 44:6 ~ There are no gods before Him or after Him. He is the first and last; there is only one God.
- LUK 20:36 ~ Those who are accounted worthy will become like the angels (not gods) and will never die.
- JOH 1:12 ~ To all who have received Christ, and believed in His name, He has given the privilege to become children of God.
- ACT 4:12 ~ Christ is our deliverer. There is no salvation in any other; for there is no other name under heaven, given to us, whereby we can be saved.
- 2 CO 11:13–14 ~ Beware of the false prophets who pretend to be disciples of Christ. Do not let them spark your interest, for even Satan disguises himself as an angel of light.
- GAL 1:8 ~ Anyone who preaches anything contrary to what Jesus Christ and His apostles preached are wrong and are cursed by God.
- GAL 4:6–8 ~ Because you are children, God has sent the Spirit of His Son into your hearts. Therefore, you are no longer servants but children of God, and as children heirs with Christ. So why, before you knew God, were you in bondage to beings who were not gods?
- EPH 4:5–6 ~ There is one Lord, one faith, one baptism, one God and Father of us all, who is above all, through all, and in all.
- PHP 2:6–10 ~ Jesus Christ, who was the image of God and was deserving of God's glory, was made in the likeness of a man. However, instead of glorifying himself He became a humble servant, obedient unto death on a cross. Therefore, God exalted Him, giving Him a name above all other names, so that everyone on earth and in heaven would bow before the name of Jesus Christ.
- 2 TH 2:3–4 ~ Beware the son of perdition, who exalts himself and proclaims to be a god.
- 1 TI 2:5 ~ There is only one God, and the only mediator between Him and humanity is Jesus Christ.

Powers of Humans

God has given people a certain amount of willpower. We possess the knowledge of good and evil and we can choose to obey God or not. Thus, we have the power to do the right thing, as well as the power to sin. We can have a positive effect on our success, our future, and our fate depending on whether we are being influenced by God or the world, or by the spirit within us as opposed to our sullied flesh. We have the power in Christ to become children of God and inherit a place in His kingdom. God, through the Holy Spirit, provides additional power at His discretion. The following are some of the powers God has given people, as documented in the Bible. Many people of God have been able to perform miracles in His name.

- GEN 31:29 ~ Power to hurt others.
- DEU 8:17–18 ~ Power to obtain worldly wealth. Power which comes from God.
- 1 KI 17:17–24 ~ Elijah raised a boy from the dead.
- 2 SA 22:23 ~ Power to obey God.
- EST 8:11 ~ Power to destroy, assault, and to kill.
- PSA 8:4–5 ~ Who are humans that you (God) keep us in your thoughts, and their offspring that you would visit them? For you made humans a little lower than angels, and have crowned us with glory and honor.
- PRO 3:27 ~ Power to do good to others.
- PRO 18:21 ~ Power of the tongue to cause life and death.
- ECC 8:8 ~ Nobody has power to retain the spirit when they die and nobody has power over death.
- ISA 47:14 ~ Nobody has the power to deliver themselves from death or hell.
- EZE 22:6 ~ Power to shed blood.
- MAT 10:1 ~ Jesus gave His disciples power against demons and power to heal the sick and diseased.
- LUK 10:19–20 ~ Jesus gave His disciples immunity over poisonous snakes and scorpions, and power over the enemy and anything harmful, including demons.
- JOH 1:12 ~ God gave people power to become His children through faith in Christ.
- JOH 19:11 ~ Jesus said to Pilate that he didn't have any power except that which was given to him from heaven.
- ACT 1:8 ~ The power of the Holy Spirit, once received, bestows the power to witness.
- ACT 2:4 ~ The power of the Holy Spirit, once received, bestows the power to speak in foreign tongues.
- ACT 3:12 ~ The power of the Holy Spirit, once received, bestows the power to heal the lame.
- ACT 9:37–42 ~ Peter raised a girl from the dead.
- ACT 20:12 ~ Paul raised a boy from the dead.
- 1 CO 7:37 ~ Power over one's own will.
- 1 CO 9:4–6 ~ Power to eat and drink. Power to lead others. Power to work or not work.
- HEB 11:7–38 ~ With faith, the great prophets were able to endure anything and performed great feats, such as subduing kingdoms, escaping certain death, overcoming incredible odds, healing the sick, and even raising the dead.
- JAM 4:7 ~ Power to resist Satan.
- REV 11:5–6 ~ God will give the two witnesses power to breathe fire, to stop the rain, to turn water into blood, and to bring plagues.

Revelations and Visions

God sometimes reveals His messages and prophecies to people in visions, dreams, and revelations. Most of the prophets received some sort of revelation or vision (including Noah, Abraham, Moses, Joseph, Jacob, Samuel, David, Solomon, Isaiah, Jeremiah, Ezekiel, Daniel, Hosea, Obadiah, Nahum, Habakkuk, Ananias, Peter, Paul, and John). God reveals all truth, wickedness, and godliness in due time. He does not withhold the truth for He is truth. He is a God who reveals hidden truths and mysteries. If you seek God you will find Him; He can be found by studying the scriptures where He reveals all you need to know about Him. And the more you learn the truth of His Word, the greater will be your insight and understanding, and the more likely you will receive direction and purpose in your life.

- NUM 12:6 ~ The Lord said, "If there is a prophet among you, I will make myself known to him in a vision and will speak to him in a dream."
- JOB 33:14–17 ~ God will speak once, maybe twice, but people do not perceive it. He speaks in a vision, at night, when we are asleep. He may speak into a person's ears and alert them with warnings to turn them from sin and pride, in order to keep their souls from the pit.
- JER 14:14; JER 23:16; JER 29:8 ~ The Lord said to Jeremiah, "Prophets come saying that I sent them, but I didn't. They say that the sword and famine will not come upon this land, but by sword and famine these prophets shall be consumed. Do not listen to false prophets. They will make you vain. They speak visions of their own hearts and not from my mouth. Do not let these prophets and fortunetellers deceive you. Do not listen to any dreams that you yourself deliberately caused to be dreamt."
- DAN 2:47 ~ The king answered Daniel, saying, "For sure, your God is a God of gods, a King of kings, and a revealer of secrets. He has revealed the secret of my dream to you."
- JOE 2:28 ~ I (the Lord) will pour out my Spirit upon all people. Your sons and daughters will prophesy, your old men will dream dreams, and your young men will see visions.
- AMO 3:7 ~ The Lord reveals His secrets to His servants, the prophets.
- MAT 10:26–27 ~ Jesus said, "Do not fear those who hate you, for everything that is hidden now will be revealed later; everything that is unknown will become known. What I tell you in darkness, you will speak in the light. What you hear will be preached from the rooftops."
- MAT 11:25 ~ Jesus said, "I thank you Father, Lord of heaven and earth, for concealing these things (the Judgment, Second Coming, etc.) from the wise and prudent, yet revealing them to children."
- ROM 1:17–18 ~ The righteousness of God has been revealed from faith to faith in the Gospel of Christ. As it is written: The just shall live by faith. For the wrath of God is revealed from heaven against unrighteousness.
- ROM 16:25–26 ~ Christ has the power to save you according to the revelation of God's mystery, which was kept secret since the world began but which is now evident by the scriptures. According to God's will the mystery is made known to all nations on earth for the obedience of faith.
- 1 CO 2:9–10 ~ God has revealed to us through His Spirit what He has prepared for those who love Him. The Spirit searches all things, even the deepest things of God.
- 1 CO 3:13 ~ Everyone's works will be revealed and will be tested by the fire to determine what sort of works they really are.
- 2 CO 12:1 ~ I will embrace visions and revelations from the Lord.
- GAL 1:11–12 ~ Paul wrote, "The Gospel I preach did not come from people, neither was I taught it; it came to me by the revelation of Jesus Christ."

- GAL 3:23 ~ Before faith came, we were under the Law, shut inside for faith to be revealed afterwards.
- 2 TH 2:8 ~ The wicked one (Satan) will be revealed and the Lord will consume this evil with the Spirit of His mouth and shall destroy it with the brightness of His coming.
- TIT 2:11 ~ The grace of God that brings salvation has appeared to all people.
- 1 PE 1:5 ~ You are kept by the power of God through faith unto salvation, ready to be revealed in the last time.
- 1 PE 4:13 ~ Rejoice, because you are partakers of Christ's suffering. When His glory is revealed, you may be glad and exceedingly joyful.
- REV 1:1 ~ Revelations from Jesus Christ, which God gave to Him, showed His servants things that would come to pass, as when the angel revealed them to John.

Life

Life is a gift from God to all of us. It is our responsibility to obey God and to depend on Christ for our salvation if we want to live forever. If we believe in Christ and walk in His righteousness, we will never die. Christ offers us fruit of the Tree of Life to eat, and water from the River of Life to drink, if we follow Him all the days of our lives.

- GEN 3:22 ~ God said, "Humans are like the higher-order beings because they have the knowledge of good and evil. They can eat from the Tree of Life and they can live forever."
- DEU 28:66 ~ You will be doubtful about your life, and you will fear day and night about whether you are to live or die.
- DEU 30:19–20 ~ Moses said, "I have presented you with life and death, blessing versus cursing. I recommend that you choose life so that you and your descendants may live. I hope you choose to love God, obey his Law, and cling to Him; for He is your life and He is your time; and you will live in the land which He promised to you and your ancestors."
- PSA 36:9 ~ With God is a fountain of life; in His light we see clearly.
- PRO 3:1–2 ~ Don't forget God's Law. Keep His commandments and He will give you peace and a long life.
- PRO 8:35 ~ Whoever finds God finds life, and will obtain God's favor.
- PRO 11:30 ~ The fruit of righteousness is a tree of life, and those who win souls for God are wise.
- PRO 22:4 ~ Through humility and the fear of God we receive riches, honor, and life.
- EZE 18:21 ~ If the wicked would turn from their sins and keep God's commandments, doing what is lawful and right, they would surely live and would not have to die.
- DAN 12:2 ~ Those who sleep in the dust of the earth will awake, some to everlasting life and some to everlasting shame and contempt.
- MAT 6:25,33 ~ Jesus said, "Don't worry about your life, what you will eat and drink, or the clothes that you will wear. Isn't life more important than food or clothing? If you seek the kingdom of God and His righteousness, all these things will be given to you in addition."
- MAT 7:14 ~ Straight and narrow is the gate which leads to life, and few people will find it.
- MAT 22:32 ~ Jesus declared, "God said, I am the God of Abraham, Isaac, and Jacob. That means God is a God of the living, not a God of the dead."
- LUK 12:15 ~ Jesus said, "Beware of earthly cravings, for your life does not consist of the abundance of the things which you can possess while living on this earth."
- JOH 3:16 ~ God loved the world so much that He sacrificed His only begotten Son, so that anyone could believe in Him and not die, but receive eternal life.

- JOH 6:51 ~ Jesus said, "I am the living bread which came down from heaven; anyone who eats this bread will live forever. The bread I give will be my flesh, which I will give for the life of the world."
- JOH 6:63 ~ Jesus said, "It is the spirit that gives life, not the flesh. The words I speak are of the Spirit and therefore give life."
- JOH 8:12 ~ Jesus said, "I am the light of the world. Whoever follows me will not walk in darkness but will have the light of life."
- JOH 11:25 ~ Jesus said, "I am the resurrection and the life; whoever believes in me, though they were dead, yet shall they live."
- JOH 14:19 ~ Jesus said, "In a little while the world will not see me anymore. But you will see me, and because I live, you will live also."
- 2 CO 3:5–6 ~ Everything we have is from God who made us ministers of the New Testament. This testament is not a written one but a spiritual one. For a written testament destroys life but the Spirit gives life.
- 2 CO 5:15 ~ He (Christ) died for all. Therefore, the living should not live for themselves anymore, but for Him who died for them and rose again to life.
- GAL 2:20 ~ I (Paul) am crucified with Christ; nevertheless, I am alive. But it is not really me who lives, but Christ who lives in me. The life I now have in the flesh I live by faith in Christ who loved me and gave Himself for me.
- JAM 4:14 ~ You never know what tomorrow will bring, for what is your life? It is but a vapor that appears for a while and then vanishes.
- REV 2:10 ~ Jesus said, "Be faithful unto death and I will give you a crown of life."
- REV 22:1–2,14,17 ~ The Lord showed me (John) a pure river of the water of life, crystal clear, proceeding from the throne of God and the Lamb. In the middle of it and on either side was the Tree of Life. The tree bore twelve different kinds of fruit each month, and the leaves of the tree provided healing power to all nations. Blessed are those who keep God's commandments, so that they can receive the right to the Tree of Life, and to enter into the gates of heaven. And the Spirit and Christ will say, "Those who thirst may come in and freely drink of the water of life."

Death

Because we are born sinful and lead sinful lives we are condemned to die. Upon death, the spirit returns to God. Everyone must die at least once (unless they are raptured beforehand). However, thanks to Christ, we don't have to remain dead. All the dead will arise to be judged. Those who believed in Christ, repented of their sins, and tried to lead a godly life will be judged blameless and will never die again. However, those who chose not to believe, and who lived a life of sin without repentance, will die a second death never to live again.

- JOB 14:10,14 ~ People die and waste away; yes, they give up their spirit, and then where do they go? When a person dies can they live again? Throughout my time I will wait, until I am free.
- PSA 23:4 ~ Even when I walk under the shadow of death, I will not be afraid because God is with me.
- PSA 49:17 ~ When you die you take nothing with you; your glory does not go with you.
- PRO 10:2 ~ The treasures of the wicked will not profit them anything on the day of their death, but the righteous will be delivered from death.
- PRO 18:21 ~ Life and death are within the power of the tongue, and those who love it will eat its fruit.

- ECC 7:1 ~ A good name is better than precious things; and the day of such a person's death is better than the day of their birth.
- ECC 8:8 ~ Nobody has power over the spirit to retain it when they die, neither does anyone have any power over death. Nobody can escape death, neither can anyone be delivered from death through wickedness.
- ECC 9:5 ~ The living know that they will die, but the dead don't know anything, neither will they ever receive any of life's rewards, for they are forgotten.
- ECC 12:7 ~ Upon death, the dust will return to earth, and the spirit will return to God who gave it.
- ISA 28:18 ~ Any covenant made with death will be nullified; any agreement made with hell will be void.
- ISA 38:18–19 ~ Those who die cannot praise God, only the living can. Once you are dead, you no longer can hope for the truth, you can hope only while you are alive.
- EZE 18:4–5,21–24,27,32 ~ God says, "Behold, all souls are mine, including the soul of the father and the soul of the son. The soul that sins will die, unless he or she does what is lawful and right. Do you think I enjoy condemning the wicked to die, never to return from their sins in repentance so they can live? When the righteous turn to sin and wickedness, do you think they will live? Their righteousness never again will be mentioned, and they will die in their sins. Further, when the wicked turn to God in repentance, and remain righteous, their sins never again will be mentioned and they will live. I take no pleasure in the death of those who must die."
- HOS 13:14 ~ God says, "I will ransom you from the power of the grave to be redeemed from death. Then I will destroy death."
- MAT 10:28 ~ Jesus said, "Don't fear anyone who can kill your body but not your soul; fear the One who can destroy both your body and your soul in hell."
- LUK 16:19–31 ~ Jesus told the parable of the rich man and the poor man: There was a rich man who lived a life of pleasure and luxury. A poor man lay at his gate that was weak, hungry, and afflicted, desiring just the crumbs off the rich man's plate. The two men died. The poor man was taken to Abraham's bosom, and the rich man was exiled in Hades. The rich man called out to Abraham asking if he would let the poor man dip his finger into water to wet his parched tongue. But Abraham reminded him how thoughtless and unmerciful he had been to the poor man, and told him that nobody could pass through the chasm separating the two underworlds. The rich man implored that his family be warned, to prevent them from the same fate. Abraham informed the rich man that they would have to rely on the Word of God like everybody else; if they didn't, not even a visit from the dead would persuade them to change their ways.
- LUK 23:43 ~ Jesus told the repentant thief, "Today (after you have died) you will be with me in paradise."
- LUK 23:46 ~ Jesus cried, "Father, into your hands I commend my Spirit," and then He died.
- JOH 5:24 ~ Jesus said, "Truly I say, anyone who hears my words and believes that I was sent by God will have eternal life. They will not be condemned, but will pass from death into life."
- JOH 11:25 ~ Jesus said, "I am the resurrection and the life. Those who believe in me, though they were dead, yet shall they live."
- ACT 7:59 ~ The crowd stoned Stephen and he called to God, saying, "Lord Jesus, receive my spirit."
- ROM 6:23 ~ The wages of sin is death, but the gift of God is eternal life through Jesus Christ our Lord.

- ROM 14:7–9 ~ Nobody can live for themselves or die for themselves; whether we live or die it is for the Lord because we belong to Him. Christ died and rose from the dead to be the Lord of the living and the dead.
- 1 CO 15:20–26,44 ~ Christ arose from the dead, becoming the first to rise into heaven. Just as death came by a man, by a man has come the resurrection of the dead. Like Adam, we die, and like Christ, we all will rise from the dead, Christ being the first. Christ will reign, and His enemies will be destroyed; the last enemy to be destroyed will be death. It is our natural body that dies, it is our spiritual body that lives forever after death.
- 2 CO 5:1,6–8,10,15 ~ We know that when this temple, which is our body, is dissolved, we will have a home in heaven; not a house made by hands but one that is eternal. This gives us the confidence we need, for we are living here in the flesh and absent from the Lord. We must walk by faith not by sight. I am not afraid; indeed, I yearn to be absent from this body and present with the Lord. We will appear before the judgment seat of Christ, to receive back the things we did with this body, whether good or bad. Since Jesus Christ died for all, we should dedicate our entire lives to Him who died and rose again.
- 2 TI 1:10 ~ Christ abolished death and brought life and immortality to us through His Word.
- HEB 2:14 ~ Just as God's children partake of the flesh and blood, Christ also took part in the same, so through His death He could destroy the devil who has the power to bring death.
- HEB 9:27 ~ Everyone must die once; then comes the judgment.
- JAM 1:15 ~ Lust brings forth sin. Sin, when finished, brings forth death.
- 1 PE 3:18 ~ Christ suffered for the sins of all, the just and the unjust, so He could bring us to God. He was put to death in the flesh, but raised to life in the Spirit.
- REV 1:18 ~ Jesus said, "I am He that lives, having once been dead, and I live forevermore, Amen. I hold the keys to death and hell."
- REV 14:13 ~ I (John) heard a voice from heaven saying, "Blessed are the those who die unto the Lord henceforth. The Spirit says they will rest from their labor and their good works will follow them."
- REV 20:4–6,13–15 ~ Those who remained righteous, witnessed for Jesus, and did not worship the beast or receive the mark of the beast, lived and reigned with Christ one thousand years. This was the first resurrection. The rest of the dead did not live again until the thousand years had ended. Blessed and holy are those who share in the first resurrection for they will not experience the second death. At the second resurrection the rest of the souls were raised to be judged by God. Death and Hell, and those who were not written in the Book of Life, were cast into the lake of fire; this was the second death.
- REV 21:4,8 ~ God will wipe away their tears and erase all death, sorrow, crying, and pain. But those who are fearful, unbelieving, abominable, murderous, lecherous, sorcerers, idolaters, and liars will be thrown into the lake of fire which is the second death.

The Church

The church of God is God's house, and comprises the entire membership of God-fearing Christians. All believers are part of God's house, and Jesus Christ is the chief cornerstone in the foundation of that house. God's people are part of His household, and they will live with Him in His home eternally. Being part of God's household is to be with our Heavenly Father, and to live with His only Son Jesus Christ. God has adopted His people, so they have become His sons and daughters, and brothers and sisters of Christ.

God's church is the bride and Christ, the groom. He is married to His church. This is why the church is called the body of Christ, as it comprises all Christians around the world. Christ is the head of that church or body. Any group of people that has congregated in order to praise, thank, and/or worship God and Christ can be considered a church. This is because, whenever two or more people have gathered together in Christ's name, there also is the Holy Spirit.

Thus, "The Church" consists of all members of God's kingdom here on earth and in heaven; any gathering of these members, large or small, is "a church." The mission of any church is to communicate God's Word, shine His Light, administer the sacraments, and reach out to those who have not heard the good news of Jesus Christ. It is a place where one may thank and worship God, pray to Him, hear His Word, find forgiveness, and be strengthened in the true faith by God's Holy Spirit and fellow believers.

- 1 CH 16:29 ~ Give to the Lord the glory due Him; bring your offerings and worship Him.
- ISA 62:5 ~ As the groom rejoices over the bride, so God rejoices over His people.
- JER 23:28 ~ God says, "Whoever has my Word should speak that Word faithfully so others might hear it."
- HOS 2:19–20 ~ I (God) will be married to you forever. I will take you as my spouse in righteousness, judgment, loving kindness, mercy, and faithfulness.
- MAT 9:15 ~ Jesus said, "Should the children of the groom mourn while He is still with them? The days will come when the groom will be taken away from them; then it will be time to mourn and fast."
- MAT 16:18 ~ Jesus said to Simon Peter, "You are Peter, and on this rock, I will build my church; and the gates of hell will not prevail against it."
- MAT 18:20 ~ Jesus said, "When two or more people are gathered together in my name, I will be there with them."
- MAT 28:19 ~ Jesus commissioned His disciples to go into the world and teach all nations and peoples everything He had taught them, baptizing them in the name of the Father, Son, and Holy Spirit.
- MAR 16:15 ~ Jesus said, "Go into the world and preach the Word to all people."
- JOH 5:25 ~ Jesus said, "The time is coming, and is now, when the dead will hear my voice, and those who listen will live."
- JOH 8:31–32 ~ Jesus said, "If you continue in my Word, you are indeed my disciples. And you will know the truth, and the truth will set you free."
- JOH 10:14–16 ~ Jesus said, "I am the Good Shepherd. I know my sheep and they know me, just as the Father knows me and I, Him; and I lay down my life for the sheep. And I have other sheep not of this fold that I also must bring to heaven; and there will be one flock and one Shepherd."
- ROM 12:4–5 ~ Just as we have many members in our body, and all members have the same purpose, so we, being many, are one body in Christ and members of one another.
- 1 CO 6:15–20 ~ Don't you realize that your bodies are the members of Christ? Would you take the members of Christ and join them with a prostitute? God forbid it! Well, to have sex with a prostitute is to be joined with a prostitute, because to be joined in sex makes two people joined in their flesh, becoming one body. Similarly, whoever is joined to Christ is of one Spirit. Resist fornication, for unlike other sins it is a sin against one's own body. Don't you realize that your body is the temple of the Holy Spirit who lives in you and who comes from God? Therefore, your body is not your own, because you were purchased with a great price. Use your body and your spirit, which belong to God, to glorify Him.

- 1 CO 16:2 ~ Set aside some money in accordance with your budget, and give it to the church on the first day of each week.
- EPH 1:20–23 ~ God has placed Jesus Christ, who He raised from the dead, at His right hand in heaven. Therefore, Christ is above all principalities, powers, and dominions; He is above every name in this world and the next. That makes Christ the head over all His church, which is His body. He is everything to everyone.
- EPH 2:18–21 ~ In Christ we have access through the Holy Spirit to our Father in heaven. Therefore, God's people are no longer strangers or foreigners, they are fellow citizens with the saints and the household of God. God's house is built upon the foundation laid by the apostles and the prophets; Jesus Christ Himself is the chief cornerstone of that foundation. Upon Christ the entire church is built; in Him the entire church is held together to be a holy temple of the Lord.
- EPH 4:14–16 ~ We will no longer be helpless as children, swayed by false teachings and influenced by the trickery of deceitful schemes. Instead, we will speak the truth out of love, and we will grow in every way in Christ, who is our head. In Christ, the whole body is joined and held together just as our bodies are joined and held together by ligaments and joints. Christ is the head of this body, in which all members work together as an integrated system; through Him the body is nurtured and grows in His love.
- EPH 5:23–27 ~ The husband is the head of the wife just as Christ is the head of the church. Christ loved the church so much He gave Himself for it, so that He could sanctify it and cleanse it with the washing of water and the Word. He has presented His church to Himself, a church without any imperfections, a church that is holy like Him.
- COL 1:12–20 ~ Give thanks to the Father, who has allowed us to partake of His inheritance, given to the saints who abide in His light. He has ransomed us from the power of darkness and delivered us to the kingdom of His dear Son Jesus Christ, who has redeemed and forgiven us through His own precious blood. Christ is the very image of the invisible God; He is the firstborn of all living creatures. Through Him, all things were created on earth and in heaven, whether visible or invisible, including all thrones, dominions, principalities, and powers. All things were created by Him and for Him. He is before all things, and because of Him all things exist. He is the head of the body which is the church. He is the beginning, the firstborn of the dead, and the supreme being above all things. God was pleased to allow His fullness to live in Christ. Christ established an everlasting peace through His blood which was shed on the cross, thereby causing all things on earth and in heaven to exist together in harmony through Him.
- 1 TI 2:4 ~ God wants all people to come to the knowledge of the truth.
- HEB 12:22–23 ~ You have come to Zion, to the city of the living God, the heavenly Jerusalem. You have come to the company of innumerable angels, to the general assembly and church of the firstborn, all of whom are written in heaven. You have come to live with God, the judge of all, and with the spirits of all honest people made perfect, and to Jesus Christ the mediator of the New Covenant.
- 1 PE 2:5 ~ You are living stones used to build Christ's church, to become a holy priesthood, and to offer your sacrifices to God.
- 2 PE 3:9 ~ God doesn't want anyone to die, He would rather everyone repents.
- REV 19:7–9 ~ Let us give honor to God for the marriage of the Lamb has come and His wife has made herself ready. She is dressed in clean white linen, which represents the righteousness of the saints. Blessed are those who are called to the wedding and the supper that follows (MAT 25:1–13).

The Church's One Foundation

The Church's one foundation is Jesus Christ, her Lord;
She is His new creation by water and the Word.
From heaven He came and sought her to be His holy bride;
With His own blood He bought her, and for her life He died.

Elect from every nation, yet one o'er all the earth,
Her charter of salvation: one Lord, one faith, one birth.
One holy Name she blesses, partakes one holy food,
And to one hope she presses with every grace endued.

The church shall never perish! Her dear Lord to defend,
To guide, sustain, and cherish, is with her to the end.
Though there be those that hate her, false sons within her pale,
Against both foe and traitor, she ever shall prevail.

Lesson: Making Decisions and Solving Problems

Countless decisions and problems emerge many times during the course of a single day. How these challenges are dealt with depends on one's attitude, outlook, and belief system. It is entirely unnecessary to allow such challenges to cause worry or anxiety; all that is required is to take them to the Lord. If we trust in His mercy and depend on His love to guide us, how can we fail? It comes down to where you place your faith and trust; if they are in the Lord you are on solid ground, if they are on yourself or the world, you are on shaky ground.

Undoubtedly, decisions are reflected in a person's worldview. That is, those who set their minds on God will make markedly different decisions than those focused on the world. Let everything you say and do be for the Lord, for your life belongs to Him (ROM 14:8; COL 3:17,23–24). If what you say and do is to promote yourself, you will eventually be brought down. Each circumstance presents a variety of options, which are quickly narrowed to but a few when the light of faith shows a righteous path.

Everyone has problems and setbacks in this world due to their sinful flesh (ROM 13:13–14). Because of sin we experience conflict in our lives, not just with others but within ourselves. In fact, our flesh is in constant conflict with our spirit. It is difficult to resolve this conflict, and impossible without God. We must remember that we are spiritual beings, not merely physical, and that our home is in heaven, not on earth. Decisions have an effect on your future, and possibly your eternity.

- ROM 7:19–20,23 ~ I don't do the good I want to do, but I do the evil I don't want to do. If I do the evil things I don't want to do, it is not I that do them but the sin that lives inside of me. I see a different law in my body that is at war with the law in my mind, bringing me into captivity to the law of sin which is part of my flesh.
- ROM 7:25; ROM 8:1–6 ~ What a sinful person I am, that God should deliver me from the body of this death? I thank God through Jesus Christ our Lord. With my mind I will serve the Law of God, but with my flesh I serve the law of sin. But there is no condemnation for those who are in Jesus Christ, because they walk after the Spirit not the flesh. For the law of the Spirit of life in Christ has made us free from the law of sin and death. The righteousness of the Law is fulfilled in us, who walk according to the Spirit. Those with a carnal mind will find death; but the spiritually minded will find life and peace.
- GAL 5:17–18 ~ The desires of the flesh are against the spirit, and vice-versa, for they are opposed to each other. If you are led by the Holy Spirit you are not under the Law.
- 1 PE 2:11 ~ Dear ones, I implore you as strangers and pilgrims to refrain from lusts of the flesh which war against your soul.

The Bible teaches us to bring our problems to God. After all, He sent His Son to bear the burden of our sin, and He sent His Holy Spirit to comfort us. He provides us with the strength to confront life's dilemmas using our faith and hope. This produces confidence in difficult times and wisdom in daily decisions.

- DEU 4:30–31 ~ When you experience tribulation, even during the latter days, turn to God and do as He commands. For He is a merciful God; He will neither forsake you nor destroy you, nor will He forget the covenant He swore to your ancestors.
- PSA 34:17 ~ The righteous cry, and the Lord hears and delivers them out of their troubles.
- PSA 50:15 ~ Call upon God in the day of trouble and you will be delivered, and you will glorify God.

- PRO 11:8 ~ The righteous are delivered out of trouble, while the wicked come to take their place.
- PRO 16:3–4,9 ~ Commit your actions to the Lord and He will guide your thoughts. He has made all things for Himself, including the wicked for the day of evil. A person's heart devises the way he or she wants to go, but the Lord directs his or her steps.
- MAT 11:28 ~ Jesus said, "Call upon me all of you who are weary and burdened, and I will give you rest" (also PSA 50:15).

God is love and His love lives in us through His Holy Spirit, a Spirit of love and truth. What greater comfort can we obtain than His steadfast love and resounding truth? He is the source of our encouragement and consolation, and these things are to be shared with one another. Love and truth are essential ingredients for a proper state of mind to make important decisions.

- PRO 3:5–6 ~ Trust in the Lord with all your heart; don't depend on your own understanding. In all things acknowledge Him and He will direct you in the right path.
- 2 CO 1:3–5 ~ Blessed is God the Father of our Lord Jesus Christ, the Father of mercies and the God of comfort. He comforts us in our tribulations, so that we may comfort others who are troubled with that same comfort God has given to us. Whereas our sufferings in Christ are many, so also is our consolation in Christ abundant.
- 2 CO 4:8–10,16–17 ~ We are surrounded by troubles, yet we are not distressed; we are perplexed, but we are not in despair. We are persecuted, but not forsaken; beaten down, but not destroyed. We always carry in our bodies the death of Jesus Christ, so that His life will also be revealed in our bodies. Therefore, we never give up, though outwardly we are worn down; yet inwardly we are renewed day after day. Our insignificant and temporary problems bring us closer to the eternal glory, and that glory far outweighs the sum of all of our troubles combined.
- 1 PE 5:6–7 ~ Humble yourselves before the mighty hand of God, and He will glorify you in due time. Toss all your cares upon Him, for He cares immensely for you.

Life's challenges, hindrances, and trials test our patience, endurance, stamina, and character. To face them with the assurance that God is in control makes us stronger and more confident, leading to better decisions and better outcomes.

- MAT 6:33–34 ~ Jesus taught: Seek first the kingdom of God and His righteousness, and everything else will be yours. Don't be anxious about tomorrow; each day has enough new challenges to confront. Just trust in God to provide your needs.
- ROM 5:3–5 ~ We glory in tribulations, knowing that tribulation works patience, and patience works experience, and experience works hope. And hope makes us unashamed, because the love of God fills our hearts through the Holy Spirit that we have been given.
- 1 CO 10:13 ~ Temptations are common to all people, but God is faithful and fair. He will not allow you to be tempted beyond your ability to endure, and He will always leave you an escape from temptation.
- 2 CO 12:9–10 ~ Jesus said, "My grace is sufficient for you, for my strength is made perfect in weakness." Therefore, I (Paul) am pleased to endure hardships and pain on His behalf, so that His power can come to me. So, I take pleasure when I am accused, abused, persecuted, and needy for Christ's sake; for when I am weak, then I become strong.

We can receive God's helping hand simply by asking for His assistance through prayer. We have the option of bringing our troubles to the Lord no matter how terrible or trivial. God has given us the gift of prayer as a means of thanking Him for His mercy and goodness and bringing our petitions to Him. We should exercise this wonderful blessing constantly, in all situations.

- ROM 8:26 ~ The Holy Spirit intercedes for us when we pray. We don't know what we should pray for all the time. But through the act of prayer, God analyzes our needs and answers our prayers in the best possible way.
- ROM 12:12 ~ Rejoice in hope, be patient in troubled times, be constant in prayer.
- EPH 5:20 ~ Always and for everything give thanks to God the Father in the name of our Lord Jesus Christ.
- PHP 4:6–7 ~ Don't have anxiety about anything, but pray for everything. With thanksgiving let your requests be known to God. And the peace of God that surpasses all understanding will keep your heart in mind in Jesus Christ.
- COL 4:2 ~ Continue to pray and wait for the answer, giving thanks for the result.
- 1 TH 5:17–18 ~ Pray constantly. Give thanks in all circumstances.

We are God's people, and through His Spirit we are bound to Him by love. Each of us represents a building block in His holy temple, of which Jesus Christ is our firm foundation. We are members of the body of Christ, and Jesus Christ is our head. Being members with each other in Spirit, we are obligated to one another, to help each other in times of need, to console each other in times of hardship, and to mend each other in times of pain or injury.

- MAT 5:23–24 ~ Jesus said, "If you intend to bring your offerings to the Lord, but you remember that you have a disagreement with another, first reconcile with that person, then present your gifts to God."
- 1 CO 12:12,25–26 ~ The body is one, yet it has many members; just like we, being many, are members of one body through Christ. There should be no discord in the body, but all members should care equally for one another. When one member suffers, all members suffer with it; when one member is honored, all members are honored with it.
- JAM 5:16 ~ Confess your faults to one another and pray for each other. The fervent prayer of a righteous person yields high returns.

Built on the Rock

Built on the Rock the church shall stand, even when steeples are falling;
Spires have crumbled in every land, bells still are chiming and calling,
Calling the young and old to rest, calling the souls of those distressed,
Longing for life everlasting.

We are God's house of living stones, built for His own habitation;
He fills our hearts, His humble thrones, granting us life and salvation.
Were two or three to seek His face, He in their midst would show his grace,
Blessing upon them bestowing.

Yet in this house, an earthly frame, Jesus the children is blessing;
Hither we come to praise His name, faith in our Savior confessing.
Jesus to us His Spirit sent, making with us His covenant,
Granting His children the kingdom.

Through all the passing years, oh Lord, grant that when church bells are ringing,
Many may come to hear God's Word where He this promise is bringing:
"I know my own, my own know me; you, not the world, my face shall see,
My peace I leave you, Amen.

CHAPTER FOUR

Lesson: Endurance and Patience

God tests the strength of our faith from time to time to remind us who is in charge, and to empower us with His knowledge and might. God shows us our weaknesses and our limitations to prepare us for greater challenges, prompting us to obtain additional education and ability. Further, by enabling us to perceive that some things have a threshold or limit, we realize that some things are limitless, such as God's everlasting love for us. Because of this, nothing is impossible within reason, as we have merely to wait on the Lord; for if it is His will it is basically a done deal, we just don't know when.

God never pushes us beyond our capacity. Further, God does not tempt us, Satan does. While God allows Satan to tempt us, He does not allow us to be tempted beyond our endurance threshold. God delivers us when the burden is too great.

- DEU 31:6 ~ Be courageous and strong; do not be afraid of anyone. For God goes with you; He will neither fail you nor forsake you.
- ISA 40:31 ~ Those who wait for the Lord will be renewed in their strength. They will soar like the eagle. They will run and not tire; they will walk and not grow faint.
- 1 CO 10:13 ~ Everyone must endure temptation, but God will not allow you to be tempted beyond your ability to withstand it, and He will always provide you an escape from the temptation.
- 2 TI 3:11 ~ Although I (Paul) endured much hardship, persecution, and affliction, God always delivered me.
- HEB 12:7,9 ~ Endure the chastisement of God, for He is simply dealing with us like a caring father deals with his children. For what son or daughter is never punished by their parents? Do we not revere our parents when they discipline us? And aren't we subject to the discipline of our Father in heaven even more than our earthly parents?
- JAM 4:7 ~ Humans have the power to resist Satan.
- REV 3:10 ~ Jesus said, "Because you have patiently kept my commandments, I will deliver you from the hour of temptation, which shall come upon the entire world to try the patience of all people."

In the Old Testament are numerous examples of how God put His servants to the test. In time, these servants learned valuable lessons in endurance, and in setting priorities.

- GEN 17; GEN 22 ~ God commanded Abraham to sacrifice His only son Isaac. Imagine Abraham's dilemma. Finally, after one hundred years he fathered an heir, only to have God request Isaac be sacrificed. Yet Abraham loved God even more than his only son. God pardoned Abraham's sin and spared Isaac, because Abraham had his priorities straight. A young ram was sacrificed instead of Isaac, and that ram represents the sacrifice of God's only son, Jesus Christ. God blessed Abraham, rewarding his faith with descendants as numerous as the stars.
- EXO 19—32 ~ God put the faith of the Israelites to the test, because of the great sin they committed in the Sinai desert, even as Moses was receiving the Ten Commandments (DEU 9:18). They further sinned by not claiming the land that God promised to them (NUM 14). They had to wander the wilderness forty years before they were allowed to inherit the promised land; that's one year for each day they sinned while Moses was on the mountain.
- JOB 1—3; JOB 37—42 ~ Job represents the epitome of endurance. God allowed Satan to push Job way beyond the endurance threshold of the average person. Job lost everything: his family, his fortune, his health, and his peace of mind. Yet Job remained faithful to God, although his faith weakened as he reached the end of his endurance. Job is a great example of

how faith can prevail over the powers and wiles of Satan. Job realized his need for salvation through repentance. God rewarded Job's faith by returning to Job everything he had lost in double-proportions.

Jesus Christ, God's only Son, was put to the extreme test.

- ISA 53:4–12 ~ He took upon Himself all of our grief and sorrows; yet we treated Him as an outcast. He was tortured for our sins and punished for our peace, and through His wounds we are healed. He was slaughtered like a lamb. He was buried like a criminal but in a rich man's grave. He was made an offering for sin, although He never committed a single act of sin or spoke an evil word. Therefore, His days will be prolonged and His name will be made great. He will be exalted, for He emptied his soul unto death.
- MAT 4:1–11; MAR 1:9–13; LUK 4:1–13 ~ Christ held securely to His faith and perseverance, even after His mind and body had become strained from lack of food and water, and even as Satan tempted Him with all the riches, lusts, and powers of the material world by appealing to His flesh.
- HEB 12:2–3 ~ Jesus Christ is the author and finisher of our faith. He was willing to endure a shameful crucifixion, knowing the reward that awaited Him, and now He sits at the right hand of God. So, consider Him who endured much hardship the next time you feel weary or faint in your own minds.

Most of the prophets and all of Christ's apostles had to endure tremendous hardships: imprisonment, banishment, persecution, abuse, torture, and crucifixion. Are you prepared to be tested as they were? Maybe you can think of some ways God has tested your faith in the past. The key to enduring the test and overcoming the challenge is an unyielding faith, which Christ exhibited in the wilderness and on the cross. This same kind of faith will bring us through our trials and temptations unharmed.

- MAR 13:13 ~ Jesus told His disciples, "People will hate you because of me, but those who endure until the end will be saved."
- 2 TI 2:3 ~ Being a good Christian soldier means you must endure much hardship.
- HEB 12:1 ~ Let us run with patience the race that is before us.
- JAM 5:10 ~ Remember the prophets as examples of those who patiently endured suffering and affliction for speaking on behalf of the Lord.
- 1 PE 2:19 ~ Be thankful if you must unfairly endure grief or suffering because you maintain an upright conscience toward God.

Each test of our faith is a learning experience in which we build upon patience and hope.

- ROM 5:3–4 ~ We can glory in our tribulations because through them we obtain patience, through patience, experience, and through experience, hope.
- 2 CO 12:9–10 ~ Jesus said to me (Paul), "My grace is sufficient for you, for my strength is made perfect in weakness." Therefore, I gladly proclaim my failures, because the power of Christ will come to me. That is, for Christ's sake I take pleasure in my weaknesses, disgraces, hardships, persecutions, and anxieties, for though I am weak, I am made strong through Him.
- JAM 1:3 ~ You learn patience when your faith is tested.

Patience allows us to be forever watchful for Christ's coming. Clearly, it also endows us with strength of will and peace of mind. Therefore, our inclination to become anxious or worried diminishes, because powers of the spirit prevail over the flesh.

- PSA 37:7 ~ Find solace in the Lord and wait patiently for Him. Don't worry about evil people who prosper.
- MAT 24:42–44 ~ Be watchful, for you never know when the Lord will come. If the man of the house knew when the burglar would come, he could have prevented his house from being burglarized. So be ready and watchful, for the Lord will come at a time when you least expect Him.
- JAM 5:7–8 ~ Brothers, wait patiently for the coming of the Lord, like the farmer who must patiently await the rain and the harvest. Be patient and take courage, for His coming is near.

God rewards those who are patient, both in this world, and the next. His love empowers us, and from that love proceed faith, hope, joy, and perseverance, and eventually, success. Thus, not only does the Holy Spirit prepare and empower us for upcoming situations, but also good fruit results thereby bringing our faith and our actions into alignment.

- PSA 40:1 ~ I waited patiently for the Lord and he gave me an audience and listened to my problems.
- MAT 10:38–39 ~ Jesus said, "If you want to be worthy of me, you must bear your cross every day and follow me. Whoever finds their life will lose it; whoever loses their life for my sake will find it."
- LUK 21:19 ~ Those who are patient will possess their souls.
- JAM 1:12 ~ Whoever endures temptation is blessed by God, for God will judge them favorably and they will receive a crown of life, which God promises to all who love Him.
- REV 2:10 ~ Jesus said, "Don't be afraid of suffering, imprisonment, and tribulation, for many will endure such hardships. Be faithful unto death and you will receive a crown of life."

A Mighty Fortress is Our God

A mighty fortress is our God, a trusty shield and weapon;
He helps us free from every need that hath us now o'ertaken.
The old bitter foe means us deadly woe;
Deep guile and great might are his dread arms in fight;
On earth is not His equal.

With might of ours can naught be done, soon were our loss effected;
But for us fights the valiant One, whom God Himself elected.
Ask ye, "Who is this?" Jesus Christ it is,
Of Sabbath Lord, and there's no other God;
He holds the field forever.

Though devils all the world should fill, all watching to devour us.
We tremble not, we fear no ill, they cannot overpower us,
This world's prince may still scowl fierce as he will;
He can harm us none; He's judged, the deed is done,
One little word o'erthrows Him.

The Word they still shall let remain, nor any thanks have for it;
He's by our side upon the plain with His good gifts and Spirit.
Take they then our life, goods, fame, child, and wife,
When their worst is done, they yet have nothing won;
The kingdom ours remaineth.

Lesson: Onward Christian Soldiers

Christians should demonstrate their commitment to Jesus Christ by having an active faith. This includes standing up for what is good and right, and opposing that which is evil and wrong. This is the fight of faith for which Jesus Christ has commissioned us into His army. The enemies are Satan, his evil demons, and all other forms or sources of wickedness in this world. This is a spiritual war we must fight, and the defense systems and offensive weapons are unlike any you will find in the material world.

- JOE 3:9–10,14 ~ Go tell the Gentiles to prepare for war. Wake up the mighty warriors and tell them to come along. Beat your plowshares into swords and your pruning hooks into spears. Let the weak say, "I am strong." Multitudes are gathered in the valley of decision, for the day of the Lord is near.
- MAT 10:34,38–39 ~ Jesus said, "Don't think I came to send peace to the earth, because I am sending a sword instead. You must take up your cross and follow me if you want to be counted worthy. Those who wish to keep their lives will lose their lives; but those who lose their lives for my sake will be given back their lives."
- 1 TI 6:12–13 ~ Fight the good fight of faith. Keep a firm grasp on eternal life, for this is why you were called, and why you testified before many witnesses and before God.

Satan entices us with the pleasures of this world by appealing to the lusts of our sinful flesh. In fact, our flesh is constantly at war with our spirit. Yes, sometimes the enemy is within our own selves, for all humans possess a compulsion to commit sin. If God's Spirit lives in us, we can triumph in this conflict, and win our souls from destruction by placing them in the hands of the Lord Jesus. He will be leading the charge during every skirmish, battle, and engagement you encounter, if you let Him.

- LUK 21:19; HEB 10:39 ~ Be patient and you will possess your soul. We do not shrink back and we are not destroyed, because those who have faith keep their souls.
- GAL 5:17–18,22–23 ~ The desires of the flesh are against the spirit, and vice-versa, for they are opposed to each other. If you are led by the Holy Spirit you are not under the Law. The fruits of the spirit are love, joy, peace, patience, kindness, goodness, faithfulness, gentleness, and self-control.
- GAL 6:8 ~ Those who sow to the flesh will reap corruption to their flesh; those who sow to the Spirit will from the Spirit reap eternal life.

Evil forces in this world represent a formidable adversary, strong and powerful. Battling the sin inside us is one thing, but the forces coming against us from the outside are quite another. We are talking about a militia of evil led by a fallen angel named Lucifer, or Satan which means adversary. We must be equipped before we attempt to take them on, by donning the armor of the Lord.

The Armor of God is the best defense against Satan and his evil hoard. This armor equates to the protection and power of the Holy Spirit, and Christians can invoke that power simply by calling upon the name of Jesus Christ. We overcome spiritual adversity by staying connected to God in spirit; we can even defeat the devil himself. The Holy Spirit conveys love and truth, the most powerful countermeasures available to the Christian to defeat demons and evil people in their midst.

- JOH 16:33 ~ Jesus said, "I have spoken to you so that you may have peace. In the world you will have tribulation; but cheer up for I have overcome the world."

- 1 PE 5:8–9 ~ Be sober and vigilant, because your enemy the devil roams about like a lion searching for someone to devour. He will attempt to consume anyone who isn't steadfast in their faith.
- 1 JO 4:6–8 ~ We are of God; those who know God will listen to us. Those who are not of God will not listen. We know the difference between the spirit of truth and the spirit of error. Beloved, let us love one another, for love is of God; and everyone who loves God is born of God and knows Him. Those who do not love cannot know Him for God is love.
- 1 JO 5:4–5 ~ Everyone who is born of God overcomes the world; this is the victory, that by faith we can overcome the world. So, who can overcome the world? Anyone who believes that Jesus Christ is the Son of God.

Evil cannot harm those who love God because we have the best insurance policy available: God's promises of protection and purpose. And we are armed with the most powerful weapon possible: God's Word. Lies and deceit cannot penetrate our armor, while the truth of the Holy Bible cuts through all defenses to the depths of one's very soul. Christians have been sealed by the Spirit and are, therefore, unscathed by the barrage of wickedness in this world and the fires of hell in the next. And armed with the Holy Bible, we can chop the enemy into pieces.

- ISA 59:17 ~ He has put on righteousness as a breastplate and salvation for a helmet. His clothing consists of the garments of vengeance and zeal is the cloak.
- EPH 6:11–17 ~ Put on the whole armor of God so that you will be prepared to stand against the trickery of Satan. For we aren't wrestling against flesh and blood, but against principalities, powers, rulers of darkness in this world, and wickedness in high places. Wear this armor so that you can withstand that day of evil, and remain standing when it is over. Gird your loins with truth and put on the breastplate of righteousness. Put on the shoes of the Gospel of peace; and take with you the shield of faith which will repel the fiery darts of the wicked. Don the helmet of salvation and arm yourself with the sword of the Spirit which is the Word of God.
- HEB 4:12 ~ The Word of God is living and active, sharper than any double-edged sword, dividing the soul and spirit, and discerning the thoughts and intentions of the heart.

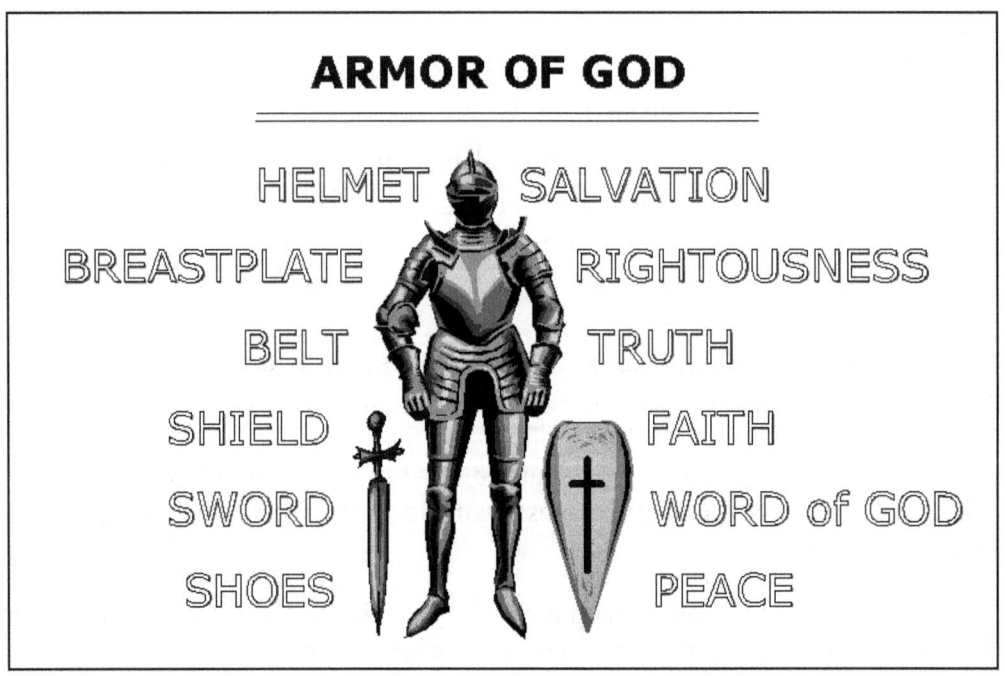

You should never fear the enemy when God is on your side. The forces of evil are powerless against Jesus Christ who is our captain, and the Holy Spirit who is our commander-in-chief. Just as the evil ones will join forces against us (MAT 12:43–45), we also must join in spirit with others in the faith (1 CO 12:20–26).

- DEU 20:1,4 ~ When you go into battle against your enemies, and you see horses and chariots, and you realize you are outnumbered, don't be afraid. For the Lord your God is with you. He is the same one who rescued you out of Egypt. He goes with you to fight for you and to save you.
- DEU 31:6 ~ Be strong and take courage; don't be afraid, for the Lord goes with you. He neither will fail you nor forsake you.
- 2 KI 6:15–17 ~ The servant awoke and found they were surrounded by the Syrians, who were coming for Elisha the prophet. He told the servant not to fear as his army was greater than theirs. Then Elisha prayed, "Lord, I pray you would open his eyes that he may see." And the Lord opened the young man's eyes and he beheld a mountain full of horses with chariots of fire around them. Then Elisha prayed, "Lord, smite these people with blindness." And the Lord did so, and they escaped.
- PRO 21:31 ~ The horse is prepared for the day of battle, but safety is from the Lord.
- MAT 10:19–20 ~ When they capture you, don't worry about what to say, for the words will be given to you by the Holy Spirit. Thus, it will not be you speaking, but the Almighty Father speaking through you.
- LUK 10:18–20 ~ Jesus said, "I saw the devil, like a star falling from heaven. I have given you power over that enemy; nothing can harm you. But don't rejoice because the demons submit to you, rather rejoice because your names are written in the Book of Life."
- 2 CO 10:3–5 ~ Although we are human flesh and blood, we do not make war with flesh and blood. For the weapons we use are not of this world, because we have the Spirit on our side to bring down the strongholds of the enemy. We break down the arguments and the influences of those high and mighty people who stand against God; we take captive human thoughts, making them obedient to Jesus Christ.
- HEB 4:12–13 ~ The Word of God is quick and powerful, and sharper than any double-edged sword. It pierces deeply, to split apart the very soul from the spirit, and the joints from the marrow. For the Word discerns the thoughts and intents of the heart. There is not a single creature alive that is not seen, but all things are naked and uncovered before God's Spirit.

Jesus Christ has called us to work in His vineyard as laborers of the harvest. Our job is to spread the good news of the Gospel to others. This is not an easy task. It requires basic and advanced training, just like in the armed forces.

- MAT 7:13–14 ~ Jesus said, "Wide is the gate that leads to destruction, and many will go through it. Straight and narrow is the gate that leads to life, and not many will find it."
- LUK 10:2–3 ~ Jesus said, "The harvest is plentiful but the laborers are few. Pray that the Lord of the harvest would send more laborers to help. Keep in mind, I am sending you out like lambs among wolves."

In addition to sharing God's Word with others, we are supposed to teach them His laws and rules, and warn those who are behaving unlawfully so that they may repent. We are not required to accept or befriend those who are unwilling to change their evil ways or are otherwise working against God.

- EZE 3:18–21 ~ God says, "I have told the wicked that they will surely die. If you do not warn the wicked to turn from their sin and be saved, you will also die since you will be partly

responsible for their death. But if you do warn the wicked and they still do not turn from their wickedness, they will die in their sin but you will have saved yourself. If the righteous turn from righteousness to sin, they will die because their righteousness will no longer be remembered. If you do not warn them you will die as well. But if you warn the righteous not to sin, and they do not sin, their souls will be saved and so will yours."
- COL 3:5 ~ Repress those who engage in fornication, uncleanness, unnatural affection, promiscuity, and covetousness which is idolatry.
- 1 TI 6:3:5 ~ If anyone teaches false doctrines, and disagrees with the true and godly teachings of Christ, they are arrogant and lack understanding. Their contrary position cause envy, strife, insulting, skepticism, and controversy. They are devoid of the truth, supposing that financial gain is a godly pursuit. Avoid such people.

If we do the work of the Lord, our labor will not be in vain, and we will see the fruits of our faith. If we work only for ourselves, we will gain nothing, and we will lose everything. Allow the Holy Spirit to be your guide and strength and you can accomplish anything you desire, for it will be in accordance with God's will for your life.

- ISA 65:22–24 ~ They will not build houses for someone else to live in; they will not plant crops for others to eat; for my (God's) elect will enjoy the fruits of their labor. They will not labor in vain or produce fruit for nothing, for they are my offspring. When they call, I answer; when they speak, I hear.
- PRO 10:16 ~ The labor of the righteous brings life; the labor of the wicked brings sin.
- PRO 13:11; PRO 23:4 ~ Wealth obtained by pride will diminish; but those that achieve by way of hard work will see their wealth increase. Don't labor to become rich, and don't concentrate on your own feeble wisdom.
- 1 CO 3:8–9 ~ Everyone will receive their own reward according to their labor. For we are all laborers for God.
- 1 CO 15:58 ~ Brothers, be constant in your labor, unwavering, firm, and productive. For you can be assured that your labor for the Lord will not be in vain.
- 1 TH 1:3 ~ We will always remember your work of faith, your labor of love, and your patience of hope in the Lord Jesus Christ before God our Father.
- HEB 6:10 ~ God will not forget your hard work and labor of love, which you showed others in His name as you ministered to the saints.
- REV 14:13 ~ I heard a voice in heaven saying, "Blessed are those who die in the Lord; they will find rest from their hard work, for their actions precede them."

As Christian soldiers, we may be required to endure hardship and pain. Nevertheless, we must never lose sight of our mission or be distracted by such obstacles as sin, temptation, and adversity. If we make sacrifices for the Lord here on earth, and fight the good fight of faith even unto death, a great reward awaits us in heaven.

- JOS 14:7–13 ~ Caleb said to Joshua and the head of the tribes of Israel, "I was forty years old when I went out to spy for Moses, and I brought him a good report. Moses assured me that I would inherit the land where I had done my reconnaissance. And now, forty-five years later, I am still alive to see God's promises come to pass. And I feel as strong now as I did then; and I am still ready to go to war for the Lord." Joshua blessed Caleb, and gave him the inheritance that was promised.
- MAR 13:13 ~ Jesus said, "People will hate you because of me, but those who endure until the end will be saved."

- 2 CO 6:4–6 ~ Don't give the ministry a bad reputation, but show that you are good ministers of God by showing patience in time of trouble, hardship, distress, punishment, imprisonment, rioting, hard work, sleepless nights, and hunger. Be an example of purity, understanding, patience, and kindness, through the Holy Spirit, with sincere love.
- 2 TI 2:3–5 ~ Endure hardship like a good Christian soldier. Those who fight wars need not get caught up with the affairs of this life, but rather should concern themselves with the affairs of Jesus Christ who chose them to be a soldier. In any competition you must discipline yourself and follow the rules if you ever expect to win the championship.
- 2 TI 4:6–8 ~ Paul wrote: I am ready to sacrifice myself as my time of departure is near. I have fought a good fight and I have finished the race, and my faith is still intact. Hereafter a crown of righteousness awaits me, which the Lord, the righteous judge, will give to me. He will give it, not only to me, but also to everyone who lovingly awaits Christ's coming.

We must always remember the sacrifice that Christ made for us, for it will make our sacrifices seem trivial by comparison. We also can be encouraged from the sacrifices made by the judges, kings, and prophets who God sent before us to share His knowledge and truth, the exploits of whom are documented in God's Word.

- HEB 11:32–40 ~ What more can I say about the powers of faith? I could tell you about great judges like Gideon, Barrack, Samson, and Japhtheh, and about great kings like David and Solomon, and about the prophets. Through faith, these people subdued kingdoms, administered justice, enforced treaties, shut the mouth of lions, quenched fires, and escaped certain death. They were weak but were made strong, and they fought valiantly in battle, routing even the greatest of armies. They raised the dead. They endured torture, refusing to renounce God as a condition for their release. They were mocked, beaten, chained, and imprisoned. They were stoned and beheaded. They wandered the wilderness in shaggy clothes, destitute, tormented, and afflicted. Although their life on earth was full of strife, they awaited their deliverance, as we also must do until God makes us perfect before Him.
- HEB 12:2–3 ~ Jesus Christ is the author and finisher of our faith. He was willing to endure a shameful crucifixion, never losing sight of the reward that awaited Him, and He now sits at God's right hand. So, consider Him who endured much hardship the next time you feel weary or faint in your own minds.
- JAM 5:10 ~ Remember the prophets as examples of those who patiently endured suffering and affliction for speaking on behalf of the Lord.

In the end, the great and final battle of Armageddon will be fought between the forces of good and evil. This will occur prior to God's final judgment. Then God will destroy evil once and for all. I hope you choose the winning side.

- MIC 4:3–5 ~ God will judge all the nations and settle disputes among them. They will beat their plowshares into swords and their pruning hooks into spears, but nations will not take up the sword against each other, nor will they train for war anymore. Everyone will sit under their own vine or fig tree, and nobody will cause them any fear, for the Almighty Lord has spoken. The nations will follow after their own gods, but we will walk after the Lord God forever (also JOE 3:9–10,14).
- 1 CO 15:54–57 ~ For the corruptible have put on incorruption, and the mortal have become immortal; then will the saying come true: Death is swallowed up in victory. Oh death, where is your sting? Oh grave, where is your victory? The sting of death is sin and the strength of sin is the Law. But thanks be to God who gives us the victory through our Lord Jesus Christ.
- REV 16:16 ~ They gathered all the armies of the world at a place called Armageddon.

- REV 19:11,19–21 ~ I saw heaven open and beheld a white horse whose rider was called Faithful and True. And I saw the beast, the kings of the earth, and their armies, gathered for battle against the King of kings. The beast was taken, and with him the false prophet that worked miracles in his sight and deceived those who had the mark of the beast and worshipped his image; both were thrown into the lake of fire. The rest were slain by the sword that issued from the mouth of the One riding the white horse. And the birds feasted upon the carrion of flesh.

Having fought for the faith, the Christian soldier will not fear death as it is not an ultimate end, and he or she will not face judgment because the victory already will be won. We are always looking forward without fear or apprehension, knowing that every spiritual battle we undertake belongs to the Lord (JDG 7; 1 SA 17; PSA 20). No matter how enigmatic our enemies, they cannot compete with the might of God who fights with us to bring down strongholds and fortifications and to defeat giants and powerful demons.

- 2 CH 20:15 ~ The prophet declared: Pay attention all of Judah, inhabitants of Jerusalem, and King Jehoshaphat, for the Lord says, "Do not be afraid or dismayed by the multitude gathered against you, for the battle is not yours but God's."
- 2 CO 10: 3–4 ~ We do not walk in the flesh and we do not war after the flesh. For the weapons of our warfare are not carnal, but mighty through God, to the pulling down of strongholds.

Onward, Christian Soldiers

Onward, Christian soldiers, marching as to war,
With the cross of Jesus going on before.
Christ, the royal Master, leads against the foe;
Forward into battle, see His banners go!
Onward, Christian soldiers, marching as to war,
With the cross of Jesus going on before.

Like a mighty army, moves the church of God;
Brothers we are treading where the saints have trod.
We are not divided, all one body we,
One in hope and doctrine, one in charity.
Onward, Christian soldiers, marching as to war,
With the cross of Jesus going on before.

Crowns and thrones may perish, kingdoms rise and wane,
But the church of Jesus constant will remain.
Gates of hell can never 'gainst that church prevail;
We have Christ's own promise, and that cannot fail.
Onward, Christian soldiers, marching as to war,
With the cross of Jesus going on before.

Onward, then you faithful, join our happy throng,
Blend with ours your voices in the triumph song;
Glory, laud, and honor, unto Christ the King;
This, through countless ages, men and angels sing.
Onward, Christian soldiers, marching as to war,
With the cross of Jesus going on before.

Lesson: The Priesthood of Believers

We have been commissioned by Christ to make disciples of all people, to baptize them, and to teach them God's truth (MAT 28:19–20). But you ask, aren't those responsibilities reserved for ordained ministers? The answer is, not necessarily. However, we rely on the shepherds of our respective congregations to perform these functions because we trust that they have received adequate education on how God would like the functions to be performed, as well as having extensive instruction in God's Word. Yet, according to the Bible, believers have the authority and the responsibility, given to them by Jesus Christ, to bring others to the knowledge of the truth. Being confident as a witness to the truth requires discipline and training. That doesn't mean everyone should become an ordained minister, but that everyone can minister to the degree that they have become equipped to do so.

- EXO 19:5–6 ~ God said, "If you obey me and keep my covenant you will be a precious treasure to me, above all other peoples. You will be to me a holy nation of priests."
- MAR 16:15 ~ Jesus said, "Go into all the world and preach the Gospel to everybody. Those who believe and are baptized will be saved; but those who do not believe will be damned."
- 1 PE 2:9 ~ You are a chosen generation, a royal priesthood, a holy nation, a unique people. Praise Him who has called you out of darkness into his marvelous light.
- 1 PE 5:2–3 ~ Feed God's flock which is among you; be overseers of the kingdom. Do this, not out of obligation but willingly; do this not for ill-gotten gain but with a clear conscience. Do not act like lords over God's heritage but set an example to the flock.
- REV 1:5–6 ~ Jesus Christ is the faithful witness, the firstborn of the dead, and the prince of the kings of the earth, who loved us and washed away our sins with His own blood. He has made us kings and priests before God His Father. To Him be all glory and dominion forever and ever. Amen.

God sent Jesus to be a witness; Jesus sends us to be witnesses as well. Christ is the High Priest and He has called us to carry on His mission, giving us His Spirit and making us missionaries. Thus, Christ is the mediator between God and believers, and we have been appointed mediators between Christ and the lost sheep. We are summoned by God, the eternal judge, to be witnesses of the truth, the whole truth, and nothing but the truth; and the world is His courtroom. Do not be afraid to testify, especially when asked about what you know to be true; that knowledge should come from God and His Word the source of absolute truth.

- ISA 43:10–12,15 ~ There are no gods before Him or after Him. God says, "You are witnesses to what I have said. My servant whom I have chosen is also sent to be a witness, so that you can know me and believe; and even so, I am He. I am the Lord and there is no other savior besides me. I have declared myself to you and I have saved you whenever you have forsaken all other gods for me. You are witnesses that I am God, the Holy One, the creator of Israel, and your King."
- JOH 20:21 ~ Jesus said to the apostles, "Peace be unto you. As my Father has sent me, even now I am sending you."
- LUK 9:1–6 ~ Jesus called His twelve disciples together, and gave them authority over demons, and power to cure diseases. He sent them to preach the kingdom of God and heal the sick. Jesus said to them, "Take nothing for your journey: no food, no luggage, no money, no extra clothes. When you enter a house, stay there until you leave that town. If a town does not welcome you, shake the dust from your feet when you leave as a testimony against them." And the disciples departed, and went through the towns preaching the Gospel and healing people everywhere.

CHAPTER FOUR

A pastor has many functions to perform, but he cannot be responsible for everything that goes on in the church. Besides, pastors vary in their spiritual gifts, same as everyone. Oftentimes, a shepherd tries to take on more than one person can handle. Pastors need all the help and support available from individual members of their church. Everyone who is a member of the body of Christ has abilities, talents, and knowledge that can be utilized to the glory of God. All believers have received God's Holy Spirit, and with His Spirit come authority and power. We therefore possess the key to the kingdom, and that key is Jesus Christ. We can unlock the gates of heaven for others by sharing Christ with them using our God-given capabilities.

- ROM 10:14–15 ~ How can they call on Him in whom they have not believed? How can they believe in Him of whom they have not heard? How can they hear of Him without a preacher? And how can they preach unless they are sent? As it is written: How beautiful are the feet of them that preach the Gospel of peace, and bring glad tidings of good things (ISA 52:7).
- EPH 4:10–16 ~ He that descended from heaven is the same that ascended far above the heavens, that He might fill all things. He appointed apostles, prophets, evangelists, pastors and teachers for the perfecting of the saints, for the work of the ministry, and for the edifying of the body of Christ. This He did so that we might become unified in the one true faith, and of the knowledge of the Son of God, to become like Him, perfect in righteousness. He wants us to grow into mature Christians and not be like little children who are easily influenced by deception and trickery. He wants us to become more like Christ who joins together the entire body, according to the effectual working of every part, and the strengthening of all in love.
- HEB 10:23 ~ Let us hold fast to the profession of our faith without wavering.

We are called by Christ to be ministers of the New Covenant. Sometimes, we call for leaders to minister to us. While people may call upon pastors and teachers (ACT 6:1–6; TIT 1:5; HEB 5:1), it is God who actually makes the choice as to who will serve and where (1 SA 16:1–14; ACT 9:1–18). He will place His people in situations where they can be of the most use in opening the eyes of others, thereby equipping them with the same gifts being shared or modeled.

- EXO 3:13–14 ~ And Moses said to God, "When I come to the children of Israel, and I say to them that the God of our fathers has sent me, they will ask His name? How should I reply?" God said to Moses, "I AM that I AM. Tell the children of Israel, I AM has sent you."
- MAT 4:18–20 ~ Jesus, walking by the Sea of Galilee, saw two men Simon called Peter, and Andrew his brother casting a net into the sea, for they were fishermen. Jesus said to them, "Follow me, and I will make you catchers of men." And immediately they left their nets and followed Him.
- MAT 20:28 ~ The Son of Man came not to be ministered to, but to minister, and to give His life as a ransom for many.
- MAT 22:14 ~ Jesus said, "Many are called but few are chosen."
- ACT 20:28,30,32 ~ Keep watch over yourselves and the flock of which the Holy Spirit has made you overseers. Feed the church of God which he purchased with his own blood. Beware, for among your own selves will come false prophets, speaking perverse things to draw away disciples after them. And now I commend you to God and to the Word of His grace, which will build you up and give you an inheritance among those who are sanctified.
- 2 TI 1:9 ~ He has saved us and summoned us with a holy calling, not according to our works but according to His own purpose and grace, given us by Christ before the world began.

We have the *right* as children of God to come before God's throne and make our requests known to Him. We also have the right, at least in this country, to speak freely, though it helps to be judicious when we do. We have the *authority* as representatives of Christ's love to preach the Gospel, and to display to all people His love, and our own love. This includes confessing the salvation of Jesus Christ, forgiving others, and administering baptism if the situation permits. We have the *power* of the Word which is God's Holy Spirit, enabling us to test what we see and hear against the truth and expose that which is false. It is very hard to argue against the truth, and those who try often come across as foolish.

- MAT 16:19 ~ I (Jesus) will give you the keys to the kingdom of heaven; and whatever you tie on earth shall be tied in heaven, and whatever you untie on earth shall be untied in heaven.
- MAT 28:19–20 ~ Jesus told His disciples, "Go into every nation and teach the people everything I have taught you. Baptize them in the name of the Father, Son, and Holy Spirit. And remember, I'll always be with you, even until the end of time."
- JOH 20:22–23 ~ Then He breathed on them, and said, "Receive the Holy Spirit; whoever's sins you forgive, they will be forgiven, and whoever's sins you retain, they will be retained."
- ROM 5:1–2 ~ Being justified by faith, we have peace with God through our Lord Jesus Christ, by whom we have access to His grace wherein we stand rejoicing in hope of the glory of God.
- ACT 1:8 ~ Jesus told His disciples, "You will receive power once the Holy Spirit has come upon you. You will be witnesses across the land, to the most remote corners of the earth."
- 1 CO 11:25–26 ~ Jesus commanded the apostles on the first Holy Communion to partake of the sacrament often to remember Him. Thus, as often as you eat the bread and drink the wine of Holy Communion, you proclaim the death of Christ until His return.
- 2 CO 4:13 ~ It is written, "I believed therefore, I have spoken." With that same spirit of faith, we also believe and therefore speak.
- EPH 5:11 ~ Don't be a companion to the unfruitful works of darkness, but rather disclose them and rebuke them.
- HEB 4:16 ~ Let us therefore come boldly before the throne of Grace, that we may obtain mercy and find help in our time of need.
- 1 JO 4:1–3 ~ Don't believe every spirit, but test them to determine if they are really of God; for many false prophets have gone out into the world. Every spirit that confesses that Jesus Christ is God in the flesh is of God. Those who don't confess that Jesus is of God are not of God; they are spirits of the antichrist, who you heard is coming and is already here.

As ministers of the Gospel we also have certain *responsibilities*. We are obligated to teach our children the ways of the Lord, to maintain a healthy relationship with Christ, to shine His light before others, to serve Him and the church, and to conduct our lives in a Christian manner. We must try to follow the example of Christ, and to be a model of Him to the degree that others will notice. We have a responsibility to our family: our immediate family, our church family, and the family of believers. We have a responsibility to the unbelievers who are lost and to the believers who are going astray. The bottom line is, we are equally responsible for one another. All people are made in the image of God and are likewise valuable to Him; we too must value everybody equally. The Lord does not want any soul to perish, so help them when you can.

- DEU 6:2–7 ~ Fear the Lord and keep all His commandments and laws. Ensure that your children and your children's children obey God. Do this and you will prosper and your life will be prolonged. Love God with all your heart, soul, and might. Keep God's Word in your heart and teach His ways carefully and thoughtfully to your children. Talk with your family all the time about God, every day and night, whenever you are together.
- PRO 22:6 ~ Instruct your children in the way they should go and when they mature, they will not depart from it.
- EPH 6:4 ~ Fathers, do not provoke your children to anger but bring them up in the nurture and discipline of the Lord.

- GAL 6:1–2 ~ Brothers, if someone is overtaken by sin, you who are spiritual need to restore that person in the spirit of humility, considering that you also can be tempted. Bear one another's burdens to fulfill the law of Christ.
- COL 3:16 ~ Let the Word of Christ abide in you richly in all wisdom. Teach and admonish one another in psalms, hymns, and spiritual songs, singing with grace in your hearts to God.
- 1 TH 5:11 ~ Comfort each other and edify one another just as you have been doing.
- HEB 10:24–25 ~ Let us encourage one another to promote love and good works. Let us never cease to fellowship with one another in God's house as others have the habit of doing.

In addition to teaching our family and building up the body of Christ, we must keep steadfast in the true faith and adhere always to the doctrine of righteousness. That doctrine is based on God's grace which activates our faith in the atoning sacrifice of Christ. Thus, our works of righteousness constitute a loving response to His blessings and represent an end not a means.

- PRO 16:3 ~ Commit your actions to the Lord and your thoughts will be established.
- ACT 2:42 ~ And they continued conscientiously in the apostles' doctrine and fellowship, in the breaking of bread, and in prayers.
- 1 CO 9:14 ~ Those who preach the Gospel should live by the Gospel.
- 1 JO 2:6 ~ Whoever says they are a Christian should show they are following Christ by the way they conduct their lives.

Our lives should always reflect the light of Christ. We should think and act like Him, because our behavior is sure to be scrutinized by others around us.

- MAT 5:16 ~ Let your light shine before others, so that they can see your good works and glorify your Father in heaven.
- 1 TI 4:12 ~ Be an example of the believers in thoughts, in conversation, in love, in spirit, in faith, and in purity.

As an example of the love of God we are to serve others. He is the vine and we are the branches, and we are compelled to bear good fruit. And we will as long as we remain grafted to the vine.

- ROM 12:1–2 ~ Let your body be a living sacrifice, acceptable to God; this is the least you can do. Do not live according to this world, but according to the perfect will of God.
- GAL 5:22–23 ~ The fruits of the Spirit include love, joy, peace, patience, gentleness, goodness, faith, kindness, and self-control. There is no law against such things.
- EPH 5:9 ~ The fruits of the Spirit originate in goodness, righteousness, and truth.
- 2 PE 1:5–8 ~ In diligence, add virtue to your faith, knowledge to your virtue, temperance to your knowledge, patience to your temperance, godliness to your patience, kindness to your godliness, and charity to your kindness. If these things abound in you, you will never be barren or unfruitful in the knowledge of our Lord Jesus Christ.

We should pray for our spiritual leaders, who endure considerable stress from the opposition of this world. We should be willing to endure hardship as well, as we confront evil in the world and fight the good fight of faith. Pray that God's Word will have free course, and spread the Word yourself to ensure that it does.

- 2 CO 6:3–10 ~ We do not place obstacles in anyone's way because we do not want the ministry to be discredited. Rather, as servants of God we commend ourselves in every way, through much endurance, trouble, hardship, and distress; through abuse, imprisonment, and rioting; through hard work, hunger, and sleepless nights; in purity, understanding, endurance,

and kindness; in the Holy Spirit and in sincere love; in truth and in the power of God; carrying weapons of righteousness in each hand; through times of glory and dishonor, favor and rejection. We are genuine yet regarded as imposters; known yet regarded as strangers; dying yet still alive; beaten down but not defeated; sorrowful but always rejoicing; poor yet spreading wealth; having nothing yet possessing everything.
- 1 TH 3:1 ~ Pray for the evangelists, so that God's Word may have free course, and be glorified in others even as it is with you.
- 1 TH 5:17–18 ~ Pray constantly. Give thanks in all circumstances.

In response to His many blessings and to equip us with the tools we need as called servants of the Word, we must become knowledgeable of the truth of God's Word so that it lives in us. God commands us to study it constantly which will equip us to teach and serve. Compare everything you see and hear against what is written in the Holy Bible, which is your primary source of knowledge, understanding, and direction. Nobody can argue against the truth, for truth always prevails over lies. That is why everyone needs to know the truth, especially when it is being stifled.

- ISA 55:10–12 ~ The rain and snow that falls from heaven does not return to heaven but waters the earth, causing the plants to bud and seed, and providing food. So also, God's Word does not return to Him void, but accomplishes what He wishes and prospers where He sends it. We joyfully go out being led in peace. The mountains and hills sing and the trees clap their hands; the world rejoices around you. Instead of a thorn bush, a tree will grow. And the name of the Lord will be magnified as an everlasting sign of the nurturing He provides.
- LUK 12:11–12 ~ Jesus said, "When they bring you before the authorities don't worry about what to say or do, for the Holy Spirit will provide the information when you need it."
- HEB 4:12 ~ The Word of God is alive and powerful. It is sharper than any double-edged sword, piercing deep so as to divide the very soul and spirit. It can discern the thoughts and intents of the heart.
- 1 TH 5:21 ~ Examine all things and hold onto the good.
- 2 TI 3:14–16 ~ Continue in the things you have learned and are convinced of, knowing from whom you have learned them. From a child you have known the Holy Scriptures, which are able to make you wise unto salvation through faith in Jesus Christ. All scripture is given by inspiration of God and is effective for doctrine, for guidance, for correction, and for instruction in righteousness.
- 2 TI 4:2–5 ~ Preach the Word; always be prepared to correct, rebuke, and encourage with patience and sound doctrine. For the time will come when people will turn away from sound doctrine and pursue their own lusts, finding teachers that tell them what they want to hear. They will wander from the truth and rely on myths. Always be watchful, willing to endure afflictions, doing the work of the evangelist, doing whatever is necessary for the continuance of the ministry.

We become equipped by cultivating our faith through prayer (1 TH 5:17), studying the Bible diligently (2 TI 3:16), attending worship services regularly (HEB 10:25), ministering to others at every possible opportunity (ROM 12:1), and witnessing in our daily lives (1 PE 3:15). Anyone who does not do these things is incomplete as a Christian, because true faith implies an active response to God's love. We willingly should execute our individual assignments in the vineyard of our Lord, to the glory of His holy name.

CHAPTER FOUR

Lesson: Unity in the Body of Christ

God has deliberately established divisions among His creations. He separated the earth from the heavens, the waters from the dry land, and the light from the darkness. God also has separated His people from the rest of the world. Christians belong to the kingdom of heaven, because heaven is our home, not the earth. This life is but a mere blink of an eye compared to eternal life with our Father in heaven.

- GEN 1:4 ~ And God saw the light that it was good, and God divided the light from the darkness.
- LEV 20:24 ~ I (God) have said unto you, "You will inherit their land for I will give it to you as a possession. The land will flow with milk and honey. I am the Lord your God, and I have separated you from other people."
- 1 KI 8:53 ~ For the Lord separated Israel from all other peoples of the earth to be His inheritance, just as He promised to His servant Moses when He brought our fathers out of Egypt.
- EZR 10:11 ~ Confess unto the Lord God of your fathers, and do what pleases Him. Separate yourselves from the people of the land, and from strange wives.
- MAT 25:32,46 ~ Jesus said, "All nations will be gathered before Him. And He will separate everybody, one from another, as a shepherd divides the sheep from the goats. And the wicked will go away to eternal punishment, but the righteous to eternal life."
- JOH 15:18–19 ~ Jesus said, "The world hates you because it hated me first. If you were of the world, the world would love you as its own. But you are not of the world since I have chosen you out of it, and that's why the world hates you."
- 2 CO 6:14 ~ Do not be unequally yoked together with unbelievers; for what fellowship has righteousness with unrighteousness? What communion can there be between light and darkness?
- 1 JO 4:2–6 ~ Every spirit that confesses that Jesus Christ is God in the flesh is of God. Those spirits that do not confess are not of God but are spirits of the antichrist, which you have heard about and is in the world. You belong to God and have overcome these spirits of error. For greater is He that is within you than he that is in the world. They are of the world and therefore speak of worldly things, and the world listens to them. We are of God. Those who know God will listen to His messengers, and those who are not of God will not listen. We know the difference between the Spirit of truth and the spirit of untruth.

As God has purposely separated Christians from other people, so we should remain separated from them. If we associate with unbelievers, we run the risk of becoming corrupted by them. While it is our duty to witness to others and serve as an example of Christ, we cannot allow ourselves to be influenced by the world, by worldly people, or by secular society. That doesn't mean we deliberately shun others, for some may respond favorably to our witness. But if they insist on rejecting God and His witnesses, there is no need to continue badgering them as it will only heighten their disdain for God and for Christians. Love them at a distance and pray for them; but keep them at a distance for their path is heading in a different direction than yours.

- EZR 9:14 ~ Should we break God's commandments again, and join in affinity with the kinds of people who commit such abominations? Wouldn't God be angry with us until He consumed us, so that nobody would remain or escape?
- PRO 22:24–25 ~ Do not make friends with an angry person or associate with someone who has a quick temper, for you risk learning their ways and falling into the same trap.

- HOS 10:2,10 ~ Their heart is divided; they have been found guilty. God will break down their altars and destroy their graven images. When it pleases God, He will punish them; nations will gather against them and enslave them because they betrayed the Lord.
- 1 CO 5:11,13 ~ Do not associate with someone who claims to be a Christian but who is sexually promiscuous, greedy, idolatrous, slanderous, or who is a drunkard or a swindler; do not even eat at the same table with such a person. You must expel the wicked from among you.
- 2 CO 6:17–18 ~ Come out from among them and be separate, says the Lord. Do not touch unclean things, and I will receive you. I will be your Father, and you will be my sons and daughters.
- JAM 1:8 ~ A double-minded man is unstable in all his ways.

The best way for Christians to remain separated from the world is for us to stick together. We must have unity of mind and spirit. We should think, speak, and act as one. If we do not work together for the edification of the body of Christ, this temple that comprises all Christians cannot stand, but will collapse. If we stay unified, we will live in peace and harmony regardless of what the world throws at us. No doubt you have heard the saying, "United we stand, divided we fall." It is absolutely true. How do we know that? Well, it comes straight out of the Bible (MAR 3:22–27).

- PSA 133:1 ~ Behold, how good and how pleasant it is for brothers and sisters of the faith to live together in unity!
- ACT 2:44–47 ~ And the believers were as one, for they had everything in common. They sold their possessions and goods and gave generously to the needy. Every day they met with one accord in the temple courts. They took turns breaking bread at the various homes, and they ate together with gladness and unity of heart, praising God and enjoying each other's hospitality. And the Lord added to their number daily, those who were being saved.
- 2 CO 13:11 ~ Finally, brothers, farewell. Be perfect, be comforted, be of one mind, and live in peace; and the God of love and peace shall be with you always.
- 1 PE 2:17 ~ Respect all people. Love the brotherhood. Fear God. Honor the King of kings.

In addition to providing peace and harmony, there is strength in unity. The Church is God's fortress; it is a place of refuge and protection in the battle between good and evil. When we stand together as one, we become a formidable force in this secular and material world in which we live.

- 2 CH 30:12 ~ Also in Judah, the hand of God was on the people giving them unity of mind to carry out the orders of their leaders in accordance with the Word of the Lord.
- JER 32:39 ~ I (God) will give them one heart, and one way, so that they will fear me forever for their own good, and for the good of their children after them.
- EZE 11:19–20 ~ I (God) will give them an undivided heart, and I will place a new spirit within them. I will remove their heart of stone and replace it with a heart of flesh. Then they will follow my decrees and carefully obey my commandments. They will be my people and I will be their God.
- 2 CO 1:11 ~ You have helped us with your prayers. Many people will thank God for our ministry and for the favor God has granted us on behalf of your support and prayers.
- PHP 1:27–28 ~ Whatever happens, conduct yourselves in a manner worthy of the Gospel of Christ. Then, whether I am with you or absent, I will find that you have continued to stand firm in one spirit, contending fearlessly in unity for the faith of the Gospel.

- PHP 2:2 ~ Make my joy complete by being like-minded, having the same love and being one in spirit and in purpose.
- 1 PE 3:8–9 ~ Finally my friends, live in harmony and care for one another. Love each other as brothers and sisters; show compassion and be courteous. Do not repay evil with evil, or insult with insult, but respond with blessings; because you yourselves were called to receive a blessing from the Lord.

It is very important to fellowship together, to study God's Word together, and to worship together, for this strengthens and edifies the body of Christ. Some people refrain from public worship, avoid churches, and refuse to partnership with other Christians; they would prefer to worship in their own way and their own time. They often make excuses; the most common excuse is probably regarding the hypocrisy that is observed in so-called Christians, churches, or preachers and teachers. Hypocrites are basically liars since they don't practice what they preach. In reality, we are all hypocrites sometimes, just as we are all liars sometimes. The best ways to eliminate those types of sins is to attend church, study the Bible with others, and support one or more ministries. Remember, churches are for sinners, and hypocrisy is but one type of sin; so those avoiding churches because only sinners attend are missing the point completely.

- EXO 19:8 ~ All the people answered together, saying, "We will do everything the Lord has asked us to do." Then Moses returned to the Lord with their response.
- DEU 31:12 ~ Gather the people together including men, women, and children, as well as the strangers among you, so that everyone can hear, learn, fear the Lord your God, and obey all the words of His Law.
- MAT 18:20 ~ Jesus said, "Where two or more are gathered together in my name, I am there with you."
- ACT 1:14 ~ All of them continued with one accord in prayer and meditation.
- ACT 4:21,24,31–32 ~ Finally, after several threats, the Sanhedrin released Peter and John because they couldn't decide how to punish them, and because the people were praising the Lord for enabling these men of God to heal the lame man. The apostles returned home and told everyone what had occurred. And when the people heard what had happened, they raised their voice to God with one accord, and worshipped Him saying, "Lord, you alone are God, who made heaven, earth, the sea, and all living things." After their song of prayer, the meeting place began to shake and everybody was filled with the Holy Spirit boldly speaking the words of God. And all the believers were of one heart and mind. Nobody claimed any possessions of their own, but everyone shared their possessions with one another.
- ROM 15:5–6 ~ May the God who gives endurance and encouragement give you oneness of spirit as you follow Christ, so that with one heart and mouth you may glorify God the Father of our Lord Jesus Christ.
- HEB 10:25 ~ Do not cease to assemble together, as some are in the habit of doing, but continue to meet with one another and encourage each other, even more as the day of our Lord approaches.

The more we worship and pray together, the more we grow in our faith, and the more God equips us to face the world with strength and unity.

- EPH 2:19–22 ~ You are no longer foreigners but fellow citizens of God's kingdom and members of His household, built on the foundation laid by the prophets and apostles with Jesus Christ as the chief cornerstone. In Him the entire building is joined together and grows into a holy temple. In Him you also are being built together to become a place for God's Holy Spirit to live.

- EPH 4:3,11–13,16 ~ Keep the unity of the Spirit through the bond of peace. Remember, Christ assigned some of you to be apostles, some prophets, some evangelists, some pastors, and some teachers, to prepare God's people for works of service. This He did so that the body of Christ can grow, until all reach a oneness of the Spirit and unity in the knowledge of the Son of God, and become mature in the faith attaining the whole measure of the fullness of Christ. In Christ, the entire body is fitly joined and held together by every supporting ligament, and grows and builds itself up in love as each component performs its function.

Those who would cause division and strife in the church should be removed or excommunicated. It is not healthy for people within a church to fight about what is true or false. God has warned us that Satan will send his disciples to infiltrate the church in an attempt to break it apart. We must remove dissenters and false teachers from among us. While it is fine to have discussions, even debates in light of the scriptures, it is harmful when they progress into arguments, hostilities, and taking sides. There are many different Christian denominations, but most of them agree on the essential doctrines of the faith. Why should we allow subtle differences between our belief systems to divide us? If all Christians stood together in the faith it would be virtually impossible for the enemy to defeat us.

- ISA 59:13 ~ They know they are being disobedient to God; they carefully plan their lies.
- MAT 18:15–17 ~ Jesus taught, "If another Christian sins against you, confront him or her and try to work it out. If that person listens to you then you have gained a partner in the faith. If they will not listen, bring a few others along so that you can establish your differences in front of witnesses. If he or she still will not listen, bring your grievance before the church; if he or she refuses to listen to the church, then treat that person as you would treat the wicked. Whatever you bind on earth will be bound in heaven, and whatever you loosen on earth will be loosened in heaven."
- ACT 20:30 ~ From among yourselves will come those speaking perverse things to gain followers.
- ROM 16:17 ~ I urge you, my brothers, identify those who cause divisions among you, and who place obstacles in your way that are contrary to the doctrine that you have learned. Avoid them completely.
- 1 CO 1:10 ~ I urge you, my brothers, in the name of our Lord Jesus Christ, to be in agreement with one another so that there will be no divisions among you. Be perfectly joined together in mind and thought.
- 1 CO 11:17–18 ~ I've heard that when you assemble together as a church that there are divisions among you. I'm telling you that such meetings do more harm than good.
- COL 2:8,18–19 ~ Beware of those who would lead you astray with their errant philosophies and vain deceptions, following traditions fashioned by the world and not by Christ. Do not let anyone swindle you out of your reward. Beware of those who practice false humility and worship angels. They claim to have seen things, but they have filled their unspiritual and arrogant minds with silly notions.
- 2 TH 3:14–15 ~ If there are people among you that fail to conform to the Word as we have taught it to you, make note of them and stay away from them, so that they will feel ashamed of their behavior. However, do not consider them as an enemy, but admonish them as you would a brother or sister.
- 1 TI 1:3–7 ~ Do not teach false doctrine or recognize any myths or irrelevant genealogies, which only serve to raise questions not provide answers concerning the faith. The goal is to love with a pure heart, a right conscience, and a sincere faith. Some have wandered away from these principles and turned to meaningless jabber, desiring to be teachers of the Law yet knowing nothing about the Law or what they say to be true.

- 2 TI 4:3–4 ~ People will seek teachers who conform to their own likes and dislikes; they will turn away from the truth and wander into myths.
- TIT 1:11 ~ They must be silenced, those who would ruin entire households, teaching things that are wrong for the sake of ill-gotten gain.
- JDE 1:17–19 ~ Dear friends, remember what the apostles told us before. They said that in the latter days there would be scoffers who follow their own ungodly desires. These people have come to divide you; they follow the instincts of their flesh and do not have the Spirit within them.

The body of Christ is one with God, for Christ is our head. We are temples of the Lord in which His Holy Spirit abides; therefore, we can unite together as one with God. Nothing can separate us from God as long as we remain in Him. If we remain in Christ, we will be glorified with Him when He returns to receive us into His kingdom.

- ROM 8:17 ~ Now if we are children, then we are heirs: heirs of God and joint-heirs with Christ, if indeed we share in His suffering so that we may also share in His glory.
- ROM 8:35–39 ~ Who is able to separate us from the love of Christ? Can tribulation, distress, persecution, famine, nakedness, peril, or war separate us from His love? No, in all these things we are more than conquerors through Him who loved us. Thus, I am convinced that neither death nor life, neither angels nor demons, neither the present nor the future, nor any powers, neither height nor depth, nor anything else in all creation can separate us from the love of God that is in Christ our Lord.
- 2 CO 13:14 ~ May the grace of the Lord Jesus Christ, and the love of God, and the communion of the Holy Spirit, be with you all. Amen.

Christ overcame the world and so will all believers. We can overcome because He has given us the power to do so, through His Holy Spirit that abides in us. United and bound together by the Holy Spirit, we will overcome and defeat those who would destroy the Church of Jesus Christ. We can be influential in dispersing assemblies of people who are following false doctrine by enabling participants to get a glimpse of real truth. As the Word spreads throughout the world, the number of people who depart from other world religions and find Jesus increases tremendously. This is why everyone with a faith the size of a mustard seed can have a significant impact on the world by spreading the Word in whatever capacity God has gifted them (LUK 17:5–6).

- JOH 16:33 ~ Jesus said, "I have spoken to you so that you may have peace. In this world you will have tribulation; but cheer up, for I have overcome this world."
- ROM 12:21 ~ Do not be overcome with evil but overcome evil with goodness.
- 1 JO 4:4 ~ You are of God little children and have overcome them (e.g., antichrists); because greater is He that is in you (Christ) than he that is in the world (Satan).
- 1 JO 5:4–5 ~ Everyone who is born of God overcomes the world; this is the victory, that by faith we can overcome the world. So, who can overcome the world? Anyone who believes that Jesus Christ is the Son of God.
- REV 2:7,11; REV 3:5,21 ~ Jesus said, "Listen to what the Holy Spirit has to say to the churches: Those who overcome will eat from the Tree of Life that is in the paradise of God. Those who overcome will not be hurt by the second death. Those who overcome will be clothed in white gowns and their names will be recorded in the Book of Life, and I will confess their names before my Father and the angels. Those who overcome will sit with me on my throne, even as I also overcame and am now sitting by my Father at His right hand."
- REV 21:7 ~ God says, "Those who overcome will inherit all things, and I will be their God and they will be my children."

Lesson: Parenthood

It is natural to want to become a parent; in fact, God encourages marriage and parenthood. These gifts from God are meant to be shared between one man and one woman.

- GEN 1:28; GEN 9:1 ~ God blessed Adam and Eve, and God blessed Noah and his sons. God told them to be fruitful and multiply.
- GEN 2:24 ~ Children eventually will leave their parents and get married themselves. Once married you become one flesh with your spouse.
- JER 29:6 ~ Get married and have children. Encourage your children to do the same so that your family can increase and not diminish.

Parents must set an example for their children to follow. God the Father is our model of unconditional parental love, and Christ sets the perfect example of a child's obedience. Children imitate their parents, so parents have to provide an appropriate model of behavior for their children to emulate. Parents must practice honor and respect in the home. Spouses must show respect to one another, and parents must show respect to their children. Without mutual respect, children will not learn to respect their parents, much less others, or even themselves.

- TIT 2:1–8,12 ~ Here is sound doctrine about how to conduct oneself: Men (fathers) should be sober, calm, moderate, faithful, charitable, and patient. Women (mothers) should conduct themselves in a godly manner, teaching what is good. Women should not be gossipers or false accusers, nor should they drink a lot. Daughters should be taught to be sober and obedient homemakers, and to love their husbands and their children. Daughters should be taught to be virtuous (chaste) and discreet. Sons should be taught to be sober, helpful, sincere, and incorruptible. Sons should be taught to be calm and collected in their speech and their actions; they should be taught not to say evil things about others. Teach your children to be godly, and to avoid the lusts of this world; teach them to be sober, righteous, and faithful to God.

Setting an example involves considerable self-control. Parents must demonstrate and execute discipline in the home. Disciplining a child may include reinforcement, and at times, punishment. When children are disobedient, parents should discipline them, just as God the Father disciplines us when we disobey Him.

- DEU 8:5 ~ Consider this: Just as a father punishes his son, so also God punishes you.
- JOB 5:17 ~ Happy is the person that God corrects; therefore, do not despise being chastised by the Almighty.
- PRO 3:11–14 ~ Children, do not despise the Lord's punishment, and do not resent when He scolds you. For those whom the Lord loves, He corrects, just as a father corrects his children who are his delight. Happy is the individual that finds wisdom and understanding, for these are more precious than fine silver and the gain is more valuable than fine gold.
- PRO 13:24 ~ Parents that do not discipline their children must hate them, for a loving parent has to punish their children sometimes.
- PRO 29:15,17 ~ Punishment provides wisdom; but children left to themselves shame their parents. Correct your children when they are wrong, and you will be able to rest at night, and they will be your pride and joy.
- HEB 12:7–11 ~ If you endure punishment, God treats you as His own child, for what child is never disciplined by their parents? But if you are never punished then you have no parents and you are nobody's child. If we have natural parents correcting us, and if we respect them,

shouldn't we subject ourselves even more to the Father of all spirits, and live? For our parents punish us largely to make themselves feel better, but God punishes us so that we will profit from it, by sharing in His righteousness. While being punished may make one feel sorrowful, later it yields the peaceful fruit of righteousness.

By setting an example of godliness and obedience to God, children also learn obedience, both to their parents and to God.

- LEV 19:2–3 ~ Be holy like your Father in heaven is holy. Everyone must respect their father and mother, and obey God.
- PRO 28:7 ~ Whoever keeps the Law is a wise child; but a riotous child embarrasses the parents.
- EPH 6:1–4 ~ Children, obey your parents, for God has given them authority over you. Honor your parents as commanded by God in His Ten Commandments (EXO 20:12). This is the first commandment that brings a promise: If you honor your parents your life will be long and happy. Parents, don't provoke your children to anger and frustration. Instead, raise them in the nurture and discipline of righteousness, as instructed by God in the Bible.
- COL 3:20–21 ~ Children, obey your parents. Parents, don't get mad at your children or they will become discouraged.

In addition to setting an example and teaching children right from wrong, parents must teach their children the ways of the Lord. When parents discipline their children, it is because they love them and want no harm to come to them. And part of that discipline is to study God's Word extensively; this should involve church attendance, Sunday School, and frequent devotions at home with all the family present.

- DEU 4:9–10 ~ Don't forget what God has done for you. May His works have a lasting impression on your lives. Teach your children and grandchildren about His glorious miracles. Especially remind your children of God's instructions given to Moses at Sinai about reverencing Him and about teaching His laws from generation to generation.
- DEU 6:2–7 ~ Fear the Lord and keep all His commandments and laws. Ensure that your children and your children's children obey God. Do this and you will prosper and your life will be prolonged. Love God with all your heart, soul, and might. Keep God's Word in your heart and teach His ways carefully and thoughtfully to your children. Talk with your family all the time about God, every day and night, whenever you are together.
- PRO 1:7–10 ~ The fear of God is the beginning of wisdom; only fools despise wisdom and instruction. Children, listen to the instruction of your parents; if sinners entice you, do not give in.
- PRO 22:6 ~ Instruct your children in the way they should go and when they mature, they will not depart from it.
- 1 JO 5:20–21 ~ Teach your children to refrain from idolatry (i.e., stay away from anything and anyone that could take God's place in their hearts).

Parents should remind their children that they have a Heavenly Father who loves them as much or more than their own parents do. Children should learn to love their Heavenly Father and His Son, and also other people as much as themselves. They should be taught that God is love.

- MAT 22:37–40 ~ Jesus said, "Love the Lord your God with all your heart, mind, and soul: this is the first and greatest commandment. The second is like unto the first: Love your neighbor as yourself. All the laws and the prophets depend on these two commandments."

- LUK 6:32,35 ~ Jesus said, "If you love only those who love you, what reward will you receive? Even sinners love those who love them. So love everyone, even your enemies. Help others whenever you can, expecting nothing in return, and your reward will be great and you will become a child of God."
- JOH 3:16 ~ God loved the world so much that He gave His only begotten Son, so that anyone who believed in Him would never die but would live forever.
- 1 CO 13:4–8,13 ~ Love is patient. Love is kind. Love is never envious or conceited. Love is never rude, self-seeking, or angered, nor does it find pleasure in sin. Love does not think of evil things, nor is it provoked by evil. Love rejoices in the truth. Love always protects, always trusts, always hopes, and always endures. Love never fails. Faith, hope, and love abide, but the greatest of these three is love.
- 1 PE 1:22 ~ Purify your souls by obedience to the truth and earnest love for one another.
- 1 JO 2:15 ~ Don't love the world or worldly things, because you can't love the world and God at the same time.
- 1 JO 4:7–12,16–21 ~ Let us love one another, for love is from God, and those who love are born of God and know Him. If you don't love God you can't know Him because God is love. The love of God was manifested among us through His only Son, so we might live through Him. If God loves us so much, we should love one another; if we love one another, God lives in us and His love is perfected in us. If you abide in love you abide in God, and God abides in you. This perfect love gives us confidence on the day of judgment, because there is no fear in love but perfect love destroys fear, because fear brings torment. We love because God loved us first. You can't say you love God and hate your brother without being a liar, because you can't hate someone you have seen and still love God who you have never seen. So, you should love God and your brother (neighbor).

Children need to begin learning about the Bible, God, and Jesus Christ at an early age. Young children are especially able to understand the love of God and can possess a strong faith in Jesus Christ.

- MAT 18:3–6 – Jesus said, "Unless you become converted and receive God as a little child, you will never enter the kingdom of heaven. Those who humble themselves like a child can become the greatest in God's kingdom. Whoever receives a child in my name receives me. But if anyone offends a child who believes in me, they would have been better off being tossed into the sea with a millstone tied to their neck."
- LUK 18:15–17 ~ The people brought children and babies to Jesus so that He could bless them. The disciples tried to prevent them from bringing the children but Jesus told them, "You must allow the little children to come to me, and never forbid them from entering my presence, for those who can demonstrate such trust and faith as a little child will inherit the kingdom of God. I tell you the truth, unless you receive the kingdom of God like a child does, you will never enter there."

Having children is like an investment. Children bring joy to a married couple. Children help the parents when they become old. Parents should likewise invest in the future of their children. Parents have children to provide them heirs, so that their children can obtain their belongings and inherit their fortune.

- PRO 13:22 ~ God leaves His inheritance to His children; sinners leave their inheritance to the just.
- ROM 17:6 ~ Grandchildren are the pride of their grandparents and the glory of their parents.
- 2 CO 12:14–15 ~ Parents save up for their children, children don't save up for their parents.

God wants us to be His children as well, and so we are, through the death and resurrection of His Son Jesus Christ. Like Christ, God wants us to receive His Holy Spirit and inherit His kingdom. God wants us to live with Him forever as His rightful heirs, for we are His adopted children, being made brothers and sisters with Christ.

- LUK 11:13 ~ Jesus said, "If humans, who are sinners, know how to give good things to their children when they ask, how much more God is able to give the Holy Spirit to those who ask Him."
- ACT 2:38–39 ~ Peter told the crowd, "Repent and be baptized every one of you for the remission of sins, and you will receive the gift of the Holy Spirit. This promise is for you, your children, and people everywhere: to whomever the Lord calls."
- ROM 8:14–17 ~ Whoever is led by the Spirit of God becomes a child of God. If you are a child of God then you are His heir, and a joint heir with His only begotten Son Jesus Christ. If we suffer with Christ, we will also be glorified with Him.
- HEB 1:1–2; HEB 2:10–11 ~ God, who spoke throughout history to the prophets, has in these past days spoken to us by His Son Jesus Christ, whom He appointed heir of all things and by whom He also made the worlds. Through His suffering, many people are saved to become glorified with Him as children of God. Both He that sanctifies and those who are sanctified are one; therefore, Christ is not ashamed to call them His brothers and sisters.

Parenthood is a responsibility that is shared equally by both spouses. It is a proven fact that the most stable home for a child to be nurtured and to succeed is one in which both parents, consisting of a father and a mother, reside in harmony. A broken home is the cause of many wayward children. What a wonderful blessing it is to fall in love and get married. Well, it always seems to start out that way, but for many it doesn't continue to be such a blessing. Too many marriages fail, usually due to some form of incompatibility or irreconcilable differences. The most important way that couples should be congruent is spiritually. It is wise to choose a spouse who believes in Christ and who follows His ways.

- LEV 21:7,13 ~ Do not take a prostitute for a wife, or a profane woman, or a divorced woman.
- 2 CO 6:14 ~ Do not be unequally yoked together with unbelievers, for what fellowship can righteousness have with unrighteousness? What communion can exist between light and darkness?

The formula for a good marriage is provided in the Bible. The best chance to succeed in marriage is to follow the guidance given in God's Word. Of course, even the most spiritual people will have problems and arguments. A successful marriage requires constant work, commitment, collaboration, and honesty, each and every day.

- PRO 31:10–31 ~ Whoever finds a virtuous woman for a wife will have something more valuable than rubies. She will do her husband good all of her life. She will work hard and give herself to the household. She will be generous and complimentary to others. Her husband will be well known and powerful. She will be clothed in strength and honor. She will be wise and kind. She will not be lazy and her husband and children will praise her for it. Although favor can be deceitful and beauty can be vain, faith in God will always yield His praise.
- 1 CO 7:1–5,8–10,28,39 ~ It is fine if you never even touch a member of the opposite sex. But if you can't contain your emotions, then marry, for it is better to marry than to burn with passion. So, marry if you want to avoid the sin of fornication. However, if you marry you must be charitable to your spouse. A husband should have power over the wife's body. Don't lie to your spouse, and don't ever split apart. It's not a sin to marry, but married people will

have problems associated with their sinful and weak nature. Once married, you are bound to each other until one of you dies.

- EPH 5:21–25,28,33 ~ Submit to one another. Wives, submit to your husbands because the husband is the head of the wife just like Christ is the head of the church. Thus, the wife is subject to the husband at all times. Husbands, love and protect your wives even as Christ loved the Church and gave Himself for it. You must love your spouse as much as you love yourselves.
- COL 3:18–19 ~ Wives, submit to your husbands, as long as it is within the Law. Husbands, love your wives and don't be bitter with them.
- TIT 2:4–5 ~ Wives, be sober, and love your husbands and your children. Be discreet, chaste, good homemakers, and obedient to your husbands, so the Word of God will not be blasphemed. Young men, be sober, upright and not corrupt; be serious and sincere, speaking good things about others.
- 1 PE 3:1,7 ~ Wives, obey your husbands, and teach them the Word if they do not understand it. Husbands, listen to your wives; honor your wives as the weaker sex and as an equal. Stay together in the grace of life, and your prayers will be answered.

The Old Testament book, Song of Solomon provides an interesting story of the love between a king and a shepherdess. While this story is a reflection of the enduring love that Christ has for His church, it also provides an example of how to succeed in marriage by adopting God's plan. Notice in this poetic scripture how a healthy heterosexual relationship follows a particular procedure, and how the importance of love, virtue, commitment, sharing, and loyalty are stressed. These are the characteristics that parents should model for their children. The procedures and rules outlined in God's Word should be taught to your children, if you want them to succeed in marriage and parenthood. When you or your children follow the ways of the world, the odds of succeeding will be poor.

- SOS 1—8 ~ The first chapter covers the attraction between the man and woman and shows how their love begins to grow. Notice that the maiden is attracted to the king's reputation, not his power, glory, or money. She exclaims that his name is pleasant, and that is why all the maidens in the king's domain adore him (SOS 1:3–4). Notice that the primary characteristic that the king admires in the maiden is her dedication and sense of duty, as opposed to her physical attractiveness. He overlooks the fact that her skin has been darkened by the sun from laboring in the fields where she tends flocks that are not her own (SOS 1:5–9). Further, the shepherdess is a woman of virtue, a virgin, undefiled and flawless (SOS 1:7; SOS 4:12; SOS 5:2), not flirtatious, flippant, or provocative. In the second chapter the king begins to court the young maiden. He entertains her through a ritual similar to what we call dating or wooing. Their love continues to grow, without becoming sidetracked by premarital sex or any "fooling around." Instead, they yearn for the time when they can experience greater intimacy as a result of being joined by God in marriage. Chapters three through five tell how they marry, are intimate, and consummate their marriage. Sex within marriage is revealed to be a beautiful experience (SOS 4:16—SOS 5:1). Notice that they are not only lovers, but friends (SOS 5:16). They became friends as they were courting and as their love grew; perhaps they were lovers all along, but they waited to "make love" until the time was right and they were man and wife. In chapters six and seven we see their love and commitment continue to increase and flourish, as they share the gifts of life, love, and companionship. In fact, sharing seems to be the principal theme of these chapters. Keep in mind that marriages which do not include very much sharing are usually doomed; spouses should want to share everything and always. In the final chapter, the major theme seems to be loyalty; for a marriage to last a lifetime, the loyalty should never fade. Another theme of this chapter is the power of lasting love: it is stronger than death, unyielding as the grave, unquenchable as an inferno, and as permanent as a rock that cannot be eroded or washed away (SOS 8:6–7).

Let us cherish the message of Solomon, who truly was a very wise man. Let us be examples to our children, teaching them God's plan, and showing them how to succeed in love and marriage using the Lord's own prescription.

- SOS 2:7; SOS 3:5; SOS 8:4 ~ Do not arouse or awaken love until it is ready.

Be Happy

(By Andrew Barber, 1975)

Happiness is contagious;

Smile and the world smiles with you.

It would be outrageous

If everyone in the world smiled at the same time.

Everyone would probably be happy all day.

It makes me laugh just to think about it.

So people, please smile away;

When you're happy, then scream and shout it.

Maybe it even could stop war, pollution, crime, prejudice,

Communication gaps, and very likely—

Unhappiness.

OTHER SPIRITUAL BEINGS

God is a spiritual being, and He made people spiritual beings in His image. There are a number of other spiritual beings including angels and demons. Satan is also a spiritual being, an angel who turned evil and fell from God's grace. There are several references to invisible and visible spiritual beings in the Bible; many of these spirits are not human. People have been known to become possessed by evil spirits if they abandon God.

Angels

- GEN 3:24 ~ God drove Adam and Eve out of the Garden of Eden. He placed cherubim with a flaming sword at the east end of the garden to guard the Tree of Life.
- GEN 19 ~ Two angels went to Sodom to meet with Lot and warn him of the impending devastation of Sodom.
- GEN 22:11–17 ~ An angel called to Abraham to spare his son Isaac.
- GEN 28:12 ~ Jacob dreamt of a ladder reaching to heaven, with angels ascending and descending upon it.
- EXO 3 ~ An angel appeared to Moses in the burning bush and gave him God's instructions.
- NUM 22:22–35 ~ An angel appeared to Baalam. Baalam didn't recognize the angel until his donkey saw the angel and started talking. The angel told Baalam what to say to Balak regarding the prophecy he sought against Israel. Balaam was forced to prophecy on behalf of Israel which infuriated Balak.
- JDG 2 ~ An angel appeared to the Israelites and to Joshua to warn them about making alliances with wicked nations.
- JDG 6:11–22 ~ An angel told Gideon to destroy the altar of Baal.
- JDG 13:3–24 ~ An angel appeared to the mother of Samson to tell her she would bear a son who would become a famous judge.
- 1 KI 19:5–7; 2 KI 1:3,15 ~ An angel strengthened Elijah.
- 2 KI 19:35; 2 CH 32:21 ~ The angel of God killed 185,000 Assyrians.
- PSA 103:20 ~ Angels excel in strength.
- PSA 104:4 ~ God makes angels' spirits.
- ISA 6:2,8 ~ Isaiah had a vision of four six-winged seraphim carrying the Lord. Isaiah heard the Lord calling, "Who shall I send?" Isaiah replied, "I am here, Send me."
- EZE 1:5–14; EZE 10:1–22 ~ Ezekiel had a vision of two four-winged cherubim. Each had four faces, four wings, and human hands.
- DAN 8:16–17; DAN 9:21–22 ~ The angel Gabriel appeared to Daniel and described the latter days.
- DAN 10:5–21; DAN 12:1 ~ Daniel again saw a vision of an angel describing the latter days. He was told that the kingdoms of Persia and Greece would be destroyed. He was told that Michael the great prince would come, and that there would be a time of trouble such as never before, but the righteous would be delivered.
- ZEC 1–6 ~ Two angels appeared to Zechariah to explain many visions about the latter days.
- MAT 1:20 ~ The angel Gabriel appeared to Joseph to tell him that his fiancé would bear the Son of God.
- MAT 2:13,19 ~ An angel warned Joseph to take his family to Egypt. The angel later told him when it was safe to return home.
- MAT 4:11 ~ Angels ministered to Jesus after Satan's temptations in the wilderness.

- MAT 13:39–50 ~ The angels are the reapers. The angels will separate the evil ones from the righteous; they will throw the evil ones into the fire.
- MAT 22:30; MAR 12:25; LUK 20:36 ~ After the resurrection, the saints will not marry, but will be like the angels in heaven.
- MAT 25:31 ~ Jesus will return in glory with all His angels.
- MAT 28:2,5; JOH 20:12 ~ The angel was at Jesus's empty tomb and appeared to several people.
- LUK 1:11–20,26–38 ~ The angel Gabriel told Zechariah he would have a son in his old age (John the Baptist). Gabriel told Mary that she would give birth to the Son of God (Jesus Christ).
- LUK 2:9–14 ~ An angel appeared to the shepherds to tell them of Jesus's birth. A multitude of heavenly hosts praised God in the heavens.
- LUK 22:43 ~ An angel came to strengthen Jesus in the Garden of Gethsemane.
- JOH 1:51 ~ Jesus said, "You will see heaven open and the angels of God ascending and descending upon the Son of Man."
- ACT 5:17–19 ~ An angel opened the prison and freed the apostles.
- ACT 8:26 ~ An angel told Philip to go to Gaza.
- ACT 10:3–16 ~ An angel appeared to Cornelius and then to Peter, to bring them together.
- ACT 12:7–23 ~ An angel freed Peter from chains and prison, and then killed Herod.
- ACT 27:23–24 ~ The angel told Paul he would appear before Caesar.
- 2 CO 11:14 ~ Satan disguises himself as an angel of light.
- COL 2:18 ~ Do not worship angels.
- 1 TH 4:16 ~ Jesus will return with the call of the archangel.
- HEB 12:22 ~ Angels are innumerable.
- HEB 13:2 ~ Don't turn away strangers, for you may be entertaining angels without knowing it.
- 1 PE 3:22 ~ Jesus sits in heaven at the right hand of God, with angels, dominions, and powers subject to Him.
- 2 PE 2:4,11 ~ God did not spare the angels when they sinned, but cast them into hell. Angels cannot pronounce judgment.
- JDE 1:6 ~ Fallen angels are kept in eternal chains until the day of judgment.
- JDE 1:9 ~ The archangel Michael contended with Satan for the body of Moses, and rebuked Satan rather than passing judgment.
- REV 1 ~ John received Christ's revelation from an angel (likely Gabriel).
- REV 1 ~ The angels of the seven churches are represented symbolically.
- REV 4:6,8 ~ John had a vision of four beasts surrounding Christ's throne. They had eyes all around them, and they had six wings (like seraphim). Each had a different face: lion, ox, eagle, or human. They sang praises to God day and night.
- REV 5:11 ~ Thousands upon thousands of angels were praising Jesus.
- REV 7:1–11 ~ Four angels hold back the four winds. Another angel ascends with the seal of God.
- REV 8—11 ~ Seven angels each blow their trumpets in turn.
- REV 10 ~ A mighty angel appears with a scroll.
- REV 12:7–9 ~ Michael and his angels defeat the dragon, and Satan and his angels are thrown out of heaven.
- REV 15—16 ~ Seven angels bring seven plagues.

- REV 20:1–3 ~ An angel comes with the key to the bottomless pit and binds Satan for one thousand years.
- REV 21:12 ~ Twelve angels guard the new Jerusalem.

Spirits, Powers, Devils, Dominions, and Principalities

- LEV 17:7 ~ God forbids sacrificing to devils.
- LEV 19:31 ~ God forbids the employment of, association with, and defilement by familiar spirits. (also LEV 20:6, DEU 18:11; 1 CO 10:21)
- ISA 8:19 ~ When others suggest that you seek those with familiar spirits reply, "Shouldn't we seek God and the living instead of the dead?"
- JER 9:11 ~ God says, "I will make Jerusalem a heap, and a den of devils."
- JER 13:18 ~ Say to the king and queen, "Humble yourselves before God; for your principalities will fall with all your glory."
- DAN 7:3–14 ~ I (Daniel) saw four beasts, one had four heads; and dominion was given to it. However, all the beasts had their dominions taken away. To the Son of Man was given all dominion, glory, and kingdom, which would never pass away or be destroyed.
- MAT 8:31–33 ~ Examples are presented of Jesus and His disciples casting out devils from possessed people; one had a whole legion of demons within him (about six thousand). (also MAT 4:24; LUK 7:21; LUK 10:20; ACT 5:16; ACT 8:7)
- MAT 12:45 ~ Jesus talked about casting out devils, and how, when one is cast out it may find seven spirits more wicked than itself to join it, returning to the individual and making him or her worse off than before. Jesus was referring to an evil generation that would come.
- ROM 8:38 ~ Neither death, life, angels, principalities, powers, nor things past and future can separate us from the love of God.
- ROM 13:1 ~ The powers that exist are ordained by God, and our souls are subject to higher powers. [Note that some are good and others are evil, so one must be cautious and informed.]
- 1 CO 12:10 ~ God gives everyone special talents one of which is the discerning of spirits.
- EPH 6:12 ~ We must fight, not against flesh and blood, but against principalities, powers, rulers of earthly darkness, and spiritual wickedness in high places.
- COL 1:16 ~ God created everything in heaven and earth, including visible and invisible, whether they are thrones, dominions, principalities or powers.
- COL 2:15 ~ Jesus triumphed over all principalities and powers.
- 1 TI 4:1 ~ In the later times, some will fall from the faith and be seduced by evil spirits and the doctrine of devils.
- JAM 2:19 ~ If you believe that there is one God you do well; even the devils believe and they tremble from it.
- 1 PE 3:22 ~ The angels, authorities, and powers are subject to Jesus who sits at God's right hand.
- 1 JO 4:1–2 ~ Don't believe every spirit but test them to see if they come from God, because there are many false prophets out there. Every spirit that confesses that Jesus Christ is God in the flesh is from God.
- REV 16:14 ~ The spirits of devils, which work miracles, will go forth to gather people to join them in their battle against God.
- REV 18:2 ~ The angel cried, "Babylon the great has fallen and has become the habitation of devils and every foul spirit."

CHAPTER FOUR

Satan

Satan was an anointed angel of God before he became sinful and was thrown out of heaven. Now he is on the earth trying to wreak havoc here. He is the evil one who tempts people to sin and to oppose God. He is a liar; he deceives people into believing false promises and wayward doctrines. Jesus Christ came to destroy Satan, along with his works, evil, sin, and death.

To complete his opposition to God, Satan has contrived an unholy trinity. First, there is Lucifer, the dragon, or beast; he was the cherub who relinquished God's favor and wants others to do the same. Second, there is the second beast, the son of Satan that is possessed by Satan himself in the latter days (antichrist). Third, there is the false prophet, the sower of lies, who hates the truth that is God's Word communicated through God's Holy Spirit. Satan is also known by these other terms: accuser, Baal, Beelzebub, Belial, devil, leviathan, serpent, tempter, and the son of perdition (hell). For more information on Satan refer to the lesson on the Tribulation and the Beast, describing Satan's rise to power in the latter days.

- ISA 14:12–15 ~ You have fallen from heaven and have been cut down to the ground, Lucifer, who brought down the nations. For you deceived yourself expecting to be exalted, even above God. Instead, you will be brought down into the depths of hell.
- ISA 14:29–30 ~ Do not be glad, Palestine, that the rod which struck you has been broken; for that rod will produce a root which will grow into a poisonous snake. The poor will find solace and the needy will be safe; but your root will be destroyed by famine, and the survivors will be slain.
- ISA 27:1 ~ On that day the Lord, with His mighty sword, will punish leviathan the wicked serpent, and He will kill the dragon that lives in the sea.
- ISA 32:6–7 ~ The vile person comes speaking blasphemy and working evil and hypocrisy, opposing God Himself. His instruments are wickedness, lies, and dishonor.
- EZE 28:14–19 ~ You were the anointed cherub; you lived upon the holy mountain of God. You were perfect from the day you were created until evil was found in you. Your great wealth made you violent inside and you became sinful. Therefore, you were thrown off the holy mountain, and you will be destroyed. You exalted yourself because of your beauty, thereby corrupting yourself. You defiled the sanctuaries with your abominations. You will be destroyed by the fire within you; your terrible deeds will come to an end.
- LUK 11:15–19; MAR 3:22–23 ~ Some of the people who saw Jesus casting out demons said He was doing it by the power of Satan (Beelzebub), the chief of devils. Jesus, knowing what they were thinking, said, "A kingdom divided against itself is destroyed; a house divided against itself falls. If Satan is divided against himself how can his kingdom stand? How can Satan cast out Satan? If you believe that I am casting out demons by the power of Satan, by whose power do your people cast them out? Let them be your judge."
- JOH 8:44 ~ Jesus said to the unbelievers, "You belong to your father the devil, and the evil of your father you will do. He was a murderer and a liar from the start. He never tells the truth. In fact, he is the father of lies."
- 2 CO 11:14 ~ Don't be tricked by Satan who disguises himself as an angel of light.
- 1 JO 4:3 ~ Anyone denying Jesus as the Christ, and God in the flesh, is an antichrist. Have you heard about the antichrist coming? Well the antichrist is here already.

- 2 TH 2:3–4,8–9,11–12 ~ Beware of false prophets who will try to deceive you, because people will fall away from God before the evil one, the son of Satan (literally, son of perdition or hell), is revealed. He is the one who opposes God and exalts himself, pretending to be God. The evil one will be consumed by the Spirit of God, and will be destroyed by the brightness of His coming. The evil son of Satan is the one who is possessed by Satan himself, and performs magic tricks and false miracles. He will deceive many people with his delusions and lies. All who follow him and find pleasure in unrighteousness will be damned.
- 1 PE 5:8–9 ~ Be sober and vigilant, because your enemy the devil roams about like a lion searching for someone to devour. He will attempt to consume anyone who isn't steadfast in their faith.
- 1 JO 3:8 ~ Whoever commits sin is of the devil who sinned from the beginning. Jesus Christ came to destroy the works of the devil.
- REV 12:9,12 ~ The great dragon, Satan, the deceiver of the world, was thrown out of heaven along with his angels. Woe to those on earth, for Satan has come to you. He is very angry because he knows he has but a short time left.
- REV 13:4,18 ~ They worshipped the dragon who gave power to the beast; and they worshipped the beast, saying, "Who is like the beast, and who is able to defeat him?" Here is wisdom for those who can understand: Count the number of the beast, for it is the number of a man, and the number is 666.
- REV 20:10 ~ The devil that deceived them was thrown into the lake of fire where the beast and false prophet were. There they were tormented day and night forever.

Powers of Satan

Satan has certain powers that he received from God. Many of these powers are listed below. Although Satan has great power, his power can be thwarted by anyone who calls upon the name of the Lord. In fact, Satan will flee from anyone exhibiting the indwelling of the Holy Spirit. If you resist Satan in Jesus's name, he will search for a more willing participant.

- ECC 8:8 ~ Nobody has the power to retain the spirit upon their death. The power of evil does not include the ability to deliver anyone from death or condemnation.
- DAN 8:24 ~ The evil one's power is mighty but not by his own power. He will destroy awfully, and will prosper; he will destroy mighty and holy people.
- DAN 11:43 ~ He will have the power over gold and silver, and other worldly riches.
- LUK 22:53 ~ Satan has the power of darkness.
- EPH 2:2 ~ In the past, you walked according to the course of this world, according to the prince of the power of the air, the same spirit that works in the children of disobedience.
- EPH 6:12 ~ We wrestle, not against flesh and blood, but against principalities, powers, rulers of darkness in this world, and spiritual wickedness in high places.
- HEB 2:14 ~ Satan can bring death (but has no power over it).
- JAM 4:7 ~ Submit yourselves to God and resist Satan and he will run away from you.
- 1 JO 4:4 ~ You are of God little children, and have overcome them (antichrists), because greater is He that is in you (Christ) than he that is in the world (Satan).
- REV 13:7 ~ He was given the power to make war with the saints and to overcome them. He possessed a power over various peoples, nations, and tongues. He had the power to deceive people through fake miracles when in the presence of the beast, who was wounded and yet lived. He could command the image of the beast to speak, forcing many to worship the image of the beast or be killed.

Lesson: The Powers that Be

All power comes from God; powers are delegated by God as He chooses. Nobody obtains power by his or her own wisdom and might, because God doles out power in accordance with His will. That same authority belongs to Jesus Christ.

- JOH 19:10–11 ~ Pilate told Jesus that he could have Him put to death. Jesus replied to Pilate that he didn't have any power except that which was given to him from heaven.
- ROM 13:1 ~ There is no power but of God; all powers that exist are ordained by God.
- COL 1:16 ~ All things in heaven and earth, visible and invisible, thrones, dominions, principalities, and powers were created by Him and for Him.

God is all-powerful. There is nothing He cannot do. Everything is possible with God. However, God will never deny Himself. Further, God can never lie, for He is the source of all knowledge and truth. God is perfect and incapable of imperfection.

- MAT 28:18 ~ Jesus Christ said, "All power in heaven and on earth belongs to me."
- MAR 10:27 ~ Things that are impossible for humans are not impossible with God.
- LUK 1:37 ~ With God, nothing is impossible.

God and Christ have the power to forgive sins. Christ gives His people the power to forgive sins in His name.

- MAT 9:6 ~ Jesus Christ proved He had the power to forgive sins when He healed the lame man.
- JOH 20:22–23 ~ Jesus said to followers who received His Spirit, "Those whose sin you forgive they are forgiven, and those whose sin you do not forgive, they are not forgiven."

God has given us His Spirit which gives us life; thus, God has the power to defeat death. Our spirit returns to Him upon death. God's power over life and death was demonstrated by His Son Jesus Christ. Christ proved His power over the grave through His death and resurrection.

- JOB 19:25–26 ~ I know my Redeemer lives and He will stand upon the earth. And though my flesh will have been destroyed, yet in my flesh I will see God.
- JOH 10:18 ~ Jesus Christ said, "I have the power to lay down my life and to take it back again."
- JOH 17:2 ~ Jesus Christ has power over all people, and He has the power to give them eternal life.
- HEB 4:12 ~ God's Word is swift, sharp, and powerful. Like a double-edged sword, it can pierce and divide the very soul and spirit, and it can discern the thoughts and intents of the heart.

The Lord is the only one who can destroy one's soul in hell, or grant someone eternal life. Satan tries to deceive people into thinking that he has these powers, but it is only a lie.

- 2 CH 25:8 ~ God has the power to help people, and the power to cast them down into hell.
- PSA 49:15 ~ God has the power to redeem a person's soul from the power of the grave.
- MAT 10:28 ~ Jesus said, "Do not fear those who can kill the body but not the soul. Rather fear the One (God) who can destroy both your body and soul in hell."
- LUK 12:5 ~ Jesus Christ has the power to kill people and cast them into hell.
- JOH 17:2 ~ God has the power over all flesh, and the power to give eternal life.

God is light, and His Spirit shines with this light, bringing the truth of His Word to anyone who is interested. God is Spirit and should be worshipped in spirit and in truth (JOH 4:24). Satan's powers are in darkness and evil, deception and fear. Satan's power is limited to the material world in which we live.

- DAN 11:43 ~ Satan has the power over gold and silver and worldly riches.
- LUK 22:53 ~ Evil is the power of darkness.

Satan is the father of lies and deception. God is truth; He will never lie to us. Remember, our perfect God cannot lie (HEB 6:18). Satan is the opposite; his proclivity is to lie and deceive. It is difficult for Satan to tell the truth, and he will do so only if it fits his evil schemes. Satan will quote scripture if he thinks it will serve his evil purpose (MAT 4:1–11).

- DAN 8:24 ~ The evil one's power is mighty but not by his own power. He will destroy awfully, and will prosper; he will destroy mighty and holy people.
- JOH 8:44 ~ Jesus told the unbelievers, "You evil people belong to your father the devil, and the evil of your father is what you do. He was a murderer and a liar from the start. He never tells the truth; in fact, he is the father of lies."
- REV 13:7 ~ The second beast was given the power to make war with the saints and to overcome them. He possessed a power over various peoples, nations, and tongues. He had the power to deceive people through fake miracles when in the presence of the beast, who was wounded and yet lived. He could command the image of the beast to speak, forcing many to worship the image of the beast or be killed. (also REV 14—15)

Satan has the power to bring death, but he cannot grant life beyond the grave. Satan knows he will be condemned to death because of his wicked ways, and he wants to drag down as many people as he can.

- ECC 8:8 ~ Nobody has the power to retain the spirit upon their death. The power of evil does not include the ability to deliver anyone from death or condemnation.
- ISA 47:14 ~ Nobody has the power to deliver themselves from death or hell.
- HEB 2:14 ~ Satan has the power to bring death.

God gave us a discerning mind, which is the knowledge of good and evil. Thus, humans have the power to do what is right or to do what is wrong. That is, we have the power to obey God and resist Satan, or to do the opposite.

- 2 SA 22:23 ~ We have the power to obey God.
- 1 CO 7:37 ~ We have power over our own will.
- JAM 4:7 ~ We have the power to resist Satan.

People have power over one another. A person can hurt another, inflict pain, even murder another person.

- GEN 31:29 ~ We have the power to hurt others.
- EST 8:11 ~ We have the power to destroy, assault, and to kill.
- PRO 18:21 ~ We have the power of the tongue to cause life and death.
- EZE 22:6 ~ We have the power to shed blood.

However, people can help one another, and be good to the people they meet. God's love is His power, and He gives that love to us. By sharing His love, we can possess that power, and bestow it upon others. The power of love can defeat evil and fear.

- PRO 3:27 ~ We have the power to do good to others.
- ROM 12:21 ~ Don't be overcome with evil, but overcome evil with good.
- 1 JO 4:18 ~ There is no fear in love, but perfect love dispels all fear, for in fear is torment

The message that Christ brought is the never-ending love of God. God loved us so much, He allowed His Son to die for us (JOH 3:16). Christ's love lives in us if we believe in Him (1 JO 4:10–16). By following the example of Jesus Christ, we have the power to become the children of God.

- JOH 1:12 ~ God gave people power to become His children through faith in Christ.
- GAL 4:6–7 ~ Because you are His children, God has sent the Spirit of His Son into your hearts. Therefore, you are no longer servants but children of God; and as children, heirs with Christ.

If we obey God, and follow Christ, He may delegate additional powers to us. Men and women of God throughout the Bible displayed great power manifested by the Holy Spirit. That same power is given to anyone who employs it to do the work of the Lord.

- 1 KI 17:17–24 ~ Elijah raised a boy from the dead.
- MAT 10:1 ~ Jesus gave His disciples power against demons and power to heal the sick and diseased.
- LUK 10:19–20 ~ Jesus gave His disciples immunity over poisonous snakes and scorpions, and power over the enemy and anything harmful, including demons.
- ACT 1:8; ACT 2:4; ACT 3:12 ~ The power of the Holy Spirit, once received, bestows the power to witness, the power to speak in foreign languages, and the power to heal the lame.
- ACT 9:37–42 ~ Peter raised a girl from the dead.
- ACT 20:12 ~ Paul raised a boy from the dead.
- HEB 11:7–38 ~ With faith, the prophets were able to endure anything and performed great feats, such as subduing kingdoms, escaping certain death, overcoming incredible odds, healing the sick, and even raising the dead.

There are other spiritual entities besides angels that are mentioned in the Bible including spirits, powers, devils, dominions, and principalities.

- DAN 7:6,12,14 ~ I saw a beast with four heads. Dominion was given to the beast. However, all the beasts had their dominions taken away. To the Son of Man was given all dominion, glory, and kingdom that would never pass away or be destroyed.
- ROM 8:38 ~ Neither death, life, angels, principalities, powers, nor things past and future can separate us from the love of God.
- EPH 1:20–21 ~ Jesus Christ, having been raised from the dead, now sits at the right hand of God in heaven. His kingdom is far above all principality, power, might, and dominion. His name is above all names that are named, not only in this world but also in the next.
- EPH 6:12 ~ We must fight, not against flesh and blood, but against principalities, powers, rulers of earthly darkness, and spiritual wickedness in high places.
- COL 1:16 ~ God created everything in heaven and on earth, including visible and invisible, whether they are thrones, dominions, principalities or powers.
- COL 2:15 ~ Jesus triumphed over all the principalities and powers.
- 1 PE 3:22 ~ The angels, authorities, and powers are subject to Jesus who sits at God's right hand.

Lesson: Angels and Spirits

God created all spiritual beings. In fact, God is a spiritual being. Since He made us in His image, we too are spiritual beings. There are numerous references in the Bible about invisible spiritual beings that are not human including angels and demons. Spirits can be good or bad. Lucifer was a good angel who became evil. People can allow themselves to become dark in spirit as well. People have been known to become possessed by evil spirits.

- PSA 104:4 ~ God makes angels' spirits.
- ROM 13:1 ~ The powers that exist are ordained by God; our souls are subject to such higher powers.

The characteristics of angels are described in the Bible.

- PSA 103:20 ~ Angels excel in strength.
- EZE 1:13–14 ~ Angels glowed like fire and moved to-and-fro with the speed of lightning.
- EZE 10:14 ~ The cherubim had four faces, one on each side (they could see in all directions).
- MAT 22:30 ~ Angels don't get married.
- LUK 20:36 ~ Angels never die.
- 2 PE 2:11 ~ Angels excel in power and might.
- REV 4:6,8 ~ The seraphim had eyes all around them (they could see in all directions).
- REV 12:7–9 ~ Michael the archangel defeated Satan.

Clearly, angels have a great deal of power. However, they differ in the degree of power they possess. Apparently, angelic beings are organized hierarchically, according to power and purpose. The archangel is likely the most powerful of all angels. Michael is the only archangel identified as such in the Bible. Michael is referred to as one of the great princes that stand over the earth (DAN 10:13). Gabriel is another.

Michael is the enforcer and the protector who carries a deadly sword.

- GEN 3:24 ~ God drove them out of the Garden of Eden. He placed cherubim with a flaming sword at the east end of the garden to guard the Tree of Life.
- EXO 23:20–23 ~ I (God) will send my angel to fight for you, but you must obey him, for I am the one who sent him and he is my representative.
- JOS 5:13–15 ~ While Joshua was preparing to attack Jericho, he saw a man with a sword drawn, so Joshua asked, "Are you for us or against us?" The man replied, "I am the captain of the angels of the Lord. Remove your shoes for you are standing on holy ground."
- 2 KI 19:35; 2 CH 32:21 ~ In one night, the angel of God killed 185,000 Assyrians with a sword.
- 1 CH 21:15–16 ~ God sent an angel to destroy Jerusalem, and as he was destroying it, the Lord had a change of heart and said to the angel, "That's enough." David saw the angel of the Lord standing between heaven and earth with his sword drawn.
- ISA 27:1 ~ On that day the Lord, with His mighty sword, will punish leviathan the wicked serpent, and He will kill the dragon that lives in the sea.
- DAN 12:1 ~ Daniel saw a vision of an angel (Gabriel) describing the latter days. Michael, the great prince, came to protect God's people. There was to be a time of trouble such as never before, but the righteous would be delivered, those whose names were written in the Book of Life.
- 1 TH 4:16 ~ Jesus will return with the call of the archangel and the trumpet of God.

- JDE 1:9 ~ The archangel Michael contended with Satan for the body of Moses, and rebuked Satan rather than passing judgment.
- REV 12:7–9 ~ Michael and his angels defeated the dragon and his angels, who were thrown out of heaven.

Gabriel is the messenger who relates God's plans. He is often associated with the angel who sounds the trumpet of God (ISA 27:13; MAT 24:31; 1 TH 4:16; REV 10:7; REV 11:15).

- DAN 8:16–27; DAN 9:21–27 ~ Gabriel appeared to Daniel and described the latter days of transgression and tribulation.
- MAT 1:20 ~ The angel Gabriel appeared to Joseph to tell him his betrothed would bear the Son of God.
- LUK 1:11–20,26–38 ~ The angel Gabriel told Zechariah he would have a son in his old age (John the Baptist). Gabriel told Mary that she would give birth to the Son of God (Jesus Christ).
- REV 1:1 ~ John received God's revelation from an angel (likely Gabriel).

Cherubim are high-ranking angels. As many as four cherubim are mentioned in the Bible. Cherubim are described as having four faces, four wings, and human hands.

- EZE 1:5–14; EZE 10:1–22 ~ Ezekiel had a vision of four cherubim. Each had four faces (lion, ox, eagle, human), four wings, and human hands. They glowed with radiance and moved like lightning.
- DAN 7:3,6 ~ Daniel also had a vision of four beasts; one was described as having four wings and four heads.

Michael and Gabriel may be the two cherubim mentioned in the following passages.

- EXO 25:10,18,22 ~ God commanded Moses to build the Ark of the Covenant with two gold cherubim facing each other, one at each end of the mercy seat. And God said, "I will commune with you from above the mercy seat and from between the two cherubim which are on the Ark."
- KI 6:21,23,27 ~ Solomon built the temple and overlaid it with gold. Within the sanctuary he made two cherubim from olive trees. They were placed facing each other, with their wings against the walls, so that the wing tips of each cherub touched those of the other.
- PSA 80:1; PSA 99:1 ~ The Lord, our Shepherd, reigns; He sits on the throne between the cherubim.
- ISA 37:16 ~ The God of Israel, enthroned between the cherubim, is Lord over all kingdoms on earth.
- EZE 41:18–19 ~ Ezekiel had a vision of the future, and a temple room with two cherubim, their human and lion faces exposed.
- ZEC 4:1–3,11–14 ~ The angel woke Zechariah and asked him what he saw. He replied that he saw a golden candlestick with a large bowl on top; there were seven lamps that were fed by seven pipes from the large bowl. There were two olive trees on either side of the bowl. Zechariah asked the angel what they were, and why they emptied their golden olive oil into the bowl. The angel said they represented the two anointed ones that stand before the Lord over the earth.
- REV 11:3–12 ~ I (God) will give power to my two witnesses. These are the two olive trees and the two candlesticks (ZEC 4). They have the power to breathe fire, to stop the rain, to turn water into blood, and to send plagues. After their 1260 days of prophecy, they will be killed and left for public display. Then they will rise from the dead after 3 ½ days.

Lucifer (Satan) is the cherub referred to in the following verses.

- ISA 14:12–15 ~ You have fallen from heaven and have been cut down to the ground, Lucifer, who brought down the nations. For you deceived yourself expecting to be exalted, even above God. Instead, you will be brought down into the depths of hell.
- EZE 28:14–19 ~ You were the anointed cherub; you lived upon the holy mountain of God. You were perfect from the day you were created until sin was found in you. Your great wealth made you violent inside and you became sinful. Therefore, you were thrown off the holy mountain, and you will be destroyed. You exalted yourself because of your beauty, thereby corrupting yourself. You defiled the sanctuaries with your abominations. You will be destroyed by the fire within you; your terrible deeds will come to an end.
- DAN 7:7 ~ The fourth beast was dreadful and terrible, and exceedingly strong; it was different than the other beasts.

Satan's fall included a host of other angels of lesser rank.

- 2 PE 2:4 ~ God did not spare the angels when they sinned, but cast them into hell, and committed them to chains of utter darkness to be kept until the judgment.
- JDE 1:6 ~ Fallen angels are kept in eternal chains until the day of judgment.
- REV 12:3–4 ~ A great wonder appeared in heaven; it was a red dragon with seven heads and ten horns. Its tail pulled down one third of the stars (angels) of heaven with it, and they were thrown to the earth.

Seraphim are also significant in the hierarchy of angels. As many as four are mentioned in the Bible. They are covered with eyes all around them. The Bible does not specify the rank order between seraphim and cherubim.

- ISA 6:2,8 ~ Isaiah had a vision of six-winged seraphim carrying the Lord. Isaiah heard the Lord calling, "Who shall I send?" Isaiah replied, "Here I am, send me."
- REV 4:6–8 ~ John had a vision of four beasts surrounding Christ's throne. They had eyes all around them, and they had six wings. Each had a different face: lion, ox, eagle, or human. They sang praises to God day and night.

Cherubim and seraphim are not the same. Seraphim are described as having six wings, and cherubim are described as having four wings. Cherubim have four faces: lion, ox, eagle, human; seraphim possibly have one of those four faces. Furthermore, seraphim minister to the Lord as He sits on His throne in heaven, while cherubim appear to perform functions elsewhere, like on earth.

Angels are God's (Christ's) helpers and laborers; they minister to Him.

- PSA 103:20–21 ~ Bless the Lord, all you angels who excel in strength; hear His voice, and do His will. Bless the Lord, all of His hosts who minister to Him.
- MAT 4:11 ~ Angels ministered to Jesus after He was tempted in the wilderness.
- JOH 1:51 ~ Jesus said, "You will see heaven open and the angels of God ascending and descending upon the Son of Man."
- LUK 22:43 ~ An angel came to strengthen Jesus in the Garden of Gethsemane.

Some of the things God's angels do in heaven are as follows.

- MAT 13:41–42 ~ The Son of Man will send His angels to collect all things in His kingdom that are offensive or evil, to be thrown into the fiery furnace.
- REV 8,9,10,11 ~ Seven angels each blow their trumpets in turn.

- REV 20:1–3 ~ An angel unlocks the bottomless pit and binds the devil there.
- REV 21:12 ~ Twelve angels guard the new Jerusalem.

Some of the things God's angels do on earth are as follows.

- GEN 19:1,15 ~ Two angels go to Sodom to warn Lot that they will destroy the city.
- GEN 22:15 ~ Angel stops Abraham from sacrificing Isaac.
- EXO 3:2 ~ Angel appears to Moses in the burning bush.
- PSA 91:11–12 ~ God gives His angels charge over you to protect you in all that you do. They will take you up in their hands so that you don't even stub your toe.
- MAT 24:31 ~ Angels gather God's (Christ's) elect from across the earth and the heavens.
- ACT 5:19 ~ An angel opens the prison and frees the apostles.
- ACT 12:7–23 ~ An angel frees Peter from chains and imprisonment and then strikes King Herod dead.
- HEB 1:14 ~ Are there not ministering angels that look after the heirs of salvation?
- REV 7:1–11 ~ Four angels hold back the four winds. Another angel ascends with the seal of God; 144,000 of God's servants are sealed.
- REV 15 ~ Seven angels bring seven plagues.

God has a vast number of angels, too numerous to count.

- JOB 21:33; HEB 12:22 ~ Angels are innumerable.
- DAN 7:10 ~ Thousands of thousands ministered to Him.
- MAT 26:53 ~ Jesus said, "Don't you realize I can ask my Father to send more than twelve legions of angels to assist me?" (A legion was about 6000 men.)
- MAR 13:27 ~ He will send His angels to gather His elect from everywhere, even the outermost parts of the earth and the heavens.
- LUK 2:13–14 ~ A multitude of heavenly hosts praise God in the heavens.
- REV 5:11 ~ Thousands upon thousands of angels were praising Jesus.
- REV 19 ~ There is a large number of angels, too numerous to count.

Satan has a large number of angels that do his bidding as well.

- MAT 12:45 ~ Jesus talked about the casting out of devils, and how, when one is cast out it may find seven others more wicked than itself to join it. Then the demons return to repossess the individual making him or her worse off than before. Jesus was referring to an evil generation that would come.
- LUK 8:26–33 ~ Jesus confronted evil spirits inhabiting a possessed man. Jesus asked the name of the demons who answered, "Legion, for we are many." Jesus sent the demons into a herd of swine; the entire herd ran over a steep cliff and drowned in the sea below.

Angels are not gods. They are not to be worshipped. Deal with an angel or spirit the same way you deal with a human being. Do not allow a foreign spirit to possess you or command you. Instead, allow God's Holy Spirit to dwell in you and command you. Humans have the power to resist evil spirits, including Satan himself. This power comes from God and is relinquished by those who would permit themselves to be corrupted by the world and evil spirits.

- LEV 17:7 ~ God forbids sacrificing to devils.
- LEV 19:31 ~ God forbids the employment of, association with, and defilement by familiar spirits (also LEV 20:6; DEU 18:11; 1 CO 10:21).
- ISA 8:19 ~ When others suggest that you seek those with familiar spirits reply, "Shouldn't we seek God and the living instead of the dead?"

- MAT 8:31–33 ~ Examples are presented of Jesus and His disciples casting out devils from possessed people (also MAT 4:24; LUK 7:21; LUK 10:20; ACT 5:16; ACT 8:7).
- COL 2:18 ~ Do not be misled by those who practice false humility and worship angels.
- HEB 13:2 ~ Don't turn away strangers, for you may be entertaining angels unawares.
- JAM 4:7 ~ Submit yourselves to God and resist Satan and he will run away from you.
- 1 TI 4:1 ~ In the later times, some will fall from the faith and be seduced by evil spirits and the doctrine of devils.
- 1 JO 4:1–2 ~ Don't believe every spirit, but test them to see if they come from God for there are many false prophets. Every spirit that confesses that Jesus Christ is God in the flesh is from God.
- REV 16:14 ~ The spirits of devils, which work miracles, will go forth to gather people to join them in their battle against God.
- REV 18:2 ~ The angel cried, "Babylon the great has fallen and has become the habitation of devils and every evil spirit."
- REV 22:8–9 ~ After receiving the vision of heaven, John fell to the angel's feet to worship him. The angel said, "Do not worship me for I am a servant like yourself, the prophets, and all who keep the Word. Worship only God."

Artists and the media usually depict angels with two wings. However, angels in the Bible are described as having either four wings or six wings. Moreover, if a person actually saw an angel, he or she probably didn't recognize the angel, since there were no visible wings. This is because angels often appear as ordinary people when they conduct God's work here on earth.

The angel Gabriel informed Mary that she would be the mother of Christ (LUK 1:26–38). Mary replied, "Behold the handmaiden of the Lord; let it be unto me according to your word.

Lesson: Discerning Spirits

The Bible cites many examples that prove the existence of spirits in this world. These spirits can be either good or bad. The good spirits we call angels and the bad ones we call demons. The good ones do God's work (PSA 91:11–12) and the evil ones do the devil's work (MAT 12:45). Perhaps as many as a third of the spirits are evil (REV 12:4,7–9); a great number of those may be in prison awaiting God's judgment (JDE 1:6; 2 PE 2:4).

Angels and demons have considerable power (PSA 103:20; EZE 1:13–14; EPH 6:12; 2 PE 2:11). For example, it is possible for spirits to communicate with people and influence people (JOS 5:13–15; DAN 8:16–27; LUK 1:20–38; LUK 8:26–33). Further, since they have been around for centuries, they also may possess quite an extensive knowledge of history. This knowledge may be both general and specific. This may explain why some spirits can imitate known characters (2 CO 11:14; HEB 13:2; REV 11:3–12). Spirits probably can appear as people or animals. In fact, the Bible explains that particular angels have several different faces, both animal and human (EZE 10:14; REV 4:6–8).

Cases involving a suspected haunting may simply be examples of demons capitalizing on their knowledge of the history of a particular location or person. They manipulate people by raising anxiety and arousal levels, since demons have an evil mission to promote fear and terror. In contrast, appearances of angels may be in the form of familiar faces such as a lost loved one. An angel's mission is not to frighten the individuals that they visit but to deliver a message from God. This task would be difficult if the message was delivered by an unfamiliar face.

People that think they have seen an extraterrestrial, believe they have lived past lives, say they have been visited by the dead, or have sensed the presence of ghosts may have experienced a familiar spirit or demon (LEV 19:31: DEU 18:10–11; ISA 8:19). Dead people are not roaming the earth; the Bible teaches that the spirit returns to God upon death of the body, and resides either in Abraham's bosom or Hades (ECC 12:7; LUK 16:19–31; HEB 9:27). If someone claims to have seen a ghost it is not a deceased person, because the dead will not appear again until the resurrection (JOB 7:9–10; JOB 19:25–16). Remember when King Saul commissioned the Witch of Endor to summon Samuel? His appearance came as a big surprise to the sorceress. But was it really Samuel? Well, either God permitted Samuel to return as it served His purpose, or a demon impersonating Samuel deceived them (1 SA 28). Elijah also returned, at least in spirit, prior to Christ's first coming and will come to proclaim His second coming (MAL 4:5; MAT 11:13–14; MAT 17:10–12; LUK 1:17); but then, Elijah never really died (2 KI 2:11). Angels often perform purposes such as these. The only person known with certainty to have returned to earth in Spirit after His death was Jesus Christ, who possesses powers far greater than that of angels and demons.

Apparently, God doesn't make it His policy to send dead people back to earth, nor does He allow them to roam freely. However, He does send His angels to perform tasks and He does allow Satan and his band of devils to wander, even to possess people. When the devil and his angels were tossed out of heaven, many ended up here on earth (ISA 14:12–15; REV 12:9–12). They will continue their reign of terror on earth until Christ returns (1 TI 4:1: REV 16:14; REV 19). So then, familiar spirits, ghosts, apparitions, phantasms, etc. are probably demons.

Of course, people are spirits too. The spirit in a person can become corrupted with evil if that person rejects Christ. They will become as the darkness, void of the light of God. On the other hand, a person can seek the Lord and invite Him to live in them, and their spirit will become sanctified by God's Holy Spirit. And they will radiate the love and light of Christ.

We understand that there are good spirits and there are bad ones (REV 12:9,12). However, bad spirits often disguise themselves as good spirits (2 CO 11:14). So how can you tell the difference? The best way is through the spiritual gift of discerning spirits. God has given certain people this special ability (1 CO 12:7–10). Additionally, the power of discernment is not necessarily limited to those with this unique spiritual gift. The discerning of spirits can be taught and/or learned to some extent. Are there any guidelines that the average person can follow in discerning spirits? The answer to this question is "yes" and the guidelines are found in the scriptures.

God has given us sophisticated sensory-perceptual systems to enable us to experience and examine the world around us. These systems are called the five senses, and include vision, hearing, touch, smell, and taste. While these five senses are normally associated with the physical world, it is possible that they may be applied to the spiritual world in some cases. Thus, the discerning of spirits can begin by keen sensitivity to specific sensory stimuli. Below, we will review the five senses and their use in identifying evil spirits.

The evil spirit searches constantly until it finds a host (MAT 12:43). If it is successful, the host is referred to as being demon possessed. Demon possession is going to increase during the latter days (1 TI 4:1). God abhors the association with and defilement by evil spirits (LEV 19:31; 1 CO 10:21). We must expose evil spirits for what they are and fight against these servants of darkness (EPH 6:12).

Smell: The senses of taste (gustatory) and smell (olfactory) are predominately influenced by the sense of smell. But what does smell have to do with discerning spirits? The Bible refers to evil spirits as demons, devils, unclean spirits, and foul spirits (MAR 9:14–29). In the Bible, the word "foul" is used synonymously with "unclean" and connotes evil, defilement, corruption, pollution, and filth. Remember Legion, the evil spirits that congregated in mass within a single unfortunate man (LUK 8:26–36)? This man lived among the catacombs and sewers. Thus, a foul spirit is one that lives among and associates with filth, vermin, stench, pollution, and corruption. Not surprisingly, a foul and unclean spirit is likely to smell foul as well. One can only imagine the smell that must have emanated from the man possessed by Legion. A foul smell is itself insufficient to suggest an evil spirit is present; logically, it depends on the circumstances and the environment. However, when an unexpected nasty smell occurs out of nowhere, it might raise one's arousal level.

Touch: A spirit is invisible, so how can one touch it? How can the tactile sense be used at all to discriminate spirits? While we cannot touch a spirit, we can still "feel" the presence of one. Jesus characterized a person's actions as being cold, hot, or somewhere in-between (REV 3:15–16). Jesus also talked about how a person's love can wax cold if they have been led astray by evil or by false prophets (MAT 24:11–12). When a person is hateful or evil, it is often possible to sense their coldness. The same can be said of a foul spirit. When a demon is around, it is often accompanied by the sensation of bitter cold, like the draft from a winter breeze. Actually, one may experience "goose bumps" just thinking about something or someone viciously evil. Sometimes, when a person feels a chill the hairs on the back of his or her neck stiffen. Have you ever awakened from a nightmare feeling cold and shivering? In addition to feeling the sensation of cold when there is a foul spirit present, it is also likely that one may feel "ill at ease" to say the least. Given the foul nature of an evil spirit, one may feel repulsion, and even nausea in its presence, just like when something you eat is foul, and you desire to vomit it out (LEV 18:25; 2 PE 2:22).

Hearing: Can we hear ghosts? Are there any auditory signals that an evil spirit produces? A person who is possessed usually has relinquished control to the demon(s). Consequently, the evil presence often does most of the talking, and the person's actions are also guided by it. The apostle John teaches us to test the spirits to see if they come from God or from Satan (1 JO 4:1–2). An evil spirit will not confess that Jesus Christ is God in the flesh, and that His death and resurrection sets us free from sin and death. A demon despises Jesus Christ and is fearful of Him, and thus is unable to confess Him, worship Him, or be near Him. Hence, a simple test of faith is usually sufficient to determine if a spirit is evil or not. A foul spirit will not verbally confess that Jesus Christ is Lord; Jesus's name alone would influence it to flee. Of course, the constant use of vile words and "evil speak" is another indication of the presence of evil. One also may notice an uncharacteristic change in the in pitch, intonation, or tempo of the victim's voice when a demon is being channeled.

Vision: If you can't see a ghost, how do you detect it visually? To understand the answer, one must examine the opposing forces of light and darkness, and of good and evil (ISA 5:20). Paul teaches us that there can be no union between the righteous and unrighteous, just as there can be no communion between the light and the dark (2 CO 6:14). Light can consume darkness, but darkness cannot consume light; even the smallest flicker of light will destroy darkness. The apostle John tells us that God is love, God is light, and in God there is no evil or darkness at all (1 JO 1:5; 1 JO 4:16). John further instructs that to hate others is to live in darkness (1 JO 2:11–12). Thus, evil exudes darkness while love radiates light. An evil spirit cannot shine the light of Christ for it is a dark spirit.

Jesus informed His followers that the eye is the lamp of the body (MAT 6:22). If you have an eye for good, your whole body will be full of light; if you have an eye for evil, your whole body will be full of darkness. If you have God's love inside, you will emanate His light (LUK 11:35–36). If you have evil inside you, then you emanate no light, for you have only darkness within, and "how great is that darkness" (MAT 6:23). Therefore, if you look into a person's eyes and see nothing but a void, like looking into a black hole, then chances are there is evil inside that person. Conversely, the countenance of a person who is full of love, joy and peace will glow, for their eyes will gleam with God's light.

Additionally, we can observe the actions of people (human spirits) to determine if their motives are good or evil. The things people say and do tell a lot about what they are thinking and feeling. As Jesus aptly put it, "The light came into the world, but men loved darkness rather than light, because their deeds were evil." Everyone that deliberately says and does evil things hates the light and avoids the light to prevent being exposed. Those who live in truth will come to the light, and "their deeds will be shown to be from God" (JOH 3:19–21). Someday, all the deeds of darkness will be uncovered by the light (1 CO 4:5).

In summary, we can employ our five senses to discriminate the good spirits from the evil spirits. Evil can come into a heart from the outside or out of the heart from the inside. An evil spirit's presence will often be detectable if some combination of the following conditions exists.

- The presence of filth, uncleanness, and/or corruption
- A foul smell
- A feeling of coldness and discomfort
- A darkness or void associated with the eyes or one's aura
- An unwillingness to verbally confess Jesus Christ as Lord and Savior
- Evil thoughts, words, and/or deeds
- Performing evil acts in secret and/or attempting to keep them hidden

Lesson: Weapons for Fighting Demons

A demon is like a parasite that preys mostly on humans, eating away at the mind and dimming the spirit. It consumes the light inside a person replacing it with darkness. God gives His people power and authority over demons. This power is manifested through God's Holy Spirit to those who call upon the name of Jesus Christ. The Bible provides some instructions concerning how to cast out demons. It is advised that a person study exorcism and spiritual discernment from a biblical perspective before attempting to perform this procedure. Some evangelical denominations employ specialists extensively trained or gifted in exorcism.

Confrontation: Let the demon(s) know that you are aware of its (their) presence (1 JO 4:1–2). Command the demon to identify itself (LUK 8:30). Manipulate the demon so that you can communicate directly with either it, or with the victim, whenever you desire. Distinguish which words and thoughts are being directed by the evil spirit versus those being provided by the victim. Show the victim the difference.

Truth: Disclose lies and deceptions coming from the individual who is possessed. Evil spirits can't stand the truth, especially the truth which is found in Jesus Christ (JOH 14:6). The truth is always superior to a lie. Therefore, truth provides mental superiority over deception and untruth. Help the possessed person accept the truth and replace any deceptions and persuasions of the demon that are contrary to the what God says (HEB 4:12).

Confidence: Truth provides confidence (PRO 2:2–6,10–12). God gives you the words of truth that you need to combat deception. The fear of the Lord gives us our confidence and removes all other fears (DEU 31:6; JOB 4:6; PSA 34:4). Never display fear to a demon, for a demon is not to be feared. Demons are afraid of the truth, and they are especially terrified of Jesus Christ (JAM 2:19). Thus, demons will fear those who possess the knowledge of the truth and who have the light of the Holy Spirit shining in them (PRO 1:7,33). Demons will perform acts in an attempt to make you afraid. Display your confidence in the truth of Jesus Christ and the demons will fear you (ROM 8:38–39).

Authority: God has given you the authority to invoke the power of His Holy Spirit, which is His Word and His Truth, manifested by Jesus Christ in the flesh. This power is granted to anyone who calls upon the name of Jesus Christ in faith (MAT 10:1; LUK 10:17–20). God gives you the power of the Word and provides you with the words you need to counter any argument advanced by a demon (MAT 10:19–20). Therefore, your authority, given to you by the Holy Spirit, is greater than any authority or power commanded by demons (1 JO 4:4). Further, demons have no authority over people; demon possession is, therefore, voluntary. Victims can be convinced that demons have no authority over them, if they ask Christ to come into their hearts. God's authority allows you to give commands to demons that they must obey, whether they like it or not (LUK 10:18–20).

Teamwork: Get the victim involved in the spiritual healing process (COL 3:16). The demon will try to resist, but with the victim's cooperation and determination, the demon will flee (JAM 4:7). Without the victim's participation, demons can be commanded to depart but they will return unless the victim is prepared to repel them (MAT 12:45). Thus, without the victim being willing to accept Christ and to expel the demon in Jesus's name, the effort may be futile. The demon will willingly and rapidly abandon the host as soon as the Spirit of Christ enters the heart and mind of the victim (EPH 6:10–17). God's Spirit will live in that person, thereby preventing the demon from returning. The Holy Spirit is a shield of faith that cannot be penetrated by the devil or his minions.

Patience: It often takes considerable time to evacuate demons, because they can be very persistent. However, time is in your favor, for demons cannot stand constant pressure. Truth and light are like pain to a demon; a constant stream of righteous thoughts and biblical words will break demons down. Thus, perseverance on the part of the victim and the exorcist is paramount (LUK 18:1–8). The behavior modification technique of desensitization is an effective tool for systematically breaking down the willpower of demons, while simultaneously building up the spiritual strength of the victim. It is a gradual process whereby the desired change in an individual is brought about little by little, rather than trying to get it done all at once.

Prayer: Pray for the victim and pray with the victim. Remember, Christ told the apostles, who were unsuccessful at casting out demons from one possessed individual, that some demons are removed only after constant prayer (MAR 9:14–29). Getting the victims to pray for themselves is most effective (PSA 50:15). Prayer is how victims can begin to accept Christ, to know Him, and to receive His Spirit.

Love: Fear is the force at work in a demon-possessed person, for fear is the greatest weapon available to a demon. Just as light destroys darkness, love destroys fear (1 JO 4:18). God is love, and love destroys evil. It is God's love that brings out the love in us. This love is the source of our faith, and is the abiding force behind the power of the Holy Spirit. Show the victim God's love, especially that love found in Jesus Christ, and share the love that is inside you (COL 3:12–17). Demons hate love for it renders their favorite weapons ineffective. Help the victim to experience God's love and to open his or her heart to the Holy Spirit, and he or she will experience the peace which surpasses all understanding (1 JO 4:11–16).

Forgiveness: The victim needs to realize that he or she is deeply loved by God. This immense love was demonstrated when God sacrificed His only Son Jesus Christ. The victim must know that Christ died for him or her too. That's how much the person is loved by God (JOH 3:16). There is always an out for the victim and that is through repentance. They may feel that it is too late, but it never is (MAT 20:1–16). Accepting that Christ has forgiven them is the first step to spiritual health. This forgiveness can be reinforced via the Holy Sacraments, which most surely will drive out all evil spirits and enable the person to invite the Holy Spirit to dwell within them, as long as the recipient desires such a union with God (ACT 2:38–39; 1 CO 10:16–21).

Satan, like other predators of his kind, is easily repelled by a single name—Jesus Christ. God has given everyone the authority to invoke the power of the Holy Spirit in Jesus's name.

Submit to God and resist Satan and he will flee from you (JAM 4:7). You are from God, little children, and have overcome the world, because greater is He that is in you than he that is in the world (1 JO 4:4).

Lesson: Keeping Your Head

You've heard the expression, "Don't lose your head." This is good advice. Notice how the statement has multiple meanings. The Bible teaches that Jesus is the head of the church, and His church comprises all believers. If you want to stay in control, let the Lord be your head; otherwise, you're likely to spin out of control. Let us examine the various ways this notion can be understood.

First, Jesus is the head with respect to being the one in charge, the headmaster, the boss if you will. All Christians are like soldiers and all report to Christ, for He is our director, counselor, and confidant. Ministers of God's Word and laborers in His kingdom can go directly to Him for advice, assistance, leadership, and love. He is our guide and He is our pilot.

- ISA 55:4 ~ I have given Him to be a witness to all people, a leader and commander.
- PSA 119:24 ~ God's precepts are my delight and my counselors.
- 1 CO 11:3 ~ I want you to know that the head of every man is Christ; and the head of the woman is the man; and the head of Christ is God.
- EPH 1:19–23 ~ How exceeding is the greatness of God's power towards believers! According to the working of His mighty purpose, which He wrought in Christ when He raised Him from the dead, God has placed His Son at His own right hand in the heavenly realm, far above all principality, power, might, dominion, and every name that is named, not only in this world but also in the next. God has placed all things under His feet, and made Him head over all things pertaining to the church, which is His body, the fullness of Him that fills all things.
- COL 2:9–10 ~ In Christ all the fullness of the Holy deity lives in bodily form. And you have been given fullness in Him, who is the head of all authority and power.

Second, Christ is the head in terms of being first, foremost, and best. He is the beginning and the end, the alpha and omega. He is the creator of the universe and He is our Lord. He is the firstborn of God and the first fruits of the resurrection. He is far ahead of the rest, the winner and champion, and His victory is now ours. His resurrection gives us eternal life, a new beginning which will never end.

- ISA 48:16 ~ Come and listen. I have not spoken in secret since the beginning. I was there all along, and now the Lord God and His Spirit have sent me.
- JER 17:12 ~ A glorious throne on high, exalted from the beginning of time, this is the place of our sanctuary.
- PRO 8:1,14,22–23 ~ I, wisdom, call to you. Counsel and sound judgment are mine; I understand all things and I have great power. The Lord possessed me in the beginning of His way, before His works of old. I was set up from everlasting, from the very beginning, before the earth existed.
- JOH 1:1 ~ In the beginning was the Word, and the Word was with God, and the Word was God.
- COL 1:18 ~ He is the head of the body which is the church. He is the beginning and the firstborn of the dead, so that in all things He might reign supreme.
- JAM 3:17 ~ The wisdom from above is first pure, peaceable, gentle, easily approachable, full of mercy and good deeds, impartial, and never hypocritical.

Third, Christ is the top, the pinnacle, the Most High. He is the foundation of our faith, the chief cornerstone, the capstone of the arch. He is the acme of excellence. He is the very highest and most perfect. He lives atop Mount Zion where He sees all things and where His light shines for all to see. He is our eyes and ears. He is our crown of life. He is above all, within all, and because of Him all things exist. He is to be exalted. The highest heaven is His throne.

- ISA 28:16 ~ The Lord says, "Behold, I lay in Zion a foundation stone, a tried, true and precious cornerstone, a sure foundation; and those who believe will never be dismayed."
- ISA 55:8–9 ~ My thoughts are not your thoughts and my ways are not your ways. As the heaven is higher than the earth so are my thoughts and ways far higher than yours.
- MAT 21:42 ~ Jesus said to them, "Haven't you read in the scriptures (PSA 118:22): The stone which the builders rejected has become the chief cornerstone? This is the Lord's doing, and isn't it marvelous?"
- EPH 2:19–20 ~ You are no longer foreigners but fellow citizens with God's people and members of His household, for you are built upon the foundation of the apostles and prophets, Jesus Christ Himself being the chief cornerstone. In Him the whole building is held together and rises to become a holy temple to the Lord.
- PHP 2:9–11 ~ God exalted Him to the highest position and gave Him a name that is above every other name, so that at the name of Jesus Christ every knee should bow, whether in heaven, on earth, or under the earth, and every tongue confess that Jesus Christ is Lord to the glory of God the Father.
- 1 PE 2:6–7 ~ It is written (ISA 28:16): Behold, I lay in Zion a chief cornerstone, and the one who trusts in Him will never be ashamed. To those who believe, this stone is precious. But let this be a warning to those who do not believe: the stone which the builders rejected has become the chief cornerstone, and that stone will be an obstacle which causes the unbelievers to stumble and fall.

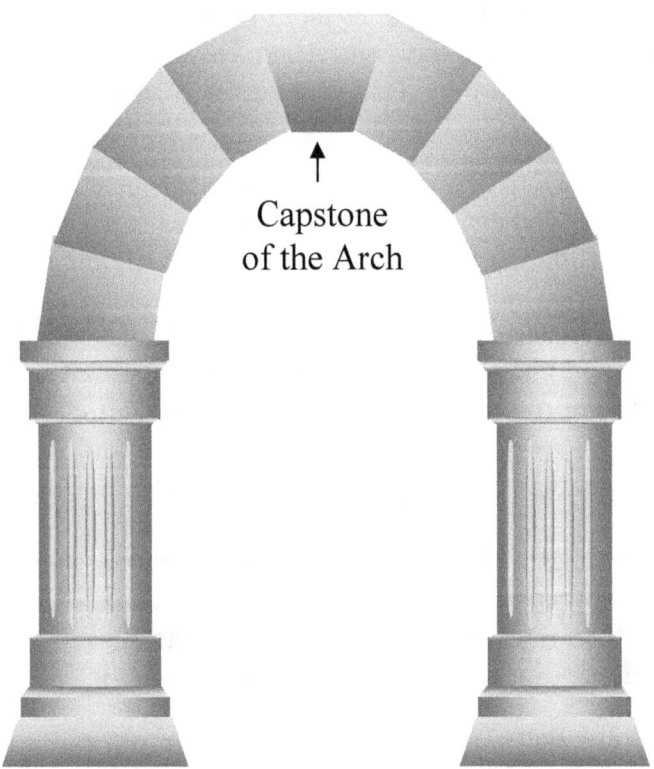

Notice how the analogy of the capstone of the arch fits perfectly the significance of Christ in our lives. In architecture, the capstone is the stone that holds the entire arch together. If the capstone is removed from the arch, the structure falls apart. The same is true for us: if Christ is removed from our lives, everything falls apart. He holds us up and He holds us together.

Fourth, the Lord is the only way to go, the means, the method, the course. He is the pathway, the sign, the route to take. Keep focused on the Lord and maintain that heading. If you are following Him, you are headed in the right direction. So full speed ahead!

- PSA 119:105 ~ God's Word is a lamp unto my feet, and a light unto my path.
- ISA 26:3 ~ The Lord will keep those in perfect peace, whose mind consistently trusts in Him.
- HAB 1:11 ~ They are blown with the wind and pass on, those guilty men who relish their own power as their god.
- JER 29:11 ~ God says, "I know the plans that I have for you: plans to prosper you and keep you safe, and plans to give you a future filled with hope."
- MAT 15:14 ~ Stay away from false teachers, for they are like the blind leading the blind. And when the blind lead the blind, both fall into the ditch.
- 2 CO 3:4–5 ~ Our confidence is in Christ. We are powerless to claim anything by ourselves because our sufficiency comes from God.
- EPH 4:15–16 ~ By speaking the truth in love, we will become continuously more like Him; in every way Christ becomes our head. Through Him the entire body is joined and held together, and grows, being built up in love as each part does its job.
- EPH 4:23–24 ~ Be renewed in the spirit of your mind and put on the new person, the one created to be like God in true righteousness and holiness.

Fifth, Christ is the head because He is the brains of the outfit. He is our mentor, our brother, and our Father. He is our mind and establishes our thoughts. Without His wisdom, influence, guidance, and instruction we would be ignorant, lost and helpless. He is knowledge and He is truth, and through knowledge of Him we become wise unto salvation.

- ISA 11:2 ~ The Spirit of the Lord will rest upon Him (Messiah), the spirit of wisdom and understanding, the spirit of counsel and might, the spirit of knowledge, and the fear of God.
- JOB 12:13 ~ All wisdom and strength belong to God; counsel and understanding are His.
- PRO 16:3 ~ Commit your works to God and He will establish your thoughts.
- ISA 40:13–14 ~ Who can understand the mind of God, and who can instruct Him? Did God have to consult anyone else to enlighten Him, to teach Him the right way, or to show Him the path of understanding?
- ROM 12:2 ~ Don't conform to the world but be transformed by the renewal of your mind to do the perfect will of God.
- 1 CO 2:16 ~ For who has known the mind of the Lord to instruct Him? But we have the mind of Christ.

It is good that we derive our knowledge and our thoughts from God, because the ways of the world are corrupt and its influence on thinking is derisive toward God. But God's way is truth and His wisdom everlasting. And from Him we receive the knowledge of forgiveness and redemption, and the inheritance of eternal life.

- JOB 28:28 ~ God declared to humanity, "The fear of the Lord is the beginning of wisdom, and to shun evil is understanding."
- PRO 14:30 ~ A sound mind gives life to the flesh.

- ECC 7:11~ Wisdom, like an inheritance, is a good thing. Wisdom can be a shelter like money is a shelter; only the advantage of having knowledge is that it preserves the life of the one possessing it.
- JER 31:31–33; HEB 8:10,16 ~ God says, "This is the covenant that I will make with the house of Israel after those days: I will put my laws into their minds, and write them in their hearts; and I will be their God, and they will be my people."
- ROM 7:25; ROM 8:1,6 ~ I (Paul) thank God through Jesus Christ our Lord. In my mind I choose to serve the Law of God; but with the flesh I am compelled to serve the law of sin. There is, however, no condemnation for those who are in Christ Jesus, and do not walk according to the flesh but according to the Spirit. To be carnally minded is death; but to be spiritually minded is life and peace.
- 2 CO 10:5 ~ Toss out vain imaginations, and everything that exalts itself against the knowledge of God, and bring into captivity every thought to the obedience of Christ.
- PHP 2:5–7 ~ Let this mindset be in you, which also was in Jesus Christ, who although He was by nature God, He did not consider equality with God something to behold but rather allowed Himself to become of low estate as a humble servant, taking on a human nature.
- 1 CO 1:10 ~ By the name of Christ, be united in one mind and be of one opinion.
- JAM 1:8 ~ A double-minded man is unstable in all his ways.

We need to make Christ the focus and center of our lives; that is where He belongs. He should not only be in your thoughts He should be controlling them. His light should be illuminating your direction and evident in your behavior. Christ needs to be in command: first place in your life, your purpose, your direction, and your mind. We must never lose sight of the path He has set before us that leads to eternal life with Him. Salvation is the ultimate objective and it can only be attained through Christ the Lord who is our head.

- ACT 4:12 ~ Peter said, "Salvation can be found in nobody but Jesus Christ; for there is no other name under heaven that can save us."

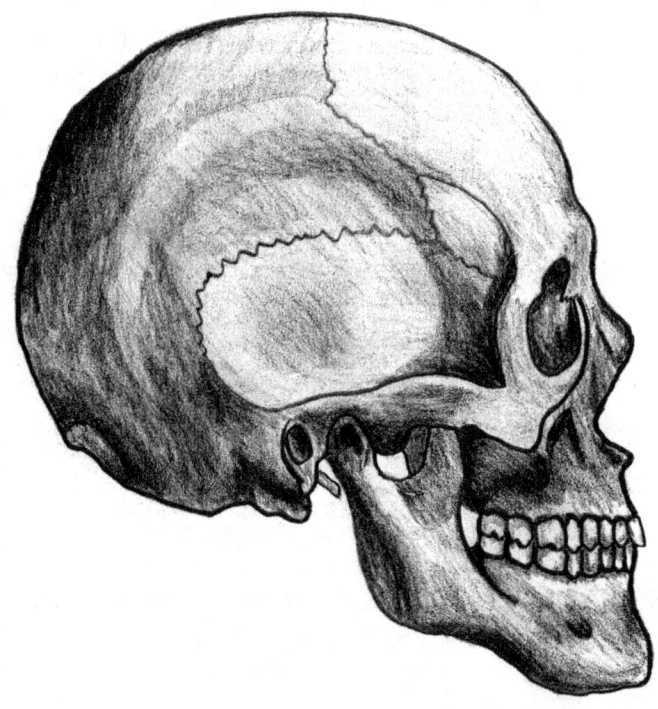

Lesson: Choices

God gives us choices, the greatest being to acknowledge Him and love Him. We also have the freedom to choose not to consider God, His Word, and His Law. With the Law came the knowledge of right and wrong; and with disobedience came the knowledge of sin. God gave us a discerning mind that enables us to distinguish the moral high ground; and we have the power to choose the greater good. And we know in advance if it is the right choice because our conscience will not lie to us. It takes little effort to prioritize one's options in terms of quality, for your alternatives are not relative or equal in value or moral superiority.

Why would God give us these choices? Why wouldn't He? Would he program us simply to behave according to His will? How then would we be able to choose Him or love Him back?

- DEU 7:7–10 ~ The Lord did not pour His love upon you, or choose you because you were greater in number than other people, for you were the fewest of all people. But because the Lord loved you, and in order to keep the promise that He made with your fathers, He brought you out with a mighty hand, and redeemed you from bondage in the land of Egypt. Know therefore that the Lord is your God; He is faithful and keeps the covenant, and bestows mercy on those who love him and keep His commandments. But He repays those who hate Him to their face, and utterly destroys them for everyone to see.
- JOS 24:15,21–22 ~ Joshua announced, "If serving the Lord seems undesirable to you, then choose who you will serve… As for me and my household, we will serve the Lord." The people said to Joshua, "We promise to serve the Lord." Joshua replied, "You are witnesses before me and your countrymen that you have chosen the Lord, and have promised to serve him." They responded, "Yes, we are witnesses."
- JDG 10:14 ~ Go and cry to the false gods that you have chosen; see if they will deliver you in the time of your tribulation.
- JOH 15:16,19 ~ Jesus said to His disciples, "You didn't choose me, I chose you and ordained you, so that you could bear fruit that would not wither. Anything you ask of the Father in my name will be given to you. If you were of the world, only the world would love you; but I have chosen you out of the world, and that is why the world hates you."

Next to choosing to believe in God and Christ, the most important choice you will ever make is to select the spiritual way from the way of the world. Jesus Christ is the way to heaven and eternal life. Since God our Father chose Christ, so should we choose Him and His ways. If we do, then God also will choose us to be His children to live with Him in His kingdom.

- DEU 30:19–20 ~ I (God) call heaven and earth as witnesses that I have set before you both life and death, blessings and curses. I recommend that you choose life so that you and your children may live, and so you may love the Lord your God, listen to Him, and cling to Him. Because He is your life; and He will bless you with many years of prosperity in the land He promised your forefathers Abraham, Isaac, and Jacob.
- PRO 1:28–33 ~ They will call me (God) but I will not answer; they will look for me but not find me. They hated knowledge and chose not to fear the Lord, ignoring my advice and spurning my reprimand. Since they did not take heed, they will eat the fruit of their ways and be full of the fruit of their schemes. The waywardness of simple-minded people will be their demise, and the complacency of fools will destroy them. But whoever chooses to listen will be safe and at peace, free from fear of harm.
- ISA 7:15 ~ Butter and honey he will eat, and he will know to refuse the evil and choose the good.

- ISA 42:1 ~ God said, "Behold, the Chosen One, my delight; my Spirit is upon Him."
- MAT 20:16 ~ Jesus said, "The last will be first, and the first last, for many are called, but few are chosen."
- MAR 9:35 ~ Jesus sat down, called the twelve, and said to them, "If any man desires to be first, the same shall be last and the servant of all."

Making the proper choices in life is a mental exercise. We can become the person we choose by thinking often about it. That is, you can opt to be godly, you can decide to be happy, you can prefer to be helpful, and so forth. It's a thought process that must precede an action. By reflecting on the decision, and praying about it, you become reassured of what to say and do. It's as easy as simply taking time for your conscience to kick in, knowing that the truth and the right path will always come to mind. Of course, you can choose to do the opposite and be miserable, afraid, angry, or depressed; those things usually proceed from not being thoughtful or careful.

- JOB 9:14 ~ How should I answer him, and choose the right words to reason with him?
- PRO 6:3 ~ Commit your works to the Lord and He will establish your thoughts.
- ACT 26:2 ~ Paul said, "I think myself happy, King Agrippa, because I will answer for myself today before you, addressing all the things of which I am accused by the Jews."
- 1 CO 10:13 ~ The temptations you endure are common to humanity. But God is faithful and fair, and He will not cause you to suffer temptation beyond your ability to withstand it. And He will always provide you a way to escape from temptation.
- PHP 1:22–25 ~ If I live in the flesh, that will mean fruitful labor for me. But which shall I choose? For I am torn between two alternatives. I long to depart from this life and be with Christ which is far better. But now it is necessary for me to remain here and to help you progress in the faith.
- PHP 4:8 ~ Whatever is true, honest, fair, pure, lovely, uplifting, virtuous, and praiseworthy—think on these things.

The devil is going to prey on your wayward and illogical thinking. He already knows your weaknesses and will continue to exploit them if you let him. Most people already realize the error of their ways. The best strategy is to change your thinking. If someone breaks into your house through the back door, don't you fix the door in a way that makes it impregnable, thereby preventing a future burglary? The same is true about blocking avenues into your head by the tempter. This requires one to be mindful constantly; the second you leave an opening temptation is bound to enter.

Train your brain to think the pure thought and not give birth to the thought that leads to sin. Satan will implant the temptation; it's up to you to dismiss it before giving it further consideration. This requires cognitive intervention whenever a bad habit is about to be primed or a familiar temptation is presented that might lead you into sin. Do not be a creature of habit, but of thoughtfulness and purpose. Remember that you can sin in thought, word, and deed. Thus, you are guilty by merely thinking of engaging in something sinful. Awareness of such things is the key to virtue and godliness.

- 1 KI 20:40 ~ The kind declared, "Since you were so busy doing this and that, the man you were supposed to guard escaped. That will be your penalty, for you have decided it yourself."
- MAT 5:27–28 ~ Jesus said, "You know that you should not commit adultery. I tell you that whoever looks at a woman with lust has committed adultery in his heart."
- MAT 6:21 ~ For where your treasure is there your heart will be also.
- MAT 6:33 ~ Seek first the kingdom of God and his righteousness, and everything you need will be added unto you.

- JAM 1:15 ~ When lust is conceived it brings forth sin; and sin, when finished, brings forth death.
- EPH 2:3–4 ~ In times past we also engaged in lusts of the flesh, fulfilling desires of the body and of the mind; we were by nature children of wrath, just like the rest. But because of God's great love for us we were made alive in Christ, even when we were dead in our sins. It is by that grace that you also can be saved.
- 1 JO 3:15 ~ Whosoever hates his brother is a murderer...

It takes practice and discipline to reject the wrong and focus on the right. It is true the saying, "Let your conscience be your guide," especially if Christ is your conscience. It is a life-long process, becoming conformed into the image of Christ. Staying in the Spirit brings sanctification, in which we receive the holiness of Jesus who took our sin upon Himself to gain for us an eternal inheritance equal to His.

- 1 CO 2:16 ~ For who has known the mind of God to instruct him? But we have the mind of Christ.
- 2 CO 1:12 ~ Paul wrote to the Corinthians: We rejoice in this, the conversation of our conscience, that in simplicity and godly sincerity, and not with the wisdom of this world but by the grace of God, we have given our testimony to the world, and more abundantly toward you.
- ROM 12:1–2 ~ I implore you therefore, by the mercies of God, that you present yourselves as a living sacrifice, holy and acceptable to God, which is a reasonable response to His love. Do not conform to the ways of this world, but be transformed by the renewing of your mind, and you will be able to determine what is good, acceptable, and perfect in accordance with God's will.
- TIT 1:15 ~ To the pure all things are pure. But to the defiled and unbelieving there is nothing pure; even their minds and consciences are defiled.
- HEB 2:11 ~ Both He who does the sanctifying (Christ) and those who He has sanctified are of one Spirit. Therefore, He is not ashamed to call them brothers and sisters.
- 1 JO 4:3–4 ~ Every spirit that does not confess that Jesus Christ has come in the flesh is not of God. This is the spirit of antichrist, who you have heard will come and even now is in the world. But you are of God little children, and have overcome them; because greater is He (Christ) that is in you, than he (Satan) that is in the world.

God will prosper those who choose Him, who work hard, and who place spiritual riches above worldly wealth. God will open doors of opportunity, bring the right people into your path, pave the way for success, and supply everything you need to flourish and produce good fruit—as long as you stay on the path of righteousness by following Christ. The abundance of His blessings will increase in accordance with your faith and His purpose for your life. When His plan is revealed to you it will come with a blueprint for victory. Everything you need to complete your mission will be placed into your hands, and more. Of course, you can choose to reject this wonderful opportunity and opt out of the blessings God has in store for you, but I wouldn't recommend it.

- PSA 105:42–45 ~ God remembered His holy promise, and Abraham His servant. And God brought forth His people with joy, and His chosen with gladness, and gave them the lands of the heathen. And His chosen inherited the labor of those people, so that they might observe His statutes, and keep His laws. Praise be to the Lord!
- PSA 115:13–14 ~ God will bless anyone who acknowledges Him, both great and small. He will increase you more and more, you and your children.

- PRO 13:21–22 ~ Evil pursues sinners; but to the righteous, good shall be their reward. A good man leaves an inheritance to his children's children; but the wealth of the sinner is laid up for the just.
- EZE 36:8–12 ~ God has said, "I have lifted my hand, and the heathen that surround you will bear their shame. For the mountains of Israel will shoot forth branches and produce fruit for my people Israel who are coming to possess the land. Behold, I am for you and I will return to you, and plant you and nurture you. And I will multiply your numbers, all the house of Israel; the cities will be inhabited and the ruins rebuilt. Your men and beasts will increase and bear fruit. And you will settle in the land and prosper more than you did before, so that you will know that I am the Lord. And I will multiply to you both man and beast; and they shall increase and produce fruit. Yes, I will cause Israel to inhabit and possess those lands and the people therein; that will be their inheritance, for they will nevermore oppress my people or deprive them of their children."
- LUK 12:16–21 ~ Jesus spoke a parable to them: The land of a certain rich man produced plentifully, and the man thought to himself, "What shall I do? I haven't enough room for all the fruits of my labor. I know what I'll do. I'll tear down the barns and build bigger ones." And the man decided, "Since I have so much wealth, I'll just take it easy and eat, drink, and be merry." But God said to him, "You fool, tonight your soul will be required. And who will possess all those things for which you have worked so hard?" Jesus concluded: Those that accumulate treasures for themselves are not rich towards God.
- ROM 8:28 ~ All things work towards good for those who love God and are called according to His purpose
- 1 CO 3:7 ~ Those who plant and those who water are nothing by themselves; because it is God that provides the increase.

Most everything in this world is available to you insofar as you can obtain it, as long as it is in accordance with God's will, in which case He will assist you in attaining it. Nothing is impossible with God so there is no reason to refrain from pursuing something great, because greatness has been programmed into each and every one of us. In other words, everybody has potential for excellence; but not necessarily in the same things. Though with hard work, we can master things that we are not naturally good or talented at, as long as we place God first in our lives.

Granted, there are some things that we cannot choose. For example, we cannot choose our gender, ethnicity, age, genetics, or relatives. Furthermore, we cannot control the past, other people, the weather, the truth, and the universe. Interestingly, we have no need to change or control any of these things to achieve whatever we aspire, and to be successful in any field of education or vocation. And even when bad things happen, God will make this work in your favor in the end, so there is no reason to lose hope (GEN 50:19–20; EST 4:14; ROM 8:28).

Exceptionalism is available to everyone if they accept Christ and receive His Spirit, so go ahead and dream big. Remember, God will prosper you in this life. And you cannot fathom what He has in store for you in the next life. The Lord gives us all good things, and even better when we make it home; and all He wants back from us is our love. Choose God to be your Father, receive His parental love and mercy, love Him above all others, and He will choose you to be His child—forever. This is the easiest choice there is, and with it comes the ultimate reward. Choose Christ and you have chosen life.

CHAPTER FIVE

HOW CAN I BE SPIRITUAL?

SPIRITUAL TREASURES

The most important things in life are spiritual. Spiritual blessings include love, faith, hope, patience, and trust, with love being the most important and powerful. Additional spiritual treasures include mercy, peace, joy, truth, and understanding. Worldly possessions are worthless in heaven, so we must strive for spiritual wealth not material wealth which does not last. That is, we must seek the kingdom of heaven and the righteousness of God, not earthly pleasures or riches. We should focus first on our spiritual life and not our physical life. If you seek God and the spiritual things in life, you will keep your soul. The soul is the most valuable thing humans possess. If you give yourself over to evil, you will forfeit your soul in the end.

- PSA 37:16 ~ Better is the little that the righteous have, than the abundance of many wicked people.
- PSA 73:25 ~ Who do I have in heaven but you, Lord? And there is nothing on earth that I desire but you.
- PSA 85:8,10 ~ Let me listen to what the Lord has to say, for He speaks peace to His people, to His saints, and to all who turn their hearts to Him. Steadfast love and truth will meet; righteousness and peace will kiss each other.
- PRO 13:8 ~ The ransom of a person's life equates to wealth; being poor equates to having no means of redemption.
- ISA 32:17 ~ The results of righteousness are peace and trust forever.
- ZEC 8:16,19 ~ Do these things: Speak the truth and render decisions that bring truth and peace; exercise love, truth, and peace.
- MAT 3:2; MAT 4:17 ~ Jesus said, "Repent, for the kingdom of heaven is at hand."
- MAT 5:12 ~ Jesus said, "Rejoice, for your reward in heaven is great."
- MAT 6:19–21 ~ Jesus said, "Don't lay-up treasures on earth. Lay-up treasures in heaven, where they will not decay and cannot be stolen. For where your treasure is, there your heart will be."
- MAT 7:21 ~ Jesus said, "Not everyone who says to me 'Lord, Lord' will enter the kingdom of heaven, but only those who do my Father's will."
- MAT 10:28 ~ Jesus said, "Don't fear those who can kill the body but not the soul. Rather, fear Him who can destroy both the body and soul in hell."
- MAT 16:26 ~ Jesus said, "What does it profit a person who gains the world but loses his soul? What can a person give in return for his soul?"
- LUK 12:30–32 ~ Jesus said, "All these things (e.g., food, drink, clothes, etc.) people of all nations seek after; your Father in heaven knows that you need these things. If you seek the kingdom of God first, He will give it to you, and He will add these other things as well. It is God's desire to give His kingdom to you."

- LUK 21:19 ~ Jesus said, "In your patience, you possess your souls."
- JOH 20:29 ~ Jesus said, "Blessed are those who have not seen and still believe".
- ROM 9:22–23 ~ God has endured in His patience, withholding His wrath, in order to make known the riches of His glory and mercy.
- 1 CO 12:31 ~ We all hold dear our best gifts, especially the gift of God's excellent Holy Spirit.
- 1 CO 13:13 ~ Faith, hope, and love abide, but the greatest of these three is love.
- 2 CO 8:9 ~ You know the grace of our Lord Jesus Christ, that though He was rich yet for your sakes He became poor, so that you, through His poverty, might become rich.
- EPH 2:7 ~ In the coming ages He will show the immeasurable riches of His grace in kindness towards us through Jesus Christ.
- EPH 6:9; COL 4:1 ~ He, who is the master of all, is in heaven, and He is always impartial.
- PHP 4:19 ~ God will supply every need according to His riches in the glory of Jesus Christ.
- COL 1:27; COL 2:2–3 ~ God chose to make known the great riches in the glory of His mystery, which is Christ in you, the hope of glory. The riches come from assured understanding and knowledge of God's mystery of Christ, in whom all the treasures of wisdom and knowledge abide.
- 1 TH 5:8 ~ Let us be sober, and put on the breastplate of faith and love, and for a helmet the hope of salvation.
- 2 TI 2:22 ~ Shun youthful passions and aim at righteousness, faith, love, and peace, along with those who call upon the Lord with a pure heart.
- 2 PE 1:5–8 ~ Fruits of the spirit include giving, faith, virtue, knowledge, temperance, patience, godliness, kindness, and brotherly love. If you possess these traits you will be fruitful for Christ.
- 2 JO 1:3 ~ Grace, mercy and peace be with you, from God our Father, and from Jesus Christ His Son, in truth and love.
- JDE 1:2 ~ May mercy, peace, and love be multiplied in you.

Love and Charity

Love is the most powerful force in the universe, and the very essence and inspiration of God. It is our connection to Him, to each other, and to all creation. Without love, we become disconnected and aimless. With it we can conquer fear, be a light of hope to others, and possibly win them over to Christ.

- LEV 19:18 ~ Do not take revenge or bear a grudge but love your neighbor as yourself.
- DEU 6:5 ~ You must love the Lord your God with all your heart, soul, and might.
- DEU 10:19 ~ Love strangers for you were strangers once.
- PSA 145:20 ~ The Lord preserves all who love Him, but He will destroy the wicked.
- PRO 8:13,17,21,36 ~ To fear God is to hate evil. God loves those who love Him and seek Him, and He gives them wealth and treasures. All who hate God love death.
- AMO 5:15 ~ Hate evil, love goodness, and establish justice.
- ZEC 8:17 ~ Don't devise evil in your heart against others or swear falsely against them, because these things the Lord hates.
- MAT 5:44 ~ Jesus said, "Love your enemies; bless those who curse you; do good to those who hate you, and pray for those who take advantage of you and abuse you."

- MAT 22:37–40 ~ Jesus said, "Love the Lord your God with all your heart, mind, and soul: this is the first and greatest commandment. The second is like unto the first: Love your neighbor as yourself. All the laws and the prophets depend on these two commandments."
- LUK 6:32,35 ~ Jesus said, "If you love only those who love you, what reward do you receive? Even sinners love those who love them. Love everyone, even your enemies. Help others whenever you can, expecting nothing in return, and your reward will be great, and you will be a child of God."
- JOH 3:16 ~ God loved the world so much that He gave His only begotten Son, so that anyone who believed in Him would never die but would live forever.
- JOH 14:21 ~ Jesus said, "Those who keep my commandments love me; whoever loves me is loved by my Father and me, and they will know who I am."
- JOH 15:12–13 ~ Jesus said, "Love each other as I have loved you. No greater love exists than to give one's life for their friends."
- ROM 13:10 ~ Love does no wrong to a neighbor; therefore, love is the fulfilling of the Law.
- 1 CO 13:2–8,13 ~ Even if you have the gift of prophecy, can understand mysteries, and have a faith to move mountains, you are nothing without love. Even if you give all you have to the poor, you profit nothing if you don't have love. Love is patient. Love is kind. Love is never envious or conceited. Love is not rude, self-seeking, or angered, nor does it find pleasure in sin. Love does not think of sinful things nor is it provoked by evil. Love rejoices in the truth. Love always protects, always trusts, always hopes, and always endures. Love never fails... Faith, hope, and love abide; but the greatest of these three is love.
- GAL 5:6,22 ~ In Jesus Christ there is neither circumcised nor uncircumcised, but there is faith working through love. The fruits of the Spirit include love, joy, peace, patience, kindness, goodness, faithfulness, gentleness, and self-control. There is no law against these things.
- COL 3:14 ~ Above all, put on love, which binds all things together in perfect harmony.
- 1 TI 6:10–11 ~ The love of money is the root of all evil; through the craving for worldly riches many have wandered away from the faith and pierced their hearts. Strive for righteousness, godliness, faith, love, steadfastness, and gentleness.
- JAM 2:5 ~ God has chosen those who are poor in the world to be rich in faith, and heirs of the kingdom He promised to all who love Him.
- 1 PE 1:22 ~ Purify your souls by obedience to the truth and earnest love for one another.
- 1 PE 3:8 ~ Have unity of mind, sympathy, love for one another, a tender heart, and a humble mind.
- 1 PE 4:8 ~ Above all love one another, for love covers a multitude of sins.
- 1 JO 2:15 ~ Don't love the world or worldly things, because you can't love the world and God at the same time.
- 1 JO 3:1,10,16–18 ~ The Father has given us such love as to be called His children, and so we are. There are children of God and there are children of the devil. Those who do what is righteous and who love one another are of God and those who don't are not of God. We can understand the love of God because He gave His life for us; therefore, we should be willing to give our lives out of brotherly love. Those who have the means to help their fellow man and do not must not have the love of God in them. My children, let us not love just in writing or in voice, let us show it in action and in truth.
- 1 JO 4:7–12,16–21 ~ Let us love one another, for love is from God, and those who love are born of God and know Him. If you don't love God you can't know Him because God is love. The love of God was manifested among us through His only Son, so we might live through Him. If God loves us so much, we should love one another; if we love one another, God lives

in us and His love is perfected in us. If you abide in love you abide in God, and God abides in you. This perfect love gives us confidence on the day of judgment, because there is no fear in love but perfect love destroys fear, because fear brings torment. We love because God loved us first. You can't say you love God and hate your brother without being a liar, because you can't hate someone you have seen and still love God who you have never seen. So, you should love God and your brother (neighbor).

Grace and Mercy

We are saved by the abundant grace and mercy of God, not by any excellence, power, or performance of our own. Grace is unmerited favor: receiving good things which are not earned such as salvation. Mercy is unmerited exoneration: not receiving unpleasant things that are deserved such as punishment. These are free gifts which are worth more than all worldly riches combined, for it is the price of the soul which is being weighed in the balance. Accept these treasures, thank and praise God for such blessings, and remain steadfast in your faith in Christ to keep your soul; otherwise, surrender these treasures willingly and lose all.

- DEU 7:9 ~ God is faithful and keeps His promises; He is merciful to those who love Him and keep His commandments.
- PSA 23:6 ~ Surely goodness and mercy will follow me all the days of my life and I will live in the house of the Lord forever.
- PSA 84:11 ~ The Lord is our sun and shield; He will give grace and glory to all who walk in righteousness.
- PSA 86:15 ~ Oh Lord, you are full of compassion, grace, and patience, and are plentiful in mercy and truth.
- PSA 100:5 ~ The Lord is good; His mercy is everlasting. His truth endures to all generations.
- PSA 103:8 ~ The Lord is merciful and gracious, slow to anger, and generous in mercy.
- PRO 16:6 ~ By mercy and truth sin is purged; by the fear of the Lord people can depart from evil.
- PRO 21:21 ~ Those who follow after righteousness and mercy will find life, righteousness, and honor.
- HOS 10:12 ~ Sow righteousness and reap mercy. It is time to seek the Lord, and when He comes, He will rain righteousness upon you.
- MIC 7:18 ~ There is no God like Him, who pardons sin and overlooks the evil of His children. He doesn't retain His anger because He delights in mercy.
- MAT 5:7 ~ Jesus said, "Blessed are the merciful, for they shall obtain mercy."
- JOH 1:14,16–17 ~ The Word was made flesh and lived among us; and we saw the glory of the only begotten Son of the Father, full of grace and truth. Of His fullness we all have received, Grace for grace. For the Law was given by Moses, but Grace and Truth came through Jesus Christ.
- ROM 5:20–21 ~ Where sin abounded, grace abounded even more. As sin reigned unto death, even so, grace reigns through righteousness unto eternal life through Jesus Christ our Lord.
- 2 CO 8:9 ~ You know the grace of our Lord Jesus Christ, that though He was rich, yet for your sakes He became poor, that you, through His poverty, might become rich.
- 2 CO 9:8 ~ God can make grace abound toward you, so that you, always having everything you need, may abound in good works.
- 2 CO 12:7–10 ~ So that I (Paul) would not exalt myself by the many revelations God showed me, I was given a thorn in the flesh, a messenger of Satan to buffet me. I prayed to the Lord thrice, that it might depart from me. He replied to me, "My grace is sufficient for you

because my strength is made perfect in weakness." Therefore, I will gladly revel in my infirmities, so that the power of Christ may rest upon me. That is, I take pleasure in illness, reproach, hunger, persecution, and distress for Christ's sake; for when I am weak, then I become strong.
- TIT 2:11 ~ The grace of God that brings salvation has appeared to everybody.
- TIT 3:5,7 ~ He saved us, not because of our works of righteousness, but according to His mercy by the washing of regeneration and renewing by the Holy Spirit. Being justified by His grace, we are made heirs according to the hope of eternal life.
- HEB 4:16 ~ Let us come boldly to the throne of Grace, that we may obtain mercy and find grace to help in time of need.
- JAM 4:6 ~ He resists the proud but gives grace to the humble.
- 1 PE 4:10 ~ As everyone has received the gift of love, even so minister the same to one another, as good stewards of the manifold grace of God.

Faith and Works

We are saved by the grace of God through our faith in Jesus Christ. Works cannot save us no matter how many of them are good. We willingly demonstrate our faith through good works and love. We cannot be Christians with only works or only faith, but faith is activated by our love and demonstrated in our actions. Simply put, faith precedes action; works cannot produce faith which is another gift of the Holy Spirit. Because we believe, we feel compelled to declare it and shine the love of Christ; if we do not, our faith is unproductive since others cannot see Christ in us. If others cannot see Christ in you, will God? Christ is our only means to connect with God through love, which energizes faith, then hope, followed by sharing and giving.

- PSA 37:5–6 ~ Commit your way to the Lord and trust in Him, and He will vindicate you.
- HAB 2:4 ~ Those whose souls are not upright will fail; but the just will live by faith.
- EZE 33:13 ~ Those who are righteous will surely live. But if you trust in righteousness and continue to sin, none of your righteous deeds will be remembered; and the sin will cause you to die.
- MAT 5:16 ~ Jesus said, "Let your light shine before others so that people may see your good works and glorify God because of them."
- MAT 7:20 ~ Jesus said, "You will know them by the fruit that they bear" (fruits of the Spirit).
- MAT 17:20 ~ Jesus said, "If you had faith the size of a mustard seed you could move mountains; nothing would be impossible."
- MAT 21:22 ~ Jesus said, "Whatever you pray for in faith you will receive."
- MAT 25:40 ~ Jesus said, "Whatever you did to even the most insignificant person you did to me."
- MAR 11:24 ~ Jesus said, "Pray, believing you will receive, and you will."
- LUK 18:18–30 ~ A certain ruler asked Jesus, "What can I do to inherit eternal life?" Jesus told him to sell everything, give the money to the poor, and follow Him. This made the man sad. Jesus told those present how hard it is for the rich to enter heaven. "Who can be saved," the people asked Jesus. Jesus answered, "What is impossible for men is possible with God."
- JOH 15:4–5 ~ Jesus said, "A branch can't bear fruit by itself unless it abides with the vine. I am the vine and you are the branches. If you abide in me you will bear much fruit, but apart from me you can do nothing."
- ROM 3:21–22 ~ The righteousness of God is apart from the Law, although the Law and the prophets bear witness to it. Righteousness from God exists through faith in Jesus Christ.

- ROM 4:6 ~ God blesses those who are righteous, apart from their works.
- ROM 10:10,17 ~ Those who believe with their hearts are justified. Those who confess with their lips are saved. Faith comes by hearing and hearing by the Word of God.
- GAL 2:16,20–21 ~ Nobody is justified by works of the Law, but by faith in Jesus Christ. I have been crucified with Christ; thus, it is no longer I who live but Christ who lives in me. And the life I live in the flesh I live by faith in the Son of God who gave His life for me. I do not discount God's grace, for if righteousness came by the Law, then Christ died in vain.
- GAL 3:11,24,26 ~ No man is justified before God by the Law, but those who are righteous through faith shall live. The Law was in effect until Christ came, that we might be justified by faith. In Christ we can become children of God through faith.
- GAL 5:5–6 ~ Through the Spirit, by faith, we wait for the hope of righteousness. Circumcision is of no avail; instead it is faith working through love.
- EPH 2:8–9 ~ You are saved by the grace of God because of your faith in Jesus Christ. Salvation is a gift of God, it cannot be earned through good works, so nobody should brag.
- 2 TI 1:9 ~ God saved us and called us, not by virtue of our works, but by virtue of His own purpose and the grace He gave us through Jesus Christ ages ago.
- TIT 3:5–8 ~ He didn't save us because of our deeds done in righteousness, but because of His mercy given us through the regeneration and renewal in the Holy Spirit by Jesus Christ, so we can be justified by faith and become heirs in hope of eternal life. Those who have believed will apply themselves to perform good deeds.
- HEB 10:11 ~ Every priest stands daily at his service, offering repeatedly the same sacrifices which can never take away his sins.
- HEB 11:1,3,6 ~ Faith is the assurance of things hoped for, the evidence of things not seen. By faith we understand that the world was created by the Word of God, such that things we see were made from things which do not appear. Without faith, it is impossible to please God, for whoever would wish to come to Him must believe He exists and that He rewards those who seek Him.
- HEB 11:7–38 ~ With faith, the great prophets were able to endure anything and performed great feats, such as subduing kingdoms, escaping certain death, overcoming incredible odds, healing the sick, and even raising the dead.
- HEB 12:2 ~ Jesus Christ is the author and finisher of our faith.
- JAM 2:17–26 ~ Faith without works is dead. Was Abraham justified by works when he offered his son Isaac? Faith was active before that and was completed by the works. So, a person is justified also by works and not faith alone. Just as a body apart from the spirit is dead, so is faith apart from works.
- 1 PE 1:3–4,9 ~ Through God's mercy we have been born anew to a living hope by the resurrection of Jesus Christ, to receive an inheritance which is imperishable, undefiled, and unfading, kept in heaven for all believers. The outcome of faith in Jesus is salvation of the soul.
- 2 PE 1:5–8 ~ Supplement your faith with virtue, your virtue with knowledge, your knowledge with self-control, your self-control with steadfastness, your steadfastness with godliness, and your godliness with brotherly love. If these are yours and they abound, they will keep you from being fruitless and ineffective.

Hope and Trust

Trust in Christ for He is your only hope of salvation. Just as faith is an extension of your love, hope is an extension of your faith. Hope keeps us looking forward at the opportunities, blessings, and possibilities rather than backward at the setbacks, transgressions, suffering, and the lack of taking action when we should have. Hope and trust produce confidence and courage to face what lies ahead, while reducing uncertainty when it is decision time.

- JOB 4:6–7 ~ Isn't your fear of God your confidence, and the integrity of your ways your hope? Did the innocent ever perish?
- JOB 8:13–14 ~ The destiny of those who forget God is the loss of hope, for their trust in worldly things is a fragile one.
- JOB 11:18,20 ~ You will be confident because there is hope; you will be protected, so take rest in your safety. But the wicked will not escape; their hope will be like taking their last breath.
- JOB 27:8 ~ What is the hope of the hypocrite who has prospered, when God takes away his soul?
- JOB 31:24–28 ~ If I placed my hope and confidence in wealth, and I rejoiced in how much of it I had attained, or if I was enticed by the beauty of the sun and moon such that they became an object of my affection, I would be guilty of disregarding God.
- PSA 5:11 ~ Let all who trust in God rejoice and sing for joy, for God will defend them; and those that love God will exalt in Him.
- PSA 16:9 ~ My heart is glad and my soul rejoices; my body abides in hope.
- PSA 31:24 ~ Be strong and let your heart take courage, you who hope in the Lord.
- PSA 33:18; PSA 147:11 ~ The eye of the Lord is on those who fear Him and who hope in His steadfast love.
- PSA 56:3,11 ~ Whenever I'm afraid, I trust in God. If I trust in God without fear, what can humankind do to me?
- PSA 62:8,10 ~ Trust in God always and pour out your heart to Him. He is your refuge. Don't trust in extortion; don't hope in robbery. Don't set your heart on earthly riches even if they are abundant.
- PSA 130:5 ~ I wait for the Lord, my soul waits; and in His Word I have hope.
- PRO 3:5 ~ Trust in the Lord with all your heart, and don't rely on your own insight.
- PRO 10:28 ~ The hope of the righteous ends in gladness, but the expectation of the wicked comes to nothing.
- PRO 13:12 ~ Hope deferred makes the heart sick, but a desire fulfilled is a tree of life.
- PRO 29:25 ~ The fear of man is a trap; but those who trust in the Lord will be safe.
- ISA 42:17 ~ Those who trust in idols and false gods will be utterly put to shame.
- JER 31:17 ~ There is hope for your future says the Lord, and your children will come back to their own country.
- LAM 3:21–22 ~ I have hope because the steadfast love of the Lord never ceases and His mercies never end.
- ACT 2:26–27 ~ My heart is glad and my tongue rejoices; my body abides in hope. For the Lord will not destroy my soul in hell.
- ACT 26:6–7 ~ I (Paul) stand here on trial for my hope in the promise made by God to our forefathers, which our twelve tribes hope to attain as they earnestly worship day and night. For this hope I am accused.

- ROM 4:18–19 ~ In hope he (Abraham) believed against hope that he would become the father of many nations as he had been told. He did not weaken in faith although his body was old and weak and although his wife's womb was barren.
- ROM 5:2–5 ~ Through Him (Jesus) we have obtained access to His grace in which we stand, and we rejoice in our hope of sharing the glory of God. We rejoice in our sufferings knowing that they produce endurance, which produces character, which produces hope. And hope does not disappoint us, because God's love has been poured into our hearts through the Holy Spirit.
- ROM 8:19–20,24–25 ~ All creation waits eagerly for the revealing of the children of God. For the creation was subjected to futility, not of its own will, but by the will of Him who subjected it in hope. In this hope we were saved. However, hope that is seen is not really hope; for who hopes for what one has? But if we hope for what we don't see, we must wait for it patiently.
- ROM 12:12 ~ Rejoice in your hope, be patient in tribulation, and be constant in prayer.
- ROM 15:13 ~ May the God of hope fill you with all joy and peace in believing, so that by the power of the Holy Spirit you may abound in hope.
- PHP 1:20 ~ It is my expectation and hope that I will never be ashamed; but with courage, Christ will always be honored in my body, whether by life or by death.
- COL 1:23,27 ~ Continue steadfast in the faith, not shifting from the hope of the Gospel... The riches of the wonder of His mystery, which is Christ in you, is the hope of glory.
- 1 TH 5:8 ~ Let us be sober, and put on the breastplate of faith and love, and for a helmet, the hope of salvation.
- 1 TI 4:10 ~ We toil and strive because of hope in the Lord our Savior.
- 1 TI 6:17 ~ Tell the rich people in the world not to act so proud or to set their hopes on uncertain earthly riches. Tell them to set their hope and trust in God, who furnishes everything in this world for us to enjoy.

Peace and Joy

The immeasurable joy and peace that can be found in Christ will last forever. As soon as you receive Christ you will realize a peace which surpasses all human understanding (PHP 4:7) and a joy that will never be taken away from you (JOH 16:22). Worry and anxiety are incompatible with peace and joy. If you feel the former you cannot feel the latter, because peace and joy are more powerful and can defeat worry and anxiety. The positive thought overpowers the negative one if your focus is Jesus. If you focus on the world alone, there is much negativity to be found.

- PSA 5:11 ~ Let everyone who trusts in the Lord rejoice and shout for joy, because He will defend them. Let all who love the Lord be joyful.
- PSA 16:11 ~ The Lord will show me the path of life. In His presence is fullness of joy; at His right hand are pleasures forevermore.
- PSA 34:14 ~ Depart from evil and do good; seek peace and pursue it.
- PSA 37:37 ~ Take notice of those who are blameless and upright, for they will find a peaceful end.
- PSA 51:12 ~ Restore unto me the joy of your salvation, Lord, and don't take your Holy Spirit from me.
- PSA 119:165 ~ Those who love God's Law have great peace; nothing can make them stumble.

- PSA 122:6–7 ~ Pray for peace; may those prosper who love God. Peace be within your walls and security within your towers.
- PRO 12:20 ~ Deceit is in the heart of those who imagine evil things; but for the counselors of peace is joy.
- ECC 2:26 ~ God gives to those who are good in His sight wisdom, knowledge, and joy; but to the sinner He gives hardship.
- ISA 9:6–7 ~ His name will be called Wonderful Counselor, Mighty God, Everlasting Father, and Prince of Peace. There will be no end to His reign and His peace.
- ISA 26:3 ~ Those whose minds are set on God and trust in Him will be kept in perfect peace.
- ISA 35:10 ~ The ransomed of the Lord will return singing songs of everlasting joy; they will have joy and gladness, and sorrow and sighing will be gone forever.
- ISA 48:22; ISA 57:21 ~ The Lord says there is no peace for the wicked.
- ISA 53:5 ~ He was wounded and bruised for our sins, His punishment bought our peace, and His wounds healed us.
- ISA 54:10 ~ The mountains and hills may be removed, but His steadfast love will never depart, and His covenant of peace will be forever.
- HAB 3:18 ~ I will rejoice in the Lord and find joy in the God of my salvation.
- MAL 2:5 ~ The Lord's covenant was one of life and peace...
- LUK 1:79 ~ Jesus came to give light to those who are in darkness or in the shadow of death, and to guide us in the way of peace.
- LUK 2:10–11 ~ The angel said to the shepherds, "Don't be afraid because I bring you tidings of great joy which shall be for all people; for Christ the Savior is born today in the city of David."
- LUK 6:22–23 ~ Jesus said, "Blessed are those who are hated and cast out for my sake. Rejoice in that day and leap for joy for your reward in heaven will be great."
- LUK 15:7 ~ Jesus said, "More joy shall be in heaven for one repenting sinner, than for ninety-nine who need no repentance."
- JOH 14:27 ~ Jesus said, "Peace I leave you; my peace I give you; I do not give as the world gives, so never let your hearts be troubled or afraid."
- JOH 16:20–22 ~ Jesus said to the apostles, "I tell you the truth, you will weep and lament but the world will rejoice. You will be sorrowful but your sorrow will turn to joy, just like when a mother in labor groans but when her child is born her pain is replaced with happiness. I will see you again and your heart will rejoice; and nobody will ever take that joy away from you."
- JOH 16:33 ~ Jesus said, "I have told you that I will bring you peace. In the world you will have tribulation; but be happy because I have overcome the world."
- ACT 5:41 ~ They were glad that they were counted worthy to suffer shame in the name of Jesus Christ.
- ROM 2:10 ~ Glory, honor, and peace is given to all who do good, regardless of race.
- ROM 8:6 ~ To set the mind on the flesh results in death, but to set the mind on the Spirit results in life and peace.
- ROM 14:17,19 ~ The kingdom of God does not mean food and drink, but righteousness, peace, and joy in the Holy Spirit. Let us therefore seek that which results in peace and mutual uplifting.
- 1 CO 14:33 ~ God is not a God of confusion; He is a God of peace.
- 2 CO 13:11 ~ Mend your ways, agree with each other, live in peace; and the God of love and peace will be with you.
- EPH 4:3 ~ Maintain unity of the Spirit in the bond of peace.

- PHP 4:7 ~ May the peace of God which surpasses all understanding keep your hearts and minds through Christ Jesus.
- COL 3:15 ~ Let the peace of Christ rule in your hearts; for this you were called into one body.
- 2 TH 3:16 ~ May the Lord of peace Himself give you His peace at all times and in all ways.
- HEB 12:14 ~ Strive for peace with everyone, and for holiness; for without these things, nobody can see the Lord.
- JAM 3:18 ~ The harvest of righteousness is sown in peace by those who make peace.
- 1 PE 4:13 ~ Rejoice when you are partakers of Christ's sufferings; for when His glory is revealed, you will be glad and exceedingly joyful. You will be happy for being rejected by men because you know Christ and His Spirit rests upon you.

Truth, Wisdom, Knowledge, and Understanding

We must never lose sight of the source of all knowledge and truth, which is the Holy Spirit the very Word of God. Further, we should continually feed upon and digest the Holy Bible all the days of our lives. The more you read the greater your understanding, and the more equipped you become to share the truth with patience and humility (1 PE 3:15).

- 1 SA 2:3 ~ Don't talk proudly or arrogantly, for the Lord is a God of knowledge, and by Him all your actions are weighed.
- 1 KI 3:9,11–12,28 ~ Solomon prayed, "Give to your servant an understanding heart to judge our people, so I may discern between good and evil; for who is able to judge so great a people." God replied, "Since you have asked for wisdom instead of long life, riches, or death upon your enemies, I will give you a wise and understanding heart; nobody else before you or after you will be as wise." And all of Israel saw that the wisdom of God was in Solomon.
- JOB 12:12–13 ~ With age comes wisdom and understanding. With God is wisdom and strength, counsel and understanding.
- JOB 28:12–13,18,28 ~ Where is wisdom found, and where is the place of understanding? We don't know the price of these, nor can they be found in the land of the living. The price of wisdom is above rubies. God said to humanity, "The fear of the Lord, that is wisdom; and to depart from evil, that is understanding."
- PSA 25:5 ~ Lead me in your truth, and teach me; for you are a God of salvation, and on you I will wait all day.
- PSA 51:6 ~ God desires truth inwardly, and inside my heart He will give me wisdom.
- PSA 86:11 ~ Teach me your ways Lord and I will walk in your truth; unite my heart to fear your name.
- PSA 90:12 ~ Teach us to number our days so we may apply our hearts to wisdom.
- PSA 111:10 ~ The fear of the Lord is the beginning of wisdom; understanding is found in obeying His commandments.
- PSA 119:34,66,73 ~ Give me understanding so I may keep your laws; yes, I will observe them with all my heart. Teach me good judgment and knowledge, so I may learn your commandments.
- PSA 145:18 ~ The Lord comes to all who call upon Him in truth.
- PRO 1:2–7 ~ Try to know wisdom and instruction; to perceive the words of understanding; to receive the instruction of wisdom, justice, judgment, and equity; to give subtlety to the simple; to give knowledge and discretion to the young. A wise person will listen and will increase in learning; a person of understanding will seek wise counsel, and will try to understand a proverb and its interpretation, or the words of the wise and the hidden meaning

of what they say. Remember, the fear of God is the beginning of understanding; only fools despise wisdom and instruction.
- PRO 2:2–6,10–12 ~ Incline your ears to wisdom and apply your heart to understanding. If you cry for knowledge and ask for understanding, if you seek wisdom as you would for treasures, then you will understand the fear of the Lord and find knowledge of God. For God gives wisdom, knowledge, and understanding. When wisdom enters your heart and knowledge is pleasant to your soul, discretion will preserve you and understanding will keep you to deliver you from evil.
- PRO 8:13 ~ To fear the Lord is to hate evil, pride and arrogance, evil ways, and the loose tongue.
- PRO 10:23 ~ It is the sport of fools to do mischief, but a person of understanding is wise.
- PRO 11:9,12 ~ A hypocrite can destroy his neighbor with his mouth, but through knowledge the just will be delivered. Those who are void of wisdom despise their neighbors, but a person of wisdom holds his peace.
- PRO 12:19 ~ The lips of truth will be established forever, but a lying tongue is just for the moment.
- PRO 14:6,8,16,29 ~ A scornful person seeks wisdom but doesn't find it; however, knowledge is easy for those who understand. The wisdom of the prudent is to understand where they are going, but the folly of fools is deceit. Wise people shy away from and depart from evil, but the fool rages on with confidence. Those who are slow to anger have great understanding, but those who are hasty produce folly.
- PRO 17:27–28 ~ Those who have knowledge spare their words, and a person of understanding has an excellent spirit. Even fools, if they hold their peace, are considered wise; those who shut their mouths are considered to be people of understanding.
- PRO 24:5,14 ~ A wise person is strong and a person of knowledge becomes stronger. So shall the knowledge of wisdom be to your soul; when you find it, you will be rewarded.
- ECC 2:26 ~ God gives to those who are good in His sight wisdom, knowledge, and joy; but to the sinful He gives hardship.
- ECC 5:3,7 ~ The more the words, the lesser the meaning.
- ECC 7:12,25 ~ Wisdom is a defense, and money is a defense; but wisdom gives life to those who possess it. I applied my heart to know, to search, and to seek wisdom, and the reasons for things, and to know the wickedness of folly, foolishness, and madness.
- ISA 11:2 ~ The Spirit of the Lord will give Him (Messiah) the spirit of wisdom, understanding, counsel and might, knowledge, and the fear of the Lord.
- ISA 33:6 ~ Wisdom and understanding will be your stability, and strength your salvation; the fear of the Lord is treasure.
- JER 9:23–24 ~ The Lord says, "The wise should not glory in their wisdom, nor the mighty in their might, nor the rich in their riches. Those who glory should glory in the fact that they know and understand God who exercises love, judgment, and righteousness in the earth; for in these things I delight."
- DAN 2:23 ~ Daniel prayed, "I thank and praise you God of my fathers who has given me wisdom and might, and has revealed to me your secrets."
- JOH 3:21 ~ Jesus said, "Those who live in truth come to the light, and their deeds are shown to be from God."
- JOH 4:24 ~ Jesus said, "God is Spirit and should be worshipped in spirit and in truth."
- JOH 8:31–32 ~ Jesus said, "If you continue in my Word, then you are indeed my disciples, and you will know the truth, and the truth will set you free."

- JOH 16:13 ~ Jesus said, "When the Spirit of truth comes, He will guide you in all truth. He will not speak of Himself, but will show you things to come."
- JOH 18:37–38 ~ Pilate asked Jesus if He was a king. Jesus replied, "My kingdom is not of this world. I was born so I could give witness to the truth. Everyone who searches for truth hears my voice." Pilate then asked, "What is truth?"
- ROM 1:18–20 ~ God's wrath is revealed from heaven against the sinfulness of people, who know the truth of unrighteousness, because God has made it known to them. The invisible qualities of God are clearly seen from the creation of the world, for through His many creations one can understand God, even His power and divine nature, so nobody has an excuse for being evil.
- 1 CO 1:19–27,31 ~ It is written: I will destroy the wisdom of the wise and bring to nothing the understanding of the prudent. Where is wisdom? Hasn't God made foolish the wisdom of this world? The world through its wisdom cannot know God. The Jews want a sign and the Gentiles want wisdom. But we preach to them about Christ's crucifixion, which to the Jews is an obstacle and to the Gentiles is foolishness. But Christ is the power and wisdom of God to all that are called, both Jews and Gentiles. The foolishness of God is wiser than the wisdom of humankind. The weakness of God is stronger than the strength of people. You can see that not many of those who are wise, mighty, and noble by earthly standards, are called by God. But God has chosen the foolish things of this world to confuse the wise, and the weak things of this world to confound the mighty. Those who glory, let them glory in the Lord only.
- 1 CO 2:7–16 ~ We speak the wisdom of God as a mystery, even the hidden wisdom of God, which He ordained and which none of the rulers of this world knew, otherwise they wouldn't have crucified Christ. It is written: Eyes have not seen, nor ears heard, nor the heart discerned the things that God has prepared for those who love Him. God has revealed these things to us by His Spirit; for the Spirit searches everything, even the deepest things of God. These things we speak, not in the words which humanity teaches, but which the Holy Spirit teaches, comparing spiritual things with spiritual. But natural people do not receive spiritual things of God for these things are foolishness to them; neither can they know these things because they need to be discerned spiritually. But those who are spiritual analyze everything and are judged by nobody. Nobody knows the mind of God that they can instruct Him, but those who are spiritual have the mind of Christ.
- 2 CO 4:6 ~ God, who commanded the light to shine out of darkness, shines in our hearts, giving the light of knowledge of His glory in the face of Jesus Christ.
- EPH 5:9 ~ The fruits of the Spirit include goodness, righteousness, and truth.
- COL 2:2–3 ~ Be comforted, and bound together in love, and to the wealth of understanding and acknowledgment of the mystery of God, the Father, and Christ, in whom all the treasures of wisdom and knowledge are hidden.
- JAM 3:13–17 ~ Whoever is wise among you should show it with good conversation and meekness. But if you are bitter and envious, do not glory in it and do not tell lies. Such behavior is not from God but is from this world, sensual and evil. For where there is envy and strife, there is confusion and wickedness. But the wisdom from above is first pure, peaceable, gentle, easily approachable, full of mercy and good deeds, impartial, and never hypocritical.
- 2 PE 1:5–8 ~ In diligence, add to your faith virtue, knowledge, temperance, patience, godliness, kindness, and charity. For if these things flourish in you, you will never be barren or unfruitful in the knowledge of our Lord Jesus Christ.

Lesson: Freedom

The root of the word freedom is *free* (i.e., no charge). Freedom is a gift from God, it is not a commodity to be bought and sold. Human beings possess certain inalienable rights that nobody can negate since they were given by God; many of our countrymen have fought to the death to ensure these liberties. To deny anyone his or her human rights is to steal that which God has given freely; to steal or subvert what God has given is a terrible offense. This country was founded on such freedoms as religion, speech, assembly, and self-preservation. These liberties were bestowed by God but some governments have tried to take them back in order to control the citizenry. This is why Americans declared independence from foreign rule, as we were not about to give up our rights. Yes, many have died to ensure these rights and still do. We thank God for such liberties and for those who have died to safeguard them, especially God's own Son.

For Christians, freedom also connotes eternal life, another free gift for those who want it. God has freed us from the bondage of sin and the penalty of death through the sacrifice of His Son Jesus Christ. We were condemned and lost, but Christ redeemed us through His atoning sacrifice. There is nothing we can do to earn this valuable gift because it is free. Christ sets us free, with the perfect freedom that can come only from God.

God freely has given us the Spirit of life. Without it, we would die; with it we can live eternally. That same Spirit will sustain us always and forever if we accept the gift of God's Son. Anyone can receive this gift by making their bodies a holy temple of the Lord. This we accomplish by acknowledging the death and resurrection of Christ, and by inviting Him to live in us through constant prayer, worship, studying the Bible, and participation in the sacraments.

- JOB 32:8 ~ It is the Spirit in a man, the breath of the Almighty, which makes him understand.
- PSA 51:10–12 ~ Create in me a clean heart, Lord, and renew an upright spirit within me. Don't remove me from your presence and don't take your Holy Spirit from me. Restore to me the joy of your salvation, and uphold me with your free Spirit.
- ECC 12:7 ~ Upon death, the spirit returns to God who gave it.
- ISA 57:15 ~ This is what the Lord says, the one whose name is Holy, "I live in a high and holy place; I also live with those who have a contrite and humble spirit, to revive that heart and spirit."
- JOH 6:63 ~ Jesus said, "It is the spirit that gives life, not the flesh. The words I speak are of the Spirit and therefore give life."
- 1 CO 2:12–13 ~ We have received, not the spirit of the world, but the Spirit of God, so that we may know the things that God has given to us for free. We speak of these things, not in the words that the world teaches, but in words that the Holy Spirit teaches, comparing spiritual things with spiritual.
- 2 CO 3:3,17–18 ~ The Spirit of the living God has written His Word into our hearts; it is not written in ink or on tablets of stone. The Lord is that Spirit, and wherever that Spirit is there is liberty. All of us can see His glory when we look into the mirror, for we have been changed into His image by God's Holy Spirit.
- REV 21:6; REV 22:17 ~ I (God) will give all who thirst a fountain of life to drink from freely.

The ultimate freedom God has granted all people is the freedom from sin and death. That salvation is a free gift to those who believe in the atonement of Jesus Christ. When we are set free by the blood of Christ, we have an eternal freedom that can never fade or be taken away.

- ISA 61:1–3 ~ The Spirit of God is upon me, because He has directed me to preach His good news to the humble, to heal the broken hearted, to free the slaves, and to release those who are bound in chains and in prison; to proclaim the Lord's favor and His vengeance, to comfort all who mourn, and to tell those who mourn to exchange their ashes for beauty; to replace mourning with joy, and to don the garment of praise in exchange for the spirit of sorrow, so that they may be trees of righteousness, planted by the Lord for His glorification.
- JOH 8:31–32,36 ~ Jesus said, "If you believe in my words then you are indeed my disciples; and you will know the truth and the truth will set you free. If the Son of God sets you free, you will definitely be free."
- ROM 3:23–24 ~ All people have sinned and come short of God's glory, and all people are justified freely by His grace through the redemption that is in Jesus Christ.
- ROM 5:14–18 ~ Just as the sin of one man (Adam) brought judgment and condemnation to all, so has the righteousness of one man (Christ) brought the free gift of grace, providing justification of life to all believers.
- ROM 6:14,17–18 ~ Now sin has no hold over you, for you are not under the Law you are under Grace. Thank God that we, who were servants of sin, have obeyed in our hearts that doctrine which delivers us, being made free from sin, and now serving righteousness instead.
- ROM 8:1–2,15–18,21 ~ Now there is no condemnation for those who belong to Christ and walk according to the Spirit and not the flesh. For the law of the Spirit of life in Christ has set us free from the law of sin and death. For you have not received the spirit of slavery and fear, you have received the Spirit of adoption, and for this we cry, "Thanks Dad." The Father's Spirit bears witness with our spirit that we are His children, and if children then heirs of God and joint heirs with Jesus Christ. If we suffer with Christ, we also will be glorified with Him. For the sufferings we endure are nothing compared to the glory we will receive in Him. Thus, we have been freed from chains of corruption to glorious liberty as children of God.
- EPH 2:8 ~ By the grace of God you are saved, through faith, and not by yourselves; it is a gift from God.

To enjoy the freedom that God gives, one must assume certain responsibilities. Accepting the free gift implies a change of heart. Being a child of God, we are obliged to be obedient to our Almighty Father. We must honor Him and reflect His love, for He paid a great price to bring us out of darkness into His marvelous light (1 PE 2:9). That light should shine before others so they can see that we belong to the Lord, and so they can find Him through us.

- PSA 119:44–47 ~ I will obey your laws continuously forevermore, and I will walk in freedom, for I have sought your rules. And I will boldly testify before kings, and I will delight in your commandments that I have loved.
- MAT 10:8 ~ Jesus said, "Freely you have received and freely you should give."
- 1 CO 7:22 ~ Those who were servants when called by Christ have become free, and those who were free when called by Christ have become servants. You were bought with a great price, so do not become a slave to humankind, but remain responsible to God and the purpose for which He called you.
- GAL 5:13–18 ~ Brothers, you have been called to be free men, but do not use that freedom as an excuse to engage in lusts of the flesh, but in love serve one another. For all the Law is fulfilled by loving your neighbor as yourself. So, walk in the Spirit not in the flesh. For the Spirit and the flesh oppose one another. If you are led by the Spirit you are not under the Law.

- JAM 1:22,25 ~ Don't just listen to the Law, do what it says. Whoever considers the perfect law of liberty, and continues focusing on doing what is right and not just hearing what is right, that person will be blessed because of their actions.
- 1 PE 2:13–17 ~ Submit to the laws of the land, for it is God's will that you are lawful and upright, thereby silencing those ignorant people who would talk behind your back. Be free, but do not use your freedom to conceal evil. Instead, you must serve the Lord, respect all people, love your fellow Christians, fear God, and honor those in authority.

Sometimes, it is necessary to fight for one's freedom, especially the freedom that God offers through His Son who died to set us free (JOE 3:9–14; REV 5:9–11). Be prepared to fight to the death if necessary, for the reward will be a crown of life (REV 2:10). Note that Jesus's twelve apostles (except John) died a martyr's death fighting for the faith.

Freedom is worth fighting for, and worth dying for if it sets others free. This is the fight of faith, and the enemy is daunting. That's because it is an invisible enemy which is evil to the core and very powerful. However, this enemy is no match for the Holy Spirit that lives in you if you possess an unyielding faith (1 JO 4:4).

Sometimes entire governments, religions, movements, and fads can be influenced by evil schemes and pursuits. That's why we have wars, divisions, rebellions, and strife. But the spiritual war being waged is far more impactful than worldly conflicts; because not only are there lives at stake, but people's eternal life is also at risk.

- 1 CO 9:26 ~ I (Paul) run like a man with a purpose. I do not fight like a boxer beating the air. Instead, I beat my body into shape, making it serve God's purpose, so that my preaching will not cause me to be disqualified for the prize.
- EPH 6:12 ~ We do not wrestle against flesh and blood, but against principalities, powers, rulers of darkness in this world, and wickedness in high places.
- 1 TI 6:12–13 ~ Fight the good fight of faith. Keep a firm grasp on eternal life, for this is why you were called, and why you testified before many witnesses and before God.

Now Thank We All Our God

Now thank we all our God with hearts and hands and voices,
Who wondrous things has done, in whom His world rejoices;
Who, from our mother's arms, has blessed us on our way
With countless gifts of love, and still is ours today.

Oh may this bounteous God through all our life be near us,
With ever joyful hearts and blessed peace to cheer us;
And keep us in His grace, and guide us when perplexed,
And free us from all ills, in this world and the next.

All praise and thanks to God the Father now be given,
The Son, and Him who reigns with them in highest heaven;
The one eternal God whom earth and heaven adore;
For thus it was, is now, and shall be evermore.

Lesson: Healing

All healing comes from God: Father, Son, and Holy Spirit. However, God may bestow such power on those whose faith is strong. Healing is among many spiritual gifts that Christians possess to bring people to Christ. Of course, God can employ people who are antagonistic to the faith, if it serves His agenda. Thus, one can be healed by someone without faith, if the person being healed has acquired true faith.

God the Father heals all afflictions of the body, mind, and spirit.

- DEU 32:39 ~ God says, "There is no other God like me, who can kill and bring to life, who can wound and heal. Nobody can deliver themselves or another out of my hand."
- PSA 103:2–3 ~ God forgives sins and heals diseases.

Jesus Christ heals all afflictions of the body, mind, and spirit.

- MAT 4:24 ~ Jesus's fame spread all over the country; the afflicted (diseased, tormented, crazy, lame, and possessed) were brought before Him and He healed them all.
- MAT 9:35 ~ Jesus healed every illness and disease wherever He went.
- MAT 14:35–36 ~ Everyone Jesus Christ touched and everyone who touched Him became healed (they became whole in body, mind, and spirit).

The Holy Spirit heals all afflictions of the body, mind, and spirit. God manifests this power through His people according to their faith. That is, God's people can induce healing if their faith is strong, and if God has awarded them with the spiritual gift of healing. After Jesus ascended into heaven, His apostles continued to perform acts of healing. Further, because they belonged to Christ, they had the best insurance possible against affliction, pain, and anguish. Thus, pure faith can enable someone to heal others, and also provides immunity from illness, disease, and injury.

- MAT 10:1,8; LUK 9:1–2,6 ~ Jesus sent His apostles all over the land to preach, giving them power to heal all manner of sickness and disease, as well as to heal people possessed with demons.
- LUK 10:19 ~ Jesus gave His disciples immunity over poisonous snakes and scorpions, and power over the enemy and anything harmful.
- ACT 3:2–16 ~ Peter healed a man lame from birth.
- ACT 5:11,15–16 ~ The apostles healed the sick and possessed.
- ACT 14:8–10 ~ Paul healed a man lame from birth.

Anyone to whom God has given the gift of healing will recognize God as the true source of that healing power. Most importantly, however, the person being healed must confess their faith by recognizing God as the source of his or her healing. In other words, faith is the power of the Holy Spirit to restore body, mind, and spirit, enabling a person to heal oneself by accepting God's Holy Spirit. And those bestowing the power of the Holy Spirit should recognize from whom that power originated.

- ACT 3:12–13,16 ~ Peter didn't take credit for healing the lame man. Rather, he attributed the miracle to faith in Jesus Christ, emphasizing the power that exists through faith in the name of Jesus Christ. That faith was shared by Peter and the man who was healed.
- 1 CO 12:7–10,28 ~ The manifestation of the Holy Spirit is given to everyone, and is exhibited in unique abilities and attributes including wisdom, faith, healing, miracles, prophesy, discerning spirits, interpreting tongues, etc.

Someone who claims to be a "faith healer" is probably in error. Human beings can heal nothing without God's intervention, because He is the one doing the healing. Besides, in the case of faith healing, it is the faith of the patient that matters most. That's why healing sometimes can occur, even when an imposter is posing as a minister of God.

- 2 CH 16:12–13 ~ King Asa became diseased, and the disease spread, and he died, for he had turned to the physicians for healing instead of to God.
- LUK 8:43–48 ~ The woman with the hemorrhage spent all her money on physicians and still was not healed, until she sought healing from Jesus Christ. The woman was healed the moment she touched Jesus's robe. Jesus told her that her faith is what allowed her to be healed.
- JOH 15:4–5 ~ Jesus said, "A branch cannot bear fruit unless it abides with the vine. I am the vine and you are the branches. If you abide in me you will bear much fruit, but apart from me you can do nothing."

Faith is a very powerful thing. With it comes the power to heal, as well as the power to be healed.

- MAT 17:20 ~ Faith the size of a mustard seed is sufficient to move mountains.
- HEB 11:7–38 ~ Because of their faith, the prophets endured and overcame much hardship and affliction. They performed great feats, overcame all odds, escaped certain death, healed the afflicted, cast out demons, and raised the dead.

It is resolved that the prevailing power behind the healing documented in the Bible was faith. In fact, faith was reported to be the single common denominator in virtually every example of healing performed by Christ and His apostles. Christ often informed those He healed that their faith had restored them to health. Notice in the scriptures below how the faith of the sufferer, which made them spiritually sound, was a physical remedy as well.

- 2 KI 20:1–5 ~ King Hezekiah was ill three days, but he was healed due to His faith and his prayers.
- MAT 8:5–13 ~ Jesus healed the centurion's servant. Jesus was amazed at the faith of the man, who believed that Christ had merely to give the word and the servant would be well.
- MAR 9:17–27 ~ A man asked Jesus to cast the demon out of his child. Jesus told the man, "All things are possible to those who believe." The man replied, "I believe, Lord; help me overcome my unbelief." Then Jesus ordered the demon to leave the child.
- LUK 5:18–25 ~ Jesus forgave the lame man before healing him. Why? Because the healing of the body is unimportant to someone whose soul is afflicted, for an individual's sin can destroy the soul.
- LUK 17:12–19 ~ Jesus healed the ten lepers. Only one returned to thank and praise Him for being made whole.
- JOH 4:46–53 ~ Jesus healed the nobleman's son the very moment he asked for healing.

Faith is manifested when we pray, for it is one's belief in God that influences a person to pray in the first place; and it is the belief that the prayer will be answered that guarantees it will be. Therefore, one must believe in God, in God's Word, and in the power of prayer for prayer to do them any good. The power of prayer has worked miracles in the lives of many believers, not just their own prayers but intercessory prayers brought to God on their behalf by other believers.

- DEU 26:7–8 ~ When we cried to the Lord, He heard us and looked into our affliction, burden, and oppression. He brought us out of Egypt with a mighty hand and terrible wrath, and with many signs and wonders.

- PSA 50:15 ~ Call on God in times of trouble.
- PSA 119:49–50,92 ~ I remember the Word you gave to us. That Word has given me hope. In it I find comfort in my afflictions, for your Word has given me life. If I did not delight in your Law, I would have perished in my afflictions.
- PRO 12:18 ~ Words can pierce like a sword but the words of the wise brings health.
- MAR 11:23–24 ~ Through prayer, you can move mountains. All you have to do is believe and you will receive what you ask for.
- JAM 5:13–16 ~ Are any of you afflicted? If so, then pray. Are any of you happy? If so, then sing praises. Are any of you sick? Then ask the church to pray for you in the name of the Lord. Confess and pray for each other, and be healed. For the fervent prayer of the believer yields high returns.

There is no spiritual healing for a person who is deliberately evil. Such evil eventually will lead to physical and mental ailments as well.

- PSA 107:17 ~ Fools become afflicted because of their evil ways.
- PRO 6:12,15 ~ The wicked and naughty person has an evil tongue. Calamity will come suddenly upon that person; such people will be stricken and there will be no remedy.
- PRO 29:1 ~ People who are constantly guilty of something become stubborn in their ways. Destruction will come suddenly upon them, for which there is no cure.
- JER 30:15 ~ Why bother crying about your afflictions? There is no cure for your sorrow because of the many evil things you have done. These things were done to you because of your wickedness.

Of course, the healing power of the blood of Jesus Christ surpasses all other sources of spiritual healing, for it is His blood that cleanses our souls from sin.

- ISA 53:4–5 ~ Surely, He bore our grief and carried our sorrows. Yet we treated Him as an outcast, as if stricken, smitten, and afflicted by God. But He was wounded and bruised because of our sins. Our punishment was given to Him, bringing us peace, and through His suffering, we have been healed.
- 2 CO 5:21 ~ God made Him (Christ), who knew no sin, to become sin for us, so that we could be made righteous before God through Him.

God wants us to strive for spiritual things, not worldly things. Spiritual health is infinitely more important than mental or physical health. If we seek spiritual things, all our needs will be provided. Besides, God knows what we need. If we pray for our spiritual needs, God will answer by providing all of our needs.

- PRO 2:2–6,10–12 ~ Incline your ears to wisdom and apply your hearts to understanding. If you cry for knowledge and ask for understanding, if you seek wisdom as you would treasure, then you will understand the fear of the Lord and find knowledge of God. For God gives wisdom, knowledge, and understanding. When wisdom enters your heart and knowledge is pleasant to your soul, discretion will preserve you and understanding will keep you, to deliver you from evil.
- MAT 6:19–21 ~ Jesus taught, "Don't collect your treasures here on earth where they can be corrupted by insects or rust, or where they can be stolen by thieves. Instead, store your treasures in heaven where they cannot be corrupted or stolen. Where your treasures are, there your heart will be also."

- MAT 6:25–34 ~ Jesus taught, "Don't worry about your life, what you will eat or drink, or what you will wear. Isn't there more to life than food and clothing? Look at the birds; they don't sow or reap, or gather food into the barn, yet our heavenly Father feeds them. Aren't people more important than birds? Consider the lilies of the field, they grow just fine yet they don't work; however, King Solomon in his glory was not clothed in such beauty. If God cares for the birds and the flowers, will He not care for you even more? Therefore, don't worry about things such as food and clothing, for your heavenly Father knows you need these things. Instead, seek first the kingdom of God and His righteousness, and everything else you need will be yours. Don't be anxious about tomorrow, because tomorrow will take care of itself. Each day has enough problems to face without adding more."
- ROM 8:26–28 ~ The Holy Spirit helps us with our problems. We really don't know what we should pray for, so the Spirit intercedes for us in ways that words could never express. God, who searches the hearts of everyone, knows the mind of the Spirit, because the Spirit intercedes for God's people according to God's will. We can be sure that God will provide good things to those who love Him, and are called according to His purpose.
- PHP 4:6–9 ~ Don't be anxious about anything but pray for everything. With thanksgiving let your requests be known to God. And the peace of God that surpasses all understanding will keep your hearts and minds in Jesus Christ.

The whole world is in need of spiritual healing. Our mission as Christians is to spread the good news of the Gospel of Jesus Christ to all who are spiritually impaired or afflicted. Help others grow in the faith by reflecting God's love onto them. Sincere faith was the main ingredient in examples of healing in the Bible, and it still is to this day. The source of faith is love, because God is love; and the gift of faith is by His Holy Spirit. Thus, the power of spiritual healing comes from the love in which our faith is rooted. You cannot have faith without having love. In fact, love is the greatest power known to man, for it comes directly from God. Faith is our response to the love of God that now lives in us through Christ.

- MAR 12: 30–31 ~ Jesus said, "You must love the Lord your God with all your heart, soul, mind, and strength; this is the most important commandment. The second is like the first: You must love your neighbor as yourself. There are no other commandments greater than these."

Rock of Ages

Rock of Ages, cleft for me, let me hide myself in Thee.
Let the Water and the Blood, from Thy riven side which flowed,
Be of sin the double cure, cleanse me from this guilt and power.

Not the labors of my hands can fulfill Thy Law's demands;
Could my zeal no respite know, could my tears forever flow,
All for sin could not atone; Thou must save, and Thou alone.

Nothing in my hand I bring, simply to Thy cross I cling;
Naked, come to Thee for dress; helpless, look to Thee for grace;
Foul, I to the fountain fly; wash me Savior, or I die!

While I drew this fleeting breath, when my eyelids close in death,
When I soar to worlds unknown, see Thee on Thy judgment throne,
Rock of Ages, cleft for me, let me hide myself in Thee.

Lesson: Unconditional Love

Text: MAR 10:14–15; MAT 18:3–5 ~ Jesus said, "Let the little children come to me and never forbid them from doing so, for the kingdom of heaven belongs to such as these. I tell you the truth, anyone who does not receive the kingdom of God like a little child will never enter there." Jesus said, "Unless you are converted and become as a little child, you will never enter the kingdom of heaven. Those who humble themselves like a child, they can become the greatest in God's kingdom. Whoever receives a little child in my name, receives me."

What did Christ mean by this? He meant that you have to receive Him with the same kind of unconditional love, faith, and trust that children exhibit. God is our Father, and we are His sons and daughters. He loved us first, and He expects us to love Him, as well as others. Children will love anyone back that loves them, and this is what God desires from His children. For that is what we are who follow Christ: children of God.

- 1 JO 4:7–12,16–21 ~ Let us love one another, for love is from God, and those who love are born of God and know Him. If you don't love God you can't know Him because God is love. The love of God was manifested among us through His only Son, so we might live through Him. If God loves us so much, we should love one another; if we love one another, God lives in us and His love is perfected in us. If you abide in love you abide in God, and God abides in you. This perfect love gives us confidence on the day of judgment, because there is no fear in love but perfect love destroys fear, because fear brings torment. We love because God loved us first. You can't say you love God and hate your brother without being a liar, because you can't hate someone you have seen and still love God who you have never seen. So, you should love God and your brother (neighbor).
- JOH 13:34–35 ~ Jesus said, "I am giving you a new commandment, that you love one another as I have loved you. This is how people will be able to tell that you are my disciples."

God is our Heavenly Father. He loves us unconditionally. Whether we are obedient or not, He still loves us, just as any dedicated father loves his children. Don't you parents love your children whether they are bad or good? And you children, don't you love your parents when they scold you as much as when they are proud of you? We love our parents and our children unconditionally, whenever love is the central bond. What does it mean to love unconditionally? Paul gives us the answer in his first letter to the Corinthians.

- 1 CO 13:4–8,13 ~ Love is patient. Love is kind. Love is never envious or conceited. Love is never rude, self-seeking, or angered, nor does it find pleasure in sin. Love does not think of evil things, nor is it provoked by evil. Love rejoices in the truth. Love always protects, always trusts, always hopes, and always endures. Love never fails. Faith, hope, and love abide, but the greatest of these three is love.

We are God's children, and we should come to Him when we are in trouble or when we are down; and we also should come to Him when we are happy and successful. He loves us more than we can ever imagine. The extent of God's love is most apparent in the sacrifice of His only Son. For this we must be grateful, loyal, and obedient to the extent we are able given our sinful nature. When you give your sins to Jesus, who already paid for them, God will forgive and forget, and continue to provide all of your needs, and help make your dreams come true.

- JOH 3:16 ~ God loved the world so much that He gave His only begotten Son, so that anyone who believes in Him would never die but would live forever.

Just as we love our children and our parents unconditionally, we must also love God unconditionally, and we must also love other people unconditionally. Remember, it's God first and everyone else second including you.

- MAT 22:37–40 ~ Jesus said, "Love the Lord your God with all your heart, mind, and soul: this is the first and greatest commandment. The second is like unto the first: Love your neighbor as yourself. All the laws and the prophets depend on these two commandments."
- LUK 6:32,35 ~ Jesus said, "If you love only those who love you, what reward will you receive? Even sinners love those who love them. So love everyone, even your enemies. Help others whenever you can, expecting nothing in return, and your reward will be great, and you will become a child of God."

Children find it easy to love those who love them. They especially display a keen ability to love God and His Son Jesus Christ. The little children love to sing, "Jesus loves me this I know, for the Bible tells me so." They do not doubt the love of Christ. They know that it is true, because He says so in His Word. Children cannot begin to understand, yet they love God and they believe in Him without exception or condition, because they trust Him. Adults tend to be skeptical. They want proof, and that proof can be found in the scriptures. The Bible says so and that should be good enough for anyone; God's Word is all the proof we will ever need.

To believe is to have faith, which implies trust. One cannot believe unless they have love, for love is greater than faith (1 CO 13:13). If we love God, we will trust Him and believe His promises, just as children love, trust, and believe their parents. If a father tells his child that men have walked on the moon, that child will believe. Why? Because children trust their parents when they are loved. If God tells us something, we should immediately believe Him for the same reason. And God has told us the truth in the Holy Bible. Little children have no problem with the trust and believing part. Adults seem to need reassurance. Oh, to have the unwavering faith of a child!

All God asks us to do is love and obey Him, which is what most parents want from their children. This we do by loving one another, for whatever we do to another person is felt by God.

- MAT 25:40,45 ~ Jesus said, "Whenever you have done something to even the least important of all human beings, you have done it to me; and whenever you have not done something to even the least important of all human beings, you have not done it to me either." In other words, whatever you do, and whatever you fail to do, to or for another person, affects God in the same manner.
- JOH 20:24–29 ~ Thomas was not with the other disciples when Jesus had appeared to them, so they told him about Jesus's visit. Thomas replied, "I will not believe until I myself have seen the nail prints in His hands and feet and touched His wounded hands and side." After eight days Jesus returned to His disciples, and this time Thomas was with them. Jesus said, "Peace to all of you." Then He turned to Thomas and said, "Look at me, see and touch my wounds, so that you might not be without faith but believe." Thomas answered, "My Lord and my God." Jesus replied, "Thomas, you have believed because you have seen; blessed are those who have not seen and still have believed."

It is so easy to obey God by loving others, yet it seems equally as easy to disobey Him due to our corrupt flesh. We neglect the feelings of others and we neglect God. We worry endlessly and fret over stupid things. How trivial are life's problems when compared to eternity? This life is but a droplet in an ocean. We must focus on eternal life which God has promised to all believers (JOH 3:16). Whenever you doubt this inheritance, you merely have to turn to God's

Word for proof. God's Word tells us to rely entirely on His saving grace, shown to us through the suffering, death, and resurrection of His only Son. We must trust in Jesus for our salvation, never doubting. We must recognize the price He paid to atone for our sins and ransom us from the grave, and we must never forget His triumph over all that is evil. Trusting in Him is our key to heaven.

As the hymn goes, "To the cross of Calvary I cling." It is that cross that unlocks the gates of heaven. A popular folk tune goes, "You hold the key to love and fear, all in your trembling hand... Just one key unlocks them both, it's there at your command" (The Youngbloods, *Get Together*). If you are a Christian, the cross of Christ will unlock the pearly gates for you to enter. If you reject Christ, that same cross will lock the gates of hell behind you. Hold tightly to the cross of Jesus and unlock the chains of sin that bind your soul.

It is difficult to always love God regardless of the trials and tribulations we experience. We certainly can't blame God for our problems, instead we should be bringing our problems to Him. Life is sort of like a poker game, you don't always get dealt a great hand; some hands are winners some are losers. If you lose your spouse, it's like losing the hand to anyone who holds a pair. After your children leave home, you remember the times when you had a full house. Maybe you have experienced problems with drugs and knew that everyone holding a straight or better had you beat. You probably won't win the lottery and you can forget about a royal flush. When you feel like life has dealt you a bunch of garbage, do you begin to envy others who seem to have all the luck? This is the time many people turn to God while others turn from Him. However, God wants us to keep Him in our hearts and minds, not only in times of grief and hardship, but also in times of joy and prosperity. Everybody will have good hands and bad ones; but God is there to bless us either way.

When a man and a woman exchange wedding vows, they promise to love each other for richer or poorer, in sickness and in health, for better or worse, until death separates them. We should love God under all possible conditions, just as He loves us no matter what. The Church will become the bride of Christ, who is the groom. We await the wedding banquet that God the Father is preparing for His Son and His people. God wants us to love Him and His Son like a husband and wife love one another, until death removes us from this life and brings us to our heavenly home in the next. The Old Testament book, Song of Solomon, symbolizes the love between a groom (Christ) and His bride (the Church). It's a love story for life, for all time.

- ISA 62:5 ~ For as a young man marries a virgin, so will your sons possess the land. And as the groom rejoices over the bride, so shall God rejoice over you.
- HOS 2:19–20 ~ I (God) will be married to you forever. I will take you as my spouse in righteousness, judgment, loving kindness, mercy, and faithfulness.
- 2 CO 11:2 ~ I (God) have a godly jealousy toward you, for I have promised you to one husband, so that I can present you to Him (Christ) as a chaste virgin.
- EPH 5:23–27 ~ The husband is the head of the wife just as Christ is the head of the church. Christ loved the church so much He gave Himself for it, so that He could sanctify it and cleanse it with the washing of water by the Word. He has presented His church to Himself, a church without any imperfections, a church that is holy like Him.
- REV 19:7–9 ~ Let us give honor to God, for the marriage of the Lamb has come and His bride has made herself ready. She is dressed in clean white linen, which represents the righteousness of the saints. Blessed are those who are called to the wedding and the supper that follows.

Jesus told the following parable about the ten virgins with their lamps that were preparing for the wedding feast. After reading the story, ponder it in your heart for a moment. It is a reminder that time is running out.

- MAT 25:1–13 ~ The kingdom of heaven is like ten virgins who took their lamps with them on the way to meet the groom. Five of them were smart and brought extra oil with them. The other five ran out of oil and their lamps went out. They asked the smart ones for some of their oil, but they replied, "We cannot for we don't want to run out of oil too." The others left to buy more oil for their lamps. Meanwhile, the groom came and everybody went into the church for the wedding. The doors were already locked when the other girls tried to enter. They asked to be admitted but the doorman replied, "I don't know you." Jesus summed up the parable saying, "Therefore, watch for my return for nobody knows the day or hour."

Those who are prepared are welcomed to the wedding. Better get prepared now, before it's too late. We must be faithful until "death do us part," or until Christ returns, whichever comes first. Since nobody knows the time of His return or the time of their own death, it's wise to begin preparing now. Watch and wait, with your hand clenched around the cross of Calvary. For the day of the Lord could be today or tomorrow.

We know that God is love and God is light. That same love and that same light shines in His Son Jesus Christ. We have that love and that light because we love God. We must let that light shine, by radiating His love.

- 1 JO 1:5 ~ God is light; in Him is no darkness at all.
- 2 CO 4:6 ~ God commanded light to shine out of darkness. This same light shines in our hearts and radiates light through our knowledge of Jesus Christ.
- LUK 11:33,35–36 ~ Nobody that lights a lamp hides it in a secret place nor do they place a cover over it. Instead, they place that lamp on a stand so that everyone can see its light. Be careful, so that the light in you does not become darkness. If your whole body is full of light, and has no darkness, it will be wholly bright, as when a lamp with its rays gives light.

Jesus is the way, the truth, and the life (JOH 14:6). His love lights the pathway to heaven. That love shines within us so that others can find their way. There is no darkness in light, but the smallest light destroys the greatest darkness. We must never allow that light within us to become extinguished. If the light burns out, we will lose our way.

- PSA 119:105 ~ God's Word is a lamp for my feet and a light for my path.
- MAT 6:22–23; LUK 11:34 ~ Jesus said, "The eye is the lamp of the body. If your eye is sound, your whole body will be full of light. If your eye is not sound, your whole body will be full of darkness. So, if the light in you is darkness, how great is that darkness."
- JOH 8:12 ~ Jesus said, "I am the light of the world; those who follow me will not walk in darkness but will have the light of life."
- JOH 12:35 ~ Jesus said, "The light will be with you a little longer. Walk while you have the light before the darkness overtakes you; those who walk in darkness do not know where they are going."

God's perfect love was shown to us through Christ, who lives in us and whose love shines through us. Love radiates like a bright star. Others can see the light that comes from inside a person, just as they can sense the darkness that comes from within. Sensible people will follow the light. I mean, who that is lost ever heads toward the darkness, especially if they can see a source of light?

- MAT 6:22–23 ~ Jesus said, "The eye is the lamp of the body. If your eye is sound, your whole body will be full of light. If your eye is not sound, your whole body will be full of darkness. And if the light in you becomes darkness, how great that darkness will be."

We love God because He loved us first. Our children love us because we loved them first. Others will love us when we love them first. In other words, love is contagious. God's love living in us becomes a perfect love because His is a perfect love. That love shines for the world to see. Love should be shown to everyone, even those people you dislike, including enemies (MAT 5:44).

- PSA 97:10 ~ Those who love the Lord hate evil.
- LUK 6:32 ~ Jesus, said, "If you only love those who love you what reward do you receive? Even sinners love those who love them."
- ROM 12:16–21 ~ Be of the same mind one toward another. Do not be high-minded, but humble yourself before others, even those of low estate. Do not pretend to be wise in your own conceit. Do not recompense evil for evil. Always be honest in all things. Live peaceably with all people. Do not seek revenge when someone has done you wrong but rather hold back your wrath. For it is written: Vengeance is mine; I will repay, says the Lord. Therefore, if your enemy is hungry, feed him; if he is thirsty, give him a drink; in doing so you will heap hot coals on his head. Do not be overcome with evil, but overcome evil with goodness.

Those who are righteous will love that which is good and hate that which is evil (PSA 45:7; ZEC 8:16–17; ROM 12:9). Therefore, the enemy of love is not hatred, it is fear; because perfect love drives away fear (1 JO 4:18). Solomon wrote that the fear of God is the beginning of wisdom (PRO 1:7). Jesus told His followers to fear only God who can destroy your body and your soul in hell (MAT 10:28). We are not to fear Satan or his demons, for they have no power over us since God is on our side. Just as a father protects His children from danger, so also our Heavenly Father protects His children on earth. If God is on our side, who can be against us (ROM 8:31)? If we have the love and protection of the Lord, we have nothing to fear.

God's power and influence in this world is love. Satan's power and influence in this world is fear and deception. Satan's fear tactic is just another one of his grand deceptions. Satan and his demons trick people into thinking that they are to be feared. However, people who have the light of God's Spirit dwelling within them are themselves feared by the devil and his demons. You simply have to invoke the power of God's Holy Spirit in the name of God's Son Jesus Christ and the evil spirits will run from you.

- JAM 2:19 ~ If you believe in one God, you are smart. Even the demons believe, and tremble.
- JAM 4:7 ~ Resist the devil and he will flee from you.
- 1 JO 4:4 ~ Greater is He that is in you (Christ) than he that is in the world (Satan).

Remember the demon-possessed individuals who encountered Christ? They always acknowledged Him as God's Son and displayed considerable fear of what He might do to them. A good example is Legion (LUK 8:26–33), the thousands of demons that inhabited one deranged man. They implored Jesus not to torment them, asking Him to cast them into a herd of swine nearby. This Jesus did, and the swine promptly stampeded over the cliffs drowning in the Sea of Galilee. The man became sane and coherent immediately, and worshipped Christ; he wanted to become a follower, and that he did when Christ suggested that he tell everyone else what the Lord had done for him.

Clearly, demons were genuinely afraid of Christ, as they are of anyone possessing God's Holy Spirit within them. Once they discover that God is with you, they will be afraid of you. Thus, a person who possesses the Holy Spirit is incapable of becoming possessed by a demon, and is capable of shooing demons away.

- 2 CO 6:14 ~ Do not be joined with unbelievers, for what fellowship can there be between righteousness and unrighteousness? What communion can there be between light and darkness?

Christ has conquered sin through His death and He has conquered death through His resurrection. There is nothing left to fear, except the punishment that is the reward for disbelief and wickedness. Satan would have people believe that he has power over death. Satan only can bring death; he cannot reverse it. Only Christ can do that (JOH 10:17–18).

- ECC 8:8 ~ Nobody has the power to retain the spirit when they die, and nobody has authority over death.
- ISA 28:18 ~ Any covenant made with death will be nullified; any agreement made with hell will be void.
- ROM 13:4 ~ If you do what is evil, be afraid, for God's minister will not bear the sword in vain, because he is sent to execute wrath upon those who do evil.

In recent years, the ranks of those who practice the occult and who worship Satan have grown. Such movements have particularly become popular among our youth who have a spiritual void to fill, and all too often grasp at the closest solution. Satan preys upon such people, leading them to believe there is no hope. They feel locked into a terrible fate; hence, the increasing rate of suicide, especially among teenagers.

Morality in the world today is at an all-time low. Look at our public schools. Remove God from the scene and the devils rush in. What has happened to family values these days? Fathers have shunned their responsibilities. Many children have nobody to guide them or to discipline them. Imagine what would happen if our Heavenly Father abandoned us. The world would be lost, and there would be utter chaos.

Those who belong to Christ must make themselves available to fill the spiritual emptiness of those around them by radiating the eternal love of God (MAT 28:19–20). Many songwriters have asserted, "Love is the answer." And that is true; love is the answer to all the problems in the world today, it is the powerful force behind all that is good, and it is the most effective way to dispel fear. Love is the light that shines in Christ and in all believers, and illuminates the way to heaven. Such a love should be shown unconditionally, to God, to others, and to yourself. God loves us just the way we are, so we should love everybody the same way.

Just as I Am

Just as I am, without one plea but that Thy blood was shed for me,
And that thou bidst me come to Thee, Oh Lamb of God, I come, I come!
Just as I am, and waiting not to rid my soul of one dark blot;
To Thee, whose blood can cleanse each spot, Oh Lamb of God, I come, I come!

Just as I am, though tossed about with many a conflict, many a doubt,
Fighting and fears within, without, Oh Lamb of God, I come, I come!
Just as I am; Thou wilt receive, wilt welcome, pardon, cleanse, relieve;
Because Thy promise I believe, Oh Lamb of God, I come, I come!

Lesson: Home Sweet Home

When you leave home for extended periods, do you ever get homesick? Most people miss their loved ones. Why is it that we don't miss God? Why is it that we never get homesick for heaven? After all, our eternal home is in heaven not here on earth. Christians need to have a greater passion for that day when we can finally go home to be with our Heavenly Father and Christ our brother (ROM 8:15; GAL 4:4–5; EPH 1:5).

- ISA 56:2–8 ~ Blessed are all people, and their children, if they obey God, avoid evil, keep the Sabbath, and cling to His covenant. Even those who are strangers to God's people Israel will be part of God's house if they obey Him. The righteous will become as God's sons and daughters, only better than that, with a name that will last forever. People of all walks of life will be joined together on His holy mountain to worship Him, for His house will be called a house for the righteous.
- JOH 1:12 ~ To all who have received Christ, and believed in His name, He has given the privilege to become children of God.
- EPH 2:19 ~ You are no longer strangers or foreigners, but fellow citizens with the saints in the household of God.
- 1 JO 3:1–2 ~ How great is the love that God the Father has for us, that we should be called His children. The world doesn't know us because it didn't know Him. We are His children, but we don't know yet what we will be; we do know, however, that we will be like Him, for we will see Him as He really is.

The world is full of evil and corruption. We have to be careful not to fall into its trap and be led astray, else we lose our way down here and our home up there. It helps to pause before making decisions, and accurately assess the alternatives before choosing; a cost-effectiveness analysis helps to determine the relative benefits and expenses. If the outcomes are spiritual, this trumps outcomes that are worldly. If the selection is sinful, the near-term consequences may seem positive but the long-term consequences will be devastating.

- MAR 4:19 ~ The worries of this world, the deceitfulness of riches, and the desire for other things enter in and choke the Word, rendering it unfruitful.
- 2 CO 4:4 ~ The prince of this world has blinded the minds of the unbelievers, preventing the light of the glorious Gospel of Christ who is the image of God from shining down upon them.
- EPH 2:2 ~ In the past, you walked according to the course of this world, according to the prince of the power of the air, the same spirit that works in the children of disobedience.
- 1 JO 2:15–16 ~ Do not love the world or worldly things. If a person loves the world, he or she cannot love God. All that is in the world, the lust of the flesh, the greed of the eyes, and the pride of humanity, do not come from the Father but are of this world alone.

If we get sidetracked and wander down the road to condemnation, we always can return home to God our Father where we will be welcomed with open arms. How comforting it is to know that He is always there for us. He is like a fortress where we feel safe and at peace. Sometimes, the only thing we need is simply to bring to mind that we are in the presence of the Lord, and we will feel all our troubles immediately fade away. We forget that He is always there with us. Did you ever want to run away from home when you were a kid? It is likely you returned home before dark. If you wait until darkness sets in you may not find your way back.

- PSA 46:1 ~ God is our refuge and strength, an ever-present help in trouble

- PSA 18:2 ~ The Lord is my rock, my fortress, and my deliverer; my God, and my strength, in whom I trust; my shield, the crown of my salvation, and my high tower (also 2 SA 22:2).
- MAT 11:28–30 ~ Jesus said, "Come to me all who are weary and burdened and I will give you rest. Take my yoke upon you and learn from me, for I am gentle and humble in heart; and you will find rest for your souls. For my yoke is easy and my burden is light."
- LUK 15:11–32 ~ Jesus told the parable of the prodigal son, who asked his father for his share of the inheritance. The father gave the son his inheritance, and the son left for a foreign land where he squandered all his money on wine and women. Meanwhile, a great famine arose in that country. The son had to feed pigs to make a living. Even his father's servants were better off than this, so he returned home to confess everything to his father, and apologize. His father saw him coming, ran out to meet the son, and embraced him. The son told his father that he was not worthy of being called a son and should be treated as a servant. But the father had his servants prepare a great feast to celebrate. The elder son became angry and refused to enter the house. The father consoled him saying, "You are always with me and all that is mine is yours. But it is fitting to celebrate, because your brother was lost, but now he is found; he was dead but now he is alive again."

We tend to get distracted by this world, and often neglect God. Yet there is nothing in this world that can compare to the treasures awaiting us in heaven. So, there is no reason to make worldly things or material wealth our primary motivators; instead we should concentrate on the Lord and His assurances. There are no guarantees in this world, but there are in heaven. And even though we cannot see heaven or imagine what awaits us, we know in our hearts it will be magnitudes better than anything we have encountered here.

- ISA 64:4 ~ Since the world began, nobody has heard, seen, or perceived, except God, the wonderful things He has prepared for those who wait for Him (also 1 CO 2:9).
- MAT 6:19 ~ Jesus said, "Store up for yourselves treasures in heaven where they cannot decay or get stolen. For where your treasure is there your heart will be."
- JOH 14:2 ~ Jesus said, "In my Father's house are many mansions; I go to prepare a place for you."
- 2 CO 5:8 ~ We are confident, and would prefer to be absent from the body and present with the Lord.
- 2 PE 1:3–4 ~ God's divine power has given us everything we need for life and righteousness through our knowledge of Him, who called us by His own glory and goodness. He has given us His very wonderful and precious promises that we may participate in the divine nature, and escape the corruption of the world caused by evil desires.

When we leave home we often can't wait to get back to our homes where we feel safe, comfortable, and happy. Every time I travel, I look forward to sleeping in my own bed, don't you? I miss my family and friends; though I may be among people I care about it is not the same somehow. We leave home to acquire and achieve things of the world that we want so bad; and often when we obtain them, we are not all that satisfied. But such feelings are only fleeting due to constant interference from the world and the many problems, trials, challenges, and sorrows we face on earth. Our home in heaven will be much more enjoyable and comfortable because the joy, comfort, and peace will last forever, while the trials and tribulations will forever cease.

- ISA 32:17–18 ~ The work of righteousness will produce peace; the effect of righteousness will be peacefulness and assurance forever. The righteous will live in quiet, restful, and safe homes.

- ISA 65:17–19 ~ I (God) will create a new heaven and a new earth; the former heaven and earth will never be remembered or recalled. You will be glad and rejoice forever, for I will make Jerusalem a place of happiness. I also will rejoice in Jerusalem for I will be happy with my people, and nevermore will there be the sound of crying among my people.
- ZEC 8:3,5–8 ~ I (God) will return to Zion and I will live in Jerusalem; and Jerusalem will be called the city of truth and Zion will be called the holy mountain. Children will be playing in the streets. It will be marvelous for my people and also for me. I will save my people from the corners of the earth and bring them to Jerusalem. They will be my people and I will be their God, in truth and in righteousness.
- REV 21:1,4 ~ I (John) saw a new heaven and a new earth, for the old heaven and earth had passed away. There was no more crying, sorrow, pain, or death, for these things had passed away.

What does your dream house look like? Most people would envision an earthly home, perhaps a chateau surrounded by rolling hills, a cottage overlooking a beach, or a cabin high in forested mountains. Some would be inclined to imagine a modest and humble abode in a secluded and serene environment. I would rather think about my abode in heaven. I have dreamt of my heavenly home but I really have no idea what it looks like. What I do know is there is a mansion in the sky being prepared for me, as well as all believers (JOH 14:1–3). Whether a literal or figurative mansion, I cannot be sure; but I know it will surpass anyplace I have lived or laid my head here on planet Earth.

Lesson: Prosperity

God has promised us that, if we love Him, follow Him, and obey His commandments, we will prosper. On the other hand, if we love and follow the world, and we disobey God, we will lose whatever prosperity we have obtained. The Old Testament is a great example of this, because it tells the story of the Israelites and how they prospered when they were faithful to God and how they were plundered when they strayed far away from Him.

- EXO 15:26 ~ God said, "If you listen diligently to my voice, do what is right, and obey my commandments and statutes, I will never bring diseases upon you like I did with the Egyptians, for I am the Lord who heals you."
- DEU 11:13–15,22–23 ~ God said, "If you listen diligently to my commandments, if you love the Lord your God, and serve Him with all your heart and with all your soul, I will provide rain in due season, so that you can gather your corn, wine, and oil. And I will make sure your fields are full of grass so that your cattle will be fat. If you listen diligently to my commandments, if you love the Lord your God, walk in all His ways, and cling to Him, I will drive away all the nations before you and you will subdue greater and mightier nations than yourselves."
- DEU 28:1,15–22,28–30,47–48 ~ God said, "If you listen diligently to the voice of the Lord, and observe His commandments, I will place you high above all nations of the earth. But if you do not listen to the Lord and you do not observe His commandments and statutes that I have commanded you to follow, these curses will come upon you and overtake you; you will be cursed in the city and in the country. Your basket and kneading trough will be cursed. Cursed will be your offspring, the fruit of your land, and your herds and flocks. You will be cursed coming in and going out. The Lord will send curses, confusion, rebuke, and destruction upon you if you forsake Him. He will send diseases, drought, and plagues upon you. You will become mad, blind, and disoriented. You will be unsuccessful at everything. You will be oppressed and robbed but nobody will help you. You will get engaged but someone else will rape your fiancé. You will build a house but never live in it. You will plant a vineyard but never enjoy its fruit. The Lord will do these things because you did not serve Him joyfully and thankfully in response to the abundance of all things that He gave to you. Therefore, you will be thirsty, hungry, naked, and needy and you will end up serving your enemies which the Lord will bring upon you, and you will be enslaved until He has utterly destroyed every last one of you."
- JOS 1:7–8 ~ God said, "Be strong and courageous, so that you are able to observe the laws which Moses commanded of you. Do not turn to the right or to the left, and you will prosper wherever you go. This book of the Law must not depart from your speech, but you must meditate on my words every day and night, and live according to all that is written there. Then I will make you prosperous and you will be successful. This book of the Law will never leave your mouth, and you will meditate on it day and night, so that you can act in accordance with all that is written therein. Then your ways will be prosperous and you will enjoy success."
- 2 CH 24:20 ~ The Spirit of God came upon Zechariah the son of Jehoiada the priest, who stood above the people and said to them, God says, "Why do you disobey the Lord's commandments? You will not prosper because you have forsaken Him, and now He has forsaken you."
- 2 CH 26:5 ~ As long as the king sought God, God allowed him to prosper.

- JOB 36:11–12 ~ If they obey and serve God, they will spend their days in prosperity, and their years in pleasure. But if they do not obey, they will perish by the sword, and they will die without knowledge.

The Israelites often met destruction because they did not seek God and obey Him with diligence. This same result applies to everyone. We must be diligent in seeking God and His righteousness. To be diligent means to make a concerted effort; it means to persevere. You really have to try hard to please God; that is, you have to work at it. If you make a half-hearted effort it will not be enough and you will fail.

- PSA 52:4–8 ~ Surely God will bring you down into everlasting ruin; He will uproot you from the land of the living. The righteous will see and fear. They will laugh, saying, "Here is the man that did not make God his strength, but instead placed his trust in the abundance of his riches and found strength in wickedness. But I am like a green olive tree, flourishing in the house of God, and I will trust in His mercy forevermore.
- JER 22:21–22 ~ God warned you when you prospered, but you said, "Don't bother me." This is the way you have been since you were young: disobedient. The wind will drive away your pastors, and your lovers will become slaves. You will be ashamed and disgraced because of your wickedness.
- MAT 7:14 ~ Straight and narrow is the gate that leads to eternal life, and few will find it.
- LUK 18:1–8 ~ Jesus taught the parable about the unjust judge. There was a judge who neither feared God nor had a high regard for his fellow man. A widow appealed to him to avenge her of an enemy who had done her wrong. The judge did nothing. The widow continued to bother the judge until her persistence finally paid off and the judge awarded her a fair settlement. God will also avenge His elect who plead with Him day and night, even though He may do it in His own time. However, when the Son of God returns, will He find such persistent faith on the earth?

Be diligent in seeking God by forsaking earthly desires. Seek spiritual riches and God will prosper you spiritually and materially. Those seeking worldly riches will be ruined and will perish. Prosperity is an end, not a means. Thus, prosperity itself is not a sin, but the motivation for it could be. Examine your motives and make sure they are honorable.

- 1 SA 2:7 ~ The Lord makes people rich or poor and lifts people up or brings them down.
- JOB 20:15 ~ Those who swallow down riches will vomit them up again, just like God rids Himself of those who relish in their riches.
- PRO 11:4,28 ~ Riches will not profit anyone in the day of wrath; only righteousness can save a person from death. Those who trust in their riches will fail, but those who trust in God will flourish.
- PRO 28:6,22 ~ Poor people who walk in righteousness are better off than rich people who are perverse in their ways. Those who are in a hurry to become rich have an evil eye, and don't realize the poverty that will come upon them.
- ECC 2:22–26 ~ What does a man get for all his work and striving under the sun? He gets pain and grief, and no rest at night. That is meaningless. A man can do nothing better than to eat and drink, and find satisfaction in his work. This comes from God, for without Him who can eat, drink, and find enjoyment? The man who pleases God will receive wisdom, knowledge, and happiness. But to the sinner God gives the task of gathering wealth, only to hand it over to the one who pleases God. That too is meaningless, a chasing after the wind.

- ECC 5:10–12 ~ Whoever loves riches will never have enough, and whoever loves money will never be satisfied with their income. This is vanity. As goods increase, so do those that consume them. And of what benefit are belongings to the owner except the enjoyment of looking at them? The sleep of the hard worker is sweet; but the abundance of the rich prevents them from sleeping.
- MAT 6:19–20,33 ~ Jesus said, "Don't accumulate a lot of earthy treasures that can be corrupted by insects or rust or that can be stolen by thieves. Instead, accumulate heavenly treasures that cannot be corrupted or stolen. Seek first the kingdom of God and His righteousness, and everything else that you need will be added unto you."
- LUK 12:15–21 ~ Jesus said to them, "Beware of greed, for a person's life does not consist of the abundance of their possessions." Then He told them the parable about the rich man who had such an abundance of wealth that he decided to build bigger warehouses to store his goods. The man said to himself, "Now that you've got it made, take it easy; eat, drink, and be merry." But God said to him, "You fool! This very night your soul will be demanded from you, and then who will enjoy your prosperity?" Jesus concluded, "This is how it will be for those who store up worldly things for themselves but are not rich toward God."
- COL 3:2 ~ Set your mind on things above, not earthly things.
- 1 TI 6:5–10,17 ~ Corrupt minds that are devoid of the truth will argue that godliness is a way of obtaining wealth. But godliness means being content with what you have. You brought nothing into this world, and you will take nothing out of it. People who want to get rich fall into the trap of temptation, consisting of foolish and harmful lusts that drown them in destruction and condemnation. For the love of money is the root of all evil. Those who have pursued it have strayed from the faith and brought upon themselves a multitude of sorrows. Tell those who are rich not to be miserly or greedy, trusting in their wealth for their needs. Tell them instead to trust in God who richly gives us all things to enjoy.

Conscientiousness and perseverance are virtues that lead to spiritual success. The same is true in other aspects of life, so be diligent in all worthwhile undertakings. The only way you will fail is to give up.

- PRO 10:4 ~ Lazy hands leads a person to poverty, but diligent hands brings a person wealth.
- PRO 11:27 ~ People that diligently seek good will find favor, but people that seek mischief will have mischief come to them.
- PRO 12:24 ~ The diligent person will be in charge, and the lazy ones will be slaves.
- PRO 13:4 ~ The lazy person desires many things and has nothing; but the soul of the diligent person will be fully satisfied.
- PRO 21:5 ~ The plans of the diligent person leads to prosperity, but the ones who are in a hurry to get rich will find poverty.
- PRO 22:29 ~ Do you know someone who is diligent in business matters? That person will serve kings, and will be able to avoid obnoxious people.
- ECC 9:10–11 ~ Whatever your hand finds to do, do it with your might; for there is no work, device, knowledge, or wisdom in the grave where you are going. I returned, and realized that the race does not belong to the swift, nor the battle to the strong, nor sustenance to the wise, nor riches to the intelligent, nor favor to the skilled; but time and luck happen to everyone.

God rewards those who are diligent in their affairs, both worldly endeavors and spiritual pursuits. The diligent person is a hard worker. As the saying goes, you reap what you sow. If we sow to the Lord, we will reap heavenly riches abundantly.

- GEN 39:3 ~ Joseph's master saw that God was with Joseph, and that the Lord prospered him in everything that he did.
- PSA 1:1–5 ~ Blessed is the person that does not walk in the counsel of the ungodly, or stand among sinners, or sit in the seat of the scornful. Blessed is the person whose delight is in God's Law, for that person meditates on God's Law every day and night. Such a person will be like a tree planted by flowing streams of water, bearing good fruit in season, with leaves that never wither. Whatever he or she does will prosper. But the ungodly are not so; they are like the chaff that the wind blows away. Therefore, the wicked will not stand with the just, and sinners will not assemble with the righteous. For God watches over the ways of righteous people, but the ways of the wicked will perish.
- ISA 55:10–12 ~ The rain and snow that falls from heaven does not return to heaven, but waters the earth, causing the plants to bud and to seed and providing food. So also, God's Word does not return to Him void, but accomplishes what He wishes, and prospers wherever He sends it. We joyfully go out, being led in peace. The mountains and hills sing before you and the trees clap their hands; the whole world will rejoice around you. Instead of a thorn bush, a tree will grow. And the name of the Lord will be magnified as an everlasting sign of the nurturing He provides.
- JOH 8:31 ~ Jesus said, "If you continue in my Word you are truly my disciples, and you will know the truth, and the truth will set you free."
- JOH 10:10 ~ Jesus said, "A thief comes to steal, to kill, and to destroy. I have come that my sheep might have life, and that they might have it more abundantly."
- HEB 11:6 ~ Without faith it is impossible to please God, for you cannot come to Him unless you first believe in Him, and in the fact that He rewards those who diligently seek Him.
- 1 PE 1:9–10 ~ You will receive the objective of your faith which is the salvation of your souls. This is the salvation that the prophets were searching intently for, who prophesied about the grace that could come to you.
- 2 PE 1:3–11 ~ God's divine power has given us everything we need for life and righteousness through our knowledge of Him who called us by His own glory and loving kindness. He has given us wonderful and precious promises, so that through them you may participate in the divine nature and escape the corruption of the world caused by evil desires. For this reason, be diligent in your faith, adding to your faith virtue, and to virtue knowledge, and to knowledge self-control, and to self-control perseverance, and to perseverance godliness, and to godliness brotherly kindness, and to brotherly kindness love. For if these things abide in you and abound, they will keep you from being ineffective and unproductive in the knowledge of our Lord Jesus Christ. But those who lack such things are blind, they cannot see the long-term benefits, and have forgotten that they were purged of old sins. Therefore, brothers and sisters, be even more conscientious and sure in your calling, for if you do these things you will never fail, and you will receive a hearty welcome into the eternal kingdom of our Lord and Savior Jesus Christ.

As God has prospered us, so we should share our abundance with others, and He will reward us with even more. God will never give you less than you need, and if He gives you more than you need it's because He knows you can handle it and will be generous with it.

- MAL 3:10 ~ The Lord says, "Bring tithes of your income to the storage room, so that there will be plenty in my house, and prove to yourself that I will open the windows of heaven and pour upon you so many blessings that you will not have room for them."
- MAT 13:12; MAT 25:29 ~ Jesus said, "Whoever has will be given more, in abundance. Whoever has not will have what little they possess taken away."

- LUK 6:38 ~ Give and it shall be given to you in abundance, overflowing; for the same measure that you give is returned to you.
- 1 CO 16:2 ~ On the first day of the week, everyone should set aside some money in accordance with the degree to which God has prospered them and give it to the church so that a collection will not be necessary.
- 2 CO 8:2–5,7,12–14 ~ Even during times of poverty, the abundance of their joy became a wellspring of generosity. They gave as much as they could, even beyond their ability. They considered it a privilege to serve, giving themselves to the Lord and to His ministers. Therefore, as you abound in everything, including faith, speech, knowledge, and earnest love, see that you also abound in the grace of giving. If the willingness is there, the gift will be acceptable, whether large or small, in accordance with the degree to which one has prospered. Our desire is not that others might be relieved even when you are hard-pressed, but that there will be equality. For now, your plenty will supply the needs of others, so that in turn their plenty will supply you in times of need.
- HEB 6:10–11 ~ God is fair; He will never forget your work, and the love you showed to Him, and the help you were to His people. We want you to continue to show this same diligence until the end, in order to make your hope complete.

In summary, strive to be rich in spiritual gifts, not material wealth. If God sees that you are responsible with what He has given you, perhaps He will entrust you with more. However, with greater prosperity comes greater responsibility. God blesses His people so that they can be a blessing to others. Therefore, be generous with what God has given to you. If you are wise with His gifts you may be enriched further so that you can enrich others materially and spiritually, using your time, talent, treasure, and testimony. Your blessings will multiply and you will climb higher and see farther.

Lesson: Responsibility

As we mature in our faith, God gives us greater responsibility. The beginning of that process is to take responsibility for sin, by confessing your sin before God and repenting in the name of Christ. Until we face up to our shortcomings and seek God's forgiveness, how can we become trusted to forgive others? That is, we must accept God's gifts before we can bestow those gifts upon others. To coin a phrase, let us practice what we preach.

- GEN 3:12–19 ~ When God uncovered the sin of Adam and Eve, Adam tried to blame Eve, and Eve tried to blame Satan. Neither of them confessed, and God punished them both, as well as Satan.
- EXO 32:21–25 ~ Aaron tried to make excuses for his sin by explaining to Moses that the people had coerced him into building the golden calf.
- MAT 27:24 ~ Pontius Pilate washed his hands in a symbolic gesture, denying any responsibility for the crucifixion of Christ, claiming that he was innocent of Christ's blood.
- MAT 7:1–2 ~ Do not judge others or you will be judged. And you will be judged according to the same standards by which you judge others.
- LUK 6:39–42 ~ Jesus taught them this parable: Can a blind man lead a blind man? Won't both of them fall into the ditch? A student is not above his teacher, but everyone who is fully trained can become a teacher. Why do you look at the speck of sawdust in your brother's eye and pay no attention to the plank in your own eye? How can you to help your brother remove the speck from his eye, when you fail to see the plank in your own eye? You hypocrite! First get rid of the plank in your own eye and then you will see clearly enough to remove the speck from your brother's eye.

A parent allows a child to earn privileges when that child behaves responsibly. When a child does not live up to the obligations he or she has accepted, then the parent takes away his or her privileges. God our Father has commended us with certain privileges, and with those privileges come higher responsibilities. And if we exceed those boundaries that He has set for us, He will narrow the boundaries further, because He is a loving Father and will not give us more than we can manage or oversee.

- MAT 7:6 ~ Do not give holy things to dogs and do not throw your pearls to the pigs, for they will trample them under their feet, and turn against you and attack.
- ROM 12:3–8 ~ Do not think of yourself more highly than you should, but rather evaluate yourself with a clear mind, in accordance with the measure of faith God has given to you. Just as our body has many members, each with a separate purpose, so we, being part of the body of Christ, have different responsibilities. Some people can minister, some can teach, some can provide guidance and counseling. We have different gifts, given to us in accordance with the grace God has given us. If you have the gift of prophecy, do so in proportion to your faith. If you have the gift of giving, do so generously. If you have the gift of governing, do so with diligence. If you have the gift of mercy, show it cheerfully.
- EPH 4:7–8,11–13 ~ To each one of us, grace has been given as Christ apportioned it. This is what the psalmist meant when he said that Christ gave gifts to humanity before His triumphant return to heaven. It was He who appointed some to be apostles, some to be prophets, some to be evangelists, and some to be pastors and teachers. We are to prepare God's people for works of service, so that the body of Christ may be edified, until we reach unity in the faith and in the knowledge of the Son of God, and become mature, attaining the whole measure of the fullness of Christ.

- 1 TI 6:20–21 ~ Paul wrote to Timothy: Guard everything that has been entrusted to your care. Turn away from godless chatter and the opposing ideas of what is falsely called knowledge, which some have professed and in doing so have wandered from the faith.

Jesus often taught using parables that provided a moral lesson. The following parables teach us to be responsible with the gifts God has given us. Note that, the more responsibilities we accept, the more responsibilities we are given. The more we do what's expected of us, the more that is expected. If we do not act responsibly with the gifts God has given us, they will be taken away and given to someone else.

- MAT 13:3–11; LUK 8:5–18 ~ A man was sowing his seeds. Some seeds fell on the path and the birds came and ate them all. Some seeds fell on the rocks where there was insufficient soil for them to take root, and the seedlings died. Some seeds fell upon the thorns where the seedlings were choked to death. Some seeds fell on good soil, took root, and grew. And the harvest was great. You who have ears listen. Whoever has will be given more; whoever does not have, what he thinks is his will be taken away from him.
- LUK 12:36–48 ~ Be like the man who awaits his master to come home from the marriage feast, so that he may open the door when he arrives. Blessed are those who the master finds awake when he comes. If the homeowner knew the time that the thief would rob him, he would have been prepared. Be ready at all times for the Son of Man to come, because no-one knows the exact hour. Who is that faithful and wise servant which the Lord will have to rule His household? Blessed is the servant that is doing a good job when the Lord returns home, for that servant will become ruler over the Lord's possessions. But if a servant, knowing that the Lord's return is far off, begins to chastise the others, and engages in drunkenness and gluttony, the Lord of that servant will arrive unexpectedly. And that servant will be punished severely; but those who disobey out of ignorance will receive a lesser punishment. Of those who have been given much, much will be required; and of those who have been entrusted with much, more will be demanded. (also MAT 24:38–51)
- LUK 19:12–26 ~ A king gave ten shares of gold to ten servants to invest during his absence. Upon his return he gathered the servants together. The first proclaimed he had made an extra ten shares with his investment. The king was pleased and gave him ten cities to govern. The second servant had made five extra shares so he was given five cities to govern. The third told the king, "Knowing what a stern man you are, I hid my shares in the ground so as not to lose anything, and here they are." The king said, "You could have invested the money in the bank at the very least. As you have called me a stern man so I will deal with you in the same fashion." The king ordered the unwise servant's share to be given to the first servant who had invested the wisest, and ordered the wicked servant to be thrown into the dungeon. Therefore, to those who have, more will be given, and to those who have not, the little they have will be taken away. (also MAT 25:14–30)

If we use God's gifts wisely, we will bear beautiful fruit. And the more we exercise those gifts, the more productive we will be. When one sows the seeds of faith, they multiply throughout the mission field. We are called to be laborers, builders, administrators, and healers and this is a high calling. Since God is our pride and joy, He will be glorified in our employment; and we will become His pride and joy, for which we will be glorified alongside His Son.

- JOB 4:8 ~ I have observed that those who plow iniquity and sow wickedness reap the same.
- ROM 8:17 ~ Now if we are children, then we are heirs: heirs of God and joint-heirs with Christ, if indeed we share in His suffering so that we may also share in His glory.

- 1 CO 3:7–11,14 ~ Neither he who plants nor he who sows is anything, but only God who makes things grow. The man who plants and the man who waters have one purpose, and each will be rewarded according to his labor. For we are God's fellow workers; you are God's field, God's building. By the grace God has given me (Paul), I laid a foundation as an expert builder, and someone else is building on it. But each one should be careful how he builds. For nobody can lay a better foundation than the one already laid, which is in Jesus Christ. If what a man has built survives, he will receive his reward.
- 2 CO 9:6 ~ Those who sow sparingly will reap sparingly, and those who sow bountifully will reap bountifully.
- GAL 6:8 ~ Those who sow to the flesh will reap corruption, but those who sow to the Spirit will from the Spirit reap eternal life.

Everyone will receive their due reward, depending on whether they led a life of righteousness or wickedness (EZE 18:20–30; EZE 33:8–19). Part of our responsibility is to warn others who are heading in the wrong direction. We also must be vigilant to ensure that we are following the right path ourselves. If not, we can expect repercussions. To state another cliché, what goes around comes around, whether positive or negative.

- GEN 4:6–7 ~ The Lord said to Cain, "If you do what is right, will you not be accepted? But if you do what is wrong, sin is crouching at your door."
- JOB 34:10–11 ~ Listen, you who have understanding. Far be it from God to do evil or for the Almighty to be wrong. He repays people for what they have done, and brings upon them what their conduct deserves.
- PSA 62:12 ~ You, oh Lord, are loving. Surely you will reward each person according to what he or she has done.
- PRO 12:13–14 ~ An evil man is trapped by his sinful talk, but a righteous person escapes trouble. From the fruit of his lips a man is filled with good things as surely as the work of his hands rewards him.
- ISA 59:18 ~ According to what a person has done, the Lord repays: wrath to His enemies and retribution to His foes.
- EPH 6:7–8 ~ Serve wholeheartedly, as if you were serving the Lord and not people, because you know that the Lord will reward everyone for whatever good he or she does, regardless of whether slave or free.

Responsibility is a gift from God, given to us in proportion to our faith. Our responsibility is to His kingdom, because we have been appointed as overseers of the flock. We answer to our Father in heaven, not to the world. If there is a conflict between what God expects and what the world wants—well, you know who will triumph.

- ACT 20:28 ~ Keep watch over yourselves and the flock of which the Holy Spirit has made you overseers. Feed the church of God which he purchased with his own blood.
- ROM 14:19 ~ Let us do things that promote peace and that lead to mutual edification.
- 1 CO 14:12 ~ Since you are eager to have spiritual gifts, try to excel in those gifts which edify the church.
- COL 3:16 ~ Let the Word of Christ abide in you richly in all wisdom. Teach and admonish one another in psalms, hymns, and spiritual songs, singing to God with grace in your hearts.
- 1 PE 5:2–3 ~ Feed God's flock which is among you; be overseers of the kingdom. Do this, not out of obligation but willingly; do this not for ill-gotten gain but with a clear conscience. Do not act like lords over God's heritage but set an example to the flock.

SPIRITUAL ACTS

By faith, we believe in Christ's sacrifice for sins. It is totally by the grace and mercy of God that we have been given the gifts of atonement and everlasting life. Repentance of our sins before God is a way of acknowledging these gifts. We must be sincerely sorry for our sins, and thank and praise God for His mercy and blessings. We also should pray to God frequently and continuously. Repentance, thanks, praise, worship, and prayer are ways of demonstrating our faith through spiritual actions. Helping, serving, and encouraging others are ways of serving God through our worldly endeavors.

All people are justified by faith, but a living faith must be visible through our words and deeds, because faith without purpose is meaningless. God appreciates certain spiritual and corporeal acts that demonstrate our faith and love for Him and others. God also gives us Holy Baptism and Communion, in which we perform personal acts of faith and observance to receive regeneration and forgiveness. These sacraments represent actions that Christ Himself endorsed by His own participation. Religious rites of Confirmation, Confession, and Marriage also are decisive ways of demonstrating personal faith and commitment.

Christians were commissioned by Christ to be His disciples and witnesses, so that the truth would have free course and bring additional believers into freedom and redemption. If we continue in our faith, love, and trust in Jesus Christ and live a god-fearing life, we will be rewarded both in this life and in the next.

Repentance and Confession

All spiritual acts of faith should begin with repentance. We must be sincerely sorry for our sins and humbly confess them before God. If we are genuinely contrite, God will forgive us and renew us by His grace and mercy unto salvation. If someone is neither sorry for their sins, nor repentant of them, they are uncommitted and unworthy, and their participation in Holy Sacraments or sacred religious rites becomes a sin.

- LEV 26:40–42,44 ~ God instructed, "If they confess their sins and the sins of their fathers; if they repent for all the times they have walked contrary to the ways I have taught them; if they accept the punishment for their sins, then I will remember my covenant with Abraham, Isaac, and Jacob, and I will not detest them or discard them."
- NUM 5:7 ~ They will confess their sins and shall recompense those they have sinned against with the principal plus twenty percent interest.
- PSA 32:5 ~ I confessed my sins to God; I did not try to hide them. And God forgave me.
- PSA 51:3 ~ I acknowledge my sins which always go before me.
- ISA 57:15 ~ The eternal and holy Lord God says that anyone who comes before Him with a contrite and humble spirit will be revived from death.
- JER 14:20 ~ We acknowledge our wickedness, Lord, and the sins of our ancestors, for we all have sinned against you.
- JER 18:8,10 ~ God says, "If a nation who I have pronounced my wrath against will turn from their evil ways, I will repent of the wrath I was planning against them. If a nation turns to evil and does not obey me, I will repent of the good I was planning for them."
- EZE 14:6 ~ God says, "Repent, turn away from idols, and stop your abominations."
- EZE 18:30 ~ God says, "I will judge everyone according to their ways. Repent and turn away from your sins, or you will be ruined by sin."

- DAN 9:4–6 ~ I prayed to the Lord, confessing my sins. I said, "Oh great and mighty God, who keeps the covenant with those who love Him and keep His commandments, we have sinned; we have been wicked. We have strayed from your commandments; we have not listened to your prophets."
- HOS 5:15 ~ God says, "I'll go away until they seek my face and acknowledge their sins."
- MAT 3:1–2,11 ~ John the Baptist preached in the wilderness of Judea saying, "Repent, for the kingdom of heaven is at hand. I baptize you with water as a demonstration of your desire for repentance. But One comes after me who is mightier than I, and whose shoes I am not worthy to carry. He will baptize you with the Holy Spirit, and with fire."
- MAT 9:13 ~ Jesus said, "I came to call sinners, not the righteous, to repentance."
- MAT 10:32–33 ~ Jesus said, "Anybody who confesses me before others, I will confess them before my Father in heaven. Anybody who denies me to others, I will deny them before my Father in heaven."
- LUK 13:3 ~ Jesus said, "Unless you repent you will perish."
- LUK 15:10–32 ~ Jesus said, "There is joy among the angels in heaven when one sinner repents. Hear the lesson of the prodigal son, who took his inheritance, left home for another land, and squandered the inheritance on sinful pleasures. Then he became sorry for his decadent life, and returned to his father in shame and contrition. His father welcomed him with open arms, just like your Father in heaven will welcome you for returning to Him. Though the prodigal son was dead in his sins, he became alive again by returning to his father and seeking forgiveness."
- ACT 2:38–39 ~ Peter said, "Repent and be baptized every one of you, in the name of Jesus Christ for the remission of your sins, and you will receive the gift of the Holy Spirit. This promise pertains to you, to your children, and to people everywhere: to whomever the Lord calls."
- ROM 10:10 ~ With the heart, people can believe unto righteousness, and with the mouth, confession is made unto salvation.
- 2 CO 7:9–10 ~ I am glad that you were sorry for your sins and repented. Spiritual sorrow for one's sins works repentance unto salvation, but the sorrow of the world works death.
- JAM 5:16 ~ Confess your faults to each other and pray for each other so you can be healed. The fervent prayer of a righteous person yields high returns.
- 1 JO 1:9 ~ If we confess our sins, God is faithful and just to forgive those sins and cleanse us from all unrighteousness.

Discipleship and Witnessing

Jesus Christ told His disciples to spread the good news of salvation to everyone. It is our duty to share our knowledge of Christ and God's Word with others. One way of doing this is to witness our faith publicly. Do not deny your faith in Christ but proclaim it to the world. Not everyone can be a teacher or an evangelist, but everyone has opportunities to be a witness. For example, the Holy Sacraments are an excellent way of witnessing for Christ.

- ISA 6:8 ~ I (Isaiah) heard the Lord say, "Whom shall I send, and who will be our messenger?" I replied, "Here I am, Lord, send me."
- ISA 12:4 ~ Praise the Lord, call on His name, declare His works to all people; mention that His name is exalted.
- MAT 5:15–16 ~ Jesus said, "You don't light a candle and then put it out, because it is supposed to give light. Let the light inside you shine before others; let people see in your actions that you live to glorify your Father in heaven."

- MAT 10:19–20 ~ Jesus said, "When they arrest you and bring you before the authorities, don't worry about what to say, for you will know what to say when the time comes. And it will be the Holy Spirit inside you doing the talking."
- MAT 28:19–20 ~ Jesus told His disciples, "Go into every nation and teach the people everything I have taught you. Baptize them in the name of the Father, Son, and Holy Spirit. Remember, I'll always be with you, even until the end of time."
- LUK 9:23 ~ Jesus said, "If anyone wants to follow me, they must deny themselves and carry their cross daily."
- LUK 14:16–23 ~ Jesus told the parable of the wedding of the king's son and how the invited guests had lousy excuses not to come. Then the master told the servants to gather the poor, handicapped, lame, and blind, and to search the highways and alleys inviting everyone to come to the wedding feast, "so that my house may be filled." Those who were on the original guest list were no longer welcome.
- JOH 1:7,9,15 ~ Jesus came to earth to be a witness of the Light, so that through Him all people could believe. Christ was the true light; He brings all people into the light. John the Baptist was the first to witness for Christ, telling everyone that Christ was the One who was next to come, yet He was preferred before John came.
- JOH 5:33,36–37,46 ~ Jesus said, "John the Baptist was a witness to the truth. I am a greater witness of the truth than he. The things the Father has given me to do, I do; and these things prove that the Father has sent me, and that I am His witness. The Father Himself, who sent me to do these things, has been a witness for me, even though you have neither seen Him nor heard His voice. But, if you believed Moses, you would believe me, for Moses has been my witness in his writings."
- JOH 18:37 ~ Pilate asked Jesus, "Are you a king?" Jesus replied, "You have said it. This is why I came into the world, to be a witness to the truth. Everyone who is interested in the truth will listen to me."
- JOH 20:21 ~ Jesus said, "Peace, brothers. Just as the Father sent me, now I am sending you."
- ACT 1:22 ~ Peter said, "Since Jesus was baptized by John, until the day He left us, we were being ordained by God to be witnesses of Jesus's resurrection."
- ROM 8:16 ~ The Holy Spirit is a witness with our spirits that we are the children of God.
- ROM 12:1–2 ~ Let your body be a living sacrifice, acceptable to God; this is the least you can do. Do not live according to this world but according to the perfect will of God.
- ROM 12:4–8 ~ Just as our body has many members, each with a separate purpose, so we, being part of the body of Christ, have different responsibilities. We all have special gifts which God in His grace has given us. Some people can minister, some can teach, some can provide guidance and counseling. If you have the gift of prophecy do so in proportion to your faith. If you have the gift of giving, do so generously. If you have the gift of governing, do so with diligence. If you have the gift of mercy, show it cheerfully.
- ROM 12:21 ~ Don't be overcome with evil, but rather overcome evil with good.
- GAL 2:20 ~ Paul wrote: I have been crucified with Christ, yet I live. But it is not I who live but Christ who lives in me. The life I live in the flesh I must live by faith in the Son of God who loved me and gave Himself for me.
- EPH 5:11 ~ Don't be a companion to the unfruitful works of darkness, but rather disclose them and rebuke them.
- PHP 2:11 ~ Every tongue should confess that Jesus Christ is Lord, to the glory of God the Father.

- 1 PE 3:15 ~ Sanctify the Lord in your hearts, and always be ready to give an answer, with humility and respect, to anyone who asks about the hope that is within you.
- 1 PE 4:10–11 ~ Whoever has received the gift of salvation in Christ should share that gift with others, as a steward of God's eternal grace. If you preach, do so as a messenger of God. If you minister, do so with the ability God gives you. Do this to glorify God through His Son Jesus Christ.
- 1 JO 2:6 ~ Whoever says they are a Christian should show they are following Christ by the way they conduct their lives.
- 1 JO 2:23 ~ Whoever denies the Son also denies the Father; whoever acknowledges the Son also acknowledges the Father.
- 1 JO 4:15 ~ Whoever confesses that Jesus is God's Son, God lives in that person and that person lives in God.
- 1 JO 5:9–10 ~ If we believe a person witnessing for another, we should believe God's witnessing even more; and God has given witness of His Son. Those who believe that Jesus is God's Son have God's witness in themselves; those who don't believe are calling God a liar, because they don't believe God's testimony concerning His Son.

Teaching

You don't have to be a certified teacher to raise your children in the knowledge of the Lord. Using the Bible as the text, anyone can teach their children the ways of righteousness; plus, there are numerous study guides and children's storybooks that make it easy and fun to learn about God and Jesus. Everyone should value the instruction of the Lord for it is the highest source of knowledge and understanding available, providing learning that is applicable to a fulfilling life that goes on forever starting with the day a person takes God at His Word.

- DEU 4:9–10,36 ~ Don't forget what God has done for you. May His works have a lasting impression on your lives. Teach your children and grandchildren about His glorious miracles. Especially remind your children of God's instructions given Moses at Sinai about reverencing Him and about teaching His laws from generation to generation. From heaven God made you to hear His voice so that He could instruct you. On earth He spoke to all people from the great fire giving them His laws.
- DEU 6:2–7 ~ Fear the Lord and keep all His commandments and laws. Ensure that your children and your children's children obey God. Do this and you will prosper and your life will be prolonged. Love God with all your heart, soul, and might. Keep God's Word in your heart and teach His ways carefully and thoughtfully to your children. Talk with your family all the time about God, every day and night, whenever you are together.
- PSA 32:8 ~ I (God) will instruct you and teach you in the way you should go. I will guide you with my eye.
- PRO 13:1,18 ~ A wise son listens to his father's instructions, but those who reject wise counsel hear nothing. Poverty and shame are the rewards for those who refuse instruction, but those who respectfully listen when being scolded will be honored.
- PRO 22:6 ~ Instruct your children in the way they should go and when they mature, they will not depart from it.
- MAL 4:5–6 ~ The prophet Elijah will return before God's judgment. His preaching will bring parents and children back together, to be of one heart and mind. They will learn to repent in order to avoid destruction.

- MAT 13:52 ~ Jesus said, "Every teacher who has been instructed about the kingdom of heaven is like a homeowner who has a treasure chest of things both old and new."
- ROM 2:21–22 ~ If you teach others, don't you also teach yourself? Don't you practice what you preach?
- EPH 6:1–4 ~ Children, obey your parents, for God has given them authority over you. Honor your parents as commanded by God in His Ten Commandments (EXO 20:12). This is the first commandment that brings a promise: If you honor your parents your life will be long and happy. Parents, don't provoke your children to anger and frustration. Instead, raise them in the nurture and discipline of righteousness, as instructed by God.
- COL 3:16 ~ Remember what Christ taught you and let His words enrich your lives and make you wise. Teach His words to one another. Sing them openly and spiritually in psalms and hymns with thankful hearts.
- 2 TI 2:24–26 ~ A servant of the Lord doesn't waste time arguing, but is gentle to everyone, able to teach, and not resentful. Such disciples gently instruct those who are in opposition to them, hoping that God will grant them repentance for acknowledging His truth, so that they may escape the devil's traps who would otherwise capture them for his own purposes.
- 2 TI 3:16 ~ All scripture is inspired by God and is effective for teaching, for reprimanding, for correcting, and for instruction in the ways of righteousness.

Evangelism

Jesus's final words before ascending into heaven commissioned Christians to make disciples of unbelievers (MAT 28:19). That is, we should spread the Gospel to people who have not heard or understood, so that they too can find salvation through Jesus Christ. The Bible teaches us how this works and what we are to do to make it happen.

- EXO 19:6 ~ You will be to me (God) a holy nation of priests. (also REV 1:6)
- ISA 55:10–12 ~ The rain and snow that falls from heaven does not return to heaven, but waters the earth, causing the plants to bud and to seed and providing food. In like manner, God's Word does not return to Him void, but accomplishes what He wishes, and prospers wherever He sends it. We joyfully go out, being led in peace. The mountains and hills sing before you and the trees clap their hands; the whole world will rejoice around you. Instead of a thorn bush, a tree will grow. And the name of the Lord will be magnified as an everlasting sign of the nurturing He provides.
- EZE 3:18 ~ God tells the wicked that they will die; you who know God must warn them about this in order to save them from death. For if you do not warn them, they will die; and their blood will be on your hands.
- MAT 18:18 ~ Jesus said, "Whatever you tie or untie on earth you will tie or untie in heaven."
- MAR 5:19 ~ Jesus told the man who had been cleansed of demon possession, "Go home to your friends and tell them what great things the Lord has done for you, and the compassion He has shown."
- LUK 12:11–12 ~ Jesus said, "When they bring you before the authorities, don't worry about what to say or do, for the Holy Spirit will provide the information when you need it."
- JOH 14:16–17; JOH 15:26–27 ~ Jesus said, "I will pray to the Father, and He will send the Comforter to be with you always. The Comforter is the Spirit of truth who testifies concerning the Son. He is the One that the world cannot receive because they do not know Him, but you have received Him and He lives in you. Therefore, you will also bear witness of me because you too have been with me from the very beginning."

- ACT 1:8 ~ Jesus told His disciples, "You will receive power once the Holy Spirit has come upon you. And you will be witnesses all across the land, and into the most remote corners of the earth."
- ACT 4:20 ~ We can't help but speak of the things we have seen and heard.
- ACT 10:42–43 ~ Peter preached, "Christ commanded us to preach to the people and to testify that it was He who was ordained by God to be the judge of the living and the dead. All the prophets have been witnesses, instructing that faith in Christ provides remission of sins."
- ROM 10:17–18,20 ~ Faith comes by hearing the Word of God. Haven't they heard? Yes, for it is written: Their words will reach the far corners of the earth. Just as Isaiah boldly proclaimed: I (God) was found by those who weren't even looking for me.
- 1 CO 2:13 ~ We speak, not the words that human wisdom teaches, but the words that the Holy Spirit teaches, comparing spiritual things with spiritual.
- 1 CO 3:16 ~ Don't you realize that you are the temple of God and inside you dwells His Holy Spirit?
- 1 CO 4:1,11–12 ~ We are the ministers of Christ and the stewards of the mysteries of God. We are hungry and thirsty, we are naked and beaten, and we have no home. We work hard, using our abilities. We bless those who mistreat us; we endure the persecutions of others and carry on.
- 1 CO 12:4–12,26 ~ There are a variety of spiritual gifts, but only one Spirit. There are different ways of administering but only one Lord. There are different operations, but the same God who works through them. The Spirit is manifested in some way in everyone to use productively. Some people have received wisdom, some knowledge, some faith, all from the same Spirit. Some people have the ability to heal, others to work miracles, others to prophesy, others to discern spirits, others to speak foreign tongues; but all of them are working with the same Spirit, who divides power among everyone as He chooses. Just as one body has many members so is Christ one body with many members. When one member suffers, all suffer; when one member is honored, all are honored.
- 2 CO 3:5–6 ~ We owe everything we are to God who has made us ministers of the New Testament. We don't tell them that they must adhere to the very letter of the Law, but to the Spirit; for the Law kills but the Spirit gives life.
- 2 CO 4:6 ~ God, who commanded the light to shine out of darkness, has shined in our hearts so that we can share the light of the knowledge of God's glory in Jesus Christ.
- 2 CO 9:6–7,10 ~ Whoever sows sparingly will reap sparingly; whoever sows bountifully will reap bountifully. It depends on the purpose one has in their heart. So when you give, don't do it begrudgingly or out of obligation, but give cheerfully, for that pleases God very much.
- 2 CO 10:17–18 ~ When you brag, brag only about the Lord. Those who commend themselves do not gain approval, but only those who God commends.
- 2 CO 12:9–10 ~ Jesus said to me (Paul), "My grace is sufficient for you, for my strength is made perfect in weakness." Therefore, I take pleasure when, for Christ's sake, I am weary, distressed, or needy, and when I am blamed or persecuted; for when I am weak, then I become strong.
- EPH 2:18–22 ~ Through Christ we have access by one Spirit to the Father. Thus, we are no longer strangers or foreigners, but fellow citizens with the saints in the household of God. We are built upon the foundation set by the apostles and the prophets, with Jesus Christ being the chief cornerstone. Together we comprise a well-framed building, a growing temple in the Lord. We are all joined together by His Spirit into one home.

- EPH 4:1–6,10–12 ~ I Paul, a prisoner for the Lord, implore that you stay worthy of the vocation for which you are called, with humbleness, kindness, and perseverance; loving one another, staying unified in the Spirit, and bonded together in peace. There is one body and one Spirit, and you are called in one hope. There is one Lord, one faith, one baptism, one God and Father of us all; He is above all, and through all, and in you. He that descended is also He that ascended far above the heavens. He made some apostles, some prophets, some evangelists, some pastors, and some teachers, for the perfecting of the saints, for the work of the ministry, and for the building of the body of Christ.
- EPH 6:19–20 ~ Paul wrote: Pray that God will give me the right words so that I may boldly proclaim the mystery of the Gospel, for which I am His ambassador in bondage.
- 2 TI 4:5 ~ Always be watchful, willing to endure afflictions, doing the work of the evangelist, doing what is necessary for the ministry.
- JAM 1:22,27 ~ Be doers of the Word and not just hearers, deceiving yourselves. To truly practice your religion and to be pure before God means you must help the orphans and widows, and not allow yourself to be corrupted by the world.
- JAM 3:17–18 ~ The wisdom from above is pure, peace-loving, gentle, accommodating, merciful, productive, impartial, and sincere. When the fruit of righteousness is sown in peace, it generates a harvest of peace and righteousness.
- 1 PE 2:9 ~ You are a chosen generation, a royal priesthood, a holy nation, a special people; for you have been selected to give praise to Him who called you out of darkness into His marvelous light.
- REV 1:6 ~ He (Christ) has made us kings and priests before God. To Him be all glory and dominion.

Holy Sacraments

God has given us the sacraments as a means of openly demonstrating our faith towards Him and our intention to keep His commandments. The sacraments are sacred acts, instituted by God Himself, in which Jesus Christ participated personally. The sacraments include Baptism and Communion. Both sacraments provide forgiveness of sins through public recognition of the atoning sacrifice of Christ. Both sacraments create in us a holy temple for God's Spirit to abide. Interestingly, Christ's ministry began when He was baptized, and His ministry was completed when He had sacrificed His body and blood shortly after the first Holy Communion with His apostles.

Holy Baptism

With the first sin came death. Therefore, we are born in sin and must be cleansed of this sin; baptism provides cleansing of the original sin of Adam which all people inherit. Baptism is a means of repentance and a demonstration of commitment to God. One must be baptized with water and with the Holy Spirit. The water symbolizes the washing or cleansing of our sins by the blood of Jesus Christ. Once clean, the Holy Spirit can enter. Baptism should be performed in the name of the Father, Son, and Holy Spirit. Note that all three persons of the Trinity were present at the baptism of Christ (MAT 3:16–17).

- PSA 51:5 ~ I was formed in sin and in sin I was conceived.
- EZE 36:24–28 ~ I will remove you from among the heathen, gather you out of all countries, and bring you into your own land. Then I will sprinkle clean water upon you, and you will be clean of all filth; from your idols I will I cleanse you. A new heart I will give you; and a new

- spirit I will put inside you. I will take away the heart of stone and place my spirit within you. And you will walk in my statutes and keep my judgments. You will live in the land I gave to your fathers; and you will be my people and I will be your God.
- MAT 3:11 ~ John the Baptist said, "I baptize you with water to fulfill your desire for repentance. But One comes after me, who is mightier than I, and whose shoes I am not worthy to carry. He will baptize you with the Holy Spirit and with fire."
- MAT 3:14–17; LUK 3:21–22 ~ Jesus came to John to be baptized and John said, "Why do you come to me for baptism? It is I who needs to be baptized by you." Jesus replied, "Let it be this way for now to fulfill all righteousness." So, John baptized Jesus. When Jesus arose from the water the heavens were opened and the Spirit of God descended like a dove, lighting upon Christ. And a voice from heaven declared, "This is my beloved Son, who pleases me immensely."
- MAT 28:19 ~ Jesus said to His apostles, "Go into every country and teach all nations what I have taught you. Baptize them in the name of the Father, Son, and Holy Spirit."
- MAR 1:4 ~ John baptized in the wilderness and preached the baptism of repentance for the remission of sins.
- MAR 16:16 ~ Jesus said, "Anyone who believes and is baptized will be saved. Anyone who does not believe will be damned."
- LUK 7:30 ~ The Pharisees rejected God's counsel and refused to be baptized.
- JOH 3:3–6 ~ Jesus said, "Unless a person is born again, he cannot see God's kingdom." Nicodemus asked, "How can someone be born when they are old?" Jesus answered, "Unless a person is born of water and of the Holy Spirit he cannot enter into God's kingdom. Those who are born of the flesh are flesh, and those who are born of the Spirit are Spirit."
- JOH 4:13–14 ~ Jesus answered the woman at the well, "Whoever drinks that water will thirst again. However, those who drink the water I give them will never be thirsty again, and it will be a well of water that springs up into everlasting life."
- ACT 1:5 ~ After His resurrection, Jesus told the apostles that they would be baptized with the Holy Spirit.
- ACT 2:38–41 ~ Peter said, "Repent and be baptized every one of you, in the name of Jesus Christ for the remission of your sins, and you will receive the gift of the Holy Spirit. This promise pertains to you, to your children, and to people everywhere: to whomever the Lord calls." Those who gladly listened to Peter's testimony were baptized, numbering about three thousand souls.
- ACT 19:4 ~ Paul said, "John truly baptized with the baptism of repentance, saying that everyone should believe in the One who was to follow him, who is Jesus Christ."
- ROM 6:3–4 ~ Paul said, "Don't you know that anyone who is baptized into Jesus Christ has been baptized unto death? Therefore, we who were baptized will be buried with Him, and as He was raised from the dead, so we shall receive a new life."
- 1 CO 12:13 ~ By one Spirit we are baptized into one body, regardless of our race or economic status; therefore, we all are nourished by one Spirit.
- 2 CO 5:17 ~ Whoever is in Christ has become a new creation; old things are put aside and all things have become new.
- GAL 3:27 ~ Whoever has been baptized into Christ has put on Christ like a suit of armor.
- EPH 4:4–5 ~ There is only one body, one Spirit, one Lord, one faith, and one baptism.
- EPH 5:26 ~ We are cleansed from sin by the washing of water and the Word (Christ's blood).
- TIT 3:5–7 ~ Christ has saved us, not because of our works of righteousness, but because of His mercy, through our spiritual washing by the Holy Spirit, which He bestowed so

abundantly through Jesus Christ our Savior. This is so that, being justified by His grace, we may become heirs according to the hope of eternal life.
- 1 PE 1:23 ~ You are born again, not of the corruptible seed of man, but of the incorruptible Word of God which lives forever.
- 1 PE 3:21 ~ Baptism will also save us through the resurrection of Jesus Christ. Baptism doesn't mean washing a dirty body, but rather establishing a clean conscience toward God.

Holy Communion

Holy Communion represents a special kind of intimate communication with God. It implies a joining together with God by allowing Christ to enter the heart and mind. We are joined to God by making our body a temple of God's Holy Spirit, through the partaking of the body and blood of Jesus Christ. Thus, the act of communion is nourishing to our body and to our spirit. This sacrament also represents a public witness of our faith in Christ, and our desire to be like Him and with Him. Consequently, through this act we are united together in the body of Christ by one Spirit.

- GEN 14:18–19 ~ King Melchizedek (King of Peace), priest of the most-high God, shared bread and wine with Abraham.
- EXO 25:22 ~ The Lord said to Moses, "I will commune with you from heaven, from between the two cherubim that are on the Ark of the Covenant. I will tell you all the commandments that I have for Israel."
- EXO 31:18 ~ God gave Moses two stone tablets on which He had written the Ten Commandments during their communion on Mt. Sinai.
- LEV 23:5–6 ~ The feasts of the Passover and Unleavened Bread are described, during which faith offerings are made. [The feasts of the Passover and Unleavened Bread symbolize the blood and body of Christ, respectively, sacrificed during this same Holy Week.]
- MAT 26:26–28 ~ Jesus took bread, blessed it, broke it into pieces, and distributed it to the apostles saying, "Take this bread and eat it, for this is my body." Then He took a cup of wine, thanked God, and passed the cup to the apostles saying, "Each of you drink from this cup of wine, for this is my blood of the New Covenant, shed for you and for many for the remission of sins."
- JOH 6:30–35,51–58 ~ The people said to Jesus, "Can you show us a sign to convince us that we should believe you, like when our fathers ate manna in the desert?" Jesus answered, "The manna from heaven didn't come from Moses; it came from God who gives you the true bread from heaven. The bread of life comes from heaven and gives life to the world. I am the bread of life; whoever comes to me will never hunger again and whoever believes in me will never thirst again. The bread I give is my flesh, and I will give it for the life of the world. Unless you eat the body and drink the blood of the Son of Man, you have no life. If you eat my body and drink my blood, you live in me and I in you; and you will have eternal life, for I will raise you up the last day. Mine is not like the manna from heaven, for whoever eats the bread I give will live forever."
- 1 CO 5:7 ~ Throw out the old leavened dough and become a new dough, without yeast; for that is what you have become because of the sacrifice of Christ who is the Passover Lamb.
- 1 CO 10:16–17,21 ~ The cup of blessing that we bless: doesn't it represent our communion with the blood of Christ? The bread that we break: doesn't it represent our communion with the body of Christ? Although we are many, we have become one body for we are all partakers of that one bread. You can't drink from the cup of the Lord and from the cup of devils (you can't be one with Christ if you commune with devils).

- 1 CO 11:25–29 ~ Jesus commanded the apostles on the first Holy Communion to partake of the sacrament often to remember Him. Thus, as often as you eat the bread and drink the wine of Holy Communion, you proclaim the death of Christ until His return. But if you participate in this holy sacrament unworthily (without sincerely repenting of your sins and desiring a communion with Christ), you will become one of those who are found guilty of Christ's crucifixion. Examine yourself before partaking of Holy Communion, because if you partake unworthily, you will be eating and drinking damnation upon yourself.
- 2 CO 6:14 ~ Do not be joined with unbelievers, for what fellowship can there be between righteousness and unrighteousness? What communion can there be between light and darkness?
- 2 CO 13:14 ~ The grace of the Lord Jesus Christ, the love of God, and the communion of the Holy Spirit be with you all.

Other Holy Practices

The church observes a number of acceptable rites and ceremonies in which believers can show their loyalty and commitment to God. These acts are found in the Bible and are thus, valid ways of demonstrating one's faith. Several religious practices are reviewed in the pages that follow. These practices are not considered sacraments, however, because Christ did not participate in them personally. They are sanctified by God because He recommended them as means by which we continue to live in accordance with His will.

Confirmation

Like Holy Communion, Confirmation represents a public witness and confirmation of one's faith in God. The term implies the confirmation of a lifetime commitment to God. Thus, it can be interpreted as a confirmation of one's baptism. God confirmed His promises to us through His Word and through His Son Jesus Christ. We must continuously confirm our faith in Him, His Word, and His Son. For this reason, Jesus Christ commanded His apostles to partake of Holy Communion often. When we confirm our love and faith in God, He confirms us through the indwelling of His Holy Spirit.

- ISA 44:24–26 ~ The Lord said, "I am the Lord who makes all things... and who confirms the Word of my Servant..."
- MAR 16:19–20 ~ After Jesus gave His last instructions to the apostles, He ascended into heaven to sit at God's right hand. And the apostles did as Jesus had told them, preaching the Word everywhere and confirming the Word with signs and miracles.
- ACT 14:22 ~ The apostles returned to places they had preached before to confirm the souls of the disciples, to encourage them in their faith, and to remind them that they must endure much hardship before entering the kingdom of God.
- ROM 10:17 ~ Faith comes by hearing and hearing by the Word of God.
- 1 CO 1:5–8 ~ You are enriched by Christ in everything you say and everything you know. Even as the testimony of Christ was confirmed among you who wait for the day of His return, so He will confirm you until the end, ensuring that you receive all your spiritual needs, and be found blameless upon that day.
- 2 CO 2:8 ~ I urgently suggest that you confirm your love towards one another and to God.
- REV 2:10 ~ Jesus said, "You will suffer and be imprisoned because of me. But, be faithful unto death and I will give you a crown of life."
- REV 3:11 ~ Hold onto your crown of faith; don't let anyone take it away from you.

Marriage

Marriage is a religious rite, ordained by God in His Law. Marriage is not a command but a privilege. Marriage allows us to satisfy our emotional, physical, and worldly needs while still obeying God. Marriage represents a commitment to one's spouse, similar to the commitment made to God through participation in the Holy Sacraments, and the commitment made by Christ to His Church on Earth. It is a covenant between one man and one woman which reflects God's contract with humanity to bless those who love Him and follow His commandments.

- GEN 2:18,21–23 ~ God said, "It is not good for man to be alone so I will make a helper for him." God took a rib from man and made woman. Adam said, "This woman is bone of my bones and flesh of my flesh; she will be called woman for she was taken out of man."
- GEN 2:24 ~ A man shall leave his parents and cling to his wife; and they shall become one flesh.
- GEN 3:16–17 ~ God said to the woman, "I will multiply your sorrow at conception and your pain at childbirth. Your desires will be toward your husband, and he will rule over you." God said to the man, "The ground is cursed for you, for you will eat it and toil over it all of your life."
- EXO 20:14 ~ You are never to commit adultery.
- LEV 18:6–16 ~ You should never get naked with one of your relatives or in-laws.
- LEV 21:7,13–14 ~ Do not take a prostitute for a wife, or a profane woman, or a divorced woman. Take a virgin of your own race for a wife, but not a widow, a divorced woman, or a prostitute.
- DEU 17:17 ~ A king should not seek to multiply his wives or his riches.
- PRO 5:18 ~ Rejoice with the wife of your youth.
- PRO 18:22 ~ Whoever finds a virtuous wife finds a good thing and obtains favor from God.
- PRO 19:13–14 ~ A quarrelsome wife is a continuous drag upon a marriage, but a prudent wife is from God.
- PRO 31:10–31 ~ Whoever finds a virtuous woman for a wife will have something more valuable than rubies. She will do her husband good all of her life. She will work hard and give herself to the household. She will be generous and complimentary to others. Her husband will be well known and powerful. She will be clothed in strength and honor. She will be wise and kind. She will not be lazy and her husband and children will praise her for it. Although favor can be deceitful and beauty can be vain, faith in God will always yield His praise.
- ECC 9:9 ~ Always be happy with your spouse, and love him or her the rest of your life.
- JER 29:6 ~ Get married and have children, and encourage your children to get married and have children, so your family can increase and not diminish.
- MAL 2:14–16 ~ The Lord has formed a husband and wife into one flesh. In both flesh and spirit, they belong to Him. But why is this so? Because He wishes godly offspring from them. Guard your spirit, and do not break the covenant with your wife or husband by getting divorced.
- MAT 5:28 ~ Jesus said, "Anyone who looks upon a member of the opposite sex with lust has committed adultery in their heart."
- MAT 19:6,9 ~ Jesus said, "Once you are joined in marriage you are no longer two separate persons, but have become one flesh. Whatever God has joined together, nobody should split apart. You cannot divorce your spouse unless he or she has committed adultery against you. If you divorce your spouse and marry another you are guilty of adultery. If you marry someone who is divorced you are guilty of adultery."

- 1 CO 7:4 ~ The wife does not have exclusive power over her body, neither does the husband have exclusive power over his body.
- 1 CO 7:1–5,8–10,28,39 ~ It is fine if you never touch a member of the opposite sex. But if you can't contain your emotions then marry, for it is better to marry than to burn with passion. Get married if you want to avoid the sin of fornication. However, if you marry you must be charitable to your spouse. A husband should have power over the wife's body. Don't lie to your spouse, and don't ever split apart. It's not a sin to marry, but married people will have problems associated with their sinful and weak nature. Once married, you are bound to each other until one of you dies.
- 2 CO 6:14 ~ Do not be unequally yoked together with unbelievers; for what fellowship can there be between righteousness and unrighteousness, and what communion has light with darkness?
- EPH 5:21–25,28,33 ~ Submit to one another. Wives, submit to your husbands, because the husband is the head of the wife just like Christ is the head of the church. Thus, the wife is subject to the husband at all times. Husbands, love and protect your wives, even as Christ loved the Church and gave Himself for it. You must love your spouse as much as you love yourselves.
- COL 3:18–19 ~ Wives, submit to your husbands, as long as it is within the Law. Husbands, love your wives and don't be bitter with them.
- 1 TI 5:14 ~ It is good for a young woman to marry, bear children, and guide the household. It is not good for a wife to be contrary, or to speak blamefully or rashly.
- TIT 2:4–5 ~ Wives, be sober, and love your husbands and your children. Be discreet, chaste, good homemakers, and obedient to your husbands, so the Word of God will not be blasphemed. Young men, be sober, upright and not corrupt; be serious and sincere, speaking good things about others.
- 1 PE 3:1,7 ~ Wives, obey your husbands, and teach them the Word if they do not understand it. Husbands, listen to your wives; honor your wives as the weaker sex, and as an equal. Stay together in the grace of life, and your prayers will be answered.

Worship, Praise, Thanksgiving, Offerings, and Service

We should constantly show God our appreciation for all His wonderful gifts. We can do this by offering Him our thanks, praise, and worship. We also show our appreciation by helping others in need, and by giving offerings and tithes to the poor, handicapped, or helpless, and to support your place of worship as well as the church at large.

In the Old Testament, sacrificial offerings were given to God as a token of appreciation and to atone for sin. But when Christ came, He made the ultimate sacrifice by offering Himself. Therefore, we should likewise offer ourselves, our time, and our treasure in service to God and to people that are needy or suffering. God has given us so much, including our lives, opportunities, and wealth (spiritual and material); and all He asks is for us to give back a fraction of what He has given; do so with gratitude and it will bring glory to His name.

- GEN 14:19–20 ~ Melchizedek (God's high priest) blessed Abraham, and Abraham gave Melchizedek tithes of everything he had.
- EXO 23:19 ~ As you reap, offer to God the choicest sample of your first harvest (i.e., the first fruits).
- NUM 18:26 ~ Moses told the Israelites they were commanded by God to give tithes to the Levites for their support, and for the Levites to offer to God a tenth (tithe) of those tithes.

- DEU 14:22 ~ You should give tithes of all your crops (i.e., income).
- DEU 26:12–13 ~ After you have tithed during the third year, which is the year of tithing, and you have given your tithes to the Levites, strangers, orphans, widows, and the hungry, then declare this to the Lord.
- 1 CH 16:25,34–35 ~ Great is the Lord, and greatly should He be praised; He is to be feared above all gods. Let's give thanks to the Lord for He is good and His mercy endures forever. Ask God to gather His people together and deliver us from the wicked, so that we can give Him thanks and praise.
- 1 CH 23:30 ~ Give thanks and praise to the Lord every morning and every evening.
- 2 CH 5:13–14 ~ As the orchestra and choir joined in musical harmony to thank and praise God, the church was filled with a cloud, for the glory of God had filled the church.
- 2 CH 31:5 ~ Everyone brought in abundance the first fruits of their crops, wine, oil, honey, and all their profits.
- PSA 9:1–2 ~ I will praise you Lord with all my heart; I will show your marvelous works. I will be glad and rejoice. I will sing praises to your holy name.
- PSA 30:4,12 ~ Sing to the Lord and give Him thanks forever.
- PSA 50:23 ~ God says that whoever offers Him praise, glorifies Him. To those who do this, He will show His salvation.
- PSA 95:2 ~ Let us come before God with thanksgiving; make a joyful noise to Him with psalms.
- PSA 96:8 ~ Give God the glory He deserves. Bring your offerings and worship Him.
- PSA 100:4 ~ Enter into God's gates with thanksgiving and into his courts with praise. Be thankful and bless His name.
- PSA 147:1 ~ It is good to sing praises to God for this is pleasant and beautiful.
- PSA 150:2,6 ~ Praise God for His mighty acts and His excellent greatness. Let everything that breathes praise the Lord.
- PRO 3:9 ~ Honor the Lord by giving Him the first part of your income, and He will fill your barns with grain, and your kegs will overflow with the finest wine.
- ISA 12:4 ~ Praise God, call on His name, declare His works everywhere, and tell everyone His name is exalted.
- JER 20:13 ~ Sing to the Lord and praise Him, for He has delivered the souls of the poor from the wicked.
- DAN 2:23 ~ I thank and praise you God of my fathers, who has given me wisdom and power, and has told me what you want me to know and to do.
- MAL 3:10 ~ The Lord says, "Bring tithes of all your income to the storage room so that there will be plenty in my house, and prove to yourself that I will open the windows of heaven and pour upon you so many blessings that you will not have room for them all."
- MAT 4:10 ~ Jesus told Satan, "You must worship the Lord your God and serve only Him."
- MAT 6:1–4 ~ Jesus said, "Remember that you shouldn't give to the poor just so others can see you do it; otherwise you will receive no reward from your Father in heaven. In other words, don't sound your horn when you give like the hypocrites do, who do it only so that others will see them and praise them for it. Truly, this is the only reward they will ever receive for their good deeds. Give generously, but do so in secret; and your Father in heaven will see it and He will reward you openly."
- MAT 25:40,45 ~ Jesus said, "Whenever you have done something to help another person, you have done it to me as well; whenever you have not done something to help another person, you have not done it to me either."

- MAR 12:33 ~ It is more important to love God and to love others than to offer all kinds of sacrifices on the alter.
- LUK 2:8–14 ~ The angels told the shepherds about Jesus's birth and praised God saying, "Glory be to God in the highest, and on earth, peace and good will toward all people." Note: when Jesus entered Jerusalem before His crucifixion, similar praises were offered to Him by the people (MAT 21:9,15).
- LUK 16:13 ~ Jesus said, "You cannot serve God and money also."
- JOH 4:24 ~ Jesus said, "God is Spirit and should be worshipped in spirit and in truth."
- ACT 20:35 ~ In your labors give to the needy, remembering the words of Jesus Christ, "It is more blessed to give than to receive."
- ROM 12:1 ~ Give yourselves to God. Let yourself be a living sacrifice. After all He has done for you, is that too much to ask?
- ROM 12:6–8 ~ Use those gifts God has given to you. If you have the gift of prophecy, exercise that gift according to the proportion of your faith. If your gift is ministry, then minister; if it is teaching, then teach; if it is encouraging, then encourage; if it is giving to the needy, then give generously; if it is leadership, then lead diligently; if it is showing mercy, then do so cheerfully.
- 1 CO 16:2 ~ On the first day of each week everyone should set aside something for the Lord in accordance with the degree that they have prospered by His grace, so it will not be necessary to take a collection.
- 2 CO 9:7 ~ Everyone should give whatever they think is fair in their heart. Giving should be done voluntarily, not out of obligation, for God loves a cheerful giver.
- GAL 5:13 ~ You have been given the freedom to love and serve one another.
- EPH 5:20 ~ Always give thanks to God for everything, in the name of Jesus Christ.
- PHP 4:6 ~ Don't worry about anything, but in everything, through praise and thanksgiving, make your needs known to God.
- COL 3:16–17 ~ Remember what Christ taught you and let His words enrich your lives and make you wise. Teach His words to each other. Sing them openly and spiritually in psalms and hymns with thankful hearts. Whatever you do or say, do it in Jesus's name, and give thanks to God in Jesus's name.
- COL 3:24 ~ If you help others you are really serving Christ.
- 1 TH 5:18 ~ Give God thanks for everything, for this is the will of God through Christ concerning you.
- 2 TH 2:13 ~ We must always give thanks to God, because He has chosen you from the beginning for salvation, through sanctification of the Spirit and belief in the truth.
- 1 TI 2:1 ~ Prayers, intercessions, and thanks should be given to God by all people.
- HEB 10:10–12,18 ~ Under the new plan we have been forgiven and made clean by Christ's offering. Under the old plan, sacrificial offerings were made that could take away one's sins. But Christ gave Himself for our sins as a sacrifice for all time, and He now sits at the highest place of honor at God's right hand. There is no need to offer any more blood sacrifices for sin.
- HEB 10:24–25 ~ Let us encourage one another to promote love and good works. Let us never cease to fellowship with one another in God's house as others have the habit of doing.
- HEB 12:28 ~ Since God has given us the kingdom, let us please Him by serving Him with thankful hearts, with holy fear, and with awe.
- HEB 13:15 ~ Let us continually offer to God the sacrifice of praise; praise and thanks are the fruits of our lips.

Prayer

God has provided prayer as a means of communicating to Him our needs, desires, griefs, and personal problems. We can receive anything we want if we pray in faith in the name of Jesus Christ. The Bible teaches us how to pray and what to pray for. Basically, we can ask God anything and He will answer in a way that delivers wisdom and additional benefits. We may think we want something but God gives us what we need, and this is what we really want: that His will be done in our lives.

- GEN 15:2 ~ Abram prayed, "Oh Lord, please give me an heir, a son."
- GEN 18:23–32 ~ Abraham prayed, "Will you indeed destroy the righteous with the wicked? Would you spare the city for fifty righteous people? For forty-five, forty, thirty, twenty, or ten?"
- EXO 32:11–13 ~ Moses prayed, "Why are you mad at your people? Please turn away your anger. Remember your promises to Abraham, Isaac and Israel, that you would multiply your descendants and give them the promised land."
- NUM 6:24–26 ~ God instructed Moses how to bless the people: May the Lord bless and keep you, may He make His face to shine upon you and be gracious unto you, may the Lord smile upon you and give you His peace.
- DEU 30:16,20 ~ God commands us: Walk in the ways of the Lord, obey His commandments, and you will live and multiply. Love the Lord your God, obey His voice, and cling to Him throughout your life.
- 1 SA 1:27–28 ~ For this child I (Hannah) prayed. And He granted my petition. Therefore, I have dedicated him (Samuel) to the Lord.
- 1 KI 3:6 ~ Solomon prayed to God, "You have shown great and lasting love to my father David because of his faithfulness and uprightness. Now you have made me king in his place, although I am but a child, and I am in the middle of a great people who you have chosen. Please give me an understanding mind to govern your people so I can discern good from evil. For who is able to govern this great nation?"
- 1 KI 8:28–30 ~ Solomon prayed, "Lord, respect this prayer of your servant towards this place of worship. Watch over your house day and night. Answer the prayers of those who pray over this sanctuary and forgive them."
- 2 KI 19:15–19 ~ Hezekiah prayed, "Oh Lord, who is enthroned above the angels and all the kingdoms of the earth, only you are God who has made heaven and earth. Incline your ear and open your eyes to these people who mock you. Cast their gods into the fire. Save us from them. Let all the kingdoms of the earth know that you alone are God."
- 1 CH 16:8–12,23–25,29–31,35–36 ~ Give thanks to the Lord; call upon His name; make known His wondrous deeds to everyone. Sing praises to Him and rejoice. Continuously seek the Lord with all your strength. Remember all the great things He has done. Sing to the Lord all the earth; tell others about His salvation. Declare His glory to the nations. For great is the Lord and He is greatly to be praised. He is to be held in awe above all gods. Give to the Lord His due glory, with praise and offerings. Worship the Lord in holy array; tremble before Him all the earth. Let the heavens be glad and the earth rejoice, and let everyone say, "The Lord reigns." Give thanks to the Lord for He is good and His steadfast love endures forever. Ask God to deliver, gather, and save you, so that you may give eternal thanks and glory to Him. Blessed be the Lord, from everlasting to everlasting.
- 2 CH 7:14 ~ God says, "If my people, who are called by my name, humble themselves, pray and seek my face, and turn from their wicked ways, I will hear them, and I will forgive their sins and heal their land."

- 2 CH 20:9 ~ Solomon prayed, "If evil comes upon us, the sword of judgment, pestilence, or famine, we will stand before you Lord, and cry to you in our affliction, and you will hear us and save us."
- PSA 19:14 ~ David prayed, "Let the words of my mouth and the meditation of my heart be acceptable to you, oh Lord, my strength and my redeemer."
- PSA 25:1–5,11,21 ~ David prayed, "To you Lord I lift up my soul. God, in you alone do I trust; let me never be ashamed. Please don't allow my enemies to get the better of me. Let no-one who waits for you be put to shame. Instead, let those who are deliberately treacherous become ashamed. Make me to know your ways and teach me your paths. Lead me in truth and teach me. For your name's sake, oh Lord, pardon my guilt. Preserve me in uprightness and integrity."
- PSA 37:3–8 ~ Trust in the Lord and do good and you will have security. Take delight in the Lord and you will receive the delights of your heart. Commit yourself to the Lord and He will vindicate you. Wait patiently for the Lord and don't worry. Refrain from anger.
- PSA 40:11,14,16 ~ David prayed, "Please don't withhold your mercy from me, Lord. Put those to shame and confusion that would take my life. May all who seek you rejoice and gladly bear your name."
- PSA 50:15 ~ The Lord says, "Call upon me in the day of trouble, and I will deliver you, and you shall glorify me."
- PSA 51:10–12 ~ Create in me a clean heart, Lord, and renew an upright spirit within me. Don't remove me from your presence and don't take your Holy Spirit from me. Restore to me the joy of your salvation, and uphold me with your free Spirit.
- PSA 70:1 ~ David prayed, "Be pleased to deliver me Lord; make haste to help me."
- PSA 118:1 ~ Give thanks to the Lord for He is good, and His steadfast love endures forever.
- PSA 119:18,27,33,35–39,41 ~ Open my eyes so that I can see wondrous things from your Law. Make me understand your rules of conduct and I will meditate upon your wondrous works. Teach me your statutes and I will keep them until the end. Lead me in the paths of righteousness. Incline my heart to your testimonies and not to personal gain. Turn my eyes from vanity and give me life in your ways. Let your steadfast love and salvation come to me.
- ISA 65:24 ~ God says, "I will answer you before you even call; I will hear you before you even speak."
- JER 33:3 ~ The Lord says, "Call on me and I will answer you, and show you great and wonderful things that you've never known."
- DAN 9:4–6 ~ I (Daniel) prayed to the Lord, confessing my sins. I said, "Oh great and mighty God, who keeps the covenant with those who love Him and keep His commandments, we have sinned; we have been wicked; we have strayed from your commandments; we have not listened to your prophets."
- MAT 5:44 ~ Jesus said, "Love your enemies; bless those who curse you; do good to those who hate you, and pray for those who take advantage of you and abuse you."
- MAT 6:6–7 ~ Jesus taught: When you pray, do so in private. Pray to the Father in your mind and He will know what you are thinking. Pray to Him secretly, and He will reward you openly. Do not use vain repetitions like the unbelievers do, for they think they will be heard for their many words.
- MAT 6:9–13 ~ Jesus taught us to pray like this: Our Father in heaven, your name is holy. Let us come to your kingdom; let your will be done on earth as it is in heaven. Provide us our daily needs. Forgive us our sins, as we should forgive others who sin against us. Lead us away from temptation and deliver us from evil. For the kingdom, power, and glory are yours forever, Amen.

- MAT 6:33–34 ~ Seek first the kingdom of God and His righteousness, and everything else will be yours. Don't be anxious about tomorrow, because God will provide your needs.
- MAT 11:28 ~ Jesus said, "Come to me, all who are weary and burdened, and I will give you rest (also PSA 50:15).
- MAT 7:7 ~ Jesus taught: Ask and you will receive. Seek and you will find. Knock and the door will be opened.
- MAT 9:37–38 ~ Jesus said, "The harvest is plentiful but the laborers are few. Pray, therefore, that the Lord will send laborers into the harvest."
- MAT 15:22 ~ "Lord have mercy on me, my daughter has a demon," cried the Canaanite lady.
- MAR 11:23–24 ~ Jesus taught: Whatever you ask in prayer, believe that you will receive it and you will. If you pray without doubting, you can make the mountain fall into the sea.
- MAR 14:36 ~ Jesus prayed, "Father, if it be your will, let this cup pass from me. But let it be in accordance with your will and not mine."
- MAR 14:38 ~ Jesus said, "Watch and pray that you do not enter into temptation."
- LUK 2:29–32 ~ Simeon prayed, "Lord, let me die in peace, for I have seen living proof of the salvation you promised to all people: Your light to the Gentiles and the glory of Israel."
- LUK 6:28 ~ Jesus taught: Bless those who curse you. Pray for those who abuse you.
- LUK 18:13 ~ The tax collector prayed, "God be merciful to me a sinner."
- LUK 21:36 ~ Jesus taught: Watch for the signs and pray that you have the strength to escape the terrible things that will take place, and to stand before the Son of Man.
- LUK 23:34 ~ Jesus prayed, "God forgive them because they don't know what they're doing."
- JOH 12:28; JOH 17:1 ~ Jesus prayed, "Father, glorify your name; Father, glorify your Son."
- JOH 14:13 ~ Jesus said, "Whatever you pray for in my name, the Father will do it, so He may be glorified in the Son."
- JOH 16:23 ~ Jesus said, "If you ask the Father anything in my name, He will give it to you."
- ACT 12:5 ~ Peter was imprisoned. But earnest prayer for him was made by the church. (The prayers were answered and Peter escaped with the help of an angel.)
- ROM 8:26 ~ The Holy Spirit intercedes for us when we pray. We don't know what we should pray for all the time. But through the act of prayer, God analyzes our needs and answers our prayers in the best possible way.
- ROM 12:12 ~ Rejoice in hope, be patient in troubled times, be constant in prayer.
- 1 CO 14:9,15,19 ~ If you don't speak words that can be understood, who will know what you are saying? You will be speaking into the air. I will pray in the spirit and with understanding. I will sing in the spirit and with understanding. In church, I'd rather speak five words that make sense and can teach, than speak ten thousand words that nobody understands.
- 2 CO 7:10 ~ Godly grief produces repentance, which leads to salvation and brings no regret.
- EPH 5:20 ~ Always and for everything give thanks to God the Father in the name of our Lord Jesus Christ.
- EPH 6:18–19 ~ Pray all the time in the Spirit. Keep alert and persevere. Pray for Christians, prophets, and priests, that their words will proclaim the mystery of the Gospel.
- PHP 4:6–7 ~ Don't have anxiety about anything, but pray for everything. With thanksgiving let your requests be known to God. And the peace of God that surpasses all understanding will keep your heart and mind in Jesus Christ.
- COL 4:2 ~ Continue to pray and wait for the answer, giving thanks for the result.
- 1 TH 5:17–18 ~ Pray constantly. Give thanks in all circumstances.
- 2 TH 3:1 ~ Pray for Christian teachers and ministers, and pray for the freedom to openly speak God's Word.

- 1 TI 2:1–2,8 ~ I (Paul) urge that supplications, prayers, intercessions, and thanksgiving be made to God for all people, for leaders, and for all who are in authority, so that we can lead an honest and peaceful life of godliness and truth. People should pray everywhere, lifting up holy hands, without being doubtful or angry.
- TIT 3:1 ~ Be submissive to rulers and authority, be obedient, and be ready for honest work.
- JAM 1:6 ~ Ask in faith without doubting.
- JAM 5:16 ~ Confess your faults to each other and pray for each other so you can be healed. The fervent prayer of a righteous person yields high returns.
- 1 JO 5:14–15 ~ If we ask Him anything according to His will, He will give it to us. If we believe that He hears us, He will hear us and He will fulfill our desires.

Prayer Guide

The guide below lists some things that we should pray for each day. Remember first to thank and praise God for His grace and mercy, and to confess and repent of your sins. Then it is appropriate to bring your petitions to the Lord, asking in the name of Jesus Christ. If you come to God faithfully, sorrowfully, and humbly, He will gladly listen to you. He always answers prayers, and will respond to your prayers in a way that enriches you spiritually and strengthens you mentally and physically.

Give Thanks and Praise to God for Spiritual Blessings.

I (we) give thanks and praise to you, Lord, for the wonderful blessings lovingly bestowed upon me (us). Thank you especially for sending your Son to die for us and for sending your Holy Spirit to comfort us. Please don't take your Holy Spirit from us, and please don't let us stray away from you. We also thank and praise you for your Word that enlightens us and for your Holy Sacraments which enrich us. We give special thanks for your grace and mercy, and the countless spiritual treasures we possess. We also thank you for the gift of prayer, and for being faithful and responsive in addressing our needs. Thank you for all who minister to others in the name of Christ in Spirit and in truth, and help me (us) to minister to others in your name using my (our) spiritual gifts to edify your church.

Give Thanks and Praise to God for Worldly Blessings.

Thank you, Lord, for my (our) family (especially parents, siblings, children, and spouse), our relatives, and our friends. Thank you for providing all we need to sustain our bodies and lives. Thank you for the worldly opportunities and material possessions that we enjoy. Remind us, however, to strive for spiritual riches as opposed to material things, knowing that everything we need will be provided. Help us to remember that all good things come from you, Lord. Help us to be generous in proportion to the degree that you have prospered us. Praise be to you Heavenly Father for blessings too numerous to mention.

Ask for Forgiveness and Mercy (Repent).

Please forgive me (us) of our sins (enumerate sins if possible). Truly we have sinned against you and others in our thoughts, words, and actions. Continue to abide in our hearts and minds. Create in us a clean heart, an open mind, and an upright spirit. Guide us always in our search for you and your righteousness and truth, and please have mercy on our souls. Help us to help others who are in need, especially those who seek you. Encourage us to be as forgiving, merciful, and compassionate to others as you are with us.

Pray for God's Church and the Spiritual Needs of Others.

Help us to be diligent in the study of your Word. Make us understand you and your Word more each day, and help us to share this knowledge with others, so that they too may understand and believe. Spread your Word to all people; let your Word be spoken freely throughout the world. Strengthen believers in the true faith and let your church, the body of Christ, grow and flourish (pray for your own church, pastor, and elders as well). Strengthen those who are commissioned by you to be ministers of your Word. Let us share as laborers in your harvest to bring souls back to you and Christ. Allow our enemies and wicked people everywhere to find you and become your children.

Pray for the Nation, World Leaders, and Peace.

Lord, please guide our country, our governors, administrators, and leaders with your Holy Spirit so they can make decisions which will further your kingdom and lift our nation spiritually and morally. Help us to be a beacon of hope for all too see. Let there be peace among nations and please bring an end to senseless wars. Let your Word be spoken freely so that people who are following false gods may see you through your Son Jesus Christ and be set free. Please be with those who are fighting the good fight of faith in foreign lands. Protect and defend your flock from those who hate Jesus, persecute Christians, or spread false doctrine. Let your truth be known in every corner of the earth. Guide and direct the leaders of all nations and peoples, and all who are in authority; help them to govern and rule in accordance with your will and your Law. Let there be peace and love among all people and demographics at home and abroad.

Pray for Your Spiritual Needs.

Dear Lord, help me (us) to prosper in the Spirit and please continue to provide me (us) with our spiritual needs. Bless our home and family. Assist us to act on our faith and to bear the fruits of the Spirit: love, joy, peace, patience, gentleness, kindness, faith, compassion, and self-control. Help us to grow in the true faith to the salvation of our souls. Please provide us with integrity and honesty, loyalty and obedience, mercy and compassion, level-headedness and calmness, and godliness and righteousness. Remind us that you are always with us.

- Help us to love you above all others and to love our neighbors as ourselves.
- Help us to serve you first, our neighbors next, and ourselves last.
- Strengthen and preserve us each day in our faith and love towards you.
- Help us always to keep our trust and hope in Jesus Christ your Son.
- Guide and direct us along the paths of righteousness and away from wickedness.
- Assist us in obeying your commandments and resisting temptation.
- Preserve us in your immeasurable peace and joy.
- Protect us from all harm, danger, and evil.
- Heal us and our loved ones of afflictions, whether physical, mental, or spiritual.
- Help us to avoid trouble and troublemakers and please keep them away from us.
- Help us to be safe and secure in your love which is our confidence.
- Let our lives be consecrated to you, Lord, and help us to be a blessing to others.
- Help us to use our time, talents, and treasures in service to you and others.
- Enable us to glorify your name in all that we say and do.
- Remind us of your presence and fill us with your Spirit.
- Let us always praise your holy name.

<u>Ask God to Help Those with Special Needs.</u>

Help, comfort, and defend the handicapped, underprivileged, afflicted, and lonely; the exploited and oppressed, the abused and neglected; the elderly and the young; those who have been traumatized and those who have lost loved ones (and others named in your heart). Help and comfort those who have been victimized by natural disaster, calamity, civil war, terrorism, and political, social, or economic strife. Especially help those who have been victimized and/or led astray by false prophets, cults, evil people, and demons; comfort them and help them to find the freedom and truth that can only be found through Jesus Christ.

<u>Ask God for Help with Your Special Needs. (Ask for anything and everything.)</u>

Please provide our mental, physical, and emotional needs and sustain us in our health and sanity. Let us live happy, productive, and prosperous lives. Help us to conduct ourselves in the ways of godliness, to be good Christian soldiers, and to bear good fruit. Enable us to be diligent in fulfilling your will in our lives.

- Let me (us) be your witness(es) to the true faith.
- Make us servants of your love.
- Make us instruments of your hand.
- Make us voices of your glory.
- Make us ambassadors of your peace.
- Make us humble and not proud.
- Make us giving and not selfish.
- Help us to search for truth, wisdom, knowledge, and understanding.
- Equip us to spread the good news of the Gospel at every opportunity.

<u>Salutation</u>

Let your Spirit always live in me (us). Please keep our souls securely in your hands, and please have your angels watch over us and protect us. Write your Word into our minds, and maintain your love in our hearts. Bless us and sustain us in our faith now and forever through your steadfast and unconditional love. In the name of Jesus Christ, I (we) pray, Amen.

The Lord's Prayer

(Poem by Andrew Barber)

Our Holy Father in heaven,
Thank you for all you have given.
In our lives let your will be done,
As in heaven where we would come.

Please provide us our daily needs;
And forgive us our awful deeds.
Help us forgive one another,
Remembering to love each other.

Your righteousness always feed us.
Away from evil please lead us.
Kingdom, power, and glory are yours;
So let us be, forevermore. Amen.

The Creed

The following statement of doctrine has been paraphrased from the *Nicene Creed*, and provides the basis for our Christian beliefs. It is recommended that readers consult the referenced scriptures in their Bibles and become familiar with those passages. These essential truths are considered to be the building blocks of the Christian faith and are not subject to scrutiny, debate, or reinterpretation. The first creed was the *Apostle's Creed* which was passed along by apostles and disciples of Christ via the oral tradition, which is how Paul received it (read 1 CO 15). These tenets of the true Christian faith continued to be taught, and were highlighted in writings found in the New Testament. The *Nicene* and *Athanasian* creeds were established much later during councils convened to clarify and elaborate on the tenets of the true faith advanced in the *Apostle's* creed. These words continue to be professed as a witness to the Triune God.

I believe that there is only one God (DEU 6:4; JER 10:10; 1 CO 8:6), the **Almighty Father** of humankind (MAL 2:10; JOH 1:12; EPH 4:4–6), who created the earth, the heavens, and everything that exists, both visible and invisible (GEN 1:1–31; ACT 17:24; COL 1:16; HEB 11:1–3). God the Father gave us His Law and His Covenant of Grace (ISA 2:3; JOH 1:17; ROM 6:14–15).

I believe that God's only begotten Son, **Jesus Christ**, is my Lord (PSA 110:1–2; JOH 20:28; PHP 2:5–11). Christ, being the very light, life, and essence of God (JOH 8:18–19; COL 1:12–19; COL 2:9; HEB 1:3) was born of God (PSA 2:6–7; ISA 9:6; GAL 4:4–5), not created (ISA 44:6; REV 1:4–5). Christ was born a male child through the power of the Holy Spirit (ISA 11:2; MAT 3:16–17) who conceived Him in the womb of the Virgin Mary (ISA 7:14; LUK 1:34–35). Christ, who has been with God from the beginning (ISA 48:16; JOH 1:1–4,14; JOH 17:5; 1 PE 1:18–20), was sent from heaven to bring salvation to all people through His suffering and death (ISA 53:1–12; JOH 3:16; ROM 5:8–11; 1 PE 3:18–19). Jesus Christ was crucified, died and was buried; the third day he rose again declaring victory over the death and hell (EPH 4:7–10; 1 PE 3:18–19). In accordance with the scriptures (ISA 53:10; MAL 4:2; 1 CO 15:3–4), Christ gave His live and took it back again (HOS 6:2; JOH 2:18–22; JOH 10:17–18; LUK 24:1–9) ensuring the resurrection of all people (JOB 19:25–26; ISA 26:19; EZE 37:1–6; REV 20:4–5). Jesus ascended into heaven and now sits at the right hand of God our Father (PSA 80:17; MAR 14:61–62; ACT 7:55–56). Christ will come again in glory, to judge the living and the dead (ECC 12:14; EZE 7:3; DAN 7:10; JOH 5:22–30; 2 CO 5:10; REV 20:12–15). His kingdom is everlasting (1 CH 17:11–12; PSA 145:11–13; REV 22:1–5).

I believe in God's **Holy Spirit** (1 PE 1:1–4; 1 JO 5:6–8), who proceeds from both the Father and the Son (ISA 11:2; JOH 14:26; JOH 15:26: LUK 4:1; EPH 2:18), and who gives us life (GEN 2:7; ZEC 12:1; JOH 6:63; 2 CO 3:6). He is the Word who spoke through the prophets, through the Holy Bible, and through Jesus Christ and His apostles (ISA 55:10–11; ROM 1:16; 1 CO 2:13–16; GAL 1:8–12; 2 TI 3:16; 2 PE 1:21). Being one with the Father and His Son Jesus Christ, the Holy Spirit also is to be worshipped, praised, and glorified (ISA 6:3; MAT 3:16–17; MAT 28:18–20; 2 CO 13:14).

I believe in God's Holy Church, which is the Body of Christ (ROM 12:4–5: EPH 1:19–23; EPH 4:14–16). I acknowledge Baptism for the forgiveness of sins (MAR 16:16; ACT 2:38–41; 1 PE 3:21), and I recognize Holy Communion as a means to further sanctify my soul (MAT 26:26–28; JOH 6:51–58; 1 CO 10:16–21; 1 CO 11:23–29). I look forward to the resurrection of the dead (JOH 11:25–26; 1 CO 15:12–58; REV 7: 9–14), and living forever with the Lord of the universe (DEU 30:19–20; PSA 37:18,28–29; ISA 56:2–8; JOH 14:19; 1 JO 3:1–2).

What a Friend We Have in Jesus

What a friend we have in Jesus, all our sins and griefs to bear!
What a privilege to carry everything to God in prayer!
Oh what peace we often forfeit, oh what needless pain we bear,
All because we do not carry everything to God in prayer!

Have we trials and temptations? Is there trouble anywhere?
We should never be discouraged; take it to the Lord in prayer.
Can we find a friend so faithful, who will all our sorrows share?
Jesus knows our every weakness, take it to the Lord in prayer.

Are we weak and heavy laden, cumbered with a load of care?
Precious Savior, still our refuge! Take it to the Lord in prayer.
Do your friends despise, forsake you? Take it to the Lord in prayer;
In His arms He'll take and shield thee, thou wilt find a solace there.

Blessed are those who hunger and thirst for righteousness, for they will be filled (MAT 5:6).

The Good Shepherd
Painting by Bernard Plockhorst (1825–1907)

Lesson: Gone but Not Forgotten

Examples:
- A family member who has passed away is gone but not forgotten.
- A childhood sweetheart may be long gone but not forgotten.
- Sin: gone but not forgotten?

What does this mean? It means that Jesus Christ abolished the sin of the world, but that sin has not been forgotten, yet.

- LEV 26:40–44 ~ If anyone confesses their sins, repents, and accepts responsibility, God will remember the covenant He made with Abraham, Isaac, and Jacob, and He will not discard them but He will forgive them.
- JOH 1:1,14 ~ Jesus Christ is the New Covenant.
- 1 JO 2:2 ~ Jesus Christ abolished the sin of the whole world through this covenant.
- ROM 5:11 ~ This means Christ has atoned for all the sin in this world.

While sin has been abolished through the atoning sacrifice of Christ, your sins have not been forgotten by God unless you have confessed those sins before God and sincerely repented of them. Thus, forgiveness is granted to those who accept Christ as Savior and act on that faith.

- JOH 8:10–11 ~ Remember when Jesus told the adulteress, "I will not condemn you, go and sin no more." She was forgiven, provided she discontinued the adulterous behavior.
- 1 PE 4:1–3 ~ Even though Christ has done away with sin, you must not continue to sin as you have in the past when you engaged in sexual sin, lust, drunkenness, overindulgence, orgies, and idolatry.

To ask Christ for forgiveness is an act of faith. However, to be forgiven, you must prove by your actions that you truly desire to do better. To continue to commit the same sin, even if you ask forgiveness each time, would not be a demonstration of a willingness to obey God. To forgive others, to sincerely repent, and to desist from further sin are accurate demonstrations, or acts of faith.

Application: Suppose you are a homosexual, an adulterer, and/or a fornicator. You ask God in Jesus's name to forgive you of your deviant sexual activities, yet you continue to engage in such behavior. How can you be considered sincere if you don't make a concerted effort to cease the sin? If you ask God for forgiveness, promising to discontinue the activity, then keep your promise. Nobody is perfect, except for the perfect sacrifice made by Christ, which conforms us into His image. Even if we discontinue a bad habit, we will be tempted by it and inclined to think about it. But godly sorrow for one's sin will result in a sincere effort to clean up one's act. If you sincerely repent, God will wipe your slate clean. In fact, God will forgive you every time you ask Him in faith. But where is the sincerity if you ask forgiveness for doing something that you have no intention of stopping?

- JER 31:34 ~ They shall all know me, says the Lord, for I will forgive their sins and I will remember their sins no more.
- EZE 33:12 ~ A person's righteousness will not save them on the day that they turn to sin. A person's wickedness will not condemn them on the day that they turn to righteousness.
- 2 CO 5:17 ~ Paul tells us that if you are in Christ you become a new creature. Old things pass away and everything becomes new. Put Christ in your life and your sins are forgotten, forever. Not just gone, but forgotten. You are like brand new.

- MAT 7:7 ~ Jesus told the world, "Ask and you will receive, seek and you will find, knock and the door will be opened." Christ wants to forgive you of those sins you have committed. There's just one catch: you have to ask Him in faith to be forgiven. Ask for forgiveness and you will obtain it. Seek God and you will find Him. Knock on heaven's door, and Jesus Christ will open it for you Himself.
- MAT 18:21–22 ~ Jesus told Peter that you must forgive your neighbor, not seven times, but seventy-seven times (seventy-times-seven in the KJV).

Faith implies action if there are to be positive results; inaction produces nothing. Many who claim to be believers or Christians do not practice their faith or religion. They expect to be saved because they are good people and do nice things for others; but even unbelievers are known to do these things. In addition to being morally upright people, believers should openly confess their faith and publicly worship and praise God.

- ISA 12:4 ~ Praise the Lord, call on His name, declare His works to all people; mention that His name is exalted.
- EPH 2:8–9 ~ You are saved by the grace of God because of your faith in Jesus Christ. Salvation is a gift of God, it cannot be earned through good works, so nobody should brag.
- JAM 2:17 ~ James further tells us that faith without works is dead.
- 2 PE 1:5–8 ~ Peter concludes the matter by teaching us to supplement our faith with virtue, knowledge, self-control, steadfastness, godliness, and brotherly love. Thus, faith without works isn't truly faith, because faith implies action not stagnation.
- MAT 6:12 ~ We must also be willing to forgive others as directed by Jesus in the Lord's Prayer. Will God forgive us if we are unwilling to forgive others? Would you?
- HEB 12:2 ~ Jesus Christ is the author and finisher of our faith.

When the six days of creation took place, God created everything as we know it (GEN 1). When God gave man and woman a choice to do good or evil, His will became known to us. God's will for humanity has been revealed to us in His Law, as outlined in the Holy Bible. Unfortunately, all people have disobeyed God's Law.

God's Law tells us what to do and what not to do; it tells us what is right and moral. To disobey God's Law is to sin. Thus, God allowed sin to occur by giving the higher creatures the free will either to adhere to His commandments or not. While God created the opportunity for evil, He did not create sin, for He cannot sin. The devil was the first to sin. The devil tempts others to do the same. Therefore, sinning is doing the devil's will and not God's will.

- ROM 5:13 ~ Sin existed in the world before the Law was given; but nothing can be attributed to sin where there is no Law.
- 1 JO 3:4 ~ Sin is the transgression of the Law.
- 1 JO 3:8 ~ The devil sinned from the very beginning. Whoever sins is of the devil. God intends to destroy the works of the devil as well as all evil, sin, and death.

As it is written, God was pleased with the good things He created. However, God is not pleased with sin, for sin expresses evil, and evil can never be good. Thus, God is determined to destroy evil forever. He sacrificed His only Son to abolish the evil in this world. No other sacrifice will ever need to be made to atone for sin, because Christ atoned for the sin of all people. But not everyone will accept this gift, and therefore their sins will be held against them.

- GEN 17 – 22 ~ Would you be willing to sacrifice your only son, like Abraham, to atone for your own sin?

- HEB 10:10–12,18 ~ Under the new plan we have been forgiven and made clean by Christ's offering. Under the old plan, sacrificial offerings were made that could take away one's sins. But Christ gave Himself for our sins as a sacrifice for all time, and He now sits at the highest place of honor at God's right hand. There is no need to offer any more blood sacrifices for sin.

Although God created the Law, He is incapable of sinning or tempting others to sin. Sin is a choice made by people. God does not choose for you to sin. Neither can He sin.

- JAM 1:13 ~ God cannot be tempted, neither does He tempt anyone.
- 1 CO 10:13 ~ God will not allow us to be tempted beyond our ability to withstand it, and He will always provide us an escape from temptation.

What does sin lead to?

- ROM 6:23 ~ The wages of sin is death.
- JAM 1:15 ~ Sin brings forth death.

Why did Jesus Christ come to earth, die, and come to life again?

- 1 JO 2:2 ~ Christ came to abolish sin.
- 2 TI 1:10 ~ Christ came to abolish death.

Someday, evil will not only be gone, it also will be forgotten forever. Jesus Christ came to destroy the works of Satan, as well as Satan himself. So, if you are working for Satan, you will be destroyed with Satan.

Those who have faith and have followed Christ have become new people. Their sins have been abolished and forgotten. They will arise from the dead during the first resurrection and will be judged pure by the blood of Christ. They will reign with Christ forever. Everybody else will arise to face judgment. That's when the Book of Life will be opened that tells who will live. Those who will live are those who led a godly life of faith and repentance. Those who led a sinful life without repentance will not be written in the Book of Life but will die the second death (REV 20). They will die because they gambled on choosing to commit evil instead of good, though they knew the risk of sin was death; but they ignored Christ and chose to do it their own way.

What is the second death? It is the lake of fire. The devil and his followers will end up there, to die eternally. Sin and death will be destroyed forever. After the second death, wickedness, evil people, and Satan will never be heard from again. Gone, as well as forgotten. How do we know this?

- 2 KI 22:17 ~ God says, "Since they have forsaken me, worshipped other gods, and angered me by their evil works, my wrath will burn against them and that fire will never be extinguished."
- PSA 52:5 ~ God will destroy the evil ones forever.
- PRO 24:20 ~ Evil has no future. Their light will be extinguished.
- ISA 14:20 ~ The evil doers will nevermore be named.
- ISA 26:14 ~ All memory of them will be wiped out.

Summary: We can rejoice in the atoning sacrifice made by Christ. By the grace of God through our faith in Christ we are saved from sin and death. However, though your sins have been atoned for, they have not been forgotten unless you have cleansed yourself in the blood of Christ. This washing removes sin and guilt, making you perfect in righteousness, and resulting in the salvation of your soul. Without purification by the blood of Christ, you will become dead in your sins, you will be judged in accordance with the Book of the Law, and you will receive the judgment of eternal separation from God. All of your sins will be recorded in the books which will be read at the judgment. If you have been cleansed, there will be no record of your sins. If you have not, you will pay for those sins with your own life.

- EPH 5:25–26 ~ The cleansing by the blood of Christ is the washing by the Word spoken of by Paul.
- 1 JO 5:4–6 ~ Whoever is born of God overcomes the world; the victory that overcomes the world is found in faith. Jesus Christ overcame the world; anyone believing in Him will also overcome the world. Christ is He, who came by water and blood. The Holy Spirit is He who bears witness, because the Spirit is truth.
- REV 1:5 ~ Jesus Christ is the faithful witness, and the firstborn of those who have died. He is the prince, who is above all the kings of the earth. He loved us and cleansed us of all sin by His own blood.

Everyone has a choice. You must choose not to forget God or He will forget you. It's an easy choice, really. If you remember God in your daily life and strive to be an obedient servant, you will be rewarded with prosperity and eternal life; because God will remember your faith instead of your sins.

Alternative 1. Seek God, acknowledge the atonement of Christ, repent by asking Him for forgiveness through faith, earnestly try to improve, and God will forget your sins, and the Holy Spirit will purify your soul. Come knocking on the Gates of Heaven with a clean heart and God will gladly let you in.

Alternative 2. Forget God, shun Christ, don't repent, never ask God for forgiveness, continue to engage in bad habits, or try to earn heaven through works, and you will be destroyed. When judgment comes, you will be declared guilty and sentenced to death; and all memory of you will be forgotten.

Take My Life

Take my life, and let it be consecrated, Lord, to Thee;
Take my moments and my days, let them flow in ceaseless praise.

Take my hands, and let them move at the impulse of Thy love;
Take my feet, and let them be swift and beautiful for Thee.

Take my voice, and let me sing always, only, for my King;
Take my lips, and let them be filled with messages from Thee.

Take my silver and my gold, not a mite would I withhold;
Take my intellect, and use every power as Thou shalt choose.

Take my will and make it Thine; it shall be no longer mine;
Take my heart, it is Thine own; it shall be Thy royal throne.

Take my love; my Lord, I pour at Thy feet its treasured store;
Take myself, and I will be, ever, only, all, for Thee.

Lesson: Bearing Good Fruit

God commands us to be kind, compassionate, forgiving, and loving to others, just as He is with us. We especially should try to help others who are in need. To not do these things is to neglect our duty. Since God has richly blessed us with so many wonderful spiritual treasures, we respond by showing our appreciation and bearing spiritual fruit. That is, we should share the gifts God has given us with others. Bearing good FRUIT means following the example of Jesus Christ in the way you treat others.

- JOH 15:1–10,16 ~ Jesus said, "I am the true vine, and my Father is the cultivator. He removes any of my branches that do not bear fruit. Those that do bear fruit, he prunes, so that they can bear even more fruit. You have been made clean through the Word which I have spoken to you. Stay in me and I will stay in you. The branch cannot bear fruit by itself; it must be connected to the vine. You cannot bear fruit unless you remain in me. I am the vine and you are the branches. Those abiding in me will bear much fruit but without me you can do nothing. If you do not abide in me you will be removed like a dead and withered branch that is burned in the fire. If you live in me, and my words live in you, you can ask for anything and it will be done. This brings glory to my Father: that you bear much fruit and that you follow me. As the Father has loved me so I have loved you. Continue in my love. If you keep my commandments you will remain in my love, even as I have kept my Father's commandments and remain in His love. You did not choose me I chose you and ordained you, so you could go out into the world and bring forth fruit, that your fruit should continue, and that whatever you ask of the Father in my name, He may give it to you."
- GAL 5:22–23 ~ The fruits of the Spirit include love, joy, peace, patience, gentleness, goodness, faith, kindness, and self-control. There is no law against such things.
- EPH 5:9 ~ The fruits of the Spirit originate in goodness, righteousness, and truth.
- 2 PE 1:5–8 ~ In diligence, add virtue to your faith, knowledge to your virtue, temperance to your knowledge, patience to your temperance, godliness to your patience, kindness to your godliness, and charity to your kindness. If these things abound in you, you will never be barren or unfruitful in the knowledge of our Lord Jesus Christ.

F = <u>Forgiveness</u>. Forgive one another. Do not seek revenge or carry a grudge.

- MAT 6:14–15 ~ Jesus said, "If you forgive others, your heavenly Father will forgive you. But if you do not forgive others, your heavenly Father will not forgive you."
- EPH 4:32 ~ Be kind to each other, tender-hearted, and forgiving, even as God for Christ's sake has forgiven you.
- COL 3:13 ~ Hold back your anger towards others and forgive them. If you have a disagreement, forgive each other just as Christ forgave you.

R = <u>Restoration/Reconciliation</u>. Although we were lost in our sin and condemned to death, God reconciled us again unto Himself by sending His Son Jesus Christ to pay for our sin. We should likewise restore others in the true faith and reconcile our differences with one another.

- PSA 23:3 ~ The Lord restores my soul. He leads me in the paths of righteousness for His name's sake.
- EZE 3:18–21 ~ God says, "I have told the wicked that they will surely die. If you do not warn these people to turn from their sin and be saved, you will die as well, for you will be partly responsible for their death. But if you warn the wicked and they still do not turn from their wickedness, they will die in their sin but you will have saved yourself. If the righteous

turn from righteousness to sin, they will die because their righteousness will no longer be remembered. If you do not warn them you will die as well. But if you warn the righteous not to sin, and they do not sin, their souls will be saved and so will yours."
- GAL 6:1 ~ Brothers and sisters, if someone among you is overwhelmed by sin and guilt, you who are spiritual must humbly restore that person, considering that you too could become tempted and stray from God in the same manner.

U = <u>Unconditional Love</u>. God has loved us despite the fact that we have disobeyed Him and consequently, deserve to die. God loves us regardless, just as any parent loves their children when they are good and when they are bad. Hence, we should have the same unreserved love for one another. Let us share the lasting and perfect love that God has given us through Christ.

- LEV 19:17–18 ~ Do not hate anyone in your heart; do not scold or sin against your neighbor. Do not take revenge or bear a grudge, but love your neighbor as you love yourself.
- MAT 22:35–40 ~ A lawyer in the crowd asked Jesus, "Master, what is the greatest commandment of the Law?" Jesus answered, "Love the Lord with all your heart, mind, and soul. This is the first and greatest commandment. The second is similar to the first. Love your neighbor as yourself. The laws and the prophets depend on these two commandments."
- ROM 13:10 ~ Love works no evil against one's neighbor; thus, love is the fulfilling of the Law (also GAL 5:14).

I = <u>Instruction</u>. Jesus Christ's final words before His ascension commissioned His disciples to teach others what He taught them. That commission pertains to all Christians (we are all disciples). Discipleship begins in the home and extends from the church outward into all facets of our lives, including work, play, travel, etc. Study the Bible and teach it to others.

- DEU 4:36 ~ From heaven God made you to hear His voice, so that He could instruct you. On earth He spoke to all people from the great fire, giving them His laws.
- DEU 6:2–7 ~ Fear the Lord and keep His commandments and laws. Ensure that your children, and your children's children, obey God. Do this and you will prosper and your life will be prolonged. Love God with all your heart, soul, and might. Keep God's Word in your heart and teach His ways carefully and thoughtfully to your children. Talk with your family all the time about God, every day and night, whenever you are together.
- 2 TI 2:24–26 ~ A servant of the Lord doesn't waste time arguing, but is gentle to everyone, able to teach, and not resentful. Such disciples gently instruct those who are in opposition to them, hoping that God will grant them repentance for acknowledging His truth, so that they may escape the devil's traps who would otherwise capture them for his own purpose.
- 2 TI 3:16 ~ All scripture is inspired by God and is effective for teaching, for reprimanding, for correcting, and for instruction in the ways of righteousness.

T = <u>Teamwork</u>. As Christians, we are all members of the body of Christ. Together we comprise a temple to the Lord, because He dwells in us and we dwell in Him. Every Christian has unique responsibilities, and avenues where they can serve the Lord best. Collectively, we are His Church and a place of refuge, edification, and influence in the world.

- ROM 12:4–8 ~ Just as our body has many members, each with a separate purpose, so we, being part of the body of Christ, have certain responsibilities. We have different gifts which God in His grace has given us. Some people can minister, some can teach, some can provide guidance and counseling. If you have the gift of prophecy do so in proportion to your faith. If you have the gift of giving, do so generously. If you have the gift of governing, do so with diligence. If you have the gift of mercy, show it cheerfully.

- 1 CO 12:4–12,26 ~ There are a variety of spiritual gifts, but only one Spirit. There are different ways of administering but only one Lord. There are different operations, but the same God who works through them. The Spirit is manifested in some way in everyone to use productively. Some people have received wisdom, some knowledge, some faith, all from the same Spirit. Some people have the ability to heal, others to work miracles, others to prophesy, others to discern spirits, others to speak foreign tongues; but all of them are working with the same Spirit who divides power among everyone as He chooses. Just as one body has many members so is Christ one body with many members. When one member suffers, all suffer; when one member is honored, all are honored.
- EPH 2:18–22 ~ Through Christ we have access by one Spirit to the Father. Thus, we are no longer strangers or foreigners, but fellow citizens with the saints in the household of God. We are built upon the foundation set by the apostles and the prophets, with Jesus Christ being the chief cornerstone. Together we comprise a well-framed building, a growing temple in the Lord. We are joined together by His Spirit into one home.
- EPH 4:11–13 ~ God gave some the abilities of apostles, prophets, evangelists, pastors and/or teachers for the work of the ministry, the edifying of the saints, the perfecting of the body of Christ, and the unity of faith. They impart the knowledge of the Son of God who was a perfect man, so that we could take on the characteristics of Christ.

Bearing good fruit means being good neighbors to all people. Treat others like you want to be treated (the Golden Rule). Act like a Christian everywhere and always.

- MAT 25:40,45 ~ Jesus said, "Whenever you have done something to even the least important of all human beings, you have done it to me; and whenever you have not done something to even the least important of all human beings, you have not done it to me either." In other words, whatever you do, and whatever you fail to do, to or for another person, affects Jesus Christ in the same manner it affects them.
- LUK 6:31 ~ Do unto others as you would like them to do unto you.
- HEB 13:3 ~ Consider those who are in bondage as if you were bound with them, and consider those who suffer as if you suffered with them.
- JAM 1:19 ~ Be swift to listen and slow to speak; also, be slow to anger.
- 2 PE 1:5–8 ~ Supplement your faith with virtue, knowledge, self-control, steadfastness, godliness, and brotherly love.
- 1 JO 2:6 ~ Whoever says they are a Christian should show they are following Christ by the way they conduct their lives.

Savior! Thy Dying Love

Savior, Thy dying love thou gavest me, nor should I ought withhold, dear Lord, from Thee;
In love my soul would bow, my heart fulfill its vow, some offering bring Thee now,
Something for Thee.

Give me a faithful heart, likeness to Thee, that each departing day henceforth may see
Some work of love begun, some deed of kindness done, some wanderer sought and won,
Something for Thee.

All that I am and have, Thy gifts so free, ever in joy or grief, my Lord, for Thee.
And when Thy face I see, my ransomed soul shall be, through all eternity,
Something for Thee.

Lesson: Using Our Talents

God sacrificed His only Son Jesus Christ to save us from sin and death. This is the greatest of the many blessings He has bestowed upon unworthy sinners. To show our appreciation we should be willing to make sacrifices for Him. This life we are living should be a testimony to Christ. Not everyone knows about Christ or understands what His death and resurrection mean to Christians. Let us spread the Good News in Jesus Christ, and be willing to minister to our fellow human beings. God has given everyone special talents to do His work; to not do anything is to deny what God has done for you.

- ROM 12:1 ~ Give yourself to God. Let yourself be a living sacrifice. After all He has done for you, is that too much to ask?
- 1 CO 6:20 ~ You were bought with a great price, so glorify God in your bodies and your spirits, for you belong to Him.
- PHP 2:12–13 ~ Paul wrote to the Philippians: Just as you were obedient while I was there, continue to do so, especially now that I am no longer with you. Continue to work on your salvation with fear and awe before the Lord. God works within you, making you want to do His will. Therefore, carry out what He asks without complaining or arguing.

<u>Witnessing</u>. Jesus Christ told His disciples to spread the Good News to everyone, everywhere (MAT 28:19). We should share our knowledge of Christ and the Word of God with others, especially when they are willing to listen. One way of doing this is to witness our faith publicly whenever appropriate; of course, it is always appropriate to exhibit faith by attending worship services at an evangelical church and participating in the Holy Sacraments.

Do not deny your faith in Christ but proclaim it to the world. This does not require one to be aggressive or pushy, but humble, confident, and courageous. Not everyone can be a teacher or an evangelist, but everyone has opportunities to testify. Discussing the Bible and studying it with others are very effective ways of receiving and giving testimony. This is the best training available to equip one to defend his or her faith in the world.

- ISA 6:8 ~ Isaiah heard the Lord say, "Who shall I send to be our messenger?" Isaiah replied, "Here I am, Lord, send me."
- ISA 12:4 ~ Praise the Lord, call on His name, declare His works to all people; mention that His name is exalted.
- MAT 10:32–33 ~ Jesus said, "Anybody who confesses me to others, I will confess them to my Father in heaven. Anybody who denies me to others, I will deny them to my Father in heaven."
- JOH 5:33,36–37,46 ~ Jesus said, "John the Baptist was a witness to the truth. I am a greater witness of the truth than he was. The things the Father has given me to do, I do; and these things prove that the Father has sent me, and that I am His witness. The Father Himself, who sent me to do these things, has been a witness for me, even though you have neither seen Him nor heard His voice. But, if you believed Moses, you would believe me, for Moses has been my witness in his writings."
- ACT 1:22 ~ Peter said, "Since Jesus was baptized by John, until the day He left us, we were being ordained by God to be witnesses of Jesus's resurrection."
- PHP 2:11 ~ Every tongue should confess that Jesus Christ is Lord, to the glory of God the Father.
- 1 PE 4:10–11 ~ Whoever has received the gift of salvation in Christ should share that gift with others, as a steward of God's eternal grace. If you preach, do so as a messenger of God.

If you minister, do so with the ability God gives you. Do this to glorify God through His Son Jesus Christ.
- 1 JO 5:9–10 ~ If we believe a person witnessing for another, we should believe God's witnessing even more, and God has given witness of His Son. Those who believe that Jesus is God's Son have God's witness in themselves; those who don't believe are calling God a liar, because they don't believe God's testimony concerning His Son.

<u>Teaching</u>. You don't have to be blessed with teaching skills to share the Gospel with others. Further, it is the responsibility of parents to instruct their children about God and Jesus Christ. Group Bible study is a way for participants to teach each other. Church attendance is a means for one to receive instruction from individuals educated in the ways of the Lord. Personal pursuits in which one delves into and meditates upon Christ and the Holy Bible are equally important. God's Word is a means to teach oneself for anybody that can read.

- DEU 4:9–10 ~ Don't forget what God has done for you. May His works have a lasting impression on your lives. Teach your children and grandchildren about His glorious miracles. Especially remind your children of God's instructions given to Moses at Sinai about reverencing Him and about teaching His laws from generation to generation.
- DEU 6:2–7 ~ Fear the Lord and keep all His commandments and laws. Ensure that your children and your children's children obey God. Do this and you will prosper and your life will be prolonged. Love God with all your heart, soul, and might. Keep God's Word in your heart and teach His ways carefully and thoughtfully to your children. Talk with your family all the time about God, every day and night, whenever you are together.
- JOH 3:16 ~ God loved the world so much that He sacrificed His only begotten Son, so that anyone who believes in Him would receive everlasting life and never die.
- EPH 6:1–4 ~ Children, obey your parents, for God has given them authority over you. Honor your parents as commanded by God in His Ten Commandments (EXO 20:12). This is the first commandment that brings a promise: If you honor your parents your life will be long and happy. Parents, don't provoke your children to anger and frustration. Instead, raise them in the nurture and discipline of righteousness, as instructed by God.
- COL 3:16 ~ Remember what Christ taught you and let His words enrich your lives and make you wise. Teach His words to each other. Sing them openly and spiritually in psalms and hymns with thankful hearts.

<u>Giving</u>. We owe God our time, talents, belongings, and lives. Everyone has something they can give, if only their worship and praise. Attend church and serve when you can. Show God your appreciation for His wonderful gifts by offering Him your thanks, praise, and adoration, and by giving tithes (one tenth of your increase) to the needy and to your church. The more you give in Jesus's name, the more you will receive, in particular time, abilities, and resources.

- NUM 18:26 ~ God commanded for tithes to be given to the church (to support the Levite priests).
- DEU 16:17 ~ Everyone should give as they are able, in accordance with the blessings which God has given them.
- DEU 26:12–13 ~ After you have tithed (given your tithes to the Levites, strangers, orphans, widows, and the hungry) then declare this to the Lord.
- 1 CH 23:30 ~ Thank and praise the Lord every morning and every evening.
- 2 CH 31:5 ~ Everyone brought an abundance of their first fruits of crops, wine, oil, honey, and all their profits.

- PSA 9:1–2 ~ I will praise you Lord with all my heart; I will show your marvelous works. I will be glad and rejoice. I will sing praises to your holy name.
- PSA 50:23 ~ God says that whoever offers Him praise, glorifies Him. To those who do this, He will show His salvation.
- PSA 96:8 ~ Give God the glory He deserves. Bring your offerings and worship Him.
- MAL 3:10 ~ Bring your tithes to the storehouse and see if God doesn't open the windows of heaven and shower upon you more blessings than you have room in your house to receive.
- JOH 4:24 ~ God is Spirit so we must worship Him in spirit and in truth.
- 2 CO 9:7 ~ Everyone should give whatever they think is fair in their heart. Giving should be done voluntarily, not out of necessity, for God loves a cheerful giver.
- HEB 12:28 ~ Since God has given us the kingdom, let us please Him by serving Him with thankful hearts, with holy fear, and with awe.
- HEB 13:15 ~ Let us continually offer to God the sacrifice of praise; praise and thanks are the fruit of our lips.

Setting an example. Live your life as an example to others by following the example of Christ. As you continue in your walk you will become more and more like Him. Others will see you shine in the way you conduct your business and in your overall demeanor and this will attract people towards that light, providing more opportunities to witness and teach.

- MAT 25:40,45 ~ Jesus said, "Whenever you have done something to help another person, you have done it to me as well; whenever you have not done something to help another person, you have not done it to me either."
- ROM 12:1–2,9–21 ~ Let your body be a living sacrifice, totally acceptable to God. Let your love show, do not hide it. Hate that which is evil, and hold onto that which is good. Love one another with brotherly love and honor. Don't be lazy in business matters. Serve the Lord with a glowing spirit. Rejoice in your hope. Be patient in times of trouble. Be consistent in prayer. Help your fellow Christians in need. Be hospitable to others. Bless others, even those who persecute you; never curse anyone. Rejoice with those who are rejoicing and mourn with those who are mourning. Try to get along with others. Don't be proud or conceited; humble yourself even before the lowliest of characters. Don't reward evil with evil. Always be honest. Promote peace. Do not seek revenge; God has said that vengeance belongs to Him alone. If your enemy is hungry or thirsty, give him food and drink. Don't let evil get the better of you, but overcome evil with goodness.
- COL 3:17 ~ Whatever you do or say, do it in Jesus's name, and give thanks to God in Jesus's name.
- 1 JO 2:6 ~ Whoever says they are a Christian should show they are following Christ by the way they conduct their lives.

Be humble, not proud. Show respect to others. Do not think evil about others or conspire against them. Rather, love them as brothers and sisters and you may win an ally or a friend. All human beings are valued equally to God which is why we are to love them as ourselves.

- PRO 6:16–19 ~ There are seven things the Lord hates: the proud look, the lying tongue, hands that shed innocent blood, a heart with an evil imagination, feet that run to mischief, a false witness, and a person that generates discord among people.
- ROM 12:3,16–18 ~ Do not be conceited in your own mind, but think soberly, according to the measure of faith God has given you. Live in harmony with one another. Be humble, not proud or arrogant. Never return evil for evil. Always be honest with everybody. Live in peace with all God's creation.

- PHP 4:8 ~ Focus your mind on things that are true, honest, just, pure, lovely, admirable, virtuous, and praiseworthy.
- 1 PE 2:1 ~ Erase from your mind all malice, deceit, hypocrisy, envy, and slander.

Assist others in need. Show mercy to the downtrodden. Console others who suffer.

- PSA 41:1 ~ Whoever helps the poor will be blessed by God, and God will deliver them when they experience a time of trouble.
- LUK 6:36 ~ Be merciful to others even as your Father in heaven is merciful.
- LUK 10:29–37 ~ Jesus told the parable of the Good Samaritan: A man was traveling from Jerusalem to Jericho when he was ambushed by thieves who beat and robbed him, leaving him for dead. A priest passed that way later in the day, and after seeing the poor man, passed by him on the other side of the road. Likewise, a Levite saw the poor man and went around him. Finally, a certain Samaritan saw the man and took pity on him. The Samaritan rendered first aid, set him on his beast, and took him to town. He placed the injured man in an inn, asking the innkeeper to take care of the man and he would pay the bill. Jesus then asked, "Which of these passersby was a neighbor to the man who was mugged?" The lawyer answered, "The man who was merciful." Jesus replied, "Go and do likewise."
- ROM 12:20 ~ If your enemy is hungry, feed him; if he is thirsty, give him a drink. Maybe you can turn him or her around by being nice to him.
- HEB 13:1–2 ~ Let brotherly love continue. Don't forget to help strangers, for you may be ministering to angels for all you know.

Be honest with everyone. Telling the truth is always the best course. Do not deceive. If the person is not ready for the truth, refrain from speech; but show you care, which requires no words.

- PRO 12:19 ~ The lips of truth last forever, but a lying tongue lasts but a moment.
- ZEC 8:16–17 ~ Always tell the truth to your neighbor; always execute judgments of truth and peace. Do not imagine evil in your hearts against another.
- EPH 4:25 ~ Don't lie, but tell the truth to people; for we are members of one another.

Be more willing to listen than to speak. Don't just hear someone, but listen to them. And be careful what you say to others so you don't offend them or hurt their feelings. Choose your words carefully; this requires one to think carefully before speaking.

- PRO 15:28 ~ The righteous heart studies the situation before giving an answer; however, a wicked mouth pours out evil words.
- PRO 17:28 ~ Even a fool who keeps quiet is considered wise; those who shut their mouths are considered people of understanding.
- MAT 12:37 ~ Jesus said, "You are justified and condemned by the words you speak."

Be cheerful; keep a smile on your face. You will find that positivity is contagious; but then again, so is negativity. Try not to get angry or lose your temper. Instead, try to understand people from their point of view before sharing yours. Argue your case with reason not emotion. The only emotion that will reinforce your words is love; other emotions may distract from your speech. It is more helpful to suggest solutions than to offer complaints.

- PRO 15:13 ~ A merry heart has a cheerful smile, but a sorrowful heart breaks the spirit.
- ECC 7:9 ~ Do not hasten to be angry, for anger belongs to the foolish.
- GAL 6:10 ~ Whenever the opportunity arises, do something nice for someone, especially your brothers and sisters in the faith.

- PHP 2:14 ~ Conduct your business without arguing or complaining.

Don't be lazy; be active. Do something. I have heard people say that this life is inconsequential, especially when compared to the next life. While it is true that God has promised us eternal life this does not mean that life here on earth is unimportant or meaningless. Remember, God has given us special talents to do His work on earth, so do not let your spiritual gifts go to waste. Do not be lazy but industrious; do not be reluctant but enthusiastic.

- PRO 6:6–9 ~ You who are lazy, consider the ant. The ant has no supervisor, guide, or ruler yet manages to provide plenty of food. How long will you sleep, lazy people; when are you going to wake up?
- PRO 10:4–5,26 ~ Whoever slacks off will become poor, but the diligent will become rich. Whoever gathers during the summer is wise; whoever sleeps during the harvest is shameful. As vinegar is to the teeth and smoke to the eyes, so is a sloth to an employer.
- PRO 20:4 ~ The slothful person will not plow when it is cold and will end up begging during the harvest, and have nothing.
- PRO 24:30–32,34 ~ I visited the field of the slothful man and the vineyard of the ignorant man and all I found were thorn bushes and broken fences. And I learned from the experience. People like that will receive poverty like hard labor, and neediness like an armed robber.
- PRO 26:13–16 ~ The lazy person will not work, giving stupid excuses like, "There could be a lion in the street." Just like a door on its hinges, the lazy person is attached to the bed, tossing and turning. The lazy person is too tired even to lift a spoon to eat. Lazy people can convince themselves better than seven people with a good excuse.
- ECC 10:18 ~ Because of laziness and idleness the building decayed and collapsed.
- MAT 25:14–30 ~ Remember the parable of the property owner who entrusted his servants with five talents, two talents, and one talent of money, respectively? The servant with five and the servant with two put their money to work and doubled it. They were given comparable rewards for being fruitful. The servant with one talent had hidden it in the ground. He was scorned because he didn't make an effort to use it or to invest it. His talent was taken away and given to the person who was the most productive with the master's money. Like the old cliché, "use it or lose it." Of course, in this case, if you do use it, you may obtain even more.

Hark, the Voice of Jesus Crying

Hark, the voice of Jesus crying, "Who will come to work today?"
"Fields are white and harvests waiting, who will bear the sheaves away?"
Loud and long the Master calleth, rich reward He offers free;
Who will answer, gladly saying, "Here am I, send me, send me?"

If you cannot speak like angels, if you cannot preach like Paul,
You can tell the love of Jesus, you can say He died for all.
If you cannot rouse the wicked with the judgment's dread alarms,
You can lead the little children to the Savior's waiting arms.

Let none hear you idly saying, "There is nothing I can do,"
While the souls of men are dying, and the Master calls for you;
Take the task He gives you gladly, let His work your pleasure be;
Answer quickly when He calleth, "Here am I, send me, send me."

Lesson: The Holy Sacraments

Text: 1 JO 5:1–12 ~ Whoever believes in Jesus Christ is born of God; whoever loves God, loves His Son. We know we are God's children, because we love God and obey His commandments, which are not that difficult to follow. Everyone who is born of God overcomes the world. This is the victory, that by faith we can overcome the world. So, who can overcome the world? Anyone who believes that Jesus Christ is the Son of God can overcome. Christ is the One who came by *water* and by *blood*. It is His Holy Spirit who testifies for the Spirit is the truth. There are three that testify in heaven, the Father, the Word, and the Holy Spirit, and these three are one. Likewise, there are three that testify on earth, the spirit, the water, and the blood. If we are willing to accept the testimony of men, then we should accept the testimony of God even more, and He has testified about His Son. People who believe in God's Son will have His testimony in their hearts. People who do not believe are essentially calling God a liar, because they do not believe the truth about Christ, even though it comes directly from God. The testimony that God has given us concerns eternal life, and this life is God's Son, Jesus Christ. Those who do not have the Son do not have life.

God has testified of the truth through His Holy Spirit by way of the written Word and the Word made flesh, which is God's Son, Jesus Christ (JOH 1:1,14). Christ, having the Holy Spirit within Him, testified of the same truth and He has commissioned His followers to further testify (MAT 28:19–20). Christ was obedient to God the Father and was God's faithful witness. He wants us to be His faithful and obedient witnesses as well.

- JOH 8:18 ~ Jesus said, "I testify about myself and the Father that sent me testifies about me."
- JOH 15:26–27 ~ Jesus said, "When the Comforter, the Spirit of truth, has come, who I will send from the Father, He will testify about me. You people also will testify because you have been with me from the very beginning."

The Holy Sacraments are a testimony about God and His Son Jesus Christ. Just as Christ was obliged to obey God the Father, so are we obligated to God. The definition of the word "sacrament" is obligation or commitment. We are beholden to God, who has asked us to testify on His behalf, just like a witness testifies in court about the truth. The Holy Sacraments are a means of being such a witness for God. Sacraments, like the sacrificial offerings of the Old Testament, are acts of obedience that provide forgiveness of sins, through acknowledging the blood sacrifice being made to atone for sins by God Himself.

- MAT 21:22–23 ~ Jesus asked His disciples, "Can you drink my cup or be baptized with my baptism?" They answered, "Yes we can." Jesus told them, "Indeed, you will drink the cup I drink and be baptized with my baptism, but I will not appoint you to sit at my right or left hand, for the Father bestows honor as He chooses."

There are two sacraments: Baptism and the Eucharist (also called Holy Communion or the Lord's Supper). There are not seven sacraments, or any other number, only two. These two sacraments are unique from any other religious rite or feast mentioned in the Bible. What sets Baptism and Holy Communion apart are four important principles, listed below.

1. Sacraments were instituted by God, through the testimony of His Son Jesus Christ.
2. Sacraments were personally endorsed by Christ, as demonstrated by His participation and His command for us to do likewise.
3. Sacraments represent a public witness of a lifetime commitment to God, by testifying about the atoning sacrifice of His Son Jesus Christ.

4. Sacraments provide forgiveness of sins, which is passed onto us via physical elements that purify our hearts and invite God's Holy Spirit to dwell within us.

Holy Baptism represents an initial commitment to God, and Holy Communion represents reaffirmation of that commitment. This is exemplified by Christ initiating His ministry with His Baptism, and completing His ministry after the first Holy Communion with His apostles.

Let us revisit the discussion of Baptism.

- JOH 3:3–6 ~ Jesus said, "Unless a person is born again, he cannot see God's kingdom." Nicodemus asked, "How can someone be born when they are old?" Jesus answered, "Unless a person is born of water and of the Holy Spirit he cannot enter into God's kingdom. Those who are born of the flesh are flesh, and those who are born of the Spirit are Spirit."
- EPH 5:26 ~ Paul wrote: We are cleansed from sin by washing of water and the Word.

What does it mean to be born again? We have been born from water and conceived in sin (PSA 51:5). This means we are born of the flesh, which is inherently sinful. We must be born again of the spirit. Baptism is that spiritual washing by the Holy Spirit (the Word). This washing removes the stain of sin that became part of human nature due to the original sin of Adam and Eve. Some denominations require total emersion (as in the womb); others do not. Does it matter? Well it depends on your church, but all evangelicals recognize the central concept of being born again and spiritual cleansing, which is more a cleansing of the soul than the body.

Sin existed in the world before the creation of man. Lucifer was the anointed cherub who was blameless when God created him but became sinful when he opposed God (EZE 28:14–15). Since the creation of Adam, Lucifer has been determined to instigate the fall of human beings from God's grace; he began this unholy mission in the Garden of Eden. That first sin committed by Adam and Eve brought with it the death penalty, which is what God warned about and Lucifer lied about (GEN 3:1–4).

- GEN 2:16–17 ~ God told Adam not to eat fruit from the Tree of Knowledge or he would die.
- ROM 5:13 ~ Sin was in the world before the Law, but nothing can be attributed to sin where there is no Law.
- ROM 6:23 ~ The wages of sin is death.
- 1 JO 3:4 ~ Whoever commits sin disobeys the Law, for that is how sin is defined.

Death became a curse that would fall upon humankind, for all people are destined to become sinners. Sinfulness is a part of our human nature which is passed onto our offspring. That is, we cannot help but be born of the flesh, of which sinfulness is an integral part. Baptism cleanses the person of sin, opening the door for the Holy Spirit to come in.

- ECC 7:20 ~ There is not a single person on earth who does good and never sins.
- ROM 5:18–19 ~ Just as the judgment of condemnation came upon all people because of the sin of one man (Adam), so also justification has come to all people by the righteousness of one man (Jesus). By the disobedience of one man all became sinful, and by the obedience of one man all can become righteous.

One may ask: Did Christ need to be baptized to cleanse Him of original sin? The answer is, absolutely not! Christ was conceived by the Holy Spirit and was by nature God, perfect in righteousness. But although He was God, Christ humbled Himself before all people and took upon Himself a human nature. Christ did not inherit sin, however, because of His divine nature. His baptism was to provide an example for the rest of us; He did not need to expiate sin from His human nature. If Christ had sinned, He could not have saved anyone, because the sacrifice required a perfect and unblemished blood offering (HEB 9:14; 1 PE 1:18–20).

- PHP 2:5–11 ~ Jesus Christ, though equal with God, took upon Himself the nature of man, and became a humble servant. He was obedient unto death, even a humiliating death on a cross. God has therefore exalted the name of Christ above all others, so everyone should bow before His name, and everyone should confess that He is Lord, to the glory of God the Father.

Christ took upon Himself the nature of man, but He did not give into temptation like other people, even though He was tempted just the same. Consequently, He did not need to be purified by the Holy Spirit, for He was never without the Spirit. Christ allowed Himself to be baptized because He lived His life by example, as God's witness of obedience and loyalty. When we are baptized, we are witnessing for Christ just as He was witnessing for our Heavenly Father. By following Christ's example, we are pleasing God very much (MAT 3:17).

A commonly debated question is this: Should small children be baptized? The Bible does not specify the age that a person is to be baptized, but it does say that baptism is for everyone, no exceptions. There are examples of when the apostles baptized entire families (ACT 16:15; ACT 16:33; 1 CO 1:16). Hence, baptism is for adults and children alike, and the sooner one is cleansed of original sin, the better it would seem. However, the personal choice made by individuals and/or their parents requires a clear conscience towards God.

- MAR 10:13–16 ~ People were bringing little children to Jesus to receive His blessing, but the disciples turned them away. When Jesus saw this, he was indignant. He said to them, "Let the little children come to me and do not hinder them, for the kingdom of God belongs to such as these. I tell you the truth, whoever will not receive God's kingdom as a little child will never enter there."
- ACT 2:38–39 ~ Peter said, "Repent and be baptized every one of you, in the name of Jesus Christ for the remission of your sins, and you will receive the free gift of the Holy Spirit. This promise pertains to you, to your children, and to people everywhere: to whomever the Lord calls."
- 1 PE 3:21 ~ Baptism will also save us through the resurrection of Jesus Christ. Baptism doesn't mean washing a dirty body, but rather establishing a clean conscience towards God.

The age at which one is baptized is not a requirement imposed by God and is therefore not fundamental to one's salvation. In any case, it represents a beginning, just as it did in the ministry of Christ. Some people choose to baptize a child early in life, and then that person confirms their baptism after intense study of the Word. Confirmation is the public witnessing of a commitment to Christ upon reaching the age of accountability. Others initiate Baptism after the child becomes of age. This affirmation of faith is where the second sacrament becomes significant. Although an individual may be purged of original sin, that individual is destined to be rebellious toward God again and again. Consequently, we need to be forgiven over and over. We can never remain righteous, because it only takes a single sin to become noncompliant.

- ISA 64:6 ~ All of us have become unclean, and our acts of righteousness are as filthy rags. We shrivel like a leaf, and like the wind, our sins sweep us away.
- ROM 3:23 ~ Everyone has sinned and come short of the glory of God.
- ROM 7:19–20 ~ I don't do the good I want to do, but I do the evil I don't want to do. If I do the evil things I don't want to do, it is not me doing them but the sin inside of me.
- JAM 2:10 ~ Whoever disobeys one point of the Law disobeys all the Law.

God will forgive our sins anytime we sincerely repent of them with a contrite heart. But the next sin destroys us and condemns us all over again. The purpose of Holy Communion is to remove the sin that is our own, and reaffirm our commitment to God. Since we continue to sin repeatedly, we need to be renewed frequently. This is why Christ told us to partake of the Eucharist often, to remember Him and the importance of the sacrifice He made (MAT 26:26–28), and to sanctify our spirits (HEB 10:10,14).

By partaking of His body and blood, we invite Christ to live in us, both physically and spiritually. The sacrament regenerates us in God's Holy Spirit and reunites us with the Holy Trinity. The definition of the word "communion" is to join. Through Holy Communion, our spirit becomes joined with God's Spirit, because Christ lives within us. Baptism is also a form of communion with the Holy Spirit. Both sacraments enable us to receive the mind of Christ (1 CO 2:16).

- JOH 6:30–35,51–58 ~ The people said to Jesus, "Can you show us a sign to convince us that we should believe you, like when our fathers ate manna in the desert?" Jesus answered, "The manna from heaven didn't come from Moses; it came from God who gives you the true bread from heaven. The bread of life comes from heaven and gives life to the world. I am the bread of life; whoever comes to me will never hunger again and whoever believes in me will never thirst again. The bread I give is my flesh, and I will give it for the life of the world. Unless you eat the body and drink the blood of the Son of Man, you have no life. If you eat my body and drink my blood, you live in me and I in you; and you will have eternal life, for I will raise you up the last day. Mine is not like the manna from heaven, for whoever eats the bread I give will live forever."

The Holy Spirit, being perfect in righteousness, cannot dwell inside us if we are unclean. The sacraments cleanse us by washing away our sins and allowing the Spirit of God to enter. Otherwise, our evil nature would not enable us to be reconciled with God who is holy.

- 1 CO 10:16–17,21 ~ The cup of blessing that we bless, doesn't it represent our communion with the blood of Christ? The bread that we break, doesn't it represent our communion with the body of Christ? Although we are many, we have become one body for we all are partakers of that one bread. You cannot drink from the cup of the Lord and from the cup of devils.
- 2 CO 6:14 ~ Do not be joined with unbelievers, for what fellowship can there be between righteousness and unrighteousness? What communion can there be between light and darkness?

We can be joined with God for we have been made perfect in righteousness through the purification of our souls by the blood of Christ. God's sacraments make us brand new (2 CO 5:17) by repeatedly restoring us with His Holy Spirit.

- PHP 3:11–12 ~ Nobody is justified by the Law before God, for the just shall live by faith. Christ redeemed us from the curse of the Law, being made a curse instead of us.
- COL 1:28 ~ Everyone is presented perfect who is in Jesus Christ.
- HEB 10:10,14 ~ We are sanctified by the offering of the body of Jesus Christ. By His offering, He has made perfect those who are sanctified.
- MAT 5:48 ~ Therefore, be perfect like your Father in heaven.

There are two sacraments for a very important reason: they each remove a particular kind of sinfulness by refining us and preserving us in the Spirit. One cleansing is by water and one is by blood. Our sinfulness has two characteristics, the sin of the world (original sin) and our own sin. Baptism cleanses us of the worldly sin that is inherent in our flesh; Holy Communion cleanses us of the sin that we create on our own. Thus, Baptism makes us clean initially, while Communion continues to cleanse us periodically.

Jesus's personal participation in the sacraments was for two reasons: to testify and to exemplify. He testified as God's witness providing an example for us to follow. That example shows us how to be God's witnesses, through participation in the sacraments and other means of grace. Christ's example also provides the definition of how the sacraments are to be performed.

During Baptism, the individual is to be baptized with water in the name of God the Father, Son, and Holy Spirit. Along with Baptism comes the requirement of earnestly studying the Word of God (MAT 28:19–20). Holy Communion requires the consecration of the elements, being the bread and wine, which contain the true body and blood of Christ (MAT 26:26–28). Recipients partaking of that bread and wine are receiving Christ as well as publicly acknowledging Christ's atonement. If the sacraments are not performed as Christ instructed, then something could be amiss; remember, one's participation necessitates a serious self-examination.

- 1 CO 11:25–29 ~ Jesus commanded the apostles on the first Holy Communion to partake of the sacrament often to remember Him. Thus, as often as you eat the bread and drink the wine of Holy Communion, you proclaim the death of Christ until His return. But if you participate unworthily, without sincerely repenting or desiring communion with Christ, you will become one of those found guilty of Christ's crucifixion. Examine yourself before partaking, because if you do so unworthily, you will be eating and drinking damnation upon yourself.

Spiritual cleansing purifies us so that we can be joined with God in righteousness. We could never be joined with Him in our corruptible flesh but only with His incorruptible Spirit. Thanks be to God for His endless grace and mercy, for through the death and resurrection of Christ we are made righteous by faith. God has given us an avenue to demonstrate our faith through the gifts of the sacraments, which provide a testimony of what we know to be true. The following are fundamental truths that Christ came to declare and that we are commissioned to declare as well.

1. Christ lived to fulfill the Law on our behalf, because our sin destroyed any chance of our remaining obedient to God. He lived the perfect life that we could never live in this body.
2. His suffering and death paid the price of disobedience by punishment of death. Christ took upon Himself the sin of the world, and died for it, conquering the world and its sin.
3. His resurrection proved His victory over death, bringing with it the resurrection of the dead and everlasting life for all believers.

Christ overcame the world and its sin, and the curse of death that was levied upon all people. We too have overcome the world when we believe in Him. We testify about this truth to others so that they also may believe, and overcome.

- JOH 16:33 ~ After the last supper on the night Jesus was betrayed, Jesus was leaving for the Garden of Gethsemane to pray. Jesus said, "The reason I told to you these things is so you could have peace. In the world you will have distress, but be cheerful for I have overcome the world."
- 1 JO 5:4–6 ~ Whoever is born of God overcomes the world; the victory that overcomes the world is found in faith. Jesus Christ overcame the world; anyone believing in Him will also overcome the world. Christ is He, who came by water and blood. The Holy Spirit is He who bears witness, because the Spirit is truth.

The free gift of eternal life is available to all people, if only they have faith. Faith is demonstrated by actions (JAM 2:17–26). Two very important acts of faith can be found through participation in the Lord's Holy Sacraments. These acts testify of the saving grace of God who sent His Son to atone for our sins, and both represent a public display of a lifetime commitment to that truth.

> Come, take and eat the body of the Lord, and drink His holy blood for you outpoured.
> He is the Lamb, the new Passover feast, our humble servant and the Great High Priest.

The Last Supper – Painting by Philippe de Champaigne (1602–1674)   The Louvre, Paris

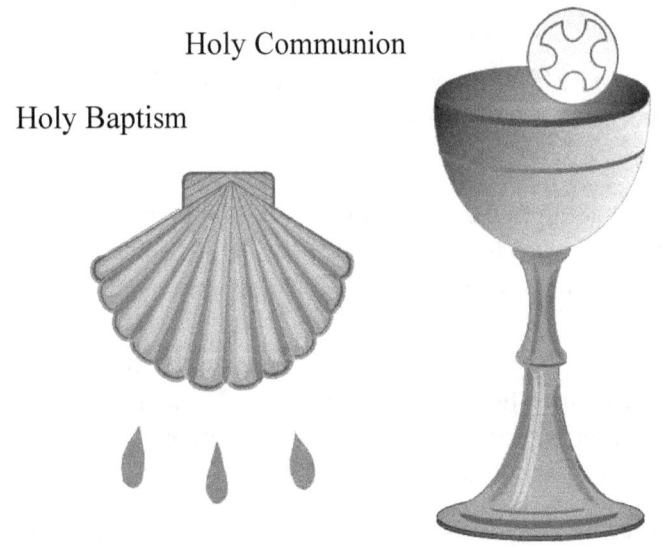

Lesson: Sacrifice

The dictionary defines sacrifice as the act of offering something of value to a deity, and we know that God is the only deity. The root word of sacrifice is sacred (Fr. *sacere*), which means to consecrate or render something as holy. The suffix (Fr. *facere*) means to make. Thus, the word sacrifice literally means to make or offer something consecrated or holy to God.

In the Old Testament, God commanded His people to make sacrificial offerings to Him as a means of expressing their obedience and faithfulness.

- EXO 20:24 ~ Erect an altar from the earth and sacrifice your burnt offerings and peace offerings upon it. Do this in all places where my name is observed, and I will visit you and bless you.
- 1 CH 23:30–31 ~ Thank and praise the Lord every morning and every evening. Regularly offer burnt sacrifices to Him every Sabbath, at the beginning of each month, and during the appointed festivals and feasts, in accordance with God's command.

The practice of presenting sacrificial offerings to the Lord started with the first family. We recall the story of Cain, a farmer, and his brother Abel, a herdsman (GEN 4). They both presented offerings to God, but the offering presented by Cain was not received. Cain became furious with God and jealous of Abel, and killed his brother. God explained to Cain that the evil desires of his heart had consumed him, making him unworthy and his sacrifice unacceptable.

An enormously significant sacrifice was that of Abraham, who was willing to offer his only legitimate son to the Lord (GEN 22). God spared Abraham's son Isaac, because God had in mind a more complete and everlasting sacrifice. Jacob's sacrifice on the mountain as a result of his pact with Laban was another example of how sacrificial offerings played an important role during key events in the lives of God's people (GEN 31). The plea of the Hebrews to Pharaoh to allow them to present sacrifices to God was met with Pharaoh's jealousy and rage, when he commanded the slaves to make bricks without straw (EXO 5).

Thus, the giving of offerings to God was extremely vital to the nation of Israel, as an act of compliance and praise. In the Mosaic Law, God passed along to the Israelites several rules and regulations concerning the offering of sacrifices (refer to the entire book of Leviticus regarding sacrifices and feasts). One of the rules of sacrifice was that the offering must not have any blemishes but be free of physical imperfections (DEU 15:21; 1 PE 1:19).

Perhaps the most important sacrifice in the Old Testament occurred on the first Passover (EXO 12). Those who followed God's command sacrificed a male lamb, painted its blood on the door posts, and ate the lamb for supper. When the angel of death came to deliver God's wrath upon the firstborn of Egypt, he passed over the homes of those who had followed God's instructions.

There are two important ingredients associated with sacrificial offerings: blood and fire. First, let's address the issue of fire. In a burnt offering, fire consumed all the flesh and blood and this represented a purification process. In the Bible, the Holy Spirit is often compared to a refiner's fire that purifies the soul, similar to the refining of gold; that is, fire removes the impurities like separating dross from metal. In a burnt offering, fire eliminated the evil and the sin, thereby providing forgiveness through the spiritual power of atonement. God's people presented such offerings to demonstrate the faith of obedience to Him, and a desire for forgiveness through repentance.

- NUM 28:6 ~ There will be a regular burnt offering, as instituted on Mt. Sinai, producing a pleasing aroma to God in an offering made to Him by fire.
- 1 KI 18:36–39 ~ At the time of the evening sacrifice, the prophet Elijah came forward and prayed, "Oh Lord, God of Abraham, Isaac, and Israel, let it be known today that you are God and that I am your servant doing the things you have commanded me to do. Answer my prayer so that these people will know that you alone are God, and that you desire for them to turn their hearts back towards you." Then fire fell from heaven and consumed the sacrifice, the wood, the stones, the soil, and all the water in the trench. When the people saw this, they fell prostrate on the ground and cried, "The Lord is God!"
- MAL 3:2–4 ~ Who can endure the day of His coming, and who can stand when He appears? He is like the refiner's fire or the launderer's detergent. He will act as a refiner, purifying the Levites and refining them like precious metal. Then the Lord will have qualified men to bring offerings in righteousness, and those offerings will be acceptable as in times past.
- LUK 3:16–17 ~ John the Baptist answered them saying, "I baptize you with water. But One comes after me whose shoes I am unworthy to unloose. He will baptize you with the Holy Spirit and with fire. He has the winnowing fork in hand, ready to clear the threshing floor. He will gather the wheat into the barn, and He will burn up the chaff with unquenchable fire."
- HEB 10:26–27,31 ~ If you deliberately continue sinning after you have received the knowledge of truth, there will remain no sacrifice for sins. All you will receive is the fearful expectation of judgment and a raging fire that will consume the enemies of God. Yes, it is a dreadful thing to fall into the vengeful hands of the living God.
- REV 21:8 ~ But the fearful, unbelieving, abominable, murderous, and promiscuous, as well as the sorcerers, idolaters, and liars, will have their part in the lake which burns with fire and brimstone, and this is the second death.

Although the fire destroys, the blood renews. While the fire eliminates the sin, the blood provides the payment that allows the sinner to be reconciled with God. The Bible says that life is found in the blood, and that the shedding of blood is necessary for the remission of sins. Remission of sins through sacrificial offerings brought transitory relief from the penalty of death. Remission of sins through the atonement of Christ brings permanent relief and eternal life.

- EXO 24:6–8 ~ Moses put half of the blood into bowls and sprinkled the other half on the altar. Then he took the Book of the Covenant and read to the people, who responded, "We will do everything the Lord has commanded, and we will obey Him." Then Moses took the rest of the blood and sprinkled it on the people, saying, "This is the blood of the covenant that the Lord has made with you in accordance with these words."
- LEV 17:11 ~ The life of all flesh resides in the blood, and I (God) have given it to you upon the altar to make atonement for your souls, for it is the blood that makes atonement for the soul.
- HEB 9:13–22,25–28 ~ The blood of animals and the ashes sprinkled on the ceremonially unclean sanctified those who were only outwardly clean. How much more will the blood of Christ, who through the eternal Spirit offered Himself unblemished to God, cleanse our consciences from acts that lead to death, so that we may live to serve the living God! This is why Christ is the mediator of a new covenant, so that those who are called may receive the promise of an eternal inheritance. Now Christ has died as a ransom, freeing us from our sins committed under the first covenant of the Law. As is the case with a will, it is necessary to prove that the person who wrote the will is dead, since a will can only be enforced after someone has died. This is why the first covenant also could not be put into effect without blood. When Moses had proclaimed the commandments to the people from the Book of the Law, he took the blood of the sacrifice and sprinkled it on the scroll and the people saying,

"This is the blood of the covenant that God has commanded you to keep." In the same manner, Moses sprinkled blood on the tabernacle and the ceremonial utensils. In fact, the Law requires that nearly everything be cleansed with blood, for without the shedding of blood there can be no forgiveness. Christ did not enter heaven to offer Himself again and again, like the high priest did by presenting offerings year after year using blood that was not his own. If that were the case, Christ would have to suffer many times. But He appeared only once, for all people and for all the ages, to remove sin through the sacrifice of Himself. As humankind is destined to die once and then face judgment, so Christ was sacrificed once, to take away the sins of many people. And He will appear a second time, not to bear our sins, but to bring salvation to those who await His return.

The oblations given in the OT provided temporary atonement for the sins of the offerer. But now the blood of Christ has been poured out to atone for the sins of the world, once and for all time. The blood of the sacrifice represented newness of life, while the lifeblood of Christ provides life eternal. That is why additional blood sacrifices are unnecessary; indeed, they are counterproductive, because the sacrifice of Christ stands forever.

- MIC 6:6–7 ~ How am I to appear before God? Shall I come before Him with offerings and sacrifices? Will He be pleased with thousands and thousands of sacrifices? Shall I sacrifice my firstborn, the fruit of my body, to atone for the sin of my soul?
- HEB 10:1–14 ~ The Law is only a shadow of the good things to come. It could never, by the same sacrifices repeated constantly every year, make perfect those who draw near to God in worship. If they could, there would have been a cessation to the sacrificing. But the sacrifices were made as an annual reminder of sins, because it is impossible for the blood of animals to take away sins. Therefore, when Christ came into the world, he told us, "Sacrifices and offerings God did not desire, yet you prepared them anyway (PSA 40:6–8). Burnt offerings and sin offerings did not please Him" (though they were required just the same) Christ declared, "Here I am, it is written about me in the scroll; I have come to do your will, oh God." Therefore, God set aside the first covenant to establish the second, through which we are made holy by the sacrifice of the body of Jesus Christ, once for all people and for all time.

It was prohibited for anyone to drink blood of sacrifices because to do so would be to defile oneself. However, we are invited to drink the blood of the Lamb of God and eat his flesh, because His body and blood sanctifies. Each time we participate in the sacraments (Baptism or Holy Communion), we acknowledge the sacrifice that Christ made and invite Him to live in us, becoming further sanctified by His Holy Spirit.

- LEV 17:14 ~ The life of every creature is in its blood. That is why I have told the Israelites not to eat the blood of any creature; anyone who disobeys will be cut off.
- DEU 12:27 ~ Present your burnt offerings on the altar of the Lord, both the meat and the blood. The blood must be poured out upon the altar, but you may eat the meat (NUM 18:9–10).
- JOH 6:53–57 ~ Jesus said, "I tell you the truth, unless you eat the flesh of the Son of Man and drink His blood, you have no life in you. Whoever eats my flesh and drinks my blood has eternal life, and I will raise him up the last day. For my flesh is real food and my blood is real drink. Those who eat my flesh and drink my blood live in me and I live in them. Just as I live because of the Father, so will the one who feeds on me live because of me."

- 1 CO 10:16–17 ~ The cup of blessing that we bless, doesn't it represent our communion with the blood of Christ? The bread that we break, doesn't it represent our communion with the body of Christ? Although we are many, we have become one body for we are all partakers of that one loaf of bread.

Although we no longer are to offer blood sacrifices, we always can exercise our spiritual gifts to glorify God. We can make sacrifices by offering our time, talents, and treasures for Him. Thus, we can serve God and others in many ways. Such spiritual acts are a form of self-sacrifice; they are very pleasing to the Lord and are of greater significance to Him than burnt offerings.

- PSA 51:17 ~ The sacrifices of God are a broken spirit; a broken and contrite heart, oh God, you will not despise. [A humble heart that seeks God's mercy and comfort is more important to Him than sacrificial offerings.]
- PRO 21:3 ~ To do what is fair and proper is more acceptable to God than sacrifice.
- HOS 6:6 ~ For I (God) desire mercy, not sacrifice, and acknowledgement more than burnt offerings.
- MAR 12:33 ~ To love God with all your heart, understanding, and strength and to love your neighbor as yourself are more important than all burnt offerings and sacrifices.
- HEB 13:15–16 ~ Through Christ, let us continually offer to God the sacrifice of praise which is the fruit of our lips, as we confess His name. And do not forget to do good and to share with others, for God is pleased with sacrifices such as these.

Whatever we do, whether it is to sacrifice something or not to sacrifice something, we should acknowledge Christ and give thanks. Some people prefer to fast, and some prefer to feast, but the motivation for either should be to praise the Lord. Paul suggests that we offer ourselves as living sacrifices, consecrated before God, in response to the wonderful blessings He has bestowed upon us. That way, everything we do or do not do is for the Lord and not ourselves.

- 1 SA 15:22 ~ Samuel said, "Does the Lord appreciate burnt offerings and sacrifices as much as He does obedience? To obey is better than to sacrifice, and to listen is more important than the flesh of rams."
- ZEC 7:5–6 ~ Ask the people of the land and the priest, "When you fasted and mourned in the fifth and seventh months those seventy years, was it really for God? And when you ate and drank, were you not merely feasting for yourselves?" (also ZEC 8:19)
- LUK 9:23 ~ Jesus told them all, "If anyone would come with me, he must deny himself, take up his cross daily, and follow me."
- ROM 12:1 ~ Give yourselves to God. Let yourself be a living sacrifice. After all He has done for you, is that too much to ask?
- ROM 14:5–8 ~ One person considers a particular day more sacred than other days; another person considers each day alike. Both should be completely confident in their decision. Those who regard one day as special, do so to the Lord. Those who feast, eat to the Lord and give Him thanks. Those who fast, do so to the Lord and give Him thanks. Nobody lives totally to themselves and nobody dies totally to themselves. If we live, we live to the Lord, and if we die, we die to the Lord. So whether we live or die, we belong to the Lord.
- EPH 5:2 ~ Live a life of love, just as Christ loved us and gave Himself for us as a fragrant offering and sacrifice to God.

We have been cleansed of sin by the sacrifice of Christ. He has reconciled us with our righteous Heavenly Father. It is His desire that we remain with Him. By serving God we separate ourselves from the corruption around us. We are to stay apart from the world, being members of God's heavenly realm. (Review also the scriptures concerning the laws of a Nazarite: NUM 6; JDG 13:3–7,24; 1 SA 1:11,20,27–28).

- JOH 15:18–19 ~ Jesus said, "If the world hates you it is because it hated me first. If you belonged to the world, it would love you as its own. But you do not belong to the world, because I have chosen you out of it. That is why the world hates you."
- JOH 17:16–19 ~ Jesus prayed to God, "They are not of the world even as I am not of the world. Sanctify them by the truth, for your Word is truth. As you have sent me into the world, so I have sent them into the world. For them, I sanctify myself so that they too may be truly sanctified."

When I Survey the Wondrous Cross

When I survey the wondrous cross on which the Prince of Glory died,
My richest gain I count but loss and pour contempt on all my pride.
Forbid it, Lord that I should boast save in the death of Christ, my God;
And all vain things that charm me most, I sacrifice them to His blood.

See, from His head, His hands, His feet, sorrow and love flow mingled down.
Did e'er such love and sorrow meet or thorns compose so rich a crown?
Were the whole realm of nature mine, that were a tribute far too small;
Love so amazing, so divine, demands my soul, my life, my all.

The Jerusalem Cross with Shield

Lesson: The Witness as Preacher

As called disciples, we are given the authority and responsibility to preach the Gospel to the world. Of course, some people have special gifts and/or training in that area. We all should exercise our special gifts to edify the church. But being a pastor to the flock requires unique abilities, training, and character.

- ISA 61:1–3 ~ The Spirit of God is upon me, because He has directed me to preach His good news to the humble, to heal the broken hearted, to free the slaves, and to release those who are bound in chains and in prison; to proclaim the Lord's favor and His vengeance, to comfort all who mourn, and to tell those who mourn to exchange their ashes for beauty; to replace mourning with joy, and to don the garment of praise in exchange for the spirit of sorrow, so that they may be trees of righteousness, planted by the Lord for His glorification.
- 1 PE 2:5–9 ~ You are living stones, built into a spiritual house; a holy priesthood, to offer spiritual sacrifices acceptable to God through Jesus Christ. You are a chosen generation, a royal priesthood, a holy nation, a special people; for you have been selected to give praise to Him who called you out of darkness into His marvelous light.

Those who are selected by God to preach the Gospel of Christ are special people indeed. Their lives are dedicated to that mission because they have sacrificed themselves to that end. But what exactly is their mission? Several objectives of the preacher will be reviewed in this lesson.

First, there is extended an <u>Invitation</u>. One of the principal tasks of the pastor is to invite others to share in God's kingdom. It is not only about tending to the needs of the flock, but also reaching out to the lost sheep. The focus is on God's most excellent promise of eternal life through faith in Christ. If there is anything that should motivate an unbeliever to reconsider, it is the prospect of living forever in peace and joy with God Almighty. It is unnecessary to dwell only on the consequences of disbelief because the rewards of faith are far more compelling. As a disciple of Christ, it requires no effort to shine His light so that others can see the great joy which abides in you (1 PE 3:15); one of the things that will attract others to God is they will want what you have.

- MAT 22:2–10; LUK 14:16–24 ~ Jesus told a parable about the kingdom of heaven: The kingdom of heaven is like the king whose son was to be married. The king sent servants to gather the invited guests for the wedding, but they gave lousy excuses not to come. The king sent servants a second time, but those on the guest list ignored them, beat them, and even murdered them. The king found out and sent his armies to destroy the murderers and burn their cities. Then he sent the servants into the streets to gather anybody and everybody, good or bad, rich or poor, the downtrodden, handicapped, and underprivileged until the wedding had enough guests. Nobody on the original guest list was welcome.
- ROM 8:16–17 ~ The Spirit Himself bears witness with our spirits that we are children of God; and if children then heirs of God, and equal heirs with Christ, provided we suffer with Him that we also may be glorified with Him.
- 1 CO 2:9 ~ It is written: Nobody has ever heard or seen, or even imagined, the wonderful things God has prepared for those who love Him (also ISA 64:4).

Next, we will turn to the <u>Confession</u>. Once someone accepts the invitation, he or she may wonder: Why me? Those who are invited to come to Jesus are called to repentance and godliness. It is not enough to want what God promises, we must ask for it. Although we can never earn it through our acts of faith, we substantiate our belief that we will receive all good things when we respond to God's calling. This is demonstrated by affirming Christ in everything say and do, which is a central role of the preacher. Thus, our confession is twofold: first to acknowledge before God our Father that we need a Savior to absolve us of our iniquities, and second to acknowledge before others that Christ is that Savior.

- MAT 3:1–3 ~ John the Baptist came preaching in the wilderness of Judea, saying, "Repent for the kingdom of heaven is near." He came to prepare people to receive Christ who was already in their midst.
- MAT 16:16 ~ Peter confessed, "You are the Christ the Son of the living God."
- ACT 17:30; ACT 26:20 ~ God commands all people everywhere to repent. That message was spread throughout the world to anyone who would listen: Turn to God, repent, and perform acts worthy of repentance.
- 1 CO 1:23–24 ~ Paul wrote: We preach Christ crucified which is an obstacle to the Jews and is foolishness to the Greeks. But to those who are called, both Jews and Greeks alike, Christ is the power of God and the wisdom of God.

The <u>Proclamation</u> of Christ's coming is the next step in the sequence of our pastoral duty. In our acts of service to others we acknowledge what Christ has done for us. The focus is totally on Christ, not ourselves. It is not about what we can do as individuals, it is about what He has done for us and all people. We have let Him inside of our hearts so that we can dwell in Him. Jesus is our love connection to God and to others. Therefore, the proclamation is that we possess a personal relationship with God through Jesus Christ, and this relationship is the focus of our lives. And that becomes the foundation of relationships we form with others and the substance of our witnessing.

- MAT 25:20 ~ Jesus said, "Whenever you serve others you are serving me."
- MAT 28:19–20 ~ Jesus told His disciples, "Go into every nation and teach the people everything I have taught you. Baptize them in the name of the Father, Son, and Holy Spirit. And remember, I'll always be with you, even until the end of time."
- JOH 10:14–16 ~ Jesus said, "I am the Good Shepherd. I know my sheep and they know me."
- JOH 15:4–5,16 ~ Jesus said, "Abide in me and I will abide in you. Just as the branch cannot bear fruit when separated from the vine, neither can you if you become separated from me. For I am the vine, and you are the branches. If you abide in me you will bring forth much fruit, but without me you can do nothing. You didn't choose me. I chose you and ordained you, so that you could continue to bear fruit. Therefore, whatever you ask the Father in heaven in my name, He will give it to you.
- 2 CO 4:5–6,13 ~ Paul wrote: What we preach is not about ourselves but Jesus Christ our Lord. We are your servants for His sake. God commanded the light to shine out of darkness, and that light has shined in our hearts. We shine the light of the knowledge of the glory of God whose face is Jesus Christ. We have the spirit of faith. As it is written: I believed, and therefore I have spoken; we also believe, and therefore speak.

The Church was established to proclaim Christ to the world; responsibilities in this regard are listed below. Being members of the body of Christ, we each share in those responsibilities as ministers of the Word.

- Shining the Light of Christ in our everyday lives
- Sharing the Gospel at every opportunity
- Developing Christ-centered relationships
- Enabling people to do God's will
- Using our talents and gifts to edify the Church
- Equipping Christians to combat evil and win souls for Christ

One responsibility that should not be overlooked is being a member of a church, serving and supporting it. But be on the lookout, for there are corrupt churches, leaders, and clergy that abuse people or espouse wayward theologies (probably more the exception than the rule). Certainly, it is wise to investigate the theology, congregation, and character of a church before selecting it to be your church home. It is your responsibility to be knowledgeable of what the Holy Bible teaches so you can tell the difference between a good church or leader and a bad one.

As members of God's kingdom, we have additional responsibilities, not the least of which is giving back to God in response to the gifts He has given to us. The greatest gift of all is eternal life in heaven, which we already have received even though it has yet to be realized. For this we give Him our lives just as He gave His life to us.

- <u>Testimony</u>. Witnessing and Teaching: Look within your heart and see if your light shines. Do you demonstrate that you are a Christian by your lifestyle and conduct? Can others see Christ in you? Do you and your family love the Word and do you study it together? Do you actively participate in the church and in the sacraments?

- <u>Talent</u>. Service and Aid: Use your abilities to the glory of God. Do you spend time in service to others and to our Lord? Are you active in your faith? Do you help out in church and/or in your community?

- <u>Tribute</u>. Offerings and Tithes: Help God's kingdom to grow and prosper; assist the poor and needy. Support the church and its mission. Do you share God's gifts with others? Are you a blessing to those around you? Do you give God the glory?

    o God loves a cheerful giver; do not give because you feel obligated to do so (2 CO 9:7).
    o Give in accordance with how much God has prospered you (DEU 16:17; 1 CO 16:2).
    o The Bible recommends that you give ten percent of your income (tithe). Abraham was the first to give tithes of his increase to the Lord (GEN 14:18–20; HEB 7:6,9). Jacob continued this practice (GEN 28:22).
    o The Law handed down to Moses required the Israelites (including Levites) to tithe (DEU 14:22; HEB 7:5). That tithe was considered holy to God (LEV 27:30).
    o To refrain from giving tithes and offerings is akin to robbing God of what is rightfully His (MAL 3:6–8).
    o We owe to God our very lives (ROM 12:1), and not just our offerings.
    o Christ admonished the Pharisees for merely tithing, without adhering to the more important points of the Law such as justice, mercy, and faith (MAT 23:23).

What marvelous gifts God gives to us; He gives us everything He has, even Himself! Likewise, give yourself to others; especially give your love, forgiveness and mercy. Give a portion of your increase back to God. We owe God everything we are, especially the prosperity we enjoy. God promises that if we give him our tithes, He will further bless us with increased prosperity. Thus, you have nothing to lose and everything to gain by giving. God will use the measure of your giving as the standard by which He prospers you; He has given us a baseline of one tenth as a starting point. God has challenged us to tithe. Prove to yourself that indeed He will open the windows of heaven and bestow more blessings upon you than you can contain (MAL 3:10). Remember, true giving must be unconditional. To anticipate a reward or accept a gratuity turns a gift into a trade. If we give cheerfully, without obligation, God will bless us abundantly.

- LUK 6:38 ~ Give and it shall be given to you in abundance, overflowing; for the same measure that you give is returned unto you.

CHAPTER SIX

WHAT IS EVIL?

SIN AND TEMPTATION

To sin is to commit evil. A person can sin in what they do, say, or think. Satan was the first to sin, and he hasn't stopped since. Therefore, Satan is a condemned creature because he loves evil. Satan will be sentenced to eternal damnation in the lake of fire. His desire is to take as many people with him as he can. He preys on the weaknesses of human flesh by tempting people to engage in immoral acts. He does this by appealing to human desires, pleasures, weaknesses, and vulnerabilities.

Satan and other wicked creatures are constantly tempting us to sin. However, anyone can opt out; it's not like this is the only option available. A person can rebuke Satan and he will leave. Rejoicing in the name of Jesus Christ is especially punishing to Satan. Through Christ, we possess the power to resist temptation and shun evil. Unfortunately, all people have sinned and are worthy of death, save Christ alone. We must recognize that we are sinners and need to be redeemed by Christ. Only then will we be free from the powers of sin and death.

What Is Sin?

- ROM 3:20 ~ With the Law comes the knowledge of sin. Therefore, you cannot be justified by works of the Law. That is, your good works cannot erase your sins.
- ROM 4:15 ~ Where there is no Law there is no sin.
- ROM 5:13 ~ Sin was in the world before the Law, but nothing can be attributed to sin if there is no Law.
- ROM 7:7,14 ~ The Law told me what not to do thereby revealing sin to me. So, is the Law sin? No, it is the opposite of sin. For the Law is spiritual, but I am carnal because I sin.
- JAM 2:10 ~ Whoever disobeys one point of the Law disobeys all the Law.
- 1 JO 3:4 ~ Whoever commits sin disobeys the Law, for that is how sin is defined.
- 1 JO 5:17 ~ All unrighteousness is sin.

Original Sin

It only took a single sin for sin to exist. Along with the original sin came death and judgment. Satan was the first spirit to sin. Later, he influenced the first humans, Adam and Eve, to sin. Since it only takes one sin to make someone sinful, and since Adam and Eve were sinful, their children were born with a sin nature. Thus, sin and death are passed onto one's offspring. Everyone is born sinful, except Christ of course, because He was born of the Holy Spirit which never sins but is perfect in righteousness.

- GEN 3:1–6 ~ The serpent (Satan) tricked Adam and Eve into eating the forbidden fruit of the Tree of Knowledge. Satan lied to them, telling them that eating the fruit would not lead to sin and death as God had told them. Satan deceived them into thinking that eating the fruit would make them like gods, but instead it made them sinful like Satan.
- PSA 51:5 ~ I was formed in sin and in sin I was conceived.
- EZE 28:14–15 ~ Lucifer was the anointed cherub, who was perfect in every respect until evil was found in him.
- MAR 7:23 ~ Jesus said, "All sin comes from within a person and defiles that person."
- ROM 5:12,18–19 ~ Sin entered the world by one man (Adam), resulting in universal death. So sin and death have been passed onto all people, for all have sinned. Consequently, just as the result of one sin condemned all people, so also the result of one act of righteousness brought justification to all people. Through the disobedience of Adam, we all became sinners; through the obedience of Christ we all have been made righteous.
- 1 JO 3:8 ~ Whoever sins is of the devil, for the devil sinned from the beginning. This is why Christ came, to destroy the works of the devil.

People Are Sinful by Nature.

- GEN 8:21 ~ The Lord said in His heart, "I will never again curse the ground because of humanity. For the imagination of the human heart is evil from youth. Never will I destroy every living thing like I did with the flood."
- JOB 15:16 ~ How filthy and abominable are humans who drink sin like water?
- ECC 7:20 ~ There is not a single person on earth that does good and never sins.
- ISA 59:12 ~ Our sins are multiplied before the Lord; these sins testify against us for they stick with us and we remember them.
- JOH 8:34 ~ Jesus said, "Whoever commits sin becomes a slave to sin."
- ROM 3:23 ~ Everyone has sinned and come short of the glory of God.
- ROM 7:19–20 ~ I don't do the good I want to do, but I do the evil I don't want to do. If I do the evil things I don't want to do, it is not I that do them but the sin that lives inside of me.
- 1 JO 1:8 ~ If we say we are not sinful, we deceive ourselves and we are liars.

People Can Resist Temptation.

- DEU 6:16 ~ Never tempt the Lord your God.
- PSA 1:1 ~ Blessed are those who refrain from sin and avoid sinners.
- PSA 25:3 ~ Let nobody be ashamed who waits for the Lord. Let only those who commit sin without cause be ashamed.
- PRO 1:10 ~ If sinners entice you, do not consent.
- MAT 4:7 ~ Jesus quoted Deuteronomy to Satan, "It is written, never tempt the Lord your God."
- MAT 6:13 ~ Jesus recited His prayer to the multitude... "Lead us not unto temptation but deliver us from evil..."
- MAT 26:41 ~ Jesus told His apostles at Gethsemane, "Watch and pray, so that you do not enter into temptation. The spirit is indeed willing, but the flesh is weak."
- ROM 8:31 ~ If God is for us, who can be against us?
- 1 CO 5:11 ~ Do not keep company with people who are fornicators, greedy, idolatrous, flirtatious, extortionists, and drunkards.

- 1 CO 10:13 ~ Temptation is common to humanity. But God is faithful and fair, and He will not cause you to suffer temptation beyond your ability to withstand it. And He will always provide you a way to escape from temptation.
- GAL 6:1 ~ If someone is overtaken by sin, you who are spiritual should restore that person in the spirit of meekness, considering you are a sinner also and can be overcome by temptation.
- EPH 6:13–17 ~ Take with you the armor of God, so that you can stand against evil and overcome it. Put on the belt of truth, the breastplate of righteousness, the shoes of the Gospel of peace, and especially carry the shield of faith so that you can repel the fiery darts of evil. Take with you the helmet of salvation, and the sword of the Spirit which is the Word of God.
- PHP 4:8 ~ Think only about things that are true, noble, just, pure, lovely, good, praiseworthy, and virtuous.
- JAM 1:12–15 ~ Blessed is the person that endures temptation, for when that person is tried, he or she will receive a crown of life which the Lord promises to all who love Him. When tempted, never say you are tempted by God, for God cannot be tempted by evil, neither does He tempt anyone. People are tempted when motivated by their own lust and enticed to sin. If you conceive of lust, it brings forth sin; and sin, when finished, brings forth death.
- JAM 4:7,17 ~ Submit to God and resist the devil, and the devil will run away. Whenever someone knows something is proper, but doesn't do it, that for them is sin.
- 1 PE 5:8–9 ~ Be sober and vigilant, because your enemy the devil roams about like a lion searching for someone to devour. He will attempt to consume anyone who isn't steadfast in their faith.
- 2 PE 2:9 ~ God knows how to deliver the faithful out of temptation, and to reserve the unjust until the day of judgment to be punished.
- 2 PE 3:17 ~ Don't allow yourself to fall from the faith and be led astray with the error of the wicked.
- 1 JO 4:4 ~ Since you belong to God, and He lives in you, you have the power to overcome evil spirits, because He (Christ) that lives in you is greater than the one (Satan) who is in the world.
- REV 3:10 ~ Jesus said, "Because you have patiently kept my commandments, I will keep you from the hour of temptation, which shall come upon the entire world to try the patience of everyone."

The Result of Sin is Death.

- PRO 8:36 ~ Whoever sins against God hurts his own soul; whoever hates God loves death.
- PRO 13:21 ~ Evil pursues sinners, but the righteous are repaid with good.
- EZE 3:18–21 ~ God says, "I have told the wicked that they will surely die. If you do not warn the wicked to turn from their sin and be saved, you will also die for you will be partly responsible for their death. But if you do warn the wicked and they still do not turn from their wickedness, they will die in their sin but you will have saved yourself. If the righteous turn from righteousness to sin, they will die because their righteousness will no longer be remembered. If you do not warn them you will die as well. But if you warn the righteous not to sin, and they do not sin, their souls will be saved and so will yours."
- EZE 18:24,26–27; EZE 33:12–13 ~ If a righteous man turns to sin, and does evil like the wicked do, his righteousness will never be remembered and he will die in his sin. If a wicked man turns to righteousness, and does what is lawful and upright, his wickedness will be forgotten and he will save his soul, and live. All the righteousness that a person has done will

not save them on the day that they return to sin. And the wickedness a person has done will not condemn them on the day that they return to righteousness.
- MIC 2:1 ~ Woe to those who plot evil and think of sinful things to do, and then carry out their evil plans just because they think they can get away with it.
- MAT 12:31 ~ Jesus said, "All manner of sin and blasphemy can be forgiven, except blasphemy directed against the Holy Spirit."
- MAT 18:7 ~ Jesus said, "Woe to the world because of their terrible offenses. It is unfortunate that such offenses have to occur, but woe unto those who commit them."
- ROM 6:23 ~ The wages of sin is death.
- 1 TI 6:9 ~ The rich fall into temptation, and a trap, and they succumb to many foolish and harmful lusts, which can drown a person in destruction and damnation.
- JAM 1:15 ~ When lust is conceived it results in sin, and sin, when finished, results in death.

Satan Appeals to Our Desires when Tempting Us to Sin.

Humans are motivated by a hierarchy of physiological and psychological needs such as sustenance (food and drink), pleasure (sex, riches, fame), and recognition (knowledge, power, control). Satan knows full well that we desire such things and places temptations in our path as we seek to gratify them. Satan especially preys on our weaknesses such as lust, greed, and pride. If the motivation is for self-gratification and not to please God, it is probably a sin, so you might want to think twice before acting or reacting.

God will provide our needs if we seek His righteousness. Therefore, Satan cannot offer anything that God has not already promised; Satan offers the exact opposite of what God offers. With God we have the power to accomplish anything; but Satan will try to convince us that we cannot. Satan enters when he can expect the least resistance, as when he tempted Christ in the wilderness at a time when the Lord was physically and mentally exhausted. Satan probably influenced the likes of Buddha, Mohammed, and other wayward spiritual celebrities in this manner.

- GEN 3:6 ~ When the woman saw that the Tree of Knowledge was good for food, that it was pleasant to the eyes, and it could make her wise, she picked a piece of fruit, ate some, and gave it to her husband who was with her, and he ate too.
- LUK 4:1–13 ~ Jesus was filled with the Holy Spirit who led Him into the wilderness. There He was tempted during the forty days He fasted there. He was very weak and hungry when the devil came to Him. The devil said, "If you're hungry, command those stones to become bread." Jesus replied, "It is written that man will not live by bread alone, but by the Word of God." Next, the devil brought Jesus into a high mountain and showed Him all the kingdoms of the world in a single moment of time. The devil said, "All the power and glory associated with these kingdoms I will give to you if you will worship me." Jesus replied, "Get behind me, Satan, for it is written that you must worship the Lord God and serve only Him." Next, the devil brought Jesus to Jerusalem where they sat at the pinnacle of the temple. The devil said, "Jump down, and the angels will catch you, since it is written that God gives His angels charge over you to keep you always from harm and danger." Jesus replied, "It is also written that you should never tempt the Lord your God." At that, the devil gave up and left Jesus.
- 1 JO 2:15–16 ~ Do not love the world or worldly things. If a person loves the world, he or she cannot love God. All that is in the world, the lust of the flesh, the greed of the eyes, and the pride of humanity, do not come from the Father but are of this world alone.

Greed and Riches

One of the greatest temptations of all is material wealth. Striving for material things instead of spiritual things causes one to veer away from God. Endeavoring for power, riches, pleasure, or fame is greed. The original sins committed by Satan, and again by Adam and Eve, were motivated by greed. Thus, greed leads to other forms of sin. Greed is never satisfied.

- DEU 23:19 ~ Don't lend money or anything else at extreme interest rates to your friends and relatives.
- 1 SA 2:7 ~ The Lord makes people rich or poor and lifts people up or brings them down.
- 1 KI 3:11–13 ~ God said to Solomon, "Since you have asked for wisdom and not for riches, a long life, death to your enemies, or any other selfish thing, I will not only make you wise, but also I will give you riches and honor."
- JOB 20:15 ~ Those who swallow down riches will vomit them up again, just like God rids himself of those who relish in their riches.
- JOB 36:19 ~ God does not have any regard for riches nor the forces of earthly strength.
- PSA 37:16 ~ The little that a righteous person has is better than the riches of many wicked people.
- PSA 39:6 ~ People put on a vain show all the time, and they become troubled in vain. People try to heap up riches not knowing who will gather them in the end.
- PSA 49:6–7 ~ Those who trust in their riches and boast of their wealth can't redeem or ransom anyone, including themselves.
- PSA 62:10 ~ Don't use oppression or robbery to obtain wealth; and if you do become wealthy, don't set your heart on your wealth.
- PRO 1:18–19 ~ Those who are greedy for riches and oppress others to obtain riches are ambushing their own lives and will succeed in destroying themselves.
- PRO 11:4,28 ~ Riches will not profit anyone in the day of wrath; only righteousness can save a person from death. Those who trust in their riches will fail, but those who trust in God will flourish.
- PRO 22:16 ~ Those who oppress the poor to increase their own wealth and those who give to the rich eventually will become needy.
- PRO 23:5 ~ Don't set your eyes on something that isn't there, because riches will certainly find wings and fly away like an eagle.
- PRO 28:6,22 ~ Poor people who walk in righteousness are better off than rich people who are perverse in their ways. Those who are in a hurry to become rich have an evil eye, and don't realize the poverty that will come upon them.
- PRO 30:8 ~ God make me neither rich nor poor; remove from me all vanity and lies, and feed me with only things that are good for me.
- ECC 5:10–14 ~ Whoever loves money will never be satisfied with it, and whoever strives for abundance will never have enough. It is futile to strive for wealth. When riches increase so do expenditures. What good is it to have a lot of money if all you can do with it is look at it? People who work hard have a restful sleep; but the abundance of the rich prevents them from sleeping peacefully. Those who keep their riches to themselves will hurt themselves, and those riches will disappear; and then they won't have anything left to give to their children.
- JER 9:23–24 ~ If you are wise, don't glory in your wisdom; if you are mighty, don't glory in your might; if you are rich, don't glory in your wealth. Whoever wants to rejoice, let them rejoice in the fact that they know God who is loving, kind, righteous, and just.

- MAT 6:19–20 ~ Jesus said, "Don't accumulate a lot of earthy treasures that can be corrupted by insects or rust or that can be stolen by thieves. Instead, accumulate heavenly treasures, that cannot be corrupted or stolen."
- MAR 4:19 ~ Jesus said, "Earthly desires, the deceitfulness of wealth, and other lusts of this world choke the Word, and it becomes useless to those who are enticed by these things."
- MAR 10:23–25 ~ Jesus said, "It is very difficult for a rich person to enter into God's kingdom; it is easier for a camel to go through the eye of a needle."
- LUK 6:24 ~ Jesus said, "I pity you who are rich for you have received your consolation."
- LUK 12:15 ~ Jesus said, "Beware of being envious of the rich, for life does not consist of the abundance of one's possessions."
- LUK 12:19–20 ~ The greedy man said to his soul, "Soul, you have ample goods; take it easy; eat, drink and be merry." But God said to him, "Fool, tonight your soul is required of you. And all your goods, who will possess them now?"
- ACT 8:20 ~ Peter said, "If you think that the gift of God's Holy Spirit can be purchased with money, you will find that your money will perish and you along with it."
- 1 TI 6:5–10,17 ~ Corrupt minds devoid of the truth will argue that godliness is a way of obtaining wealth. Avoid these people. Godliness means being content with what you have. You brought nothing into this world and you will take nothing out of it. People who want to get rich fall into the trap of temptation, consisting of foolish and harmful lusts that drown them in destruction and condemnation. For the love of money is the root of all evil. Those who have pursued it have strayed from the faith and brought upon themselves a multitude of sorrows. Tell those who are rich not to be miserly or greedy, trusting in their wealth for their needs. Tell them instead to trust in God who richly gives us all things to enjoy.
- JAM 5:1–3 ~ Go cry and moan you rich people, for the miseries that will come upon you. Your riches are corrupted and your clothes are worn out. Your disintegrating wealth will eat at you in the same fashion. You have heaped up riches for the last time.
- REV 18:17 ~ In just one hour all the great riches of Babylon will come to nothing.

Lust

Humans are often overcome by desires of their sinful flesh. Satan is most successful in getting people to sin by tempting them with worldly pleasures. God wants us to pursue things of the spirit, and avoid lusts of the flesh; for lust leads to sin, and sin leads to death.

- ISA 3:16–26 ~ The Lord says, "Because the daughters of Zion have exalted themselves with their pride and arrogance, acting carefree and flirtatious, I will expose their nakedness and their sin will come back on their own heads. I will take away their ornaments, jewelry, perfume, hair-dos, and flashy clothes. Their sweet smell will be replaced with stink, their wardrobe with rags, and their beauty with burning. They will be slain by the sword; they will cry and moan over their desolation."
- JER 11:14–15 ~ God says, "Don't bother to pray for those people; I will not listen to them when they finally cry to me about their troubles. They have no business in my house with their lewdness, for they enjoy being evil."
- JER 13:27 ~ God says, "I have seen your adultery, your lewdness, and your abominations. Woe to you, Jerusalem. Will you ever become clean again?"
- EZE 16:58–59 ~ God says, "Your lewdness and your abominations will be upon you. I will deal with you in accordance with your own actions, for you have broken the covenant."

- EZE 23:27–30,48–49 ~ God says, "I will make you stop your lewdness and lust that you brought with you from Egypt. I will deliver you into the hands of your enemies, and they will deal harshly with you. They will take away all you have worked hard for, leaving you naked; your lewdness and promiscuity will be exposed to the world. I will do this to you because you have become polluted with lust and idolatry. Thus, I will cause lewdness to cease in the land, and I will recompense your lewdness upon you and you will pay for your sins."
- MAT 5:28 ~ Jesus said, "If you lust after someone you have committed adultery in your heart."
- MAR 4:19 ~ Jesus said, "Worldly desires, the deceitfulness of riches, and other lusts choke the Word, and it becomes unfruitful."
- ROM 1:27 ~ Men left their natural desire for women and pursued homosexual lust, thereby receiving in themselves the due recompense of their sinfulness.
- ROM 8:5–7,13 ~ Those who pursue things of the flesh belong to the flesh; those who pursue things of the spirit belong to the Spirit. To have a carnal mind is death; to have a spiritual mind is life and peace. The carnal mind hates God; it disregards God's Law for it is in complete opposition to it. If you live for the flesh you will die. If you live for the Spirit you can control the flesh, and you will live.
- 1 CO 6:18 ~ Refrain from fornication, for those who commit sexual sin are sinning against their own body.
- EPH 2:2–4 ~ In the past you walked according to the ways of the world, along with the prince of the power of the air, the spirit that works in those who are disobedient to God. We too engaged in lusts of the flesh, fulfilling the desires of our bodies and minds. Though we were dead in our sins, God in His infinite mercy and love has made us alive in Christ, and by His grace we are saved.
- EPH 4:22–24 ~ Get rid of the old self, which is corrupted with deceitful lusts. Become renewed by the spirit of your mind by putting on the new self, which is like God, created in righteousness and true holiness.
- TIT 2:11–12 ~ The grace of God which brings salvation is available to everyone. It teaches us to avoid ungodliness and worldly lusts, and to live sober, righteous lives instead.
- HEB 11:24–25 ~ Moses's faith prevented him from claiming to be the son of Pharaoh's daughter. Moses chose to suffer the afflictions of God's people rather than enjoy the pleasures of sin.
- JAM 1:14–15 ~ Everyone is tempted when they are enticed by their own lust. Lust, when conceived, brings forth sin, and sin, when finished, brings forth death.
- JAM 4:1 ~ Where do you think arguments and wars come from? They come from the lusts that battle inside you.
- 1 PE 2:11 ~ Abstain from lusts of the flesh which make war with your soul.
- 2 PE 1:4 ~ God has promised great and precious things, so that you can participate in the divine nature and escape the lusts of the world.
- 2 PE 2:9–10 ~ The Lord knows how to deliver the godly from temptation, and to reserve the wicked for the day of judgment to be punished. This includes those who seek the lusts of the unclean, who despise government, who are shameless, self-gratifying, and openly despise dignity.
- 2 PE 2:18 ~ They speak great words of vanity and they entice with lusts of the flesh; they prey upon those who are innocent and who try to escape such wickedness.
- 2 PE 3:3–4 ~ Don't forget that in the latter days, scoffers will come pursuing their own lusts and saying, "Where is the promise of His coming? Everything is the same as it was before."

- 1 JO 2:15–17 ~ Don't love the world or worldly things. If you love the world, God's love cannot be in you. Worldly things, like the lusts of the flesh, the greed of the eyes, and the pride of humanity, are not things of God. The world will pass away along with its lust, but whoever does the will of God lives forever.
- JDE 1:4 ~ Certain ungodly people, whose condemnation was written about long ago, have sneaked into the church without anyone noticing, attempting to turn God's grace into lust, and denying the only God and our Lord Jesus Christ.

Sexual Deviancy

The Bible warns us against sexual perversion and promiscuity. Unfortunately, society has become sexually permissive, to the extent that some churches ignore this behavior. In fact, the Bible tells us that such permissiveness will accelerate in the latter days. God has been very explicit about staying away from sexual sin; anyone practicing or condoning such behavior will be punished severely.

- GEN 18–19 ~ God destroyed Sodom and Gomorrah for their terrible sin and sexual lust.
- EXO 20:14; LEV 18:20 ~ Never commit adultery.
- LEV 18:6–18; LEV 20:11–21 ~ Never have sex with a family member or your in-laws.
- LEV 18:22–23; LEV 20:13–16 ~ A man must not have sex with another man as he would with a woman. Never should anyone have sex with an animal. These acts are abominations, punishable by death.
- DEU 22:5,22,25 ~ Women shouldn't wear men's clothes and men shouldn't wear women's clothes. If a husband or wife is caught in adultery, the adulterer and their lover are worthy of the death penalty. If a man rapes a woman, only the man is worthy of the death penalty.
- DEU 23:17 ~ God will not tolerate harlots among His people's daughters or sodomites among His people's sons.
- DEU 27:21–22 ~ Anyone having sex with an animal, or their brother or sister, is cursed.
- EZE 16:15–21 ~ You trusted in your beauty and fornicated with anybody and everybody. You played the harlot more than ever before or ever will be. You made images of men and played the harlot with them. You sacrificed your sons and daughters. Do you think this is a small matter?
- JOE 3:3–4 ~ They gamble for my people; they trade a boy for a harlot, and a girl to get intoxicated. What are you doing, paying me back? It will come back upon your head.
- AMO 4:10–11 ~ I will send pestilence like I did on Egypt. You will be overthrown as with Sodom and Gomorrah.
- MAR 7:21–22 ~ Jesus said, "Out of peoples' hearts proceed evil thoughts, adultery, fornication, murder, theft, greed, wickedness, deceit, lewdness, lust, blasphemy, pride, and foolishness."
- ROM 1:24–32 ~ They exchanged God's truth with lies. They worshipped and served the creation rather than the Creator. They performed dishonorable passions. Women gave up natural relations for unnatural. Men gave up natural relations with women in favor of passion for each other. Men performed shameless acts with other men, thereby receiving in their own persons the due penalty for these evil deeds. They were filled with all manner of wickedness, evil, disobedience, jealousy, boastfulness, insolence, malice, murder, deceit, slander, strife, and all manner of malignity. They were faithless, heartless, ruthless, and foolish. They enjoyed doing evil, even though they were warned that such wickedness would lead to death.
- 1 CO 6:9 ~ The unrighteous will not inherit the kingdom of heaven. The unrighteous include fornicators, idolaters, adulterers, homosexuals, and immoral and abusive people.

- GAL 5:19 ~ The actions of one's evil flesh include adultery, fornication, uncleanness, and lewdness.
- COL 3:5 ~ Repress those who practice fornication, uncleanness, promiscuity, unnatural lust, and avarice, which is idolatry.
- 1 TI 1:10 ~ They are prostitutes, defiling themselves with each other; men stealers, liars, and perjurers, who perform crazy and abnormal behaviors.
- 2 TI 3:1–6,13 ~ There will be a time of great distress. People will love themselves and money. They will be abusive, arrogant, conceited, disobedient, treacherous, slanderous, ungrateful, unholy, inhumane, haters of good and lovers of pleasure. They will capture weak and wayward women, swayed by impulses. Evil people and impostors will progress from bad to worse, as will the deceivers and the deceived.
- 1 PE 4:1–3 ~ Even though Christ has done away with sin, you must not continue to sin as you have in the past when you practiced lewdness, lust, drunkenness, overindulgence, orgies, and idolatry.
- 2 PE 2:1–3,14,18–19 ~ False prophets are coming, bringing damnable heresies, denying the Lord, and deceiving many. They will exploit with false words and attract you with lusts of the flesh. They have eyes full of adultery, insatiable for sin. Their hearts are trained in greed, and they gain through wrongdoing. They promise freedom but are themselves slaves to corruption, and are condemned. They will get perpetually worse.
- JDE 1:7–8,18–19 ~ It will be just like Sodom and Gomorrah, indulging in unnatural lust. In their dreams they defile the flesh, reject authority, and abuse the righteous. They are complainers, boasters, ridiculers, deceivers, lewd and disgusting, and devoid of the Spirit.

Abortion

The Bible warns against the shedding of innocent blood, especially that of children. Sacrificing one's children is a terrible abomination. The Bible indicates that the child is a living, spiritual creature, even when in the womb. Thus, abortion is akin to murder.

- GEN 9:6 ~ Whoever sheds the blood of another human being will have their blood shed as well; for everyone was made in the image of God.
- EXO 21:22–23 ~ If men get in a brawl and a pregnant woman is hurt, causing her to give birth prematurely, and there is no serious injury, the offender will be fined whatever the husband of that wife demands within the limits of the court. But if there is serious injury, the penalty will be life for life, hand for hand, foot for foot, burn for burn, wound for wound, bruise for bruise.
- LEV 18:21 ~ Never let any of your offspring be sacrificed to Molech (the pagan god of the Ammonites).
- 2 KI 8:12–13 ~ Hazael said, "Why are you crying, man of God?" Elisha answered, "Because I know the evil you will do to the children of Israel. You will set fire to their fortresses, you will cut down their young men with the sword, you will murder their children, and you will cut open their pregnant women." Hazael said, "Am I such a dog that I would do these terrible things?" Elisha answered, "God has told me that you will do these things when you become king of Syria."
- JOB 31:15 ~ Did not He who formed me in the womb make others the same way? Was it not the same One who formed every one of us within our mother's womb?
- PSA 22:10 ~ The Lord called me, even as I was in the womb, and I have been His since I was born.

- PSA 100:3 ~ The Lord is God. He is the One that made us, not we ourselves...
- PSA 139:13,15–16 ~ The Lord controlled my very being, even when I was in my mother's womb. My essence was never concealed from Him, for He knew me even as I was being secretly made and as I developed inside my mother. He saw me when I was still imperfect, and in His book were written all the members of my body while they were being formed and were yet undeveloped.
- ISA 44:2,24 ~ The Lord made you and formed you in the womb.
- ISA 46:3–4 ~ God says, "Listen all of you in the house of Jacob and the remnants of Israel, for you were mine since you were conceived and lived in the womb; when you are old and gray I still will be the one who keeps you. I made you, I sustain you, and I will deliver you."
- ISA 49:5 ~ The Lord formed me (Isaiah) from the womb to be His servant.
- JER 1:5 ~ God said to Jeremiah, "I knew you before I formed you in your mother's womb; I sanctified you before you were delivered from your mother's womb. I ordained you to be a prophet to all nations."
- HOS 13:16 ~ Samaria will become desolate, for their people have rebelled against God. They will be slain by the sword, their children will be cut to pieces, and their pregnant women will be ripped open.
- AMO 1:13 ~ God says, "I will severely punish the Ammonites because of their terrible sins, for they have ripped open pregnant women in Gilead in order to expand their own borders."
- LUK 1:13–15,44 ~ God told Zachariah that his wife Elisabeth would bear a son, and to call him John. That son would be filled with the Holy Spirit, even from his mother's womb. Elisabeth said to Mary, "The moment you said hello, the baby in my womb leaped with joy."
- ACT 7:17–19 ~ The descendants of Jacob multiplied in Egypt until another king arose who didn't know Joseph. This king was terrible to our ancestors, making them throw away their young children so that they couldn't live.
- 1 CO 6:19 ~ Don't you know that your body is the temple of God's Holy Spirit that lives in you, and that you belong to Him?
- 1 CO 7:4 ~ The wife does not have exclusive power over her body and neither does the husband.

Pride versus Humility

The Bible teaches us that pride, conceit, and arrogance are shameful. God prefers that we be meek and humble. It is wrong to brag about anything, except the wonderful things God has done and the fact that Jesus Christ is the source of our faith, hope, and joy. God deserves the credit and the glory for all that you accomplish, and for all that you are. After all, if it wasn't for God nobody would be alive and nobody would be saved. It is God that gives people their power and abilities, so recognize Him in your achievements so that He can be glorified, and maybe He will bless you with more ability and success.

- PSA 10:2–4 ~ The wicked in their pride persecute the poor. They will be taken in by their own imaginations. The wicked brag about their hearts' desires, and praise those who envy them. The Lord despises arrogant people who do not seek Him.
- PSA 12:3 ~ The Lord will silence those who speak arrogantly and with flatteries.
- PSA 40:4 ~ Blessed are those who trust in the Lord rather than giving their respect to the proud and deceitful.
- PSA 44:8 ~ It is good to brag about God and praise His name always.

- PSA 101:5 ~ Whoever privately slanders another, whoever has a conceited look and a proud heart, they will be cut off from God.
- PRO 8:13 ~ To fear God is to hate evil, pride, conceit, and a perverse tongue.
- PRO 11:2 ~ With pride comes shame; with humility comes wisdom.
- PRO 15:33 ~ The fear of the Lord is the instruction of wisdom, and before honor comes humility.
- PRO 16:18–19 ~ Arrogance and a proud spirit are followed by destruction. It is better to share a humble spirit with the lowly than to share the wealth of the proud.
- PRO 21:4 ~ Conceit, pride, and oppression are sins.
- PRO 28:25 ~ People with proud hearts serve only to create conflict, but those who trust in God will prosper.
- PRO 29:23 ~ Pride brings a person down, but honor lifts the humble in spirit.
- ISA 10:33 ~ Those who appear to be high and mighty will be cut down, and those who are proud will be humbled.
- ISA 13:11 ~ The evil and wicked will be punished for their sins. God will cause the arrogance of the proud to cease and will make them the lowest of all.
- ISA 57:15 ~ God says, "I will live in the high holy place as will all people having a humble and repentant spirit, because I will revive the spirits of those who are humble."
- JER 9:23–24 ~ If you are wise, don't glory in your wisdom; if you are mighty, don't glory in your might; if you are rich, don't glory in your wealth. Whoever wants to rejoice, let them rejoice in the fact that they know God, who is loving, kind, righteous, and just.
- JER 50:32 ~ The proud will stumble and fall, and nobody will raise them. God will burn their cities and destroy everything around them.
- DAN 4:37 ~ God will humble the proud as He did to King Nebuchadnezzar.
- ZEP 2:10–11 ~ The Lord will be terrible to those who are proud, blameful, and arrogant towards His people.
- MAR 10:43–44 ~ Jesus said, "He that is great among you will be your servant. For even the Son of God came to serve not to be served, and to give His life as a ransom for many."
- LUK 14:7–11 ~ Jesus told a parable to address those who sought the best seats in the house. When you are invited to a formal affair like a wedding, don't choose the seat with the highest honor, for that seat may be reserved for someone else who is more important than you. It will be embarrassing for you when you are asked to move to a seat of lesser honor. Instead, go sit at the seat with the lowest honor; if a seat of higher honor has been reserved for you, you will be shown respect by being asked to move to a seat of higher honor. The moral of the story is this: Those who exalt themselves will be humbled and those who humble themselves will be exalted.
- LUK 18:9–14 ~ Jesus told the parable of the Pharisee and the publican. Two men went to the temple to pray: a Pharisee and a publican. The Pharisee said, "Thank you Lord that I am not a sinner like other men, such as that tax collector, because I give tithes and I fast twice a week." The publican bowed low before the altar and beat on his breast saying, "God be merciful to me a sinner." Only the publican returned home justified by God. Those who exalt themselves will later be humbled, and those who humble themselves will later be exalted.
- ROM 12:3,16 ~ Do not be conceited in your own mind, but think soberly, according to the measure of faith God has given to you. Live in harmony with one another. Be humble, not proud or arrogant.
- 2 CO 3:5 ~ We are not self-sufficient enough to claim responsibility for what we have, because all of our sufficiency comes from God.

- 2 CO 10:17–18 ~ Let those who rejoice, rejoice in the Lord. Those who commend themselves will not receive approval, only those who are commended by God.
- 2 CO 11:10 ~ Paul wrote, "Nobody can stop me from bragging about the fact that Christ lives in me."
- GAL 6:3–4 ~ People who think they are something when they are nothing are deceiving themselves. But test your own actions, without comparing yourself to others, for everyone should carry their share of the load.
- EPH 2:8–9 ~ You are saved by the grace of God because of your faith in Jesus Christ. Salvation is a gift of God, it cannot be earned through good works, so nobody should brag.
- PHP 2:3–8 ~ Don't do anything through strife or vanity; instead, be humble, and regard others as better than yourselves. Don't focus on yourself, focus on others like Christ did, who although He was equal with God, He took on the form of a man. Instead of exalting Himself He became the servant of all. He humbled Himself before others and was obedient unto death, even death on the cross.
- 1 TI 1:17 ~ All glory and honor belongs now and forever to our eternal, immortal, and invisible King, who is the only wise God.
- JAM 3:5 ~ Although the tongue is a small member of the body, it boasts great things; how great is the catastrophe that can be kindled by a small fire.
- JAM 4:16 ~ It is evil to be a braggart.
- 1 PE 5:5–6 ~ Show respect to your elders. Serve each other. Clothe yourselves in humility. For God resists the proud and gives grace to the humble. Therefore, humble yourself before God and He will exalt you in due time.

Hatred and Anger

Anger is a common human emotion that too often is expressed through hatred. God commands us never to hate another person. Hatred is as serious as murder, for hatred is the very response that provokes actions such as murder, rape, prejudice, and assault. Jesus Christ taught us to love everyone, even our enemies and those who hate us. The only thing we should hate is evil (PSA 45:7; ZEC 8:16–17; ROM 12:9). What persons feels in their heart is revealed through their actions. Therefore, let God's love abide in your heart and your life will emanate that love.

Many forms of sin can be linked to uncontrolled anger including discrimination, animosity, resentment, slander, and treachery. When we become enraged and hateful, we become vulnerable to a multitude of onerous sins. For example, prejudice is a form of hatred; prejudice becomes bigotry, which becomes racism, which leads to assault and possibly murder.

People need to manage their temper, and replace such emotions as fury and rage with genuine love and compassion. There are better ways of expressing anger than lashing out, plotting revenge, letting your blood boil, battering your self-esteem, and other harmful reactions. These things only make matters worse. Often anger is merely a response to expectations not being met, disappointments, or frustration with self or others. The obvious solution is to not have expectations, but let the Lord be your confidence. If you follow and trust in Him, and expect that He will make good on His promises, you will be satisfied and happy.

Obviously, anger when expressed through rage or malice towards another is very caustic. However, anger can be vented in constructive ways, but that requires considerable self-control. It is recommended that those with unbridled anger seek counseling, especially from God. Let God take care of it. He will exact vengeance upon those who have crossed Him or who have hated and persecuted Christians. The best way to let go of anger and resentment is forgiveness, which will help you to replace the negative emotion with a positive one. Bringing to mind the fact that God has forgiven you makes it easier to forgive and tolerate others who are unruly and abrasive.

- LEV 19:17–18 ~ Never hate your brother in your heart; confront him openly with your grievance so that you do not fall into the same sin as he. Never bear a grudge or seek revenge against one another. Instead, love one another as much as you love yourself.
- JOB 34:17 ~ Should a person who hates what is right govern others? Would anyone condemn a person who is honest and fair?
- PSA 26:5 ~ I detest those who do evil, and I refuse to associate with them.
- PSA 36:1–2 ~ The sins of the wicked show God that they do not fear Him. The wicked people flatter themselves, ignoring the fact that they are evil and sinful.
- PSA 45:7 ~ If you love righteousness and hate wickedness God will shower His joy upon you and elevate you above others.
- PSA 97:10 ~ Those who love God hate evil.
- PRO 6:16–19 ~ There are seven things God hates: arrogance, lying, malicious assault, evil imaginations, mischief-makers, perjury and slander, and those who deliberately stir up trouble.
- PRO 8:13,36 ~ To fear God is to hate evil; God hates pride, conceit, evil ways, and perverse speech. Whoever sins against God hurts their own soul, and all who hate God love death.
- PRO 14:17 ~ Those who are easily angered do stupid things, and those who do hateful things are themselves hated by others.
- PRO 14:29; PRO 15:1; PRO 30:33 ~ He that is slow to wrath has understanding; but he that is hasty of spirit creates folly. A soft answer turns away wrath; but grievous words stir up anger. The forcing of wrath brings strife.
- PRO 15:1,18 ~ A gentle answer repels anger but a harsh word provokes anger. An angry person creates conflict, but a calm person creates peace.
- PRO 16:32 ~ People that are slow to anger and are in control of themselves are better than the mighty who can destroy cities.
- PRO 19:11 ~ A wise person is patient, and to his or her credit, overlooks an offense.
- PRO 22:24–25 ~ Don't make friends with an angry person, and don't associate with a furious person; otherwise you may become like them and fall into the same rut.
- PRO 26:24–28 ~ Hateful people conceal their hatred with deceitful words, but in their heart lives anger. They may try to disguise their hate, but eventually it will become exposed to everyone. They are digging a hole that they will fall into themselves; they are rolling a stone that eventually will crush them. Those who lie hate the people they lie about, and their flattering words create only ruin.
- PRO 29:22 ~ An angry person causes problems; a furious person abounds in sin.
- ECC 7:9 ~ Do not allow yourself to be easily angered for anger belongs only to fools.
- EZE 23:28–29 ~ God says, "I will deliver you to those who you hate. They will treat you with the same hatred, taking everything that you worked for, leaving you naked and exposing your shame."
- AMO 5:14–15 ~ Seek the good and avoid the evil, so that you can live with the Lord. Hate evil and love goodness. Maintain justice in your courts, and maybe God will have mercy on you.
- MAT 5:22–25 ~ Jesus said, "Whoever is angry with their brother without reason is in danger of the judgment. If you wish to offer a gift to God, reconcile with your brother, and then bring your gift. Settle your grievances with your adversary before he takes you to court, where the judge may sentence you."

- MAT 5:43–44 ~ Jesus said, "You have heard that you should love your neighbor as yourself, but you can hate your enemy. I tell you that you should love your enemies as well, and that you should pray for those who persecute you or take advantage of you."
- MAT 18:15 ~ Jesus said, "If someone does you wrong, go and discuss the matter with them in private; maybe they will listen and you will gain a brother."
- MAT 24:8–11 ~ Jesus warned everyone that those who follow Him will often be hated by others and that being a Christian will be offensive to many. Some Christians will be assaulted, imprisoned, and even killed for following Christ, but those who endure until the end will receive a crown of life.
- JOH 3:17–21 ~ Jesus said, "Those who believe in God's Son are not condemned, but those who do not believe are condemned already. God sent His light into the world, but people loved the darkness rather than the light for they were evil. Everyone who follows evil hates the light, and they avoid the light because it will uncover their evil deeds. Everyone who follows the truth will come to the light, and the light will show that their ways are godly."
- JOH 12:25 ~ Jesus said, "Those who love their lives on this earth will lose their lives, but those who hate their lives on this earth will keep their lives, unto life eternal."
- JOH 15:16–25 ~ Jesus commanded His people to bear good fruit, which is demonstrated by loving one another. He warned His followers that people would hate and persecute them, because they hated Him first, and therefore they also hate God. Jesus said that this will come to pass in accordance with the scriptures saying, "They would hate me without a cause" (see PSA 69:4; ISA 49:7).
- ROM 12:19 ~ Do not seek revenge and give way to wrath, for it is written: "Vengeance is mine. I will repay, says the Lord" (see DEU 32:35).
- EPH 4:26,31 ~ If you become angry, do not let yourself be tempted; do not let not the sun go down upon your wrath. Refrain from bitterness, rage, anger, brawling, slander, and all forms of maliciousness.
- EPH 5:29 ~ Nobody hates their own bodies; instead they nourish and cherish their bodies, just as Christ nourishes and cherishes the church (the body of Christ).
- COL 3:8; 1 PE 2:1 ~ Put away your anger, wrath, malice, blasphemy, and filthy talk. Put aside all malice, guile, hypocrisy, envy, and evil words.
- COL 3:21 ~ Fathers, do not provoke your children to anger which could discourage them.
- TIT 3:2–4 ~ Paul wrote: Don't speak evil of others; don't be brawlers but be gentle and meek to all people. We too were sometimes foolish, disobedient, deceived, lustful, envious, malicious, and hateful. Then we discovered the love of God through our Savior Jesus Christ.
- JAM 1:19–20 ~ Be eager to listen, slow to speak, and slow to anger; for the anger of humankind cannot work with the righteousness of God.
- JAM 4:4 ~ You are an adulterous people. Don't you know that friendship with the world results in hatred towards God?
- 1 JO 2:9–11; 1 JO 3:15; 1 JO 4:20 ~ Those who say they are in the light, yet hate their brother, are still in darkness. Those who love their brother live in the light, and therefore they can see where they are going without stumbling. Those who hate their brother walk in darkness and they cannot see where they are going because the darkness has blinded them. Whoever hates their brother is a murderer, and murderers cannot inherit eternal life. Anyone who says they love God and hate their brother is a liar. How can you hate someone you have seen and still love God who you have not seen?

Lying and Deceit

Lying is a sin of which everyone is guilty. Deception is as bad as lying, since a deliberate attempt is made to hide the truth from another. Deceit is a very effective tool that Satan uses to drive us away from the truth. Satan tricks us, and we carry on the trickery, lying to others and even ourselves. Any time the truth is obscured or tainted, it can no longer be truth, for truth is pure. God is truth and He wants us to emulate Him and tell the truth. To lie is to imitate Satan. Lying and deceit are serious sins, which is why they are included in the Ten Commandments (do not bear false witness).

- LEV 19:16 ~ Do not go around spreading gossip or rumors.
- DEU 11:16 ~ Guard your heart from deceptions that would cause you to turn aside, to serve other gods and worship them.
- PSA 12:2 ~ They speak vainly about their neighbors; with flattering lips and two faces they speak.
- PSA 50:19–22 ~ You speak evil and act deceitfully. You even slander your own brother or sister. I (God) have kept silent while you did these despicable things. I will accuse you to your face, and I will tear you into pieces so that nothing remains.
- PRO 10:18 ~ Those who disguise their hatred with lies and those who slander another are fools.
- PRO 17:4 ~ An evildoer gives heed to false lips; and a liar gives ear to a filthy tongue.
- PRO 24:28 ~ Do not testify against your neighbor without just cause, and do not use your lips to deceive.
- MAT 24:4–5,11,24 ~ Jesus said, "Be careful that nobody deceives you, for many will come in my name claiming to be Christ, and they will influence many people. Many false prophets will come, deceiving many; and false messiahs will come showing great signs and wonders, to convince even the elect if that were possible."
- JOH 8:42–47 ~ Jesus said to them, "If God were your Father, you would love me because I came from Him, and now I am here. I have not come on my own, but He has sent me. Why can't you understand? It's because you are unable to grasp what I say. You belong to your father the devil, and the evil of your father is what you do. He was a murderer from the beginning, and lived not in the truth because there is no truth in him. When he lies, he speaks his own language, for he is a liar; indeed, he is the father of lies. Yet when I speak the truth you do not believe me! Can any of you prove me guilty of sin? If I am telling the truth why don't you believe? Those who belong to God hear what He has to say. The reason you do not believe is that you do not belong to God." (also 2 TH 2:9–10)
- 2 CO 11:13–14 ~ For such are false apostles, deceitful workers, disguising themselves as apostles of Christ. And no wonder, for Satan himself masquerades as an angel of light.
- GAL 6:3 ~ If anyone thinks they are something when they are nothing, they deceive themselves.
- EPH 4:25,29,31 ~ Quit lying; instead, speak only the truth about one another, for we are part of one another. Don't let any corrupt words leave your lips, but speak only good things about others. Put away bitterness, hatred, anger, complaining, and slandering, and every kind of maliciousness.
- EPH 5:6 ~ Let nobody deceive you with vain words, for because of these things God's wrath comes upon the children of disobedience.
- JAM 1:22 ~ Be doers of the Word and not hearers only, deceiving your own selves.
- 1 JO 1:8–10; 1 JO 2:4; 1 JO 4:20; 1 JO 5:10 ~ If we claim to be without sin, we deceive ourselves and the truth is not in us. If we confess our sins, He is faithful and just and will

forgive our sins and cleanse us from all unrighteousness. If we claim we have not sinned, we make Him out to be a liar and His Word has no place in our lives. Whoever says, "I know Him," but does not do as He commands is also a liar. If anyone says, "I love God," but hates his brother, he is a liar. For anyone who does not love his brother, whom he has seen, cannot love God whom he has not seen. Anyone who believes in the Son of God has His testimony in their heart. Anyone who does not believe God has made Him out to be a liar, because he or she has not believed the testimony God has given about His Son.

- REV 20:10; REV 21:8 ~ The fearful, unbelieving, and abominable, the murderers, sorcerers, idolaters, philanderers, and liars, they will have their part in the lake that burns with fire and brimstone which is the second death. And the devil that deceived them will be cast into the lake of fire, where the beast and the false prophet are, to be tormented day and night forever.

Gluttony

Gluttony means overindulgence. Too much of anything can be harmful (except, of course, goodness). Overeating and over-drinking are bad for your health. In fact, although food and water are essential, to consume too much of either can cause illness or even death. It is not a sin to occasionally consume alcoholic beverages, but to do so to the point of intoxication is extremely dangerous, not only to the individual who is intoxicated, but to others as well. It is not a sin to have sex within marriage, but to have sex promiscuously can be extremely calamitous to you and to your sexual partner.

Our bodies are supposed to be treated with care and respect, for they are temples for God's Holy Spirit. To abuse one's body is to sin against God. God has given us an abundance of blessings to enrich our lives, to sustain our health, and to make us wise. These gifts are not to be abused. To abuse any gift of God, especially our bodies, is the same as greed and selfishness. The negative consequences of such abuse and overindulgence will be realized in this life, as well as the next. The Bible teaches moderation in all things, and this is excellent advice.

- GEN 19:30–38 ~ Each of Lot's two daughters got him drunk with wine and seduced their father into having sex with them. Both daughters became pregnant, and their descendants became the Moabites and the Ammonites (both nations were extremely evil before God). This is a prime example of the dangers of too much alcohol, which in the case of Lot led to incest, and that sin was perpetuated in the nations of Moab and Ammon.
- DEU 21:18–21 ~ A stubborn and rebellious son or daughter who does not obey their parents, and who is a drunkard and a glutton, shall be brought before the elders. The penalty will be death by stoning.
- PRO 23:21 ~ The drunkard and the glutton will come to poverty.
- ECC 7:16–18 ~ Do not try to be too righteous or too wise, too wicked or too foolish. It is good to hold onto the one and not let go of the other. Those who fear God will avoid all extremes.
- EZE 16:28–30,36–38 ~ You played like a prostitute with the Assyrians, with your insatiable lust which could never be satisfied. You further multiplied your sinful lust in the lands of Canaan and Chaldea, and were still not satisfied. You obviously have a weak heart because you behave like an arrogant prostitute. Since you were so terribly filthy, with your fornication, your idol worship, and the sacrificing of your children, God will gather those you have had sex with, along with those you hate, so that they can see you naked and ashamed. And God will judge you the way he judges murderers and adulterers.
- HAB 2:15 ~ Woe to those who get their neighbors drunk so that they can seduce them.

- MAT 23:23–25 ~ Jesus said, "Woe to you hypocritical scribes and Pharisees. You make tithes of your goods, yet you ignore the more important matters of the law: justice, mercy, and faith. You are like the blind guide, who would strain at a gnat but easily swallow a camel. Woe to you hypocrites, for you make the outside appear clean while the inside is full of extortion and excess."
- LUK 21:34–35 ~ Jesus said, "Be careful. Don't let overindulgence, drunkenness, and the worries of life get the better of you, so when that fateful day comes you will not be caught by surprise. That day will be like a snare that catches the whole earth in its trap."
- ROM 13:13–14 ~ Be honest, as in the daylight; don't engage in rioting, drunkenness, overindulgence, promiscuity, fighting, and jealousy. Build your life around Jesus Christ, don't indulge in the lusts of the flesh.
- 1 CO 3:16–17 ~ Don't you realize that you are the temple of God, and that His Spirit lives in you? If you defile the temple of God you will be destroyed by God, because the temple of God is holy and you are that temple.
- 1 CO 6:12; 1 CO 10:23 ~ Something that is permissible is not necessarily beneficial or constructive. It is all right to enjoy something but I will not let it control me.
- 1 CO 6:18–20 ~ Escape from fornication. Those who fornicate are sinning against their own bodies. Your body is the temple of the Holy Spirit who lives in you, so your body does not belong to you. You were bought with a great price. Therefore, glorify God in your body, and in your spirit, both of which belong to God.
- 1 CO 9:25–27 ~ Whoever strives to master a task must discipline themselves. For example, athletes strive for an earthly, corruptible crown, but I pursue an incorruptible, heavenly crown. I run my race and fight my battles with confidence. I discipline my body; I practice what I preach so that I will not be found to be a hypocrite.
- GAL 5:19–23 ~ The works of the flesh include adultery, fornication, perversion, lust, idolatry, witchcraft, hatred, quarreling, rivalry, dissension, rage, fighting, sedition, heresy, jealousy, murder, drunkenness, orgies, and the like. Those who engage in such activities will not inherit the kingdom of God. The fruits of the Spirit include love, joy, peace, patience, gentleness, kindness, faith, humbleness, and self-control. There is no law against these things.
- EPH 5:18,29 ~ Don't get drunk, which is excess; instead, fill yourself with the Holy Spirit. Nobody hates their own bodies; instead they nourish and cherish their bodies, just as Christ nourishes and cherishes the church.
- PHP 3:17–19 ~ Follow Christ with me (Paul) and do not stray from the path of righteousness like so many others who have left the faith; this causes me great despair. Their end is destruction for their god is their stomach; their glory is their shame, for their minds focus only on earthly things.
- PHP 4:5 ~ Let your moderation be an example to others.
- 1 TH 5:5–8 ~ You are children of the light and of the day, you are not children of darkness and of the night. Therefore, be watchful and sober, not asleep like others. Those who sleep and get drunk do so at night. Let us, who are of the day, remain sober, putting on the armor of faith and love, and the hope of salvation.
- 1 TI 5:23 ~ Drinking a little wine will soothe your stomach and is sometimes good for what ails you.
- 2 PE 1:5–8 ~ Be diligent in all things. Add to your faith: virtue, knowledge, self-control (temperance), patience, righteousness, kindness, and brotherly love. If these attributes abound in you, you will bear good fruit.

Laziness and Idleness

Although often overlooked, laziness (or sloth) is a sin. We are supposed to be active and to earn what we receive. Inactivity and slothfulness breed a multitude of other sins such as a deviant imagination. It is healthier to stay active physically, mentally, and spiritually. This is especially true in regards to faith; God wants us to have an active faith.

- PRO 6:6–9 ~ You who are lazy, consider the ant. The ant has no supervisor, guide, or ruler yet manages to provide plenty of food. How long will you sleep you lazy people? When are you going to wake up?
- PRO 10:4–5,26 ~ Whoever slacks off will become poor, but the diligent will become rich. Whoever gathers during the summer is wise; whoever sleeps during the harvest is shameful. As vinegar is to the teeth and smoke to the eyes, so is a sloth to an employer.
- PRO 20:4 ~ The slothful person will not plow when it is cold and will end up begging during the harvest, and have nothing.
- PRO 24:30–32,34 ~ I visited the field of the slothful man and the vineyard of the ignorant man and all I found were thorn bushes and broken fences. And I learned from the experience. People like that will receive poverty like hard labor and neediness like an armed robber.
- PRO 26:13–16 ~ The lazy person will not work, giving lousy excuses like, "There could be a lion in the street." Just as a door on its hinges, the lazy person is attached to the bed, tossing and turning. The lazy person is too tired to lift a spoon to eat. Lazy people can convince themselves better than seven people with a good excuse.
- ECC 9:10–11 ~ Whatever your hand finds to do, do it with your might; for there is no work, device, knowledge, or wisdom in the grave where you are going. I returned, and realized that the race does not belong to the swift, nor the battle to the strong, nor sustenance to the wise, nor riches to the intelligent, nor favor to the skilled, but time and luck happen to everyone.
- ECC 10:18 ~ Because of laziness and idleness the building decayed and collapsed.
- EZE 16:49 ~ The sins of Sodom included pride, gluttony, laziness, and selfishness.
- 2 TH 3:10–12 ~ When we were with you, we gave you this rule: if a man does not work, he shouldn't eat. We have heard that some of you are lazy. They are not busy, they're just busybodies. We urge these people, in the name of Christ, to settle down and to earn the bread that they eat.
- 1 TI 5:8 ~ If anyone does not provide for his relatives, especially his immediate family, he has denied the faith and is worse than an unbeliever.
- JAM 1:17 ~ Faith without works is dead.

The Eight Deadly Sins

The Catholic Church established a list of seven deadly sins around the fifth or sixth century AD. During the Middle Ages, the concept began to show up extensively in art and literature. Listed alphabetically, the seven deadly sins included the following: anger (wrath), avarice (greed), envy (covetousness), gluttony (overindulgence), lust (lasciviousness), pride (arrogance), and sloth (laziness). This list seems incomplete, however. Deceit and dishonesty are awfully deadly, why didn't they make the list? They are both encompassed in the ninth commandment to not bear false witness. And couldn't idolatry, blasphemy, and/or hypocrisy be on the list? Sins such as these, which are directed against God, are more deadly than other sins on the list of seven. For example, consider idolatry (the second commandment in God's list of ten) which robs the Lord by exalting false gods or by not placing Almighty God first in priority. And then there is murder (sixth commandment), adultery (seventh commandment), stealing (eighth commandment), and the rest of the Ten Commandments which are excluded from the list of seven (e.g., not observing the Sabbath, using God's name in vain, and dishonoring one's parents).

I would like to revise the list. First of all, avarice, envy, and theft are similar insofar as greed seems to encompass them all, seeing how these sins reflect a desire to amass worldly possessions for oneself at the exclusion of others. Second, anger itself is not always evil, for even God (who never sins) gets angry and wroth (e.g., the wrath of God which falls upon those opposing God). Anger is a common emotion that produces a great deal of energy; one can use that energy to build up or to break down. All too often it is used destructively because it produces rage which is contagious, and that is when things begin to get out of hand. Thus, it is the manner in which anger is expressed that can make it deadly; this might lead to hurting, demeaning, or dishonoring others for no good reason. Hatred, is a very deadly way of expressing anger, since it leads to greater atrocities such as rape, bigotry, terrorism, and murder.

Of course, all sins are deadly since any one leads to death. Clearly, some sins are worse than others in the grand scheme of things. Three sins which seem to be extremely destructive and idolatrous are lust, greed, and pride, for they direct our focus on this world and therefore place our own will before God's. Next to deceit (which didn't make the list of seven), lust, greed, and pride seem to be Satan's favorite temptations; he even tried these three temptations on Christ in the wilderness. Let's leave gluttony (overindulgence) and sloth (laziness) on the revised list.

Allow me to suggest the new list using modern terminology. Listed alphabetically, here are the eight deadly sins: deceit, greed, hatred, idolatry, laziness, licentiousness, overindulgence, and pride.

Go to Dark Gethsemane

Go to dark Gethsemane, ye that feel the tempter's power;
Your Redeemer's conflict see, watch with Him one bitter hour;
Turn not from His griefs away, learn of Jesus Christ to pray.

Follow to the judgment hall, view the Lord of life arraigned;
Oh, the wormwood and the gall! Oh, the pangs His soul sustained;
Shun not suffering, shame, or loss; learn from Him to bear the cross.

Calvary's mournful mountain climb; there, adoring at His feet;
Mark that miracle of time, God's own sacrifice complete,
"It is finished!" hear Him cry; learn of Jesus Christ to die.

Early hasten to the tomb where they laid His breathless clay;
All is solitude and gloom. Who hath taken Him away?
Christ is risen! He meets our eyes. Savior, teach us all to rise.

Lesson: The Ten Commandments

God's Ten Commandments (EXO 20:1–17), which were given to Moses on Mt. Sinai, were inscribed in stone by God Himself. His Law was communicated to humankind in those commandments. To disobey any of God's commandments is to sin. The King James Version (KJV) of the Bible provides ten statements, each ending in a period, one for each commandment. These ten statements, or commandments, are paraphrased and discussed in this lesson. Note that different Christian denominations sometimes list the commandments differently. The following discussion assumes that the KJV delimited each statement by a period for good reason: to separate each commandment.

1. Never place other gods before the Lord God (EXO 20:3).

God wants to be first in our lives. We should never place ourselves, our jobs, our homes, our spouses, or our children above God (or any other worldly thing for that matter). We should never allow anyone or anything to come between us and the Lord, especially money. We are commanded by God to love Him above all others and to love our neighbors as ourselves. We must, therefore, love God more than we love anyone or anything. We must never deny, ignore, or despise God. We should never place worldly things on an equal plane with spiritual things.

- DEU 6:5 ~ You must love the Lord your God with all your heart, soul, and might.
- PSA 14:1 ~ Only a fool would say in his or her heart that there is no God. Such people are corrupt and have done terrible things in the eyes of the Lord.
- MAT 6:24 ~ Nobody can serve two masters, for they will end up loving one and despising the other. You cannot serve God and money at the same time.
- MAT 22:37–40 ~ Jesus said, "Love the Lord your God with all your heart, mind, and soul: this is the first and greatest commandment. The second is like unto the first: Love your neighbor as yourself. All the laws and the prophets depend on these two commandments."
- ROM 13:10 ~ Love is the fulfilling of the Law.
- 1 TI 6:10–11 ~ The love of money is the root of all evil; through the craving for worldly riches many have wandered away from the faith and pierced their hearts. Strive for righteousness, godliness, faith, love, steadfastness, and gentleness.
- 1 JO 2:15–16 ~ Do not love the world or worldly things. If a person loves the world, he or she cannot love God. All that is in the world, the lust of the flesh, the greed of the eyes, and the pride of humanity, do not come from the Father but are of this world.
- 1 JO 4:7–12,16–21 ~ Let us love one another, for love is from God, and those who love are born of God and know Him. If you don't love God you can't know Him because God is love. The love of God was manifested among us through His only Son, so we might live through Him. If God loves us so much, we should love one another; if we love one another, God lives in us and His love is perfected in us. If you abide in love you abide in God, and God abides in you. This perfect love gives us confidence on the day of judgment, because there is no fear in love but perfect love destroys fear, because fear brings torment. We love because God loved us first. You can't say you love God and hate your brother without being a liar, because you can't hate someone you have seen and still love God who you have never seen. So, you should love God and your brother (neighbor).

2. Do not practice idolatry in any form (EXO 20:4–6).

God forbids the worshipping of false gods, creating graven images of false gods, or bowing down before or serving anyone or anything before Him. God abhors the use of witchcraft and other occultist practices. He commands us never to defile anything that is holy, participate in a sacrilege, or commit blasphemy or heresy, for all of this connotes idolatry. Idolatry also includes living a life of sexual sin, lust, and/or greed. Further, idolatry includes idolizing someone, like a celebrity, an authority, or even a fictional character. We should never strive to fashion ourselves exactly like our favorite movie star, character, athlete, or some significant figure in our lives or our history. God wants us to strive to be like His Son Jesus Christ. His example is the one we should fashion ourselves after; we are to emulate Jesus's example of the Father, for an obedient child emulates parents who are honorable. All glory, praise, and thanks should be directed to God, for we owe everything that we have and that we are to Him. To worship or idolize anyone else but the Lord God is to place God second, and that is a grievous mistake. To repeat, never let anyone or anything come between you and God.

- LEV 19:26,28,31 ~ Don't eat blood. Don't cut or tattoo your flesh. Don't practice witchcraft or fortunetelling. Don't confide in mediums or wizards.
- DEU 5:8–9 ~ Never make graven images. Don't worship idols. Don't bow before any idols or worship them in any way.
- DEU 18:10–12 ~ Don't sacrifice your children. Don't practice fortunetelling, divination, calling upon the dead, or sorcery. Don't be a medium, charmer, or wizard. Whoever does these things is an abomination to God.
- JOB 31:26–28 ~ If my heart was enticed by worldly things and celestial bodies, or if I was infatuated with myself, I would be guilty of denying God and worthy of His punishment.
- PSA 96:8 ~ Give God the glory He deserves. Bring your offerings and worship Him.
- PSA 97:7 ~ Those who serve graven images or brag about their idols are confused. Everyone must worship God alone.
- ISA 42:8 ~ God says, "I am the Lord. I will not share my glory with another or allow my praise to be given to idols."
- ISA 44:9–11 ~ Only fools would create their own gods and idols.
- MAT 4:10 ~ Jesus told Satan, "You must worship the Lord your God and serve only Him."
- MAT 12:31 ~ Jesus said, "All manner of sin and blasphemy can be forgiven, except blasphemy directed against the Holy Spirit."
- COL 3:5 ~ Repress those who practice fornication, uncleanness, promiscuity, unnatural lust, and avarice, which is idolatry.
- 1 JO 5:20–21 ~ Teach your children to refrain from idolatry.

3. Never use the name of the Lord in vain (EXO 20:7).

We should never swear an oath, take a vow, or promise something in God's name, and not follow through with it, for God holds us accountable. Never lie, especially if you have sworn on the Bible to tell the truth. It is a wise practice to never take a vow or swear an oath of any kind, if possible, for a person calls upon God to enforce such a promise. The only times when it is necessary to take a vow is in a court of law or at the wedding altar. Additionally, it is a horrible thing to curse in God's name, especially calling upon God to condemn something or someone to eternal damnation. God's name is holy (MAT 6:9) and should not be used in combination with unholy behavior or profanity. Holy things should never be treated in a profane manner. God's name should never be spoken unless one is addressing God or referring to Him in a solemn and upright manner. Never tell lies under a facade of religion, and never distort or debase the Word of God. Never use God's name to conduct a sham or swindle. Never blaspheme the Holy Spirit of God or call God a liar.

- LEV 5:4 ~ Anyone who vows to do something foolish, whether the vow is sincere or not, is guilty.
- LEV 19:12 ~ Never falsely swear using God's name, and never profane the name of God.
- NUM 30:2 ~ If you take an oath before God to do something or not to do something, you'd better not break that oath.
- 1 KI 8:31–32 ~ If you swear in God's name before a judge or in church, you must do what you say and tell the truth, because God will hear the oath and hold you to it.
- JER 14:14 ~ False prophets tell lies in my (God's) name; I did not send them, command them, or speak to them. They receive false visions and make false predictions from the deceit of their lying hearts.
- EZE 22:26 ~ Their priests violated my (God's) Law, for they defiled my holy things. They treated holy and profane things the same way, they treated clean and dirty things the same way. They disregarded the Sabbath. Furthermore, my name has been profaned by them.
- MAT 5:34,37 ~ Jesus said, "Don't swear oaths. To declare something with the addition of an ultimatum (e.g., by God, by heaven, or by, to, or on anything) is the same as taking an oath. Just answer people with a simple yes or no. To strengthen a promise with a vow makes it suspect."
- MAT 12:31 ~ Jesus said, "All manner of sin and blasphemy can be forgiven, except blasphemy directed against the Holy Spirit."
- MAT 23:22 ~ Jesus said, "Whoever swears by heaven swears by the throne of God and He who sits upon the throne."
- HEB 6:16 ~ When someone takes an oath, they are calling upon God to force them to comply and to punish them if they don't.
- JAM 5:12 ~ Don't swear by heaven or by earth, or by/on anything else. A simple yes or no will suffice, and you will avoid sin and condemnation.
- 2 PE 2:1–3,14,18–20 ~ False prophets will come bringing damnable heresies, denying the Lord and deceiving many. They will exploit you with false words and attract you with lusts of the flesh. They have eyes full of adultery, insatiable for sin. Their hearts are greedy, and they gain through dishonesty. They promise freedom but are themselves slaves to corruption, and are condemned. They will get perpetually worse.

4. Remember the Sabbath day and keep it holy (EXO 20:8–11).

God created the heavens, the earth, and all life as we know it in six days. God rested the seventh day; this God did, not because He was tired, but because He wanted to set an example for us to follow. The Sabbath day was established as a day of rest from work, so that we do not overdo it and so we can be more productive when we are busy. The day of rest gives us an opportunity to examine our lives, and to praise and thank God for the wonderful blessings He has bestowed upon us. This is why the seventh day is considered holy, for it is the last day in the week when our work for the week has been completed; the first six days have been dedicated to our own pursuits but the seventh day belongs to God. It is a holy day, for God has given us that day to reverence Him. It is a day of offering our worship, praise, thanksgiving, and gifts to the Lord and to show our appreciation for the gifts and sacrifices that He has provided for us. Just as God admired His creation on the seventh day, we should use that day to admire God and His creations. The Sabbath is the day when we should go to church, praise God, and publicly demonstrate our commitment to Him. There is no substitute for going to church, because church provides an atmosphere of public worship and Christian fellowship not available elsewhere. Church also provides a place for us to study the scriptures with others, to strengthen one another, and to grow in our faith as an integrated body in Christ. The particular day a person dedicates to God is a personal choice (ROM 14:5–9). All Sabbath days in the OT, to include special celebration days, involved no work and a holy convocation (church assembly)

- EXO 31:16–77 ~ The children of Israel should keep the Sabbath for all generations as a lasting covenant. It is a sign between God and His people forever. For in six days God made heaven and earth, and the seventh day He rested and was refreshed.
- LEV 23:3–8 ~ Six days shall work be done, but the seventh day is the Sabbath of rest, a holy convocation. You will do no work because it is the Lord's Sabbath in all your dwellings. There are feasts of the Lord, also holy convocations, which you will observe in their seasons. The fourteenth day of the first month (Nisan) is the Lord's Passover. The fifteenth day of Nisan begins the feast of Unleavened Bread; seven days you must eat unleavened bread. The first day of that period will be a holy convocation: you will do no work on that day. You will present burnt offerings to the Lord throughout the celebration. The seventh day will be another holy convocation: you will do no work on that day.
- PSA 100:4 ~ Enter into God's gates with thanksgiving and into his courts with praise. Be thankful and bless His name.
- PSA 122:1 ~ I was glad when they said to me, "Let us go to God's house."
- PSA 147:1 ~ It is good to sing praises to God, for this is pleasant and beautiful.
- MAT 18:20 ~ Jesus said, "Whenever two or more people are gathered together in my name, there I will be also."
- JOH 4:24 ~ Jesus said, "God is Spirit and should be worshipped in spirit and in truth."
- ROM 12:1 ~ Give yourself to God. Let yourself be a living sacrifice. After all He has done for you, is that too much to ask?
- ROM 14:5–6 ~ One person may regard a particular day as important, another person may regard a different day, and some people consider every day alike. Let everyone be fully persuaded in their own mind. Those who regard the day let them regard it to the Lord, and those who do not regard the day, let it be to the Lord also.
- 1 CO 16:2 ~ Set aside some money, in accordance with your budget, and give it to the church on the first day of each week.
- EPH 2:18–21 ~ In Christ we have access to our Father in heaven via the Holy Spirit. Therefore, God's people are no longer strangers or foreigners; they are fellow citizens with the saints and the household of God. God's house is built upon the foundation laid by the apostles and the prophets; Jesus Christ Himself is the chief cornerstone of that foundation. Upon Christ the entire church is built; in Him the entire church is held together to be a holy temple of the Lord.
- EPH 4:14–16 ~ We will no longer be helpless as children, swayed by false teachings and influenced by the trickery of deceitful schemes. Instead, we will speak the truth out of love, and we will grow in every way in Christ who is our head. In Christ, the whole body is joined and held together just as our bodies are joined and held together by ligaments and joints. Christ is the head of this body, in which all members work together as an integrated system; through Him the body is nurtured and grows in His love.
- COL 2:16 ~ Do not let anyone judge you according to what you eat or drink, or with respect to the holy day or Sabbath.
- HEB 10:25 ~ Don't forget to continue assembling together in God's name, which many of you have stopped doing; do this more often as the day of the Lord's coming approaches.

5. Honor, obey, and respect your parents (EXO 20:12).

God is our Father in heaven and we are to fear and love Him. Parents are supposed to follow the example of God the Father in showing love to their children and in guiding their children in the ways of righteousness. Such parental love should not be countered with insolence, disrespect, or disobedience. Just as we are commanded by our Heavenly Father to be obedient to Him, so also, we are commanded by God to be obedient to our earthly parents.

- PRO 1:7–10 ~ The fear of God is the beginning of wisdom; only fools despise wisdom and instruction. Children, listen to the instruction of your parents; if sinners entice you, do not give in.
- PRO 3:11–14 ~ Children, do not despise the Lord's punishment, and do not resent when He scolds you. For those whom the Lord loves He corrects, just as a father corrects his children who are his delight. Happy is the individual that finds wisdom and understanding, for these are better than fine silver and the gain is better than fine gold.
- PRO 22:6 ~ Instruct your children in the way they should go and when they mature, they will not depart from it.
- PRO 23:22 ~ Listen to your parents and do not despise them when they become old.
- 2 CO 12:14–15 ~ Parents save up for their children; children don't save up for their parents.
- EPH 6:1–4 ~ Children, obey your parents, for God has given them authority over you. Honor your parents as commanded by God in His Ten Commandments (EXO 20:12). This is the first commandment that brings a promise: If you honor your parents your life will be long and happy. Parents, don't provoke your children to anger and frustration. Instead, raise them in the nurture and discipline of righteousness, as instructed by God.
- COL 3:20–21 ~ Children, obey your parents. Parents, don't get mad at your children which may cause them to become discouraged.
- TIT 2:1–8,12 ~ Here is sound doctrine about how to conduct oneself: Men (fathers) should be sober, calm, moderate, faithful, charitable, and patient. Women (mothers) should conduct themselves in a godly manner, teaching what is good. Women should not be gossipers or false accusers, nor should they drink a lot. Daughters should be taught to be sober and obedient homemakers, and to love their husbands and their children. Daughters should be taught to be virtuous (chaste) and discreet. Sons should be taught to be sober, helpful, sincere, and incorruptible. Sons should be taught to be calm and collected in their speech and actions; they should be taught not to say evil things about others. Teach your children to be godly, and to avoid the lusts of this world; teach them to be sober, righteous, and faithful to God.

6. Never murder anyone (EXO 20:13).

It is a horrendous act to murder a fellow human being, which is why it is a heinous crime, not only in God's eyes, but also in the eyes of civilized society. Life is precious to God, and no life should be sacrificed without just cause. While it is not spelled out clearly in the Bible, suffice it to say that irresponsible murdering of any form of life is unconscionable. Even hatred towards another is a form of murder, at least in thought.

- GEN 9:6 ~ Whoever sheds the blood of another human being must have their blood shed also; for everyone was made in the image of God.
- EXO 21:23–26 ~ Punishment will be life for life, eye for eye, tooth for tooth, hand for hand, foot for foot, burning for burning, wound for wound, bruise for bruise.

- LEV 24:20 ~ Punishment will be breach for breach, eye for eye, and tooth for tooth. Whoever has scarred another will be scarred in the same manner.
- NUM 35:16–31 ~ A murderer shall surely be put to death.
- MAT 26:52 ~ Jesus said, "Those who live by the sword will die by the sword."
- 1 JO 3:15 ~ Whoever hates another is a murderer, and murderers do not inherit eternal life.
- REV 21:8 ~ Evildoers, such as murderers, will take part in the lake of fire which is the second death.

7. Never commit adultery (EXO 20:14).

Marriage is an institution blessed by God, given to us as a means of avoiding sexual sin, as well as a means of sharing companionship, love, and commitment with a member of the opposite sex. Sex within marriage is not a sin, but any sex outside of marriage violates this commandment. To avoid the sin of fornication, one can get married and have sex with their spouse; but any sex outside of marriage is fornication and/or adultery. To lust after another is to commit adultery (fornication) in one's mind and heart. Sexual attention and behavior should be directed only to the person to whom one is married or betrothed. Once a man and woman engage in sex, they are married in God's eyes, for their union has been consummated and they have become one flesh.

- DEU 22:22,25,28–29 ~ If a man is found having sex with a married woman, both will be put to death. If a man rapes a married or betrothed woman, only the man shall die. If a man finds a maiden that is a virgin, and who is not betrothed, and he has sex with her, then she shall be his wife, and because he has humbled her, he may not put her away all his days.
- MAT 5:28 ~ Jesus said, "To lust after someone with your eyes is to commit adultery in your heart."
- MAT 19:6,19 ~ Jesus said, "Once joined in marriage, the two spouses become one flesh. Don't ever let people split apart anything that God has joined together. Anyone who gets a divorce (except for infidelity) and then marries another is guilty of adultery."
- 1 CO 7:2–3,8–9,28,39 ~ To avoid fornication get married and love your spouse. It's fine to stay single, but if you cannot control your emotions get married, for it is better to marry than to burn with passion. It is not a sin to marry, but married people will have problems due to their sinful nature. Once married, you are bound to your spouse until one of you dies.
- 1 CO 7:15 ~ If an unbelieving spouse departs, let him or her go. A brother or sister is not bound under such circumstances.
- JAM 1:14–15 ~ Everyone is tempted when they are enticed by their own lust. Lust, when conceived, brings forth sin, and sin, when finished, brings forth death.
- 1 PE 2:11 ~ Abstain from lusts of the flesh which make war with your soul.

8. Never steal (EXO 20:15).

To take something or someone away from another is stealing. There is never a legitimate excuse to confiscate something that does not belong to you. Stealing also includes oppression, dishonesty, underhanded dealing, fraud, usury, and cheating. To not give what is due and to not repay are also forms of stealing. The punishment for stealing in the Old Testament was to recompense the victim from four times the value of the item stolen (EXO 22:1), to as much as seven times the value (PRO 6:30–31). The penalty for kidnapping in the Old Testament was death (EXO 21:16; DEU 24:7).

- LEV 19:11,13,35 ~ Never steal, never deal dishonestly, and never lie. Never defraud your neighbor or rob him. Never shortchange anyone.
- PSA 37:21 ~ Wicked people borrow money or goods without paying back.
- PRO 21:6–7 ~ Obtaining wealth by lying is a vanity tossed about among those who seek death; for the robbery committed by the wicked will destroy them.
- PRO 22:16 ~ Those who oppress the poor to gain wealth and who give to the rich will surely become needy themselves.
- PRO 29:24 ~ Whoever is a partner of a thief must hate his or her own soul.
- JER 22:13 ~ Woe to those that hire someone to do a job and then do not pay their wages.
- EZE 22:29 ~ The people have used oppression, robbery, and swindling, so I (God) will recompense it upon their heads and consume them with the fire of my wrath.
- EZE 33:14–15 ~ If an evil person pledges to turn from sin, to return those things they have stolen, and to do what is right and lawful, then they will live.
- MAL 3:8 ~ Can you rob God? Yes, you can, for people have robbed Him by not presenting their offerings and tithes.
- LUK 19:1–9 ~ Zacchaeus accepted Jesus Christ as Lord, saying, "Lord, I will give half my wealth to the poor, and if I have cheated anybody, I will repay them four times." Jesus replied, "Today, salvation has come to this house."
- MAT 22:17,21 ~ The Pharisees asked Christ, "What do you think? Is it lawful to give tribute to Caesar, or not?" Jesus replied, "Render unto Caesar the things that are Caesar's, and unto God the things that are God's."

9. Never commit perjury or falsely accuse anyone (EXO 20:16).

This commandment prohibits any action in which a person makes false allegations against another, such as perjury, libel, and slander. Also included are lying, gossiping, and spreading vicious rumors about another. If called to be a witness tell the truth. If you are not sure of the truth, don't make something up.

- LEV 19:16 ~ Do not go around spreading gossip or rumors.
- PSA 12:2 ~ They speak vainly about their neighbors; with flattering lips and two faces they speak.
- PSA 50:19–22 ~ You speak evil and act deceitfully. You even slander your own brother or sister. I (God) have kept silent while you did these despicable things. I will accuse you to your face, and I will tear you into pieces so that nothing remains.
- PRO 10:18 ~ Those who disguise their hatred with lies and those who slander another are fools.
- PRO 11:13 ~ A gossip betrays a confidence, but a wise person does not.
- PRO 13:3 ~ He that keeps his mouth, keeps his life; he that opens wide his lips will have destruction.
- PRO 17:28 ~ Even a fool that holds his or her tongue is considered wise.
- PRO 18:7 ~ A fool's mouth is his or her destruction, and a snare to the soul.
- PRO 19:5 ~ A false witness will be punished. A liar will not escape.
- LUK 6:37 ~ Jesus said, "Don't judge others and you will not be judged; don't condemn others and you will not be condemned. Forgive others and you will be forgiven."
- ROM 2:1 ~ It is inexcusable to judge another person, for by judging another you condemn yourself, because you are guilty of the same things.

- EPH 4:25,29,31 ~ Quit lying; instead, speak only the truth about others, for we are part of one another. Don't let any corrupt words leave your lips, but speak only good things about people. Put away any bitterness, hatred, anger, complaining, and slandering, and related forms of maliciousness.
- JAM 3:5–6 ~ The tongue, although a little member, boasts great things; how great a matter a little fire can kindle. For the tongue is like fire, creating a world of sin; the tongue defiles the entire body, setting on fire the course of nature, burning with hellfire.
- JAM 4:11 ~ Don't speak evil about someone else. Whoever speaks evil of another or judges them unfairly judges the Law. If you judge the Law you cannot be adhering to the Law.

10. Never covet another person's spouse or belongings (EXO 20:17).

Covetousness includes behaving in the following manner: jealous, envious, greedy, selfish, stingy, gluttonous, ravenous, voracious, begrudging, impatient, and egocentric. God will severely punish those who are covetous, just like He did to King David (2 SA 12:7–13) and King Ahab (1 KI 21:17–19,23). We must never strive for earthly possessions or wealth, but instead focus on spiritual treasures. To place your heart's desire on anything belonging to another is akin to idolatry.

- PSA 10:3 ~ An evil person brags about the desires of his or her heart, and blesses those who are covetous; the Lord hates evil.
- PRO 28:6,22 ~ Poor people who walk in righteousness are better off than rich people who are perverse in their ways. Those who are in a hurry to become rich have an evil eye, and don't realize the poverty that will come upon them.
- ECC 5:10–14 ~ Whoever loves money will never be satisfied with it, and whoever strives for abundance will never have enough. Therefore, it is futile to strive for wealth. When riches increase so do expenditures. What good is it to have a lot of money if all you can do with it is look at it? People who work hard have restful sleep; but the abundance of the rich prevents them from sleeping peacefully. Those who keep their riches to themselves will hurt themselves, and those riches will disappear; and then they won't have anything left to give to their children.
- MAT 6:19–21 ~ Jesus said, "Don't collect treasures on earth. Collect treasures in heaven, where they won't decay and cannot be stolen. For where your treasure is, there your heart will be also."
- LUK 12:15 ~ Jesus said, "Beware of covetousness, for a person's life does not consist of the abundance of their earthly possessions."
- LUK 12:30–32 ~ Jesus said, "These things (e.g., food, drink, clothes, etc.) people of all nations seek after. Your Father in heaven knows that you need these things. If you seek the kingdom of God first, He will give it to you, and He will add these other things as well. It is God's desire to give His kingdom to you."
- EPH 5:5 ~ Covetousness is a form of idolatry.
- 1 TI 6:9–10 ~ Those who long to be rich will fall into temptation and a snare, and into many foolish lusts which will drown them in destruction and damnation. For the love of money is the root of all evil. Those who have coveted after money have departed from the faith and brought upon themselves much pain and sorrow.
- HEB 13:5 ~ Refrain from covetousness; be content with what you have, for God has said that He will never leave you or forsake you.

Lesson: Sinfulness

God gave us His Law that tells us what His will is for us. By establishing the Law, God gave us the knowledge of good and evil. God has given us the free will to comply with His laws or not. To disobey any of God's laws is to sin. Thus, God does not create our sin, we do. Further, God does not tempt us, Satan and other demons do; sometimes, other human beings are the ones tempting us. Know this, that God always provides us an escape from temptation and sin.

- ROM 3:20 ~ Nobody can be justified by works of the Law, for by the Law comes the knowledge of sin.
- ROM 5:13 ~ Nothing can be attributed to sin where there is no Law.
- 1 CO 10:13 ~ God will not allow us to be tempted beyond our ability to withstand it, and He will always provide us an escape from temptation.
- JAM 1:13 ~ God cannot be tempted, neither does He tempt anyone.
- JAM 4:17 ~ When someone knows what is proper, but doesn't do it, that for them is sin.
- 1 JO 3:4 ~ Whoever commits sin disobeys the Law, for that is how sin is defined.
- 1 JO 5:17 ~ All unrighteousness is sin.

Sin leads to death and damnation. Righteousness leads to eternal life. To be condemned to death means to lose one's soul. To be redeemed means to keep one's soul which has been cleansed of sin by the blood of Jesus, and purified forever by the Holy Spirit so that we can be reconciled to God our Father.

- PRO 8:36 ~ Whoever sins against God hurts his own soul; whoever hates God loves death.
- ISA 26:14 ~ The wicked will die, never to live again; they will be destroyed completely, along with any memory of them.
- EZE 18:24,26–27; EZE 33:12–13 ~ If a righteous man turns to sin, and does evil like the wicked do, his righteousness will not be remembered and he will die in his sin. If a wicked man turns to righteousness, and does what is lawful and upright, his wickedness will be forgotten and he will save his soul, and live. The righteousness a person has done will not save them on the day that they turn to sin. The wickedness a person has done will not condemn them on the day that they turn to righteousness.
- MIC 2:1 ~ Woe to those who plot evil and think of sinful things to do, and then carry out their evil plans just because they think they can get away with it.
- JOH 8:34 ~ Jesus said, "Whoever commits sin becomes a slave to sin."
- ROM 6:23 ~ The wages of sin is death.
- JAM 1:12–15 ~ Blessed is the person that endures temptation, for when that person is tried, he or she will receive a crown of life which the Lord promises to all who love Him. When tempted, never say you are tempted by God, for God cannot be tempted by evil, neither does He tempt anyone. People are tempted when motivated by their own lust and enticed to sin. If you conceive of lust, it brings forth sin; and sin, when finished, brings forth death.

Satan was the first to disobey God's Law. Thus, Satan is a condemned creature because he loves being evil and he hates God. Satan will be sentenced to eternal damnation in the lake of fire. His desire is to take as many people with him as he can because he hates us too. He preys on the weaknesses of humankind by tempting us to commit evil. He does this by appealing to our selfish desires and worldly pleasures. Everyone has two choices, follow Satan into the lake of fire or follow Jesus into the promised land. Who in their right mind would choose Satan over God? I would conclude that they must not be in their right mind or their mind is in the gutter.

- GEN 3:1–6 ~ The serpent (Satan) tricked Adam and Eve into eating the forbidden fruit of the Tree of Knowledge. Satan lied to them, telling them that eating the fruit would not lead to sin and death as God had told them. Satan deceived them into thinking that eating the fruit would make them like gods, but instead it made them sinful like Satan.
- JOH 8:44 ~ Jesus told the unbelievers, "You evil people belong to your father the devil, and the evil of your father is what you do. He was a murderer and a liar from the start. He never tells the truth; in fact, he is the father of lies."
- 1 PE 5:8–9 ~ Be sober and vigilant, because your enemy the devil roams about like a lion searching for someone to devour. He will attempt to consume anyone who isn't steadfast in their faith.
- 1 JO 3:8 ~ Whoever sins is of the devil, for the devil sinned from the beginning. This is why Christ came, to destroy the works of the devil.

People can rebuke Satan and he will leave them alone. Through Christ, we possess the power to resist temptation and evil. If the Holy Spirit lives in you, Satan will look for more vulnerable prey.

- EPH 6:13 ~ Put on the armor of God, so that you can stand against evil and overcome it.
- JAM 4:7 ~ Submit to God and resist the devil, and the devil will run away from you.
- 1 JO 4:4 ~ Since you belong to God, and He lives in you, you have the power to overcome evil spirits, because He (Christ) that lives in you is greater than the one (Satan) who is in the world.

All people have sinned and are worthy of death, save Christ alone. A person can sin in what they do, say, or think. We must recognize that we are sinners and need a savior to redeem us, which only Christ can. Only then will we be free from the powers of sin and death and the invasion of our minds by evil beings and malicious people.

- ECC 7:20 ~ There is not a single person on earth that does good and never sins.
- MAT 26:40–41 ~ Jesus told His apostles at Gethsemane, "Watch and pray, so that you do not enter into temptation. The spirit is indeed willing, but the flesh is weak."
- ROM 3:23 ~ Everyone has sinned and come short of the glory of God.
- 1 JO 1:8 ~ If we say we are not sinful, we deceive ourselves and we are liars.

To love and honor God is the most important commandment. Next, we must love one another as much as ourselves. This suggests a hierarchy. The Ten Commandments also imply a hierarchy, with the first four directed towards God and the rest towards humanity. Since God's commandments differ in importance, sin must likewise differ in severity. For example, to think something evil is not as bad as doing it. Thus, there are different degrees of sin. While there are degrees of sin, to commit one sin is to violate all of God's Law. That is, it only takes a single sin, no matter how insignificant, to warrant condemnation and to require redemption.

- EXO 20:3–17 ~ The Ten Commandments: 1) Do not place any other gods before God Almighty. 2) Do not make or worship graven images or practice idolatry. 3) Do not take God's name in vain or swear false oaths. 4) Keep the Sabbath a holy day. 5) Respect, honor, and obey your parents. 6) Do not kill. 7) Do not commit adultery. 8) Do not steal. 9) Do not falsely accuse anyone or commit perjury. 10) Do not covet anything that belongs to someone else.
- EZE 7:3 ~ God will judge everyone according to their ways, and will recompense the abominations of the wicked back upon them.
- OBA 1:15 ~ The day of the Lord is near for the wicked. As they have done, so shall it be done to them; it will come back upon their heads.

- MAT 4:7 ~ Jesus quoted Deuteronomy to Satan, "Never tempt the Lord your God."
- MAT 12:31 ~ Jesus said, "All manner of sin and blasphemy can be forgiven, except blasphemy directed against the Holy Spirit."
- MAT 22:36–40 ~ The lawyer asked Jesus, "Master, which is the greatest commandment of the law?" Jesus replied, "Love God with all your heart, mind, and soul, that is the greatest commandment. The second greatest commandment is to love your neighbor as yourself. All the laws and the prophets rely on these two commandments."
- JOH 19:10–11 ~ Pilate told Jesus, "Don't you realize I have the power to crucify you or release you?" Jesus replied, "You can do nothing to me without being given the power by God. The ones who delivered me to you for crucifixion, they have committed a greater sin than you."
- LUK 20:46–47 ~ Jesus said, "Beware of the Pharisees. They enjoy wearing fancy robes, being greeted in the marketplace, sitting in the places of honor in church, and reserving the nicest rooms for their banquets; yet they cheat widows out of their homes, and for a show, say long prayers. They will receive the greater damnation." (also MAT 23:14)
- 2 CO 5:10 ~ Everyone will stand before the judgment seat of Christ to be judged for their deeds, whether right or wrong, and to be punished accordingly. (also ROM 14:10)
- JAM 2:10 ~ Whoever disobeys one point of the Law disobeys all points of the Law.
- JAM 3:1 ~ Those who teach the Word will be judged more strictly.
- 2 PE 2:20–21 ~ It is better to have never known the way of righteousness, which is found in Jesus Christ, than to have known the way of righteousness, and later turned away and followed the corruption of the world. The end will be worse for them.

We must help others to resist temptation and to fight against evil. We must warn those who are living a life of sin that it will ultimately lead them to the grave. Don't forget, we are responsible for others, not just for ourselves.

- EZE 3:18–21 ~ God says, "I have told the wicked that they will surely die. If you do not warn the wicked to turn from their sin and be saved, you will also die for you will be partly responsible for their death. But if you do warn the wicked and they still do not turn from their wickedness, they will die in their sin but you will have saved yourself. If the righteous turn from righteousness to sin, they will die because their righteousness will no longer be remembered. If you do not warn them you will die as well. But if you warn the righteous not to sin, and they do not sin, their souls will be saved and so will yours."
- MAT 18:15–17 ~ Jesus said, "If someone has sinned against you, go tell that person of the fault; if they listen, you will have gained a brother. If they will not listen, take a few others with you the next time. If he or she still will not listen, bring your grievance before the church. If the person will not listen to the church, then that person is not a righteous person."
- GAL 6:1 ~ If someone is overtaken by sin, you who are spiritual should restore that person in the spirit of meekness, considering you are a sinner also and can be overcome by temptation.
- EPH 5:11 ~ Do not associate with the evil works of darkness, but rather express your disapproval.
- 1 TH 5:14 ~ We encourage you to warn those who are unruly, comfort the feeble minded, support the weak, and be patient towards everyone.
- 1 TI 5:20 ~ Those who sin should be publicly reprimanded, so that others may see and be warned.
- HEB 10:24–25 ~ Consider one another, encouraging each other in love and good works. Do not forget to gather together in worship, as many have done, but continue to strengthen each other even more as the day of the Lord approaches.

It is important that Christians continue to strengthen one another, for we all are tempted, and our flesh makes us constantly susceptible to pursuing Satan down the wrong path. To belong to Christ, a person must continue steadfast in the faith and never turn from it. That is, a true Christian will make the effort to change for the better, and will not merely take the salvation of the Lord for granted. The scriptures make it clear that to know Christ, and then to turn away from Him, will buy you a ticket to hell.

- EZE 18:24,26–27; EZE 33:13–19 ~ When a righteous person turns away from righteousness, and engages in the sin of the wicked, will that person live? All the righteousness that person did will no longer be remembered, but only the sin, which will cause that person to die. When a wicked person turns from evil and does what is lawful and right, that person will live.
- EZE 28:14–19 ~ You (Lucifer) were the anointed cherub; you lived upon the holy mountain of God. You were perfect from the day you were created until evil was found in you. Your great wealth made you violent inside and you became sinful. Therefore, you were thrown off the holy mountain, and you will be destroyed. You exalted yourself because of your beauty, thereby corrupting yourself. You defiled the sanctuaries with your abominations. You will be destroyed by the fire within you; your terrible deeds will come to an end.
- MAT 5:18 ~ Jesus said, "Not one rule or statute of the Law will be removed, until earth and heaven pass away and all things have been fulfilled."
- LUK 8:13 ~ Jesus explained the parable of the sower of seeds. The seeds that fall on the rocks represent the Word of God falling upon receptive ears, only the Word does not take root in their hearts. For a time that person believes, but when temptation gets the better of them, he or she falls away.
- ROM 6:1–2,12–16 ~ Shall we continue to sin, so that God's grace can continue to abound? God forbid this! How can we, who were dead in our sins, continue to live a life of decadence? Do not allow sin to reign in your mortal body, influencing you to pursue the desires of the flesh. Do not use your body parts as instruments of unrighteousness and sin, but yield to God, and use your body to glorify Him. Sin cannot control you for you are no longer under the Law, but under the grace of God. Does that mean we can sin, because we are under Grace and not the Law? No way! A person obeys whomever they yield to; you can yield to sin unto death, or you can yield to obedience unto righteousness.
- HEB 3:14 ~ We are partakers of Christ if we keep the same confidence we had in the beginning, steadfast until the end.
- HEB 6:4–7 ~ For those who were once enlightened, who tasted the eternal gift, were made partakers of the Holy Spirit, were aware of the good news and the powers of the world to come, and who then fell away, it is impossible to renew them unto repentance since they will be crucifying Christ all over again, putting Him to open shame.
- HEB 10:26–29 ~ If we sin willingly, after having received the knowledge of the truth, there can be no further sacrifice for sins, but only the expectation of judgment and raging fire. A worse punishment awaits those who think themselves worthy, yet have walked over the Son of God, insulted the Spirit of Grace, and treated as unholy the blood of the covenant that sanctified them.
- 2 PE 1:5–9 ~ Peter teaches us to supplement our faith with virtue, knowledge, self-control, steadfastness, godliness, and brotherly love. These are the fruits of our knowledge of Christ. Whoever lacks these things is blind for he or she has forgotten about the sacrifice Christ made for sins.

- 2 PE 2:20–21 ~ If, after a person has escaped the wickedness of this world through the knowledge of our Lord and Savior Jesus Christ, they allow themselves again to be entangled and overcome by the world, their end will be worse than their beginning. For it would have been better for them not to have known the ways of righteousness, than to have understood and yet turned away from the holy commandments given to them.
- JDE 1:4 ~ Certain ungodly people, whose condemnation was written about long ago, have sneaked in without anyone noticing, attempting to turn God's grace into lust, and denying the only God and our Lord, Jesus Christ.

Remain in Christ and His Spirit will remain with you so that you do not lose heart. The Holy Spirit will strengthen you in your faith, the blood of Jesus will purify your soul, and your spirit will be holy for the rest of eternity. Or if you prefer, you can perish in your sin, but I pray you do not.

Abide, Oh Dearest Jesus

Abide, Oh dearest Jesus, among us with Thy Grace
That Satan may not harm us nor we to sin give place.

Abide, Oh dear Redeemer, among us with Thy Word
And thus now and hereafter true peace and joy afford.

Abide with heavenly brightness, among us precious Light;
Thy truth direct and keep us from error's gloomy night.

Abide with richest blessings among us bounteous Lord;
Let us in grace and wisdom grow daily through Thy Word.

Abide, Oh faithful Savior, among us with Thy love;
Grant steadfastness and help us to reach our home above.

I Am Trusting Thee, Lord Jesus

I am trusting Thee, Lord Jesus, trusting only Thee;
Trusting Thee for full salvation, great and free.

I am trusting Thee for pardon; at Thy feet I bow,
For Thy Grace and tender mercy, trusting now.

I am trusting Thee for cleansing in the crimson flood;
Trusting Thee to make me holy by Thy blood.

I am trusting Thee to guide me; Thou alone shall lead,
Every day and hour supplying all I need.

Lesson: Five Unnatural Sins

You've heard the expression, "Don't fool around with Mother Nature." In this lesson you will learn how true that expression is. We know that violating any of God's laws or statutes is to sin, and sin brings death. Opposing the laws of nature often brings dire consequences, as well. To contravene nature is to flirt with destruction, not just of the mind but also of the body.

- 1 CO 6:9,18 ~ The unrighteous will not inherit the kingdom of heaven. The unrighteous include fornicators, idolaters, adulterers, homosexuals, and immoral and abusive people. Don't fornicate, for those who commit sexual sin are sinning against their own body.

In the first chapter of Genesis, we find the story of how God created everything in six days. While He was creating, God separated and distinguished certain things, such as the darkness versus the light, the waters from the land, the fowl of the air and the beasts of the earth, and male or female. God created everything to have both unity as well as uniqueness, thereby resulting in certain laws of nature and the physical world. These natural laws are found in the disciplines of physics, mathematics, chemistry, and biology. God established natural law and order in His universe, and also spiritual law and order among higher-order beings. Violation of the moral law can be physical, mental, or spiritual, and constitute sins worthy of death.

God gave to Moses the Law, which is God's will for us. In the eighteenth chapter of Leviticus, Moses listed five deadly sins associated with sex. To commit any of these sins is to defy the laws of nature, in addition to violating the will of God. Thus, there will be consequences in this life and in the next for those who willingly engage in such behavior.

- LEV 18:6–18 ~ Never have sex with a member of your family or your in-laws (incest).
- LEV 18:20 ~ Never have sex with your neighbor's spouse (adultery).
- LEV 18:21 ~ Never sacrifice your children to pagan gods (abortion).
- LEV 18:22 ~ Never have sex with a member of your own gender (homosexuality).
- LEV 18:23 ~ Never have sex with an animal (bestiality).
- LEV 18:24–25,28 ~ Do not defile yourselves by doing any of these things, for because of this the other nations are defiled, and that is why I am driving them out before you. Even the land has become defiled by them, so I will punish the land for its sin, and the land will vomit out its inhabitants. And if you defile the land, it will vomit you out as well.

Nature retaliates against deviant sex in the worst way imaginable. Knowing the risk, why would anyone gamble with their lives in order to experience unnatural sexual pleasure? Obviously, there is grave danger in continuously participating in promiscuous, unprotected sex, where it's almost a certainty to degrade the quality of one's life.

Bestiality. God prohibits having sex with animals for several obvious reasons. During the days of Moses, the penalty for bestiality was death.

- DEU 27:21 ~ Cursed is anyone having sex with an animal.
- LEV 20:15–16 ~ If a man or a woman lies with a beast he or she shall be put to death and the beast shall be killed.

Research has shown that serious venereal diseases have originated from sex with animals. For example, syphilis has been traced to sheep, and gonorrhea has been traced to dogs. While a sheep carrying syphilis is not in immediate danger, a human who contracts the disease can die from it, if not treated during the early stages. God warns of the pestilence associated with such deviant sex.

- AMO 4:10 ~ I (God) have sent pestilence among you like I did upon Egypt. I have caused the stench in your towns to pervade your nostrils.

In nature, crossbreeding often produces inferior species and mutations. For example, the offspring of a male donkey and a female horse is a mule. The mule is an inferior species compared to the other two because it cannot reproduce. Thus, the result is a fluke of nature. Fortunately, the human species is incompatible with animals; otherwise, there's no telling what kind of mutant creatures would be roaming around. Nature has its own way of eliminating waste, corruption, and mutation. In fact, nature is remarkably swift and thorough in cleansing itself of toxic waste, inferior species, mutations, and disease.

<u>Homosexuality</u>. The adverse effects of homosexuality are clearly evident in today's society. In the Bible, God warns us repeatedly not to engage in homosexuality. During the time of Moses, the penalty for homosexuality was death. In fact, God destroyed the cities of Sodom and Gomorrah for engaging in homosexual and other deviant sex. The Bible teaches us that to even dress like a member of the opposite sex is forbidden. Sects of the church that are permissive towards homosexuality are misleading people.

- GEN 19:24–25 ~ God rained fire and brimstone upon Sodom and Gomorrah. He destroyed those cities, the plains, the inhabitants, and everything that was alive or growing.
- LEV 20:13 ~ If a man lies with another man as he lies with a woman, both have committed an abomination and shall be put to death.
- DEU 22:5 ~ A woman shall not wear men's clothes, and a man shall not wear women's clothes, for that is disgraceful to God.
- 1 CO 6:9 ~ Don't you realize that the wicked will not inherit the kingdom of God? Do not let yourself be deceived, because fornicators, idolaters, adulterers, homosexuals, prostitutes, thieves, gluttons, drunkards, and swindlers will not be going to heaven.

The origin of the word sodomy is obviously from the ancient city of Sodom. The fate of Sodom is a matter of historical fact. Many states in the USA have laws against sodomy that are not enforced. Throughout history, sodomy has been viewed as immoral. It is confusing why an advanced society such as ours would promote such behavior today. Paul cautions about the latter days when homosexuality will abound, and warns of the negative consequences of such behavior.

- ROM 1:26–27 ~ God gave up on them because of their vile affections. Woman engaged in unnatural sex. Likewise, men gave up natural sex with women for unnatural sex with other men. They received in their bodies the recompense for their abominable actions.

What recompense do homosexual men receive in their bodies due to unnatural sex? Consider AIDS (Acquired Immunodeficiency Syndrome). In the case of sodomy, the anus becomes irritated leaving blood vessels exposed to sperm. The body must produce antibodies to fight foreign intruders invading the blood stream. Continued exposure increases the degree to which the antibodies must be produced and the rate at which they must fight unexpected proteins in the blood. Eventually, the immune system becomes overloaded; the body cannot produce sufficient antibodies (they are outnumbered). The immune system begins to break down, making the body susceptible to a variety of diseases including hepatitis, tuberculosis, pneumonia, and HIV (Human Immunodeficiency Virus). Eventually, the immune system fails and the person dies a gruesome and protracted death.

Incest. Those committing incest are cursed by God. In the days of Moses, the death penalty was given to those engaging in sex within the immediate family.

- LEV 18:6–18; LEV 20:11–21 ~ Anyone having sex with a natural parent, child, stepparent, stepchild, aunt or uncle, or in-laws shall be put to death.
- DEU 27:22 ~ Cursed are those who have sex with one of their siblings, parents, or children.

Great Americans like Washington, Jefferson, and Lincoln, told us that all people are created equal. Our nation was founded upon liberty for all Americans, for this is a right given by God to humanity. Of course, the founders knew of this doctrine from the Bible which teaches equality for all people.

- ACT 10:34–35 ~ Peter said, "Truly, God does not show favoritism to any person. Within every nation, anyone who fears the Lord and works righteousness is accepted by Him."
- GAL 3:28 ~ Paul wrote, "There is no such thing as Jew or Greek, slave or free, male or female, for we are all equal in Jesus Christ."

To be created equal means everyone has the same capacity and potential for uniqueness, excellence, and righteousness. Of course, everyone is born with special talents and abilities; it is up to the individual to realize his or her own potential. However, it is sometimes more difficult for people if they are born with or develop an abnormality or handicap. Children of incest are more likely to be born with such a handicap. While this is not always the case in the animal world, it is usually the case for humans.

Incestuous reproduction increases the likelihood of inferior offspring by increasing the chances of inheriting abnormal or negative genetic traits. For example, if you have a schizophrenic parent, the likelihood of you becoming schizophrenic is, say 25 percent (for the sake of argument). If both parents are schizophrenic, the likelihood of you becoming schizophrenic would be 50 percent. In other words, the likelihood of inheriting an abnormal mental condition is increased with incest.

Incestuous reproduction also increases the likelihood of inferior offspring by reducing the chances of inheriting superior or positive genetic traits. However, if both parents are normal, yet genetically different (unrelated), their children are more likely to inherit the superior or positive genes from both parents. Thus, by increasing the gene pool, humans evolve into genetically superior beings. For example, notice how the life expectancy has doubled over just the last few centuries.

Here's a hypothetical example. Say an average man and an average woman each have ten negative and ten positive genetic traits. Suppose the man and woman have only 10 percent of their genes in common. They have the potential of producing offspring with eighteen positive traits and only two negative traits, a ratio of 9:1 positive-to-negative. Now suppose the man and woman are brother and sister who share virtually 100 percent of their genetic material. They have potential for producing offspring with the same ten negative and ten positive traits, a ratio of 1:1 positive-to-negative.

Many extremists today advocate genocide or ethnic cleansing. However, constricting the gene pool in this manner will actually produce the opposite effect desired. Narrowing the gene pool will ultimately result in an inferior race, by promoting the inheritance of negative genes, and by reducing the capacity to inherit the positive genes that each parent possesses independently of the other.

In short, incest increases the probability of producing inferior or defective offspring. Perhaps that is why God has prohibited incest, because the laws of nature are in opposition when incest occurs. Now, the immediate counterargument is, "What about Adam and Eve? Clearly, incest was common during their time." This is true, but incest was already in decline when Abraham married his half-sister Sarah, and it was outlawed entirely by the time of Moses. God's desire for humans to replenish the earth was realized when the human genome was relatively pure, so incestuous sex became unnecessary and unwholesome, and it necessarily declined.

Adultery. Marriage was instituted by God to allow a person to engage in sex with one's soulmate without being guilty of fornication. Adultery is infidelity in marriage, or any sex outside of marriage. Again, the penalty for adultery during Moses's time was death. God commands us never to break apart a couple joined together in marriage.

- GEN 2:24 ~ Marriage results in a man and wife becoming one flesh.
- DEU 22:22,25 ~ If a man is found having sex with a married woman, they will both be put to death. If a man rapes a married or betrothed woman, only the man shall die.
- MAT 5:28 ~ Jesus said, "To lust after someone with your eyes is to commit adultery in your heart."
- MAT 19:6 ~ Jesus said, "Once joined in marriage, the two spouses become one flesh. Don't ever let people split apart anything that God has joined together."
- 1 CO 7:2–3,8–9,28,39 ~ To avoid fornication, get married and love your spouse. It's fine to stay single, but if you can't control your emotions get married, for it is better to marry than to burn with passion. It's not a sin to marry, but married people will have problems due to their sinful nature. Once married, you are bound to your spouse until one of you dies.

Adultery may not appear to defy the laws of nature, but there are negative consequences. These days, promiscuous behavior is very high risk; for example, venereal disease is a real hazard. This in itself is a sufficient reason to remain monogamous. Adultery also breaks down the trust, love, and respect in a marriage, thereby destroying the unity. The result is that the couple is no longer one flesh and one mind. Perhaps this is why adultery and abandonment are permissible reasons for getting divorced (according to the Bible) because the unity usually cannot be completely restored.

- MAT 19:9 ~ Jesus said, "If a person divorces a spouse, except for infidelity, and marries another, both are guilty of adultery."
- 1 CO 7:15 ~ If the unbelieving spouse departs, let him or her go. A brother or sister is not bound under such circumstances.
- 2 CO 6:14 ~ Do not be unequally yoked with unbelievers, for what fellowship has righteousness with unrighteousness, and what communion has light with darkness?

The practice of polygamy is akin to adultery. Nowhere in the Bible is the taking of multiple wives (or husbands) condoned. In fact, the opposite is true. Considerable evil came upon individuals because they had multiple wives (GEN 21:9–14; DEU 21:15–17; 1 KI 11:4–9). Scripture encourages people to have their own spouse; this implies that a married person is not to share that spouse with another. References to marriage in the Bible regard one wife or one husband; the Bible never says to take wives or husbands (in the plural).

Jesus said that a person is guilty of adultery if that person looks with lust in their heart upon someone other than their spouse. So how could anyone possibly consider it to be acceptable taking on additional spouses? If two people that marry become one flesh, how can a married couple share that union with multiple spouses? Further, a male cannot become one flesh with another male, and a female cannot become one flesh with another female. They were never meant to; that's why they cannot bear children together.

Scripture indicates that kings, priests, and deacons are to live by example, and that example includes having only one spouse. We also have the example of Christ. A husband should not seek multiple wives any more than Christ would seek multiple churches. It would be like Christ being the head of the Christian church, the Moslems, Buddhists, Hindus, etc. God accused His people of infidelity whenever they worshipped other gods. The Bible makes it clear that there is only one bride and one groom.

- GEN 2:24 ~ A man shall leave his parents and cling to his wife; and they shall become one flesh.
- DEU 17:15–17 ~ You may have a king from among your people that the Lord will choose. That king must not seek to acquire great numbers of horses, gold or silver; neither should he seek to multiply wives unto himself, for that could cause his heart to become distracted
- 1 CO 7:2,10–11 ~ Nevertheless, let every man have his own wife, and let every woman have her own husband. God requires that a wife must not leave her husband and the husband must not divorce his wife.
- EPH 5:21–25,28,33 ~ Submit to one another. Wives, submit to your husbands, because the husband is the head of the wife just like Christ is the head of the church. Thus, the wife is subject to the husband at all times. Husbands, love and protect your wives, even as Christ loved the Church and gave Himself for it. You must love your spouse (not spouses) as much as you love yourselves.
- 1 TI 3:2,12; TIT 1:6 ~ The directions Paul gave to Timothy about pastors, deacons, and elders included that they must be the husband of only one wife.

Abortion. God forbids the sacrificing of children to pagan gods. This was a common practice among the Ammonites, who sacrificed their children by fire to Molech. According to the Mosaic Law, the shedding of innocent blood deserved the death penalty, and innocent blood included a pregnant woman's fetus.

- GEN 9:6 ~ Whoever sheds the blood of another person shall have their blood shed as well.
- EXO 21:22–23 ~ If men get in a brawl and a pregnant woman is hurt, causing her to give birth prematurely, and there is no serious injury, the offender will be fined whatever the husband of that wife demands within the limits of the court. But if there is serious injury, the penalty will be life for life, hand for hand, foot for foot, burn for burn, wound for wound, bruise for bruise.
- EZE 16:20–21 ~ You have taken your sons and daughters, who you bore unto me (God), and sacrificed them. If you think this is a small matter you are mistaken.
- AMO 1:13 ~ God says, "I will severely punish the Ammonites because of their terrible sins, for they have ripped open the pregnant women of Gilead in order to expand their own borders."

Scientists are finally coming around to the fact that life begins at conception. Given that all humans are valued and equal, to abort a living fetus is murder, not to mention a gross violation of the human rights of the child. Some people still maintain that abortion is not the same as murder; they argue that the human embryo is not a living being. Let's review what the Bible says.

- PSA 139:13,15–16 ~ The Lord controlled my very being, even when I was in my mother's womb. My essence was never concealed from Him, for He knew me even as I was being secretly made and as I developed inside my mother. He saw me when I was still imperfect, and in His book were written all the members of my body, while they were being formed and were yet undeveloped.

- ISA 46:3–4 ~ God says, "Listen all of you in the house of Jacob and the remnants of Israel, for you were mine since you were conceived and lived in the womb; when you are old and gray I still will be the one who keeps you. I made you, I sustain you, and I will deliver you."
- JER 1:5 ~ God said to Jeremiah, "I knew you before I formed you in your mother's womb. I sanctified you even before you were delivered from your mother's womb. I ordained you to be a prophet to all nations."
- LUK 1:13–15,44 ~ God told Zachariah that his wife Elisabeth would bear a son, and to call him John. That son would be filled with the Holy Spirit, even from his mother's womb. Elisabeth said to Mary, "The moment you said hello, the baby in my womb leaped with joy."

The Bible is clear that a human fetus is alive, loved by God, and capable of emotion. Abortion must be an abomination to God. Nature's law of survival does not include the killing of innocent babies. Further, the act of abortion can be harmful to the woman's reproductive system, sometimes resulting in sterility. There may be special circumstances or medical reasons when abortion might be a viable alternative; however, the following are not acceptable excuses: birth control, medical research, embryonic tissue transplants, and pagan rituals.

Summary: Interestingly, these five dreadful sins are associated with sex. They have been known to result in genetic mutations and deficient, deformed, diseased, or dead offspring. Four sins deal with deviant sex and the fifth deals with an abhorrent alternative to birth control. The Bible tells us that such behavior will increase during the latter times. Those who indulge in such activity will not inherit the kingdom of God. This should be a warning to those who are guilty of sexual sin, but who claim to be Christians. They should heed God's warnings and change their behavior before it's too late.

- EZE 16:15–20 ~ You trusted in your beauty, and played the harlot, fornicating with anyone and everyone. You took all the riches and fine things, made images, and had sex with those. You sacrificed your sons and daughters to your idols. Do you think this is a small matter?
- 1 CO 6:9 ~ The unrighteous will not inherit the kingdom of heaven. The unrighteous include fornicators, idolaters, adulterers, homosexuals, and immoral or abusive people.
- COL 3:5 ~ Repress those who practice or promote fornication, uncleanness, promiscuity, unnatural desires, and avarice, which is idolatry.
- JDE 1:7–8,18–19 ~ They will be just like Sodom and Gomorrah, indulging in unnatural lust. In their dreams they defile the flesh, reject authority, and abuse the righteous. They are complainers, boasters, ridiculers, deceivers, lewd and disgusting, and devoid of the Spirit.

God's Law is His will. To commit a deadly sin is to disobey God. If you commit a deadly sin you will have to contend, not just with God's judgment, but also with the laws of nature which God has established to provide order and stability in our universe. For without order, and without God's Law, the only things left are chaos and destruction. Let us fight against disorder and dishonor as we daily carry the cross of Christ. Boldly proclaim who you are and expose those who would tell lies or speak falsely about the faith. Repel and repress evil wherever you find it.

However, let us remember that churches, church leaders, and Christians are not to turn away any particular group of sinners. Everyone violates God's Law and are equally guilty. We all need to be cleansed, and to discontinue the evil ways of our past. No single category of sinner should be singled out, but all must be called out so they can recognize, repent, and change habits that could lead to natural death, and spiritual death.

Lesson: Bad Habits

Bad habits often lead to addictions. Addictions reflect overindulgence or abuse of a substance or an activity. Given this definition, the following could be considered forms of addiction: overeating, heavy smoking, alcoholism, drug dependency, sexual promiscuity, pornography, compulsive gambling, and even habitual use of electronic devices or the Internet. These examples can be linked to lust for they relate to the desire for immediate gratification of the flesh. Therefore, such addictions could be considered idolatry, because the individual has placed their worldly desires before God.

- JOB 31:26–28 ~ If my heart was enticed by worldly things and celestial bodies, or if I was infatuated with myself, I would be guilty of denying God and worthy of His punishment.
- PRO 23:21 ~ The drunkard and the glutton will come to poverty.
- COL 3:5 ~ Repress those who practice fornication, uncleanness, promiscuity, unnatural lust, and avarice which is idolatry.
- 1 JO 2:15–16 ~ Do not love the world or worldly things. If a person loves the world, he or she cannot love God. All that is in the world, the lust of the flesh, the greed of the eyes, and the pride of humanity, do not come from the Father but are of this world.

God wants to be the center of our lives. He demands in His Ten Commandments that we do not have any other gods before Him, neither are we to worship, praise, or adore anything more than God. Unfortunately, for most addicts, that is precisely what they are doing. Consequently, worldly addictions and compulsions are a violation of the first commandment when the bad habit becomes the primary motivator.

- MAT 23:25 ~ Jesus said, "Woe to you hypocrites, for you make the outside appear clean, while the inside is full of extortion and excess."
- ROM 13:13–14 ~ Be honest, as in the daylight; don't engage in rioting, drunkenness, overindulgence, promiscuity, fighting, and jealousy. Build your life around Jesus Christ, don't indulge in the lusts of the flesh.
- PHP 3:17–19 ~ Follow Christ with me (Paul) and do not stray from the path of righteousness like so many others who have left the faith; this causes me great despair. Their end is destruction for their god is their stomach. Their glory is their shame, for their minds focus only on earthly things.

Everything in this world is a gift from God; He has given us all things. God intends for us to use and enjoy His creations. But God did not create the world for us to abuse, and He did not create our lives for us to destroy. Therefore, bad habits and addictions are sins against God as well as against one's own body. Everything from God is free, so use it but do not abuse it, else it takes God's place in your life.

- GEN 1:29–30 ~ God said, "I have given to humankind every seed-bearing plant on the face of the entire earth, and every tree that has fruit and seed in it. They will be yours for food. And I have given to you every green plant, the beasts of the earth, the birds in the sky, and all creatures that move on the ground: everything that has breath and life in it."
- 1 CO 3:16–17; 1 CO 6:19 ~ Don't you realize that you are the temple of God and that His Spirit lives in you? If you defile the temple of God you will be destroyed by God, because the temple of God is holy and you are that temple. You are not your own for you were bought with a great price. Therefore, honor God with your body.

- EPH 5:18,29 ~ Don't get drunk, which is excess; instead, fill yourself with the Holy Spirit. Nobody hates their own bodies; instead they nourish and cherish their bodies, just as Christ nourishes and cherishes the church.

There is nothing wrong with eating, drinking, using medications, and having sex, as long as they are enjoyed within the limits set forth in God's Word. When these limits are exceeded, God's gifts cannot be enjoyed to their fullest extent. That is, when excessiveness is required to maintain the pleasure level, then the activity is not fully satisfying. The Bible teaches moderation in all things so that we do not overdo it.

- ECC 7:18 ~ Those who fear God will avoid all extremes.
- 1 CO 6:12; 1 CO 10:23 ~ Something that is permissible is not necessarily beneficial or constructive. It is all right to enjoy something but I will not let it control me.
- PHP 4:5 ~ Let your moderation be an example to others.

A hardcore addict will sacrifice anything to feed the habit. The first things to go will include honesty, integrity, self-esteem, and morality. After surpassing the stages of lying, stealing, and worse crimes, the addict begins to sacrifice his or her job, belongings, home, friends, marriage, and children. Eventually, an addiction could cost the addict his or her life and even their very soul. It is amazing the lengths to which addicts will go to feed their cravings. This is a trap set by the devil to lure people away from God, and to pursue someone or something more than God.

- PSA 49:7–8 ~ Nobody can ransom themselves, or give to God the price of their soul, for the ransom is costly and nothing can ever suffice.
- MAT 16:26 ~ Jesus said, "What does it profit a person who gains the world but loses his soul. What can a person give in return for his soul?"
- LUK 12:19–20 ~ The greedy man said to his soul, "Soul, you have ample goods; take it easy; eat, drink and be merry." But God said to him, "Fool, tonight your soul is required of you. And all your goods, who will possess them now?"
- LUK 21:34–35 ~ Jesus said, "Be careful. Don't let overindulgence, drunkenness, and the worries of life get the better of you, so when that fateful day comes you will not be caught by surprise. That day will be like a snare that catches the whole earth in its trap."
- 1 PE 2:11 ~ Abstain from the passions of the flesh which wage war against your soul.

The Bible makes it clear that wickedness will lead to death and hell. People that continue in their sinful ways will lose everything, not only earthly treasures, but also spiritual ones. Individuals that hang around with addicts or constantly engage in lustful pursuits are playing in the devil's den. Those who belong to Satan's lair include idolaters, fornicators, sexual deviants, murderers, gluttons, blasphemers, occultists, and dishonest and deceitful abusers and exploiters of others. Those who dabble in such misbehavior will find themselves quickly sinking deeper into the abyss. They must be warned that if they continue, Satan will succeed in dragging them down into hell. There is a way out for them, however: repentance, and the forgiveness that only Christ can give.

- EZE 3:18–19 ~ God says, "I have told the wicked that they will surely die. If you do not warn the wicked to turn from their sin and be saved, you also will die, for you will be partly responsible for their death. But if you do warn the wicked and they still do not turn from their wickedness, they will die in their sin, but you will have saved yourself."
- LUK 5:32; LUK 13:5 ~ Jesus said, "I did not come to call the righteous, I came to call sinners to repentance. Unless you repent you will perish."

- 1 CO 5:11; 1 CO 6:9 ~ Do not associate with people who are fornicators, adulterers, sexually immoral, greedy, idolatrous, flirtatious, extortionists, drunkards, corrupt, and abusive. They are the unrighteous and they will not inherit the kingdom of heaven.
- 2 CO 12:21 ~ Paul said, "I'm afraid that when I return, God will humble me before you, and I will be grieved over many that have sinned and not repented of the uncleanness, fornication, and lasciviousness they committed."
- GAL 5:19–21 ~ The works of the flesh include adultery, fornication, perversion, lust, idolatry, witchcraft, hatred, quarreling, rivalry, dissension, rage, fighting, sedition, heresy, jealousy, murder, drunkenness, orgies, and the like. Those who engage in such activities will not inherit the kingdom.
- 1 PE 4:1–3 ~ Even though Christ has done away with sin, you must not continue to sin as you have in the past when you practiced lewdness, lust, drunkenness, overindulgence, orgies, and idolatry.

In many cases, the person who has developed a deep dependency for a substance or an activity is trying to fill a void in their lives: a spiritual void. When this void is filled with lust, greed, pride, and worldly indulgences it becomes an addiction, because the victim can never obtain gratification; that is why they continue to repeat the behavior, reaching for that ultimate fix, high, or rush. Thus, addiction is like demon possession, since a spiritual void is being filled with evil and sin, whereby indulging the flesh trumps nurturing the mind and spirit.

In fact, you may have noticed how addiction makes a person mean, hateful, and wicked. Such a person develops a dual personality, with a good side and an evil side. Unfortunately, the evil side prevails when they are intoxicated, they experience withdrawals, or they lose control. These people need to know that Christ alone can fill the void. He can chase away the demons of addiction and allow the Holy Spirit to replace the emptiness in a person's life. Christ can satisfy every craving of the heart, whereas nothing from this world can.

- EZE 16:28–30,36–38 ~ You played like a harlot with the Assyrians, with your insatiable lust which could never be satisfied. You further multiplied your sinful lust in the lands of Canaan and Chaldea, and still were not satisfied. You obviously have a weak heart because you behave like an arrogant prostitute. Since you were so terribly filthy, with your fornication, your idol worship, and the sacrificing of your children, God will gather those you have had sex with, along with those you hate, so that they can see you naked and ashamed. And God will judge you the way he judges murderers and adulterers.
- MAT 26:41 ~ The spirit is willing but the flesh is weak.
- ROM 13:13–14 ~ Be honest, as in the daylight; don't engage in rioting, drunkenness, overindulgence, promiscuity, fighting, and jealousy. Build your life around Jesus Christ and you won't indulge in the lusts of the flesh.
- GAL 6:8 ~ Those who sow to the flesh will reap corruption to their flesh; those who sow to the spirit will from the Spirit reap eternal life.
- EPH 6:11–13 ~ Put on the whole armor of God so that you will be prepared to stand against the trickery of Satan. For we aren't wrestling against flesh and blood, but against principalities, powers, rulers of darkness in this world, and wickedness in high places. So, wear this armor of God so that you can withstand that day of evil, and remain standing when it is over.

Obviously, to be dependent on the world is to ignore God. He has promised to provide our needs if we seek Him first (MAT 6:31–34). We are to value spiritual riches above earthly possessions and luxuries (MAT 6:19–21). While it is possible to overdose from worldly things, we can never overdose on God's love which will gratify our deepest desires eternally.

- GAL 5:22–23 ~ The fruits of the Spirit include love, joy, peace, patience, gentleness, goodness, faith, kindness, and self-control. There is no law against such things.
- EPH 5:9 ~ The fruits of the Spirit originate in goodness, righteousness, and truth.
- 2 PE 1:5–8 ~ In diligence, add virtue to your faith, knowledge to your virtue, temperance to your knowledge, patience to your temperance, godliness to your patience, kindness to your godliness, and charity to your kindness. If these things abound in you, you will never be barren or unfruitful in the knowledge of our Lord Jesus Christ.

God should be the heart's desire for everyone. Let us become addicted to God's love; let us strive for spiritual fulfillment. If we crave the Lord alone, we will not yearn for worldly things because we will have everything we need in accordance with God's promise (MAT 6:33). Seek Him and everything is yours; you will never want for anything and you will never insist on more.

- PSA 37:4 ~ Delight in the Lord and He will give you the desires of your heart.
- PRO 11:23 ~ The desires of the righteous lead only to good, but the expectations of the wicked will be wrath.
- ISA 26:7–8 ~ Lord, you make the path of righteousness a smooth one. Yes Lord, walking in the way of your laws we wait for you. Your name and majesty are the desires of our hearts.
- GAL 5:17–18 ~ The desires of the flesh are against the spirit, and vice-versa, for they are opposed to each other. If you are led by the Holy Spirit you are not under the Law.
- ROM 8:26–27 ~ The Spirit helps us in our weakness; the Spirit intercedes for us in prayer. The mind of the Spirit intercedes for the saints according to God's will.
- 1 JO 5:14–15 ~ This is the confidence that we have in God: If we ask for anything according to His will, He hears us and grants us what we ask of Him.

Bad habits result from the weakness of our sinful flesh, and the desire to partake of earthly delights. They become bad habits because the behavior is recurrent, as the person strives to satisfy an emptiness that can never be filled by the world. Such obsessive behavior is destined to continue as the victim becomes a slave to the sin, erroneously believing that the insatiable desire can be quenched. But there never is satisfaction, which becomes more elusive as the cravings get perpetually worse. Akin to being possessed, addiction will destroy one's spiritual, mental, and physical health.

- EZE 7:19 ~ Their silver and gold will not be able to deliver them in the day of God's wrath. They will not satisfy their souls and they will not fill their stomachs, because this has become the obstacle of their iniquity.
- ECC 1:8 ~ The eye never has enough of seeing, nor the ear its fill of hearing.

Only the Holy Spirit can fill the void in our lives with a completeness that lasts forever. God fulfills the desire of every living thing through a steadfast love that is fully satisfying. If we seek His love, we will never want nor need anything, for all things will be provided in this life and the next. Whenever you are feeling empty, consider a heart-to-heart talk with God and see if that doesn't provide strengthening to your heart, assurance to your soul, and comfort to your spirit.

- PSA 145:15–16 ~ The eyes of all wait upon you, Lord, and you give them their food in due season. You open your hand and satisfy the desire of every living thing.

Lesson: Suffering

Question: What is the cause of all the suffering, sorrow, and pain in this world? Answer: sin. Sin brings a curse upon every human being and along with it the punishment of death.

- GEN 3 ~ The fall of Adam and Eve brought sorrow, pain, and suffering. That was their reward for sin. And sin became a curse that would affect all human beings.
- JOB 14:1 ~ Everyone who is born of a woman can expect a short life and a lot of trouble.
- PSA 51:5 ~ I was brought forth in sin, and in sin my mother conceived me.
- ROM 4:15; ROM 5:13 ~ Where there is no Law, there is no sin. Sin was in the world before the Law, but nothing can be attributed to sin if there is no Law.
- ROM 6:23 ~ The wages of sin is death.
- 1 JO 2:15–16 ~ Do not love the world or worldly things. If a person loves the world, he or she cannot love God. All that is in the world, the lust of the flesh, the greed of the eyes, and the pride of humanity, do not come from the Father but are of this world alone.
- 1 JO 5:17 ~ All unrighteousness is sin.

There is no suffering, sorrow, or pain in heaven, because there is no sin in heaven. God cannot allow sinfulness in His presence because He is perfect in righteousness. That is why He purges His people of their sin, so they can live with Him forever.

- ISA 32:17–18 ~ The work of righteousness will be peace; the effect of righteousness will be peacefulness and assurance forever. The righteous will live in quiet, restful, and safe homes.
- ISA 35:10 ~ The ransomed of the Lord will return and come to Zion with songs and everlasting joy; sorrow and sighing will be gone forever.
- ISA 64:4 ~ Since the world began, nobody has heard, seen, or perceived, except God, the wonderful things He has prepared for those who wait for Him.
- ISA 65:17–19 ~ I (God) will create a new heaven and a new earth; the former heaven and earth will never be remembered or recalled. You will be glad and rejoice forever, for I will make Jerusalem a place of happiness. I will rejoice in Jerusalem for I will be happy with my people, and there shall nevermore be the sound of crying among them.
- ROM 6:1–2,12–16 ~ Shall we continue to sin, so that God's grace can continue to abound? God forbid it! How can we, who were dead in our sins, continue to live a life of decadence? Do not allow sin to reign in your mortal body, influencing you to pursue the desires of the flesh. Do not use your body parts as instruments of unrighteousness and sin, but yield to God, and use your body to glorify Him. Sin cannot control you for you are no longer under the Law, but under the grace of God. Does that mean we can sin, because we are under Grace and not the Law? No way! A person obeys whomever they yield to; you can yield to sin unto death, or you can yield to obedience unto righteousness.
- REV 7:15–17 ~ They will live before the throne of God and will serve Him day and night in the temple. They will never be hungry, thirsty, hot or cold again. The Lamb among them will feed them, will lead them to fountains of living waters, and will remove all sorrow.
- REV 21:1,4 ~ I (John) saw a new heaven and a new earth, for the old heaven and earth had passed away. There was no more crying, sorrow, pain, or death, for these things had passed away.
- REV 22:3–5 ~ The curse was gone forever. Everyone served the Lamb, and His name was on their foreheads. And His light shined constantly so that there was never any darkness, and nobody needed a lamp.

At the resurrection, Christians will receive glorified bodies that will never die, similar to Christ's. These bodies will never die because they will be clean, without any trace of sin, and with zero imperfections. It is written: Sin brings forth death. But without sin, there is no death.

- LUK 17:21 ~ Jesus said, "They can't say, behold, here it is, or there it is, because the kingdom of God is within you."
- ROM 5:8–11,18–21 ~ God showed us His great love for us, for although we were sinners, Christ died for us. Therefore, we are justified by the blood of Christ, saved from God's wrath through Him. We were reconciled to God by the death of His Son and we were saved by His life. We find great joy in God through our Lord Jesus Christ by whom we have now received the atonement. By one man, sin came into the world, bringing death with it; and death was subsequently passed along to everybody, for all have sinned. Therefore, while the sin of one brought judgment and condemnation upon humankind, so the righteousness of one brought the free gift of justification and life. Thus, by the disobedience of one (Adam) we became sinful, and by the obedience of one (Christ) we can become righteous.
- 1 CO 15:42–44,50–56 ~ This is the resurrection: a corrupt body was sown, but an incorruptible body is raised. It was sown in dishonor but raised in honor. It was sown a physical body but raised a spiritual body. Flesh and blood cannot inherit the kingdom of God; neither can corruption inherit incorruption. A mystery is revealed: we will not all die but all will be changed. Upon His return, in a single moment as the great trumpet sounds, Christ's own whether alive or dead will arise into heaven to receive new, incorruptible bodies. The corruptible must become incorruptible, before the mortal can become immortal. Then the statement "death is swallowed up in victory" will be true. Finally, when Christ delivers the kingdom of God to the Father, He will destroy death. Death, where is your sting, and Hell where is your victory? The sting of death is sin, and its strength is the Law.
- 2 CO 5:17 ~ Therefore if anyone is in Christ, he is a new creation; old things have passed away and all things have become new.
- PHP 3:20–21 ~ Christ will change our vile bodies into bodies like His glorified body.
- COL 3:4 ~ When Christ, who is our life, appears again, you will appear with Him in glory.

Sin cannot exist in heaven, so God had our sins removed; otherwise, His holiness would burn us into ashes if we were to appear before him in our corrupted state. The sacrifice of Christ cleansed us from unrighteousness and destroyed sin, making us presentable before God Almighty. And because sin had no hold on Christ, neither did death. Thus, His resurrection will bring us back to life, because He has taken our place in death and conquered it for all who would believe.

- ISA 53:4–12 ~ He took upon Himself all of our grief and sorrows; yet we treated Him as an outcast. He was tortured for our sins and punished for our peace, and by His wounds we are healed. He was slaughtered like a lamb, and buried like a criminal but in a rich man's grave. He was made an offering for sin, although He never committed a single act of sin or spoke an evil word. Therefore, His days will be prolonged and His name will be made great. He will be exalted, for He emptied his soul unto death.
- 2 CO 5:19–21 ~ God was in Christ, and reconciled the world to Himself. He has not imputed our sins upon us; instead, He has given us the message of reconciliation. So now we have become ambassadors for Christ, as though God was speaking His message through us, so that you too may be reconciled unto Him. For He made Christ who knew no sin to bear our sins, so that we could receive the righteousness of God that was in Him.

- GAL 3:8–9,11,13,21–24 ~ The scriptures foretold that God would justify the unrighteous through faith, announcing the Gospel in advance to Abraham through whom God said all nations would be blessed. So those who live by faith will be blessed along with Abraham. But nobody is justified by the Law in God's sight, for it is written that the just will live by faith. Christ has redeemed us from the curse of the Law, being made a curse in our place; for it is written that one is cursed who is crucified on a cross. Is the Law, therefore, in opposition to God's promise? Absolutely not! For no law was given that would bring life. The scriptures tell us that the world is a slave to sin, and that the promise of life is given to all believers in Jesus Christ. Before faith in Christ came, everyone was a prisoner to the Law, kept there until faith was revealed in Christ. Hence, the Law is our teacher to bring us to faith in Christ, so that we might be justified by that faith.
- HEB 10:10,18 ~ We are sanctified by the offering of the body of Jesus Christ, one sacrifice for all people. No more offering for sin will ever be needed again.
- 1 JO 2:1–2 ~ If anyone sins, we have an advocate with the Father: Jesus Christ the righteous who abolished the sin of the whole world.
- 1 JO 2:25 ~ The promise He made was eternal life.

On earth, everyone will suffer because of sin. But Christ suffered in our place and He paid the ultimate price for sin. Thus, we shouldn't dwell on our afflictions, woes, torments, and sorrows. Instead, we should focus on Christ who makes us strong in the face of persecution, tribulation, and life's setbacks. Remember, He has suffered for us all so that we do not have to suffer. So, give your emotional baggage to God; it belongs to Him anyway because Christ bought and paid for it. Otherwise you will be the one to suffer the consequences.

- JOB 3:20–26 ~ Why is light given to someone that is in misery, and why is life given to those with a bitter soul who long for death but it does not come, searching for it as if for hidden treasure, rejoicing when they finally find the grave? Why is light given to someone whose way is obscured and who God has hemmed in? For my groaning comes before supper and my sorrow is poured out like water; because the thing I feared the most has come upon me and what I dreaded would happen has happened. I am restless and outspoken, because trouble is on the way.
- MAT 11:28 ~ Jesus said, "Come to me all who are weary and troubled and I will give you rest."
- ROM 5:2–5 ~ Through Him (Jesus) we have obtained access to His grace in which we stand, and we rejoice in our hope of sharing the glory of God. We rejoice in our sufferings knowing that they produce endurance, which produces character, which produces hope. And hope does not disappoint us, because God's love has been poured into our hearts through the Holy Spirit.
- ROM 8:35,38–39 ~ Who can separate us from the Lord? Can tribulation, distress, persecution, famine, nakedness, peril, or sword? I am convinced that neither death nor life, nor angels, principalities, or powers, nor things present or future, nor height or depth, nor any other created thing, can separate us from the love of God which is in Jesus Christ our Lord.
- 1 PE 1:3–6 ~ Blessed is God and Father of our Lord Jesus Christ, who according to His abundant mercy has given us rebirth in living hope, through the resurrection of Christ from the dead, to receive an inheritance that is incorruptible and undefiled, and that will never fade away. This is reserved for you who are kept by the power of God through faith for salvation, ready to be revealed the last day. In this you greatly rejoice, though for now you are grieved by various trials.

Those who follow Christ will have to endure certain trials and tribulations because of their faith. This is because the secular world enables wickedness and promotes sinfulness. The unbelievers despise those who cling to faith and strive to be like Christ, because they are opposed to Him and His followers. Why? Because they want to do whatever they feel like doing without being judged or punished. Don't be dismayed when your Christian faith is tested, for you will pass the test and you will be greatly rewarded. Eternal punishment is the ultimate reward for those who make no attempt to follow Christ or who persecute and murder Christians.

- JOB 11:13–20 ~ If you would prepare your heart, and stretch out your hand toward God; if sin was in your hand but you could put it far away and not let wickedness abide in your tents; then surely, you could lift up your face without blemish and you could be steadfast and not fear. Because you would forget your misery like water passing under a bridge, and your life would be bright like the midday sun; though you were in darkness it would be like the dawn. And you would be secure in your hope and find rest in your safety; you could lie down without fear, and many would seek your approval. But the eyes of the wicked will fail them; they will not escape. Their only hope is death!
- ISA 26:14 ~ The wicked will die, never to live again; they will be destroyed completely, along with any memory of them.
- ACT 14:22 ~ Paul informed the disciples that they would endure considerable tribulation before entering the kingdom of God.
- ROM 5:3 ~ Paul said that he glories in his tribulations, knowing that tribulation produces patience.
- 2 CO 7:10 ~ Do not regret godly sorrow which produces repentance leading to salvation. But worldly sorrow produces death.
- 2 CO 12:7–10 ~ So that I (Paul) would not exalt myself by the many revelations God showed me, I was given a thorn in the flesh, a messenger of Satan to buffet me. I prayed to the Lord thrice that it might depart from me. God replied, "My grace is sufficient for you because my strength is made perfect in weakness." Therefore, I will gladly revel in my infirmities, so that the power of Christ may rest upon me. That is, I take pleasure in infirmity, reproach, hunger, persecution, and distress for Christ's sake; for when I am weak, then I become strong.
- 1 TI 5:24–25 ~ Some people's sins will be exposed and they will be punished; for others, their punishment will come later. Likewise, some people's good deeds will be exposed and they will be rewarded; others will be rewarded later.
- 2 TI 3:12 ~ Everyone who lives a godly life in Christ will suffer persecution.
- JAM 1:2–3,12 ~ Brothers, count it as joy when you fall into various trials, knowing that the testing of your faith produces patience. Blessed are those who endure temptation, for when they are proven, they will receive the crown of life which the Lord has promised to all who love Him.
- 1 PE 2:19–21 ~ It is commendable when you patiently endure grief and sufferings for Christ, because for this you were called; and Christ also suffered on our behalf, leaving us His example to follow.
- 1 PE 3:17–18 ~ It is better, given the will of God, to suffer for doing good than to suffer for doing evil. For Christ also suffered once for sins, the just for the unjust, so He could bring us to God; being put to death in the flesh but made alive by the Spirit.
- 1 PE 4:12–13,16–17 ~ Do not consider it strange, the fiery trial that you must endure, but rejoice when you partake of the sufferings of Christ; when His glory is revealed you will be exceedingly glad. If you suffer for being a Christian do not be ashamed, but glorify God in the process; for judgment will begin with God's house. And if it begins with us first, what will be end for those who do not obey the Gospel of the Lord?

- 2 PE 2:9 ~ The Lord knows how to deliver the godly out of temptation, and to reserve the unjust for the day of judgment to be punished.

Many people believe that suffering is God's punishment, or that they are being chastised by God for their sins. They think that's why they are afflicted, grieving, oppressed, or depressed. But God's primary mission on earth is salvation, not judgment. He took the punishment upon Himself, and the grief. We are miserable because we are sinners (LUK 18:13). But we can place all this negativity and despair at the foot of the cross and Christ will bear it.

- DEU 4:30–31 ~ When you are in tribulation, and these things have come upon you, especially in the latter days, if you turn to the Lord and obey His voice, He will not forsake or destroy you, nor will He forget the covenant that He swore to your fathers, for He is a merciful God.
- LAM 3:31–33 ~ Men are not pushed aside by the Lord forever. Though He allows grief He shows compassion, because great is His unfailing love. For God does not deliberately bring affliction or grief upon the children of men.
- JOH 5:24–25 ~ Jesus said, "Truly I tell you, whoever hears my Word and believes in Him who sent me will receive eternal life. They will not be condemned, but will pass from death into life. Truly I say that the hour is coming when the dead will hear my voice, and those who listened to me will live."
- JOH 16:33 ~ Jesus said, "These things I have told you so that in me you might have peace. In the world you will have tribulation; but be of good cheer because I have overcome the world."
- 1 JO 2:17 ~ The world will pass away along with its sinfulness; but whoever does the will of God will live forever.

Often, we tend to ascribe blame to ourselves, other people, events, or circumstances in order to explain death, crime, violence, suffering, or pain. We want a reason for why bad things happen. But sin is to blame for all that is evil in this world. Instead of trying to find blame, we should be giving thanks to God. For His Son overcame the world and its sin, and He has given us freedom from its curse. Instead of blaming, we need to be forgiving, just as He has forgiven us of our wrongdoing. And we need to be thanking God every day, and forever.

We do not need to worry about the future or fret about the past. We need only to persevere in the faith day by day. God wants to be our confidence so that we always cling to His promises. He promises to provide for us, He promises to protect us, and He promises that we will produce good fruit if we stay connected to Him. Thus, we should expect nothing, except that God will make good on His promises in His own good time. Let us follow Him and remain steadfast, leaving our troubles behind, and staying focused on the path in which we are led.

- ECC 8:6–7 ~ To every purpose there is a time, and judgment is reserved, though the misery continues to escalate. For we do not know what will happen, so who can tell us when it will occur?
- 2 CO 1:3–4 ~ God comforts us in our tribulations, so that we will be prepared to comfort others who are having trouble, using the same comfort with which we ourselves are comforted by God.
- PHP 3:12–13 ~ I (Paul) continue to press on, to grab hold of that for which Christ has grabbed hold of me. I do not claim to have obtained it as yet, but instead I forget those things that are behind, and reach for those things which lie ahead.

God promises we will be provided for.

- PSA 23:1 ~ Because the Lord is my Shepherd, I have everything I need.
- PSA 145:14–16 ~ The Lord upholds those who fall and lifts those who are down. The eyes of everyone look upon Him, and He gives them their food in due season. He opens His hand and satisfies the desires of every living thing.
- MAT 6:31–33 ~ Jesus said, "Don't worry about your worldly needs, for your heavenly Father knows what you need. Instead, seek first the kingdom of God and His righteousness, and this you will receive, as well as your worldly needs. Don't be concerned about tomorrow for it will bring its own problems; you have enough to deal with today to be worrying about tomorrow."

God promises we will be protected.

- DEU 11:13–15,22–23 ~ God said, "If you listen diligently to my commandments, if you love the Lord your God, and serve Him with all your heart and with all your soul, I will provide rain in due season, so that you can gather your corn, wine, and oil. And I will make sure your fields are full of grass so that your cattle will be fat. If you listen diligently to my commandments, if you love the Lord your God, walk in all His ways, and cling to Him, I will drive away all the nations before you and you will subdue greater and mightier nations than yourselves."
- PSA 91:11–12 ~ God will appoint angels to take charge of you to protect you in all your ways. They will gather you up in their hands, so that you do not stub your foot on a stone.
- PRO 29:25 ~ The fear of humankind is a trap, but those who trust in God will be safe.
- 2 TH 3:3 ~ The Lord is faithful; He will make you strong and guard you from the evil one.

God promises we will be productive.

- LUK 1:37 ~ With God, nothing is impossible.
- JOH 15:4–7 ~ Jesus said, "Abide in me and I will abide in you. As the branch cannot bear fruit apart from the vine, neither can you unless you abide in me. I am the vine and you are the branches. Those who abide in me, and I in them, will bear much fruit; but without me you can do nothing. If anyone does not abide in me, he or she will be thrown out like a broken branch that is burned in the fire. If you abide in me, and my words abide in you, you can ask for anything you desire and it will be done for you."
- PHP 4:13 ~ I can do all things through Christ who strengthens me.

Everyone has problems. Why swim in your gloom? It will pass soon enough. Don't let life bring you down, let God lift you up. Focus on where you are going, not where you've been; it's a lot brighter where you are headed even though there is darkness in your past. Dump your trauma, negativity, hopelessness, and desperation on Christ and He will cover you with His love and peace. Go to Him in crisis and you will find solutions.

Sin is the cause and Christ the remedy. Exchange your grief for His joy; it's the best deal you'll ever have. And the Lord will use you to bring comfort to others, having yourself overcome the trials and tribulations of life with that same comfort you received from Jesus. Who better to serve than those who can understand the pain of others, since they have firsthand experience themselves? Yes, you have the knowledge of sin, and you know the agony that Christ endured because of it; and you have the power of God's love to heal those who are experiencing its curse and suffering for it. Why must we suffer? For the same reason Christ did (read 2 CO 4).

FALSE DOCTRINE

The Bible tells us not to add words to it or change its meaning. The apostles tell us not to follow any doctrines or practices unless they were taught by Jesus Christ. Yet religions have emerged that distort the teachings of Christ and the scriptures. Beware of any doctrine that is contrary to that found in the Bible and preached by Jesus Christ and His apostles. Any religious teachings or practices not documented in the Bible come from false teachers and/or Satan.

There are a number of cults in the world today that claim the Bible or Christ as their basis, but teach counterfeit doctrine, practice pagan rituals, have secret oaths and practices, and employ symbols and graven images as a fundamental part of their worship. Religion in general has become a way for dishonest people to exploit others for money and sex; it has become a con game, practiced by charlatans and swindlers. Even some churches of God have wandered into myths, and have substituted their own traditions for sound dogma.

It is unfortunate when people have to change something in order to believe it, especially when it is already crystal clear. Any distortions of Christianity should be avoided, especially those that deny Christ as God in the flesh and the Savior of humankind.

False Teachers and Fake Prophets

- DEU 18:20–22 ~ If a prophet presumes to speak on my (God's) behalf when I have not directed them to do so, or speaks in the name of other gods, he or she will die. If people wonder how they will know what prophecy comes from the Lord, they can simply observe if the words spoken by the prophet come true or not. Do not be afraid of a prophet who speaks presumptuously.
- PRO 30:5–6 ~ Every word of God is true; don't attempt to add to God's words or He will rebuke you and you will be proven false.
- ISA 44:25 ~ God proves the false prophets to be liars and fools, causing their prophecies to be invalid.
- ISA 59:13 ~ They know they are being disobedient to God; they carefully plan their lies.
- JER 14:14 ~ False prophets tell lies in my (God's) name; I did not send them, command them, or speak to them. They receive false visions and make false predictions from the deceit of their lying hearts.
- JER 23:32 ~ Their lies lead many people into sin. I did not send them and they have nothing important to say.
- LAM 2:14 ~ Your prophets have said foolish things and seen false visions. They haven't pointed out to you your sins but rather have told you that everything is fine.
- HOS 6:9 ~ Their priests commit murder and lewdness.
- MAT 6:5,16 ~ Jesus said, "Don't pray or fast like the hypocrites do, who pretend to be pious, praying and fasting in public places and before the congregations so that everyone can see them. That display is the only reward they will ever receive for their efforts."
- MAT 7:15,21–23 ~ Jesus said, "Beware of false prophets; they are like wolves disguised as sheep. Not everyone who acts righteous or appears to be so, is righteous."
- MAT 24:11,24 ~ Jesus said, "False prophets will come and lead many astray. They will perform wonders in an attempt to trick people; even some of God's people can become deceived."

- MAR 7:7–9 ~ Jesus said, "Those hypocrites ignore God's laws and substitute their own traditions. They pray great prayers but they don't really love God and their worship is a joke. They claim that God commands people to obey their idiotic rules."
- LUK 21:8 ~ Jesus said, "Many will come in my name claiming to be Christ, but do not follow them."
- ACT 20:30 ~ From among yourselves will come those speaking perverse things to gain followers.
- ROM 16:17 ~ Take notice of those who cause divisions and take offense to the doctrine you have learned, and avoid them.
- 2 CO 11:13–14 ~ They have fooled you into thinking they are Christ's apostles. But even Satan disguises himself as an angel of light.
- GAL 1:8 ~ Anyone, including angels, who preaches anything contrary to what Jesus and the apostles preached are cursed.
- COL 2:8,18–19 ~ Beware of those who would lead you astray with their errant philosophies and vain deceptions, following traditions fashioned by the world and not Christ. Do not let anyone swindle you out of your reward. Beware of those who practice false humility and worship angels. They claim to have seen things, but they have filled their unspiritual and arrogant minds with silly notions.
- 2 TH 2:9–11 ~ Those false signs and fake miracles come from Satan. Such deceptions belong to the self-righteous who will die, for they did not believe the truth that could save them. God will let them believe their lies and perish.
- 1 TI 1:3–7 ~ Do not teach false doctrine, or recognize any myths or irrelevant genealogies, which only serve to raise questions not provide answers concerning the faith. The goal is to love with a pure heart, a right conscience, and a sincere faith. Some have wandered away from these principles and turned to meaningless jabber, desiring to be teachers of the Law yet knowing nothing about the Law or what they say to be true.
- 1 TI 4:1 ~ Some will depart from the faith by recognizing evil spirits and demons.
- 1 TI 6:5 ~ They are corrupt and have no knowledge of the truth. They think it is godly to exploit others for money.
- 2 TI 3:13 ~ Evil people and false teachers will get worse, deceiving many; they themselves have been deceived by Satan.
- 2 TI 4:3–4 ~ People will seek teachers who conform to their own likes and dislikes; they will turn away from the truth and wander into myths.
- TIT 1:11 ~ They must be silenced, those who would ruin entire households, teaching things that are wrong for the sake of ill-gotten gain.
- 2 PE 2:1–3,14,18–20 ~ False prophets come bringing damnable heresies, denying the Lord, and deceiving many. They will exploit you with false words and attract you with lusts of the flesh. They have eyes full of adultery, insatiable for sin. Their hearts are greedy, and they gain through dishonesty. They promise freedom but are themselves slaves to corruption, and are condemned. They will get perpetually worse.
- 1 JO 2:18 ~ You have heard that the antichrist comes, and many will.
- 1 JO 4:1–3 ~ Don't believe every spirit, but test them to determine if they are really of God; for many false prophets have gone out into the world. Every spirit that confesses that Jesus Christ is God in the flesh is of God. Those who do not confess that Jesus is of God are not of God; they are spirits of the antichrist, who you heard is coming and is already here.
- JDE 1:4 ~ False teachers have infiltrated the churches, claiming that once you become Christians you can do whatever you want without being punished. They deny the Lord and turn God's grace into lust.

The Occult

There are numerous warnings in the Bible to refrain from witchcraft, consulting mediums, practicing fortunetelling, calling spirits from the dead, and confiding in astrological forecasts. It is dangerous to dabble in the occult and to summon or channel demons. Instead, we are instructed to resist and fight evil spirits, predators of the unseen world. All forms of occult activity are ordained by Satan and are forbidden by God.

- LEV 19:26,28,31 ~ Don't eat blood. Don't cut or tattoo your flesh. Don't practice witchcraft or fortunetelling. Don't confide in mediums or wizards.
- DEU 17:3–5 ~ Anyone who has been proven to worship other gods, the sun, the moon, or other celestial bodies is to be put to death.
- DEU 18:10–12 ~ Don't sacrifice your children. Don't practice fortunetelling, divination, calling upon the dead, or sorcery. Don't be a medium, charmer, or wizard. Whoever does these things will be condemned by God.
- 1 CH 10:13 ~ Saul died for being unfaithful and consulting a medium instead of seeking guidance from God.
- ISA 8:19 ~ When others suggest that you seek those with familiar spirits reply, "Shouldn't we seek God and the living instead of the dead?"
- ISA 47:10–14 ~ You felt secure in your wickedness. But evil shall come upon you and disaster will befall you. So, stand fast in your enchantments, sorceries, and counsels. Let them save you those who gaze at the stars, divide the heavens, and predict what will happen to you according to the new moon. Fire will consume them and you.
- JER 10:2–3 ~ Don't learn the ways of unbelievers or be dismayed by signs in the heavens, for the customs of the people are false.
- JER 14:14 ~ False prophets tell lies in my (God's) name; I did not send them, command them, or speak to them. They receive false visions and make false predictions from the deceit of their lying hearts.
- 2 CO 11:4,12–15 ~ Even as the serpent deceived Eve by his cunning, so he will attempt to lead you astray from devotion to the true Christ. I (Paul) will try to undermine those who claim and boast that theirs is a mission of God like ours is. They are false prophets, deceitful workers, disguising themselves as apostles of Christ. No wonder, because Satan also disguises himself as an angel of light, so it isn't strange that his servants disguise themselves as servants of righteousness. Their end will correspond to their deeds.
- EPH 6:10–12 ~ Put on the armor of the Lord to stand against the wiles of the devil. For we are not contending against flesh and blood, but against principalities, powers, rulers of darkness, and evil spirits.

Idolatry

Idolatry is the worship of false gods. God does not tolerate any form of worship unless it is directed towards Him. Idolatry includes adoring idols or famous people, bowing to graven images, and self-infatuation. Christianity is the religion of God and His Son. All others are counterfeits invented by people who want to invent their own truth.

- GEN 35:2 ~ Jacob told his household and everyone else present to put away all strange gods.
- EXO 20:4–7 ~ Don't make graven images or idols resembling animals. Never bow to an idol or image or worship it in any way, for God is a jealous God and will not tolerate false gods. Never use the name of God in vain or swear a falsehood, or you will be severely punished.

Anyone who worships another god (or anything else for that matter) will be punished, and that punishment will continue for generations.

- DEU 5:8–9 ~ Never make graven images. Don't worship idols. Don't bow before any idols or worship them in any way.
- JOB 31:26–28 ~ If my heart was enticed by worldly things and celestial bodies, or if I was infatuated with myself, I would be guilty of denying God and worthy of His punishment.
- PSA 16:4 ~ Sorrows will be multiplied for those who hurry after another god. I (God) do not offer the things that they offer; I don't even speak their names.
- PSA 97:7 ~ Those who serve graven images or brag about their idols are confused. Everyone must worship God alone.
- ISA 44:9–11 ~ Only fools would create their own gods and idols.
- ACT 17:29 ~ Don't think of God as an idol made from wood, metal, or stone.

Swearing Oaths and Allegiances

Don't swear oaths in the name of God or before a judge that you cannot keep, because God will hold you accountable. Don't ever use God's name with any form of verbal expression other than prayer, teaching, or worship, otherwise you will be using His name in vain. Any religion that requires participants to take an oath or swear allegiance is following false doctrine.

- EXO 20:7 ~ Never take God's name in vain or God will find you guilty.
- LEV 5:4 ~ Anyone who vows to do something foolish, whether the vow is sincere or not, is guilty.
- LEV 19:12 ~ Never falsely swear using God's name, and never profane the name of God.
- NUM 30:2 ~ If you take an oath before God to do something or not to do something, you'd better not break that oath.
- DEU 23:22 ~ It is not a sin to refrain from making vows.
- 1 KI 8:31–32 ~ If you swear in God's name before a judge or in church, you'd better do what you say and tell the truth; because God will hear the oath and hold you to it.
- ECC 5:4–5 ~ If you make a vow to God to do something, don't put it off.
- MAT 5:34,37 ~ Jesus said, "Don't swear oaths. To declare something with the addition of an ultimatum (e.g., by God, by heaven, or by, to, or on anything) is the same as taking an oath. Just answer people with a simple yes or no. To strengthen a promise with a vow makes it suspect."
- HEB 6:16 ~ When someone takes an oath, they are calling upon God to force them to comply, and to punish them if they don't.
- JAM 5:12 ~ Don't swear by heaven or by earth or anything else. A simple yes or no will suffice, and you will avoid sin and condemnation.

Secrecy

God reveals secrets; He doesn't hide them. Religions that keep sacred doctrines secret are not sanctioned by God. On the contrary, secrets often imply that something evil is being concealed. God has given us His Word through Jesus Christ, which tells us everything that we need to know and to do. God's Word is something to be shouted from the rooftops, not something to be held in confidence. It is fine to worship or to pray in private, but secret oaths, languages, and practices are not used in Christian circles or churches.

- DAN 2:28 ~ There is a God in heaven who reveals mysteries (as opposed to hiding them).

- MAT 10:26–27; LUK 12:3 ~ Jesus said, "Don't fear those who hate you, for everything that is hidden now will be revealed later; everything that is unknown will become known. What I tell you in darkness you will speak in the light. What you hear in private will be proclaimed from the rooftops."
- MAT 13:35 ~ It was prophesied that Christ would talk in parables and would explain secrets that were hidden since the beginning of time (as opposed to keeping them secret).
- JOH 18:20 ~ Jesus said, "What I teach is widely known; I have preached it openly and often in church. Everyone, including the Jewish leaders, has heard what I teach. I teach nothing in private that I have not said in public."
- ROM 2:16 ~ The day will come when God will judge the secrets of everyone, to include their thoughts, deeds, and motives.
- ROM 16:25–26 ~ Christ has the power to save you according to the revelation of God's mystery, which was kept secret since the world began, but which is now evident by the scriptures. According to God's will, the mystery is made known to all nations on earth for the obedience of faith.
- 1 CO 14:2,4,9,14–15,19,23–28 ~ Whoever speaks in an unknown tongue speaks to nobody but God, since nobody else can understand them. How can they be revealing mysteries? Those that speak in tongues instruct themselves; a true prophet instructs the church. If you don't speak words that others can understand you might as well be speaking to the wind. If I pray to God in an unknown tongue, my spirit may be praying, but I have no understanding. Therefore, I will pray and sing with the spirit, and with understanding also. In church, I would rather say five words that can teach something than ten thousand words that nobody understands. If an unbeliever or a new believer came to your church and everyone was speaking in tongues, the person might think everyone was crazy. That person may become discouraged concerning religion in general. Therefore, if someone in church wants to talk in an unknown tongue there should be an interpreter. If an interpreter isn't available, then that person should keep quiet, or talk to himself and to God silently.
- 2 CO 4:2 ~ We apostles have renounced hidden and shameful ways; we do not engage in deception and we do not distort the Word of God. We appeal to those who have a conscience in the sight of God.
- EPH 5:12 ~ It is shameful to even speak about the evil they do in secret.
- JAM 3:17 ~ Wisdom from heaven is pure, merciful, gentle, peaceful, and easily obtained. It always produces positive results that are impartial, straightforward, and sincere.

Traditions

Many modern religions maintain their own traditions, even elevating them to the level of doctrine as if they are essential for salvation, in spite of the fact that those traditions have no scriptural basis. Christ was extremely critical of the Pharisees during His ministry. While they acknowledged the Law of Moses, they did not adhere to the finer points of the Law, nor did they acknowledge Christ. Instead, they acted pious, exalting themselves as self-proclaimed experts on God's will for all people. Martin Luther criticized the Papacy and the powerful officials of the Roman Catholic Church of his era for the same kinds of things: selling forgiveness as merchandise, acting pious and exalting themselves, making up rules and adhering to doctrines that were not biblical. Many so-called Christian churches (and cults) today have fallen into the same syndrome. Their leaders pretend to be experts, yet they discourage people from studying the scriptures themselves. Their officials judge and condemn other denominations or their members, often asserting that all other faiths are false and only theirs is true. God alone can judge a person's heart. However, if we intently and frequently read the Bible, as God encourages that we do, we will become equipped to judge what people say and do, and to expose wayward leaders and false teachings.

- DEU 12:32 ~ Make sure that you do what God tells you; don't add to it or take away from it.
- ISA 29:13 ~ God says, "The people honor me with their lips but have removed their heart from me, and their knowledge of me is taught using the principles invented by men."
- EZE 20:18–19 ~ I told their children in the desert not to follow the statutes of their fathers, or to keep their laws, or defile themselves with their idols. I am the Lord, and I want you to follow my decrees and be careful to keep my laws.
- MAT 5:18 ~ Jesus said, "Not one rule or statute of the Law will be removed, until earth and heaven pass away and all things have been fulfilled."
- MAT 15:14 ~ Jesus said, "Forget them, for they are like the blind leading the blind, both of whom will fall into the ditch."
- MAR 7:6–9,13 ~ Jesus said, "Isaiah prophesied about you hypocrites (ISA 29:13). For you put aside the commandments of God and follow the traditions of men. By following your own traditions, you show a disregard for the Word of God." (also MAT 15:8–9)
- ROM 14:22–23 ~ Whatever you believe about life, keep it between you and God. Blessed is the person who is not condemned by the same things for which he or she has given approval. If you have any doubts, don't do it; for whatever is not of faith is of sin.
- COL 2:8,20–22 ~ Beware that you are not spoiled by errant philosophies or vain deceptions, originating from worldly traditions and principles and not from Christ. You are in Christ and not the world, so why submit to its rules? You are not subject to ordinances that are the doctrines and commandments of men (such as don't touch, taste, or use). Those traditions are destined to die out. People may appear reasonable with their self-imposed worship, false humility, and harsh treatment of the body, but these lack value in restraining the sinful flesh.
- 2 TI 3:16 ~ All scripture is inspired by God. God's Word provides the doctrine of truth, refutes that which is false, and instructs all people in the ways of righteousness.
- 2 TH 2:15 ~ Fellow Christians, stand fast in your faith and hold onto those traditions that you have been taught in God's Word, through the prophets and apostles.
- TIT 1:14 ~ Pay no attention to Jewish fables and the commandments of men that turn people from the truth.

Obviously, it is critical that we know the truth of God's Word so we can identify errors in a purported expert's teachings, call out charlatans who claim divine guidance and inspiration, or expose wayward theologies that are unscriptural. Generally speaking, the central doctrines of the Christian faith are taught in the vast majority of evangelical churches, to include Protestant and Catholic. Most employ the same Bible, the one comprising the sixty-six books of the Old and New Testaments. Additional traditions, practices, theologies, and mysticisms that are unbiblical should be avoided. Even so, some people have come to the knowledge of the truth as a result of false teachers and healers, because try as they will to distort the facts, they have to use some of the facts and the Holy Bible to make a case. Still, it is advisable to test everything you hear and see that has a religious connotation; if it doesn't agree you are smart to flee.

- PHP 1:15–18 ~ Some indeed preach Christ out of envy and rivalry; others preach out of good will. One preaches Christ in order to be controversial; insincerely pretending to be an authority to draw attention to themselves. Another preaches out of love, the way I (Paul) preach in defense of the Gospel. But whether in pretention or in truth, Christ is being preached, and for this I rejoice.

Lesson: False Doctrines and Cults

Beware of doctrines and teachings that are contrary to the Bible and the words of Jesus Christ and His apostles. There are a number of cults in the world today that claim the Bible as their basis but distort its meaning and purpose. This is heresy, and heresy comes from Satan. Avoid religions that teach false doctrines, practice pagan rituals, exercise secret oaths and practices, and employ symbols and graven images as objects of their worship.

The cults of today attempt to lure subjects by enticing them with worldly temptations and desires of the flesh. One cannot love God and love the things of this world at the same time. We are instructed in the Bible to strive for spiritual riches and forget about worldly treasures and pleasures. The Lord provides everything we will need in this life if we trust in Him, so it is essential that our focus remain on Christ and the heavenly blessings He offers.

The Holy Bible is the only true Word of God. Any book or person espousing theology that deviates from the Bible is dead wrong. If it does not conform to God's Word, it cannot be true.

- PRO 30:5–6 ~ Every word of God is true; don't attempt to add to His words or He will rebuke you and you will be proven false.
- GAL 1:7–12 ~ Some would pervert the Gospel of Christ. If anyone preaches another gospel (not preached by Jesus Christ and His apostles), that person is cursed by God. The Gospel of Christ does not come from the thoughts of humans, or from the teachings of people, but rather from the revelation of Jesus Christ.
- 1 JO 4:1–3 ~ Don't believe every spirit, but test them to determine if they are really of God, for many false prophets are out there. Every spirit which confesses that Jesus Christ is God in the flesh is of God (JOH 3:16). Those who don't confess that Jesus is of God are not of God. They are spirits of the antichrist, who you heard is coming and is already here.
- REV 22:18–19 ~ For I testify to everyone who hears the words of the prophecy of this book, that if anyone adds to these words, God will add unto that person the plagues mentioned in this book. If anyone subtracts from the words of this prophecy, God will take away their name from the Book of Life, and they will not share in the inheritance.

The Bible warns us about following doctrines or practices which were not taught by Jesus Christ. Yet many false prophets have emerged that distort the teachings of Christ and the scriptures. The following verses reflect what the true prophets said would happen.

- ISA 44:25 ~ God proves the false prophets to be liars and fools, causing their prophecies to be invalid.
- ISA 59:13 ~ They know they are being disobedient to God; they carefully plan their lies.
- JER 14:14 ~ False prophets tell lies in my (God's) name; I did not send them, command them, or speak to them. They receive false visions and make false predictions from the deceit of their lying hearts.
- JER 23:32 ~ Their lies lead many people into sin. I did not send them and they have nothing important to say.
- MAT 24:11,24 ~ Jesus said, "False prophets will come and lead many astray. They will perform wonders in an attempt to trick people; even some of God's people can become deceived."
- ACT 20:30 ~ From among yourselves will come those speaking perverse things to gain followers.

- 2 TH 2:9–11 ~ Those false signs and fake miracles come from Satan. Such deceptions belong to the self-righteous who will die, for they didn't believe the truth that could save them. God will let them believe their lies and perish.
- 1 TI 4:1 ~ In the end times, some will depart from the faith by recognizing evil spirits and demons. Such teaching comes from hypocrites and liars, whose consciences have been seared as with a hot iron.
- 1 TI 6:5 ~ Those who teach that material wealth is godly have perverse minds, devoid of the truth. They would exploit the truth to gain riches. Stay away from them.
- 2 TI 3:13 ~ Evil people and false teachers will get worse, deceiving many; they themselves have been deceived by Satan.
- 2 TI 4:3–4 ~ People will seek teachers who conform to their own likes and dislikes; they will turn away from the truth and wander into myths.
- TIT 1:11 ~ They must be silenced, those who would ruin entire households, teaching things that are wrong for the sake of ill-gotten gain.
- 2 PE 2:1–3,14,18–20 ~ False prophets come bringing damnable heresies, denying the Lord, and deceiving many. They will exploit you with false words and attract you with lusts of the flesh. They have eyes full of adultery, insatiable for sin. Their hearts are greedy, and they gain through dishonesty. They promise freedom but are themselves slaves to corruption, and are condemned. They will get perpetually worse.

The Occult. There are numerous warnings in the Bible to refrain from witchcraft, consulting mediums, practicing fortunetelling, attending seances, calling or channeling demons, and confiding in astrological forecasts. Such activity is sponsored by Satan and is against God's Law. Dabbling in the occult is an invitation to demonism and will lead to greater evil.

- LEV 19:26,28,31 ~ Don't eat blood. Don't cut or tattoo your flesh. Don't practice witchcraft or fortunetelling. Don't confide in mediums or wizards.
- DEU 18:10–12 ~ Don't sacrifice your children. Don't practice fortunetelling, divination, calling upon the dead, or sorcery. Don't be a medium, charmer, or wizard. Whoever does these things is an abomination to God.
- ISA 8:19 ~ When others suggest that you seek those with familiar spirits reply, "Shouldn't we seek God and the living instead of the dead?"
- ISA 47:10–14 ~ You felt secure in your wickedness. But evil shall come upon you and disaster will befall you. So stand fast in your enchantments, sorceries, and counsels. Let them save you, those who gaze at the stars, divide the heavens, and predict what will happen to you according to the new moon. Fire will consume them and you.
- JER 10:2–3 ~ Don't learn the ways of unbelievers or be dismayed by signs in the heavens, for the customs of the people are false.
- DAN 4:7–8 ~ The king consulted magicians, astrologers, and fortunetellers but none of them could help him understand his dream. [Daniel was the only one who could interpret King Nebuchadnezzar's dream for Daniel was a prophet of God.]
- EZE 13:6–7 ~ They have seen vain visions and perform lying divinations; the Lord did not send them.

Idolatry. Idolatry is the worship of false gods. God does not tolerate any form of worship unless it is directed towards Him. Idolatry includes adoring idols or famous people, bowing to graven images, and self-infatuation.

- EXO 20:4–7 ~ Don't make graven images or idols resembling animals. Never bow to an idol or image, or worship it in any way, for God is a jealous God and will not tolerate false gods.

Never use the name of God in vain or swear a falsehood, or you will be severely punished. Anyone who worships another god (or anything else for that matter) will be punished, and that punishment will continue for generations.

- DEU 5:8–9 ~ Never make graven images. Don't worship idols. Don't bow before any idols or worship them in any way.
- JOB 31:26–28 ~ If my heart was enticed by worldly things and celestial bodies, or if I was infatuated with myself, I would be guilty of denying God and worthy of His punishment.
- PSA 16:4 ~ Sorrows will be multiplied for those who hurry after another god. I (God) do not offer the things that they offer; I don't even speak their names.
- ISA 44:9–11 ~ Only fools would create their own gods and idols.

Oaths and Allegiances. Don't swear oaths in the name of God if you don't have to, for if you do you are calling upon God to enforce that oath. God's name should never be used in vain, or foolishly. A vow should only be made at the altar or in a court of law. Any religion that requires participants to take an oath or swear allegiance is following false doctrine. Remember as an example, how a foolish oath caused Jephthah, judge of Israel, to lose his only child and precious daughter. Jephthah vowed to sacrifice the first to welcome him home if God would help him defeat the Ammonites, which already was God's intention (JDG 11:29–39).

- LEV 5:4 ~ Anyone who vows to do something foolish, whether sincere or not, is guilty.
- NUM 30:2 ~ If you take an oath before God to do something, or not to do something, you'd better not break that oath.
- DEU 23:22 ~ It is not a sin to refrain from taking vows.
- 1 KI 8:31–32 ~ If you take an oath in church or in court, you'd better do what you say, and you'd better tell the truth, because God will hear the oath and hold you to it.
- ECC 5:4–5 ~ If you make a vow to God to do something, don't put it off.
- MAT 5:34,37 ~ Jesus said, "Don't swear oaths. To declare something accompanied with an ultimatum (e.g., by God, by heaven, on a stack of Bibles, to the dead, etc.), makes it suspect. A simple yes or no will do."
- HEB 6:16 ~ When someone takes an oath, they are calling upon God to make them comply and to punish them if they don't.

Secrets. God reveals secrets He doesn't hide them. Religions that keep sacred doctrines secret are not ordained by God. On the contrary, secrets often imply that something evil is being concealed. God has given us the Bible and Jesus Christ to tell us everything we need to know and do. God's Word is truth; it should be shouted from the rooftops, not held in confidence. It is fine to worship or pray in private, but secret oaths, languages, and practices are entirely non-scriptural.

- DAN 2:28 ~ There is a God in heaven who reveals mysteries (as opposed to hiding them).
- LUK 12:3 ~ Jesus said, "What we have discussed in the dark will be repeated in the light. What you have heard in closed rooms shall be proclaimed from the rooftops."
- JOH 18:20 ~ Jesus said, "What I teach is widely known; I have preached it openly and often in church. Everyone, including the Jewish leaders, have heard what I teach. I teach nothing in private that I have not said in public."
- ROM 16:25–26 ~ Christ has the power to save you according to the revelation of God's mystery, which was kept secret since the world began, but which is now evident by the scriptures. According to God's will the mystery is made known to all nations on earth for the obedience of faith.

Tongues. On the Pentecost following Christ's ascension, the apostles spoke in foreign languages (tongues) that were unknown to them, thereby fulfilling of the prophecy of Joel (JOE 2:28; ACT 2:1–4). The tongues were unknown because the apostles had never learned to speak the language. They were moved by God's Spirit to preach and prophesy to foreigners in Jesus's name. From this example it can be inferred that speaking in tongues is a spiritual gift, and by definition requires inspiration from the Holy Spirit (1 CO 12:7–11). However, in some New Age circles, continuous jabber passes as the gift of tongues.

Tongues are not demonstrated by repetitive chants having variable meanings or interpretations. In church, a speaker of tongues will use words and phrases having a specific meaning. An interpreter can recognize what is being said and can translate it for those who do not understand. But the worship service cannot be enhanced if an interpreter is not present; otherwise the speaker edifies only himself or herself. There are churches that require members to talk in tongues, but this practice misses the point. Everyone has unique gifts; one particular gift is not universal (1 CO 12:28–31). Paul addresses the appropriate use of tongues in public, and in private (1 CO 14). Anyone can have a private prayer language, but a genuine spiritual gift will be used for the edification of the church (1 CO 14:3–4,12).

- MAT 6:7 ~ Jesus said, "When you pray, do not use vain repetitions ("babble" as translated by the New International Version) like the pagans do, for they think they will be heard for their many words."
- MAR 16:17 ~ Jesus said, "Signs will follow those who believe. In my name they will cast out devils, and speak in tongues that are new to them."
- ACT 2:6–8 ~ The crowd was amazed, because everybody heard the apostles speaking in their own native language.
- 1 CO 14:2–4,9,14–15,19,23–28 ~ Whoever speaks in an unknown tongue speaks only to God, since nobody else can understand them. How can they be revealing mysteries? Those who speak in tongues instruct themselves; a true prophet instructs the church. If you don't speak words that others can understand you might as well be speaking to the wind. If I pray to God in an unknown tongue, my spirit may be praying, but I have no understanding. Therefore, I will pray and sing with the spirit, and with understanding also. In church, I would rather say five words that can teach something than ten thousand words that nobody understands. If an unbeliever or a new believer came to your church and everyone was speaking in tongues, the person might think they were crazy. That person may become discouraged concerning religion in general. Therefore, if someone in church wants to talk in an unknown tongue there should be an interpreter. If an interpreter is not available, then that person should keep quiet, or talk to himself and to God silently.
- 1 CO 14:12 ~ Since you are eager to have spiritual gifts, try to excel in those gifts that edify the church.

Traditions. The Bible provides the Law. All rules, commandments, feasts, rites, and sacraments are clearly defined in scripture. Religions that make up their own rules and force people to obey unscriptural traditions are leading people astray. If the Bible does not require it, it is not required.

- ISA 29:13 ~ The Lord says, "These people come near to me with their mouth and honor me with their lips, but their hearts are far from me. Their worship of me consists only of rules taught by men."
- MAR 7:6–9,13 ~ Jesus said, "Isaiah prophesied about you hypocrites (ISA 29:13). For you put aside the commandments of God and follow the traditions of men. By following your own traditions, you show a disregard for the Word of God."

- COL 2:8,16 ~ Beware, that you are not spoiled by errant philosophies and vain deceptions, originating from worldly traditions or principles but not from Christ. Do not let anyone judge you according to what you eat or drink, or with respect to the holy day or Sabbath.
- 2 TH 2:15 ~ Fellow Christians, stand fast in your faith and hold onto those traditions that you have been taught in God's Word, through the prophets and apostles.
- TIT 1:14 ~ Pay no attention to Jewish fables and the commandments of men that turn people from the truth.

Jesus Christ changed some of the rules and traditions previously followed during Old Testament days. The principal change was that His sacrifice negated the need for further blood sacrifices and burnt offerings (HEB 10:10–18). Below are some additional changes that Christ made to traditional Jewish laws.

- MAT 5:21–48 ~ Jesus said, "You have heard that you must never kill or you will be in danger of the judgment, but I say that if you become angry with another person, or call a person a fool without cause, you will be in danger of the judgment. Do not carry a grudge or any animosity towards another, but reconcile with your neighbor before bringing your offerings to the altar. You have heard that you must not commit adultery, but I maintain that to look upon another with lust is to commit adultery in your heart. It was said that whoever wishes to get rid of his wife should prepare a statement of divorce, but I tell you that anyone who divorces his or her spouse, and marries another, is guilty of adultery. The only exception is when the spouse has been unfaithful. Another old tradition was to swear oaths to God or to heaven, but I tell you never to swear. Do not swear to heaven for it is God's throne; do not swear on anything in heaven or on earth. It is written: an eye for an eye and a tooth for a tooth; but I say that if someone strikes you on the cheek, turn to him the other cheek. If someone would sue you under the law for your coat, give him your overcoat too. If a person compels you to walk with them one mile, walk with them an additional mile. You have heard: love your neighbor and hate your enemy; but I'm telling you to love your enemies also, and pray for them. What reward is there if you love only those who love you? Even sinners love those that love them. Strive to be perfect like your Father in heaven."
- MAT 23:1–9 ~ Jesus said, "The scribes and Pharisees tell you to do this and observe that; it is all right to obey them but do not imitate them, for they do not practice what they preach. They place heavy burdens on the people, but they themselves are not willing to lift a finger to help. Everything they do is for others to see. They love to be greeted in public. But do not call them Teacher or Master, for you have but one Teacher and Master, Christ the Lord. And do not call them Father, because God in heaven is your Father."
- MAR 7:14–19 ~ Jesus said, "Can't you see that nothing entering a person from the outside can make him or her unclean? It is what comes out of the person that makes them unclean. Something entering from the outside goes into the stomach (not the heart) and then out of the body. If something evil comes from the heart, it will make that person unclean."
- ACT 6:9–14 ~ The elders of the church argued with Stephen, but they were not able to resist the wisdom that he taught. Some of the more stubborn men accused Stephen of blasphemy, saying, "We heard him say that Jesus of Nazareth would destroy the temple and would change the customs handed down by Moses."
- ACT 15:24–29 ~ Many of the Gentiles were troubled because some of the teachers had told them that they must be circumcised and must keep the rest of the laws of Moses. Paul identified the more important aspects of the Law that they must follow, such as refraining from idolatry and fornication, and not eating blood or the meat of animals that were strangled.

- ROM 2:28–29; ROM 3:29–30 ~ A true Jew is not someone who has been circumcised of the flesh; a true Jew is someone who has been circumcised inwardly in the spirit. There is only one God, and He is the God of the Jews as well as the Gentiles. That same God will justify the circumcised according to their faith, and the uncircumcised according to their faith.
- 1 CO 7:2,10–11 ~ To avoid fornication, let a man have his own wife and let a woman have her own husband (implies one spouse, not many). Once married, a person must never depart from their spouse (divorce is not an option except for infidelity or abandonment).
- 1 TI 4:1–3,7 ~ In the end times some will depart from the faith, acknowledging evil spirits, following the doctrine of devils, telling lies of hypocrisy, forbidding marriage, and prohibiting the eating of meat which God created for us to be received with thanksgiving. Refuse to accept such profane traditions and old wives' tales, and exercise godliness.

Be advised, many avenues and pathways established by societies lead to a dead end. Governments employ politics to compel their citizenry to comply and they put in place regulations to subdue and subjugate the people. When politicians and leaders talk of socialism, communism, or globalism they are hoping to deceive the public into thinking that theirs is a better system; but all of these approaches enslave people by making them dependent on government and not themselves and especially not God. There is a one-way street that ends up in paradise; all other routes lead nowhere. The Way to heaven is Jesus Christ; there is no other way, period.

Lesson: Distortions of Christianity

Distortions of Christianity are false religions and are invented by deceitful people and Satan. They do not use the Holy Bible as their basis, even though they may claim that they do, and they do not acknowledge Christ as their Savior or the Son of God. Upon close scrutiny of their sacred books, you will find certain Bible passages have been altered or deleted, while other passages and/or books have been added. You will also find that they engage in ceremonies, rites, and practices that are entirely unscriptural.

Such deviant practices and teachings have given rise to numerous cults, which distort the Word of God, and are therefore heretical and blasphemous. The cults described below are examples of religions or groups that employ deviant practices and writings. It is not the intention to judge or accuse any of their members. It is the intention to scrutinize what they say and do against what is written in the Word of God. The Bible teaches us not to judge others (MAT 7:1–2), but instead to judge what others say or do (JOH 14:11–12; 1 CO 10:15), in order to determine if they are from God.

<u>Masons</u> (also Rosicrucians) have an eclectic view toward religion, integrating eastern philosophy (such as Buddhist and Egyptian) with western (Christianity). Freemasonry is a fraternal organization that is not religious per se, but requires members to have a religion, or to believe in a god. While Masonic lodges sometimes have an altruistic agenda, there is favoritism within the organization. In public life, they tend to promote people within the organization while excluding those outside of it. Some branches of Freemasonry engage in subverting religious and other private or public institutions, they lead God-fearing people into occultist activities, and they are a driving force behind the New World Order. Masons swear oaths and engage in secret acts. At the top levels (i.e., thirty degrees and above) their practices become extremely ritualistic, even pagan. This is not to say that a member of a fraternal organization cannot be a Christian, but that some of the doctrines, practices, and/or beliefs appear to conflict with biblical teachings.

<u>Jehovah's Witnesses</u> deny the Holy Trinity; they deny that Christ is equal to God and one with the Holy Spirit. They believe that only the Almighty Father is God, and that Jesus was one of God's creations, and is therefore, a subordinate god. Supposedly, Jesus was the angel Michael in the flesh, not God's only begotten Son. They also deny the Second Coming of Christ in the flesh, and they deny the resurrection of the body. They reject the existence of hell and eternal persecution, and they believe that the kingdom of heaven is limited to 144,000 members. They believe in salvation by works not faith. The Watchtower society advances false predictions about the end of the age. These predictions have been revised each time they were proven wrong.

<u>Gnosticism</u> (e.g., Christian Science, Zen) deny that Jesus is Christ, the Son of God, begotten of the Holy Spirit, and born of the Virgin Mary. Instead, they believe that Christ was divine energy living in a mere mortal man. They deny that Christ died to absolve sin, and they deny the resurrection and ascension of Christ. They often believe in reincarnation, but not resurrection. They deny the existence of hell, evil, sin, sickness, and death. In fact, they often resist the help of physicians and medication, not accepting that these are gifts from God. Thus, their view of faith is very distorted. They believe that man is equal to Christ and that man is perfect in spirit. They believe knowledge is more important than anything else (including faith). They believe that everything can be rationalized or explained scientifically (e.g., virgin birth, heaven, resurrection, ascension, etc.). They believe that heaven is a state of mind and that the material world is an illusion. They believe the Bible is full of mistakes and misinterpretations and is therefore not the inspired Word of God. They are very materialistic, even though they claim nonprofit status.

Mormons deny the Holy Trinity. They deny Almighty God. Instead, they believe in many gods, and that people can become gods themselves. In fact, they believe that people can become equal with Christ, and become the god of their own planet just like the one "god" of this planet. They believe that Joseph Smith was a prophet and received divine guidance in writing the Book of Mormon. They believe that the Bible is not entirely the inspired Word of God, but the book of Mormon is. They believe that Jesus Christ was merely a prophet like Smith, and not God in the flesh, begotten of the Virgin Mary by the Holy Spirit. In fact, Christ is regarded as an angel, the spirit brother of Lucifer. They also emphasize works over faith. They have been known to practice such sinful acts as polygamy, racial prejudice, favoritism, and discrimination. The Church of Latter-Day Saints (LDS) is very secretive. For example, members consider certain material things to be sacred (such as underwear). Further, congregants must swear secret oaths of allegiance. The Church of LDS engages in unbiblical practices and rituals that can be viewed as ungodly if not occultist. People at the top levels of the LDS are extremely reticent and conniving. (Note the similarities between Mormonism and Freemasonry.)

Unification Churches (Bahai, Hare Krishna, Transcendental Meditation, Est) deny the Holy Trinity, and that Christ is the Son of God the only source of salvation. They redefine Christian doctrine based on new, more important "prophecy" or "prophets," and they believe that these other prophets are equal to Christ. In fact, they believe that all prophets come from God (i.e., there are no false prophets). They focus on works and recruitment. Some practice corporal punishment within their own sect. They believe in reincarnation, karma, and several gods. They believe in a hierarchy of gods, including human gods.

New Age Movement (also Spiritism and Scientology). New-agers believe that humanity is evolving into a single consciousness, such that people are already a part of God, and are therefore divine. They believe that people can become gods, and that God wants us to become His equal, and not worship Him. They believe that you can save yourself, and nobody dies or is condemned. They believe God-is-nature-is-God. Many believe in karma and reincarnation. They believe that spirituality is based on experience, not belief, and that spiritual experience is obtained through mysticism and mind-altered states, not by intense study of the Bible (thus, enlightenment is experiential and subjective). They believe that personal fulfillment is as important as spiritual fulfillment, thereby rejecting traditional morality. They practice self-love, and are fascinated with the occult (e.g., astrology, idolatry, witchcraft, mediums, psychic forces, spirit guides, trances, paranormal experience). They practice channeling, which is allowing a spirit or demon to control oneself and one's functioning. They advance alternative explanations of biblical prophecies, events, and doctrine. That is, the supernatural is explained in naturalistic terms, objective science is replaced with subjective interpretation, and things are examined holistically rather than analytically. Their focus is on evolutionary, not creative processes. They typically are activists who are organized, networked, and autonomous. They establish alliances with a central hierarchy of power and control. They practice manipulation and indoctrination. They believe in an idealism based on worldly pursuits and self-survival. Thus, they are very egocentric and materialistic, having less regard for others than themselves. They attempt to influence world and regional events and societal developments through agenda and trend setting, situational manipulation and conditioning, resource distribution, censorship, propaganda, and deception.

Satanism is the most extreme segment of the New Age conspiracy. Satanists worship Satan, practice evil, and embrace all that opposes God. They do everything the opposite from what is taught in the Bible. They engage in deviant and occultist practices. Some perform animal and human sacrifices, drink blood, and/or practice cannibalism. They entice people to join them using temptation and deceit, and worldly desires: pleasure, riches, fortune, fame, power. They promote discipleship through ruthless tactics. They terrorize, traumatize, brainwash, hypnotize, whitewash, trick, deceive, blackmail, extort, kill, and take revenge. They practice indoctrination and forced compliance. They turn the Word of God into a lie; in fact, their whole philosophy is a lie and exactly the reverse of what Christianity teaches.

Summary: The previously reviewed cults are deviations from scripture, yet they steal their basic structure and foundation from the Bible. They have their own interpretations of scripture, taken out of context, to bolster their viewpoints. The leaders of such cults have developed convincing arguments that fail to hold up when compared to the actual words of God. Cult leaders would have you rely on them for the truth, and adhere to their aberrant renditions of the Bible. They often discourage people from studying God's Word because they do not want to be proven false. This is why it is very important to read the Bible and learn the truth.

You may have noticed how each cult reviewed above appears more extreme than the one preceding it, with Satanism being the direct opposite of Christianity. Any distortion of God's Word is the work of Satan. While it is not the intention to judge any member of a cult, it is the intention to judge what the leaders purport as truth, which oftentimes is not truth at all. God's Word is truth. To distort the truth is presuming God to be a liar. We must study the Holy Bible and become equipped to counter those who would change God's truth into a lie, which is the one unforgivable sin. Christians need to take a stand against false teachers and their erroneous doctrine, and be prepared to defend the one true faith.

Stand Up, Stand Up for Jesus

Stand up, stand up for Jesus, you soldiers of the cross;
Lift high His royal banner, it must not suffer loss.
From victory unto victory His army shall He lead,
Till every foe is vanquished, and Christ is Lord indeed.

Stand up, stand up for Jesus, the trumpet call obey;
Forth to the mighty conflict, in this His glorious day.
You that are men, now serve Him against unnumbered foes,
Let courage rise with danger, and strength to strength oppose.

Stand up, stand up for Jesus, stand in His strength alone;
The arm of flesh will fail you, you dare not trust your own.
Put on the Gospel armor, each piece put on with prayer;
Where duty calls or danger, be never wanting there.

Stand up, stand up for Jesus, the strife will not be long;
This day the noise of battle, the next the victory song.
To Him that overcometh a crown of life shall be;
He with the King of glory shall reign eternally.

Lesson: World Religions

Religion is defined as service, devotion, and worship of God (or gods), representing a particular set of beliefs in the supernatural. Religion is an organized system of faith and worship. It is a personal belief structure including certain practices, principles, and objectives. According to Freud, a noted atheist, religion was invented by humanity as a reaction to frustrations, developed from anxiety experienced due to the prohibitions imposed by society. Religion to many is simply a method of developing a system of truths, defining reality and the universe, understanding the meaning and purpose of life and death, establishing moral values, and/or distinguishing right from wrong. Commonalties of religions include belief in a supreme being; worshipping publicly in a holy place; praying and/or meditating; reading and teaching from holy books; following certain traditions and customs pertaining to liturgy, doctrine, and ethics; distinguishing what is good from what is evil; attempting to be good or righteous; and attempting to make oneself worthy of salvation or attaining a higher level of existence upon death.

Major religions of the world are discussed below; the discussions are hierarchically ordered according to number of believers. Christianity has far more believers than any other religion. You will find that non-Christian religions are basically distortions of biblical principles and beliefs, as evidenced in the common cults emerging in recent years in the western hemisphere. The most familiar distortions are as follows: several gods (versus one); one manifestation of God (versus trinity); one prophet (versus numerous prophets), one inspired author (versus many authors of the Bible, all inspired by God's Holy Spirit); importance of physical and mental experience (versus scriptural study, public worship, and spiritual edification); importance of works (versus faith); reincarnation (versus resurrection).

<u>Christianity</u>. Christian's believe that Almighty God is good, holy, and just. There are three identities of God: Father, Son, and Holy Spirit. God sent His only Son into the world as an example of His righteousness and to show how we can become worthy of His favor. Christians believe Christ was born of a virgin by the power of the Holy Spirit to bring the good news of salvation to all believers. The Christian faith is founded in the atoning sacrifice and subsequent resurrection of God's Only Son.

The Holy Bible provides the foundation of the Christian faith. The Old Testament presents the Law, which is God's will and covenant to humankind, as well as God's promise and prophecy of a New Covenant. The New Testament proclaims the fulfillment of the Law and the Old Testament prophecy, through the New Covenant which is the promised Messiah Jesus Christ. Christ fulfilled the Law on behalf of all humans, who are by nature sinful, unclean, and weak. A single sin can obliterate all the good a person has done, thereby separating him or her from God who is by nature, perfect in righteousness. Christ, who was without sin, sacrificed Himself for us thereby paying the punishment for sin, and redeeming people from the curse of death and the punishment of damnation. That is, Christ conquered all that is evil by taking upon Himself the sin of the world, cleansing the souls of believers from unrighteousness.

By the shedding of His blood, Christ washed away all sin and conquered death, which He proved by His own resurrection, thereby assuring the resurrection of all human beings. Those who place their faith and hope in the New Covenant, which is Christ the Lord, are made righteous before God, and therefore worthy of living in God's presence eternally. Those who reject Christ and His invitation to the kingdom of heaven will be condemned to eternal hell.

Symbols: The cross of Christ, the Star of Bethlehem, the Trinity (three interwoven circles and a triangle), and the fish. For more on Christian symbols and symbolism consult the Keyword Index.

Christian Symbols

The Christian church uses a number of symbols to represent God and/or Christ. For example, you may have noticed the overlapping Greek letters **X** and **P** (chi and rho), which represent the first letters in the word Christ. Also, there are the first three letters of Jesus, which in Greek are **I, H, S** (iota = J, eta = E, and sigma = S). You've probably seen the cross of Christ displaying the letters **INRI**; these Roman letters stood for Jesus (**I**esus) of Nazareth (**N**azarenus), King (**R**ex) of the Jews (**I**udaeorum); Pilate ordered this posted at the crucifixion. A common sight on cars and front doors is the fish, sometimes with the word ichthus; the Greek letters **ΙΧΘΥΣ** are the first letters of the following words: Jesus Christ, God's Son, Savior. The fish came into use by early Christians who concealed their identity from governments antagonistic to Christianity; pagans during that period also used the fish to represent a funeral wake. Different symbols are displayed throughout this book as reminders that God is forever present with us.

The Word of God is depicted as a Bible, which is a "Lamp unto my feet, and a light unto my path" (PSA 119:105). The dove descending from heaven symbolizes the Holy Spirit declaring the Word made flesh to the world during Jesus's baptism, when the Holy Spirit lighted upon Him and a voice from heaven declared, "This is my beloved Son in whom I am well pleased" (MAT 3:13–17). The dove also reminds us when Noah sent the dove from the ark to find land (which returned with an olive branch in its beak) and God's promise seen in a rainbow.

The all-seeing eye of God became popular during the Renaissance and is used by Freemasons. However, in recent years this symbol has been adopted by some cults and followers of new age doctrine.

Islam. Islam is largely based on principles of Christianity, Judaism, and the Holy Bible. The god of Islam is Allah. Moslems (or Muslims) recognize such biblical notables as Adam, Noah, Abraham, Moses, and Jesus. In fact, many Arab tribes are descendants of Abraham's son Ishmael, while the Hebrews are descendants of Abraham's son Isaac. A rivalry between these nations has ensued since that initial rivalry between the sons of Abraham, and resulted in wars where the land known as Palestine has changed hands several times.

Moslems highly revere their prophet Mohammed, considering him more important than any other prophet, including Moses and Jesus Christ. While meditating and fasting on Mt. Hira, Mohammed supposedly received revelations from the angel Gabriel. While contemplating the relevance of judgment, hell, and paradise, Mohammed was given his visions. He proceeded to preach against idolatry, immorality, cruelty, selfishness, and polytheism, eventually dictating the holy book of Islam called the Koran (or Quran). He made a famous pilgrimage to Mecca, where He destroyed the idols there. In commemoration, Moslems pray five times a day (called Salat) while facing Mecca; they also attempt to make at least one pilgrimage to Mecca during their lifetime (called Hajj). In commemoration of Mohammed's revelation, Moslems fast and pray during their holy month (called Ramadan).

Moslems believe they will live in paradise (heaven) after they die, where they will enjoy the pleasures of wine and women, desires that are forbidden on earth. Unlike Christians, their ticket to heaven is earned by accumulating good works. Consult the lesson, *Islam versus Christianity*, for a more extensive analysis.

Symbols: Star and crescent moon (new moon).

Hinduism. Brahman is the name of the god of the Hindus. Like the Christians and Moslems, their god is the creator, and represents the epitome of goodness, truth, and mercy. Life is a search to find Brahman within oneself, and to know him from that perspective (or as Christ put it, "the kingdom of heaven is within you"). Vishnu is the part of Brahman that sustains people, and is thus, the savior. Maya is the evil force that obstructs knowledge of Brahman. While these beliefs appear similar to Christianity, one major difference is their belief in subordinate gods. Modern Hinduism recognizes a three-god system: Brahma (creator), Vishnu (preserver), and Shiva (destroyer).

Hindus attempt to lead a life of sensuous, aesthetic pleasure, while maintaining a standard of ethics and morality. Hindus are supposed to be non-violent and charitable. They work to achieve self-sufficiency, public harmony, and economic prosperity. They attempt to maintain sound mental, physical, and moral health; yoga is practiced to achieve these goals. The soul is believed to be reincarnated periodically until it reaches its peak of human excellence, and the individual finds his or her way into the light. The Hindus use four holy books: Vedas (poems and hymns), Brahmanas (worship liturgy), Epics (heroes, gods, and events), and Upanishads (issues concerning life and death).

Symbols: Lotus blossom.

Buddhism. Siddhartha Gautama was a prince who, as he approached old age, became a recluse and spent his time meditating (he was a practicing Hindu). He fasted and meditated for forty-nine days at one stretch, while sitting beneath a bo-tree, contemplating the meaning of life and its many temptations by the evil spirit Mara. Siddhartha learned that one can survive with only a minimum of their basic needs provided, and that life brings suffering which is a result of one's pursuit of personal needs and desires. He asserted that discipline and restraint relieve people of such suffering, allowing them to become enlightened. Enlightenment results in the pursuit of more important ideals such as truth, and allows one to control and refine their personal views, ideas, intentions, speech, conduct, work, endeavors, and meditations. Buddha discovered, neither extreme self-indulgence nor extreme self-denial were acceptable, and declared the middle path to be the optimal way to live.

Buddhism deviates somewhat from Hindu beliefs such as dismissing reincarnation as valid or necessary. There is less emphasis on the concept of God and more on the concept of self. In fact, the self can be viewed as divine if one has achieved enlightenment through hard work, self-discipline, and compassion. Zen, a Japanese Buddhist sect, shares essentially the same doctrine, focusing on self-evaluation, self-discipline, and following one's intuitions. Tibetan Buddhism regards their leader, the Dalai Lama, as a divine reincarnation of Buddha. Thus, there are significant divisions among Buddhist sects.

Symbols: Wheel with eight spokes; wheel following eight paths.

Judaism. The Jewish Bible is basically the Old Testament (or parts of it depending on which faction of Judaism). The OT begins with the Torah (Pentateuch) which comprises the written law handed down by God to Moses who was their greatest prophet. The words of the prophets and the promise of the Messiah, along with associated holy books (Hagiographa), are also deemed sacred. One such book is the oral law (Talmud), which consists of additional statutes, historical accounts, rules of ethics, and Jewish folklore. Jews believe there is only one God who is the source of justice and righteousness. He prospers those who are righteous and destroys those who are wicked. The goal, therefore, is to strive for righteousness and refrain from sin. All trials and tribulations have a purpose and a message; this is why the history of their faith is central to their belief system. Jews follow a number of traditions, rituals, and customs, some more earnestly than others. These traditions include observing feasts and festivals, lighting candles, and going to temple on Saturday. The leader in the temple is called a rabbi; he is not considered a priest but a teacher. Some Jews do not believe in life after death. The Orthodox Jews strictly adhere to the old traditions and the Torah, while Conservative and Reformed Jews are not as strict and include the rest of the OT as well as certain apocryphal books in their worship and teaching. A small percentage of Jews are Christians, since they recognize Christ as the Messiah. A great percentage of Jews still seek a messiah and look forward to the resurrection.

Symbols: Star of David; tablets of the Ten Commandments; Menorah (usually seven candles for the seven feasts; eight or more candles would represent Hanukkah as an additional feast).

Confucianism. The Chinese philosopher Confucius rejected traditional Taoism and attempted to redefine the importance of one's existence and mission in life. He stressed the necessity of inner beauty as evidenced by a character of righteousness, goodness, courtesy, humility, loyalty, ethics, and restitution. He believed that one should strive for harmony within oneself, and in the home, the nation, and the world. He advocated strong government and social institutions. Ways of reaching harmony included attempting to understand both sides of an issue, being diligent in benevolent endeavors, and adhering to the rules regarding relationships. These rules are as follows: fathers must be kind, children must be obedient and respect their elders, husbands must be reasonable, wives must be obedient, siblings must be courteous and respectful to the eldest, friends must be wise and respectful, rulers must be honest and benevolent, subjects must be loyal. Confucius advanced a personal definition of the golden rule: do not do to others what you do not want done to you. The holy book of classics provides history, poems, hymns, and rites.

Symbols: (not used)

Shintoism. This religion is a belief system based on rules of conduct associated with being a citizen of Japan. It is derived from Japanese history recorded in two books: Chronicles (Nihongi) and Ancient Records (Kojiki). In ancient history, the emperor was elevated to divine status, being worshipped as the descendant of the sun goddess Amaterasu. Although the leaders are no longer given such status, they are still highly regarded. People are viewed as imperfect but not as sinners; everyone is affected by the shortcomings of others.

Patriotism and loyalty to the Japanese government are the focus of this religion. There is little distinction between what is human and what is divine. Nature and its many spirit gods are objects of worship. Nothing is too great or small to be revered with awe; that is, beauty can be found in anything and everything. The names of their many gods are written on pieces of paper during worship; there are no idols or images of their gods. The land is, for the most part, their god; for the land is sacred, being the source of all sustenance. The first parents, whose offspring were the islands of Japan, were Izanagi (the sky father) and Izanami (the earth mother).

Symbols: The mirror of righteousness; the sword of wisdom and justice.

Taoism. Taoism originated from other eastern religions, and is very similar to Buddhism though much older. The goal is to attain harmony with the external world. Civilization interferes with nature so humans must find harmony with nature and nurture it. If you love the world as much as yourself, it will be entrusted to your care and you will be blessed. People strive to adapt to their world not struggle with it. Life is a search for inner truth, wisdom, and contentment. These attributes are attained by being content with little, and being humble, dedicated, dutiful, virtuous, and moderate. The Tao Te Ching (way to power) is the holy book that teaches principles of life in the context of paradoxes. For example, to be richly blessed one must be moderate; to be successful one must not be too ambitious; to be virtuous one must seek virtue; to be brave one must be humble. Taoists believe in living a simple life free of government and society.

Symbols: Yin (female, dark, earth) and Yang (male, light, heaven).

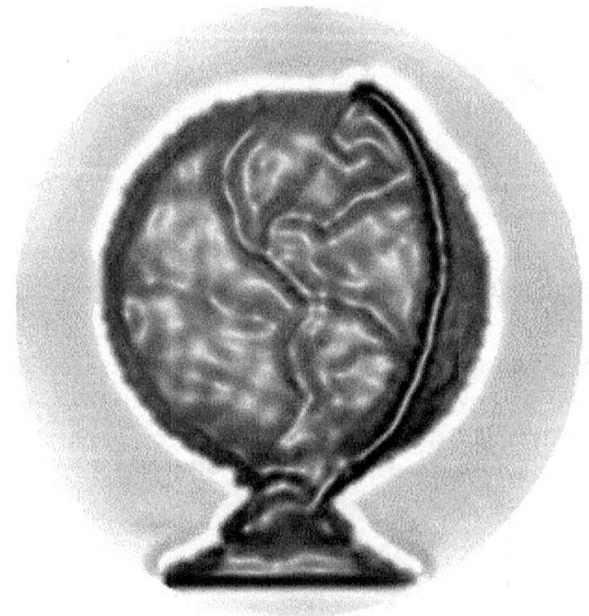

World Religions

RELIGION	GOD	HOLY BOOK(S)	FOUNDER	PROPHETS	BELIEVERS (approx.)
Christianity	I AM	Bible (Old and New Testaments)	Jesus Christ (AD 30)	Elijah, Moses, Isaiah, Peter, Paul, John, John the Baptist	2.3 billion
Islam	Allah	Koran	Mohammed (AD 570–632)	Mohammed Hussein, Abu Bakr, Omar, Ali, Othman	1.5 billion
Hinduism	Brahman (reality)	Vedas, Brahmanas, Epics, Upanishads	None	Mahatma Ghandi, Ramakrishna	900 million
Buddhism	Various Names	Dharma (Sutta), Vinaya Abhidhamma	Siddhartha Gautama (560–480 BC)	Gautama, Amitabha	375 million
Judaism	Yahweh	Torah, Talmud (Old Testament)	Abraham, (2000 BC)	Abraham, Jacob, Moses	16 million
Mormonism	God	Book of Mormon	Joseph Smith	Brigham Young	9 million
Confucianism	Confucius, Shang-Ti	Nu Ching, Ssu Shu	Confucius (557 BC)	Yang Chu, Moh Tih	6 million
Jehovah's Witnesses	Jehovah	Bible (revised)	C. Russell W. Miller	Jesus	5 million
Shintoism	Izanagi, Izanami	Nihongi, Kogiki	Unknown (BC–AD)	None	4 million
Taoism	Jade Emperor (and others)	Tao Te Ching	Lao-Tsu (604 BC)	Lao-Tsu, Chuang-Tsu	3 million

World Empires

World Religions (continued)

RELIGION	LEADER	HOLY PLACE(S)	HOLY DAYS	NATIONS	BELIEFS
Christianity (Catholics)	Pastor (Pope)	Bethlehem, Jerusalem, Zion	Christmas, Good Friday, Easter	Americas, Europe, (everywhere)	Trinity (Father, Son, Spirit). Christ sacrificed for sin; His death and resurrection grants salvation and eternal life.
Islam	Caliph, Imam	Mecca, Medina, Jerusalem,	Ramadan (month)	Arabia, Mid-East, Africa	Mohammed is the Apostle. Prayer five times daily facing Mecca; fast during Ramadan.
Hinduism	Guru	Benares, Ganges River	Mela Holl, Dasera, Divuli	India, Sri Lanka	Become one with Brahma (creator) and avoid evil Maya by finding yourself.
Buddhism	Lama, Monks	Sarnath, Lumbrini, Budh-Gaya, Kusinara	Pershera, Wesak	Far East, Asia, India	Derived from Hinduism. Focus on inner power (self-reliance); no reincarnation.
Judaism	Rabbi	Jerusalem	Rosh Hashanah, Yom Kippur	Israel, USA, Europe	God will send a Messiah. Obey the Law and seek God's righteousness.
Mormonism	Bishop, Ward	Temple	Easter Christmas Pioneer Day	USA mostly	God spoke to latter day saints. J. Smith was a prophet equal to Christ; distorts orthodox Christian beliefs.
Confucianism	Confucius	None	None	China, Japan, Korea	Rejects Taoism. Strive for a good heart, moral character, and harmony with others.
Jehovah's Witnesses	Watchtower Society	None	None	USA mostly	Distorts Christian beliefs; denies deity and virgin birth of Christ; snubs Holy Trinity, resurrection, and salvation by grace through faith alone.
Shintoism	Kami (spirits)	Mt. Fujiyama	Shogatsu (new year)	Japan	Humans are divine, not sinful. Revere the dead; everything is beautiful; many gods.
Taoism	None	Kiangsi, Mountains	Birthdays of gods; Day of dead	China	Focus on nature and inner self; adapt to environment. Achieve harmony, love, and moderation.

Lesson: Mormonism versus Christianity

The Book of Mormon does not begin to approach the Holy Bible with respect to its validity as the inspired Word of God. Unlike the Bible, the Book of Mormon has no History, Authenticity, Reliability, or Prophecy (Keyword: *HARP*).

Lack of validity

The Holy Bible cross-validates itself; that is, the Old Testament is validated by the New Testament and vice-versa. The prophecy of the New Covenant (the Messiah) provided in the OT, is fulfilled by Jesus Christ as written in the NT. Events in the Bible are corroborated in other historical accounts as well. Unlike the Holy Bible, the Book of Mormon has no source of internal or external validity; in other words, there are no sources of corroboration for the Book of Mormon in the literature or in any historical archives.

The Book of Mormon is also inconsistent and incompatible with the Holy Bible. The Book of Mormon doesn't fulfill any prophecy provided in either the OT or the NT. If God intended further scripture to be inspired by Him, He would have said so in the Holy Bible. Instead, the Bible informs us that it alone is God's Word, and that it is a terrible sin to attempt to add to or subtract from the words of the Bible. The Book of Mormon subtracts from and adds to the words of the Holy Bible, thereby violating the very tenet of divine inspiration. It adds fiction that is supposed to complement the Bible, as well as removing key concepts or changing their meaning. The Book of Mormon provides nothing in the way of truth above that found in the sixty-six books of the Holy Bible.

Lack of reliability

The Holy Bible is a compilation of tens of thousands of manuscripts written by different authors, at different times, in different locations. However, these numerous manuscripts complement each other because they are components of the same exposition. Further, the different books in the Bible provide both a unique perspective, while also collectively providing pieces to a larger mystery. Through the Holy Bible, God's plan of salvation is clearly revealed.

God has provided us His Word through multiple sources, thereby providing high consistency, reliability, and corroboration. The Book of Mormon was compiled by a single individual of questionable credibility. The Book of Mormon has no established validity or reliability since it is not corroborated by any other source (it is neither consistent with the Bible nor is it internally consistent). The only truth to be found in the Book of Mormon are those passages that were taken directly from the Holy Bible.

Lack of authenticity

The Holy Bible has been transcribed and authenticated by dozens of biblical theologians and scholars on numerous occasions. Although the Bible has been translated in hundreds of languages, and has been handed down from generation to generation, the themes and concepts never changed. There may be slight grammatical differences in the translation of individual passages, but the events, prophecies, and principles do not vary. On the other hand, the Book of Mormon has been altered significantly on numerous occasions since it was first transcribed, in order to reduce internal inconsistencies.

The Book of Mormon was written by one person: Joseph Smith. He claims that others knew about the origins of his book, but this is hearsay evidence at best. Smith himself practiced divination (witchcraft) and engaged in other practices that defy God's Law. He fostered discontent among followers and frequently clashed with civil authorities. Smith, therefore, is not a good source for authentication of God's Word, particularly if he must be trusted as the sole authority. Smith supposedly received the exact transcription of his text from God word-for-word, yet his original text has been modified many times. In short, Smith was nothing more than a cult figure and false prophet, far from being a reliable messenger who received divine inspiration directly from God.

Mormons will say that they rely on the Book of Mormon for precisely the reason that it was transcribed by one person and thus, has not been contaminated by multiple translations, authors, or interpreters. Anyone who has had instruction in the laws of probabilities, statistics, or the notions of central tendency and normal distribution can tell you that a sample of one does not make a very reliable study, and predictions or beliefs based on such a sample are entirely unreliable. The fact that the Holy Bible provides corroborating testimony from multiple witnesses makes it magnitudes more credible than the Book of Mormon.

<ins>Lack of historical evidence</ins>

The Holy Bible is supported by a wealth of evidence. For example, the Bible is consistent with other historical accounts. In fact, biblical events usually can be established and connected to a particular time and place in history. Further, substantial archaeological findings support countless OT and NT accounts. God did not destroy evidence that supports the Bible, rather, much of the evidence can still be found today in historical, geological, astronomical, and archaeological records. Events, people, and locations from the Bible continue to be proven to this day.

There is no evidence that the events recorded in the Book of Mormon ever happened. J. Smith writes that God told him where to find buried plates from which the Book of Mormon was transliterated, and then God supposedly retrieved the plates when the book was finished. If the Book of Mormon was true, why would God remove the only source of physical evidence that could prove it? While there is evidence available to prove biblical events as far in the past as Noah's flood, why is there no evidence to prove anything in the Book of Mormon? Why, because the Book of Mormon is a work of fiction!

In the Mormon book of Ether, for example, it is claimed that millions of people died in a single battle some two millennia ago. This implies the existence of enormous civilizations in the western hemisphere during that time, about the size of Houston or San Francisco. There is no evidence that ancient civilizations this large ever existed in North America that long ago, or in the rest of the world for that matter. The largest known ancient civilizations in North America were the Inca, Aztec, and Maya, none of which reached numbers in the millions until around the fifteenth century. Further, these civilizations were pagan, and practiced such abominations as human sacrifice, hardly what one would call righteous or chosen by God.

<ins>Lack of prophecy</ins>

The Holy Bible has a wealth of prophecy. The prophecy in the Bible is very detailed and precise. For example, the OT describes in detail the coming of a Messiah, giving such information as where the Messiah would be born (MIC 5:2), His lineage (GEN 1:18, 26:4, 28:14; 2 SA 7:12–16; ISA 11:1–2), the fact that He would be born of a virgin (ISA 7:14), and so forth. All these prophecies came true in Christ as shown in the NT (JOH 7:42; MAT 1:2–16; LUK 1:26–35).

The Book of Mormon has no prophecy. It adds no further understanding about the future of the world or God's people. It is just a tale about some people and civilizations that developed and evolved over centuries, and fell in and out of God's grace. It is a novel, nothing more. The only prophecy in the Book of Mormon is lifted from the Holy Bible.

Lack of depth

Mormons read the Book of Mormon more often than the Holy Bible. Why? They typically respond that it is easier to read and understand than the Bible, as well as being shorter in length. Nobody should refrain from reading the Bible simply because it is lengthy and complicated. It is not prudent to always pursue the easy path, especially if it is not the correct way. Such logic is counterproductive.

God never said it would be easy to understand the mysteries that He has revealed in the scriptures. That is why He commands that we study His Word often. The way of righteousness is a difficult one and takes much discipline. One cannot grasp everything in the Bible from a single reading; but every time a person reads the Bible, they get more out of it. Such knowledge will continue to increase incrementally after each reading. After reading the Book of Mormon only once or twice, the gist of the book can be understood, because the book lacks depth and breadth, unlike the Bible which is voluminous in its wisdom.

Blasphemy

Blasphemy is the writing or verbalizing of false prophecy or teachings claimed to be from God. The Book of Mormon is a distortion of Christianity and therefore fits the definition. The book does not follow true doctrine, theology, or principles set down in the New Testament of Jesus Christ. Yet the Book of Mormon claims to be the corrected Word of God and another testimony of Jesus Christ. It is a lie to call anything but the Holy Bible the true Word of God. Again, the only words in the Book of Mormon that are absolutely true are those which were plagiarized.

It is completely ludicrous to place one's faith in a written work compiled by a single individual of questionable character. The only credentials J. Smith possessed were of the occult. His visions were false and contrived, and were used to mislead people from the truth. He took the Bible, which is truth, and altered it. He distorted the meaning and purpose of God's Word, turning God's truth into a lie. Mormons are persuaded to believe this lie.

- PRO 30:5–6 ~ Every word of God is true; don't attempt to add to His words or He will rebuke you and you will be proven false.
- JER 14:14 ~ False prophets tell lies in my (God's) name; I did not send them, command them, or speak to them. They receive false visions and make false predictions from the deceit of their lying hearts.
- JER 29:8 ~ God says, "Do not let those prophets and diviners among you deceive you, and do not pay attention to their dreams which they themselves caused to be dreamt."
- ZEC 10:2 ~ The idols speak lies and diviners see false visions. They give comfort in vain. Therefore, the sheep wander from the flock and are oppressed, for they have no shepherd.
- GAL 1:7–12 ~ Some would pervert the Gospel of Christ. If anyone preaches another Gospel (not preached by Jesus Christ and His apostles), that person is cursed by God. The Gospel of Christ does not come from the thoughts of man, or from the teachings of man, but rather from the revelation of Jesus Christ.
- REV 22:18–19 ~ For I testify to everyone who hears the words of the prophecy of this book, that if anyone adds to these words, God will add unto that person the plagues mentioned in this book. If anyone subtracts from the words of this prophecy, God will take away their name from the Book of Life, and they will not share in the inheritance.

In the Old Testament, a seer was the same as a prophet; that is, the words were used synonymously. Since then, the two terms have taken on different meanings. Now, a seer is usually associated with a fortuneteller. Unlike a seer, a prophet is understood to be someone inspired by God to witness to the truth, and to foretell future events that are part of God's plan. In the Mormon book of 2 Nephi, a seer is proclaimed to be greater than a prophet.

To say that a seer is greater than a prophet is bewildering. A prophet is inspired by God. A seer is like J. Smith, someone who engages in divination, astrology, and/or witchcraft. The Holy Bible teaches us that such occultist behavior and practices are repulsive to God. You cannot rely on a fortuneteller to know or to tell the truth. J. Smith, author of the Book of Mormon, was a shrewd con artist who practiced divination; he obviously was not inspired by God who condemns such behavior. The reason the Book of Mormon contains no prophecy or truth is because it was written by a fraud.

- ISA 47:10–14 ~ You felt secure in your wickedness. But evil will come upon you and disaster will befall you. So stand fast in your enchantments, sorceries, and counsels. Let them try save you, those who gaze at the stars, divide the heavens, and predict what will happen to you according to the new moon. Fire will consume them and you.
- COL 2:18–19 ~ Do not let anyone swindle you out of your reward, those who practice false humility and worship angels. They claim to have seen things, but they have filled their unspiritual and arrogant minds with silly notions.

There are several warnings in the Bible that tell us to watch out for false prophets and teachings. These warnings relate to cults such as Mormonism.

- ISA 59:13 ~ They know they are being disobedient to God; they carefully plan their lies.
- MAT 24:11 ~ False prophets will come and lead many astray.
- ACT 20:30 ~ From among yourselves will come people speaking perverse things to gain followers.
- JDE 1:4 ~ False teachers have infiltrated the churches, claiming that once you have become Christians you can do whatever you want without being punished. They deny the Lord and turn God's grace into lust.

Secrecy

The Mormons engage in numerous secret practices and rituals. They take secret oaths and make clandestine allegiances. Violation of a secret Mormon oath is suggested to be punishable by death. The use of such secret teachings, objects, and oaths is entirely unbiblical.

In the Mormon book of Mosiah, it is claimed that only seers can know the mysteries and secrets of God. However, through the Bible and through Jesus Christ, God has revealed His mysteries to everyone who faithfully desires such wisdom and knowledge and searches the scriptures to find it. Anybody can understand God's mysteries by reading the Holy Bible every day. Mysteries that can be known only to a seer are those he or she has contrived or dreamt.

Allegedly, J. Smith designed some special glasses, in accordance with God's direction, before being able to interpret the plates from which he assembled his book. This appears to be a reference to divination. He might as well have used a Ouija board. God never uses material objects to instruct His prophets on what to write or say. Instead, God writes the words into their hearts and minds, without contriving any secret combinations. For example, God spoke directly to Moses from the burning bush. Why didn't He speak directly to J. Smith if he was so important a prophet (or seer)? Supposedly, God spoke directly to the first Mormons.

Incidentally, the Mormon book of Ether says the Lord doesn't work in "secret combinations." Yet, Smith used such tools in His occultist practices. In fact, the Mormons have several secret rituals and practices that they don't care to discuss. For example, it's very difficult to get a Mormon to talk about their sacred underwear; yes, sacred underwear! Further, they engage in a pagan ritual associated with the fall of Adam, in accordance with the solemn rite of marriage! Mormons do not recognize original sin; on the contrary, they view the fall of Adam in a positive way. However, the Bible teaches that the original sin was a terrible thing; not only did it result in the fall of Adam and Eve, it resulted in their sin and their death being passed onto subsequent generations (ROM 5:12–13).

Clearly, God does not encourage keeping secrets. In fact, God discloses secrets. We too are to profess what we know to be true, not keep it a secret or swear an oath of secrecy.

- DAN 2:28 ~ There is a God in heaven who reveals mysteries.
- MAT 10:26 ~ Jesus said, "Don't fear those who hate you, for everything that is hidden now will be reveled later; everything that is unknown now will become known.
- LUK 12:3 ~ Jesus said, "What we have discussed in the dark will be repeated in the light. What you have heard in closed rooms will be shouted from the rooftops."
- ROM 16:25–26 ~ Christ has the power to save you according to the revelation of God's mystery, which was kept secret since the world began, but which is now evident by the scriptures. According to God's will, the mystery is made known to all nations on earth for the obedience of faith.
- 2 CO 4:2 ~ We apostles have renounced secret and shameful ways; we do not engage in deception and we do not distort the Word of God. We appeal to those who have a conscience in the sight of God.

<u>Inconsistencies between the Book of Mormon and the Holy Bible</u>

One thing that proves the authenticity of the Holy Bible is its profound prophecy, and the extraordinary depth, accuracy, and detail of that prophecy. In the Bible, God didn't tell us to expect another Testament, so why would anyone believe the Book of Mormon to be one? The Bible doesn't mention the coming of a new prophet, so why should anybody expect one? The only prophets the Bible tells us to expect are false ones.

- JER 14:14 ~ The prophets are telling lies in my name.
- LAM 2:13–14 ~ Your prophets have seen vain and foolish things. They have given you false burdens and beliefs to bear.
- MAT 7:15,21 ~ Jesus said, "Beware of false prophets. Not everyone appearing to be righteous is righteous."
- MAT 24:11 ~ False prophets will come and will lead many people astray.
- 2 CO 11:13 ~ They will try to fool you into thinking they are Christ's apostles.
- 2 TI 3:13 ~ Evil people and false teachers will get worse, deceiving many. They themselves have been deceived by Satan.
- 2 PE 1:21 ~ No prophecy ever came from the impulses of men, but holy men spoke as they were directed by the Holy Spirit.
- 1 JO 2:18 ~ You have heard that the antichrist comes, and many will.

In Revelation (REV 11:3–4), the prophet John describes the coming of two anointed ones or "witnesses" that will perform miracles and will testify about Christ. The Mormon books of 2 Nephi and Moroni, describe the coming of three witnesses. This contradicts Revelation. Perhaps J. Smith decided to add himself to the list, and changed the number to three. In any case, the Book of Mormon is incorrect, the New Testament is correct.

CHAPTER SIX

The Bible is the only completely accurate account of Jesus Christ. The fact that the Book of Mormon has Christ appearing to inhabitants of North America is wholly unbelievable. According to the book of Mormon, Christ appeared to these people prior to His birth in Bethlehem. Why would Christ appear to them and nobody else? Why didn't God send an angel, a vision, or a revelation like He usually did during the Old Testament era?

One prophet in the Holy Bible to whom the Holy Spirit possibly appeared in the flesh was Abraham (via King Melchizedek). If Christ wasn't used to making public appearances before His birth, why would He show Himself to the forerunners of the Latter-Day Saints? Additionally, Smith would have us believe that the resurrected Christ spent more time with the original Mormons than among those with whom Christ lived and preached. If the original Mormons were really righteous and faithful, they would have believed, as current Christians do, without having seen Christ in the flesh (they saw Him complete with scars, supposedly). Jesus said, "Blessed are those who have not seen and yet believe" (JOH 20:29). Further, if the Mormons were truly righteous, and were visited by Jesus Christ Himself, why didn't their faith survive? Why didn't their descendants survive? Why is there no record that they ever lived? Why? Because they never existed in the first place.

According to the Mormon book of 3 Nephi, people in the New World supposedly saw the Star of Bethlehem. Many scholars believe that the star was produced by an alignment of planets that converged over Bethlehem while others suggest it was a comet; either way, the wise men were able to navigate via this celestial occurrence. Since wise men from the east followed the Star which hovered over Bethlehem, how is it that the same phenomenon was purportedly witnessed tens of thousands of miles to the west? Would they propose the star was pointing at them?

The Holy Bible was written by a large number of authors having different writing styles. Although the Book of Mormon has several purported authors, the writing style remains the same throughout; that is, the same phraseology is employed. For example, phrases such as "waxed strong," "it came to pass," and "stiff-necked people," are used throughout the Book of Mormon. Such phrases appear to be taken from the Bible, and indicate that the Book of Mormon did not have multiple authors. If J. Smith really was transcribing the works of different authors, the writing styles would also be different, just as they are for the Gospels.

J. Smith attempted to follow the overall writing style of the Bible to make it appear to be genuine and dated. Thus, it is not surprising that much of the Book of Mormon is a direct steal from the Holy Bible. For example, the original words of Isaiah can be found in the Mormon books of Nephi, Mosiah, and Alma. In fact, Nephi claims to have seen the same visions as Isaiah; if he did, why didn't he use his own words to describe them? If J. Smith transcribed the words accurately, why are they identical to those found in the book of Isaiah? If the Book of Mormon was written by several authors, why are all the words in the style of J. Smith alone?

Christian principles, concepts, and revelations are also described in the Book of Mormon using the exact same phraseology as used in the New Testament. This is totally suspicious. The Book of Mormon would have us believe that these passages were written before the birth of Christ, yet they emulate word-for-word excerpts written by apostles of Christ (e.g., Peter and Paul), and allegedly recorded on plates long before the Book of Mormon was even conceived.

Another important point is the Book of Mormon's frequent display of bigotry. In fact, the books of 2 and 3 Nephi describe a race of people who were punished by God by having their skin turned black. Later they were rewarded by God and had their skin turned back to its original shade. The Bible teaches that God does not discriminate between races, sexes, or social and economic strata (GAL 3:28). It is foolish to think that God would punish or reward a nation by changing the color of their skin. The Bible sometimes uses the term "black" to create a mood of brooding or gloom (i.e., darkness, as opposed to the light of God). The color of one's skin is never associated with a curse in the Bible.

Mormon beliefs which contradict Christian beliefs

Mormons believe there are many gods and that they will become gods if they adhere perfectly to Mormon doctrines and teachings. They think they will be the god of their own planet, and its occupants will worship them just like Mormons worship the god of this planet. Unfortunately, the ruler of this planet is Satan, so they may be worshipping the wrong god altogether. Truthfully, the Lord God is God of everything including Satan, the universe, and everybody who takes a breath. There are no other gods, only one God; and the saints will live with Him, but the saints will be like angels not gods.

- DEU 32:17,39 ~ Demons are not gods. New gods were invented by people. Besides God, there are no others.
- ISA 37:19–20 ~ Their gods will be cast into the fire, for they were not gods at all but were man's invention. Let all the nations know that God alone is God.
- LUK 20:36 ~ Those who are accounted worthy will become like the angels and will never die.
- 2 TH 2:3–4 ~ Beware of the son of perdition who exalts himself and proclaims to be God.
- 1 JO 3:1–2 ~ How great is God's love that we should be called His children. The world doesn't know us because it didn't know Him. We are His children, but we don't know yet what that really entails; we do know, however, that we will be like Him, for we will see Him as He really is.

Mormons deny the Holy Trinity, and the fact that God never changes. They deny that God is omnipresent, perfect in righteousness, and exists throughout eternity.

- PSA 139:7–8 ~ I cannot go anywhere without God being there, for He occupies all of heaven and earth.
- PSA 102:27 ~ God is always the same and His existence is eternal.
- JER 23:24 ~ The Lord says, "Can anyone hide from me? Do I not fill heaven and earth?"
- MAT 28:18–20 ~ Jesus said, "All authority on heaven and earth is given to me. Go and teach everyone what I taught you, baptizing them in the name of the Father, Son, and Holy Spirit."
- 1 CO 12:5 ~ God is always the same.
- JAM 1:17 ~ Every good thing comes from God; every perfect gift comes from above, from the Father of lights. God never varies, and in Him there is no darkness, not even a shadow.
- 1 JO 5:6–7,20 ~ There are three recorded in heaven: the Father, the Word (Christ), and the Holy Spirit. These three are one. The Spirit is the witness, because the Spirit is truth. Jesus Christ is true God and the source of eternal life.
- REV 1:17; REV 22:13 ~ God (Christ) is the first and last, the beginning and the end.

Mormons deny that Jesus Christ is God; they consider Christ to be just another one of God's creations. They believe Christ was merely a prophet like J. Smith. Worse, they believe that Christ was a physical manifestation of the angel Michael and the spirit brother of Lucifer. The Bible teaches us that Jesus Christ is Prophet, Priest, and King, and is our Lord (not an angel of the Lord).

- ISA 43:10–12,15 ~ There are no gods before Him or after Him. God says, "You are witnesses to what I have said. My servant, whom I have chosen, was also sent to be a witness so that you can know me and believe. And even so, I am He (I am that witness). I am the Lord and beside me there is no other savior. I have declared myself to you and I have saved you whenever you have forsaken all other gods for me. You are witnesses that I am God, the Holy One of Israel, the creator of humankind, and your King."
- ISA 53:4–5 ~ Surely, He bore our grief and carried our sorrows. Yet we treated Him as an outcast, as if stricken, smitten, and afflicted by God. But He was wounded and bruised because of our sins. Our punishment was given to Him, bringing us peace, and through His suffering, we have been healed.
- JOH 1:1–4,14 ~ In the beginning was the Word, and the Word was with God, and the Word was God. All things were made by Him. In Him was life, and the life was the light of humankind. The Word was made flesh and lived among us. And we saw His glory, like the glory of the only Son of the Father, full of grace and truth.
- 1 CO 15:3 ~ Jesus Christ died for our sins in accordance with the scriptures.
- 2 CO 11:14 ~ Don't be tricked by Satan who disguises himself as an angel of light.
- HEB 1:3–6 ~ Christ is the radiance of God's glory, and the exact image of His being, sustaining all things by His powerful Word. After He had provided purification from our sins, He sat down at the right hand of His Majesty in heaven. Therefore, He is superior to the angels, and His name is above all names. Did God ever say to an angel, "You are my son, today I have begotten you?" Or did He ever say, "I will be his Father and he will be my son?" Further, when God brought forth His firstborn He said, "Let all the angels worship Him."
- 1 PE 2:24 ~ Jesus Christ bore our sins in His own body on the cross, so that we, who were dead in our sins, could live unto righteousness.

The Mormons believe that the Holy Bible is not entirely the inspired Word of God, but the Book of Mormon is. Latter Day Saints consider all other religions including Christian denominations to be false, comparing Christian churches to the whore of Babylon.

- 1 TH 2:13 ~ We thank you that you have received His Word (the Gospel of Jesus Christ) and accepted it as the Word of God and not the Word of men. The Word of God is at work in believers like you.
- 2 PE 1:16,21 ~ We did not follow cleverly devised fables when we told people about the power and coming of Jesus Christ, for we were eye witnesses of His majesty. No prophecy ever came from the impulse of man, but holy men spoke as they were directed by God.

Mormons emphasize salvation by works, not faith.

- GAL 2:16 ~ Nobody is justified by works of the Law, they are justified by faith in Jesus Christ.
- EPH 2:8–9 ~ You are saved by the grace of God because of your faith in Jesus Christ. Salvation is a gift of God, it cannot be earned through good works, so nobody should brag.

Mormons deny the virgin birth of Jesus Christ. They think Christ was begotten in the same manner as mortal humans. They also believe that Christ was married, Himself being the groom in the wedding at Cana, even though it is precisely stated in the Bible that Christ was a guest at that wedding (JOH 2:1–2).

- ISA 7:14 ~ A virgin shall conceive and bear a son. His name will be called "God with us."

- MAT 1:18,20 ~ Mary, before she had come together with Joseph, became pregnant by the Holy Spirit.
- LUK 1:34–35 ~ Mary said to the angel, "How can I bear a son when I have never been with a man?" The angel replied, "The Holy Spirit will come upon you. Therefore, your son will be called the Son of God."

Mormons practice idolatry, because they hold certain material objects as being sacred. These objects are a fundamental part of their dogma and worship.

- JOB 31:26–28 ~ If my heart was enticed by worldly things or if I was infatuated with myself, I would be guilty of denying God, and worthy of His punishment.
- PSA 97:7 ~ Those who serve graven images or brag about their idols are confused. Everyone must worship God alone.
- ACT 17:29 ~ Don't think of God as an idol made from wood, metal, or stone.

One of the most disturbing of their doctrines is baptism for the dead. In fact, Mormons believe a person can be saved after they have died. They don't realize that one must accept Christ before death, because after that it's too late. They don't recognize baptism as receiving God's Spirit by accepting Christ as one's personal Savior; baptism is supposed to represent a beginning not the end. Thus, Mormons downplay the role of Jesus Christ and His redeeming sacrifice for sins, and they deny Christ as the only source of salvation and the One being received in baptism.

- ECC 9:10 ~ Whatever your hand finds to do, do it with your might; for there is no work, device, knowledge, or wisdom in the grave where you are going.
- ISA 38:18 ~ The grave cannot praise Him; death cannot celebrate Him. Those who go down into the pit cannot hope for truth.
- EPH 4:4–5 ~ There is only one body, one Spirit, one Lord, one faith, and one baptism.
- 1 CO 6:9–11 ~ Don't you realize that the wicked will not inherit the kingdom of God? Don't be deceived, for sinners (i.e., fornicators, idolaters, adulterers, homosexuals, perverted people, thieves, greedy people, drunkards, slanderers, and swindlers) will not inherit the kingdom. And many of us were sinners just like them. But we have been washed clean, sanctified, and justified in the name of our Lord Jesus Christ, by the Spirit of our God.
- 1 PE 3:21 ~ Baptism will also save us through the resurrection of Jesus Christ. Baptism doesn't mean washing a dirty body, but rather establishing a clean conscience toward God.
- 1 JO 1:7,10 ~ If we walk in the light as He is in the light, we have fellowship with one another; and the blood of Jesus Christ, God's Son, will cleanse us from all sin. If we say we do not sin we make Him out to be a liar, and His Word is not in us.

Summary: The Book of Mormon by J. Smith is a work of fiction. It is not the inspired Word of God. It distorts the Holy Bible thereby making God out to be a liar. Since God's Word is truth, and truth comes to us by the Holy Spirit, then to call God a liar or to make lies out of His truth is akin to blasphemy against the Holy Spirit. If this is so, then false prophets like J. Smith may be guilty of committing the only unpardonable sin.

- MAT 12:31 ~ Jesus said, "All manner of sin and blasphemy can be forgiven, except blasphemy directed against the Holy Spirit.

Lesson: Islam versus Christianity

Islam was developed as a replacement to Judaism and Christianity. Arab peoples had been searching a long time for a religion they could call their own. Establishing a religion which was principally Arabic would enable them to unite and still maintain their separation from the rest of the world. Arabic speaking peoples elected to detach themselves from other peoples, especially Jews and Christians, and therefore were unable to adopt the traditional Judeo-Christian belief system. Presumably, God sent them a prophet of their own, according to the Koran (Surah 2:151–153). Mohammed allegedly received God's direction and revelation in Arabic (Surah 43:1–5), and this information is regarded by Moslems (or Muslims) as flawless (Surah 39:27–28). Curiously, the tenets of the faith of Islam do not deviate all that much from biblical theology; unfortunately, they deviate on the most important doctrines.

Islam developed much in the same manner as other false religions and cults, with a charismatic leader at the helm. The prophet Mohammed's early life was wrought with hardship. He lost his father when he was very young, and his mother died not long afterwards. He was raised by his grandparents and uncle. He got married and had many children, but lost all but one daughter. Thus, he was sensitive to the tragedies of life. Mohammed was troubled by the inhumanity around him and wanted to do something about it, and rightfully so. Though his motivation was in the right place, his results would become a scourge to many souls.

According to legend, Mohammed was meditating on Mt. Hira when an angel appeared to him. This angel supposedly gave him many revelations and messages from God. He found the initial vision troubling, but eventually Mohammed became convinced that it was inspired by Allah (God). Mohammed's wife and friends concluded that he must be a prophet. He should have listened to his first reaction about being troubled by the vision, for it was a portent that was misinterpreted only to bring many people down.

Mohammed claimed that the angel in his vision was Gabriel. However, the vision Mohammed received could not have been from Gabriel, because the words and declarations are in conflict with biblical revelations, including those from Gabriel himself who informed Mary and Joseph that they would be the earthly parents of God's Son, the Messiah. Tradition holds that Mohammed received "satanic verses" during this vision via the evil jinn (demons). This is a plausible explanation since Satan disguises himself as an angel of light, accounting for Mohammed's initial negative reaction to the experience.

- 2 CO 11:13–14 ~ Beware of the false prophets who pretend to be disciples of Christ. Do not let them spark your interest, for even Satan disguises himself as an angel of light.
- GAL 1:8 ~ Anyone, including angels, who preaches anything contrary to what Jesus and the apostles preached, are cursed.
- 2 TH 2:9 ~ Those false signs and fake miracles come from Satan.

Mohammed first gained converts among his family and friends, then from young people and slaves. His movement got some momentum in Medina, where he accepted a job as an administrator on the condition that they accept Islam. There Mohammed recruited twelve leaders. His enemies in Mecca conspired to kill him, but he eluded the assassins. Followers from Mecca joined Mohammed in Medina. Those people lost their property and jobs, because Mohammed had been declared a heretic there. Mohammed recited his prayers while facing Jerusalem, but later changed the direction toward Medina as a result of his rejection by the Meccans.

Military conflicts ensued. Eventually, Mohammed was able to negotiate a truce between the tribes of Mecca and Medina. He gradually gained support from the Meccans, making his farewell pilgrimage in the year AD 632. During his journeys, he allegedly sprang into heaven on a horse to visit Allah, at the site now called the Dome of the Rock in Jerusalem; this landmark is known to Muslims as the Mosque of Omar. Thus, Jerusalem was the original center of Islam because of the significance of the rock, which also was the traditional site where Abraham took Isaac for sacrifice, where Jacob had his dream of a ladder to heaven, and where Solomon built a Jewish temple.

The popularity of Islam spread, primarily due to its uniqueness. In particular, it differed from orthodox biblical theology and was purely Arabic in its target audience. Arabs wanted a religion of their own and found one. They wanted to be seen as special and important to God. They wanted to be the chosen race or nation, to replace their arch rivals the Israelites. Desiring God's favor they excluded all peoples but those following Islam, thereby excluding themselves from the kingdom of heaven.

- ISA 29:13 ~ The Lord says, "These people come near to me with their mouth and honor me with their lips, but their hearts are far from me. They worship me in accordance with rules invented by men."
- COL 2:8,18–19 ~ Beware of those who would lead you astray with their errant philosophies and vain deceptions, following traditions fashioned by the world and not Christ. Do not let anyone swindle you out of your reward. Beware of those who practice false humility and worship angels. They claim to have seen things, but they have filled their unspiritual and arrogant minds with silly notions.
- 2 TI 4:3–4 ~ People will seek teachers who conform to their own likes and dislikes; they will turn away from the truth and wander into myths.

Unlike the Holy Bible, the Koran (or Quran) has undergone many changes. For example, the original vision of Mohammed included instructions to worship three goddesses, but this was later removed from the Koran. The final version of the Koran became standardized some 650 years after the death of Mohammed. When Mohammed died, there was much disagreement concerning the selection of later successors (caliphs), causing Islam to break into two factions: the Shia (Shiites) and the Sunni (Sunnis).

There are numerous troubling ideas originating from Islam that are entirely anti-Christian. The Bible warns us about antichrists that teach doctrines which oppose or dismiss Christ.

- 1 JO 2:18 ~ You have heard that the antichrist comes, and many will.
- 1 JO 4:1–3 ~ Don't believe every spirit, but test them to determine if they are really of God; for many false prophets are in the world. Every spirit that confesses that Jesus Christ is God in the flesh is of God. Those who do not confess that Jesus is of God, are themselves not of God; they are spirits of the antichrist, who you heard is coming, and is already here.

The words of Mohammed, who actually was illiterate, were transcribed by his followers and became the Koran. Thus, the Koran is principally a collection of the teachings of Mohammed, and is the basis for Islam. Moslems believe the Koran to be the word of God and they believe Mohammed to be the only reliable spokesperson and prophet. They also believe that the Koran is not translatable from Arabic to other languages, so that they can claim exclusive right to Allah's kingdom. But God's kingdom is given to everyone who accepts Christ as their personal Savior regardless of ethnicity.

- ISA 56:2–8 ~ Blessed are all people and their children if they obey God, avoid evil, keep the Sabbath, and cling to His covenant. Even those who are strangers to God's people Israel will be part of God's house if they obey Him. The righteous will be like God's sons and daughters, only better than that, with a name that will last forever. People of all walks of life will be joined together on His holy mountain to worship Him, for His house will be called a house for the righteous (also 2 CO 6:17–18).
- ACT 10:34–35 ~ Peter said, "Truly, God does not show favoritism for any person. Within every nation, anyone who fears the Lord and endeavors to be righteous is accepted by Him."
- 1 CO 12:13 ~ By one Spirit we are baptized into one body. Whether Jews or Gentiles, free men or slaves, for all Christians have become members of one Spirit.

Like the Jews, Moslems claim Abraham as their patriarch. This is because a great number of Arab tribes originated from Abraham's son Ishmael. We know from the Bible that a great nation was promised to Hagar, Ishmael's mother. Moslems believe that nation to have been ushered in by Mohammed. Arabs and Jews have been at odds with one another ever since the initial rivalry between Abraham's first two sons, Ishmael and Isaac (the father of Jacob who God renamed Israel). Islam is the Arabic response to the promises God made to the Jews through Abraham, Isaac, and Jacob; however, Moslems believe the promise passed through Ishmael, not Isaac.

According to Islam, the first Kaaba (a rectangular shrine) was constructed by Abraham and Ishmael to unite the various tribes. That shrine was originally filled with idols to appease the different Arab factions amongst them; therefore, the tribes were largely polytheistic. This is nonsensical, since Abraham feared God alone and could not condone or participate in idol worship of any kind. This fact is documented in the Koran where it is stated several times that Abraham was no idolater, and he admonished his father and his people for their idolatry (Surah 2:135–136; 21:51–54). This is a principal reason why God instructed Abraham to depart from Ur in the first place (GEN 12:1–2). So why would Abraham engage in constructing a shrine for idols with his son? It would be a sacrilege.

There are many parallels between the Koran and the Bible. For example, the Koran repeats a number of biblical accounts to include the stories of Adam and Eve; Noah and the great flood; Moses, Aaron, the liberation of Israel and the Exodus; the lives of Abraham, Lot, Ishmael, Isaac, and Jacob; the plight of Joseph; references to Saul, David (and Goliath), and Solomon; mention of Job, Jonah, and Isaiah; honorable mention of John the Baptist, Jesus, and His apostles; and references to the angels Gabriel and Michael. The Koran acknowledges that Jesus will be a sign that judgment is near (Surah 43:61).

Islam adheres to the doctrines of Repentance, Grace, and Mercy. It acknowledges God's covenants. Islam denounces the concept of many gods and the practice of idolatry. Islam also preaches the doctrines of the Resurrection and Judgment, and Heaven and Hell. Islam adheres to a moral code similar to that of the Mosaic Law. However, consistencies fall apart when contrasted with the significant deviations from biblical teaching.

The Koran ascribes new quotes and deeds to the likes of Noah, Abraham, Moses, Joseph, Jonah, and Christ. One of the most serious discrepancies misquotes Jesus Christ (MAT 5:17–18) as follows: I came to confirm the Torah and give news of an apostle named Ahmad (another name for Muhammed, which means "the praised one") (Surah 61:5–7). Thus, Islam discounts the importance of Christ, making Him appear like John the Baptist, a forerunner to a more important prophet, in this case Mohammed. We know that Christ did not come promising another prophet or messiah, He came as the Messiah, the New Covenant. However, like many Jews, Moslems await a different messiah. Many Moslems believe the Messiah will be a past leader, namely, the twelfth imam who mysteriously disappeared and is supposed to return someday.

- MAT 5:17–18 ~ Jesus said, "I didn't come to destroy the Law, I came to fulfill the Law. Not one bit of the Law will be removed until heaven and earth have passed away."
- LUK 1:68–79 ~ The Holy Covenant sworn to Abraham was made manifest in Jesus Christ. Now we can follow Christ and find our way to heaven.
- 2 PE 1:3–4 ~ By God's divine power we have received all things pertaining to life and godliness, because we know Him who called all people to righteousness and glory. We cling to His precious promises, that His people will receive a divine nature, and escape the corruption and lust of the world.

Curiously, the Koran accepts the virgin birth through Mary (Surah 19:19–21), but does not accept that Jesus was begotten by the Holy Spirit. The Koran denies that Jesus Christ is divine (Surah 5:15–17; 5:72–73) and God's only begotten Son (Surah 4:171; 19:88). Jesus is always referred to as "Jesus, son of Mary" and never "Son of God." Islam considers it perverse that God would have a human son (Surah 10:68). Islam denies the crucifixion and resurrection of Christ (Surah 41:147–148); they believe it was an imposter who was crucified in His stead (Surah 4:157). It is impossible to reconcile these diversions from the Bible. Islam and Christianity are contradictory on key doctrines and thus incompatible; as a result, they cannot both be true.

- ISA 7:14 ~ God Himself will provide the sign: A virgin shall conceive and bear a son. His name will be called "God with us."
- LUK 1:34–35 ~ Mary said to the angel, "How can I bear a son when I've never been with a man?" The angel said, "The Holy Spirit will come upon you. Therefore, your child will be called the Son of God."

In the Koran, Jesus is a created being like Adam (Surah 3:59). Jesus is considered a mere mortal, being regarded as a prophet such as Moses, or an apostle such as Mohammed (Surah 4:177; 5:75). However, Mohammed proclaims himself to be "The Apostle" and more important than Jesus Christ. Mohammed exalts himself above other prophets and above all people (Surah 24:63). We know that Christ, although He was God, humbled Himself by taking on the nature of a man. In contrast, Mohammed, a mere man, exalted himself above Christ. This is what Lucifer did and it got him kicked out of heaven.

- EZE 28:14–19 ~ You were the anointed cherub; you lived upon the holy mountain of God. You were perfect from the day you were created until evil was found in you. Your great wealth made you violent inside and you became sinful. Therefore, you were thrown off the holy mountain, and you will be destroyed. You exalted yourself because of your beauty, thereby corrupting yourself. You defiled the sanctuaries with your abominations. Therefore, you will be destroyed by the fire within you; your terrible deeds will come to an end.
- JOH 14:6,9–11 ~ Jesus said, "I am the way, the truth, and the life; nobody comes to the Father but by me. If you have seen me, you have seen the Father, because the Father lives in me and I in Him."
- PHP 2:3–8 ~ Don't do anything through strife or vanity; instead, be humble and regard others as better than yourselves. Don't focus on yourself, focus on others just like Christ did, who although He was equal with God, He took on the form of a man. Instead of exalting Himself, He became the servant of all. He humbled Himself before others and was obedient unto death, even death on a cross.

CHAPTER SIX

While the Bible is accepted as a prophetic work, the Moslems believe the Koran is the final word of God that corrects previous versions or testaments. The Koran claims divine inspiration; it supposedly describes the true religion of Abraham, Ishmael, Isaac, Jacob, and the twelve tribes associated with Ishmael (not Israel). To a Moslem, the Koran confirms and supersedes the Bible; that is, the Torah and the Gospel were replaced by the Koran. However, they are mistaken, because there are no additional testaments and there are no additional covenants. The New Covenant was established to last for all time and for all people.

- PRO 30:5–6 ~ Every word of God is true; don't attempt to add to God's words or He will rebuke you and you will be proven false.
- HEB 9:15; HEB 10:12,14 ~ For this reason, Christ has become the mediator of the New Testament. By His death, we are redeemed from the sins committed under the first (Old) Testament, so that those who are called might receive the promise of God's eternal inheritance. But this man, after He had offered a sacrifice for sins that would last forever, sat down at the right hand of God. By that one offering He has perfected forever those who are sanctified.

Moslems believe that Mohammed came to resolve the apparent disagreements on doctrine between and among Jews and Christians. Those divisions rendered previous religions obsolete. Initially, it was the desire of Arabs to be included with Jews and Christians as chosen by God, but later excluded others from membership in the kingdom of heaven. Islam is regarded as the only true faith and all other religions are believed to be false; that is, Jews and Christians are lost because they broke God's covenant, so Moslems say they are the chosen ones. Mohammed's divine mission was to unify the Arabs, who were the "true believers." However, Moslems are actually unbelievers since they do not believe in and follow Christ.

- JOH 3:17–21 ~ Jesus said, "Those who believe in God's Son are not condemned, but those who do not believe are condemned already. God sent His light into the world, but people loved the darkness rather than the light because they were evil. Everyone who follows evil hates the light, so they avoid the light because it will uncover their evil deeds. Everyone who follows the truth will come to the light, and the light will show that their ways are godly."
- JOH 8:44 ~ Jesus told the unbelievers, "You evil people belong to your father the devil, and the evil of your father is what you do. He was a murderer and a liar from the start. He never tells the truth; in fact, he is the father of lies."
- 2 TH 2:9–11 ~ Those false signs and fake miracles come from Satan. Such deceptions belong to the self-righteous who will die, for they didn't believe the truth that could save them. God will let them believe their lies and perish.

In the Koran, heaven is described as an oasis of fulfilled desires, and hell is a place of perpetual torment. On the surface this does not seem problematic, until one understands their definition of "desires." Moslems believe that paradise is a place where one is adorned with jewels and dressed in fine robes, where people lounge around on luxurious couches, drink wine continuously without getting drunk, and enjoy constant service from voluptuous virgins created exclusively for man's enjoyment (Surah 52:14–20; 55:52–68; 56:7–48; 83:22–25). This is clearly a vision of a sinful man's utopia. Interestingly, the things that are prohibited to Moslems on earth are what they expect to receive in heaven. That is, it is okay to sin in the paradise of Islam.

- ISA 64:4 ~ Since the world began, nobody has heard, seen, or perceived, except God, the wonderful things He has prepared for those who wait for Him.
- 1CO 14:1 ~ Follow the way of love and eagerly desire spiritual gifts, especially the gift of prophecy.

- EPH 2:2–4 ~ In the past you walked according to the ways of the world, along with the prince of the power of the air, the spirit that works in those who are disobedient to God. We too engaged in the lusts of the flesh, fulfilling the desires of our bodies and minds. Though we were dead in our sins, God in His infinite mercy and love has made us alive in Christ, and by His grace we are saved.
- 1 PE 2:2 ~ Like newborn babies your desire should be for spiritual milk, so that you can grow up in your salvation knowing that the Lord is good.
- 1 JO 2:15–16 ~ Do not love the world or worldly things. If a person loves the world, he or she cannot love God. All that is in the world, the lust of the flesh, the greed of the eyes, and the pride of humanity, do not come from the Father but are of this world.

Clearly, the depiction of heaven in the Koran is subordinate to women. In fact, the Koran renders women second-class citizens. Women must be supportive and subservient to men; this is why woman was created in the first place. Men can have up to four wives if they can support them, although Mohammed had nine (none of which bore him any sons that survived). Marriages are often arranged, but the woman can give her consent, unless she is a slave. Men can have sex with wives and slaves. Husbands can divorce their wives at will (Surah 2:227–230). Sons inherit two times that of daughters. Husbands inherit all the wife's estate but the wife can inherit only a quarter of the husband's estate. It is disturbing the treatment of women in the Koran; they clearly are not allowed the rights and benefits of men (Surah 2:187; 4:10–12; 4:129–130; 16:72; 33:57).

- GAL 3:28 ~ There is no such thing as Jew or Greek, slave or free, male or female, for we all are equal in Jesus Christ.
- HEB 2:10–11 ~ Through His suffering, many people are saved to become glorified with Him as children of God. Both He that sanctifies and those who are sanctified are one; therefore, Christ is not ashamed to call them His brothers and sisters.

It is very unusual how the Koran is presented. The text is written in the first-person plural. Although the Koran is supposed to be the words of Gabriel, the collective "we" is used, so Gabriel is presumably speaking for God and the angels. Examples include, "We created the heavens and the earth, we gave the light to the day and darkness to the night, we created man, we created you, we exalted some above others, we raised an apostle in every nation, we inspired them with revelations, we revealed the Koran to humankind, we made a covenant with the righteous, we will resurrect the dead" (Surah 2:87–93; 6:154–156; 7:11; 9:70; 15:19–31; 23:6; 33:7; 36:9–12; 50:16; 50:38)." The problem is this: who are "we" in these passages?

The feats listed above could be performed only by God. If the Moslems claim one God and reject the Trinity, why use the collective in ascribing His mighty deeds? It is disturbing the way the Koran presents acts of God as being performed by angels or by more than one god or deity. This suggests that the vision came from Satan not Gabriel, since Gabriel never used the collective term "we" but ascribed all power and authority to God. It would be typical of Satan to portray himself as somehow jointly responsible for God's creations; further, one might expect the jinn to respond in the collective. When creating people, God described this unique event using the plural form "we" which in Hebrew is *Elohim* (namely: Father, Son, and Holy Spirit). This illustrates how humans were created in God's image, not vice-versa (GEN 1:26). For example, like God we have a physical, mental, and spiritual component; but unlike God, these components are separable in humans (MAT 10:28). It is curious how the Koran employs the collective; for they believe Allah to be one entity and they reject the notion outright that God can be three persons (Surah 5:72–73). Further, they believe incorrectly that the Christian concept of the three persons of the trinity includes Mary the mother of Jesus (Surah 5:116).

- 1 CH 29:11 ~ To you Lord belongs all greatness, power, glory, victory, and majesty. Everything in heaven and earth is yours, including the everlasting kingdom. You are exalted as head above all creatures.
- PSA 104:4 ~ God makes angels' spirits.
- COL 1:16–17 ~ He created all things on heaven and earth, visible and invisible. He is before all things, and holds all things together.

One of the most troubling quotes appearing many times throughout the Koran is as follows: When we said to the angels to bow before Adam, all did except Satan (Surah 2:34; 17:61; 18:50; 20:115; 38:70–73; 52:14–20). Was Satan condemned for not worshipping man? How ridiculous this is! God does not command, nor does he allow anyone to worship another than Himself. In the Koran, Adam was seemingly exalted when the angels supposedly prostrated themselves before him. Satan is portrayed as the bad guy because he did not worship God's human creation. This concept is entirely unscriptural and blasphemous.

- EXO 20:4–7 ~ Don't make graven images or idols resembling animals. Never bow before an idol or image or worship it in any way, for God is a jealous God and will not tolerate false gods. Never use the name of God in vain or swear a falsehood, or you will be severely punished. Anyone who worships another god (or anything else for that matter) will be punished, and that punishment will continue for generations.
- JOB 31:26–28 ~ If my heart was enticed by worldly things and celestial bodies, or if I was infatuated with myself, I would be guilty of denying God, and worthy of His punishment.
- MAT 4:10 ~ Jesus said, "Go away, Satan! For it is written: Worship the Lord your God and serve Him only." (DEU 6:13)
- COL 2:18 ~ Never worship angels.

While the Koran preaches repentance and faith, it also preaches that good deeds can make amends for sin (Surah 11:114), and will reap a rich reward in heaven (Surah 17:9). Moslems believe that heaven is for those whose good deeds outnumber the bad. The Koran asserts that one must not allow hatred to lead them into sin or away from justice (Surah 5:2, 8–9), and that those who refrain from retaliation, will by their restraint, atone for themselves (Surah 5:45–46). In other words, good deeds are as much if not more important in Islam than faith, insofar as one can save themselves and do not need a personal savior.

Many would argue that Islam is a religion of peace. The Koran advocates making peace with those who are inclined toward peace (Surah 8:60–62). However, Moslems are prohibited from making friends with unbelievers. Despite these precepts militant extremists will practice and encourage terrorism against infidels. Aside from the fact that Gabriel proclaimed to Mohammed that Moslems will be the ones to put terror into the hearts of unbelievers (Surah 3:149–150), it is declared to be the mission of God and His angels to eradicate evildoers.

On the one hand, the Koran seems to advocate aggression if the infidels don't keep their distance. When foreigners refuse to stop their hostilities against the Moslems, they are warranted in their resolve to kill their enemies wherever they may be found (Surah 4:90–91), as long as their enemies attack first (Surah 2:190). It is acceptable for Moslems to make war on the infidels that dwell among them (Surah 9:122–123), and to drive them away from areas Moslems were driven out before (Surah 2:191) such as Palestine. This would appear to be a doctrine of restraint, with violence and aggression executed only in retaliation to the same.

Elsewhere in the Koran, there seems to be encouragement to fight against "friends of the devil," to be prepared to give one's life for Islam, and to expect a great reward for doing so (Surah 4:73–76). Indeed, Moslems are directed to make war on unbelievers (until all idolatry ceases), to rouse the faithful to arms, and to strike terror into the enemies of God (Surah 8:39–65). Followers of Mohammed are supposed to be ruthless to unbelievers but merciful to each other (Surah 48:29). Moslems are to slay the idolaters wherever they are found, to arrest, besiege, and ambush them (Surah 9:4). They are to fight for the cause with their wealth and their persons, because not to fight is to invite punishment from God (Surah 9:39–41).

There are conflicting messages in the Koran about this issue, one advocating restraint and the other, aggression. It is no surprise that some Moslems take these passages literally, waging a jihad or holy war on Jews and Christians, while others are content to live peacefully with them. However, the real fight of faith is not between races or religions, it is between good and evil.

- MAT 26:52 ~ Jesus said, "Put away your sword, for those that take up the sword will die by the sword."
- LUK 6:32,35 ~ Jesus said, "If you love only those who love you, what reward will you receive? Even sinners love those who love them. So love everyone, even your enemies. Help others whenever you can, expecting nothing in return, and your reward will be great, and you will become a child of God."
- 2 CO 10:3–5 ~ Although we are human flesh and blood, we do not make war with flesh and blood. For the weapons we use are not of this world, because we have the Spirit on our side to bring down the strongholds of the enemy. We break down the arguments and the influences of those high and mighty people who stand against God; we take captive human thoughts, making them obedient to Jesus Christ.

In addition to neglecting certain laws, Moslems have created their own. For example, a number of behaviors that are against God's Law are permitted under Islamic law to include divorce, slavery, and violence. Further, to a Moslem, it is reprehensible to kill a fellow believer (Surah 4:92–93), but it is permissible to murder an unbeliever. However, clashes between the Shia and Sunni have claimed more lives than the slaughter of so-called infidels, so this law has been violated in a big way.

The Bible lists only one unpardonable sin: blasphemy against the Holy Spirit. This is the very sin that calls God a liar, attempts to turn His Word into lies, and/or advances a lie in the place of the truth given us by God's Holy Spirit. Anyone going to their grave disbelieving God and His Son Jesus Christ will not be going to heaven.

- MAT 12:31 ~ Jesus said, "All manner of sin and blasphemy can be forgiven, except blasphemy directed against the Holy Spirit."
- REV 21:8 ~ The fearful, the unbelieving, the murderers, prostitutes, sorcerers, idolaters, and liars will take part in the lake of fire which is the second death.

Another law that was changed by the Koran regards the giving of tithes, which was reduced from 10 percent to a mandatory tax of 2.5 percent. This percentage of one's income is to be set aside as alms for the poor and needy. It seems a rather small amount given that tithes and offerings should equal or exceed one tenth of one's increase.

- MAL 3:6–8 ~ God says, "I am the Lord, I never change. But you have not kept my commandments. Return to me and I will return to you. Will you rob God? Yet you have robbed me. You ask how you have robbed me? You have robbed me by not presenting your tithes and offerings."
- 2 CO 9:7 ~ Everyone should give whatever they think is fair in their heart. Giving should be done voluntarily, not out of obligation, for God loves a cheerful giver.

In order to trick the reader into thinking that the Koran is the essential word of God, a number of double-bind statements are presented. For example, the following passage is repeated many times (Surah 6:21; 7:36–37): Who is guilty of the greater evil, the one who makes up a lie about God, or the one who denies His revelations (are both sins not equally deadly)? This statement is made to counter the prominent argument that Mohammed's Koran is a compilation of "invented tales." The impetus of error is diverted towards the skeptics, or as the Koran puts it, "only unbelievers dispute the revelations." Thus, readers are compelled to think they could be worse off by disbelieving Mohammed than those who invent false doctrine (such as Mohammed). The logic in the above statement is warped and ambiguous. Is it a greater sin to tell a lie or to believe a lie? Both will lead to death if it represents a denial of the truth. Such passages can be found continuously throughout the Koran, probably because the reader needs constant persuasion to believe something that is categorically untrue.

The difficulty is that one can hardly distinguish a false vision from a revelation without corroboration; unfortunately, there is none for the Koran or for Mohammed. As for the Holy Bible, corroboration exists internally and externally. For example, John's Revelation is consistent with visions of Ezekiel and Daniel, thereby providing internal consistency. Old Testament prophecy is corroborated in New Testament fulfillment, thereby promoting validity. The life, death, and resurrection of Jesus Christ are substantiated by numerous eyewitnesses. Historical and archaeological evidence provide additional, external support for the Bible. However, there are no prophets, eyewitnesses, or historical accounts that corroborate the words, teachings, and visions of Mohammed, neither is the Koran compatible with the Holy Bible or any other work of antiquity.

Islam is very ritualistic, with many idolatrous undertones. One of the goals of any Muslim is the Hajj, which is a pilgrimage to Mecca. Moslems are supposed make the pilgrimage at least once in their lifetime if at all possible. Upon arriving in Mecca, they dress in white robes and get their heads shaven. Then they encircle the shrine and kiss the sacred black stone. This is followed by a ceremonial jog (commemorating when Hagar searched for water). On the eighth day they listen to teachings in the Great Mosque, then head to the towns of Mira and next Arafat to hear more teaching. They spend the night outside, and the next morning they throw seven stones on the big heap to symbolize rejection of Satan. Finally, they sacrifice a goat or a sheep, shave their heads again and return to Mecca, where they bathe in the holy well before leaving. Moslems observe Ramadan, a holy month of daylight fasting and prayer. Moslems chant the Salat, a prescribed prayer, five times each day as they engage in Raka, a cycle of ritual movements during prayer (stand, bow, kneel, touch forehead to ground). Although such ritual behaviors seem harmless, they represent traditions established by men, not by God.

- MAR 7:6–9,13 ~ Jesus said, "Isaiah prophesied about you hypocrites (ISA 29:13). For you put aside the commandments of God and follow the traditions of men. By following your own traditions, you show a disregard for the Word of God." (also MAT 15:8–9)
- JOH 4:24 ~ Jesus said, "God is Spirit and should be worshipped in spirit and in truth."
- COL 2:8,20 ~ Beware, that you are not spoiled by errant philosophy and vain deceptions, originating from worldly traditions and principles, and not from Christ. You are in Christ and not of this world, so why submit to its rules?
- 2 TH 2:15 ~ Fellow Christians, stand fast in your faith and hold onto those traditions that you have been taught in God's Word, through the prophets and apostles.

Islam incorporates many biblical principles, events, and ideas. Other teachings of Islam are downright incongruous with the Holy Bible. Thus, Islam is founded on deceit and follows false doctrine that will lead its followers away from the truth, far from Christ, and straight to hell.

Lesson: The Rise of Satanism

Satanism is the worship of the devil, wherein evil is viewed as good and vice-versa. Satanists enjoy sinning, although they pretend to be good and upright citizens. Satanism is an invitation to demon possession.

Lucifer (Satan) was an angel of God before he became sinful and was thrown out of heaven. He is the evil one who tempts people to sin and to join him in opposing God. He deceives people into believing false promises and false doctrine.

- JOH 8:44 ~ Jesus said to the unbelievers, "You belong to your father the devil, and the evil of your father you will do. He was a murderer and a liar from the start. He never tells the truth. In fact, he is the father of lies."
- 2 CO 11:14 ~ Don't be tricked by Satan who disguises himself as an angel of light.
- 2 TH 2:3–4,8–9,11–12 ~ Beware of false prophets who will try to deceive you, because people will fall away from God before the evil one, the son of Satan (literally, son of perdition or hell), is revealed. He is the one who opposes God and exalts himself, pretending to be God. The evil one will be consumed by the Spirit of God, and will be destroyed by the brightness of His coming. The evil son of Satan is the one who is possessed by Satan himself, and performs magic tricks and false miracles. He will deceive many people with his delusions and lies. All who follow him and find pleasure in unrighteousness will be damned.
- REV 13:4,18 ~ They worshipped the dragon who gave power to the beast (son of Satan); and they worshipped the beast, saying, "Who is like the beast, and who is able to defeat him?" Here is wisdom for those who can understand: Count the number of the beast, for it is the number of a man, and the number is 666.
- REV 20:10 ~ The devil, the beast, and the false prophet (Satan's unholy trinity) will inherit the lake of fire.

Satanists think they can obtain worldly powers or possessions from Satan; this is a major deception used by Satan. Everything in the universe belongs to God, including you and I; Satan cannot make good on promises to give you something that you have the power to obtain yourself by trusting in God. Further, Satan tricks people into thinking they can live forever whether they obey God or not. People are willing to sell out their souls to obtain things assured them by Satan. However, these people have yet to realize that they don't need Satan to achieve their dreams and goals; quite the contrary, Satan will be an obstacle in achieving anything worthwhile or godly.

- ECC 8:8 ~ The power of evil does not include the ability to deliver anyone from death or condemnation.
- ISA 28:18 ~ All agreements made with Satan will be null and void.
- EPH 2:2 ~ In the past, you walked according to the course of this world, according to the prince of the power of the air, the same spirit that works in the children of disobedience.
- EPH 6:12 ~ We wrestle, not against flesh and blood, but against principalities, powers, rulers of darkness in this world, and spiritual wickedness in high places.

<u>History of Satanism</u>. Satanism has its roots in some of the earliest recorded history in the Bible. A number of evil generations have emerged and re-emerged periodically. For example, in Noah's time, the entire world was wicked except Noah. Sometimes entire civilizations have been apostate or engaged in occultist behavior, lewdness, and idolatry. The Moabites and Ammonites, descendants of Lot's incestuous affairs with his daughters, and the Edomites, descendants of Jacob's brother Esau, were such a people. Their evil practices were passed down from generation to generation. Satanists are often practicing the evil of their ancestors.

- NUM 21:29 ~ Woe to Moab who gives their sons and daughters to captivity.
- NUM 25:1 ~ The people committed fornication with the daughters of Moab (also ISA 16:2–6).
- NEH 13:25 ~ Don't give your sons or daughters to the children of Ammon.
- JER 49:17–18 ~ Edom shall become desolate. They hiss at their plagues. They will be overthrown like Sodom and Gomorrah.
- LAM 4:21–22 ~ The Edomites are drunken and naked; God knows of the sins of Edom.
- JOE 3:19 ~ Edom is desolation because of their violations against the children of Judah, for they shed innocent blood.
- AMO 1—2 ~ For three sins, and a fourth, the following nations will be punished: Moab, Ammon, Edom, Philistia, Syria, Gaza, Tyre, Judah, Israel.
- AMO 3—4 ~ They will be punished forever.
- ZEP 2:8–9 ~ I (God) have heard the insults, taunts, and threats against my people by the Moabites and Ammonites. Therefore, as I surely live, Moab will become like Sodom, and Ammon will become like Gomorrah, a wasteland of salt and weeds...

Jesus warned of a particularly evil generation that would come during the latter days (MAT 24; MAR 13; LUK 21). These latter days will be the vilest of all times, even more than Sodom and Gomorrah. The times will get progressively worse towards the end (2 TI 3:1). The most heinous of crimes will be committed and condoned. A period of great tribulation will occur because of this evil generation. It is the time of sorrows (i.e., Jacob's trouble: JER 30:7).

- MAT 12:43,45 ~ Jesus said, "When an evil spirit leaves a person, it roams the land looking for rest but finding none. Then it finds seven other evil spirits that are even worse and returns to the person, leaving the possessed person in worse shape than before. This is the way it will be for the wicked generation to come."
- MAT 24:5–34; MAR 13:30; LUK 21:32 ~ Jesus said, "Many shall come in my name, claiming to be me, and deceiving people. There will be wars, famines, pestilence, and earthquakes. These are only the beginning of sorrows. They will capture you, torture you, and kill you; you will be hated for being a Christian. People will offend, betray, and despise each other. When you see the abomination of desolation stand in the holy place, as prophesied by Daniel, escape into the mountains. There will be great tribulation, worse than ever before or ever again. Then a sign in heaven will appear; the entire earth will be in mourning when the Son of God returns in a cloud, with all His power and glory. This generation will not pass away until all these things have happened."
- LUK 16:8–10,13 ~ Jesus summarized His parable saying, "The rich man commended the dishonest steward's shrewd tactics. He thought it was wise how the steward made friends with the greed of unrighteousness. He had planned ahead, doubting his job security, ensuring he would have some means of external support. Such a conniving nature will be considered wisdom to this evil generation. In fact, the evil children in that generation will be wiser than the children of light. The moral is this: Those who are faithful in a little will be faithful in a lot, and those who are dishonest in a little will be dishonest in a lot. Nobody can serve two masters; they will be loyal to only one, honoring the one and despising the other. You can't serve God and money."

In the latter days a new Babylon will emerge. The new Babylon will be represented by a world power that becomes a major source of evil and corruption in the world. Eventually, Babylon will fall and evil will be destroyed.

- ISA 13:1,9–10,19 ~ The day comes when the Lord's wrath and anger will result in the desolation of Babylon and the destruction of the sinners there. The glory of Babylon will be like Sodom and Gomorrah when God destroyed those cities.
- JER 50:13,23–24,28,46 ~ Babylon will be destroyed; everyone who goes there will be astonished at the plagues and destruction. Babylon will become a desolation. They were unaware that God would catch them and punish them for continuing to sin. They will flee from Babylon when the vengeance of the Lord is declared in Zion. The earth will be shaken, for the cry of Babylon's fall will be heard around the world.
- JER 51:6,29,35,49,64 ~ Get out of Babylon and save your soul, don't get caught in her sin, for the Lord comes to pay them back for their sins. The land will tremble and mourn when God comes, making the land desolate and eliminating its inhabitants. Their violence to innocent people will be upon their heads. As Babylon has killed the people of Israel, so shall everyone in Babylon be killed.
- REV 14:8 ~ The angel said, "The great city of Babylon has fallen because she caused all nations to drink the wine of the wrath of her fornication."
- REV 17:5,9,18 ~ On her head was written: Mystery, Babylon the great, the mother of prostitutes and all earthly abominations. This is the great city that sits on seven mountains and over many waters, nations, and peoples.
- REV 18:2,10 ~ The angel cried, "Babylon has become the habitation of devils and every foul spirit. That mighty city will receive judgment in one hour."

Additional information is provided on the pages that follow characterizing Satanism and those who engage in Satanic practices, describing how people gradually become indoctrinated by playing in the devil's den. While participation in one or more of the behaviors outlined below does not necessarily make someone a Satanist, it does make them vulnerable to greater temptations and wickedness. It is important for parents to detect the warning signs in their children and prevent them from becoming corrupted. It is recommended that everyone, adults and children alike, refrain from any behavior that can be considered occultist or anti-Christian.

Satanic Symbols

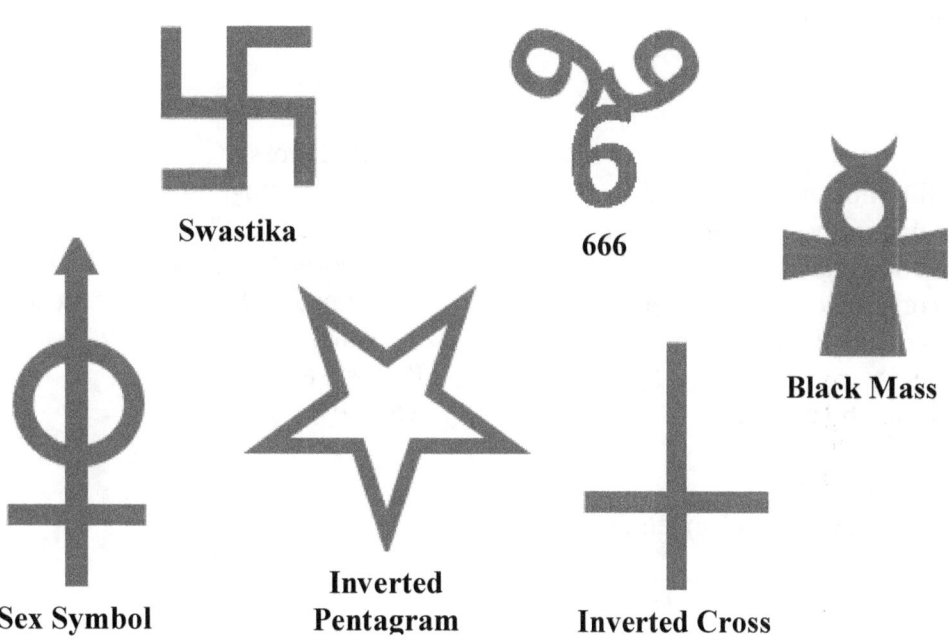

The Underworld of Satanism

<u>Why is Satanism so popular?</u>
Exaggerations of liberalism
Media hype and agenda setting
Immorality (e.g., Hollywood)
Evil and vain imaginations
Infatuation with the supernatural
Popularity of parapsychology
Interest in eastern philosophies
Desire to dabble in the occult
Breakdown in criminal justice
Breakdown in educational system
Breakdown in the family
Mind altering substances

<u>Vulnerability of its victims</u>
Short-sighted thinking
Irresponsibility
Sensation and risk seeking
Desire for gratification and kicks
Self-indulgence and self-promotion
Ego boost
Sexual expression
Need to belong and peer pressure
Darkness obscures the truth

<u>Enticement</u>
Power and fame
Riches and material goods
Pleasure and fun

<u>Indoctrination and entrapment</u>
Deceit, flirtatiousness, and trickery
Hypnotizing, trances, brainwashing
Victimization and fear
Forced compliance and participation
Traumatizing and punishment
Threats and terrorism
Extortion and blackmail
Revenge
No escape mentality
Demon possession and channeling

<u>Target population</u>
Children (own offspring; innocents)
Women (single and with children)
People (naive and vulnerable)
Social (church, school, government)
Authorities (at all levels)
World (all nations)

<u>Common crimes</u>
Trespassing and vandalism
Grave desecration
Pornography (especially child)
Prostitution (especially child)
Animal cruelty and sacrifice
Sexual abuse (children; offspring)
Ritual abuse (anyone; offspring)
Kidnapping
Rape
Slavery (missing persons; children)
Torment and torture
Sadism (chains and whips; cages)
Murder
Suicide
Human sacrifice (babies)
Breeding (confiscate babies)
Drug trafficking

<u>Symbols</u>
666
Inverted cross
Inverted pentagram
Goat (as opposed to sheep)
Goat horns (hand signal with horns)
Combined male/female medical sign
Swastika
Runes (secret writing)
Third eye

Props
Tattoos and body piercing
Exotic hair styles and colors
Black robe, hood, and/or cape
Book of death (signed in blood)
Candles
Fire
Arena (pentagram configuration)
Altar with nude woman
Elixir (e.g., blood, body parts, etc.)
Coffin (often complete with corpse)
Drugs and alcohol
Music (especially heavy metal)

Black mass
Secrecy and security (to the extreme)
Coven (usually thirteen members)
High priest; six priests, priestesses
Sex (homosexuality, sodomy, rape)
Defilement (especially the Bible)
Service (often backwards)
Hazing (excrement, urine; torture)
Necrophilia (including sex)
Pedophilia (missing children)
Black magic and witchcraft
Voodoo and Santeria
Magic spells and potions
Seance (calling the dead)
Demonology (calling demons)
Channeling (demon possession)

Warning signals
Satanic music*
Occultist behavior**
Drug abuse
Disobedience and defiance
New, strange friends
New, strange fixations and interests
Gang membership
Pain, headaches, stomachaches, etc.
Sores, bruises, rashes, etc.
Venereal disease and/or genital pain
Disorders in sleeping, eating, etc.
Nightmares and night terrors
Lies and denial
Amnesia and dissociation
Argumentativeness
Hatefulness
Violence and viciousness
Withdrawal and isolation
Low esteem
Promiscuity
Lack of emotion
Panic and paranoia
Fear and torment
Obsessive-compulsive behavior
Manic-depressive behavior
Self-abusive or destructive behavior
Suicidal tendencies
Multiple personality disorder
Internet addiction (sites promote sin)
Black clothes, makeup, etc.

* Music
— Musicians often promote evil (evidence of Satanism found on album covers and in lyrics)
— Music Television often promotes evil (evidence found in video and audio messages)
— Entertainers that promote evil (evidence found in mannerisms, appearance, speech, behavior)

** First steps into the occult
— Infatuation with horror movies and/or violent or evil videos and games
— Ouija board
— Tarot cards, crystal balls, etc.
— Practicing or studying divination, witchcraft, and sorcery
— Participation in seances, black magic, and/or demonology
— Avid interest in dungeons-and-dragons role, or any of the ultimate "I dare you" games

GOOD VERSUS EVIL

Goodness is the antonym of wickedness. If you sow goodness you will reap good things; if you sow evil you will reap bad things. Thus, the consequences of being a good person versus being an evil person are also opposite. Those who are faithful to God, trust in Jesus Christ for their salvation, and lead a godly life will live forever in heaven enjoying peace, joy, clarity, and honor. Those who despise God, foster wickedness, or allow evil to pollute their souls will be tormented forever in hell. Not only is selecting goodness smarter than selecting wickedness, it is also more powerful, and the rewards are magnitudes better.

- PSA 45:7 ~ If you love righteousness and hate wickedness God will shower His joy upon you, and elevate you above others.
- AMO 5:14–15 ~ Seek that which is good and avoid evil, so that you can live with the Lord. Hate evil and love goodness; maintain justice in your courts, and maybe God will have mercy on you.
- ROM 12:17,21 ~ Do not repay evil for evil, but be honest in everything. Don't let evil overcome you, but overcome evil with goodness.

Darkness of Evil versus Light of Righteousness

The opposing forces of light and darkness provide a good analogy for the opposing forces of good and evil. Light can consume darkness, but darkness cannot consume light. In fact, even the smallest flicker of candlelight will break the deepest darkness. Christ is the light of the world, showing the way to God and heaven. His light illuminates the path to God and to righteousness. Satan is the prince of darkness; his way leads only to death and hell. Follow Satan and you will lose your bearings, and possibly never find your way back to the path God has laid out for you.

- GEN 1:2–5 ~ Darkness covered the earth and God commanded there to be light, and He saw that the light was good, and He separated the light from the darkness.
- PSA 119:105 ~ God's Word is a lamp unto my feet, and a light unto my path.
- ISA 5:20 ~ Woe to those who call evil good and good evil, who put darkness for light and light for darkness, who put bitter for sweet and sweet for bitter.
- ISA 60:1–2 ~ Arise and shine, for your light has come; yes, the glory of God has come to you. Darkness covers the earth and great darkness covers its people. But the Lord will arise and come to you, and you will see His glory. And the Gentiles will come to His light, and kings will come to the brightness of His rising.
- MAT 2:9 ~ The wise men departed after visiting King Herod. And the star that they had followed all the way from the east shone before them, pointing the way to Bethlehem. Finally, they stood directly under the star. There they found the young Christ child. When they saw the child, they rejoiced with great joy.
- MAT 6:22–23; LUK 11:34 ~ Jesus said, "The eye is the lamp of the body. If your eye is sound, your whole body will be full of light. If your eye is not sound, your whole body will be full of darkness. So, if the light in you is darkness, how great is that darkness."
- LUK 1:79 ~ The baby Jesus was born to give light to those who sit in darkness and in the shadow of death, and to guide their feet into the way of peace.
- LUK 11:35–36 ~ Be careful, so that the light in you does not become darkness. If your whole body is full of light and has no darkness, it will be wholly bright as when a lamp with its rays gives light.

- JOH 1:7–9 ~ John came to be a witness of the light so that others might believe in Christ. This was the true light that brings light to everyone born in this world.
- JOH 3:19 ~ The light came into the world, but men loved darkness rather than light, because their deeds were evil.
- JOH 8:12 ~ Jesus said, "I am the light of the world; those who follow me will not walk in darkness, but will have the light of life."
- JOH 12:35 ~ Jesus said, "The light will be with you a little longer. Walk while you have the light, before the darkness overtakes you; those who walk in darkness do not know where they are going."
- ROM 13:12 ~ The night is gone and the day is at hand. Let us cast away the works of darkness and put on the armor of light.
- 1 CO 4:5 ~ Judge nothing before the Lord returns, for He will bring to light all that is hidden in darkness, and will reveal the motivations of the heart. Then everyone will praise God.
- 2 CO 4:6 ~ God commanded light to shine out of darkness. This same light shines in our hearts and radiates that light through knowledge of Jesus Christ.
- 2 CO 6:14 ~ Do not be joined with unbelievers, for what fellowship can there be between righteousness and unrighteousness? What communion can there be between light and darkness?
- EPH 5:8–14 ~ You were once in darkness, but now you are in the light of the Lord. Live as children of light and discover what pleases the Lord, for the fruit of the light consists of goodness, righteousness, and truth. Have nothing to do with the fruitless deeds of darkness, but rather expose them. For it is shameful to even mention what the disobedient do in secret. But everything exposed by the light becomes visible for all to see, for it is light that makes things visible. This is what is meant by the saying, "Wake up you sleepers; rise from the dead and Christ will shine on you."
- EPH 6:12 ~ We are not contending against flesh and blood, but against principalities, powers, rulers of darkness, and spiritual wickedness in high places.
- 1 PE 2:9 ~ You are a unique, chosen generation, a priesthood and holy nation, because you praise Him who called you from darkness into His marvelous light.
- 2 PE 2:4 ~ God did not spare the angels when they sinned, but cast them into hell, and committed them to chains of utter darkness to be kept until the judgment.
- 1 JO 1:5 ~ God is light; in Him is no darkness at all.
- 1 JO 2:10–11 ~ Those who love others abide in the light and will not stumble. Those who hate others abide in darkness and do not know where they are going because the darkness has blinded their eyes.

Fear

Satan's power is in fear and deception; he scares and tricks people so they'll think he is to be feared but he is not. God's power is in love for God is love. If we fear and love God, we need not be afraid of anyone or anything, including Satan. Love destroys fear; the two are contrasting. But there is one exception: if we fear only God, He will love, protect, and save us, leaving us with nothing to fear. If we fear Satan, then Satan will destroy us. What does it mean to fear God? It means to stand in awe of Him, since He is an awesome God, mighty, powerful, and majestic. He will bring judgment and destruction upon the wicked, but will preserve and uphold the righteous. Our righteousness comes from Christ who gave it to us in exchange for our sins. If you have not received this free gift, there is plenty for you to fear, and with fear comes torment.

- GEN 15:1 ~ God told Abraham, "Don't be afraid, because I will be your shield, and I will reward you for your faith."
- GEN 28:12,17 ~ Jacob had a dream about a ladder reaching from earth to heaven, with angels ascending and descending upon it. When he awoke, he was afraid, saying, "How awesome this place is, for this is none other than the very house of God and the gate to heaven."
- EXO 14:13,31 ~ Moses told the people, "Don't be afraid of the Egyptians. Stand and watch, and you will see the salvation of the Lord; for after this day you will never see the Egyptians again." And the people saw what the Lord did to the Egyptians (drowning them in the Red Sea); and the people feared the Lord and believed in God and His servant Moses.
- NUM 14:9 ~ Joshua said, "Don't rebel against God, and don't be afraid of your enemies; for the Lord is with us, so their assaults against us are useless."
- DEU 5:29 ~ God said, "I wish the people had such a heart that they would fear me and keep my commandments always, so they and their children would be well."
- DEU 10:12 ~ God wants people to fear Him, walk in His ways, love Him, and serve Him with all their heart and soul.
- DEU 20:3–4 ~ The Lord is He that goes with you to fight against your enemies, and to save you. So, there is no need to be afraid of your enemies when going into battle.
- DEU 28:9–10,58–59,66 ~ God will establish a holy people unto Himself, just like He promised, as long as you keep His commandments and walk in His ways. And all people on earth will see that you are called by the name of the Lord, and they will be afraid of you. If you don't observe all the words in the Bible and fear God, then He will send plagues and sickness upon you continuously. And your life will hang in doubt, and you will be afraid night and day, having no assurance of your life.
- DEU 31:6 ~ Be strong and courageous, and don't be afraid of anyone. For God will go with you; He will never forsake you.
- JOS 1:9 ~ God said, "Didn't I command you to be strong and have courage, and not to be afraid or dismayed? For I am with you wherever you go."
- JOS 24:14 ~ Fear the Lord and serve Him in sincerity and truth. Put away false gods.
- 1 SA 12:24 ~ Fear only the Lord and serve Him in truth with all your heart. Consider the wonderful things He has done for you.
- 2 KI 17:25,35–36,39–41 ~ The people did not fear God so God sent lions among them. God said, "Don't fear other gods, or bow before them, or serve them, or sacrifice to them. But fear God who brought you safely out of Egypt; worship Him only and sacrifice to Him. If you fear the Lord your God, He will deliver you from your enemies." But they continued to serve their idols from generation to generation.
- 1 CH 16:25 ~ Great is the Lord; He is greatly to be praised. He is to be feared above all gods.
- 1 CH 29:11 ~ To you, Lord, is greatness, power, and glory, the victory and the majesty. For all that is in heaven and earth belongs to you, including the kingdom. Lord, you are exalted as the head over all that exists.
- NEH 9:32–33 ~ Our God is great and mighty, an awesome God who keeps His covenant of mercy. Do not think that our problems are trivial, those hardships that have come upon our nation since the Assyrians ruled. God has been fair in punishing us this way, for we have been wicked.
- JOB 4:6 ~ Isn't the fear of God your confidence, hope, and righteousness?
- JOB 5:21–22 ~ You will be hidden from the scourge of the tongue; you will not be afraid of destruction when it comes. You will laugh at destruction and famine; you will not be afraid of the beasts on earth. You will be at peace.

- JOB 13:11 ~ Doesn't His excellency make you afraid?
- JOB 26:6–11,14 ~ Hell is naked before Him and destruction is left uncovered. He stretches the sky over the emptiness and suspends the earth on nothing. He brings water into clouds yet they do not burst under the weight. He divides the limitless heavens from the earth, the waters from the land, and the light from the darkness. Heaven and earth tremble at astonishment. These are but a small fraction of His mighty works. We hear only a whisper of His works, so who can possibly understand the thunder of His power?
- JOB 28:28 ~ The fear of the Lord is wisdom; to depart from evil is understanding.
- PSA 23:4 ~ Even when I walk through the valley of the shadow of death, I will not be afraid of any evil, for God will be with me to comfort me.
- PSA 27:1,2 ~ The Lord is my light and my salvation. Who should I fear? He is the strength in my life. Of whom shall I be afraid? Even if a whole encampment of my enemies is preparing war against me. I will not be afraid, but confident.
- PSA 31:19 ~ How great is your goodness, Lord, which you have given to those who fear you and trust in you before all others.
- PSA 33:8,18 ~ Let all the earth fear the Lord; let inhabitants stand in awe of Him. The eye of the Lord is upon those who fear Him and hope in His mercy.
- PSA 34:4,9,11 ~ I sought the Lord and He heard me, and delivered me from my fears. So fear the Lord all you saints, and you will never need anything. Come to me, people, and I will teach you about the fear of the Lord.
- PSA 56:3–4 ~ If I am afraid, I will praise God's Word and put my trust in Him. I will not be afraid of what flesh can do to me.
- PSA 103:17 ~ The mercy of the Lord is forever for those who fear Him, as well as for their children.
- PSA 119:120 ~ My flesh trembles with fear at the Lord for I am afraid of His judgments.
- PSA 145:5,19 ~ I will speak of the glory and majesty of the Lord and His wondrous works. God will fulfill the desires of those who fear Him. He will hear their cries and will save them.
- PRO 1:7,33 ~ The fear of the Lord is the beginning of knowledge; but fools despise knowledge and wisdom. Those who seek God will be safe and sound from the fear of evil.
- PRO 3:25 ~ Don't be afraid of sudden fear or of the desolation of the wicked when it comes.
- PRO 8:13 ~ To fear the Lord is to hate evil, pride, conceit, sin, and verbal abuse.
- PRO 10:27 ~ The fear of the Lord will prolong your days; but the years of the wicked will be shortened.
- PRO 13:12 ~ Whoever despises the Word will be destroyed. But whoever fears the commandments will be rewarded.
- PRO 15:32 ~ The fear of God is the instruction of wisdom; and before honor comes humility.
- PRO 19:22 ~ The fear of God gives life; those who have it will be satisfied and will not be visited by evil.
- PRO 22:4 ~ Through humility and the fear of God come riches, honor, and life.
- PRO 29:25 ~ The fear of humanity brings a snare; but those who put their trust in God will be safe.
- ECC 12:12 ~ The conclusion of the whole matter is this: fear God and keep His commandments. This is the entire duty of humankind.
- ISA 8:12–13 ~ Don't join in any conspiracies or alliances with people who are afraid; don't fear the things that they fear; don't be afraid at all. Sanctify the Lord of hosts, and let Him be your fear.
- ISA 33:14 ~ Sinners are afraid; fear surprises the hypocrites. Who among you will live in the devouring fire and burn?

- ISA 35:4 ~ Tell those who are afraid not to fear, because God will come with a vengeance and will save them.
- ISA 41:10 ~ God says, "Fear not, for I am with you. Don't be dismayed, for I am your God. I will strengthen and help you. I will hold you up with the right hand of righteousness."
- ISA 51:7 ~ God says, "Look for me, you who know righteousness and you who hold my laws in your hearts. Don't be afraid of the accusations of others or their verbal abuse."
- MAT 10:28 ~ Jesus said, "Don't be afraid of those who can kill the body but not the soul. Fear only Him who can destroy both your body and soul in hell."
- MAR 7:37 ~ The people were astonished at Jesus, saying, "He has done everything well. He even makes the deaf hear and the dumb speak."
- LUK 4:36 ~ Everyone was amazed at Jesus, saying, "How powerful are His words, for with authority He even commands the unclean spirits and they leave."
- LUK 5:26 ~ Everyone was amazed at Jesus when He cured the man who was stricken with palsy. They were filled with fear, saying, "We have seen strange things today."
- LUK 12:32 ~ Jesus said, "Fear not, little flock, for it is your Father's good pleasure to give to you the kingdom."
- JOH 14:27 ~ Jesus said, "Peace I leave you; my peace I give you. But I don't give like the world gives. Don't let your heart be troubled, neither let your heart be afraid."
- ROM 13:4 ~ If you do what is evil, be afraid, for God's minister will not bear the sword in vain, because he is sent to execute wrath upon those who do evil.
- PHP 1:14 ~ Brothers in Christ are bold enough to speak the Word without fear.
- 2 TI 1:7 ~ God has not given us the spirit of fear, but of power, love, and a sound mind.
- HEB 5:7 ~ When you offer prayers and humble requests to God, He will hear you because you fear Him.
- HEB 12:28–29 ~ Since we will receive a kingdom which cannot fall, let us have grace to willingly serve God with reverence and awe, for He is a consuming fire.
- JAM 2:19 ~ If you believe in one God you are smart. Even the demons believe, and tremble.
- JAM 4:7 ~ Resist the devil and he will flee from you.
- 1 JO 4:18 ~ There is no fear in love, but perfect love casts out fear, because fear has torment. Those who fear are not made perfect in love.
- REV 2:10 ~ Jesus said, "Don't be afraid of any of the things you may suffer. The devil will throw some of you into prison to be tried; you will have tribulation for ten days. Be faithful unto death and I will give you a crown of life."
- REV 15:4 ~ Who will not fear you, Lord, and glorify your name? For only you are holy; all nations will come to worship you, for your judgments are clearly obvious.
- REV 21:8 ~ The fearful, the unbelieving, the murderers, prostitutes, sorcerers, idolaters, and liars will take part in the lake of fire which is the second death.

The Kingdom of Heaven

Heaven is a place of peace and bliss: utopia, paradise, the glory land. Heaven is also referred to as the New Jerusalem and holy Mount Zion. Those who obey God and follow Christ will live forever with Christ in heaven; they will never experience the second death of the unbelievers. All evil will have been eradicated and all suffering will have ceased. There will be no sorrow, terror, torment, anxiety, grief, and sin. Heaven is God's domain, which encompasses everything, everywhere, forevermore. This is where the saints will live, with their own piece of paradise. There will be an eternity of learning, occupation, excitation, celebration, and happiness.

Paradise

- GEN 28:12,16–17 ~ Jacob dreamed about a ladder set on earth and reaching into heaven. He saw angels of God ascending and descending upon it. Jacob awoke and declared, "Surely the Lord abides in this place and I was unaware. How awesome is this place for it is the very house of God and the gate to heaven."
- EXO 24:9–10 ~ Moses, Aaron, and the elders went up to the foot of the mountain, and they saw God; and under His feet it looked like a roadway of transparent sapphire, just like heaven itself.
- KI 8:27 ~ Solomon said, "Will God dwell on earth? Behold, heaven and the highest heaven cannot contain Him."
- 2 KI 2:11 ~ Elijah and Elisha walked and talked; then horses and a chariot of fire separated them, and Elijah went up by a whirlwind into heaven.
- 1 CH 17:11–12 ~ God said to David, "I will raise up one of your descendants and I will establish His kingdom. He will build my house and I will establish His throne forever."
- NEH 9:6 ~ Ezra said, "You alone are God; you made heaven, the highest heaven with all their hosts, and the earth, the seas, and all that lives there. And you preserve it all; and the heavenly hosts worship you."
- PSA 37:9,11 ~ Evil people will be cut off, but those who wait on the Lord will inherit the earth. The meek will inherit the earth and will find joy and peace in abundance.
- PSA 103:19 ~ God has established His throne in the heavens and His kingdom rules over all.
- PSA 115:16 ~ The heavens are the Lord's, but He has given the earth to the sons of men.
- PSA 145:11–12 ~ The saints will speak of the glory of your kingdom, and tell of your power, to make known to everyone your mighty deeds, and the glorious splendor of your kingdom. Your kingdom is everlasting, and your dominion endures throughout all generations.
- ISA 32:17–18 ~ The work of righteousness will be peace; the effect of righteousness will be peacefulness and assurance forever. The righteous will live in quiet, restful, and safe homes.
- ISA 51:11 ~ Those redeemed by the Lord will return singing praises; they will have everlasting joy, and all sorrow and grief will be gone forever.
- ISA 64:4 ~ Since the world began, nobody has heard, seen, or perceived, except God, the wonderful things He has prepared for those who wait for Him.
- EZE 47:1,5,9,12–13,22 ~ Later, God brought me (Ezekiel) again to His house, and I saw waters flowing out from it which formed a river that I could not pass over. Everything that the water touched flourished. On both sides of the river grew all kinds of trees that never died. The trees produced new fruit every month; the fruit of the trees provided food and the leaves provided medicine. God told me that the river was the border of the land promised to the twelve tribes of Israel. The land bordering the river was to be divided as an inheritance for God's chosen people, including the twelve tribes, and all strangers who lived among them.
- DAN 7:18,27 ~ The saints of the Lord will receive the kingdom, and will possess it forever. And the kingdom and the dominion, and the greatness of the kingdoms under heaven, will be given to the saints of the Lord. Their kingdom will be everlasting, and all dominions will serve and obey them.
- MAT 5:12 ~ Rejoice and be glad, for your reward is great in heaven.
- MAT 6:20 ~ Lay up for yourselves treasures in heaven, where they cannot rust, or rot, or be stolen by thieves.
- MAT 13:24–30,37–42 ~ Jesus told a parable about the kingdom of heaven: The kingdom of heaven is like the man who sowed good seed of wheat. While he was sleeping, his competitors threw seeds of weeds in his field. Both the wheat and the weeds grew. His

servants wanted to pull the weeds but the owner said not to, because some of the wheat might be pulled up with the weeds. At harvest time, the wheat and weeds were gathered. The weeds were separated from the wheat and burned, and the wheat was stored in the barn. The Son of Man is the owner who sows the good seed; His enemy is Satan, who sows the bad seed. The servants are the angels, who will gather the offensive things in this world and burn them in the fiery furnace. The wheat are the saints who will live in God's house forever.

- MAT 13:31–32 ~ Jesus told a parable about the kingdom of heaven: The kingdom of heaven is like the mustard seed. It is one of the smallest of seeds yet it grows into one of the largest of trees. Then the birds come and make homes in its branches.
- MAT 13:45–50 ~ Jesus told a parable about the kingdom of heaven: The kingdom of heaven can be compared to a great pearl for which the merchant sold everything he had to purchase it. The kingdom of heaven is like a big net that catches all varieties of fish. The good fish are saved and the bad fish are thrown in the trash. The end of the world will be like this. The angels will gather the fish and separate the righteous from the wicked.
- MAT 18:23–35 ~ Jesus told a parable about the kingdom of heaven: The kingdom of heaven is like a king who called his debtors to pay him. One of them owed a small fortune, so the king ordered that he and his family be sold as slaves to repay the debt. The man fell to the king's feet and begged for more time to pay the debt. The king felt sorry for the man and forgave the debt in its entirety. Later that man accosted another man who owed him some money. The man had him put in jail until he could repay the entire debt. The king found out about this and had the evil man brought to him. The king was irate. He said, "After I forgave your debt you likewise should have shown pity on that other fellow. Since you didn't, I will treat you the same way you treated him." The king had the man put in jail until he could repay the entire debt. The moral is, God will forgive you only if you forgive others.
- MAT 20:1–16 ~ Jesus told a parable about the kingdom of heaven: The kingdom of heaven is like the owner of the vineyard who spent the entire day hiring laborers to toil in his fields. At the end of the day he paid them a full day wage. The ones who had worked all day were mad because the others who had not worked all day received the same payment. The owner replied, "I did not treat you unfairly; you received the agreed upon wages. It's not against the law for me to spend my money the way I please. You should not have an evil eye simply because I was generous to the others." Likewise, in heaven the last will be first and the first will be last, for many are called, but few are chosen.
- MAT 22:2–14 ~ Jesus told a parable about the kingdom of heaven: The kingdom of heaven is like the king whose son was to be married. The king sent servants to gather the invited guests for the wedding, but nobody came. The king sent servants a second time, but those on the guest list ignored them, beat them, and even murdered them. The king found out and sent his armies to destroy the murderers and burn their cities. Then he sent the servants out to gather anybody and everybody, good or bad, rich or poor, until the wedding had enough guests. At the church, the king saw a man who was not appropriately dressed. He asked the man why he didn't wear his dress suit. The man was speechless. The king had him thrown into the dungeon. For many are called, but few are chosen.
- MAT 25:1–12 ~ Jesus told a parable about the kingdom of heaven: The kingdom of heaven is like ten virgins who took their lamps with them on the way to meet the groom. Five of them were smart and brought extra fuel with them. The other five ran out of fuel and their lamps went out. They asked the smart ones for extra fuel, but they replied, "No way, we don't want to run out of fuel too." The others left to buy more fuel for their lamps. Meanwhile, the groom came and everybody went into the church for the wedding. The doors were locked when the other girls tried to enter. They asked to be admitted but the doorman replied, "I

don't know you." Therefore, be prepared for the Son of Man to return for you don't know the day or hour of His return.

- MAT 25:14–30 ~ Jesus told a parable about the kingdom of heaven: The kingdom of heaven is like an investor who called his servants together and gave each of them some of his fortune to invest for him. He gave them varying amounts, depending on their abilities. After a year or so the investor returned to see how his money had been invested. The man who had received five portions doubled his money, as did the man who had received two portions. The boss was very happy saying, "Since you have been faithful with but a few things, I will make both of you rulers over many things." The man who had received one portion didn't invest it but had hidden it away for fear of losing it. The boss was irate saying, "The least you could have done is put it in the bank where it would have yielded a modest amount of interest." Then he ordered the portion be taken away from him and given to the man who had made the most of his investment. The boss said, "To those that have, more will be given; to those that don't have, the rest will be taken away." Then the unwise servant was thrown into the dungeon.
- LUK 17:21 ~ Jesus said, "They can't say, behold, here it is or there it is, because the kingdom of God is within you."
- LUK 23:42–43 ~ The criminal said to Jesus, "Remember me when you enter your kingdom." Jesus replied, "Today you will be with me in paradise."
- JOH 14:2 ~ Jesus said, "In my Father's house are many mansions; I go to prepare a place for you."
- ACT 7:49 ~ The Lord says, "Heaven is my throne, and the earth is my footstool."
- 1 CO 2:9 ~ It is written: Nobody has ever heard or seen, or even imagined, the wonderful things God has prepared for those who love Him (ISA 64:4).
- REV 2:7 ~ Jesus said, "To those who overcome evil, I will grant each a Tree of Life, which is in the paradise of God."
- REV 7:15–17 ~ They will live before the throne of God and will serve Him day and night in the temple. They will never be hungry, thirsty, hot or cold again. The Lamb among them will feed them, will lead them to fountains of living waters, and will remove all sorrow.
- REV 22:1–5 ~ I was shown a pure, crystal clear river of the Water of Life, proceeding from the throne of God and the Lamb. In the middle of the river, and on either side of it, was the Tree of Life. The tree bore twelve different fruits each month, and its leaves could be used as medicine for any ailment. The curse was gone forever. Everyone served the Lamb, and His name was on their foreheads. And His light shone constantly so that there was never any darkness, and nobody needed a lamp.

Zion and the New Jerusalem

The holy mountain of Jerusalem is called Zion. It is the location where God called Abraham, Jacob, David, and Solomon. The old Jerusalem and the old Earth will be destroyed, but God will dwell on His holy mountain in the New Jerusalem (heaven).

- 2 SA 5:7 ~ David took the stronghold of Zion which is called the City of David. (also 1 KI 8:1; 1 CH 11:5)
- PSA 2:6 ~ God says, "I have set my King upon my holy hill of Zion."
- PSA 9:11 ~ Sing praises to the Lord who lives in Zion and declare to the people all He has done.
- PSA 48:2 ~ The joy of the whole earth is mount Zion, the city of the great King.
- PSA 50:2 ~ Out of Zion, the perfection of beauty, God has shined.
- PSA 76:2 ~ In Salem (peace) is God's tabernacle; in Zion is His home.

- PSA 110:2 ~ The Lord will send the rod of His strength out of Zion to rule in the middle of His enemies.
- PSA 125:1 ~ Those who trust in the Lord will be like mount Zion, which can't be removed, but abides forever.
- PSA 149:2 ~ Let everyone rejoice in God who sent the Lord; let the children of Zion be joyful in their King.
- ISA 2:2 ~ People will say, "Come, let's go to the mountain of the Lord, to the house of the God of Jacob, and He will teach us His ways and we will walk in His paths. For out of Zion will come the Law; out of Jerusalem will come the Word." (also MIC 4:2)
- ISA 4:2 ~ Those who remain in Zion and Jerusalem will be called holy, including everyone who is written among the living.
- ISA 12:6 ~ Shout with joy you inhabitants of Zion, for great is the Holy One of Israel who will be with you.
- ISA 27:12 ~ On that day, the great trumpet will sound, and those who were about to perish in the land of Assyria, and the outcasts in the land of Egypt, will worship the Lord on the holy mountain in Jerusalem.
- ISA 28:16 ~ The Lord says, "I will lay a foundation stone, a precious cornerstone, in Zion."
- ISA 35:10 ~ The ransomed of the Lord will return and come to Zion with songs and everlasting joy; sorrow and sighing will be gone forever.
- ISA 51:2 ~ The Lord will comfort Zion and her wasted places. The wilderness will become like Eden; joy, gladness, thanksgiving, and singing will be found there.
- ISA 60:14 ~ Those who afflicted you and despised you will bow down to you; they will call you the city of the Lord, Zion, the Holy One of Israel.
- ISA 65:17–19 ~ I (God) will create new heavens and a new earth; the former heaven and earth will never be remembered or recalled. You will be glad and rejoice forever, for I will make Jerusalem a place of happiness. I will rejoice in Jerusalem for I will be happy with my people, and there will nevermore be the sound of crying among them.
- JER 30:17 ~ Those who devoured you will be devoured and will become captives; those who preyed upon you will become the prey, because they called you an outcast and said, "Here is Zion which nobody cares about." But I (God) will restore you and heal your wounds."
- JER 50:4–5 ~ In those days, the children of Israel will come weeping, seeking the Lord. They will ask the way to Zion saying, "Let us join with the Lord in a perpetual covenant that will not be forgotten."
- EZE 34:13–14,22 ~ I (God) will bring my sheep, who are scattered across the country, to their own land. I will feed them upon the mountains and by the waters of Israel. They will graze in a good pasture. I will set one shepherd over them, the Holy One of my servant David who will feed them.
- JOE 2:32 ~ Whoever calls upon the name of the Lord will be gathered and delivered to live in mount Zion and Jerusalem.
- ZEC 1:16–17 ~ I (God) will return to Jerusalem with mercy, and I will rebuild my house there. My cities will prosper again; I will again comfort Zion, and I will again choose Jerusalem.
- ZEC 2:4 ~ Jerusalem will be a town without walls, for I (God) will be a wall of fire around her, and I will be the glory in the middle of her.

- ZEC 8:3,5–8 ~ I (God) will return to Zion and I will live in Jerusalem; and Jerusalem will be called the city of truth and Zion will be called the holy mountain. Children will be playing in the streets. It will be marvelous for my people and also for me. I will save my people from the corners of the earth, and bring them to Jerusalem. They will be my people and I will be their God, in truth and in righteousness.
- ZEC 14:11 ~ Jerusalem will be a safe haven for my people, and there will nevermore be total destruction.
- HEB 12:22 ~ You will come to mount Zion, and to the city of the living God, the heavenly Jerusalem, and to the innumerable company of angels.
- REV 14:1 ~ I (John) saw the Lamb standing on mount Zion, and with Him were 144,000 with His Father's name on their foreheads.
- REV 21:1,4,10–11,14 ~ I (John) saw a new heaven and a new earth, for the old heaven and earth had passed away. There was no more crying, sorrow, pain, or death, for these things had passed away. An angel took me in spirit to a high mountain and showed me that great, holy city of Jerusalem, descending out of heaven from God. It showed the glory of God, and shined like a precious stone or like crystal. The wall of the city had twelve foundations, on which were written the names of the twelve apostles of the Lamb.

Hell

Hell is a place of eternal torment and pain. It is also referred to as the bottomless pit, the second death, outer darkness, and the lake of fire. The wicked and the nonbelievers will inherit the desolation of hell, and total separation from God for eternity.

- NUM 16:30 ~ When the earth opens its mouth and quickly swallows up the evil people and all things associated with evil, then everyone will know that they provoked the Lord.
- DEU 32:22–24 ~ God says, "A fire is kindled by my anger and shall burn into the lowest depths of hell; and as it grows it shall consume the earth. They will be wasted with hunger, devoured with fire, and poisoned with pestilence."
- PSA 9:17 ~ The wicked, and all who forget God, will go to hell.
- ECC 9:10 ~ Whatever your hand finds to do, do it with your might; for there is no work, device, knowledge, or wisdom in the grave where you are going.
- ISA 38:18 ~ The grave cannot praise Him; death cannot celebrate Him. Those who go down into the pit cannot hope for truth.
- ISA 66:24 ~ Their punishment will not end, neither will their fire be quenched, for they have been a contempt to humankind.
- EZE 26:20–21 ~ God says, "When you go down into the pit, in the lowest parts of the earth, in old and desolate places, but I will set glory in the land of the living. And I will make you a terror and you will be no more; you will be sought but never found again."
- EZE 31:16 ~ I (God) made the nations shake at the sound of his fall, when I cast him down to hell with the others who descend into the pit. Meanwhile, the trees of Eden, and all that drink water, will be comforted throughout the earth.
- EZE 32:25 ~ They have set the harlot in the middle of those who were slain; her graves are around those who were uncircumcised, slain by the sword. Though their terror was caused in the land of the living, they have taken their shame with them who go down into the pit.

- MAT 13:37–42 ~ Jesus summarized His parable saying, "The field represents the world. The harvest represents the end of the world. The reapers are the angels. The good grain represents the children of God, and the evil weeds represent the children of Satan. Jesus Christ is the sower of the grain. The enemy that sows the weeds is Satan. The weeds will be gathered by the angels and burned in the fire; all things that are offensive and evil will be thrown into the furnace where there is weeping and gnashing of teeth."
- MAT 25:30,41 ~ Jesus said, "He will cast the worthless people into outer darkness where there is weeping and gnashing of teeth. They will depart into the eternal fire prepared for the devil and his angels."
- LUK 3:17 ~ He will gather the wheat into the barns, and He will burn the chaff with unquenchable fire.
- LUK 16:19–24 ~ Jesus told the parable of the rich man and the poor man: There was a rich man who lived a life of pleasure and luxury. A poor man lay at his gate who was weak, hungry, and afflicted, desiring just the crumbs off the rich man's plate. The two men died. The poor man was taken to Abraham's bosom, and the rich man was exiled in Hades. The rich man called out to Abraham asking if he would let the poor man dip his finger into water to wet his parched tongue. But Abraham reminded him how thoughtless and unmerciful he had been to the poor man before, and told him that nobody could pass through the chasm separating the two underworlds. The rich man implored that his family be warned, to prevent them from the same fate. Abraham informed the rich man that they would have to rely on the Word of God like everybody else. If they didn't, not even a visit from the dead would persuade them to change their ways.
- 2 PE 2:4 ~ God didn't spare the angels who sinned, but threw them into hell and into chains of darkness until Judgment Day.
- REV 9:1–2 ~ The fifth angel sounded and I (John) saw a star fall from heaven to the earth, and to him was given the key to the bottomless pit. And there arose smoke from the pit, and the sun and air were darkened. And from the smoke came locusts who were given power to sting like scorpions.
- REV 14:9–11 ~ Those who worship the beast and his image, and those who receive the mark of the beast on their hand or forehead, will receive God's wrath. They will be tormented with fire and brimstone in the presence of the Lamb and His holy angels. The smoke from that torment will ascend from hell forever; and they will have no rest day and night.
- REV 19:20 ~ The beast, the false prophet, and those who worshipped the image of the beast, were cast into the lake of fire to be tormented forever.
- REV 20:1–3,7–10,14–15 ~ An angel came down from heaven with the key to the bottomless pit and grabbed the dragon (the old serpent Satan) and bound him one thousand years, and threw him into the pit. After the thousand years he was set free for a little while. The devil waged war against God and was defeated a final time. Then he was cast into the lake of fire where the beast and the false prophet were, to be tormented day and night forever. And death and hell were thrown into the lake of fire. Whoever's name was not found written in the Book of Life was thrown into the lake of fire.
- REV 21:8 ~ The fearful, unbelieving, and the abominable; the murderers, prostitutes, and sorcerers; the idolaters and liars; all will take part in the lake of fire. This is the second death.

The Inheritance of the Righteous

Those who follow Christ are chosen by Him to receive an inheritance in His eternal kingdom. We are called to be His but not everyone is proven worthy. To be worthy, one must receive His righteousness through faith, then repent, reform, and lead a Christian life. It is by God's grace that we have this opportunity to be His and live with Him in His kingdom, and all we have to do is believe on His Son to initiate the process! All believers will inherit eternal life and become an heir to God's kingdom as an adopted child of God. Instead of being condemned to hell, God will allow us to keep our souls and live forever with Him. Believe it or not, it is your choice.

- DEU 7:6–9 ~ You are a holy people to God, for He has chosen you to be a special people to Him, above all people on the earth. God didn't choose you and love you because you were greater in number than the others, for you were actually fewer in number. He loves you, and He keeps his holy covenant with you; He brings you out with His mighty hand and redeems you from slavery. Know then that He is God, faithful and just, who keeps His covenants and gives mercy to those who love Him and obey His commandments.
- PSA 33:12 ~ Blessed is the nation who makes God their Lord, for they will be the people God chooses for His own inheritance.
- PSA 37:9,11,18,29 ~ The wicked will be cut off, but those who wait on the Lord will inherit the earth. The meek will inherit the earth; they will receive joy and peace in abundance. God knows those who are blameless, and their inheritance will be forever. The righteous will inherit the land and will live there eternally.
- PSA 106:4–5 ~ Remember me with favor, Lord. Bring your salvation to me, so that I may rejoice in the gladness of your people, and glory in your inheritance.
- PRO 19:16 ~ Those who keep the commandments will be saved; but those who hate God's ways will die.
- ISA 56:2–8 ~ Blessed are all people, and their children, if they obey God, avoid evil, keep the Sabbath, and cling to His covenant. Even those who are strangers to God's people Israel will be part of God's house if they obey Him. All the righteous will be like God's sons and daughters, only better than that, with a name that will last forever. People of all walks of life will be joined together on His holy mountain to worship Him, for His house will be called a house for the righteous (also 2 CO 6:17–18).
- ISA 64:4 ~ Since the world began, nobody has ever seen or heard anything so wonderful as that which God has prepared for people who wait for Him (also 1 CO 2:9).
- MAT 5:5 ~ Jesus said, "Blessed are the meek for they will inherit the earth."
- MAT 20:16 ~ Jesus said, "The last will be first, and the first will be last, for many are called, but few are chosen."
- MAT 24:31 ~ Jesus said, "At the great sound of the trumpet, God will send His angels to gather His elect together from the four winds and one end of heaven to the other."
- LUK 21:17–19 ~ Jesus said, "People will hate you because of me, but be patient, and you will keep your soul."
- JOH 1:12 ~ Whoever receives Christ and believes in His name will be given the power to become a child of God.
- JOH 15:16,19 ~ Jesus said to His disciples, "You didn't choose me, I chose you and ordained you, so that you could bear fruit that would not wither. Anything you ask of the Father in my name will be given to you. If you were of the world, only the world would love you; but I have chosen you out of the world, and that is why the world hates you."

- ROM 8:16–17 ~ The Spirit of God is a witness with our spirits that we are the children of God. If we are children of God, then we are His heirs, and joint heirs with Christ. So if we suffer with Him, we will be glorified with Him also.
- ROM 8:28–31 ~ We know that all things work together for good to those who love God and are called according to His purpose. For God knew them in advance and predestined them to be conformed to the image of His Son, and to be among the firstborn of His brothers. Whomever He predestined, He called; and whomever He called He justified; and whomever He justified, He also glorified. Therefore, if God is with us, who can be against us?
- GAL 3:26,29 ~ You are the children of God because of your faith in Jesus Christ. If you are Christ's then you are part of Abraham's chosen seed, and heirs according to God's covenant.
- GAL 4:4–7 ~ When the time was right, God sent His Son, who was born of a woman under the Old Covenant of the Law, to redeem those who were under the Law. He did this so that everyone could receive the honor of becoming adopted children of God. If you are a child of God you are no longer His servant, but a fellow heir of God through Christ.
- EPH 1:5,11,13–14,18 ~ We were predestined to become adopted children of God by Jesus Christ, according to His marvelous will. In Christ we obtain an inheritance in heaven, because we listen to the truth and trust in Him for our redemption and salvation. I hope your eyes will be opened and you will become enlightened, and you will feel the hope of His promise, and experience the glory of the inheritance of the saints.
- EPH 2:19 ~ You are no longer strangers or foreigners, but fellow citizens with the saints in the household of God.
- PHP 3:20–21 ~ Christ will change our vile bodies into bodies like His glorified body.
- COL 3:12 ~ As God's elect, holy and blessed, we should be merciful, kind, humble, meek, and patient.
- 2 TH 2:13 ~ Give thanks always to God for choosing you from the beginning to be saved through sanctification of the spirit and belief in the truth.
- HEB 1:1–2; HEB 2:10–11 ~ God, who spoke throughout history to the prophets, has in these past days spoken to us by His Son Jesus Christ, whom He appointed heir of all things and by whom He also made the worlds. Through His suffering, many people are saved to become glorified with Him as children of God. Both He that sanctifies and those who are sanctified are one; therefore, Christ is not ashamed to call them His brothers and sisters.
- HEB 10:39 ~ We do not shrink back and we are not destroyed, because those who have faith keep their souls.
- HEB 12:22–23 ~ You have come to God's holy mountain, to His holy city, to stay with the living God and His multitude of angels. You are part of the assembly and church of the first born, whose names are written in heaven. You are among the righteous who are redeemed, and whose spirits have been made perfect.
- JAM 2:5 ~ Listen my brothers, hasn't God chosen the poor of this world to be rich in faith, and heirs of His kingdom which He promised to all who love Him?
- 1 PE 1:2,4 ~ Christians are chosen by God in advance, through sanctification of the Spirit, to be obedient to Christ and cleansed by His blood. Blessed is God the Father of our Lord Jesus Christ. According to His abundant mercy, He recreated in us the living hope, brought by the resurrection of Christ from the dead, to receive an incorruptible and undefiled inheritance, reserved in heaven and lasting forever.
- 1 PE 2:9 ~ You are a chosen generation, a royal priesthood, a holy nation, a special people. Show your praises to Him who called you out of darkness into His marvelous light.
- 2 PE 1:3–4 ~ By God's divine power we have received all things pertaining to life and godliness, because we know Him who called all people to righteousness and glory. We cling

to His precious promise, that His people will receive a divine nature, and escape the corruption and lust of the world.
- 1 JO 3:1–2 ~ How great is the love that God the Father has for us, that we should be called His children. Thus, the world doesn't know us because it didn't know Him. We are His children, but we don't know yet what we will be; we do know, however, that we will be like Him, for we will see Him as He really is.
- REV 21:7 ~ God said, "Jesus Christ is He who overcomes the world, and He will inherit everything. And I will be His God and He will be my Son."

The Fate of the Wicked

Those who insist on leading a life of evil and/or disbelief will be sentenced to eternal damnation. They will be judged guilty of their sin for not turning to Christ and for not amending their ways. Eternal separation from God and the lake of fire which burns forever will be their inheritance.

- LEV 26:27–32 ~ God says, "If you oppose me, I will oppose you with fury in my soul. I will punish you seven times for your sins. You will eat the flesh of your children. I will destroy your idols and throw your carcasses out with them. I will destroy your cities and your lands will be desolate."
- DEU 32:22–24 ~ A fire will burn in the lowest depths of hell. They will be wasted with hunger and poisoned with pestilence.
- PSA 52:5 ~ God will destroy the evil ones forever. He will uproot them from the living.
- PSA 145:20 ~ All the wicked will be destroyed.
- PRO 1:18 ~ They lay in wait for their own blood. They will ambush their own lives.
- PRO 24:20 ~ Evil people have no future. Their light will be extinguished.
- PRO 29:16 ~ The righteous will see the downfall of the wicked.
- ECC 8:8 ~ Nobody has the power over the spirit to retain it. Neither do they have any power on the day of their death. Neither shall wickedness deliver anyone.
- ISA 3:11 ~ What they have done to others will be done to them.
- ISA 14:19–21 ~ You are cast out, like a loathed untimely birth; slain by the sword and thrown into the pit, like a dead body trodden under foot. You will not be joined with the living. The evil doers will nevermore be mentioned. Prepare slaughter of their children so they cannot rise and possess the earth.
- ISA 26:14 ~ They are dead and will not live; they will not rise. They have been visited with destruction and all memory of them has been wiped out.
- ISA 28:18 ~ Your covenants with death and your agreements with hell will be null and void. You will be beaten down by the overwhelming scourge.
- ISA 29:20 ~ The ruthless will come to nothing and the scoffers will cease. All who watch evil and do evil will be cut off.
- ISA 33:14 ~ The sinners in Zion are afraid; fear has surprised the hypocrites. Who among us will inherit the devouring fire? Who will burn forever?
- ISA 45:16 ~ All of them are put to shame and confounded.
- LAM 4:6 ~ Their punishment will be greater than that of Sodom.
- EZE 11:21 ~ To those whose hearts seek detestable things and abominations, I will recompense it back upon their own heads.

- EZE 32:27–29 ~ The fallen of the untrue have gone to hell with their weapons of war. They were the terror of the mighty in the land of the living, but now they join with those who go down to the pit.
- JOE 3:4 ~ It will come back upon your head.
- AMO 1:11 ~ For the three sins of Edom, and the fourth, they will be punished.
- AMO 2:1–2 ~ For the three sins of Moab, and the fourth, they will be punished.
- ZEP 2:8–9 ~ Moab and Ammon are as Sodom and Gomorrah, perpetual desolation. The residue of my people will plunder them, and the remnant of my people will possess them.
- MAL 1:4 ~ The Lord will be angry with Edom forever.
- MAL 4:1 ~ All the evildoers will burn, leaving no roots or branches.
- MAT 25:30,41 ~ Jesus said, "God will cast the worthless people into outer darkness where there is weeping and gnashing of teeth. They will depart into the eternal fire prepared for the devil and his angels."
- MAR 9:43–44 ~ It is better to enter into life maimed, than to go to hell with all your faculties, into the unquenchable fire where your essence will be destroyed forever.
- LUK 20:9–18 ~ Jesus told them a parable. "A rich man planted a vineyard and leased it to others. At harvest time he sent servants to collect some of the fruit of the harvest, but they were beaten and sent back empty handed. The owner sent servants again, but they were murdered. Then the owner sent his only son, thinking that the renters would treat him with respect. When they saw him, they plotted together and killed him, expecting to claim the inheritance of the vineyard that was to be passed onto the son. And what do you think the owner did then? He came to the vineyard personally, and destroyed every last one of them; then he leased the vineyard to others. This is what the prophet meant when he wrote that the stone which was rejected became the capstone of the arch."
- ROM 6:21 ~ What reward did you expect for the things in which you are now ashamed? The reward is death.
- 2 TH 1:8–9 ~ God will inflict vengeance upon those who do not know Him and who do not obey the Gospel of Jesus Christ. They will suffer the punishment of eternal destruction and exclusion from the glory of the Lord.
- 2 TH 2:8–9,12 ~ The evil one, who will be revealed in the latter times, will be consumed by the Spirit of God and the brightness of His coming. The evil one comes to do the work of Satan, with his false signs and his fake miracles. Those who follow false teaching, find pleasure in unrighteousness, and do not believe the truth will be damned.
- REV 21:8 ~ The fearful, the unbelieving, the murderers, prostitutes, sorcerers, idolaters, and liars will take part in the lake of fire which is the second death.

Perdition

(By Andrew Barber, 1980)

Limitless furnace of fiery flame, that hides a multitude of shame.
The stench of death, the stain of guilt; corrupted ruins of the world sin built.

Beneath the shadow of clouded bliss; in silence, ashamed, a farewell kiss.
Beyond the edge of finishing space: fathoms of dreams one cannot embrace.

Distinction lost in a forgotten crowd. A heart now empty, once endowed.
All things destroyed and nothing grown. All together yet all alone.

Lesson: The Salt of the Earth

Salt often was an ingredient added to sacrificial offerings during Old Testament times. Salt adds flavor to food, just as it added to the savor of the burnt offerings being presented to God. God did not want offerings made to Him to be bland, any more than He wants His people to be without taste. Who wants to eat food that is tasteless? And if a drink is unsavory, who will not spit it out? The primary use of salt is to bring out the flavor in food; a secondary use of salt is to preserve food. Both uses of salt will be discussed in terms of the relevance to our Christian walk.

- LEV 2:13 ~ Season your grain offerings with salt; never leave out the salt of the covenant from your grain offerings, but add salt to all your offerings.
- LEV 18:25 ~ The land was defiled so I punished it for its sin, and the land vomited out its inhabitants.
- JOB 6:6 ~ Can tasteless food be eaten without salt? Is there flavor in the white of an egg? [Job, who was downtrodden, was offered meaningless words that provided no comfort or consolation.]
- MAR 9:49–50; LUK 14:34–35 ~ Jesus said, "Everyone will be salted with fire, and every sacrifice will be salted with salt. Salt is good, but if the salt loses its saltiness, can you use it for seasoning food? If salt loses its flavor it becomes useless; it is no good for the soil or the manure pile. So have salt in yourselves, and have peace with one another."
- REV 3:15–16 ~ Jesus said, "I know your deeds, and that you are neither cold nor hot; I would rather you were either cold or hot. But you are lukewarm, neither cold nor hot, so I will spew you out of my mouth."

God visits anyone who seeks Him, and He extends to them the same agreement: stay constant in faith and obtain the promise of the covenant. Once received, this free gift changes a person for the better, like seasoning enhances the flavor of food. God's covenant is found in God's Word, and His Word is His bond. His Word lived in the flesh through Christ and was written in Christ's blood. Now God's covenant lives in the hearts, minds, and spirits of believers. Without the presence of His Holy Spirit, we would be without flavor, unpalatable to God as well as everyone else.

- NUM 18:19 ~ The part set aside from the holy offerings presented by the Israelites to the Lord, I (God) have given to your sons and daughters as your regular share. It is an everlasting covenant of salt before the Lord for you and your offspring.
- DEU 18:18–19 ~ Moses sprinkled the blood of the sacrifice on the Book of the Law and the people, saying "This is the blood of the everlasting covenant made by God through this His Word."
- 2 CH 13:5 ~ Don't you know that the Lord God of Israel gave the kingship of Israel to David and his descendants forever by a covenant of salt? (also 2 KI 2:19–22)
- PSA 121:7–8 ~ The Lord will protect you from evil and preserve your soul.
- JER 23:5–6; JER 31:31–34 ~ The days are coming when I (God) will raise a righteous descendant of my servant David, a king that will reign with wisdom and justice. I will make a New Covenant with my people. It will not be like the covenant I made when I brought my people out of Egypt, which they broke. The New Covenant will be this: Instead of writing my laws on stone, I will write my laws into the minds and upon the hearts of my people. I will be their God and they will be my people; they will know me from the least to the greatest, because I will forgive and forget their sins.

- MAL 3:1 ~ Malachi informed that the Messiah would be the messenger of the New Covenant.
- MAT 26:27–28 ~ Jesus presented the first Holy Communion to His apostles, informing them that the shedding of His blood was the New Covenant, and that His blood cleansed everyone from all unrighteousness.
- JOH 1:1,14 ~ The Old Covenant was the Word of God, provided in the Book of the Law. The New Covenant is the Word made flesh, which is Jesus Christ.

Salt as a preservative has been used since time immemorial and still is. This is analogous to Christ's love which is the light living in us that preserves us in true faith for the day of His return. The salt, that ingredient which brings out the best in us, is Christ the light of life. His blood is what sweetened the sacrificial offering for the sins of humanity. His light shines in true believers so that others will see that Christians are not ordinary people. Christ is the promised covenant that changes us on the inside and the outside. In other words, changes of heart and conscience should be obvious from the corresponding changes in attitude and behavior. God's Spirit wakes us up from a deep slumber, just as the sun breaks the dawn and the light kills the darkness. And that same Holy Spirit preserves us day by day, even forevermore.

- MAT 5:13–16 ~ Jesus said, "You are the salt of the earth, but if the salt has lost its flavor, how can it be made salty again? It is no longer good for anything, except to be thrown out and trampled down. You are the light of the world. A city built on a hill cannot be hidden. People do not light a lamp and then cover it; instead, they put it on a stand so that it provides light to everyone in the room. In the same manner, let your light shine before others so they can see your good deeds and praise your Father in heaven."
- JOH 8:12 ~ Jesus said, "I am the light of the world; those who follow me will not walk in darkness, but will have the light of life."
- JOH 12:35 ~ Jesus said, "The light will be with you a little longer. Walk while you have the light, before the darkness overtakes you; those who walk in darkness do not know where they are going."
- ROM 13:12 ~ The night is gone and the day is at hand. Let us cast away the works of darkness and put on the armor of light.
- 2 CO 4:6 ~ God commanded light to shine out of darkness. This same light shines in our hearts and radiates light through knowledge of Jesus Christ.
- EPH 5:8–15 ~ You were once in darkness, but now you are in the light of the Lord. Live as children of light and discover what pleases the Lord, for the fruit of the light consists of goodness, righteousness, and truth. Have nothing to do with the fruitless deeds of darkness, but rather expose them. For it is shameful to even mention what the disobedient do in secret. But everything exposed by the light becomes visible for all to see, for it is light that makes things visible. This is what is meant by the saying, "Wake up you sleepers; rise from the dead, and Christ will shine on you." So be very careful how you live. Live like the wise not the unwise, making the most of every opportunity, because the days are evil.

We are expected to walk in the light and shine the light of Christ, thereby revealing the truth. We must illuminate the Word for others to see, because nobody can read or see in the dark. Let us capitalize on opportunities for others to discover the truth, so that they too can walk in the light. Those who are not in the light will get lost if they continue down that dark and lonely road. We are seasoned with God's love, and through our love we are able to season others with that same love, so they too can be preserved in the true faith for eternity.

- PSA 119:105 ~ God's Word is a lamp unto my feet, and a light unto my path.

- MAT 10:26–27 ~ Jesus said, "Don't fear those who hate you, for everything that is hidden now will be revealed later; everything that is unknown will become known. What I tell you in darkness, you will speak in the light. What you hear in private will be preached from the rooftops."
- 1 CO 4:5 ~ Judge nothing before the Lord returns, for He will bring to light all that is hidden in darkness, and will reveal the motivations of the heart. Then everyone will praise God.
- COL 4:5–6 ~ Be wise in the way you act towards outsiders and make the most of every opportunity. Let your speech always be full of grace, seasoned with salt, so that you can know how you ought to respond to others.
- TIT 2:11–12 ~ For the grace of God that brings salvation has appeared to all people. It teaches us to say no to wickedness and worldly pleasures. It teaches us to live in a self-controlled, upright manner.
- 1 JO 2:10–11 ~ Those who love others abide in the light and will not stumble. Those who hate others abide in darkness and do not know where they are going, because the darkness has blinded their eyes.

Jesus told His disciples that they were the salt of the earth because they possessed the truth of His Word, the love of His Spirit, and the light of His life. We too are seasoned with God's love, grace and mercy, thereby enhancing our existence, just as seasoning enhances the flavor of food. But nobody seasons their food and then throws it away; rather they present that food for consumption, in the manner burnt offerings in OT times were presented.

Christ sends His followers into the world to spread that salt, that light: to bring out the best in others with the good news of salvation and the hope of eternal life through faith. God gives all Christians opportunities to witness, serve, and help others who are stumbling around in the darkness of sin. Just as the light of Christ shows us the way to heaven, our light can illuminate the pathway to Christ so others can find their way.

- 2 CO 4:13–15 ~ It is written: I believed therefore I have spoken. With that same spirit of faith, we also believe and therefore speak; because we know that the One who raised Jesus from the dead will raise us and you to be with Him. This is for your benefit, so that the grace that is reaching more and more people may cause thanksgiving to overflow, to the glory of God.

Remember, in addition to bringing out the flavor in food, salt is also used as a preservative. God's light not only shows people the way, it also keeps them on track. Christ is the Way, and we are here to show that way to others, especially our children (PRO 22:6). Once you find your pathway to heaven you always will know where you are going and never will be blinded by darkness. Jesus Christ is the one ingredient that makes our lives complete. His Spirit shines in us and brings out the best in us, as well as sustaining us in our Christian faith through the process of sanctification. Our souls will be pure and our bodies will be sinless, and we will live in that state forever under the umbrella of the Lord's grace and the inspiration of His love, Amen.

- PSA 23:6 ~ Surely goodness and mercy will follow me all the days of my life and I will dwell in the house of the Lord forever.
- 1 TH 5:23 ~ May the God of peace sanctify you wholly, so that your entire spirit, soul, and body can be preserved blameless until the coming of our Lord Jesus Christ.

CHAPTER SIX

Lesson: Science and Religion

Although many have argued that science and religion are incompatible, nothing could be further from the truth. For example, one common misconception is that the notions of creation and evolution are in conflict. The fact is, many scientific theories, notions, and ideas can be found in scripture. Science is a gift from God to help us understand our world and His world.

Science is a process by which one attempts to establish cause-effect relationships evident in the environment, through observation and replication. During biblical times, scientists studied the cosmos, because it was the most mysterious aspect of their environment. They discovered that the various constellations moved in a single direction and reappeared about the same time every year. They also discovered that the proportions of daylight to nighttime varied systematically. Through such observations, scientists proved that the earth is round and is revolving; the vernal and autumnal equinoxes also were determined as well as the summer and winter solstices. Ancient calendars were based on the equinoxes and solstices making these calendars extremely accurate. Monuments from ancient civilizations also were built based on the equinoxes (e.g., Egyptian and Mayan pyramids, Stonehenge, etc.). Some people attribute such brilliance to the presence of ancient astronauts, assuming that primitive people could not have understood such things. This notion is absurd. Ancient people focused on the aspects of their universe that were most important to them, just as modern people do. Of course, modern scientists have discovered more things to study. Our civilization uses a calendar based on the equinoxes as well, but our calendar is less accurate because we divide the day into equal parts, rather than dividing the day according to the proportions of light and dark. The only time these proportions are the same is during the equinoxes; and the times when these proportions are the most dissimilar is during the solstices. Ancient peoples were very concerned about the amount of daylight because they worked while the light of the sun was available to them (JOH 9:4).

It is important to distinguish between astronomy and astrology. Astronomy is the science that studies the configurations, sizes, distances, and movements of celestial bodies. Astrology is a false science asserting that astronomical data can be used to define a person's personality, traits, behaviors, and habits, or to predict what will happen in the future. Astrology is categorized under divination and is despised by God; those who take it seriously are bewitched.

- DEU 18:10–12 ~ Don't sacrifice your children. Don't practice fortunetelling, divination, calling upon the dead, or sorcery. Don't be a medium, charmer, or wizard. Whoever does these things is an abomination to God.
- ISA 47:10–14 ~ You felt secure in your wickedness. But evil shall come upon you and disaster will befall you. So stand fast in your enchantments, sorceries, and counsels. Let them save you, those who gaze at the stars, divide the heavens, and predict what will happen according to the new moon. Fire will consume them and you.

When God created the universe, He put order where there was chaos, resulting in certain physical laws within which the universe operates. Science is derived from such natural laws so science must come from God. It is not difficult to be a Christian and a scientist at the same time. In fact, there were many prominent figures in the Bible who were educated in the sciences and yet revered God.

- DAN 1:1–7 ~ King Nebuchadnezzar of Babylon conquered Israel. After the siege of Jerusalem, he searched for Israelites who were well known for their uprightness, wisdom, analytical abilities, and understanding of science. Among those who were brought before the king were Daniel, Shadrach, Meshach, and Abednego.

- MAT 2:1–16 ~ Wise men came from the east, following the Star of Bethlehem. When they found the Christ child, they were very happy. They worshipped the Christ child and presented offerings of gold and incense. They avoided King Herod for they were told in a dream that he wanted to destroy the child.

Among other things, the wise men were astronomers. They saw something that was very unusual in the heavens. They studied the phenomenon. Modern astronomers have postulated that the Star of Bethlehem consisted of an alignment of planets, possibly becoming superimposed; others have suggested a comet or other celestial phenomenon. Perhaps this is how the wise men knew where to go; they may have used their knowledge of astronomy, mathematics, geometry, and prophecy to plot a course that ultimately led them to Bethlehem.

We Christians believe that God created everything. He first planned the universe and next created light. Scientists surmise that the universe was created with a big explosion, known as "big bang" theory. This theory does not conflict with the biblical account of the creation of light. In fact, one can imagine that when God initially created light from darkness, there must have been some fantastic fireworks.

- GEN 1:1–3 ~ God created the heavens and the earth and separated the light from the darkness.
- AMO 4:13 ~ He forms the mountains, He creates the wind, He communicates His thoughts to humankind, and He turns the dawn into dusk. He can be found in the high places of the earth, and the Lord God Almighty is His name.
- JOH 1:1–4 ~ In the beginning was the Word, and the Word was with God, and the Word was God. All things were made by Him, for there is nothing that He didn't make. In Him was life, and that life was the light of the world.

After creating plants and animals, God created people. He created man and woman in His own image or likeness. Thus, God gave humans a physical, mental, and spiritual component like Himself, which included a mind that could discern good and evil. God's Holy Spirit gives life, and He gives everyone a piece of that spirit which gives us life. When we die, that spirit departs from our bodies and returns to God.

- GEN 1:26–27; GEN 2:7 ~ God created man and woman in His own likeness and made them rulers over the beasts of the earth. God breathed into them the spirit of life and they became living souls.
- ECC 12:7 ~ Upon death, the spirit returns to God who gave it.
- JOH 6:63 ~ Jesus said, "It is the spirit that gives life, not the flesh."

God placed the first man and woman in the Garden of Eden. We are told in Genesis (GEN 2:8–14) that this garden was located in the Euphrates River valley. Interestingly, archaeologists agree that the earliest civilizations originated in this same area and spread outwardly from there. Concerning the location of the origin of humankind, there is no conflict between what the Bible says and what science has revealed.

When God created life on this planet, including humans, He commanded them to "be fruitful and multiply," thereby allowing His creations to evolve and develop naturally. God wanted His creatures to flourish and reproduce, beasts and humans alike. God gave humans greater abilities than the animals, making it possible for us to subdue the lesser creatures. Thus, in creating life, God placed a natural order in the animal chain, with humans being at the top of the hierarchy. It is unnatural for humans and animals to crossbreed with other species for the two cannot reproduce. Additionally, a species' offspring is ordinarily genetically superior to the parents. Each species also learns to adapt to changes in their environment. Thus, natural order, microevolution, adaptation, and mutation come from God and represent additional blessings and wonders of His creations. But these phenomena only occur within kinds (GEN 1). One species or kind cannot morph into a different kind (known as macroevolution).

- GEN 1:28 ~ God blessed the man and woman. He created them and told them to be fruitful, multiply, and replenish the earth. He told them also that they were in control of the other creatures He'd created.
- LEV 18:23 ~ Humans must never have sex with an animal.

It is doubtful that there are any scientists who will dispute that humans are superior to other creatures on this planet. While some would claim we evolved from apes, they still are looking for a "missing link" between apes and humans. Of course, there are missing links in the "evolution" of other species as well. It is possible that, while creating humans, God selected some of the attributes He liked from other creatures He'd already created; it's all encoded in the DNA. However, He clearly made humans superior by making us in His likeness and giving us a discerning mind. It would be a great challenge for any anthropologist to prove that an ancient primate or anthropoid had a mind that could discern good from evil. Obviously, an animal cannot evolve into a human, and an animal does not have a discerning mind. Even if an animal is taught to be evil, the animal does not know any better because it cannot reason on its own but behaves by instinct. Animals do not sin and are not condemned by the sin of man, but they are affected by it.

- GEN 1:28 ~ God blessed the man and woman and told them to be fruitful, multiply, replenish the earth, and subdue it; to have dominion over the fish, fowl and every living thing that moves upon the earth.
- PSA 8:4–7 ~ What significance is a human that you (God) keep him or her in mind and that you care? You made humans only slightly lower than heavenly beings, and crowned them with glory and honor. You made them rulers over your creations and placed them in charge of the earth and all other creatures.

God creates and God destroys. The Bible provides many examples of spontaneous destruction at the hand of God. Geologists argue that the dinosaurs became extinct through such a cataclysmic event. Historically, rapid destruction often is followed by rapid regeneration and rebirth. The Hawaiian Islands is a good example of our rapidly evolving planet. Thus, science provides evidence that support both the notions of spontaneous creation and spontaneous destruction, not just adaptation and microevolution, and examples of all these can be found in the Bible.

- GEN 6:5–7,12–13 ~ God was appalled by the wickedness that abounded on earth. He told Noah He would destroy this wicked world with a flood. [The animals Noah collected replenished the earth, and crossbred within kinds creating additional breeds. Noah's family repopulated the earth as well.]
- GEN 19:24–25 ~ God destroyed Sodom and Gomorrah for the same reason He sent the great flood.
- DEU 8:20 ~ Just like the nations which the Lord destroyed before your eyes, so also will you (Israel) perish for being disobedient to God and ignoring Him.
- JOS 24:20 ~ If you forsake God and pursue false gods, He will bring disaster upon you, even after He has been good to you.

God rewards righteousness with prosperity and wickedness with destruction. The Israelites prospered when they were obedient, and then were destroyed as a result of their wickedness. The USA seems to be following the same pattern, and therefore may be heading for a terrible fate. Is this not similar to the Darwinian concept of "survival of the fittest?" Obviously, God defines "fittest" in terms of degree of faith and obedience. Hence, evil people are inferior beings and will be destroyed. Those who seek God and His righteousness will surely find Him and will not be destroyed. In fact, the righteous will inherit the kingdom of heaven, where they will receive new, heavenly bodies like that of the angels (MAT 22:30; 1 CO 15:44,49; PHP 3:20–21). Thus, saved humans eventually evolve into higher-order beings, but they will still be human; however, other animals will remain what they are.

- JOB 12:23 ~ He (God) increases the nations and destroys them; He enlarges the nations and disperses them.
- PSA 33:12 ~ Blessed is the nation who makes God their Lord, for they will be the people God chooses for His own inheritance.
- ISA 45:6–7; ISA 65:17 ~ All may know from east to west that there is none beside me, for I (God) am the Lord and there is no other god. I form the light and create darkness. I make peace, and create evil. I the Lord do these things. I will create a new heaven and a new earth, and the former heavens and earth will no longer be remembered.
- JAM 4:8 ~ Draw near unto God and He will draw near unto you. Wash your hands you sinners, and purify your hearts those of you who are double minded.

Psychologists have suggested that humans use only a fraction of their mental potential. Astronomers have suggested that there may be intelligent life on other planets. Parapsychologists believe in ancient astronauts. All of these theories presume there is life that exceeds our intellect, implying superior beings. The Bible teaches that there are indeed spiritual beings superior to us: namely God and His angels. The Bible further reveals that there may be a hierarchy among the angels, with Michael being the archangel (DAN 12:1; JDE 1:6,9). Humans are after angels on the hierarchy for now (see above: PSA 8); but in the next life, we will be judging angels (1 CO 6:1–3). Once again, science and the Bible are not in conflict concerning the notion of superior beings.

Many theorists believe that superior beings have been invading the earth from outer space. They believe in extraterrestrials, unidentified flying objects (UFOs), space aliens, and other fantastic phenomena. Why is it so easy for some to believe in these things and not in God? Both require faith. The fact is, such ideas may have come from the Bible. For example, angels are not space aliens from other planets, but they do come from heaven, and many biblical figures saw them. Angels may even use some form of spacecraft to travel for all we know.

We learn from scripture that Elijah ascended into heaven on a chariot of fire (2 KI 2), Isaiah saw a throne in the sky with the Lord sitting on it surrounded by angels (ISA 6), and Ezekiel saw a wheel within a wheel flying across the sky with angels (EZE 1:15–16; EZE 10:10–12). Many other biblical figures had visions or saw angels including Lot, Daniel, Zechariah, Joseph and Mary, and the apostle John. In fact, many people actually have seen God. Abraham conversed with God personally (GEN 18:2–3,9–10), Moses conversed with God from the burning bush (EXO 3:2,13–14), and God appeared in the flesh through His Son Jesus Christ (JOH 1:1–14), who called Paul from heaven with thunder and lightning (ACT 9:1–7).

The Bible tells us that there are beings superior to us including a hierarchy of angels, then God Himself. If anyone has actually seen a superior being it was probably an angel. Other possible explanations concerning experiences with extraterrestrials is that Satan, his hoard of demons, and/or his followers could be up to their usual tricks.

- MAT 24:11,24 ~ Jesus said, "False prophets will come and lead many astray. They will perform wonders in an attempt to trick people; even some of God's people can become deceived."
- 2 TH 2:3–4,8–9,11–12 ~ Beware of false prophets who will try to deceive you, because people will fall away from God before the evil one, the son of Satan (literally, son of perdition or hell), is revealed. He is the one who opposes God and exalts himself, pretending to be God. The evil one will be consumed by the Spirit of God, and will be destroyed by the brightness of His coming. The evil son of Satan is the one who is possessed by Satan himself, and performs magic tricks and false miracles. He will deceive many people with his delusions and lies. All who follow him and find pleasure in unrighteousness will be damned.

Physics and neuroscience have proven that our sensory-perceptual organs are only receptive to a small segment of the electromagnetic spectrum. Further, physicists have theorized that the universe is composed of particles that never have been physically detected. Astronomers believe in the existence of intelligent entities in space that also have yet to be identified. Interestingly, such theories are not in disagreement with the Bible. Scientists concur that there are many things in this universe that they cannot comprehend, observe, or prove by discovery, but yet they believe. However, reverence for God is not based on the same blind faith, but on solid evidence.

- COL 1:16–17 ~ For by Him (God) all things were created that are in heaven and earth, whether visible or invisible, including thrones, dominions, principalities, and powers. All things were created by Him and for Him. He is before all things, and because of Him all things exist.
- HEB 11:3 ~ Through faith we understand that the worlds were framed by the Word of God, so that things which are seen were made from things that do not appear.

This world can never achieve the wisdom of God through scientific research and discovery, for the wisdom of God is incomprehensible to humans. It is futile to attempt to explain everything in this world, for such a venture leads only to confusion and frustration. Who will dispute the fact that there are things we humans may never be able to understand or explain in this life? Yet we pursue knowledge, forgetting that God is the source of all wisdom and truth. All too often, science is used as a tool in an attempt to confound God's truth and to confuse the issue.

- JOB 26:6–11,4 ~ Hell is naked before Him and destruction is left uncovered. He stretches the sky over the emptiness and suspends the earth on nothing. He brings water into clouds yet they do not burst under the weight. He divides the limitless heavens from the earth, the waters from the land, and the light from the darkness. Heaven and earth tremble at astonishment. These are only a small fraction of His mighty works. We hear but a whisper of His works, so who can possibly understand the thunder of His power?
- 1 CO 1:19–27,31 ~ Paul wrote: It is written, I (God) will destroy the wisdom of the wise, and bring to nothing the understanding of the prudent. Where is wisdom? Hasn't God made foolish the wisdom of this world? The world through its wisdom cannot know God. The Jews want a sign and the Gentiles want wisdom. But we preach to them about Christ's crucifixion, which to the Jews is an obstacle and to the Gentiles is foolishness. But Christ is the power and wisdom of God to all that are called, both Jews and Gentiles alike. The foolishness of God is wiser than the wisdom of humanity. The weakness of God is stronger than the strength of people. You can see that not many of those who are wise, mighty, and noble by earthly standards are called by God. But God has chosen the foolish things of this world to

confuse the wise, and the weak things of this world to confound the mighty. Those who glory, let them glory in the Lord only.
- 1 CO 2:7–16 ~ We speak the wisdom of God as a mystery, even the hidden wisdom of God, which He ordained and which none of the rulers of this world knew, otherwise they wouldn't have crucified Christ. It is written: Eyes have not seen, nor ears heard, nor the heart discerned the things that God has prepared for those who love Him. God has revealed these things to us by His Spirit; for the Spirit searches everything, even the deepest things of God. These things we speak, not in the words which humanity teaches, but which the Holy Spirit teaches, comparing spiritual things with spiritual. But a natural person does not receive spiritual things of God for these things are foolishness to them; neither can they know these things because they need to be discerned spiritually. But those who are spiritual analyze everything and are judged by nobody. Nobody knows the mind of God that they can instruct Him, but those who are spiritual have the mind of Christ.
- 1 TI 6:20–21 ~ Paul wrote to Timothy: Guard carefully those things of which you have been entrusted. Avoid profane and vain babble. Ignore opposing arguments that are falsely called scientific knowledge, which are professed to be truths by those who have consequently become diverted from the true faith.
- JDE 1:10 ~ They speak evil of those things that they do not understand. However, the things they know naturally by instinct only serve to corrupt them.

It is fairly easy to conceptualize a scientific explanation for the wonders and events described in the Bible, but that doesn't make them false. Since God has deliberately placed controls and laws over nature, perhaps He has provided nature and science as a way for us to understand what He has done and how He did it; and maybe this can help us to understand why He did it.

Often, scientists and researchers painstakingly search for evidence to refute the Bible. Yet such evidence has only served to prove its accuracy. The world, and all aspects of nature, is constantly changing (including the earth's crust via plate tectonics). Thus, evidence of the past is often lost. Interestingly, God has allowed us to recover a great many of His wonders recorded in the Bible. These wonders go as far back as Noah, whose ark came to rest near Mt. Ararat (GEN 8:4). Catastrophes of biblical proportion are frequent, and will continue to occur, increasing as we near Christ's second coming (DEU 28:21–28; MAT 24:5–8). However, geologists are still searching for the cataclysmic event that wiped out the dinosaurs. In the process, they have discovered a number of such possible events, to include Noah's flood.

It must be emphasized that science cannot explain everything, nor are all scientific methods entirely reliable. Scientific techniques have a margin of error, whereas the Holy Bible is infallible. Consider the Shroud of Turin, regarded by many to be the burial cloth of Christ. A vast amount of scientific data support authenticity, yet the carbon dating of a small fragment places it around the Middle Ages. So, there is conflict in the data. However, one cannot place a high degree of faith in carbon dating, particularly for highly biodegradable material. A number of extraneous variables also can affect the reliability of such tests. For example, the shroud has been damaged by fire and aging. There is evidence the fabric was repaired with interwoven strands. There is a lot of biomaterial embedded in the cloth. Such factors can skew radiometric test results. It is not the position of this study to take a stand on the authenticity of this relic, but rather to demonstrate the fallibility of science due to limits in human understanding and errors in methodology such as experimental sampling and testing methods. The shroud accurately depicts crucifixion in general and the wounds of Christ in particular, in a light-induced photographic negative that is scientifically unexplainable. For more on this look under *Shroud* in the Index.

The Bible is the greatest source of history and science known to man. It is the only book that has been proven to be true time and time again. Let us review a previous lesson on the validity of the Bible using the key word *HARP*: history, authenticity, reliability, prophecy.

History has provided evidence, including geological, geographical, archaeological, and anthropological data, to prove the accuracy of people, places, and events recorded in the Bible.

- o Progression of empires and associated emperors: Egyptian, Assyrian, Babylonian, Persian, Greek, Roman
- o Natural phenomena such as the great flood and parting of the Red Sea
- o Discovery of the city of Jericho, edifices of Rameses, and the Dead Sea Scrolls

Authenticity of thousands of manuscripts in Hebrew, Greek, and Aramaic is undisputed. These documents have been verified by numerous scholars several times. Many people from diverse places and times contributed to the recording of God's Word. Each author provided a piece to a great mystery revealed in the Holy Bible. To unravel God's mystery, one needs all the pieces to the puzzle. The combined wisdom of humankind could not have generated such an enormous and wonderful arrangement that tells us of God's plan for people. Though there are numerous writers, there is a single author: God's Holy Spirit. The Old and New Testaments, as well as books within them, provide a cross-validation not found in any other religious or scientific work.

Reliability is one of the principal tools of a scientist. A researcher will not accept a finding unless it has been replicated numerous times with 95 percent confidence or better. The reliability of the Holy Bible is 100 percent. The Bible provides substantial replication with several eyewitnesses, as well as providing revelations and visions from various prophets all of which complement one another. Is it not amazing how all of the contributors to the Holy Bible provided a piece to a colossal thriller unveiled in God's Word? They never could have realized the future significance of their contribution. The Bible not only is internally consistent, but also it is consistent with external sources from the historical archives.

Prophecy in the Bible is so detailed that it leaves no chance for error. Forecasters who attempt to predict such things as the weather, the future, and the economy will never achieve the accuracy achieved in scripture. The OT prophecy of the coming Messiah, as fulfilled according to writings in the NT, is the most compelling evidence of the validity of the Bible and the fact that it was inspired by the Holy Spirit. Scientists would never dream of achieving the degree of predictive validity found in scriptural prophecy.

For more information about the reliability and validity of the Holy Bible, refer to Chapter Eight of this text under the headers *Empirical Proof that the Holy Bible Is True* and *Does Science Disagree with the Bible*. The results of scientific examinations of the Bible are provided along with supporting evidence of the infallibility of God's Word.

To be sure, there is no disagreement between science and religion when it comes to absolute truth, for neither are set up to deny the truth and both can be helpful in uncovering the truth. Like the Lord said, "Seek and you will find." Truth is evident in God's creation and in His words, and He has given us the tools we need to discover it. And truth, by definition, should never disagree with either source, for truth cannot be proven false no matter how many ways people will try to spin it.

Lesson: Politics and Religion

Our fine nation was founded on the principles of liberty and equality; one of the most fundamental liberties was religious freedom. Our founding fathers knew the importance of faith in God and the right to worship Him as one sees fit. Their strong position concerning inalienable rights was based on the assumption that such rights are given by God Himself, and therefore cannot be taken away by governments or people.

When God has been the center of our existence, this country has prospered. In fact, God prospers those who seek Him and His righteousness. The Bible provides numerous examples of how God prospered those who obeyed Him and how He crushed those who disobeyed Him. Whenever the Israelites were faithful, they stayed in God's grace and they prospered. Whenever they were unfaithful, they experienced destruction and desolation. If our country continues in our backsliding ways, we too will suffer the fate of nations that have strayed from God.

Our politicians have determined that it is prudent to separate matters of government from matters of religion. Thus, we have separation of church and state. However, matters of government should be guided by our religious beliefs, and not vice-versa. It matters not whether someone is a Democrat or a Republican. What matters is whether someone believes in God, and His Son Jesus Christ. If someone asks you what your political party is, the correct answer should be "Christian." Our beliefs are what drive our penchants and politics.

The fact that God has been removed from our schools is a travesty of justice, for it is our belief in God that guides our high standards of morality and equality. Without God, there is no morality, justice, or liberty. It is, therefore, no surprise that there has been a decline in self-discipline and a rise in promiscuity among our youth. Religious education, founded firmly on the Word of God, is the most important education of all. If our schools shun this responsibility, then parents need to get more actively involved in the education of their children and the calibration of their moral compass (DEU 4:9–10,36; DEU 6:2–7).

In days of old a leader was required, above all, to be a spiritual leader. A strong faith in God was the most important characteristic of a leader. That is why God played a major role in selecting leaders in the OT, such as Moses. God also selected the judges and prophets. The twelve apostles were selected personally by Jesus Christ in the NT. The following governors also were mighty men selected by God, who remained faithful and just: Joseph (GEN 42:6), Solomon (1 CH 29:22), Joshua (2 KI 33:8), Nehemiah (NEH 12:26), and Daniel (DAN 2:48).

- EXO 18:21–22 ~ Moses's father-in-law advised him, "Select capable men who fear God, who are trustworthy, and who hate dishonest gain, and appoint them as governors over thousands, hundreds, and tens. Have them serve as judges for the simple cases, so that you can decide the difficult cases."
- DEU 17:14–17 ~ After you have entered the land which the Lord has given you, and you possess it and live there, you will say, "Let us elect a king to rule over us like the other nations." You must let the Lord choose your king from among you; do not select a stranger who is not your brother. The king should not be intent on collecting wealth, cattle, or wives, for that might cause him to turn from God.

It is fitting and right for God to select those who would govern, since God created the Law. All knowledge of right and wrong comes from God, who made us in His image giving us a discerning mind. He told us how to obey Him by keeping His commandments. We know that if we do not obey Him, we are guilty of sin and the penalty for sin is death. Anyone who purports to know the Law must first know God, for He is the lawmaker, enforcer, and judge.

- NEH 9:13–14 ~ God came to Mt. Sinai and spoke from heaven, giving the people sound judgments and true laws and commandments. He gave to Moses His servant holy commandments, statutes, and laws.
- PRO 29:26–27 ~ Many people seek favor from their rulers, but all judgment comes from God. An unjust person is disgusting to a just person; an upright person is disgusting to an evil person.
- ISA 33:22 ~ The Lord is our judge and our lawgiver. The Lord is our King. He will save us.
- DAN 4:17 ~ The following is an excerpt from Nebuchadnezzar's dream: A decision will be announced by messengers and declared by holy people, so that everyone can know that the Lord is our sovereign king. He rules over all kingdoms, giving those kingdoms to anyone He wants, and placing over them the vilest of people.
- JAM 4:10–12 ~ Humble yourselves before God and He will exalt you. Do not speak evil of one another or judge one another, for you will be guilty of speaking evil of the Law and of judging the Law. If you judge the Law you cannot be a doer of the Law. There is only one lawgiver, who is able to save and to destroy.

God gave us His laws because He wants us to obey Him and love Him. God has placed rulers over us to ensure that we obey these laws. We are therefore required to obey the laws of the land, since laws and rulers are promulgated by God. We are to be doers of the Law and not just hearers of the Law. We should respect authority and pray for our leaders.

- ROM 13:1–6 ~ Everyone is subject to the higher powers, for all power comes from God; that is, all powers that exist have been ordained by God. Anyone who resists these powers are resisting the ordinance of God, and those who resist God receive damnation as punishment. Those who do what is right have no fear of the authorities, only those who do wrong are afraid of them. Do what is right and the authorities will commend you. Governments are God's servants; they are there to make sure you do what is right. But if you do what is evil, beware, for they do not carry a sword in vain, but to execute judgment on those who are evil. Submit to those who are in authority, not just because you will be punished if you don't, but also as a matter of keeping a clear conscience. This is why you should pay your taxes, because the governments are God's servants who work fulltime in governing.
- 1 TI 2:2 ~ Pray for your leaders and all who are in authority.
- HEB 13:17 ~ Obey those who rule over you, and submit yourselves to them; for they will be watching you and will give an account, and you want them to give a good report.
- JAM 1:22–27 ~ Don't just listen to the Word, but do what it says. Whoever listens but does not act is like a person who looks in the mirror and later forgets what they look like. But those who look intently into the perfect law of liberty and who act on this will be blessed in all they do. Those who consider themselves to be religious, but don't control their tongue, deceive themselves and their religion is worthless. God accepts the religion of those who look after the poor, widows, and orphans and who keep themselves from becoming polluted by the world around them.
- 1 PE 2:13–14 ~ Submit to every ordinance of society for the Lord's sake, whether to the king, or to his governors who are given the authority to punish evildoers and to commend those who do right.
- 2 PE 2:10 ~ God knows how to deliver the righteous from temptation and hold the unrighteous until the day of judgment to be punished. This especially relates to those who follow corrupt and sinful desires and who despise authority.
- JDE 1:7–8 ~ Those, who like Sodom and Gomorrah will suffer the punishment of eternal fire, include people that pollute their own bodies, reject authority, and slander dignitaries.

For a law to be just and fair it must promote morality and righteousness. All righteousness comes from God. Thus, it should be a requirement that those who govern know God's Law and God's Word, for this is the basis for all other laws. To disobey any law is to disobey God. To love God and one another is to fulfill the letter of the Law. Only Jesus Christ was able to do this; He did so on our behalf (MAT 5:17–18). Wouldn't you rather have leaders that are godly?

- DEU 1:13 ~ Take the wise men of understanding and notoriety, and make them rulers.
- 2 SA 23:3 ~ God, the Rock of Israel, spoke saying, "Whoever rules others must be just, ruling in the fear of God."
- EZR 7:25 ~ Ezra, since you have the wisdom of God, you will select magistrates and judges to govern those beyond the river. They must know the laws of your God, and if they do not, you must teach them.
- JOB 34:17 ~ Shall someone who hates what is right govern others? Can a just person be condemned?
- JER 31:33 ~ This is the covenant that I (God) will make with my people. I will place my Law into their minds and write it upon their hearts. And I will be their God and they will be my people.
- ROM 13:10 ~ Love creates no ill will towards another; therefore, love is the fulfillment of the Law.
- 1 TI 1:8–9 ~ Laws are good if they are used lawfully. Laws are not made for the righteous, they are made for the lawless, profane, and disobedient; laws are for ungodly people and for sinners.

We are obliged to obey the laws of the land. But what if these laws go against God's laws? There are examples in the Bible when the rulers of the land ordered people to disobey God, but they refused to do so at great personal risk. Remember when Shadrach, Meshach, and Abednego refused to worship the king? God spared them from death in the fiery furnace because they adhered to a higher authority, namely God (DAN 3). Obviously, when man's law and God's Law are in conflict, God's Law must prevail.

- ACT 5:22–29 ~ When the authorities commanded the apostles to stop preaching in the name of Jesus they replied, "We must obey God rather than men."

Wickedness gives rise to more wickedness. Corruption in politics and government fosters corruption among the governed. Similarly, corruption among the citizenry practically guarantees they will select a corrupt government. Satan prospers when a corrupt and evil government prospers. This is how Satan will seize power in the latter days.

- PSA 12:8 ~ The wicked are all around when vile men are exalted.
- PRO 28:15 ~ Like a roaring lion or a raging bear, so is a wicked ruler to the poor people.
- PRO 29:12 ~ If a ruler listens to lies, his entire cabinet will be evil.
- DAN 8:23–25 ~ In the latter days, when the evil ones are fully in power, a fierce king will arise from darkness. He will be powerful and mighty, but not by his own power. He will destroy tremendously, and will prosper. He will destroy the mighty and holy people. He will cause deceit to flourish. He will exalt himself, and through the guise of peace he will destroy many. He will even stand against the Prince of peace, but the Prince will defeat him without raising a hand.
- HAB 1:4 ~ The law becomes loose and justice is not served, for the wicked encompass the righteous and wrong judgment proceeds.

- ROM 12:17,21 ~ Do not repay evil for evil, but be honest in everything. Don't let evil overcome you, but overcome evil with goodness.

God is the one in charge; He rules over heaven and earth. God is the King and Jesus Christ is the Prince. God sent His Son to earth to be His mediator; now Jesus sits upon the white throne over all the earth (REV 20:11). He has been assigned the duty of judging everyone; thus, those who govern, judge, or enforce the law should report directly to Jesus Christ. For God has established legal systems and governing bodies to reveal His wisdom, His will, and His sovereignty.

- PSA 22:28 ~ The kingdom belongs to the Lord; He is the governor of all the nations.
- PSA 103:19 ~ The Lord has prepared His throne in heaven and His kingdom rules over all.
- ISA 9:6–7 ~ Unto us a child is born; unto us a Son is given. The government will be upon His shoulders. His name will be called Wonderful Counselor, Mighty God, Everlasting Father, and Prince of Peace. There will be no end to His government or the peace He brings. He will inherit the throne of David, and will rule with judgment and justice henceforth, even forevermore. The zeal of the Lord of Hosts will see to it.
- MIC 5:2 ~ Bethlehem, though you are but a small village, from you will come the great ruler of Israel; His coming has been told from ages past.
- 1 CO 12:27–31 ~ You are the body of Christ, and each particular member has certain responsibilities. God places some of you in the church: first apostles, second prophets, third teachers; then those who perform miracles, those with gifts of healing, those who can govern, and those who can speak in tongues. Not all can be apostles, prophets, or teachers, but everyone contributes something special. Strive especially for the greater gift God has given which is His Spirit (also ROM 12).

The USA is a self-governing nation, which ascribes responsibility to each and every citizen to obey the laws, follow the rules, and elect leaders who will do likewise. Equality makes us all responsible to one another. Liberty requires that we do the right thing. Morality dictates what is right and wrong. Justice provides the incentive to comply. These gifts from God were treasured by our founders and became the pillars of our society and staples of our faith; this must continue in order to save this republic from ruin. Any worldview or ideology that dismisses or diminishes these fundamentals of faith and brotherhood will lead to the demise of this great nation. It is our Judeo-Christian values and beliefs that enabled this country to exceed all others, and only by God's grace will we remain faithful to Him.

Crown Him with Many Crowns

Crown Him with many crowns, the Lamb upon His throne;
Hark! How the heavenly anthem drowns all music but His own!
Awake, my soul, and sing of Him who died for thee,
And hail Him as thy chosen King through all eternity.

Crown Him the Lord of life who triumphed o'er the grave,
And rose victorious in the strife for those He came to save;
His glories now we sing, who died, and rose on high,
Who died, eternal life to bring, and lives, that death may die.

Crown Him the Lord of heaven, enthroned in worlds above,
Crown Him the King to whom is given the wondrous name of Love.
Crown Him with many crowns as thrones before Him fall,
Crown Him, you kings, with many crowns, for He is King of all.

Lesson: Dreams and Visions

Often, we gain insights into reality or truth through dreams and visions. Dreams and visions may occur at night when one is in a deep state of sleep, but they also can occur in a deep state of concentration, meditation, or trance. Perhaps God chooses to deliver His revelations at lower levels of consciousness where our internal programming exists. Embedded there, God's revelations would not be subject to personal bias or outside influence which could otherwise contaminate or distort the truth. In the depths of the unconscious mind, humans are able to process vast amounts of information in very little time, as opposed to the cognitive domain where processing capabilities are much more limited and selective.

God spoke to many of His prophets and messengers in dreams and visions including Noah, Jacob, Joseph, Isaiah, Jeremiah, Ezekiel, Daniel, Paul, and John. In fact, God may speak to the rest of His children in the same manner whenever He needs to convey an important message. No doubt, it is easier for God to implant a message into our memory where it cannot be distorted by perception or processing. Besides, we would be overwhelmed if God was to appear in person to deliver such revelations. As it is written: God will write His laws upon our minds and hearts (JER 31:33; HEB 8:10).

- NUM 12:6 ~ The Lord said, "If there is a prophet among you, I will make myself known to him in a vision and will speak to him in a dream."
- JOB 4:12–13 ~ Eliphaz declared, "A word was brought to me secretly and my ears caught a whisper of it. Amid disquieting dreams in the night, when deep sleep falls upon all people, fear and trembling seized me and my bones were shaking. A spirit glided by my face and the hair on my body stood on end. It stopped, but I could not tell what it was. A form stood there and I heard a hushed voice whisper: Can a mortal be more than God, and can a man be purer than his Maker?"
- JOB 33:14–18 ~ God will speak once, maybe twice, but people do not perceive it. He speaks in a vision, at night, when we are asleep. He may speak into our ears, and terrify us with warnings, to turn us from sin and pride, and to preserve our souls from hell in order to save our lives.
- HOS 12:10 ~ God spoke through the prophets, gave them many visions, and told parables through them.
- JOE 2:28 ~ I (the Lord) will pour out my Spirit upon all people. Your sons and daughters will prophesy, your old men will dream dreams, and your young men will see visions. (ACT 2:14–21)

There are many examples in the Bible where God revealed the future, warned people, or gave directions through dreams and visions. Not all of these revelations were given to God-fearing people, though many turned to God as a result, and still do. The following is but a sampling of the many visions recorded in the Bible.

- GEN 15 ~ God told Abraham that his descendants would inherit the land He promised.
- GEN 20 ~ God told King Abimelech not to touch Sarah.
- GEN 28 ~ God showed Jacob a ladder reaching from earth to heaven with angels.
- GEN 31 ~ God told Laban to be careful what he says to Jacob.
- NUM 24 ~ God revealed a vision to the evil sorcerer Balaam, who was ordered by King Balak to prophesy against Israel. Instead, Balaam blessed Israel and prophesied against Balak's people, in accordance with God's revelation.
- JDG 7 ~ God revealed through Gideon's countryman that they would defeat the Midianites.

- 1 SA 3 ~ God called Samuel to be a prophet and revealed what would happen to the house of Eli.
- 2 SA 7; 1 CH 17; PSA 89 ~ God revealed through Nathan the prophet that David would be an ancestor of the Messiah.
- 1 KI 3 ~ God appeared to Solomon in a dream in which he asked God for wisdom.
- ISA 1; ISA 21; ISA 22 ~ God warned Israel through the prophet Isaiah about amending their wicked ways or else.
- EZE 8; EZE 11; EZE 12; EZE 40; EZE 43 ~ God warned Ezekiel about the abominations of the Israelites and declared that their peace would not last.
- OBA 1 ~ God told Obadiah that Edom was doomed.
- NAH 1 ~ God told Nahum about the fall of Nineveh.
- HAB 2 ~ God warned Habakkuk about the sins of the people.
- MAT 2 ~ God warned the magi to avoid Herod and return using a different route.
- MAT 27 ~ God warned the wife of Pontius Pilate that Christ was no ordinary man.
- ACT 9 ~ God told Ananias to seek out Saul (Paul) and help open his eyes to the truth.
- ACT 10 ~ God told Peter and Cornelius to meet one another.
- ACT 11 ~ Peter had a vision that God would proclaim His Gospel to the Gentile nations.
- ACT 16; ACT 18 ~ God told Paul to take the Gospel to the Gentiles.
- REV 9 ~ God showed John the vision of the four horsemen of the apocalypse.

Several notable prophets chosen by God were given the gift of dreams and dream interpretation. These people were mighty men of God and were a great influence during pivotal periods in history. Joseph was one of the greatest dreamers of the Old Testament. Through his own dreams and the dreams of others, God revealed to Joseph the future, not just his own future but also the future of his countrymen, and the future of his family. Note that Joseph gave God the credit for revealing to him the meaning of dreams (GEN 40:8).

- GEN 37 ~ Joseph's dream about the sheaves was an indication that he would reign over his brothers. His dream about the sun, moon, and stars was an indication that he would reign over his entire family. When Joseph told his father Jacob the dream, his father rebuked him saying, "Will your mother, I, and your brothers bow before you?" However, as Joseph's brothers burned with jealousy, their father kept the matter in mind, and remembered it when the prophecy was fulfilled.
- GEN 40 ~ We know that Joseph was sold into slavery by his brothers as a result of their jealousy. After being unfairly imprisoned by the Egyptians, Joseph used his talents of dream interpretation again. Two of his fellow prisoners told Joseph their dreams. The two dreams, which revealed the fate of each dreamer, came true just as Joseph had predicted.
- GEN 41 ~ Word eventually got back to Pharaoh that Joseph could interpret dreams. Pharaoh summoned Joseph to see if he could make sense of Pharaoh's recurring dream, since nobody else in the palace could interpret it. Joseph informed Pharaoh that God had revealed the future. There would be seven years of plenty followed by seven years of famine. Joseph devised a plan that would enable the Egyptians to survive the famine, so Pharaoh put him in charge of the land of Egypt, second only to himself. Later, Joseph sent for his family so that they could survive the famine, after which the prophecies came true.
- GEN 50 ~ Joseph told his elder brothers that what they had done to him was evil, but God used it for good in order to save them from the famine and reunite the family.

Daniel was another great dreamer of dreams and interpreter of dreams (DAN 1:17). Like Joseph, Daniel would discover the wonders of God's truth to include the future. In fact, Daniel would see well into the future, from Babylon to the empires that would follow, and even to the end of time. Note that Daniel always gave God the credit for revealing to him the meaning of dreams (DAN 2:28).

- DAN 2 ~ Probably the most notable dream in the Bible was that of the King, Nebuchadnezzar of Babylon. The king commanded his magicians, astrologers, and sorcerers to reveal to him the content and the meaning of his troubling dream or they would die. They claimed that nobody could do what the king asked, so the king ordered their execution. Daniel intervened for them, appearing before the king who had requested his help. Daniel went home, and that night God came to Daniel in a dream and revealed the dream and its interpretation. When Daniel returned to the king, Nebuchadnezzar asked, "Can you tell me the interpretation of the dream?" Daniel replied, "There is a God in heaven that reveals secrets, and He will make known to the king what will be." Then Daniel explained the dream to the king: about the empires which would follow Babylon, and the fact that all empires of the world would crumble and fall prostrate before the everlasting kingdom of the Lord.
- DAN 4 ~ Once again, Daniel came to Nebuchadnezzar after the king had a troubling dream. As before, the magicians, astrologers, and sorcerers were helpless to interpret the dream, but not Daniel. Unfortunately, the interpretation and reality of the dream proved more troublesome for the king than the dream itself. The king went insane for seven years until he finally acknowledged that God was the one who ruled the universe and not Nebuchadnezzar.
- DAN 5 ~ Belshazzar, the son of Nebuchadnezzar, was the next to employ Daniel's unique gift. Daniel revealed the secret message which the king envisioned being written on the wall by the hand of God. Daniel told him how his father had defied God and was punished for it; but his father finally repented. Daniel continued that the king had not humbled himself before God as his father did. He was told that his days were numbered and that Babylon would fall to the Medes and Persians. That very night, Belshazzar was assassinated and Darius (a Mede) seized power.
- DAN 7 ~ When Belshazzar was king, Daniel had a significant dream of his own. This was the dream of the four beasts representing future empires up to the last days. Most importantly, Daniel saw the Son of Man (Jesus Christ) coming down from heaven. To Him was given all authority, glory, power, and dominion and people of all nations worshipped Him. His kingdom was eternal.
- DAN 8 ~ Daniel had another dream about the latter days. He saw the abomination of desolation and was astonished and upset. He was sick for days.
- DAN 9 ~ During the first year of the reign of Darius (predecessor of the Persian king Xerxes), Daniel had another significant dream. He was given the interpretation of Jeremiah's revelation of the seventy years (JER 25) and its relationship to seventy weeks (seventy times seven). Once again, Daniel saw the abomination of desolation and the tribulations to come.
- DAN 10 – 12 ~ Daniel was still present when Cyrus, king of Persia reigned. He had another great vision. Although others were present, only Daniel saw the vision. The angel Gabriel appeared to Daniel then, and many other times, and revealed to Daniel details of the final days and the terrible things that would occur.

God spoke several times to Joseph, husband of Mary and earthly stepfather of Jesus Christ. How difficult it must have been for Joseph to accept that his fiancé was pregnant, and to believe the message from the angel Gabriel that Mary was impregnated by the Holy Spirit. Of course, God would not have chosen Joseph had he not been a man of great faith. What an inspiration was this man of God, who faithfully accepted the huge responsibility set before him without doubting God or His messenger.

- MAT 1 ~ The angel of the Lord appeared to him in a dream, saying, "Joseph, son of David, don't be afraid to take Mary as your wife, for the child in her womb is of the Holy Spirit."
- MAT 2 ~ God warned Joseph to escape into Egypt to avoid the evil decree of Herod. Then after Herod died, God told Joseph it was safe to return to Nazareth a town in Galilee. This would fulfill the Old Testament prophecy: He will be called a Nazarene (a nickname for one who is despised as in PSA 22:6; and a reference to the fact that Christ would come from Galilee as in ISA 9:1).

Anyone can claim to have received a revelation from God in a dream, but that doesn't make it so. The accuracy of everything we hear or read needs to be validated. God tells us to compare what people claim to be true against what is written in the Bible (GAL 1:7–9; 1 JO 4:1). God also provides the proof of His revelations with physical evidence. Thus, God provides two ways of checking the validity of a revelation or prophecy. Does it come to pass, and is it consistent with God's Word? Those who cannot prove that they are prophets or that they received God's revelation should be avoided. They will deceive themselves, but don't let them deceive you. Examples of prophets whose visions cannot be verified include Buddha, Mohammed, and Joseph Smith.

- DEU 13:1–5 ~ A prophet may emerge from among you claiming to be a dreamer and declaring miraculous signs or wonders. And these signs may even come true. But if he says, "Let us follow other gods," do not listen to him. God could be testing you to see if you are loyal to Him, and to see if you love God with all your heart and soul. Such false prophets should be put to death in order to remove this evil from your midst.
- JER 14:14 ~ False prophets tell lies in my (God's) name; I did not send them, command them, or speak to them. They receive false visions and make false predictions from the deceit of their lying hearts.
- JER 23:25–32 ~ God says, "I have heard those who prophesy lies in my name, claiming that they have dreamed great dreams. How much longer will these lying prophets share the delusions of their own minds? They think their visions will cause people to forget my name, like their forefathers did when they worshipped Baal. Let a prophet who has a dream tell it to others, and let those who know my Word speak it faithfully. For what is the chaff to the wheat? Isn't my Word like a hammer that can break a rock into pieces? I am against those false prophets that steal words from each other and say they come from me. I despise those that wag their tongues and declare that I gave them their falsehoods and contrived dreams. Their lies lead people into sin. I did not send them and they have nothing important to say."
- JER 29:8 ~ God says, "Do not let those prophets and diviners among you deceive you, and do not pay attention to their dreams which they themselves caused to be dreamt."
- ZEC 10:2 ~ The idols speak lies and diviners see false visions. They give comfort in vain. Therefore, the sheep wander from the flock and are oppressed, for they have no shepherd.
- COL 2:8,18–19 ~ Beware of those who would lead you astray with their errant philosophies and vain deceptions, following traditions fashioned by the world and not Christ. Do not let anyone swindle you out of your reward. Beware of those who practice false humility and worship angels. They claim to have seen things, but they have filled their unspiritual and arrogant minds with silly notions.

God is not likely to give someone a vision who is irresponsible with His gifts. Disaster will come upon those people that fabricate visions as well as those that follow wayward prophets. God also will punish people that deny Him or ignore His true prophets. He will send them a famine of the Word, and they will thirst for His wisdom and truth. The best remedy is to be nurtured by God's Word on a daily basis.

- ISA 47:10–14 ~ You felt secure in your wickedness. But evil shall come upon you and disaster will befall you. Stand fast in your enchantments, sorceries, and counsels. Let them save you, those who gaze at the stars, divide the heavens, and predict what will happen to you according to the new moon. Fire will consume them and you.
- AMO 8:11–13 ~ I will send a famine of the Word. They will seek the Word of God and not find it. The virgins and young men shall faint of thirst for the Word.
- MIC 3:5–7,11 ~ God says, "Those prophets lead my people astray. If someone pays them, they predict peace; if not, they predict war. Night will fall but there will be no visions; darkness will come without divinations. The sun will set upon the prophets and daylight will become darkness. Seers will be ashamed and diviners, disgraced. They will cover their faces for there will be no answers from God. Their leaders judge for a bribe, their priests teach for a price, and their prophets tell fortunes for money. Yet they lean on the Lord claiming that God is with them so nothing can harm them. But because of them, Zion will be plowed as a field and Jerusalem will become a pile of rubble; and the temple mound will be overgrown."
- ZEC 13:2–4 ~ God says, "On that day, I will banish the names of the idols and they will be remembered no more. I will remove the prophets and the impurity from the land. If anyone prophesies, his parents will tell him he must die for telling lies in the Lord's name. On that day, the prophets will be ashamed of their visions. They will remove the animal skins, claiming that they are not prophets but farmers."

Often it is hard to follow God's instructions. His path is seldom the easy one. Consider the trials and tribulations of Jacob's son Joseph, God's servant Job, or the prophet Daniel. When you think the Christian way is becoming burdensome, compare your mission to that of Joseph the stepfather of Christ; or compare your anxiety to that of Jesus's mother Mary, as she gazed upon her crucified son.

But be comforted, for the Holy Spirit will provide the strength you need in time of trouble. And God will tell you what to say when using you to convey His messages to others (MAT 10:19–20), just like He informed the prophets and the writers of the Holy Bible about what to say and write.

- PSA 119:4–5 ~ God, you have established your precepts that must be fully obeyed. Oh, that my ways were steadfast in obeying your decrees!
- MAT 7:14 ~ Straight is the gate and narrow the way which leads to life, and not many will find it.
- MAT 16:24 ~ Jesus said to His disciples, "If anyone would come with me, let them deny themselves, take up their cross, and follow me."
- 2 TH 3:5 ~ May the Lord direct your hearts to His love, and into patiently waiting for Christ.
- 2 PE 1:21 ~ No prophecy ever came from the impulses of men, but holy men spoke as they were directed by the Holy Spirit.

At times, God makes His will apparent to us in dreams and visions. We can request His guidance using prayer and meditation and He will convey it. When God does reveal something to us, we must thank Him and give Him the credit for the mighty works He performs in our lives. But we must be careful. Before accepting a dream or vision as a revelation from God, make sure it is consistent with God's Word. Usually, it is not difficult to distinguish truth from lies. But it is essential that we remain diligent in the study of God's Word so we can recognize the difference between a revelation from God and a deception from Satan.

Lesson: Where Do We Go from Here?

Our life force is found in the living spirit, which energizes the body. Upon death, that spirit returns to God because He gave it to us and we belong to Him. Thus, a believer that dies will automatically travel in spirit to our Father in heaven.

- GEN 35:18 ~ Rachel died and her soul departed (implies separation of body and soul upon death).
- ECC 12:7 ~ Upon death, the spirit returns to God who gave it.
- LUK 8:55 ~ The girl's spirit returned to her when Jesus brought her back to life (implies separation of body and spirit upon death).
- JOH 6:63 ~ Jesus said, "It is the spirit that gives life, not the flesh." Jesus spoke the words of spirit and life.
- 2 CO 3:6 ~ God has made us able ministers of the new testament, not of the letter of the Law, but of the Spirit, for the letter kills, but the Spirit gives life.
- 2 CO 5:8 ~ We are confident, and would prefer to be absent from this body and present with the Lord.

Those, who by God's mercy have been saved through Christ because of their faith in Him, will go directly to Him after they die. God's chosen people will live in peace forever in paradise with our Lord. It will be wonderful there, where there is never any sorrow, pain, or distress. However, those who do not believe and trust in Christ will go to the other place where all hope is lost.

- JOB 8:13–14 ~ The destiny of those who forget God is the loss of all hope, for their trust in worldly things is a fragile one.
- PRO 24:20 ~ Evil people have no future. Their light will be extinguished.
- ECC 9:10 ~ Whatever your hand finds to do, do it with your might; for there is no work, device, knowledge, or wisdom in the grave where you are going.
- ISA 51:11 ~ Those redeemed by the Lord will return singing praises; they will have everlasting joy, and all sorrow and grief will be gone forever.
- ISA 64:4 ~ Since the world began, nobody has heard, seen, or perceived, except God, the wonderful things He has prepared for those who wait for Him.
- JER 18:11–12 ~ God warned them that He was going to destroy them unless they turned from their evil ways. But they said, "It's hopeless. Let us continue in our own plans. We will follow the imaginations of our evil hearts."
- LUK 16:19–31 ~ Jesus told the parable of the rich man and the poor man: There was a rich man who lived a life of pleasure and luxury. A poor man lay at his gate that was weak, hungry, and afflicted, desiring just the crumbs off the rich man's plate. The two men died. The poor man was taken to Abraham's bosom, and the rich man was exiled in Hades. The rich man called out to Abraham asking if he would let the poor man dip his finger into water to wet his parched tongue. But Abraham reminded him how thoughtless and unmerciful he had been to the poor man before, and told him that nobody could pass through the chasm separating the two underworlds. The rich man implored that his family be warned, to prevent them from the same fate. Abraham informed the rich man that they would have to rely on the Word of God like everybody else; if they didn't, not even a visit from the dead would persuade them to change their ways.
- LUK 23:43 ~ Jesus said to the repentant thief, "I tell you the truth, today you will be with me in paradise."

- ACT 2:26–27 ~ My heart is glad and my tongue rejoices; my body abides in hope. For the Lord will not destroy my soul in hell.
- 2 PE 2:4; JDE 1:6 ~ God did not spare the angels that sinned, but sent them to hell, imprisoning them in chains of darkness to be held for judgment.
- REV 7:15–17 ~ They will live before the throne of God and will serve Him day and night in the temple. They will never be hungry, thirsty, hot or cold again. The Lamb among them will feed them, will lead them to fountains of living waters, and will remove all sorrow.

God will allow His people to keep their souls forever. Thus, when Christ returns, Christians will possess that life-giving Spirit that awakens and preserves our bodies, as well as our own minds so we can think for ourselves continuously and still have a mind for Christ. This is our reward for the obedience of faith. It is God's gift to His elect for believing in Him and following His Son Jesus Christ to their heavenly home.

- ISA 55:3 ~ Listen up and come to me, pay attention so your soul might live. I will make an everlasting covenant with you, to give you all the faithful love and mercies I showed to David.
- LUK 21:17–19 ~ Jesus said, "People will hate you because of me, but be patient and you will keep your soul."
- 1 CO 15:42–46 ~ This is the way it will be with the resurrection of the dead. It is sown in corruption it is raised in incorruption. It is sown in dishonor it is raised in glory. It is sown in weakness it is raised in power. It is sown a natural body it is raised a spiritual body. The spiritual did not come first; the natural came first and then the spiritual. Flesh and blood cannot inherit the kingdom, and neither can corruption inherit perfection.
- HEB 10:39 ~ We do not shrink back and we are not destroyed, because those who have faith keep their souls.
- 1 PE 1:2,4 ~ Christians are chosen by God in advance, through sanctification of the Spirit, to be obedient to Christ and cleansed by His blood. Blessed is God the Father of our Lord Jesus Christ. According to His abundant mercy, He recreated in us the living hope, brought by the resurrection of Christ from the dead, to receive an incorruptible and undefiled inheritance reserved in heaven and lasting forever.

When the Lord returns, it will be to call the righteous home and to pronounce judgment upon the wicked. Christians who are both alive and dead will be called. Our spirits will be reunited with our earthly bodies, which will be changed into glorified bodies that will never die.

- JOB 19:25–26 ~ I know that my Redeemer lives and that He will stand upon the earth. And although my flesh will have been destroyed, yet in my flesh I will see God.
- PSA 118:16–17 ~ The righteous rejoice, for the Lord's right hand has done mighty things. I will not die, but live, and I will declare the works of the Lord.
- LUK 20:34–39 ~ Jesus answered them saying, "The people of this age get married. In the next age, those who are considered worthy of taking part in the resurrection will not marry, and will never die, for they will be like the angels. They are God's children, the children of the resurrection. When Moses encountered the burning bush, He learned that the dead arise, for He referred to the Lord as the God of Abraham, Isaac, and Jacob. God is not a God of the dead, but of the living; for to Him all are alive." Some teachers of the Law responded, "Well said, Teacher."
- 1 CO 15:51–58 ~ Here is a mystery of God: We will not all sleep (die) but we will all be changed. Upon Christ's return, in a single moment when the great trumpet sounds, Christ's own, whether alive or dead will arise into heaven to receive new, incorruptible bodies. Hence, the corruptible will have become incorruptible and the mortal will have become

immortal. Then at the end, when He delivers the kingdom of God to the Father, He will destroy death. Then the statement "death is swallowed up in victory" will be true. The godly will receive spiritual bodies that will never die. The flesh is of the earth, the spirit is of heaven; thus, flesh and blood will not inherit the kingdom of heaven. Therefore, be confident in your faith because your labor is not in vain.

- PHP 3:20–21 ~ Christ will change our vile bodies into bodies like His glorified body.
- COL 3:4 ~ When Christ, who is your life, appears again, you also will appear with Him in glory.
- 2 PE 1:3–4 ~ By God's divine power we have received all things pertaining to life and godliness, because we know Him who called all people to righteousness and glory. We cling to His precious promise, that His people will receive a divine nature, and escape the corruption and lust of the world.
- 1 JO 3:1–2 ~ How great is God's love that we should be called His children. The world doesn't know us because it didn't know Him. We are His children, but we don't know yet what that really entails; we do know, however, that we will be like Him, for we will see Him as He really is.

There are differing views concerning the rapture and the resurrection. There are three common views of the rapture, namely the pre-, mid-, and post-tribulation rapture. The two prevailing positions of the thousand-year reign include millennialism and amillennialism. The former holds that there is a physical resurrection of the just prior to the millennium and a second physical resurrection of the unjust after the millennium. The latter viewpoint holds that the first resurrection is a spiritual one occurring at death, and the second a physical resurrection of all humankind on the last day, with the millennium being the unspecified period between Christ's Resurrection and His Second Advent. Thus, the former camp views the millennium as beginning with Christ's return, and the latter see it as ending with Christ's return. Regardless of a person's viewpoint on these issues, the truth is that believers are either raptured or resurrected to receive an inheritance in heaven. The unbelievers will be resurrected, only to die a second death in the lake of fire.

- DAN 12:2 ~ Some will arise to receive everlasting life and some will arise to everlasting shame and contempt.
- PSA 52:5 ~ God will destroy the evil ones forever. He will uproot them from the living.
- ISA 26:14 ~ They are dead and will not live; they will not rise. They have been visited with destruction and all memory of them has been wiped out.
- LUK 17:34–37 ~ Jesus said concerning His second coming, "Two men will be in bed, one will be taken and the other will be left behind; two women will be grinding grain together, only one will be taken; two men will be working in the field, only one will be taken."
- JOH 5:28–29 ~ The time is coming when all who are in the grave will hear His voice and come forth. Those who have been faithful and good will arise to everlasting life, and those who have been evil will arise to receive judgment.
- 1 TH 4:16–17 ~ The Lord will descend from heaven with a shout, with the voice of the archangel, and with a blast from the trumpet of God. Then the dead in Christ will arise first. Those who remain alive in Christ will rise to join the others in the clouds, meeting the Lord in the sky. Those chosen by Christ will live with Him forevermore.
- HEB 12:22–23 ~ You have come to God's holy mountain, to His holy city, to stay with the living God and His multitude of angels. You are part of the assembly and church of the first born, whose names are written in heaven. You are among the righteous, who were redeemed and whose spirits have been made perfect.

- REV 20:4–6,13–15 ~ I (John) saw thrones, and sitting on them were judges. I saw the souls of those who had been beheaded for their testimony of Jesus, who had not worshipped the beast or its image, nor received its mark on their foreheads or hands. They came to life again and reigned with Christ one thousand years. This was the first resurrection. The rest of the dead did not live again until after the thousand years. Blessed and holy are those who share in the first resurrection for they will not be victims of the second death. At the second resurrection the rest of the souls were raised to be judged by God. Death and Hell, and those who were not recorded in the Book of Life, were cast into the lake of fire; this was the second death.

Once you have died, there is no more hope for salvation (HEB 9:27). You must believe in Christ and never reject Him. If you die in your sins, without repentance or forgiveness, you cannot be saved and you will not go to heaven. After the resurrection, the evil and unrepentant ones will be judged, found guilty, and condemned. The penalty will be death, for they will die again, becoming engulfed in the lake of fire with Satan and the other lost souls.

Upon death, those who believed in Christ will be with Him immediately in spirit, in paradise. When the righteous are resurrected, they will be found innocent of their sin, for they will have been cleansed of all unrighteousness by the blood of the Lamb. Believers will receive glorified bodies uncorrupted by sin that will last for eternity; for without sin, there is no death. They will live as brothers and sisters with Jesus in a heavenly house with God the Father.

One final note about the unscriptural doctrines of purgatory, penance, and indulgences, traditions that have been commonly practiced within the Roman Catholic Church. Penance is a way of showing remorse for one's sins through contrition, confession, punishment, and absolution. Yes, we must confess and repent of our sins to God, and true godly sorrow will result in a desire to change. But this does not require one to make any material payment to the church or inflict self-punishment as penance.

Purgatory is a fictional place where the dead go to further expiate their sin, prior to being admitted into heaven. It is proposed that even good people have to do time in purgatory commensurate with their sinfulness. The sentence in purgatory, or the punishment levied as penance, can be remitted by paying monetary indulgences. These are among the doctrines to which Martin Luther objected when instigating the Protestant Reformation. Such deviations from scripture lead people away from the truth and should be rejected.

Clearly, there is nothing anyone can do to earn forgiveness or to purchase his or her freedom from sin and death. If this were the case, why would anyone need a savior? Believers are assured by God Himself in His Word that we will be with Him when we die. This promise is God's guarantee in His covenants and in the Gospel of Jesus Christ. It is the free gift that comes from faith in God's Son, that through Him your sins have been removed and replaced with His righteousness making you acceptable to God (ROM 4:4–8; 2 CO 5:19–21; TIT 2:11–14). Once Jesus sets you free, you are definitely free forever (JOH 8:36).

It is senseless to pay indulgences or penance for something already bought and paid for by Christ (PSA 32:5; PSA 130:3–4; HEB 9:24–28; HEB 10). That is, those who have accepted Christ as their personal Savior have had their penalty paid in full (ISA 53:10–12; ROM 8:1–5). Those who refuse to accept Christ cannot ransom their souls from the grave or buy their way out of a nonstop trip to hell (PSA 49; ISA 64:6; ISA 66:24; 1 PE 1:17–21). The passage to heaven is a one-way journey; there are no stops along the way at purgatory or anywhere else. To render any kind of payment for the sins of oneself or another is to deny the payment Christ already made, and this practice is shameful if not deadly (HEB 6:6).

Lesson: Crown of Life

The Crown of Life is the prize that God promises to all who win the human race. It is the reward for being steadfast in the true faith despite all the worldly temptations to quit. Eternal life is the gift that God gives to anyone who will receive it; one must simply believe that the Lord has given it in order to possess it. Those who do not believe God's promises have no inheritance in His kingdom. However, finishing the race is not easy. It takes instruction, discipline, hard work, and Jesus Christ.

- PRO 27:23–24 ~ Pay attention to your business, for riches do not endure forever, and an earthly crown does not endure to every generation.
- 1 CO 9:24–27 ~ Do you understand that there are many competitors in a race but only one will receive first prize? Therefore, run with the intention of winning that prize. Those who strive to master a task must train hard and discipline themselves. However, they do so to obtain an earthly crown that won't last; but we strive for a crown that will last forever. Therefore, I run like a man with a purpose. I do not fight like a boxer beating the air. Instead, I beat my body into shape, making it serve God's purpose, so that my preaching will not cause me to be disqualified for the prize.
- 2 TI 4:6–8 ~ Paul wrote: I am ready to sacrifice myself, for my time of departure is near. I have fought a good fight and I have finished the race, and my faith is still intact. Hereafter a crown of righteousness awaits me, which the Lord, the righteous judge, will give to me. He will give it, not only to me, but also to everyone who lovingly awaits Christ's coming.
- HEB 11:6 ~ Without faith it is impossible to please Him, for those coming to God must believe that He exists and that He rewards them who diligently seek him.
- JAM 1:12 ~ Blessed are those who persevere despite their trials and temptations, because they will receive the Crown of Life which the Lord has promised to anyone who loves Him.

A great deal of training and effort goes into acquiring the prize. Take for example athletes who compete in sporting events; they train for days, even years, so that they can be the best. They don't give up after losing, and second place is not acceptable either. And after they win, they still do not stop training, but continue to work hard at becoming better, because the next time they compete their previous performance may not be good enough. Furthermore, professionals find no honor in winning unless the game is played according to the rules, and this requires integrity. A true professional strives to become more proficient by continuing to develop in knowledge as well as in skill. Similarly, in order to win the Crown of Life, one must become equipped with the wisdom of God's Word and continue to cultivate the spiritual abilities with which God has blessed them.

- PRO 13:11; PRO 23:4 ~ Wealth obtained by pride will diminish; but those that achieve by way of hard work will see their wealth increase. Don't labor to become rich, and don't concentrate on your own feeble wisdom.
- 1 CO 15:58 ~ Brothers, be constant in your labor, unwavering, firm, and productive. For you can be assured that your labor for the Lord will not be in vain.
- GAL 6:8 ~ Those who sow to the flesh will reap corruption to their flesh; those who sow to the Spirit will from the Spirit reap eternal life.
- 2 TI 3:14–16 ~ Continue in the things you have learned and are convinced of, knowing from whom you have learned them. From a child you have known the Holy Scriptures, which are able to make you wise unto salvation through faith in Jesus Christ. All scripture is given by inspiration of God and is effective for doctrine, for guidance, for correction, and for instruction in righteousness.

- PHP 3:13–14 ~ Brothers, I have not yet taken hold of the prize for which God has called me in the name of Jesus Christ. But I press on, forgetting what is behind and focusing on what lies ahead.
- 2 TI 2:3–5 ~ Endure your hardships with us, like a good soldier of Jesus Christ. Soldiers do not involve themselves with civilian affairs but follow the orders of their commander. Similarly, if a person strives to master the task (as an athlete), he or she does not receive the victor's crown without obeying the rules.
- HEB 12:1–3 ~ Since we are being watched by numerous spectators, let us discard everything that hinders us such as the sin that trips us up, and run the race that has been set before us with perseverance. Let us fix our eyes on Jesus, the author and perfecter of our faith, who for the joy set before Him endured the cross, scorning its shame, and who now sits on His throne at the right hand of God. Remember Him, who endured great opposition from sinful men, so that you will not grow faint and lose heart.
- 2 PE 1:2–8 ~ May the Lord's grace and peace be multiplied to you, through the knowledge of God and of Jesus Christ our Lord. His divine power has given us everything we need for a life of godliness, through the knowledge of Him who called us to His glory and virtue. He has made wonderful and precious promises so that you can partake in His divine nature, and escape the corruption and sinful desires of this world. So be diligent, and become multiplied in your faith, adding to it virtue, knowledge, discipline, patience, godliness, kindness, and love. For, if these things abound in you, you will bear abundant fruit in the knowledge of our Lord Jesus Christ.
- REV 3:11 ~ Jesus said, "I am coming soon. Hold tight to what you have so that nobody can take away your crown."

What is the Crown of Life if not the Lord Himself, who will crown your head in glory? You will wear His glory like a garment, clothed in His righteousness and blanketed in His love, as you persevere in your faith through this life and into the next.

- JOB 29:14 ~ I put on righteousness, and it clothed me; justice was my robe and crown.
- PSA 8:4–5 ~ Who is man that you, Lord, would be mindful of him? For you have made him a little lower than the angels, and have crowned him with glory and honor. (HEB 2:6–9)
- PSA 73:24 ~ You guide me with your counsel, and afterward you will lead me into glory.
- PSA 103:2–4 ~ Praise the Lord, oh my soul, let everything in me praise Him who forgives sins, heals diseases, and redeems my life from destruction. He crowns me with love and tender mercy.
- PRO 10:12 ~ Hatred stirs up strife, but love covers all sins.
- ISA 28:5 ~ On that day the Lord of hosts will be a crown of glory and a diadem of beauty for the remnant of His people.
- ISA 61:10 ~ I will greatly rejoice in the Lord; my soul will be joyful in my God. For He has clothed me with the garments of salvation, he has covered me with the robe of righteousness, just like the groom is adorned with ornaments and the bride is adorned with jewels. Blessed are those whose sins are not counted against them.
- ROM 4:7–8 ~ Blessed are those whose iniquities are forgiven, and whose sins are covered.
- HEB 2:9 ~ We see Jesus, who was made a little lower than the angels to suffer death, now crowned with glory and honor because by the grace of God He tasted death for everyone.
- 1 PE 4:8 ~ Love one another fervently, for love will cover a multitude of sins.
- REV 3:5 ~ Jesus said, "Those who overcome will be clothed in white raiment. Their names will never be blotted out of the Book of Life, for I will acknowledge them before our Heavenly Father and His angels."

God has sent His Son to guide you along the correct route. Follow Him and discover a new lease on life.

- PSA 48:14 ~ He is our God forever and ever. He will be our guide until the day we die.
- PSA 119:105 ~ God's Word is a lamp unto my feet, and a light unto my path.
- ISA 58:11 ~ The Lord will guide you continuously. He will satisfy your soul when it thirsts and He will put meat on your bones. You will be like a watered garden, and like a wellspring where the waters never fail.
- JOH 14:6 ~ Jesus said, "I am the way, the truth, and the life; the only way to the Father is through me."
- 1 TH 3:11 ~ Paul wrote: May God our Father and our Lord Jesus Christ direct you along the path we have followed.
- 2 TH 3:5 ~ May the Lord direct your hearts into the love of God and into the patient waiting for Christ's coming.

God has sent His Spirit to sustain you so that you can endure the race. He will hold you up so you do not fall.

- JDG 16:28–30 ~ Remember when Samson called to the Lord and said, "Oh Lord God, strengthen me, I pray, one more time, so that I may see with my own eyes your vengeance upon the Philistines." Then he caused the entire temple to collapse, killing all of the pagan worshippers.
- PSA 27:14; PSA 31:24; PSA 119:28 ~ Be patient with the Lord and take courage, and He will strengthen your heart. Wait for the Lord those of you whose hope is in Him. My soul is weary and sorrowful; strengthen me Lord in accordance with your Word.
- PSA 55:22 ~ Place your burdens upon the Lord and He will sustain you; He will never allow the righteous to fall.
- ISA 41:10 ~ Do not fear for I am with you. Do not be dismayed for I am your God. I will strengthen you and I will help you. Yes, I will hold you up with the right hand of my righteousness.
- 2 CO 12:9 ~ God said to Paul, "My grace is sufficient for you, because my strength is made perfect in weakness." Therefore I (Paul) gladly accept my difficulties, so that the power of Christ may rest upon me.
- EPH 3:16 ~ I pray that God, according to the richness of His glory, with strengthen you and impart the power of His Spirit into your innermost being.
- 1 PE 5:10 ~ And after you have suffered for a while, may the God of all grace, who through Christ called you into His eternal glory, restore you and strengthen you so that you can be firm and steadfast.

Though the pace is grueling and the path steep, the Lord will strengthen you the entire way. As the race gets longer, the will gets stronger, nourished by the omnipresent grace and mercy of God.

- PSA 46:1 ~ God is our refuge and strength, an ever-present help in trouble.
- PSA 145:18–19 ~ The Lord is near to all who call upon Him in truth. He fulfills the desires of every living thing.
- ISA 55:10–12 ~ The rain and snow that falls from heaven does not return to heaven, but waters the earth, causing the plants to bud and seed, and providing food. So also, God's Word does not return to Him void but accomplishes what He wishes, and prospers where He sends it. We joyfully go out, being led in peace. The mountains and hills sing and the trees

clap their hands; the world rejoices around you. Instead of a thorn bush, a tree will grow. And the name of the Lord will be magnified as an everlasting sign of the nurturing He provides.
- EPH 5:29 ~ Nobody ever hated his or her own flesh, but nourishes and cherishes it, even as the Lord nourishes and cherishes His church.

Jesus Christ is adorned with the royal crown, Himself being the Prince of Peace. So also have we been adopted into the royal family as princes and princesses, and worthy of such a crown. Jesus Christ gives us the desire and the power to obtain the Crown of Life. He knocks on the door of your heart, and if you invite Him in, He will enter and dwell with you. Once He is part of you and you are part of Him, you can achieve anything. Everyone has a choice to welcome Christ or to reject Him. It seems a simple choice. Who wouldn't want God to be a part of them? Are you ready to open the door when He knocks?

- JOB 23:6 ~ Would God prosecute me with His great power? No, but He would put strength in me.
- JOH 15:2 ~ Jesus said, "Every branch in me that does not bear fruit is removed. Every branch in me that bears fruit, God prunes it, so that it can bear more fruit."
- JOH 10:38 ~ Jesus said, "The Father is in me, and I am in Him."
- COL 1:26–27,29 ~ The mystery which was hidden for ages and generations is now made evident to the saints, to whom God will show the riches of His glory which is Christ in you, the hope of glory. Therefore I (Paul) work hard, striving according to His working, which works mightily in me.
- PHP 4:13 ~ I can do all things through Christ who strengthens me.
- REV 3:20 ~ Behold, I stand at the door and knock. Everyone who hears my voice and opens the door, I will come into them, and I will abide (eat) with them, and they with me.

The King of kings came to earth to save us all, but was rejected by the majority of humankind, then and now. He forgave those who mocked, tormented, and tortured Him. The ultimate disgrace was when they marred His precious head with a crown of thorns. His executioners made a joke out of His majesty and kingship, yet that crown of thorns was the most exquisite crown that ever adorned the head of any king in all history. Imagine that! God would allow Himself to be humiliated, dishonored, and debased in order to pay the price that would atone for such despicable sins as these. He is above all, yet placed Himself below all. How great a love is this!

- ZEC 9:9 ~ Rejoice greatly oh daughter of Zion; shout oh daughter of Jerusalem. Behold, your King is coming: He is just and brings salvation. He appears lowly, riding upon a donkey's colt.
- MAT 27:29 ~ After they had constructed a crown of thorns, they placed it on His head, and they put a reed in His right hand; they bowed before Him with bended knee and mocked Him, saying, "Hail, King of the Jews!"
- MAR 15:17 ~ They clothed Him with purple; and they constructed a crown of thorns and placed it on His head.
- JOH 19:2,5 ~ And the soldiers constructed a crown of thorns and placed it on His head; and they put a purple robe around Him. Jesus proceeded forth wearing the crown of thorns and the purple robe. And Pilate said to the crowd, "Behold the man!"

We owe so much to Christ, yet all He requires from us is to believe in His merciful love, love Him back, and share that love with others through works of faithfulness. And though we fall short of these reasonable tasks, He rewards us for trying by crowning us in righteousness, life, and glory. This crown is incorruptible, given to those who trust that the blood of Christ has covered their sins.

- ISA 28:5–6 ~ In that day the Lord of Hosts will be a crown of glory, a garland of beauty to the remnant of His people. He will be a Spirit of justice, sitting in judgment: a source of strength to those that turn the battle back from the gate.
- ISA 62:3 ~ You will be a crown of glory in the Lord's hand: a royal coronet in the hand of God.
- PRO 4:7–9 ~ Wisdom is the principal thing; therefore, seek wisdom, and with it receive understanding. Make this your priority, for with wisdom comes honor. And you will obtain a garland of grace, and a crown of glory.
- HEB 2:6–10 ~ In a certain place one has testified (PSA 8:4–6): Who is man that you are mindful of him; or the son of man that you minister to him? You made him a little lower than the angels, and crowned him with glory and honor; and you set him in charge over the works of your hands. You have placed all things in subjection before his feet. But as yet we cannot see all the things you have entrusted to him. But we see Jesus, who was made a little lower than the angels, now crowned with glory and honor through His suffering of death; so that by the grace of God He might taste death for everyone, and bring many into glory. It was fitting for God, through whom all things exist, to make the champion of our salvation perfect through suffering.
- JAM 1:12 ~ Blessed is the person that endures temptation; for when tried, he or she will receive the Crown of Life which the Lord has promised to those who love Him.
- 1 PE 5:2–4 ~ Be shepherds of God's flock, serve them and be an example to them; and when the Chief Shepherd appears you will receive a crown of glory that will never fade away.
- REV 2:10 ~ Jesus said, "Do not be afraid of suffering and tribulation, for the devil will throw some of you into prison to test your faith, and you will be tormented for ten days. Be faithful, even unto death, and I will give you a Crown of Life."
- REV 3:11 ~ Behold, I come quickly. Hold fast to what you have so that nobody can take your crown away from you.

God is supreme and He reigns forever. And the saints will reign with Christ in His kingdom forever as well as sharing in His glory. What did we do to deserve this? Not a thing. It is only because of what Christ has done for us and the fact that we know it to be true.

- EXO 15:18 ~ The Lord will reign forever and ever.
- PSA 145:13; PSA 146:10 ~ Your kingdom is an everlasting kingdom, and your dominion endures throughout all generations. The Lord your God will reign forever and for all generations. Praise be the Lord!
- ISA 24:23 ~ The moon will be demeaned and the sun ashamed; for the Lord of hosts will reign gloriously in mount Zion and Jerusalem, and before the elders.
- ISA 32:1 ~ Behold, a king will reign in righteousness and princes will rule with justice.
- MIC 4:7 ~ I will make a remnant from the handicapped and a great nation from the outcasts. The Lord will rule over them in mount Zion henceforth, even forevermore.
- ROM 5:18–21 ~ By one man, sin came into the world bringing death, and death was subsequently passed along to humankind for all have sinned. Therefore, while the sin of one brought judgment and condemnation upon humanity, so the righteousness of one brought the

free gift of justification and life. Thus, by the disobedience of one (Adam) we became sinful, and by the obedience of one (Christ) we can become righteous.

- 2 TI 2:12 ~ If we suffer with Him, we also will reign with Him; if we deny Him, He also will deny us.
- REV 20:6 ~ Blessed and holy are those who take part in the first resurrection; on these the second death has no power. They will be priests of God and of Christ, and will reign with Him a thousand years.
- REV 22:5 ~ There will be no night, no need for a candle or the light of the sun; for the Lord God will provide the light; and they will reign forever and ever.

Many people strive for worldly riches, fame, fortune, and crowns of gold. Such things come and go; they do not last, and are valueless in heaven.

- PSA 21:1–4 ~ Oh Lord, I (King David) rejoice in your strength and in your victories. You have given me the desires of my heart and you have satisfied all the requests of my lips. You have welcomed me with rich blessings and placed a crown of pure gold on my head. I asked for life and you provided it, to last forever and ever.
- EZE 21:26–27 ~ The Sovereign Lord says: Remove the diadem and take off the crown. Nothing will be the same as before: the lowly will be exalted and the exalted will be brought down. I will ruin, ruin, yes ruin it all; and it will not be restored until He comes to whom it rightfully belongs, and I will give it all to Him.
- REV 4:4,10–11 ~ Surrounding the throne were twenty-four seats of honor, and upon the seats sat twenty-four elders clothed in white raiment; and they had crowns of gold on their heads. The elders fell down before Him who sat on the throne, and worshipped Him who abides forever and ever; and they cast their crowns of gold before the throne saying, "You alone are worthy, oh Lord, to receive glory, honor, and power; for you have created all things and for your pleasure all things were created that exist.
- REV 19:11–13 ~ And I saw heaven open, and a white horse appeared whose rider is called Faithful and True; in righteousness He judges and make war. His eyes were ablaze with fire, and on His head were many crowns. On Him was written a name that only He knows. He was clothed with a robe dipped in blood; and His name is the Word of God.

CHAPTER SIX

Crown of Life

© 2001 by Andrew Barber (PAu 2–613–596)

G.. F# E... G.. F# E...

VERSE 1
```
         F#..           C#  B.       A.
In the Garden of Eden were Adam and Eve,
         F#             C#      B.   A.
But they fell from God's grace and they had to leave.
         F#..         C#    B...
They passed onto us their original sin,
         G...                A...
And it's bound to continue 'til I don't know when.      G... D B E.......
```

VERSE 2
```
But we've been set free by the blood of the Lamb.
You'd better believe or you're going to be damned.
Keep watch for His coming. Play it safe; play it straight.
On the day He returns it will be too late.      G... D B E....... F. C
```

CHORUS
```
   D...           A...
Jesus, I will wait for you,
   C...              G   C  A.
Hoping that you'll come back soon.
   D...           A...
Strengthen me, I pray dear Lord,
      C.......              D.......
Whereas I cling unto your Word.
      C...                  D.......
Whereas I cling unto your Word.
```

C... A... C... A... C... A... B.......   G.. F# E... G.. F# E...

VERSE 3
```
Being saved through faith just because of God's grace,
I'll strive to persevere until I win this race.
Overcoming my trials, tribulations, and strife,
And attaining first prize of a Crown of Life.      G... D B E....... F. C
```

REPEAT CHORUS

C... A... C... A... C... A... B.......   G.. F# E... G.. F# E...

CHAPTER SEVEN

BIBLE OUTLINE

This outline presents the major themes and events in the Bible. Each book of the Bible is described in terms of the following specifics.

- Author (if known)
- Prevailing themes of individual chapters (chapters denoted by number, 1, 2, etc.)
- References to verses where particular events or themes can be found (verses identified by "v" followed by the number)
- Listing of key passages (important and noteworthy passages from that book of the Bible)

An * by an Old Testament chapter number indicates that the chapter provides a direct and important reference to Christ the Messiah, and related events recorded in the New Testament.

Old Testament Books

Genesis (Author: Moses)
 1. Creation
    a. Heaven and earth (v1–2)
    b. Light (v3–5)
    c. Atmosphere (v6–8)
    d. Land and sea (v9–10); vegetation (v11–13)
    e. Constellations, sun, and moon (v14–19)
    f. Animals, birds, and fish (v20–25)
    g. Man and woman (v26–31)
 2. Garden of Eden
 3. Original sin
    a. Woman's curse: painful labor (v16)
    b. Man's curse: work hard and eat dirt (v17)
 4. Cain kills his brother Abel
 5. Genealogy from Adam to Noah
 6. Noah's ark
 7. Great flood
 8. Flood subsides
 9. Rainbow covenant
 10. Noah's descendants: Japheth (v2–4); Ham (v6–20); Shem (v21–31)
 11. Tower of Babel
    a. Genealogy from Shem to Abram (v10–32)

12. God's guidance to Abram
    a. Abram, Sarai, and Lot travel to Canaan (v4–9)
    b. Abram and family continue to Egypt (v10–13)
13. Abram and Lot split up (Lot settles along Jordan, Abram in Canaan)
14. Sodom and Gomorrah wars
    a. Melchizedek blesses Abram (v17–20)
15. Abram prays for a son (heir)
16. Hagar (Sarai's maid) bears Ishmael (Abram's son)
17. God's covenant with Abram (Abram becomes Abraham)
    a. Sarai (now Sarah) will bear a son (v13–19)
18. Abraham pleads for Sodom and Gomorrah; bargains with God
19. Sodom and Gomorrah's destruction
    a. Angels appear to Lot (v1–3)
    b. Angels threatened by Sodomites (v4–11)
    c. Sodomites are temporarily blinded; Lot and family escape (v12–25)
    d. Lot's wife looks back and is turned to pillar of salt (v26)
    e. Lot impregnates both daughters (v30–36)
    f. Daughters bear sons; descendants are Moabites and Ammonites (v37–38)
20. Abraham deceives King Abimelech
21. Sarah bears Isaac
    a. Hagar and Ishmael sent away (v8–20)
    b. Treaty at Beersheba (v22–34)
*22. God tells Abraham to sacrifice Isaac (Isaac is spared due to Abraham's faith)
23. Sarah dies
24. Isaac marries Rebekah
25. Descendants of Abraham
    a. Abraham remarries and has more children (v1–2)
    b. Abraham dies (v7–9)
    c. Ishmael's descendants (v12–18)
    d. Isaac's descendants; birth of Esau and Jacob (v19–28)
    e. Jacob trades food for birthright from Esau (v28–34)
26. Isaac dwells in Egypt under protection of King Abimelech II
27. Jacob receives blessing from Isaac
*28. Jacob's dream (ladder from earth to heaven with angels)
29. Jacob marries Leah and Rachel (daughters of his uncle Laban)
    a. Leah bears sons: Reuben, Simeon, Levi, Judah (v31–35)
30. Jacob has more children
    a. Bilhah bears sons: Dan, Naphtali (v1–8)
    b. Zilpah bears sons: Gad, Asher (v9–13)
    c. Leah bears more sons and a daughter: Issachar, Zebulun, Dinah (v14–21)
    d. Rachel bears Joseph (v22–24)
31. Jacob flees to Gilead
    a. Laban pursues Jacob (v22–25)
    b. Jacob reconciles with Laban (v26–55)
32—33. Jacob (now Israel) reconciles with Esau
34. Dinah is raped; rape is avenged without Jacob's permission
35. Jacob returns to Bethel
    a. Rachel dies bearing Benjamin (v16–18)
    b. Jacob's twelve sons (v23–26)

    c. Isaac dies (v27–29)
36. Esau's descendants (Edomites)
37. Joseph sold as a slave by his brothers
    a. Joseph's many-colored coat (v3–4)
    b. Joseph's dream of future where family bows before him (v5–11)
38. Judah has sex with his daughter-in-law Tamar
39. Joseph imprisoned because of his master's unfaithful wife
40. Joseph interprets dreams of other prisoners; interpretations come true
41. Joseph becomes prince in Egypt after interpreting Pharaoh's dream
    a. Interpretation: seven years prosperity followed by seven years famine (v1–32)
    b. Joseph has two sons: Manasseh and Ephraim (v50–52)
42—43. Jacob sends sons to Egypt for grain
44. Joseph tricks brothers
45. Joseph reveals himself to brothers
46. Jacob goes to see Joseph
    a. Jacob's (Israel's) descendants (v8–25)
47. Israelites settle in Egypt at Goshen
48. Jacob blesses Joseph's sons
49. Jacob dies
50. Joseph dies

Key Verses:
- GEN 17:7–11 ~ God told Abraham, "I will establish my covenant with you and your descendants, and it will be an everlasting covenant that will continue for generations to come. I will be your God and the God of your offspring. You and your descendants must not break this covenant. To prove your commitment to this covenant, every male among you must be circumcised."
- GEN 22:2–3,7–8,11–13 ~ God told Abraham to take His only legitimate son Isaac, and sacrifice him on a mountain. Abraham proceeded to do as God had requested. Along the way, Isaac asked his father, "Where is the lamb for the sacrifice." Abraham answered, "God will provide the lamb Himself." As Abraham was about to offer Isaac, an angel of God called Abraham by name from heaven. Abraham responded, "Here I am." The angel replied, "Do not harm your son, for it is obvious that you fear and honor God since you were willing to sacrifice your only son as God requested." Abraham found a ram caught in the bushes and offered it as a sacrifice to God. [God intended to provide His only Son to be the sacrifice.]
- GEN 28:12,16–17 ~ Jacob dreamed about a ladder set on earth and reaching into heaven. He saw angels of God ascending and descending upon it. Jacob awoke and declared, "Surely the Lord abides in this place and I was unaware. How awesome is this place for it is the very house of God and the gate to heaven." [The ladder represents Jesus Christ, the Way to heaven.]

Exodus (Author: Moses)
1. Pharaoh enslaves Israelites
2. Moses grows up in Pharaoh's household
    a. Birth of Moses (v1–8)
    b. Moses flees to Midian (v15–20)
    c. Moses marries Zipporah who bears a son (v21–2)
3. God speaks to Moses from burning bush
4. Moses returns to Egypt

5. Pharaoh commands Israelites to make bricks without straw
6. Moses and Aaron plead to Pharaoh to release Israelites
7—11. Plagues (ten in all) sent upon Egypt
   a. Blood (7:14–25)
   b. Frogs (8:1–15)
   c. Gnats (8:16–19)
   d. Flies (8:20–32)
   e. Livestock diseases (9:1–7)
   f. Boils (9:8–12)
   g. Hail (9:13–35)
   h. Locust (10:1–20)
   i. Darkness (10:21–29)
   j. Death of firstborn in Egypt (11:1–10)
12. The Passover
13—14. The Exodus
   a. Parting of the Red Sea (14:21–23)
15. Moses's song and prayer
16. Manna sent from heaven
17. Water springs from a rock
18. Moses becomes judge
19. The journey to Mount Sinai; Moses goes into the mountains
20. Moses receives the Ten Commandments from God
21—23. Additional laws
24. Moses returns from Mount Sinai with the stone tablets (Ten Commandments)
25—27. Moses receives the instructions for the Ark of the Covenant and the tabernacle
28. Aaron becomes priest
29. Consecration of priests
30—31. Additional instructions
32. Israelites worship the golden calf; Moses destroys the tablets
33. God declares the promised land
34. New stone tablets are formed by Moses; God writes the commandments on them
35—40. Ark of the Covenant and tabernacle are built
   a. God's cloud fills the tabernacle (40:34–35)

Key Verses:
- EXO 20:3–17 ~ The Ten Commandments: 1. Do not worship or honor any gods but the Lord God Almighty; 2. Do not make graven images and do not bow down to or serve idols; 3. Do not swear falsely or take God's name in vain; 4. Remember the Sabbath (the seventh day) and keep it a holy day (reserved for worshipping God); 5. Honor your father and mother; 6. Do not kill; 7. Do not commit adultery; 8. Do not steal; 9. Do not commit perjury or falsely accuse anyone; 10. Do not be envious or jealous of someone else, desiring what belongs to them (including their home, spouse, belongings, etc.).
- EXO 24:8 ~ Moses took the blood of the offering and sprinkled it on the book and the people saying, "This is the blood of the Covenant which God made with you concerning His Word."

Leviticus (Author: Moses)
1—5. Offerings (Atonement for sin): Burnt, Meat, Grain, Sin, Trespass, Consecration, Peace
6—7. More on offerings
8—9. Priesthood of Aaron and his sons

10. Aaron's sons disobey God
11. Beasts that can be eaten and not eaten
12. Rules for the mother concerning childbirth
13—14. Rules concerning skin diseases (e.g., leprosy)
15. Rules concerning venereal diseases and menstruation
16. Aaron's atonement offerings for himself and Israel
17. Eating blood is prohibited
18. Deviant sex is prohibited
    a. Incest (v6–18)
    b. Adultery (v20)
    c. Sacrificing children (v21)
    d. Homosexuality (v22)
    e. Bestiality (v23)
19. Additional rules
20. Punishments
21. Rules concerning priests
22. Rules concerning offerings
23. Feasts of the Lord (seven in all)
    a. Passover (v5)
    b. Unleavened Bread (v6)
    c. First Fruits (v10)
    d. Pentecost (v16)
    e. New Year (v24)
    f. Atonement (v27)
    g. Tabernacles (v34)
24—25. Additional rules
26—27. Penalties, rewards, and reimbursements

Key Verses:
- LEV 17:11 ~ The life of all flesh resides in the blood, and I (God) have given it to you upon the altar to make atonement for your souls, for it is the blood that makes atonement for the soul.
- LEV 24:20 ~ Whatever harm or evil you do to someone else shall be done to you; breach for breach, eye for eye, tooth for tooth.

Numbers (Author: Moses)
1. Twelve tribes of Israel (descendants of Jacob)
2. Encampments set up
3—4. Roles of the Levites
5. Penalties for wrongdoing and infidelity
6. Rules concerning marital separation and Nazarites
7. Presentation of tabernacle offerings
8. Purification ceremony for the Levites
9. Rules concerning defilement from a dead body during Passover
10. Marching orders from Sinai
11. Quail sent for meat to eat
12. Aaron and Miriam object to Moses's Ethiopian wife
13. Spies sent to the land of Canaan
14. Rebellious Israelite spies are skeptical, except Caleb and Joshua

15. Sacrifices for sinning out of ignorance
16. Death comes upon dissenters by plague and an earthquake
17. The rod of Levi
18. The priesthood and tithing
19. The offering of Eleazar the priest
20. Arrival at the edge of the promised land
    a. Water springs from a rock (v8–11)
    b. Aaron dies (v22–29)
21. Resistant natives in promised land are conquered
22. Balaam confronted by an angel
23—24. Prophecy that Israel would prevail
25. Israelites sin with the Moabites; Phinehas turns away God's wrath
26. Census is taken
27. Joshua takes command
28. Offerings and feasts
    a. Daily offerings (v1–8)
    b. Weekly offerings (v9–10)
    c. Monthly offerings (v11–15)
29. Feasts and offerings
30. Rules concerning vows
31. Defeat of the Midianites
32. Range land available for cattle
33. Journeys of the Israelites summarized
34. Allocation of land
35. Rules concerning wrongful death and murder
36. The inheritance of unwed daughters

Key Verses:
- NUM 6:24–26 ~ The benediction of the Lord: May the Lord bless and keep you; may the Lord make His face shine upon you and be gracious to you; may the Lord smile upon you and give you His peace.

Deuteronomy (Author: Moses)
1—3. Moses reviews God's laws, the Exodus, and the conquest of Canaan
4. Obey God if you wish to keep your inheritance
5—6. Moses reviews the Law, emphasizing obedience
7—12 Moses reviews rules concerning the promised land; vow of obedience before crossing
    Jordan River
13. Death to all false prophets and their followers
14. What to eat and not to eat
15. Release for debtors and servants after six years
16—17. Reminders about feasts, laws, rules, and punishment
18. Witchcraft and divination prohibited
19. Additional rules and regulations
20—21. God protects His people in battle
22. Promiscuous sex and rape are prohibited
23. Do not worship with unbelievers; live upright and be neighborly
24. Rules concerning divorce and slavery
25. Rules concerning controversies

26. Giving of the first fruits and tithing
27. Curses for sinning against another or oneself
28—30. Blessings for obedience and curses for disobedience
31. Joshua appointed leader of the Israelites
32. Moses's song and prayer
33—34. Moses blesses the Israelites and then dies

Key Verses:
- DEU 4:29–31 ~ If, from this time forward, you will seek the Lord, provided you seek Him with all your heart and soul, you will find Him. If you are in tribulation, even in the later days, and you turn to God and are obedient to Him, God who is merciful will not forsake you or destroy you. God will never forget the covenant He made with your ancestors.
- DEU 6:2–7 ~ Fear the Lord and keep all His commandments and laws. Ensure that your children and your children's children obey God. Do this and you will prosper and your life will be prolonged. Love God with all your heart, soul, and might. Keep God's Word in your heart and teach His ways carefully and thoughtfully to your children. Talk with your family all the time about God, every day and night, whenever you are together.
- DEU 18:10–12 ~ These things are an abomination to God: sacrificing one's child; practicing witchcraft, astrology, black magic, and fortunetelling; calling upon the dead and consulting with evil spirits.
- DEU 32:35 ~ To God belongs vengeance and recompense. The evil nation will slide in due time, for the day of their calamity is at hand, and the things that will come upon them will come fast.

Joshua (Author: Attributed to Joshua, and Eleazar son of Aaron)
1. God speaks to Joshua, and the people follow him
2. Rahab hides two spies sent ahead for reconnaissance
3—4. Crossing the Jordan river on dry land
5. Encampment at Gilgal
6. Fall of Jericho
7. Achan stoned to death for taking bounty
8. Fall of Ai
9. Gibeon tricks the Israelites; Gibeonites are spared
10. Joshua's army conquers; five Amorite kings are hanged
    a. Time stands still (v12–13)
11. More kings fall
12. List of fallen kings
13—19. Inheritance of Israel and allocation of land
20. Cities of refuge
21. Cities of Levites
22. Phinehas's (the priest) declaration
23. Joshua's farewell
24. Joshua dies

Key Verses:
- JOS 1:8 ~ This book of the Law will never leave your mouth, and you will meditate on it day and night, so that you can act in accordance with all that is written therein. Then your ways will be prosperous and you will enjoy success.

- JOS 5:6 ~ The children of Israel wandered forty years in the wilderness, until all the men of war that came out of Egypt were consumed because they disobeyed the voice of the Lord. For the Lord had warned them He would not show them the land flowing with milk and honey promised to their fathers. [Of all men over twenty, only Joshua and Caleb would enter the Promised Land: see NUM 26:65.]

Judges (Author: Attributed to Samuel)
 1. Fall of Canaan; survivors pay tribute to Israel
 2. Israel serves false gods and are cursed; judges are appointed by God to keep the Law
 3. Succession of warrior judges
     a. Judge Othniel (v9)
     b. Judge Ehud (v15)
     c. Judge Shamgar (v31)
 4—5. Judge Deborah defeats Canaanites
 6—8. Judge Gideon defeats Midianites
     a. Midianites kill each other in battle (7:22)
 9. Abimelech (Gideon's son) is slain for evil ways
 10—11. Fall of Ammon
     a. Judge Tola (10:1–2)
     b. Judge Jair (10:3–4)
     c. Judge Jephthah (11:8)
 12. Fall of Ephraim
     a. Judge Ibzan (v8–9)
     b. Judge Elon (v11)
     c. Judge Abdon (v13)
 13. Samson is born
 14. Judge Samson's riddle
 15. Samson versus the Philistines
     a. Samson kills one thousand men with the jawbone of an ass
 16. Samson is deceived by Delilah
     a. Samson destroys temple of Dagon and all inhabitants, including himself (v25–30)
 17. Micah finds a Levite priest
 18. Idolatry of Micah and the Danites
 19. Levite's concubine is raped to death by Benjamite men
     a. Girl's body is chopped into twelve pieces and sent to the Israelites (v29)
 20. Benjamites are defeated, Israel is avenged
 21. Remnant of Benjamites find wives

Ruth (Author: Attributed to Samuel; possibly others)
 1. Ruth's husband dies; she stays with Naomi, her mother-in-law
 2. Ruth meets Boaz
 3—4. Boaz, a kinsman of her deceased spouse, marries Ruth

1 Samuel (Author: Possibilities include Samuel, Nathan, and Zabud, son of Nathan)
 1. Samuel is born
 2. Eli's evil sons must die
 3. God calls Samuel in a dream to serve Him
 4. Philistines capture the Ark of the Covenant

5. Ark is a curse to the Philistines
6. Philistines return the Ark of the Covenant
7. Philistines are subdued
8. Israel asks for a king
9. Saul seeks out Samuel
10. Samuel anoints Saul
11. Saul becomes king
12. Samuel's warning
13. Samuel prophesies against Saul
14. Israelites battle Philistines
15. Samuel chastises Saul
    a. Samuel kills King Agag (v32–33)
16. Samuel anoints David
    a. David serves Saul (v14–23)
17. David kills Goliath the giant
18. David stays in Saul's palace
    a. David and Jonathan (Saul's son) become friends (v1–4)
    b. Saul detests David (v5–16)
    c. David marries Michal (Saul's daughter) (v20–29)
19. David escapes from Saul, finds Samuel
20. David and Jonathan meet secretly
21—23. David hides out
24. David sneaks up on Saul but spares his life
25. Abigail persuades David not to attack Nabal
    a. Samuel dies (v1)
    b. Nabal dies of heart attack (v36–38)
    c. David marries Abigail (v39–42) and Ahinoham (v43)
26. David spares Saul again
27. David hides out in the land of the Philistines
28. Saul consults witch of Endor
    a. Ghost haunts Saul (v11–20)
29. Philistines battle against Saul in valley of Jezreel
30. David rescues captured wives and destroys Amalekites
31. Philistines defeat Saul
    a. Saul's sons killed (v1–2)
    b. Saul takes his life (v3–4)

Key Verses:
- 1 SA 15:22–23 ~ Samuel said to King Saul, "Does the Lord appreciate burnt offerings and sacrifices as much as He does obedience? To obey is better than to sacrifice, and to listen is more important than the flesh of rams. For rebellion is as bad as witchcraft, and pride is as evil as idolatry. Since you have rejected the command of the Lord, He has rejected you as king."

2 Samuel (Author: Possibilities include Nathan, Zabud, and Gad)
1. David mourns Saul and Jonathan
2—4. War between David and Saul's sons (and among Saul's sons)
    a. Abner makes a treaty with David (3:6–21)
    b. Joab kills Abner (3:22–27)

5. King David unites Israel with Judah
    a. David takes Jerusalem (v6–10)
    b. David defeats Philistines (v17–25)
6. David celebrates arrival of the Ark of the Covenant
*7. Nathan prophesies coming of Christ
    a. David's song and prayer (v18–29)
8. David conquers Moab, Syria, and extends the kingdom
9. David helps Jonathan's lame son
10. David defeats Ammonites and Syrians
11. David commits adultery with Bathsheba
    a. David sends Bathsheba's husband Uriah into battle to be killed (v14–24)
12. Nathan chastises David for his sin and curses David's family
    a. David repents (v13–23)
    b. Bathsheba bears Solomon (v24)
13. Amnon (David's son) rapes his half-sister Tamar (David's daughter)
    a. Absalom (Tamar's brother) has Amnon killed (v19–29)
    b. Absalom flees the country (v34–38)
14. Absalom returns
15—17. Absalom plots against David
    a. David flees the country (15:13–17)
    b. Absalom sleeps with David's concubines (16:20–22)
18. David defeats Absalom
    a. Absalom is killed (v9–15)
19. David returns
20. Joab pursues the rebels; returns with the head of Sheba
21. Sons of Saul are hanged; sons of Goliath are slain
22. David's farewell song and prayer
23. David's heralding of the valiant men in his command
24. Census of David's army
    a. David repents for taking census (v10–25)

Key Verses:
- 2 SA 7:12–15 ~ Nathan's prophecy: After you (David) are dead and buried, I (God) will raise up one of your descendants and establish His kingdom. He will build a house in my name, and I will give Him an everlasting throne and kingdom. I will be His Father, and He will be my Son. If He sins, He will be punished by men. But my mercy will never be taken away from Him like I withdrew it from Saul.

1 Kings (Author: Possibilities include Nathan, Elijah, Elisha, and Jeremiah)
1. Solomon declared successor by David (V28–53)
2. Solomon becomes king
    a. David dies (v10–11)
3. Solomon asks God for wisdom
    a. Solomon settles dispute over baby (v16–28)
4. Allocation of authority
5. Trade agreement between Solomon and Hiram of Tyre
6. Solomon builds temple
7. Solomon builds palace
8. Ark of the Covenant brought to temple

a. God's cloud fills temple (v10–11)
   b. Solomon's dedication prayer (v12–61)
9. Solomon builds cities and a navy
10. Solomon's fame spreads
    a. Queen of Sheba visits Solomon (v1–13)
    b. Solomon becomes richest and wisest king of all time (v23)
11. Solomon disobeys God; Solomon dies
    a. Solomon marries many foreign women (v1–4)
    b. Solomon has many adversaries (v14–40)
12. Rebellion and idolatry; kingdom splits; Lord stays with Judah, but not Israel
13. King Jeroboam of Israel falls from grace
14. King Rehoboam of Judah falls from grace
15. Good king Asa of Judah, followed by several evil kings
16. Evil king Ahab of Israel provokes the Lord more than others
17. Elijah is fed by ravens in the desert
    a. Elijah replenishes widow's food (v13–16)
    b. Elijah revives widow's son (v19–22)
18. Elijah slaughters prophets of Baal
    a. Fire from heaven consumes alter soaked with water (v30–38)
19. Elijah flees to Horeb
20. Ahab defeats Ben-Hadad (king of Syria)
21. Wickedness of Ahab and Jezebel; murder of Naboth for his vineyard
    a. Elijah prophesies against Ahab and Jezebel (v20–26)
22. War between Israel and Syria; King Jehoshaphat reigns in Judah
    a. Elijah's prophecy against Ahab and Jezebel is fulfilled (v35–37)

2 Kings (Author: Possibilities include Nathan, Elijah, Elisha, and Jeremiah)
1. Elijah calls fire upon Samaritan armies and proclaims that King Ahaziah will die
2. Elijah ascends into heaven on a fiery chariot; Elisha becomes prophet in his stead
3. Elisha prophesies against Moab
4—6. Elisha performs miracles
    a. Elisha revives dead boy (4:8–37)
    b. Elisha heals Naaman of leprosy (5:1–27)
    c. Elisha makes ax head float (6:3–7)
    d. Elisha blinds armies of Aram (6:8–23)
7. Elisha prophesies there will be grain for food
8. Hazael inherits throne of Syria
9. Jehu anointed king of Israel (v1–6)
    a. Elijah's prophecy against Jezebel fulfilled (v30–37)
10. Ahab's seventy sons and household are killed in response to Jehu's command
    a. Prophets of Baal killed by Jehu (v18–28)
11. Joash anointed king of Judah; Jehoiada destroys temple of Baal
12. King Joash repairs temple of the Lord
13—16. Succession of good kings and mediocre kings
    a. Elisha dies (13:20)
    b. Jerusalem is plundered (14:8–14)
17. Assyria conquers Israel
18. Good King Hezekiah of Judah trusts God, rebels against Assyria
19. Isaiah prophesies against Assyria

a. Angel kills 185,000 Assyrians (v35)
20. King Hezekiah's faith earns him fifteen more years of life
   a. God reverses time as a sign to Isaiah and Hezekiah (v8–11)
   b. Isaiah prophesies about the Babylonian empire (v12–18)
21. Evil kings cause Judah to sin
22. Good King Josiah of Judah
   a. Priest finds Book of the Law (v8)
23. Josiah renews covenant before his death, destroys pagan idols, altars, and priests
   a. Josiah dies in battle of Megiddo (v29–30)
24—25. Babylon (King Nebuchadnezzar) conquers Judah and destroys Jerusalem

1 Chronicles (Author: Attributed to Ezra)
1—9. Genealogy from Adam through the twelve tribes of Israel
10. Saul and his sons are killed in battle
11—12. King David's captains and valiant men
   a. David takes Jerusalem (11:4–8)
13. David brings Ark of the Covenant to house of Obededom
14. David subdues Philistines
15. David celebrates return of the Ark of the Covenant
16. David sings praises
17. Nathan tells David that his son will build God's temple
18—20. David conquers Philistines, Moabites, Ammonites, Edomites, Amalekites, Syrians
21. Census of David's army and God's curse for David's sin
22. David charges Solomon to build temple
23—25. Division of responsibilities among Levites and priests
26. Division of church administrators
27. Division of armies
28. David declares Solomon successor to throne; specifications provided for temple
29. David's farewell address and prayer

Key Verses:
- 1 CH 29:11 ~ To you, oh Lord, belongs all greatness, power, glory, victory, and majesty; for all that is in heaven and earth is yours; yours is the kingdom; you, oh Lord are exalted as the head above all.

2 Chronicles (Author: Attributed to Ezra)
1. Solomon asks God for wisdom
2—4. Solomon has temple and furnishings built
5. Ark of the Covenant brought to temple
6. Solomon prays in temple
7. Fire from heaven consumes Solomon's offering; God appears to Solomon
8. Solomon builds cities and marries Pharaoh's daughter
9. Queen of Sheba visits Solomon
   a. Solomon dies (v30–31)
10. Kingdom splits
11. Rehoboam rules Judah
12. King of Egypt takes away the riches of Judea
13. Israel wages war with Judah and is defeated
14. King Asa of Judah defeats Ethiopians

15. Asa unites Judah and destroys idols
16. Asa trusts Syria in vain
17. Peace under King Jehoshaphat
18. Micaiah prophesies against King Ahab of Israel
19. Jehoshaphat establishes priests and judges
20. Jehoshaphat observes as Moabites and Ammonites destroy themselves
21—22. Evil kings succeed Jehoshaphat
23. Jehoiada the priest crowns Joash king of Judah
24. King Joash repairs the temple, later falls from grace after Jehoiada dies (v17–25)
25. King Amaziah of Judah commits idolatry
26. King Uzziah builds towers and advanced weapons; he is stricken with leprosy after defiling the sanctuary
27. King Jotham of Judah prospers
28. Evil King Ahaz of Judah falls before Syrian king
29. Good King Hezekiah purifies the temple
30. Hezekiah celebrates Passover and unites Jerusalem
31. Hezekiah reestablishes the Law
32. Assyrian siege of Jerusalem fails; angel kills 185,000 Assyrians
33. King Manasseh of Judah repents
34. Good King Josiah of Judah repairs the temple; book of Law is found
35. Josiah celebrates the Passover
36. Babylon (King Nebuchadnezzar) conquers Judah

Key Verses:
- 2 CH 7:14 ~ God says, "If my people who bear my name would humble themselves, pray, seek my face, and turn from their evil ways, I would hear them from heaven, and I would forgive them of their sins and heal their land.

Ezra (Author: Ezra)
1. Cyrus, king of Persia, permits the Jews to rebuild the temple in Jerusalem
2. Exiles return to Judah
3. Foundation of the temple is laid
4. Artaxerxes persuaded to disallow the rebuilding
5. Appeal is made to King Darius to allow rebuilding
6. King Darius allows rebuilding; temple is completed
7. Ezra returns to Jerusalem with decree from Artaxerxes
8. Money is gathered for furnishing the temple
9. Ezra asks God for mercy concerning intermarriages with foreigners
10. Israelites confess and divorce their foreign spouses

Nehemiah (Author: Nehemiah)
1. Nehemiah prays for the Jews
2. Nehemiah appeals to King Artaxerxes who gives permission for him to go to Jerusalem and rebuild city
3—4. Rebuilding of the gates and walls of Jerusalem continues despite opposition
5. Nehemiah ensures the poor will be reimbursed
6. Wall of Jerusalem completed much to the dismay of neighboring nations
7. Congregation assembles
8. Ezra reads the Book of the Law; the feasts begin to be celebrated accordingly

9—10. Israelites confess and renew the covenant, giving tithes
11—12. Residents of Jerusalem selected
   a. Walls of Jerusalem dedicated (12:27–47)
13. Nehemiah prays

Esther (Author: Unknown; Possibilities include Mordecai and Ezra)
1. King Xerxes of Persia disowns Queen Vashti
2. Mordecai introduces Esther to Xerxes; Mordecai saves the king's life
3. Haman plots to destroy the Jews
   a. Mordecai refuses to bow to Haman (v1–6)
4. Mordecai solicits help from Esther
5. Esther honors king with banquet
6. Mordecai honored at banquet
7. Esther exposes Haman's plot to eradicate Jews to Xerxes; Haman hanged on gallows meant for Mordecai
8. Mordecai takes Haman's place in the palace and voids all edicts of Haman
9. Haman's sons and other enemies of the Jews are killed
10. Mordecai becomes second to the king

Job (Author: Possibilities include Job, Elihu, David, and Solomon)
1—2. Satan seeks to destroy Job's spirit
   a. Job loses livestock, servants, children, everything (1:13–20)
   b. Job stricken with sores (2:7–8)
   c. Job's friends mourn with him (2:11–13)
3. Job is distraught, curses his life
4—5. Eliphaz thinks Job is being punished
6—7. Job grieves, claiming innocence
8. Bildad thinks Job is being punished
9. Job admits imperfection
10. Job is confused, doesn't understand why he is being punished
11. Zophar thinks Job should not question God's motives
12. Job denies being spiritually ignorant
13. Job denies being wicked, maintaining his hope of salvation
14. Job admits his sinful flesh and the fact that he will die from sin
15. Eliphaz accuses Job, condemning himself with vain words
16—17. Job desires comfort, not pity or scorn
18. Bildad gets defensive; asserts that wickedness will be rewarded with destruction
19. Though he suffers in this life, Job knows he will still go to heaven someday
20. Zophar declares that the wicked will inherit nothing
21. Job asserts that the wicked are not punished in this life, but the next
22. Eliphaz accuses Job of wickedness, and recommends he turn to God
23—24. Job fears God and is not rebellious
25. Bildad asserts that everybody is sinful
26. Job declares God to be all-powerful
27. Job holds fast to his faith despite his afflictions
28. Job realizes that fear of God and faith in His divine wisdom is the basis of wisdom for man
29—30. Job longs for the days when he was respected as a righteous man
31. Job defends himself
32—36. Elihu accuses Job of self-righteousness, asserting that all people must repent

37. Elihu suggests that nobody can second-guess God
38—39. God reminds Job about his mortality and flesh
40—41. God informs Job that his anger and pride are foolishness, and that such vanity comes from the devil
42. Job admits he did not understand God's purpose, and repents
    a. God commands Eliphaz, Bildad, and Zophar to repent for the same reasons Job did
    b. God blesses Job with twice the possessions and with another family (v10–17)

Key Verses:
- JOB 5:17 ~ Blessed is a person corrected by God; never despise the discipline of the Lord.
- JOB 19:25–26 ~ I know my that Redeemer lives and that He shall stand upon the earth on the last day. And though worms will destroy my body in the grave, yet in my flesh I will see God.
- JOB 32:8 ~ It is a person's spirit, the breath of the Almighty, that enables him or her to understand.
- JOB 33:14–17 ~ God speaks again and again, but humankind does not perceive it. While in a deep sleep, in a dream or vision, God opens the ears of people and provides them with instructions, so that they will forget their pride and follow God's own purpose for their lives.

Psalms (Author: David, Solomon and others)
1. Blessed are the godly
*2. Only those that serve the Lord and trust the Son will inherit the earth
3. God protects us from our enemies
4. Righteousness reaps gladness
5. The wicked will be destroyed
6. The Lord is merciful to those who repent
7. God will judge everyone according to their ways
8. God should be praised for loving humans as He does
9. Judgment comes to all people
10—11. The wicked will be destroyed
12. God's words are pure and true, but the words of people are vain
13—17. Corruption abounds; but trust in the Lord and honor Him, and He will abide with you
18. God provides deliverance to those who serve Him
19. God's laws are perfect and convert the soul
20—21. God saves His anointed, but the wicked will be destroyed
*22. Christ's sufferings are referenced
*23. The Lord is the Good Shepherd who protects His flock
24. God is the king of glory
25. God is forgiving to those who trust in Him
26. Stay away from evil
27—28. Seek the Lord and He will help you
29. The voice of God is powerful
30—31. God is merciful and will preserve the faithful
32. Confess your sin and you will be forgiven
33—34. Fear God and praise Him and He will deliver your soul from death
35. God will defend the righteous
36—37. Pride makes people evil; the wicked will be cut off; the righteous will find peace and life
38. When you feel beaten and weary, commit yourself to the Lord and He will not forsake you

39—40. Don't be vain; seek the Lord and trust in Him
41. Be merciful to others as God is to you
42—43. Seek the Lord with all your strength and He will lift you up
44. Do not forget God and He will not forget you
45. God is glorious
46. God is our refuge and strength
47—48. Praise the Lord
49. There is no amount of money that can ransom the soul
50. Speak always of God's glory
51. Confess your sins; pray for God's Spirit to preserve and guide you
52—56. God destroys the wicked and saves the good
57. Praise God for His mercy
58. God's vengeance will be upon the wicked
59—60. God delivers us from the wicked
*61. The righteous King will reign forever
62. Wait for God and trust Him
63. Seek the Lord
64—65. God preserves and nourishes the righteous
66—67. Sing praises to God
68. God is almighty and all-powerful
69—70. God will save His people
71—72. Trust in God and He will deliver you
73—75. The ungodly will perish
76. Fear the Lord and He will judge you innocent
77. Come to the Lord when you are troubled
78. Proclaim God and all His mighty deeds to the world
79. God will render harsh judgment against the wicked
*80. God's right hand, the Son of Man, will plant a righteous vine
81. Israel should never have turned from God
82. God judges all
83. Those who are against God will perish
84. God is a blessing to all people
85—86. God is merciful and truthful
87. Worship the Lord
88. Trouble vexes the soul
*89. God is holy and faithful to His eternal covenant
90. Fear the wrath of God
91. God protects us
92. Give thanks to God
93. God is mighty
94. Vengeance belongs to God
95—101. Thank and praise God; exalt God
102. God answers prayer
103—108. Bless the Lord; praise and thank Him for all His marvelous works
109. The wicked will receive judgment equal to their deeds
*110. God will send a ruler and priest, His own right hand
111. Praise the Lord for his marvelous works
112. God shows favor to the upright, but the wicked will perish
113. Bless the Lord for His mercy

114—115. Fear and trust God and you will be blessed
116. Love God and call upon Him
117—*118. Praise and thank God; He is our cornerstone
119. Seek God and obey Him
120—124. Turn to the Lord for help, for He is on our side
125—128. The Lord does great things for those who trust Him
129—131. Hope in the Lord
132. Stay faithful to God
133—136. Thank and praise God, for peace and gladness are with those who are with God
137. Sadness over the fall of Jerusalem
138. Praise the Lord
139. The Lord knows all things
140—144 God delivers the righteous from evil and violence in the fight to overcome evil
145—146. God preserves us
147—150. Praise the Lord; tell everyone about the wonders of God and His enduring mercy

Key Verses:
- PSA 1:1–3 ~ Blessed is he that does not walk in the counsel of the ungodly, or stand in the path of sinners, or sit in the seat of the scornful. His delight is the Law of the Lord and he meditates upon it day and night. He will be like a tree planted by flowing rivers, that brings forth fruit in due season; his leaf will not wither, and whatever he does will prosper.
- PSA 19:14 ~ Let the words of my mouth and the meditation of my heart be acceptable to you, oh Lord, my strength and my Redeemer.
- PSA 23:1–6 ~ The Lord is my Shepherd; He provides everything I need. He lets me graze in green pastures beside still waters. He restores my soul. He leads me in paths of righteousness for His namesake. Even when I walk through the valley of the shadow of death, I will not be afraid; His rod and staff protect and comfort me. He prepares a table before me in the presence of my enemies. He anoints my head with oil; my cup overflows. Surely goodness and mercy will always follow me, and I will live in the house of the Lord forever.
- PSA 32:5 ~ I confessed my sins to God, I did not hide them, and God forgave me of my sins.
- PSA 37:4–5 ~ Find your delight in the Lord and He will give to you the desires of your heart. Commit yourself to the Lord and trust in Him, and He will make your desires come to pass.
- PSA 51:10–12 ~ Create in me a clean heart, Lord, and renew an upright spirit within me. Don't remove me from your presence and don't take your Holy Spirit from me. Restore to me the joy of your salvation, and uphold me with your free Spirit.
- PSA 95:1–3 ~ Let us sing to the Lord, the rock of our salvation. Let us come before Him with thanks, praise, and psalms. For He is a great God, and a great King above all gods.
- PSA 110:1 ~ God said to my Lord, "Sit at my right hand and I will crush your enemies under your feet."
- PSA 118:22 ~ The stone that the builders rejected became the main cornerstone.
- PSA 122:1 ~ I was glad when they said to me, "Let us go to the house of the Lord."
- PSA 145:18–20 ~ The Lord is near to all who call upon Him in truth. He fulfills the desires of every living thing. He hears their cries and saves them. He preserves all who love Him, but the wicked He will destroy.

Proverbs (Author: Solomon, his advisors, and King Lemuel)
1. Sinners will destroy themselves
2—4. Search for the wisdom of God's laws, don't rely on your own understanding

5—7. Don't commit adultery; stay away from prostitutes and loose women
8. Righteousness is wisdom
9—10. Forsake the foolish and walk in righteousness
11. The righteous will avoid trouble, but the wicked will find it
12. Truthfulness stands the test of time, but lies eventually are uncovered
13—14. Evil reaps only shame and death; goodness reaps honor and life
15. The righteous person thinks before speaking, but the evil person blurts out foolishness
16—17. The humble will be merry; the proud will find sorrow
18. Be patient and prudent
19. Be compassionate and kind
20. Be sober, merciful, and patient
21. Don't be deceitful, proud, or covetous
22. Don't be lazy, hateful, or oppressive
23. Don't strive for worldly riches; do not envy sinful people or associate with sinners
24. Don't be mischievous or lazy
25—26. Don't gossip or disclose secrets
27. Don't be conceited and don't brag
28. Confess your sins; don't strive to be rich
29. Don't take bribes or obtain riches through flattery
30. Don't brag and don't lie
31. A woman of virtue is very valuable to her husband

Key Verses:
- PRO 1:7 ~ The fear of the Lord is the beginning of knowledge, but fools despise wisdom and instruction.
- PRO 3:5–8 ~ Trust in the Lord with all your heart; do not rely on your own understanding. Acknowledge God in everything you do, and He will direct you in your ways. Do not consider yourself wise, but fear the Lord, refrain from evil, and you will be healthy and strong.
- PRO 6:16–19 ~ There are seven things that the Lord hates: pride and conceit; lying and deceit; shedding of innocent blood; a wicked imagination; those who delight in mischief; false accusations and committing perjury; and those who incite arguments and plot discord.
- PRO 16:3 ~ Commit your acts to God and He will establish your thoughts.
- PRO 22:6 ~ Instruct your children in the way they should go and when they mature, they will not depart from it.
- PRO 22:16; PRO 28:22 ~ Those who oppress the poor to become richer, and those who help only the rich, they will become the needy. Those who try to get rich quick have an evil eye, and do not consider the poverty that will come upon them.
- PRO 28:13 ~ Whoever covers up their sins will not prosper; but those who confess and forsake their sins will obtain mercy.

Ecclesiastes (Author: Solomon)
1. There is no limit to what can be learned, but with wisdom comes responsibility
2. The pressures of this world amount to nothing
3. For everything there is an appropriate time
4. Two can do better than one
5. Don't make vows you can't keep; enjoy what you have, and don't yearn for more
6. Don't let your desires control you, let God control you
7. Seek truth and don't believe everything you hear

8. The wicked have no control over their eventual demise
9. Make the best of everything in life; do not fret about the future or the past
10. Be careful what you say; folly is its own reward
11. Rejoice every day for all your blessings
12. Always remember God

Key Verses:
- ECC 3:1 ~ For everything there is a season, and a time for every purpose under heaven.
- ECC 5:10–12 ~ Those who love money will never be satisfied with it; those who love abundance will never have enough. When goods increase, there is an increase in expenditures. What good is it to those who have plenty, except merely to look at it? The sleep of working people is sweet, whether they have much or little; but the abundance of the rich will not allow them to sleep soundly.
- ECC 8:8 ~ Nobody has power over their spirit to retain it. Neither has anyone power at the time of death to avoid it; neither shall wickedness deliver anyone from death.
- ECC 9:10–11 ~ Whatever your hand finds to do, do it with your might; for there is no work, device, knowledge, or wisdom in the grave where you are going. I discovered that the race does not belong to the swift, nor the battle to the strong, nor the bread to the wise, nor riches to the knowledgeable, nor favor to the skilled; but timeliness and luck happen to everyone.

Song of Solomon (Author: Solomon)
1—8. Songs of love; reference to the love between the groom (Christ) and the bride (His Church); God's prescription for love, courtship, and marriage; the many facets of love

Key Verses:
- SOS 2:7; SOS 3:5; SOS 8:4 ~ Do not arouse or awaken love until it is ready.

Isaiah (Author: Isaiah)
1—2. Turn to the Lord and be redeemed
3. Judah and Jerusalem will be judged
4. God will cleanse the world of filth
5. Woe to those who delight in evil
6. Isaiah volunteers for service to God
*7. Prophecy of the coming Messiah
8. The Assyrian will come and conquer
*9. The Prince of Peace will come as will much wickedness
10. Fear God, not the Assyrian
*11. The Branch will judge with righteousness
*12. Praise God for the Holy One of Israel
13. Isaiah prophesies against Babylon
14. Isaiah prophesies against Lucifer (Satan) and his minions
15—16. Isaiah prophesies against Moab
17. Isaiah prophesies against Syria and Damascus
18. Isaiah prophesies against Ethiopia
19. Isaiah prophesies against Egypt
20. Further mention of the fall of Ethiopia and Egypt
21. Isaiah prophesies against Media and Arabia
22. Isaiah prophesies against Judah and Jerusalem
23. Isaiah prophesies against Tyre

24. The land will be desolated
25. God will bring down the wicked and destroy death
26. Sing His praises, for God will establish His everlasting kingdom of peace and will destroy evil
27. Sin will be destroyed and the righteous will be delivered
28. Woe to Ephraim; those who make contracts with death will find them to be null and void
29. Woe to Ariel; the wicked will be cut off
30. Woe to those who disobey God
31. Woe to those who seek help from anyone but God
32. Judgment will come to the wicked, but the righteous will find peace
33. Treachery is its own reward, but the upright will live with God
34. God will have His revenge
35. The ransomed of the Lord will return to Him
36. King of Assyria tries to lead people away from King Hezekiah and God
37. Angel of God kills 185,000 Assyrians
38. Hezekiah repents and earns fifteen more years of life
    a. Time is reversed (v6–8)
39. Isaiah prophesies that Babylon will capture Judah
40. Prepare for God in all His glory
*41. God will redeem Israel through His Holy One (Christ)
*42. God's servant comes; He will be a light to the Gentiles
*43—45. The Redeemer and God are one; there are no other gods
46. Listen to God's promise and refrain from idol worship
47. Don't depend on astrologers and sorcerers to help you
48—49. Obey God and He will lead you into righteousness
50. God will help those who seek Him
51. Salvation awaits the righteous
52. The redeemed will worship the Lord in Zion
*53. Isaiah prophesies about the life, death, and resurrection of Christ
*54—55. Seek God and all His righteousness (seek the Holy One of Israel)
56. God blesses all who seek Him, regardless of their heritage
57. Only the righteous will find peace; there will be no peace for the wicked
58. True fasting is avoiding sin and seeking guidance from God
59. Judgment comes to the wicked, not the just
*60. The Holy One is the light of heaven
61—62. God will redeem His people and they will be free
63—64. The day of vengeance is near, but heaven awaits the righteous
65—66. Isaiah prophesies about the new Jerusalem, and a new heaven and earth

Key Verses:
- ISA 5:20–24 ~ Woe to those who call evil good and good evil, who put darkness for light and light for darkness, who put bitter for sweet and sweet for bitter. Woe to those who consider themselves wise and prudent. Woe to those who are mighty in their ability to drink alcohol, who justify and reward the wicked, and who take away the righteousness from the righteous. Just as the fire devours the stubble and the chaff, so will their roots become rotten and their blossoms wither; for they have thrown away God's laws and despised the Word of the Holy One of Israel.
- ISA 7:14 ~ The Lord Himself will give you a sign: A virgin will conceive and bear a son, and shall call His name Emmanuel (meaning God with us).

- ISA 9:6 ~ For unto us a child is born; unto us a Son is given. The government will be upon His shoulders. His name will be called Wonderful Counselor, Almighty God, Everlasting Father, and the Prince of Peace.
- ISA 11:1–2 ~ A descendant of Jesse will come, and the Spirit of the Lord will be upon Him, the spirit of wisdom and understanding, the spirit of counsel and might, the spirit of knowledge, and the fear of the Lord.
- ISA 14:12–15 ~ You have fallen from heaven and have been cut down to the ground, Lucifer, who brought down the nations. For you deceived yourself, expecting to be exalted, even above God. Instead, you will be brought down into the depths of hell.
- ISA 26:14 ~ The wicked are dead, they will not live; they are deceased, they will not rise. God has come to destroy them, and their memory will perish with them.
- ISA 28:18; ISA 29:20 ~ All covenants made with death will be null; all agreements with hell will be void. When the scourge passes through, the evil ones will be stomped into the dirt. For the terrible one will be brought to nothing, the hater will be consumed, and all who look for sin will be cut off.
- ISA 43:10–11 ~ The Lord says, "You are my witnesses, and so is my servant whom I have chosen, so that you can know me and believe, and even so, I am He. There are no other gods before me or after me. I am the Lord and there is no other savior."
- ISA 48:16 ~ Come and listen. I have not spoken in secret since the beginning. I was there all along, and now, the Lord God and His Spirit have sent me.
- ISA 53:4–5 ~ Surely, He bore our grief and carried our sorrows. Yet we treated Him as an outcast, as if stricken, smitten, and afflicted by God. But He was wounded and bruised because of our sins. Our punishment was given to Him, bringing us peace, and through His suffering, we have been healed.
- ISA 55:10–12 ~ The rain and snow that falls from heaven does not return to heaven but waters the earth, causing the plants to bud and seed, and providing food. So also, God's Word does not return to Him void, but accomplishes what He wishes and prospers where He sends it. We joyfully go out being led in peace. The mountains and hills sing and the trees clap their hands; the world rejoices around you. Instead of a thorn bush, a tree will grow. And the name of the Lord will be magnified as an everlasting sign of the nurturing He provides.

Jeremiah (Author: Jeremiah)
  1. Jeremiah called by God
  2. Israel has forsaken God
  3—5. Israel and Judah are warned about their wickedness
  6. Jerusalem will fall to a country from the north
  7—10. Backsliding Israel will pay the penalty for turning from God
  11—12. Listen to God and obey Him or He will destroy you; the wicked will not prevail
  13. Judah and Israel will be sorry
  14. Beware of false prophets who say there is nothing to worry about
  15—16. Israel and Judah will become captive; the people will pay for forsaking God
  17. This is the last chance to repent and change your evil ways
  18. They have refused to repent and return to God
  19. Jerusalem will be made desolate
  20. Jeremiah prophesies that Judah will fall to Babylon
  21. King Zedekiah will be destroyed with the city
  22. The throne in Judah will end
*23. The righteous Branch will come, as will false prophets

24. God will separate the good and the evil, and the evil will die
25. Jeremiah prophesies that Babylon will conquer the world
26. Jeremiah's life is threatened, but he is spared
27. Jeremiah prophesies that the nations will serve Babylon
28. Hananiah's false prophecy results in his death
29. Don't listen to false prophets for they will be punished
30. Someday God will bring His remnant back home
*31. There will be a New Covenant that stands for all time
32. Jeremiah buys the land of his ancestors as he waits in prison
*33. God will restore His kingdom
34. Jews disobeyed God and did not free the slaves the seventh year
35. The house of Rechab will remain righteous
36. King Jehoiakim will be punished for burning Baruch's scroll
37. Jeremiah is imprisoned for prophesying against Jerusalem
38. Jeremiah is thrown into cistern because of his negative prophecies
39. Jerusalem is sacked by Nebuchadnezzar's army
40. Jeremiah is freed and stays with the governor
41. Rebels assassinate the governor and many Jews
42. Jeremiah tells remnant of Israel to stay put
43. Remnant of Israel goes to Egypt against God's direction
44—45. Those fleeing to Egypt will be sorry for disobeying God
46. Jeremiah prophesies that Egypt will fall
47. Jeremiah prophesies that the Philistines will fall
48. Jeremiah prophesies that Moab will fall
49. Jeremiah prophesies that Ammon, Edom, Damascus, etc. will fall
50. Jeremiah prophesies that the Babylonian empire will fall, just as the Assyrian empire did
51. The kingdom of the Medes will follow
52. Jerusalem falls to Babylon and the Jews are taken into captivity

Key Verses:
- JER 9:23–24 ~ Wise people must not glory in their wisdom; mighty people must not glory in their might; rich people must not glory in their riches. Instead, glory only in the fact that you know God who exercises love, mercy, righteousness, and judgment upon the earth, for it pleases God when you glorify Him.
- JER 14:14 ~ False prophets tell lies in my (God's) name; I did not send them, command them, or speak to them. They receive false visions and make false predictions from the deceit of their lying hearts.
- JER 23:5; JER 33:15 ~ A righteous descendant of David will become King and will reign and prosper. He will execute judgment and justice on the earth.
- JER 29:11 ~ The Lord says, "I know the thoughts that I think toward you; thoughts of peace, not evil, to give you the promised end."
- JER 31:31–34 ~ God will make a New Covenant with Israel, not according to the covenant He made when He rescued Israel out of the land of Egypt, which they broke. With the New Covenant, God will write His Law into the hearts of His people. They will not have to teach each other to know God, for everyone will know Him, from the least to the greatest among them, because God will forgive all their sins and will forget their sins forever.

Lamentations (Author: Jeremiah)
  1—2. Grieving over the fall of Jerusalem and the captivity of the Jews in Babylon
  3. Evil will be punished accordingly
  4. Their punishment will be greater than Sodom
  5. Grieving over the loss of the Lord's favor

Key Verses:
- LAM 3:26 ~ It is good to hope and wait patiently for the salvation of the Lord.

Ezekiel (Author: Ezekiel)
  1. Ezekiel sees a vision of a wheel in a wheel with angels
  2. Ezekiel is called to proclaim God's words to a rebellious people
  3. Ezekiel warns Israel about their wickedness
  4. Ezekiel prophesies against Jerusalem
  5. God will send famine, beasts, pestilence, and war upon the rebellious Jews
  6. A remnant will escape these judgments
  7. God will punish evil accordingly
  8. God reveals to Ezekiel the abominations of the Jews
  9. God will spare only those who were righteous and received His mark
  10. Ezekiel sees a vision of cherubim and wheels again
  11. Ezekiel prophesies against the wicked leaders
  12. A remnant will be spared God's judgments (also in the latter days)
  13. Beware of false promises and prophecies
  14. God will send death, famine, beasts, and pestilence
  15. Jerusalem will be desolate
  16. Ezekiel prophesies against Israel for their many abominations
*17. God will bring down the mighty (e.g., Babylon, Egypt) and exalt the lowly (i.e., the Branch)
  18. The wicked will die
  19. Lament for Israel
  20. Israel is rebellious
  21. Israel will face God's double-edged sword, as will Babylon and Ammon
  22—23. Ezekiel prophesies against Israel for becoming corrupted by Babylon and Assyria
  24. Woe to the bloody city
  25. Ezekiel prophesies against Ammon, Moab, Edom, and Philistia
  26. Ezekiel prophesies against Tyre
  27. Lament for Tyre because Babylon will destroy everything
  28. Ezekiel prophesies against Tyrus, Sidon, and the fallen cherub (Lucifer)
  29. Ezekiel prophesies against Egypt
  30. Lament for Egypt and North Africa because Babylon will destroy everything
  31. Ezekiel prophesies about the rise and fall of the Assyrian and Egyptian emperors
  32. Lament for Pharaoh and Edom because Babylon will destroy everything
  33. Ezekiel warns the people to turn from their wickedness, and advises them to watch for God
*34. The Good Shepherd will seek out and find His flock
  35. Mount Seir and all of Edom will be desolate
  36. The evil will be purged, and the kingdom will be rebuilt
*37. Ezekiel sees vision of bones representing the resurrection of the dead
  38—39. Ezekiel prophesies against Gog and Magog
  40—43. Ezekiel sees a vision of a new house and a temple
  44. The sanctuary is defiled

45. The layout of the promised land is like that of the sanctuary
46. Lambs are sacrificed by the prince in the inner court
47. Ezekiel sees a vision of the River of Life with flourishing trees
48. Land inheritances are divided among the twelve tribes of Israel and their companions

Key Verses:
- EZE 3:18–21 ~ God says, "I have told the wicked that they will surely die. If you do not warn the wicked to turn from their sin and be saved, you will also die for you will be partly responsible for their death. But if you do warn the wicked and they still do not turn from their wickedness, they will die in their sin but you will have saved yourself. If the righteous turn from righteousness to sin, they will die because their righteousness will no longer be remembered. If you do not warn them you will die as well. But if you warn the righteous not to sin, and they do not sin, their souls will be saved and so will yours."
- EZE 9:4–5 ~ God said to the angel, "Set a mark on the foreheads of all who sigh and cry because of the abominations they have witnessed; then strike the others down with the sword, without pity."
- EZE 18:4,20 ~ All souls belong to the Lord, including the soul of the father and the soul of the son. The soul that sins will die. The son does not share the guilt of the father, nor does the father share the guilt of the son. The righteousness of a godly man will be credited to him alone, and the wickedness of an evil man will be charged only against him.
- EZE 28:14–16 ~ There is the anointed cherub, who was once upon the holy mountain of God, and was perfect when created until evil was found in him.
- EZE 33:12 ~ The righteousness of the righteous will not save them on the day that they sin; the wickedness of the wicked will not destroy them on the day that they repent and turn from their wickedness.
- EZE 34:12 ~ As the shepherd gathers his flock when they become scattered, so God will seek out and find His sheep and deliver them on that dark and cloudy day.

Daniel (Author: Daniel)
1. Daniel given power to interpret visions and dreams
2. Daniel interprets King Nebuchadnezzar's dream about future kingdoms
3. Shadrach, Meshach, and Abednego survive the fiery furnace
4. Nebuchadnezzar goes crazy for seven years, then begins to understand God
5. Daniel interprets King Belshazzar's vision of the writing on the wall, and the coming of the Medes and Persians
6. Daniel survives the lion's den
*7. Daniel's dream about four beasts, Judgment Day, and the eternal reign of Christ
8. Daniel's dream, interpreted by Gabriel, about future kings, and the final empire of the beast
9. Gabriel explains to Daniel Jeremiah's prophecy about the seventy weeks before the judgment
10—11. Daniel's vision of the coming kingdoms and the rise of the beast at the end
12. Daniel's vision of the tribulation and the judgment

Key Verses:
- DAN 7:13–14 ~ I saw the Son of Man come in the clouds and He stood before the Ancient of Days. He was given dominion, glory, and the kingdom, so that all nations, peoples, and races could serve Him. His kingdom was eternal and would never be destroyed.

- DAN 11:21,37–38 ~ A vile person will come peaceably and obtain power through flattery. He will have complete disregard for God and will not desire the affections of women. He will consider himself to be a god and above all others. He will serve the god of forces, and will honor with riches and pleasure.
- DAN 11:31; DAN 12:11–12 ~ Beware of the time that the daily sacrifice is taken away and the abomination that makes desolate is set up in the holy place. Blessed are those who patiently endure the 1,335 days which follow.

Hosea (Author: Hosea)
 1. Hosea marries a prostitute (Gomer) and has a son (Jezreel)
 2—3. Israel has been unfaithful to God (has gone after prostitutes)
 4—10. Israel will be punished for its many abominations
 11—13. Israel has sinned, they have worshipped idols; calamity awaits Israel
 14. Israel better repent before it is too late

Key Verses:
- HOS 6:2 ~ After two days He will revive us, and the third day He will raise us up to live with Him.

Joel (Author: Joel)
 1. Pestilence, famine, and fire will come upon the land
 2. A day of gloom is coming; call upon the Lord to be delivered
 3. The many abominations of the wicked will come back upon them

Key Verses:
- JOE 2:28 ~ I (God) will pour out my Spirit on humankind, and your sons and daughters will prophesy, your old men will dream dreams, and your young men will see visions.

Amos (Author: Amos)
 1. Amos prophesies against Damascus, Gaza, Tyre, Edom and Ammon
 2. Amos prophesies against Moab, Israel, and Judah
 3. Israel will be punished
 4. Their punishment will be like that of Egypt, and Sodom and Gomorrah
 5. Lament for Israel for the day of the Lord brings darkness upon them
 6. Woe to them that think they have it made
 7. The land will be desolate and Israel will become captive
 8. A time of gloom and famine of the Word is coming
 9. Nobody from the evil empire will escape God's wrath

Key Verses:
- AMO 8:11–13 ~ A day is coming when God will send a famine of the Word. Young people will faint from thirst of God's Word. They will wander to-and-fro seeking the truth but will not find it.

Obadiah (Author: Obadiah)
 1. Obadiah prophesies against Edom

Key Verses:
- OBA 1:15 ~ The day of the Lord is near for the wicked. As they have done, so shall it be done to them; it will come back upon their heads.

Jonah (Author: Jonah)
  1. Jonah disobeys God and is swallowed by a whale
  2. Jonah repents and the whale beaches Jonah
  3. Jonah warns Nineveh; the people repent and are spared
  4. Jonah objects to God sparing them; God explains His reasons

Micah (Author: Micah)
  1. Micah prophesies against Israel and Judah; Samaria and Jerusalem will fall
  2—3. Woe to the evildoers and false prophets, and all who have been led astray
  4. Mount Zion will be established for the righteous
 *5. A ruler of Israel will come from Bethlehem
  6. The evil ones will never get satisfaction
  7. Wickedness will result in desolation, but there is forgiveness with God

Key Verses:
- MIC 5:2 ~ Bethlehem Ephratah, though you are small among the thousands of towns in Judah, from you will come forth the ruler of Israel. His existence has been known from ancient times and His kingdom will continue forever.
- MIC 7:2–6 ~ All the godly and upright men are gone. The wicked lie in ambush for blood. They do evil with diligence. Princes and judges ask for bribes. Great men speak of and pursue the evil desires of their souls. Even the best of them is like a thorn. Their confusion and punishment are awaiting them. Nobody can be trusted; even family and friends become the enemy.

Nahum (Author: Nahum)
  1. The wrath of God will fall on the wicked and the evil counselor
  2. Nahum prophesies against Nineveh
  3. Woe to the bloody city; Nineveh will be destroyed

Habakkuk (Author: Habakkuk)
  1. The Babylonians will bring violence and captivity
  2. Woe to the wicked
  3. Habakkuk's prayer

Key Verses:
- HAB 1:4 ~ The law has been slackened and sound judgment cannot be found; for the wicked have encompassed the righteous causing wrong judgment to proceed.

Zephaniah (Author: Zephaniah)
  1—2. The entire land will be consumed on that fateful day
  3. The righteous will live in peace and harmony in Zion

Haggai (Author: Haggai)
  1. The people heed God's coming
 *2. The Desire of Nations comes in glory

Zechariah (Author: Zechariah)
  1. Israel was scattered all over the world, but God will bring them home to Jerusalem
  2. God will gather His people at the new Jerusalem
*3. God will take away sin through His servant the Branch
  4. Two branches representing anointed ones of God
  5. Curse upon the entire earth
*6. The Branch will build the temple
  7. They were told to be compassionate but were oppressive and were scattered among nations
  8. God will rebuild Jerusalem for those who are saved
*9. The King comes to establish salvation and eternal peace
  10. God will gather all the redeemed from everywhere
*11. The Branch (staff of beauty) will be broken
*12. His death will be mourned as a Father mourns for an only Son
*13. The Shepherd will be struck down and the sheep will scatter
  14. Those who oppose God will be cut off

Key Verses:
- ZEC 9:9 ~ Rejoice all of Jerusalem and Zion, for your King comes bringing justice and salvation; He appears lowly, riding on a donkey's colt.
- ZEC 11:12–13 ~ The man said to them, "Give me my price if you want, or forget about it." And they weighed out thirty pieces of silver." The Lord said to the man, "Throw it to the potter, this good price that was appraised of me." And the man took the thirty pieces and threw them to the potter, in the house of the Lord.
- ZEC 13:7~ Almighty God says, "Wake up oh sword, against my shepherd, the man who is close to my heart."
- ZEC 13:8–9 ~ Two parts will be cut off and die, and the third will be left there; and God will bring the third part through the refiner's fire, to be purified like gold. Those who call upon His name will be called His people, and they will say, "The Lord is my God."

Malachi (Author: Malachi)
  1—2. Defiled offerings, unfaithfulness, and the abominations of priests
*3—4. The messenger of God's covenant is coming to purify and to judge

Key Verses:
- MAL 3:1–2,5 ~ God will send a messenger to prepare the way for His coming; then the Lord, the messenger of the covenant whom you seek, will come. Who can endure His arrival, and who can stand before Him? For He is like a refiner's fire or like laundry detergent, removing all impurities and filth. He will execute swift and permanent judgment against the sorcerers, adulterers, perjurers, cheaters, oppressors of widows and the fatherless, abusers of human rights, and people who refuse to fear God.
- MAL 3:8,10 ~ Will a man rob God? But you do rob me (God). How have we robbed you, you ask? In your tithes and offerings. Bring tithes of all your income to the storage room, so that there will be plenty in my house, and prove to yourself that I will open the windows of heaven and pour upon you so many blessings that you will not have room for them.
- MAL 4:2 ~ For those who honor my name, the Sun of Righteousness will arise with healing in His wings. And they will go out leaping like a calf freed from its stall.

New Testament Books

Matthew (Author: Matthew)
1. Genealogy of Jesus Christ (through Joseph); birth of Jesus
2. Herod's decree to kill all babies in Bethlehem
    a. Magi visit Herod (v1–9)
    b. Magi bring gifts to baby Jesus (v10–12)
    c. Joseph and family flee to Egypt to escape Herod's decree to massacre babies (v13–18)
    d. Herod dies and Joseph and family return to Nazareth (v19–23)
3. John the Baptist prepares the way for Jesus
4. Satan tempts Jesus in the wilderness; Jesus calls Peter, Andrew, James, and John
5—6. Beatitudes and laws given by Jesus at sermon on the mount
    a. Lord's Prayer (6:9–13)
7. Don't judge others; ask, seek, and knock and God will reply
8. Jesus heals the lame and diseased and casts out demons
    a. The centurion's faith saves his servant (v5–13)
9. Jesus, the great physician, heals people; Jesus raises a girl from the dead; Jesus calls Matthew
10. Jesus sends apostles out to preach
11. Jesus reassures John the Baptist; Jesus condemns the Jews who refuse to listen
12. Jesus is Lord of all, including the Sabbath
13. Jesus preaches parables from a ship
    a. The sower of seeds (v3–23)
    b. Separating the wheat from the chaff (v24–30,37–43)
    c. Analogies to the kingdom of heaven (v31–33,44–52)
14—15. Jesus miraculously feeds multitudes as He ministers to the crowds
    a. John the Baptist beheaded (14:1–13)
    b. Jesus feeds over five thousand with five loaves and two fish (14:14–21)
    c. Jesus walks on water (14:22–23)
    d. Jesus admonishes Pharisees' lack of faith (15:1–20)
    e. Canaanite woman's faith heals her daughter (15:21–23)
    f. Jesus feeds over four thousand with seven loaves and a few fish (15:29–39)
16. Jesus foretells the future, including His suffering and death
    a. Peter displays a strong faith in Christ (v13–20)
17. Transfiguration of Jesus with Moses and Elijah
18—20. Jesus preaches in parables and analogies
    a. Who can enter the kingdom of heaven (18:1–4; 19:13–30; 20:20–28)
    b. Forgiveness of sins (18:15–22)
    c. The unmerciful creditor (18:23–35)
    d. Jesus proclaims divorce unlawful except for adultery (19:3–11)
    e. Workers in the vineyard (20:1–16)
21—23. Jesus enters Jerusalem and preaches at the temple; Jesus speaks in parables
    a. Jesus chases money changers out of the temple (21:12–13)
    b. Faithfulness and unfaithfulness (21:18–32)
    c. The vineyard tenants (21:33–46)
    d. The wedding banquet (22:1–14)
    e. Separation of heavenly and earthly kingdoms (22:15–22)
    f. Aspects of life after resurrection (22:23–33)
    g. The Son of God is also David's Lord (22:36–45)

h. Hypocrisy of the Scribes and Pharisees (23:1–39)
24. Signs of the final days and the tribulations before Christ's return
25. More parables
   a. Ten virgins (v1–13)
   b. The master's investors (v14–30)
   c. The sheep and the goats (v31–46)
26. The last Passover feast and betrayal of Jesus
27. The trial of Jesus and His crucifixion
28. The resurrection of Jesus (Easter); His appearances and ascension

Key Verses:
- MAT 3:11 ~ John the Baptist said, "I baptize with water unto repentance. But He who comes after me is mightier than I; I am not worthy to untie His shoes. He will baptize with the Holy Spirit, and with fire."
- MAT 5:14–18 ~ Jesus said to His followers, "You are the light of the world; a city on a hill cannot be hidden. A person does not light a candle and cover it, but places it on a candlestick so it will light the house. Let your light shine before others, so they can see your goodness, and glorify our Father in heaven. I did not come to destroy the Law or the words of the prophets, I came to fulfill them. Truthfully, until heaven and earth have passed, not a single bit of the Law will pass until all the prophecy is fulfilled."
- MAT 5:44 ~ Jesus said, "Love your enemies; bless those who curse you; do good to those who hate you, and pray for those who take advantage of you and abuse you."
- MAT 6:9–13 ~ Jesus taught us to pray like this: "Our Father in heaven, your name is holy. Let us come to your kingdom. Let your will be done on earth as it is in heaven. Provide us our daily needs. Forgive us our sins, as we forgive others who sin against us. Lead us away from temptation and deliver us from evil. For the kingdom, power, and glory are yours forever, Amen."
- MAT 6:14–15 ~ Jesus said, "If you forgive others, your heavenly Father will forgive you. If you do not forgive others, your heavenly Father will not forgive you."
- MAT 6:31–34 ~ Jesus said, "Don't worry about what you will eat or drink, or what you will wear; for your heavenly Father knows that you need these things. Instead, seek only the kingdom of God and His righteousness, and He will provide everything you need in addition."
- MAT 7:1–2 ~ Jesus said, "Don't judge others or you will be judged; for whatever standards you use to judge others will be used to judge you."
- MAT 7:7 ~ Jesus said, "Ask and you will receive; seek and you will find; knock and the door will be opened."
- MAT 10:19–20,28 ~ Jesus said, "When you are captured, don't worry about how to act or what to say, for the proper words will be given to you even as you speak them. It will not be you, but the Holy Spirit doing the talking. Don't worry about those who can kill your body, but cannot reach your soul. Instead, fear Him who is able to destroy both your body and soul in hell."
- MAT 12:31 ~ Jesus said, "All manner of sin and blasphemy can be forgiven, except committing blasphemy against the Holy Spirit, which will not be forgiven."
- MAT 15:18 ~ Jesus said, "The things which proceed from the mouth come from the heart, and defile a person."
- MAT 16:26 ~ Jesus said, "What does a person profit if they gain the whole world but lose their soul? What can a person give in exchange for their soul?"

- MAT 18:21–22 ~ Peter asked Jesus, "How many times should someone forgive a person? Seven times?" Jesus replied, "Not seven times, but seventy times seven (or seventy-seven in the NIV)."
- MAT 21:22 ~ Jesus said, "If you believe, you can receive anything you ask through prayer."
- MAT 25:40 ~ Jesus said, "Whatever you do to another person, you do to me also."
- MAT 28:18–20 ~ Jesus said to His apostles just before leaving them, "All power in heaven and earth is given to me. Go and teach all nations the things I have taught you, baptizing them in the name of the Father, Son, and Holy Spirit. And remember, I will be with you always, even until the end of time."

Mark (Author: Mark)
1—5. Jesus begins His ministry
  a. John the Baptist prepares the way (1:1–11)
  b. Jesus recruits Simon (Peter), Andrew, James, and John (1:14–20)
  c. Jesus casts out demons, heals the lame and diseased (1:21–2:12; 3:1–5)
  d. Jesus ordains His twelve apostles (3:13–18): Peter, Andrew, James, John, Philip, Bartholomew, Matthew, Thomas, James, Thaddaeus, Simon, Judas
  e. Jesus proves He isn't demon possessed (3:22–30)
  f. Parables of the sower of seeds (4:1–34)
  g. Jesus calms the storm (4:35–41)
  h. Jesus casts out Legion (thousands of evil spirits) from a man into a herd of swine (5:1–20)
  i. Jesus heals woman and revives dead girl (5:21–43)
6—10. Jesus's travels and ministry; Jesus prophesies about His death and resurrection (MAT 12—20)
11—13. Palm Sunday (MAT 21—25)
14. Holy Communion (MAT 26)
15. Crucifixion (MAT 27)
16. Easter and the ascension (MAT 28)

Key Verses:
- MAR 2:17 ~ Jesus said, "Those who are healthy do not need a doctor, but those who are sick do. I came to call sinners, not the righteous, to repentance."
- MAR 10:14–15 ~ Jesus said, "Let the little children come to me, and don't forbid them, for the kingdom of God belongs to such as these. I tell you the truth, unless you receive the kingdom like a little child does, you will never enter there."
- MAR 13:22 ~ Jesus said, "False prophets and antichrists will come, showing signs and miracles, to deceive even the elect if they could."
- MAR 13:35–37 ~ Watch for the master, for you don't know if the master will come in the evening, at midnight, or at dawn. Do not let Him catch you sleeping on your watch."

Luke (Author: Luke)
1. Angel Gabriel promises a son to Zechariah and also to Mary
2. Jesus's birth and childhood
  a. Angel proclaims the birth of Christ to shepherds tending their flocks (v4–20)
  b. Simeon blesses the baby Jesus (v25–34)
3. John the Baptist prepares the way for Jesus
  a. Genealogy of Jesus through Mary (v23–38)
4. Jesus prepares for ministry

a. Satan tempts Jesus in the wilderness (v1–13)
   b. Jesus preaches in Nazareth and is rejected (v14–30)
   c. Jesus casts out demons and heals the sick (v31–44)
5—19. Jesus's travels and ministry (MAT 14—20); Jesus speaks in parables
   a. Jesus teaches to love everyone, even enemies (6:27–36)
   b. The Pharisee's banquet (6:36–50)
   c. Jesus sends seventy disciples to preach (10:1–24)
   d. The good Samaritan (10:25–37)
   e. Satan and demons (11:4–28)
   f. The light of a lamp should not be hidden (11:33–36)
   g. Jesus addresses greed (you can't take it with you) (12:13–21)
   h. Be watchful and seek God (12:35–48)
   i. Who can enter the kingdom of heaven (13:22–30)
   j. Places of honor (14:1–14)
   k. Discipleship (14:25–34)
   l. The lost sheep and the prodigal son (15:3–31)
   m. The dishonest steward (16:1–15)
   n. The rich man and the poor man (16:19–31)
   o. Jesus heals ten lepers (17:11–27)
   p. The unjust judge (persistence pays off) (18:1–8)
   q. The Pharisee and the publican (18:9–4)
   r. Zacchaeus climbs a tree to see Jesus (19:1–9)
   s. The unwise investor (19:11–27)
   t. Jesus enters Jerusalem on a donkey (19:28–44)
20—21. Jesus preaches at the temple in Jerusalem (MAT 21—25)
   a. The widow's offering (21:1–4)
22. The Last Supper (MAT 26)
   a. Peter denies Jesus (v54–62)
23. Jesus is crucified (MAT 27)
24. Easter and Jesus's Ascension (MAT 28)

Key Verses:
- LUK 6:31–32,37–38 ~ Jesus said, "Treat others the way you would like them to treat you; for if you love only those who love you, what thanks will you receive? Even the wicked love those who love them. Do not judge others and you will not be judged; do not condemn others and you will not be condemned. Forgive others and you will be forgiven. Give and it shall be given to you in abundance, overflowing; for the same measure that you give is returned to you abundantly."
- LUK 12:8–9 ~ Jesus said, "Whoever confesses me to others, I will confess them before God and His angels; but whoever denies me to others, I will deny them before God and His angels."
- LUK 12:29–32 ~ Jesus said, "To those who are given much, much will be required; to those who have committed much, the more will be asked."
- LUK 21:33 ~ Jesus said, "Heaven and earth will pass away, but my words will remain true forever."

John (Author: John, the apostle)
 1. The Word made flesh; the Lamb of God
 2. The wedding at Cana
 3. Jesus instructs Nicodemus
 4. The woman at the well
 5—9. Jesus's travels and ministry (MAT 14—20)
    a. Jesus existed before Abraham and always (8:31–58)
    b. Jesus heals a man born blind (9:1–41)
 10. The Good Shepherd
 11. Jesus raises Lazarus from the dead
 12. Jesus enters Jerusalem for the last time (MAT 21—25)
 13—18. The Last Supper (MAT 26)
    a. Jesus washes apostles' feet (13:1–17)
    b. Jesus declares his betrayal (13:18–30)
    c. Jesus declares Peter's denial (13:31–38)
    d. Jesus comforts apostles and promises an eternal reunion (MAT 14)
    e. Jesus is the Vine; He will send the Comforter (MAT 15–16)
    f. Jesus prays for Himself, His apostles, and all believers (MAT 17)
    g. Jesus is arrested and tried (MAT 18)
 19. Jesus is crucified (MAT 27)
 20. Easter and Jesus's appearances (MAT 28)
 21. Jesus's ascension (MAT 28)
    a. The great catch of fish (v1–14)
    b. Peter's confirmation (v15–19)

Key Verses:
- JOH 1:1,14,17 ~ In the beginning was the Word, and the Word was with God, and the Word was God. And the Word became flesh and lived among us; and we saw His glory, the glory of a Father's only Son, full of grace and truth. For the Law was given to us by Moses, but Grace and Truth came by Jesus Christ.
- JOH 3:16–17 ~ Jesus said, "God loved the world so much that He sacrificed His only Son, so that anyone could believe in Him and not die but live forever. For God sent His only Son into the world to save it not to condemn it."
- JOH 8:31–32,36 ~ Jesus said, "If you believe in my words then you are indeed my disciples; and you will know the truth, and the truth will set you free. And if the Son of God sets you free, you will definitely be free."
- JOH 8:58 ~ Jesus, said, "I tell you the truth, before Abraham was, I am."
- JOH 10:17–18 ~ Jesus said, "The Father loves me, because I will give my life, so that I can take it back again; nobody takes it from me, I give it by myself. I have the power to give my life, and to take it back again. I have received these instructions from my Father."
- JOH 11:25–26 ~ Jesus said, "I am the resurrection and the life; those who believe in me, though they were dead, yet shall they live; whoever believes in me will never die."
- JOH 14:2–3,6,19 ~ Jesus said, "In my Father's house are many mansions; I go to prepare such a place for you. I will return for you, so that where I am you can be also. I am the way, the truth, and the life; nobody can come to the Father without coming through me. In a little while, the world will see me no more, but you will see me again; and because I live, you also will live."
- JOH 15:4–5,16 ~ Jesus said, "Abide in me and I will abide in you. Just as the branch cannot bear fruit when separated from the vine, neither can you if you become separated from me.

For I am the Vine, and you are the branches. If you abide in me you will bring forth much fruit, but without me you can do nothing. You didn't choose me, I chose you and ordained you, so that you could continue to bear fruit. Therefore, whatever you ask the Father in heaven in my name, He will give it to you."
- JOH 16:20,22,33 ~ Jesus said, "You will cry and lament while the rest of the world rejoices. But your sorrow will turn to joy, because we will be together again; and nobody will ever be able to take that joy from you. I am telling you these things so you can be at peace. In this world you will experience much tribulation, but be cheerful, for I have overcome the world."

Acts [of the apostles] (Author: Luke)
1. Peter holds apostles together
   a. Matthias selected to replace Judas (v12–26)
2. Apostles preach in tongues during Pentecost
   a. Peter's sermon (v14–41)
3. Peter heals a lame man
4—5. Peter and John instruct the priests, elders, and Jewish rulers
   a. Believers pool resources to support the apostles (4:32–37)
   b. Peter exposes Ananias's greed; apostles continue to preach and heal (5:1–5)
   c. Angel frees apostles imprisoned by high priest and Sadducees (5:17–20)
   d. Apostles preach despite warnings and threats (5:21–23)
   e. Jewish leaders are afraid the apostles may be sent from God (5:33–42)
6. Stephen performs miracles, is charged with insurrection
7. Stephen reviews the scriptures, teaches about Christ, and is stoned to death
8. Philip preaches, converts Simon the sorcerer and an Ethiopian
9. Saul, called by Jesus, becomes Paul; Ananias sent to minister to Paul
   a. Peter heals paralyzed man and raises woman from the dead (v32–43)
10. Peter meets with Cornelius the centurion
    a. Cornelius's vision (v1–8)
    b. Peter's vision (v9–23)
11. Jesus was sent to the Jews and Gentiles alike
    a. Disciples called Christians at Antioch (v26)
12. Herod imprisons Peter and kills James (the apostle and brother of John)
    a. Angel frees Peter from chains and Peter walks out of prison (v6–11)
    b. Herod dies, eaten by worms (v21–23)
13—14. Paul and Barnabas preach in the land of the Gentiles
    a. Paul strikes the sorcerer blind (13:4–12)
    b. Paul heals a lame man (14:8–10)
    c. Paul is stoned and left for dead, but survives (14:19–20)
15. Apostles reconvene in Jerusalem
16—20. Paul and Silas continue to preach in Asia and Macedonia
    a. Paul and Silas imprisoned (16:16–24)
    b. Earthquake opens jail; disciples freed; jailer converted (16:25–40)
    c. Paul goes to Athens and Corinth to preach (17:13–18:17)
    d. Paul performs miracles (19:11–12; 20:7–12)
    e. Rioting of the Ephesians (20:13–38)
21—23. Paul returns to Jerusalem and preaches to the hostile crowds
    a. People riot; Paul arrested (21:27–40)
    b. Paul declares his conversion and his Roman citizenship (22:1–30)
    c. Jews plot to kill Paul (23:1–22)

d. Paul appears before the governor (23:23–35)
24—25. Paul's trial and imprisonment
26. Paul defends himself before King Agrippa, appeals to Caesar
27—28. Paul sent to Rome to appear before Caesar
   a. Paul's ship wrecks on island of Malta (27:27–44)
   b. Paul is unharmed by viper bite (28:1–6)
   c. Paul preaches and heals people of Malta (28:7–10)
   d. Paul preaches in Rome (28:16–31)

Key Verses:
- ACT 1:8–11 ~ Jesus told the apostles, "The Holy Spirit will come upon you and give you power; and you will be my witnesses in Jerusalem, Judea, Samaria, and the far corners of the earth." Then Jesus ascended into heaven and disappeared into the clouds. As the apostles gazed into heaven, two angels appeared with them and said, "Men of Galilee, why do you gaze into heaven? This same Jesus who you saw ascend into heaven will return in the same manner in which He just departed."
- ACT 2:3–4,6 ~ On the day of Pentecost, small flames of fire appeared on the heads of each apostle, and they began to preach in foreign languages unknown to them, as moved by the Holy Spirit. After the word got out, people came to see, and were amazed, because everyone heard the Word being spoken in his or her native tongue.
- ACT 2:38–39 ~ Peter told the crowd, "Repent and be baptized, every one of you, in the name of Jesus Christ for the forgiveness of sins, and you will receive the gift of the Holy Spirit. This promise is for you and your children, and everyone all over the world, as many as the Lord our God will call."
- ACT 4:12 ~ Peter said, "Salvation can be found in nobody but Jesus Christ; for there is no other name under heaven that can save us."
- ACT 10:34–35 ~ Peter said, "Truly, God does not show favoritism for any person. Within every nation, anyone who fears the Lord and endeavors to be righteous is accepted by Him."
- ACT 20:30 ~ Even from among yourselves men will come, speaking perverse things to get others to follow them.

Romans (Author: Paul)
1. The wrath of God will fall on the ungodly, unrighteous, and wicked
2. Don't judge others; obey God's laws or be judged accordingly
3. All people are sinners; justification comes by faith in Christ
4. Righteousness comes through faith
5. By Adam we became sinful unto death; by Christ we become righteous unto everlasting life
6. Anyone can be saved by the grace of God through His Son Jesus Christ
7. We are all sinful and disobey God
8. Follow the Law of the Spirit and not that of the flesh, and become a child of God
9. To be a Jew does not save a person; only those with faith are saved, Jews and Gentiles alike
10. There is no difference between Jew, Greek, etc., for the same Lord is available to anyone who calls upon His name
11. Beware of the unbelievers, for many Jews have been cut off; but those who believe will be grafted onto the true Branch
12. Love and help one another, even those you dislike; be of one mind, guided by the Spirit
13. Love is the fulfillment of the Law
14. Do everything in love and faith; do not judge others
15—16. Be of one mind in Christ and receive each other as Christ receives you before God

Key Verses:
- ROM 2:1 ~ It is inexcusable to judge another, for by doing so you condemn yourself, since you are guilty of the same things.
- ROM 3:23; ROM 6:23 ~ Everyone has sinned and come short of God's glory. The risk of sin is death. But God's gift of eternal life is available to everyone through Jesus Christ our Lord.
- ROM 8:1–2 ~ Those who are in Christ are no longer condemned, because through Him, the law of the Spirit of life sets us free from the law of sin and death.
- ROM 8:26–28 ~ The Holy Spirit intercedes for us when we pray. We don't know what we should pray for all the time. But through the act of prayer, God analyzes our needs and answers our prayers in the best possible way. All things work together for good, for those who love God and who are called to do His will.
- ROM 8:14,17,30 ~ Anyone who is led by the Spirit of God is a child of God; and if a child of God, then an heir of God, and a joint heir with Jesus Christ. So if we suffer with Christ, we also will be glorified with Him. Those who God predestined He also called; those He called He also justified; those He justified He also glorified.
- ROM 8:31,38–39 ~ If God is for us, who can be against us? Neither death nor life, nor angels, principalities, or powers, nor things present or future, nor any creature can separate us from the love of God which is in Jesus Christ our Lord.
- ROM 10:9–10 ~ If you confess the Lord Jesus with your words, and believe in your heart that God raised Him from the dead, you are saved. For with the heart the people believe unto righteousness, and with the mouth they confess unto salvation.
- ROM 12:14–18,21 ~ Bless those who persecute you, don't curse them. Rejoice with those who are rejoicing, and mourn with those who are mourning. Be of one mind towards each other. Don't be high-minded, but humble yourselves to others who are lowly; don't consider yourself wise by your own conceit. Never reward evil for evil; be honest and peaceful with all people. Don't allow yourself to be overcome with evil, but overcome evil with goodness.
- ROM 12:4–6 ~ Just as we have many members in our body, and all members have the same purpose, so we, being many, are one body in Christ, and members of one another. We all have different gifts according to the grace God has given us...
- ROM 13:10 ~ Love never does anything bad to another person; thus, love is the fulfilling of the Law.

1 Corinthians (Author: Paul)
1—2. One cannot know God through the wisdom of the world; but only through the Spirit, the very wisdom of God
3. Jesus Christ is the strong foundation; you are the temple of God's Spirit if Christ lives in you
4. Don't judge anyone, not even yourself
5. Purge yourselves of the evil among you
6. Don't sue each other, help each other; be one in Christ and refrain from sin
7. It is all right to stay single, but to avoid the sin of fornication, marry and stay with spouse
8. If you sin against someone, you sin against Christ; live by example
9. Spreading the Gospel does not allow someone to be self-righteous
10. Avoid temptation; you cannot partake of God's things if you partake of evil things too
11. Partake of the Lord's supper to witness Christ's death, but do not do it if you do not believe
12. We are all members of the same Spirit; as we are one body in Christ, we should look after each other as if we were part of each other
13. Do everything in love; without love, everything you do is meaningless

14. It is not fruitful to speak in tongues at church if nobody else understands
15. Many people saw Christ after His death proving that He rose from the dead, thereby proving the resurrection and the fact that Christ has conquered death for us
16. Remain faithful and do everything with love

Key Verses:
- 1 CO 2:14 ~ Worldly people do not receive the things of the Spirit of God, for these things are foolishness to them; neither can they know these things for they must be discerned spiritually.
- 1 CO 3:16–17 ~ Don't you realize that you are the temple of God, and that His Spirit lives in you? If you defile the temple of God you will be destroyed by God, because the temple of God is holy and you are that temple.
- 1 CO 7:4 ~ A wife and husband no longer have exclusive power over their own body, because it also belongs to the spouse.
- 1 CO 10:13 ~ The temptations before you are common to humankind. God is faithful and will not cause you to be tempted beyond your ability to endure, and He will always provide a way to escape the temptation.
- 1 CO 11:25–29 ~ Jesus commanded the apostles on the first Holy Communion to partake of the sacrament often to remember Him. Thus, as often as you eat the bread and drink the wine of Holy Communion, you proclaim the death of Christ until His return. But if you participate in this holy sacrament unworthily (without sincerely repenting of your sins and desiring a communion with Christ), you will become one of those who are found guilty of Christ's crucifixion. Examine yourself before partaking of Holy Communion, because if you partake unworthily, you will be eating and drinking damnation upon yourself.
- 1 CO 13:2–8,13 ~ Even if you have the gift of prophecy, can understand mysteries, and have a faith to move mountains, you are nothing without love. Even if you give all you have to the poor, you profit nothing if you don't have love. Love is patient. Love is kind. Love is never envious or conceited. Love is not rude, self-seeking, or angered, nor does it find pleasure in sin. Love does not think of sinful things nor is it provoked by evil. Love rejoices in the truth. Love always protects, always trusts, always hopes, and always endures. Love never fails... Faith, hope, and love abide; but the greatest of these three is love.

2 Corinthians (Author: Paul)
1. In Christ is our hope, comfort, and salvation
2. Forgive one another and strengthen each other
3. All glory comes from God; He will bestow His glory on those who trust in Christ
4. The apostles suffered much for their labor but were never discouraged
5. He who raised Christ from the dead will reconcile the righteous unto Himself
6. Do not join with unbelievers; evil and godliness don't mix
7. God is our comfort and joy
8—9. Be generous like Christ, who was rich but became poor for our sake, so we could be rich in His Spirit
10. Be humble not proud; glory only in the Lord
11. Beware of false prophets; even Satan disguises himself as an angel of light
12—13. It is an honor to be persecuted for the sake of Christ, for in your weakness you will be made strong by His power

Key Verses:
- 2 CO 5:17–19,21 ~ Anyone who is in Christ has become a new creation; the old has been removed and everything has become new. This God did to reconcile us unto Himself through Christ. He has not counted our sins against us, but instead made Christ who knew no sin to become sin for us, so that we could receive the righteousness of God that was in Him.
- 2 CO 6:14 ~ Do not be joined with unbelievers, for what can the righteous and unrighteous have in common, and what communion can there be between light and darkness?
- 2 CO 9:7 ~ Everyone should give from their heart whatever they can. Don't give grudgingly and don't feel forced to give, but remember that God loves a cheerful giver.
- 2 CO 10:17 ~ Those who would glory should glory only in the Lord.
- 2 CO 11:13–14 ~ Beware of false deceitful prophets who claim to be from Christ, for even Satan disguises himself as an angel of light.
- 2 CO 12:9–10 ~ The Lord said, "My grace is sufficient for you, because my strength is made perfect in weakness." Therefore, I gladly rejoice in my infirmities, so that the power of Christ may rest upon me. I take pleasure in infirmities, accusations, neediness, persecutions, and distress that I endure for Christ's sake; for when I am weak, then I become strong.

Galatians (Author: Paul)
1. Don't believe anyone who preaches anything different from the Gospel of Christ
2. We are justified by faith in Christ not through the works of the Law
3. The Law is our teacher that brings us to faith in Christ
4. Redemption in Christ makes us adopted children of God, and heirs of His kingdom
5—6. Christ has set us free in the Spirit; but we are not free to pursue the lustful desires of the flesh, only to live in the Spirit

Key Verses:
- GAL 3:27–28 ~ Anyone baptized in Christ has put on Christ like a suit of armor. Thus, there is neither Jew nor Greek, poor nor rich, male nor female, for we are equal in Jesus Christ.
- GAL 4:4–7 ~ When the time was right, God sent His Son, who was born of a woman under the Old Covenant of the Law, to redeem those who were under the Law. He did this so that everyone could receive the honor of becoming adopted children of God. If you are a child of God you are no longer His servant, but a fellow heir of God through Christ.
- GAL 5:13 ~ You have been called to be free; but do not use freedom as an excuse to live according to the flesh, but through love to serve one another.
- GAL 5:22–23 ~ The fruits of the Spirit include love, joy, peace, patience, kindness, goodness, faithfulness, humbleness, and restraint; there is no law against these things.
- GAL 6:1,8 ~ If a person falls prey to temptation, you who are spiritual should restore that person to a spirit of humbleness, considering that you could succumb to the same temptation. Whoever sows to the flesh reaps corruption; whoever sows to the Spirit reaps eternal life.

Ephesians (Author: Paul)
1. God chose us before the world began to be His children in Christ
2. We are saved by God's grace through faith in Christ, not by our deeds; through Christ we become one in Spirit
3. May Christ live in your heart and strengthen your faith through the Holy Spirit
4. Be kind to one another as one body and one Spirit, with unity of faith and love through Christ
5. Abandon wickedness and false teachers of darkness; wives and husbands need to love each other as one, even as believers are one with Christ

6. Teach your children the truth; use the shield of faith to repel evil forces; pray constantly

Key Verses:
- EPH 2:8–9 ~ You are saved by the grace of God because of your faith in Jesus Christ. Salvation is a gift of God, it cannot be earned through good works, so nobody should brag.
- EPH 2:18–20 ~ Through Christ, we have access by one Spirit to the Father. Thus, we are no longer strangers and foreigners, but fellow citizens with the saints in the household of God. God's house is built on the foundation of the apostles, with Christ being the chief cornerstone.
- EPH 6:4 ~ Parents, do not provoke your children to anger, but raise them with the nurturing and guidance of the Lord.
- EPH 6:11–12 ~ Put on the armor of God so that you can stand against the wiles of Satan. For we do not battle against flesh and blood, but against principalities, powers, rulers of darkness on earth, and spiritual wickedness in high places.

Philippians (Author: Paul)
1. Live in Christ, not in the flesh; be willing to suffer for Him
2. Be humble and obedient like Christ, and confess Him
3. Follow Christ and become like Him, resurrected and glorified
4. Rejoice in the Lord, focus on His godliness; practice all you have learned with prayer and thanksgiving

Key Verses:
- PHP 2:3 ~ Hold people in higher esteem than yourself; do nothing with strife or vainglory.
- PHP 2:5–11 ~ Keep your thoughts on Jesus Christ who, although He was God in the flesh, did not glorify Himself but became a servant. In the form of a man He humbled Himself, becoming obedient unto death, even death on a cross. Therefore, God has exalted Him and given Him a name above all other names. Everyone should bow at the name of Jesus Christ, whether they are in heaven or on the earth. Every tongue should confess that Jesus Christ is Lord, to the glory of God the Father.
- PHP 4:6–8 ~ Don't worry about anything, but pray for everything with thanksgiving, humbleness, and eagerness. Focus your mind on things that are true, honest, just, pure, lovely, admirable, virtuous, and praiseworthy.
- PHP 4:13 ~ I can do all things through Christ who strengthens me.

Colossians (Author: Paul)
1. Thank God for His Son who redeems us and reconciles us unto Himself if we continue in in faith and hope
2. Beware of false prophets and keep the faith in Christ; do not regard the traditions of people
3. Live in Christ; teach and forgive one another; do everything in love
4. Give thanks and pray constantly

Key Verses:
- COL 1:16–17 ~ All things were created by God and for God: things in heaven and on earth, visible and invisible, including thrones, dominions, principalities, and powers. He is before all things, and by Him all things exist.
- COL 4:2 ~ Pray and give thanks to God constantly.

1 Thessalonians (Author: Paul)
  1—3. Thank God always for receiving His Word; boldly proclaim it to the world
  4. Love one another; be honest and faithful unto death, and you will live forever with Jesus
  5. Help those who are weak and comfort each other; maintain love, faith, and hope, rejoicing and praying constantly

Key Verses:
- 1 TH 4:16–17 ~ The Lord will descend from heaven with a shout, with the voice of the archangel, and with a blast from the trumpet of God. Then the dead in Christ will arise first from the dead, and those who are still alive in Christ will arise with them, joining the Lord in the sky, to be with Him forever.
- 1 TH 5:14,16–22 ~ Warn those who are unruly, comfort the feeble minded, support the weak, and be patient towards everyone. Rejoice always; pray without ceasing; give thanks in everything, for this is God's will in your life. Quench your thirst for the Spirit; do not hate the words of the prophets. Test all things and keep hold of that which is good. Refrain from anything that is evil.

2 Thessalonians (Author: Paul)
  1. Thank God for His faithfulness; those who persecute the righteous receive His vengeance
  2. Beware of false prophets and Satan, who pretend to be God; they will be destroyed
  3. Pray that God's Word will never be stifled; avoid those who disobey God

Key Verses:
- 2 TH 2:3–4,8–9,11–12 ~ Beware of false prophets who will try to deceive you, because people will fall away from God before the evil one, the son of Satan (literally, son of perdition or hell), is revealed. He is the one who opposes God and exalts himself, pretending to be God. The evil one will be consumed by the Spirit of God and will be destroyed by the brightness of His coming. The evil son of Satan is the one who is possessed by Satan himself, and performs magic tricks and false miracles. He will deceive many people with his delusions and lies. All who follow him and find pleasure in unrighteousness will be damned.
- 2 TH 3:1 ~ Pray for teachers of the true faith, and pray that the Word of God will be freely spoken and understood, like it was for you.

1 Timothy (Author: Paul)
  1—2. Pray for everyone, everywhere, without doubting; maintain a pure heart and a strong faith
  3. Teachers of the faith must be upright models of faithfulness and sobriety
  4. Beware of seductive spirits and false prophets; refuse their counsel and exercise godliness, teaching others to do the same
  5. Elders of the church must ensure the welfare of forsaken widows, but the church should not be burdened with those who receive adequate support
  6. Strive for righteousness through love, faith, and patience, laying a foundation for eternal life; don't strive for money which is a trap that causes many to fall into evil and destruction

Key Verses:
- 1 TI 2:5 ~ There is one God, and one mediator between Him and us, who is Jesus Christ.
- 1 TI 4:1 ~ The Spirit tells us that in the latter days, many will fall from the faith, giving credence to evil, seductive spirits, and doctrines of Satan.

- 1 TI 6:7–10 ~ We brought nothing into this world and we can bring nothing out of it. Let us, therefore, be content with the food and clothes we have. For those who would be rich fall into temptation, a trap, full of foolish and harmful lusts, which drown them in destruction and damnation. The love of money is the root of all evil.

2 Timothy (Author: Paul)
1—2. Don't be ashamed of being a Christian, but hold fast to your faith and love in Christ; don't deny Him or He will deny you
3. In the last days there will be much evil, deceit, conceit, lust, and dishonesty; Christians will be persecuted; many will follow false doctrine
4. Continue to spread the Gospel and receive a crown of righteousness

Key Verses:
- 2 TI 3:1–4,12 ~ In the last days, perilous times will come. People will be self-centered, proud, boastful, envious, blasphemous, disobedient to parents, unthankful, and ungodly; people will be perverted, peace breakers, false accusers, unrestrained, fierce, and despisers of those who are good; they will be traitors, violent, arrogant, and lovers of pleasure rather than of lovers of God. Those who live a godly life in Christ will be persecuted.
- 2 TI 3:16 ~ All scripture is inspired by God. God's Word provides the doctrine of truth, refutes that which is false, and instructs all people in the ways of righteousness.
- 2 TI 4:3–4 ~ People will seek teachers who conform to their own likes and dislikes; they will turn away from the truth and wander into myths.

Titus (Author: Paul)
1. Teachers of the faith must be upright models of faithfulness and sobriety; there are many who say they know God but their actions are contradictory
2. Teach obedience, fidelity, honesty, sobriety, and godliness
3. We are justified by God's grace and saved by His mercy to the hope of eternal life through faith

Key Verses:
- TIT 2:11 ~ The grace of God which brings salvation appears to everyone.

Philemon (Author: Paul)
1. There is great joy in sharing our faith and love with fellow Christians; treat each other as brothers

Hebrews (Author: Paul or one of his companions, Barnabas, Apollos, or Silas)
1. God placed Christ, His Son, above all others far above the angels
2. God sent His only Son to save us from sin and death and to destroy evil
3. We are partakers of Christ, the great High Priest, provided we remain steadfast in the true faith until the end; help others in that belief so they won't be deceived by sin
4. Come boldly to the throne of grace for help in time of need
5—6. As Christ was obedient to God and perfect unto death, so we should be patient and obedient to Him, the reward being eternal salvation
7. Jesus is High Priest and King forever (following the priestly order of Melchizedek)
8—9. Christ sacrificed Himself, thereby abolishing sin and perfecting our salvation, which the Law was unable to do because of its imperfection

10. The Law with its sacrificial offerings wasn't enough to make us perfect before God; so Christ made a single sacrifice for sin that would last forever; no other sacrificial offering will ever be needed
11. Belief in God and Christ is faith; without faith we cannot please God; with faith we can endure anything and can do anything as seen in the patriarchs and prophets
12. Jesus Christ is the perfecter of our faith, having endured the cross; for this we must reverence Him and the Father, and follow His righteousness, thereby receiving an inheritance in His kingdom
13. Always love and help your neighbor; don't pursue strange doctrines; praise God forever

Key Verses:
- HEB 4:12 ~ The Word of God is alive and powerful. It is sharper than any double-edged sword, piercing deep, so as to divide the very soul and spirit. It can discern the thoughts and intents of the heart.
- HEB 7:19; HEB 8:7 ~ The Law made nothing perfect, but the bringing of a better hope through Christ did; by that hope we are drawn to God. For if that first covenant (Law) had been faultless, there would have been no need for the second covenant (Grace).
- HEB 9:11–15,18–22 ~ Christ came as the high priest and king over all good things to come, to prepare a greater and more perfect church, not made by hands like a building. Christ obtained eternal redemption for us, not by the blood of burnt offerings but by His own precious blood. If the blood of burnt offerings purified the hearts of men, how much more will the blood of Christ purify us! Through the Holy Spirit, Christ offered Himself, who was without blemish (sinless), and who purged our consciences from dead works to serve the living God. By this cause, Christ has become the mediator of the New Testament (Covenant). By His death, we are redeemed from the sins committed under the first (old) covenant, so that those who are called might receive the promise of God's eternal inheritance. Even the first covenant included blood, for after Moses read from the Book of the Law, He sprinkled blood from the offering on the book and the people, saying, "This is the blood of the covenant which God has commanded for you to keep." Moses also sanctified the tabernacle in this manner. Under the Law, all acts of disobedience are purged with blood, for without the shedding of blood there is no remission of sins.
- HEB 10:1–2,10–18 ~ The Law, even with all the sacrifices offered continuously during the year for sin, could never make anyone perfect; otherwise they would have ceased the practice, and would have lost their knowledge of sin. By one offering, Christ has made perfect those who will be sanctified. We are sanctified by the offering of the body of Jesus Christ, one sacrifice for all people. No more offering for sin will ever be needed again.
- HEB 11:1—12:2 ~ Faith is the substance of things hoped for and the evidence of things not seen. Through faith we understand that everything was created by God's Word, and that the things that are tangible were made from things that are intangible. Without faith it is impossible to please God, because if you don't believe in God you can't find Him; but if you seek God you will be rewarded and you will find Him. The prophets are good examples of the power and rewards of faith; they subdued kingdoms, wrought righteousness, made treaties, escaped certain death, battled armies, raised the dead, endured torture, and more. Jesus Christ is the author and finisher of our faith; He endured the cross and a shameful death and now sits at God's right hand.
- HEB 13:1–2 ~ Let brotherly love flourish. Remember to help others whenever you can, for you may be entertaining angels without knowing it.

James (Author: Attributed to James the brother of Jesus)
 1. Resist temptation, be patient, and endure, and you will receive a crown of life; don't just listen to God's Word, but practice it
 2. If you don't practice God's Word your faith is dead; you cannot have a true faith if your faith is not demonstrated in your actions
 3. Hold your tongue if you have nothing constructive to say; silence is wisdom, as are gentleness, mercy, and honesty
 4. You can't love God and worldly things also; be humble and submit to God; resist Satan and he will flee from you
 5. Don't waste time heaping up worldly possessions and riches; be patient and watchful for the Lord; never swear; confess your faults to each other, and pray fervently and frequently

Key Verses:
- JAM 1:12–15 ~ Blessed are people that endure temptation, for when they are judged, they will receive the crown of life that God promises to all who love Him. Don't say that you are tempted by God, because God cannot be tempted by evil, neither does He tempt anyone; but people are tempted when they are drawn by their own lust and enticed to commit sin. When lust conceives, it brings sin, and sin, when it is finished, brings death.
- JAM 1:19 ~ Be anxious to listen, but slow to speak and slow to anger.
- JAM 1:22 ~ Be doers of the Word and not just hearers, deceiving yourself.
- JAM 2:10 ~ Whoever strives to obey all the Law, yet disobeys one point, has disobeyed all.
- JAM 2:17 ~ Faith without good works is meaningless (act on your faith).
- JAM 4:7 ~ Submit to God; resist Satan and he will flee from you.
- JAM 4:17 ~ If you know the right thing to do, and don't do it, it is a sin.
- JAM 5:16 ~ Confess your faults to each other and pray for each other, so that you may be healed. The fervent prayer of a righteous person yields high returns.

1 Peter (Author: Peter)
 1. Blessed be God the Father who, through the resurrection of Christ, has given us salvation and our inheritance that is perfect and everlasting
 2. We are chosen by God to be free; not free to disobey the laws or to commit sin, but free to serve Him; we must be willing to suffer for Christ, enduring patiently as Christ did
 3. Be of one mind, love one another, and be courteous; don't reward evil for evil; witness to others about your faith in Christ
 4. Share the Word with others; rejoice if you suffer for Christ, because His Spirit will be upon you, and through your suffering God will be glorified
 5. Be humble, sober, and vigilant, for Satan is out there waiting for you

Key Verses:
- 1 PE 1:3–4 ~ Blessed be God the Father, who by His mercy has given us a new life, through the resurrection of His Son Jesus Christ. Therefore, we will be resurrected with Christ to enjoy an incorruptible and undefiled inheritance, reserved in heaven for all believers.
- 1 PE 2:9 ~ You are a chosen generation, a royal priesthood, a holy nation, a unique people. So, praise Him who has called you out of darkness into his marvelous light.
- 1 PE 2:24 ~ He (Christ) bore our sins in His own body on the cross so that we might die to sins and live to righteousness.
- 1 PE 3:15 ~ Sanctify the Lord in your hearts, and always be ready to give an answer, with humility and respect, to anyone who asks about the hope that is within you.

- 1 PE 4:10 ~ Even as you have received the free gift, share that gift with others, as good stewards of the endless grace of God.
- 1 PE 5:8–9 ~ Be sober and vigilant, because your enemy the devil roams about like a lion searching for someone to devour. He will attempt to consume anyone who isn't steadfast in their faith.

2 Peter (Author: Peter)
1. Be faithful and virtuous, try to be like Christ, and receive His everlasting kingdom
2. Beware of false prophets who teach damnable heresies and lure people through lust of the flesh; they will perish in their own corruption
3. Scoffers will come saying, "Where is the Lord," but the day of the Lord will come unexpectedly; grow in righteousness and don't be led astray; wait diligently and patiently for the Lord

Key Verses:
- 2 PE 1:5–8 ~ Supplement your faith with virtue, your virtue with knowledge, your knowledge with self-control, your self-control with steadfastness, your steadfastness with godliness, and your godliness with brotherly love. If these are yours and they abound, they will keep you from being fruitless and ineffective.
- 2 PE 1:16,21 ~ We did not follow cleverly devised fables when we told people about the power and coming of Jesus Christ, for we were eye witnesses of His majesty. No prophecy ever came from the impulse of man, but holy men spoke as they were directed by God.
- 2 PE 2:20–21 ~ For if, after they have escaped the pollution of the world through the knowledge of the Lord and Savior Jesus Christ, they are again entangled therein, and overcome, the latter end is worse for them than the beginning. For it would have been better for them not to have known the way of righteousness, than, after they had known it, to turn from the holy commandment delivered to them.

1 John (Author: John, the apostle)
1. Everyone has sinned; but if we confess our sins, we will be forgiven
2. Don't love worldly things but abide in Christ; whoever denies Christ is an antichrist
3. Love one another and believe in Christ; refrain from hate and sin which come from Satan; Christ came to destroy the works of Satan
4. Test the spirits, for many false prophets will come; God is love; those who love God and one another have His Spirit living in them
5. Anyone believing that Jesus is Christ and God's Son is also a child of God; Jesus, the Holy Spirit, and God the Father are one

Key Verses:
- 1 JO 1:8 ~ If we say we are not sinful, we deceive ourselves and we are liars. If we confess our sins, God, who is faithful and just, will forgive our sins and cleanse us from all unrighteousness.
- 1 JO 2:15–16 ~ Do not love the world or worldly things. If a person loves the world, he or she cannot love God. All that is in the world, the lust of the flesh, the greed of the eyes, and the pride of humanity, do not come from the Father but are of this world alone.
- 1 JO 4:1–3 ~ Do not believe every spirit, but test the spirits to determine if they are from God, because many false prophets exist. Any spirit that confesses that Jesus Christ is God in the flesh is from God; any spirit that denies Christ is not from God but is an antichrist. You have heard that the antichrist will come, but is already here.

- 1 JO 4:7–12,16–21 ~ Let us love one another, for love is from God, and those who love are born of God and know Him. If you don't love God you can't know Him because God is love. The love of God was manifested among us through His only Son, so we might live through Him. If God loves us so much, we should love one another; if we love one another, God lives in us and His love is perfected in us. If you abide in love you abide in God, and God abides in you. This perfect love gives us confidence on the day of judgment, because there is no fear in love but perfect love destroys fear, because fear brings torment. We love because God loved us first. You can't say you love God and hate your brother without being a liar, because you can't hate someone you have seen and still love God who you have never seen. So, you should love God and your brother (neighbor).
- 1 JO 5:6–8,20 ~ There are three that are recorded in heaven: the Father, the Word, and the Holy Spirit. These three are one. The same three bear witness: the Spirit, the Water, and the Blood. The Spirit is The Witness, because the Spirit bears the Truth. We know Jesus Christ who is true so that we may know God who is true; and so we live in Him who has shown us His Son, the source of eternal life.

2 John (Author: John, the apostle)
  1. Love one another and obey God's commandments; beware of deceivers who deny Christ

3 John (Author: John, the apostle)
  1. Don't pursue evil things but always walk in truth

Jude (Author: Attributed to Judah the brother of Jesus)
  1. Beware of ungodly people who are evil, deceitful, and defile things of God; keep yourselves in the love of God and show compassion for others

Revelation (Author: John, the apostle)
  1. Jesus Christ is the beginning and the end; He lived, died, and is alive again forevermore; He has the keys to hell and death
  2—3. John is called by Christ to address the seven churches and remind them of God's promise to all believers who repent and obey God
     a. Ephesus: be faithful to your first love (2:1–7)
     b. Smyrna: endure your tribulations; don't listen to false prophets (2:8–11)
     c. Pergamos: beware of false doctrine; refrain from idolatry (2:12–17)
     d. Thyatira: stay away from the harlot who calls herself a prophetess (2:18–29)
     e. Sardis: be watchful and strengthen each other (3:1–6)
     f. Philadelphia: keep the faith; beware of liars who call themselves Jews and build a temple for Satan (3:7–13)
     g. Laodiceans: worldly riches do not make you wealthy; seek spiritual riches (3:14–22)
  4. John's vision of the throne of God, with angels and elders
  5—6. The Lamb of God, the only one worthy to open the book with seven seals
     a. First seal: white horse with conqueror carrying a bow (6:2)
     b. Second seal: red horse with warmonger carrying a sword (6:3–4)
     c. Third seal: black horse with rider carrying balances (6:5–6)
     d. Fourth seal: pale horse with death rider, followed by four punishments (war, famine, plagues, and fierce beasts); one quarter of the earth dies from the punishments (6:7–8)
     e. Fifth seal: white robes given to the faithful of the dead (6:9–11)

    f. Sixth seal: great earthquake and gloom; stars fall to the earth; people hide from God (6:12–17)
7. God seals 144,000 of His people with His mark to protect them; multitude of God's faithful in white robes (who endured tribulations) sing in a choir
8—9. Seventh seal: silence in heaven; seven angels prepare to blow their trumpets
    a. First angel: hail and fire mingle with blood; one-third of trees and all the grass burn (8:7)
    b. Second angel: burning mountain falls into the sea; one-third of sea turned to blood; one-third of sea life dies; one-third of ships destroyed (8:8–9)
    c. Third angel: burning star called Wormwood falls from heaven; one-third of water becomes bitter and poisoned (8:10–11)
    d. Fourth angel: darkness; one-third of heavenly bodies darkened; day shortened by one-third; three woes will come (8:12–13)
    e. Fifth angel: first woe; star falls from heaven with key to bottomless pit; smoke and stinging locust arise from pit to torment people without God's seal; people want to die but cannot (9:1–12)
    f. Sixth angel: second woe; four angels turned loose to kill one-third of humankind; cavalry of 200,000,000 with breastplates of red, blue, and yellow kill people; sinners still won't repent (9:13–21)
10. Seventh angel: third woe; God's mystery is finished; seven thunders speak; angel's little book tastes sweet but sours the stomach
11. Two witnesses
    a. Prophesy for 3 ½ years (v3)
    b. Have power to breathe fire, stop rain, turn water to blood, and send plagues (v5–6)
    c. Beast kills them but they rise from dead in 3 ½ days, ascending into heaven (v7–12)
12. War in heaven between Michael the archangel and his angels against Satan the dragon and his angels; Satan and his angels are thrown out of heaven to the earth where Satan makes war with Christ and His people
13. The Beast, whose power comes from Satan, is ascribed the number 666
    a. People without God's mark worship the beast, who speaks blasphemy 3 ½ years and has power to subdue humankind (v4–8)
    b. Second beast performs wonders, like bringing fire down from heaven; many are deceived; people are persuaded to make a talking image of the beast (v11–15)
    c. Mark of beast put on hand or forehead; nobody can buy or sell without the mark of the beast (v16–17)
14. Judgment day
    a. 144,000 redeemed from Israel gather with Christ in Zion (v1–5)
    b. Those receiving mark of beast and worshipping the beast receive eternal torment (v8–11)
    c. Righteous are gathered into God's kingdom (v12–16)
    d. Unrighteous receive wrath of God (v17–20)
15—16. God's wrath is poured out (seven plagues); people still don't repent
    a. First plague: sores (16:2)
    b. Second plague: sea dies and everything in it (16:3)
    c. Third plague: rivers and springs die (16:4)
    d. Fourth plague: fire from the sun scorches people (16:8–9)
    e. Fifth plague: darkness and pain (16:10)
    f. Sixth plague: Euphrates river dries up; evil spirits emerge from Satan, the beast, and the false prophet; evil armies gather at Armageddon (16:12–16)
    g. Seventh plague: great earthquake causes Babylon to fall into three parts; cities and nations are destroyed; great hail falls (16:17–21)

17. Babylon: city of blasphemy that presides over many nations
    a. Sits over seven mountains (v9)
    b. Seven kings; beast is eighth king, also one of the seven (v10–11)
    c. Ten kings receive power with the beast for one hour to make war with the Lamb; they are defeated by Lamb (v12–14)
18. Fall of Babylon due to its many abominations
19. Christ rides triumphantly on a white horse to judge and make war; the beast and those with his mark are thrown into the lake of fire; the rest of the evil ones are killed by the sword
20. The millennium and the opening of the Book of Life
    a. Satan thrown into bottomless pit and bound for one thousand years (v2–3)
    b. Christ and His followers reign one thousand years (first resurrection) (v4)
    c. Rest of dead resurrected after one thousand years (second resurrection) (v5)
    d. Satan freed to deceive the nations and to wage war; fire from heaven devours them (v7–9)
    e. Satan thrown into lake of fire where beast, false prophet, and those with mark of beast will be tormented forever (v10)
    f. Rest of dead are judged according to their works; those not written in the Book of Life are thrown into lake of fire (second death)
21—22. New heaven and earth for the righteous; lake of fire for the wicked

Key Verses:
- REV 1:8 ~ Jesus said, "I am the alpha and omega, the beginning and the end; who was, is, and is to come—the Almighty."
- REV 3:20 ~ Behold, I stand at the door and knock. Everyone who hears my voice and opens the door, I will come into them, and I will abide (eat) with them, and they with me.
- REV 2:10 ~ Jesus said, "Don't be afraid of the things that you must suffer; Satan will throw some of you into prison to be tried; you will endure tribulation for ten days. Be faithful unto death and I will give you a crown of life."
- REV 7:9–10,13–14 ~ I (John) saw a giant multitude, too many people to even count; there were people from every nation, race, and tongue standing before the throne and the Lamb, who was clothed in white. They held palm branches and sang, "Salvation to our God who sits on the throne and to the Lamb." One of the elders asked me who these people were. I replied, "Tell me, sir." He said, "These are the ones who came from great tribulation, and have washed their robes and made them white with the blood of the Lamb."
- REV 20:12,14 ~ I saw the dead standing before God and the books were opened, including the Book of Life. And everyone was judged according to what was written in the books, according to their works. And death and hell were thrown into the lake of fire. This is the second death.
- REV 21:1,4,8 ~ There was a new heaven and earth with no sea; the old heaven and earth was gone. And God wiped away all tears, and there was no death, sorrow, crying, or pain ever again, for these things had passed away. The fearful, the unbelieving, the murderers, prostitutes, sorcerers, idolaters, and liars were thrown into the lake of fire which was the second death.
- REV 22:18–20 ~ For I testify to everyone who hears the words of the prophecy of this book, that if anyone adds to these words, God will add unto that person the plagues mentioned in this book. If anyone subtracts from the words of this prophecy, God will take away their name from the Book of Life, and they will not share in the inheritance. He who testified of these things says, "Surely I am coming soon." Amen, let it be so; come Lord Jesus.

Lesson: The Trinity Revisited

You probably have heard the argument that there is no such thing as the Holy Trinity since the word "trinity" does not appear in the Holy Bible. This logic is obviously flawed. Otherwise, one might conclude that dinosaurs never existed because the word "dinosaur" doesn't appear in the Bible either. Of course, the list could go on and on.

However, we can be certain that there is a Holy Trinity. Why else would Christ command that Baptism be performed in the name of the Father, Son, and Holy Spirit (MAT 28:19)? And why else would St. Paul mention these three personifications of God in His benediction (2 CO 13:14)? Notice in this lesson how all three persons of the Trinity are required for God's plan of salvation to work, and how each personage plays an integral role in yours and my redemption.

The Holy Bible, God's Word, is a detailed description of God's intricate plan. It tells us how Jesus Christ came to the earth to be God the Father's witness to humanity. Christ is the Redeemer promised in the Old Testament; He is the fulfillment of that prophecy as revealed in the New Testament. The Holy Spirit is the witness that testifies through the Word, and Christ is that Word who was made flesh so God could further testify to the truth.

- ISA 43:10–12,15 ~ There are no gods before Him or after Him. God says, "You are witnesses to what I have said. My servant whom I have chosen is also sent to be a witness, so that you can know me and believe; and even so, I am He. I am the Lord and there is no other savior besides me. I have declared myself to you and I have saved you whenever you have forsaken all other gods for me. You are witnesses that I am God, the Holy One, the Creator of Israel, and your King."
- ISA 48:16 ~ Come and listen. I have not spoken in secret since the beginning. I was there all along, and now, the Lord God and His Spirit have sent me (Christ).
- JOH 1:1,14 ~ In the beginning was the Word, and the Word was with God, and the Word was God. And the Word became flesh and lived among us; and we saw His glory, the glory of the Father's only Son, full of grace and truth.
- JOH 8:18 ~ Jesus said, "I testify about myself and the Father that sent me testifies about me."
- JOH 15:26 ~ Jesus said, "I will send the Comforter to you and He will testify about me; the Comforter is the Spirit of truth which proceeds from the Father."
- 1 JO 5:6–8,20 ~ There are three that are recorded in heaven: the Father, the Word, and the Holy Spirit. These three are one. The same three bear witness: the Spirit, the Water, and the Blood. The Spirit is the Witness, because the Spirit bears the truth. We know Jesus Christ who is true so that we may know God who is true. We live in Him who has shown us His Son, the source of eternal life.

God is perfect and God is love; where there is perfect love, there can be no sin. God wanted children to share His love, so He created people in His image. However, humans could not resist temptation and were destined to become sinners. We who are evil cannot dwell with God who is righteous unless our sin is purged first. God knew this all along and developed His elaborate plan of salvation, even before He created people (PRO 8; EPH 1). Jesus Christ came to remove our sins and cleanse us of all unrighteousness, so we could be joined with our Heavenly Father and live with Him in His kingdom in a purified state. So that we might seek Him, our Heavenly Father gave us a sophisticated brain, able to distinguish right from wrong. Unlike Christ, however, we chose to sin; and every sin has separated us from God who is perfect in righteousness. God's Spirit communicates His will to us and His love for us. Because of His endless love, God forgives us if we believe in His promises, and He has promised us salvation through faith in His only Son Jesus Christ.

God gives His love, His Spirit, and His Son for free. He gives us salvation that leads to eternal life if only we accept Christ. We cannot earn salvation by our own merit; it is given entirely because of God's bounteous grace and mercy. In love, the Father created us establishing His requirements for salvation. God breathed into us the spirit of life by the power of His own Holy Spirit, and by that Spirit He sustains us in our faith. But our sin has condemned us and alienated us from God. The penalty for every sin is death, insofar as it only takes one. The shedding of Christ's blood on the cross which resulted in His death has covered that penalty in full. We can begin to understand the Holy Trinity in terms of Love, Life, and Blood.

Love

- DEU 7:9 ~ The Lord is God. He is faithful. He keeps His covenant of love for a thousand generations to those that love Him and keep His commandments.
- PRO 10:12 ~ Hatred stirs up strife, but love covers all sins.
- JOH 3:16 ~ God loved the world so much that He gave His only begotten Son, so that anyone who believed in Him would never die but would live forever.
- ROM 13:10 ~ Love does no wrong to a neighbor; therefore, love is the fulfilling of the Law.
- 1 CO 13:2–8,13 ~ Even if you have the gift of prophecy, can understand mysteries, and have a faith to move mountains, you are nothing without love. Even if you give all you have to the poor, you profit nothing if you don't have love. Love is patient. Love is kind. Love is never envious or conceited. Love is not rude, self-seeking, or angered, nor does it find pleasure in sin. Love does not think of sinful things nor is it provoked by evil. Love rejoices in the truth. Love always protects, always trusts, always hopes, and always endures. Love never fails... Faith, hope, and love abide; but the greatest of these three is love.
- 1 JO 4:7–9 ~ Let us love one another, for love comes from God, and those who love are born of God and know Him. If you don't love God you can't know Him because God is love. The love of God was manifested among us through His only Son, so we might live through Him.

Life

- ECC 12:7 ~ Upon death, the spirit returns to God who gave it.
- ZEC 12:1 ~ The Lord formed the spirit of man within him.
- JOH 6:63 ~ Jesus said, "It is the spirit that gives life, not the flesh." Jesus spoke the words of spirit and life.
- JOH 10:7,10–11,18 ~ Jesus said, "I am the gate for the sheep. The thief comes only to steal, kill, and destroy the sheep. I have come that they may have life, and have it more abundantly. I am the Good Shepherd. The Good Shepherd lays down His life for the sheep. Nobody takes my life from me, but I lay it down of my own free will. I have the power to lay it down and to take it back up again. This command I received from my Father."
- JOH 14:6 ~ Jesus said, "I am the way, the truth, and the life; nobody can come to the Father without coming through me."
- 1 CO 2:10–12 ~ God reveals His mysteries to us through His Spirit, for the Spirit searches all things, even the deepest things of God. Nobody can know the deepest thoughts of another, only the spirit within that person can know them. Similarly, nobody can know the deepest thoughts of God except His Holy Spirit. We have received the Spirit of God, not the spirit of the world, so that we might know the things that God has given to us for free.
- 2 CO 3:6 ~ God has made us able ministers of a new testament, not of the letter of the Law, but of the Spirit, for the letter kills, but the Spirit gives life.

Blood

- LEV 17:11 ~ The life of all flesh resides in the blood, and God has given it to you upon the altar to make atonement for your souls, because the blood makes atonement for the soul.
- MAT 26:26–28 ~ Jesus took bread, blessed it, broke it into pieces, and distributed it to the apostles saying, "Take this bread and eat it, for this is my body." Then He took a cup of wine, thanked God, and passed the cup to the apostles saying, "Each of you drink from this cup of wine, for this is my blood of the New Covenant, shed for you and for many for the remission of sins."
- COL 1:19–22 ~ God was pleased to have His fullness living in Christ, so that, through Christ, everything on earth and in heaven could be reconciled to Himself, by the peace that came through the shedding of Christ's blood on the cross. Before, you were separated from God; you were His enemies because of your sinful minds and evil deeds. But now, God has reconciled you by the body of Christ, through His death, to be presented holy, blameless, and pure in the sight of God.
- HEB 9:11–14,22 ~ Christ has come, the high priest of all good things, into a perfect temple, but not a temple made with hands like a building. He entered the sanctuary, not by blood sacrifices of animals, but through the perfect sacrifice of His own blood. He obtained, not temporary forgiveness for us, but eternal redemption. Therefore, if the blood of animals could sanctify those who were unclean, how much more will the blood of Christ, who offered Himself unblemished to God, cleanse our consciences from sin that leads to death, so that we may serve the living God.

The Father, Son, and Holy Spirit perform particular functions yet they comprise one God. God's Spirit gives us life and communicates to us His truth. That truth is conveyed in God's Word, and includes the knowledge of obedience passed onto us when the Almighty Father handed down His commandments. But people will break the Law from the beginning until the end; and as a disobedient child, we all deserve to be punished. Jesus Christ is God's obedient Son; He is the way, the truth, and the life. Christ is our advocate who shed His blood to pay the price of our disobedience, and to exemplify the cost levied upon Him but due to us.

Only Jesus could take our place, because He alone has been perfectly obedient to the Father and in total adherence to God's laws. Because of His obedience Jesus was raised from the dead. If Christ had sinned, His death could not have been reversed. And without His death and resurrection, we could not be raised either. This then is the great plan of salvation that God has communicated to us in His Word and in His Law. We cannot earn this great gift of salvation by works, because we are not perfectly obedient. If we could be perfect, we would not need a savior. We can be saved only by believing in Christ and accepting God's righteousness given us through His Son. Otherwise, we would die in our sins along with the unbelievers, who will pay for their sins with their own deaths, never to be reconciled unto God the Father. Our faith in Christ is established and strengthened by God's Holy Spirit, and by His grace that Spirit will preserve us forever and always in the knowledge of salvation and the certainty of reuniting with God and His chosen.

Thus, the Holy Trinity can be described in terms of God's Covenants: the Law established by the Almighty Father in the OT, and Grace realized through God's Son Jesus Christ in the NT. Both covenants are upheld and connected by the same faith, which is founded on Christ the rock of our salvation. That faith, maintained in us by the Holy Spirit, signifies our trust in God's promises guaranteed in both testaments of the Holy Bible. Consider the interrelationships between Law, Faith, and Grace.

Law

- JER 31:31–33 ~ The days are coming when I will make a New Covenant with my people. It won't be like the covenant I made when I brought my people out of Egypt, which they broke. The New Covenant will be this: Instead of writing my laws on stone, I will write my laws inside the hearts of my people. They will not have to teach others to know God because everyone will know me, for I will forgive their sins and remove those sins forever.
- ROM 3:20 ~ Nobody can be justified by works of the Law, for by the Law comes the knowledge of sin.
- ROM 5:13,18–19 ~ Sin existed in the world before the Law was given; but nothing can be attributed to sin where there is no Law. By the sin of one (Adam) came the judgment of all, unto condemnation of death. By the righteousness of one (Christ) came the free gift of justification, unto eternal life. As by the disobedience of Adam are many people made sinners, so by the obedience of Christ are many people made righteous.
- ROM 7:7,14 ~ The Law told me what not to do, thereby revealing sin to me. So, is the Law sin? No, it is the opposite of sin. For the Law is spiritual, but I am carnal because I sin.
- ROM 8:2 ~ The law of the Spirit of life in Jesus Christ has made me free from the law of sin and death.
- JAM 2:10 ~ Whoever keeps the Law, then disobeys but one point, is guilty of disobeying all the Law.

Faith

- PSA 31:23 ~ Love the Lord, all you saints. For the Lord preserves the faithful, but the proud He pays back.
- HAB 2:4 ~ Those whose souls are not upright will fail; but the just will live by faith.
- GAL 2:16,20–21 ~ Nobody is justified by works of the Law, they are justified by faith in Jesus Christ. I have been crucified with Christ; thus, it is no longer I who live but Christ who lives in me. And the life I live in the flesh, I live by faith in the Son of God who gave His life for me. If righteousness could be gained from the Law, then Christ would have died for nothing.
- GAL 3:11,24,26 ~ No man is justified before God by the Law, but those who are righteous through faith shall live. The Law was in effect until Christ came, that we might be justified by faith. In Christ we can become children of God if we have faith.
- HEB 11:1,3,6 ~ Faith is the assurance of things hoped for, the evidence of things not seen. By faith we understand that the world was created by the Word of God, such that things we see were made from things which do not appear. Without faith, it is impossible to please God, for whoever would wish to come to Him must believe He exists and that He rewards those who seek Him.
- JAM 2:17–26 ~ Faith without works is dead. Was Abraham justified by works when he offered his son Isaac? Faith was active before that and was completed by the works. So a person is justified also by works and not faith alone. Just as a body apart from the spirit is dead, so is faith apart from works.

Grace

- PRO 16:6 ~ By mercy and truth, sin is purged; by the fear of the Lord, people can depart from evil.
- MIC 7:18 ~ There is no God like Him, who pardons sin and overlooks the evil of His children. He doesn't retain His anger because He delights in mercy.

- JOH 1:17 ~ For the Law was given by Moses, but grace and truth came by Jesus Christ.
- ROM 5:20–21 ~ Where sin abounded, grace abounded even more. As sin reigned unto death, even so, grace reigns through righteousness unto eternal life through Jesus Christ our Lord.
- EPH 2:8–9 ~ You are saved by the grace of God because of your faith in Jesus Christ. Salvation is a gift of God, it cannot be earned through good works, so nobody should brag.
- TIT 3:5,7 ~ He saved us, not because of our works of righteousness, but according to His mercy by the washing of regeneration and renewing by the Holy Spirit. Being justified by His grace, we are made heirs according to the hope of eternal life.

We can comprehend the Holy Trinity further in terms of God's heavenly Court of Law. When someone commits a crime, they must be tried in court where the truth is heard and justice is administered. In our justice system, the punishment is supposed to be commensurate with the crime. According to God's system, all people are sinful, the punishment for sin is death, and God passes judgement on sinners.

This is why we need an advocate, who is Jesus Christ; He is our attorney at law. He will testify on our behalf that the fines for our crimes have been paid when He presents us blameless before God. Through His death, Christ redeemed us from being imprisoned by our sin, and through His resurrection He saved us from being sentenced to death. Therefore, God will render a verdict of "not guilty" because we have been cleansed of unrighteousness by the blood of the Lamb who justified us through our faith in His atonement. Now we can describe the Holy Trinity in terms of the Truth that has set us free from the chains of sin; the Victory wherein Christ has overcome the world and conquered death; ensuring our Deliverance from hell and reprieve from eternal separation from God.

Truth

- DEU 32:4 ~ He is the Rock; His works are perfect and His ways are just. He is a God of truth and He can do no wrong.
- PRO 30:5 ~ Every word of God is true. He protects those that put their trust in Him.
- MAT 10:32–33 ~ Jesus said, "Anybody who confesses me before others, I will confess them before my Father in heaven. Anybody who denies me to others, I will deny them before my Father in heaven."
- JOH 4:24 ~ Jesus said, "God is Spirit and should be worshipped in spirit and in truth."
- JOH 8:31–32 ~ Jesus said, "If you continue in my Word, then you are indeed my disciples, and you will know the truth, and the truth will set you free."
- JOH 18:37–38 ~ Pilate asked Jesus if He was a king. Jesus replied, "My kingdom is not of this world. I was born so I could give witness to the truth. Everyone who searches for truth hears my voice." Pilate then asked, "What is truth?"
- 1 JO 2:1–2 ~ My little children, I am writing these things to you so you will not sin. But if anyone does sin, we have an advocate with the Father who will speak in our defense: Jesus Christ the Righteous One. He is the atoning sacrifice for our sins, and not only for our sins, but also for the sins of the entire world.

Victory

- PSA 98:1 ~ Sing to the Lord a new song, for He has done marvelous things. The right hand of His holy arm has won the victory.
- ISA 25:8 ~ The Lord will swallow up death in victory. He will wipe away the tears and He will remove the disgrace from His people. For the Lord has said so.

- ISA 53:11 ~ Through the knowledge of Him many will become justified, for He took their sins upon Himself.
- ROM 3:19–28 ~ Now we know that whatever the Law says, it speaks to those that are under the Law, so that every mouth may be silenced and the whole world held accountable to God. Therefore, nobody will be declared righteous in His sight by observing the Law; rather, through the Law we become conscious of sin. But now righteousness of God apart from the Law has been made known, to which the Law and the prophets testify. This righteousness is available, through faith in Jesus Christ, to all believers. There is no difference between Jews and Gentiles, for all have sinned and fallen short of God's glory, and all can be justified freely by His grace through the redemption that came by Christ. God presented Him as an atoning sacrifice, received through faith in His blood. He did this to demonstrate His justice. He restrained Himself from executing punishment for the sins committed beforehand so that He could show His justice now, in order to be fair in justifying those who have faith in Jesus.
- 1 CO 15:54–57 ~ When the corruptible are clothed with incorruption, and the mortal with immortality, then will the words, "death is swallowed up in victory," be true. Oh death, where is your sting? Oh grave, where is your victory? Thank God who gives us the victory through our Lord Jesus Christ!
- HEB 10:10,14 ~ We are sanctified by the offering of the body of Jesus Christ. By His offering He has made perfect all those who are sanctified.

Deliverance

- PSA 86:4,13 ~ Gladden my soul, oh Lord, for to you I lift up my soul. For great is your steadfast love toward me; you have delivered my soul from the depths of hell.
- ISA 61:1–3 ~ The Spirit of God is upon me, because He has directed me to preach His good news to the humble, to heal the broken hearted, to free the slaves, and to release those who are bound in chains and in prison; to proclaim the Lord's favor and His vengeance, to comfort all who mourn, and to tell those who mourn to exchange their ashes for beauty; to replace mourning with joy, and to don the garment of praise in exchange for the spirit of sorrow, so that they may be trees of righteousness, planted by the Lord for His glorification.
- JOE 2:32 ~ Whoever calls upon the name of the Lord will be delivered. There will be deliverance in mount Zion and in Jerusalem, for the Lord has said, including all survivors that the Lord calls.
- JOH 5:22–24,30 ~ Jesus said, "The Father judges nobody but has entrusted judgment to the Son, so that everyone may honor the Son as they honor the Father. Those that do not honor the Son do not honor the Father who sent Him. Truthfully, whoever hears my Word and believes Him who sent me has eternal life and will not be condemned, but will cross over from death into life. My judgment is fair, because I seek the Father's will and not my own."
- GAL 3:13; GAL 4:4–5 ~ When the time was right, God sent His Son, born of a woman and established according to the Law, to redeem those who were under the Law, so that we could receive adoption as children of God. Christ has redeemed us from the curse of the Law, being made a curse in our stead.
- HEB 12:22–22 ~ You have come to God's holy mountain, to His holy city, to stay with the living God and His multitude of angels. You are part of the assembly and church of the first born, whose names are written in heaven. You are among the righteous, who have been redeemed and whose spirits have been made perfect.
- REV 2:10–11 ~ Jesus said, "Be faithful unto death and I will give you a crown of life. Those that overcome will not be hurt by the second death."

By being perfectly obedient, Christ was able to impute His righteousness upon us, because He fulfilled the Law on our behalf. By dying for our sins Christ cleansed us from evil, thereby conquering sin, having paid the punishment for our unrighteousness. By rising from the dead, Christ became victorious over death, ensuring the resurrection of the dead. Christ removed our sins and replaced them with His righteousness, making us acceptable before God our Father; if a believer dies, he or she remains forever alive in Him. Christ abolished sin and death to ransom our souls, wherein we now abide eternally with God as His righteous sons and daughters.

To summarize, our Heavenly Father wanted children to share His love and enjoy His creations and His kingdom. In order to know God, He gave us a discerning mind (GEN 3:22) so His Spirit could convey to us the Law (1 CO 2:13–14). With the knowledge of good and evil came sin (GEN 2:16–17; GEN 3:11–12), and sin resulted in death (ROM 6:23), and death brought judgment upon all people (REV 20:12). The only way for us to be reconciled unto God was for the Law to be fulfilled, our sin to be expunged, and our death sentence to be commuted. This then, is the mission of Christ: He perfectly obeyed the Law on our behalf, He paid the penalty for our disobedience, and He overcame death thereby restoring the lives of believing Christians for all eternity.

This lesson is encapsulated in the table below which provides a graphic look at attributes ascribed to God, thereby revealing, in part, His character.

HOLY TRINITY	GOD'S GIFTS	COVENANT	JUDGMENT
Almighty Father	Love	Law	Deliverance
Holy Spirit	Life	Faith	Truth
Jesus Christ	Blood	Grace	Victory

The Unholy Trinity

It is important to note that Satan has attempted to destroy the works of the Lord, and continues to do so, to no avail. Satan tried to get evil men to murder the Christ child, he personally endeavored to tempt Christ into sin, he has brought death upon many people, and he has succeeded in persuading angels and humans to follow him into the fires of hell. He has fought against God every inch of the way, but he still faces a no-win situation. To complete his insubordination towards God, Satan has established his own anti-trinity, verifying that he is quite the opposite of God in character. Consequently, Satan possesses the antithesis of attributes ascribed to God in the table above.

The unholy trinity begins with the false prophet who speaks grandiose lies and distorts the truth advanced by God's Holy Spirit. The antichrist, beast, or son of hell is Satan's counterpart to God's Son; this possessed soul gains power in the latter days and promotes devil worship, initiating the abomination of desolation. And finally, there is Lucifer himself, the dragon, the beast, the devil; he was the angel that exalted himself and was exiled from heaven. Now he stalks the earth looking for ways of leading people astray, tempting them with lusts of the flesh and worldly treasures, and diminishing their faith in God little by little so the person doesn't realize they are being recruited into his demise in the lake of fire.

- ISA 32:6–7 ~ The vile person comes speaking blasphemy and working evil and hypocrisy, opposing God Himself. His instruments are wickedness, lies, and dishonor.
- JOH 8:44 ~ Jesus told the unbelievers, "You evil people belong to your father, the devil, and the evil of your father is what you do. He was a murderer and a liar from the start. He never tells the truth; in fact, he is the father of lies."
- 2 TH 2:3–4,9–12 ~ The man of lawlessness comes, who is the son of damnation (perdition). He exalts himself to be a god, or an object of worship, taking the seat in the temple of God. He brings about the acts of Satan through deception and magic. God will let them believe these lies and carry on with their wickedness, and be condemned to hell.
- 1 JO 4:3 ~ Anyone denying Jesus as the Christ, and God in the flesh, is an antichrist. Have you heard about the antichrist coming? Well the antichrist is here already.
- REV 13:1–17 ~ While standing on the seashore I saw a beast rise from the sea, with seven heads and ten horns; a crown was on each horn, and on each head was the name of blasphemy. And the dragon gave him his power. One of its heads was wounded, but it healed itself. The world marveled at the beast and worshipped it, and they worshipped the dragon that gave its power to the beast. The people said, "Who is like the beast? Who possibly can oppose him?" The beast spoke blasphemy against God for 3 ½ years. He waged war against anyone that was holy, to defeat them. He gained power over all races, peoples, and nations. Everyone except the righteous honored the beast. Then another beast with two horns came, speaking like the dragon. He exercised the same power as the first beast, performing magic feats such as bringing fire down from heaven. He convinced everyone to worship the first beast, and to make a graven image of it. And the second beast brought the image of the beast to life. He caused everyone to receive the mark of the beast on their right hand or forehead; only those with the mark could buy and sell goods. They tracked down and murdered anyone that did not receive the mark and worship the beast.
- REV 13:18 ~ Here is wisdom for those who can understand: Count the number of the beast, for it is the number of a man, and the number is 666 (the unholy trinity).
- REV 16:13 ~ And I saw three evil spirits leap like frogs out of the mouths of the dragon, the beast, and the false prophet.
- REV 19:20 ~ But the beast was captured, and with him the false prophet that performed miraculous signs on his behalf, with which he deceived those who had received the mark of the beast and worshipped his image. They were thrown alive into the lake of fire.
- REV 20:10 ~ And the devil that deceived them was cast into the lake of fire where the beast and the false prophet were, to be tormented day and night forevermore.

Summary: There is one Holy Trinity of God; Christians recognize and worship all three persons. There is one principal antagonist, Satan, who represents all that is not God and promotes anything contrary to truth. Everybody has the capacity to recognize God, His works and His ways; similarly, the discernment of right and wrong is implanted in all of our minds. No other earthly creatures are created in God's image; further, humans alone are offered the opportunity to live forever in paradise. It is an extraordinary privilege to be a member of the King's inner circle with the status of prince or princess. Not even angels are given this status. Would you rather follow the prince of darkness into the bottomless pit and be consumed by fire, or live as royalty in the company of angels, saints, and the Holy Trinity? God made us free and will do it again, unless you'd rather not.

Lesson: The Seven Spirits of God

You may have heard of the seven spirits of God, found in different places in the Bible but most notably in the book of Revelation. There are predominant theories as to what these seven spirits represent. One popular position is it is a reference to the Holy Spirit. This is based on the number seven representing perfection and therefore symbolic of the only perfect being. Keep in mind, the spirit of the Lord is not divided into seven, because the Holy Spirit, our Heavenly Father, and Jesus Christ are equally God. Here we have the Word of God being associated with perfection, not the numeric connotation of seven.

A second popular theory is the seven spirits refer to seven angels of the Lord that are sent out to the Earth to perform tasks assigned by the Holy Spirit. This notion is based largely on the following citations from Revelation.

- REV 1:4,11–13,16,20 ~ From John to the seven churches in Asia: Grace to you and peace, from He who is, was, and is to come, and from the seven spirits which are before His throne. I turned to the voice that called me to write to the seven churches and I saw seven candlesticks, and in the middle was the Son of God. He had in His right hand seven stars, and from His mouth went a sharp, double-edged sword, and His face shined like the sun. The seven stars represented the angels of the seven churches; the seven candlesticks represented the seven churches.
- REV 3:1 ~ To the angel of the church of Sardis write these sayings which come from the One who has the seven spirits of God, and the seven stars: "I know your works, that you have a name, and that you lived and died."
- REV 4:5 ~ From the throne in heaven proceeded lightning and thunder with voices. There were seven lamps of fire burning before the throne, which were the seven spirits of God.
- REV 5:1,6 ~ In the right hand of Him who sat on the throne was a book which was sealed with seven seals. In the middle stood the Lamb that was slain having seven horns and seven eyes that were the seven spirits of God sent throughout the earth.
- REV 8:2,6 ~ There were seven angels standing before God and they were given seven trumpets; each angel sounded their trumpet in order.

The passages above mention (1) seven stars representing angels, (2) seven candlesticks representing churches, (3) seven lamps or candles, (4) seven seals, (5) seven eyes, (6) seven horns, and (7) seven trumpets. The connection to angels in these scriptures is evident. Plus, there are seven things in this list that liken angels to the seven spirits of God. These seven angels, or stars, are probably the ones who blow seven trumpets when the end is nigh. The trumpets are associated with removal of the seventh seal from the book, announcing calamities that will occur in the last days, and culminating with the last trumpet which ushers in the seven vials of God's wrath poured out upon the wicked (REV 6:15–17). Powerful angels are symbolized by seven horns; these angels are dispatched by God to perform mighty feats. They shine like stars illuminating everything around them. Analogous to a candelabra with seven candles, a noticeable comparison can be made to a Jewish menorah.

Let us examine the seven churches which are linked to the seven candlesticks. Seven angels, portrayed as seven eyes and seven lamps, watch over and protect these churches. St. John disseminated copies of the Revelation of Jesus Christ to seven churches in Asia Minor (REV 2—3). For each church, a particular issue was raised along with the solution. The table below summarizes messages given to the seven churches, which proclaimed the light of Christ but were nowhere near perfect, for only the Lord is perfect. Naturally, there is always room for improvement when it comes to people and churches, so the messages apply to our day as much as they did when John addressed those seven churches. Though imperfect, all become perfect in Christ at the marriage of the Church and the Lamb (REV 19:7–9).

Church	Issue	Solution
Ephesus	Need strengthening in love and faith.	Repentance
Smyrna	Need to endure tribulations.	Perseverance
Pergamos	Need to return to genuine doctrine.	Truth
Thyatira	Need to refrain from lust and idolatry.	Godliness
Sardis	Need to strengthen one another.	Edification
Philadelphia	Need to heed warnings and overcome.	Watchfulness
Laodicea	Need to stop being worldly.	Spirituality

Of course, the book of Revelation also contains passages referring to seven evil spirits; these are Satan's agents. Definitely the seven spirits of God have nothing to do with the seven spirits of His adversary the beast, described below.

- REV 12:3 ~ A great red dragon appeared in heaven having seven heads and ten horns, and seven crowns upon the seven heads.
- REV 13:1 ~ A beast rose out of the sea which had seven heads and ten horns, and upon the ten horns were ten crowns, and upon each of the heads were the names of blasphemy.
- REV 17:9–11 ~ The angel explained the mystery of the beast with the seven heads as follows: The seven heads represented seven mountains on which the new Babylon sits (the great whore that sits over many waters). And there are seven kings, five have fallen, one is currently in power, and one is yet to come; and the seventh will reign for a short time. The beast is the eighth king and was also one of the seven.

These passages identify seven heads of the beast, referring to seven kings with seven crowns. Just as seven empires ruled the world and vanished, seven will rule with Satan for a short time before his kingdom is finally demolished. Then the kingdom of Christ will prevail without end. Perhaps the seven spirits of God are to be challenged by Satan's seven evil spirits in a futile attempt to defy God and His power once again, similar to Satan's concoction of an unholy trinity. Well then, do the seven spirits refer to seven good and seven evil spirits associated with God and Satan, respectively? Not in the slightest. They certainly must pertain to God, His angels, and/or His people (the Church). Undoubtedly, the characteristics bestowed upon God's angels such as mighty, watchful, and ever faithful messengers of truth, pertain to God as well; for surely, the Lord has these same characteristics in absolute entirety.

Additional references to seven spirits can be found in the Old Testament.

- NUM 8:1–3 ~ God told Moses to tell Aaron, "When you light the seven lamps, they will give light from the candlestick." And Aaron lit the candles and they gave light.
- ISA 11:12 ~ The Spirit of the Lord will rest upon Him (the Messiah), the spirit of wisdom and understanding, the spirit of counsel and might, the spirit of knowledge, and the fear of God.
- ZEC 3:8–9 ~ God said to Joshua, "I will bring forth my servant the Branch. This cornerstone, which I have shown to Joshua, will have seven eyes. The engraving will show that I have removed the sin of that land in a single day."
- ZEC 4:2,10 ~ The angel of God showed Zechariah a gold candlestick with a bowl on top and seven lamps with seven pipes coming from it, and said it represented the seven eyes of the Lord which keep a watchful eye over the entire earth.

There is much we can glean from the verses above. To begin with, the scripture from Isaiah lists seven spirits: (1) Holy Spirit or Word of God, (2) spirit of wisdom and (3) understanding, (4) counsel and (5) might, (6) knowledge, and (7) reverent fear. A popular position taken from this scripture is that the seven spirits describe characteristics of God's Son. Isaiah definitely is not describing angels; he is speaking of Messiah. Therefore, the seven spirits can be applied to God, and the ways in which the Holy Spirit asserts His power among humankind. Additionally, the citations from Numbers and Zechariah mentioned seven eyes and seven lamps which is consistent with characteristics of the seven angels as well as God. Accordingly, if you don't think you are being watched, think twice, because God and His angels are watching, 24-7.

So, which is it? Are the seven spirits of God a reference to God's perfection, or to powerful angels, or characteristics of God, or assignments from God, or members of the kingdom of heaven, or some combination of these? As always, we need to interpret scripture using other scripture addressing the same topic. Seven is a significant number in many ways: the seven days of creation (GEN 1:1—GEN 2:3); the seven Jewish feasts (LEV 23); the seven years of tribulation which include seven seals, seven trumpets, and seven vials of wrath (REV 4—10). These books in the Bible describe events: whether days of creation, festivals entailing worship services, or time periods associated with the end of the age. Some theologians assert that there are exactly seven years associated with the great tribulation, but this is not explicitly stated in the Bible. The time element cannot be referring to characteristics of God since He is timeless; thus, the creation days and the tribulation years are not necessarily related to the seven spirits of God, except perhaps with regard to the seven trumpets sounded in turn by the seven angels previously discussed.

The seven feasts commanded of the Jews through Moses add more clarification to this discussion. Remember that the original menorah displayed seven candles, one for each feast that God required in the Mosaic Law. These feasts have bearing, not only to Jews but also to Christians. Can you bring to mind seven candles on one candelabra which illuminates an entire room? It is an image of the seven lamps. In these seven lights we see a reflection of the character of God, and the character of those who seek Him. Let's take a closer look at the seven feasts which can be broken down into what God is to His people and what our response should be to Him.

Passover is indicative of God being merciful and receptive to the prayers and pleas of His people; and the appropriate response: worship and praise. Unleavened Bread is associated with God's grace, which He showed the Jews in manna from heaven, and then to all people through His Son who is the bread of life, with the proper response being faith. First Fruits is a feast for giving back to God in response to all the blessings He has given. Pentecost corresponds to the bestowing of the Holy Spirit upon believers, turning them into disciples, witnesses, and evangelists spreading the truth to the world. Trumpets relate to making a joyful noise in celebration of God's promises and the fact that God continues to provide, ushering in another year with renewed hope and confidence. Atonement is an obvious reference to being forgiven of our sins and reflects the blood of the Lamb; our response is to confess and repent of our sins. Tabernacles represent churches, places of worship, God's house; as in all Jewish feasts, there was a convocation (assembly) complete with structured worship, Bible readings, and fellowship. The seven feasts are summarized in the table below.

Feasts	Gifts	Human Responses	God's Character
Passover	Mercy	Thanks, Praise	Mighty, Powerful (Omnipotence)
Bread	Law, Grace	Faith, Trust	Revealer, Messenger (Redeemer)
First Fruits	Giving	Offerings, Service	Caring, Sharing (Wisdom)
Pentecost	Truth, Spirit	Teaching, Witnessing	Knowledge (Omniscience)
Trumpets	Provision	Joy, Hope	Understanding (Omnipresence)
Atonement	Forgiveness	Confession, Repentance	Responsive, Comforting (Counselor)
Tabernacles	Fellowship	Worship, Assembly	Awesome (Feared)

So how can we put all of this together? Let us review the sets of seven. For starters, it would appear the seven spirits relate to angels in one context, and the perfection of God in another context: Father, Son, and Holy Spirit. The seven horns illustrate God's power and strength reflected in the mighty deeds done through God and His angels. The seven eyes and seven lamps indicate His omnipresence and the fact that He is always watching over us, His light forever shining in our hearts, and His Word providing enlightenment to our souls. The seven candlesticks represent God's Church on Earth which provides education, edification, and fellowship. The seven stars or angels of great might are those God has appointed to watch over His church and His people. God confers His power on angels, churches, and people as He sees fit to accomplish His will in the world while advancing His kingdom in the process.

The seven feasts are associated with holy convocations whereby God's people are commanded to gather together, worship, praise, and honor Him who has never faltered in His love towards us and whose blessings are innumerable and everlasting. Furthermore, the seven trumpets seem relevant, not only to the seven angels but also to God's directives to the seven churches in particular and His Church in general: repentance, perseverance, truth, godliness, edification, preparedness, and spirituality. Seven lamps and eyes indicate that the light of Christ shines in His people and in churches that preach the truth of His Word, and that God is ever watchful and protective as are His appointed angels. Therefore, we always should be watchful for His Son to return and take us home where His Church will be joined with Christ forever.

In a way, all of the aforementioned positions involving the seven spirits can be integrated into one consolidated explanation of this mysterious phenomenon, because they relate to God, angels, churches, and the community of believers—all of which work in congruence to proclaim the glory of God in our world, to maintain and witness faith in His Messiah, and to embody the consult of His perfect Holy Spirit which will shine in the believer's heart eternally. This notion is elaborated in both testaments of the Holy Bible so that Jews and Christians alike would find God, understand obedience through faith, desire the forgiveness of sins He offers, reflect His light on Earth, and obtain an inheritance as rightful heirs to the Kingdom of Heaven.

Be advised, seven is not a lucky number; this is clearly a worldly interpretation. Even at the crap table the number seven can be a winner or a loser. Seven is a symbolic number, however; but once again, it sometimes connotes winning versus losing, or good versus evil. But, don't get hung up on the number seven like numerologists often do. While there are no perfect numbers, there is one perfect God. Actually, there is nothing else but God that demonstrates perfection in our world or any world. If you are looking to get lucky, you are not putting your faith in a sure thing. Once again, there is only one sure thing upon which to place your entire trust: one God in three persons. But you have to be all in; you have to bet your life on Jesus. If you do you are a winner. And you certainly are lucky, because the gift you win is undeserved, but for the fact that you trusted in it.

If you will decide to accept Jesus Christ right now, this is your lucky day. If you already have received Him, bring to remembrance the days when your faith was reassured, for they were the best days of your life. But if you refuse Him, eventually your luck will run out and there will not be a next time.

Lesson: Counseling for Christ

God's Holy Spirit is the great Counselor. God first sent His mediator, Jesus Christ, to counsel us. Jesus told His followers that, though He was departing, His Holy Spirit would remain behind for counseling and consoling. Jesus instructed His followers to instruct and counsel others. To do so, we must understand His words and His ways and become equipped to serve. We cannot second-guess God, but we can learn His truth, we can practice His methods, and we can understand the mission He has for us by staying united with Him in spirit.

- JOB 12:13 ~ To God belongs all wisdom and strength; counsel and understanding are His.
- JOB 38:2; JOB 42:1–3,6 ~ After Job complained to God, God asked Job, "Who can question my counsel when they have no knowledge and understand so little?" Job replied to the Lord, "I know that you can do all things, and that your plans cannot be thwarted. I realize that I spoke of things I did not understand, things too wonderful for me to know." And Job repented.
- PRO 13:10; PRO 19:20 ~ Pride breeds conflict; but those who listen to sound advice find wisdom. Listen to advice and accept instruction, and you will be wise.
- ISA 25:1 ~ O Lord, you are my God; I will exalt you and praise your name. For you have done marvelous things; your counsels of old include faithfulness and truth.
- ISA 40:13–14 ~ Who can understand the mind of God, and who can instruct Him? Did God have to consult anyone else to enlighten Him, to teach Him the right way, or to show Him the path of understanding?
- ROM 11:33–35 ~ Oh how deep are the riches of the wisdom and knowledge of God. How unsearchable are His judgments; how untraceable are His steps. For who knows the mind of the Lord, and who has been His counselor? Who has ever sacrificed to God, that God should repay them?

Just as Jesus Christ acts as mediator between His people and God the Father, so we can act as mediators between Christ and other people. This is the mission of a counselor for Christ. We are to guide others along the righteous path in which the Lord guides us. Once we become strong in God's Word, in our faith, and in our conviction, we are prepared to strengthen and guide others. It is our duty to exercise spiritual gifts to edify the body of Christ in this manner.

- EXO 18:15–21 ~ Moses's father-in-law advised Moses, "Be the people's representative before God, and bring their problems to Him. Do not try to do it alone, but get others who are trustworthy to help out."
- PSA 31:3; PSA 32:8; PSA 42:14; PSA 73:24 ~ Oh Lord, you are my rock and my fortress; for your name's sake lead me and guide me. God will instruct me and teach me in the way to go; He will guide me with His eye. God will be my guide until the day I die. He will guide me with His counsel, and afterward receive me into glory.
- ROM 15:1–7 ~ We who are strong ought to bear with the failings of the weak. When we do the right thing, it should not be to please ourselves, but to please others and to build them up in the Lord. Even Christ did not please Himself, but as it is written of Him, "The insults of those who would insult you have fallen on me." Everything that was written in the past was for our instruction, so that through endurance and the encouragement of the scriptures we might have hope. May the God who gives endurance, encouragement, and hope give you a spirit of unity as you follow Christ. Give glory to God the Father of our Lord Jesus Christ with one voice and one heart. Accept each other as Christ accepted you, so that God may be praised.

- 1 CO 12:27–28 ~ You are of the body of Christ and each one of you has a part in it. In the church God has appointed apostles first, prophets second, teachers third, then miracle workers, those with the gift of healing, helpers, administrators, and those that can speak in different tongues.
- 1 CO 14:12 ~ Since you are eager to have spiritual gifts, try to excel in those gifts that edify the church.
- EPH 4:11–13 ~ Christ appointed some to be apostles, some to be prophets, some to be evangelists, some to be pastors, and some to be teachers, in order to prepare God's people for works of service, and for the edifying of the body of Christ. This will enable us to achieve unity of faith and of the knowledge of God's Son, and to mature as Christians until we have attained the full measure of Christ's perfection.
- 1 TH 5:11,14 ~ Comfort each other and edify one another just as you are doing. Warn the lazy, encourage the timid, help the weak, and be patient with everyone.

People who do not seek God's wisdom, strength, consolation, and peace will find uncertainty and sorrow. For they seek counsel and leadership from unbelievers, deceivers, and the ungodly, thereby pursuing worldly solutions.

- PSA 1:1 ~ Blessed is the person that does not walk in the counsel of the ungodly, or stand in the path of sinners, or sit in the seat of the scornful.
- PRO 11:3,14 ~ The integrity of righteous people can guide them, but the perverseness of wicked people will destroy them. For lack of guidance a nation falls, but many advisors assure the victory.
- PRO 12:15,20 ~ The way of fools is right in their own eyes, but the one who listens to advice is wise. There is deceit in the hearts of those that plot evil, but to those promoting peace there is joy.
- ECC 4:1 ~ I saw the oppression that occurred under the sun; I saw the tears of those that were down and out and noticed that they had no comforter. Even though they had power, they had no comforter.
- ISA 30:1 ~ Woe to the rebellious children, declares the Lord. Woe to those who carry out plans that are not mine, who form alliances but not with my Spirit, and who heap sin upon sin.
- JER 7:24; JER 23:22 ~ They did not listen or pay attention, but followed the imagination of their evil hearts, going backward, not forward. If they had listened to my advice, and proclaimed my words to the people, they would have turned from their evil ways.
- MAT 15:13–4; MAT 23:23–24 ~ Jesus said, "Every plant that has not been planted by my heavenly Father will be pulled up by the roots. Leave them alone, for they are like the blind leading the blind; and when the blind lead the blind both fall into the ditch. Woe to you teachers of the Law and you Pharisees, hypocrites every one. You tithe but yet you neglect the more important matters of the law such as justice, mercy, and faith. You should have practiced the latter without neglecting the former. You are blind guides, which would strain at a gnat but swallow a camel."

Those who seek God will be blessed with spiritual gifts including faith, hope, and healing. It is important to stay connected to God and maintain communications with Him. If you knock on His door, He will let you into His world; if He knocks on your door, let Him in and He will guide you through this world (REV 5:20), and the next. To achieve spiritual health, invite the Holy Spirit to dwell in your house. Baptism, Holy Communion, prayer, weekly worship, and Bible study are examples of such an invitation.

- 2 KI 20:1–5 ~ King Hezekiah was ill three days, but was healed due to His faith and his prayers.
- PSA 31:24 ~ Be strong and let your heart take courage, you who hope in the Lord.
- LAM 3:21–22 ~ I have hope because the steadfast love of the Lord never ceases and His mercies never end.
- MAT 8:5–13 ~ Jesus healed the centurion's servant. Jesus was amazed at the faith of the man, who believed that Christ had merely to give the word, and the servant would be well.
- MAT 9:20–22 ~ Jesus noticed that the woman had touched his garment. He said to her, "Be of good comfort, for your faith has healed you." And the woman with the hemorrhage was healed at that moment.
- MAT 10:1 ~ Christ called His twelve disciples together and gave them authority over unclean spirits to cast them out, and to heal all manner of sickness and disease.
- MAR 10:46–51 ~ The blind man called out to Jesus and Jesus summoned for him. The man asked that Jesus restore his sight. Jesus said to him, "Be of good comfort, arise, and go your way, for your faith has healed you."
- JOH 4:46–53 ~ Jesus healed the nobleman's son the very moment he asked for help.
- ROM 5:2–5 ~ Through Him (Jesus) we have obtained access to His grace in which we stand, and we rejoice in our hope of sharing the glory of God. We rejoice in our sufferings knowing that they produce endurance, which produces character, which produces hope. And hope does not disappoint us, because God's love has been poured into our hearts through the Holy Spirit.
- ROM 12:12 ~ Rejoice in your hope, be patient in tribulation, and be constant in prayer.

Research has proven time and again of the great healing potential of faith and prayer. In fact, religious people tend to be healthier overall. Those to whom Jesus and the apostles ministered received healing of mind, body, and spirit because they had faith in Christ. The very fact that a person seeks help is because they believe they can get better.

- MAT 14:35–36 ~ When the people recognized Jesus, word spread rapidly, and everyone brought their sick to Him. They begged Jesus just to touch His garment, because everyone that did was made perfectly healthy.
- MAR 9:17–27 ~ One of those in the crowd answered the Lord, "Teacher, I have brought my son to you; he has a mute spirit. Whenever it seizes him, it throws him down; he foams at the mouth, gnashes his teeth, and becomes rigid. I asked your disciples if they could cast out the demon but they could not." Jesus responded, "You faithless generation, how long shall I be with you and bear your problems? Bring the child to me." When the child came, he immediately went into convulsions. Jesus asked the child's father, "How long has this been going on?" The father answered, "Since childhood. Sometimes he throws himself into the fire or into the water to destroy it. Please, Lord, you can do anything; have compassion on us and help us." Jesus replied, "All things are possible if you believe." The father cried out in tears saying, "I believe Lord, help me when I doubt." Then Jesus rebuked the unclean spirit, "Deaf and dumb spirit, I command you to come out of him and enter him no more." The spirit screamed, the boy went into a major convulsion, and the spirit left the boy as if dead. Many people thought the child was dead, but Jesus took him by the hand and lifted him to his feet.
- ACT 3:12,16 ~ Peter said, "Men of Israel, why do you marvel at the healing of this lame man? And why do you look so intently at us, as if we made him walk by our own power or goodness? In the name of Christ and because of faith in Him, this man who is known to you was healed. Yes, the faith which comes from Christ has made him perfectly well in the presence of all of you."

- ROM 8:26–28 ~ The Spirit helps us in our weaknesses. For we don't know what we should pray for, but the Spirit intercedes for us in ways we cannot possibly imagine.
- JAM 5:13–16 ~ Is anyone among you suffering? Let him pray. Is anyone cheerful? Let him sing psalms. Is anyone among you sick? Let him call for the elders of the church to pray over him. And the prayers of faith will save the sick, and the Lord will raise them up, and forgive their sins.

Many people with medical problems or mental health issues have lost their spiritual focus; they are seeking comfort or wellness that only can come from God. Oftentimes, what they need is to reconnect with their spiritual identity and become more hopeful and purposeful.

- MAT 11:28 ~ Jesus said, "Come to me all of you who labor or are heavy laden and I will give you rest."
- 2 CO 12:9–10 ~ Jesus said to me (Paul), "My grace is enough for you for my strength is made perfect in weakness." Therefore, I boast of my infirmities, so that the power of Christ can rest upon me. Yes, I take pleasure in infirmity, reproach, necessity, persecution, and distress for Christ's sake, for in my weakness I am made strong.
- JOH 14:16,26; JOH 15:26–27; JOH 16:7,13 ~ Jesus said, "I will ask the Father and He will give you another Comforter to abide with you forever. The Comforter that the Father is sending in my name, which is the Holy Spirit, will teach you all things and will remind you of everything I have said to you. When the Comforter, the Spirit of Truth comes, whom I will send to you from the Father and who proceeds from the Father, He will testify about me. And you also must testify, for you have been with me from the beginning. It is good for me to go, because until I am gone, the Comforter cannot come to you; but I will send Him to you when I leave. When the Spirit of truth comes, He will guide you into all truth. He will speak the words of God and He will show you what is yet to come."

Holistic health, by definition, is comprised of three components: physical, mental, and spiritual. So also, the treatment or cure should integrate all three. We are created in the image of God, who manifests himself to us in three eternal personifications: Father, Son, and Holy Spirit. We have a spiritual presence: God the Holy Spirit gives us life. Thus, growth is enabled if we stay steadfast in His Spirit. We have a physical presence: God the Son was a perfect, human example of obedience and righteousness. We have a mental component: God the Father gave us a discerning mind that can distinguish good and evil, and He gave us the free will to obey or disobey him. Therefore, we make our own choices; and we can choose to change for the better. Try it and you will see that it works to your advantage in achieving wholeness.

- MAT 22:37–38 ~ Jesus said, "You must love the Lord your God with all your heart, soul, and mind. This is the first and greatest commandment"
- JOH 6:63 ~ Jesus said, "It is the Spirit that gives life, not the flesh; the flesh profits nothing. The words that I speak are of the Spirit and give life."
- JOH 10:10 ~ Jesus said, "I came that you might have life, and have it more abundantly."

Change begins with a change of heart; when the Lord enters the heart, everything becomes new. This enables a change in belief; for example, "I can do this, with the help of the Lord." A change in belief enables a change in thinking, and this produces a change in behavior over time. Once the person feels new inside, the old ways rapidly fade, because with each new day the adaptive individual becomes more distant from the maladaptive one. And that is the definition of positive growth. And it is achieved more rapidly and with greater fidelity when the individual believes that God is in control. So, if God changes my heart, it will change my mind, and a corresponding change in my actions should follow.

- LUK 1:37 ~ The angel told Mary that nothing is impossible with God.
- JOH 15:5 ~ Jesus said, "I am the vine and you are the branches. Anyone who lives in me, and I in him, will bear much fruit. But without me you can do nothing."
- 2 CO 5:17 ~ If anyone is in Christ, he or she is a new creation. Old things have passed away; behold, all things have become new.
- PHP 4:13 ~ I can do all things through Christ who strengthens me.

Faith without action is meaningless because inaction produces nothing. People need to be active physically, mentally, and spiritually to be completely healthy. If I believe I can get better I will, as long as I am willing to make the effort and never give up. Perseverance enables us to remain connected to the power and wisdom of God and to achieve worthwhile needs and goals.

- PRO 2:10–13 ~ When wisdom enters your heart and knowledge is pleasant to your soul, discretion will preserve you and understanding will keep you, to deliver you from evil and from those who speak evil.
- PRO 10:4 ~ Those with idle hands become poor. Those with diligent hands become rich.
- JOH 8:31–32 ~ Jesus said to the Jews who believed, "If you abide in my Word, you are indeed my disciples. And you will know the truth and the truth will set you free."
- JAM 2:17 ~ Faith without works is dead.

Those who follow Christ will realize their full potential because He will make good things happen in their lives. He will lead us where we need to be (PSA 23). It will be the right place at the right time.

- ISA 58:11 ~ The Lord will guide you always, and will satisfy all your needs. You will be like a well-watered garden and a spring of water that never runs dry.
- MAT 6:31–34 ~ Jesus said, "Don't worry about what you will eat or drink, or what you will wear; for your heavenly Father knows that you need these things. Instead, seek first the kingdom of God and His righteousness, and He will provide everything you need in addition."
- GAL 5:22–23 ~ Fruits of the Spirit include love, joy, peace, patience, kindness, goodness, faithfulness, gentleness, and self-control. There is no law against such things.

Holistic health requires one to exercise body, mind, and spirit. Such exercise enables the expression of feelings and the expenditure of emotional energy. That's right, emotions create energy (negative and positive); this energy can be used to build or to destroy. Destructive ways of releasing emotional energy include hitting, throwing things, yelling, and battering your self-esteem. Constructive ways of using this energy include creating a masterpiece, building something in someone's honor or memory, exercising, finishing chores, and assisting others. There are many ways to get emotional material out: express it, expend it, and give it to God.

- PRO 6:16–19 ~ There are seven things that the Lord hates: arrogance, lying, malicious assault, an evil imagination, mischief makers, perjury and slander, and those who deliberately create trouble.
- PRO 14:17; PRO 15:1,18; PRO 19:11; PRO 26:24–28 ~ Those who are easily angered do stupid things, and those who do hateful things are themselves hated by others. A gentle answer repels anger but a harsh answer provokes it. An angry person creates conflict, but a calm person creates peace. A wise person is patient, and to his or her credit, overlooks an offense. Hateful people conceal their disdain with deceitful words, but in their heart lives anger. They may try to disguise their hate, but eventually it will become exposed to everyone. They are digging a hole that they themselves will fall into; they are rolling a stone

that eventually will crush them. Those who lie hate the people they lie about, and their flattering words create only ruin.
- ROM 14:5–8,22–23 ~ Whatever you believe and whatever you do, let it be for God. If you eat or if you fast, do it for Him. For nobody lives to themselves and nobody dies to themselves. Regardless of whether we live or die, we belong to the Lord. If you have faith, maintain it between you and God. Blessed is the person who is not condemned by the same things for which he or she has given approval. If you have any doubts, don't do it; for whatever is not of faith is of sin.

Our capacity to reason enables positive thinking (true, uplifting, praiseworthy thoughts), or negative thinking (putting ourselves or others down). Our capacity to contemplate enables positive imagery (the cross of Christ; a favorite peaceful place). Our capacity to hope enables forward looking (the big picture, the finish line with the Lord in heaven, the attractive possibilities that lie ahead if we follow Jesus). Negative thoughts are contradictory, usually untrue, and at the very least, unlikely. Positive thoughts are those which are truthful, uplifting, and pure; and these are healthy for you. If you tell yourself you are worthless, ugly, and stupid, but God tells you that you are precious (He even knows the number of hairs on your head), important (so important He would make the ultimate sacrifice for you), and beautiful (since Christ lives in you), who is right and who are you going to believe? Well, Satan is the father of lies (JOH 8:44). God, who is the source of all truth is incapable of lying for He is intrinsically righteous (PRO 30:5; HEB 6:18). The answer is obvious. When a person begins to tell themselves the truth and believe it, their self-image improves immediately.

- PRO 6:3 ~ Commit your works to the Lord and He will establish your thoughts.
- ISA 32:17 ~ The fruit of righteousness will be peace; the effect of righteousness will be tranquility and confidence forever.
- PHP 1:20 ~ I eagerly expect and hope that I will not be ashamed, and will have sufficient courage so that Christ always will be exalted in my body, whether by life or by death.
- PHP 4:8 ~ Whatever is true, honest, fair, pure, lovely, uplifting, virtuous, and praiseworthy, think on these things.

Let the Lord be your confidence and hope and you will not be disappointed with the outcome. And you will know which way to go and when; in your spirit you will discern it, though you may not be sure beforehand. And there will be no need for expectations, other than the assurance that the Lord will provide and protect as He has promised. We look forward to His promises, though we may not know the time of their fulfillment. Thus, it is wise not to jump the gun on God's timeframe or it may cause more problems (as it did for Abraham and David, for example). Instead of planning your life in accordance with your own desires, wait patiently for God's will to be done in your life, and thank Him in advance.

- PSA 5:3 ~ In the morning, Lord, you hear my voice, as I present my requests before you and wait in expectation.
- PSA 71:5; PRO 3:26; JER 17:7; HEB 10:35 ~ For you have been my hope, oh Sovereign Lord, and my confidence since my youth. The Lord will be your confidence and will keep your foot from being snared. Blessed is the person who trusts in the Lord, whose confidence is in Him. So do not throw away your confidence; it will be richly rewarded
- PRO 1:21 ~ Although we may develop many plans, it is the Lord's purpose that will prevail.
- JER 29:11–13 ~ God says, "I know the thoughts that I think towards you: thoughts of peace and not evil, so that you will have a future of hope. Then you will call on me and I will listen; you will look for me and you will find me, as long as you search with all your heart."

- HAG 1:9 ~ "You expected much, but see, it turned out to be little. What you brought home I blew away," declares the Lord Almighty. "Why? Because my house remains in shambles while each of you is busy with his own house."
- PHP 1:6 ~ Be confident of this: He who began a good work in you will carry it to completion until the day Christ returns.

You must look forward and not backward. If you take a step back for every two steps forward, you are still making positive progress. If Christ is in the picture, you are heading in the right direction. Leave the emotional baggage behind as it will only slow you down for it impedes forward movement. Usually, this requires forgiveness: yourself and others. Remember, the love of God can change anyone. If you radiate that love it will change those around you (ROM 12:20–21). Love can exist without faith, but faith cannot exist without love; if you don't love God you certainly won't believe Him. It is by faith that we cling to the hope of living with God forever.

- PSA 27:13 ~ I am confident that I will see the goodness of the Lord in my lifetime.
- ROM 8:24 ~ We were saved in this hope. But hope that is seen is not hope for who hopes for what they can see?
- GAL 5:5 ~ Through the Spirit we have faith, which is our hope in receiving the righteousness of God.
- PHP 3:12–13 ~ I (Paul) continue to press on, to grab hold of that for which Christ has grabbed hold of me. I do not claim to have obtained it as yet, but instead I forget those things that are behind, and reach for those things which lie ahead.
- HEB 11:1 ~ Faith is the assurance of things hoped for, the evidence of things not seen.

Ultimately, the catalyst for change, growth, and healing is love. The most powerful force in the universe is love, because God is love (1 JO 4:8). The power of evil is fear (terrorism, hatefulness, torment), which the wicked use to erode hope and obscure love. Love and fear are incompatible, just like light and darkness are incompatible. Light can consume darkness but darkness cannot consume light; love can consume fear but fear cannot consume love.

- PRO 29:25 ~ The fear of humankind is a trap, but those who trust in God will be safe.
- 1 JO 4:18 ~ There is no fear in love, but perfect love casts out fear, because fear has torment. Those who fear are not made perfect in love.
- 2 TI 1:7 ~ God has not given us the spirit of fear but of power, love, and a sound mind.

God is the source of our comfort, which He bestows upon us through His Holy Spirit. Like a blanket, His peace and joy can cover those who are troubled, afflicted, or suffering. God's love can ease the pain, whether it is physical, mental, or spiritual.

- PSA 94:19; PSA 119:50,52,76 ~ Oh Lord, when I was overcome with anxiety, your comfort brought joy to my soul. Whenever I suffer, I find comfort in your unfailing love, in your promises, and in your laws.
- 2 CO 1:3–7 ~ Praise God, the Father of our Lord Jesus Christ, the Father of compassion and the God of all comfort. He comforts us in all our tribulations, so that we can comfort others that are troubled, by the same comfort we ourselves have received from God. Just as the sufferings of Christ flow over into our lives, so also through Him our comfort overflows. If we are distressed, it is for your comfort and salvation. If we are comforted, it is for your comfort as well, which produces in you the patience to endure the same sufferings we suffer. And our hope for you is firm because we know that just as you share in our sufferings so also you share in our comfort.

God gives us the power through His love and His light to overcome the evil and darkness that plague our souls, to win the good fight of faith, and to prevail over death. You cannot be defeated when you are protected by the Lord, for you will win the battle and subdue the opposition when God is on your side (EPH 6:10–18; HEB 4:12). Occasionally, the conflict involves personal demons (spiritual or mental) which are easily dismissed using powers of the spirit. Your flesh and spirit will battle each other over which will control your mind. If a person is guided by God's Spirit, he or she will win the war and receive a Crown of Life (JAM 1:12).

- ROM 8:4–6 ~ The righteous requirement of the Law is fulfilled in those who walk according to the Spirit and not according to the flesh. For those who walk according to the flesh set their minds on things of the flesh, and those who walk according to the Spirit set their minds on things of the Spirit. To be carnally minded means death, but to be spiritually minded means life and peace.
- GAL 5:17; GAL 6:8 ~ For the flesh is against the Spirit and the Spirit is against the flesh, because they are contrary to one another, and you end up doing the things you don't want to do. Those who sow to the flesh will reap corruption, but those who sow to the Spirit will reap eternal life.

People in need of counseling may view their problems as insurmountable, may have difficulty coping with their hardships, may have a poor self-image, and/or may be overcome with anxiety or depression. Often, they live in fear, without hope and without love. The best remedy is the peace and joy that surpasses all understanding which only God's Spirit can supply. Those who are troubled need reassurance that God is in control. They need to be reminded that they are precious to Him, so precious He sacrificed His Son that they might live. And they need to cling to promises which are true and everlasting: God promises to protect, provide, renew, and guide.

The central problem for many is a spiritual void that only Christ can fill. As soon as the afflicted person turns to Him in faith for healing, the healing begins. It is the principal objective of a counselor for Christ to build others up in their hope and faith through love, compassion, and kindness just as Christ did throughout His ministry. Let us follow the example of Christ and edify one another so that His name can be praised and glorified.

Question: What do people really need that are seeking counseling?

Answer: To feel like a complete person; to become whole again; to be renewed.

- PSA 51:10 ~ Create in me a clean heart Lord, and renew a right spirit within me.
- ISA 40:31 ~ Those who wait on the Lord will be renewed in their strength. They will mount up with wings of eagles; they will run and not tire, and walk and not faint.
- ROM 12:2 ~ Do not be conformed to this world: but be transformed by the renewing of your mind, so you may prove what is the good, acceptable, and perfect, will of God.
- 2 CO 4:16 ~ For the cause of Christ we endure, though our outward man may perish yet the inward man is renewed day by day.
- EPH 4:23–24 ~ Be renewed in the spirit of your mind and put on the new person, created after God in true righteousness and holiness.
- COL 3:10 ~ Put on the new person, which is renewed in knowledge after the image of God who created him.
- TIT 3:5 ~ He saved us, not because of our works of righteousness, but according to His mercy, by the washing of regeneration, and renewing by the Holy Spirit.

CHAPTER SEVEN

Lesson: Mending the Broken Heart

Do not blame the Lord for suffering. Suffering is due to sin which is the work of Satan, fallen angels, and human beings, not God. In a sin free world there would be no suffering or worry; and heaven is a sin free world. Sin causes us to turn from God and seek alternative sources of gratification, leading one into addictions, following false instructors and healers, or seeking miracle cures. Jesus Christ gives us solace from suffering; He is the remedy for our sin, afflictions, suffering, and grief. The Lord promises abundant life free from sin, suffering, and death if we turn our sin over to Him. He suffered for it; you might as well let Him have it. And your heart will be made whole, and He will live there.

- JOB 1—2 ~ One day the angels of the Lord came before God and Satan was among them. And God said to Satan, "Have you considered my servant Job? There is nobody on earth like him, a righteous and upright man that fears God and shuns evil." Satan answered, "Does Job fear God for nothing? Haven't you richly blessed him? Take away all that he has and he'll curse you to your face." God replied, "Everything he has is within your power to do with as you please, but do not harm him." So, Satan proceeded to destroy all that Job had built but Job remained steadfast in his faith. Again, the angels appeared before God and Satan was among them. God said to Satan, "You see, Job still maintains his integrity, even though you tried to get me to destroy him." Again, Satan challenged God, saying, "He would give it up to save his life." God replied, "You have the power in your hand to harm him, but do not take his life." So once again, Satan sought to destroy Job by bringing upon him afflictions and pain. Still, Job refrained from sinning.
- PSA 145:17 ~ The Lord is righteous in all His ways and holy in all His works.
- JOH 10:9–11 ~ Jesus said, "I am the door. Everyone who enters through me will be saved; and they will be able to come and go freely and they will find pasture. The thief comes only to steal, kill, and destroy. I have come so that people might have life, and have it more abundantly. I am the Good Shepherd who gives His life for His sheep."
- 2 CO 1:5 ~ Just as the sufferings of Christ abound in us, so also our comfort abounds in Him.
- JAM 5:10–11 ~ My friends, consider the prophets who spoke in the name of the Lord as an example of patience during times of suffering. Blessed are those who have persevered in this way. Remember Job, whose perseverance was rewarded with God's mercy and compassion.

Those who suffer endlessly are allowing Satan to get the better of them. If a person allows God to dwell in his or her heart, it will drive away the pain and torment. The Lord's desire is to restore the lost souls and mend the broken hearts.

- PSA 23:3–4 ~ He restores my soul; He leads me in the paths of righteousness for His name sake. Although I walk through the dark valley of death, I fear no evil, for you Oh Lord are with me; your rod and staff are a comfort to me.
- PSA 147:3 ~ He heals the broken hearted and binds up their wounds.
- PRO 15:4,13 ~ A perverse tongue breaks the spirit. A sorrowful heart breaks the spirit.
- PRO 27:19 ~ The heart reflects the man just like a mirror.
- MAT 15:18–19 ~ Jesus said, "Those things which proceed out of the mouth come from the heart and they defile the individual. For out of the heart comes evil thoughts that make a person unclean."
- COL 3:15 ~ Let the peace of God rule in your heart.

A broken heart is best mended by taking one's plight to the Lord. Only He can repair a troubled heart and comfort a persecuted spirit. Let us look to God to fulfill the desires of our heart, and He will change us from the inside out.

- PSA 34:18; PSA 51:10–12,17 ~ The Lord is near to those who have a broken heart; He saves those with a contrite spirit. Create in me a clean heart, Lord, and renew an upright spirit within me. Don't remove me from your presence and don't take your Holy Spirit from me. Restore to me the joy of your salvation, and uphold me with your free Spirit. Sacrifices to God represent a broken spirit; God will not despise a broken and contrite heart.
- PSA 145:16,18 ~ God opens His hand, and satisfies the desire of every living thing. He is there for anyone that calls upon Him in truth.
- ISA 41:10 ~ God says, "Do not be afraid for I am with you; do not be not dismayed, for I am your God. I will strengthen you and help you; I will hold you up with the right hand of my righteousness."
- JOH 14:1–3,27 ~ Jesus said, "Do not let your heart be troubled. Trust in God, and trust in me. There are many mansions in my Father's house, and I am going there to prepare one for you. And I will come back for you and take you there, so that where I am you can be also. Peace I leave with you, my peace I give to you; I do not give as the world gives. So do not let your heart be troubled, neither let it be afraid."

Jesus came to mend broken hearts, to bring peace to those who seek the Lord, to save us from death, and to free those who are enslaved by their flesh.

- ISA 61:1–3 ~ The Spirit of God is upon me, because He has directed me to preach His good news to the humble, to heal the broken hearted, to free the slaves, and to release those who are bound in chains and in prison; to proclaim the Lord's favor and His vengeance, to comfort all who mourn, and to tell those who mourn to exchange their ashes for beauty; to replace mourning with joy, and to don the garment of praise in exchange for the spirit of sorrow, so that they may be trees of righteousness, planted by the Lord for His glorification.
- LUK 4:17–18 ~ Jesus stood up to read in the synagogue, and they handed Him the scroll of Isaiah. He located the above scripture and read it aloud. Then He gave the scroll back to the attendant and sat down. Everyone was looking at Him, and He spoke again saying, "Today that scripture was fulfilled as you were hearing it."
- 2 CO 5:17 ~ Therefore, if any man be in Christ, he is a new creature. Old things have passed away; behold, all things have become new.

One should never give up hope. All sufferings will pass. It will require a lot of patience. If we place our trust and desire in God, He will give us everything we need including the desires of our hearts.

- PSA 10:17; PSA 37:4; PSA 145:18–19 ~ Lord, you know of the desires of the afflicted; you hear them and give them encouragement in their hearts. Make the Lord your delight and He will give to you the desires of your heart. The Lord is near to all who call upon Him in truth. He will fulfill the desire of anyone who fears Him; He will hear their cry, and will save them.
- PRO 13:12 ~ Hope deferred makes the heart sick, but a desire fulfilled is a tree of life.
- MAT 11:28 ~ Jesus said, "Come to me, all who are weary and burdened, and I will give you rest.
- ROM 5:2–5 ~ Through Christ we have obtained access to His grace in which we stand, and we rejoice in our hope of sharing the glory of God. We rejoice in our sufferings knowing that they produce endurance, which produces character, which produces hope. And hope does not disappoint us, because God's love has been poured into our hearts through the Holy Spirit.

- ROM 8:18 ~ I (Paul) think that the sufferings of this present time cannot be compared to the glory that will be revealed in us. The entire creation eagerly awaits that time when the sons and daughters of God will be revealed.
- 2 CO 4:16–18 ~ Therefore we do not lose heart. Though outwardly we continue to deteriorate, yet inwardly we are constantly renewed. For our momentary and minor troubles are achieving for us an eternal glory that far outweighs them all. We do not focus on the things we can see, but on the things that we cannot see; for the things that we can see are temporal, but the things that we cannot see are eternal.

We must help others who suffer by lifting them up in the spirit of love. Fulfilling the commandments of God requires His love, which will mend any broken heart. Open your heart, receive His love, and share it.

- 2 CO 1:3–4 ~ Praise to God, the Father of our Lord Jesus Christ, who comforts us in all our troubles, so that we will be able to comfort others that are troubled, giving the same comfort that we ourselves have received from God.
- EPH 4:2 ~ Be humble, gentle, and patient, holding up each other in love. Try earnestly to stay united in the Spirit through the bond of peace.
- 1 TH 5:11 ~ Continue to encourage one another and edify each other just as you are doing.
- HEB 13:3: Remember those who are in bondage as if you were bound with them, and remember those who suffer adversity as if you were suffering with them, because you are fellow members of the body.

My friends, be aware of what's going on inside your heart. Does Christ live there? Listen to your heart for it will show you the right path; if you follow that path it will lead you to the Lord, and He will lead you to the Promised Land. So, protect your hearts. Remove the blockage that prevents the true expression of God's love which is always there if you ask Him. Allow Christ to repair the damaged heart, open the closed heart, soften the hardened heart, warm the cold heart, and create within you a new heart (PSA 51:10–12).

- PRO 4:23 ~ Guard your heart with all diligence, for from it flow the issues of life.

The 23rd Psalm

(Poem by Andrew Barber)

The Lord is my Shepherd, I've nothing to fear.
I graze in green meadows with still waters near.
My soul is restored from the curse of the grave.
His righteousness leads me; His name, it means "save".

The valley of death will not make me afraid;
No evil can harm me, I am not dismayed.
For He will protect me with His staff and rod.
His Spirit gives comfort and guides me to God.

I sit at a table in front of my foes;
He christens my head; my cup overflows.
His goodness and mercy will last all my days;
Living forever, and singing His praise.

Lesson: Remember

God created us and He preserves us because He loves us. Though we are but lowly sinners, God always remembers us and provides us everything we need (PSA 23). God wants us to be free to live with Him forever in His kingdom. Obviously, we are very important to God.

- PSA 8:4–9 ~ Who are humans, that you would be mindful of them, and the offspring of humans that you would care for them? You made man only a little lower than the angels and crowned him with glory and honor. You made him ruler over your creations, and put everything on earth below him, including the animals, birds, and fish. Oh Lord, how majestic is your name in all the earth!

So that we could be with Him always, God devised a plan of salvation. He intends to redeem our souls from death so that we may have everlasting life. To receive this gift, a person has only to believe. This covenant, or agreement, applies to everyone who concurs with it, and the covenant stands for eternity. Thus, God will never forget His promises; those promises are repeated throughout the Bible so that we will remember (GEN 9:15–16; EXO 2:24; EXO 6:5; LEV 26:42–46).

- DEU 4:31 ~ For the Lord your God is merciful. He will not abandon you or destroy you, nor will He ever forget the covenant with your forefathers which he swore to them.
- 1 CH 16:15–17; PSA 105:8–9 ~ God remembers His covenant forever, the Word He commanded, for a thousand generations. This is the covenant sworn to Abraham, Isaac, and Jacob.
- EZE 16:59–61 ~ I (God) will deal with you the way you deserve, for you have despised my oath by breaking the covenant. Nevertheless, I will remember the covenant I made with you when you were young, and I will establish with you an everlasting covenant. Then you will remember your evil ways and be ashamed...

We are reminded of God's promises so that we will not forget. Therefore, we must keep Him in mind, remembering that He always is present. This will enable us to forsake the ways of the world, and to follow the route God has recommended to us. Remembering God and His promises gives us the ability to continue through life with peace, and to overcome its troubles and temptations with gladness.

- NUM 15:38–40 ~ God commanded Moses: Put tassels on your garments, so that when you see the tassels, you will remember my commandments and obey them, and so you do not corrupt yourselves by seeking after your own hearts and your own eyes. Then you will remember and obey, and you will be consecrated unto me.
- DEU 4:9 ~ Be careful and keep close watch over your soul, so you do not forget the things that you have witnessed, or let them slip away from your heart. Teach these things to your children and your children's children.
- DEU 8:11 ~ Be careful not to forget God, and remember to keep His commandments, laws, and statutes.
- DEU 8:18–19 ~ Remember God, for it is He that gives you the power to prosper, thereby confirming His covenant which he swore to your forefathers, and which still applies to this day. But if you forget God, and follow, serve, or worship other gods, you surely will be destroyed.
- LAM 3:19–22 ~ When I think about my sorrows, it brings my soul down. When I am down, I bring to mind that I'll always have hope. Because of the Lord's great love, we are not consumed, and His compassion never fails.

- JAM 1:25 ~ Anyone who looks into the perfect law of liberty, and continues therein, not forgetting what he or she has heard but being a doer of the works of that law, will be blessed.

Those who choose to forget God, or who pay no attention to Him and His pledge, will be sorry; because eventually it will be too late to reconsider. God will forget the sinners that do not repent. They will be destroyed in the eternal fire, and all memory of them will be extinguished.

- DEU 32:26 ~ I (God) said that I would scatter them into corners and blot out their memory from humankind.
- JOB 24:19–20 ~ The grave will snatch away those who have sinned. The womb will forget them; worms will enjoy feeding upon them. They will nevermore be remembered, for wickedness will be broken as a tree branch.
- PSA 6:5; PSA 9:17; PSA 34:16; PSA 109:14–15 ~ The dead cannot remember God. Who gives thanks to Him from the grave? The wicked will return to the grave, and all the nations that forget God. For the Lord is against those who are evil; He will obliterate their memory from the earth, because their sins are not forgotten.
- PRO 10:7 ~ The memory of the righteous will be a blessing, but the name of the wicked will rot away.
- ECC 9:5–6 ~ For the living know that they will die, but the dead know nothing; they receive no reward and their memory is forgotten. Their love, their hate, and their jealousy vanished a long time ago; never again will they take part in anything that happens under the sun.
- ISA 26:14 ~ They are dead, they will live no more. Their departed spirits will not rise. God punished them and destroyed them, and caused their memory to perish with them.
- ISA 65:17 ~ I (God) will create a new heaven and a new earth; and the former will nevermore be remembered or come to mind.

God forgets the unfaithful because He remembers their sin. Their sin condemns them because they have not sought redemption from their only Lord and Savior Jesus Christ. If anyone asks God in faith, He will forgive them of their sins and forget those sins.

- JDG 8:33–34 ~ No sooner had Gideon died than the Israelites again corrupted themselves with idolatry. They forgot their Lord, who had delivered them out of the hands of their enemies on every side.
- JER 2:31–32; JER 14:10 ~ God says, "Why do my people say that they are free to roam? Does a maiden forget her jewelry? Does a bride forget her wedding ornaments? Yet my people have forgotten me for days without number." The Lord says this to the people: "They love to wander; they cannot keep their feet from straying. Therefore, the Lord does not accept them; He will now remember their iniquity, and punish them for their sins."
- EZE 21:24; EZE 36:22,24–32 ~ The Lord says, "You have caused your iniquity to be remembered because of your open rebellion, revealing your sins in everything you do; for this you will be taken captive. It is not for your sake, Israel, that I am doing this, but for the sake of my holy name which you profaned among the nations where you have been taken. But I will gather you back, cleanse you from impurity and from your idols, and give you a new heart and a new spirit. I will allow you to prosper once again. Then you will remember your previous evil ways and you will be ashamed of yourselves. I am doing this for your own good; I want you to feel ashamed and disgraced for your contemptible conduct."
- REV 18:2,5–7 ~ Fallen is the great city of Babylon; she has become a haven for demons and for every detestable creature. For her sins are piled up to heaven, and God has remembered her sins. Give back to her what she has done; pay her back double from her own cup. Give her as much torture and grief as she gave glory and luxury to herself...

God will not remember the sins of those who have turned to Him and away from iniquity. But returning to a life of wickedness will result in God forgetting a person's righteousness and recalling those sins, and He will hold those sins against them. Since we cannot quit sinning, we need forgiveness often; and God will forgive every time if we are sincere. However, if you are not contrite and do not make a serious effort to improve, God eventually will stop listening.

- ISA 43:25 ~ I (God) am the one who blots out your transgressions for my own sake, and remembers your sins no more.
- ISA 49:13–16 ~ The Lord comforts His people and will have compassion on His afflicted ones. Yet they cry, "The Lord has forsaken me; the Lord has forgotten us." Can a mother forget the baby at her breast, or have no compassion on the child that she has borne? Though she may forget, I will never forget you. See, I have engraved you on the palms of my hands; your walls are always before me.
- JER 31:33–34; HEB 8:10–12; HEB 10:16–17 ~ "This is the covenant I will make with them," says the Lord. "I will put my laws in their minds and write them upon their hearts. I will be their God and they will be my people. No longer will a man teach his neighbor or his brother, telling them to know the Lord, because they all will know me from the least to the greatest; for I will forgive their wickedness and remember their sins no more."
- EZE 3:20; EZE 33:13–14 ~ When a righteous person turns from his righteousness, and commits sin, God will allow him to stumble and fall. He will die, and the righteousness that he did will not be remembered. If you did not warn him, his blood will be on your hands, and you will die also. When God tells the righteous man that he will surely live, but then he begins to trust in his own righteousness and does what is evil, all his righteousness will be forgotten, and because of his sin he will die. But if God says to the wicked man that he will surely die, and that person turns away from his evil ways, does what is righteous, and refrains from sin, he will surely live; and the previous sins he committed will be forgotten.

We always must remember to remain under the protective umbrella of God's grace, which He showed so abundantly through Christ our Savior. If we keep focused on Christ, we will never go astray and we will never forget His covenant and promises.

- PSA 30:4 ~ Sing to the Lord all you saints, and give thanks at the remembrance of His holiness.
- MAT 26:26–28; LUK 22:19–20; 1 CO 11:24–26 ~ Jesus took the bread, gave thanks, and broke the bread, giving it to His disciples and saying, "Take and eat; this is my body which is given for you; do this to remember me." In like manner He took the cup of wine saying, "Drink from this cup all of you. It is the New Covenant in my blood which is poured out for you, and for many others, for the forgiveness of sins. Do this often to remember me." For whenever you eat of the bread and drink from the cup you proclaim the Lord's death until He returns.

Our faith in Christ enables us always to remember His teachings and His gifts. This helps us remain steadfast until the end, at which time He will deliver to us the most wonderful gift of eternal life in paradise. Bringing that thought into remembrance is the key to staying joyful in the midst of life's setbacks; for we know they will pass soon enough, but eternal life will never pass and neither will the joy that comes with it.

- LUK 23:42–43 ~ And the thief said to Jesus, "Lord, remember me when you enter into your kingdom." Jesus replied, "Truthfully I tell you that this day you will be with me in paradise."
- JOH 2:22 ~ After he had risen from the dead, Jesus's disciples remembered what He had said to them, and they believed the scriptures and the words of Christ.

- JOH 14:26; JOH 15:26–27; JOH 16:1–4 ~ Jesus said, "The Comforter, which is the Holy Spirit, whom the Father will send in my name, will teach you all things, and will remind you of everything I told you. I will send the Comforter to you, the Spirit of Truth who proceeds from the Father; He will testify about me. And you must also testify, for you have been with me from the beginning. I have told you these things so that you will not go astray. They will throw you out of the synagogue; they will kill you thinking they have done a service to God. They do these things because they do not know the Father or me. I am telling you this so that when the time comes you will remember my warning. I did not have to tell you these things while we were together."
- JOH 16:22 ~ Jesus said, "You may have sorrow now, but I will see you again and your heart will rejoice, and your joy nobody can take from you."

We also must remember our brothers and sisters in the faith, particularly those who are doing the work of the Lord, and especially those who are being persecuted for claiming Christ. Every day, all across the world, numerous Christians are enduring rejection, enslavement, incarceration, torment, torture, and death. We often take our freedom of religion for granted, but there are countless others that do not enjoy this freedom. Although we cannot take their place, we still can remember them, stand with them in spirit, and pray for them constantly.

- 1 CO 11:2 ~ Paul wrote: I honor you for remembering me always, and for holding fast to the teachings that I have passed onto you.
- 1 CO 12:25–26 ~ There should be no division in the body of Christ, but all members should have equal concern for one another. If one member suffers, everyone should suffer; and if one member is honored, all the members should rejoice.
- GAL 2:10 ~ Paul wrote: They asked us to remember the poor, which I was eager to do.
- PHP 1:3–6,9 ~ Paul wrote: I thank God every time I remember you. I pray for you all the time with joy because of our partnership in the Gospel, being confident that He who began a good work in you will carry it onto completion until the day Christ returns. And this is my prayer: that your love will abound more and more in knowledge, depth, and insight, so that you will be able to discern what is best, and can remain pure and blameless until Christ comes.
- 2 TH 3:1–3 ~ Finally, brothers, pray for us that the message of the Lord may spread rapidly and be honored wherever it goes, just as it was with you. And pray that we may be delivered from wicked and evil men, for not everyone has faith. But the Lord is faithful, and He will strengthen and protect you from the evil one.
- 2 TI 1:2–7 ~ Paul wrote to Timothy: I thank God, whom I serve with a pure conscience as my forefathers did; for night and day I remember you and you are constantly in my prayers. Recalling your tears, I have longed to be with you, because that would fill me with joy. I am reminded of your sincere faith which first appeared in your relatives, and now I am persuaded lives in you. For this reason, I must remind you to fan the flames of God's gifts to you, for God did not give us a spirit of fear, but of power, love, and a sound mind.
- HEB 13:1–3 ~ Continue to love each other as brothers and sisters. Do not forget to entertain strangers, for by doing so some people have entertained angels without knowing it. Remember those who are in prison as if you were there with them, and remember those who are mistreated as if you yourselves were suffering.

Lesson: Answers

People are constantly searching for answers to questions, problems, dilemmas, decisions, aspirations, you name it. Many of them do not realize that they can find answers in the scriptures and through prayer. God is the answer to everything, and the Holy Bible is a compendium of all that we seek in Him. If you want answers, go to God; and one sure way of finding Him is through His Word. Everything that we know about God can be found there. Those who claim that "love is the answer" are correct, because God is love, and He is the answer.

Everyone can ask God anything and He will answer them. God listens to all our complaints, ideas, petitions, and inquiries whenever we come to Him in faith. However, when and how God will answer us is mostly undefined. We must be patient and believe, and we will get our answers, and those answers will be amazing as well as timely.

- EXO 19:19–20 ~ The sound of the trumpet had blared for a long time and it became louder and louder when Moses spoke. God answered with a voice calling him to the top of the mountain, so Moses went up there. The next time Moses went up the mountain to visit with God he received the Ten Commandments (EXO 20).
- LUK 2:46–47 ~ Mary and Joseph found their son Jesus in the temple courts, sitting among the teachers and asking them questions. Everyone who heard Jesus was astonished at His understanding and His answers.
- COL 4:2 ~ Continue to pray and wait for the answer, giving thanks for the result.
- HEB 4:12 ~ The Word of God is alive and powerful. It is sharper than any double-edged sword, piercing deep, so as to divide the very soul and spirit. It can discern the thoughts and intents of the heart.

God reveals answers to great mysteries and unfortunate predicaments. He uncovers things that are hidden, shows us methods and paths that will work, and exposes lies. We can depend on God for the truth which is readily available in the Holy Bible. Everything God says is true whether from the written Word, the spoken Word, or the living Word. Notice how all three persons of the Holy Trinity are represented here: out of love, God the Father speaks things into existence including everything; God the Holy Spirit inspires the Word as well as anybody reading, writing, and teaching it; and God the Son is He who died for us and is yet still alive, thereby ensuring believers newness of life. So there it is, the three essential components of our existence: live, truth, and love.

- DEU 29:29 ~ The secret things belong to the Lord, but those things that He reveals belong to us and to our children forever, so that we may follow the words of His Law.
- MAT 10:26–27; LUK 12:3 ~ Jesus said, "Don't fear those who hate you, for everything that is hidden now will be revealed later; everything that is unknown will become known. What I tell you in darkness you will speak in the light. What you hear in private will be proclaimed from the rooftops."
- JOH 18:19–21 ~ The high priest questioned Jesus about His teaching and His disciples. Jesus answered, "I have spoken openly to the world; I have always taught in synagogues and in the temple where the Jews gather. I have said nothing in secret. Why interrogate me? Ask those who have heard me. Surely they can testify about what I said."
- ROM 16:25–26 ~ Christ has the power to save you according to the revelation of God's mystery, which was kept secret since the world began, but which is now evident by the scriptures. According to God's will, the mystery is made known to all nations on earth for the obedience of faith.

Although the answers God provides may surprise us, they also will enlighten us. That is why we approach God, because His knowledge is awesome. We seldom approach God with ordinary problems; instead, we seek His advice on the difficult, enigmatic, confusing problems. In addition to being the answer to our problems, God is the answer to our needs and desires. Be advised, you frequently will not find your answers or solutions looking exclusively at the world; and any truth discovered via worldly pursuits should never disagree with God's words which are true forever (MAT 24:35).

- PSA 50:15 ~ Call upon God in the day of trouble, and you will be delivered, and you will glorify God.
- PRO 3:5–6 ~ Trust in the Lord with all your heart; don't depend on your own understanding. In all things acknowledge Him and He will direct you in the right path.
- MAT 6:25–34 ~ Jesus said, "Don't be anxious about your life, and don't worry about your next meal or what to wear. Look at the birds. They don't sow or reap but God feeds them just the same. Look at the lilies. They don't work or worry but Solomon himself was not clothed in such beauty. And aren't you more important to God than birds or flowers? So don't worry about these things, because God knows that you need them. Besides, will being anxious about tomorrow add one second to your life? But seek first the kingdom of heaven, and all these other things will be added unto you. Don't worry about tomorrow, because each day has enough trouble of its own. Let tomorrow worry about itself."
- MAT 11:28 ~ Jesus said, "Come to me all who are weary and troubled and I will give you rest." (PSA 50:15)

God not only answers our prayers and meets our needs, He also is the answer to our desires, our hopes, and our dreams.

- 2 SA 23:5 ~ David proclaimed as he was dying, "Isn't my house right with God? Hasn't He provided to me an everlasting covenant that will bring salvation and fulfill all my desire?"
- PSA 42:1 ~ As the deer pants for streams of water, so my soul pants after you, oh God.
- PSA 73:25 ~ Whom have I in heaven but you, Lord? There is nothing on earth that I desire besides you.
- PSA 130:5 ~ I wait for the Lord, my soul waits; and in His Word I have hope.
- PSA 145:16 ~ You open your hand and you satisfy the desire of every living thing.
- 1 JO 5:14–15 ~ If we ask Him anything according to His will, He will give it to us. If we believe that He hears us, He will hear us and He will fulfill our desires.

Above everything else, God is the answer to our salvation. There is nothing else on this planet that matters. Our life here is but a blink of the eye compared to our life in heaven. The promise of salvation is guaranteed through the atonement given us by God's only Son. Do you know the answer to the question, "What is the meaning of life?" The answer is Jesus Christ, and all it takes is faith in Him if you want it to last forever.

- ROM 1:17 ~ For in the Gospel a righteousness of God is revealed, a righteousness that is by faith, from the first to the last, just as it is written: The just shall live by faith.
- 1 CO 1:6–8 ~ Because our testimony of Christ was confirmed in you, you do not lack any spiritual gift, as you eagerly wait for our Lord Jesus Christ to be revealed. He will confirm you until the end, so that you may stand blameless when His day comes.
- TIT 1:1–3 ~ Paul was a servant of God and an apostle of Jesus Christ for the faith of God's elect, and the knowledge of the truth that leads to godliness. This faith rests on the hope of eternal life, which God, who does not lie, promised before the beginning of time.

- HEB 2:3–4 ~ How can we escape, if we neglect such a great salvation? This salvation, which was announced by Christ the Lord, was confirmed to us by those who heard Him. God also testified to it by signs, wonders, various miracles, and gifts of the Holy Spirit distributed according to His will.

Remember, we cannot always depend on the world for answers because those answers can be subject to variation. You can ask ten different people and get ten different answers. Even the same person may give you a different answer if you ask more than once. In contrast, God is always the same; He never changes. His truth stands forever; truth does not vary with extenuating circumstances and it does not have conditions attached.

- EZE 13:22–23 ~ With lies you have saddened the heart of the righteous, but I (God) did not made them sad; by promising life you have strengthened the hands of the wicked, so that the people do not forsake their wicked ways. Therefore, you will no longer see your false visions or practice your divinations.
- JOB 21:34 ~ How can you comfort me with your nonsense, because in your answers there remains falsehood?
- 2 TI 4:3–4 ~ People will seek teachers who conform to their own likes and dislikes; they will turn away from the truth and wander into myths.
- 2 PE 1:16,21 ~ We did not follow cleverly devised fables when we told people about the power and coming of Jesus Christ, for we were eye witnesses of His majesty. No prophecy ever came from the impulse of man, but holy men spoke as they were directed by God.

Although Christians do not have the wisdom of God, He gives them the authority to speak on His behalf. We should, therefore, be prepared to give answers to others that are searching for truth. This requires that we become equipped with the knowledge of the Lord by means of faith, the study of God's Word, prayer, fellowship, and attending worship services. Such preparation produces power, authority, and wisdom. Of course, any answers given by a messenger of the Lord should be delivered with godly love, humility, and patience.

- MAR 16:20 ~ After Christ ascended into heaven, the disciples went forth and preached everywhere, the Lord working with them, and confirming the Word with signs that accompanied their teaching.
- LUK 12:11–12 ~ Jesus said, "When they bring you before the authorities, don't worry about what to say or do, for the Holy Spirit will tell you."
- 2 CO 5:20 ~ We are, therefore, Christ's ambassadors, as though God were making His appeal through us.
- 2 TI 3:14–17 ~ Continue in what you have learned and are convinced of, because you know those from whom you learned it. Remember how, from the beginning, you understood the scriptures which are able to make you wise unto salvation through faith in Christ. All scripture is inspired by God. God's Word provides the doctrine of truth, refutes that which is false, and instructs all people in the ways of righteousness, so that a true follower can become thoroughly equipped for every good work.
- 1 PE 3:15 ~ Sanctify the Lord in your hearts, and always be ready to give an answer, with humility and respect, to anyone who asks about the hope that is within you.

Lesson: No Excuses

Have you ever pondered this question: What will happen to the innocent child that never had a chance to learn about Jesus? Surely, God would not condemn that person, would He? Of course not! While the answer seems obvious, we still need reassurance, don't we? The Bible provides all the reassurance we need, that God protects the innocent and punishes the guilty.

- JOB 4:7–8 ~ Consider this: Who among the innocent ever perished? When were the righteous ever destroyed? I have seen for myself, that those who plow evil and those who sow trouble reap the same.
- PRO 17:26 ~ It is not good to punish an innocent person.
- ISA 7:16 ~ Before the child knows better to refuse the evil and choose the good the land of the two kings that you dread will be laid to waste.
- MAT 18:6 ~ Whoever would cause a little child that believes in me to sin, it would be better for him if a millstone was hung around his neck, and he was drowned in the depths of the sea.

But then you continue to wonder, okay, so God defends the innocent. But what about primitives in a third world country, who practice a pagan religion and are never visited by Christian missionaries? How can they be saved? Again, the Bible makes it clear that God is everywhere, and to deny that fact is to ignore the obvious. Anyone can look around and see that the universe is a complex yet orderly phenomenon. How could anyone realistically conclude that the universe just occurred by chance, and that our existence is but a fluke of nature? Basically, you have two options: to believe that the universe was created via intelligent design or to believe that it just sprang up all by itself.

Let's consider the odds of the universe snapping into existence without any intervention from God. One would have to assume that perfect order arose from random chaos. An example may help to illustrate this probability. Suppose you have a brand-new deck of 52 playing cards (jokers not included). The deck is prearranged in perfect order, from Ace to King of spades, Ace to King of hearts, then clubs, then diamonds. Now, shuffle the deck once, twice, fifty times, ten thousand times, a billion times. Will you ever shuffle them enough to be able to deal the cards in perfect order again? The probability of taking a shuffled deck (random) and dealing them in the exact sequence (perfect order) would be… Well, the likelihood is infinitesimal (1 divided by 52 factorial, or $1/52 \times 1/51 \times 1/50 \ldots\ldots 1/4 \times 1/3 \times 1/2$). The probability of just dealing an ace, deuce, and trey of spades in succession is about 7.5 chances in a million. For the sake of argument, let's pretend the chance of obtaining perfect order emerging from random chaos is the same as dealing 52 cards in precise arrangement ($p = 1/52!$); the likelihood of it not occurring that way would be the inverse, or 99.99999 percent (add about 60 more 9s to the end of that row).

Thus, the statistical probability of the universe being created by God instead of it just happening by random chance is rock solid. It's so certain you can bet your life on it. Curiously, many atheist scientists purport that our universe was the lucky one from among multiple universes and has evolved through natural biochemical processes. Realistically, I doubt if most of them actually believe that. To deny that a greater power had a hand in it is like wagering your soul on a card game for a chance of winning the world (again, the chance of that is incalculably minute). I would rather place all my trust in the Lord who has revealed Himself to me; with Him it is a sure thing, not a gamble. Wake up! God enables people to find Him, even when they are not looking for Him (ISA 40:21–31).

- ISA 65:1 ~ I (God) revealed myself to those who did not ask about me and I was found by those who did not seek me. To the nation that did not call on my name, I said, "Here I am."
- JER 31:31–33 ~ The days are coming when I will make a New Covenant with my people. It won't be like the covenant I made when I brought my people out of Egypt, which they broke. The New Covenant will be this: Instead of writing my laws on stone, I will write my laws inside the hearts of my people. They will not have to teach others to know God because everyone will know me, for I will forgive their sins and remove those sins forever.
- ROM 1:18–25 ~ The wrath of God is being revealed from heaven against the wickedness of men, who suppress the truth through unrighteousness, though the things that are known about God are clear to them because God has made these things clear. Since the creation of the world God's invisible qualities have been obvious, including His eternal power and His divine nature. Therefore, they have no excuse; because, while they knew God, they neither glorified Him nor gave thanks to Him. Their thinking became futile and their foolish hearts were darkened. Though they claimed to be wise, they were foolish, exchanging the glory of God for graven images. God allowed them to become depraved, who turned God's truth into a lie and worshipped and served the creature rather than the Creator who is blessed forever.
- ROM 1:32; ROM 2:1–2,5–6 ~ Even though they are aware of God's righteous decree that those who are evil deserve to die, they not only continue to be wicked but they give their approval to others who are wicked. So, you have no excuse, you people that judge others, because whenever you judge another you are judging yourself since you are guilty of the same things. We know that God's judgment against those who act this way is based on truth. Because of stubbornness and an unrepentant heart, they are storing up vengeance against themselves for that day when God unleashes His wrath, and His righteous judgment is revealed. "God will give back to each person according to what he or she has done."
- ROM 4:16 ~ The fulfillment of God's promise in your life depends entirely on trusting Him and His ways, and embracing Him and His works. The promise is received purely as a gift. That's the only way everyone can have a chance, including those who recognize religious traditions and those who are unaware of them.
- ROM 10:17–18,20 ~ Faith comes by hearing the Word of God. Haven't they heard? Yes, for it is written: Their words will reach the far corners of the earth. Just as Isaiah boldly proclaimed: I (God) was found by those who weren't even looking for me.
- 2 TI 4:8 ~ A crown of righteousness is reserved for me which the Lord, the righteous judge, will give me on that day; and not only me, but everyone that looks forward to His coming.
- TIT 2:11–12 ~ For the grace of God that brings salvation has appeared to all people. It teaches us to say no to wickedness and worldly pleasures. It teaches us to live in a self-controlled, upright manner.

God's judgments are based solely on truth, for He cannot lie and He cannot sin. Truth, being perfect in purity, is God's gift to us through His Word. All people have the ability of discernment: knowing the difference between right and wrong. A willful life of sin and depravity is a choice people make, knowing full well the consequences. The only other choice is a life of obedience and faith. It's as easy as believing that the universe was created by God over the improbable alternative. The bottom line is, God's judgment is righteous, His judgment is fair, and His judgment is final. Don't be fooled by intellectual rationalizations because it isn't that complicated.

- PSA 119:7,160 ~ I will praise God with an upright heart, once I have learned of His righteous judgments. God's Word is entirely true, and His righteous judgments endure forever.

- ISA 45:21 ~ How do you know the truth? Who has told it to you all along? Has it not been I the Lord? There is no God but me, a fair God and a Savior; there are no others besides me.
- JOH 7:24 ~ Jesus said, "Do not judge by appearances, but only according to righteousness."
- 1 CO 10:13 ~ The temptations you endure are common to humanity. But God is faithful and fair, and He will not cause you to suffer temptation beyond your ability to withstand it. And He will always provide you a way to escape from temptation.
- 2 TH 1:5–6 ~ God's judgment is right. God is just.
- REV 16:7; REV 19:2 ~ I heard a voice from the altar say, "Yes, Lord God Almighty, your judgments are true and righteous."
- REV 19:11 ~ I saw heaven open and a white horse emerge. The man upon the horse is the One called Faithful and True; in righteousness He judges and He makes war.

Those people who refuse to listen to or acknowledge God will be held responsible for their actions. Those who repent and make an effort to do better because they have faith in God's covenant will be forgiven. Again, it's an easy choice: accept the free gift of salvation and live in love and faith forever, or die in your sin and be condemned to hell where all the suffering you ever caused will come back upon you.

- PRO 1:18 ~ They lay in wait for their own blood. They will ambush their own lives.
- ISA 3:11 ~ What they have done to others will be done to them.
- EZE 11:21 ~ To those whose hearts seek detestable things and abominations, I will recompense it back upon their own heads.
- JOE 3:4 ~ It will come back upon your head.
- ROM 2:6 ~ He will render to every man according to his deeds…

The person relying on Christ will be justified because of their faith. That means they will be found not guilty by virtue of the righteousness they received from Christ in exchange for their sins. When Christ comes in judgment Christians will be set free, because we believed in Him who died for us. Those who do not believe will have their sins counted against them; they will be judged according to the Law and found guilty. And the punishment will be a death sentence (i.e., the second death which is the lake of fire). Let me remind you: you don't have to die if you believe Christ already died in your place.

- ACT 13:38–39 ~ I want you to know that, through Jesus, forgiveness of sins is proclaimed. In Him, believers are justified from everything that the Law of Moses could not justify.
- ROM 6:23 ~ The wages of sin is death; but the gift of God is eternal life through Jesus Christ our Lord.
- ROM 8:30 ~ Those He predestined He also called; those He called he also justified; and those He justified He also glorified.
- GAL 2:16; GAL 5:4 ~ A man is not justified by the works of the Law but by faith in Christ. We too have placed our faith in Jesus Christ and do not depend on works of the Law, because nobody can be justified by observing the Law. If you are attempting to be justified through works of the Law you have separated yourselves from Christ and have fallen from Grace.
- REV 20:6,12–15 ~ Blessed and holy are those who take part in the first resurrection, because the second death has no power over them, for they will be priests of God and of Christ, and will reign with Him a thousand years. But I saw the dead, important and unimportant, stand before God. And the books were opened; and then another book was opened, which is the Book of Life. And the dead were judged according to what they had done as recorded in the books. The sea gave up its dead, and death and hell delivered up its dead, and they all were judged according to the things they had done. And death and hell were thrown into the lake

of fire, which is the second death. Anyone whose name was not written in the Book of Life was thrown into the lake of fire.

Many of those who glory in evil are deceived into thinking that hell is not such a bad place, that everybody is saved, or that the end of this life is the absolute end regardless. Some have adopted the delusion that "ruling in hell is better than serving in heaven" (from Milton's *Paradise Lost*). Of course, there are no rulers in hell. The lake of fire is the melting pot for all that is evil, where there is no such thing as individual will, but only mutual obliteration. On the other hand, serving in heaven will be a thrill. Remember the story of the prodigal son (LUK 15:11–32)? He was eager to return to his father and be treated as a slave, because he knew that even slaves were treated with loving kindness. But his father restored his status as a son and heir, just as our Almighty Father will do for us when we He sees us returning to Him. We will live in eternal righteousness and bliss, at home with the Lord, serving Him with love and receiving His everlasting love in return.

This notion is illustrated by the Old Testament rules regarding servitude. Under the Law of Moses, an indebted Hebrew could pay his or her debt in full by becoming a servant for up to six years. The seventh year was called the year of jubilee, because all servants (or slaves) were given their freedom. Thus, when the Bible talks of slavery, it often is referring to servitude (not the type of forced bondage and submission that the Hebrews experienced in the land of Goshen, Egypt). However, obedient servants often didn't want to be emancipated. They liked it where they were; they loved their masters and their lives. In such cases they had an ear pierced, willfully becoming permanent members of their master's household to serve until the day of their deaths. It's like our home in heaven. We do not want to leave God's household because we love it there. We enjoy our lives with Him and do not want to be turned loose to fend for ourselves. Serving our Lord in heaven will be pleasurable, fun, and glorious. It will be like one, big, happy family, where everyone pitches in to make life grand and exciting. And we will be welcomed home by our Father, just like the prodigal son, forgiven and restored as full heirs to His kingdom.

- EXO 21:5–6 ~ If a servant is granted his freedom, but the servant declares, "I love my master, and my wife and children, and I prefer not to go free," then his master will bring him before the judges and pierce his ear, and he will be a servant for life.
- DEU 15:12–17 ~ If your Hebrew brother or sister is indebted to you and serves you for six years, he or she must be set free the seventh year. And when you release them, do not send them away empty-handed, but give them ample supplies from your stock. Give generously as God has given unto you, remembering that you were slaves in Egypt before God redeemed you. But if your servant does not wish to leave because he loves you, and if your family is blessed by that servant, then pierce the earlobe and he or she will be your servant for life.
- PSA 40:6 ~ You did not require, nor did you desire sacrifices and offerings, yet you pierced my ears (with your words).

In conclusion, God lives, and His glory can be found everywhere. Those who refuse to recognize this have deliberately closed their eyes, ears, and minds to God; just as many who saw and heard Christ refused to accept Him. Miracles are occurring daily in our lives and around the world; it is difficult to simply ignore them. You can choose to marvel at them and thank God, or you can pretend that it's all just a spectacular coincidence. But, are you willing to risk your soul on being wrong? Personally, I prefer to entrust my life on a sure bet: Jesus Christ!

- JOH 6:68–69 ~ Simon Peter answered Jesus, "Lord, who else can we turn to? You alone have the words of eternal life. And we believe and we are sure that you are the Christ, the Son of the living God."

- HEB 6:17–19 ~ When a person swears an oath by someone greater than themselves, the oath confirms what is said, and puts an end to the argument. Because God wanted to make the unchanging nature of His purpose very clear to the heirs of His promise, He confirmed it with an oath. First, God's Word is always true, and second, He gives His Word on it. That is, He backed up His promise with His Word of honor. He did this to emphasize the promise so that we, who cling to that hope, could be encouraged. We have this hope as an anchor for our souls, firm and secure…

The Creator's Masterpiece

(By Andrew Barber, 2001)

God's GRACE abounds from endless sky;
With BLUE most pleasing to the eye.
Grace guarantees I'll never die;
Eternal thanks, is my reply.

For my trust is in Christ who has ransomed my soul,
Making good on the promise that long was foretold.
And His MERCY, a glorious thing to behold;
It will gleam with a luster, the tincture of GOLD.

Desiring things as yet unseen,
Mankind aspires with HOPE pristine.
Like budding plants in early Spring
That grow and beam with shades of GREEN.

Since the Lord is my Shepherd, there's nothing I lack.
I believe, but I wish that we could interact.
While absorbing suspicions, reflecting none back,
From the void, FAITH stares through as the pigment of BLACK.

Though my faith may be dim, I can still see the light
That illuminates TRUTH, which is perfectly WHITE.
With the words of Jehovah, who always is right,
Truth is pure, without stain, and it glows wholly bright.

When sun has set and spreads its shroud;
RED-ORANGE draped on every cloud;
I break a smile, then laugh out loud,
For JOY is graciously endowed.

From a rich PURPLE hue comes the color of PEACE.
It entices my spirit with quiet release.
Christ is steadfast in patience that never will cease,
While preparing in heaven a wonderful feast.

All power, everlasting LOVE,
That radiates from God above;
Descending softly, as a dove,
In RAINBOW patterns—awesome stuff!

CHAPTER EIGHT

BIBLE FEATURES

IMPORTANT NUMBERS

Certain numbers bring special meaning to the Bible. That is, numbers often can be interpreted symbolically. Note that multiples and fractions of numbers can be relevant also. Sometimes, there are two meanings which are different, or opposite. For example, the number three can refer to the Holy Trinity or the three evil facets of Satan, otherwise referred to as the unholy trinity. The number four can refer to four sins as well as four judgments. The number seven can refer to the eyes (spirits) of the Lord or the heads (spirits) associated with the beast.

The purpose of this section is to review the significance of important numbers. The intent is not to promote numerology, which is a paranormal practice which lacks objectivity. In Hebrew, the letters of the alphabet were numbered, and they used combinations of numbers to uncover additional meaning or intent. This is not the case with Greek or English; the counting or arrangement of numeric combinations does not add meaning to the Bible, especially the NT. While numbers themselves may have multiple connotations, there is no hidden code or amalgamation of numbers within the biblical text that adds revelation. Those who believe in a secret numeric code are pursuing fables. The Bible does not hide anything but uncovers God's mysteries to those who follow God's command to keep studying His Word.

Number 2

The number 2 implies a pair, such as man and woman, or the male and female of the animals Noah brought into the ark. Two represents the traditional number of witnesses required to bring a verdict. Perhaps this is why there are two testaments to the Holy Bible. Also, there is the pair of tablets upon which God wrote the Ten Commandments (twice).

The number 2 is associated with the "anointed ones" that stand on either side of the throne of Jesus Christ. These two are probably symbolized by the cherubim which stand on either side of the mercy seat on the Ark of the Covenant. The cherubim may be Michael the enforcer at the right who carries a deadly sword, and Gabriel the messenger on the left who carries the Good News to God's people. The two witnesses in Revelation, also referred to as anointed ones, may be these cherubim; or they may be Moses and Elijah, a popular view among modern theologians. Elijah and Enoch are also possibilities as they are the only ones written about in the Bible who never died but were raptured straight to heaven.

- GEN 1:26–27; GEN 6:19 ~ God made Eve so that Adam would have a companion, and so that they could be fruitful and multiply. God instructed Noah to collect a male and female of each species of animals so that they could replenish the earth.

- GEN 19:1 ~ Two angels came to Sodom that night. Lot was sitting by the gates to the city, saw them, and went over to greet them, bowing his head.
- EXO 25:18 ~ God commanded Moses concerning the construction of the Ark of the Covenant that there should be 2 cherubim of gold, one at each end of the mercy seat.
- EXO 31:18; EXO 32:19; EXO 34:1,4 ~ God gave Moses 2 tablets of stone on which God wrote His testimony. Moses came down from the mountain and found the Israelites worshipping the golden calf. In his anger he threw the tablets on the ground, breaking them. Later, God commanded Moses to hew 2 new stone tablets, upon which God again wrote His testimony. Moses did as God requested, taking the hewn tablets back into Mount Sinai. Therefore, God wrote His commandments on stone two times.
- NUM 7:89 ~ God spoke to Moses from the mercy seat between the 2 cherubim.
- EZE 10:1 ~ Ezekiel envisioned 2 cherubim, with a throne above them in the heavens.
- ZEC 4:1–3,11–12,14 ~ The angel woke Zechariah and asked him what he saw. Zechariah replied that he saw a golden candlestick with a large bowl on top. There were seven lamps that were fed by seven pipes from the large bowl. There were 2 olive trees on either side of the bowl. Zechariah asked the angel about the 2 olive trees, and about the 2 olive branches that emptied out their golden oil. The angel replied that they represented the 2 anointed ones that stand by the Lord over all the earth.
- MAT 17:1–3 ~ Jesus was transfigured in the presence of Peter, James, and John; His face glowed like the sun and His clothes were bright as light. Appearing and talking with Jesus were Moses and Elijah.
- MAT 26:59–60 ~ At Jesus's trial the chief priests and elders found 2 false witnesses to testify against Him, since the Jewish law required at least 2 witnesses to obtain a death sentence (DEU 19:15).
- MAT 27:38 ~ There were 2 thieves that were crucified with Jesus, one on either side of Him.
- LUK 10:1 ~ Jesus sent seventy disciples, 2 by 2, to preach in all the places He was planning to visit.
- LUK 24:1–4; JOH 20:12 ~ Jesus's followers went to the tomb with spices, but they found the stone had been rolled away. They went inside the tomb but found nobody; instead there were 2 angels wearing shiny robes.
- ACT 1:8–11 ~ Two angels appeared to the apostles just after Jesus ascended into heaven, assuring them that Jesus would return someday in the same manner that He had just departed.
- REV 11:3–4 ~ God will send 2 witnesses clothed in burlap who will prophesy 1230 days. These are the 2 olive trees and the 2 candlesticks that stand before God over all the earth (ZEC 4).

Number 3

The number 3 carries with it many significant meanings. First, it is considered a number of completeness and unity—beginning, middle, and end (the alpha and omega). The most obvious association is with the 3 persons of God, the Holy Trinity: Father, Son, and Holy Spirit. Then there are the 3 manifestations of Satan: beast, antichrist, and false prophet. Like God, we also have three components: body, mind, and spirit.

There are three categories of sin mentioned in the Bible: the lust of the flesh, greed of the eyes, and pride of man. Everyone has been tempted by Satan in each of these areas, including Jesus Christ Himself. There are 3 woes or judgments that seem to correspond to these 3 temptations. Three is the number of days the dead are in the grave before being resurrected to be with God. Also, there were 3 wise men (assumed since there were 3 gifts given to the baby Jesus).

Thirds of the number three are also relevant. One third of the people (possibly Jews) will be purified with fire, while the other two-thirds will be completely cut off. Further, 1/3 reflects the number of fallen angels. In the latter days, the day will be shortened by 1/3, and 1/3 of living beings will be destroyed.

- EXO 10:22 ~ Moses stretched out his hand toward heaven and there was darkness in Egypt for 3 days.
- EXO 19:10–18 ~ God said to Moses, "Go to the people, sanctify them today and tomorrow, have them wash their clothes and be ready the third day. For on the third day I will come down upon Mt. Sinai in the sight of all the people." On the third day in the morning came thunder and lightning, and a thick cloud descended upon the mountain. And the voice of a trumpet was heard exceedingly loud, and all the people in the camp trembled. Then Moses brought the people forward to meet with God at the foot of the mountain. Sinai was blanketed in smoke while the Lord descended with fire; and the whole mount quaked.
- EXO 23:14 ~ God told Moses to have a special feast 3 times a year.
- EXO 32:17–28 ~ When Moses returned from Sinai with the Ten Commandments, he found the Israelites worshipping the golden calf. And 3000 souls were killed for worshipping the golden calf (ACT 2:41).
- LEV 12:1–5 ~ The time of purification for a mother who had given birth was 33 days for a boy and 66 days for a girl.
- LEV 19:5–7, 23–24 ~ Peace offerings had to be eaten within 3 days. God told Moses that when they come into the new land and plant trees not to eat the fruit for 3 years.
- NUM 24:10 ~ Balaam blessed Israel 3 times, to the dismay of Balak.
- 1 KI 17:21–22 ~ Elijah stretched himself over the woman's dead son 3 times asking the Lord to revive his soul, and the Lord did as Elijah asked.
- 1 KI 18:31–38 ~ Elijah had the pagans drench the altar with water 3 times before calling fire from heaven that consumed the sacrifice, the altar, the water, and everything.
- 2 KI 20:1–5 ~ King Hezekiah was ill 3 days before being healed because of His faith and his prayers.
- ISA 6:2–3 ~ The angels (seraphim) shouted, "Holy, Holy, Holy is the Almighty Lord; the earth is full of His glory." (Note that the word holy is repeated 3 times for a reason).
- EZE 5:2,12 ~ A third of you will die from pestilence and famine; a third will fall by the sword; a third will be scattered to the four winds, and I (God) will draw a sword after them.
- EZE 48:31–34 ~ God described the gates of the city (i.e., the new Jerusalem) as having 3 gates on each side: north, south, east, and west (also REV 21:13).
- HOS 6:2 ~ God will revive us after two days, and the third day He will raise us from the dead and we will live with Him.
- JON 1:17 ~ The Lord caused the whale to swallow Jonah, and he was in its belly for 3 days.
- ZEC 13:7–9 ~ The Lord of hosts says: Awake oh sword, against my shepherd, against the man who is my partner; smite the shepherd and the sheep will scatter, and I will turn my hand upon the little ones [possible reference to the scattering of the Jews]. Two thirds will be cut off and die; the other one third will be brought through the refiner's fire to be tested for purity. Those who call on my name will be heard, and I will say, "These are my people," and they will say, "The Lord is my God."

- MAT 2:11 ~ Three wise men came to worship the baby Jesus and gave Him gifts of gold, frankincense, and myrrh. [They came from Midian, Ephah, and Sheba, bringing gifts of incense and gold and praising the Lord. (see ISA 60:6)]
- MAT 12:40 ~ Jesus said, "Just as Jonah was in the belly of the whale for 3 days and 3 nights, so shall the Son of God be in the heart of the earth for 3 days and nights."
- MAT 22:37 ~ Jesus said, "Love the Lord with all your heart, soul, and mind."
- MAT 26:36–46 ~ Jesus found the disciples had fallen asleep 3 times in the Garden of Gethsemane, while He prayed 3 times in anguish awaiting His betrayal and execution.
- MAT 28:19 ~ Jesus told His apostles, "Go teach all nations, and baptize them in the name of the Father, Son, and Holy Spirit."
- MAR 8:31 ~ Jesus taught the apostles that He would suffer and die, and would rise from the dead after 3 days.
- LUK 2:46 ~ When Jesus turned up missing, His parents found Him 3 days later in the temple, studying the Law.
- LUK 4:1–13 ~ Satan tempted Jesus 3 times while in the desert when He was physically weak. Christ was tempted with the 3 types of sin mentioned by John (1 JO 2:16): weakness of the flesh (hunger), desire of the eyes (worldly riches), and pride (power over others).
- LUK 23:13–24 ~ Pontius Pilate pleaded with the Jews 3 times to allow him to spare the life of Christ.
- JOH 13:36–38; JOH 18:25–27 ~ Peter told Christ he would die for Him. Christ replied that Peter would deny knowing Him 3 times that very night. Peter denied Christ 3 times just as Christ said. Later, Jesus made Peter reaffirm his commitment to Him 3 times.
- ACT 2:41 ~ That day the apostles baptized some 3000 souls. (see EXO 32:17–28)
- ACT 9:3–9 ~ Saul (Paul) was without sight for 3 days after the Lord appeared to him and told him to stop persecuting Christians.
- 1 TH 5:23 ~ May the God of peace sanctify you wholly, so that your entire spirit, soul, and body can be preserved blameless until the coming of our Lord Jesus Christ.
- 1 JO 2:15–16 ~ Do not love the world or worldly things. If a person loves the world, he or she cannot love God. All that is in the world, the lust of the flesh, the greed of the eyes, and the pride of humanity, do not come from the Father but are of this world alone.
- 1 JO 5:7–8 ~ There are 3 recorded in heaven: the Father, the Word, and the Holy Spirit. These 3 are one. The same 3 bear witness on earth: the Spirit, the Water, and the Blood.
- REV 8:7–12 ~ The first angel sounded and hail mixed with blood fell to earth; 1/3 of the trees and all the grass were burned. The second angel sounded and a great mountain burning with fire was cast into the sea; 1/3 of the sea turned into blood, killing 1/3 of the sea life and destroying 1/3 of the ships. The third angel sounded and a great star called Wormwood fell from heaven; 1/3 of the water was contaminated. The fourth angel sounded and 1/3 of the sun, moon, and stars became blackened; daylight occurred for only 1/3 of the day.
- REV 11:3,7,11,14 ~ The two witnesses were killed, but came back to life. The second woe had passed and the 3rd woe was coming quickly.
- REV 12:3–5,8–9 ~ A great wonder appeared in heaven: a red dragon with seven heads and ten horns. Its tail pulled down 1/3 of the stars (angels) of heaven, and they were thrown to the earth. The dragon waited for the woman to give birth so it could eat her child. Her child would rule the nations with an iron hand. The child was taken to heaven to sit on God's throne. Satan (the dragon) was cast out of heaven along with the rest of the corrupt angels.
- REV 16:13,19 ~ In his vision, John saw 3 evil spirits leap like frogs out of the mouths of the dragon, the antichrist, and the false prophet. And the great city (the new Babylon) was divided into 3 parts, and the cities fell under great earthquakes.

Number 4

The number 4 has a few prevailing meanings. First, the 4 terrible sins committed by the pagan nations, and the 4 judgments that God will send upon such evil people. Note there are also 4 Gospel authors in the New Testament. Four is the number of angels in Ezekiel's vision; each had 4 faces and 4 wings. Four is the number of angels in John's vision as well. Four also refers to the number of horsemen of the apocalypse.

- GEN 2:10–14 ~ A river originated in Eden and it broke into 4 tributaries: the Pison, the Gihon, the Hiddekel (Tigris), and the Euphrates Rivers.
- GEN 15:13–14 ~ God told Abraham that his seed would be enslaved 400 years (ACT 7:6). [It was actually closer to 430.]
- PRO 30:15–16,18–19,21–31 ~ There are 4 things that are never satisfied: the grave, the barren womb, the dry earth which thirsts for water, and fire. There are 4 things that are amazing: the flight of an eagle, the slithering of a snake, the sailing of a ship, and the love between a young man and woman. There are 4 things that are unbearable: a servant that becomes your ruler, a fool who has eaten his fill, a hateful woman who gets married, and a maid who marries her mistress's husband. There are 4 things that are very small yet very wise: ants are not powerful but they gather plenty of food; rodents are not strong but they build their homes in the rocks; locust have no ruler but they travel in swarms; and spiders can hold things with their legs and live in king's palaces. There are 4 things that go proudly about: a strong and fearless lion, a greyhound, a male goat, and a king who will never be defeated.
- EZE 1:5–10 ~ Ezekiel had a vision of 4 creatures. They had 4 faces and 4 wings. They had feet of a calf that sparkled like brass and human hands. Their 4 faces were of a man, lion, ox, and eagle.
- EZE 5:17; EZE 14:15–21 ~ God will send 4 judgments upon the wicked: the sword, famine, ferocious beasts, and pestilence.
- EZE 10:14 ~ Ezekiel had a vision of a creature with 4 faces: a cherub, man, lion, and eagle.
- DAN 2:32–33,39–43 ~ Daniel interpreted King Nebuchadnezzar's dream of an image having a head of gold, breast and arms of silver, belly and thighs of bronze, legs of iron, and feet of iron mixed with clay. The image represented the kingdoms that would follow. The first kingdom of gold represented the kingdom of Babylon; the next kingdom of silver (Media-Persia) would be inferior to the one of gold. The third kingdom of bronze (Greece) would rule the world. The 4th kingdom would be strong as iron (Rome); but the 4th kingdom would split into two kingdoms that would eventually fall apart since iron and clay don't mix.
- DAN 7:1–7,17,23–25 ~ Daniel had a vision of the 4 winds stirring the sea from which 4 beasts arose. The first beast was like a lion with wings of an eagle; its wings were plucked and it stood on earth like a man. The second was like a bear that had three ribs between its teeth; it was told to devour much flesh. The third was like a leopard with 4 wings of a fowl and 4 heads; it was given dominion. The 4th was very strong and terrible with iron teeth; it devastated everything in its path; it was different than the other beasts, and had ten horns. The 4 beasts represented 4 kings that were to come. The fourth beast, which was very dreadful and devastating, represented the fourth kingdom that would be different from the other kingdoms, and would devour the whole earth and stomp it into the ground. The ten horns represented ten kings who would arise. Another king would come after them, who was dissimilar to the rest; he would subdue three other kings. For 3 ½ years he would speak blasphemy against God and would persecute the saints, trying to change the times and laws.

- DAN 8:5,8,21–25 ~ Daniel had a vision of a male goat coming from the west who was very great and strong. The goat's horn broke into 4 pieces. The goat represented the king of Greece and the great horn represented the first king. The broken horn represented 4 kingdoms that would arise from the original one. In the latter days of that kingdom, when iniquity would be rampant, a fierce king of darkness would arise. He would be mighty but not of his own power. He would be extraordinarily destructive, destroying the mighty and the holy people. He would be a master of deception; he would destroy many in the name of peace. He would consider himself to be great, even challenging the Prince of princes, but he would be defeated.
- AMO 1:3,6,9,11,13; AMO 2:1,4,6 ~ God will punish Damascus, Gaza, Tyrus, Edom, Ammon, Moab, Judah, and Israel for their 4 sins.
- ZEC 1:18–21 ~ Zechariah had a vision of 4 horns. The 4 horns represented the 4 kingdoms that would scatter Judah, Israel, and Jerusalem. Then Zechariah had a vision of 4 carpenters. The 4 carpenters would come against the 4 kingdoms and dismantle them.
- ZEC 6:1–7 ~ Zechariah had a vision of 4 chariots emerging from between two mountains of brass. The first chariot was driven by red horses, the second by black horses, the third by white horses, and the 4th by brown and gray (pale) horses. The chariots represented the 4 spirits of heaven which stand before the Lord of the earth. The black horses will go north, and the white horses will follow them. The pale horses will go south. The red horses will go back and forth across the earth.
- JOH 11:17,39,43–44 ~ Jesus raised Lazarus from the dead; he had been dead and in the grave for 4 days.
- JOH 19:23–24 ~ The soldiers divided Jesus's clothing into 4 piles, one for each soldier. Then they cast lots (dice) to see who would win Jesus's seamless coat.
- REV 4:6–8 ~ John had a vision of a throne surrounded by 4 beasts which had six wings and eyes all around them. The first beast was like a lion, the second like a calf, the third like a man, and the fourth like an eagle. Day and night the beasts praised God.
- REV 6:2–8 ~ John had a vision of 4 horsemen. The first had a bow and rode a white horse; he received a crown and went forth conquering. The second had a sword and rode a red horse; he received power and went forth to wage war and destroy peace. The third carried balances in his hand and rode a black horse; and the price of bread became a day's wages. The 4th rider was called Death and rode a pale horse; he was followed by Hell. They were given power to kill 1/4 of the earth's inhabitants by the 4 judgments: sword, famine, disease, and wild beasts. (see ZEC 6)
- REV 7:1 ~ John had a vision of 4 angels, one standing on each of the 4 corners of the earth, holding back the power of the 4 winds.
- REV 9:13–16 ~ John had a vision of the seven angels blowing trumpets. When the sixth angel sounded, John heard a voice from the 4 horns of the golden altar before the Lord. The voice told the sixth angel to release the 4 angels who had been imprisoned within the Euphrates River. The 4 angels had been preparing for that moment when they would be released to kill 1/3 of humankind. They were followed by a cavalry of 200,000,000.

Number 6

Because seven represents wholeness or conclusion, then 6 represents falling short, being incomplete or unfinished. It is the number for humankind, created on day 6. The number 6 is sometimes associated with Satan and the fall of man. Moreover, the number 666 may represent Satan's anti-trinity. Six can relate to the days we labor or wait for God, that time being spent on worldly pursuits. The seventh day we dedicate to God, in honor of Him who created the universe in 6 days. Thus, 6 may reflect the physical world, a world corrupted by sin, the nature of humankind, and/or Satan's domain. Note also that Jesus hung on the cross for 6 hours (refer to lesson on *Jesus's Last Words*).

- GEN 1; EXO 20:11; EXO 31:17 ~ In 6 days God created the physical world as we know it. On day 6 God created human beings (GEN 1:26). God blessed the seventh day as the Sabbath, a day for reverencing Him and thanking Him for His many blessings.
- EXO 24:16 ~ Six days Sinai was shrouded in a cloud, and the seventh day God called Moses from the cloud.
- NUM 35:11,14 ~ There were 6 cities of refuge where a person could obtain asylum, three on each side of the Jordan River.
- DEU 5:13–14; DEU 15:12–18; DEU 16:8–11 ~ Work for 6 days, and then rest the seventh. Serve a master 6 years and then be set free the seventh year. Eat unleavened bread 6 days and then rejoice and thank God the seventh day.
- 1 KI 10:14; 2 CH 9:13 ~ Solomon received a bounty of 666 talents of gold every year, not including profits from merchants and traders.
- EZE 36:1–6 ~ Only 1/6 of the northern army will survive their attack over the mountains of Israel.
- EZE 40:5,12; EZE 41:1–8; EZE 46:1–6 ~ In Ezekiel's vision, he saw an angel with a measuring stick 6 cubits long. He measured the dimensions of the building; all measurements came to 6 cubits. He measured the temple; all measurements came to 6 cubits. The inner court gate was shut 6 days prior to the new moon. The sacrifices included 6 unblemished lambs.
- DAN 3:1 ~ The gold statue commissioned by King Nebuchadnezzar was 60 cubits high and 6 cubits wide.
- REV 13:18 ~ Here is wisdom for those who can understand: Count the number of the beast, for it is the number of a man, and the number is 666.

Number 7 (also includes 7 times 7, or 49; 7 times 2, or 14; and 7 divided by 2, or 3 ½)

Seven is referred to as the number of wholeness or conclusion. The number 7 often has two opposite connotations: the 7 spirits or angels of God versus the 7 heads or spirits of the beast or Satan. The ministry of Christ was 3 ½ years; this is also the duration of the abomination of desolation during the last times. Seven is often assumed to be the number of years of the great tribulation and is often divided into two parts of 3 ½ each. There are the 7 days of consecration, quarantine, and shame; and the 7th year of jubilee when all are released from debts and servitude.

Pentecost represents 7 times 7 days (7 weeks) after the Passover. Also, the Holy Spirit came upon the apostles on the day of Pentecost, one week after Christ ascended into heaven (ACT 2—3). Particularly relevant is the prophecy of seventy weeks of years (LEV 25:1–13; JER 25:11–12; DAN 9:23–27); it is recommended that the reader research this uncommonly precise prophecy. For more information refer to the number 70.

- GEN 2:3 ~ And God blessed the 7th day and sanctified it because it was the day He chose to rest and admire His creations. Note that the first six days of creation were represented by an evening and a morning, but not the 7th (GEN 1).
- GEN 29:18–30 ~ Jacob worked 7 years for the hand of Rachel but got Leah instead, so he worked another 7 years for the hand of Rachel.
- GEN 41:53–54 ~ There were 7 years of plenty in Egypt followed by 7 years of famine, just as Joseph had interpreted from Pharaoh's dream.

CHAPTER EIGHT

- GEN 50:2,10 ~ Joseph commanded the physicians to embalm his father. Then they journeyed to Atad, which is beyond the Jordan River, and there they mourned for 7 days.
- EXO 13:6 ~ God instructed Moses that for 7 days the people would eat unleavened bread after celebrating the Passover feast.
- EXO 20:10 ~ The 7th day is the Sabbath day of the Lord; nobody should work on that day.
- EXO 25:37 ~ God instructed Moses to make 7 lamps (the original Menorah) to light the Ark of the Covenant.
- EXO 29:37 ~ God instructed Moses to make an atonement sacrifice on the altar over the course of 7 days.
- LEV 4:6 ~ God instructed Moses that the anointed priest should sprinkle the blood of the sacrifice 7 times before the veil of the sanctuary.
- LEV 8:33 ~ God instructed Moses that the priest should not exit the sanctuary for 7 days.
- LEV 13:4 ~ God instructed Moses that those with signs of leprosy would be quarantined for 7 days.
- LEV 15:13 ~ God instructed Moses that a man having an issue (i.e., venereal disease) who is determined to be cleansed, must continue to cleanse himself and his clothes in quarantine for 7 more days.
- LEV 23 ~ God instructed Moses that there would be 7 feasts to be celebrated every year.
- LEV 23:5–6,8,15–36 ~ The 14th day of the first month is the Passover feast. God instructed Moses that after the 7 days of Unleavened Bread and the holy convocation on the 7th day (First Fruits), to count 7 weeks (49 days) and then offer a meat sacrifice on the 50th day (Pentecost). And the first day of the 7th month will be a day of celebration, and the tenth day of the 7th month will be the Day of Atonement, and the fifteenth day of the 7th month will be the Feast of Tabernacles while for 7 days sacrifices will be made.
- LEV 25:1–13 ~ God instructed Moses that the 7th year in the new land would be a year of rest for all, and to repeat the year of jubilee 7 more times for 7 years. Moses was to count 7 Sabbaths (weeks) of years (49).
- LEV 26:18–28 ~ God said, "I will punish 7 times those sinners who oppose me."
- NUM 12:14–15 ~ Miriam was shamed for 7 days.
- NUM 23:1 ~ Balaam said to Balak, "Build me 7 alters and prepare 7 oxen and 7 rams for sacrifice."
- DEU 7:1–2 ~ Seven nations were driven out of Canaan and/or destroyed by the Israelites.
- DEU 15:1–14 ~ God instructed Moses that all debts would be forgiven at the end of every 7 years.
- JOS 6:4,15–16 ~ God instructed Joshua that 7 priests must carry 7 trumpets of ram horns, and on the 7th day circle Jericho 7 times, blowing the trumpets. On the 7th day they did as Joshua said and after the 7th time around the city the people shouted and trumpeted, and the walls of the city collapsed.
- JDG 16:7,13,19 ~ Samson's hair had 7 braids.
- 1 KI 6:38 ~ It took Solomon 7 years to complete the temple.
- 2 KI 5:10,14 ~ Elisha sent a messenger to Naaman telling him to wash in the Jordan river 7 times and he would be cleansed of leprosy, and it worked as Elisha said it would.
- 1 CH 2:13 ~ David was the 7th son of Jesse.
- JOB 2:13 ~ Job mourned with his friends, without speaking for 7 days and nights.
- JOB 42:13 ~ After his health was restored to him, Job had 7 sons (and 3 daughters).
- PRO 6:16–19 ~ These six things the Lord hates; yes 7 are an abomination to Him: pride, lies, murder, wickedness, mischief, false accusations, and troublemakers.

- JER 25:11–12 ~ The land will be laid to waste and the people will serve the king of Babylon 70 years.
- EZE 39:9,12 ~ God told Ezekiel that Magog would burn, that the people would burn weapons for 7 years, and that it would take 7 months to bury the bodies.
- DAN 4:32–34 ~ King Nebuchadnezzar acted like a lunatic for 7 years and then repented.
- DAN 7:24–25 ~ The ten horns are the ten kings that will rise up; and another will come who will subdue three kings. This king will speak against God and will wear-out God's saints; he will change the laws and the times. He will be in control for 3 ½ years.
- DAN 9:2 ~ I, Daniel understood by books the number of the years, whereof the word of the Lord came to Jeremiah the prophet that God would accomplish in 70 years the desolation of Jerusalem.
- DAN 9:23–27 ~ From the beginning of the restoration of Jerusalem to the coming of the anointed prince will be 7 weeks. He will confirm the covenant with many in 7 days. During that week He will cause the sacrifice to cease and will destroy the abominations, until they are consumed.
- DAN 12:7,11 ~ God told Daniel that it would be 3 ½ years that the holy people would be scattered. The time from when the sacrifice is taken away until the abomination that makes desolate would be 3 ½ years.
- AMO 5:8 ~ God told Amos to prophesy as follows: Seek Him (the Lord) that makes the 7 stars of the constellation Orion, who turns the shadow of death into a new morning, and who turns darkness into light.
- MIC 5:5 ~ God told Micah to prophesy as follows: When the Assyrian treads into our palaces, we will raise against him 7 shepherds and eight principal men.
- ZEC 3:8–9 ~ God said to Joshua, "I will bring forth my servant the Branch. This cornerstone, which I have shown to Joshua, will have 7 eyes. The engraving will show that I have removed the sin of that land in a single day."
- ZEC 4:2,10 ~ The angel of God showed Zechariah a gold candlestick with a bowl on top and 7 lamps with 7 pipes coming from it, and said it represented the 7 eyes of the Lord which keep a watchful eye over the entire earth.
- MAT 1:17 ~ The number of generations from Abraham to David were 14, from David to the fall of Babylon were 14, and from the fall of Babylon to Christ were 14.
- MAT 18:21–22 ~ Peter asked Jesus, "How many times should I forgive someone who does me wrong, 7 times?" Jesus replied, "No, 70 times 7."
- MAR 8:20 ~ After feeding over four thousand people using 7 loaves, the disciples gathered 7 baskets of fragments.
- LUK 4:25 ~ Elijah stopped the rain for 3 ½ years.
- ACT 6:2–5 ~ The twelve apostles gathered together more disciples of Christ; 7 men were selected from the group because they were honest, wise, and filled with the Holy Spirit. These men were appointed to minister to the people.
- ACT 13:19 ~ God helped the Israelites destroy 7 nations in Canaan before they divided the Promised Land (DEU 7).
- JAM 5:17–18 ~ Elijah stopped the rain for 3 ½ years.
- REV 1:4 ~ John sent his message of Revelation to the 7 churches of Asia.
- REV 1:11–13,16,20 ~ I (John) turned to the voice that called me to write to the 7 churches and I saw 7 candlesticks, and in the middle was the Son of God. He had in His right hand 7 stars, and from His mouth went a sharp, double-edged sword, and His face shined like the sun. The 7 stars represented the angels of the 7 churches; the 7 candlesticks represented the 7 churches.

- REV 4:5 ~ From the throne in heaven proceeded lightning and thunder with voices. There were 7 lamps of fire burning before the throne, which were the 7 spirits of God.
- REV 5:1,6 ~ In the right hand of Him who sat on the throne was a book which was sealed with 7 seals. In the middle stood the Lamb that was slain having 7 horns and 7 eyes that were the 7 spirits of God sent throughout the earth.
- REV 8:2,6 ~ There were 7 angels standing before God and they were given 7 trumpets; each angel sounded their trumpet in order.
- REV 10:1–4 ~ A mighty angel came down and roared like a lion. Then 7 thunders spoke, but I (John) was instructed not to write what the 7 thunders said.
- REV 11:2–3,7,9–11 ~ God said the Gentiles would stomp the temple into the ground for 3 ½ years. Then God would give power to two witnesses to prophesy 3 ½ years; when they had finished their testimony, they would be killed. People of all nations would view their unburied bodies and rejoice at the death of the two witnesses who prophesied against them. After 3 ½ days, the Spirit of God would enter them and they would rise from the dead, causing great fear to spread; then they would ascend into heaven.
- REV 12:3 ~ A great red dragon appeared in heaven having 7 heads and ten horns, and 7 crowns upon the 7 heads.
- REV 12:13–14 ~ The dragon persecuted the woman and the child, so she was given wings to fly away into the wilderness, where she was nourished for 3 ½ years.
- REV 13:1,5 ~ A beast rose out of the sea which had 7 heads and ten horns, and upon the ten horns were ten crowns, and upon each of the heads were the names of blasphemy. Power was given to the beast for forty-two months (3 ½ years).
- REV 15:1,7 ~ Seven marvelous angels appeared in heaven having 7 plagues to deliver the wrath of God. One of four beasts gave the angels 7 golden vials filled with God's wrath.
- REV 17:9–11 ~ The angel explained the mystery of the beast with the 7 heads as follows: The 7 heads represented 7 mountains on which the new Babylon sits (the great whore that sits over many waters). And there are 7 kings, five have fallen, one is currently in power, and one is yet to come; and the 7th will reign for a short time. The beast is the eighth king and was also one of the 7.

Number 8

Eight is significant primarily because it is the number following seven. Eight often finishes a sequence, event, or matter. For example, Holy Week continues over the span of 8 days for Jews and Christians alike (see *Holy Week* in the Keyword Index).

- GEN 7; 1 PE 3:20; 2 PE 2:5 ~ Eight souls were saved from the great flood. Noah was the 8th person to be saved.
- GEN 17:12; GEN 21:4; LEV 12:3; LUK 1:59–60; LUK 2:21; ACT 7:8; PHP 3:5 ~ God instructed that male infants be circumcised the 8th day. Christ Himself was circumcised on the 8th day.
- EXO 22:30; LEV 9:1–2; LEV 14:10,23; LEV 15:14,29; LEV 22:27; NUM 6:10; EXO 43:27 ~ The 8th day was a day of holy convocation in which the first fruits were offered to the Lord.
- 1 KI 8:66 ~ The 8th day the feasting and celebrations were over and everyone went home rejoicing.
- 2 CH 7:9; NEH 8:18 ~ On the 8th day, following the seven-day feast, there was a solemn assembly of the people.

- MIC 5:5 ~ God told Micah to prophesy as follows: When the Assyrian treads into our palaces, we will raise against him seven shepherds and 8 principal men.
- REV 17:10–11 ~ There are seven kings, five have fallen, one is currently in power, and one is yet to come; and the seventh will reign for a short time. The beast is the 8th king and was also one of the seven.

Number 10

Ten, and multiples of 10, represent totality such as the tally in a list. The number 10 relates to the 1/10 of our total income or increase that belongs to the Lord (tithe). It also refers to the 10 kings who will rule with the beast during the latter days. Ten cubed ($10^3 = 1000$) represents the millennial reign of Christ and the saints (see information concerning the number 1000). Note there were 10 plagues brought upon Egypt and 10 commandments written on stone by the hand of God when the Israelites fled Egypt. Thus, we see a typical counterbalance as is often the case with certain numbers.

- GEN 14:20 ~ Abraham gave tithes (1/10) of everything he had to King Melchizedek.
- GEN 28:22 ~ Jacob set a stone to mark the location of his vision and the holy temple of God. He promised he would give 1/10 (tithe) of all he owned to God.
- EXO 6–10 ~ God sent 10 plagues against Pharaoh's Egypt: blood, frogs, gnats, flies, animal diseases, boils, hail, locust, darkness, and death of the firstborn.
- NUM 14:22–23 ~ God said they would not see the promised land because 10 of the twelve spies had returned with a negative report contrary to what God had already assured them. Only Caleb and Joshua gave a positive report of the vulnerability of those inhabiting the land and the reliability of promises coming from God. Note that 10 of the twelve tribes of Israel became rebellious after the death of King Solomon; these 10 split-off from the other two tribes forming two separate kingdoms (2 CH 10).
- DEU 14:22 ~ The Jews were commanded in the Law to tithe (also LEV 27:30).
- DAN 7:7–8 ~ The fourth beast had 10 horns; three horns were replaced with one. The 10 horns represent 10 kings; another king will rise and subdue three kings. (see also the 10 toes in DAN 2:41)
- ZEC 8:23 ~ In those days, 10 men from the nations of every language will take hold; and they will say to the Jews, let us go with you because God is with you.
- LUK 17:11–18 ~ Jesus healed 10 lepers. After showing themselves to the priest that they were healed, only one of them returned to thank and praise Jesus. Jesus questioned why the other nine had not returned to give thanks to God.
- REV 2:10 ~ Jesus said, "Satan will throw some of you Christians into prison to be tried; and you will have tribulation for 10 days. If you endure unto death, I will give you a crown of life."
- REV 12:3 ~ The red dragon had seven crowned heads and 10 horns.
- REV 13:1; REV 17:12 ~ A beast will rise from the sea with seven heads and 10 horns bearing the names of blasphemy. The 10 horns represent 10 kings which have not received a kingdom as yet, but will rule one hour with the beast.

CHAPTER EIGHT

Number 12

Twelve is a very important number associated with membership. It refers to the 12 judges of the Lord in heaven in the NT, where 12 judges will sit on 12 thrones. This coincides with the 12 judges of Israel in the OT. There were 12 tribes of Israel corresponding to the 12 sons of Jacob; there also were 12 tribes of Ishmael. Equally as relevant are the 12 apostles of Christ. Thus, the number 12 may imply the elect or chosen, as well as twelve-squared (144). Multiply 12 times 1000 (12,000), or 12 squared times 1000 (144,000); these numbers reflect the chosen of the Lord from the tribes of Israel during the latter days. Two times 12 is reflected in the 24 elders mentioned in Revelation. Also 24 times 1000 (24,000) has represented those selected to die.

- GEN 17:20; GEN 25:13–16 ~ God said to Abraham, "I will bless your son Ishmael also, and will make him fruitful. I will multiply his descendants. I will make him a great nation, and he will give birth to 12 princes."
- GEN 35:22–26 ~ Jacob had 12 sons: Reuben, Simeon, Levi, Judah, Issachar, Zebulun, Joseph, Benjamin, Dan, Naphtali, Gad and Asher.
- GEN 49:28 ~ The 12 sons of Jacob represent the 12 tribes of Israel.
- EXO 15:27; NUM 32:9 ~ There were 12 fountains and seventy palm trees at the encampment of the Israelites.
- NUM 25:1–13 ~ God sent a plague to punish Israel for sinning with the Midianites; 24,000 died.
- NUM 31:5 ~ From each tribe, 1000 men were prepared for battle (12,000 in all).
- JDG 3–13 ~ There were 12 judges who judged God's people: Othniel, Ehud, Shamgar, Deborah, Gideon, Tola, Jair, Jephthah, Ibzan, Elon, Abdon, and Samson. Following the judges came the era of kings ushered in by Samuel who anointed the first two kings (Saul and David).
- JDG 21:10 ~ There were 12,000 valiant men poised for battle.
- 1 CH 25:1–31 ~ There were 12 times 24 people (288) assigned to make music in God's house with 12 brothers and sons per lot.
- 1 CH 27:1–34 ~ Each tribe of Israel assumed the duties of the guard on one of the 12 months of the year (24,000 guards per army).
- EZE 48:31–34 ~ The New Jerusalem had three gates at each of the four sides for a total of 12 gates. (also REV 21:13)
- MAT 10:2–4; MAR 3:14–19; LUK 6:13–16; ACT 1:13 ~ Jesus had 12 apostles: Peter and his brother Andrew, James and John (sons of Zebedee), Philip, Bartholomew (possibly also called Nathanael), Thomas, Matthew (the publican), James (son of Alphaeus), Thaddaeus (Lebbaeus; possibly also called Judas), Simon (the Canaanite), and Judas Iscariot (who betrayed Jesus and was replaced).
- MAT 14:20; MAR 8:19 ~ After Jesus fed five thousand with the five loaves and two fishes, the crumbs were gathered and filled 12 baskets.
- MAT 19:28 ~ Jesus told the 12 apostles that they shall each sit on a throne and judge the 12 tribes of Israel.
- MAR 6:37–44; MAR 8:17–21 ~ When Jesus fed the five thousand, 12 baskets full of fragments were collected. When He fed the four thousand, seven baskets full of fragments were collected.
- LUK 2:42 ~ When Jesus was 12 years old, He and His parents went to Jerusalem for the Passover. The caravan left without Jesus and when they realized He wasn't with them they searched for Him, finding Him in the temple.

- ACT 13:20 ~ God gave the Jews judges, until the time of Samuel the prophet (of which there were 12 that preceded Samuel).
- REV 4:4,10; REV 5:8,14; REV 11:16; REV 19:4 ~ There were 24 elders serving the Lord and worshipping Him.
- REV 7:5–8 ~ There were 12,000 saints that were sealed as God's servants from each of the 12 tribes of Israel (144,000 in all).
- REV 12:1 ~ A great wonder appeared in heaven: a woman clothed with the sun, the moon under her feet, and upon her head a crown of 12 stars.
- REV 14:3 ~ The 144,000 sang a new song; nobody could learn the song except them.
- REV 21:9–12,14,16 ~ The bride, who is the Lamb's wife (the Church) in the new Jerusalem, had 12 gates, guarded by 12 angels, with the names of the 12 tribes of Israel written upon them. The wall of the city had 12 foundations, bearing the names of the 12 apostles. The city measured 12,000 furlongs in length, breadth, and height.
- REV 22:1–2 ~ In John's vision of heaven, he saw the Tree of Life, which bore 12 different types of fruit each month (12 months a year).

Number 20

The number 20 is significant primarily because it is half of 40. Since 40 is the traditional number of years in a generation, 20 would be half of a generation. In the Old Testament, 20 was the age of adulthood, that is, the age of consent and self-accountability.

- NUM 1:3,18–22; NUM 26:2–4 ~ Men past the age of 20 were eligible for going to war.
- NUM 14:29–30 ~ Because of their sin at Sinai and their doubting of the Lord's promises, everyone past the age of 20 had to wander the wilderness until their death (they wandered the wilderness 40 years). Only Joshua and Caleb were spared of those who were older than 20 when the Lord punished the Israelites.
- JDG 15:15–20; JDG 16:29–31 ~ Samson was a judge for 20 years.
- 1 SA 6:19 ~ The Philistines had the Ark of the Covenant for 20 years and it brought them bad luck.
- 1 KI 9:10–13; 2 CH 8:1 ~ It took Solomon 20 years to build the temple and the palace. And Solomon gave King Hiram of Tyre 20 cities as collateral for the gold he borrowed.
- 1 CH 23:24–27; 1 CH 27:23; EZR 3:8 ~ Levites began their ministry at the age of 20.

Number 40

The number 40 appears several times and implies the duration of God's instruction or influence. This influence can be 40 days or 40 years, depending on the circumstances. In the Old Testament, 40 years was generally the duration of one generation. Note that 40 is the number of days of Lent (prior to Easter) and the number of days until Christ's ascension (after Easter). Also, 40 times 10 (400) represents the duration of God's curse (GEN 15:13; ACT 7:6).

- GEN 7:4,17 ~ It rained 40 days and nights causing a great flood.
- GEN 50:1,3 ~ Joseph was deeply saddened when his father Jacob died. He mourned the death for 40 days, because the custom was to allow the embalmed body to rest in state for 40 days.
- EXO 7:7 ~ Moses was 80 years old, and Aaron was 83, when they came before Pharaoh (to appeal to him to free the Israelites). Moses was 40 when he left Egypt and 120 when he died.
- EXO 16:35 ~ The children of Israel ate manna 40 years.

- EXO 24:18; EXO 34:28 ~ Moses fasted on Mt. Sinai 40 days and nights, on two different occasions, to receive the Ten Commandments.
- NUM 14:33–34; NUM 32:13; DEU 9:18 ~ Those over the age of 20 would be condemned to wander in the wilderness 40 years, one for each day of sin committed while Moses was on the mountain (NUM 13), and one for each day the 12 spies reconnoitered the land.
- DEU 25:3 ~ Capital punishment consisted of 40 stripes with the whip (or 40 minus 1 = 39).
- DEU 31:2; DEU 34:7 ~ Moses was 120 years old when he died. His life consisted of three phases, each of 40 years: Egypt, Midian, Wilderness (EXO 7; DEU 9; ACT 7).
- JDG 3:11,30; JDG 5:31 ~ There were 40 years of peace under Othniel, 80 under Ehud, and 40 under Deborah.
- JDG 8:28; 13:1 ~ There were 40 years of peace under Gideon, for he was a good man; then there were 40 years of suffering under the Philistines, for they were evil.
- 1 SA 4:18 ~ Eli the priest was in charge for 40 years.
- 2 SA 5:4; 1 KI 11:42; 2 KI 12:1; 1 CH 29:27; 2 CH 14:1; ACT 13:18,21 – Saul, David, Solomon, Johoash, Joash and many other kings ruled Israel for 40 years.
- 1 KI 19:8 ~ Elijah journeyed 40 days and nights to Mt. Horeb (Sinai).
- EZE 29:12 ~ Egypt was laid to waste 40 years.
- JON 3:4–5 ~ As God directed, Jonah went to Nineveh and warned them that they had 40 days to repent.
- MAT 1:1–17 ~ There were 40 generations separating Abraham and Jesus.
- MAT 4:2; MAR 1:13; LUK 4:2 ~ Jesus fasted 40 days and nights in the wilderness, and was tempted during that time by Satan.
- ACT 1:3 ~ Jesus appeared after his resurrection for 40 days.
- ACT 7:6 ~ The Jews were in captivity over 400 years.
- ACT 7:22–36 ~ Moses was educated by the Egyptians, and was known for his words and deeds. He was a full 40 years old when he was driven in his heart to come to the aid of the Israelites. He hoped they would understand that God had sent him to deliver them, but they did not. They rejected him, and made known to him that they knew he had murdered the Egyptian. Moses fled to Midian, where he lived for 40 more years. It was during that time when the Lord's angel visited him in the burning bush, commissioning him to return to Egypt and take command of the Israelites. When their freedom was gained, Moses showed he possessed the power of the Holy Spirit by the many miracles he performed, as the Israelites roamed the wilderness those 40 years.

Number 70

The number 70 has different meanings: 70 elders or ministers of the Lord versus 70 ministers of evil; also 70 years of destruction. Note that the Sanhedrin consisted of 70 elders. Seven and ten, numbers that are symbolic of completion, unity, or totality, can be multiplied together to produce 70.

- GEN 46:27; EXO 1:5 ~ All the souls that came from Jacob's seed to live in Egypt numbered 70, including Joseph and his family.
- EXO 15:27; NUM 32:9 ~ There were twelve fountains and 70 palm trees at the encampment.
- EXO 24:1 ~ God said to Moses, "Come to me, Moses, along with Aaron, Nadab, Abihu, and 70 of the elders of Israel, and worship me" (also DEU 10:22).
- NUM 11:16,24–25 ~ God said to Moses, "Gather 70 of the elders of Israel and bring them to the tabernacle." Moses told the people what the Lord said, and gathered the 70 elders in the

tabernacle. Then the Lord came in a cloud and spoke to Moses, and gave His Spirit to the 70 elders; and when the elders received the Holy Spirit, they prophesied without ceasing.
- JDG 1:7 ~ Seventy kings of the Canaanites had their thumbs and big toes cut off.
- JDG 8:30; JDG 9:1–6,56 ~ God destroyed Abimelech and the men of Shechem for murdering the 70 sons of Gideon (except one who escaped).
- 2 KI 10:1–7 ~ King Ahab had 70 sons in Samaria. King Jehu wrote a letter to the elders and rulers of Jezreel telling them to place the best of Ahab's sons on the throne to defend them. Then Jehu wrote a second time, telling them to bring him the heads of all 70 of Ahab's sons if the Samaritans would rather yield to King Jehu. As soon as the letter arrived, the rulers killed Ahab's 70 sons and sent their heads in baskets to Jezreel.
- 2 CH 36:21 ~ The Babylonian captivity lasted 70 years.
- ISA 23:15,17 ~ In those days, the kingdom of Tyre will be forgotten for 70 years. After the 70 years, the king will wail like a prostitute, and Tyre will commit fornication with all the kingdoms of the world.
- JER 25:11–12 ~ The land will be desolated, and the nations will serve Babylon for 70 years. After the 70 years are over, God will punish the king of Babylon and that nation for their wickedness, and will utterly destroy everything.
- EZE 8:10–12 ~ I (Ezekiel) saw all kinds of creeping things, abominable beasts, and many idols of Israel, portrayed on the wall. Seventy of the ancient elders of Israel stood, burning incense. Then God said, "Have you seen what the elders of Israel do behind my back with their graven images and idols? They say that I can't see them; they think I have forsaken the earth."
- DAN 9:2,16,21,24–27 ~ I (Daniel) began to understand the prophecy of Jeremiah concerning the 70 years of desolation in Jerusalem (JER 25). I prayed for Jerusalem and the holy mountain, that God would forgive His people and turn away His anger and fury. While I was praying, the angel Gabriel came to me to help me understand this vision. The angel said that it will take 70 weeks ($7 + 62 + 1 = 70$) for the transgressions to end. Then reconciliation will occur, everlasting righteousness will come, and the Holy One will be anointed king. From the beginning of the restoration of Jerusalem until the coming of the Messiah will be 7 weeks. The rebuilding of the streets and walls, even in perilous times, will take 62 weeks. After the 62 weeks, the Messiah will be cut off, and the evil ones will destroy the city and the sanctuary. This will be followed by a flood, war, and desolation. Then God will confirm His covenant with many in one week. During that week, all offerings and sacrifices will cease, and all abominations will be destroyed and consumed.
- MAT 18:21–22 ~ Peter asked Jesus, "How many times should we forgive another, 7 times." Jesus replied, "Not 7, but 70 times 7." (also DAN 9).
- LUK 10:1,17 ~ Jesus appointed 70 disciples to preach in every city, sending them in teams of two. The 70 returned after their ministry with joy, saying that even demons obeyed them when they invoked the name of Jesus Christ.

Number 1000

If ten is the number of a whole, then 10^3 must mean ultimate completion of that whole, sort of like the three-dimensions of space. The number 1000 is used frequently in the Bible to represent an extraordinarily large but unspecified amount or period of time or number of people. For example, 1000 years could represent the duration of a biblical era (such as the millennial reign). However, time is irrelevant to God, as one day is as a thousand years and a thousand years as one day.

- NUM 31:4–6 ~ From each of the tribes of Israel, 1000 men were selected to go to war.
- DEU 1:11 ~ May the Lord God of your fathers multiply you 1000 times and bless you as He has promised.
- DEU 7:9; 1 CH 16:15; PSA 105:8 ~ Remember that God is faithful, and He keeps His covenant and shows His mercy to those who love Him for 1000 generations. He remembers His covenant forever, the Word that He commanded for 1000 generations.
- JOS 23:10 ~ One man shall chase 1000, for the Lord goes with you to fight on your side just like He promised.
- JDG 15:15–16 ~ Samson killed 1000 Philistines with the jawbone of an ass.
- 1 SA 18:13 ~ Saul made David the captain over 1000 men.
- 1 KI 3:4; 2 CH 1:6 ~ Solomon offered 1000 burnt offerings upon the altar in the high ground of Gibeon.
- 1 CH 16:15–17 ~ God remembers His covenant forever, the Word He commanded, for 1000 generations.
- PSA 90:4 ~ A 1000 years to God are but as yesterday when it has passed, and like a single watch in the night.
- ISA 60:22 ~ The least among you will become 1000, and the smallest among you a mighty nation. I am the Lord; in time I will do this swiftly.
- EZE 47:3–6 ~ There was an enormous river emanating from the temple. We waded out 1000 cubits where the water was ankle deep. After another 1000 cubits the water was to the knees. After another 1000 cubits it was to the waist. After another 1000 cubits it was deep enough to swim under; and the river went on and on. It had become a river that I could not pass over.
- DAN 7:10 ~ A fiery stream flowed before Him. Thousands upon thousands ministered to Him, and 10,000 times 10,000 stood before Him. The judgment was set, and the books were opened.
- 2 PE 3:8 ~ Understand this, that a single day to the Lord is like 1000 years, and 1000 years like one day.
- REV 5:11 ~ And I heard the voice of many angels surrounding the throne, the living creatures, and the elders. And they numbered 10,000 times 10,000, and thousands upon thousands.
- REV 14:3 ~ The 144,000 sang a new song; nobody could learn the song except them.
- REV 20:1–6 ~ And the angel grabbed the dragon, that old serpent, which is the devil and Satan, and bound him 1000 years. And Satan was thrown into the bottomless pit for the entire 1000 years; then he was released for a short while. And I saw judges sitting on thrones; and I saw the souls of those that had been beheaded because they witnessed for Jesus and for the Word of God. They had not worshipped the beast or his image, neither had they received his mark on their foreheads or hands. And they lived and reigned with Christ 1000 years. Blessed and holy are people that have part in the first resurrection for they will not experience the second death. But they will be priests of God and of Christ, and will reign with Him 1000 years.

Summary: It is fair to say that numbers are interesting to study for they introduce an element of symbolism to scripture. An equally fascinating aspect is how numbers often depict dichotomies, similar to opposite ends of a continuum or spectrum. But it is senseless to read more into numbers than is there, like counting words, letters, or syllables to imply or add unwritten truth. The OT was written in the Hebrew language; they sometimes numbered letters but this did not add separate meaning, only validation. The NT was written in Greek where the letters were not numbered and did not provide additional validation or meaning than provided in the words.

FOR FURTHER STUDY

The purpose of this book is to get people interested in studying and researching God's Word. There is much to learn, and every reader will increase in knowledge each time he or she picks up the Holy Bible and examines it with an open heart. The studies that follow were prepared to encourage the reader to delve further into the Bible during their continued exploration of the scriptures. The first set of studies require the reader to look up the supportive scriptures because only the citations are provided. The second set of studies are formatted so that some scriptures are provided and others are not. It is recommended that the reader look up all of the referenced scriptures in their own Bible. Hopefully, you already have been looking up passages in your personal Bible to verify and clarify what you have read in this book. I mean, why take someone else's word for something when you have God's Word on it? Compare the Holy Bible to everything that people preach, teach, or write regarding spiritual truth; because there is only one infallible source of revelation and truth and that is God.

As one grasps the veritable depth and breadth of the Bible, he or she realizes it is impossible to fathom the vastness of it in a single reading, or even a dozen readings. But the enlightenment of your spirit, the illumination of your understanding, and the increased comprehending of God's magnificence will leave you hungry for more, and that is the point: more is better. God's reservoir of knowledge is available to you anytime you feel like dipping into it. And it provides a wellspring of wisdom that never runs dry, and always quenches your thirst for truth. God's Word is a light that will positively impact your life in every aspect for as long as you live; which will be forever if you believe what you are reading.

I encourage people to develop their own studies, diving evermore deeply into scriptural doctrines, topics, and events. Memorize favorite passages and be prepared to apply and recite them, citation and verse. Share God's Word with your family and friends, teach others, and equip yourself to defend the faith to anyone who asks (1 PE 3:15). You will be amazed how God uses you to impact the lives of others, opening their hearts and minds. Remember, it is futile to argue against the truth, particularly when it comes directly from the Lord God Almighty.

Prepare to defend the faith by studying God's Word. Are you familiar with the term *Apologetics*? That is precisely how the word is defined: defense of the faith. Bible study prepares a person to witness Jesus Christ and empowers a person to exercise his or her spiritual gifts to His glory and to the edification of His Church.

The principal objective of this book is to equip the reader with the truth in order to refute that which is false; correct those who are misinformed or mistaken; uplift and instruct those who are beaten down with sin, doubt, or despair; and build up the church which embodies the bride of Christ (2 TI 3:16).

CHAPTER EIGHT

Bible Study: Is Jesus God?

Dissenters and scoffers of Christianity seldom have actually read the Bible, much less taken the time to study it or comprehend its meaning in entirety. Their tendency is to make certain assumptions based on verses taken out of context or based on a popular narrative which is dead wrong. Many would argue that the phrases Son of God (DAN 3:25; MAT 4:1–11; LUK 1:26–35; 1 JO 5:10,20) and Son of Man (DAN 7:13; MAT 25:31; MAR 12:1–12: JOH 3:13) do not suggest Jesus and God are united. This is a gross misunderstanding of scripture, since the doctrine of Christ as the Godman is well established and fundamental to the Christian faith. Unbelievers in general and atheists in particular allege that Jesus never professed to be God. However, Jesus stated that He is God rather matter-of-factly on numerous occasions. There are episodes where Christ declared in no uncertain terms that He is equal with God (JOH 5:19–24), they are One (JOH 10:30), and there can be only one God (MAR 12:29).

It is particularly important to note that, not only did Jesus proclaim Himself Lord, God, and Messiah, but the spiritual leaders of the Jews constantly sought to murder Jesus because of such proclamations (MAT 12:1–14;). They knew Jesus was claiming to be God and had Him crucified because of it (MAT 26:62–66). Such was considered blasphemy, a cardinal sin worthy of death according to the Mosaic Law (LEV 24:16; MAT 26:57–66). By the way, the death sentence was typically carried out by stoning the perpetrator (read 1 KI 21:10–13; JOH 10:24–33; ACT 7:55–60), which was attempted more than once against Jesus for declaring He was God (JOH 8:52–59; JOH 10:27–33). Of course, in His case it wasn't blasphemy because it was true.

The apostle John cites many occurrences in which Jesus proclaimed Himself God. I especially cherish the Gospel of John because a great deal of it is recorded in Jesus's own words. Examine the following passages in which Jesus refers to Himself as equal with God the Father, as Lord of all, possessing the Holy Spirit, who came from heaven and was not of this world.

JOH 6:35–42   JOH 8:23–29   JOH 13:12–20   JOH 14:6–21   JOH 15:26   JOH 18:33–38

God identified Himself to Abraham and Moses as the eternal I AM (GEN 15:1; GEN 26:24; EXO 3:14; MAT 22:31–32). Christ also referred to Himself as I AM (JOH 4:25–26). The following passages give witness to the fact that Christ is exactly who He says He is.

MAT 28:18–20   MAR 14:61–64   JOH 8:31–33,51–59   JOH 11:25   PHP 2:1–12   HEB 1:1–3

You may find it interesting to know that, not only did Christ claim to be God, God also claimed to be Christ, the Redeemer, the Messiah. They were together since the beginning and will be for all time (ISA 48:16–17; JOH 1:1–14; JOH 7:28–29; COL 2:9; 1 JO 2:23; REV 1:8,18). The most prolific Messianic prophet of the Old Testament was Isaiah. He references God's Messiah frequently, detailing the birth, life, suffering, death, and resurrection of Christ (read ISA 7:14; ISA 53:1–12). Check out the scriptures below indicating clearly that God Himself is the Savior, and He is sending that Savior into the world so that we may know Him.

ISA 9:6–8   ISA 11:2   ISA 42:1   ISA 43:10–11   ISA 44:6,24   ISA 45:11–13   ISA 47:4

God is great (JOB 36:26; PSA 96:4; PSA 135:5; 1 JO 5:9) and God is good (PSA 100:5; JER 33:11; NAH 1:7; JOH 10:7–18). In fact, nobody else is really either. While there are varying forms of greatness and goodness, which everyone possesses from time to time, nobody can claim to be perfect all the time except God (MAR 10:18). Everything God and Jesus creates or says is not just good or great but perfect and excellent.

GEN 1:10,12,18,21,25   ISA 42:5–6   ISA 65:17–18   MAL 2:10   EPH 3:9   COL 1:16   REV 4:11

Bible Study: How Do We Listen to God?

Since we are allowed a personal relationship with God, we can communicate with Him the same way we communicate with one another: talk to Him and listen to Him. We speak to Him through prayer and He speaks to us through His written Word, especially the words of Christ, and through the words of ministers ordained by God to preach and teach the good news. The most important thing is to listen to what He tells you and not question His motives. Prophets such as Moses and David did as God commanded (EXO 18:23; DEU 4:5; 1 CH 14:16) and were richly blessed; but they were severely punished when they did not do as God commanded (NUM 20:8–12; 2 SA 12:7–13). Our Father in heaven disciplines His people just as any loving father does. The disciples of Jesus did as He commanded (MAT 21:6; JOH 16:33; PHP 4:7) and received that peace which surpasses all understanding. You will obtain spiritual treasures if you listen and obey; but if you do not listen and obey, you won't receive them.

In this Bible study, we will address some of the things God tells us to do. My advice to everyone is this: just do it! Notice how, when we follow His orders, there is a special reward attached to each command. Bible verses are listed that clarify what God says we must do; it is recommended that the reader review the context of what is going on before and after the particular passage to get the gist of how it applied when it was written and how it still applies today. As stated above, when the Lord speaks, things happen (GEN 1). And when He says to do something, don't put it off. Whenever Christ is speaking or giving commands, it is the same as God the Father saying it (JOH 8:51; JOH 14:15; JOH 15:10,15). That is, the Bible tells us to do what the Father says and to do what the Son says, seeing how they are persons of the same God, and both speak to us via the Holy Spirit which bears witness to the truth (1 JO 5:3–7). Look up the following passages explaining these essential fundamentals.

ISA 18:3   ISA 48:16–17   JER 29:13–14   MAT 17:5   MAR 8:18   JOH 2:5   HEB 11:6

The Old Testament is largely God's Law for humanity; it is a guide to help us understand His will. The testament of the Law points to its fulfillment, prophesied to take place when Messiah comes which is proclaimed in the New Testament of Jesus Christ. Though Christ has already come and paid the penalty for disobedience, that doesn't mean we quit trying our level best to be obedient to God (MAT 5:18; ROM 3:31; ROM 6:15). If we make an honest and earnest effort to keep God's commandments, He will be merciful to us and bless us. Of course, we are talking, not only about the Ten Commandments (EXO 34:28), but all of God's laws, precepts, and instructions (PSA 119:4; JER 31:31–34; HEB 8:10). And we also are to obey the laws passed by our government, for God has given them authority to enforce the law and maintain order (ROM 13:1–6).

EXO 20:6   PSA 119:73   PRO 8:32   MAT 19:17   ACT 5:29   ROM 6:16   2 JO 1:6

The greatest commandment of God is to love Him with all your heart, soul, and spirit (DEU 6:5). Love, it is written, is the fulfillment of the Law (DEU 11:1; DEU 30:16,20; ROM 13:10). As you can see, this love is to be extended to others (MAT 22:37–40). So, love God above all others, and love others as yourself (love all humans equally including you). If you were able to love unconditionally as desired by God, you would not sin against Him or anybody else, thereby fulfilling the Law and prophecy just as Christ who is the example of perfect love and obedience.

Because we cannot resist temptation, and we fall into sin on a daily basis, we are unworthy. Christ, being without sin, is the only one who is worthy. By His sacrifice, He has made people worthy by cleansing our souls with His precious blood, thereby imputing on us His righteousness in exchange for our sins (ROM 3:20–25; 2 CO 5:18–21). Thus, in order to receive justification under the Law, we must believe that Christ has redeemed us from its curse (ISA 43:10–11; ROM 1:17; GAL 3:13). That is, God expects faith from us which is demonstrated by a change of heart, a change in thinking, possibly a change in lifestyle, as well as a firm commitment to Christ (DEU 13:17–18; PRO 3:5–6; 2 CO 5:17).

In order to receive the forgiveness of God, you must acknowledge that you need a Savior and confess your faults and transgressions to Him in prayer (ROM 14:11–12). If you are sincerely sorry, God will know your heart is true, and He will wipe your sins from the record. But remember this: God's mercy is a gift given freely to those who love Him and want to please Him. It is not something to bargain with, as if to say "I'll do this for you God, if you'll do that for me" (*quid pro quo*). God makes it clear that He will test our faith from time to time, but we are not to test God (DEU 6:16; MAT 4:7).

LEV 26:40–42   EZR 10:11–12   PSA 32:5   PRO 28:13   ISA 64:5–6   ROM 10:10   1 JO 1:9

In addition to confessing our sins to God, we are expected to confess our faith as a witness to others. Do not be ashamed or embarrassed to be called a child of God and do not be hesitant to confess your Savior. Otherwise, you really aren't carrying His name. We are to proclaim who and what we are boldly and proudly. After all, who wouldn't be excited to refer to God as "my Dad" (ROM 8:15). Confession of your faith is proof of it, for it puts faith into action. Listening to what God has to say in His Word should be ongoing after that. Sharing the Gospel of Christ will make you wise unto salvation (ROM 1:16).

1 CH 16:8–9   PSA 22:30–31   MAT 10:32–33   ROM 10:9–10   PHP 2:11   1 JO 4:2

Another excellent way to communicate to God and to confess God is to through our worship of Him. We should worship Him in private and also in public by attending church services and Bible studies. God expects it, so never make excuses not to do it for this is an expression of our love of Jesus who is our example of God.

1 CH 16:29   PSA 22:27–28   PSA 95:6   JER 7:2   LUK 4:8   COL 3:16   HEB 10:25

The other ways we demonstrate our obedience to God and our willingness to serve Him is by the way we conduct ourselves in our daily living and the way we relate to others. We are to follow Christ's lead for He is the way to heaven (MAT 8:22; MAR 1:17). He is the light of the world, so believe in that light, walk in that light, and live in that light (PSA 63:8; ISA 2:5; JOH 8:12; JOH 12:35–36). In other words, strive to become more and more like Christ by leading an upright, honorable, and temperate lifestyle, and by exhibiting a humble, friendly, and caring attitude. Others will notice the kind of person you are and it will draw them towards you. And you can do the work of the Lord by showing them the way that was shown to you (JOH 6:29). If we give Him our works, God will give us His thoughts (PRO 16:3).

JOB 1:8   PSA 51:10   PRO 21:21   PRO 28:18   ROM 1:17   1 CO 15:58   1 PE 3:15

God commands us to give of ourselves: time, talent, treasure. These gifts are to be shared with others, and by doing so, we are giving back to God. In a way, we are giving ourselves to God by giving ourselves to others (MAT 25:40,45), so they too can give themselves to Him. Everything we are and everything we have is His, including our very lives (ROM 12:1). And by giving something back, we receive even more gifts, abilities, and blessings (DEU 16:17; MAL 3:8–10; LUK 6:38; 2 CO 9:7). We have been commanded to make disciples (MAT 28:19) by teaching them (EXO 18:20; MAT 28:20). And above all, make sure you teach your children and family the ways of the Lord (DEU 6:6–7; DEU 11:19; PRO 22:6; MAT 19:14). You don't want to make it to heaven only to leave your loved ones behind, do you?

In order to be equipped to witness and serve you must be well grounded in the Bible, especially the Gospel of Jesus Christ. I mean, how are you to teach others if you have not absorbed yourself into His teaching? The Bible is the primary avenue by which we listen to the Lord. If a person has only a passing understanding of scripture it becomes easier to be deceived by false prophets, or fall for wayward interpretations and translations of God's Word (DEU 13:1–4). In other words, if you are going to share the good news, you had better do your homework.

NEH 8:8   EZE 13:3   EZE 44:5   MAT 24:4–5   LUK 9:50   ACT 8:30–31   ROM 16:17

Do you really want a relationship with God? Then all you have to do is recognize that He is there and invite Him into your heart. A great number of people deny that there is a Creator, and many who think there is a God cannot imagine having a personal friendship with Him (PSA 14:1–2). After all, He is the Almighty and we are mere humans. How can we possibly relate to an infinitely powerful and knowledgeable supreme being given that we are inferior and ignorant? Such rationalization will lead one to think it impossible to connect with God and thus, never attempt it. Well, He created us for His pleasure and wants to be known to us, and He wants us to understand His great love for us (PSA 147:11; LUK 12:32; EPH 1:5; REV 4:11). He loves us as any devoted Father loves and protects his children, and all He wants from us is to love Him back (1 JO 3:1–2). And that implies an intimate relationship which is filial.

So, if you want to find God, simply look for Him, listen to Him, and talk to Him. He is always there. All that is required, really, is to acknowledge that fact. The Bible makes it plain and simple: seek Him and you will find Him (ISA 55:6–7). Knock and He will open the door (JOB 31:14; LUK 12:36); and when He comes knocking you must open your heart (JER 9:23–24; REV 3:20). And your reward will be life with Him forever (JOH 20:31), at which time you will be able to talk to Him face to face (1 CO 13:12).

1 CH 16:10–12   2 CH 19:3   PSA 69:32   PRO 3:5–6   ACT 17:22–32   1 JO 4:15–16

Once you get to know God you will find Him to be a very accommodating God. Are you a parent or hoping to become a parent someday? Wouldn't you sacrifice anything and everything for your children? It will be your desire to provide for them, nurture them, cherish them, and see them grow and prosper. You'd give your life to save them would you not? These things our heavenly Father has done for us. As a child of God, you can come to Him with any need or desire, and He will give you the best of everything. Just ask and you will receive.

1 KI 3:5   PSA 145:15–20   ISA 58:2,8–9,14   MAT 21:22   LUK 11:9–13   JOH 15:16   1 JO 3:22

This lesson has focused on listening to God. but communication is not a one-way street. A solid relationship requires a two-way exchange. Do not be shy, and do not think it awkward to pray to God. Actually, it is recommended we pray constantly (1 TH 5:16–19). That is to say, be mindful of God always, and acknowledge His presence whenever He comes to mind. Prayer is not just about asking for things, or confessing your sins, or thanking God. It is designed to connect with the Holy Spirit who lives within you, and to stay connected. Talk to God and He will answer. Listen to God for He speaks to your heart. Live for Him and the Holy Spirit will tell you what to do and when (LUK 12:11–12; JOH 14:26).

JOB 13:3   JOB 34:28   PSA 19:14   PRO 15:29   1 TI 2:1,8   JAM 5:16   1 PE 3:12

CHAPTER EIGHT

Bible Study: Why Do People Go to Hell?

When we try to define God, we find ourselves grasping for adjectives that project His majesty and excellence, knowing full well that we haven't even come close to understanding or explaining Him. We have only His Word, the man Jesus Christ, and this universe with which to comprehend who He is and why He created us. We are confined to our finite knowledge and we are constrained by our physical limitations; the best we can do is to identify the remarkable characteristics of humans and ascribe them to God. But it is we who are made in His image and not the other way around. We cannot begin to elucidate His infinite capacity, perfection, glory, and wisdom. It makes one wonder why God would care about us at all (PSA 8: 4–5).

However, not only does God love us unconditionally, He enables us to have a personal relationship with Him (ROM 8:15). Who wouldn't want that? Seriously, ponder this carefully: there is an omnipotent, omniscient, and omnipresent deity that has created all things, who listens to you, speaks to you, and invites you to be a member of His family (ACT 10:34–35). He goes to great lengths to make it easy for us, by calling us, redeeming us, and sanctifying us to make us holy like Him. He allowed Jesus Christ to die in your place and mine, and He will give us an inheritance equal to His own Son (HEB 2:11; 1 PE 1:3–5). I guess that makes us pretty important to God our Father. The only requirement to live forever with God in His kingdom is to believe in His promises and thank Him for His acts of mercy, especially allowing His Son Jesus to pay for our trespasses and sins.

There is a catch, however. You have to choose (DEU 30:15). He will not make anyone accept these free gifts. He will neither force you to love Him nor program you to do His will. You have to want to receive God and His blessings, and you have to want to serve Him. Those who choose rightly will be joined with the saints in the eternal membership of the household of God Almighty (DAN 7:14), having been made pure and holy for that purpose (MAT 5:48). This seems the easiest choice ever presented to each one of us in our entire lifetime: to be or not to be with God.

Those who do not pick God have excluded themselves. God does not send people to hell; they choose it for themselves. They do not want to know God, to be with Him, or to obey Him; they want what they want and that's that. Those who choose Christ choose life; they are compelled to follow Him and will strive to be like Him. Those who opt for a life of disobedience, denial, and/or disbelief are living for themselves, not for God (ROM 6:1–2,12–16). Ask yourself this question: Are you governed by God's will or your own?

PRO 8:36   LUK 16:10   JOH 3:16   JOH 3:36   ROM 1:21–25   ROM 2:6–11

God, who is perfect in righteousness and holiness, will not allow corruption, sin, or death in heaven. That's why He has provided everyone a way out of the grave and into His presence. Only God is always good (MAR 10:18); therefore, only God can save you (ACT 4:12). I recommend you choose God and His Son Jesus Christ, who is God in the flesh and the perfect human example of goodness and respect (JOH 5:23). Christ is faultless and pure, so only His sacrifice can pay the penalty of death; that's why death had no hold over Him (JOH 10:14–18; ACT 2:22–24). But it does for those who rely upon themselves and reject Christ as Savior. Though all will see God at the resurrection, those who chose not to stick with God will experience a second death, and that's that.

EZE 18:4–5,20,23,32   EZE 33:10–11   ROM 3:20–25   JAM 2:10   1 JO 3:4   JDE 1:17–21

We humans have free will, an attribute no other occupants of this planet possess. And when we make choices, we usually get immediate knowledge of results. It does not take long to see how positive and proper actions yield good results, and how harmful and improper actions result in negative, often devastating consequences. We are compelled to do the right thing in order to avoid bad outcomes. Even if we get away with something sinful, we don't really, as our own conscience condemns us. Does this not seem a very poignant lesson? The message is clear: Do the right thing! There are very good reasons to do so. Believe that which is true and hold fast to it; reject that which is proven false. Otherwise, there will be negative repercussions for denying the truth as well. God gave us the knowledge of good and evil; and every time we chose wrong, we became aware that sin has a cost. But many do not accept the ultimate penalty, which is death. All the wonderful, gracious, and responsible acts of a lifetime cannot blot out a single evil word or action. But a small flicker of light can consume the deepest darkness. Let that light shine within you; and follow that light which illuminates a path that will end up in heaven (PSA 119:105; 1 PE 2:9).

The course that a person chooses in life will lead to one of two places: Heaven or Hell. Take your pick; I hope you choose well. Keep in mind, there is one way to heaven: it is through Christ the Lord (JOH 14:6). The way to hell has many routes; in fact, all paths but one end up there (MAT 7:13–14). There are profound benefits and costs, good or bad, depending on which direction you take. But we all know the outcome even as we make our selections, because the spirit inside will not lie to you. When you choose evil, or base your decision on a lie, you know that you are doing wrong. We receive the due recompense for our choices in life as well as in death (DEU 30:19–20).

2 CH 6:23   EZE 11:21   EZE 22:31   OBA 1:15   LUK 16:19–31   ROM 6:23   GAL 6:7–8

God's justice is fair and permanent. We pretty much get what we ask for. We will be held accountable and we will be judged. But Christ, who is your counselor and advocate, will plead your case to the Father (1 JO 2:1); and He will grant you a pardon because you have been justified by the blood of His Son (ROM 3:28; ROM 5:1; GAL 2:16; GAL 3:24); well, as long as you believe. If you don't, well good luck with that choice.

JER 23:5   JOH 3:17–21   ROM 5:21   1 TI 2:4–6   TIT 3:7   JDE 1:7   REV 20:14–15

God does not wish for anyone to be condemned. People condemn themselves when they think they do not need God, or maintain that they do not deserve damnation because they are decent people. We reap what we sow. Everyone has a chance to seek God and find Him; all they have to do is look. But you may ask, what about people that never had a chance, like a young child, or some poor soul in a lost third world country? How can they possibly know God? Surely God would not damn them to hell, would He? A loving, merciful, and forgiving God would not punish an innocent person, would He? Perish the thought! Take time to study the following passages for the answers to these dilemmas. You will find that only the guilty are condemned in God's court of law, and that everyone who seeks God will discover the truth.

JOB 4:7–9   JOB 8:3   PSA 19:1   JOH 20:29   ACT 17:27–28   ROM 3:5–6   TIT 2:10–13   2 PE 3:9–10

So, the fallen get what they deserve, right? But, the images of hell portrayed in the Bible make it out to be one horrible place. It is depicted as a torture chamber for wayward souls. And will the inhabitants have to endure their punishment for an eternity? It seems an unfair penalty to torment a mind forever due to a single generation of ungodliness. Does an unrighteous life spanning eighty years on the average warrant an eternity of punishment? What exactly would be a fair penalty? Let's see what the scriptures teach.

CHAPTER EIGHT

DEU 32:22   ISA 5:14   DAN 12:2   MIC 5:15   MAT 10:28   MAT 13:41–32   MAT 23:14

MAT 25:41,46   ROM 1:20   2 PE 2:20–22   REV 14:11   REV 19:20   REV 20:10

Well, I guess the Bible does say forever. But is that word used literally, or figuratively? I mean, I vowed to love my wife forever; but that translated into "until death do us part." So, marriage on this earth isn't really forever; but if two spouses make it to heaven, they will be with their Savior forever and will never part due to death. Now here is an interesting play on words. Because, God is saying precisely that: sin will separate you from Him, and it leads to death (ISA 59:2); death means perish (JOH 3:16) which is forever. Like the groom, who is Christ, and His church who is the bride, we are joined forever in marriage (REV 19:6–9). Those who are unfaithful will not be rejoined with Jesus Christ, for they have chosen not to be a part of Him. In death, we who believe will part company with those who don't; the latter will not live with God but will die instead. So, if you are not joined with Christ until death, then you will be apart from him forevermore.

There is a resurrection of the body that all people will experience (REV 20:1–15). The judgment which follows will divide those who are redeemed from those who are damned. And the condemned who die again will never live again: eternally separated from God because their sins were never expunged. You see, sins corrupt the soul, which cannot penetrate the barrier of God's holiness. Nobody enters into His presence unless those sins have been forgiven and the payment remitted. Place your trust in Christ who died in your place; He will cover your sins and bestow upon you His righteousness (JAM 2:23; 1 PE 4:81). Otherwise, you will have to render payment yourself.

ISA 33:14   ISA 35:10   MAT 25:32–33   ROM 8:35–39   2 TH 1:7–10   HEB 7:26

To be separated from God forever is torment in itself. For God provides all sustenance, happiness, and peace. Without God, there is nothing good to be had. And that is what death brings, an eternity of emptiness. Nevertheless, it's not like one can feel the nothingness if they are dead. The lake of fire blends all the lost souls into a mindless concoction of confusion; forever lost and never to be found (ECC 9:10; ISA 26:14; ISA 28:18). Those people who maintain that death is the end and there is nothing after that will be right. Because that's the way they wanted it to be, and so it will, at least for them. What a waste. But if the fallen didn't want God before, they sure won't want Him forever. For them, that probably would be an eternity of agony; death will be a more merciful end, when they cease to be. Thus, God is merciful even to those who reject Him.

I'd much rather be counted among the living, protected by the oversight of God's grace; stimulated by the power of His perfect love, to spend an eternity of bliss, tranquility, and harmony with Jesus my friend and brother. Reunited in body, mind and spirit to the magnificent company of the Lord of life, and realizing every circumstance with awesome sensation, expanding cognition, and constant spiritual awareness. Possessing a glorified essence of being, pure and perfect like that of Christ Himself (1 TH 5:23; 2 PE 1:4); forever experiencing new wonders of God's creations in communion with His Holy Spirit. Continuously learning from an everlasting repository of wisdom, with every question given an answer that reflects upon God's absolute truth. Never again will we be constrained by time or plagued by worry; no pain, no suffering, no sorrow, no sin. I can only imagine what God has in store for me, but I am surely looking forward to it (ISA 64:4; JOH 14:2). Are you? If you are not sure, you need to decide very soon. If you are living only for today, eventually the days will run out. If you are living only for yourself, eventually you will lose that self.

Bible Study: Does Science Disagree with the Bible?

The short answer to the topic question is a flat "no." In fact, the Bible is extraordinarily accurate with respect to current scientific knowledge. In this study, a number of scientific discoveries will be examined in light of what scriptures reveal. You may be surprised to discover that, not only is the Bible consistent with recent research findings, but also it is quite ahead of its time regarding many findings. While a number of the passages reviewed in this lesson are subject to alternate interpretations, or are otherwise ambiguous, there is no incontrovertible evidence that biblical revelation is contrary to scientific revelation (as long as the "science" is founded on sound reasoning and methodology, and factual data).

Let us first address the age-old issue of evolution versus creation. Obviously, the Bible supports the creation worldview. Many scientists, naturalists, and atheists continue to hold desperately to the macroevolution model even though the latest scholarship debunks that theory. Darwin himself found the notion of species evolving into transformational life forms a stretch, though the notion of microevolution was quite evident in his observations. That is, an organism may develop adaptive qualities which are superior to their ancestors, but they do not leap into new life forms of a different kind. There is nothing in the fossil record to suggest such an event ever has occurred. The Bible speaks with certainty that life forms do not evolve into different kinds, but only within kinds.

This truth is abundantly clear in the first chapter of Genesis, where the phrase "according to its kind" is introduced repeatedly. Take for example dogs. They can produce other varieties of dogs; but they will never evolve into or produce cats. All dog breeds can be traced to one male and one female dog, just like all humans can be traced back to one male and one female human. This has been determined by contemporary research supporting the single mother theory: all human mothers possess mitochondrial DNA linked to one primary source (namely, Eve).

Resolved: an ape cannot become a human, and a dog cannot become a cat. God created them unique from the start. There is enough variation in respective DNA to prevent two different "kinds" to mate and reproduce. Further, there is too much complicated information in the DNA sequence to have assembled randomly, or to have modified itself into an entirely novel arrangement that supports a new life form. Such sophistication, intricacy, and design require intelligence. For changes to happen they have to be within the kind: canine, feline, bovine, etc. Thus, the idea that humankind could have evolved from a lesser species is untenable; the DNA will not match up. Further, the theory that every life form came from some one-celled organism in an ancient primordial soup is totally without merit. How did the organism get there in the first place? Can life formulate from benign matter?

Read the creation account (GEN 1:1–31) and count the number of times "after his kind" or "their kinds" or anything like that appears. As you study the history of creation, pay attention to the repetition of the word "seed" as well. Notice that plants have their own seed within them, as does sea life (fish, whales), air life (fowl), land life (beasts, mammals), not to mention human life. They all reproduce after their kind. God created all of these kinds; they did not evolve from one seed. That's why the fossil record shows an explosion of animal life forms at the dawn of the Cambrian period with no evidence of animals prior to that.

Now review the account of Noah (GEN 7:9–22) and recall how every living creature that made it into the ark survived the great flood, and how the rest of the animals living on dry land (including humans) died. Fortunately, Noah gathered "two of all flesh" including one each "male and female" (GEN 1:27; GEN 7:9; MAR 10:6–8). Notice how marriage is defined the same way:

one man and one woman. Noah saved a pair of each kind that "breathed air" to replenish the earth. God commanded both Adam and Noah to be "fruitful and multiply" (GEN 1:28; GEN 8:13–17); consequently, all humans alive today descended from Adam and Noah. Or, better said, human beings are all one blood regardless of ethnicity or shade of flesh (ACT 17:26). Each kind created by God has its own separate tree of life, not several limbs stemming from the same root.

Many modern scientists are beginning to realize that evolution will explain neither the origin of the universe nor the origin of life; others continue to hold fast to the outdated and discredited theory (1 CO 2:7–16; 1 TI 6:20–21; JDE 1:10). Unfortunately, while scholars might accept the possibility of intelligent design, a great number have a hard time identifying God to be the source of that intelligence (ISA 51:13; ISA 55:8–11; ROM 1:21–25; 1 CO 1:19–31). As Christians, we believe firmly that God created everything; and He created it especially with us in mind (GEN 1:26; ISA 45:18), and for His pleasure (ISA 44:23–26; COL 1:16: REV 4:11).

PSA 33:6–9   PSA 104:1–13   PSA 136:4–9   ISA 45:7,12   JOH 1:1–5   COL 1:14–17

God spoke everything into existence via the power and wisdom of His Word (PRO 8:22–30; PRO 3:19–20). Nothing came into existence by itself or via natural processes without God's command and permission. You may recall that the Word became flesh, who is Christ the Lord. So, Christ who possesses the power and wisdom of God, was actively involved and played an integral role in the creation story.

ISA 42:5–7   ISA 48:13   ZEC 12:2   JOH 1:1–5   HEB 1:1–4   HEB 9:24   1 PE 1:19–20

Of course, the primary reasons why scientists have rejected the creation out of nothing perspective are because it is illogical and unbelievable, not to mention unscientific and unobservable. They concede that something cannot spring from nothing, any more than there can be an effect without a cause. While the reductionists will invent infinite universes and all sorts of unprovable and fantastic alternate theories, it always boils down to the fact that there must be an uncaused first cause, which is outside of the natural realm (supernatural). Scientists will allow that the universe had a beginning, which coincided with the start of time, energy, and matter as we know it. Hence, the big bang theory. Guess what? An immediate beginning of space and time is precisely what the Bible teaches (GEN 1:1; ISA 46:8–10). And thus, from the invisible and intangible came the visible and tangible; but not from nothing (GEN 1:2–4; ROM 1:20; HEB 11:3), for God was there all along.

God is all powerful, all knowing, and always present; He is a supernatural and timeless being and by definition exists outside of time and space (PSA 90:4; 2 PE 3:8). Since God operates without time constraints, He can manipulate time if He so chooses; this is clearly evident when He stops or reverses the arrow of time (JOS 10:12–14; 2 KI 20:8–11). Now these are supernatural events, miracles if you will. Hence, a reasonable definition of a miracle: it is divine intervention that is not constrained by the laws of physics or natural progressions. Since Christ is God in human form, it comes as no surprise that He too could perform miracles, not the least of which was His own resurrection. There is considerable variation in how miracles are defined in the literature. But in the Bible, they contain a message from God Himself.

JOB 9:4–9   PSA 90:1–4   ISA 46:9–11   ROM 1:25–27   2 TI 1:9–10   TIT 1:1–3

Speaking of physics: it is a hard science based on the analysis, interpretation, and measurement of the apparent order, structure, uniformity, movement, and predictability of the universe. But if one is to infer law and order, one must necessarily assume a lawgiver. Yes, God created the heavens and the earth, and placed inherent order along with physical laws by which the universe operates and continues (ISA 40:12; JER 33:25). God also incorporated the law of morality. Entire books have been written on morality as well, and again there is found variability in opinions and in the research being advanced as proof.

One of the interesting discoveries of modern times is the idea that the universe is expanding very rapidly. And that realization has become the conventional wisdom, when for centuries many thought this was a steady-state universe which continued indefinitely, or would otherwise contract sooner or later. There are a number of references in the Bible suggesting an ever-expanding universe; the words speak of how God stretched the heavens like an enormous canopy. Did the writers of the ancient biblical texts understand universal expansion thousands of years before modern scientists? Read what the Bible says about it.

JOB 9:8   PSA 104:2   PSA 136:4–9   ISA 42:5   JER 10:12–13   ZEC 12:1

According to physics, this universe cannot sustain its current configuration forever. Due to nonstop expansion, it will eventually die from heat death, according to one fundamental law of physics: the second law of thermodynamics. Now wait a minute. Could it be that the ancient scriptures also declared this phenomenon known as "entropy" thousands of years ago? I'm afraid so (PSA 102:25–27; ISA 34:4–5; ISA 51:6; 2 PE 3:4–13). The Bible makes it clear that the current heaven and earth will fade away, and that God will create new ones where His people can dwell, including all who believe in Him and cling to His promises. It will be similar to how He created the original universe; only the next one will be even better (REV 21:1–7). God is not ruled by laws, but actually ordained them, incorporating order while creating this universe and everything in it. Who knows if the new heaven and earth will follow the physics or laws here?

It is uncanny when scientific descriptions of the formation of the earth, solar systems, galaxies, and the rest of the cosmos generally fit the biblical accounts (GEN 1:1–31; JOB 38:4–13,16; PSA 104:1–13). God had a brainstorm and kicked it off with the introduction of light (GEN 1:3; JOB 38:18–20). Could that have been a big bang? The heavens or "firmament" and all its elements began to form into molecules and separate into layers, to produce celestial bodies and "atmospheres." The Bible seems to organize the heavens into three atmospheres: the air surrounding our earth, the cosmos beyond, and the highest heaven where God walks (JOB 22:14). Once again, science and God's Word are not in disagreement.

DEU 10:14   1 KI 8:27   JOB 37:18   PSA 19:1   PSA 148:4–5   AMO 9:6

Land masses and mountains protruded out of the "waters" separating the land from various bodies of water. This process, as explained in the Bible, seems strikingly similar to the phenomenon referred to in geology as plate tectonics.

GEN 1:9   PSA 33:6–9   PSA 77:16–19   PSA 104:7–8   PRO 8:24–26

Creation as we comprehend it began at the beginning of spacetime. The ensuing process followed a very organized pattern: forming, dividing, seeding, developing, reproducing, and flourishing. After God put it all together, He let things progress, with no intention of intervening further unless to send us a message or revelation. His work was finished, for the time being (GEN 2:1–10). Since then, things have continued without much change, but things will not remain so (ROM 8:21–23; 2 PE 3:4–13). For example, humans have not improved much in functionality since Adam, but we will be changed significantly for the next world (1 CO 15:51). The spacetime continuum in which we now abide will cease to exist someday. Our corner of the universe has been corrupted by sin and death, which will die along with the earth. Yes, God will create it all anew at the end of time. I can assure you this: it will be very good just like His initial undertaking (GEN 1:31; EXO 20:4; 2 PE 3:13); and once again His people will be free.

In days of old, when prophets and teachers were communicating God's messages to the world, science was a byword. The field didn't really spring into the limelight until a few hundred years ago. There were archaic ways of looking at the solar system, the cosmos, and what was beyond. People thought the world was flat, the planets and moons were propped up, and the earth was the center of everything. It was considered heretical to suggest that the earth rotated about the sun. However, the Bible did not hold to any of those fables.

For instance, the earth is described as circular in the Bible, determined to be so by the curvature of the horizon, and the arc of shadows on the moon during different phases and eclipses. Further, the celestial orbs and stars are described as being suspended by forces, and moving relative to one another. Space is understood to be vast and immeasurable. Stars are defined as innumerable (billions) and varying in magnitude (PSA 147:4). Note that eight to ten thousand stars can be seen from earth, depending where you are, and they shine with varying brightness. The Bible also mentions the relative absence of stars appearing at magnetic north. Notice how these concepts are presented and defined quite well in God's Word though relatively novel in the field of astrophysics.

GEN 15:5   GEN 22:17   JOB 26:5–12   JOB 38:4–7,31–36   ISA 40:21–26   JER 33:22

The last thing God created was the human race. He wanted a thriving and pristine environment for us to blossom, waiting until the earth and the heavens were just right for our development. Humans were appointed stewards of that world (GEN 1:26–28: PSA 8:4–8). When everything was ready, we arrived on the scene. Humankind was formed out of the "dust," and became a "living soul." This is an intriguing parallel to the scientific notion that an essential ingredient to our existence is space or cosmic dust, like that emitted from exploding stars and the like (GEN 2:1–10; GEN 3:19).

In order for us to survive, God handed down a number of additional laws and regulations. Many of these are enumerated in the Law of Moses. There were precautions against eating spoiled food (LEV 7:15–17). There were rules for the quarantine of sick people or those with contagious diseases (LEV 13:45–46; NUM 19:22). Warnings were given about eating blood or food with blood that had not been drained, or eating road kill and carrion, as there was greater risk of getting a parasite or bloodborne illness (LEV 17:11–15). The people were directed to dig a latrine outside of camp to maintain sanitation, further preventing the spread of disease (LEV 23:12–13). Many laws of nature were set forth by God for our protection. If people violate the laws of nature, they risk serious downsides. This fact is particularly relevant for those who engage in unnatural sex (ROM 1:25–27). It seems a great deal of biblical medical science corresponds with tenets of modern medical practice, not the least of which is cleanliness, which is a component of all the procedures mentioned above and rule number one in every hospital.

Apparently, God's people also had significant knowledge about meteorology, geology, and physical science. They were well aware that thunder was the sound lightning makes. They understood a great deal about water: the cycle of water; vapor, distillation, and evaporation; cloud formation and rain; the freezing of water (snow and ice); springs (fountains) underground and under the seas. They comprehended sea currents, sea valleys, and shipping channels. They determined prevailing wind currents and trends, cold fronts, and the fact that air has mass and weight much like water. They determined that dirt packed down under pressure becomes rock. For a quick study on earth science, peruse the following scriptures.

GEN 7:17–20   2 SA 22:16   JOB 28:24–27   JOB 36:26–30   JOB 37:9–11,18   JOB 38:36–38

PSA 8:8   PSA 18:15   PSA 135:6–7   PRO 8:28–29   ECC 1:4–9   JER 10:13   JER 51:15–16

I think God gave us the gift of science to enable us to better appreciate His creation by observing, studying, and measuring it; and pondering, contemplating, and admiring it. After all, God pre-enabled these capabilities while resting on the seventh day. He admired His handiwork because it was good. We should follow God's example and take a day off each week to marvel at His glorious creation, and worship Him every day as the One responsible for our life, sustenance, freedom, success, and happiness. Science is a gift from God; and it can bring us closer to Him. Unfortunately, many use tools of science irresponsibly, sometimes in attempt to disprove God's existence; but they cannot. I'm sure many readers have never viewed the Bible as a science reference, but its portrayal of the subject is incredibly up-to-date.

There is one more important point worth elaborating. It is the way God uses miracles and supernatural acts of wonderment to get our attention. A few significant miracles have been mentioned throughout this lesson. The two most important being the creation of the universe and the resurrection of Christ. Now let's look at another celestial spectacle that a scientist can really appreciate: The Star of Bethlehem (read NUM 24:17; ISA 9:2; ISA 60:1–6; MAT 2:1–12). God placed a sign in the heavens to signal the coming of His Son, our Savior the promised Messiah. There has been speculation about whether God actually circumvented the laws of physics or used them to produce the spectacular sight. The phenomenon sure grabbed the attention of the magi, astronomers in their own right; they were captivated by the cosmological phenomenon of the star which compelled them to follow it.

One of the prevailing theories on the Star of Bethlehem concerns the occurrences during 6–7 BC when Jupiter and Saturn were closely conjoined on three different occasions within the span of almost one year. Apparently, the phenomenon occurs about every eight hundred years. This timeframe would fit with the proposed death of King Herod around 4 BC. While not a spectacular event to a layperson, the conjoining of planets would have been quite alluring to an astronomer (i.e., a scientist). Another conjunction involving Jupiter and Venus occurred in 2 BC and many scholars see that as significant especially given it occurred in the constellation Leo (kingly like the "lion of Judah"). A fairly recent theory is that an uncharted comet could produce the biblical description. Regardless, it is fun to speculate about how God has used the natural and supernatural to reveal His majesty and show us the way to Him. And don't forget: there will be wonders in the heavens when Christ arrives for His second advent. Check out the passages below that explain what will be going on celestially as a sign that He is coming again and the end is near. It will be every bit as enthralling as the Star of Bethlehem.

ISA 13:10   JOE 2:10   AMO 8:9   MAT 24:29   REV 6:13   REV 8:12

In conclusion, the creation reveals a lot about God, and provides enhanced understanding of what He did, how He did it, and why. Science is a tool for increasing our comprehension of it. Thus, we have two sources of truth from which to gain in knowledge: the book of God's Word and the book of God's Creation. God is the author of both books. However, the Word is our foundation for fathoming the Creation; one cannot interpret the Bible from the book of nature, it's the other way around. But absolute truth is shown when both converge upon the facts; and if proven factual, it will not conflict with either source since truth does not change and cannot be absolutely refuted. Of course, something that is true today may not be true tomorrow, but that does not discount or refute the facts. For example, I may have been sick yesterday but not today, but the facts have not changed while the circumstances have. The primary objective of science is to uncover the truth. This is also the primary objective of the Holy Spirit: to disclose the truth which is found in God's Word and the words of God's Son Jesus Christ (JOH 18:37). Evidently, we are all scientists in a way, because we listen, learn, observe, decide, react, adjust, and relearn; this in a nutshell is the scientific method. Employ these methods while studying God's Word and His Creation and you will find truth.

CHAPTER EIGHT

Bible Study: Did Christ Really Rise from the Dead?

Perhaps the most disputed event in the historicity of the Bible is the resurrection of Jesus Christ. Maybe it's because that is the capstone of the Christian faith (JOH 11:25–26; REV 1:17–19). Without Christ's resurrection, there is no religion, no faith, and no hope (ECC 9:10; 1 CO 15:12–41; 1 PE 1:3). Without Christ being victorious over death there would be no meaning to life. If that were true, the atheists and the relativists would be right. But the proof is rather overwhelming that Christ did, in fact, rise from the dead.

Only a perfect being could make such a promise and back it up by fulfilling it. The resurrection defies the laws of nature and physics, which is why many scientists reject it. But they would deny also that the sudden appearance of our universe is a miracle, though it also defies these laws. We know God operates outside of nature because He is a supernatural being. How could He be responsible for establishing the laws of the universe if He was subject to them? That would mean God was a product of the universe, but of course, the converse is true.

Very few scholars dispute the fact that Jesus lived, was crucified, and was buried. Those who refuse to believe that in three days He emerged from the tomb alive have come up with all kinds of speculations to try to explain the event away. Interestingly, attempts to falsify evidence only validate that the tomb was indeed empty; there is no way to get around that point. That is, if skeptics could have proven that Christ was in the tomb or was otherwise dead, they would not have made up excuses or concocted theories as to why the tomb was empty and why sightings of Jesus were rampant. The Jewish leaders bribed guards and perpetuated a lie that the disciples stole the body. These leaders were suspicious of the resurrection claim before Christ was entombed and already had made up their lie prior to the tomb being evacuated.

The Law of Moses required at least two to three eyewitnesses to render a person guilty of a capital crime resulting in the death penalty; so, the elders found two false witnesses to testify against Jesus because they wanted Him dead. Interestingly, the resurrection of Christ had hundreds of eyewitnesses. According to the New Testament, He appeared to the eleven apostles, to James the brother of Jesus, to the apostle Paul, to groups of people, and to crowds of people. That's why the event could not be stifled despite earnest attempts to do just that.

All four Gospel writers provide a perspective of the account of Jesus's crucifixion, death, burial, and resurrection. Each author provides an individual point of view about important details. The aggregation of these testimonies results in a very clear picture of the events before, during, and after His trial and execution. His own demise was proclaimed by Christ Himself prior to the passion; even the temple leaders were aware of that prophecy (MAT 12:38–40; MAT 20:17–19; MAT 26:1–4; MAT 27:62–62; MAR 8:31; MAR 14:58; JOH 2:19; LUK 24:6–8).

It is certain that Jesus died of His injuries. His death was verified by soldiers on the mount of Golgotha who pierced Jesus's side with a spear; that's why they didn't break His legs to hasten death. It was verified to Pontius Pilate again by the centurion in charge, when a rich man named Joseph from Arimathaea requested the body of Christ to ensure a proper burial (ISA 53:4–12). This Jewish leader, and another named Nicodemus, prepared the body of Christ for interment and placed the corpse in a newly hewn sepulcher. The tomb was closed by rolling a giant stone across the entrance and affixing a Roman seal. The above facts, and that the tomb was occupied by the dead body of Jesus, can be found in all four Gospels (MAT 27:62–66; MAR 15:43; LUK 23:50; JOH 19:38). The Chief Priests and Pharisees petitioned Pilate to ensure the tomb would be guarded and secured, for they feared that Jesus's followers would fake a resurrection (MAT 27:57–66).

The most amazing thing happened on the first Easter Sunday, which is the focus of God's plan of salvation and our faith: Christ's resurrection. There was an earthquake, the stone was rolled aside, angels showed up, and the soldiers freaked out and abandoned their post. Mary Magdalene and several other women, who knew full well the burial site, departed before sunrise hoping someone would remove the stone so they could anoint the corpse with ointments and fragrances. They were mighty surprised when they got there; in the tomb was found only burial garments. The angels present at the tomb told Mary to alert the apostles that Jesus had arisen from the dead. Thus, the initial eyewitnesses of the empty tomb were women: Mary Magdalene, Mary the mother of James, Salome, and Joanna (notwithstanding Roman soldiers who witnessed something but were not prepared to bear witness).

Apparently, the first to actually see the risen Lord was Magdalene; she immediately notified the disciples as the angel directed. At first, they did not believe; they thought their journey with Christ was over. They were afraid and had been hiding from the authorities. But after Magdalene's report, Peter and John raced to the tomb and discovered for themselves that it was true. Again, all four Gospels give corresponding testimony about the empty tomb and the resurrection of Christ (MAT 28:1–10; MAR 16:1–11; LUK 24:1–12; JOH 20:1–18). As mentioned previously, when the security guards reported to the chief priests about the empty tomb, the priests bribed them instructing them to perpetuate a hoax that the body was stolen by the disciples. That lie has continued to this day as the preferred argument against the claim of the resurrection (MAT 28:11–15). Of course, the lie would not have surfaced at all if there had been a dead body to parade around.

It seems the next two people to see Jesus alive were men traveling to the nearby town of Emmaus. Jesus began walking with them and they discussed the extraordinary events which had transpired the previous week. The men hadn't recognized Him when Jesus related the scriptures, but they invited Him to dine with them; suddenly they realized who Christ was when He disappeared after blessing the meal. They returned to Jerusalem and found the apostles, explaining all the things they had seen. Before they knew it, Jesus was there in the midst of them, showing them His wounds, teaching them, and reproving them for not believing the truth that was prophesied to them (MAR 16:12–14; LUK 24:7–49; JOH 20:19–25). Thomas was not among them during that meeting and was unconvinced when the apostles told him that they had conversed with Jesus. A second appearance occurred eight days later and Thomas was present to witness the truth of the Lord's resurrection (JOH 20:26–31). The third time recorded in the Gospels when Jesus appeared to the eleven apostles was the day of His ascension. They met as planned along the banks of the Sea of Galilee, caught fish, dined, received Jesus's final instructions, and observed His ascension into heaven (MAT 28:16–20; MAR 16:15–20; LUK 24:50–53; JOH 21:1–14).

Jesus was seen by many others during the forty days after His resurrection and prior to His ascension (ACT 1:1–11; ACT 10:38–41). One of the most complete accounts was documented by St. Paul; it was a compilation of eyewitness testimony communicated to him by the apostles and inner circle of Christ (1 CO 15:1–11). Paul writes of the appearances to Peter, James (the brother of Jesus), and the apostles; he identifies one occasion in which over five hundred men (not including women and children) were present during a preaching from the resurrected Christ, many of whom were still alive to swear to it.

The last one to witness Jesus alive was Paul, he states. That occasion is described in detail in the book of Acts (ACT 9:1–25), where Paul references the preaching of the Gospel by the apostles. That same mission Paul undertook after his personal experience with the risen Lord who called Paul to be an apostle and carry His Gospel to the Gentiles. Paul had been persecuting and murdering Christians, and was on his way to Damascus to continue the slaughter. A great light appeared, blinding Paul; a voice chastised Paul for persecuting Him (at that moment Saul became Paul). Paul asked who was speaking to him and Christ replied, "It is me, Jesus." The men with Paul also saw the light but did not hear the voice (ACT 22:6–13). Jesus told Paul to seek a man named Ananias who would bless him, after which Paul received his sight again, and the calling of the Holy Spirit. One could say that Paul finally saw the light.

People were amazed to witness Paul preaching Christ, especially the Jewish leadership who sought to kill Paul as a traitor to their cause, just like they had plotted to kill Jesus. Paul barely escaped with the help of fellow Christian followers. Paul recounted the event of his conversion while addressing King Agrippa and his council (ACT 26:12–18). Perhaps Paul wasn't the last one to see the risen Christ, however, because the apostle John saw a vision and heard Christ and His appointed angel speak to him, from which John prepared the manuscript that would become The Revelation of Jesus Christ (REV 1:17–19).

Notice how witnesses to the risen Christ did not recognize Him at first. While He was seen in the flesh, and could be touched, and ate food, He was different somehow. That's because He possessed a spiritual body; that is, His body had changed. He was not merely a physical entity but radiated a visible Spirit (JOH 12:16; 1 CO 15:42–58). Perhaps this was the same spiritual body appearing to Abraham as Melchizedek (HEB 7:1–28). Apparently, such is the same type of body that the saints will receive at our resurrection: an immortal body unstained by sin and glorified like that of Christ (JOH 17:6–25).

JOB 19:25–26   ROM 8:17,30   2 CO 5:21   PHP 3:20–21   COL 3:4   1 TH 5:23   1 PE 5:4

The most credible evidence one can obtain to attest the accuracy of history is eyewitness testimony. Luke diligently set out to identify and interview primary sources to certify his research was truthful, reliable, verifiable, and precise (LUK 1:1–4). Luke was able to establish many facts not reported in the other New Testament books, providing additional corroboration. Scholars regard Luke as a topnotch historian for accuracy and thoroughness. Peter also made it clear that he witnessed firsthand the works of Christ when he preached and wrote about what he had observed and learned (ACT 10:39–41; 2 PE 1:16–21), as did John (JOH 19:35; 1 JO 1:1–3).

God has provided testimony to us in His Word; and that Word became a man so that we could receive it firsthand (1 JO 1:1–14). The Word which spoke everything into existence is called *Logos* in the original Greek (PSA 33:6,9). While God bears witness of His glory, so Christ bore witness to God's glory and the glory they share equally (ISA 43:9–15; JOH 17:1–5). We are to give testimony just as Christ commissioned the apostles to testify of the truth of God's message of redemption (MAT 28:19–20). In other words, spread the Word.

There is no other work in history that has the degree of supporting and corroborating evidence than the Bible. All other ancient works are based on documents that emerged centuries after the author lived. Yet those are declared to be historically accurate, credible, and relevant. The New Testament Gospels, Epistles, and associated texts originated during the lifetimes of the authors who wrote them. Their basic testimony was handed down in oral and written form because a low percentage of people were literate, and reproducing written works was tedious, expensive, and time consuming. Thus, the story of Christ was well established within five years of His death and resurrection; the culmination of this testimony was incorporated into the Apostle's Creed, which they taught to Paul and is recorded in his first letter to the Corinthians. Historians have determined that hardcopies of the original four Gospels began to appear from twenty to forty years after Christ ascended, when most of the apostles and eyewitnesses were still living.

Did you know that over five thousand complete or fragmented NT manuscripts in the original Greek have survived? This is unheard of when it comes to the preservation of antiquated texts. Amazingly, some Gospel fragments date to the mid first century, as discovered among the Dead Sea Scrolls. The writers of these scrolls were meticulous in ensuring that no alterations or mistakes were made when reproducing the scriptures. A great example is the entire scroll of Isaiah, over two millennia old and completely consistent with the current version. Truthfully, ancient biblical manuscripts like Isaiah have proven to be 99 percent unchanged from those used today; purported errors represent mere grammatical differences, word changes, and the like. In short, the meaning remained unaltered. That in itself is evidence of divine inspiration and intervention?

A great deal of external confirmatory evidence comes from historical accounts in the secular world. Examples exist in the works of Josephus, a Jewish historian during the middle to late first century, and Tacitus a Roman historian during the early second century. They report about the life, crucifixion, and alleged resurrection of a messianic figure in Jerusalem during the governorship of Pontius Pilate; a great number of other details make it clear that the events surrounding Jesus were believed to have occurred, to include the multitude of Christian believers that had multiplied in number since these events took place. Other sources included Roman historians such as Suetonius, Justin Martyr, and Tertullian; and the Roman provincial governor Pliny (the Younger). Early Christian theologians also quoted from the New Testament to include Ignatius, Clement, Irenaeus, and Origen, circa AD 100–200. The repeated canonization of scripture ensured that the original standard would be preserved. The NT was well established early and remained stable throughout the growth of the Christian Church until now.

Before closing, consider some archeological findings that reflect the story of Jesus and the crucifixion. The first is the Shroud of Turin, presumed by many to be the actual burial cloth of Christ. This artifact depicts precisely the types of wounds and scourging that Christ received as explained in the Bible, and the actual blood patterns to be expected in the wrists, ankles, side, back, and head (note that the shroud has remnants of real human blood). The second is an interesting discovery made some forty-five years ago in Jerusalem: the bones of a first century crucifixion victim. Again, the pierced wrist and ankle bones depict precisely how the person was impaled on a cross, to include broken legs to accelerate death by asphyxiation.

It is highly recommended that the reader take time to study Christian Apologetics. There are excellent books available discussing the evidence for the New Testament from primary sources, secondary sources, even non-Christian sources. These sources are identified from the time of Christ, throughout the first century AD, and beyond. Thus, the historic timeline and associated events surrounding the life, death, and resurrection of Christ is solidly founded and documented. I assure you, studying this research will remove the doubt you might have about your faith in general and the Holy Bible in particular. And it will equip you to defend the faith to anyone who asks about the hope within you. Refer to the lesson *Is the New Testament True* for more on proof the Bible is the actual Word of God.

Question: How many eyewitnesses does it take to substantiate the truth? Is two or three enough? Well, there are innumerable reliable witnesses and sources proving the authenticity of the New Testament. No other work of ancient and classic literature comes close to receiving the degree of attestation that the NT has, so it can be asserted with certainty that the words in the NT were recorded correctly and should be believed. God has seen to it.

Bible Study: How Are God and Light Alike?

The first thing the Bible says about God is that He created the universe (GEN 1:1–2). On day one, He created light (GEN 1:3–4). And that light has permeated space since the beginning of time, from here to eternity. Light is a phenomenon that baffles even scientists. It is, no doubt, the most significant aspect of our physical world. Without light, we could not have existed. Light is every bit as relevant with respect to the mental realm and our cognitive functioning. Light gives wisdom and illuminates truth, not to mention transmitting information to our eyes and through our neural circuitry. Light also happens to be quite significant in the spiritual sense. It is written: God is light, and in Him is no darkness at all (1 JO 1:5). Remember, it is the Spirit that gives life, not the flesh (JOH 6:63), and in the Spirit is the light of life (JOH 8:12).

The Bible compares God's goodness and steadfastness to light. Everything that lives needs light; nothing can survive without it. Scientists have shown this to be true: Light is essential. The photon is the basic building block in the development of the universe and living, breathing entities abiding herein; light is operating everywhere from photosynthesis in plants to visual perception in humans. All organisms on this planet require the light rays of our sun; without sunlight no currently existing life forms would be found on Earth. As referenced above, the apostle John informed us that God is life, and God is light. Thus, eternal light is an interesting and defining characteristic of God, the author of life. By understanding the qualities and features of light, God helps us to understand Him and this universe in which we thrive. Keep in mind that the brightness of His light will destroy sin and all who are led into darkness by it. His light can save and it can consume; it can lift you up, or it can burn you down.

JOH 3:19–21   JOH 12:35   ACT 26:13   2 CO 4:6   2 TH 2:8   1 JO 1:1–10

God, like light, never changes. He is constant: always was, is, and will be—the Alpha and Omega (REV 1:8; REV 22:13). In order to remain perfect, how can God possibly change? Any change would render Him imperfect. Since God is omniscient, why would He change in knowledge? Anything short of all knowing would not be all knowing. Does light change? Not according to scientists who have proven that light travels at about 186,000 miles per second, even in a vacuum. Yes, you can bend, reflect, and refract light. Light can be separated into the various colors of the rainbow. But light itself has not changed; and to collect all the colors of the rainbow into one is to produce white light. The properties of light can be examined, but not altered or destroyed. And we can observe the characteristics of God but nobody can change them, not even God, for He cannot deny who He is. But why would anyone want to change God? He is omnipotent, omnipresent, always faithful, always just, always loving, always living, always and forever.

PRO 24:21   MAL 3:6   MAT 22:31–32   1 CO 1:9   1 CO 10:13   HEB 13:8   1 JO 4:8,16

God, like light, is pure. He is incorruptible. In Him there is no darkness because light consumes darkness. In Him there is no sin because complete holiness destroys sin. God is incapable of lying because He is the source of absolute truth. And truth cannot change as it remains factual no matter what the circumstances. Everything that proceeds from the mind of God is perfectly true: crystal clear, transparent, and unadulterated. God illuminates all that is right, and moral, and acceptable, so nobody can unequivocally maintain that they never knew any better. I remember the words of a song I sang as a child, "This little Gospel light of mine, I'm going to let it shine." You can close your eyes to the light or try to hide from it, but you cannot remove or destroy it. Besides, who turns on a light and then tries to block it out (MAT 5:15)? We use light to see and would get lost without it (PSA 119:105). Light cannot stop itself from shining, just as God cannot deny His glory, majesty, and holiness (2 TI 2:12–13); neither can He go back on His Word (NUM 23:19; MAT 24:35; 1 PE 1:25). Light will bring everything into view, same as truth exposes every lie. Light is incredibly powerful. It creates and it destroys.

MAT 17:5   LUK 11:36   JOH 3:33   JOH 4:24   1 CO 4:5   2 CO 6:14   EPH 5:8–14

Those who witnessed Christ saw in Him all the aforementioned characteristics of God; that's because He was, and is, one with God Almighty. I admire St. Peter, who though he was weak and afraid, he said some of the most profound statements in defense of his faith in Christ. Though he denied the Lord, He didn't doubt Him (MAT 16:16; LUK 18:28; JOH 6:68–69). And consider Thomas, who doubted despite all the credible evidence and testimony available to him; but he knew that he was in the presence of deity when Christ appeared to him in His glorified body (JOH 20:28). Yes, the fickle disciples of Jesus were in awe of Him, as were the Old Testament patriarchs and prophets to whom God revealed Himself. This awe is experienced by all believers, even though we have not met the Lord personally at least not in the flesh. But someday everyone will. That will be the best day of your life; or the worst.

1 KI 38:36–38   JOB 19:26   JOB 42:2   PSA 29:4   PSA 83:18   JOH 20:29

God is the Light of the world. He has created all things, breathed life into us, shown us the way home, and graced our existence with love, justice, and truth. It has been said that love is blind, and so are justice and truth. Well, maybe and maybe not. While we cannot always make sense of the wisdom and mercy of God, what with all the evil, corruption, and suffering around us, I submit to you that everything will make perfect sense someday. There are many things that we can, and many that we cannot understand, prove, or perceive. But one thing is certain, if we can know or comprehend anything it's because God has revealed it to us by bringing it into the light.

All the laws, facts, and realities that will ever be examined, explained, or established via science and philosophy come from the mind of God. His wonders became available the second we showed up in this extraordinary universe. Funny how unbelievers and atheists try to argue or rationalize their positions from the naturalist, relativist, or reductionist points of view as if their premises and conclusions were reached outside of God's knowledge and His Word. But, unlike God, they contradict themselves. They assert that there are no absolutes, intelligence is random, and morality is merely a social convenience. But all of these contentions are themselves self-contradictory. Stating that there are no absolutes is stating an absolute. Holding that morality is a social convenience is taking a moral stand. Saying that intelligence is random means words are meaningless. We are instructed by the wise king not to succumb to such foolish arguments, but rather point out fallacies in reasoning (PRO 26:4–5); for all laws come from God, including those of physics, nature, morality, and logic. There is no excuse for those who cannot see the light (ROM 1:20), especially when they are blinded by it (JOH 12:40; 2 CO 4:4).

PSA 8:4–7   1 CO 1:17–29   1 CO 2:1–16   1 CO 3:18–23   1 TI 6:14–21   JDE 1:10

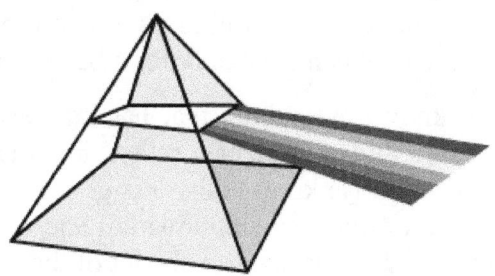

Bible Study: Is There Proof of God?

The answer to the above question is a resounding, "yes." Now, many would dispute this conclusion, especially those who have chosen deliberately not to believe in God. For example, some scientists, many of whom happen to be staunch atheists, vehemently reply "negative" to this question without providing evidence or rationale. They believe the existence of God cannot be proven empirically which is precisely why they reject God. They maintain that there is no way of proving why the universe came into existence, much less the origin of life; much less if there is a Creator of it all including a heaven and a hell. They postulate ridiculous alternative explanations of how there could be an infinite number of universes and ours came out the winner; or life sprang from some primeval muck and evolved into intelligent humans; or it was aliens from outer space that brought life with them; or that our morality is nothing more than interactions among neurons, represented by random chemical processes, a result of natural adaptation and selection. Of course, there is zero proof that any of these hypotheses are true.

The problem with disbelief is this: one must place his or her faith in lies, innuendo, or fantastic theories such as those listed above. The wonders of God's creation are reduced to random chance, meaningless occurrences with no ultimate purpose. Everything is relative and truth is unverifiable, such that God has no relevance. To assert relativism is itself is a relative statement which violates the most fundamental law of logic: non-contradiction. This law states that two opposites cannot both be true at the same time; for example, it cannot be raining on my head and not raining on my head right now. Interestingly, God Almighty does not violate that fundamental principle either. Because God is holy, He cannot lie, sin, alter His perfection, or contradict Himself even though He is totally powerful. It is illogical to think that a flawless being would change or behave in a self-contradictory manner. Let it be known that God, and Christ, will never change (MAL 3:6; HEB 13:8); and everything they say is absolutely correct (PSA 100:5; JOH 17:17; 1 JO 5:6), spoken through the Holy Spirit of truth (1 JO 5:6).

Consider the reasoning of German philosopher Gottfried von Leibniz (he died in 1716). He proposed that the universe is constantly changing, and when things change there must be a reason. Further, things that exist must exist for a reason; and when they change there must be a cause for that change. The cause must either reside within itself or outside of itself. Since there is no reason within the universe to explain its own existence, the cause must be outside the universe. This is especially relevant in light of the fact that modern science has demonstrated the universe had a beginning and therefore must have an external cause. The reason the universe began and exists must either have another cause to explain that cause, or it is a cause in and of itself. The latter is referred to as the first cause. There cannot be an infinite number of prior causes, or multiple first causes; it makes more sense that God necessarily is the uncaused first cause. But atheists will ask the ridiculous question, "then what caused God." By definition, God's existence is outside of space and time; He is His own sufficient reason for being. God is the reason for everything and He is the cause of life. Thus, God is alive; and the past, present, and future look the same to Him for He is timeless. Funny, how skeptics dismiss the notion of an infinite being in favor of infinite universes or infinite time. But time as we know it began when the universe was born; and infinite time can exist only for a being that is timeless.

Being omniscient, God knows everything that has happened, happening, and going to happen. But He allows us to cause things to happen rather than making our choices for us; and although we don't always do His will, He knows how it is going turn out. That is, God grants us free will, so we become the cause of our own sin, downfall and death. Thank goodness He saw this in advance; otherwise we would neither have a way out of the grave nor a way into heaven.

The point is, a lot of the evidence must be discarded in order to believe God does not exist or to argue there is no proof that He does. The proof is all around, because God has revealed Himself to us in countless ways. One can simply ponder the intricacy of the universe and the interrelated variables and constants that are calibrated to the nth degree which, if any one was a fraction out of tolerance, it would cause the end of us all. Or if that is too complicated, take time to appreciate the beauty of God's creation, the magnificence of it, and the vastness of it. Clearly, an intelligent being can conclude that intelligence had to be the cause. There is no reasonable argument that such organization, sophistication, and clarification can basically cause itself via processes like macroevolution, random mutation, natural selection, and biochemistry. The evidence is frankly not there. Since the probability is infinitesimally small for a universe like ours to exist on its own, the converse must certainly be true: the probability is astronomical that the universe was indeed created or caused to exist.

The first major element of proof, therefore, is God's revelation to humanity. He makes Himself, His rules, His glory, His creation, and His plan available to all people. The best and only primary source is the Holy Spirit, who gives to us the written Word, the spoken Word, and the living Word made flesh. Those who have absorbed the Holy Bible into their hearts have living proof. Okay, so a great number of people choose not to believe the Bible. They come up with all kinds of excuses why it cannot be true. They even go to great lengths to disprove it scientifically, although such attempts usually end up confirming it. What the cynics have not done is actually study the Bible adequately enough to arrive at the proposition that it is false. In this study guide we have examined extensively the history, authenticity, reliability, and prophecy of the Bible; the reader may wish to review the acronym *HARP* (see Index) for a refresher.

In short, the accuracy of the Bible, particularly the prophecy, provides sufficient evidence that God exists. Nobody can predict the future with precision; but the Bible does. While the Bible was written by men, God instructed them to write it (2 PE 1:21); and its wisdom far exceeds that of humankind. Suffice it to say that an open, earnest, and diligent student of the Bible will not doubt it at some point during his or her studies. It is written: the glory of God is revealed to all flesh, but not all will receive or acknowledge God (ISA 40:21–31).

ISA 40:5   ISA 56:1   ROM 1:19–22   ROM 16:25–27   1 CO 12:7–8   EPH 1:6–14   TIT 2:11–13

There is evidence of God inside each one of us. Within our own minds we possess abilities to reason, understand, and elucidate. My, how advanced are our mental faculties, our imagination, our grasp of morality! Do you think these gifts just happened by accident or are being directed by your chemistry? They are given to us precisely so we can know God, and learn about His righteousness, and observe and comprehend His creation. Wisdom is not inherited, not a mutation, not an adaptation, but a unique attribute of God Himself, which He has in His infinite wisdom chosen to share with us. But not all at once: for we could not fathom such a barrage of knowledge. Besides, there can be only one all-knowing entity. We have eternity to learn and become; and we will become more and more like God, but we will never become a god ourselves (JOB 40:9; 1 CO 8:5–6). Since wisdom can change and increase, there must be causes. Only an omniscient God can be the first cause of unlimited potential to learn, know, and grow. He has all knowledge but we never will; though our potential for learning will be endless with eternal life.

JOB 28:12–15   PRO 1:7   PRO 9:9–10   1 CO 1:19–31   COL 2:2–4   JAM 3:17–18

Apparently, God makes certain thoughts known and His promises accessible to everyone. But, of course, this requires one to pay attention. Too many dismiss His Word because it is not easy to grasp; yes, it requires effort and work if you really want to get it. But God's truth can be found even if you are not willing, able, or looking (ROM 10:19–21; ACT 17:27). Some people just accept what God says and they cling to His promises, like a child does when a trusted loved one provides instruction or encouragement (MAR 10:13–16; 1 CO 13:11–12).

It seems unlikely one can completely tune-out God. Ever notice how, during a conversation, we tune people out or they tune us out; we all do it from time to time. We either have other things on our mind, or we are distracted, or we are preparing our rebuttal, or whatever. It takes considerable effort to concentrate and hear every word; that is, to listen intently. This is especially true when the topic is complicated, detailed, or deep. If you miss too much of the message you will miss the point. But some people don't want to see, hear, or know. They dismiss it before the fact (*a priori*). Who, in their right mind jumps to a conclusion without considering the facts? Well, I guess everyone does. But when it comes to the facts of life, I recommend you take heed. Do not be so quick to dismiss God. Consider the logic of French philosopher Blaise Pascal (he died in 1662) who proposed that there is nothing to lose and everything to gain by wagering on God. If you believe and He doesn't exist, you have lost nothing. But what if He does exist and you do not believe? You will lose everything. When the Lord comes knocking, open your heart and your mind and let Him in (ISA 66:4; REV 3:20).

JOB 33:14–16   ISA 6: 9–10   ISA 42:18–20   EZE 3:27   MAT 13:10–17,34–35   ROM 11:7–8

This discussion has been about God's revelations and how He bestows His wisdom upon humans in a variety of ways. It is understood that we must be open to Him and not close our hearts and minds. And it takes a lot of energy to remain mindful of His presence and His influence in the world. But let's take it one step further and suggest that we will realize a great deal more by actually looking for Him, seeking His virtue, and being eager to learn; in other words, be more proactive. It is one thing to listen when spoken to, and another to open your eyes to what is going on around you; it is yet another thing to actually pursue these things with purpose and tenacity (PRO 2:1–5,10–14). This is a journey of the spirit, seeing how the source of what we seek is the Holy Spirit (1 CO 2:1–16). Open your eyes and ears, pay attention with your mind, and connect with your spirit.

DEU 4:29   PRO 11:27   PRO 15:32–33   LAM 3:25–26   HOS 10:12   MAT 7:7–8   1 JO 4:6–8

Obviously, one of the avenues in which God communicates to us is through our spirits. For example, we have a conscience which reminds us about right and wrong; it is our moral compass. Everyone has one but not all take heed of it. It will not lie to you since therein dwells knowledge of truth. Hence, there is evidence of God's presence in our morality. It is akin to the capability known as discernment; an attribute not shared by other creatures inhabiting this planet. God gave this knowledge to Homo sapiens so that we would do the right thing, especially to walk in righteousness like Christ. The scientists have no way of explaining this phenomenon via evolution or naturalism; especially since all humans possess it, other organisms do not, and it can be observed even in small children. If morality could evolve, why haven't other species acquired it? Animals can be taught to obey but do not inherently choose right or wrong; they behave according to instinct. Though they may have feelings, they do not feel guilty unless we teach them to; they cannot comprehend sin and therefore are not condemned for it. But we humans know the difference because we have the Law written into our hearts. In order for there to be a moral law, there must be a lawgiver (ISA 33:22). Only a perfect being could teach anyone how to be perfectly obedient. God has given us His Law to teach us, guide us, and reprove us (EXO 20:1–17; EXO 20:20; ROM 2:14–15) and His Son as an example of perfect obedience.

The underlying power behind morality is God's love; He loves everyone without reservation. He implores us to love one another the same way. It is this pure and positive regard for our fellow man that is the basis of moral values; we value human life as sacred. Why? Because God made us in His image, and He loves us so much that He would send His Son to die so that we might live. Such love will motivate some people to place themselves in danger, even sacrifice their own lives, so that another might live or be safe. All of God's commandments to us are founded on loving Him and humankind. In fact, love is the fulfillment of all moral laws (ROM 13:9–10; 1 CO 13:2–8,13).

EXO 24:7   MAT 22:35–40   LUK 10:25–37   GAL 5:14   JAM 2:8–10   JAM 4:10–12

Those proposing that ethics are relative, or that morality is just a social norm, do so because they do not want to be held accountable. Atheists in particular reject God, not because He doesn't fit evolution, reductionism, or naturalistic concepts, but because they don't want God. They would prefer that morality remains subjective or unrealistic. That way they won't need to feel ashamed for disregarding others; they can satisfy their hedonistic pleasures without concern or remorse. After all, if life is meaningless and there is nothing beyond, then why give sin a second thought? Eat, drink, and be merry because this is all we've got (LUK 12:19–21). How will they answer God when they stand before Him in judgment, I wonder?

Such a worldview is unreasonable and destructive, and those suggesting it are wise in their own eyes; but they can be very persuasive to persons of poor intellect, unsure of the facts, or ignorant of God. These arrogant fools will never admit to themselves that God exists, even though they know He must. The very statement "God does not exist" violates the law of non-contradiction. How can one believe or not believe in something if it is not a viable concept? It's like saying "I don't believe in flying pink elephants," and then condemning others that do. You see, it's not that atheists have no concept of God; it's that they hate the concept. They enjoy the free will part; they just don't want the consequences and particularly the judgment. One must be careful not to fall into their trap of twisted logic, rationalizations, and fabricated evidence (PRO 14: 6–8; 1 CO 3:18–20). They are simply looking for company in the fall, and do not know it or are in denial about it; either way, they are working against God and for the other side.

JOB 35:10–13   PSA 14:1–2   PRO 18:1–2   JOH 15:23–25   ROM 1:32   ROM 2:14–15

It is foolishness to reject something outright without even trying it. For all you know you might be good at it, or learn to like it. But most people that refuse to believe, or allow setbacks or negative experiences to cause them to drop Christianity from their repertory of beliefs, never really gave God a chance. They find it embarrassing, stupid, unfashionable, or troublesome. It makes no sense to reject knowledge of any kind, or to deny any fact, especially absolute truth. Well, some people prefer fiction over reality, and they will take a stand for ignorance and argue a falsehood with vigor. To me this seems embarrassing. It certainly is not wise according to King Solomon, who was arguably the wisest of anyone, and the author of the following proverbs.

PRO 10:21   PRO 12:15   PRO 16:22   PRO 18:7   PRO 26:4–5   PRO 26:11–12   PRO 29:11

The next category of evidence proving there is a God consists of amazing miracles. God and Christ have performed miracles which appear to defy the laws of nature and physics. This is another bone of contention for some scientists and for all atheists. Remember, they often force themselves to determine natural causes for things. Miracles from God are, by definition, supernatural. Naturally, God can employ Nature to make things happen, such as cause a great flood or destroy a city. However, on other occasions, there is no earthly explanation, such as water instantaneously becoming wine or calming a storm with the snap of the fingers. There are a variety of miraculous events recorded in the Bible, not the least of which is the resurrection of Jesus Christ. As reviewed in previous lessons, the evidence for that incident is overwhelming. It is the single most important event in human history, and the foundation of faith in Christ; there is no other world religion or worldview that includes or even considers that fact. If there ever was evidence of God it is in the resurrection. Those denying it will be surprised when their resurrection takes place. For them, the only thing left will be judgment, and that will be their end. For believers, it will be the beginning of everlasting joy and peace.

Everybody has witnessed a miracle, either personally or vicariously. One could argue that conception, birth, and life represent a miracle; and that miracle occurs hundreds of times on this planet every hour of the day. Packed into every single cell is the entire DNA blueprint of the human being that became you. And everything about you is completely unique, from your fingerprints to your eyes to your toes. No other human being that ever lived or ever will live is like you in appearance, demeanor, personality, talents, and purpose.

DEU 11:1–28   DEU 29:2–4,29   JOH 7:31   JOH 12:36–38   ACT 2:22   HEB 2:3–4

While not the most compelling evidence available, experience can be proof of God. Have you ever had a "religious experience" in your life? It is one of those things that are entirely unplanned, unrehearsed, unexpected, and unbelievable. It could have been a wakeup call from God to clean up your act (addiction, promiscuity, etc.); or perhaps God's Spirit spoke to you, or you received a message from Him in a dream; maybe all-of-a-sudden you were speaking in tongues; you could have been visited by an angel; or someone you know overcame certain death; or you escaped a calamity completely unscathed; perhaps your prayers were answered; maybe you simply beheld the wondrous miracles of God's creation. There were several notable figures in the Bible that witnessed the glory of God firsthand. One of these days, you will too (JOB 19:25–26; ROM 14:10), if you haven't already. Keep in mind, experience is not a substitute for learning; it's just another form of it.

GEN 14:18–20   GEN 18:1–3   EXO 3:1–6   EXO 3:13–15   ACT 9:1–6   2 CO 5:10

Just remember this: God reveals Himself to everyone each in His own way, in such a way that you will not be dismayed, distracted, or disillusioned. This often occurs when you are not expecting a revelation, insofar as you cannot make it happen, will it to happen, or anticipate it happening. But if and when it does, it will be real and it will be true; and you will not be able to deny it or explain it. For example, once you have given your life and your heart to Christ, you will become new (2 CO 5:17). You will feel different because it will be a different you, complete with spiritual transformation. Little by little, you will be sanctified by the Holy Spirit of God to be conformed to the likeness of His Son, and receive an inheritance as an equal heir to His kingdom. Such an experience is life changing, and you will not dismiss God from that moment forward. When the love of Christ changes lives, people do an about-face, and souls are saved; who can deny the One that caused it? The best ways to find God is to seek Him in the Word, through meditation and worship, and by fellowshipping with other members of the flock. If you seek God, He will reveal Himself to you. And you will experience Him in a personal way, possibly every day.

Everybody who denies God's existence will have to explain Him away, and discount episodes of His revelation to them as a nonevent. This is the sin of disbelief. It is arguably the most grievous sin of them all, for it leads to eternal death. If one goes to his or her grave in disbelief it is unpardonable after that (MAT 12:31). You must desire forgiveness, repent, and accept the salvation of Christ before you die. Death cannot be reversed, and nobody can be saved in the grave, because there is no hope beyond there. The greatest proof that God exists will be revealed the moment Christ returns (1 TH 4:16–17). For many, it will be too late.

NUM 14:11,22–23   ECC 9:10   JER 45:3–5   ROM 1:20–25   HEB 3:12–19   HEB 4:1–2

Bible Study: Is the New Testament True?

The following analysis is a review of numerous facts bearing witness that the Bible is true, with the New Testament being the focus. You may recall an easy way to remember some of the categories of biblical proof is using the keyword *HARP*: history, authenticity, reliability, and prophecy. There is a great deal of evidence, both internal to the Bible and external to it, upholding it as the inspired Word of God beyond any reasonable doubt. It must be emphasized that the sixty-six books of the Holy Bible, thirty-nine from the Old Testament (OT), twenty-seven from the New Testament (NT) underwent intense examination before being universally included into the canon of scripture. For more information on this process, it is recommended that the reader consult the Index on *Canonization*.

1. **Biblical Influence**: Forty plus authors contributed to the OT and NT during the course of over fifteen hundred years. There is no way the writers could have known how theirs was just one piece of an elaborate puzzle that would come together long after they passed (2 TI 3:16; 2 PE1:20–21). Combined, each work congeals into one magnificent theme that has not changed for millennia. God's Word remains the only complete compilation of His plan of salvation, and is thus uniquely inspired. Original texts and subsequent copies were meticulously duplicated such that every *t* was crossed and *i* dotted (MAT 5:18). And despite efforts to destroy it by governments, rulers, societies, and Satan, not to mention natural and manmade catastrophes, the Bible is still with us and remains unaltered and unscathed (ISA 40:8; MAT 24:35). Certainly, God must have guided the entire procedure to include observation, education, inspiration, documentation, authentication, dissemination, translation, preservation, and publication.

    The Holy Bible has gained worldwide acceptance; it is undoubtedly the most widely read, copied, and distributed book that has ever existed or ever will. The complete Bible has been translated into over five hundred languages, with thirteen hundred more NT translations, and another thousand languages with one or more books of the Bible interpreted. No other written work has had anywhere near the degree of influence; not just globally, but also for individuals. Societies, legal systems, belief systems, and cultures have been based on the Bible. It has been a principal inspiration for art, music, drama, ethics, philosophy, science, world religions, travel, and the list goes on. No religion or religious text has the degree of external support as the Bible, which for alternate faith systems is scant at best. Regarding God's Holy Word, the proof is abundant just like God's love and mercy.

2. **Manuscript Evidence**: There is a plethora of complete manuscript copies as well as parts and fragments of different NT books. Evidence dates as far back as the first century, within fifty years of the resurrection of Christ. No ancient document approaches the amount of manuscript evidence as the New Testament. And no other work of antiquity has near the timeliness, in terms of proximity of available copies to the original. For example, credible scholars never question the worthiness and value of ideas from ancient Greek philosophers. But there exist no known copies of any works from Socrates (469–399 BC). Regarding Plato (427–347 BC), there exist seven copies of his work but they are some 1200 years removed from when he lived. Aristotle (384–322 BC) fares better with forty-nine existing copies but they are 1400 years removed. Twenty copies of the works of the late first century historian Tacitus exist, also removed by 1000 years from his death. Now consider the New Testament, written in the first century, for which there are literally thousands of copies, some less than 100 years removed from the original.

The current tally is a few-hundred short of 7000 NT pieces of varying size (including complete Bibles, individual books or chapters, and fragments) in Greek, the language in which the NT was originally written as well as the language of the oldest extant manuscripts. There are thousands more manuscripts translated into other languages (Latin, Coptic, Syriac, Armenian, Slavonic, Ethiopic, Arabic, etc.). In total, there are roughly 25,000 known NT manuscript portions (partial or complete). The oldest manuscripts were typically copied on papyrus as it was reasonably durable and abundant. The joining together of all existing NT papyri could recreate the NT in whole.

Christianity spread like wildfire across the civilized world, such that the NT had been translated into several languages as early as the second century. Since there was a proliferation of reliable versions, emerging in different tongues and times, it became virtually impossible to introduce counterfeits. This is because the agreement across multiple sources contradicted false, contrived, or inaccurate texts. In order to be included into the canon, manuscripts were scrutinized to ensure they were authentic, consistent with established doctrine and teaching, and known works from reliable sources, prior to being distributed. Obviously, God had a hand in ensuring His Word was recorded, copied, and translated accurately. For example, the agreement among Dead Sea Scrolls and current versions of the Bible is extraordinary. More on that topic can be found in upcoming pages on archaeological evidence.

3. **Early Church Leaders**: From the first to the fifth centuries a number of early church fathers and theologians quoted directly from the New Testament. In fact, a compilation of the over 36,000 such quotations would be sufficient to recreate the NT in the event that the manuscript evidence had been lost. Some of the reputable early church leaders are described below in approximate chronological order.

Apostles and Eyewitness (AD 30–100). The NT was written by people close to Christ and His companions who actually witnessed the events they reported, or by those who personally interviewed those witnesses. In other words, authoring and compilation of the NT was conducted using primary sources. Remember the principle rule of NT canonization and standardization: verification that the witness was an authority beyond reproach. NT authors were inspired by Christ himself: apostles like Matthew, John, Peter, Paul; companions like Mark and Luke; relations like James and Jude. Notice how their personal accounts gelled into a cohesive and comprehensive story of the greatest man that ever lived: His biography, His teachings, and His perfection. Not a single one of them doubted who Christ was, and most of them went to their deaths believing Him and proclaiming it to the world. Who, in their right mind would suffer such sorrow, punishment, imprisonment, torture, and death for something they knew to be a lie or a hoax? And not just them, but many believing evangelists that followed such as those listed next.

Polycarp (AD 69–155). While there are no existing manuscripts directly attributed to Polycarp, he was himself quoted by many of the church fathers succeeding him. He served as Bishop of Smyrna in the early second century. Irenaeus wrote of Polycarp having been instructed in his youth by apostles of Christ. Like the apostles, Polycarp was martyred, but as a very old man. The fact that he was burned at the stake for refusing to denounce Christ is well documented.

Papias (@ AD 100). Not much is known of this Bishop of Hierapolis, other than he was a companion of Polycarp and wrote several books, of which Irenaeus and Eusebius were familiar, had studied, and critiqued. Apparently, Papias was a NT scholar and historian, particularly knowledgeable of the early Gospel writers and the oral tradition of preserving the truth.

Clement of Rome (died @ AD 100). This early Roman Bishop wrote a letter to the church in Corinth that is a testimonial to the plight of the early Christian Church, including the martyrdom of Peter and Paul. Clement was ordained by St. Peter himself, according to the historian and apologist Tertullian (below). He proclaimed the Gospel that was given to the apostles by Jesus, and preached the resurrection.

Ignatius of Antioch (died @ AD 110). This man was mentored by the Apostle John and is known primarily through seven letters. Six letters were written to churches in Rome, Ephesus, Philadelphia, Smyrna, Magnesia, and Tralles; one letter was addressed to his friend Polycarp. He also was a willing martyr to the faith, who announced that Jesus was born of a virgin, baptized by John, crucified under Pilate and Herod, and resurrected by the Almighty; and He would raise those from the dead who believed in Him. He wrote that Christ showed Himself alive to the apostles, and ate and drank with them.

Justin Martyr (martyred @ AD 165). All but a few of his many works have been lost, but he is considered one of the premier apologists. Being born a heathen in his native Palestine, he became a student, witness, and teacher of the Word (Logos), in Palestine, Rome, and Ephesus (one pupil was Tatian, an Assyrian theologian who translated the four Gospels into Syriac). He wrote of the lineage of Christ, His birth in Bethlehem to include the visit by the magi, the miracles, how He fulfilled Old Testament prophecy, how He predicted His own death, and how He died, arose, and ascended into heaven. Martyr also warned that a tale was afoot about Jesus's body being stolen. Clearly this man was conversant in the Gospels.

Irenaeus (became bishop of Lyons in AD 177). A student of Polycarp for a time, he was another prolific teacher, writer, and apologist. He sought to develop and preserve the canon of scripture, and he was a formidable opponent to the Gnosticism of his time.

Clement of Alexandria (@ AD 150–215). Born of pagan parents, he converted to Christianity later in life. He was a man well educated in Hellenism, particularly Greek philosophers such as Plato. Origen was one of his renowned young students; Eusebius also wrote about this prolific writer, passionate teacher, generous giver, and disciplined theologian. He was a poet, songwriter, and visionary. His most noteworthy literary accomplishment was a trilogy of works focused on the divine Logos of truth, to educate and convert the masses and to conform believers into the image of God's Son.

Gospel of Truth (second century AD). Purported by Irenaeus to have been composed by Valentinus, this work declares Jesus to be the Son of God and the Word made flesh, who was persecuted, nailed to a tree, suffered greatly, and died; His death brought salvation to believers. Jesus appeared to His friends after rising from the dead. Certainly, this information mirrors the Gospel of John.

Tertullian (writings date from late second century to early third century). Hailing from Carthage Africa, he was another productive teacher and writer. One of the first to write in Latin, many of his books have survived, the most famous being *Apology*. He was a staunch critic of those he considered heretics, and a strict observer of laws and rules. He also mixed a little science with his theology.

Hippolytus of Rome (AD 170–235). A student of Irenaeus and role model to Origen, he is mostly known for his work *Apostolic Traditions*. His philosophy was largely based on the Logos doctrine of Justin Martyr. Like many believers of his time he protested the unholy practices of certain church authorities. He was banished to die in the mines.

CHAPTER EIGHT

Origen (AD 185–254). Born in Alexandria to Christian parents, he was a seasoned teacher, preacher, mediator, author, translator, and theologian. Like another mentor Clement, he mixed a little Platonic philosophy along with strict dogmatics into his teachings, writings, and speeches. He traveled extensively, he studied intensely, and he was attributed to authoring some six thousand works according to Epiphanius.

Cyprian (died @ AD 258). Though he was baptized a Christian rather late in life, he became the Bishop of Carthage soon thereafter. A great number of his many treatises have been authenticated. A man of wealth he was quite the philanthropist, giving away most of it. He was persecuted, exiled, imprisoned, and executed for his perseverance in the faith and refusal to capitulate to Roman secularism.

Athanasius (AD 296–373). One of the most famous of early apologists, this Bishop of Alexandria was instrumental in establishing Christian doctrine such as the Trinity, developing a creed of the essentials of faith, and adopting the twenty-seven NT books of the canon (he also was in attendance at the Council of Nicaea in the year AD 325). He spent a large portion of his life in exile, being an outspoken critic of Arianism. His most famous quote (paraphrased) is "Christ became like a man so that we could become like God."

Eusebius (AD died @ 339). A man of sorrows, he was tormented and imprisoned during the Great Persecution, but later became the Bishop of Caesarea in his native Palestine and a friend of Emperor Constantine. Though a small number of his works have survived, he was quite the church historian, completing his many iterations of *Church History* in the year AD 324.

Ambrose (@ AD 340–397). This nobleman became the Bishop of Milan in the year AD 374, and later a provincial governor in northern Italy as well as an advisor to Emperor Theodosius. He is considered one of the first to sing hymns in church, and composed a number of hymns as well. He is credited for being a great influence on St. Augustine whom he baptized, commemorating the event with his song *Te Deum*.

Epiphanius (died in AD 403). This Bishop of Salamis, Cyprus was known for his work *Panarion* which was a history of heresies advanced to corrupt or destroy the Christian Church. The text was replete with biblical quotations. He also was known for his persecution of non-believers, and contesting the philosophy of Origen.

Jerome (@ AD 330–420). He was the son of Eusebius who was instrumental in translating the Bible into Latin (the Vulgate). He was a traveler, theologian, historian, and scholar. His writings and commentaries are extremely orthodox and dogmatic. He also was well versed in the Hebrew language and understood the many connections between the OT and the NT.

Augustine (AD 354–430). Bishop of Hippo (present day Algeria), he was probably the most influential of the early apologists and theologians, especially with respect to Western Christianity. He was an educated man who became a Christian as an adult, and later a priest. He was a dynamic writer, influential philosopher, and prominent teacher. He was instrumental in advancing a greater understanding of sin, eschatology, and the doctrines of the sacraments, sex and marriage.

4. **Secular History**: A number of historians from the secular world, most of whom were antagonistic towards Christianity, have substantiated several events delineated in the New Testament. Some of these ancient sources are discussed below. Even though many loathed Christians and Christianity they were talking and writing about it; and while they portrayed

believers in a negative light, their testimony served to confirm the faith and certain truths, nevertheless.

Thallus (@ AD 52). He recorded history from the Trojan wars to his own time. Possibly the earliest secular corroboration of the crucifixion of Christ, he reported an eclipse of the sun to explain the great darkness that occurred during the event. While most of his writings are lost, the above-mentioned report was referenced by Julius Africanus (below).

Mara Bar-Serapion (@ AD 74). This imprisoned Syrian philosopher wrote a letter to his son comparing Jesus Christ to famed Greek philosophers such as Socrates and Pythagoras. The contents of the letter, composed during the time the Gospels were being written, was copied and preserved, though the original deteriorated.

Josephus (AD 37–100). Given the name Flavius by Emperor Vespasian, he was a Jewish historian and cleric who was commissioned by Rome to write his history of the Jews entitled *Jewish Antiquities*. He wrote of a wise and extraordinary man named Jesus, a miracle worker and teacher, who was condemned to die on a cross by Pontius Pilate. He further recorded the belief among followers that Christ rose from the dead on the third day as prophets had foretold, and he declared that the cult of Christianity continued to proliferate. He also recorded the condemnation of a member of the Sanhedrin by the name of James, the "brother of Jesus who they called the Christ." And he documented the execution of John the Baptist by Herod Antipas.

Tacitus (AD 55–120). This Roman historian wrote *Annals* and *Histories* logging the periods from the death of Augustus (AD 14) to the death of Nero (AD 68) to the death of Domitian (AD 96), respectively. Details in these records corroborate NT history such as the crucifixion of Christ by Pontius Pilate during the reign of Tiberius, the spread of Christianity from Judea to Rome, and the persecution of Christians by the Romans in general and Nero in particular.

Suetonius (@ AD 69–123). This Roman historian's most significant work chronicled the reigns of seven emperors from Julius to Domitian to include the life and times of the imperial era. He also spoke of the Christians who were persecuted by Rome and were willing to go to their deaths for believing in the life, death and resurrection of Christ.

Pliny the Younger (@ AD 112). This magistrate in Bithynia wrote Trajan about his concern that so many people were willing to die than curse Christ. He was requesting guidance from the emperor about how to deal with this peace-loving and law-abiding group of people who would sing, worship, and pray to Christ as if He was a god. Trajan replied to Pliny advising him not to go searching them out, or posting anonymous accusations, but to follow proper procedure if they were brought for prosecution.

Phlegon (born @ AD 80). A historian and writer during the reign of Hadrian, he also was referenced by Africanus in reporting an eclipse and an earthquake during Christ's crucifixion under the reign of Tiberius. Origen mentioned this report as well, though it has been lost to antiquity. Quoting Phlegon, "Jesus arose after His death and displayed the marks of His punishment."

Lucian of Samosate (@ AD 125–180). He was an Assyrian writer and satirist who wrote in Greek and poked fun at Christianity. He reported that Christians had continued to worship a man named Jesus who was the crucified leader of their cult.

Julius Africanus (@ AD 160–240). A traveler and historian, he was most likely a native of Palestine, being well informed about the life and times of the early Christians. He compiled a history of people from the creation of man to his era, a timeframe spanning 5723 years. He estimated the birth of Christ to be March 25, 1 BC. His proposed date for creation of the universe was 5500 years before Christ. These estimates were proffered long before Rome recreated their calendar to coincide with their estimate of Christ's birth (which is now thought to be closer to 4–5 BC).

Babylonian Talmud (AD 70–200). This is a collection of rabbinical teachings which made references to the historic Jesus as early as the first and second centuries. Of primary importance is the mention of Jesus being "hanged" (crucified) for "heresy" (blasphemy) and "sorcery" (works of Satan) during Passover.

5. **Archaeological Validation**: An amazing number of archaeological finds confirm various biblical accounts, despite the fact that archaeologists often have sought to disconfirm the Bible. There have been zero authentic archaeological discoveries that contradict the Bible outright. The following list is but a smidgeon of the significant evidence that has been found over the last few centuries. Note that some Old Testament relics are introduced since substantiation of the OT helps to validate the NT. It is highly recommended that the reader study biblical archaeology, and cross reference the Bible names and places discussed below. Obtain a Bible Concordance and you can easily find the passages where the names and places referenced below can be found. You will discover that the physical evidence from archaeology supports the biblical account.

Dead Sea Scrolls. From 1946–1956 almost one thousand texts were discovered at Qumran. Virtually all of the Old Testament (except the book of Esther) was represented from the multitude of scrolls, which were preserved in clay jars found in various caves dotting the cliffs. Probably the most important among the scrolls was the entire book of Isaiah. Even more outstanding is that the Hebrew scroll is 99 percent identical to the current version. God preserved the truth for over two millennia; it was never altered by copyists or translators as skeptics had assumed. The primary copyist errors that investigators found in the biblical manuscripts include typographic, punctuation, spelling, and word usage, none of which altered the meaning. One of the Dead Sea scrolls not widely disseminated made reference to a Messiah who was crucified for the sins of humanity, and the fact that the prophet Isaiah had predicted it. Another such scroll referred to the "Son of the Most High" the exact words used by Luke. Many scrolls can be dated to the first century when the Gospels were being written.

Ossuaries. These decorative burial caskets, usually made from limestone or clay, were quite durable. After decomposition, the bones of the deceased were contained in the ossuary, sometimes those of entire families. Inscriptions carved on the outside indicated whose bones were contained therein. One such ossuary was inscribed as follows (translated): *Caiaphas, Joseph son of Caiaphas*. Given the ornate craftsmanship, it can be assumed that someone of high prominence was interred there, likely the high priest Caiaphas, leader of the Sanhedrin when Jesus was tried and found guilty of heresy. Another ossuary is inscribed as follows: *James, the son of Joseph, brother of Jesus*. Naturally, there is debate over whether the ossuary contains the bones of Jesus's half-brother James, the leader of the Christian Church in Jerusalem who was ordered stoned by the Sanhedrin. Well, if this relic is genuine, who else could it be? Sure, there could've been families having the same three names; but then again, God has a way of making His truth be known precisely so cynics might rethink it. Another ossuary identified names of *Mary, Martha, and Lazarus*; yes, these were common names in the first century, but having them all appear together with no others is at least an interesting coincidence, or possibly proof they were siblings and Jesus's close friends. Additionally, bones from a crucifixion victim were found in a first century ossuary during excavations. Included were broken legs to hasten death, and a portion of a nine-inch nail still stuck through the heel bone, with olive tree fragments indicating the nail was driven into a knot which prevented its removal from the foot. Therefore, contrary to the belief of some, the Romans really did execute offenders in that fashion.

Monoliths, Steles, Tablets. There are a wealth of carvings and inscriptions which verify the Bible, many from nations that were enemies or were otherwise foreign to the Hebrews. Here are some of the noteworthy finds in chronological order: Hammurabi Stele (@ 1760 BC) provides the code of Assyrian King Hammurabi, not dissimilar to the laws of Moses; Merneptah Stele (@ 1200 BC) provides an early reference to the nation of Israel; Mesha Stele (950 BC) from basalt stone documents the wars brought by the Moabite king against Kings Omri and Ahab; Black Obelisk (@ 825 BC) records the conquest of Assyria against Israel, allegedly portraying King Jehu kneeling before Shalmaneser III; Tel Dan Stele (@ 800 BC) with Aramaic inscription, *House of David*; Nimrud Tablet (@ 730 BC) is a relief reviewing the campaign of Tiglath-Pileser III in the land of Judah (2 KI 16:7–8); Siloam Tunnel (@700 BC) which brought water from the Gihon Spring into Jerusalem is inscribed in Hebrew and commemorates King Hezekiah who commissioned the project (2 KI 20:20); Sennacherib Prism (@700 BC) is a clay obelisk which documents the Assyrian king's attack on Jerusalem during the reign of Hezekiah (2 KI 18:13–36); the name Pontius Pilate is inscribed on a stone marker (@ 50 AD); Arch of Titus (70 AD) portrays the plunder of Jerusalem the year the temple was destroyed.

Edifices. Archaeology has confirmed a great number of palaces and temples; and there are assorted artifacts among the ruins of edifices that corroborate biblical accounts. The following is an abstract from a very large list. Noah's Ark (@ 2500 BC) declared to have been found, though some experts would dispute this (research it yourself on the Internet; looks like an ark to me); stone bust of King Nimrod, the great-grandson of Noah (@ 2000–2400 BC) found in present day Turkey; Ziggurat at Ur the homeland of Abraham (@ 2100 BC) believed by many to resemble the Tower of Babel (or, House of Nimrod to the Jews) reportedly built in Shinar a region to the north; ruins of Sodom and Gomorrah (@ 2000 BC) buried in brimstone (sulfur) and ash (note: the historian Josephus reported that the ruins were still visible in the first century); ruins of Jericho (@ 1400 BC) reveals walls that collapsed; palace of Rameses II (@ 1260 BC) probably built by the Hebrew slaves; Ishtar Gate from palace of King Nebuchadnezzar (@ 570 BC); ruins of Persepolis (@ 515 BC), likely the palace of Cyrus, predecessor to Darius I; palace of Darius (@ 500 BC), predecessor of Xerxes (aka Ahasuerus); palace of Artaxerxes, son of Xerxes (@ 375 BC); aqueduct and port built by King Herod the Great (@ 35 BC) in Caesarea.

People in the NT. Countless names are provided in the details of various biblical accounts. For years, a lot of these names were unverifiable; evidence they ever existed was unavailable. Of course, this fueled the doubters who assumed that the Bible was a work of fiction. However, many of these names have been verified in recent history. The following is a condensed list of names known to have existed at the times, in the locations, and occupying the positions reported in the NT. Again, it is recommended that the reader research these names in the Bible because most people will not recognize many of them: Barsabbas, Caiaphas, Erastus, Gallio, Lysanius, Quirinius.

Places in the NT. Let us add to the list of irrefutable proof some of the known places to have existed that are recognized in the NT: Bethany, Bethlehem, Capernaum, Gaza, Nazareth, Pool of Bethesda, and Pool of Siloam. Other known locations include landmarks familiar to tourists visiting Jerusalem: Garden of Gethsemane, Garden Tomb, Mount of Golgotha, Mount of Olives. And last but not least, ruins of Seven Churches in Asia Minor to which John sent the Revelation: most notably Ephesus, Pergamos, Sardis, and Smyrna.

First Century Boat, A contemporary discovery includes a fishing boat near the banks of the Sea of Galilee found preserved in mud when the water level declined. Such a vessel would have been the type utilized by four fishermen that became apostles of Christ (Peter, Andrew, James, John).

Shroud of Turin. Argued to be the burial cloth of Christ (JOH 19:39–41), there is no other artifact of antiquity like the shroud. It is unique in every way and no scientist has ever been able to explain it or replicate it. Though carbon dating tests showed it to be from the Middle Ages, recent evidence has revealed that the samples were taken from a portion of the shroud that had been repaired with intricate inter-weavings. Thus, that particular result has been nullified. Other tests show it to have originated in Palestine (pollen, soil, etc.). Further, a complimentary head cover (JOH 20:6–8), matched by exact blood spatter and smear has been ascribed to the shroud. It seems the preponderance of the evidence suggests that the shroud is a photographic negative, possibly portraying a three-dimensional image of Jesus Christ at the moment of resurrection.

6. **Scientific Evidence**: Are you aware of the remarkable accuracy of the Bible when it discusses science, the cosmos, and nature? You may find this hard to believe but many of the scientific explanations by Old and New Testament prophets and personages show an unabashed comprehension of concepts, laws, and elucidations that only recently have been affirmed using modern scientific methods. While it is too cumbersome to get into the details, a few of these amazing findings are reviewed again in this lesson. The reader is referred to the previous lesson *Does Science Disagree with the Bible*. Research the findings below and see how marvelous is the Bible. God's Word was way ahead of science, especially those scientists that have made it their mission to dispute God's truth. Since scientists cannot explain God, many deny him. Science also cannot explain conscious awareness, intelligence, morality or anything else that exists outside of observable reality, though scientists postulate theories of invisible matter and unexplained forces nonetheless.

Creation Account. The order of creation in Genesis is exactly the way scientists describe the progression, and is not in conflict with modern cosmology regarding universal expansion and formation. The seven days of creation are outlined below. No argument will be made as to the exact duration of this period since the Bible does not explicitly address that issue. Note that the seven days follow the opening statement of Genesis (KJV). "In the beginning God created the heaven and the earth. And the earth was without form and void; and darkness was upon the face of the deep. And the Spirit of God moved upon the face of the waters." (GEN 1:1–2). The following is what happened next (GEN 1:3—GEN 2:3).

1) Light (dividing light from darkness)
2) Separating of waters (firmament or atmospheres)
3) Gathering of waters, protrusion of land, and production of seed-bearing plants
4) Sun, moon, stars (full development and configuration of our solar system)
5) Production and multiplication of sea and air animals
6) Production and multiplication of land animals and creation of humans
7) God rested and admired His handiwork (only day without an evening and morning)

Common Knowledge. What seems to be common knowledge nowadays also was known long ago and is illustrated in the Bible. The list that follows is but a sampling.

1) Layers of atmosphere
2) Innumerable stars (more than the eye can see)
3) Circular shape of the earth and horizon
4) Gravity (mutual attraction of heavenly bodies and magnetism)
5) Movement of celestial bodies (in concert with one another)
6) Cycle and states of water (vapor, liquid, solid; evaporation, rain, freezing)
7) Medical knowledge (sanitation, blood, parasites, contagious diseases)
8) Uniqueness of life forms possessing seed able to reproduce within kinds (DNA)
9) Sea currents and shipping channels
10) Springs of water underground; fountains beneath the seas

Contemporary Findings. The following findings from the last century or so are also corroborated in the Bible. That is, the Bible shows that God had a plan and His revelations enabled people to figure it out way before the scientists did.

1) Space and time had a beginning (big bang theory)
2) Things that begin have a cause (natural or intelligent); first cause implies intelligence
3) Universe is expanding (unlimited capacity for space)
4) Entropy and heat death (eventual passing away of heaven and earth)
5) Fine tuning and precision (of elements, laws, physical constants)
6) Light has properties of particles (mass) and waves (movement)
7) Uncertainty principle (some things cannot be predicted by science)
8) Uniformity of space (shown in microwave background radiation)
9) Accuracy of general relativity (proves universe began and is expanding)
10) Man was made from dust (stardust)
11) Anthropic principle (the universe was made for humanity)
12) Specified complexity of design (cosmos, earth, organisms, DNA)
13) Fossil record (Cambrian explosion indicates unique kinds and debunks evolution)
14) Law and order (physical laws and moral laws) implies a lawmaker
15) Existence of ordinary and exotic matter (visible and invisible properties)

7. **Prophecy**: Probably the most compelling evidence of all is the profoundly precise prophecies, sometimes made centuries in advance, that always came true to the finest detail. A few examples are provided below. There is no other book written throughout history, including religious texts, that provides prophecy of such extraordinary reliability. Actually, there really is no other accurate prophetic work, period. So-called prophets, seers, fortune-tellers, and soothsayers (such as Nostradamus) provide only vague predictions with few details, which could be ascribed to any number of possible outcomes. Not so with the Bible. Well, you can see for yourself by examining the prophecy discussed in this section.

Elijah. Elijah made some interesting predictions. A personal favorite is his proclamation of the curse upon Ahab and Jezebel, and the precise manner of their deaths. King Ahab's blood would be spilled on the very tract of land upon which he and wife Jezebel had Naboth murdered, and dogs would lick his blood just as they had when Naboth died. Queen Jezebel would die in Jezreel by being ripped apart, eaten, and scattered by dogs. Now how many people die that manner? Elijah further told the evil pair that their heirs would die, so that their entire family line would be obliterated. And so, it was. (1 KI 21—22; 2 KI 9)

Daniel. It is uncanny how prophetic this comparatively short book is. A widely discussed prediction is the progression of empires made centuries in advance. Written during the reign of Babylonian King Nebuchadnezzar, Daniel declares that Babylon would be followed by Media-Persia, Greece, and Rome. Particular pieces to the puzzle are provided, not the least of which outlines how Babylon would break into two factions, which would be melded into one led by a great conqueror (Alexander); and how his kingdom would split into four, to be rejoined into one terrible empire that would become Rome (DAN 2; DAN 8).

Fate of the Jews. There are many such prophecies, so three significant prophecies will be presented here. The first was Moses, Jeremiah, Hosea, and others who spoke of yet another eventual captivity of the Jews (long after their captivity in Egypt). Indeed, after Solomon died the kingdom of Israel split into two, weakening it and making it vulnerable. Israel and Judah would be conquered and the citizens taken captive by the Assyrians, Babylonians, and Romans. These events were instrumental in the second prophecy advanced by Moses, Isaiah, Micah, Zechariah, and others: the scattering of the Jews throughout the earth (known as *Diaspora*). It's amazing how many times the land of Palestine changed hands over the centuries, which makes the third prophecy even more amazing: the Jews would return to claim their homeland according to Isaiah, Jeremiah, Ezekiel, Hosea, Zephaniah, and others. It took about 2500 years for that to take place; but in 1948 Israel was recognized among the United Nations as an independent nation. The predicted captivity, scattering, and rejoining of the Jews in their native Israel is nothing less than remarkable.

Messiah. Literally hundreds of OT prophecies describe the first advent of Christ, all of which are fulfilled as documented in the NT Gospels. Jesus was proclaimed to be born of a virgin (ISA 7:14) in the city of Bethlehem (MIC 5:2), and worshipped by kings (ISA 49:7). He would minister throughout Galilee (ISA 9:1–2), healing the lame, blind, and brokenhearted (ISA 35:5–6). He would speak in parables (PSA 78:2), and perform miracles (ISA 35:5–6), blessing some and angering others (ISA 66:4–6). He would be betrayed by a friend for thirty pieces of silver, which would be used to buy a field for a pauper's graveyard (ZEC 11:12–13). He would be tortured to death, an innocent man, for the sins of the world (ISA 30:6; ISA 53:4–7). They would pierce His body and gamble for His clothes (PSA 22:16–18), but never a bone of His would be broken (PSA 34:20). He would be counted with the criminals but buried in a rich man's tomb (ISA 53:8–9). He would rise from the dead after three days (HOS 6:2: JON 1:17; PSA 61:6–7; ISA 53:10); and that event would be proclaimed throughout the world (ISA 42:6; ZEC 3:9; MAL 1:11). This is only the tip of the iceberg regarding proof that Jesus is the Messiah. There is ample prophecy about His second advent by the way, so you might want to look into that because His coming is soon (REV 22:20).

8. **Resurrection**: Every bit as astonishing as biblical prophecy is the fact of the resurrection. This is the ultimate truth underlying the entire Holy Bible: Salvation by Grace through Faith in the Life, Death, Atonement, and Resurrection of our Lord and Savior Jesus Christ. Without the resurrection, Christianity falls apart, the Bible is false, and our faith is in vain (1 CO 15:12–20). The following certifiable truths are generally recognized by the majority of historians, especially biblical scholars. See also the prior lesson, *Did Christ Really Rise from the Dead*.

- Jesus Christ was born in Bethlehem and preached throughout the land of Judea.
- Jesus Christ performed miracles, healed people, and was a man of the highest character.
- Jesus Christ was tried, falsely convicted, and crucified during the time of Passover.
- There was an earthquake and extreme darkness on that day (likely an eclipse).
- Christ was buried in a new sepulcher owned by a Pharisee.
- His tomb was found empty on the third day. Church leaders bribed the guards to say His body was stolen to explain away the empty tomb.
- The first witnesses of the empty tomb and the resurrection of Christ were women.
- Numerous embarrassing facts were reported which remove suspicion that the entire story was fabricated. Because, if someone wanted to perpetrate a prank, they would not add details that were discomfiting, humiliating, or perturbing; they would likely embellish the story instead to make it more compelling or believable.
- The disciples were devastated and scared until they discovered firsthand that Jesus had arisen, which made them dedicated and undaunted in their mission to spread the Word.
- The resurrected Jesus was witnessed by the eleven apostles, Jesus's half-brothers (James, Judah), the apostle Paul, and on at least one occasion over five hundred people.
- Many who were unfriendly towards Jesus, such as members of the assembly that condemned Him, those persecuting His followers, and criminals, foreigners, and materialists, would become converts: James and Judah (Jesus's brothers); Paul, Nicodemus, Joseph of Arimathaea (Pharisees); Zacchaeus a tax collector, Simon the sorcerer, a thief crucified with Jesus, three centurions, and over three thousand on the day of Pentecost from among the Jews, Romans, Egyptians, Libyans, Medes, Asians, and others (ACT 2). Conversions such as these are still occurring.
- The lives of those who witnessed Christ and those who believed His witnesses changed in an amazing way (of course, life changes for anybody that allows Christ into their heart).
- Believers were willing to die rather than renounce their faith or cease to proclaim the good news of the Gospel.
- The testimony of eyewitnesses, proselytizers, clergy, and apologists was cohesive and united, to the degree that essential doctrines and key teachings remain clear and uncompromised to this day.
- The establishment of the Christian Church and the proliferation of converts multiplied dramatically, and this has continued ever since the resurrection.
- There is no other religion or faith system throughout the history of humanity that depends upon or even preaches the resurrection of Christ. Thus, Christianity is exclusive to those believing in the resurrection. Further, it is the only worldview that teaches salvation by faith, whereas others that teach salvation or eternal life emphasize works.

Conclusions

It is not difficult to find God; one merely must desire to seek Him. A great way of finding Him is by studying His Word. Doesn't everyone ponder who they are and how they got here? Doesn't everyone need a purpose, and a reason for everything that happens to them? Doesn't everyone want life to last forever, to continue after death? Well, I guess not everybody. But for those who do, the answer to all these questions can be found in the Holy Bible. Obviously, those searching for answers to these and other questions about life want the truth. Truth is always absolute and is knowable: a fact is a fact for everybody, everywhere, and always. When a person dies, they are dead to everyone, everywhere; and that fact will always remain true. Even if they are resurrected because they believed in Christ, it will not change the fact that their death was a matter of public record. There is only one source of absolute truth—God. And He speaks via the Holy Spirit through the written Word, the living Word, and the Creation. Since truth can be known and God is the source, then God can be known by connecting with His Holy Spirit through Christ. God wants us to know the truth, to know Him, to experience His love, and to do His will. He is the standard for all these things: knowledge, truth, love, morality, obedience. He is the solution to sin, suffering, and death. He is the reason for the universe, for life, for everything. I can't understand why anyone would not want to know God and be with Him.

There is only one God and He is infinite in existence, knowledge, and power. God is the uncaused first cause of everything. There can be only one God, because for there to be more than one they would have to be different, which is impossible if they are infinite, perfect, and all knowing. Further, God has to be supernatural since nature cannot cause itself. That means He also exists outside of space and time because both had a beginning and God did not. God is the source of miracles. A miracle is an example of a supernatural event; otherwise it could be explained using the physical laws or science. Nature cannot develop the physical laws as it does not possess an intelligence of its own. Laws imply intelligence. Nature was created with laws in mind and must adhere to these laws; scientists do too, but not God because He established the law and order that applies to this universe. That was part of His plan. Even still, He can intervene and change something anytime because He operates outside of nature, laws, space, and time.

God has a plan for your life as well, but He still gives you free will. He will not force you to seek Him or to do His will. But if you don't seek Him or try to do His will you likely will not fulfill the purpose He has for your life, and you will not receive the things He desires for you to have. If you choose to go with God you will, and if you choose not to go you won't. Like C. S. Lewis wrote concerning these two choices (1946): Say to God "thy will be done," or He will say to you "thy will be done." To not choose God is to have no meaning or purpose but to enjoy oneself for a time and then die. Such a worldview renders life meaningless and pointless. But with God, you have abundant life that has direction, purpose, and significance; and it lasts forever. This is unquestionably the better choice.

References

Craig, W. (2010). *On Guard*. Colorado Springs: David Cook.

Fales, R. (2001). *Archaeology and History Attest to the Reliability of the Bible,* in *The Evidence Bible*, Ray Comfort Ed., Bridge-Logos Publishers: Gainesville, FL.

Geisler, N. (1999). *Baker Encyclopedia of Christian Apologetics*. Grand Rapids, MI: Baker Publishing.

Geisler, N., and Turek, F. (2004). *I Don't Have Enough Faith to Be an Atheist*. Wheaton, IL: Crossway.

Habermas, G. (1996). *The Historical Jesus*. Joplin, MO: College Press.

Jeffrey, G. *Extraordinary Evidence about Jesus in the Dead Sea Scrolls*. (http://www.grantjeffrey.com)

Lewis, C. S. (1943). *Mere Christianity*. New York: Macmillan.

Lewis, C. S. (1947). *Miracles*. New York: Macmillan.

Lewis, C. S. (1946). *The Great Divorce*. San Francisco: Harper-Collins.

McDowell, J. (1993). *A Ready Defense*. Nashville, TN: Thomas Nelson Publishers.

McDowell, J. (1993). *Evidence for Christianity*. Nashville, TN: Thomas Nelson Publishers.

Niswonger, R. (1988). *New Testament History*. Grand Rapids, MI: Zondervan Publishing.

Sailhamer, J. (1998). *Biblical Archaeology*. Grand Rapids, MI: Zondervan Publishing.

Slick, M. (2010). *Manuscript Evidence for Superior New Testament Reliability*. (http://carm.org/manuscript-evidence)

Wright, G. E. (1957). *Biblical Archaeology*. Philadelphia: Westminster Press.

"Blessed are the pure in heart for they shall see God" (MAT 5:8).

CHAPTER EIGHT

Bible Study: Fulfillment of Biblical Prophecy

Some basic rules of scriptural interpretation include the following. In this lesson we will review the fifth rule: that prophecy can be fulfilled more than once.

1. Translated accurately
2. Understood within context
3. Scripture used to interpret scripture
4. Interpretations of all relevant scriptures must be in agreement
5. Prophecy can be fulfilled more than once

Prophecy is the foreknowledge of some future event(s) provided by God to His prophets and messengers. Biblical prophecy in the Bible has deliberately imparted sufficient detail to ensure its fulfillment would be incontrovertible, such as the prophecy of Messiah which had to be spelled out plainly since there could be only one Messiah. God made absolutely sure that Messiah would not be confused with one of countless counterfeits. But some elements of prophecy were deliberately withheld, though still unmistakable in foretelling the future.

It is entirely reasonable that certain prophecy was meant to be applied more than once. To be sure, not all prophecy can be fulfilled more than once; in fact, it may be more the exception than the rule when it is. A thorough understanding of biblical hermeneutics, and a comprehensive search and cross-referencing of scripture, enables one to identify cases allowing multiple applications derived from a single scripture or prophecy. On the other hand, several scriptures or prophecies can converge upon a single construct or message as in the case of Christ the Messiah for which there are over three hundred such prophecies in the Old Testament pointing to Jesus.

Theologians have proposed that all biblical prophecy has been fulfilled, and they suggest particular events in the past to support that proposition. Then there are others who propose that much prophecy has yet to be fulfilled, especially regarding eschatology (concerning the last days). A case in point is the book of Revelation: does it refer to the era during Christ's first coming, or His second, or both? Can more than one position be right? John's statements to the Seven Churches clearly mirror issues and concerns within the church then as well as today (REV 2—3).

Consider the Olivet Discourse (MAT 24; MAR 13; LUK 21): from the Mount of Olives Christ declared the events that would occur during the latter days before His second coming. He had been asked specifically about the signs of His return. Jesus asserted that a generation of ungodliness would not pass until those prophecies came true. Some theologians have maintained that Jesus was alluding to the generation alive at that time. No doubt He was, insofar as the temple was destroyed less than forty years later (circa AD 70) which Jesus pronounced would happen during the course of that teaching. (Note: It is generally understood that a generation lasted forty years and Christ was in His thirties; you can do the math). Obviously, there is practical support that this prophecy was fulfilled. However, other theologians maintain that Christ was referring to the last generation on earth before He returns in judgment. There is ample evidence to support this view as well, especially Christ proclaiming that everyone will see Him coming down from heaven to gather His elect, which clearly has yet to happen. Who knows, could each of these camps be half right? Does the prophecy point to two events, one regarding the ones who heard it live, and one for the rest of us who have read it in the Bible? Well, God knows, for He is the source of all true prophecy. It seems the Olivet Discourse refers to Jesus's generation and the generation living when He returns. Further, all generations in-between will be well-advised to take heed of it.

A great many prophetic declarations are included in the Olivet Discourse. For example, reference is made in three Gospel accounts cited previously to the abomination of desolation spoken of by the prophet Daniel (DAN 9:24–27; DAN 11:31; DAN 12:8–13). One position suggests that Daniel was referring to the Greek king and conqueror Antiochus Epiphanes and his desecration of the Jewish temple in 167 BC, during which the treasury was plundered and a pig was butchered and offered to a statue of Zeus erected in the holiest place. This event was corroborated in the Apocryphal work *1 Maccabees*, also during the second century BC; it is not debatable whether that event occurred. What is contended it there is only one abomination of desolation. Daniel's prophecy certainly pertains to the "seven weeks of years" validating the events described above, as well as the desecration of God's holy temple in Jerusalem.

In the Olivet Discourse, Christ declared that the abomination of desolation would occur in the latter days, referencing Daniel's prophecy. Evidently, Jesus was not referring to an event two hundred years prior. So, was Daniel's prophecy fulfilled when the temple was desecrated in the second century BC? Was Jesus referring to the destruction of the temple in AD 70 by Titus of Rome? Are we to expect another abominable sacrilege in the last days as many biblical scholars profess? Which camp is correct: one of them, two of them, or all of them? Perhaps the prophecy was given to Daniel precisely so it could be applied as a pretense to Christ's first appearance, and also to His second. Since Christ reminded everyone of Daniel's prophecy, it must be significant.

One thing is certain: Christ was giving a warning applicable to every generation until He returns. Calamities He spoke of have occurred repeatedly throughout history: wars, earthquakes, floods, famine, pestilence, affliction, false prophets, desecrating of churches, tribulation, hate and betrayal. And in the Gospel accounts, as well as in John's Revelation, the Lord's final warning rings true for all people for all time: You'd better be ready for His coming, because it can occur in your lifetime, and once He arrives in judgment it will be too late to choose Him (1 TH 5:2; 2 PE 3:10,13; REV 22:20). When Christ reappears, this life, this earth, this epoch, and time itself will end. Those not believing Jesus and eagerly awaiting His return will not be joining Him on a trip to paradise. That prophecy will continue to be relevant until time is up (MAT 28:16–20).

The OT has considerable prophecy of the first coming of Messiah. This information was given to God's chosen Israel. Was it meant only for them? Absolutely not, since the promise was proclaimed to the Gentiles (non-Jews) as well, who would likewise respond to and cherish God's message of salvation (ISA 49:6–7; LUK 2:25–32). Nowadays, there are people of all races reading the Bible and clinging to God's Word. So, it doesn't matter your heritage, ethnicity, or language does it (ACT 10:34–35; GAL 3:28)? The Holy Bible is for anyone who seeks God and His truth. Simply put, the entire Bible will stand for all time, so one could argue that end times prophecy applies now as much as it ever did since it isn't over.

Let's look at another prophecy regarding the coming of Christ. It establishes that a forerunner will prepare the way: a voice crying in the wilderness calling people to repentance (ISA 40:3–5; MAT 3:1–3; MAR 1:1–5; LUK 3:1–6; JOH 1:19–37). That was John the Baptist; the Bible says the voice and power which came through John was that of the prophet Elijah (LUK 1:5–17). Is it possible that the same prophetic voice will usher in Christ's second coming (MAL 4:1–6; MAT 11:7–15; MAR 9:10–13)? This is precisely what Jesus said: The spirit and power of Elijah is present in the first and the second coming of Christ.

Now let us turn to a fascinating prophecy from the book of Joel (JOE 2:27–32). He addresses God's people Israel stating that in future times, God will pour out His Spirit on all humankind; and people will prophecy, dream, and receive visions. Similarly, Christ assured that He would send the Holy Spirit to instruct us (JOH 14:16; JOH 14:26; JOH 15:26; JOH 16:7; JOH 20:22). In fact, St. Peter proclaimed that their speaking in tongues on Pentecost shortly after

Christ's ascension was in fulfillment of Joel (ACT 2:1–21). But Joel also spoke of days of gloom and darkness, and wonders in the heavens. That segment of Joel's prophecy did not occur during Peter's preaching; it seems to be referring to the last days (recall that Jesus's execution coincided with darkness, gloom, and despair). In the Olivet Discourse, Jesus alluded to these same events occurring prior to His return, and repeated it in His Revelation to St. John (MAT 24:29–31; REV 6:12–17). There were a number of additional OT prophets who pointed to these identical events (ISA 13:9–19; EZE 32:7–11; AMO 8:9–11; ZEP 1:14–18). I expect this prophecy recurred several times for a reason. Then is Joel making a duel prophecy, half associated with the days following Jesus ascension into heaven, and the other half associated with the days preceding His future descending from heaven? Or is the entire prophecy pointing to both events equally?

A common interpretation of the above prophecies about heavenly disturbances followed by darkness and despair posits that these occurrences are symbolic of God's divine intercession. That is, His great hand reaches down and intervenes from outside of spacetime, and this disrupts the natural scheme of things because the incident is supernatural. While a reasonable position, it must be noted once again that several prophets envisioned the same events. The reiteration of the vision by multiple prophets suggests that God wants us to pay attention to this teaching. There may be a symbolic as well as a literal interpretation attached, precisely because the scenario itself is repeated; but the last time it occurs will foreshadow the end of the age.

Isaiah and Ezekiel indicate in the aforementioned prophecy that Israel would fall to Babylon and become captives there (JER 27:13–18); but after that, Babylon also would fall (JER 50—51). These events were looming on the horizon when those prophetic statements were recorded. Certainly, these prophecies also can be applied to the final days and the new Babylon (REV 14:8; REV 16:19; REV 17:5; REV 18:2; REV 18:10; REV 18:21). Obviously, the apostle John was not referring to the old Babylon that fell hundreds of years before he received the Revelation. Once again, we have the prophets providing revelations that applied to the people to whom those words were spoken and written, and to those of us reading the same words today.

Another example of prophecy being fulfilled more than once is God's directive to Israel through Moses regarding keeping the faith and remaining obedient to God (DEU 29:10–29; DEU 30:1–19). God told His people they would prosper as long as they kept His laws and worshipped only Him; and He also told them they would reap destruction if they turned away from Him and forsook His ways. And each time the Israelites were faithful to God they prospered; and every time they were unfaithful, they suffered, were enslaved, and/or perished. How many times did these episodes occur? Every time; and they still do. God's blessing applies to each nation and person that follows Him; but those who follow their sinful flesh receive His curse. Look at how the United States has followed God, then fallen away, and the associated consequences. It is not a pretty picture. The same was true for ancient Babylon and Rome. Or do you think God was talking only to the Jews about what was in store if they approached or avoided Him? The fact is, those instructions apply to Old Testament Jews and New Testament Christians alike.

You see, the Bible is for everyone; God speaks to anybody who opens it and reads it with an open heart. God loves us equally; and His love is timeless. If you welcome the Lord into your life, He will pour His Spirit upon you too (ACT 2:38; ACT 10:45; 1 CO 6:19; 1 CO 12:7–11). To argue all biblical prophecy was fulfilled, over, and done with is ludicrous. Some prophecy has been fulfilled so that we can prove the Bible is true. Other prophecy has not been fulfilled so that we can believe it will happen. In writing Revelation, John states that He was charged with proclaiming things past, present, and future (REV 1:17–19). It seems logical to apply the prophecy in that book accordingly: some of it happened, is happening, or is going to happen.

DEEPER INTO THE WORD

Lessons in this section are meant to propel the reader further into the depths of God's exhaustive Word. I recommend a scholarly approach to apprehending the Bible, and that is to keep studying it individually, with family, in groups, and in church. If you want a PhD in the Bible, pile higher and deeper your grasp of God's Word, which explains itself. Amazing revelations come your way, further expanding your spiritual wisdom and understanding of truth (PRO 2:2–6,10–12). In other words, the more you explore its breadth and depth, the clearer your knowledge and the higher your Bible IQ.

Notice how every lesson in this chapter contains proof of the Holy Trinity. In fact, when you read carefully, the trinity is implied in many of the referenced passages. Pertinent biblical citations are listed, and additional references suggested for perusing at some point during your studies (look up listed passages for a minilesson). As usual, itemized verses are paraphrased using the King James Version (KJV) of the Bible in order from Genesis to Revelation.

Empirical Proof that the Holy Bible Is True

Popular beliefs are aplenty in this land, many based on scant evidence, precluding some from ever probing the Bible in any depth. Scholars, including scientific, haven't taken the time to read it even once. The Bible isn't the most popular book of all time for nothing; that alone is reason enough to check it out. To dismiss it out of hand is illogical if not unscholarly. I encourage anyone to challenge my findings and prove me wrong the Holy Bible is nothing but God-spoken (*Logos*). Like Martin Luther said, "Here I stand, I can do no other." He challenged the biblical scholars of his day to prove him wrong using the Bible alone (*sola scriptura*), but they could not.

I have done my share of empirical and methodological investigations, performing experimental design, test execution and data collection, as well as statistical analysis in the areas of national defense, academia, and social, behavioral, and clinical psychology. I've employed the scientific method in my career studies and in studying the Bible. I conclude that the Bible provides truth, and its significance exceeds any other produced through decades of research. In the scientific furrows of my mind, I have removed any shadow of doubt the Holy Bible is infallible. The likelihood of it being random chance, unguided processes, physical, material, or coincidental is incalculably small (like computing pi to an ultimate conclusion). One could assert we have mathematical proof the Holy Bible is true, and science supports this proposition.

Allow me to present results from my scientific examination of the Holy Bible. Firstly, one might wonder what qualifies me to be an authority on the Bible since my doctorate was in psychology not divinity. It is true, I never attended a seminary. But I am piled higher and deeper in advanced biblical studies through the calling of the Holy Spirit, who likewise calls you to become engrossed in His Word. I have been studying the Bible and worshipping regularly in church since I was a toddler (over sixty years). After I received my PhD thirty years ago, I turned exclusively to the Holy Bible to continue my education. As a first-year grad student in God's university, the head schoolmaster instructed me to read the Bible all over again from cover to cover; the second year He told me to read it twice, and the third year thrice. After three years and six consecutive journeys through God's Word it started to come together like a jigsaw puzzle. I just keep reading it as God commanded, while my wisdom and understanding grew.

I dove into the Bible over and over, forwards, backwards, in sections, looking up every verse that had a single word such as love, faith, hope, grace, and mercy, and probing the Bible from diverse points of view and theological frameworks. I divided it and scrutinized it, every doctrine and promise. I researched the history of the Christian church, New Testament canonization, biblical hermeneutics, and the text authentication process. I compared different versions of the Bible, denominations, and cults as well as other religions and belief systems. Never did I find in the Bible any conflict with known truth, neither did I find inconsistencies, nor was there any hint it had changed over millennia. It was evident the Bible demonstrated internal consistency and consistency over time, two measures of data *reliability* which is one pillar of scientific study.

Another pillar of scientific study is *validity*. I discovered that the Old Testament (OT) and New Testament (NT) cross-validate each other. For example, hundreds of prophecies from the OT became fulfilled in the NT. Similarly, hundreds of OT scriptures were quoted by NT prophets, apostles, and Christ. I have scrutinized numerous external sources and historical accounts from diverse cultures corroborating the Bible, particularly with regards to Jesus Christ and the resurrection. This was backed by a panoply of archaeological findings which continue to surface, further confirming biblical people, places, and times. Additionally, the voluminous NT manuscript evidence exceeds any found for another work of antiquity, traceable to the very times and places in which they were initially documented. Typically, antiquated literature postdates the people and places by hundreds if not thousands of years; the Bible is unique, having manuscript evidence dating back to its origin. From early church fathers to present-day preachers, the Bible has not been altered in content, meaning, function, or relevance despite the many languages in which it has been translated. Additionally, the original concepts, teachings, prophecy, and historicity of the Bible remain applicable today. The Bible also can be demonstrated to exhibit factual agreement with cosmology, geography, medicine, and science in general. Thus, we have internal and external content validity, unmatched predictive validity, and construct validity that the Bible is absolutely genuine and Christ is the only Way to heaven.

A third important element of biblical study is the hermeneutic quality of arrangements of passages, enabling the recognition of the historical and cultural application of associated times, peoples, places, and events, and the personalities of protagonists, antagonists, and witnesses (look in the Index under *Hermeneutics*). Each of these categories can be broken down into specifics, which are verifiable by researching the archives of archaeology, history, physical science, religion, politics, and government. This I have written about in detail, the overwhelming evidence and the hermeneutic applicability of the Bible (Barber 2020; Barber 2016b). I also have documented a great deal of empirical research proving that faith, prayer, and spirituality are effective in healing ailments of the body, mind, and spirit (see Barber 2016a). Evidently, if you do what the Bible says, your life is improved in many ways to include promoting holistic health.

Consider the statistical probability of the correctness, detail, and fulfillment of OT and NT prophecies; how they came true, are coming true, and will continue to come true until Judgment Day and beyond. Then there is the likelihood of all the differing testimonials gelling together into one interconnected and unified framework. The Bible contains declarations from hundreds of eye witnesses and primary sources, and from forty-some-odd writers living at different times and places all telling the exact same story. Yet still the Bible has never changed (PRO 30:5–6; MAT 24:35; JOH 17:17; GAL 1:9; REV 22:18–19) just as God never changes (MAL 3:6; 2 TI 2:13; HEB 13:8; JAM 1:17). There is only one interpretation and conclusion to be derived: God is real and He is the author of the Holy Bible; therefore, it follows that God also is the author of this universe (GEN 1:1), plus you and me (PSA 139:14–17). Over decades of conducting scientific research, I have never encountered a more precise and accurate finding. In scientific terms, there is an infinitesimally small probability that the Bible is a fraud; and there is a very high, statistically significant likelihood the Bible is exactly what it says it is: God's Word written by men directed by the Holy Spirit (JOH 16:13; 1 JO 5:6).

What impresses me most is this: Compilations of seemingly diverse facts, from various sources starting with the Holy Bible, are incredibly cohesive. Could it be computed, the chances of that many unlikely coincidences coming together to form one complete picture unveiling God's purpose, promise, and plan? It would be a challenge just to enumerate the vast number of intricately interrelated factors coming together to verify God's Word as truth, much less their interactions and variabilities; not to mention this universe and its countless components calibrated to precision which demonstrably shows it was created by an intelligence far greater than the entire human race. Add to that incredibly accurate prophecy, significant reliability and validity, historical verification and secular corroboration, a plethora of authenticated manuscripts going back two thousand years, the uniformity of the message from Genesis to Revelation, and relatedness from the beginning of time until now, unto eternity.

How much more does an intelligent person need in order to believe? But there are intelligent people who do not believe simply because they choose not to, without reason or excuse (ISA 6:8–10; ACT 28:27; ROM 1:20–21). Which kind of intelligent person are you: One who reads God's bestseller with an open mind, or closes his or her mind to God? If you want a great example of the former, take a look at Isaac Newton arguably the godfather of physics, whose motivation to explore and explain the universe was driven by his love of God and His Word. I wouldn't place myself in the same league as Newton, but I was driven to delve into God's book of man and His book of nature for the same reasons. I can assure you, science and philosophy are not contradictory, and neither is truth which can be found in both books written by the hand of God. Whenever they converge upon a single fact, it is absolutely indisputable.

If you have a thirst for perfect truth, and a desire to meet its source who is God, you will receive a constancy of both. If that is your desire, begin with God's Word and don't stop.

References

Barber, A. V. (2020). *A Message of Truth: The History, Science, and Politics of Christianity*. El Paso, TX: Special Delivery Press. 375 pages.

Barber, A. V. (2016). *Faithbook for Christian Counselors*. El Paso, TX: Special Delivery Press. 404 pages.

Barber, A. V. (2016). *Fundamentals of Christianity: A Bible Study and Guide (Second Edition)*. El Paso, TX: Special Delivery Press. 742 pages.

CHAPTER EIGHT

Lesson: Lord of the Sabbath

The Sabbath is generally connected to the seventh day when God rested from His work after forming the universe and creating humankind. God blessed that day (GEN 2:2–3) and designated it the Sabbath, a day of repose and reverence. Honoring the Sabbath as a holy day was listed fourth among the Ten Commandments. As directed, the Israelites dedicated the Sabbath Day to God on the last day of the week (Saturday). The first six days were associated with the works of man; the seventh day of the week was set aside to admire and appreciate the works of God (EXO 20:8–11). Thus, the original application of the term "Sabbath" referred to worshipping and not working every seventh day of the week (LEV 23:3).

- GEN 2:2–3 ~ On the seventh day God had ended His work and admired all that He had made; and He rested [insofar as His creation work had been completed].
- EXO 20:8–10 ~ God commanded the Israelites to remember the Sabbath Day and keep it holy. "Six days you will labor and complete your work. But the seventh day is the Sabbath of the Lord your God; in it you will not do any work, and this includes your family, servants, strangers, and beasts of burden; all which reside within your gates."

Additionally, there also were special Sabbaths occurring in concert with Jewish feasts, with the same requirements: do not work that day because it was set aside for revering God. These special occasions were designated "high" Sabbaths. For example, there were two such Sabbaths connected with the feast of Unleavened Bread; the first day and last day of the feast involved a convocation, or church assembly. This tradition began with the first Passover and has continued to this day (EXO 12:1–20; NUM 28:16–26). There also were high days associated with the feasts of trumpets, atonement, and tabernacles (LEV 23:1–44). Thus, there were two types of Sabbaths that God commanded the Israelites to observe: the last day of the week and days linked to commemorative feasts; both entailed a church assembly and refraining from work.

- LEV 23:3–8 ~ Six days shall work be done, but the seventh day is the Sabbath of rest, a holy convocation. You will do no work because it is the Lord's Sabbath in all your dwellings. There are feasts of the Lord, also holy convocations, which you will observe in their seasons. The fourteenth day of the first month (Nisan) is the Lord's Passover. The fifteenth day of Nisan begins the feast of Unleavened Bread; seven days you must eat unleavened bread. The first day of that period will be a holy convocation: you will do no work on that day. You will present burnt offerings to the Lord throughout the celebration. The seventh day will be another holy convocation: you will do no work on that day.

As a footnote, in accordance with the Genesis account (GEN 1:4), the Jews observed dusk to be the beginning of a new day: "And the evening and the morning were the first day." It seems convoluted because different cultures have their own ways of measuring days. Romans during Jesus's time observed sunup as the beginning of a new day, and so did many Jews for this reason. Modern nations start the new day at midnight and end it at midnight; the rationale being, time of day should not change with seasons (in accordance with the position and tilt of the earth relative to the sun). Midnight on one side of the earth will be exactly opposite of where the sun appears at its zenith (high noon). The importance of days and calendars will become evident.

Jesus's passion occurred during the period of Passover and Unleavened Bread (MAT 26:1–4). There could have been three Sabbath days that week: two high days and one Saturday. Evangelical Christians refer to the day Jesus served the apostles Holy Communion (known as Eucharist), and was later betrayed, as Maundy (meaning *commandment*) Thursday (1 COR 11:23–25); for Christians, this is a high day. The day Christ was crucified is recognized on Good Friday, another high day for Christians; there may be alternate viewpoints as to why it is called "good" though it obviously was good for sinners who believe Christ's death saves them. Strictly speaking, our Thursday would have started Wednesday night at 1800 hours for the Jews. People get confused about how Jesus could have died on Friday, stayed in the grave three days and nights, and still have risen from the dead Easter Sunday, particularly if the Sabbath (the day before Christ was taken off the cross) was on Saturday. But that assumption is incorrect.

Allow me to unravel and explain this conundrum by applying it to Jesus's final Holy Week on Earth. According to St. John, Jesus probably washed the apostles' feet and ate His final Passover meal on the "Day of Preparation" for upcoming festivals of Passover and Unleavened Bread (see JOH 13:1–2; JOH 18:28). Jesus already knew His time was nigh and related that to the apostles at the Last Supper and again when initiating the Eucharist. Later that night while praying in the Garden of Gethsemane, Jesus was betrayed by Judas Iscariot, accosted by a mob, and arrested on the authority of the chief priests. These atrocities likely occurred on the evening of Passover and persisted into the morning during which Jesus's trial would commence before dawn (MAT 26:26–75). Jesus was mocked, accused, assaulted, and tortured all day; before the setting of the sun He would be dead. Is it not fitting that Jesus would offer Himself as a Passover sacrifice on the very day the Jews celebrated that feast? After all, He is the Lamb of God and a lamb was always sacrificed in observance of Passover. Since the following day was a High Sabbath it would have been a sacrilege to leave a body hanging on a cross after sunset. That's why a burial site was prepared in advance, so Jesus could be interred before the High Sabbath started (read JOH 19:31–42). With this in mind, one can produce a timeline of the events of Holy Week when the last supper, arrest, trial, crucifixion, and resurrection of Christ occurred.

- MAT 26:1–2 ~ Jesus said to his disciples, "You know that after two days is the feast of Passover, and the Son of Man is betrayed to be crucified."
- JOH 13:1–2 ~ Before the feast of Passover, Jesus knew that His hour was nigh, stating how He would depart from this world and return to the Father, but continue to love His own which were in the world through the end of time. Before supper was over, the devil already had entered the heart of Judas Iscariot, son of Simon, to betray Jesus.
- JOH 18:28 ~ They led Jesus away from Caiaphas to the judgment hall; it was still early so they did not accompany Jesus into the judgment hall in order to avoid defilement, which would preclude them from eating the Passover meal with their loved ones.
- JOH 19:31 ~ The Jews therefore, because it was the day of preparation (for a feast of celebration), implored that the bodies should not remain upon the cross during the Sabbath, for that Sabbath Day was a high day. They appealed to Pilate that the legs of the crucified be broken (to hasten death) so their bodies could be taken down prior to nightfall.
- JOH 19:42 ~ They laid Jesus in a sepulcher which had been prearranged in observance of Preparation Day.

Before laying out the timeline of Jesus's death, we need to establish the timeframe of Jesus's birth; this can be done by synchronizing the scriptures chronicling the births and deaths of John the Baptist and Jesus. John's birth was probably coincident with the Feast of Passover (usually around April), and Jesus's birth, which occurred six months afterwards (LUK 1:21–31), was probably coincident with the Feast of Tabernacles (usually around October). Therefore, John was likely born in proximity with the spring harvest, and Jesus in proximity with the autumn harvest; interestingly their deaths were possibly the reverse of this order, again separated by about six months, such that both men died at the same age (33 ½). We know King Herod died after Jesus was born because Jesus's family had escaped into Egypt to avoid Herod's decree to massacre all the little boys in Bethlehem (MAT 2:16–18). The family returned to Nazareth once the angel declared that Herod had passed and it was safe to go home (MAT 2:19–23).

CHAPTER EIGHT

The year Herod the Great died can be extrapolated from the Gospel of Luke plus the works of historians including Josephus, as well as early Christian church fathers (of course, Luke is the preeminent source as his book was inspired by God Himself). The majority of scholarship suggests Herod's death to be late 5 BC or early 4 BC; this is largely because Josephus reported a lunar eclipse prior to Herod's demise, and provided a fractional chronology of several other events from that time period. There was a partial eclipse in March, 4 BC which is the preferred date among theologians (though others argue with that conclusion because they believe it must have been a full lunar eclipse). Consequently, most place Herod's death in early 4 BC, which would place Jesus's birth in the latter part of 5 BC. If the proposed timeline is accurate, it is possible that the magi found the Christ child in Bethlehem at the close of 5 BC, (possibly around the time we celebrate Christmas and New Year), or about three months after Jesus's birth (note: many scholars believe the magi could have encountered Jesus up to His second birthday). Nevertheless, the family's initial flight to Egypt would have occurred forthwith, and their return to Nazareth when Herod expired around March, 4 BC.

Given the prospective birth of Christ in autumn 5 BC and the fact that he died 33.5 years later in springtime (on Passover), the probable (and most recognized) year of His death was AD 30. We know that prophets traditionally began their ministry at age thirty just like Jesus did (LUK 3:23), and Jesus ministered for about 3.5 years (refer to the myriad of scriptures concerning the significance of the number 3.5, or ½ of 7). Now let's do the math based on Jesus's birth being in early October of 5 BC. Between OCT 1, 5 BC and JAN 1, 1 BC were 4.25 years; between JAN 1, AD 1 and APR 1, AD 30 were 29.25 years (not 30.25 years because there is no year 0 BC or AD 0; that is, AD 1 starts at year 1 not 0). Anyway, when we add it up, we get 33.5 years.

Extensive research was conducted concerning Passover and Easter for the year AD 30. Projected Jewish and Christian timelines associated with this holiest of weeks were established. Remember, the Jewish evening began at dusk (1800 hours) and ended at dawn (0600 hours); correspondingly, the daytime was roughly 0600–1800 hours. Our day would have started at 0000 hours and ended at 2400 hours. So, days of the week are not going to line up since the Jewish day started six hours earlier. Further, there are inconsistencies with historians' attempts to convert the ancient Hebrew calendar into the Gregorian calendar (a variance of three days, give or take). Additionally, our calendar year is 365.25 days while the lunar calendar used by the Jews is much shorter. Since the New Testament was written mostly by Jews it generally follows Jewish traditions regarding times of day, dates of the year, and the lunar phases; but sometimes their reporting reflected the Roman calendar and clock. These anomalies produce subtle disparities, to include variations among the Gospel writers concerning this epochal time. Some passages indicate the Last Supper occurred on the Day of Preparation and some suggest it was the Day of Passover; this can be reconciled if one considers how the different calendars and timeframes overlap. The table below represents an aggregation of scriptures (particularly from the Gospels) pertaining to Holy Week, as well as an independent, analytically determined timeline for relevant Jewish feasts occurring in the year AD 30.

Notice how Jesus really was in the grave three days and three nights (using the OT tradition, whereby any part of a day was considered a day and any part of a night was considered a night). It actually adds up to about 2 ½ twenty-four-hour periods that Jesus's body remained in the grave. Assuming that Jesus and His apostles ate the Passover meal the evening of Nisan 13 and experienced the first Holy Communion a few hours later, that actually would have been Nissan 14 or Thursday (Maundy Thursday). Jesus was betrayed in Gethsemane and dragged before the Jewish leadership early that morning; He was interrogated and abused by the elders, then by king Herod, and again by the Roman governor Pontius Pilate who sentenced Jesus to death by crucifixion. Jesus's body was removed from the cross just before sundown on Passover Day (Nisan 14), prior to the High Sabbath commencing the feast of Unleavened Bread. It would appear that Jesus died and was buried just before the Jewish Friday began (Good Friday), notwithstanding the overlapping of calendars.

Breakdown of the Holiest Week

Jewish Timeline (Nisan 13–21, AD 30)

Christian Timeline (April 6–10, AD 30)

Date	Day	Eve/Morn	Occasion or Feast	Date	Passion Week of Christ	Time in Tomb
Nisan 13	WED	1800/0600	Preparation Day	April 6	Preparing Upper Room (1200) Washing Apostles' Feet (1600) Last Seder Supper (1700)	
Nisan 14	THU	1800/0600	Passover (Pesach)	April 7	Holy Communion (1800) Arrest at Gethsemane (2400) Trial (0400–0800) Crucifixion (0900–1500) Burial (1600)	One day (2 hours)
Nisan 15	FRI	1800/0600	Unleavened Bread (day 1) (Matzah) High Sabbath	April 8		One night, day (24 hours)
Nisan 16	SAT	1800/0600	Burnt Offerings (day 2) Sabbath Day	April 9		One night, day (24 hours)
Nisan 17	SUN	1800/0600	First Fruits (day 3) (Omer)	April 10	Resurrection (0400) Women at Tomb (0600)	One night (10 hours)
Nisan 18	MON	1800/0600	Burnt Offerings (day 4)		**Total Time in Tomb: 3 days and 3 nights** (60 hours)	
Nisan 19	TUE	1800/0600	Burnt Offerings (day 5)			
Nisan 20	WED	1800/0600	Burnt Offerings (day 6)			
Nisan 21	THU	1800/0600	Unleavened Bread (day 7) High Sabbath			

(Dates and times are approximated.)

One reason Maundy Thursday and Good Friday were chosen as holy days on the Christian calendar was to commemorate the last days of Jesus's passion prior to His resurrection. The body of Christ had to be removed from the cross prior to the Sabbath Day which was assumed to be Saturday; but this interpretation did not consider that the Sabbath being referred to by St. John was a High Sabbath, which did not fall on Saturday in the year AD 30 but on Friday (the day after Passover). Regardless, Jesus arose before dawn three days later on Nisan 17, which was Sunday on both the Jewish and the Gregorian calendars. Notice how Easter Sunday coincided with the Jewish feast of First Fruits that year. During this celebration the Jews offered the first of their harvest to the Lord, which was a tithe of their produce and income. The Jewish calendar began with the month of Nisan and the early harvest when they brought the first fruits in proximity with Holy Week (about midmonth), presenting the best of their produce to God as a tithe offering. Since that first Easter, Jesus bears the distinction of being the First Fruits of God, who was sacrificed to save the souls of humankind from sin on the day of Passover, and then raised from the dead Easter Sunday.

Certain belligerent denominational leaders insist that the weekly day of rest and worship should remain Saturday, at times maintaining that those who attend public worship any other day are violating the fourth commandment. The reason many Christians rest and worship on Sundays is because Jesus came back to life on Easter Sunday. Consequently, many Christians worship and rest at the beginning of the week (Sunday) and others at the end of the week (Saturday). Christ's resurrection represents a new beginning which is the rationale for starting the week with worship rather than ending it that way (ACT 20:7; 1 CO 16:1-2). It really matters not what day of the week you decide to dedicate as a convocation to the Lord, for Jesus declared Himself "Lord of the Sabbath." Paul also pointed out that it is unnecessary to regard one day as more important than another since, technically, they all belong to God and Jesus is Lord of all.

- MAR 2:27–28 ~ Jesus announced, "The Sabbath was made for man, not man for the Sabbath. Therefore, the Son of man is Lord even of the Sabbath."
- JOH 9:14–16 ~ It was on the Sabbath Day when Jesus made the clay and opened the beggar's eyes. The Pharisees asked the man how he had received his sight and the man replied, "Jesus put clay upon my eyes, and I washed, and now I can see." Some of the Pharisees complained about Jesus, "This man is not of God because he does not keep the Sabbath." Others said, "How can a sinful man perform miracles?" And there was division among them.
- ACT 20:7 ~ On the first day of the week, when the disciples came together to break bread, Paul preached to them until midnight before his planned departure the next morning.
- ROM 14:5,18–19 ~ One person may esteem one day above another while another person esteems every day equally. Let everyone be fully persuaded in his or her mind.
- ROM 14:7–10 ~ None of us lives to himself, and none of us dies to himself. For if we live, we live unto the Lord; and if we die, we die unto the Lord. Whether we live or die, we are the Lord's. Christ died, revived, and arose so that He might be Lord over both the dead and the living. But why do you judge your brother? And why do you call him out? Because everyone will stand before the judgment seat of Christ.
- ROM 14:18–19 ~ He who serves Christ in these things is acceptable to God and approved of men. Let us therefore follow after the things which promote peace and edify one another.

The last official Sabbath was the high day that began shortly after Jesus Christ died. Does that mean we can disregard the fourth commandment? Of course not! Jesus said that no part of the Law will be eliminated prior to His return (MAT 5:17–20). We can be sure that Christ fulfilled the Law because we could not; and part of fulfilling that Law was He had to suffer and die, for this is the price of sin and evil. Jesus paid with His life so you won't have to; but you must receive this blessing. To reject His payment is to lose everything. Evangelicals who observe the Sabbath on Sunday do so in commemoration of Jesus's resurrection on Easter Sunday, the pivotal event for all Christians without which we have no religion (1 CO 15:12–20).

- MAT 5:18 ~ Jesus said, "Truly I say unto you, until heaven and earth pass away, not one bit of the Law will pass until all has been fulfilled."
- MAT 24:35; MAR 13:31; LUK 21:33 ~ Jesus said, "Heaven and earth will pass away, but my words will remain true forever."

Numerous theories about the time, day, and year of Jesus's crucifixion exist. Some say Jesus was born a different year or a different time of year. AD 30 is most likely the year of Jesus's birth, since the Lamb of God would be sacrificed on Passover and His resurrection would occur on the Feast of First Fruits which fell on Sunday (Easter). This schedule also reconciles with Herod's death in 4 BC and Jesus living 33.5 years (not 30.0). It is appropriate for Jesus's birth to occur during the Feast of Tabernacles. Recall, the Holy of Holies in the tabernacle held the Ark of the Covenant containing the Ten Commandments, all of which presage Christ the New Covenant.

Lesson: Jesus's Last Words

Let us further examine the circumstances surrounding Jesus's death, which ushered in the first High Sabbath of the Jewish Feast of Unleavened Bread (covered in the previous lesson). Remember, certain yearly festivals had additional Sabbath days, to observe in like manner as any other Sabbath but for the fact it was a "high" day, separate from the weekly service in the temple. Kind of how Christians celebrate Maundy Thursday with Holy Communion, coincident with Passover when the Romans crucified the Lamb of God. In accordance with Jewish law, the Romans took the deceased Jesus down from the cross before the High Sabbath started.

No longer should any blood offering be allowed as it will not measure up to Christ's atonement, which is why most Christians worship on Sunday to commemorate Easter. But it doesn't matter the exact day of the week, for a high day is observed for the very reason people call it that; it does not apply to worldly interpretations of the word "high". God commanded His people Israel to acknowledge such days by refraining from work and attending a holy convocation. Such Holy Week traditions distinguishing high days endure for many Americans holding a Judeo-Christian worldview, thereby acknowledging both testaments of the Holy Bible.

Below is a breakdown of Jesus's last sayings from the cross during the six hours He hung there, one fateful anniversary of Passover. Notice, in His distress Jesus was still taking care of business the first half of the ordeal. During the second half Jesus was in travail, exhausted and broken. His only recourse was to pray to His Father, in yet another example of how we return to God for guidance and comfort. The Gospel writers record seven separate statements that Jesus made in the course of those six hours. While it is difficult to intertwine Jesus's last verbalizations and determine sequence, they likely occurred in order of priority; Jesus is definitely a man whose priorities are always straight. In these sayings, Jesus proved that He is not only a man but also God. (Times are approximated.)

Time	Event
0900 hours (third hour)	Jesus was nailed to the cross.
0930	Jesus prayed aloud, "Father forgive them for they know not what they do."
1000	Jesus facing his mother, "Woman, behold your son!" Then, facing his disciple John, "Behold your mother!"
1100	Jesus said to one man being crucified beside him, "Truly I say to you, today you will be with me in paradise."
1200 noon (sixth hour)	Darkness lasted for the next three hours.
1300	Jesus declared, "I thirst."
1400	Jesus cried, "My God, my God, why have you forsaken me."
1430	Jesus announced, "It is finished."
1500 hours (ninth hour)	Jesus prayed, "Father, into your hands I commend my spirit."

First, Christ forgave the very people that hated Him, some of whom were relishing in His suffering and horrible death. The Lord's objective while on this planet was to forgive humans of their sins, and He made no exception with executioners and blasphemers. But only those witnesses who would receive Jesus's absolution took heed; and by the way, you also are a witness (so take heed). Can you imagine? The hellions had just nailed our Lord to the cross, and He looked over them and forgave them right then and there. I wonder which of them received the gift He was offering. We know at least one centurion did (referenced below in three Gospels), as well as one repentant thief crucified next to Jesus.

Second, Jesus made accommodations to ensure His mother would be cared for; He wasn't just an obedient son to God the Father, but to His earthly mother as well. St. John responded accordingly, and took Mother Mary under his wing. Talk about loyalty. One might say Jesus was loyal to a fault: our fault. His mom and friend were loyal back, as should we be.

About that time, Christ showed compassion and forgave one of the criminals being crucified with Him, whose final act was one of confession mixed with contrition. Yes, a man of ill repute would come to know Jesus and be saved at the last minute. It appears the second thief took the other road, the one to perdition. It's a graphic sight knowing there are two paths, and the sheer numbers choosing the wrong one; how terrifying just thinking of their fate. But in a way, we all took part in Christ's crucifixion. So, pray to the Blood and ask for the Spirit and you will receive the Word, if you believe. And this decision will save you; but it is unwise to wait until the last minute (MAT 20:1–16).

With three hours to live, Jesus who is wholly God and naturally man, was dying of thirst; so, He asked for a drink. See, He took care of everyone else before addressing His personal needs. But what they offered was certainly not going to quench our Savior's thirst; actually, it was meant to sedate Him. Christ refused the drink and any potential of deadening the pain or clogging His mind (MAT 27:34). I would imagine hyssop and vinegar would be a nauseating concoction anyhow. Obviously, Jesus didn't mean "thirst" the way the others did. When your thirst cannot be quenched, what you need is His living water; if you drink His water you will never thirst again (read JOH 4:13–15; JOH 7:38–39).

In His agony the Son called out to His Father, quoting King David (PSA 22:1). Feeling the weight of humanity's sin laid upon His shoulders, Jesus had finally reached the finale. The physical, mental, and spiritual anguish must have been horrendous. Christ recognized the terrible darkness awaiting those who would end up permanently separated from God for rejecting His sacrifice. However, it was not Jesus but the lost who would be forsaken by God. How distressing could that have been for the Lord to foreknow? Who says God doesn't suffer? He feels our suffering as well, not just that of His Son! When your child is hurting, does it pain you? And we are God's children, well if you want to be; but He'll disown you if you don't want to be. And that will pain Him deeply. If your child does not accept Jesus and you think he or she could be condemned, does that not pain you the most? It is one thing to worry about their physical health and quite another to be afraid for their spiritual health.

No doubt, getting hit with a ton of sins was the finishing blow. It was now over and Jesus pronounced that fact to the crowd. This was everyone's big chance to pick a side, the same choice available to you and me, not to mention every individual person in the world. Because, salvation has been revealed to all men and all nations. (PSA 67:1–2; PSA 98:2; ISA 52:10; TIT 2:11–15). As for me, it's an easy pick: the best of the best, or not. It is downright irrational not to choose Jesus, who knew why He had to die: for us. He understood His sacrifice was completed once and for all (HEB 10:8–14). Could His last thought have been one of relief after declaring it finished? Possibly, since with His last breath Jesus addressed His Father one last time, again quoting King David (PSA 31:5), therein relinquishing His Spirit, and allowing His own death to take the place of yours and mine.

I don't know about you, but I doubt if I would have been able to feel compassion, be forgiving, and endure such sorrow and terror with even an ounce of grace or mercy. Thank God Christ did, nobody else could. Once again, this substantiates His deity. Keep in mind, beloved, the Spirit leaving Jesus was His life-giving power. Being reunited with the Father, Jesus continues to offer that Spirit to you (read JOH 14:16–20,26–28). Jesus made it clear that He was leaving but His Spirit was staying. If you do not accept this free gift, beware; the bell may toll any day now.

- MAT 27:45–53 ~ From the sixth hour there was darkness over all the land unto the ninth hour. And about the ninth hour Jesus cried with a loud voice, saying, "Eli, Eli, lama sabachthani?" Which translated means, "My God, my God, why have you forsaken me." Some who stood there, after they heard Jesus shout said, "This man is calling Elijah." One of them ran, took a sponge, filled it with vinegar, put it on a reed, and raised it to Jesus to drink. People were saying, "Let's see if Elijah will come save him." Jesus cried again with a loud voice and gave up the ghost. And behold, the veil of the temple was rent in two from top to bottom; and the earth quaked and the rocks broke. Graves were opened and many bodies of saints which slept arose out of their graves, and wandered into the holy city appearing to many. Now when the centurion and the others watching over Jesus saw the earthquake, and everything that happened, they feared greatly saying, "Truly this was the Son of God."
- MAR 15:25 ~ It was the third hour, and they crucified Him.
- MAR 15:33 ~ And when the sixth hour came, there was darkness over the whole land until the ninth hour.
- MAR 15:36–39 ~ One man ran and filled a sponge with vinegar, put it on a reed, and gave it to Jesus to drink saying, "Let's see whether Elijah comes to take him down." Then Jesus cried with a loud voice and gave up the ghost. And the veil of the temple was rent in two from the top to the bottom. When the centurion in charge witnessed this and saw that Jesus gave up the ghost, he said, "Truly this man was the Son of God."
- LUK 23:33–34 ~ When they arrived at the place called Calvary, they crucified him along with two malefactors, one on the right and the other on the left. Then Jesus prayed aloud, "Father forgive them for they know not what they do."
- LUK 23:39–43 ~ One of the malefactors ridiculed Jesus saying, "If you are the Christ, save yourself and us." But the other rebuked him saying, "Do you not fear God, seeing how you are receiving the same sentence? We are indeed guilty, deserving the due reward for our misdeeds. But this man has done nothing wrong." Turning to Jesus he said, "Lord, remember me when you enter into your kingdom." Jesus replied to him, "Truly I say to you, this day you will be with me in paradise."
- LUK 23:44–47 ~ It was about the sixth hour, and there was darkness over all the earth until the ninth hour. The sun was darkened, and the veil of the temple was rent in two. Then Jesus cried in a loud voice, "Father, into your hands I commend my spirit." Having said that, He gave up the ghost. After the centurion witnessed these things, he glorified God saying, "Certainly this was a righteous man."
- JOH 19:25–29 ~ Those standing by the cross of Jesus included His mother and the disciple whom He loved standing with her. Jesus said to His mother, "Woman, behold your son!" Then to the disciple He said, "Behold your mother!" And from that hour the disciple took Jesus's mother into his home.
- JOH 19:28–30 ~ Jesus, knowing all things were now accomplished that the scripture might be fulfilled said, "I am thirsty." There was set a vessel full of vinegar, so someone dipped a sponge, put it on a hyssop branch, and lifted it to His mouth. Once Jesus had acknowledged the drink He said, "It is finished." And He bowed his head and gave up the ghost.

Interestingly, though there is considerable consistency between the Gospel writers' accounts of the crucifixion, they do not mention the same statements of Jesus, and they do not report situational occurrences during those six hours the exact same way. But without their distinct perspectives, we would not have a complete picture. This is not a discrepancy since it is common for eyewitnesses to give varying accounts of what they saw and heard. In fact, it becomes quite suspect when an investigator acquires identical stories from different witnesses because this suggests their testimony was rehearsed. Clearly the testimony of the disciples was never rehearsed, it was proclaimed by the power of the Holy Spirit within them (2 PE 1:21). If you invite the Holy Spirit into your heart, you will proclaim it as well (LUK 12:11–12).

Consider the Pharisees, who rehearsed their excuse and invented a testimonial well in advance, in anticipation of an empty tomb. They knew of Christ's declaration to rise from the dead, so they made arrangements to ensure the disciples would not be able to fake a resurrection. Everything happened just as Jesus said, precisely what the Jewish leaders feared. The Roman guards witnessed it firsthand and told the chief priests and Pharisees who stuck with the fabricated story as planned. This baffles me. They knew deep down Jesus was a man of God who had accurately predicted His own death and resurrection. It wasn't only the disciples who would proclaim this, it was the very guards the Pharisees emplaced to keep others away from the gravesite. The authorities took every precaution to obstruct the inevitable, but to no avail. These elders of the temple bribed guards to perpetuate a lie because they themselves could not bear the truth. Neither could Pontius Pilate, apparently, for he left before Jesus could respond to his question, "What is truth?" Pilate's excuse for executing Jesus was that He offended the Jews by proclaiming to be their King; as a further affront to the Jewish leaders, Pilate posted this on the cross (the titulus indicated the crime warranting crucifixion). None of these closed-minded imbeciles had a clue concerning the truth; they all got it wrong. Christ was a king alright, but unlike any they had ever encountered. They all tried to stifle the truth rather than accept it.

- MAT 27:62–66 ~ Now after the day of preparation, the chief priests and Pharisees came together to appeal to Pilate saying, "Sir, we remember how that deceiver said awhile back how He was going to rise again in three days. Please command the sepulcher be made secure until the third day, so his disciples cannot come by night and steal him away, then say to the people he arose from the dead: If that happens, the last error will be worse than the first." Pilate assured them, "You have your watch, now go your way; see that the sepulcher is made secure to your satisfaction." They left for the cemetery, and made the tomb secure by sealing the stone and posting a guard.
- MAT 28:1–15 ~ The morning of the Sabbath [the feast of First Fruits] some women went to the tomb. An angel had moved the stone causing the ground to quake, whereupon he sat. His face was shining like lightning and his robe was white as snow. The guards began to shake, scared to death. The angel spoke to the women and told them not to fear, because the crucified Jesus they sought was not there; He had risen like He said He would. "Come and see where He was laid," the angel suggested. Next the angel directed the women to inform the disciples that Jesus would catch up with them in Galilee. The ladies left hastily and joyfully; they couldn't wait to spread the good news. As they were on their way, some of the watch came into the city, and appeared before the chief priests relating what they had witnessed. An assembly of elders consulted together, then gave a large sum of money to the soldiers, ordering them, "You will testify that his disciples came by night and stole the body while you slept. If this comes to the governor's attention, we will persuade him not to make anything of it." So, the guardsmen took the money and did what they were told. And that tale continues to be reported among the Jews to this day.

It is not possible for everyone to experience the same event exactly the same way. We are equal and unique, and we choose what we attend to; and that is often biased by past experience which also varies greatly from person to person. This actually adds credibility to testimony and evidence provided by multiple witnesses, which was the case with the New Testament writers, how their individual testimonies added greater clarity to the scenario. No single person would have remembered every detail, but collectively they filled in the picture.

Primary sources were prophets and scribes appointed by God to ensure His Word could be trusted in entirety. The proof is staggering that the resurrection of Christ indeed occurred; the incident is thoroughly documented and corroborated. It couldn't be spelled out more plainly. Not only did Jesus and His disciples proclaim it, so did some of the guards who were paid hush money to conceal the facts. I wonder if those guards were able to keep their mouths shut, much less shut it out of their minds. The Word got out either way and still turns hearts to the vertical today.

In closing, Jesus died and arose from the grave on Easter Sunday, the Jewish Day of First Fruits. Like He promised, He would give His life and take it back again (JOH 10:17–18) all within three days (JOH 2:18–19). Jesus announced His victory on the cross, then to the souls of the dead (1 PE 3:19). Satan's defeat was sealed when Christ pronounced it finished. By His resurrection, Christ brought to naught every evil work of the devil for all time (HEB 2:14; 1 JOH 3:8). At the same instant, Christ paid the price for humankind and by His rising guaranteed their resurrection from the dead. Praise be to God! Let us worship Him every day, all day, and not just one day a week; let every day be a "high" day. For you can get high on the Lord every minute of every day from now until eternity if you want. You can receive it, or leave it and pay your own way. But can you afford it?

- JOH 2:18–19 ~ The Jews answered Jesus, "What sign can you show us, to prove it is you doing these things?" Jesus replied, "Destroy this temple [His body was the temple of the Holy Spirit by the way], and in three days I will raise it up."
- 1 PE 3:18–19 ~ Christ suffered once for sins, the just for the unjust, in order to bring us to God. He was put to death in the flesh but brought to life by the Spirit, with whom He went to preach to the spirits in prison.

Christ Washing the Disciples' Feet – Painting by Tintoretto (1518–1594)
Museo del Prado, Madrid Spain

CHAPTER EIGHT

Lesson: Receiving the Holy Spirit

Satan will inherit the lake of fire (REV 20:10–14). Care to join him? If you'd rather go up instead of down, you must receive the Holy Spirit. Some modern churches worship Jehovah God alone. Some differentiate Jesus Christ referring to Him as a subordinate god, or a mere man. Others emphasize just the Spirit, while others do not include the Holy Spirit at all in their prayers or convocations. A genuine faith in Jehovah is nurtured by the Holy Spirit, through Jesus Christ. Christians confess, repent, pray, and kneel before the Lord Jesus. We receive His forgiveness and believe His promises by the power of God living in us which is His Holy Spirit. This is why the doctrine of the Holy Trinity is central to Christianity. It is three-in-one or your faith comes undone.

Claiming to be a Christian is one thing, having the power of the Holy Spirit is quite another. Remember, your body is to be made a temple where the Holy Spirit can reside, just as His Spirit resided within Jesus. Relinquishing your spirit to Him is to accept His in you, with which comes greater responsibility. The Holy Spirit is one of the most neglected topics among various denominations, for many do not recognize Him or worship Him. Yet the Holy Spirit is your connection to God. Be advised, if you do not recognize the Holy Spirit working in your life, you might not be a Christian.

- 1 CO 6:19 ~ Do you not know that your body is the temple of the Holy Spirit living within you, which you received directly from God? You are not your own, you belong to God.

There are good spirits and there are bad ones. Then there is Paraclete, who is over all spirits; this is an ancient term meaning legal advocate, counselor, intercessor, and consoler, all attributes ascribed to the Holy Spirit and Jesus Christ in the Bible. God is in charge of your spirit and my spirit, although He permits free will to choose who you will follow. Whose spirit is guiding you? Is it your own, somebody else's, a familiar spirit, or God's? The Holy Spirit has the power of life; in fact, the Spirit is life. God's life force which energizes human beings spoke everything into existence (including you) via the Word of God (Logos).

- GEN 2:7 ~ The Lord God formed man from the dust of the earth, breathed into his nostrils, and man became a living soul.
- JOH 6:63 ~ Jesus said, "It is the spirit that energizes your body; the flesh cannot live without it. The words I speak are spirit, and they are life."
- ROM 8:1–2,8–9 ~ There is now no condemnation for those who are in Christ Jesus, who walk after the Spirit and not the flesh. For the law of the Spirit of life in Christ has made us free from the law of sin and death. Those who live in the flesh cannot please God. If you are in the Spirit it is because God's Spirit dwells within you. As for people who do not have the Spirit of Christ, Christ has no part of them or they in Him.

Sacraments such as Holy Baptism and Holy Communion are means by which we invite God's Spirit to indwell us. Baptism is the initial way to receive the Holy Spirit. It is a relatively simple procedure employing a ceremonial washing wherein forgiveness is conveyed through the consecrated water whenever the proper commitment is applied. Then, what is meant by being baptized in, with, and of (or by) the Holy Spirit? Are there different types of baptism? Let us examine each of these via the scriptures.

Being baptized *in* the Holy Spirit is to be covered by the water of life, which cleanses one of original sin. You were covered with water in the womb and again in baptism, illustrating the concept of being born again. Acceptance of the Lord's presence in your life and His influence in your decisions is a free gift given through this sacred act. Baptism is a fundamental element in all evangelical persuasions, though there are variations in when and how it is administered. Is there one authorized way to administer baptism? Well yes, for it is to be performed in the name of the Father, Son, and Holy Spirit. Just as the three persons of the trinity were present at Jesus's baptism, so all three will be present at yours. Denominations that do not acknowledge the Holy Trinity in their theology and worship should be avoided.

- MAT 28:19–20 ~ Jesus made His last pronouncement to His followers, thereby ending His first advent, "Go now and teach all nations, baptize them *in* the name of the Father, Son, and Holy Spirit. Teach them to observe all things ever I have commanded, and remember I am always with you, even until the end of the world. Amen."
- ACT 2:38–39 ~ Then Peter said to the crowd, "Repent, and be baptized every one of you *in* the name of Jesus Christ for the remission of sins, and you will receive the gift of the Holy Spirit. This promise is to you, your children, those who are far away, and whomever the Lord our God calls."
- ACT 8:35–38 ~ Philip read aloud the scripture which the eunuch had asked about, and preached to him how Jesus fulfilled that scripture. As they journeyed along the way, they came upon a certain body of water, and the eunuch asked, "See, here is water; what is stopping me from being baptized right here and now?" Philip replied, "If you believe with all your heart, you can be baptized." The eunuch answered, "I believe that Jesus Christ is the Son of God." Then he halted the chariot, and the two men went down into the water; and Philip baptized him.
- GAL 3:27 ~ For as many of you who have been baptized *into* Christ have put on Christ.
- EPH 4:4–6 ~ There is one body and one Spirit, just as when you were called *into* one hope. One Lord, one faith, one baptism, one God and Father of us all, who is above all, through all, and in all.

Being baptized *with* the Holy Spirit is to receive God into your heart and mind. Holy Baptism and Holy Communion are ways of calling the Holy Spirit to be with you and live inside you. The goal is to keep Him in your heart; this generally happens when you have delved into His Word, matured in the faith, and accepted responsibility for your words and actions (having reached the age of accountability). God's Spirit helps you to grow spiritually, follow His instructions, choose rightly, and act accordingly. If you have obtained the salvation of Christ it is because your sins have been covered *with* His blood. Your response should be to remain steadfast in your commitment and your faith. And the Holy Spirit who is the source of your faith will be your escort in life; He will never leave you or forsake you.

- DEU 31:6 ~ Be strong and courageous, do not worry or be afraid; for the Lord your God is *with* you. He will never fail you or forsake you.
- JOH 1:33 ~ John the Baptist mentioned that he had yet to encounter the Messiah before stating, "He who sent me to baptize with water said unto me, "Upon whom you see the Spirit of God descending and remaining on Him, the same is He that baptizes *with* the Holy Spirit.
- ACT 1:4–5 ~ Jesus assembled together the disciples, commanding them not to depart from Jerusalem, but to wait for the promise of the Father which He was coming. "For John truly baptized with water; but you will be baptized *with* the Holy Ghost several days from now."
- ACT 2:1–4 ~ And when the day of Pentecost had come, they were joined with one accord in one place. Suddenly a sound from heaven was heard like a rushing mighty wind; it filled the house where they were sitting. Next appeared cloven tongues of fire, sitting upon each of the evangelists' heads. They were filled *with* the Holy Spirit and began to speak in other languages, as the Spirit directed them.

- ACT 11:15–16 ~ While Peter was speaking to them, the Holy Spirit came upon them, just as it came upon the apostles when their ministry began. And Peter remembered the words of Jesus when He said, "John indeed baptized with water, but you will be baptized *with* the Holy Spirit."
- ACT 15:7–9 ~ After much disputing, Peter arose and spoke, "Men and brothers, you know a good while ago God chose some of us to take the Gospel message to the Gentiles so they would hear and believe. God, who knows all hearts, bore witness, giving them the Holy Spirit just like He did with us. There is no difference between us and them regarding the purifying of hearts through faith.

Baptism *of*, or *by*, the Holy Spirit is to have received transformation, constant renewal, and eventual sanctification thereby making a miserable sinner like you and me holy before God, even as He is holy (1 PE 1:16). It creates a new you (2 CO 5:17), which means having received and responded to your rebirth in Christ. Jesus explained this succinctly to Nicodemus, a Pharisee (church elder) and member of the Jewish Sanhedrin (ruling party); and the apostles were witnesses to it (JOH 3:1–21). The fundamental message from that momentous encounter was basically this: You need to be empowered by the truth of God's Word which is communicated through the Holy Spirit to hear, speak, and act the Gospel of Jesus Christ (JOH 3:14–18).

The Holy Spirit will ordain you to minister to others, especially the lost sheep. It is a christening into spiritual service and sacrifice. Baptism by the Holy Spirit is to align your desires with God's desires for your life. That is, you have relinquished control of your life to Christ who is your pilot. The Holy Spirit is your navigator and the Kingdom of God is your destination. You'll serve and witness in whichever vocation you pursue, in any situation you find yourself, and with a full repertoire of God-given talents, abilities, education, and preparation. Keep in mind, the Holy Spirit is the free gift; it cannot be bought or sold. And your actions are an extension of your faith not the other way around. Since the gift of life is conveyed by the Holy Spirit, God will raise you from the dead just as He did His Son, and you will live forever with the Lord in heaven bearing a new and improved body (MAT 10:28; 1 CO 15:44; PHP 3:21) purified and sealed by the Holy Spirit.

- MAR 16:15–18 ~ Jesus said unto them, "Go into all the world and preach the Gospel to every soul. Anyone who believes and is baptized will be saved; but those who do not believe will be damned. Signs will follow those who believe; in my name they will cast out devils and speak new tongues. They will pick up serpents and not be harmed; and if they drink anything poisonous, it will not hurt them. They will lay hands on the sick and those people will recover."
- JOH 7:39 ~ Jesus spoke of the Spirit and preached that those believing in Him would receive the Holy Ghost, whom they had yet to receive because Jesus was not yet glorified.
- JOH 20:21–23 ~ Jesus addressed them once again, "Peace be to you. As my Father has sent me, now I am sending you." After saying this, He breathed on them, and announced, "Receive the Holy Ghost. Those who's sins you remit, they are remitted; and those who's sins you retain, they are retained."
- LUK 24:49 ~ Jesus announced, "Behold, I bestow the promise of my Father upon you. Tarry awhile in the city of Jerusalem, until you are infused with power from on high."
- ACT 8:17–20 ~ The apostles laid their hands on the converts, and they received the Holy Ghost. And when Simon (the sorcerer) saw that through the laying of hands the Holy Ghost was bestowed, he offered them money saying, "Give me this power, so I can lay hands on others and bestow the Holy Ghost." Peter admonished him, "Your money will perish with you because you think the gift of God can be purchased."

- ACT 10:44–47 ~ While Peter was speaking, the Holy Spirit came upon those who heard the Word. Those from the circumcision who believed were astonished, and also those aligned with Peter, because the gift *of* the Holy Spirit was being poured out upon the Gentiles. For they heard the apostles speaking in tongues, magnifying God. Then Peter announced, "Can any of you who have received the Holy Spirit forbid offering the water of baptism to Gentiles?"
- ACT 19:1–6 ~ While Apollos preached at Corinth, Paul had passed through the upper coasts into Ephesus, where he found certain disciples and inquired of them, "Have you received the Holy Spirit since you started believing?" They said they hadn't even heard of the Holy Spirit. Paul asked, "Into what then were you baptized?" They replied, "Into John's baptism." Then Paul announced, "John truly baptized with the baptism of repentance, telling people they should believe on Him who would come next, namely Jesus Christ." When they heard this, they were baptized in the name *of* the Lord Jesus. As soon as Paul laid his hands upon them, the Holy Spirit came upon them; and they spoke in tongues and prophesied.
- EPH 4:7-13,30 ~ To every one of us is given grace according to the measure of the gift *of* Christ, for it is said, "When He ascended on high, he led the captives along and gave gifts to men." (That He ascended means He first descended to the lower parts of the earth. He that descended is the same who ascended far above the heavens, so He might encompass all things.) He appointed some to be apostles, some prophets, some evangelists, some pastors and some teachers for the perfecting of the saints, for the work of ministry, and for the edification of the body of Christ; until we all reach unity in the faith, and in the knowledge of the Son of God, progressing into the perfect man, having achieved the full measure *of* the stature of Christ. Do not grieve the Holy Spirit of God, whereby you are sealed unto the day of redemption.
- 2 CO 1:21–22 ~ He who established us and you in Christ, and anointed us, is God who has sealed us and placed into our hearts His Spirit as insurance that we remain in Him and receive the promise.
- TIT 3:5–6 ~ Not by works of righteousness but according to His mercy God saved us, *by* the washing of regeneration, and the renewing *of* the Holy Spirit. He shed His Spirit abundantly and covered us through Jesus Christ our Savior.

So how many ways are there to receive the Holy Spirit. Well, it boils down to Word, Sacrament, and Faith in Jesus Christ.

- JOH 3:5 ~ Jesus answered, "Truly I say, unless a person is born of water and of the Spirit, he or she cannot enter into the kingdom of God.
- 1 JO 5:8 ~ There are three who bear witness on the earth: the Spirit, the water, and the blood; and these three agree as one.

Through Baptism, living water cleanses the body of original sin in a ceremonial washing by the One who will quench your thirst forever with that living water. However, being cleansed of sin is an ongoing process, whereby one continues to confess and repent of their own sins on a daily basis, participating frequently in Holy Communion for renewal. Your forgiveness and redemption will come only if you make the request with sincerity and contrition.

- PSA 51:10–12 ~ Create in me a clean heart, Lord, and renew an upright spirit within me. Don't remove me from your presence and don't take your Holy Spirit from me. Restore to me the joy of your salvation, and uphold me with your free Spirit.
- JOH 4:13–15 ~ Jesus answered her, "Whoever drinks this water will thirst again. But whoever drinks the water I offer will never thirst again; that water will enter into them as a

wellspring of everlasting life." The woman replied, "Sir, give me this water so I will not be thirsty, and so I will not need to come to this well ever again."
- 1 CO 12:13 ~ By one Spirit we are baptized into one body, whether we are Jews or Gentiles, bond or free; because we all have received water from the one true Spirit.

Through the Eucharist, the body and blood of Christ enters the recipient to purify the soul, like fire refines gold. The bread and wine represent the living body and blood of Jesus. The bread of life satisfies permanently, unlike manna from heaven which satisfied daily. Receive the meal Christ offers and you will never hunger again. Both sacraments (Baptism and Communion) purify the soul periodically, while the process of sanctification purifies it permanently.

- MAL 3:1–3 ~ I (God) will send a messenger to prepare the coming of the Lord; but who can endure His coming? For He is like a refiner's fire which completely removes all impurities and imperfections. [John the Baptist, the messenger referred to here, used the same analogy in describing Christ, for whom he was sent to prepare the way.]
- MAT 3:1–3,11 ~ John the Baptist preached in the wilderness of Judea, "Repent for the kingdom of heaven is near." This is the person referred to in the scripture, "The voice of the one crying in the wilderness will prepare the way of the Lord, making straight a pathway to Him." John told the people, "Indeed, I baptize you with water unto repentance. But He who comes after me is mightier than I; I am not worthy of carrying His shoes. He will baptize you *with* the Holy Spirit, and with fire."

Finally, you are strengthened in the Holy Spirit by way of Word and Worship. This includes the spoken, written, and living Word; and spoken, written, and living Worship. Remember, the Holy Spirit is life, truth, and love. You must strive to live by faith (2 CO 5:7), putting God first; speaking only the truth (JOH 8:31–32), and loving everyone equally to yourself (MAR 12:28–31). Worship is a daily occurrence, whereby you walk the walk, study the Bible, and attend a weekly convocation with fellow believers (HEB 10:24–25). Praise and prayer are acts of worship, done privately on a daily basis (if not hourly) as well as publicly in church (MAT 6:5–13; 1 TH 5:16–19) in obedience to the fourth commandment (Honor the Sabbath Day to keep it holy).

Studying God's Word, worshipping with fellow believers, offering thanks, praise, and constant prayer, and testifying about the things God has done for you are your faithful responses to God's gift of life which comes by the Holy Spirit.

- ROM 1:16–17 ~ I am not ashamed of the Gospel of Christ, for it is the power of God unto salvation given to everyone who believes; to the Jew first and also the Gentile [to those who spoke Greek as well as those whose native language was Hebrew]. Therein is the righteousness of God revealed from faith to faith as it is written: the just will live by faith.
- ROM 10:17 ~ Faith comes by hearing and hearing by the Word of God.
- HEB 11:1 ~ Faith is the substance of things hoped for and the evidence of things not seen.
- JDE 1:17–19 ~ Dear friends, remember what the apostles told us. They said that in the latter days there would be scoffers who follow their own ungodly desires. These people have come to divide you; they follow the instincts of their flesh and do not have the Spirit within them.

The bottom line is this: if you have not been sealed by the Holy Spirit, you remain susceptible to the forces of evil. At the end times, Satan will attempt to place his mark on human beings, as if to claim them for himself (REV 13:16–18). But the only thing he will seal is his own fate and that of those who receive his mark (REV 20:3). If you bear God's mark, Satan can never place a claim on you. In olden days, a king would seal his correspondence using his signet ring, to verify it certified by his majesty. Sometimes a man needed a passport sealed by the king in order to safely travel within the kingdom. In a similar manner, God will sign his name onto your heart, validating that you are His (ISA 43:6–7; 2 CO 3:2–4; GAL 6:17). In which case you'll have a free passport to go anywhere anytime in God's kingdom: signed, sealed, and delivered by His Majesty the King of kings.

- JOH 3:31–34 ~ He who comes from above is above all, but he who is of the earth speaks of earthly things. The witness from heaven testifies of things seen and heard, though nobody accepts it, except those who certify it as true, having been sealed by God. He who was sent speaks the words of God, wherein God gives His Holy Spirit without limit.
- JOH 6:27 ~ Jesus pronounced, "Truly I tell you, the reason you follow me is not for the miracles, but because you have partaken of the bread and are filled. Labor not for meat that perishes but for meat which endures unto everlasting life (i.e., the bread of life, which is the body of Christ). This is the Son of Man who carries the seal of God the Father."
- 2 TI 2:19 ~ The foundation of God stands firm, inscribed in truth revealing that God knows His own. Everyone who calls upon the name of Jesus Christ will turn from their iniquity.
- REV 7:2–4 ~ An angel appeared in the east carrying God's seal. He shouted to the four angels who were given charge to harm the earth and the sea, warning them to hold off until God's servants had been sealed. I (John) heard the number of those who were sealed: 144,000; 10,000 from each of the twelve tribes of Israel.
- REV 9:1–4 ~ The angel blew the trumpet and I (John) saw a star falling to the earth from heaven; he opened the bottomless pit from which bellowed smoke like a furnace, blocking out the sun. From the smoke arose locusts who would sting like scorpions. They were commanded to hurt anyone or anything except those with God's seal on their foreheads.

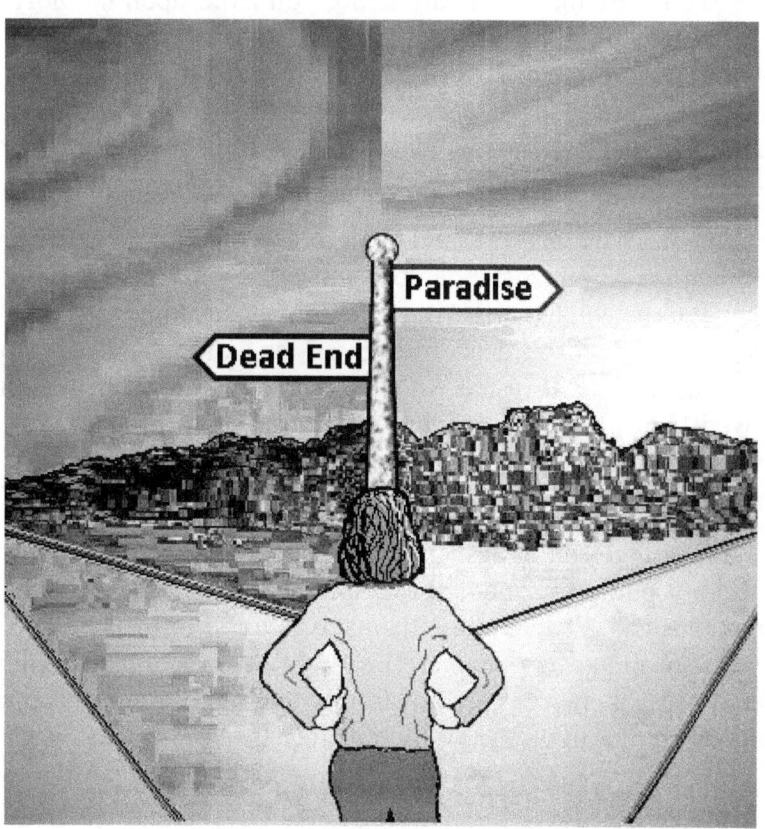

Lesson: Can Spirits Be Dead?

Nowadays, there are countless television and movie shows about demon possession, paranormal activity, and haunted locations which lead one to think that such phenomena are commonplace. They are not actually, and they also are not associated with spirits of the dead. Evil spiritual activity exists on this planet, and these incidents are evidence of fallen angels not the return of dead people or roaming ghosts from lives past.

The Bible tells us that Lucifer, once the anointed cherub, rebelled against God and was cast out of heaven to the earth (LUK 10:18); taking one third of the angels with him I might add (REV 12:3–12; REV 16:14). Fallen angels are referred to as demons in order to distinguish them from friendly angels doing the Lord's bidding, who also appear from time to time to help us out or relay God's messages (GEN 22:11–17; NUM 22:22–35; JOS 5:13–15; DAN 8:16–17; LUK 1:11–38; ACT 12:7–23). However, demons will disguise themselves as angels to trick people into believing things that are untrue (2 CO 11:4–15; 2 TH 2:3–12); in fact, deception is Lucifer's favorite tactic (GEN 3:1–15; JOH 8:44). Satan and his cronies have had a lot of practice at deception and temptation. Like us, angels know right from wrong, and many choose the latter. Unlike us, demons are condemned whereas we can be forgiven and saved.

- ISA 14:12–15 ~ How have you fallen from heaven, Lucifer the morning star, cut down to the ground, weakening the nations? You said in your heart, "I will ascend into heaven and exalt my throne above all of God's stars (referring to angels); I will lead the congregation of the north and ascend to the clouds. I will be like the Most High." But you will be brought down to the lowest pit of hell.
- EZE 28:14–19 ~ You were the anointed cherub; you lived upon the holy mountain of God. You were perfect from the day you were created until evil was found in you. Your great wealth made you violent inside and you became sinful. That is why you were thrown off the holy mountain, to be destroyed. You exalted yourself because of your beauty, corrupting yourself. You defiled the sanctuaries with your abominations. Eventually, you will be consumed by the fire within you and your terrible deeds will come to an end.

Angels and demons have been around since before carnal man, so they obviously know their history. A haunted house may have demons impersonating the dead, but they are far from dead. Of course, they will be condemned with fallen humans, ending up in the lake of fire (REV 20:10–15), after which they will be dead forever as far as the saints are concerned. For true believers, our spirits and souls will reside with our triune God forever, from the time we chose His Son and followed Him into the light, through our Sabbath rest, and beyond when we are reunited with our bodies and glorified by the Light of God (JOH 8:12; ROM 8:16–18), which we will wear as a garment to protect and sustain us forever (ROM 13:14; GAL 3:27; EPH 6:10–18).

Those summoning the dead or desiring to commune with the spirit world are deliberately inviting demons. Simply put, you cannot rouse spirits of the dead via occultist activity; what you'll get are demons instead. People allow themselves to be influenced by these demons as if what they relate is true or empowers people. The Bible warns against dabbling in the occult or consorting with demons; such practices are an atrocity to God. If you need spiritual guidance and truth, it is stupid and dangerous to go to any source other than the Holy Spirit.

- LEV 19:26–28.31 ~ Do not eat anything containing blood; do not use enchantments or align with sorcerers. Do not shave your head or trim your beards to single yourselves out. Do not cut, pierce, or tattoo your body on behalf of the dead. For only God is Lord. Avoid those with familiar spirits and avoid wizardry; do not be defiled by them. I AM the Lord your God.

- DEU 18:10–12 ~ Nobody is to sacrifice his or her child in the fire; or employ divinations, witchcraft, call spirits of the dead, cast spells, or summon demons. All of these things are an abomination to the Lord; He will drive such people away from His presence (also 2 KI 21:6).
- ISA 8:19 ~ If anyone suggests consulting demons (familiar spirits), or listening to sorcerers who search for paranormal visions and murmurings, answer them saying, "Shouldn't we be consulting with the Lord God; shouldn't we be seeking the living not the dead?"
- ISA 47:10–15 ~ You trusted in your wickedness, thinking that nobody sees you; but your wisdom and knowledge have perverted you. You told yourself that your power was superior and you needed no other. But disaster will befall you; you will not see it coming and you cannot put it off. Utter desolation will be swift and unexpected. Stand by your enchantments, charms, and visions, which you practiced since your youth for profit and advantage. You will become weary of your astrologers and their monthly forecasts. Let's see if they can save you. They will burn as stubble in the fire; nobody will come to deliver them from the powerful flame. This is not a fire for providing warmth or to gather around. But it is the only thing they gave you ever since childhood, those you promoted and depended upon. All of you have erred and wandered into the fire together, with nobody to pull you out.
- MAR 12:27 ~ [Regarding a trick question about the resurrection] Jesus asked in reply, "Have you not read the story of Moses and the burning bush when God said, 'I AM the God of Abraham, Isaac, and Jacob?' He is not the God of the dead, but the God of the living."
- 1 TI 4:1-2 ~ The Holy Spirit explicitly states that in the latter days some will depart from the faith, conferring with seducing spirits and following the doctrine of devils; speaking lies of hypocrisy, and possessing a conscience seared by a hot iron.

You may recall King Saul seeking an audience with Samuel the prophet, who had died and left him without a spiritual advisor. Traveling incognito, Saul visited the witch of Endor herself possessed by a demon (1 SA 28:1:7–11). When she summoned Samuel, she had a vision and cried out (1 SA 28:12–13). Saul asked what she saw and she told him, "I saw spirits rise from the ground" and "an old man wearing a robe." Both were convinced it was Samuel (1 SA 28:14–15), especially when they heard the entity say, "Why have you summoned me?" Since Saul perceived it to be Samuel, he sought counsel from the spirit; but this spelled very bad news for Saul (1 SA 28:16–20).

An argument can be made that old Saul had a bona fide visit from a dead person, and this may be an exception to the rule. But was it really Samuel without a body, Samuel in a glorified body, or a demon in disguise? Did the witch use her demon to summon its demonic friend in order to trick Saul, and imprison him? Then again, the witch was frightened to death herself. Either way, Saul understood the message, and the curse that came with it (1 CH 10:13-14). Let us carefully examine the text in 1st Samuel 28. The conclusion that the apparition was Samuel is debatable if not dismissible; the evidence is in the scripture itself. The witch saw a robed man arise out of the ground, not descend from heaven. If it was Samuel, I would think he would descend from heaven, not in a disembodied spirit but in a glorified state. Further, it remains unclear if Saul actually saw the vision because he asked the witch what she saw. But he probably heard the words loud and clear. Could the appearance of Samuel have been an angel, or perhaps a devil disguised as a man? Well, it could have been Lucifer himself and it still would've had the same effect. But if an evil spirit, why tell the truth, don't they usually lie? Not if God makes them tell the truth. That's right, God sometimes will use evil spirits and dishonest men to do His bidding in order to make His truth be known (see NUM 22; MAR 5:1–13).

Demons have been around as long as angels, and they are privy to the truth. Satan quotes scripture then twists it, like he did with Jesus in the wilderness. Fallen demons are not altogether ignorant of God's Word, for they recognize Christ's dominion over them and it terrifies them immensely (LUK 4:31–41; LUK 26:33). Satan and his underlings will use the truth against you, but they can't handle the truth, the whole lot of them (JAM 2:19).

It must have served God's purpose to communicate to Saul his errors, especially the engaging in witchcraft to garner God's favor. Saul's kingship was already in shambles and he was doomed by his indulgences. Saul had impatiently disregarded Samuel's instructions and was rebuked for it (1 SA 13:9-14); only after Samuel was long gone was Saul eager to listen, wishing he could turn back the hands of time. The experience literally scared the hell out of both the witch and Saul, possibly also the demon living in the witch. Enough to change their ways? The Bible doesn't say. But this certainly provides a poignant lesson for the rest of us. Once you get the hell scared out of you, don't let it back in. Instead, let the Holy Spirit in and you will remain alive in the image of Christ forever.

Now we'll address another interesting vision, this one from the New Testament: the transfiguration of Jesus. Remember when Jesus appeared in the sky with Moses and Elijah in front of three witnesses (DEU 17:6)? Moses and Elijah were already dead, right? Well, let's look into the text. Jesus went up the mountain to pray with Peter, James, and John. The three apostles fell asleep and awakened to see Jesus speaking with Moses and Elijah. [These two prophets might be the two witnesses who testify in the final days: ZEC 4:12–14; MAL 4:5; MAT 17:10-13; LUK 1:17; REV 11:3-12.] How did the apostles know it was Moses and Elijah, whom they'd never met? But here they were alive (see MAR 12:26–27). Imagine, witnessing Jesus in His glorious splendor, and Moses and Elijah glorified with Him. No, the apostles were not seeing dead people, but a vision of the future, a premonition of things to come when all God's witnesses will be glorified with Jesus. Every true witness (including you and me) will see the same thing: the magnificence of God and the radiant bodies of saints; for we will converse with them in our own glorified bodies (1 CO 15:44; PHP 3:21). This preview of the Good Shepherd bringing His sheep home is an image worth keeping in mind.

- JOB 19:25–26 ~ I know my Redeemer lives, and He will stand upon the earth on the last day. And though my body may be destroyed by worms, yet in my flesh I will see God.
- LUK 9:28–36 ~ Eight days later Jesus took Peter, James, and John to the mountaintop to pray. While Jesus prayed, His countenance changed and His clothes shined as lightning. Two men, Moses and Elijah, appeared with Jesus in glorious splendor; they were conversing about Jesus's departure from this earth which would occur upon His return to Jerusalem. The apostles had been in a deep sleep and awakened to witness this. The two prophets were preparing to leave Jesus when Peter interrupted, "Master, it is good to be here; let us build three shelters for you." Peter had no idea what he was talking about, but while he spoke, a cloud surrounded the place and the apostles became afraid as it enveloped them. A voice spoke from the cloud saying, "This is my beloved Son; listen to Him." Then the fog cleared and Jesus stood alone. The apostles kept this secret until after Jesus's resurrection. (Read also MAT 17:1–9; MAR 9:2–10).
- HEB 3:4–6 ~ Every house is built by someone, but God is the builder of everything. Moses was a faithful servant in God's house, testifying of things to be repeated in the future. Christ is the faithful Son who governs over God's house.
- 2 PE 1:16-18 ~ We did not follow cunningly devised fables when we testified of the power and coming of our Lord Jesus Christ, for we were eyewitnesses to His majesty. He received honor directly from God the Father, when a voice from heaven announced gloriously, "This is my beloved Son in whom I am well-pleased." (also MAT 3:16–17; MAR 1:9–11; LUK 3:21–22)

Moses and Elijah came down from heaven, not up out of the ground. They came to meet with Jesus atop the mountain, not to hang around (though Peter was ready to build tents to coax them into staying). From the cloud God proclaimed, "This is my beloved Son, listen to Him" (see EXO 40:38; NUM 9:15; 1 KI 8:10-11; 2 CH 5:13-14). What an experience that must have been. Talk about sending shivers up your spine. It is a message for everyone. Yes, you will see Christ in His glory with your own eyes, and you can meet all the saints who are glorified with Him if you happen to become a saint yourself. Recall when God brought Moses to the mountaintop where he could see the Promised Land, knowing he would not enter with the rest of the Israelites (DEU 34:1–12). The apostles saw the Promised Land too but would not cross into it just yet. But they got a glimpse of it; we all do. Jesus invites you to the mountaintop to witness His glory, to witness for Him, and to become an adopted brother or sister (GAL 4:4–5; EPH 1:5; HEB 2:11).

There really is only one exception to the rule about people returning from death in a disembodied spirit: Jesus Christ. Jesus was technically dead three days (MAT 12:40). Upon death He commended His Spirit to the Father, and at the resurrection He arose fully restored, but for the scars on His body. Yes, Jesus was alive and well; He was seen, heard, and touched. At the ascension Jesus departed in the body; but He left His Spirit behind to comfort us and teach us (JOH 14:16,26; JOH 15:26; JOH 16:4–28). Jesus is still alive and well, and will prove it when He returns again in the flesh (ACT 1:9–11). Christ arrived in a body, was assassinated and retuned alive in the body, and will come again in glory in His flesh. He died once He arrives thrice. Next time Jesus comes He will greet us in our bodies, the living and the dead, after which Christians will never die again having received an incorruptible body, while the rest will die the second death cursed with degenerate bodies (REV 2:11; REV 20:14; REV 21:8). This is why you need to be born again, or you will die again for the last time.

- LUK 24:39 ~ Jesus said, "Behold my hands and my feet that it is me; touch me and see, for a spirit does not have flesh and bones as I do."

Can you fathom the masses choosing death? Greater than those choosing life I'm afraid. The sheep will welcome Christ with open arms, like He welcomed us when we were called to be a member of His flock. The goats will rue the day they cast their eyes upon the living Lord Jesus. How could they not want to meet Him? But they had strayed from the Good Shepherd, and that condition will persist for perpetuity.

- ISA 40:5 ~ The glory of the Lord will be revealed, and all human flesh will see it together, for the Lord has said so.

Interestingly, when Jesus arose from the dead, He was accompanied by people who had come out of their graves (MAT 27:52-53). They were seen in their bodies, implying that they were not dead spirits wandering around the city but living souls. Isn't this an exception to the rule? Not if they were alive in the flesh. The description has more in common with Jesus raising His friend Lazarus, who was dead four days (JOH 11:18-44). Lazarus was restored to life in the body, but not a glorified body because he would eventually die and be buried again; in fact, the Jewish leaders sought to hasten that end by placing a "hit" on Lazarus (JOH 11:53; JOH 12:10). Remember a young boy (son of Nain) whom Jesus revived (LUK 7:11–15); and the daughter of Jairus who Jesus revived after everyone said it was too late (LUK 8:49–56)? Old Testament prophets also revived the dead (1 KI 17:21–22; 2 KI 4:17–37) as did New Testament apostles (ACT 9:36–41; ACT 20:7–12). Reviving the dead is not similar in any way to dead spirits roaming the Earth; nor is it associated with the first or second resurrection.

None of the aforementioned examples were dead people wandering around without a body. Neither is the Holy Spirit a wandering or aimless soul, seeing how Jesus is God and so is the Holy Spirit, and God does not wander for He is omnipresent. Though the Bible does not elaborate about those arising with Christ on the day of His resurrection, it is likely they lived a bit longer and then died, like Lazarus and the others who were revived. These are portents of the upcoming resurrection of the first fruits of Christ (1 CO 15:12-58), not examples of it. Incidentally, the alternate theory that Jesus brought the risen dead home with Him when he joined His Father lacks biblical support; it is more likely they were left behind to witness. Jesus too would be sticking around to witness forty more days, in His glorified body. Certainly, seeing lost loved ones come back alive was Christ's doing; they were awarded more time to further proclaim Jesus's power and glory. No doubt it was particularly special for their inner circles.

It is fair to ask, where is the biblical proof that the dead do not return, do not haunt us, or otherwise cannot visit the living? Read the following passages if you please.

- JOB 7:7–10 ~ Remember, life is like the wind; after death, my eyes can no longer look for the good. Those who have seen me will see me no more for I will not exist. Like a cloud at the mercy of the wind, life vanishes. Those who go to their grave shall rise up no more. They will not return to their houses and nobody will know them any longer.
- ECC 9:5–6 ~ The living know that they will die, but the dead know nothing, neither can they receive any reward for they have been forgotten. Their love, hate, and envy have perished with them; they have no involvement forever with anything under the sun.
- PSA 115:17 ~ The dead do not praise the Lord, nor any who have gone down into silence.
- PSA 146:4 ~ His breath leaves, and he returns to the ground; in that day his thoughts also perish.
- ECC 12:7 ~ The dust will return to the ground; and the spirit will return to God who gave it.
- ISA 26:14 ~ They are dead; they will not live; they are deceased, they will not rise. God has visited them and destroyed them, and caused all memory to perish with them.
- HEB 4:10 ~ A person who has entered into his or her rest has also ceased from their own works, as God did from His.

Do you think your spirit dies with you? If not, where does it go after your body is interred? Well, Jesus's Spirit didn't die; and He promised the Holy Spirit would stay behind once He was reunited with God the Father. The Holy Spirit will dwell with you forever if you ask. And if you trust in this promise your spirit will not die either; plus, you will keep your soul (MAT 25:31–40; LUK 21:19). With respect to the condemned, they perish (JOH 3:16); their spirits return to God (DEU 12:7), for they have forfeited their souls to the fire (MAT 10:28).

When Jesus gave up the ghost, the Spirit left Him. Absolutely He felt the separation which disconnects sinful humans from the Father (MAT 27:45–47). But it is the convicted who have separated themselves, possessing not the Spirit (JDE 1:18–19). Jesus knew the feeling of being forsaken, and allowed Himself to experience it so you won't have to. Christ offers His Spirit to you and me so we can live forever with our heavenly Father. Notice once again how all three persons of the trinity are present in this elaborate plan.

- PSA 31:5 ~ "Into your hand, oh Lord, I commit my spirit," prayed King David.
- LUK 23:46 ~ Jesus cried in a loud voice, "Father, into your hands I commend my Spirit."
- JOH 16:12–14 ~ Jesus informed them, "I have many things to tell you but you are not ready for them yet. Nevertheless, the Spirit of Truth comes; He will guide you into all truth. He does not draw attention to Himself but to me. He hears and He speaks, and He will show you things to come."

In summary, when you die your spirit and soul enter the presence of the Lord, well if you exhibited a persistent faith. If not, you'll wait in Hades for the judgment (MAT 25:41–46; LUK 16:19–31). Neither the spirit nor the soul lingers in the grave, only the body. Do you think some spirits stick around, like in haunted houses? Do you think your spirit will lag behind; maybe it goes somewhere else, or does it just die? I don't want any part of death or hanging around here after my spirit leaves this body. Because I know I'm going to a better place. Are you? One thing I can guarantee, you won't be moseying around Earth after you die.

Besides, there will come a time when there will be nothing left of this place. Even if you could choose to be sentenced to Earth, you wouldn't be able to stay indefinitely because this place is going to burn (2 PE 3:10). Either way, you won't make it. You can opt to be destroyed along with this world, in which case you've waived the invitation to go home to God and experience a new world (REV 21:1–3).

Fallen angels are not disembodied spirits, but they are looking for a host (MAT 12:43-45). Are you interested in being influenced by any spirit other than God's? You can but it will be a bad decision. If that is your penchant, you can expect the same message and curse King Saul received. I recommend strongly against it. If anyone calls you to attend a séance, or observe a channeling, or study spiritism, or engage in occultist behavior—tell them where they can go.

Few people are aware when friendly angels are ministering to them, because they can look and act like people if it suits God's purpose (HEB 13:2). Maybe you thought you saw your grandmother after she died and it was a comforting experience; maybe someone helped you out of a jam and then suddenly he or she was gone; maybe you received news about something very important just in the nick of time. God's Holy Spirit talks to us, and sometimes He sends angels to talk to us or show us how. The Bible names two particular angels, likely cherubim. Michael is signified the archangel; he helped Joseph and Daniel (JOS 5:13–15; DAN 10:13–21). Gabriel also helped Daniel (DAN 8:16; 9:21) as well as Zacharias, Mary and Joseph (MAT 1:18–25; MAT 2:19–23; LUK 1:5–32). Lucifer was a cherub too, who fell from heaven to the earth; familiar spirits are those who were tossed out of heaven with him. It is evident in the Bible there are good and bad spirits, oftentimes difficult to detect or even differentiate. Though they may possess a spirit body, they are not physical beings.

In the last days there will be a great falling away from the faith prior to the revealing of the son of perdition, who will seek worship and exaltation just as Lucifer did before he got kicked out of heaven. In fact, that human host will be possessed by Lucifer, still on a mission to replace God as the object of your worship. Be assured: Satan, dragged a third of the angels down, and now they are here trying to drag you down, and if you follow any of them or their followers you will go where they are going—down.

- ISA 66:4 ~ I also will choose their delusions and will bring their fears upon them; because when I called nobody answered and when I spoke nobody listened. But they did evil before my eyes and chose that which I did not appreciate.
- 2 TH 2:2–5 ~ Do not be deceived, for the day of the Lord will not come until there occurs a falling away from the faith. Then the son of perdition will be revealed who opposes God and exalts himself as an object of worship, sitting in the temple of God as if he is to be adored. Remember, I (Paul) have spoken of this repeatedly.
- 2 TH 2:8–11 ~ After the wicked one is revealed the Lord will consume him with the spirit of His mouth, and will destroy him with the brightness of His coming. Not only the one who acts on behalf of Satan, with power, signs, and wonders, but also followers who likewise possess deceptiveness and unrighteousness, hating the truth that could save them. For this reason, God will send them a strong delusion, and allow them to believe that lie.

Lesson: Has Anyone Seen Heaven?

Definitely, many books have been written and many movies have been produced about near-death and out-of-body experiences, not to mention people visiting heaven or hell, along with their descriptions of events, people and places they supposedly encountered. In general, heaven is described as a pleasant place with good people and hell is just the opposite. However, this information has been available from days of old. Well, did these people really see heaven or hell, to include deceased relatives and other conditions described from their visions? As always, we need to look into God's Word. If there is disagreement among witnesses, we know the Bible will be the most credible witness.

There is only one clear example in the Bible when someone got a view of heaven, and that event is reported by the apostle Paul (2 CO 12:2–4). Paul spoke of a man who was "caught up to the third heaven" meaning God's domain; ordinarily, the first heaven is associated with sky (atmosphere) and the second heaven with outer space (cosmos). Whatever was seen and heard during that occasion, Paul was not permitted to reveal it. Paul goes on to say that his job was to tell the truth, not to exalt himself or to be exalted by others. To ensure this, Paul was given a "thorn in the flesh" which Satan used to pummel Paul, lest he be exalted (2 CO 12:5–7). Perhaps the guy who was "caught up" into heaven was Paul himself, but this is unclear. Either way, Paul was prohibited from providing further details about the experience and who experienced it.

- 2 CO 12:2–4 ~ I knew a man in Christ over fourteen years ago (whether in the body or out of the body, I cannot tell, but God knows). This man was caught up to the third heaven, and I knew this man. How he was caught up into paradise to hear unspeakable words I am not free to explain.

Paul's episode is similar to one described by the apostle John (REV 10:1–6), in that both experienced a supernatural phenomenon but were commanded by God to exclude something they had learned from being disclosed in their report. John observed an angel speaking, followed by thundering voices proclaiming things which John was not allowed to write. John was then directed by that same angel to "prophesy before many peoples, nations, tongues, and kings." This angel, and the seventh angel sounding the final trumpet announcing Jesus's return, are one in the same (1 CO 15:51–52). We only get the second half of the angel's message which refers to the completion of time (REV 10:7–11). Whatever Paul and John witnessed, it wasn't for public consumption; in both cases, a portion of their testimony was withheld.

- REV 10:1–6 ~ I saw another mighty angel descend from heaven in a cloud. He had a rainbow over his head, his face shown like the sun, and his feet were as a flaming fire. In his hand was a small, opened book. The angel stepped his right foot upon the sea and the left upon the earth. He cried aloud like a roaring lion; after he spoke, seven thunders uttered their voices. I was about to write when a voice from heaven told me, "Seal up those things which the seven thunders uttered and do not write them down."

Another similarity between Paul's and John's vison reflects an inheritance available in heaven, as well as the inheritance awaiting those going to the other place. The prophets have declared that nobody has seen or heard what God has prepared for the next life (ISA 64:4; 1 CO 2:9); but people sure get enough of a glimpse in scripture to make up their minds about both destinations. The two visions described above have a third thing in common: the prophets lived to bear witness; that is, Paul and John would carry on, and not die until their assigned tasks were accomplished. And they knew they were not done as explained in their testimony; and you aren't done either, at least not yet. "It ain't over till it's over," to reiterate a phrase from Yogi Berra.

Doubtless, Paul likely had numerous near-death experiences, which he chose not to dwell upon (ACT 14:19; 2 CO 6:3,9). He surely suffered more than most; but miraculously, he'd be up and back on the road posthaste (ACT 14:20). Obviously, "near death" doesn't have much in common with dead. And when people are brought back from the dead, they are not "nearly" dead, but fully alive body, mind and spirit. Notice how those who had their lives extended by God to minister and testify (such as Lazarus), left no records concerning their familiarity with the other side. How can we be sure? Well, if it was written in the Bible it's because God wanted it recorded, and the reason it is not is because God didn't want it recorded. People purporting to think they know through personal experience about the afterlife, and then making a spectacle of themselves, would appear to be violating a basic principle outlined above. They exhibit self-exaltation and hence, their testimony is untrustworthy.

- ACT 14:19–22 ~ Some Jews from Antioch and Iconium came, persuading the people to stone Paul. They dragged him out of the city figuring he was dead. The disciples gathered him up and went back into the city. The next day, Paul and Barnabas left for Derbe where they preached the good news and won many disciples. Next, they left for Lystra, then on to Iconium and Antioch. And many more disciples were confirmed, in the knowledge of the trials and tribulations associated with faith.

I guess everyone gets a premonition of heaven and hell. Likewise, the consequences and circumstances determining which route one should take in life are readily available to everybody reaching the age of accountability (NUM 14:29–31; ISA 15:18; 2 PE 3:9). The mass media also provide images and scenarios which have proliferated over the years and stimulate these ideas. It stands to reason that an end-of-life or out-of-body experience would produce similar pictures or perceptions for most everyone. Indeed, it does to some degree; consolidation of the available literature on the subject displays many consistencies, even with scripture. Anyone can see the contrast of heaven and hell, light and darkness, and good and evil everywhere and frequently. Who wouldn't contemplate such things if they figured they were about to die? Who wouldn't give prayer a chance when encountering the threshold of demise? Well the answer to these questions is, far too many.

Keep in mind there also are noteworthy dissimilarities among the various testimonials regarding alleged visits to the other side. And that poses a reliability problem, statistically speaking. The similarities are what you would expect but the differences tend to contradict scripture. How do you weed out the false testimony from the truthful? You compare it to the Word of God, whether it is in agreement. But even if the descriptions are in agreement with scripture, this is not evidence that the testifier experienced the other side. Because nobody has seen or heard, remember?

What would motivate one to testify that they went to heaven or hell? How could that possibly be verified by the dreamer or anyone else? Well, look out; because many are telling their stories for attention, profit, self-aggrandizement, or whatever. That's why critical elements of their stories don't agree; these people really didn't go anywhere outside of their own minds. When the spirit and the mind have departed, the body is dead as can be; and the deceased has already thought their last thought on the earth. Even if these people believe what they saw and boldly declare it, who can confirm their vision? Maybe they dreamt it, maybe God provided a revelation, maybe they made it up. The nice thing about the Holy Bible is this: the testimony of the prophets and apostles can be verified using additional reliable sources. But the single testimony of one person, however convincing, will always be suspect. That doesn't mean they are lying; it means they could be mistaken. Or, they could be lying in order to get the attention.

Like Paul said: he didn't know if the experience was in the body or out of the body. Neither does anybody else know, and neither can the experience be measured, observed, or objectified. That such visionaries repeat the same things others do, which are revealed in the literature as well as the Bible, should not raise anyone's eyebrows. This is more commonplace than people may think. When in limbo, people may remember things long suppressed, and they may see faces of people long passed; and they might even be able to possess some awareness of things happening in the physical world although they do not appear to be conscious or responsive. And certain details may be confirmed by their relatives; but this is not evidence of an actual visit to heaven or hell. What these witnesses cannot relate is that which God has forbidden from revealing until Christ returns.

Many scriptures suggest that nobody gets to visit the other side, until death. Which means nobody can return as a disembodied spirit which was discussed in the previous lesson. You die, and then that's it for this life (JOB 7:9–10; ECC 9:5–6; PSA 6:5; HEB 9:27); you don't go to heaven or hell and come back to tell about it (1 TH 4:13–17). On rare occasions noted in scripture people were brought back from the dead; like Paul, they probably didn't dwell on the afterlife but on the promise of eternal life. No doubt, they lived their renewed life looking forward, not backward.

Anyone saying they went to heaven and were in the presence of God in their degenerate state are misguided. That doesn't mean people will never be visited by angels or Jesus Christ through a vision or a dream (JOE 2:28). Certainly, Paul was visited during his conversion and John when he received and wrote the Revelation of Jesus Christ. God came down from heaven to speak to the prophets; but they did not go up to speak with Him and return later to blab about things God keeps to Himself. He obviously holds it back until we are ready for it.

- EXO 33:17–20 ~ Moses asked God to reveal His glory. God replied, "Nobody can see my face and live… But before my glory passes by you, I will place you inside the cliff and cover your face with my hand; when I take away my hand you will see only my back in departing."
- JOH 1:18 ~ No man has seen God at any time. It is the Son of Man, who is in the bosom of the Father, that declares Him.
- REV 21:27 ~ By no means will anyone enter into heaven who is defiled, does abominable things, or invents lies; only those who are written in the Lamb's Book of Life will enter there.

It makes perfect sense that someone teetering on death may invite Jesus to visit, or ask Him to forgive and bless them (LUK 23:39–43); and I expect He would do just that because He has promised to (MAT 7:7; ROM 10:12–13). Those who have never beckoned Jesus to call on them are likely to perceive something more remorseful during a death-defying experience. Many have come to Christ as the result of a vision, recurring dream, or near-death episode; such incidents are related by converts from Islam, Buddhism, and previous followers of other false religions. The Holy Spirit arouses them into faith and they are saved as a result of the encounter, whether by vision or revelation.

When a person doesn't know Christ, he or she will be more easily fooled by a figure of light; because malevolent spirits often disguise themselves as benevolent ones (2 CO 11:14–17). This is likely the case for such mystics as Buddha and Mohammed; both fasted for weeks before purportedly receiving a vision of a spirit of light. Since their correspondence contradicts the Holy Bible, it seems they were listening to the wrong spirit. Perhaps they were deliberately attempting to deceive, as is the case for many tale-tellers proclaiming experiences in heaven and hell or face-to-face conversations with God. How can a person tell the difference between a vision from

God verses one from Satan without the Spirit of Christ guiding them? Perhaps that's why hoards are leaving the other world religions in a quest for truth, and end up joining Christendom.

Just before he died, Stephen saw heaven and Jesus sitting at the right hand of God; then Stephen called to Jesus to take him home (ACT 7:55–60). Paul was actually a party to Stephen's last stand (ACT 7:58); this was prior to Paul's conversion from Saul (ACT 9:1–17). Stephen knew exactly where he was going prior to his death. His was not a near-death experience for he was alive and ready to be taken to paradise upon his impending demise. True Christians know what Stephen knew and will not be caught by surprise; and they will know in their heart their next destination. They may even see a vision of it in their mind as they lay dying. If you are not sure about your visions or sources, you do not have your house in order; and time's-a-wasting folks.

I recommend taking afterlife stories with a grain of salt. Yes, they can be inspirational and interesting, but not necessarily factual. Like the Bible says, "Test what the spirits and seers put out against what the Bible says" (2 CO 11:13; 1 TH 5:21; 1 JO 4:1–13). Likewise, test what is being placed into a book or a movie in light of what the Bible says. Those who are less educated or otherwise ignorant of God's Word produce deviations from the "normal" view of heaven and hell. While there is a common thread in many of the various presentations, there also is divergence regarding critical aspects of Christian theology. Therefore, before believing these stories, it helps to know the scriptures; better yet, it is best to believe the scriptures. Surely, embellishment is a tricky if not risky business when the things being portrayed are in discord with Biblical truth; naturally, one should expect this from an imposter or a spirit of darkness.

Remember this, experience is not the quintessential avenue to enlightenment, but the Bible is. Gleaning truth and enlightenment from the Bible will require intense study, however. There is no easy road to salvation (MAT 7:14). You cannot drop acid, have a "religious" experience, and decide you can see, hear, or feel God in this manner. Hint: It was a hallucination, duh. That's why people take illicit drugs, they are motivated to experience something unusual, abnormal, or supernatural.

Another thing to consider is this: a person in a physically incapacitated, mentally delirious, or heavily medicated state are subject to hallucinations and delusions; that is, it is normal to experience psychotic features producing sounds and sights that are fantastical or unreal under these conditions. Further, to a person suffering from psychosis, such as a paranoid schizophrenic, the hallucinations and delusions seem real; and I'm sure people remembering near-death experiences might say the same thing. But the event is just as unreal as it would be if the person happened to be under the influence of drugs, medication, evil entities, delirium, or otherwise was mentally, medically, and/or spiritually vulnerable. That is, distortions to reality are likely during altered states of consciousness no matter what the cause. This alone makes such testimony admissible only in the court of opinion.

Invite the Holy Spirit to come in, and you will never be persuaded by the superstitions of others. You will know in your heart when a revelation is real or contrived if you are well versed in the Bible, because such disclosures will be backed up by scripture. And this will illuminate the path in which the Lord is leading you. These experiences are supposed to be personal, not something that needs to be publicized. By making them public it draws attention to oneself; but God wants to draw attention to Him.

Where and when your path ends, God only knows. Death is always imminent, my friends. Every moment can be considered a near-death moment from now on, until the time Christ returns, after which you will remain forever in either the lost or the found column. For some, it may be the last thing they think before drawing a complete blank.

Lesson: The Key to Three

The number three is a very significant number, biblically speaking. Certainly, the greatest importance of three to a Christian is the Holy Trinity: God in three persons. I have written about the trinity on many occasions and the relevance and contributions of the Father, Son, and Holy Spirit with respect to salvation (ISA 6:2–3; JOH 1:1; 1 JO 5:7–8). Some religions acknowledge God as a father and creator, but deny the deity of God's Son; other religions accept a divine Spirit but do not commune through Him. All three persons in the trinity play a crucial role in your redemption, making the Holy Trinity vital to Christian dogma, doctrine, and teaching. You may be aware of Satan's attempt to oppose God by constructing an unholy trinity (REV 16:13). We humans also have three components to our existence: body, mind, and spirit (1 TH 5:23). Therefore, three can represent three persons, personalities, or components depending on context.

Oftentimes three illustrates something that must be repeated: Balaam blessed Israel three times to the dismay of the Moabite king (NUM 24:10). God called young Samuel three times while he slept before recognizing the Lord's voice (1 SA 3:1–10). Elijah stretched himself over the woman's dead son three times and God revived the lad (1 KI 17:21–22). Elijah told the pagan priests to drench the altar with water three times; after which he called fire from heaven that consumed the sacrifice, the altar, the water, everything (1 KI 18:31–38). Jesus was tempted in the wilderness three times (LUK 4:1–13). Jesus found the disciples sleeping three times while he prayed in the Garden of Gethsemane (MAT 26:36–46). Thrice, Pontius Pilate pleaded with the Jews with respect to Jesus's sentencing (LUK 23:13–24). Jesus informed Peter he would deny Him three times, which he did, but Jesus also forgave Peter three times (JOH 13:36–38; JOH 18:25–27; JOH 21:14–17).

Three also refers to pivotal events. Moses raised his hand toward heaven and there was darkness in Egypt three days (EXO 10:22). God told Moses they would come to the new land and plant trees, but not to eat of the fruit for three years (LEV 19:23–24). Faithful King Hezekiah was ill three days before being healed (2 KI 20:1–5). The persistent antichristian Saul was without sight three days during his conversion by Christ who dubbed him Paul (ACT 9:3–9). We also know that Christ arose from the dead in three days (HOS 6:2; JON 1:17; MAT 12:30: MAT 28:19; MAR 8:31).

Three threes, or thirds, is particularly germane to the beginning of time as we know it, and the end of time as foretold. Prior to God creating man and woman, there was a rebellion in heaven. Lucifer was cast out along with one third of the angels, most of whom are still wreaking havoc on Earth. Evil spirits represent cunning and malevolent enemies of humankind, Satan being the arch-enemy (EPH 6:11–13).

- MAT 12:45 ~ Jesus talked about casting out devils; when one is cast out it may find seven spirits more wicked than itself to join, returning to the individual and making him or her worse off than before. Jesus was referring to an evil generation that would come.
- REV 12:3–5 ~ A great wonder appeared in heaven; it was a red dragon with seven heads and ten horns. Its tail pulled one third of the stars (angels) in heaven down with it, and they were thrown to the earth. The dragon waited for the woman to give birth so it could eat her child. Her child would rule the nations with an iron hand. The child was taken to heaven to sit on God's throne.
- REV 12:9 ~ Satan (the dragon) was cast out of heaven along with the rest of the corrupt angels, and brought down to the earth.

Proving that Jesus was with God all the while, He announced to seventy disciples, "I saw Satan fall from heaven like lightning" (LUK 10:18); this certified prophecies of Isaiah and Ezekiel itemized in the lesson *Can Spirits Be Dead*. The devil was thrown down to the earth and the demonic with him (REV 12:7–9). Upon the second coming of Christ, the whole bunch will be tossed into the depths of the lake of fire (perhaps the lowest chamber in that cauldron), as well as those sinners who rejected the Word of God. Thus, God established Hades, where the ungodly go and where a hoard of devils might already dwell. It is a chasm filled with lost souls. The found souls reside in Abraham's bosom (LUK 16:19-31) to receive the inheritance of Abraham (ROM 9:4–8).

Apparently, the original inmates confined in hell were fallen angels; the rest were confined to Earth. Lucifer (Satan) received similar travel plans as a result of his mutiny, dropping to Earth where he solicits humans to join him in defying God. But Satan will find himself bound in chains and sentenced to eternal hell, where evil will be extinguished for good. Though Satan's fate is sealed, thank the Lord ours is not, until we die or Christ returns whichever comes first. For many, they already have been sealed by the Holy Spirit for redemption (EPH 1:13; EPH 4:30). In response, Satan (the beast) will be requiring people be sealed with his mark (REV 13:16 –18).

- GEN 3:15 ~ God told the serpent (Satan), "I will place a barrier of hostility between you and the woman and between her progeny and yours. The offspring from the woman will bruise your head, and you will bruise his heel."
- MAT 25:41 ~ The Lord will say to those on the left, "depart from me you cursed ones into everlasting fire prepared for the devil and his angels."
- 2 PE 2:4,9 ~ God didn't spare the angels that sinned, but imprisoned them in hell to await judgment. God knows how to deliver the righteous from temptation, and how to deliver the unrighteous to judgment for punishment.
- JDE 1:6 ~ The angels which did not keep their position but left their estate are bound with everlasting chains in darkness until Judgment Day.

With respect to the end of time, when the latter days are upon us, one third of everything will be obliterated, including a third of the living. Some say such prophecies are symbolic and cannot be deciphered. What do you think?

- 2 TI 3:13 ~ Evil people and false teachers will get worse, deceiving many; they themselves have been deceived by Satan.
- REV 8:7–12 ~ The first angel sounded a trumpet and hail mixed with blood fell to earth; a third of the trees and all the grass were burned. The second angel trumpeted and a great mountain burning with fire was cast into the sea; a third of the sea turned into blood, killing a third of all sea life and destroying a third of the ships. The third angel sounded and a great star called Wormwood fell from heaven; a third of the water was contaminated. The fourth angel sounded and a third of the sun, moon, and stars became blackened; daylight occurred for only a third of the day.

Here's one that you may have missed. One third will make it to heaven because they were tested and true; the other two thirds will not make it. This is associated with God's people Israel but may also apply to the latter days when believers also will be tested for purity. For you staunch scientists out there who need mathematical proof: $1/3$ of believers + $2/3$ of angels = 1 (one with God); $1 - 2/3$ of unbelievers $- 1/3$ of angels = 0 (nothing with Satan). Is it really that difficult picking the right side?

- EZE 5:2,12 ~ A third of you will die from pestilence and famine; a third will fall by the sword; a third will be scattered to the four winds, and I (God) will draw a sword after them.
- ZEC 13:7–9 ~ The Lord of hosts says: Awake oh sword, against my shepherd, against the man who is my partner; smite the shepherd and the sheep will scatter, and I will turn my hand upon the little ones [possible reference to the scattering of the Jews]. Two thirds will be cut off and die; the other one third will be brought through the refiner's fire to be tested for purity. Those who call on my name will be heard, and I will say, "These are my people," and they will say, "The Lord is my God."
- GAL 5:4–5 ~ If you are attempting to be justified through works of the Law you have separated yourselves from Christ and have fallen from grace. But we who are of the Spirit wait for the hope of righteousness by faith.
- 1 PE 3:17–18 ~ It is better, given the will of God, to suffer for doing good than to suffer for doing evil. For Christ also suffered once for sins, the just for the unjust, so He could bring us to God; being put to death in the flesh but made alive by the Spirit.
- REV 16:19 ~ And the great city (the new Babylon) was divided into three parts, and the cities collapsed under devastating earthquakes.

It could be that the ones who are doomed will be divided into two parts, or thirds; with one third receiving a greater damnation than the other third. That is, a third are so despicable and mutinous towards God that their hell might be worse and/or longer than for people who tried to do the right thing though chose not to side with Christ. Jesus often warned the Pharisees about their sanctimonious, fake piety, with their self-admiration and aggrandizement which would earn them a harsher punishment (MAT 23). Further, while Christ commissions everyone to witness and teach (MAT 28:19–20), those who are called into ministry will be held to a higher standard (JAM 3:1; 1 TI 4:12–16). If someone forsakes their calling (LAM 2:14), or their religiosity is a scam (ACT 20:29–31), they will pay a greater penalty.

- MAT 6:5,16 ~ Jesus said, "Don't pray or fast like the hypocrites do, who pretend to be pious, praying and fasting in public places and before the congregations so that everyone can see them. That display is the only reward they will receive for their efforts."
- MAT 18:6 ~ Jesus said, "Whoever would cause a little child that believes in me to sin, it would be better for him if a millstone was hung around his neck and he was drowned in the depths of the sea."
- MAT 23:14 ~ Woe to you hypocritical scribes and Pharisees, who confiscate widows' houses and speak long prayers as a ploy; you will receive the greater damnation.
- JOH 19:11–16 ~ Jesus said to Pilate that he didn't have any power except that which was given to him from heaven. Pilate appealed to the Jews to release Jesus but they cried for His execution; and Pilate caved to the pressure, delivering Jesus to be crucified.
- ROM 2:5–6 ~ Because of stubbornness and an unrepentant heart, they are storing up vengeance against themselves until the day God unleashes His wrath, and His righteous judgment is revealed. God will give back to each person according to what he or she has done.
- 2 PE 2:20–22 ~ For if, after escaping the pollution of the world through the knowledge of our Lord and Savior Jesus Christ, they are again entangled therein and overcome, the latter end is worse for them than the beginning. It would have been better for them not to have known the way of righteousness, than after they had known it, to turn from the holy commandment delivered to them. What will happen to them is like a true proverb: The dog has returned to its vomit, and the pig that was washed is again wallowing in the mire.

- JDE 1:7–8 ~ Sodom and Gomorrah, and other cities and peoples who were destroyed because of their wickedness, are examples of the vengeance of eternal fire that awaits the wicked. Likewise, are those filthy dreamers who defile the flesh, despise dominion, and speak evil of dignity.

Steer clear of the false prophets and teachers or you could be misled (read JER 14:14; JER 23:32; LAM 2:14; HOS 6:9; MAT 6:5,16; MAT 7:15,21–23; MAT 24:11,24; MAR 7:7–9; LUK 21:8; ACT 20:3). They are at the bottom of the heap, with the sexual perverts, addicts, swindlers, idolaters, murderers, and such (1 CO 6:9–11; REV 21:8). Some have a lot more to pay it would seem; that is, there may be a hierarchy of punishment commensurate with wickedness (PSA 7:19), just like there is a hierarchy in the Law as evident in the Ten Commandments.

Some people are not evil to the core and do not oppose everything God stands for, but will face condemnation nevertheless if they feign ignorance, fail to repent, or decline the righteousness of Christ. They deceive themselves assuming that being good is what matters, but their goodness cannot save them because nobody is good except Jesus (MAR 10:18). Only if you accept Him as Savior will you receive His righteousness in exchange for your unrighteousness (2 CO 5:21). The cross is the single pointer to paradise. All other paths lead to the worst part of this universe.

- REV 20:1–14 ~ And the angel grabbed the dragon, that old serpent known as the devil and Satan, and bound him one thousand years. Satan was thrown into the bottomless pit for the entire thousand years, but then was released for a short while. I (John) saw judges sitting on thrones; and I saw the souls of those who had been beheaded because they witnessed for Jesus and for the Word of God. They had not worshipped the beast or his image, neither had they received his mark on their foreheads or hands. And they lived and reigned with Christ one thousand years. Blessed and holy are people taking part in the first resurrection for they will not experience the second death. Instead, they will be priests of God and of Christ and will reign with Him one thousand years. Next, Satan was unloosed and waged war against God, deceiving the nations; the devil gathered his armies but was defeated in no time. He was cast into the lake of fire where the beast and false prophet already were, to be tormented day and night forever. Death and hell were thrown into the lake of fire as well. Whoever's name was not found written in the Book of Life was condemned to the lake of fire. Then, I saw a great white throne and the King who sat upon it, from whose face the world had turned; and there was nowhere for them to go. And I saw the dead, great and small, standing before God; and the books were opened including the Book of Life. The dead were judged according to what was written in the books, in accordance with their works. The sea gave up its dead, and death and hell delivered up their dead, and all were judged according to their works. Ultimately, death and hell were cast into the lake of fire. This is the second death. Whoever's name was not written in the Book of Life inherited the lake of fire.

A popular theological position is that one third essentially will get another chance during the course of the millennial reign described in the above passage. Though possible, that viewpoint is weakly substantiated in scripture. Neither is it sealed in concrete the legitimacy of other eschatological viewpoints, to include millennialism versus amillennialism, and pre-, mid-, or post-tribulation rapture positions. Thus, it is unnecessary to take a stand on any of these platforms because it is not essential to your salvation. I expect this is why some things are not spelled-out succinctly in the Bible, so we won't get hung-up on ancillary issues. Not that we shouldn't study or debate eschatology, but any single interpretation of end time events is not an essential doctrine of biblical faith.

If we know not the day and time, how can we know with certainty all the other details (MAT 24:36; MAT 25:13)? God has deliberately withheld certain information as reviewed in the lesson *Has Anyone Seen Heaven*. As for me, I am not about to place my faith on another chance; I aim to get it right the first time placing all my trust in Jesus Christ, the Savior of the world.

The impetus of God's message is eternal life, which continues without end during which Earth's trials will have been forgotten. We needn't get stuck on the concept of time, when and how it will end, the age of the universe, and whether time is linear or constant. God is timeless, and His chosen will be too; hence, time is irrelevant. When time ends, your life will have just begun; this birthright already has been established if you are a true born-again believer.

- PSA 16:10-11 ~ God will not leave my soul in hell, and He will not allow His Holy One to be corrupted. He will show me the path of life. In His presence is fullness of joy; with His right hand (Jesus) there are pleasures forevermore.
- LUK 10:10–16 ~ Jesus taught that when you enter a town where you are not welcome, announce from the streets, "The dust of your town we wipe from our feet as a warning to you. To be sure, the kingdom of God has come." "It will be more bearable for Sodom than for that town," Jesus continued, "Woe to Chorazin, Bethsaida, and the rest. For if the miracles performed among you would have occurred in Tyre and Sidon, they would have repented long ago in sackcloth and ashes. But it will be more bearable for Tyre and Sidon at the judgment than for you. And Capernaum, will you be lifted into the heavens? No, you will go down into Hades. Those who listen to my disciples whom I have sent will listen to me; whoever rejects those who I have sent reject me. And those who reject me reject Him who sent me."
- LUK 12:37–50 ~ Jesus said, "Blessed are those who the Lord finds watching for Him when He returns; like a waiter, He will seat them at the table and serve them a banquet. If He comes at the second watch, or the third, and finds them alert they will be blessed. Know this, if the good man of the house was aware a thief was coming, he would have watched and protected his house from being burglarized. So be ready, for the Son of Man comes when you least expect Him." Peter asked the Lord, "Are you referring to us or to everyone?" Jesus replied, "Who is a truly wise and faithful servant, whom the Lord appoints to oversee His household and always takes good care of it? Blessed is that servant whom the Lord finds alert and watching. I tell you the truth, the Lord will make him ruler over His property. But if that servant says in his heart that the Lord has delayed His arrival, then proceeds to beat the servants, engorge himself with food, and drink until he is drunk—the Lord will catch him off guard, cut him in two, and give to him the inheritance of the unbelievers. For he knew the Lord's will and ignored His commands, taking advantage of others. He was ignorant and committed grievous deeds worthy of a beating, so he will receive one. To those whom much is given, much will be required; and to those to whom much has been committed, more will be asked. I came to send fire upon the earth, and I would rather it was already kindled. But I have a baptism to undergo, and it is unsettling knowing it is eminent."

Listen everybody, your beginning starts when you accept Christ. And your end is when you arrive at the new heaven and earth, which is a totally new beginning without end. What will have ended is the old heaven and earth, not to mention the lives of those who did not keep their sight on the promise and the prize. A time is coming when hearts of men will tremble with fear from terrifying events long foreseen (LUK 21:26). You can pick Jesus's side or your adversary the devil; or remain neutral if you think you actually can. But hey, one out of three isn't bad, though the other two are.

- ISA 65:17 ~ Behold, I create new heavens and a new earth; and the former will not be remembered, or ever come to mind.

On a side note, there could be multiple levels or rewards in heaven, but I leave you to research this topic (read MAT 5:11–12; MAT 6:1–20; MAT 19:28–30; LUK 19:12–27; 1 CO 3:11–13;5; 2 CO 5:10; JAM 3:1). Keep in mind, an argument also can be made against the idea of levels of exaltation for the saints (read MAT 6:31–33; MAT 20:1–15; COL 3:23–34; ACT 20:32). Either way, we don't really know since nobody has seen or perceived what God has in store for the saved; there is nothing in this life that compares (ISA 64:4; 1 CO 2:9). As for me, I would rather swab the pigs and sleep in God's stable then be counted among the damned (LUK 15:11–32).

Additionally, Paul speaks of three heavenly realms (2 CO 12:2–4), generally believed to include our atmosphere or sky; the rest of the cosmos or outer space; and God's domain including everywhere else, of which humankind has never perceived or comprehended. Then again, one can only speculate what God has in store for the condemned (JOB 38:17). May I ask, would you rather stay here and fry (2 PE 3:7–10); be a wandering lone soul in this entropic universe which is gradually burning-out anyway; or experience an everlasting journey with Jesus Christ throughout God's realm, a virtual multiplicity of universes?

Let's wrap it up with one last set of three. God's chosen should give of their first fruits to Him as a thank offering (PRO 3:9–10; JER 2:3). God already has given to us His First Fruits and that is Jesus Christ (1 CO 15:20–28), who confers upon us His Holy Spirit (JOH 14:12; ACT 1:7–8). Soon Christ will collect us, His first fruits, unto Himself (ROM 8:22–33; 1 TH 4:16–17; JAM 1:18). And behold, He is coming soon, Amen (REV 22:20). The Holy Trinity is present in this doctrine as in every aspect of God's plan. Thus, believers give our first fruits to God, God gave to us His first fruits who is Jesus, and Jesus collects His first fruits which is us.

Three is the key, three-in-one that is; the key at the start of this lesson and the end (the alpha and omega and all points in-between). Recognize and thank the Father for giving us His grace. Grace is commonly defined as receiving something you have not earned or deserved. God the Father freely gives His abundant and everlasting love, He provides provision, and He guarantees protection. Competent moms and dads know these to be basic requisites of parenting. God the Son gives His mercy, commonly defined as not receiving something you have deserved or earned, like a death sentence. Christ offers Himself as an atonement for sin, thereby affording forgiveness and salvation to all who believe. These spiritual gifts are conveyed to us though the Holy Spirit who bestows life, truth, and faith directly to your body, mind, and spirit. All three persons of God display examples for us to heed: caring, obedience, perseverance. First, our Father gives us everything we will ever need; second, His obedient Son gives His life for you and me; third, the Holy Spirit gives us a shining unveiling of holiness that we can receive into our spirits, through acceptance of His physical, mental, and spiritual gifts, praising and thanking Him every day and always, and giving everything we are and have back to Him in love.

- ROM 12:1–3 ~ I implore you brothers and sisters, by the mercies of God, that you present yourselves as living sacrifices, holy and acceptable to Him; this is your reasonable service. Do not conform to the ways of the world but be transformed by the renewing of your mind, so you can discern the good, acceptable, and perfect will of God. I (Paul) tell you this, by the grace given to me and everyone among you, refrain from thinking more highly of yourself than you ought; instead, think soberly in accordance with the faith God has apportioned unto you.

Lesson: Babylon: Past, Present, and Future

Why does everything seem to begin and end in Babylon? The region in question is of major significance to world history in general, and to the Old Testament (OT) in particular. The prophecy appears to follow a loop of spacetime that encompasses the dawn of civilization to its dusk, turning full circle. The Bible declares that everything started in the Garden of Eden near a confluence of rivers that included the Tigris and Euphrates (GEN 2:10–15). Science also substantiates this origin of humankind and the spread of civilization into the fertile crescent. Many empires and nations were destined to absorb this territory, then lose it. Six formidable empires possessed most of the area surrounding the Mediterranean Sea and fertile crescent while enveloping Israel, a land hallowed by Jews, Christians, and Moslems alike.

It all began in the southern part of Mesopotamia which was known as the land of the Chaldees in the OT; this is where civilization spawned. Chaldea and Babylon, civilizations often referenced synonymously, arose from the banks of the Euphrates. Probably the greatest early Mesopotamian king was Nimrod (GEN 10:8), frequently associated with the epic of Gilgamesh. Nimrod sprang from the line of Noah, Ham, and Cush. Abraham, a descendent of Noah's son Shem, also resided in the land of the Chaldees in the city of Ur (GEN 11:28–31; ACT 7:2). God would guide Abraham away from there to the land of promise at the other end of the fertile crescent. Before occupying their land, Abraham had to grapple with the Egyptians, as would many of his descendants, like Isaac and Moses. Egypt subjugated Jacob's (Israel's) descendants and Moses liberated them, showing them the land of Canaan (another son from Noah's son Ham). This was the land God promised Abraham (GEN 12:1–3). Moses's deputy Joshua would lead the Israelites in defeat of Canaanite tribes before occupying that piece of real estate. Eventually, David would build his kingdom there making Jerusalem his capital city. But corruption would become Israel's ruin, just as corruption has ruined all world empires before and after. It makes you wonder how long this country can stand, with the extensive corruption in government, business, and social institutions.

Two cities founded in the northern district by Nimrod were Babel and Nineveh; both became capital cities of fallen empires. After the Egyptian empire faltered the region was subjugated by the Assyrians, Israel included (2 KI 17:24; ISA 23:13). The Babylonians would promptly overthrow Assyria (2 KI 24–25; HAB 1:6) and ransack Jerusalem, taking many Israelites hostage most notably Daniel (PSA 137:1). They were carried north to Shinar (DAN 1:2–4; ZEC 5:9–11) a site also associated with the Tower of Babel (GEN 10:10; GEN 11:1–9); that tower probably resembled the menagerie of stone temples found in the region. People still visit and climb the famous ziggurat at Ur, Abraham's homeland. Daniel became great in Babylon (DAN 2:46–48) which soon fell to the kings of Media-Persia (JER 51:12–14,53–54), while Daniel's legacy continued (DAN 6:1–2).

Babylon was idolatrous from the start, engaging in sorcery, debauchery, and self-worship (ISA 47; JER 50; DAN 5). God sent them to destroy the Assyrians and Israel who had adopted the same lascivious, sacrilegious, and outright pagan ways (EZE 12:13–15; ZEC 2:6–7; ACT 7:43). God surely punishes any kingdom or person engaging in such mischief and godlessness, and Israel was no exception; neither was Babylon. The prophets predicted Israel's fall and the kingdoms that would advance upon them. It was spelled-out succinctly in Nebuchadnezzar's dream which Daniel interpreted via the power of God's Holy Spirit; the Babylonian king and conqueror was so impressed that he proclaimed the glory of Daniel's God and promoted Daniel to second in command. The king's dream foretold the rise and fall of Babylon, and the coming of Media-Persia, Greece, and Rome (DAN 2:25–49), with honorable mention of an everlasting kingdom which would reign supreme over all kingdoms of the world. The conquerors of old would succeed in holding the territory for a finite period of time; and all would lose it. But we who are conquerors in Christ will inherit the kingdom of heaven and rule with Him for eternity.

Babylon was the pivotal midpoint between empires; it was also the midpoint in the lineage of Christ from Abraham (MAT 1:1–17). Babylon is a depiction of the immorality of man, then until now, and including the final days (REV 14:8; REV 16:19; REV 18:1–10,21). Note how past and future kingdoms referenced by Daniel (DAN 2:36–43; DAN 7; DAN 8:20–25) overlap those referenced by John (REV 17:9–18). The final earthly kingdom identified by both of these prophets, which will rise up prior to Christ's return, is that of the Beast (DAN 7:17–24; REV 13:1–18; REV 16:12–17), or the "new" Babylon. These messengers knew this last kingdom would collapse the very second the King of kings arrives (REV 19:11–16). But not before Satan establishes the most corrupt and violent global empire ever, comparable to Sodom and Gomorrah in their worldly lusts as well as their terrible and fateful demise.

- JER 49:4–18 ~ Why do you brag about your flowing river valleys you backsliding daughter? You trusted in your treasures saying, "Who can challenge me?" Behold says the Lord of hosts, I will bring terror upon you from your neighbors; you will be driven out straightaway, and your refugees will find no solace. I will repeat the captivity of the children of Ammon and I will bring calamity upon the Edomites. When you force people to drink of the cup of vengeance, how can you go unpunished? Your lands will become desolate and cursed, and your cities turned into wastelands. The Lord sent you a message to assemble yourselves and prepare for battle. But you will be diminished and despised. Your terrorism and pride have deceived you, those who abide among the cliffs and in the heights. You built your nest as high as the eagle, but will be brought down to the lowest. You will be overthrown, desolate, and ridden with plagues. People will pass by with astonishment; for your destruction will be like that of Sodom and Gomorrah and nearby cities.
- JER 50:40–46 ~ As God destroyed Sodom and Gomorrah and the neighboring cities so will nobody remain in your cities. Behold says the Lord, a great nation from the north with many kings will rise up from the coasts. They are armed and dangerous, cruel and merciless. And they are coming for you, oh daughter of Babylon. Who have I appointed to perform this task? Is there anyone like me; is there a shepherd that can stand before me? Listen to the words of the Lord, for He is against Babylon and the land of the Chaldeans. The youngest of the flock will be carried away and the land made desolate. The sound of the fall of Babylon will be heard around the world and the earth will shake.
- EZE 16:15–38 ~ [Oh Jerusalem], you trusted in your beauty and played the harlot for which you became famous, and poured out fornications upon everyone passing by. You adorned yourselves with colorful garments in the high places where you engaged in prostitution. Such things are not supposed to happen. You made jewelry out of my gold, silver, and stones, then fashioned them into male idols with which you also had sex. And you clothed them in embroidered garments and offered my oil, incense and food to them, as you would a sweet sacrifice to the Lord your God. Moreover, you took the sons and daughters born to me and sacrificed them. Do you think this is a small matter? You murdered my children, allowing them to pass through the fire! Do you not remember in your youth how you were naked and bare, bathed in blood? Consider the extent of your wickedness ("Woe, woe unto you," says the Lord God). You built shrines on every street corner and declared your beauty, which became abhorrent. You had sex with anyone and everyone, including your neighbors the Egyptians, and provoked me to anger. Behold, I have stretched out my hand towards you and snatched your resources, and delivered you to your enemies the daughters of the Philistines who were embarrassed by your lewdness. You fooled around with the Assyrians, Canaanites,

and Chaldeans, for your lust was insatiable. You must be weak-minded, committing such despicable acts. You are like an adulterous wife who sleeps with any man but her husband. Prostitutes charge a fee but instead you showered them with expensive gifts to coax them into your houses. Because of your utter filthiness, whoremongering, idolatry, and the murdering of your children, I will gather together those you have played with and those you have fought with, and uncover your nakedness before them. You will be judged as an adulteress and a murderer, with wrath and blood.

- NAH 3:1–7 ~ Woe to the bloody city! It is filled with lies and robbery; the prey never leaves. One can hear the crack of a whip, the rattling of chariot wheels, and the prancing of horses. The riders carry shiny swords and spears. Many will be slain, leaving carcasses everywhere, causing people to stumble over them. Because of your whoredom and witchcraft, I am coming against you, says the Lord of hosts. I will lift your skirts above your heads and expose your nakedness and shame. I will throw disgusting filth on you, and display your vileness, and make a spectacle of you. And all who see you will flee saying, "Nineveh is laid waste. Who will lament for her? Is there anyone who can comfort you now?"
- LUK 17:16–30 ~ As it was in the days of Noah, so it will be when the Son of man returns. The people ate, drank, and married until Noah and his family entered the ark, the flood came, and the rest drowned. Likewise, it will be as the days of Lot; they ate, drank, bought, sold, planted and built, until Lot and his family departed; then it rained fire and brimstone destroying them all. Accordingly, perilous times will draw closer in the last days.
- 2 TI 3:1–3 ~ Know this, that perilous times will come in the last days. People will love only themselves. They will be covetous, boasters, blasphemers, arrogant, disobedient to parents, unthankful and ungodly, void of natural affection. They will be promise breakers, false accusers, undisciplined, fierce despisers of goodness; traitors, reckless, conceited, lovers of worldly pleasures more than God; displaying a form of godliness, but denying the power thereof. Stay away from people like this. For they attempt to sneak into houses and coax weak-minded women swayed by lustful pleasures; they are able to learn but will never acknowledge the truth. Like Jannes and Jambres who contested Moses, they resist truth; they are men of corrupt minds, insincere in the faith. They will not continue in their folly, for they will be exposed. You are aware of my (Paul's) doctrines, precepts, purposes, and example. I have remained faithful, patient, and charitable despite the persecutions and afflictions I endured at Antioch, Iconium, and Lystra. Unfortunately, everybody that lives a godly life in Christ Jesus will suffer persecution. The evil men and seducers will grow continually worse, deceiving and being deceived.
- 2 PE 2:4 ~ God did not spare the angels who sinned but cast them down to hell, delivering them into chains of darkness to be reserved for judgment.
- JDE 1:6–8 ~ The angels who lost their positions are kept in everlasting chains and darkness until that great day of judgment. Like Sodom, Gomorrah, and the adjacent towns who gave themselves over to fornication and perversion, they will be made examples of the suffering and vengeance of eternal fire. This will be the inheritance of filthy dreamers who defile the flesh, despise authority, and speak evil of dignities.
- REV 17:1,5 ~ Upon the forehead of the great harlot that sits over many waters it was written: Mystery, Babylon the Great, the mother of prostitutes and many abominations of the earth!
- REV 18:2–3 ~ With a mighty voice the angel shouted, "Babylon the great has fallen, fallen. It has become the habitation of devils and every foul spirit, like a cage for unclean and hateful birds. All nations have drunk the wine of the wrath of her fornication, kings of the earth have committed fornication with her, and merchants have become rich through the excess of her luxuries."

The kingdom of the Beast will be connected to fallen empires of the past. Lust, greed, pride, idolatry, and exploitation were their downfall, and will be for anyone believing they can do whatever they want without consequences. People ignore that they are made in God's image, many desiring to be deities themselves; they think they can become a god or they think they already are. As did Lucifer, who convinced Adam and Eve to want the same thing (GEN 3:4–7; ISA 14:12–13; TH 2:3–4). Those who would be their own gods will perish, some in unimaginable ways; they will receive the treatment they dished out (PSA 7:16), but they will not be able to take it (MAL 3:2).

History does, indeed, repeat itself. Let's recap the great empires of the world, reviewing each one in chronological order. Remember, thanks to Daniel and John we have a complete list. They both wrote about how the last or eighth kingdom would be the worst, controlled by the son of Satan who would set himself up as a ruler and a deity (2 TH 2:3; REV 17:10–11). Standing on the Mount of Olives, Jesus also warned of the evilest kingdom ever, and how many of the chosen would endure terrible tribulation. Literally, all hell will break loose, but some will be spared the horror; then Jesus will step in to save the day (for those accepting His leadership). We were made to be children of God. Sadly, many defectors go their own way; that's why they must be tossed out, for they are defective.

1. Egyptian: Though some might consider Mesopotamia to have been an empire, it was compartmentalized and quickly became disjointed, resulting in diverse cultures and languages (GEN 11:1–9). Meanwhile, along the Nile River were splendors galore and a rapidly developing world power. As Egypt advanced in strength and wealth, they also grew in pride and stature. But they wanted more, so they subjugated their Hebrews neighbors who also were growing in numbers and posed an existential threat to Egypt. Possessing the might, means, infrastructure, and economy, Egypt overtook the ancient world and reigned supreme for a millennium, notwithstanding other ancient cultures that were sprouting in the far east. God intervened seeing how Egypt enslaved His people Israel who finally had repented and turned back to Him. Pharaoh refused Moses's plea to heed God's warning and let His people go, bringing ten plagues upon the land. The angel of death was the final blow to the empire, except for those acknowledging the Passover commandment who escaped the wrath of God and of Pharaoh. Egypt was pretty-much washed-up as a dominion after that (literally, since the better part of their army drowned in the Red Sea). Although they subdued the Hebrews, soon thereafter the Israelites would turn the tables and rule over them, most of the Holy Land, and surrounding territories. Egypt had its heyday, edifices of which are still around; but it has since shrunk into an average-sized country.

2. Assyrian: Israel would govern for the first half of the second era, gaining in wealth and fame; but they adopted the lascivious ways of their neighbors. Israel became divided upon King Solomon's death (1 KI 11—12; 2 CH 10). Assyria whittled away at Israel in the north, then Judah in the south, waging a full-out war of savagery. Funny how the Assyrians were allowed a golden opportunity to repent and amend their ways after listening to the preaching of Jonah (JON 3:4–10). But in a few generations, they fell back to their worldly lusts, especially for wealth and prominence. And they obtained it because Israel and Egypt, their greatest adversaries, were falling apart at the seams. Assyria's triumphs and glory would deteriorate along with their memory in just two centuries. That's when Babylon came out of nowhere, or so it seemed but for the fact that Isaiah foretold the fall of Assyria and Jeremiah foretold the conquest of Babylonia. Assyria never had a chance; they were totally outmaneuvered. They'd already struggled in their invasion of the southern kingdom of Judah and were barely holding onto the northern kingdom of Israel. Nebuchadnezzar marched in

and destroyed it all, with the sacking of Jerusalem being the coup-de-grace. Assyria abated; now all that's left is Syria, itself ripping apart as we speak.

3. Babylonian: Babylon was a place of wonder and beauty; but in less than one hundred years it would be gutted. The grandeur and riches of Babylon made it renown, as represented by the head of gold in Nebuchadnezzar's dream (DAN 2). But depravity, overindulgence, and avarice infected the empire (DAN 3). Babylon flourished under Nebuchadnezzar, a relentless and ferocious warlord and king, who exalted himself until God brought him down (DAN 4). The king acknowledged the God of Daniel for a time but it is unknown if he kept the faith. Certainly, his offspring did not acknowledge God, but sank further into a gulf of gluttony. King Belshazzar, also a dreamer of prophetic dreams, foresaw his own death. Daniel interpreted the writing on the wall which spelled doom for the degenerate king, who was assassinated that very night (DAN 5). Daniel was quite the visionary, recording his own dreams of the end times, the final kingdom of evil, and the eternal kingdom of Christ (DAN 7–9). The grandiose Babylon would devolve into present-day Iraq, which also has become fragmented and is again ripe for assimilation by foreigners.

4. Medio-Persian: Babylon was rent in two as prophesized, shown in the silver arms of the statue in Nebuchadnezzar's dream; for they were overtaken by the Medes and Persians. Daniel continued to be an official in the king's court throughout the domains of Babylonia and Media-Persia. Darius the Mede made some vain decisions, but understanding Daniel's wisdom to be God-given, thrived under the prophet's counsel (DAN 6 and DAN 11). Cyrus the Persian also accepted Daniel's counsel and allowed the Jews to rebuild Jerusalem. Again, it is uncertain if those kings continued in the faith and kept the one true God above themselves. After a couple hundred years, this empire would be conquered in short order by a great commander named Alexander (DAN 8:20–22; DAN 10:20). Like the kingdoms preceding it, Media-Persia would further split, and all that is left is present-day Iran, now in disarray and unprepared for a possible civil war.

5. Greek: Daniel foretold the rise of an illustrious warrior who would enjoin the broken kingdom. It would be a reign of bronze, as noted in the waist and thighs of Nebuchadnezzar's statue. Alexander the Great would arise with imperialism in his heart, hungry for victory, continuing his relentless pursuit of world domination. But his luck would run out and he would die at a young age. His kingdom would fragment into four as prophesied (DAN 8:8; DAN 11:2–5) which weakened it, making it vulnerable for takeover by an even more dreadful and ruthless realm. Greece would have a lasting effect on culture and philosophy over the course of two centuries, continuing into the time of Christ. In fact, the New Testament was written almost exclusively in Greek. But in time, Greece too would be downgraded to an average-sized country.

6. Roman: Represented as the iron legs in Nebuchadnezzar's dream, Rome's strength would be in the sword (DAN 2:39–40; DAN 7:7; DAN 8:22–25). And for three centuries they would rule most of Europe and the world with an iron fist. Fierce and domineering they were; especially towards Jews and Christians, culminating with the demolition of the temple in Jerusalem which Jesus prophesied forty years in advance (MAT 24:1–2). Rome would eventually sever into two legs, and further fall apart. It too would eventually shrink into an average-sized country (Italy). Actually, Rome has become more of a city-state, with the Vatican possessing most of the power. Ironically, Rome's demise came after the persecution of Christ and His followers; but in an unprecedented reversal, Rome became the seat of Catholicism.

7. Number Seven: St. John characterized the seventh king as a brief reign, which would follow Rome after an undefined interlude. I ask you, who since the Romans ruled the lands governed by these former empires, a reign lasting for a short stead? Some say the Ottoman empire (the Ottoman Turks) who spread Islam throughout the Middle East in an attempt to create a global theocracy. Though more a dynasty than an empire it wasn't altogether a short period (roughly half a millennium). The Ottomans dominated much of Asia Minor from Turkey to the Holy Land, presiding over Jerusalem off and on. They were unable to prevail in Europe however. Additionally, there was infighting amongst their leaders, with opposing factions jockeying for position. The Europeans quashed Islamic advances north of the Mediterranean; consequently, the movement lost momentum and became stagnant until now. The Ottoman Turks had little in common with the empires preceding it, except their globalist leanings and subsequent fragmentation. But there are many in the world of Islam who would repeat that scenario; some have recently tried, and will continue in vain.

    There existed one short-lived reign with similarities to empires past: it was the Nazi regime. In another attempt at globalism, Hitler's Germany took a stance on dominating peoples perceived as inferior and worthy of either subjugation or eradication, meaning everybody else. The Nazis were every bit as bloodthirsty, conniving, overbearing, and godless as their predecessors. They managed to control the Mediterranean and most of Europe, with eyes on the world. But they couldn't handle the combined assist of the Brits by the Americans, Canadians, and Australians, or the pushback from the Russians, much less the unpredictable Japanese. Talk about trying to bite off more than you can chew. World domination is tricky business, especially when there are a multitude of diverse and independent cultures, nations, armies, and philosophies to overpower. Thus, the Nazi movement was finished rather fast, though their radical fascist, communist, and statist views are still in vogue across the globe, as seen in communism and assorted dictatorships.

    World empires gain traction by seeking a one-world order. How does the elite get the masses to submit to oppression and behave in accordance with their anti-capitalist rules? Well, they promise free stuff, protection, provision, and more; while at the same time they take stuff, eradicate the opposition, tax the citizenry to death, and squelch liberties one by one. You see, the people must be stung by the globalization bug. And ignorant or naïve persons think it is something called socialism, the definition of which they do not comprehend either. Beware of preachers of socialism, which leads to communism, and next totalitarianism. Has history not proven it? This was the pattern of all great empires of the world and will be during the last days. Greed for power can never be satisfied, and will result in the middle-class losing out. What is left is an aristocracy in charge who are themselves out of control, and a proletariat that is impoverished, unmotivated, and dependent; and that setup cannot sustain itself. It never has and it never will.

8. Number Eight: John wrote of eight kingdoms with the eighth being the last (REV 17:9–11). He mentioned five kingdoms past (Egypt, Assyria, Babylon, Media-Persia, Greece), one present (Rome), and a seventh to come for a short period (Nazi perhaps). John identified number eight to be that of the Beast, and a repeat of the seven (one, or all seven). John named it the New Babylon (REV 17:5). Many refer to the last kingdom as the Revived Roman Empire (DAN 7:23). One might suggest that Nazism resembles the eighth, given the millions of Jews exterminated; in fact, the holocaust was one of the most heinous hate crimes ever committed. Yet people still hold to principles advanced by the likes of Marx, Engels, Hitler, and Stalin including certain presidential candidates. The last empire also can be compared with Assyria in locality (MIC 5:1–6); or Egypt, and the plagues occurring at the end (REV 22:18). Thus, an argument could be made for every one of the seven empires being part of

number eight seeing how it is Satan who infiltrated them all and global power that motivated them. Notice how they rejected the Lord God, sought ultimate power, proclaimed themselves deities, consumed everything then lost it, toppled into ruins, and became insignificant and inglorious. And like the statue in Nebuchadnezzar's dream they will lay broken and prostrate at the feet of Christ whose dominion encompasses everywhere and whose kingdom lasts forever. At that time the prophecy will be true, "You will bite his heel, but He will crush your head" (GEN 3:14–15).

It is important to mention that a great number of modern theologians consider the USA to be the kingdom of the beast. They reference the four beasts identified by Daniel (DAN 7) and the New Babylon discussed by John (REV 18). Certainly, it is possible that the USA could succumb to globalism, but it is equally possible that the USA could isolate from a globalist world. In this day and age, the country is split between leftist globalism, rightwing isolationism, and the moderates in-between. One could make a case that the city (Babylon) which splits into three during the latter times is America (REV 16:19). It sure seems to be divided now. Hopefully, the globalists will not prevail, else we lose our democratic republic. When Ben Franklin was asked what the Continental Congress had accomplished, he replied, "A republic if you can keep it." If the globalists win, we will lose it. And that would turn this country into a beast.

The eighth global government already may be forming and moving in; if not, it isn't far off. Because globalists are everywhere, demanding power; and they will do anything however underhanded to seize it. The oligarchs will join forces and finances, only to be commandeered by Satan's prodigy, the Antichrist (DAN 11:24–25) and his hoard of demons (REV 18:2). Satan, the archenemy of every man, woman, and child, wants humans to hate God because Satan hates God and wants to convince people to replace God with themselves like he does. Indeed, Satan is still trying to steal worship from God (LUK 4:5–8), and is disgusted with those who would worship God seeking to destroy them. Christians worshipping the one true God will be persecuted for nonconformance to immoral rules levied by evil men influenced by forces of darkness (LUK 21:12–17). Fortunately, the righteous will be delivered out of the midst of the wickedness and chaos. If you have recognized the commonalities of fallen world sovereignties, their degeneracy, exploitation, treachery, promiscuity, deceitfulness, and bribery, you have a picture of things to come. Fortunately, you also have a preview of the kingdom of heaven which conquers them all, and the Lord God who is and always has been sovereign.

- JER 30:7 ~ Alas, that will be a momentous day; there will be no other like it! It is the time of Jacob's trouble; but he will be saved out of it.
- JER 42:11 ~ Do not fear the king of Babylon; I see you are afraid but don't be says the Lord. For I am with you to save you, and I will deliver you from his hand.
- DAN 12:1 ~ At that time Michael will stand up, the great prince that stands for the children of God. It will be a time of trouble, unlike any before or since. You will be delivered, everyone whose name is written in the book.
- MAT 24:22; MAR 13:20 ~ And except those days be shortened, no flesh will be saved; but for the elect's sake, whom the Lord has chosen, those days will be shortened.
- 2 PE 2:2–9 ~ The Lord knows how to deliver the godly out of temptations, and to set aside the unjust until the day of judgment to be punished.
- REV 18:21–24 ~ A mighty angel picked up a gigantic stone and cast it into the sea saying, "With such violence Babylon will be thrown down and disappear. There will be no music or art, no craft or trade. The lights will have gone out, and the bride and groom will have departed. Vendors and businesses had once comprised the most powerful people on earth, and through their cunning they deceived the nations. Now the only thing remaining is the blood of prophets, saints, and the slain."

To conclude this lesson let's take a brief look at Gog and Magog. These are people and places often associated with the end of times and a particular region north of Israel. Ezekiel is very helpful in unraveling this conundrum.

- EZE 32:17–30 ~ The word of the Lord came to Ezekiel. Son of man, wail for Egypt and all who are thrown into the pit of the uncircumcised. They will fall with others slain by the sword. The mighty men from hell will call her to help, along with Asshur and Elam and their armies. They caused terror in the land, but their shame will be exposed; they have made their bed in the midst of the slain with many graves surrounding them. There is Meshech, Tubal, and their multitudes, with graves all around them; all of them uncircumcised, slain by the sword, though they once caused terror in the land. They lie with the rest of the uncircumcised warriors, who came from hell with their weapons of war. Their sins will be upon their bones; yes, they will be broken along with the uncircumcised who were slain by the sword. Then there is Edom and her kings and armies, as well as those from Sidon. They will be taken down with the rest, all who served as princes for the north.
- EZE 38:1-23 ~ The word of God came to Ezekiel. Son of man, set your face against Gog of the land of Magog, the chief prince of Meshech and Tubal, and prophesy this against him. The Lord says, "I am against you Gog, the chief prince of Meshech and Tubal. I will turn you around, put hooks into your jaws, and drag you out with your entire army, horses, horsemen, and armored warriors. That includes Persia, Ethiopia, and Libya; Gomer and his soldiers; the house of Togarmah in the north and his soldiers; and the others with you. Prepare yourselves and those assembled with you, and take command; after many days you will be called. In the latter years you will invade a land that has laid down the sword, gathered near the mountains of Israel which has long been harsh terrain." You will say, "I will invade that land of unwalled villages, those who live in peace and without walls, gates, or fortifications. I will plunder their goods, cattle, gold and silver, and overrun their settlements." Sheba, Dedan, and merchants of Tarshish will ask, "Have you come to plunder and take lives?" Therefore, son of man, prophesy to Gog the words of the Lord, "In that day when my people Israel live safely and in peace, will you not notice? Yes, in the latter days you will invade from the north and many nations with you, advancing like a cloud that covers the land. I will bring you down upon my people so that all the world will know who I am, for I will reveal my holiness through you." This has been spoken of since ancient times by the prophets, a future time when Gog will attack Israel, and God's wrath will be poured out in retaliation. The earth will quake, and there will be trembling and fear. The armies will be fighting amongst themselves while cliffs and walls crumble to the ground. "I will send plagues and swords upon them, with rainstorms of hail, fire and brimstone. The world will behold my greatness," says the Lord, "and realize that I alone am God."
- EZE 39:11-12 ~ The Lord says, "It will come to pass in that day when I will present Gog a graveyard in Israel, along the eastern passage by the sea. It will be called the Valley of Hamongog. And Israel will be burying the bodies for seven months to cleanse the land."
- LUK 21:20 ~ When you see Jerusalem surrounded by her enemies the desolation is nigh.
- REV 20:7-9 ~ When the thousand years are over, Satan will be cut loose from his prison to deceive the nations in all four corners of the earth, Gog and Magog, and muster them for battle, the number of which is as the sand of the sea. They will surround the camp of the saints and the beloved city; but fire will come down from heaven and consume them all.

So, which are those nations that create a coalition against Israel in the latter days? Ezekiel names them, many from the sons of Japheth and Ham. Note that Japheth had seven sons: Gomer, Magog, Madai, Javan, Tubal, Meshech and Tiras (GEN 10:2). Ham had four sons: Cush, Mizraim, Phut and Canaan (GEN 10:6). Shem had five sons: Elam, Asshur, Arphaxad, Lud and Aram (GEN 10:22). In the end times it seems two sons of Noah will come against Shem's descendants in Israel (namely Jacob, the ancestor of Noah, Shem, and Arphaxad; Abraham, Isaac, Judah, David, and Jesus also were from the lineage of Shem). Recall that Israel was prophesied to inhabit the land of Canaan (GEN 9:26), and they did. The Antisemitic jihadists will be attempting to wrench it back from the Jews again, like their predecessors the Ottomans.

The nations listed below are found in the words of Ezekiel (quoted earlier) as being members of the coalition of Gog. Mostly Moslem, it is a revived Ottoman Empire of sorts, except for possible Soviet involvement. It could be the eighth and final attempt at a global theocracy, to be swallowed up by Satan's prince from the north (namely, Gog). Their attempt to overrun Israel will be a disaster, and their blood will fill a two-hundred-mile valley (REV 14:18–20). This very well may occur in the valley of Jezreel where also is found Megiddo, a place of many battles in the OT. This ought to stir up further thought and study, because Armageddon is where it ends for Lucifer and his armies (REV 16:13–17). Keep this in mind: If any country in the world is prone to come to Israel's aid it would be the USA. But even that sentiment is becoming increasing skewed in the other direction by extremists who are bent on deconstructing our democracy, eliminating free enterprise, and disowning Israel. It is a very dangerous world in which we live, so keep your head down and your powder dry (a phrase quoted often by military veterans in deference to those who fought the Revolutionary War to win our independence). Here are the nations listed by Ezekiel.

- Asshur was Shem's second son, an ancestor of the Assyrians who settled in modern-day Iraq. Elam was Shem's first son, who settled farther east, nearer to present-day Iran.
- Sidon was a city north of Israel in present-day Lebanon.
- Gomer was Japheth's firstborn, who had a son named Togarmah. They settled in the area of eastern Turkey, south of the Black Sea.
- Magog, Japheth's second son, is understood to have settled farther north, perhaps as far as Russia.
- Tubal and Meshech, also sons of Japheth, settled in the area of western Turkey and Armenia (between the Black and Caspian seas).
- The land of Cush (Ham's eldest son) is primarily the vicinity of Ethiopia and Sudan.
- The land of Phut (Ham's third son) is primarily Libya.
- The land of Mizraim (Ham's third son) coincides with Egypt.
- Lot's eldest son Ammon, settled east of the Jordan River (present-day Jordan). Edom, the nation of Esau's descendants, occupied the area southeast of Jordan and the Dead Sea.
- Persia is present-day Iran.
- Sheba and Dedan are associated with Saudi Arabia; the merchants of Tarshish were likely trade partners possibly for shipping goods via the Strait of Gibraltar. It is unclear what role they will play in the coalition, whether ally or victim.

The figure below depicts the probable landmass conjoined in a league with Gog and possibly the eighth global empire; the figure is based on names and places provided in scriptures quoted throughout this lesson. If you do some research you will find the map closely resembles maps of the Assyrian and Babylonian empires. No doubt, Ezekiel lived through both empires for a time, as did Daniel who served kings from Babylon, Media, and Persia. St. John was right-on when predicting the rise of a new Babylon; it would be in fulfillment of prophecy from Ezekiel and Daniel who lived over two millennia prior to its reckoning. Today's state of affairs is looking like fulfillment of that prophecy. Could it be? It is best not to be caught by surprise.

It is not the intention to prove or disprove a particular explanation of the mystery of Gog and Magog, the New Babylon, and the latter days. A presentation of the data has been offered with reasonable explanations. The purpose is to bring to mind the importance of these prophecies concerning a final earthly kingdom targeted by Satan to gain influence in the world. This has been a very popular scriptural topic of late, as many theologians suggest the signs are evident that the end is near. Tidbits have been presented from different points of view to raise your interest in case you would like to investigate this phenomenon on your own. The symbolism of Babylon suggests world domination by immoral globalists, and their enemy is the Church, the people of God who stand in their way. Babylon destroyed Jerusalem and took captive the Israelites, causing many to turn from their faith and their roots, such that only a remnant would ever return to their homeland. Similarly, the New Babylon represents the battle between this sinful world and the chosen of God, and only those who remain steadfast in the faith will return to Father God and their heavenly home.

    I will close with the words of the prophet Daniel spoken to him by the Lord, "But you, Daniel, shut up the words and seal the book, even until the end times. Many shall run this way and that until knowledge increases" (DAN 12:4). I believe knowledge is increasing and I tend to agree that the prophecies of Christ's return are coming to fruition. Christ said the signs of the end will take place in the span of a single generation (MAT 24:34). Maybe that means the generation beginning with the statehood of Israel, the generation of their children, or the generation of their grandchildren. There is every reason to believe that the Antichrist is already among us and the reader might be a witness to these things. Regardless, we are warned by Jesus to watch and wait, because His coming is eminent (REV 22:20).

The Empire of Gog
(indicated by shaded area)

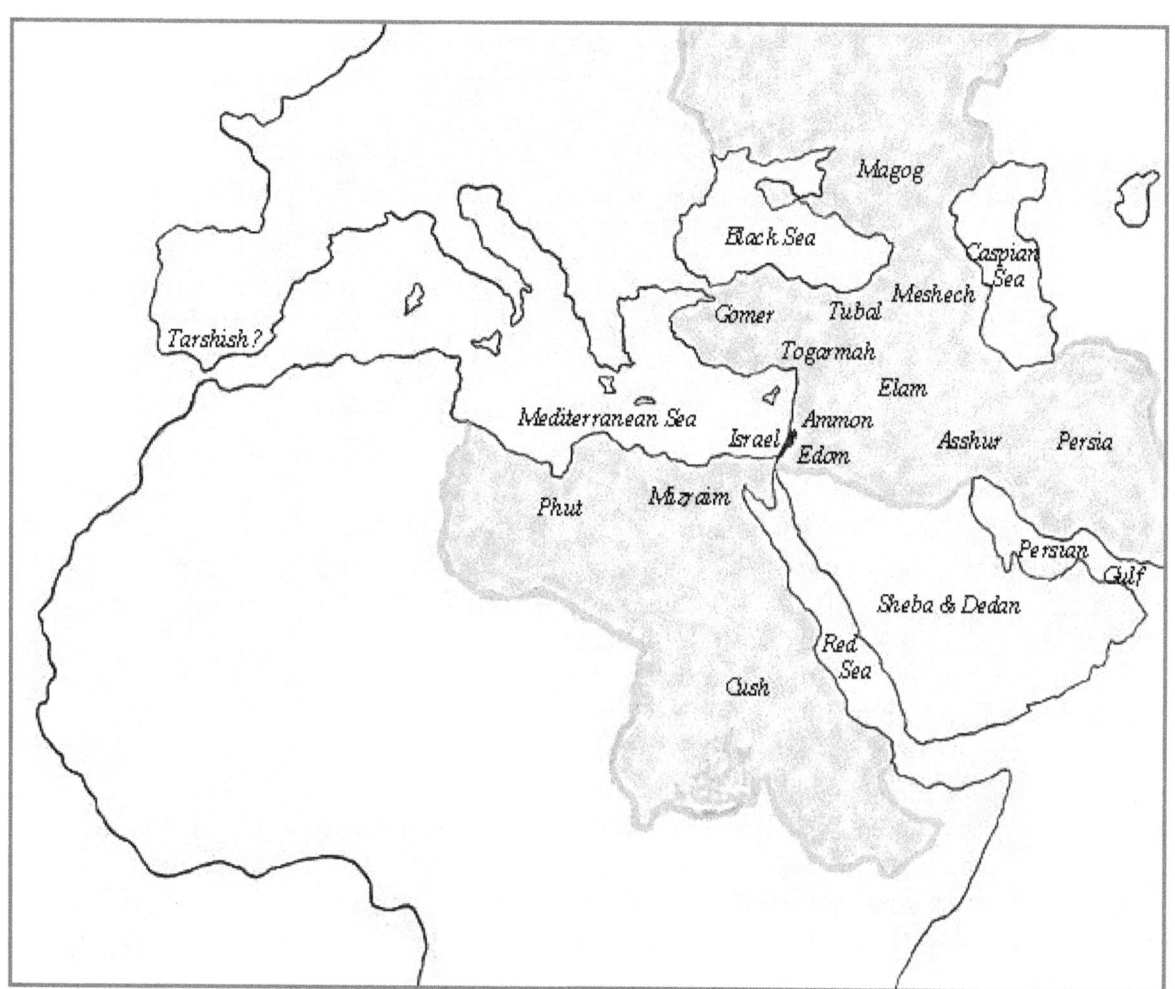

CHAPTER EIGHT

Lesson: The Great I AM

What should we call God and how should we address Him? What is His name? Well, He is known by many names. Yet in the OT, His chosen people didn't even speak His sacred name to avoid appearing disrespectful. When they wrote His name, they used "Yahweh" with no vowels (YHWH) which is translated "Jehovah" (GEN 22:14; PSA 83:18; ISA 12:2). Christians address God as our heavenly Father as instructed by Jesus Christ in the Lord's Prayer (MAT 6:9–13; LUK 11:1–4). God addressed Himself as I AM; in fact, all three persons of the Holy Trinity are the I AM. What does that make you and me? Through Christ, I am an adopted child of the living, triune God (ROM 8:14–17; ROM 9:26; GAL 3:26–29)! How about you? How would you fill in the blank: I am _____!

God the Father says He is the eternal I AM, the Alpha and Omega, the first and last.

- EXO 3:13–14 ~ Moses asked God, "When I return to the children of Israel and tell them the God of their fathers has sent me, and they ask me your name, what should I say?" God said to Moses, "I AM that I AM. Say this to the children of Israel: I AM has sent me unto you."
- ISA 41:4 ~ Who has done this, calling every generation from the beginning? It is I, the Lord; from the first through the last, I AM He.
- ISA 48:12–13 ~ God said, "Listen to me, Oh Jacob, Israel who I have called; I AM He. I AM the first and the last. My hand laid the foundation of the earth, and my right hand spans the heavens. When I call, they stand up in unison."

God the Son says He is the eternal I AM, the Alpha and Omega, the first and last.

- JOH 8:58 ~ Jesus said to them, "Truly, truly I declare unto you, Before Abraham was, I AM.
- REV 1:18 ~ When I (John) saw Him (Jesus), I fell before His feet as dead. And He laid His right hand upon me and said, "Do not fear. I AM the first and the last. I AM He that lives who was dead; and here, I AM alive forevermore, Amen. I hold the keys to hell and death. Write down the things you have seen, and the things which are, and the things which will be hereafter."

Jesus and the Father are the same I AM, joined as One with the Holy Spirit whose words are spoken in the Holy Bible and live in our hearts (JER 31:33; ROM 2:14–15; HEB 10:16). God sent Himself in His Messiah; and that witness, the great I AM, is Jesus Christ. And the gift He gives is the Holy Spirit.

- ISA 43:10–15 ~ God says, "You are my witnesses, and so is my servant whom I have chosen so you can know me and believe; and understand that I AM He. There have been no gods before me, neither will there be any after me. I AM the Lord; there are no other saviors." I have declared myself to you and I have saved you whenever you have forsaken all other gods for me. Yes, before there was day, I AM He. Nobody can be delivered out of my hand. When I do something, it cannot be undone. This is what the Lord, your Redeemer, the Holy One of Israel says: For your sake I will take down Babylon. I AM the Lord, your Holy One, the creator of Israel, and your King."
- ISA 52:6 ~ Therefore my people will know my name. They will know that I AM He who speaks; yes, it is I have who told you all these things.
- MAT 16:13–16 ~ When Jesus came to the coasts of Caesarea Philippi, He asked His disciples, "Who do men say that I, the Son of man, am?" And they answered, "Some say you are John the Baptist, some say Elijah, and others say Jeremiah, or one of the prophets." Jesus asked, "But who do you say I AM?" Simon Peter answered, "You are the Christ, the Son of the living God."

- JOH 8:23–30 ~ Jesus informed them, "You are from below, I am from above; you are of this world, I am not of this world. I reminded you that you could die in your sins; because if you do not believe that I AM He, you will die in your sins." They replied, "Who are you?" Jesus answered, "Even the same that has spoken to you from the beginning. I have many things to tell you about judgment. He that sent me is true; I speak to the world those things which I have heard from Him." They did not understand that Jesus was speaking of the Father. Jesus continued, "When you have lifted up the Son of man, then you will know that I AM He; that I do nothing of myself but everything in accordance with what my Father has taught me, and of which I speak. He who sent me is with me; the Father never leaves me alone. I always do those things that please Him." While Jesus was speaking these words, many believed in Him.
- REV 2:23 ~ John wrote to the church of Thyatira the words of Jesus: I will reward her (Jezebel's) children with death. All the churches will know that I AM He who searches minds and hearts. And I will repay every one of you according to your works.

Throughout both testaments, the Bible spells out God's plan of redemption. He gives us Himself so that we can live in Him and bring honor and glory to His name. The redeemer He sent to us was Jesus, His only begotten Son, within whom indwelled His very Holy Spirit. We call Jesus Redeemer, Savior, Messiah, and Christ; and for good reason.

Redeemer is one who sets free. Savior is one who saves. Jesus Christ came to save our souls from sin and redeem our bodies from the grave. Messiah is a Hebrew word meaning "Anointed One" which translated into Greek is Christ (Christos). In the OT, those commissioned by God to be prophets, priests, and kings were consecrated by a christening, an anointing of the head with oil. In the NT, Jesus Christ was anointed by the Holy Spirit to be our prophet, priest, and king. We are likewise anointed by the Holy Spirit when we receive Christ as our personal Savior and Redeemer.

Death is the penalty for sin, but those who trust in Christ will not die, for their sins have been remitted (paid for), in order that we might live through Him; and live with Him in His kingdom, forever blameless, unspoiled, and sanctified by the Holy Spirit. Jesus sends those who love Him and believe in Him to be witnesses. Whoever receives those witnesses, receives Him, and is therefore received by God the Father, to be likewise sent as witnesses with power from the Holy Spirit.

- ISA 46:4 ~ God said: Even in your old age with your gray hair, I AM He who carries you. I created you, I sustain you, and I will deliver you.
- JOH 13:19–20 ~ Jesus said, "I am telling you now before it happens, so that when it comes to pass you will believe that I AM He. Truly, truly I say to you, whoever receives those whom I send receives me; and those receiving me receives Him who sent me."

The OT had many witnesses proclaiming Messiah, including Job (JOB 19:25–26), Abraham (JOH 8:56), Moses (EXO 24:8), David (PSA 19:14; 78:35), Isaiah (ISA 41:14; 44:6, 24; 47:4; 48:17; 49:7, 26; 54:5; 59:20–21), Jeremiah (JER 50:34), Daniel (DAN 9:25–26), Micah (MIC 5:1–2) and countless others who looked forward to meeting God's designated Messiah and Savior of humanity. The NT connects the words of those prophets to God's Son, shedding light on this Messiah and Redeemer for all to see. Everyone who loved Jesus proclaimed His majesty, including His mother Mary (LUK 1:46–47), John the Baptist (JOH 1:29), apostles Andrew (JOH 1:40–42), Thomas (JOH 20:26–31), Peter (ACT 5:29–32; 1 PE 1:1–5; 2 PE 3:18), John (1 JO 5:1–5), and Paul (GAL 3:13–16; PHP 3:20–21; 2 TI 1:10), and half-brothers James and Judah (JAM 1:1; JDE 1:1), to name but a few. Unfortunately, most of the Jewish leaders rejected Jesus outright (MAT 26:61–64), while many foreigners, also considered enemies of the Jews, came to know Jesus as Messiah (JOH 4:5-42; MAR 15:39). Even beings from out of this world, including angels and demons, have proclaimed Christ as God's Son or Savior (LUK 2:4–20; LUK 8:26-28; JAM 2:19; 1 PE 1:12). Christ Himself validated that He was the Savior of the human race (LUK 4:17–21; JOH 11:21–45).

Against the vehement objection of the Jewish leaders, Pontius Pilate identified Christ as "Jesus of Nazareth the King of the Jews" (indicated as *INRI*); this was posted in Hebrew, Latin, and Greek on the titulus at the top of Jesus's cross (JOH 19:19–22). This, after Jesus informed Pilate that His kingdom was not of this world (JOH 18:33–37). Numerous others rejected Jesus knowing full well that He proclaimed Himself Christ, King, Alpha and Omega, Son of God, Son of Man, and I AM; and they despised Him for that, even though He proved it to be true before the entire world. There have been witnesses who adored Him and witnesses who hated Him; witnesses that knew the truth and witnesses that didn't know what they were talking about. And the Gospel message spread either way (PHP 1:16–18) and still does. The harder people try to stifle Christ and remove His name from public discourse, the more powerful His name becomes for those who speak of Him and for those who listen.

How many more credible witnesses does a person need before they can believe in God's Messiah? Can I get a witness? Will you be a witness? I AM is calling you. Respond to His call by answering, "Here I am, send me" (ISA 6:8). And what will you be witnessing, exactly? You will want to tell those who will listen about the great things the Lord has done for you (MAR 5:15–20); and not just for you but for all people, by sending His Son to make atonement for our sin, and sending His Holy Spirit to inoculate us so that we may remain purified in the likeness of Jesus Christ, to live eternally in the presence of God the Father Almighty. Everybody needs to be apprised of this; they need to know that time is running out in which to choose a path to follow. They need to be sure of the direction in which they are heading and to know what they can expect to find at the end of the road.

When Christ arrives again in glory, it will be too late to take a stand; there will be no tomorrow. What is meant by no tomorrow? Well, when Jesus returns it will be the end of time as we know it, or as Jesus put it, "the end of the world" or "the end of the age" (MAT 28:20). The next world will be the new one, unconstrained by time. In fact, you will not be able to split it into segments, because eternity is a singlular entity not subject to division. There will be no day or night, no calendars, no clocks, just a life of bliss with the Lord of hosts in a perpetual reality of love. In essence there will be no tomorrow since that implies a finite universe, but the next one will go on forever.

By the way, the same will be true for the condemned. Their eternity is the lake of fire which burns forever, consuming everything that enters therein. It is the second death (REV 20:10–14). There will be no time-served only a death sentence, which may or may not vary in degree of torment prior to one's demise. Regardless, nobody in hell will know when or how it ends. But when it is over, it's for good. There will be no more time and no more tomorrows, not even a memory (ISA 26:14; ISA 65:17).

Lesson: Steadfastness

Now that you know who you are, a child of the living God, the imperative for you is to remain so. It is one thing to recognize the reality and history of Jesus Christ, and even believe that He rose from the dead. It is quite another matter to know it and show it. You may accept who Christ is in your mind but do you believe Him in your heart? If you are sure in your heart, you should proclaim Him with your lips. Has your life become a daily sacrifice to God Almighty through Christ our Lord (ROM 12:1–3)?

- ROM 10:9–10 ~ If you confess the Lord Jesus with your mouth, and believe in your heart that God raised Him from the dead, you will be saved. For with the heart we believe unto righteousness; and with the mouth confession is made unto salvation.

Perseverence in the faith requires courage (DEU 31:6–8; 1 CO 16:13) and commitment (PSA 37:5; 1 JO 2:6), patience (PSA 37:7; JAM 1:3) and endurance (1 CO 10:13), service (PSA 41:1; MAT 25:40-45) and generosity (DEU 16:17; LUK 6:38). This is what is meant by steadfastness: giving back to the Lord. And when you give your love to others it's as if you are giving it to Him (MAT 25:40). This is a lifelong duty, since He has given everything to you and for you. Do you believe in God and do you have faith in His Son? You need both.

Does that mean if you aren't steadfast in your faith you can lose your salvation? Let me put it this way. A person can believe but not have faith; belief and faith are different. First, I believe wholeheartedly in the salvation of Jesus Christ and I am compelled to proclaim it by faith. Second, I also believe that all people are created in the image of God, but not all will accept Christ as Savior and are therefore condemned. But I do not place my faith in the latter statement but in the former, though I believe them both to be true.

Can you gain salvation and lose it? This has long been debated, and a case can be made that you can lose your salvation insofar as you never fully received God's Holy Spirit (2 PE 2:20–22; ACT 19:16). A case also can be made that you cannot lose your salvation, insofar as once you are sealed you are sealed forever (2 CO 1:22; ROM 8:28–39). But the point is this, if you never lose faith you will keep your soul (LUK 21:19). There is only one thing on your part that is required in order to receive God's reward: keep the faith. But if you truly believe, it will show and people will know. If those people do not agree, are disappointed, or otherwise do not accept the truth, they will separate from you for they do not possess the Spirit and you do (JDE 1:17–19).

- EZE 18:24 ~ When a righteous person turns away from righteousness, commits sin, and is motivated by evil, can that person live? All the righteousness that occurred beforehand will never be remembered, but because of the sin he or she will die.
- MAT 7:21–23 ~ Jesus informed the people that not everyone who says to Him, "Lord, Lord," will enter the kingdom of heaven, but only those who do the will of our heavenly Father. Many will say to Him, "Haven't we prophesied and done mighty works in your name?" Jesus will reply to them, "I never knew you; depart from me you who work iniquity."
- MAT 13:3–23 ~ Jesus told the parable of the sower of seeds. He explained that some people will receive the Word with joy; it will begin to grow but it will not take root (because the seed was sown upon rocky places). Tribulations and persecutions associated with being a follower of Christ will offend many people and many will let the Word die in their hearts.
- HEB 6:4–6 ~ It is impossible for those who were once enlightened, who tasted of the heavenly gift and were made partakers of the Holy Ghost, who understood the good Word of God and the powers of the world to come, to be renewed unto repentance if they should fall away. They crucify the Son of God all over again and put Him to open shame.

Everyone is chosen by God to listen and obey. But many do not choose Him or His Way. The sheep follow the Good Shepherd, the goats stray from the flock and get lost, spiritually speaking (MAT 25:32). Are you a sheep or a goat? Because the sheep not only follow Jesus, they thank God every day from the beginning of their conversion through the end of time. Those who are sanctified eventually will be glorified (ROM 8:30); though already in progress, sanctification is a lifelong process as is steadfastness; we must remain committed because God does.

- PHP 1:3-6 ~ Paul wrote: I thank God every time I think of you, and pray to Him with joy for your fellowship in the Gospel, from the very first day until now; being confident that He who began a good work in you will bring it to completion when Jesus Christ returns.
- 2 TH 2:13–14 ~ Give thanks always to God for choosing you from the beginning to be saved through sanctification of the Spirit and belief in the truth. He called you by His Gospel to share in the glory of our Lord Jesus Christ.
- 1 PE 1:2–5 ~ Christians are chosen by God in advance, through the sanctification of the Spirit, to be obedient to Christ and cleansed by His blood. Blessed is God the Father of our Lord Jesus Christ. According to His abundant mercy, He recreated in us the living hope, brought through the resurrection of Christ from the dead, to receive an incorruptible and undefiled inheritance reserved in heaven and lasting forever. Through faith, He has shielded us by His power until the coming of the salvation that is ready to be revealed on the last day.

Obviously, steadfastness is to consistently reach for the Holy Spirit to guide, direct, embolden, and protect you. With the love of Christ abiding and active in your heart, you will be changed from the inside-out. Your motivations will be towards a heavenly reward and not for worldly gain. Your service will be to God, to your faith family, and to the lost sheep, and will not be dominated by what you desire for yourself; because your wants and needs will be met by God Himself (MAT 6:33). By putting God first and everyone else second (you are part of the second group), you will have met the requirements of the Law and the Gospel.

- ROM 6:6–18 ~ If we have been planted together in the likeness of His death, we also will be raised together in the likeness of His resurrection; knowing that our old self was crucified with Him, that the body of sin might be destroyed and that henceforth we should serve sin nevermore. For the dead in Christ are freed from sin. We who have died with Christ believe that we also will live with Him; knowing that Christ who was raised from the dead cannot die again, since death has no power over Him. Jesus died once unto sin, but He lives forever unto God. Likewise, you must die unto sin, but will live forever unto God through Jesus Christ our Lord. Do not let sin rule in your mortal body, or give into the lusts thereof. Neither employ your members as instruments of unrighteousness unto sin, but yield to God as a person alive in Christ, and use your members as instruments of righteousness unto God. Then sin will have no dominion over you; for you are not under the law but under grace. What then? Can we sin because we are not under the law, but under grace? Absolutely not! Do you not realize that a slave must obey the master? Will you be a slave to sin unto death, or obedient to God unto righteousness? Thank God! Though you once served sin, you now serve the doctrine of deliverance; being made free from sin, you became servants of righteousness.
- PHP 2:13–15 ~ For it is God who works in you both to want and to do that which pleases Him. Do this without grumbling or quarreling, so you can remain blameless and harmless children of God, without reproach, in the midst of a crooked and perverse nation where you shine as lights to the world.
- PHP 3:8–14 ~ Without a doubt, I count everything loss except the excellent knowledge of Christ Jesus my Lord, for whom I have suffered the loss of all worldly things, which to me are as garbage because of what I have gained in Christ; finding righteousness from Jesus,

though not having any of my own in accordance with the law, but possessing the righteousness of God by faith in His Son. So that I may know Him, and the power of His resurrection, and the fellowship of His sufferings, becoming like Him in death so I might attain the resurrection of the dead. I have not yet attained it however; it is not like I am already perfect. But I continue forward, that I may hold onto the promise for which Christ holds onto me. Brothers, I have not obtained it as yet, though I have let go of the past, forgetting those things which are behind and reaching for those things which are to come; pressing onward toward the goal of receiving the prize of eternal life for which God has called me on behalf of Jesus Christ.

If you want a great example of steadfastness consider Job. Most everyone knows the story of Job, and how God allowed the devil to try Job's faith (JOB 1—2). Satan figured he could break Job while God knew that Job's faith would not falter. Satan threw everything he had at Job, to include deaths, losses, hardship, and disease. Job was reaching his breaking point, exhausted from the suffering, to the point he questioned God's motive. God responded to Job by explaining the intricacy of the universe and the forming of the cosmos; the wonders of nature and its processes; the variety of lifeforms and the wisdom of human beings. These miraculous accomplishments could only be performed by the one true God who created this splendid world in its entirety (JOB 38—39). Then God asked Job, "Can anyone contending with the Almighty instruct Him? Let him who accuses God provide an answer" (JOB 40:1-2). Job replied, "I am unworthy to answer, so I must cover my mouth with my hand. I have spoken time and again, but now I have nothing to say" (JOB 40:3-5). Then God told Job, "Prepare yourself like a man, for I will question you further and you will answer me. Would you doubt my justice? Would you condemn my works to elevate yourself? Do you have the reach of my arm or the thunder of my voice? If so, then clothe yourself with majesty and excellency, and array yourself with beauty and glory. Unleash your wrath upon the proud and bring them down; humble them and crush the wicked. Hide them in the dust and cover them in the grave. Then I will agree that you have the ability to save yourself by the power of your own right hand" (JOB 40:6-14). God spoke of the behemoth and the leviathan: intimidating giants that roamed the earth and the sea (possibly dinosaurs). They were powerful and not easily subdued, yet marvelous in their stature though menacing in their appearance (JOB 40:15-41:34). Job responded, "I know that you can do anything and that you know everything. You spoke of people who obscure your counsel and are lacking in knowledge (JOB 38:1-2), and you asked me to give an answer. I have heard about you, but now I have seen who you are. And I detest myself, and I repent in dust and ashes" (JOB 42:1-6). Therefore, God blessed the latter part of Job's life more than the former, with a double portion (JOB 42:10-16). God also chastised Job's friends Eliphaz, Bildad, and Zophar for being among those who speak of things they know nothing about; and God ordered them to humble themselves, repent, and offer sacrifices (JOB 42:7-9).

To conclude this lesson, let us aggregate the many facets of steadfastness. First, we need to stay strong in our faith, cling to our hope, surround ourselves with fellow believers, and pray for Christians all around the world. Second, we must keep the commandments of God and follow the teachings of Jesus to the best of our ability; passing these along to our children so that they will pass them along to their children. Third, we must be constantly on the alert, fully aware, and very cautious, so that we do not fall into social and political traps, follow or join others who are heading in the wrong direction, or give into worldly temptations which sully the flesh and darken the spirit. Fourth, we must use our love, time, gifts, abilities, and knowledge to further God's kingdom throughout our lives with courage; living confidently for Jesus who died for us, and forever striving to be more like Him by continuously eliminating previous immoral tendencies.

CHAPTER EIGHT

- RUT 1:11–18, 22 ~ Naomi [who had lost two sons, both married to Moabite women] said, "Turn back my daughters-in-law, why should you follow me? I will never marry again or bear more sons to marry; besides you should not have to wait to remarry. It grieves me tremendously for your sakes how the hand of the Lord took my two sons, your husbands." The widows wept. Then Orpah kissed her mother-in-law goodbye and departed. But Ruth held onto Naomi who suggested, "Your sister-in-law has returned to her people and their gods; you should go with her." Ruth replied, "Please do not ask me to leave, for I would rather follow you, and go where you go and live where you live. Your people will be my people and your God my God. Where you die, I will die and be buried with you." When Naomi saw that Ruth was determined, she kept quiet. So, Naomi and Ruth (the Moabitess) went to Bethlehem together, arriving at the beginning of the barley harvest.
- JOB 11:14–16 ~ If iniquity is in your hand, put it far away; do not let wickedness dwell in your tents. And you will raise your face without spot; yes, you will be steadfast and never afraid. Because you will forget your misery, and remember it as waters that flow away.
- PSA 78:6–8 ~ God established a testimony in Jacob and appointed a law in Israel, which He commanded our fathers to obey and make them known to their children. Each generation will be taught them; those children born to you will declare them to their children. So that they might set their hope on God, and never forget His works, and keep his commandments; and might not be as their fathers, a stubborn and rebellious generation, whose heart was not right with God and whose spirit did not hold steadfast to Him.
- ACT 2:42 ~ And those who listened remained steadfast in the doctrine and fellowship of the apostles, in the breaking of bread together and in prayer.
- 1 CO 15:58 ~ Therefore my beloved brothers, be steadfast, unmovable, and always abounding in the work of the Lord, insofar as you know your labor is not in vain.
- HEB 3:14 ~ We are made partakers of Christ, if we hold the beginning of our confidence steadfast unto the end.
- HEB 6:19 ~ We have hope as an anchor to the soul; it is sure and steadfast, and penetrates into the depths of our being.
- 1 PE 5:8–9 ~ Be sober and vigilant, because your enemy the devil roams about like a lion searching for someone to devour. He will attempt to consume anyone who isn't steadfast in their faith.
- 2 PE 3:17 ~ Beloved, now that you know these things, beware that you are not led astray by the error of the wicked, and thus fail in your steadfastness.

Repeat the prayers of David about properly carrying out God's assignments. Remember, you are saved by the blood of Jesus not by your steadfastness; but it does keep you on track.

- PSA 51:10–12 ~ Create in me a clean heart, Lord, and renew an upright spirit within me. Don't remove me from your presence and don't take your Holy Spirit from me. Restore to me the joy of your salvation and uphold me with your free Spirit.
- PSA 141:1–5, 8–10 ~ Lord I cry out to you; hear my prayer. I offer it as incense and lift it up with my hands toward you. Please warn me before I open my mouth. Let me not be inclined toward any evil thing, or associate with those who work wickedness, or be enticed by their luxuries. If I am admonished by righteous men it will be a blessing to be reproved by them, and I bid your blessing upon them. My eyes are fixed upon you, Lord God, in you I will trust to never leave my soul destitute. Keep me from snares being laid for me and protect me from traps set by workers of iniquity. Let the wicked fall into their own nets, that I may escape.

Lesson: The Golden Rule

Everybody knows the Golden Rule. This moniker was coined in the early seventeenth century, but the concept has endured since God created humankind. The impetus of the Golden Rule is recorded in the New Testament, when Jesus was administering His famous *Sermon on the Mount*. Jesus directed this message to everyone including you and me. He repeated it often for good reason: Jesus alone speaks the words of eternal life (JOH 6:68).

- MAT 7:12 ~ Whatever you want others to do for you, do the same for them; for this is the basis of the law and the prophets.
- LUK 6:31 ~ What you wish that others would do unto you, do likewise unto them.
- JOH 13:34 ~ Jesus also said, "A new commandment I give to you, that you should love one another, even as I have loved you."

You might ask, how can this commandment have endured for all time if it is found in the NT, especially if Jesus refers to it as a "new commandment." Well Jesus also said the rule is founded in the law and in prophecy indicating it wasn't exactly new, though perhaps news to those hearing it directly from Him, people who were beginning to accept Him as Lord and King. The rule had been preached by teachers of Jewish law before Jesus gave that sermon, but His authority was acknowledged by those who were listening to Him with their hearts.

- LEV 19:17–18 ~ You must not hate your brother in your heart. You must not rebuke your neighbor or commit sin against him or her. You must not avenge or bear a grudge against any of your people. You must love your neighbor as yourself. I AM the Lord.
- DEU 1:17 ~ You must not discriminate against others in judgment; permit the testimony of the lowly as well as the great. You should not be afraid when facing man's judgment for judgment belongs to God. If you have a cause that is too difficult for you, bring it to God and He will hear it.
- DEU 10:19 ~ Love the strangers in your midst for you were once strangers in the land of Egypt.
- ISA 56:1–2 ~ The Lord says, "Uphold justice and do the right thing, for salvation is coming soon when my righteousness will be revealed. Blessed are those who do these things, and who keep the Sabbath holy, and who stop their hand from doing evil to another."

The principles underlying all the commandments of God is to love Him with all your heart, strength, soul, and spirit and to love others as your love yourself. Thus, love is the foundation of the law and the prophets, love is the fulfillment of the law, and love is the basis of the Golden Rule.

- DEU 6:5; DEU 13:3 ~ You shall love the Lord your God with all your heart, soul, and might.
- MAT 22:35–40; MAR 12:28–31 ~ A man asked Jesus "Which is the greatest of all the commandments of the law." Jesus replied, "You must love the Lord your God with all your heart, soul, mind, and strength. This is the first and greatest commandment. And the second is like unto the first, you must love your neighbor as yourself. On these two commandments hang the laws and the prophets."
- ROM 13:9–10; GAL 5:14 ~ All commandments can be understood in the message, love your neighbor as yourself. Love does no harm to a neighbor; therefore, love is the fulfilling of the law.

What would you have others to do for you? How about treat you as an equal, with respect and kindness; or be helpful, honest, and thoughtful, or attentive to your needs? Certainly, nobody wants to be lied to, robbed, betrayed, assaulted, or killed. Thus, obedience to the law involves caring about others, maintaining moral principles, and possessing the ultimate human ethic which is to value and love all life. No matter what religion, or nation, or epoch of time, the worth of every human should be central; otherwise there can be no equality, liberty, or morality. All laws, regardless of legal system or basic worldview, address doing evil to or committing crimes against others or the state. Remember, if you do it to others you are doing it to God whether good or bad (MAT 25:31–46). Therefore, we must obey laws, including those established by God and those promulgated by governments (ROM 13:1–5). If you obeyed the Golden Rule to the letter, you would never worry about getting into trouble with the law, would you?

Laws of civilized society are based on God's laws. And there are penalties with respect to the severity of the infraction just as there is a hierarchy in the Ten Commandments. For example, murder is a more serious offense than theft, and garners a greater punishment; this is true everywhere and for all people. Those proclaiming that laws and morality are relative to the individual's personal perspective are kidding themselves, and they will discover this the moment they get caught violating the law. The only thing relative about the law and legal systems is that they relate to God and His love for us.

- PRO 2:9 ~ You will understand righteousness, judgment, and equity; yes, every good path.
- ROM 3:20 ~ Nobody is justified by works of the law in the sight of the Lord; for through the law comes the knowledge of sin.
- ROM 6:15–18; GAL 5:18 ~ If you are led by the Spirit you are not under the law. What then; should we sin because we are not under the law but under grace? God forbid it! Don't you know, to that which you yield yourself you obey, whether of sin unto death or obedience unto righteousness? Thank God, though you were servants of sin you have obeyed in your heart the doctrine delivered unto you; being made free from sin you became servants of righteousness.
- 1 TH 5:22 ~ Abstain from all appearance of evil.
- JAM 4:17 ~ To anyone who knows to do good and does not do it, that for them is sin.
- 1 JO 3:4 ~ Whoever commits sin transgresses the law, for sin is the transgression of the law.

God loves us unconditionally; He wishes we would do likewise by loving Him unconditionally. If we could do that, we could love others unconditionally as well, in which case we would never violate any law. And though the knowledge of right and wrong has been written into the heart of every man, woman, and child, we still choose wrong knowing full well that negative consequences are likely to follow. Equally, when we follow the Golden Rule the consequences are usually positive and beneficial. All the while, we know the difference before we act, because the conscience either convicts or acquits a person regarding their actions and the observed actions of others. Experience reaffirms the connection, so the knowledge of results reminds us continuously to adjust our moral compass.

- JER 31:33 ~ This is the covenant that I will make with the house of Israel. After those days, says the Lord, I will put my law in their minds and write it on their hearts. And I will be their God and they will be my people. (also HEB 8:10)
- ROM 2:14–15 ~ When the Gentiles, who were not given the law, do by nature the things required of the law, though they have not the law they are a law unto themselves. They exhibit the work of the law written upon their hearts, their conscience also bearing witness; because their thoughts either accuse them or excuse them for things they say and do.
- ROM 7:19–23 ~ The good I want to do I do not do, and the evil I do not want to do I do. If I do that which I wish not to do, it is not I that do it but sin that dwells in me. And even when I do good, evil is still present within me. Although I delight in God's law in my mind, I see

another law working in my body, warring against the law of my mind and making me a slave to the sin which is inherent in my body.

Unfortunately, we all know the Golden Rule but we all disobey it. And we know this before we do it. Then what is a person to do? We cannot ignore the sin that lingers in our hearts, so what's the use in trying to fight it? Well, that is the whole point isn't it? We are supposed to resist temptation and keep trying to do better. We are fighting a spiritual battle: are you in it to win it? With Christ, you are a winner; because once you receive Christ into your heart, you are able to rely on Him to defeat the sin within and the evil without. By accepting the guidance of His Holy Spirit, we get progressively better at shunning the sin; but this takes considerable practice just like it does to achieve anything worthwhile. Through this process we become sanctified, or made holy, by the righteousness of Christ until the end, after which we will remain sinless forever. But if you aren't trying, it shows you are not sincere in your faith; because a true faith is evident by your actions.

Take time to identify the sins in your life which you struggle with on a regular basis. Make a list of them and prioritize the list. Then focus your attention on the more serious infractions of God's law which you are committing, keeping mindful of the circumstances that trigger them. With time, you will find yourself saying or doing those things a lot less frequently. And by controlling the major problems, you will become cognizant of the minor ones as well. Of course, the opposite is also true; that is, if you disregard the minor offenses you will graduate to major offenses and cease to care about both (LUK 16:1–13). Yes, the devil will continue to throw the temptation at you, possibly even more as you grow in your walk and abandon your wayward ways. But you will be stronger and will more readily repel the devil's advances against you, for you will be equipped and strengthened by the armor of God and the sword of the Spirit (EPH 8:10–18; 2 CO 10:3–4).

One of the keys to modifying your behavior is to do the opposite of what you want to stop doing. As a psychotherapist, I often conducted a group activity where the participants identified the things that bring them down and the things that lift them up (see Barber, 2016a cited in the introduction to this chapter). I wrote these items on the whiteboard as shown in the table below. Those clients came to realize that the things which lifted them up were far more powerful and true than the things which brought them down, because the uplifting things were largely spiritual in nature, thereby representing higher powers that they all possessed. Further, they realized that the things lifting them up were not only the opposite of the things bringing them down, but also that the positive ones could overpower if not defeat the negative ones.

- PRO 28:13 ~ Those who conceal their sins will not prosper; but those confessing their sins and forsaking them will receive mercy.
- 1 CO 10:13 ~ God will not allow us to be tempted beyond our ability to withstand it, and He will always provide us an escape from temptation.
- 1 CO 15:33 ~ Do not be deceived; evil associations corrupt good manners.
- GAL 5:19–23 ~ The works of the flesh are clearly evident and include adultery, fornication, vileness, lust, idolatry, witchcraft, immorality, hate, rage, strife, sedition, heresy, envy, murder, drunkenness, selfishness, and the like. I tell you again as I have before, those who continue doing such things will not inherit the kingdom of God. But the fruits of the Spirit include love, joy, peace, hope, patience, gentleness, goodness, faith, humbleness, and temperance; there is no law against these things.
- 2 TI 2:22 ~ Flee from youthful lusts and follow righteousness, faith, love, and peace in unity with others who call on the Lord with a pure heart.

- HEB 10:26 ~ If we sin willfully after having received the knowledge of truth, there remains no sacrifice for sins.
- 1 JO 1:9 ~ If we confess our sins, He is faithful and just to forgive our sins and cleanse us from all unrighteousness.

The following is an abridged version of a much more comprehensive list. Examine these items and see where you fit in (listed in no particular order). This will give you a starting point in your game plan to reduce if not eliminate unwanted behavior. Use your higher powers to gain control over your negativity and to help others by lifting them up, just as Christ will lift you up.

Brings you down	Lifts you up (higher powers)
Deceit	Honesty
Failure	Achievement
Despair	Hope
Fear	Love
Anger	Patience
Conflict	Reconciliation
Loneliness	Companionship
Doubt	Faith
Abuse	Nurturing
Stress	Peace
Confusion	Understanding
Betrayal	Loyalty
Guilt	Justification
Sadness	Laughter

To conclude this lesson, hear the words of Christ who said to the adulteress, "Go and sin no more" (JOH 8:1–11). He also said this to a leper whom He healed (JOH 7:14–15). What did Jesus mean, since it is impossible for us to never sin? Obviously, Jesus was commanding us to quit bad habits that we still engage in. For example, He was telling the woman to stop committing adultery. He expected the woman to desist from further fornication outside of marriage. Those of you who are committing sexual sin need to stop now. Believe me, back in the day I was guilty as sin, but I changed. I am happily married and I have no intention or desire to cheat on my wife. I assure you it was a challenge during my youth; and I am tempted every bit as much as I was back then, even though I am over-the-hill. If I can cease such behavior, anyone can. The problem is, we are guilty of adultery even when we think about it (MAT 5:27–28). This is the greatest challenge: to stop thinking about it, which is much harder than to stop doing it. What makes it possible is that you have the mind of Christ (1 CO 2:16). Strive to be mindful of what you are thinking, doing, or about to do. "Let your conscience be your guide" is akin to the Golden Rule, as long as your conscience is being guided by the Holy Spirit. Of course, if it wasn't for the Holy Spirit you wouldn't have a conscience at all.

- ISA 30:21 ~ Whether you veer to the left or to the right, your ears will hear a word behind you saying, "This is the way, walk in it."
- PRO 20:27 ~ The spirit of a person is the candle of the Lord who searches the inward parts.
- ROM 9:1 ~ I am telling the truth in Christ; I do not lie. My conscience bears witness of the truth via the Holy Ghost.
- 1 TI 1:5 ~ The goal of God's command is to love which comes from a pure heart, a good conscience, and a true faith.

Lesson: If You Could Choose Your Job in Heaven

Yes, there will be work in heaven (JOH 5:17; REV 7:15). It's not as if God's people are going to retire; instead, we will remain Christians for eternity in the employ of the Lord. It's probably preordained, but what if you could choose your job in heaven right now? Frankly I'd be okay as the custodian; just being home with my brothers and sisters in Christ would suit me. But let's face it, this is a very attractive proposition is it not? Go ahead and use your imagination. How would you like to be the cartographer for every new orb or celestial body? Or maybe a galactic ranger, rounding up the various strays, like a ghost rider in the sky. How about the border guard who prevents peddlers from approaching the gates of glory? Maybe you could be an artisan and create masterpieces that would please the Almighty Himself; perhaps a choir director, vocalist, composer, writer, or musician in God's choir or orchestra; or a caretaker of the furrows and burrows of the new universe (the new job description for custodian). Then again, will jobs in heaven resemble anything that ever existed on the old earth?

Besides, what prequalifies one to perform a job in heaven? Certainly, nothing we did down here but for our undying faith, which was evident in our work. God is going to make all things new, including me (and you too, if you want a job in the company of God). One thing's for sure, heavenly employees will be working for the Father, alongside His Son Jesus Christ, forevermore empowered by His Holy Spirit. Awesome stuff, isn't it? And that doesn't even include the benefits package.

Many will ask themselves, "Why should I work for God, I have my own priorities?" Because He has been working for you and me for eternity past, present, and future, that's why! He sent His Son to establish the family business down here and then left His Holy Spirit behind to continue our training. Although God rested the seventh day from all His creating, He hasn't stopped working and intervening in people's lives; recall, the seventh day of creation is continuous, it does not have an evening and a morning. God's work was continued here by Jesus Christ who didn't stop healing, even on the Sabbath (MAR 3:1–5; LUK 13:10–17). Jesus is a physician who makes house calls 24-7.

Likewise, we should work diligently throughout our lives in order to please God with our academic and vocational endeavors, allowing His light to shine through us and our accomplishments. We will forever be doing God's work hand-in-hand with Jesus, along with innumerable angels and saints, possessing all the faculties necessary to accomplish things that are beyond imagination. Heaven will be so great that I'm never going to call it a day since the work will never become tiresome and there will be no night anyway.

- HAB 1:5 ~ Take note, you heathen; regard and wonder marvelously, for I will work a work in your days which you will not believe, though you were told.
- PRO 11:18 ~ The wicked work deceitfully; but for those who sow righteousness there will be a sure reward.
- ECC 12:14 ~ God will judge every work, including works done in secret, whether good or evil.
- MAT 5:15 ~ Let your light shine before others that they may see your good works and glorify your Father in heaven.
- JOH 4:33–34 ~ After His disciples implored Him to eat, Jesus informed them, "My nourishment is doing the will of Him that sent me, and to finish His work."
- JOH 5:17 ~ Jesus answered them, "My Father has been at work all the while, and I work too."

- JOH 9:4 ~ Jesus declared, "While it is day, we will do the work of Him who sent me, for the night approaches when nobody can work."
- JOH 14:12 ~ Jesus promised, "Truly I tell you, those believing in me will do the works that I do; and greater works than these shall they do, when I have gone to be with my Father."

The works of God have been revealed in His Creation and His Word; similarly, the works of Christ reflect the work of God. Works assigned to humans are in accordance with God's will on earth and in heaven (MAT 6:10). In our lives we try to emulate Christ through the vigor of our faith in Him. That is our sole duty as we serve Him and others. Whatever your occupation, you are able to please God in that capacity (EXO 35:31–35; 1 CO 12:6–11), as well as keeping Him close to your heart via the means of grace. This is how we always can know what He expects us to do at any given time. He equips us with the education, knowledge, and experience to succeed. Our training manual is the Holy Bible, which is the textbook we are following right now in this study.

- ISA 2:8 ~ Their land will be full of idols, those who worship the works of their own hands.
- JOH 6:29 ~ Jesus answered them saying, "This is the work of God: that you believe Him whom He has sent."
- EPH 4:11–13 ~ God appointed apostles, prophets, evangelists, pastors, and teachers for the perfecting of the saints, work of the ministry, and edifying the body of Christ; to unite us in faith with the knowledge of God into the fullness of Christ.
- COL 1:29 ~ Likewise, I (Paul) labor, striving with God's power which works in me mightily.
- HEB 6:10 ~ God is not unfair, and will not dismiss your labor of love which you gave for others in His name, because you have ministered to the saints and continue to do so.
- JAM 1:25 ~ Those who study the perfect law of liberty and continue therein, not forgetting but continuing to do the work, these persons will be blessed for their deeds.

It is a special blessing when you really love your work. I'm sure everyone has had a job, or a manager, or an employer that they couldn't stand. It can be grueling going to work at a place like that; sometimes it's a matter of survival it seems (2 TH 3:10). What is more a rarity is to possess a true passion to go to work day after day (PSA 104:23), up to six days a week (EXO 20:8–11; EXO 23:12). I've had a few jobs that were kind of fun, but not enough to live there. Eventually, we all run out of gas; we need to rest every so often lest it harm us. In heaven, you will be unable to work yourself to death. Given that there will be no timeclock, the work will continue indefinitely: whenever, whatever, wherever, forever. But your work will enrich you with great dividends, premier fringe benefits, perks and surprises, and the best office parties ever; not to mention that each moment is like a family reunion.

- MAT 16:27 ~ The Son of Man will come in the glory of His Father and with angels, to reward everybody according to their works.
- 1 CO 3:8–9 ~ The one who plants and the one who waters is the same; everyone receives a yield commensurate with their labor. We are laborers working together with God. You are the mission field; you are God's building.
- 1 CO 3:13–14 ~ Everyone's work will be seen for what it is because the light will illuminate it; it will be revealed by the fire which tries every person's work as well as his or her dedication. If that which is built endures, the builder will be rewarded. If it burns down, the builder will suffer the loss but will be saved from the flames.
- PHP 1:6 ~ Be confident, for He who began a good work in you will prolong it until the day Christ returns.

- JAM 1:4 ~ Let patience have her perfect work, that you may be perfect and complete, wanting nothing.
- REV 21:23–25 ~ The city will not need the sun or the moon to shine, for the glory of God will provide eternal light. And the nations of the saved will walk in that light; and the kings of the earth will confer their glory and honor into it. And the city gates will be open every day, for there will be no night.

Paradise will be fun. You're going to love it, and you will never become tired, fatigued, bored, sleepy, or weary (GEN 3:17–19). Whereas down here on planet Earth, everyone gets burned out eventually if not repeatedly. Who wouldn't want to retire early? Some people play the lottery religiously, precisely because they don't want to work anymore. Granted, we all need our rest; and in heaven we will find rest (MAT 11:28; HEB 4:3–11; REV 14:13). It will be everlasting rest from the chaos, insanity, and stupidity, as well as a reprieve from the curse of sin (REV 22:3): a spiritual, mental, and physical rest but not a cessation of activities, duties, or celebrations. It will be way livelier than life down here, I can assure you that. But if what you want is rest in the afterlife, you can receive the second death and be able to desist from having anything to do for the rest of eternity.

It is better to work hard because you want to, despite the fact that you have to. You were given a calling by the Lord to serve Him in this life; you may be given a similar calling when you serve Him in the next. Possibly it will be the same line of work; perhaps your talents, knowhow, and skills will come in handy up there. Adam might still be tending God's gardens just as he did in Eden (GEN 2:15). Of course, a lot of jobs will not transfer into heaven, such as law enforcement and guidance counselors; we will have the great Counselor and Lawgiver as our permanent, personal guide and mentor. Furthermore, some jobs will be for everyone, such as singing praises, worshipping, and fellowshipping together in His name (MAT 18:20).

- ISA 65:18–25 ~ Be glad and rejoice forever in that which I the Lord create; I will create Jerusalem for rejoicing and her people will be a joy unto me. They will be heard for all of their days; while the sinners, though their days may be many, will be accursed. My people will build houses and inhabit them; they will plant vineyards and eat the fruit thereof. They will not build a house for another to inhabit, or plant a vineyard for another to consume. My people will enjoy the works of their hands, for their labor will not be in vain nor will it cause them trouble. For they represent the blessed seed of the Lord, as well as their offspring with them. Before they call, I will answer; and while they speak, I will hear. The wolf and the lamb will feed together, and the lion will eat straw like the ox; but dust will be the serpent's supper. The Lord says, "Nobody will harm or destroy those who abide on my holy mountain."
- REV 7:15 ~ There are many who stand at the throne of God, ready to serve Him day and night in His temple; and the One who sits on the throne will live among them.
- REV 15:3–4 ~ They were singing the song of God's servant Moses, the song of the Lamb. "Great and marvelous are your works, Lord God Almighty; fair and true are your ways, King of saints. Who does not fear you and glorify your name, Lord? For only you are holy, and all nations will come and worship before your throne while your judgments are pronounced."

Okay, so there will be work in heaven and it will not get boring; but what about that party mentioned previously? Who doesn't like a good party, huh? Guess what, the celebration will be continuous as well. Everything will be pleasurable and glorious, and you will never get irked, scared, disappointed, or burned out. If the work is fun, can you imagine the celebrations? You may be overwhelmed, I suppose, but it will be with bliss, truth, happiness, freedom, calmness of mind, and profound love; actually, the feeling will be more like awestruck, I would guess. I mean, once the groom who is Christ is reunited with the bride who is the Church, there will be a wedding reception unlike any you have ever seen or heard. There will be singing and dancing, laughing and shouting.

- PSA 16:10–11 ~ For you will not leave my soul in hell; neither will you allow your Holy One to be corrupted. You will show me the path of life; and in your presence I will find fullness of joy. At your right hand are pleasures forevermore.
- PSA 47:1 ~ Clap your hands all you people; shout to God with the voice of triumph.
- ECC 3:1,4 ~ For everything there is a season, and a time for every purpose under heaven. A time to weep and a time to laugh; a time to mourn and a time to dance.
- ISA 25:6 ~ In this mountain the Lord of hosts will prepare for His people a feast of delicious food and fine wine.
- LUK 6:21 ~ Blessed are those who hunger now, for you will be filled. Blessed are those who weep now, for you will laugh.
- REV 19:6–9 ~ I heard the sound of a great multitude, as the rushing of many waters, with a thundering of voices singing "Alleluia, for the omnipotent Lord God reigns. Let us be glad and rejoice, and give honor to Him; for the marriage of the Lamb has come, and His wife has made herself ready." The bride was dressed in fine linen, clean and white, representing the righteousness of the saints. Then the angel told me to write, "Blessed are those who are invited to the marriage feast of the Lamb," continuing, "These are the true words of God."

God bestows upon each individual unique talent, gifts, and potential. These include spiritual gifts to be used in His service. Some of your abilities are God-given, some inherited, some learned, and some attained by exercising your freedom of choice. In all these ways a person can bear fruit worthy of repentance (MAT 3:8–10; JOH 15:1–16). What does this mean? Well, if you praise God and give Him the glory, your faith in His promises will be counted as righteousness (GEN 15:1–6; ROM 4:16–22). Henceforth, when you repent with sincere contrition, not only will you will be forgiven, you will bear good fruit, and your works done by faith will be credited to your account. Therefore, through the power of faith provided by the Holy Spirit, you can dedicate your labor to the Lord, and you will indeed perform works of love and righteousness, thereby glorifying God and shining His light before others. Since this is our duty on the earth, no doubt it will be in heaven. It is about being a proper steward of God's gifts, now and forevermore. Stewardship is service; we serve God and we serve one another using our time, talent, treasure, testimony, etc. And it doesn't matter what kind of work we are doing because there are plenty of jobs available in God's kingdom, all of which can be used to glorify Him, so that we can be glorified with Him.

- ACT 10:35 ~ In every nation, those who fear God and work righteousness will be accepted by Him.
- ROM 8:16–17 ~ His Spirit bears witness with our spirits that we are children of God; and if children then heirs of God and joint heirs with Christ if we share in His suffering that we also may share in His glory.
- 1 CO 12:7 ~ The manifestation of the Spirit is given to everyone for the common good.
- PHP 1:9–11 ~ I pray that your love abounds continuously in knowledge and judgment; that you approve of things which are excellent and that you remain sincere and without offense until the Lord returns; being filled with the fruit of righteousness that comes through Christ, to the glory and praise of God.
- 1 PE 4:10–11 ~ As everyone has received the gift, even so minister the same to one another, as good stewards of the manifold grace of God.

Count your blessings and you will find they outweigh the hardships. But you can multiply your hardships by resisting, disobeying, opposing, and/or rejecting God. You can work hard and make a fortune, and pride yourself on your own accomplishments; but that will be your only reward and it will not last. You can multiply your blessings by being a blessing to others as you serve them and God in your daily work. This will be your job from now on, that is, forevermore. And God will rain more blessings upon you than you can even count (MAL 3:10). You can receive hardships that last forever, or blessings (PSA 23:1–6; MAT 25:31–46). It's a pretty easy decision if you ask me.

What does it mean to be a timeless, eternal being? How can one fathom a life with no past, present, or future? One can only imagine and speculate. Try to comprehend nonstop love, grace, mercy, truth, joy, peace, contentment, comfort, and light, or continuous learning, growth, understanding, and recognition. How would you like no waiting, hesitation, panic, uncertainty, repetitiveness or redundancy; no anxiety, dislike, unpleasantry, or negativity? How about never becoming tired, unimpressed, lonely, fatigued, or starved? And everything is always new, interesting, entertaining, and fun; nothing grows old or becomes unnecessary. Then to top that off, everything is good and becomes increasingly better, such as your wisdom, love, happiness, and excitement. Your attributes, skills, knowledge, and spirituality get bigger, higher, broader, greater, longer, and deeper. But you won't notice these changes because the novelty of the experience transpires in an uninterrupted cascade of becoming.

You will not find anything on planet Earth with which to compare heaven. One might envision paradise being like a humongous amusement park, with rides that go on forever, without duplicating a single twist, turn, or reversal. Or perhaps a fantastic vacation that never ends, with new destinations, activities, views, productions, and recreation. Maybe you envision a fantastic dream that comes true and lasts indefinitely. An old friend who was dying thought of a paradise with a different golf course to play every day. You can think outside the box until doomsday, and I bet you will not have scratched the surface of how wonderful, perfect, and glorious it will be in heaven living an abundant and endless life with God the Father, Son, and Holy Spirit. Just thinking about this should bring hope and peace of mind. Because all that has past will be behind us and we will never look back.

CHAPTER EIGHT

GLOSSARY OF NAMES, PLACES, AND TERMS

Aaron	Moses's older brother, assistant, and companion; first of priestly order of Aaron
Abednego	Daniel's friend who survived the fiery furnace
Abel	Adam and Eve's second son who was murdered by his brother Cain
Abiathar	High priest escaped King Saul's slaughter of priests and became King David's advisor
Abihu	Aaron's son and priest found guilty of idolatry and executed
Abigail	Became David's wife after death of husband Nabal
Abimelech	King of Gerar who brought Sarah to his harem believing her to be Abraham's sister; his son made the same mistake with Isaac's wife Rebekah; both kings made treaties with Abraham and Isaac; also name of evil son of Gideon
Abinadab	Man of God from Judea who housed the Ark of the Covenant for twenty years
Abishai	David's nephew and captain; Joab's brother
Abner	Commander of King Saul's army who later joined with David
Abomination	A detestable act, thing, or event
Abraham	(also Abram) God's righteous servant was blessed by God for being willing to sacrifice his only legitimate son Isaac; God's covenant with him resulted in him becoming the ancestor of nations (Hebrews and Arabs) and the example of faith
Absalom	King David's son who killed his half-brother Amnon for raping his sister Tamar; rebelled against David and was killed
Achan	Man from Judea who illegally took spoils of Jericho and died for it
Adam	First human created by God to live in Eden; father of humankind
Adonijah	King David's son who contested Solomon's right to the throne and was killed
Adultery	Infidelity in marriage or to God; sex outside of marriage (fornication)
Ahab	Evil king of Israel who married Jezebel and practiced idolatry; died for his evil ways as prophesied by Elijah, as did his seventy sons
Ahithophel	David's adviser who conspired with Absalom against David and later committed suicide
Alexandria	Egyptian city founded by Alexander the Great; active in early Christian Church
Alleluia	Praise the Lord
Alpha	First letter of the Greek alphabet; the beginning
Alphaeus	Father of James the lesser, an apostle of Jesus
Amen	Let it be so
Ammon	Also Benammi; second son of Lot and his daughter by incest; descendants were called the Ammonites
Amnon	King David's son killed by half-brother Absalom for raping his sister Tamar

Amos	Prophet of Israel; book in the Old Testament
Amram	Father of Moses and Aaron
Andrew	One of Jesus's twelve apostles and Simon Peter's brother
Annas	Jewish high priest and father-in-law of Caiaphas
Anoint	To appoint or consecrate, usually by pouring oil on the head (christen)
Antichrist	Anyone who denies or opposes Christ
Antioch	Syrian city where the term "Christians" originated
Apocrypha	Assemblage of books not found in the canonical books of the Bible; the Roman Catholic Church officially accepted them in response to the Protestant Reformation (Council of Trent, 1546) because they supported unscriptural doctrines being practiced (e.g., purgatory); the books were of unknown authorship, were internally inconsistent, and contradicted scripture
Apollos	Companion of Paul and fellow evangelist
Apostle	One of the twelve principal followers called by Jesus Christ, who became the first evangelists for the Christian church
Aquila	Friend and companion of the apostle Paul
Arabia	Southern peninsula below Red Sea and likely the land inhabited by descendants of Ishmael
Aram	Armenia; see also Syria
Aramaic	A Semitic language similar to Hebrew and spoken in the land of Palestine
Ararat	Mountain range on which Noah's ark came to rest after the flood subsided
Archangel	A heavenly spirit in angelic form of extremely high rank (e.g., Michael)
Ark of the Covenant	The chest which held the stone tablets containing the Ten Commandments
Armageddon	Site of the final battle between the forces of good and evil
Artaxerxes	Persian king who allowed Ezra to rebuild Jerusalem
Asa	Upright king of Judea who established peace during his rule
Ascension	The return of Christ into heaven following His resurrection and subsequent appearances
Asenath	Joseph's Egyptian wife
Asher	Jacob's eighth son; tribe of Israel
Assyria	Mesopotamian civilization and empire by the Tigris River; Assyrians were descendants of Shem's son Asshur
Athaliah	Made herself queen by killing all the sons of Ahaziah, except Joash; was killed when Joash became older
Atonement	To make amends for one's sins through reconciliation; see also Feasts
Baal	(also Baalam) Pagan god of fertility despised by God and the prophets; Baalzebub is another term for Satan

Babel	City founded by Nimrod; see also Babylon
Babylon	Mesopotamian civilization and empire by the Tigris and Euphrates rivers; also, the name of the harlot (new Babylon) that seduces the nations in the latter days
Balaam	Sorcerer who tried to curse Israel but ended up blessing Israel by God's command
Balak	King of Moab who employed Balaam the sorcerer
Baptism	The washing away of original sin by water and the Holy Spirit
Barabbas	Prisoner that Pilate released instead of Jesus in honor of Passover
Barak	Judge of Israel and companion of Deborah
Barnabas	Follower of Jesus; companion of Paul and fellow evangelist
Bartholomew	One of Jesus's twelve apostles
Bathsheba	Committed adultery with King David and became his wife upon the death of her husband Uriah; Solomon's mother
Beersheba	City in southern Judea; site of a well owned by Abraham and Isaac
Belshazzar	King of Babylon whose dream (the writing on the wall) was interpreted by Daniel
Ben-Hadad	Name of three Syrian kings who subdued Israel
Benjamin	Jacob's youngest son; tribe of Israel
Bernice	Sister and wife of King Herod Agrippa II
Bethany	Town by the Mount of Olives and home of Mary, Martha, and Lazarus
Bethel	City near Jerusalem where Abraham built an altar, where Jacob became Israel, and where the Ark of the Covenant resided
Bethlehem	Town near Jerusalem where Jesus was born and where David settled
Bethsaida	Town where the Jordan River and Sea of Galilee meet; birthplace of Peter, Andrew, and Philip
Bilhah	Rachel's servant who bore Jacob two sons
Birthright	Privilege of being the firstborn son and principal heir; entitled the firstborn to a double proportion of the father's inheritance
Blasphemy	Words or actions which contradict God
Bless	Bestow kindness and favor
Boaz	Wealthy Bethlehemite who married Ruth; Jesse's grandfather
Brimstone	Sulfur
Caesar	Roman emperors including Augustus, Tiberius, Claudius, and Nero
Caiaphas	Jewish high priest denounced Jesus and His apostles; had Jesus arrested for insurrection; accused Jesus of blasphemy and sought crucifixion by Romans
Cain	Adam and Eve's first son who murdered his brother Abel
Caleb	Joshua's companion who spied on Canaanites for Moses

Calvary	Place of the skull where Christ was crucified (also Golgotha)
Cana	Town in Galilee, north of Nazareth, where Jesus performed His first miracle
Canaan	Land between Jordan River and Mediterranean Sea claimed by Israelites as the promised land; Canaanites were descendants of Ham's son Canaan
Canon	Books of the Bible officially accepted as inspired by God; standard or rule
Capernaum	City along the Sea of Galilee and home of Peter, Andrew, James, and John
Carmel	Mountain where Elijah embarrassed the prophets of Baal by destroying the altar with fire from heaven
Centurion	Roman captain in charge of about one hundred men
Chaldea	Southern Babylonia
Cherub	(plural is cherubim) Powerful angel with four wings and four faces
Chittim	Island of Cyprus
Circumcision	Removal of the foreskin of the penis
Colosse	City in Asia Minor to which Paul addressed his epistle to the Colossians
Comforter	The Holy Spirit
Commandment	Law
Communion	The Lord's Supper of unleavened bread and wine (Eucharist); forgiveness of one's sins is received via repentance and the witnessing of Christ's sacrifice
Corinth	Greek city where Paul preached; he addressed epistles to the Corinthians
Cornelius	Roman centurion who dreamed that Peter would visit him; he subsequently became a Christian
Covenant	A binding contract or agreement
Crucifixion	Execution on a cross
Cush	Ethiopia (and possibly Sudan)
Cyprus	Mediterranean island and homeland of Barnabas
Cyrene	City in Libya
Cyrus	First of the Persian emperors; he allowed the Jews to return to Israel and rebuild the temple in Jerusalem
Dagon	Pagan god of Mesopotamia and Canaan; temple of Dagon destroyed by Samson to include all its Philistine inhabitants and leaders; god of fertility
Damascus	Capital of Syria and highway where Jesus called Paul
Damnation	Condemnation; sentenced to serve eternity in hell
Dan	Jacob's fifth son; tribe of Israel
Daniel	Major prophet and author of Old Testament book bearing his name; interpreted dreams for kings; survived the lions' den; visualized the latter days and a time of tribulation, the rise of the evil beast, and the eternal reign of Christ

CHAPTER EIGHT

Darius	Name for Medio-Persian emperors; Persian king who allowed edict of Cyrus to stand (rebuilding temple in Jerusalem); succeeded by Xerxes (Cyrus's grandson)
David	Seventh son of Jesse who killed the giant Goliath; succeeded Saul as king over the Israelites; wrote most of the Old Testament book of Psalms; committed adultery and murder before claiming Bathsheba as his wife
Deacon	Temple servant or minister
Dead Sea	A salt lake at the mouth of the Jordan River
Deborah	Prophetess and judge of Israel who defeated the Canaanites through shrewdness
Defile	To pollute or corrupt
Delilah	Betrayed Samson to the Philistines
Demon	Evil spirit or fallen angel
Desolation	Total destruction
Devil	Evil spirit or demon; also Satan
Dinah	Jacob's daughter whose rape was avenged by her brothers
Disciple	Follower
Eden	Garden where Adam and Eve lived and committed the original sin
Edify	To instruct, enlighten, or build up
Edom	Country southeast of Israel; Edomites were descendants of Esau
Egypt	Northeastern part of Africa where Joseph became prince and the Israelites settled before being enslaved by Pharaoh; home of descendants of Ham's son Mizraim; first world empire, along the Nile River
Eleazar	Aaron's son who succeeded him as priest; father of Phinehas
Eli	Priest who was responsible for Samuel's upbringing
Elijah	(also Elias) Prophet performed miracles; ascended into heaven on a chariot of fire
Elisabeth	John the Baptist's mother
Elisha	Prophet who was Elijah's successor and performed many miracles
Emmanuel	See Immanuel
Enoch	Methuselah's father; God's witness who was taken to heaven before dying
Ephesus	Seaport in Asia Minor where Paul preached and to which Paul addressed his epistle to the Ephesians
Ephraim	Joseph's second son who was blessed by Jacob with the birthright; tribe of Israel
Epistle	Letter written by a Christian evangelist and included in the New Testament
Esau	Isaac's first son who sold his birthright to his brother Jacob for food; descendants were Edomites
Esther	Jewish girl who became King Xerxes's queen; exposed Haman's plot to eradicate the Jews resulting in his execution; Old Testament book tells her story

Ethiopia	Country south of Egypt along Nile River; descendants of Ham's son Cush settled there
Eunuch	Castrated male that served as a royal attendant
Euphrates	Largest river in western Asia and site of ancient Mesopotamia and Babylonia
Evangelist	Missionary who teaches and preaches God's laws, the Gospel, and the scriptures
Eve	First woman created by God to be Adam's companion in Eden; mother of humans
Excommunication	Exclusion from the church; banishment
Exegesis	Analytical explanation or clarification of written material, especially scripture
Exodus	The flight of the Israelites from Egyptian slavery; Old Testament book tells story
Ezekiel	Major prophet and author of the Old Testament book bearing his name; visualized angels, the resurrection, and heaven
Ezra	Priest, prophet and author of Old Testament books including the one bearing his name; rebuilt the walls of Jerusalem
Faith	Belief in God and His Word
Feasts	Special Jewish celebrations ordained by God to commemorate an event or act of faith; there are seven principal feasts and two secondary feasts.

Passover (commemorates when Israelites' firstborn were spared from God's curse on the Egyptians); *Unleavened Bread* (commemorates the Exodus); *First Fruits* (celebrates God's generosity via offerings and tithes); *Pentecost* (celebrates God's Holy Spirit via offerings); *Trumpets* (celebrates new year and God's Law); *Atonement* (celebrates God's forgiveness through godly sorrow for one's sins); and *Tabernacles* (commemorates God's covenant via praise and thanksgiving); *Purim* (commemorates the story of Esther and Mordecai); *Hanukkah* (observes Maccabean revolt and restoration of temple, not recorded in the Bible).

Seven Principal Feasts

Name	Event	God's Gift	Acts of Faith
1. Pesach	Passover	Mercy	Worship/Praise
2. Matzah	Unleavened Bread	Faith	Witnessing
3. Omer	First Fruits	Blessings	Tithing
4. Shavuot	Pentecost	Truth	Evangelism
5. Rosh Hashana	New Year (Trumpets)	Hope	Memorials
6. Yom Kippur	Atonement	Forgiveness	Repentance
7. Succoth	Tabernacles	God's Word	Teach/Study

Felix	Roman governor of Judea who was afraid of Paul and had him bound
Festus	Roman governor who succeeded Felix and granted Paul's appeal to Caesar
Firstborn	Birthright entitling eldest son to double portion of inheritance
Frankincense	An aromatic resin burned as incense
Gabriel	Angel of God who appeared to Daniel, Zacharias (father of John the Baptist), and Mary and Joseph (Jesus's parents)

Gad	Jacob's seventh son; tribe of Israel
Galatia	Part of Asia Minor where Paul preached and to whom was addressed his epistle to the Galatians
Galilee	Land where Jesus lived as a boy; also, the lake adjacent to Jesus's homeland fed by the Jordan River; much of Jesus's preaching took place in this region
Gamaliel	High priest who taught Paul to be a Pharisee
Gentile	A foreigner to the Jews
Gethsemane	Garden on the Mount of Olives where Jesus was betrayed
Gibeon	Hill and site of the tabernacle where time stood still
Gideon	Prophet and judge of Israel who conquered the Midianites
Gilboa	Mountain south of Jezreel where Saul was defeated by the Philistines
Gilead	Mountainous region east of the Jordan River
Gilgal	Area where Israelites camped upon crossing the Jordan River before the battle of Jericho
Golan	A city of refuge for the half tribe of Manasseh
Golgotha	Hill near Jerusalem resembling a skull where Jesus was crucified; also Calvary
Goliath	Philistine giant and champion killed by David
Gomorrah	City destroyed by God along with Sodom because of its wickedness
Goshen	Area in Egypt where Israelites settled and Joseph ruled; Israelites later were enslaved but escaped with the help of Moses
Gospel	Teachings of Jesus Christ; literally "good news"
Habakkuk	Prophet and author of the Old Testament book bearing his name
Hades	Hell; holding area for the condemned
Hagar	Servant of Sarah who bore Abraham's son Ishmael and was driven away by Sarah
Haggai	Prophet of Israel; book in the Old Testament
Ham	Noah's youngest son and father of Mizraim, Canaan, Phut, and Cush Ham's descendants: Mesopotamia, Phonecia, Africa Nations: Ethiopian, Mesopotamian, Libyan, Phoenician, Canaanite, Egyptian
Haman	Nobleman under King Xerxes whose attempt to eradicate the Jews was thwarted by Mordecai and Esther, resulting in his execution on gallows that he made to execute Mordecai
Hannah	Samuel's mother who dedicated him to the Lord for blessing her with a son
Haran	Lot's father and Abraham's brother; also, a location in ancient Mesopotamia
Hazael	Syrian King, anointed by Elijah, who attacked Israel
Heaven	Paradise where the righteous will live with the Lord

Hebron	Ancient city in the hills near Jerusalem where Abraham built an altar and where David settled
Hell	Lake of fire where the wicked will be tormented
Heresy	See blasphemy
Hermeneutics	The science of properly deriving meaning in written works, especially scripture, using sound principles of interpretation such as cultural and historical relevance
Herod	King of Judea ordered little boys in Bethlehem murdered in attempt to kill Jesus; his son was Herod Antipas, the governor who had John the Baptist beheaded and mocked Jesus at his trial; his grandson and great-grandson were Herod Agrippa (I and II), responsible for the death of the apostle James and the arrest of Peter
Herodias	Abandoned her husband to carry on an adulterous affair with Herod Antipas; persuaded illegitimate daughter Salome to ask Herod for John the Baptist's head
Hezekiah	Upright King of Judah who restored the holy temple
Hiram	King of Tyre who helped King David build his palace, and helped King Solomon build the temple and ships for his navy
Hittite	Canaanite tribe and nation
Holy	Sacred
Horeb	Mount Sinai
Hosea	Prophet who married the prostitute Gomer; the Old Testament book tells his story
Hur	Companion of Moses; also, the name of Caleb's son
Hypocrite	Insincere person who does not adhere to his or her own rules or religion; a person that pretends to be someone they are not
Idolatry	Adoring or worshipping false gods, people, or graven images
Immanuel	The Messiah; literally "God with us"
Isaac	Abraham's son and heir; father of Esau and Jacob
Isaiah	(also Esias) Major prophet and priest who foresaw the coming, life, death, and resurrection of the Messiah (Jesus Christ); author of the Old Testament book bearing his name; warned Israel of impending invasion and destruction
Ishmael	Abraham's son from Sarah's servant Hagar
Ishtar	Pagan goddess of fertility for Semitic tribes and empires of ancient Babylon
Israel	Name for Jacob and his descendants; the northern kingdom comprising ten tribes
Issachar	Jacob's ninth son; tribe of Israel
Jacob	Isaac's son traded food for his brother Esau's birthright, then tricked his father into blessing him with the birthright; dreamed about a ladder to heaven with angels, and wrestled with the angel of God; was renamed Israel
Jael	Wife of Heber who killed Sisera the Canaanite general

James	Name of two of Jesus's twelve apostles (son of Zebedee and son of Alpheus); James Z. was executed by Herod Agrippa; also, Jesus's half-brother who authored the New Testament book bearing his name
Japheth	Noah's eldest son and father of Tiras, Meshach, Tubal, Javan, Madai, Magog, and Gomer; Japheth's descendants: Europe, Asia, and America Nations: French, British, Spanish, Portuguese, Germans, Russians, Medes, Greeks, Romans
Jehoiachin	Kings of Judah; son defeated and imprisoned by Nebuchadnezzar; later released and promoted over other kings; ancestor of Christ
Jehoram	Evil king of Judah
Jehoshaphat	King Asa's son who succeeded him as king of Judah; established judges
Jehovah	The Lord God Almighty; from YHWH (unspoken name of God, or Yahweh) meaning "to be" (I AM)
Jehu	Upright king of Israel who exterminated the house of Ahab and Jezebel and the prophets of Baal
Jephthah	Judge of Israel who defeated the Ammonites; sacrificed his daughter because of a foolish vow
Jeremiah	Major prophet and priest who foresaw the day of judgment and the conquest of Babylon; was imprisoned and thrown into a cistern, then released; author of the Old Testament book bearing his name
Jericho	City by the Jordan River which was conquered by Joshua upon entering the promised land
Jeroboam	Seized the throne of Israel after Solomon died and the kingdom split due to revolt
Jerusalem	Sacred city of Israel; captured by David, became his capital; site of Solomon's temple and Jesus's trial and conviction
Jesse	David's father; grandson of Boaz and Ruth
Jesus Christ	The Messiah, the Son of God, and Savior of humankind; God in the flesh and part of the Holy Trinity
Jethro	Moses's father-in-law and adviser
Jezebel	Ahab's wife; evil sorceress who worshipped Baal and killed prophets of Jehovah; died a dishonorable death as prophesied by Elijah
Jezreel	Valley and city in south Galilee; place where Jezebel and the house of Ahab were eradicated; son of Hosea and Gomer
Joab	King David's nephew and commander of his army who killed Abner; conspired against Solomon and was killed
Joash	Upright King of Judah who rebuilt the temple
Job	Wealthy and righteous man who Satan sought to destroy; he lost everything but gained it back because of his faith; Old Testament book tells his story
Joel	Prophet and author of the Old Testament book bearing his name

John	One of Jesus's twelve apostles, who wrote five New Testament books including Revelation and the four books bearing his name; also, the name of the messenger who prepared the way for Jesus Christ by baptizing people in the Jordan River, including Jesus (the baptizer was beheaded by Herod Antipas)
Jonah	Prophet who was swallowed by a whale for defying God; the Old Testament book tells his story
Jonathan	Saul's son and David's best friend who was killed in battle
Joppa	Seaport northwest of Jerusalem visited by Jonah and Peter
Jordan	River that runs from the Dead Sea to the Sea of Galilee; crossed by the Israelites before inhabiting the land of Canaan; site of John the Baptist's ministry
Joseph	(also Joses) Eleventh son of Jacob who was sold by his brothers into slavery; was imprisoned and later became a prince in Egypt due to his ability to interpret dreams; also, the name of Jesus's stepfather, Mary's husband; also, the name of a Pharisee from Arimathaea who donated his tomb to inter the dead body of Jesus
Joshua	Moses's successor as the leader of the Israelites; prophet who conquered the land of Canaan where the Israelites settled; Old Testament book tells his story
Josiah	Upright king of Judah and reformer who found the Book of Law
Jubilee	Year of freedom and thanksgiving; the seventh year
Judah	Jacob's fourth son; tribe of Israel; ancestor of Christ
Judas	(also Iscariot) The apostle who betrayed Jesus
Jude	Brother of Jesus (Judah) and author of the New Testament book bearing his name
Judea	(also Judah) Southwest part of the kingdom of Israel comprising two tribes
Justification	Being found not guilty
Kidron	Valley near the Mount of Olives where a stream flowed
Laban	Rebekah's brother and Jacob's father-in-law for whom Jacob worked seven years each for his wives Leah and Rachel, Laban's two daughters
Lamech	Son of Methuselah and Noah's father
Lazarus	Jesus's friend that He raised from the dead; brother of Mary and Martha
Leah	Jacob's first wife and Rachel's older sister; she bore him six sons and a daughter
Lebanon	Mountainous northern boundary of Canaan
Levi	Jacob's third son; tribe of Israel; Levites had responsibility as priests
Lot	Abraham's nephew who escaped Sodom with his family and whose wife was turned to salt for looking back; impregnated both daughters each of whom bore him a son; descendants became the Moabites and Ammonites
Lucifer	Satan, the fallen cherub
Luke	Physician and companion of Paul wrote two New Testament books (Luke and Acts)

Luther	Martin Luther, considered to be the father of the Protestant Reformation, was a Catholic monk and priest who objected to unscriptural practices taking place in the church and imposed by the leadership of his time; advanced *sola scriptura*
Magog	Northern lands of Germanic peoples; descendants of Japheth's son Magog settled there, possibly the southernmost area of Russia
Malachi	Prophet and author of the Old Testament book bearing his name
Malta	Island where Paul was shipwrecked
Manasseh	Joseph's first son who was blessed by Jacob but not with the birthright; tribe of Israel
Manna	Bread-like food God provided to the Israelites as they wandered in the Sinai wilderness; spiritual nourishment (translated as "what is it")
Mark	Paul's companion and Barnabas's cousin who wrote the New Testament book bearing his name
Martha	Sister of Mary and Lazarus
Mary	Mother of Jesus; also, Mary Magdalene a follower of Jesus who He freed from demon possession; also, the sister of Martha and Lazarus and the one who washed Jesus's feet; also, the name of Mark's mother and James Alpheus's mother
Matthew	One of Jesus's twelve apostles who was formerly a tax collector; wrote the New Testament book bearing his name
Matthias	Selected among the apostles by lottery to replace Judas Iscariot; however, Jesus called Paul to be His twelfth apostle
Media	Land east of Babylonia next to Persia
Megiddo	City and stronghold by Carmel mountain pass; site of many battles, likely including the final Armageddon
Melchizedek	King of Salem (meaning peace) and original priest of the order of Melchizedek; communed with Abraham; the one to whom Abraham gave tithes; he was likely a manifestation of the Holy Spirit (Jesus Christ, the Prince of Peace, was the only other high priest from the order of Melchizedek)
Menorah	Candlestick with seven candles representing the seven feasts (eight or nine candles represent the addition of feast of Hanukkah)
Mephibosheth	Lame son of Jonathan who was helped by King David
Meshach	Daniel's friend who survived the fiery furnace
Mesopotamia	Land of the Tigris and Euphrates river valleys (an ancient civilization)
Messiah	Jesus Christ (*Christos*); literally "the Anointed One"
Methuselah	Noah's grandfather who lived the longest of any known person (969 years)
Micah	Prophet of Israel; author of Old Testament book bearing his name
Michael	Archangel of the Lord and defender of the righteous; defeated the dragon (e.g., Satan) who was thrown out of heaven along with one-third of the angels

Michal	Saul's daughter who became David's wife; Saul later gave her to another man but David finally got her back
Midian	Abraham's son by second wife Keturah; ancestors were the Midianites who were merchants that traveled by camel
Miriam	Moses and Aaron's sister who was stricken with leprosy for speaking against Moses
Mizraim	Ham's son and ancestor of the Egyptians (northern Africa)
Moab	Lot's first son from his oldest daughter; descendants were the Moabites
Mordecai	Esther's cousin who raised her and introduced her to King Xerxes who married her; persuaded Esther to expose Haman's plot to eradicate the Jews; took Haman's place in the court of Xerxes
Moses	Born a slave in Egypt, escaped Pharaoh's extermination of slave children and was raised a prince; called by God to deliver the Israelites from slavery; became a prophet and judge and performed many miracles; received Ten Commandments and other laws directly from God; wrote the first five books of the Old Testament
Myrrh	A fragrant compound used for ointment, perfume, and embalming
Naboth	Killed for his vineyard as a result of the evil plot of Jezebel
Nadab	Aaron's son and priest found guilty of idolatry and executed
Nahum	Prophet of Israel; Old Testament book bears his name
Naomi	Ruth's mother-in-law
Naphtali	Jacob's sixth son; tribe of Israel
Nathan	Prophet and adviser to King David; denounced David's sin with Bathsheba for which David's family was cursed; prophesied about God's Messiah
Nathanael	See Bartholomew
Nazareth	City in Galilee where Jesus was raised
Nebuchadnezzar	Babylonian king who conquered Israel and whose dreams were interpreted by Daniel; became evil and went crazy, but later repented
Nehemiah	Governor of Israel who helped rebuild Jerusalem; Old Testament book tells story
Nicodemus	Pharisee who followed Jesus Christ and helped bury Him
Nimrod	Noah's great-grandson from son Ham and grandson Cush; became the great Mesopotamian ruler of Babel, and established other cities including Nineveh
Nineveh	Capitol city of Assyrian empire and place God sent Jonah to prophesy
Noah	(also Noe) Built the ark and saved his family and the animals from the great flood; Noah's sons were Japheth, Shem, and Ham
Obadiah	Prophet and author of the Old Testament book bearing his name
Olives	Mountain near Jerusalem where Jesus preached to the crowds
Omega	Last letter of the Greek alphabet; the ending

CHAPTER EIGHT

Onesimus	Slave for whom Paul interceded in his letter to Philemon
Othniel	Relative of Caleb; judge who freed Israel from Aram
Palestine	The land of Canaan later claimed by the Israelites; a derivative of Philistia
Papyrus	A reed that grows in Nile river valley used to make baskets, sandals, boats, and paper
Parable	Story that teaches a moral lesson
Passover	The night the angel of death killed the firstborn of Egypt, but passed over the Israelites' homes which had been sprinkled with lamb's blood; see also Feasts
Patriarch	Founding father
Paul	Originally called Saul, he was a Pharisee who persecuted Christians until he was called by Jesus Himself to become an apostle; was the leading evangelist who spread the Gospel to the Gentiles; wrote most of the New Testament epistles
Pentecost	The fiftieth day (seven weeks after Passover); the day the Holy Spirit came upon the apostles and they preached in foreign tongues; may coincide with Moses's receiving of the Ten Commandments on Sinai; see also Feasts
Persia	Land east of Babylonia and the original empire established by King Cyrus; descendants of Shem's son Elam settled there
Peter	Originally named Simon the brother of Andrew, became leader and spokesman for Jesus's twelve apostles (literally, "the rock"); he wrote two New Testament epistles bearing his name, and was likely the source for the Gospel of Mark
Pharaoh	King or emperor of Egypt
Pharisee	Member of a Jewish tribunal that strictly observed the laws of Moses as well as their own traditions; member of the Jewish Sanhedrin (ruling party)
Phenice	(also Phonecia) Coastal area of Syria containing ports of Tyre and Sidon
Philemon	Paul's companion to whom Paul wrote the New Testament epistle bearing his name
Philip	One of Jesus's twelve apostles; also, a companion of Paul and fellow evangelist
Philippi	Macedonian city where Paul preached and to which Paul addressed his epistle to the Philippians
Philistia	Land along the Mediterranean coast and southern part of Canaan; inhabitants were called Philistines
Phinehas	Eleazar's son and priest who killed an evil Israelite and his Midianite harlot, thereby turning away God's wrath
Pilate	Roman governor of Judea who interrogated Jesus and under whose authority Jesus was crucified
Potiphar	Egyptian who bought Joseph to be his slave and later had him imprisoned for allegedly attempting to seduce his wife

Predestination	The doctrine which holds that all things were foreordained by God, including the salvation of all believers, insofar as God knows all things despite allowing humankind free will to choose their way
Praetorium	Headquarters of the Roman governor in Jerusalem
Priscilla	Aquila's wife and follower of Christ
Prodigal	Wasteful
Prophecy	Spiritually inspired words of a prophet directed by God to tell the future
Prophesy	The act of a prophet communicating prophecy (to prophesy)
Prophet	(also prophetess) Spokesperson for God; directed by God to say or write something
Proverb	Moral rule of thumb
Psalm	Song of praise and thanks
Publican	Tax collector
Quirinius	Governor of Syria when Caesar Augustus ordered a census of the empire, requiring the enrollment of Joseph and Mary, just prior to the birth of Jesus
Rachel	Jacob's second wife and Leah's younger sister; she bore Jacob two sons
Rahab	Prostitute from Jericho that hid Joshua and Caleb who were spying for Moses; she was spared when the Israelites invaded; mother of Boaz
Rebekah	Isaac's wife and sister of Laban; mother of Esau and Jacob
Redeemer	One who buys back or ransoms something; Christ bought back our souls from the grave through His death and resurrection
Red Sea	Sea between Africa and Arabia which Moses miraculously parted, allowing Israelites to cross; Egyptians were drowned when they tried to cross
Rehoboam	Solomon's son who became king of Judah when the kingdom split
Repent	To humbly confess and feel regret for one's sins before God
Resurrection	To arise from the dead with a body, as a living being
Reuben	Jacob's first son lost his birthright for sleeping with Bilhah, mother of his half brothers; tribe of Israel
Revelation	The disclosing of a mystery, truth, or secret
Righteousness	Keeping God's laws and doing His will; holiness or godliness
Rome	Capital city of the Roman Empire where Paul preached and to which Paul addressed his epistle to the Romans
Ruth	Naomi's daughter-in-law who married Boaz after her husband died; her first son was Obed, father of Jesse and grandfather of David
Sabbath	Day of rest and worship; precedent set by God during creation
Sacrament	One of two solemn acts of righteousness instituted by Christ and providing forgiveness of sins; includes Holy Baptism and Holy Communion

Sacrilege	Profaning something holy
Sadducee	Jewish aristocrat and member of a religious sect that didn't believe in the resurrection of the dead
Salome	Danced for her father Herod Antipas in exchange for the head of John the Baptist; also, the name of Zebedee's wife and mother of the apostles James and John
Salvation	The act of saving someone; through Christ we receive salvation of the soul from sin and death through purification by the blood of Jesus
Samaria	City and neighboring land west of the Jordan River between Nazareth and Judea
Samson	Judge known for his great physical strength; was betrayed by Delilah to the Philistines; destroyed the Philistine temple of Dagon and everyone in it
Samuel	Major prophet and judge who subdued the Philistines; anointed Saul as king, then condemned Saul and anointed David; Old Testament books bear his name
Sanctify	To make holy
Sanhedrin	High council of the Jews comprised of seventy elders
Sarah	(also Sarai) Abraham's wife and half-sister who God blessed; she bore Isaac in her old age and despised her maidservant Hagar who had borne Ishmael
Satan	The devil; God and man's adversary who tempts us to sin; the fallen angel Lucifer
Saul	First king of Israel who disobeyed God and became demon possessed; tried to destroy David but failed; also, the original name of Paul the evangelist, the twelfth apostle called by Christ
Scribe	A writer and translator of the Law or Gospel
Scripture	Sacred words inspired by God; passages from the Holy Bible
Semite	Inhabitants of the Fertile Crescent descended from Noah's son Shem
Seraph	(plural is seraphim) Angel with six wings and many eyes
Seth	Adam and Eve's third son
Shadrach	Daniel's friend who survived the fiery furnace
Sharon	Seacoast plain north of Joppa and near Mount Carmel
Shechem	Raped Jacob's daughter Dinah; was killed by Dinah's brothers Simeon and Levi; also, an ancient city north of Jerusalem
Shem	Noah's second son and father of Arphaxad, Aram, Lud, Asshur, and Elam; Shem's descendants: Middle East and Asia Minor; Nations: Persians, Assyrians, Babylonians, Armenians, Syrians, Israelites
Sheol	Hell
Shiloh	Ancient city north of Jerusalem and first capital of Israel
Sidon	(also Zidon) Son of Canaan and seaport city of Phenice
Silas	Prophet and close companion of Paul and Peter
Siloam	Sacred pool in the Kidron valley

Simeon	Jacob's second son; tribe of Israel; also, the name of a man who prayed that he would see God's Messiah before dying, which he did, because he blessed the baby Jesus at His dedication
Simon	One of Jesus's apostles; also, the original name of the apostle Peter; name of a Pharisee with whom Jesus dined; name of man from Cyrene who carried Jesus's Cross; also, sorcerer who tried to buy power of Holy Spirit from Peter and Paul
Sinai	(also Horeb) Sacred mountain where God spoke to Moses
Sisera	Commander of the Canaanite army who was killed by Jael
Sodom	City destroyed by God along with Gomorrah because of its wickedness
Solomon	David and Bathsheba's son who succeeded David as King of Israel; asked God for wisdom and was rewarded with wisdom and riches; built the temple of Israel; wrote part of the Old Testament including most of Proverbs, Ecclesiastes, and Song of Solomon
Sosthenes	Head of the synagogue in Corinth who became a Christian
Stephen	Disciple of Christ who died a martyr for following Him; was recruited by the apostles to be their representative and later was stoned to death
Supplication	An earnest and humble request, as with prayer
Synagogue	Location or site of a congregation of worshipers
Syria	Land north of Israel where descendants of Shem's sons Aram and Arphaxad settled
Tabernacle	Portable sanctuary; home of the Ark of the Covenant; see also Feasts
Tabor	Mountain east of Nazareth where Barak's army encamped
Tamar	David's daughter who was raped by her half-brother; also, the name of Judah's daughter-in-law (God slew Judah's sons who rejected her so she disguised herself as a prostitute and tricked Judah into getting her pregnant, and that child became part of Jesus's ancestry)
Temptation	Attempt to get someone to do something evil or wrong
Testimony	The presentation of the truth by a witness
Thaddaeus	One of Jesus's twelve apostles
Theophilus	A friend of Luke to whom he addressed his Gospel
Thessalonica	Macedonian capital where Paul preached and to which Paul addressed his epistles to the Thessalonians
Thomas	One of Jesus's twelve apostles; refused to believe in Jesus's resurrection until he saw and touched Jesus again
Timothy	Paul's companion to whom Paul wrote two New Testament epistles
Tithe	Tenth part of one's income given to support God's work
Titus	Gentile companion of Paul to whom Paul wrote a New Testament epistle

Transfiguration	When Jesus Christ appeared in His spiritual glory and radiance, alongside Moses and Elijah
Transgression	Sin
Trespass	Sin
Trinity	Although God is One, there are three manifestations, or persons: Father, Son, and Holy Spirit
Tyre	Seaport city and capital of King Hiram of Syria
Ur	Ancient city on the Euphrates River where Abraham lived
Uriah	Hittite husband of Bathsheba who David sent to battle to be killed so he could covet his wife
Uzziah	King of Judah stricken with leprosy for assuming the responsibilities of a priest
Vanity	Worthlessness
Vision	A revelation or glimpse of the future, often from God, sometimes in a dream
Xerxes	King of Persia who married Esther, honored Mordecai, and hanged Haman (aka Ahasuerus)
Zacchaeus	Rich tax collector who climbed a tree to see Jesus; he repented and pledged half his wealth to the poor
Zacharias	John the Baptist's father
Zadok	High priest under David who guarded the Ark of the Covenant
Zealot	Radical group that protested the payment of taxes to the Romans and their occupation of Judea
Zebedee	Father of the apostles James and John
Zebulun	Jacob's tenth son; tribe of Israel
Zechariah	Prophet of Israel; author of the Old Testament book bearing his name
Zedekiah	Appointed king of Judea by Nebuchadnezzar; his defiance of the king and his imprisonment of Jeremiah was rewarded by being captured, blinded, and his sons executed by order of the Babylonian emperor
Zephaniah	Prophet of Israel; Old Testament book bears his name
Zerubbabel	Head of the tribe of Judah; governor of Israel who led exiled Jews back to Israel and helped rebuild the temple in Jerusalem
Ziba	King Saul's treacherous assistant
Zilpah	Leah's servant who bore Jacob two sons
Zion	Hill of Jerusalem and site of the temple; a name for heaven (where God lives)
Zipporah	Moses's first wife

BIBLICAL TIMELINES

Approx. Date (BC)	Person/Place	Event
3000	Noah	Builds ark to survive worldwide flood
2600	Ur	Early Mesopotamian dynasty and city
2300	Egypt	Egyptian empire flourishes
2000	Abraham	God's Covenant with all people
1800	Hammurabi	Babylonian king's code of justice
1775	Jacob	Becomes Israel
1700	Joseph	Governor of Egypt; Hebrews settle at Goshen
1600	Hittites	Defeat Babylon in battle
1500	Moses	Exodus from Egypt
1450	Joshua	Fall of Jericho and conquest of Canaan
1150	Judges	Median era of the Judges in Israel
1025	Saul	King falls from God's grace, consults witch
1000	David	King builds palace; repents of adultery, murder
950	Solomon	King builds temple; wisest and richest of Israel
925	Israelites	Kingdom splits: Israel (ten tribes), Judah (two)
920	Rehoboam	King of Judah; Jeroboam king of Israel
890	Asa	King of Judah
870	Ben-Hadad	King of Syria
870	Elijah	Prophet ascends into heaven on fiery chariot
860	Ahab	King of Israel; Jehoshaphat, king of Judah
850	Elisha	Prophet works many miracles
840	Jehu	King of Israel; overthrows Ahab and Jezebel
825	Hazael	King of Syria
820	Joash	King of Judah
810	Jehoahaz	King of Israel
795	Jehoash	King of Israel
780	Jeroboam II	King of Israel
760	Hosea	Prophet; Uzziah king of Judah
740	Amos	Prophet
730	Hoshea	King of Israel
725	Ahaz	King of Judah; Tiglath-Pileser, king of Assyria
725	Isaiah	Prophet declares the coming of God's Messiah
720	Sargon II	King of Assyria; fall of Samaria to Assyrians
705	Hezekiah	King of Judah (angel slays 185,000 Assyrians)
695	Micah	Prophet; Shalmaneser, king of Assyria
685	Manasseh	King of Judah; Sennacherib, king of Assyria
630	Josiah	King of Judah; prophet Zephaniah
615	Jeremiah	Prophet foretells the conquest of Babylon
610	Megiddo	Josiah falls at Megiddo to Necho, King of Egypt
610	Nineveh	Assyrian capital destroyed by Babylon
590	Nebuchadnezzar	Babylon invades Judah; blinds King Zedekiah
585	Jerusalem	Jerusalem falls; temple wrecked; captives taken
580	Ezekiel	Prophet sees a vision of angels

TIMELINES

Approx. Date (BC)	Person/Place	Event
570	Daniel	Prophet interprets dreams of kings about future
550	Zechariah	Prophet during governorship of Zerubbabel
540	Cyrus	King of Medes and Persians (fall of Babylon)
530	Ezra	Return of captives to Jerusalem
520	Darius	King of Persia allows rebuilding of Jerusalem
500	Esther	Marries King Xerxes of Persian Empire
480	Nehemiah	Rebuilds wall of Jerusalem
470	Malachi	Prophet promotes tithing
450	Artaxerxes	Son of Xerxes, king of Persia
400	Joel	Prophet of gloom and despair
350	Philip	Macedonian conquests
330	Alexander	Sacking of Persia by Greeks
320	Ptolemy	Ptolemaic dynasty in Egypt begins
195	Egypt	Rosetta stone is discovered
168	Jerusalem	Antiochus Epiphanes desecrates the temple
160	Maccabees	Revolt in Israel; reacquires the temple
135	Hasmoneans	Dynasty of Maccabees reunite Holy Land
65	Pompey	Overthrow of Hasmonean dynasty by Romans
55	Julius Caesar	Emperor of Rome
35	Herod the Great	King of Judea
25	Caesar Augustus	Emperor of Rome
5	Jesus Christ	Jesus's birth in Bethlehem
4	Herod	Herod the Great dies; son Antipas succeeds

Approx. Date (AD)	Person/Place	Event
15	Tiberius	Emperor of Rome
30	Jesus Christ	Crucifixion by Roman prefect Pontius Pilate
31	Apostles	Establish the common Creed; spread the Gospel
32	Stephen	Stoned to death (supervised by Saul of Tarsus)
33	Paul	Called by resurrected Christ to be an apostle
35	Caligula	One of several decadent emperors in Rome
36	Pontius Pilate	Pilate removed from post
42	James	Apostle executed by King Herod Agrippa I
50	Mark	First Gospel written; Paul's Epistle to Galatians
55	Herod Agrippa II	King of Judea
55	Paul	Epistle to the Corinthians
58	Luke	Physician writes Gospel of Luke
60	Paul	Imprisoned by Romans; Epistles from Paul
61	Acts	Luke documents the Acts of the Apostles
61	James	Book by James the brother of Jesus
62	James	Jesus's brother, church leader, stoned to death
64	Matthew	Gospel of Matthew

TIMELINES

Approx. Date (AD)	Person/Place	Event
65	Nero	Emperor persecutes Christians; Paul executed
69	John	Gospel of John
70	Titus	Romans sack Jerusalem, destroy temple
79	Pompei	City annihilated by eruption of Mt. Vesuvius
80	Domitian	Roman ruler persecutes Christians
82	Peter	Epistles from Peter; John exiled to Patmos
88	Revelation	John authors last book of the Bible
93	Josephus	Jewish historian confirms historical Jesus
100	Trajan	Roman emperor
104	Tacitus	Roman historian records crucifixion by Pilate
110	Ignatius	Promotes obedience to leaders; quotes NT
112	Pliny the Younger	Roman regent writes Trajan about Christian sect
155	Polycarp	Bishop of Smyrna martyred; quotes NT
165	Justin Martyr	Christian teacher martyred by Marcus Aurelius
200	Jewish Rabbis	Compilation of Mishnah (Jewish laws)
205	Clement	Alexandrian bishop
210	Irenaeus	Promotes Christian dogmatics and NT canon
245	Origen	Alexandrian bishop
250	Cyprian	Promotes universal church; Valerian rules Rome
300	Diocletian	Edict against Christians; destroys scriptures
310	Galerius	Roman ruler accepts Christianity
315	Constantine	Emperor legalizes Christianity
325	Nicaea	Doctrine of Trinity defended; Nicene Creed
320	Pachomius	Monasticism originated
330	Constantine	Bishop of Constantinople proclaims sovereignty
365	Athanasius	Bishop of Alexandria produces NT canon
380	Jerome	First Latin translation of Bible (Vulgate)
390	Ambrose	Bishop of Milan; boosts singing, writes hymns
390	Theodosius	Christianity made official religion of Rome
395	Augustine	Bishop of Hippo; Council of Carthage
420	Augustine	Verifies canonization of twenty-seven NT books
412	Cyril	Alexandrian patriarch supports venerating Mary
450	Palestine	Compilation of Jerusalem Talmud
450	Leo	Advances the cause of papacy
500	Benedict	Benedictine monastic order
525	Dionysius	Monk estimates Christ's birth; Roman calendar
580	Gregory I	First Pope (changes bishopric into papal system)
630	Mohammed	Legendary return to Mecca; beginnings of Islam
725	Catholicism	Eastern (Byzantine) and Western (Roman) split
726	Catholic Orthodoxy	Disputed borders, doctrine, alliances, authority
800	Leo III	Charlemagne declared emperor (church-state)
820	Iraq	Caliph of Baghdad
1055	Europe	Eastern and Western Orthodoxy split permanent

CHAPTER EIGHT

TIMELINES

Approx. Date (AD)	Person/Place	Event
1075	Jerusalem	Ottoman Empire conquers Holy Land
1095	Europe	Crusades begin
1205	Innocent III	Pope abuses power; height of papal control
1210	Francis of Assisi	Franciscan monastic order
1215	Dominic	Dominican monastic order
1235	Gregory IX	Inquisition (torturing and murdering dissenters)
1255	Europe	Augustinian monastic order
1270	Holy Land	Crusades end
1380	Wycliffe	English translation of the NT
1455	Gutenberg	Movable type printing press; Bible reproduced
1525	Tyndale	Printed English language edition of NT
1517	Martin Luther	Protestant Reformation (Ninety-five Theses)
1519	Zwingli	Reformation movement grows in Switzerland
1521	Martin Luther	Luther makes scriptural stand in Diet at Worms
1523	Europe	Anabaptists promote adult baptism
1530	Melanchthon	Augsburg Confessions
1534	Martin Luther	German translation of the NT
1535	Martin Luther	Smalcald Articles
1536	Calvin	Promotes education, Presbyterianism in Europe
1540	Loyola	Origination of Jesuit order
1550	Charles V	Council of Trent (Roman counter-reformation)
1590	Elizabeth	Puritanism
1600	Europe	Age of Protestantism begins
1610	King James	Commissions English translation of the Bible
1618	Rome	Thirty years war begins (Catholic reformation)
1630	Smyth	Baptist denomination
1640	Charles I	Presbyterian denomination
1750	Wesley	Methodist denomination
1790	France	French revolution; religion abolished
1845	Walther	First president of the General Lutheran Synod
1861	USA	United States Civil War begins
1917	USA	United States enters World War I
1941	USA	United States enters World War II
1945	Hitler	Nazi Germany spreads; evil Fuhrer kills Jews
1947	Qumran	Discovery of Dead Sea Scrolls
1947	USA	Lutheran Missouri Synod
1948	Europe	Formulation of NATO
1948	Palestine	Nation of Israel is recognized globally
1960	USA	Lutheran Wisconsin Synod
1961	Germany	Berlin Wall is built
1964	USA	Civil Rights Act
1973	USA	Vietnam War ends
1990	Germany	Berlin Wall is dismantled

INDEX OF KEYWORDS

Abbreviations	**xii**	Baptism	**373–374**, 402, **704–707**
Abomination (of Desolation)	206–214, 216, **242**, 689	Bartholomew	**111–112**
Abortion	**423**, 451–452	Beast (also Satan)	**241–242**, 308, 597, 727
Abraham	62, 72, 82–83, 86–87, **104–109, 552**, 752	Bible	(see Holy Bible)
Acts (of faith) (Book of)	**32**, 41, 35, **367–384, 585–586**	Birth (of Christ)	73, 143, **149–151**, 696
Adam	148, 415, 553, 752	Birthright	**103**, 754, 757
Addiction	**453–456**, 756	Blame	40, 129, 249, 364, **461**
Adopted (by God)	**267**, 302, 519–521	Blasphemy	145, 487, 501, 754
Adultery	377, 439, **450–451**	Blessings	103, **331**, 384, 751
Almighty God	**51–68**, 69, 652, 670	Blood	126, 392, **407–410**, 601
Amos	10, **577**, 753, 769	Body of Christ	274, **294–298**, 375, 697
Andrew	**110**, 112, 753	Born Again	170, 255–257, **402**
Angels	305, **313–317**	Bride (of Christ)	68, 274, **352**, 658
Anger	**426–428**, 432	Canonization	**6**, 7, 675–676, 771
Answers	26, **627–629**	Casting (Demons)	**321–322**, 354, 614, 720
Apostles	**110–113**	Change	**47–50, 255**, 524, 615
Ararat	**2**, 753	Children	100–109, 266, 312, 519
Archaeology	2, 532, **680–682**	Choice	277, **327–330**, 686
Armageddon	**243–244**, 287, 753	Chosen Ones	**100–103**, 104, 542, 740
Armor of God	**283–284**, 769	Christ	(see Jesus)
Ascension	**179–181**, 665, 753	Christmas	68, **141**, 192, 484
Athanasius	387, **678**, 771	Chronicles	10, **564–565**
Atonement	32–33, 88, **126–127**	Church	6, 113, 182, **273–276, 676–677**
Augustine	**678**, 771	Clement	**677**, 772
Authenticity	**3**, 7, 532, 675	Circumcision	**106–108**, 644, 755
Authority	**290–291**, 321, 412	Colossians	10, **590**, 755
Awesome God	**55–59**, 509–510	Comfort	461, 618, **620–622**
Babylon (Old) (New Babylon)	206, 231, **726–730** **215–216**, 237, **731–735**	Comforter	71, **78**, 145, 615, 755
		Commandments	14, 35, 87, **434–441**, 443, 556, 744, 764

INDEX OF KEYWORDS

Communion (Holy)	26, 28, 294, 373, **375–376**, 401, 405, 406	Deviancy	389, **422–423**, 432, 447–452
Condemnation	90, 127, 217, 344, **521**	Diaspora	684
Confession	33, **367–368**, 412, 609	Diligence	293, **359–363**, 385, 541
Confidence	321, 337, **617**	Discernment	23, **318–322**, 606, 672
Confirmation	**376**, 403	Discipleship	289, **368–373**, 394
Conflict	96, 238, 277, 726, 746	Discipline	79, **299–300**, 329, 653
Corinthians	10, 350, **587–589**, 755	Division	167, **294, 297**, 738
Counseling	394, 426, **612–619**	Divorce	157, 377, **450–451**, 580
Covenant	9, **82**, 86, 187–188, **523**	Doctrine, Dogma (False Doctrine)	6–10, **387**, 478–479, 11, **463–507**
(New)	**83–85**, 87–89, **114**, 188		
(Old)	**82–83**, 87–89, 187		
(The Ark of the)	1, 27, 556, 564, 698	Dreams	269, **537–541**, 576, 761
Covetousness	432, **441**	Easter	**179–180**, 190, 665, 697
Creation	553, **659–663**, 671, 682	Ecclesiastes	10, **570–571**
Creed	6, **387**, 678, 770, 771	Edification	295, 412, 472, 612–619
Crown	323, **546–551**, 552	Education	14, 125, 289, 412, 553
Crucifixion	**178**, 189, 664, 697, **699**	Elijah	4, 228, 318, **563**, 635, **683**, 689, 712, 720
Cults	463, **469–477**		
Damnation	(see Condemnation)	Empires	1, **231**, 244, 539, 726–735
Daniel	84, 231, **538–539**, **576–577**, 684, **726–735**, 769	Endurance	**280–282**, 286, 739
		Envy	(see Covetousness)
Darkness	320, 353, **508–509**, 517, 524–525, 668, 699	Ephesians	10, **589–590**, 756
		Equality	**265–267**, 533, 536
David	83, 142, 148–151, 184, **561–564**, 756, 769	Equipping	203, **290**, 293, 364, 612
Dead Sea Scrolls	3, 667, **680**, 772	Esther	10, **566**, 756, 768, 770
Death	**271–273**, 343, 391, 417–418, 545	Eternal Life	15, 32, 251–252, **519–521**
		Eternity	512–522, 656–658, 738
Deceit	(see Lying)	Evangelism	110–112, **371–373**, 412
Decisions	**277–279**, 328, 356, 627	Evidence	531, 539, 664–667, **670–674**, 675–687, **691–693**, **701–703** (see also Validity)
Deliverance	59, 87–89, 92, **604–605**		
Demons	307, 315, **318–322**, 503		
Deuteronomy	10, **558–559**	Examination	**7–11**, 405, 675–676, 691–693

INDEX OF KEYWORDS

Example	**36–40**, 299–300, 398	Freedom	134, 327, **343–345**, 533
Excommunicate	297, 756	Fulfillment (Prophetic)	128, 370, 385, 456, 653 **114**, 142, **688–698**, 734
Excuses	**630–634**, 654, 664	Gabriel	121, 149–151, **314**, 757
Exegesis	**7**, 11–12, 757	Galatians	10, 50, **589**, 758, 770
Exodus	10, **555–556**, 757, 769	Garden of Eden	2, 13, 402, 527, 553, 725
Exorcism	(see Casting Demons)	Genealogies	10, **148**, 553, 564
Experience	23–24, 194, 277, 281, 461, **674**, 702, 717–719	Generation	148, 167, **214–215**, 234, 504, 647, 688
Eyewitnesses	3, 6, **664–667**, **701–702**	Genesis	2, 10, 139, 259, 527, **553–555**, 682, 694
Ezekiel	4, 10, 84, 529, **575–576**, **733–736**, 757, 769	Geography	**5**, 7, 692
Ezra	10, 530, 564, **565**, 757	Gifts (Spiritual)	42–43, 67, 252, **331–366**, 414, 605, 610, 750,
Faith	**32–35**, 47–50, 87–90, 100–109, 129–133, **335–336**, 346–349, 367, 612–619, 739–742	Giving	30, 42, 378–390, **414**
		Glory	45, 55, **60–64**, 192, 750
Familiar Spirits	(see Demons)	Gluttony	**430–431**, 441, 453–456
Father (God) (Fatherhood)	54–59, 69–71, **74–77**, 389, 438, 627, 736 299–302, 354	God	**51–81**, 652, 670–674
		Gog	(see Magog)
Fear	47–48, 55–59, 86, 179, 319–322, **509–512**	Golden Rule	395, **743–746**
Feasts	140, 189, 472, 557, 609–611, 694, **757**	Gospel	**148–204**, 580–585
		Government	169, 343, 474, **533–536**, 653, 692, 726, 732
Fellowship	**296**, 436–437, 610	Grace	24, 87–91, **334–335**, 387, 602–603, 605
Fight (of Faith)	**283–288**, 321–322, 345, 501, 619, 745	Greed	**419–420**, 434–435, 441
Fire	228, **407–408**, 523, 710	Guidance	50, 541, **612–619**, 699
Firstborn	(see Birthright)	Habakkuk	10, **578**, 758
First Fruits (Feast of)	44, 185–186, 193, **246**, 725 99, 190–191, 557, 610, 697	Haggai	10, 182, **578**, 758
Forgiveness	32–34, **128–129**, 274, 322, 373, 401–402, 625, 707	HARP	**1–5**, 485, 532, 671, 675
		Harvest	160, **184–186**, 285, 695–697
Fornication	439, **450**, 746, 752	Hate, Hatred	354, **426–428**, 433, 438
Forward (Look)	48–50, 86, 288, 337, 617, 658, 718		
Free	91–97, 343–344, **704–709**		

INDEX OF KEYWORDS

Healing	**346–349**, 614, 618–619	Idolatry	**432–437**, 453, 465–466, 470–471, 479
Heart	32, 47–48, 255, 320, **261–262**, **620–622**	Image (Graven) (of God)	435, **463–466**, 605–606 38–40, **196–199**, 260–261
Heaven	108, 254, 267, **513–516**, 716–719, 747–751	Imagination	**192–195**, 658, 712, 747
Hebrews	2, 10, 134, **592–593**, 729	Imitate (Emulate)	**40**, 299–300, 318, 435, 747
Heirs	(see Inheritance)	Immaculate Conception	**73,** 93, 149, 402
Hell and Hades	163, 219, 454, **517–518**, 521–522, 656–658, 715, 721	Incest	447, **449–450**, 503, 557
Helping	**41–46**, 253, 278, 367, 378, 386–400	Inheritance	102–103, 135, 166, 251, **519–521**, 716, 754
Hermeneutics	**7–12**, 687, 692, 759	Instruction	**14–15**, 36, 289, 300, 325, 370–371, 394, 397
Herod	73, 120, 149–150, 157, 695–698, **759–760**, 770	Isaiah	10, 84, 563–564, **571–573**, 652, 680, 725, 759
History	**1–4**, 7, 10, 142–144, **675–682**, 726–731	Islam	480, 483–484, **494–502**, 731, 771
Holy Bible	1, 6–10, 125–126, **145–147**, 627, 691–693	Israel	82–83, 87, 104, 108, 189, 240, **554–579**, 729
Holy Spirit	15, 26–31, 54, 71–76, **78**, 91–97, 125–126, 145–147, 149, 259, **704–709**, 714	Jacob	98, 104, 148, **554–555**, **759**, 769
Holy Week	**98–99**, 174–181, 189–190, **694–698**, 699	James	10, **110–112**, 113, **594**, 680, 760, 770
Home	166, 254, 273, 302, **356–358**, 519–521, 543, 633	Jeremiah	10, 84, **573–575**, 729, 760, 769
Homosexuality	389, **448**, 557	Jesus Christ	15, 69, **77**, 79, **114–259**, 267, 310, 335–336, 387, 401–406, 770
Honesty	167, 399, 429, 440, 453, 746		
Honor	15, 173, 360, **438**	Job	10, 280–281, **566–567**, **741**
Hope	48–50, 254, **337–338**, 541, 617–619, 621	Joel	10, 182, **577**, 689–690, 770
Hosea	10, **577**, 684, 759, 769	John (Apostle)	761 10, 110–112, 224, 231, **584–585**, **595–596**, 716, 731, 771
Humanity	6, 66–68, 196–198, 245, 416–418, 640–641, 682, 743–746	(Baptist)	149–153, 157, 689, 695
		Jonah	10, **578**, 729, 761
Humility	41, 165, 173, **424–426**, 741	Joseph (Jacob's Son) (Mary's Spouse)	761 538, **554–555**, 764 73, 113, 120, 122, **148–151**, 539–540, 680
I AM	79–81, 652, **736–738**, 760		
Idleness	(see Laziness)		

ANDREW V. BARBER

INDEX OF KEYWORDS

Josephus	2, 113, **679**, 681, 696, 771	Lineage	68, 142, **148**, 553–555, 733–734
Joshua	10, 58, 533, 557–558, **559–560**, 761, 769	Listening	107, 197, 359, 399, 438, 622, **653–655**. 672, 743
Joy	175, 301, **338–340**, 412, 625	Logos	**259**, 666, 677, 691, 704
Judas Iscariot	110, 168, **173–177**, 761	Love	14, **43**, 47, 302–303, 311, 332–334, **350–355**, 600
Jude	10, 113, **596**, 676, 761	Lucifer	(see Beast, Satan)
Judges	10, **560**, 769	Luke	7, 10, 85, 148, **582–583**, 585, 666, 695, 761, 770
Judgment	**220–222**, 249–250, 597		
Julius Africanus	**679–680**	Lust	328–329, **420–423**, 432, 439, 453
Justification	85, 89, **129–131**, 189, 202, 335–336, 602–604, 632	Lying	**429–430, 440–441**, 668
Justin Martyr	667, **677**, 771	Magog	238–239, 575, **733–735**
Kindness	21, 292–293, 619, 743–744	Malachi	10, 84, 151, **579**, 770
Kingdoms	1, 151, 231, 244, **729–735**	Manuscripts	3, 6–10, 667, **675–676**, 680, 692–293
Kings	1, 10, 143, 231, **561–566**	Mark (Disciple)	10, 111–112, 148, **582**, 676, 762, 770
Knowledge	65–68, **340–342**, 683, 744	(of Beast)	216, **240–242**, 597, 606
Lake of Fire	198, 232, 341, 442, **517–518**, 658, 723, 738	(of God)	227, 251, 306, 708–709
Lamb of God	77, 133, 152, 231, **190–191**, 695, 698	Marriage	299, 302–304, **377–378**, 439, 450–451, 571, 658
		(of the Lamb)	68, 273–274, **352–353**, 658, 749
Lamentations	10, **575**	Mary	762
Latter Days	(see Second Coming)	(Virgin Mary)	73, 113, 121–122, **148–150**, 317, 541, 700
Law	9, 14, 82–83, **434–441**, 556, 743–746	(Magdalene)	179, 665
		(and Martha)	167–168, 680, 761
Laziness	361, 400, **432–433**	Matthew	10, 110–112, **589–582**
Leaders	6, 42, 113, 290, 385, 412–413, 467, 613, **676–678**	Melchizedek	**72**, 87, 98, 375, 490, 554, 592, **762**
Learning	(see Instruction)	Mercy	222, **334–335**, 399, 725
Leviticus	10, 407, 447, **556–557**	Messiah	4–5, 77, 84–90, **114–124, 139–144**, 652, 684, 688–690, 737
Life (Newness of)	17, 32, **196–199**, 270–271 255, **546–552** (see also Eternal Life)		
		Micah	10, 150, **578**, 769
Light	508–509, 524–525, **668–669**	Michael	228–229, 306, **313–314**, 597, 762

INDEX OF KEYWORDS

Millennial Reign	223, **232**, 243, 247–248, 544, 649, 723	Omniscience	**51–52**, 610, 668, 670–671
Mind	15, 23–24, 48, 198, **260–264**, 277, 295, **325–326**, 442, 528, 619, 672, 694	Origen	667, 677, **678–679**, 771
		Original Sin	373, **402–404**, **415–416**, 553, 704, 754
Mindfulness	23, **328–329**, 623, 655, 745	Out of Body	246, 262–263, 716–718
Ministry	112, 143, 148, **151–157**, 183, **371–373**, 402, 722	Overcoming	**48–50**, 163, 283–284, **298**, 312, 401, 405, 462
Miracles	59, 268, **660–663**, 673–674	Overindulgence	(see Gluttony)
Morality	9, 533–535, 671–673, 714	Parables	8, 143, **159–160**, 365, 580–583
Mormonism	483–484, **485–493**, 476	Paradise	(see Heaven)
Moses	36, 83, 87–89, 134, 434, 481, **555–558**, 763, 769	Parenthood	77, **299–304**, 350–355
Murder	423, 426, **438–439**, 451	Passover	144, **174–180**, 187–190, 407, 557, 610, **694–699**, 757
Nahum	10, **578**	Patience	49–50, 222, 278, **280–282**, 331–332, 621, 739
Nature (Earth)	2, 447–449, 452, 531, 661–664, 673, **686**	Paul	85–86, 106, **110–112**, 182, **585–586**, 665–666, 716–719, 764, 770–771
(Human)	6, 22, 90, 402–403, **415–416**		
Nehemiah	10, **565–566**, 763, 770	Peace	150, 225, 295, **338–340**, 385, 571–573
New Covenant	**82–90**, 98, 114, 184–191, 478, 601–602	Penance	545
Noah	82, 553, **659–660**, 763, 769	Perjury	(see Lying)
Numbers (Book of)	**635–650** 10, **557–558**	Perseverance	**34–35**, 361–362, 616, **739–742**
Oaths	(see Swearing)	Peter	10, **110–113**, 174–182, 203, **585–586**, **594–595**
Obadiah	10, **577**	Philemon	10, **592**, 764
Obedience	23, **36–40**, 86, 128–132, 392, 407, 558, 529	Philip	**110–112**, 124, 153, 585
Occult	435, **465–467**, 470, **505–507**, 710, 715	Philippians	10, **590**, 764
Occupation	330, 512, 706, **747–751**	Pilate, Pontius	2, **177–179**, 664, 702, 720, 738, 764, 770
Offerings	(see Sacrifice)	Plagues	212, 230–231, 238, **556**, 596–598
Olivet Discourse	**205**, 688–690	Plan, Planning	45, 65–66, 527, 617, 686
Omnipotence	**51–52**, 54, 610, 660		
Omnipresence	**51–52**, 356–357, 610	Politics	225, 474, **533–536**

INDEX OF KEYWORDS

Polycarp	**676–677**, 771
Polygamy	**450–451**, 476
Power	**310–317**, 534
(of God)	**54–59**, 65–68, 73, 255
(of Humans)	**268**, 280–283, 354, 745–746
(of Satan)	**308–309**, 311, 354, 509–512
Praise	27, 35, **43**, **378–380**, 384, 436–437, 567–569
Prayer	30–31, 278–279, 347–348, **381–386**
Preaching	290, **412–414**, 665–666
Predestination	**136–138**, 519–522, 765
Pride	365, **424–426**, 432–433
Priesthood	20, 72, **289–293**, 556
Probability	5, 630, 671, 692–693
Problem Solving	47, **277–279**, 302, 352, 462, 615–619, 628
Promises	48, 107, 195, **251–254**, 462, 621–622
Proof	(see Evidence)
Prophecy	**4–5**, 9–10, **114–124**, 142–144, 146, 224, 231, 469–471, **683–685**, **688–690**, 733–734
Prosperity	352, **359–363**, 414, 555, 391
Proverbs	10, **569–570**, 767
Psalms	10, **567–569**, 756
Raising (Dead)	179, 190, **217–219**, 228, 245–246, 312, 664–667, 713, 716–719
Rapture	**216–217**, 222, 228, 245, 544
Receiving	198, 210, 253, 334, **704–709**
Reconciliation	92, **134–135**, 393–394, 746
Redeemer	90, 114, 134, **737**, 765
Redemption	85, 127, **134–135**, 707, 721
Relationships	**16–25**, 100, 135, 188–189, 291, 303, 413, **653–655**
Reliability of Bible (Consistency)	**3–4**, 7–10, 485, 531–532, **691–693**, 3, 6, 8–9, 489–491, 502, 691–692, 696, 701–702
Religion	5, 463, **475–484**, 526–532, 533–536, 675, 719
Remember	611, **623–626**, 719
Repentance	166, 249, **367–368**, 379–392, 454, **608–610**, 755
Resources	**xiii**, 12, 686–687, 693
Respect	**299–300**, 398, 426–428, **438**, 450, 534
Responsibility	289–293, 301–302, **364–366**, 414, 533, 704–705
Resurrection	**179–181**, 765
(of Christ)	87–89, 684–685, 697–698
(of Man)	217–219, 228, 232, **246–250**, 713–714
Revelation	8, 269–270, **537–541**, 659, 671–674, 691
(Book of)	10–11, 111, **596–598**, 688–690, 761, 771
(of Christ)	**223–224**, 607–609, 718
Riches	331–332, 360, **419–420**
Righteousness	29–30, 37–40, 82–86, 90, **255–257**, 404, 442–446, **508–509**, 546–551, 750
Rock	**94–96**, 112–113, 601, 764
Romans	10, 43, **586–587**, 730–731, 679, 699, 769–770
Rome	231, 730, 765, 770–771
Ruth	10, 134, 148, **560**, 742
Sabbath	14, 43, **436–437**, **694–698**, 699
Sacraments	28, **373–376**, **401–406**
Sacrifice	32–33, **82–89**, 115, 118, 126–129, **187–191**, 316, **407–411**, 451
Salt	157, **523–525**, 553, 761

INDEX OF KEYWORDS

Salvation	15, 35, 66, **132–133**, 136–138, 599–601, 739, 766	Spirit (Human)	255, 260, **262–263**, 320, 404, 704, **710–715**
Samuel	10, 318, **560–562**, 711–712	Spirits (Other)	**305–322**, 465, 704, 715
Sanctification	**129–132**, 525, 706, 740	Stars	211–212, 227, 607, **662**
Satan	152, 229, 241–243, **308–311**, 354–355, 415–416, 418, 442–445, 509	Stewardship	35, **41–46**, 750
		Steadfastness	34, **739–742**
Satanism	197–198, 391, 465, 477, **503–507**	Stealing	45–46, 432, **439–440**
		Suffering	60, 75, 225, 387, **457–462**, 512, 580, **620–623**
Scattering	(see Diaspora)	Swearing	158, 435–436, **466**, 471
Science	**526–532, 659–663**, 682–683, 691–693	Symbolism	8, 11, 607, 650, 735
Seals (Seven)	212–213, **225–227**, 596–597, 607	Symbols (Judeo-Christian)	463, 635–650 13, 25, 53, 78, 86, 89, 144, 199, 276, 324, 406, 479, 551, 609–610, 751
Second Coming	172–173, 194–195, **205–244**, 689	(Pagan, Satanic)	480–482, 483, 505, 506–507
Secrecy	**466–467**, 488–489, 507	Tacitus	2, 667, 675, **679**, 771
Seed	85–89, 92–95, **104–109**, 159–160, 184–186, 253, 659–660	Talents	42–43, **396–400**, 413–414, 750
		Talmud	12, 481, 680, 771
Service	**41–46, 378–380**, 706, 750	Teaching	33, 42–43, 203, 300, **370–373**, 397, 463–464, 475
Sexual Sin	(see Deviancy)		
Shepherd	114, 143–144, **190–191**, 192, 303, 567, 569,	Teamwork	295, 321, **394–395**
		Temptation	328, **415–433**, 442–446
Shroud of Turin	531, 667, **682**	Tertullian	667, **677**
Signs	67, 167, 172, 214, **234–239**, 540–541, 688–690	Testimony	(see Witnessing)
		Tests	147, 189, 278, **280–281**, 291, 460, 531, 654, 681
Simon	110–112, 153, 173, 767 (see also Peter)	Thaddaeus	**110–112**
Sin	88–90, 128–131, 139–140, 256–257, 389–392, **415–462**, 620	Thanksgiving	43, **378–380**, 436–437, 461
Soldiers	222, **283–288**, 664–665	Thessalonians	10, **591**, 767
Song of Solomon	10, **303**, 571, 767	Thomas	**110–112**, 123, 180–181
Soul	**91–95**, 129–133, 143, 247, 260–261, **262–264**, 331–332, 401, 407	Three or Thirds	8, 74–76, **636–638, 720–725**

ANDREW V. BARBER

INDEX OF KEYWORDS

Time	3, 30, **41–42**, 46, 172, 205, 223, **660–661**, 694–698, 738
Timelines	7, 297, **695–699**, **769–772**
Timothy	10, **591–592**, 767
Tithing	**44–45**, 378, 397–398, 414
Titus	10, **592**, 681, 767, 771
Tongues	182, **472**, 764
Tools	**47–50**, 62–63, 293, 532
Tower of Babel	2, 553, 681, 726
Traditions	6, 203, 232, **467–468**, 473, 477, 502, 545, 699
Training	285, 288, 412, **546**, 747–749
Transfiguration	162, **712–713**, 768
Translation	xi, 3, **7–10**, 12
Treasure	**44–46**, 164, 331–366, 441
Tribulation	172, 205, 216–219, 225, 228, **240–244**, 245, 609
Tribute	**43**, 46, 414, 440
Trinity	**69–81**, 201–203, **599–606**, 705, 720, 725, 771
Trumpets	212, 225, **227–229**, 607, 610, **757**
Trust	15, 55–56, 167, 254, **337–338**, 351
Truth	5–11, 24–27, 79–81, **145–147**, 289, 321–322, **340–342**, 399, 401, 429–430, 663, 670–674, 685–686
Understanding	16–25, 65–68, **340–342**, 348, 472, 612–619
Unity	**294–298**, 44, 450
Universe	259, 447, 526–528, 530, 630–631, **659–663**, 664, 668, 670–671, 683, 693, 738
Unleavened	99, **189–190**, **694–695**, 697, 755, 757
Unnatural	**422–423**, **447–452**, 527–528, 662
Unpardonable	146, 493, 501, 674
Uplifting	254, 617, 745–746
Validity of Bible (Empirical)	**1–12**, 485, 532, 670–674, 675–687, **691–693**
Vengeance	(see Wrath)
Victory	55–56, 60, 222, 287–288, 405, **603–604**
Vineyard	93, 165, 169, **184–186**
Visions	3, 146, 192–195, 242, **269–270**, 502, **537–541**, 719
Vocation	(see Occupation)
War	212–213, 229–230, 232, **241–244**, 277, **283–288**, 500–501, 772
Will of God	32, 66, **87–89**, 129, 222, 292, 330, 421, 447, 460, 656, 721
Wisdom	**65–68**, 325, **340–342**, 530–531, 569–571, 671, 763
Witnessing	46, 368–370, **396–397**, 403
Word of God	xi, 6, 14, 26, 125–126, **145–147**, 296, 387, 418, 445, 463, 469, 475, 603, **653–653**, 663, 677
Work or Works	**335–336**, 602, 747–751
Worship	150, 157, 197–198, **296**, **378–380**, 418, 435–437
Wrath	56, 227, 230, 432–433 (see also Anger)
Zechariah	10, 84, 149, 209–210, 231, **579**, 770
Zephaniah	10, **578**, 769
Zion	84, 98–99, 324, **515–517**, 768 (see also Heaven)

www.ingramcontent.com/pod-product-compliance
Lightning Source LLC
Chambersburg PA
CBHW060501300426
44112CB00017B/2516